Collection of ICC Arbitral Awards
2001 – 2007
Recueil des sentences arbitrales de la CCI

Kluwer Law International

COLLECTION OF ICC ARBITRAL AWARDS
2001 – 2007
RECUEIL DES SENTENCES ARBITRALES DE LA CCI

Jean-Jacques Arnaldez *Yves Derains* *Dominique Hascher*

International Chamber of Commerce
The world business organization

Wolters Kluwer
Law & Business

AUSTIN   BOSTON   CHICAGO   NEW YORK   THE NETHERLANDS

Published by:

Kluwer Law International
PO Box 316
2400 AH Alphen aan den Rijn
The Netherlands
Website: www.kluwerlaw.com

ICC Services – Publications
38, Cours Albert Ier
75008 Paris
France
Website: www.iccbooks.com

Sold and distributed in North, Central and South America by:
Aspen Publishers, Inc.
7201 McKinney Circle
Frederick, MD 21704
United States of America
Email: customer.care@aspenpubl.com

Sold and distributed in all other countries by:

Turpin Distribution Services Ltd.
Stratton Business Park
Pegasus Drive, Biggleswade
Bedfordshire SG18 8TQ
United Kingdom
Email: kluwerlaw@turpin-distribution.com

ICC Services – Publications
38, Cours Albert Ier
75008 Paris
France
Email: pub@iccwbo.org

Printed on acid-free paper

The *Collection of ICC Arbitral Awards 2001–2007* has already been published in the *Yearbook commercial Arbitration* and the *Journal du Droit International* (Clunet). These extracts are reproduced with the permission of the respective editors and publishers.

ISBN: 978 90 411 2877 5 (Kluwer)
ISBN: 978 92 842 0068 9 (ICC)
ICC Publication No. 699

Printed in Great Britain.

Table of Contents

Table des matières

The Authors / Les auteurs

Jean-Jacques Arnaldez

Lecturer, University Panthéon-Sorbonne (Paris 1)
Former Deputy-Registrar of the International Court of Justice (1994-2008)
Former Counsel, ICC International Court of Arbitration (1982-1994)

Yves Derains

Lawyer, Paris Bar
Former Secretary General, ICC International Court of Arbitration (1977-1981)

Dominique Hascher

Presiding Judge, Court of Appeal (Reims, Champagne)
Adjunct Professor of Law, University Panthéon-Sorbonne (Paris 1)
Former General Counsel and Deputy Secretary General of the International Court
of Arbitration of the ICC (1990-1998)

Foreword to Volume V

1. This fifth volume of the *Collection of ICC Arbitral Awards* contains the awards that have already been published between 2001 and 2007 in the *"Yearbook Commercial Arbitration"* and in the *"Journal du Droit International"* (Clunet).

2. As in the first four volumes, the year when the award was rendered may not coincide with the year when it was reported in one of these publications.

3. Some awards are reproduced both in English and in French. This is the case with awards that were originally published simultaneously in the *"Journal du Droit International"* (Clunet) and the *"Yearbook Commercial Arbitration."*

4. The Analytical Table of Volume V covers all awards contained in the five Volumes of the *Collection of ICC Arbitral Awards*. A page number preceded by "I" refers to Volume I and if preceded by "II", "III", "IV" or "V" refers to Volume II, III, IV or to Volume V. Although the extracts of awards that figure in the first four volumes are not reproduced in Volume V, the reader can therefore limit his search to the Consolidated Analytical Table of Volume V and then look up the case extract in Volumes I, II, III, IV or V as the case may be.

5. From Volume II onwards, the Consolidated Analytical Table refers to the first page of the award and not necessarily the page where the point in question is to be found, which constitutes a change from Volume I. The reader will thus be directed to start reading the case from the beginning. In some cases, the reference will already be found in the summary, which will allow the reader to go straight to the part of the commentaries which sometimes follow the award. In other cases, the reference will have to be sought in the text of the award itself or, as may be, in the commentaries that follow, the reference being followed by the sign (c).

6. At the end of Volume V, the reader will find a Table of Cross-Referenced Cases to the *"Journal du Droit International"* (Clunet), the *"Yearbook Commercial Arbitration"* and *"The International Construction Law Review,"* for each of the awards published in Volumes I to V of this Collection. This table will enable the reader, looking at a given award, to rapidly obtain complete references in one or several of these three publications.

Introduction au cinquième volume

1. Ce cinquième volume du *Recueil des sentences arbitrales de la CCI* regroupe les sentences qui ont déjà été publiées entre 2001 et 2007 au *"Yearbook Commercial Arbitration"* et au *"Journal du Droit International"* (Clunet).

2. Comme dans les quatre premiers volumes, l'année durant laquelle la sentence a été rendue peut ne pas coïncider avec l'année de sa publication dans l'une de ces publications.

3. Certaines sentences sont reproduites tant en anglais qu'en français. C'est le cas de celles qui ont été à l'origine publiées simultanément au *"Journal du Droit International"* (Clunet) et au *"Yearbook Commercial Arbitration"*.

4. La Table analytique du cinquième volume couvre l'ensemble des sentences reproduites dans les cinq volumes du *Recueil des sentences arbitrales de la CCI*. Une page précédée d'un « I » renvoie au volume I et précédée d'un « II », « III », « IV » ou « V » au volume II, III, IV ou au volume V. Dans la mesure où les extraits de sentences qui figurent dans les quatre premiers volumes ne sont pas reproduits dans le cinquième, le lecteur limitera donc ses recherches à la Table analytique consolidée du volume V, puis se reportera, selon le cas, aux volumes I, II, III, IV ou V.

5. A compter du second volume, la Table analytique consolidée renvoie à la première page de la sentence et non pas nécessairement à la page où figure la référence recherchée, ce qui constitue un changement par rapport au premier volume. Le lecteur sera ainsi conduit à commencer la lecture de l'affaire à son début. Dans certains cas, la référence se trouvera déjà dans le sommaire, ce qui lui permettra en particulier de se reporter facilement à la partie du commentaire qui suit éventuellement la sentence. Dans les autres cas, la référence devra être recherchée dans le corps même de la sentence ou dans les commentaires qui la suivent, la référence étant alors suivie de la lettre (c).

6. A la fin du volume V, le lecteur trouvera une Table de correspondance des références au *"Journal du Droit International"* (Clunet), au *"Yearbook Commercial Arbitration"* et à *"The International Construction Law Review"*, de chacune des sentences publiée aux volumes I à V. Cette table permet ainsi au lecteur d'obtenir rapidement pour une sentence donnée ses références complètes dans l'une ou plusieurs de ces trois publications.

How to use this book?

First situation: the reader knows the case number

The reader who wishes to find the award rendered in case number 8938 will consult the Table of Cross Referenced Cases and find that this award figures at page 333 of Volume IV.

Second situation: the reader is looking for a specific issue

The reader who wishes to know whether a particular question has been an issue in an ICC arbitration, will consult the Consolidated Analytical Table of Volume V which will send him to the pages of the awards published in each of the five volumes which deal with the point in question.

The reader who is looking for a particular subject, should he not know the exact terminology in French or English, can consult one of the Key Word Indexes which will give him the corresponding notion in the other language if the same issue exists in the awards published in that other language.

Third situation: the reader wishes to give the complete references of an award

The reader will consult the Table of Cross-Referenced Cases and will thus obtain for each of the awards:
– on the one hand, its complete references in the *"Journal du Droit International"* (Clunet) or *"The International Construction Law Review,"* in particular with the mention of the initials of the author whose commentaries follow the award, and also in the *"Yearbook Commercial Arbitration"*;
– on the other hand, the indication of the volume and the page where it appears in the *Collection of ICC Arbitral Awards.*

Paris, January 2009

Jean-Jacques Arnaldez   Yves Derains   Dominique Hascher

Comment utiliser ce livre?

Premier cas : le lecteur connaît le numéro de l'affaire

Le lecteur qui souhaite par exemple trouver la sentence rendue dans l'affaire 9667 se reportera à la Table de correspondance des références et constatera qu'elle est publiée à la page 579 du volume IV.

Deuxième cas : le lecteur cherche une donnée spécifique

Le lecteur qui veut savoir si une question particulière a été abordée dans un arbitrage CCI, consultera la Table analytique consolidée du volume V qui le renverra aux pages des sentences publiées dans chacun des cinq volumes où la question est évoquée.

Un lecteur qui cherche un point particulier et ignore la terminologie exacte en anglais ou en français s'aidera de l'un des deux Index des mots-clés qui lui fournira la notion correspondante dans l'autre langue dans la mesure où le point en question est traité dans les sentences publiées dans cette langue.

Troisième cas : le lecteur souhaite donner les références complètes d'une sentence

Le lecteur se reportera à la Table de correspondance des références et obtiendra au regard de chacune des sentences :
– d'une part, ses références complètes au *"Journal du Droit International"* (Clunet) ou à *"The International Construction Law Review"* avec en particulier la mention des initiales de l'auteur des observations qui la suivent, ou encore au *"Yearbook Commercial Arbitration"*;
– d'autre part, l'indication du volume et de la page de sa publication au *Recueil des sentences arbitrales de la CCI.*

Paris, janvier 2009

Jean-Jacques Arnaldez   Yves Derains   Dominique Hascher

Abbreviations / Abréviations

Arb Int   Arbitration International (London)

Bulletin ASA   Bulletin de l'Association suisse de
                                l'Arbitrage (Bâle)

Bulletin ICC/CCI   The ICC International Court of Arbitration
                                Bulletin / Bulletin de la Cour internationale
                                d'arbitrage de la CCI (Paris)

DIS   Schriftenreihe des Deutschen Instituts für
                                Schiedsgerichtswesen, Band 6, Band 8, Carl
                                Heymanns Verlag KG, Köln, Berlin, Bonn,
                                München

ICLR   The International Construction Law Review
                                (London)

JDI   Journal du Droit International (Clunet)
                                (Paris)

JIA   Journal of International Arbitration (Geneva)

Jahrbuch   Jahrbuch für die Praxis der
                                Schiedsgerichtsbarkeit, Band, 1, 2, 3, 4,
                                Verlag Recht und Wirtschaft, Heidelberg

RDAI   Revue de Droit des Affaires Internationales :
                                International Business Law Journal (Paris)

Rev. Arb.   Revue de l'Arbitrage (Paris)

YB   ICCA Yearbook Commercial Arbitration
                                (Deventer, The Netherlands)

Consolidated Analytical Table

of Awards published in

1974 – 2007

Table analytique consolidée

des sentences publiées en

1974 – 2007

Analytical Table

A

1

D

Damages

M

c

O

Q

R

S

Voie directe
See **Applicable Law, to substance**

W

Y

Table Analytique

C

Voir aussi **Règlement d'arbitrage CCI:**
           - de 1975 : article 11
           - de 1998 : article 15

F

Voir aussi **Règlement d'arbitrage CCI:**
- de 1975 : article 20
- de 1998 : articles 30 et 31
Honoraires des arbitres
Jonction de demandes

France

— **Code du travail**

- article L.517-1	I	306

— **Code civil**

- article 1108	III	561
- article 1131	III	561
- article 1133	III	562
- article 1134	III	201
	V	663, 807
- article 1135	III	202
- article 1139	I	57
- article 1142	III	206
- article 1147	V	637
- article 1149	III	181, 204
- article 1150	III	181, 204
- article 1151	III	181
- article 1152	V	703
- article 1153	I	73
	III	146, 206, 207, 306, 518
- article 1154	III	307
- article 1254	V	659
- article 1273	V	807
- article 1275	III	303, 304
- article 1276	III	306
- article 1277	III	301
- article 1315	III	516
	V	807
- article 1382	III	206
- article 1458	V	807
- article 1582	III	514
- article 1592	IV	533
- article 1648	III	147
- article 1652	I	73
- article 1690	III	302
- article 1709	V	589

I

J

Jonction de demande

K

Koweït

L

ICC Arbitral Awards

reprinted from the *Yearbook Commercial Arbitration*

2001–2007

INTERNATIONAL CHAMBER OF COMMERCE

Partial award in case no. 7146 of 1992

Parties:	Claimant: Exclusive distributor M/A-Belgium (Belgium) Defendant: Manufacturer/exclusive licensee X/B-France (France)
Place of arbitration:	Brussels, Belgium
Published in:	Unpublished
Subject matters:	– Art. 85 EC Treaty – requirement to seek advice EC Commission? (no) – application of community competition law by arbitral tribunal – exclusive distributorship contract

Facts

The present arbitration arises in the context of the relationship between two industrial groups extending back over thirty years to when M, the original manufacturer, granted a licence to manufacture certain large plants to its French branch, M-France. In its turn, M-France concluded a contract with M-Belgium, a Belgian company controlled by the original manufacturer M, for the after-sales service to plants installed in Belgium.

The original manufacturer M sold part of M-France to X, a French company, and granted X the exclusive licence to manufacture and sell the plants which had previously been built by M-France, and to supply spare parts to customers. Shortly thereafter, X concluded a service contract with M-Belgium ["the first service contract (*convention de représentation*)"], under which M-Belgium continued to provide after-sales service to the plants in Belgium. Several years later, the original manufacturer M ceded all remaining shares in M-France to X. As M-France had ceased to be part of the M group, the cession contract also terminated the licence contract concluded between the original manufacturer M and X, providing however that X would still "have all the rights under the present licence agreement with respect to orders . . .

received before [the end of that year], so That it can complete the manufacturing process, deliver and provide maintenance on such orders, including accessories and spare parts". X notified the EC Commission of the conclusion of the cession contract. After an initial denial and some amendments, the cession contract was authorized by the Commission.

X concluded a second *convention de représentation* ["the Second Service Agreement"] with M-Belgium, which is the subject matter of the present dispute. Under the Second Service Agreement, M-Belgium again obtained the exclusive right to provide after-sales service in Belgium, including the supply of spare parts, periodical revisions and maintenance. Clause 2 of the Second Service Agreement provided that M-Belgium would buy the necessary parts solely and directly from X, with some exceptions listed under "Special Cases", among which were the installation of additional equipment and the reconditioning of the plants. In these listed cases, M-Belgium would request an offer from both the original manufacturer, M, and X and would then "examine" which offer was more favourable to the customer. The Second Service Agreement further contained a dispute settlement clause providing for ICC arbitration in Brussels under Belgian law.

Both M and X subsequently merged with other companies. The M group merged with the A group, creating the M/A group; M/A-Belgium, the Belgian company which is the claimant in this arbitration, is an entirely controlled branch of this group. The X group merged with B, creating the X/B group; X/B-France, the defendant in this arbitration, is an entirely controlled French company of the X/B group.

Several years after the merger, X/B-France wrote to M/A-Belgium terminating the Second Service Agreement as of the time of the merger, on the grounds of the M group's merger with B's competitor A and the acquisition by M/A-Belgium of the Belgian Company Y, an alleged direct competitor of X/B-France. M/A-Belgium commenced ICC arbitration against the termination of the Second Service Agreement.

The present award dealt with preliminary issues of community competition law. The Arbitral Tribunal held, in a majority award, that while it was not necessary to seek the advice of the EC Commission on competition law, it was required to apply community competition law as interpreted by community institutions. The Second Service Agreement fell within the scope of Art. 85(1) EC with respect to the exclusive right to provide after-sales service but not with respect to reconditioning for which no exclusive right was provided. The exclusive distributorship contract fell under EC Regulation 1983/83 on exclusive distributorships and benefited from its category exemption. The limitation in its Art. 3 did not apply because the parties were not competitors in the specific market covered by the Second Service Agreement. Thus, neither the

M/A merger nor the acqusition of Company Y by M/A Belgium affected the validity of the Second Service Agreement under community law.

Excerpt

(. . . .)

I.   REFERRAL TO THE EC COMMISSION

[1]   "The Arbitral Tribunal first considers whether it is necessary, expedient or useful to seek the advice of the EC Commission on the issues of community competition law on which the parties disagree in this arbitration. The possibility of seeking the Commission's advice is envisaged in the present case because the Arbitral Tribunal may not address a preliminary question of interpretation of community law to the EC Court of Justice under Art. 177 EC Treaty. The Court confirmed in its decision of 23 March 1982 (case no. 102/81, *Nordsee*) that an arbitral tribunal sitting in the Community is not a national court that can refer a preliminary question to the Court of Justice.

[2]   "The Arbitral Tribunal notes that neither party has argued that the Tribunal lacks jurisdiction to settle the dispute by applying community competition law.

[3]   "Arbitrators are not public or supernational bodies charged with the obligation of applying the competition provisions; rather, they are in the same position as any judge and/or private person who must comply with such competition provisions when carrying out their tasks and/or activities.

[4]   "In the case at issue, the Tribunal is seized with a dispute concerning the termination of a contract. The contract has been alleged to be null and void and this leads to an issue of community competition law.

[5]   "By considering that it has jurisdiction, in principle, to examine the preliminary issue of community competition law, the Arbitral Tribunal accepts the parties' implicit indication and shares the opinion adopted by doctrine,[1] and confirmed by some ICC arbitral awards.[2]

[6]   "The EC Court of Justice held in its decision of 28 February 1991 (case no. 234/91, *Delimitis*) that seeking the advice of the EC Commission is not compulsory. We must then consider whether seeking the Commission's advice is expedient and/or useful.

---

1. "See Van Hecke, 2 *Miscellanea Ganshof van der Meersch* (1972) p. 957 et seq.; Kovar, *Etudes Goldman* (1983) p. 109 et seq.; Steindorff, *Fordham Corporate Law Institute* (1985) p. 409 et seq.)."
2. "Awards rendered in case no. 1397 in 1966, Clunet (1974) p. 879 and in case no. 2811 in 1978, Clunet (1979) p. 1984."

[7]   "The Arbitral Tribunal noted already that the parties disagree on this point; their only common conclusion is that the Tribunal could only consider the advice of the Commission as an expert report, although highly authoritative.

[8]   "The Arbitral Tribunal notes that seeking the advice of the Commission is provided for in the Court's jurisprudence only 'where the concrete application of Art. 85(1) [presently Art. 81(1)] or of Art. 86 [presently Art. 82] gives rise to particular difficulties, in order to obtain the economic and legal data that [the Commission] can ... supply' (*Delimitis*, para. 53). The Commission's advice is thus not provided for in relation with the application of Art. 85(3) [presently Art. 81(3)]. Moreover, the Arbitral Tribunal does not deem that there are 'particular difficulties' in the application of Art. 85(1), in the present case, which justify seeking the advice of the Commission.

[9]   "The Arbitral Tribunal further notes that the Commission's advice could only be provisional, as it would be based on the information supplied and it could be modified if supplementary information were obtained.

[10]   "Last, the Commission's advice would have in practice a quasi-decisional impact on the issues without being, either in form or substance, a formal decision of the Commission in the sense of Art. 189 EC Treaty [presently Art. 249]. Hence, the parties could not appeal to the Court of Justice [against the Commission's advice] as they could if this were a [formal] decision of the Commission. Seeking the advice of the Commission in the present proceedings does not seem, therefore, to give the parties the same jurisdictional guarantee that they would have if the Commission issued a formal decision on the validity of the Second Service Agreement.

[11]   "The Arbitral Tribunal notes that, according to the Terms of Reference ... it shall settle the dispute by applying Belgian law, 'as well as community competition law applicable in Belgium'. The Arbitral Tribunal would not fulfil its task if it preliminarily and entirely entrusted the task to settle the issues of community law to the EC Commission, especially considering that community competition law is directly applicable, as constantly held by the Court of Justice, starting with its decision of 13 July 1966 in cases nos. 56 and 58/64, *Consten* and *Grundig* (see also the decision of 30 January 1974 in case no. 127/73, *BRT v. SABAM*). Direct application must be adhered to and guaranteed by national courts and administrations as well as by private persons.[3]

[12]   "The Arbitral Tribunal holds that it is bound by community competition law and that it must apply it to the resolution of the preliminary issues raised in the present case. In doing so, and in order to guarantee uniform application

---

3. "See, recently, *Munari, Diritto del Commercio Internazionale* (1990) p. 629; *Zimmer, Zulassigkeit und Grenzen schiedsgerichterlicher Entscheidung von Kartellrechtsstreitigkeiten*, Baden Baden (1991)."

and legal certainty, the Arbitral Tribunal shall obviously take into account the manner in which these community provisions are interpreted and applied by community institutions, especially by the Commission and by the Court of Justice."

(. . . .)

II.   ARTICLE 85 EC TREATY

[13]   "According to Art. 85(1) EC Treaty, 'the following shall be prohibited as incompatible with the common market: all agreements between undertakings, decisions by associations of undertakings and concerted practices which may affect trade between Member States and which have as their object or effect the prevention, restriction or distortion of competition within the common market'. Any agreements in violation of Art. 85(1) shall be automatically void (Art. 85(2) EC Treaty). The prohibition of Art. 85(1) may be declared inapplicable under Art. 85(3), which applies to all agreements which contribute 'to improving the production or distribution of goods or to promoting technical or economic progress, while allowing consumers a fair share of the resulting benefit, and which does not: (a) impose on the undertakings concerned restrictions which are not indispensable to the attainment of these objectives; (b) afford such undertakings the possibility of eliminating competition in respect of a substantial part of the products in question'.

[14]   "The exemption of Art. 85(3) may apply to individual agreements on the basis of individual exemptions granted by the Commission, or to a *category* of agreements between undertakings, on the basis of a category exemption granted by a Regulation for the application of Art. 85(3). An agreement meeting the requirements and conditions in the Regulation granting exemption to that type of agreement is allowed with no need for a preliminary notification [to the Commission]. In the field of exclusive distributorships, Regulation 1983/83 grants automatic exemption to agreements meeting its requirements.

(. . . .)

[15]   "The Arbitral Tribunal considers that Art. 85 EC Treaty applies to all agreements between undertakings or to concerted practices which affect competition in the common market. In order to ascertain whether the Second Service Agreement is prohibited under Art. 85, the Arbitral Tribunal must examine whether it leads to a restriction of competition within the common market and, if so, whether it is not covered by an individual or collective exemption which would allow such restriction of competition in the case at issue.

[16]   "The first point to be examined when applying the general rule of Art. 85 EC Treaty, and of the Regulations concerning its application, is the definition of the market affected by the agreement between undertakings. In the present case,

the market affected by the agreement is neither the manufacturing of the (specific type of) plants concerned, nor the more limited field of the supply of spare parts for such plants. The market is specifically after-sales service (supply of spare parts being the predominant part thereof, see infra [18]) to certain plants manufactured in France by M-France/X under licence by the original manufacturer M. . . . This market is, therefore, very limited and may not be deemed to cover the general industrial branch to which the parties to the Second Service Agreement belong and in which they are normally competitors.

[17] "The constant jurisprudence of the Court of Justice, in particular its decision of 31 May 1979 (case no. 22/78, *Hugin*) and the decision of the Court of First Instance of 12 December 1991 (case no. T-30/89, *Hilti*), compels the Arbitral Tribunal to give such a restrictive interpretation of the market affected in the case at issue. In [*Hilti*], the Commission adopted the same restrictive attitude with its decision of 22 December 1987.

[18] "The Arbitral Tribunal is of the opinion that the parties are not competitors in the specific market concerned. The subject matter of the Second Service Agreement is after-sales service to certain plants. In this context, the main performance is the supply of spare parts, as has been proven to the Arbitral Tribunal. Only X could guarantee the supply of spare parts for the maintenance of the plants which had been installed either by X or by its predecessors in Belgium. X acquired an exclusive right through the licence agreement stipulated with the original manufacturer M, whose effects were maintained, as concerns after-sales service, by the cession contract. X/B-France is thus the holder of an exclusive position, with which M-Belgium (now M/A-Belgium) cannot compete, as the latter does not have the detailed drawings which are needed to carry out the repairs to the plants indicated in the Second Service Agreement. These drawings are indispensable to replace parts without stopping the plant. The fact that M-Belgium could not compete with X in the after-sales service to the plants installed in Belgium is indirectly confirmed by the statements of X/B-France . . . according to which M/A-Belgium could only become a competitor after it acquired Company Y and when it changed its objectives in this sector (on the merits of this statements see infra [under V]).

[19] "In conclusion, the Arbitral Tribunal does not find that the Second Service Agreement is an agreement between undertakings which are competitors on the specific market concerned.

[20] "The parties have discussed one aspect of the Second Service Agreement in particular, that is, the part of Clause 2, 'Special Cases', ... which explicitly provides for the installation of additional equipment and the reconditioning of the plants. In such special cases, M-Belgium 'shall examine' which supplier, either X or the original manufacturer M, 'can provide and carry out the solution more favourable to the customer'.

[21]   "The parties agree that as far as the reconditioning and the modernization of the plant are concerned, X and the original manufacturer M are potential competitors in the Belgian market. . . . However, according to M/A-Belgium, the Second Service Agreement does not affect competition in this field . . . as the reconditioning of the plants does not fall within the scope of the Agreement. . . .

[22]   "According to the Arbitral Tribunal, it does not ensue from the contractual provision at issue that M-Belgium's decisions apportioned the [Belgian] market for the reconditioning of these plants between the original manufacturer M and X. First, the Arbitral Tribunal does not accept M/A-Belgium's argument that reconditioning was not covered by the Second Service Agreement: reconditioning is explicitly mentioned in Clause 2. It is true, however, that Clause 2 does not provide for exclusivity and non-competition. M-Belgium's task in this matter is simply to 'examine' which party 'can' provide and carry out the solution more favourable to the customer. The parties are free to submit their offers to the customer, which in its turn is free to choose a supplier other than the supplier deemed ['more favourable'] by M-Belgium after its analysis (see letter of company X, rejecting M/A-Belgium's offer for the modernization of certain plants covered by the Second Service Agreement). The information which M-Belgium had to supply to both the original manufacturer M and to X allowed both parties to explore their own attitude towards the reconditioning and to decide accordingly.

[23]   "We may thus conclude that the Second Service Agreement does not restrict competition on the reconditioning and modernization of these plants. However, the Second Service Agreement 'though concluded between two non-competitors' provides for exclusive rights to after-sales service; this justifies an examination in the light of Art. 85(1) and (3), and in particular with respect to a possible category exemption under Regulation 1983/83."

III. REGULATION 1983/83

[24]   "On the issue whether the Second Service Agreement falls under the scope of Art. 85(1) EC Treaty, the parties disagree as to the application of EC Commission Regulation 1983/83 'concerning the application of Art. 85(3) EC Treaty to certain categories of exclusive distributorship agreements'. M/A-Belgium concludes on this point that the Second Service Agreement is an exclusive distributorship agreement which benefits from the category exemption provided for in Regulation 1983/83, and that the exception in Art. 3 of this Regulation does not apply. X/B-France reaches opposite conclusions on both points and again argues that the Second Service Agreement is invalid because it is

at odds with Art. 85(1). The Arbitral Tribunal shall examine these two points in proper order.

[25]   "The Second Service Agreement, which is called a *convention de représentation*, concerns in reality after-sales service to certain plants installed in Belgium. The Tribunal found that, under Clause 1 of the Agreement, service includes the supply of spare parts and maintenance. The Tribunal also established that the parties, which are competitors, have no exclusivity obligation on the reconditioning of the plants provided for in Clause 2 of the Agreement.

[26]   "Art. 1 of Regulation 1983/83 states that Art. 85(1) EC Treaty does not apply to agreements between undertakings, under which one of the parties undertakes to supply certain products only to the other party for resale in the whole or part of the common market.

[27]   "The first question which the Tribunal must examine in order to ascertain whether the Regulation applies to the Second Service Agreement is whether the Agreement is an exclusive distributorship agreement. The answer depends on the comparative evaluation of the weight of the maintenance to the plants and of the supply of spare parts in the context of the (performance under the) Second Service Agreement. We can understand Clause 1 of the Second Service Agreement, which defines the duties of the parties, only if we consider the parties' relationship in the field of after-sales service to this kind of plant in general and their relationship in the case at issue.

[28]   "The [EC] Regulation explicitly allows that an exclusive distributorship obligation may be accompanied by obligations concerning 'service to customers and guarantee' (see sixth Considering and Art. 2(3)(c)). In its communication concerning Regulation 1983/83, the Commission specified that this category exemption is not ruled out if the distributor supplies service to customers in relation with the resale of products; however, [the exemption is ruled out] if the price of this service is higher than the price of products. In the case at issue, the parties have agreed before the Arbitral Tribunal that the price of the products was noticeably higher than the price of assistance and maintenance. The Arbitral Tribunal concludes, therefore, that the Second Service Agreement falls within the scope of application of Regulation 1983/83.

[29]   "We must still examine whether the exemption which, according to the Regulation, is applicable in principle to the Second Service Agreement, is not ruled out in the present case under Art. 3 of the Regulation, which excludes that the exemption applies to agreements between competitors. The Tribunal already examined this issue [above] and concluded that the parties were not competitors in the market for spare parts for M's technology plants installed in Belgium. They were still potential competitors in the specific case of the reconditioning of plants. This latter aspect notwithstanding, the Arbitral Tribunal

found on this point that the Second Service Agreement did not impose exclusivity obligations in this matter [on the parties], as has also been shown in practice.

[30]   "The Arbitral Tribunal thus concludes that the Second Service Agreement falls within the scope of application of Regulation 1983/83 and that it benefits of the Regulation's category exemption."

IV.   ACQUISITION OF M-FRANCE BY X

[31]   "The parties have also discussed another aspect of the validity of the Second Service Agreement under community law, that is, the effect of the decision of the EC Commission, allowing the acquisition of M-France by X.

[32]   "The original manufacturer M sold all M-France shares to X by a cession contract. . . . This [cession] contract provides that X 'shall continue to have all the rights under the present licence agreement with respect to orders . . . received before the end of that year . . . so that it can complete the manufacturing process, deliver and provide maintenance on such orders, including accessories and spare parts'.

[33]   "The Arbitral Tribunal already mentioned . . . that X notified the cession contract to the Commission . . . and that the Commission, after an initial denial and certain amendments to the contract, authorized it in the version which contains the clause quoted above. The Arbitral Tribunal adds that the letter of the Commission explicitly approved the above-mentioned clause, explicitly referring to the licence agreement between the original manufacturer M and X, which 'remains in force for [for 15 years], when it will expire, having been terminated in advance in . . . (letter of the Commission)'.

[34]   "The Second Service Agreement between X and M-Belgium is only a consequence on the Belgian market of the cession contract. As the cession contract and its exclusivity provisions in favour of X were approved by the Commission, it appears to the Arbitral Tribunal that this approval extends to the Second Service Agreement, which only regulates X's exclusive rights in Belgium.

[35]   "It is clear to the Arbitral Tribunal that the original manufacturer M granted X the exclusive right to manufacture certain spare parts in France. . . . It is also evident that this exclusive right included, with the original manufacturer M's agreement, the supply of parts for the plants installed in Belgium, in application of the Second Service Agreement's predecessor, the [first] *convention de représentation* concluded between X and M-Belgium.

[36]   "The Tribunal concludes that the Second Service Agreement is valid under community law."

V.   ACQUISITION AND MERGER

[37]   "The Arbitral Tribunal shall now examine the impact of M/A-Belgium's acquisition of Company Y on the validity of the Second Service Agreement. Unlike M-Belgium, Company Y could manufacture plants of the same size as X, although, at that time, it could actually manufacture only smaller plants. . . . M/A-Belgium later changed the objectives of Company Y, so that it could manufacture the same large plants . . . and provide after-sales service to all types of plants. . . .

[38]   "The Arbitral Tribunal notes that at the time of its acquisition by M/A-Belgium, Company Y was a manufacturer of smaller plants and that consequently M/A-Belgium did not become a competitor of X on the Belgian market in the field of the supply of spare parts for the large plants referred to in the Second Service Agreement. It is only [two years later] that there could be competition in Belgium between M/A-Belgium and X/B-France. At that time, X/B-France had already terminated the Second Service Agreement. . . .

[39]   "Further, in the light of the definition of market at [16] above, we cannot consider that the parties became competitors because of the acquisition of Company Y. The Arbitral Tribunal concludes on this point that the acquisition of Company Y did not, as of [the time of the notification of the termination], make M/A-Belgium a competitor of X/B-France.

[40]   "The Arbitral Tribunal notes that X/B-France, in its termination letter, relied on the merger between the A and the M group, leading to the creation of the M/A group, as a ground for the termination of the Second Service Agreement. According to X/B-France . . . , this new entity is one of X's major competitors in [their wider field of activity] worldwide.

[41]   "M/A-Belgium first argued, in its reply to the termination letter, that the merger between A and M did not affect the Second Service Agreement and that X/B-France had continued to perform under the Agreement [for the two years prior to the termination letter]. . . . Differently, [in a later statement] M/A-Belgium maintained that the merger did not modify the situation between the parties as competitors, considering that X/B-France had an exclusive right to the supply of spare parts.

[42]   "The Arbitral Tribunal already decided on this matter, finding that X/B-France had an exclusive right for the supply of spare parts for the plants installed in Belgium. This implies that the merger between A and M could not make M/A-Belgium a competitor of X/B-France in the specific market concerned by the Second Service Agreement.

[43]   "The Arbitral Tribunal concludes that neither the A-M merger nor the acquisition of Company Y by M/A-Belgium affects the validity of the Second Service Agreement under community law."

VI. DECISION

[44] "By this partial award, the Arbitral Tribunal answers the preliminary questions of community law raised by the parties [as follows]: '(a) the Second Service Agreement falls within the scope of Art. 85(1) EC Treaty in that it grants a claimant [M/A-Belgium] the exclusive right to provide after-sales service in Belgium for the plants mentioned in the Agreement; Art. 85(1) does not apply to reconditioning, for which no exclusive right is provided in the Second Service Agreement; (b) the Second Service Agreement is an exclusive distributorship contract, to which [EC] Regulation 1983/83 applies; the limitation in Art. 3 of this Regulation does not apply as the parties are not competitors in the specific market covered by the Second Service Agreement; (c) the exemption which the Agreement enjoyed [under Regulation 1983/83] is not affected by the merger between A and M . . . nor by the acquisition of Company Y by M/A-Belgium.'"

Interim award in case no. 7645 of 1995

Parties:	Claimant: Supplier (Slovakia) Defendant: Buyer (Korea)
Place of arbitration:	Paris, France
Published in:	Excerpt in 11 ICC International Court of Arbitration Bulletin (2000, no. 2) pp. 34-46
Subject matters:	– applicability of CISG to contract – CFR contract – avoidance of contract – contractual obligation to deliver documents – delay in shipment – defects in Bill of Lading

Facts

Defendant contracted to purchase a quantity of goods from claimant. The goods were to be shipped to defendant within a specified time limit. The contract specified a latest date of shipping and a maximum age of 20 years for the shipping vessel. Claimant agreed to open a bank performance bond [L/C] payable in the event that shipping would be delayed for more than 15 days after the specified time limit. The contract and amending L/C indicated the documents to be submitted by the claimant, the most important document of which was a clean on board Bill of Lading [B/L].

Claimant's agents faxed defendant several documents requesting an extension for the latest date of shipping and a final expiration term. Defendant's bank issued an amendment fixing a new expiration date without setting an extension of the latest shipping date. By the time defendant's bank provided claimant with a second amendment extending the latest date of shipping, the extension date had passed.

Actual shipment took place five days following the latest date of shipping. Although claimant asserted that defendant was informed of the exact shipping date, no documentary evidence was provided to support this assertion. Several weeks after leaving port, the vessel collided with another vessel. Efforts to save the vessel were unsuccessful; there was no balance of profit after salvaged cargo was liquidated at forced sale.

Defendant sent claimant a communique stating that it was unable to accept the ship because the cargo was loaded after the latest date of shipping, the documents were not presented within the expiration date of the L/C and the B/L was undated. Furthermore, claimant had concealed the age of the vessel and the true shipping date giving defendant the right to avoid the contract. Claimant protested against the defendant's avoidance of the contract and insisted on payment of the purchase price.

Claimant initiated arbitration relying on the arbitration clause in the contract which provided for ICC arbitration. The contract provided that Austrian law was applicable to the dispute. Although disagreeing initially, parties later accepted the application of the United Nations Convention on Contracts for the International Sale of Goods (CISG).

Applying INCOTERMS 1990 as well as the CISG, the arbitral tribunal established that late shipment can cause two breaches of contractual obligations: no goods in conformity placed on board ship and no bill of lading. Claimant was under an obligation to deliver documents within the prescribed time limits to defendant and to give sufficient notice that the goods had been delivered on board the vessel (INCOTERMS CFR A 7). Defendant was also entitled to receive clearly dated documents. As these requirements had not been complied with, the tribunal found that defendant had validly avoided the contract, and thus claimant had no right to claim payment of the purchase price. Claimant was ordered to pay 96% of the costs of the arbitral proceedings and an indemnity for defendant's costs.

Excerpt

I. APPLICABLE LAW

1. *Does the CISG Prevail over the National Law Applicable to the Contract?*

[1] "The contract provided . . . that it was to be governed by Austrian law.

[2] "This choice of law made by the parties was not disputed by either of them. In view of the autonomy of the parties in selecting the law governing their relationship the clause is to be regarded as valid and binding upon them.

[3] "In the initial phase of the proceedings the parties advanced conflicting opinions though as to whether this reference to Austrian law would lead to the applicability of the United Nations Convention on Contracts for the International Sale of Goods of 11 April 1980, signed in Vienna [CISG], or

not. In the later phase of the proceedings the parties concurred that the CISG was indeed applicable to the extent provided in the Convention itself.

[4]   "Austria is amongst the countries having signed and ratified the CISG. No restricting declarations were made by Austria when ratifying the CISG, neither according to Art. 95 of the Convention, that it will not be bound by Art. 1(1)(b) of the CISG, nor according to Art. 92 that it will not be bound by Part II of the CISG or that it will not be bound by Part III of the CISG. In and for Austria the CISG is, therefore, applicable in its integrality.

[5]   "According to Art. 1(1)(b) the Convention applies to contracts of sale of goods between parties whose places of business are in different states when the rules of private international law lead to the application of the law of a Contracting State. This rule, which seems to have been controversial when the CISG was negotiated, which was the reason why the CISG provided for the possibility of the Contracting States, in Art. 95, to declare the non-applicability of the clause, has been accepted by Austria and has, thereby, become applicable under Austrian law.

[6]   "As it already has been seen, the choice of Austrian law by the parties as governing law of the contract is to be regarded as being valid and binding on them. By this reference to Austrian law the CISG became, based on the just discussed clause, applicable to the contractual relationship between the parties.

[7]   "The CISG is applicable to contracts of sale of goods in general, with certain exceptions according to Art. 2 of the CISG. None of these exceptions do apply in the present case, so that the CISG is applicable also in view of the nature of goods covered by the contract.

[8]   "According Art. 4 of the CISG, it governs only the formation of the contract and the rights and obligations of the seller and the buyer arising from such contract. The CISG is not concerned with the validity of the contract or of any of its provisions or of any usage. In the present case, the valid conclusion of the contract was not disputed. The issues relate to the interpretation of the contract, the obligations under the contract and the remedies available to the parties in case of breach of contract, all being topics covered by the CISG, especially in its Part III, and also in its Part I.

[9]   "Depending on the doctrine followed in the relevant country relating to the nature and effect of public international law the provisions of an international treaty either are regarded as superior to the national law or are regarded as being integrated into national law. Irrespectively of the basic approach relating to this question it seems clear that the provisions of the CISG prevail over the provisions of the otherwise applicable national law. Art. 7 of the CISG expressly provides that questions concerning matters governed by the CISG which are not expressly settled in it are to be settled in conformity with the general principles on which it is based or, in the absence

of such principles, in conformity with the law applicable by virtue of the rules of private international law. Therefore, the issues in these proceedings have to be answered first based on express provisions of the CISG, second based on the general principles which may be deduced from the CISG, third by the provisions of Austrian law and only last and fourth based on general customs and usages of the trade."

2. Application of INCOTERMS 1990 to the Contract

[10]   "In its Art. 9, the CISG specifically provides that the parties are bound by any usage to which they have agreed. In fact, if the parties refer specifically to any usage, the relevant rules become part of their contract by reference (or integration).

[11]   "In the contract, the parties have, in the document schedule clause, under the heading 'price' referred to 'CNF FO . . . Korea (INCOTERMS 1990)'.

[12]   "The 'INCOTERMS' 1990 edition published by the International Chamber of Commerce in Paris, which became effective as of 1 July 1990, do not provide for a clause 'CNF'. The parties however concurred that the clause to which they intended to refer was the clause 'CFR' – 'Cost and Freight (. . . named port of destination)'.[1]

[13]   "It would, indeed, seem that the parties, although referring to the INCOTERMS 1990, had still in mind the designation used for such clause in the prior INCOTERMS, namely 'C+F' or 'C and F', in extended terms 'cost and freight'. The middle letter 'N' used in the clause in the contract would seem to have stood for the word 'and'. The arbitral tribunal, in conformity with the opinions expressed by the parties, holds that the reference in the contract was indeed a reference to the clause 'cost and freight' – CFR – of the INCOTERMS 1990.

[14]   "The letters 'FO' which were mentioned beside the letters CNF stood, in the opinion of the arbitral tribunal, for the words 'free out' which are used to

---

1. Cost and Freight CFR according to the ICC INCOTERMS 1990 is defined as:

"'Cost and Freight' means that the seller must pay the costs and freight necessary to bring the goods to the named port of destination but the risk of loss of or damage to the goods, as well as any additional costs due to events occurring after the time the goods have been delivered on board the vessel is transferred from the seller to the buyer when the goods pass the ship's rail in the port of shipment.

The CFR term requires the seller to clear the goods for export.

This term can only be used for sea and inland waterway transport. When the ship's rail serves no practical purpose, such as in the case of roll-on/roll-off or container traffic, the CPT term is more appropriate to use."

qualify the term 'freight' under C.I.F. and C.F.R. contracts, and which mean that the expenses connected with discharging the goods from the vessel are included in the 'freight'.

[15]   ". . . . In concurrence with the opinion of the parties the arbitral tribunal holds that the reference to Incoterm clauses in one clause of the contract with no specification or restriction as to its bearing could be understood in good faith by both parties and had in fact to be understood to be a general reference, thus integrating the CFR clauses as a whole into the contract. The wording of the contract has therefore to be seen in conjunction with the provisions of the CFR clauses of the INCOTERMS 1990, which are held to have been integrated in their entirety into the contract.

(. . . .)

[16]   "According to Art. 8 of the CISG statements made by a party are to be interpreted according to its intent where the other party knew or could not have been unaware what the intent was. This rule is basically equivalent to the general principle of law on contracts to the effect that manifestations of a party of its contractual intent have to be understood and interpreted as a counterparty in good faith had to understand them.

[17]   "When parties have concluded a contract established by an extended wording, the agreement of the parties has to be analysed in first instance by interpreting the wording of the contract itself. According to Art. 8(3) of the CISG usages of the trade constitute guidelines only to establish what a reasonable person had to understand in view of the wording of the contract.

[18]   "As also seen already in [paras. [10]-[15]] above, the contract made specific reference, in its document schedule clause, to the INCOTERMS 1990, whereby the reference is to be understood to refer to the clauses 'CFR' (cost and freight . . . named port of destination), and whereby further the reference was to be understood as a general reference to such clauses and not as a reference for defining the price only (see above [paras. [10]-[15]]). According to Art. 9(1) of the CISG the parties are bound by any usage to which they have agreed. The contractual agreement between the parties has therefore to be understood as it results from their written contract in conjunction with the CFR clauses of the INCOTERMS 1990.

[19]   "Where the provisions of the contract and of the Incoterm clauses do not provide specific answers, the Rules of the CISG and, in a subordinated way, rules of its underlying principles and, even in a more subordinated way, the rules of Austrian law are determining for defining the mutual obligations of the parties based on their contract.

[20]   "According to INCOTERMS clause CFR A 4 the seller must deliver the goods on board the vessel at the port of shipment on the date or within the period stipulated, and according to INCOTERMS clauses CFR A 8 the seller

has, unless otherwise agreed, to provide the buyer without delay with the usual transport document for the agreed port of destination. The INCOTERMS CFR clauses (as the CIF clauses) do actually provide for a dual obligation of the seller, first, the seller has to actually furnish the goods and arrange for their transport (which is to lead to the actual physical delivery of the goods to the purchaser or his successor), and, second, the seller has to deliver to the purchaser the relevant transport documents which enable the purchaser to actually dispose of the goods even while being transported.

[21]   "In an English case (*Kwei Tek Chao v. British Traders and Shippers Ltd.*, 1954, 2 Q.B. 459 at p. 480, as reported in *Sasson's CIF and F.O.B. Contracts*, 3rd ed. (1984) p. 28) the nature of the CIF contract was summarized as follows:

> 'A c.i.f. contract puts a number of obligations upon the seller, some of which are in relation to the goods and some of which are in relation to the documents. So far as the goods are concerned, he must put on board at the port of shipment goods in conformity with the contract description, but he must also send forward documents, and those documents must comply with the contract. If he commits a breach the breaches may in one sense overlap, in that they flow from the same act. If there is a late shipment . . . the seller has not put on board goods which conform to the contract description. . . . He has also made it impossible to send forward a bill of lading which . . . conforms. . . . Thus the same act can cause two breaches of two independent obligations.'

[22]   "Even though in the present case the contract was not a CIF but rather a CFR contract, and although the applicable law is not the English law but rather the CISG respectively Austrian law, the opinion in the mentioned English case may be taken as an expression of an internationally recognized understanding of the CIF clause. The CIF and the CFR clause being of the same nature under the aspect here under review, what has been said relating to the CIF clause is valid also with regard to the CFR clause."

II.   THE DOCUMENTARY NATURE OF THE TRANSACTION

[23]   "It is widely admitted in published judgements and in the doctrine that the CIF – or CFR – contracts are of a documentary nature (see for others *Sasson's CIF and F.O.B. Contracts*, 3rd ed. (1984) p. 27 et seq.). For example, in an old English case of 1914 reported in *Sasson's* (p. 27) the judge declared:

> 'I am strongly of the opinion that the key to many of the difficulties arising in c.i.f. contracts is to keep firmly in mind the cardinal distinction that a c.i.f.

sale is not a sale of goods, but a sale of documents relating to goods. It is not a contract that goods shall arrive, but a contract to ship goods complying with the contract of sale, to obtain, unless the contract otherwise provides, the ordinary contract of carriage to the place of destination, and the ordinary contract of insurance of the goods on that voyage, and to tender these documents against payment of the contract price.'

[24]   "*Sasson*, also with reference to a precedent, describes the contract as a contract for the sale of goods to be performed by the delivery of documents, and emphasizes that the seller must tender documents and cannot claim performance of a CIF contract by tendering, in lieu thereof, the goods themselves at the port of destination unless of course the buyer waives compliance with the terms of the agreement (*Sasson's* p. 28). The documentary nature of CIF contracts is also emphasized by Schmitthoff, Clive M., *Schmitthoff's Export Trade*, 8th ed. (London 1986) p. 29/30. Claimant, in concurrence with the prevailing opinion, expressly acknowledged the documentary nature of the transaction.

[25]   "There can be no doubt that, in accordance with INCOTERMS clauses CFR A 8, claimant had to deliver to defendant a clean on board bill of lading (B/L), and that this constituted – besides the actual shipping of the goods – a main obligation of claimant.

[26]   "It remains to be seen what was the significance of the schedule of documents to be submitted by seller under the L/C as provided in the document schedule clause of the contract. This contractual clause provided that payment should occur by an irrevocable at sight letter of credit to be opened in favour of seller under which the seller would have to submit and deliver a specified number of documents.

[27]   " . . . [C]laimant sustains that this clause of the contract related only to the means and ways of payment of the purchase price and did not define obligations of the seller to actually submit such documents. According to claimant's view he could have chosen not to make use of or rely on the L/C opened by defendant at all and could, instead, have chosen to send the documents representing the goods and giving the power of defendant to dispose of the goods also directly, without going through the bank.

[28]   "It is true that the heading of the L/C clause of the contract reads 'payment' and that the L/C clause deals with the L/C to be opened by the purchaser and the documents to be submitted under the L/C exclusively. It is also true that parties to a contract can, in their contract, provide for alternative options for the seller to either make use of a L/C to be opened by the purchaser by presenting all the documents provided under the L/C or to furnish the relevant documents required by the contract (which do not necessarily need to be identical with those required under the L/C directly, without going through the banks, and

without making use of the L/C (Cf. e.g. Eisemann, Frédéric, and Eberth, Rolf, *Das Dokumenten-Akkreditiv im Internationalen Handelsverkehr*, 2nd ed. (Heidelberg 1979) p. 144, with further references). If the contract provides for such alternative possibilities the seller simply waives, when he chooses to submit the documents directly, the advantages it would have had under the procedure with the L/C. By delivering the relevant documents directly to the buyer, the seller then acquires a simple claim against the buyer for the purchase price, not guaranteed by any bank, which becomes usually due upon delivery of the relevant contractual documents."

1. Contractual Obligation to Submit Documents According to INCOTERMS CFR Clauses

[29] "However, when parties to an international sales contract do relate to the INCOTERMS clauses CFR they, in principle, accept conceptually the documentary nature of the transaction, as has been seen already. If parties in such a transaction define specified documents to be presented under a L/C in addition to the B/L to be delivered according to INCOTERMS clauses CFR A 8,[2] this constitutes a strong element in support of their intention to the effect that it becomes also a *contractual obligation* of the seller to submit not only the transport document provided in INCOTERMS clauses CFR A 8 but also the further documents to be presented under the L/C as specified in the contract.

[30] "In other words, the parties then by agreement add to the main document to be submitted under INCOTERMS clauses CFR A 8 additional documents considered to be relevant for the purpose of giving to the purchaser the assurance

---

2. INCOTERMS CFR A 8 reads:

"*Proof of delivery, transport document or equivalent electronic message*
The seller must: unless otherwise agreed at his own expense provide the buyer without delay with the usual transport document for the agreed port of destination.

This document (for example, a negotiable bill of lading, a non-negotiable sea waybill or an inland waterway document) must cover the contract goods, be dated within the period agreed for shipment, enable the buyer to claim the goods from the carrier at destination and, unless otherwise agreed, enable the buyer to sell the goods in transit by the transfer of the document to a subsequent buyer (the negotiable bill of lading) or by notification to the carrier.

When such a transport document is issued in several originals, a full set of originals must be presented to the buyer. If the transport document contains a reference to a charter party, the seller must also provide a copy of this latter document.

Where the seller and the buyer have agreed to communicate electronically, the document referred to in the preceding paragraphs may be replaced by an equivalent electronic data interchange (EDI) message."

that he is receiving goods in compliance with the contractual agreement and suitable for the purchaser to dispose of the goods effectively based on and with the documents being delivered to him. Especially if the goods which are object of the sale are goods being frequently traded on the international markets, a seller must be aware, when entering into the contract, that the purchaser may possibly not be interested so much in actually receiving and using the goods purchased for its own purposes but might rather be interested to trade them on. Since the documents become extremely relevant in such circumstance it would appear that the specification of documents to be submitted under an L/C to obtain payment usually is meant to also constitute a contractual obligation of the seller to deliver the documents as specified, and *all* such documents, to the purchaser.

[31] "The arbitral tribunal is of the opinion that there is a presumption to such effect in international sales transactions and that a contractual agreement to the contrary, namely to the effect that the documents specified need to be submitted only if the seller chooses to make use of the L/C, would have to be set out *specifically* in the contract. If in a written contract with extended wording no distinction is being made between the documents to be submitted under the L/C provided for in the contract, it must therefore be taken that the documents mentioned under the L/C clause are meant to have to be submitted to the purchaser in any event, irrespective of whether the seller wants to take advantage of the L/C or not.

[32] "The arbitral tribunal holds that this is how the contract between the parties had to be understood irrespectively of the fact that the documents were mentioned in a clause with the heading 'Payment' only and with relation to the L/C only. In other words, the seller had the contractual obligation to deliver timely to the purchaser all the documents as specified in the L/C clause of the contract. (Incidentally, this does not necessarily mean that the seller would also have been under an obligation to actually make use of the L/C for obtaining payment. The seller might, depending on the understanding between the parties, still have been free to choose either to make use of the L/C or to deliver directly to the purchaser the relevant documents, not passing through the banks and not presenting them under the L/C. But the seller would, if he had chosen not to make use of the L/C, nevertheless have had to submit all the documents, as they have been specified for the L/C, to the purchaser.)"

(. . . .)

2. *Did Defendant Waive Contractual Right to Receive Documents?*

[33] "It is claimant's case that defendant, by its behaviour and by its communications, waived the contractual right to receive the documents and,

accordingly, waived compliance with the terms of the agreement, and agreed to accept the physical delivery of the goods purchased at the port of destination instead of insisting on receiving the documents. Claimant goes on sustaining that he discharged his obligation to deliver the goods (in the right quantity and of the contractual quality) by shipping the goods on the [vessel name]. ... Without specifying much on what facts such waiver by defendant has to be assumed, claimant seems to base its assertion on the fact that contracts occurred between the parties in December and over the Christmas days and that on such occasion defendant allegedly had stated, shortly before the end of the first week in January that it would not be able to accept the cargo if the vessel would not leave Greece within four days. At most, such a statement, if it had been actually made and communicated officially, might have constituted a waiver by defendant to draw the legal consequences from a possible delay of shipment, provided that the vessel would actually leave Piraeus within four days. Such statement could even be interpreted, in a certain way, as the fixing of a very last additional period of time for performance by the purchaser to the seller.

[34] "Claimant wants also to interpret the telefax of defendant of the end of January as a waiver by defendant to receive the documents, but the arbitral tribunal cannot see anything in this document which would suggest that defendant would have been prepared to accept the cargo being on the ship without regard to the documents, or as an admittance to the effect that such agreement had occurred before. To the contrary, para. 2 of this fax clearly confirms the intention to cancel the contract, announcing, as a consequence, the return of the shipping documents. Even if talks did take place about the conditions under which defendant would be prepared to accept the cargo despite of the suspicion about a delay in shipment and the criticized defects in the documents, this cannot be seen to have implied an agreement of defendant to change the structure of the transaction."

3. *Did Claimant's Non-abidance of Time Limit to Deliver Documents Constitute a Breach of Contract?*

[35] "The contract dealt with the time frame, within which the shipment had to take place. ... [Two] clauses specified the time requirements with regard to the shipment only and did not deal specifically with time requirements for delivering the documents. The contractual clauses use the terms 'loading' and 'shipment'. It was explained by the parties and not contested that according to the usage of the trade the expression 'loading' stands for the activity of placing the goods in the harbour on the pier in a way suitable and ready for being carried on the ship by appropriate means, while the term 'shipping' or 'shipment' stands

for the actual stowing of the goods in the appropriate manner on and in the vessel. The time limit agreed for the 'shipment' therefore refers to the time when the stowing of the goods on and in the vessel has been completed in an appropriate manner for sailing. The periods defined in clause V of the contract therefore referred to the time when the sold goods had actually to be stowed on respectively in the vessel in the sailing port. This has not been challenged by claimant.

[36] "Art. 34 of the CISG provides that in cases in which the seller is bound to hand over documents relating to the goods, he must hand them over at the time and place and in the form required by the contract. If the seller has handed over the documents before that time, he may, up to that time, cure any lack of conformity in the documents, if the exercise of this right does not cause the buyer unreasonable inconvenience or unreasonable expense.

[37] "INCOTERMS clauses CFR A 8 specify that the transport document has to be provided 'without delay'. Since the contract did not specifically determine a time limit for delivering the documents, the contract has to be understood in the manner that the documents had to be handed over respectively delivered without delay, or within reasonable time after the time limit determined for the shipment. An indication of what might have to be understood as reasonable time in the trade could be seen in Art. 47 of the old Uniform Customs and Practise for Documentary Credits (UCP) (1983 revision in force as from 1 October 1984, which were those still applicable at the time of the conclusion of the contract). This article provides that banks should refuse documents presented to them later than 21 days after the date of issuance of the transport document.

[38] "It is left open for the time being what legal implications the determining of the expiry date of the L/C in the L/C itself might have had with regard to the *contractual* time limit available for the seller to deliver the documents. It should be remembered that the expiry date of the original L/C (before its amendment) was . . . the twentieth day after the latest date allowed for shipment.

[39] "The contract provided that shipment had to take place, in case of loading in the Black Sea, which was the case, during [that month]. The latest date allowed for shipment therefore was [the last allowed date of shipment]. The performance bond clause of the contract, however, contained provisions relating to a performance bond which was to become payable in the event that the shipment was to be delayed more than 15 days after the latest shipment time allowed in the contract.

[40] "Defendant sustains that every sale under the INCOTERMS clauses CFR is to be regarded as a 'fixed term' contract within the meaning of the term as it is used in the legal terminology in many countries, to the effect that the time limit defined in the contract is of essence and that the non-abidance

by this time limit constitutes 'ipso facto' a fundamental breach of contract within the meaning of Art. 49(1)(a) of the CISG.[3] Defendant submits some opinions of judiciaries and learned authors in support of this theory. However, the principle can, in this generalized form, not be recognized. The INCOTERMS clauses CFR do not provide anything to this effect. It is true that INCOTERMS clauses CFR A 4 provide that the delivery of the goods on board the vessel at the port of shipment has to be made by the seller on the date or within the period stipulated. The INCOTERMS clauses CFR do not, however, specify that the abidance within the time limit is an obligation of especially essential importance or that the non-abidance by the time limit gives to the purchaser unconditionally the right to avoid or terminate the contract or that the contract automatically becomes void in any case where the time limit for shipment is not respected.

[41]   "Even though there might exist a usage of the trade to the effect that *in the absence of provisions to the contrary* in the relevant contract, a CFR contract has to be understood as a fixed term contract, – which can be left open –, such usage of the trade would certainly not prevent the parties from providing to the contrary in their specific contractual agreement. When the parties have entered into an agreement in writing (within a broad sense of the word) also the question at stake here has to be determined primarily based on the wording of the agreement and the manner in which such wording had to be understood in good faith by both parties. With a view to this, the bearing of the time frame clauses of the contract has to be analysed, and the time frame determined in [the first time

---

3. Art. 49 of the CISG reads:

"(1) The buyer may declare the contract avoided:
(a) if the failure by the seller to perform any of his obligations under the contract or this Convention amounts to a fundamental breach of contract; or
(b) in case of non-delivery, if the seller does not deliver the goods within the additional period of time fixed by the buyer in accordance with paragraph (1) of Art. 47 or declares that he will not deliver within the period so fixed.
(2) However, in cases where the seller has delivered the goods, the buyer loses the right to declare the contract avoided unless he does so:
(a) in respect of late delivery, within a reasonable time after he has become aware that delivery has been made;
(b) in respect of any breach other than late delivery, within a reasonable time:
(i) after he knew or ought to have known of the breach;
(ii) after the expiration of any additional period of time fixed by the buyer in accordance with paragraph (1) of Art. 47, or after the seller has declared that he will not perform his obligations within such an additional period; or
(iii) after the expiration of any additional period of time indicated by the seller in accordance with paragraph (2) of Art. 48, or after the buyer has declared that he will not accept performances."

frame clause] can certainly not be looked at without regard to the provisions of the L/C clause which are significant for determining the issue.

[42] "The performance bond clause of the contract determined an obligation of the seller to provide for a performance bond by its bank. It is easily understandable from the wording of the contract that this performance bond was to give to the purchaser the right to be paid a penalty in case of a delay of shipment by the seller. The amount of the performance bond was, however, to become payable only in the event that the shipment would be delayed more than 15 days after the latest shipment time allowed in the contract. This is a clear indication, in the opinion of the arbitral tribunal, that the last date of shipment allowed in the [first time frame] clause in the contract was not to be understood as a fixed term, the non-abidance by which would have constituted a fundamental breach of contract within Art. 49(1)(a) of the CISG. To the contrary, the provision indicates that the purchaser was prepared to tolerate a delay up to 15 days.

[43] "Further, the provision does not say in any way that in the case the delay of shipment would have lasted more than 15 days, the contract was to become void automatically or the purchaser had the right to avoid the contract immediately. If something to such effect had been intended by the parties it is probable that they would have specified it in view of the fact that the question of a possible delay of shipment had obviously been the subject of considerations when the contract was negotiated.

[44] "This leads to the conclusion that the non-abidance by the last shipment date allowed by the contract was not to be considered as a fundamental breach of contract according to the prior mentioned provision of the CISG and that, accordingly, the purchaser would, as a consequence of a delay of shipment, not have been authorized to declare the contract avoided according to Art. 47 in conjunction with Art. 49(1)(b) of the CISG were applicable with regard to the question of delay of shipment."

III. LEGAL EFFECTS OF DELAY OF SHIPMENT

[45] "In view of the double or twofold obligation of the seller, on the one hand to ship the goods timely, on the other hand to deliver the documents without delay, a delay in performance can occur either with regard to the shipping of the goods or with regard to the delivery of the documents. As to the time of shipment, and elaborating on what has just been said, the wording of the contract and the facts around the issuance and the extension of the L/C suggests the following analysis of the situation as to the time of the shipment:

[46] "As seen, the contract provides as the last allowed date of shipment [the last allowed date of shipment]. However, the purchaser had conceded right from the outset in the contract to tolerate a delay of 15 days, i.e. through [the tolerated

delay date]. This extended time limit has to be regarded as pre-agreed tolerance. Consequently, the shipment would not have been late if it had occurred latest on [the tolerated delay date]. Based on the contract, and without regard to any extension which might have been agreed, the seller would have been in default as from [the day following the tolerated delay date] as a consequence of the delay of shipment. Had the purchaser known about the delay he would have had the possibility to proceed in accordance with Art. 47 of the CISG[4] fixing an additional period of time of reasonable length to the seller for providing for the shipment.

(. . . .)

[47] "In other words, claimant would have had a period of twenty days (one day less than the longest period allowed of twenty-one days according to Art. 47 of the old UCP) for presenting the documents to its bank, as the L/C provided the expiry date with reference to this bank.

[48] "When [claimant's agent], requested, on [the last allowed date of shipment], defendant to extend the terms of the L/C by providing [the tolerated delay date] as new latest allowed date for shipment and the end of October as new date for expiry of the L/C, this was in concurrence with the provisions of the contract. In fact, seller benefitted of a tolerance period until [the tolerated delay date] for shipping. By the extension of the L/C as requested by the seller, the purchaser would simply have acknowledged the fact of the existing tolerance period, and such extension would not have pre-supposed an amendment of the contract. The seller would have had the time until [specific date two weeks later] to present the documents to its bank, now showing a date of shipment not subsequent to [the tolerated delay date]. Seller would have had, in other words, two weeks as from the shipment to present the documents to its bank.

[49] "In other words, when claimant was requesting the extension of the last date allowed for shipping in the L/C, it did that within the frame of the contract, and no amendment to the contract was necessary, and defendant did, by

---

4. Art. 47 of the CISG reads:

"(1) The buyer may fix an additional period of time of reasonable length of performance by the seller of his obligations.

(2) Unless the buyer has received notice from the seller that he will not perform within the period so fixed, the buyer may not, during that period, resort to any remedy for breach of contract. However, the buyer is not deprived thereby of any right he may have to claim damages for delay in performance."

providing for the extension, not concede anything it was not obliged to anyway."

1. Extension of the Contractual Tolerance Period

[50]   "Claimant sustains that at the time when the parties were in contact relating to the extension of the relevant dates in the L/C and agreement was reached to the effect to amend the contract by shifting the last date allowed for shipping from. . . . , with the effect that the period of tolerance of 15 days provided in the performance bond clause of the contract was also automatically extended to [specific date]. Defendant contests this view and sustains that at the time it was agreed to extend the relevant date in the L/C, but that this never meant to extend also the contractual tolerance period for shipping.
[51]   "The factual allegations of both parties relating to their contracts at that time are rather vague.
[52]   "In the documents submitted nothing can be found in support of the position of claimant to the effect that the contractual dates would have been extended by an amendment of the contract. To the contrary, the fax messages of [claimant's agent], to defendant, . . . clearly referred to the extension of the dates in the L/C and did not mention in any way whatsoever a change of the relevant dates by amendment of the *contract*. Also in view of what has been said above, that the extension of the relevant dates in the L/C was requested by claimant within the frame of the contract, strongly supports the assumption that at that time claimant thought of the L/C and of the L/C only, because there was no need to amend the contract. The arbitral tribunal cannot follow the theory of claimant to the effect that there would have been, at the time, an agreement of the parties to extend not only the dates in the L/C but rather the relevant dates in the contract."
(. . . .)

2. Claimant's Default

[53]   "When, therefore, claimant did not the ship the goods by [the tolerated delay date], but later only, it was actually in default. At that time, defendant, had it known about the delay, could have fixed to the seller an additional period of time of reasonable length for providing for the shipping and for handing over the to the purchaser the relevant documents within the meaning of Art. 47(1) of the CISG.
[54]   "However, defendant did not know about the delay of shipment until much later."
(. . . .)

3. *Obligation of Claimant to Give Sufficient Notice:*
   INCOTERMS CFR A 7

[55]   "INCOTERMS clauses CFR A 7[5] provides specifically for the obligation of the seller to give the buyer sufficient notice that the goods have been delivered on board the vessel. It was, consequently, a contractual obligation of the seller to give to the purchaser notice of actual shipment, in the meaning of completion of the stowing of the goods on the vessel in a way enabling the vessel to sail. Claimant has not alleged to have ever given such notice to defendant and defendant was, actually, never advised on the real and actual date of shipment. Defendant has alleged that it repeatedly inquired about the situation but never received a clear and specific answer. It cannot be excluded that claimant did, in fact, purposedly not give the notice which it contractually was bound to give in the fear that the disclosure of the actual shipping date, having occurred after [the tolerated delay date] only, might be detrimental to its legal position.

[56]   "Nevertheless the delay of shipment alone and by itself would not have given the right, in the opinion of the arbitral tribunal, to defendant to declare the contract avoided, based on the following considerations.

[57]   "Had defendant known on [the day following the tolerated delay date] that shipment did not take place by [the tolerated delay date] defendant could have fixed to claimant the additional period of time for shipment, in accordance with Art. 47(1) of the CISG, as seen above. . . . Such period of time, which had to be of reasonable length, could certainly not have been less than four days. In other words, the end of the additional period could not have been before [four days following the tolerated delay date], the day on which shipment actually occurred. As a result, the seller has in fact shipped the goods within the additional period which could hypothetically have been fixed to it. This excludes the possibility to declare the contract avoided, since Art. 49(1)(b) gives the right to avoid the contract only if the performance did not take place within the additional period."

---

5. INCOTERMS CFR A 7 reads:

"*Notice to the buyer*
        The seller must: Give the buyer sufficient notice that the goods have been delivered on board the vessel as well as any other notice required in order to allow the buyer to take measures which are normally necessary to enable him to take the goods."

IV.   DO DISCREPANCIES IN DOCUMENTS SUBMITTED BY CLAIMANT CONSTITUTE BREACH OF CONTRACT?

[58]   "As considered above, the documents to be submitted by claimant were those listed in the L/C clause of the contract, as amended by the L/C, which required two more documents.

[59]   "Among the documents to be provided, the most important and crucial one was obviously the clean on board Bill of Lading, which was due to be delivered also irrespectively of the L/C clause of the contract and directly based on INCOTERMS clauses CFR A 8.

[60]   "It has to be seen whether claimant has delivered the documents in accordance with the contract, and has thereby abided by its contractual obligations, as it sustains, or not, as is sustained by defendant.

[61]   ". . . . [T]he question here is only whether the documents fulfilled the requirements of the *contract*. Nevertheless, one may look at the Uniform Customs and Practise for Documentary Credits as an auxiliary guidance as to what requirements certain documents have to fulfil according to the usages of the international trade. Obviously, the relevant UCP would be those in force at the time, which were the old UCP, 1983 revision in force as from 1 October 1984 (the new UCP, 1993 revision, having become effective on 1 January 1994 only).

[62]   "The B/L submitted by claimant was, as a matter of principle, a clean on board Bill of Lading, as was required by the contract, which has not been contested by defendant.

[63]   "Defendant has, however, criticized various alleged defects of the B/L."

[64]   The most serious defects in the B/L alleged by claimant were: a discrepancy in the contract number on the B/L and the contract number marked on the commercial invoice; an incomplete description of goods in the B/L; the B/L contained no date of issue."

1.   Requirement of Clearly Dated Documents: INCOTERMS CFR A 8

[65]   "INCOTERMS clause CFR A 8 specifically and clearly requires that the transport documents must be dated within the period agreed for shipment.

[66]   "The contract having referred to the INCOTERMS clauses CFR, it was, consequently, a contractual obligation of claimant to provide the purchaser with a dated bill of lading, or more specifically with a bill of lading evidencing the date of issue.

[67]   "This date is in fact a relevant information in so far as the B/L is, according to correct procedures, always issued only when the activity of physical stowing of the goods on the vessel is completed and the goods are shipped. The date of issue is therefore evidence for the fact that the shipment of the

goods has taken place on or before the date of issue. Since the date of shipment is in most cases an important element under international sales contracts providing for shipment of the goods by sea it is obvious that the date of issue on the B/L is a highly important element.

[68]   "The date of issue of a B/L appears also to be relevant in practice for the further trading of goods. As a matter of fact, it is often the case that a purchaser and beneficiary of a bill of lading trades on the goods, possibly even before the goods have been shipped to him. In such further trades, the date of shipment very often is again an important element of the contract. It is therefore of great relevance for the purchaser to be able to deliver to its further purchaser a bill of lading showing the date of issue, because only in such a way is he able to clearly fulfil his contractual obligations.

[69]   "The importance and essential nature of the dating of the B/L under the INCOTERMS is also stressed in two publications on INCOTERMS, (i) Eisemann, Frédéric and Melis, Werner, *INCOTERMS Ausgabe 1980, Kommentar* (Vienna) p. 149, and, (ii) Eisemann, Frédéric and Ramberg, Jan, *Die INCOTERMS Heute und Morgen*, 2nd ed. (Vienna 1980) p. 176 and esp. p. 178.

[70]   "The CISG does, understandably, not address the question of the importance of the date of a B/L. But the Austrian law, in the Austrian *Handelsgesetzbuch* – HGB –, which was enacted by taking over the German *Handelsgesetzbuch*, and is therefore identical with the latter, does deal with the requirement of dating of a B/L. In the fourth book on maritime trade (*Viertes Buch: Seehandel*, Sect. 476 et seq.), Sect. 643 HGB specifies in its subsect. 10 the indication of the place and the day of issuance as one of the legal elements of a B/L (*Konossement*). The learned authors in their commentaries on the HGB do mention that the date is not an essential requirement for the validity of the B/L as a negotiable instrument, but nevertheless stress the importance of the date especially with a view to the abidance by contractual obligations.[6]

[71]   "The arbitral tribunal holds, that defendant was entitled under the contract to receive a B/L showing the date of issue and with an unambiguous wording fully concurring with the contract and that the B/L as presented and delivered by claimant did not fulfil these requirements.

[72]   "Since the Bill of Lading was the most essential document to be furnished by the seller, the existence of non purely trivial defects in such document was of

---

6. "See, Schlegelberger, Franz, *Seehandelsrecht* (Berlin/Frankfurt 1959) p. 409 et seq.; Schaps, Georg and Abraham, Hans Bürgen, *Das Seerecht in der Bundesrepublik Deutschland*, 4th ed. (Berlin/ New York 1978) p. 762 et seq.; Prüssmann, Heinz and Rabe, Dieter, *Seehandelsrecht*, 2nd ed. (Munich 1983) p. 497 et seq."

such importance that the tender of the B/L as it was, is to be regarded as a lack of performance by claimant.

(. . . .)

[73]   "The importance and relevance of all the asserted discrepancies respectively defects in the documents need not be further analyzed in view of the fact that the defects in the bill of lading alone did render the set of documents unsuitable as means of performance by claimant.

[74]   "According to Art. 34 of the CISG[7] the seller could have cured these defects before the end of the relevant time period. However, claimant did not submit any new bill of lading later on."

V.   AVOIDANCE OF CONTRACT

(. . . .)

[75]   "Defendant sustains that the declaration of avoidance of the contract was justified, timely and effective, while claimant sustains that it was unjustified and without legal effect. Claimant mainly argues that defendant could not declare the avoidance of the contract before having fixed to claimant an additional term for performance according to Art. 47(1) of the CISG, that further the declaration of defendant was contradictory with subsequent communications of defendant and that, thirdly, the declaration of defendant was too late and therefore ineffective according to Art. 49(2) of the CISG.

[76]   "Defendant alleged that claimant, by its behaviour, committed a fundamental breach of the contract. So defendant sustains that claimant has purposely caused the shipping documents to be marked with a wrong date, that by this and by not advising defendant about the true shipping date it purposely intended to deceive defendant, that by such behaviour it prevented defendant to call timely the performance bond, that it selected and used a vessel which was older than what the contract had allowed, that the vessel selected and used was not sea worthy and in addition, that the ship was too small to carry the contractual quantity of the goods and was overloaded.

(. . . .)

---

7. Art. 34 of the CISG reads:

"If the seller is bound to hand over documents relating to the goods, he must hand them over at the time and place and in the form required by the contract. If the seller has handed over documents before that time, he may, up to that time, cure any lack of conformity in the documents, if the exercise of this right does not cause the buyer unreasonable inconvenience or unreasonable expense. However, the buyer retains any right to claim damages as provided for in this convention."

[77] "As to the delay of shipment it has been seen that it was claimant who did create a situation of uncertainty by submitting shipping documents with a wrong shipping date and by not advising defendant about the true shipping date as it would have been its obligation according to INCOTERMS clauses CFR A 7. It has also been seen that irrespectively of these circumstances and of the delay of shipment of five days defendant could not have declared avoided the contract based on the delay of shipment alone, because the shipment occurred within the hypothetical additional period of time for performance which defendant would have had to fix to claimant had defendant immediately known about the delay.

[78] "As to the delivery of the documents, there has been not only a delay but a lack of performance on the part of claimant. . . . In other words, claimant had been made aware of the fact that the documents did, in the opinion of defendant's bank, not comply with the L/C. Since the conditions of the L/C corresponded to the contractual provisions (with the adding of two additional documents) claimant was aware at that time that defendant would almost certainly not accept the documents as they were.

[79] "If one were of the opinion that at that time defendant would have had to fix to claimant an additional period of time of reasonable length within the meaning of Art. 47(1) of the CISG for delivering a set of documents complying with the contractual specifications, such period would have had to be of ten or fourteen days and would, in other words, have ended some time around mid-December. Claimant might have had legally the possibility to cure the lack of conformity in the documents in accordance with Art. 34 of the CISG by recalling the set of documents submitted and by re-delivering a new set of documents with the indication of the true shipping date and complying also otherwise with the contractual conditions. But claimant did not endeavour to replace the defective set of documents and claimant has neither alleged to have offered to defendant, during the contracts which occurred in that period between the parties through their agents, to replace the challenge documents by new ones.

[80] "In view of the fact that claimant had been made aware by defendant's bank that the documents submitted were not in order and that contacts between the parties during the period took place and that the situation was obviously discussed amongst them, it would, in the opinion of the arbitral tribunal, be an overly formalistic approach to have required defendant to formally fix an additional period for performance to claimant at that time and to deny the possibility of defendant to declare the contract avoided as a consequence of not having fixed the additional period of time.

[81] "As from about [the permitted avoidance date], the hypothetical additional period of time which might have been at the disposal of claimant to cure the lack of conformity in the documents had elapsed without claimant having

advised by that time defendant about the true shipping date, as it contractually would have been obliged to do, nor submitted a new set of documents or offered to do so. Therefore, the arbitral tribunal holds that at least after [the permitted avoidance date], defendant was entitled, according to the principles underlying the rules of Art. 49 of the CISG, to declare the contract avoided.

[82]   "When defendant did so . . . , this was done timely. As to the claimant's argument, that the declaration of avoidance by defendant was late and is therefore to be disregarded according to Art. 49(2) of the CISG, it is again to be considered that the situation of uncertainty as to the shipping date and consequently the truthfulness of the documents submitted was due to the behaviour of claimant and to a clear breach of claimant's obligations under INCOTERMS clauses CFR A 7. According to the general rules on good faith the argument of the delay of the declaration of avoidance could not be heard since the delay, had it occurred, would have to a substantial extent been caused by the behaviour of claimant itself.

(. . . .)

[83]   "The declaration of avoidance by defendant . . . had as a consequence that the contract ended and defendant automatically became entitled to damages suffered by the breach of contract by claimant, all in accordance with Art. 81(1) and Art. 74[8] et seq. of the CISG.

[84]   "Since the contract was validly avoided by defendant, and the contract terminated accordingly, there is no basis for claimant to claim the payment of the purchase price from defendant. This is an obvious conclusion but is also clearly established by Art. 81(1) of the CISG stating that the avoidance of the contract releases both parties from their obligations under it, subject to any damages which may be due.

[85]   "However, even if the avoidance declared by defendant had been unjustified or ineffective because the declaration was late or for any other reason, the claim of claimant could still not be upheld. The contract would then still be continuing, but claimant would nevertheless have no justification to claim the purchase price, since it never did adequately perform under the contract. In fact, claimant did not deliver to the purchaser, either through the bank or directly, a bill of lading and other documents being in compliance with the contract. According to a basic rule of the law on contracts, the 'exceptio non adimpleti contractus', the purchaser is not bound to pay the purchase price as long as the seller has not performed or at least adequately tendered correct performance. This principle is specified by Art. 58(1) of the CISG. Since claimant could today, under the criterium of timeliness, no longer fulfil its contractual obligations,

---

8. CISG articles in Section II on Damages.

it would definitively have no longer any claim under the contract even if the contract had not been validly avoided by defendant.

[86]   "The claim of claimant is, therefore, to be rejected."

(. . . .)

VI.   COSTS

[87]   "According to Art. 20 of the [ICC] Rules the arbitral award is to fix the costs of the arbitration and decide in what proportions the costs shall be borne by the parties.[9] In accordance with basic procedural principles followed in arbitration, the costs of the arbitration have to be borne by the succumbing party. If none of the parties prevails totally with its requests, the costs must be apportioned in proportion of the degree in which each party prevailed and/or lost with reference to the relevant amounts.

(. . . .)

[88]   ". . . . Since both, claim and counterclaim, are being rejected, claimant succumbed with roughly 96% while defendant lost with roughly 4%. The cost of the arbitration is to be allocated in the same proportion.

(. . . .)

[89]   "According to Art. 20 of the ICC Rules and the procedural principles prevailing in arbitration generally and also applicable in France, which was the seat of the arbitration, the succumbing party must indemnify the prevailing party for its expenses and costs in relation to the arbitration. The arbitral tribunal has to determine the relevant amount. In their mutual requests, both parties have specifically requested that the other party be ordered to reimburse all costs of or related to the arbitration.

(. . . .)

---

9. Art. 20 of the ICC Rules of Conciliation and Arbitration reads:

"*Decision as to costs of arbitration*
(1) The arbitrator's award shall, in addition to dealing with the merits of the case, fix the costs of the arbitration and decide which or the parties shall bear the costs or in what proportions the costs shall be borne by the parties.
(2) The costs of the arbitration shall include the arbitrator's fees and the administrative costs fixed by the Court in accordance with the scale annexed to the present Rules, the expenses, if any, of the arbitrator, the fees and expenses of any experts, and the normal legal costs incurred by the parties.
(3) The Court may fix the arbitrator's fees at a figure higher or lower than that which would result from the application of the annexed scale if in the exceptional circumstances of the case this appears to be necessary."

[90] ". . . . The arbitral tribunal in assessing the amount of compensation to be adjudicated, has considered the amount in dispute and the characteristic of the case. The tribunal has also taken into account that defendant has not unreasonably requested the assistance of counsel not only in its home country but also of another counsel in Austria which has added to its expense and justifies a somewhat larger indemnity than usual. The tribunal noted also that defendant did not prevail entirely in its claim and this would justify a reduction in the indemnity for legal costs even if only of modest proportions."

(. . . .)

Final award in case no. 8423 of 1994

Parties:	Claimant: Portuguese company Defendants: French parent company and French subsidiary
Place of arbitration:	Brussels, Belgium
Published in:	Unpublished; original in French
Subject matters:	– arbitrability of application of European competition law – co-operative joint venture – Art. 85 EC Treaty

Facts

In 1989, two Portuguese companies (the Portuguese group) entered into an association agreement with a French subsidiary of a French parent company. The agreement concerned the sale to the French subsidiary company of part of the shares in C, a Portuguese company owned by the Portuguese group, whose corporate object was the exploitation of certain plants. The French subsidiary company signed the agreement in its own name and on behalf of "all physical or legal persons in its group with which [it] may associate" for carrying out its activities (the French group); the French parent company signed the agreement as the "intervening party". The agreement contained a non-competition provision and an ICC arbitration clause.

Alleging several violations of the non-competition provision by both French companies, the Portuguese group commenced ICC arbitration. The Arbitral Tribunal first determined that the 1998 agreement was a "co-operative" joint venture as distinguished from a "concentrative" joint venture and should be examined under Art. 85 EC Treaty. The Arbitral Tribunal then found that the non-competition provision in the agreement was not incompatible with Art. 85 EC Treaty as it neither affected trade nor competition in an appreciable manner. The Arbitral Tribunal found that the French parent company was liable for breach of the non-competition provision with respect to the tender for one of the four plants at issue. In this instance the French parent company had allowed its French subsidiary, as part of a consortium, to submit an offer in a tender for the exploitation of a plant of the type explicitly mentioned in the non-competition provision and awarded damages based on the theory of loss of opportunity. In the other cases, it was found that although there had also been a breach of the non-competition provision, the Arbitral Tribunal could not establish a relationship of damage and causality with respect to that breach.

Excerpt

I. ARTICLE **85** EC TREATY

[1]   "One of the issues for the Arbitral Tribunal . . . is whether the obligation in the non-competition provision of the 1989 Agreement complies with Art. 85 EC Treaty.[1] According to paragraph 1 of this provision:

'the Portuguese group, the French group and the intervening party, the French parent company, undertake to carry out . . . the exploitation of [certain plants] in Portugal, which pertains to the present corporate object

---

1. Art. 85 (now Art. 81) EC treaty reads:

"1. The following shall be prohibited as incompatible with the common market: all agreements between undertakings, decisions by associations of undertakings and concerted practices which may affect trade between Member States and which have as their object or effect the prevention, restriction or distortion of competition within the common market, and in particular those which:
(a) directly or indirectly fix purchase or selling prices or any other trading conditions;
(b) limit or control production, markets, technical development, or investment;
(c) share markets or sources of supply;
(d) apply dissimilar conditions to equivalent transactions with other trading parties, thereby placing them at a competitive disadvantage;
(e) make the conclusion of contracts subject to acceptance by the other parties of supplementary obligations which, by their nature or according to commercial usage, have no connection with the subject of such contracts.
2. Any agreements or decisions prohibited pursuant to this Article shall be automatically void.
3. The provisions of paragraph 1 may, however, be declared inapplicable in the case of:
– any agreement or category of agreements between undertakings;
– any decision or category of decisions by associations of undertakings;
– any concerted practice or category of concerted practices, which contributes to improving the production or distribution of goods or to promoting technical or economic progress, while allowing consumers a fair share of the resulting benefit, and which does not:
(a) impose on the undertakings concerned restrictions which are not indispensable to the attainment of these objectives;
(b) afford such undertakings the possibility of eliminating competition in respect of a substantial part of the products in question."

of C, exclusively through their participation in the shares and in the management of C . . . '.

The French parent company alleges . . . that the 1989 Agreement is null and void under Art. 85 EC Treaty.

(. . . .)

[2] "Paragraph 1 of the non-competition provision is strictly limited to certain specific fields of C's activity, [that is], the exploitation of certain plants; other fields are open to competition. . . . Also, the French group undertakes to give C exclusive access to its know-how in the fields mentioned in paragraph 1 of the non-competition provision against payment of royalties by C. . . .

[3] "The first issue for the Arbitral Tribunal is whether disputes concerning the application of community competition law are arbitrable. As community law pertains to international public policy, the Arbitral Tribunal must examine this issue ex officio, even if the parties do not raise an objection. The arbitrability of disputes concerning the application of competition law and, in particular, the (in)validity of an agreement in the light of these provisions is fully recognized today by the courts.[2] The Tribunal also notes that the parties agree on this point.

[4] "The second issue for the Tribunal is whether C is either a concentrative or a co-operative joint venture, and thus whether the validity of paragraph 1 of the non-competition provision under community competiton law must be examined in the light of EC Regulation no. 4064/89 (Council Regulation (EEC) of 21 June [rectius: December] 1989 on the control of concentrations between undertakings, OJEC 1990 L 257/14) or in the light of Art. 85 EC Treaty. Regulation no. 4064/89 applies to concentrative joint ventures, whereas Art. 85 EC Treaty applies to co-operative joint ventures. The Commission has issued a Notice on

---

2. "See for France: Cour d'Appel, Paris, 19 May 1993 (Labinal), Revue de l'arbitrage 1993 p. 645; Cour d'Appel, Paris, 14 October 1993 (Velcro), Revue de l'arbitrage 1994 p. 164; for Italy, Corte d'Appello, Bologna, 21 December 1991, Yearbook 1993 p. 422; on the arbitrability of US competition law see especially Supreme Court, 2 July 1985 (Mitsubishi Motors Corp. v. Soler Chrysler-Plymouth Inc.), Yearbook 1986 p. 555, Revue de l'arbitrage 1986 p. 273; for Switzerland, Tribunal Fédéral, 28 April 1992, ATF 118 II 193, ASA Bulletin 1992 p. 368, RSDIE 1994 p. 198, Revue de l'arbitrage 1993 p. 124. On this issue in doctrine, see especially Fouchard/Gaillard/Goldman, Traité de l'arbitrage commercial international, (Paris 1996) no. 575 and the numerous references therein; Redfern/Hunter, International Commercial Arbitration, 2nd ed. (London 1991) p. 139; B. Hanotiau, 'L'arbitrage et le droit européen de la concurrence', in L'arbitrage et le droit européen, Acts of the international colloquium of CEPANI of 25 April 1997 (Brussels 1997) pp. 33-64 (for Belgium, pp. 44-45). [See also] ICC award no. 1397 of 1966, JDI 1974 p. 878; ICC award no. 2811 of 1979, JDI 1979 p. 984; ICC award no. 6106 of 1990, quoted by Fouchard/Gaillard/Goldman in note 432 at p. 364)."

the distinction between concentrative and co-operative joint ventures made in Art. 3(2) of Regulation no. 4064/89 (OJEC 1994 C 385/1). According to Art. 3(2) of Regulation no. 4064/89 and to the Notice, a concentrative joint venture cumulatively:

(a) performs on a lasting basis all the functions of an autonomous economic entity (Art. 3(2) Regulation), meaning that the joint venture 'must operate on a market, performing the functions normally carried out by other under-takings operating on the same market. In order to do so the joint venture must have sufficient financial and other resources including finance, staff, and assets (tangible and intangible) in order to operate a business activity on a lasting basis' (point 13 Notice). The Commission specifies that, in respect of intellectual property rights, it is sufficient that these rights are licensed to the joint venture for its duration (point 13 Notice);
(b) is intended to operate on a lasting basis (point 16 Notice);
(c) does not co-ordinate the behaviour of undertakings which remain independent (Art. 3(2) Regulation, point 8 Notice).

[5]   "The Tribunal holds that the conditions for a concentrative joint venture are not met in the present case and that the 1989 Agreement thus concerns a co-operative joint venture. Its compliance with community competition law must be examined under Art. 85 EC Treaty.
[6]   "The third issue for the Tribunal is thus the validity of paragraph 1 of the non-competition provision of the Agreement under Art. 85 EC Treaty. The parties, through their respective experts, reach completely diverging opinions on this point. The Portuguese group concludes that paragraph 1 is valid under Art. 85(1), while French parent company alleges that it is null and void under Art. 85(2) as it violates the provisions in Art. 85(1).
[7]   ". . . . [T]he Tribunal finds, on the grounds below, that the elements in its possession do not allow it to find that the obligations undertaken with paragraph 1 of the non-competition provision of the 1989 Agreement are incompatible with Art. 85 EC Treaty.
(. . . .)
[8]   After quoting Art. 85(1) the Tribunal continued; "When examining whether paragraph 1 of the non-competition provision agrees with Art. 85, we must first of all define the market affected by the 1989 Agreement. It appears from C's by-laws that its corporate object is 'providing management, mainte-nance and exploitation services [to certain plants]'. Providing these services is thus the market affected by the Agreement. Geographically, the market affected is the territory of the Community. It is relatively frequent that enterprises from other Member States submit offers in tenders issued by Portuguese authorities.

[9] "The application of Art. 85(1) EC Treaty depends on two conditions: trade between Member States must be affected and competition must be interfered with.

[10] "As far as affecting *trade* between Member States is concerned, the Commission Notice on agreements of minor importance (OJEC, C 231 of 12 September 1986, p. 2) states that 'agreements whose effects on trade between Member States or on competition are negligible do not fall under the ban . . . in Art. 85(1) EC Treaty. Only those agreements are prohibited which have an appreciable impact on market conditions, in that they appreciably alter the market position, in other words the sales or supply possibilities, of third undertakings and of users' (point 2 Notice).

[11] "It appears from the file of the case that the Portuguese group has no experience in the field of activity of C and that its size is negligible on a European level. The French group is only one of the groups operating in France in this specific market. Although it has strong international experience and a strong technical and financial capacity, several enterprises, both in France and in other Member States, can be its competitors in this field.

[12] "Further, according to point 3 of the above-mentioned Notice, 'the quantitative definition of appreciable given by the Commission (at point 7) is . . . no absolute yardstick; in fact, in individual cases even agreements between undertakings which exceed these limits may still have only a negligible effect on trade between Member States or on competition, and are therefore not caught by Art. 85(1)'.

[13] "In the light of the elements in its possession, the Tribunal deems that the clause at issue does not affect trade between Member States in an appreciable manner in the sense of Art. 85(1).

[14] "But does the 1989 Agreement interfere with *competition* in the sense of Art. 85(1)? The Tribunal notes that the Agreement does not aim at restricting competition; rather it aims at 'develop[ing] the relevant activities of (C's) corporate object in Portugal'. The Commission does not deem that any restriction suffices for an agreement to restrict competition; it requires that the restriction have an appreciable impact on competition. The question is thus whether the non-competition provision of the 1989 Agreement is of such nature as to restrict competition in an appreciable manner.

[15] "According to this provision of the 1989 Agreement, the Portuguese group, the French group and the French parent company undertake to carry out in Portugal the activities falling within the scope of the corporate object of C exclusively through their participation in the capital and in the management of C. Although at first sight such behaviour appears to entail a restriction of competition in the market in which C operates, since four enterprises agree not to

compete, we must determine whether this behaviour effectively restricts competition and, if it does, whether this restriction has an appreciable impact.

[16]   "It appears from the Commission's jurisprudence on this issue that:

(a) for the creation of a joint subsidiary to result per se in a restriction of competition, the associated undertakings must before their association be actual or potential competitors on the market and on the territory at issue;[3]

(b) the creation of a joint subsidiary does not restrict competition where the associated undertakings did not operate in the same field before associating or where some of them would be unable to provide the subsidiary's service independently;[4]

(c) where there are several competitors on the market, the creation of a joint subsidiary does not result in a restriction of competition.[5]

[17]   "This interpretation is further supported by the Commission in its Notice concerning the assessment of cooperative joint ventures pursuant to Art. 85 EC Treaty (93/C 43/02, OJEC Cap. 43 of 16 February 1993 p. 2), where it states that 'the assumption of potential competitive circumstances presupposes that each parent alone is in a position to fulfil the tasks assigned to the joint venture and that it does not forfeit its capabilities to do so by the creation of the joint venture' [point 18 Notice].

[18]   " ... [N]one of the parties to the 1989 Agreement, and especially the Portuguese party, was well placed in this market, which was still in its infancy, at the time of concluding the Agreement. The Portuguese group manifestly did not have the necessary technology to enter this market on its own with any chance of reasonable success. The French group and the French parent company had strong international experience but did not know the peculiarities of the Portuguese market. It cannot be deemed that the parties were actual or even potential competitors at the time of the conclusion of the Agreement. After all, C was unable to submit an offer for [certain tenders discussed below] due to lack of know-how and of the necessary technology. Clearly, the non-competition provision of the Agreement was not of such nature as to restrict competition in an appreciable manner.

---

3. "Para. 4 of judgment IV/M535 of 21 December 1994 (*Mannesmann Demag v. Delaval Stork*) OJEC 1995 C 023/4 and para. 19 of judgment IV/31340 of 17 December 1986 (*Mitchell Cotts v. Sofiltra*) OJEC 1987 L 041/31)."
4. "Para. 46 of judgment IV/30320 of 14 July 1986 (*Fibres Optiques*) OJEC 1986 L 236/30 and para. 17 of decision IV/32437/8 of 24 October 1988 (*Eurotunnel*) OJEC 1988 L 311/36."
5. "Para. 19 of the *Mitchell Cotts v. Sofiltra* judgment mentioned above."

[19] "Even if the Tribunal had reached a different conclusion, that is, if it had found that the Agreement restricted competition between the signatories, still the Agreement's impact on competition in the market concerned was largely beneficial, and it would be necessary in any case to conclude that it did not restrict competition. This is the point of view of the Commission in its above-mentioned Notice on the assessment of co-operative joint ventures, where it says that Art. 85(1) does not apply to a joint venture, even between competitors, 'when the co-operation . . . can objectively be seen as the only possibility for the parents to enter a new market . . . provided that their presence will strengthen competition or prevent it from being weakened' [point 42 Notice].

[20] "The Tribunal concludes that the data and elements in its possession do not in any way allow it to hold that the non-competition provision of the 1989 Agreement violates Art. 85(1) EC Treaty."

II. ALLEGED VIOLATIONS OF THE 1989 AGREEMENT

1. Plant I

[21] In late 1989, a Portuguese municipality issued a tender for the construction and exploitation of a certain plant. S, a company controlled by the French parent company, submitted an offer together with Z, a Portuguese company. C was also interested in submitting an offer and first approached the French subsidiary. When the French subsidiary replied that it did not have the necessary technological means, C contacted S and discovered that it had already formed a consortium with Z. S and Z were eventually granted the contract.

[22] As to the French subsidiary, the Tribunal held: "[French subsidiary] did not have the sufficient technology to submit an offer. It does not appear from the evidence of the case that it refused to provide C with its technical knowledge and know-how to allow it to submit an offer. As the French subsidiary argues, its field of activity does not allow it to compete with large consortia, which can submit offers for both the construction and the exploitation of plants. The Arbitral Tribunal also notes that neither the Portuguese group nor C ever complained to the French subsidiary with respect to this case before the commencement of the present proceedings. . . .

[23] "The only issue . . . is whether the French subsidiary is liable for the French parent company's breach of the Agreement, as the Portuguese group maintains. The French subsidiary declared, in the 1989 Agreement, that it acted both in its own name and on behalf of all physical and legal persons of its group with which it could associate. In the Tribunal's opinion, the text of the Agreement, as well as its general balance and system, shows that the French

subsidiary did not enter into an obligation on behalf of the various companies of the French parent company group, of which it was a part. First, the conditional form used in the sentence ('on behalf of all physical or legal persons of its group with which it *could* associate') shows that the parties intended that the French subsidiary could associate with other physical or legal persons of its group for performing under the Agreement, but that the French subsidiary did not mean, even if it were able to do so, to enter into an obligation on behalf of the subsidiaries of the parent company. The French subsidiary had in fact its own subsidiaries and participated in other companies . . . ; hence, this formulation was not meaningless. The Arbitral Tribunal must respect the difference which the Agreement makes between the French subsidiary and French parent company. Further, if the French subsidiary were liable for the French parent company's breaches, we do not see why the French parent company signed the Agreement separately. (. . . .)

[24]   "Second, the Arbitral Tribunal must ascertain whether the participation of S in the tender was a breach of contract by the French parent company. (. . . .)

The Arbitral Tribunal shall first dismiss French parent company's argument that the Portuguese group may not rely on the 1989 Agreement against the French parent company as the 1989 Agreement is a shareholders' agreement and the French parent company is not a shareholder in C. According to the French parent company, the mention of the French parent company in the non-competition provision of the Agreement, which is the only clause mentioning the French parent company as 'the intervening party', can be explained only in the sense of 'its participation in the capital and in the management of C'.

[25]   "The Arbitral Tribunal does not share the French parent company's thesis. According to a generally accepted principle of contract law, a contract must be interpreted according to the interpretation which an objective good faith observer could reasonably give of it. It is evident that the non-competition provision would be meaningless if the scope of the French parent company's obligation depended on its participation in the capital of C. The French parent company could then choose to compete with C by deciding not to participate in its capital, or to enter into the Agreement by participating in C's capital. In the Arbitral Tribunal's opinion, the French parent company manifestly undertook not to compete with the Portuguese group and with C in the field of the exploitation of certain plants. The 1989 Agreement is indeed an agreement between shareholders concluded between the Portuguese group and the French group; however, the non-competition provision directly concerns the French parent company, which undertakes not to compete with the company in which its subsidiary, French subsidiary, participates. The Tribunal notes that paragraph 3 of this provision . . . states that the object of the 1989 Agreement is an association agreement. . . . The French parent company's obligation cannot depend

on the name which the parties gave to their agreement. The 1989 Agreement clearly distinguishes between the French subsidiary, which participates in its own name and whose obligations are relatively numerous, since it participates in the capital of C, and French parent company, which is only an intervening party and which only undertakes to abstain from competition. The Tribunal notes that both claimant Portuguese group and defendant French subsidiary so understood the agreement which they negotiated. . . .

[26]   "The Tribunal deems that the nature of the obligation of French parent company, which French subsidiary understood, could not in good faith escape Mr X, who represented French parent company at the signing of the 1989 Agreement. If he had doubts on this point, he should have asked for information to clarify them, in particular from the representatives of his subsidiary, French subsidiary, which participated in the negotiations. He should have tried to better understand the extent of the obligation which he entered on behalf of defendant French parent company. It is perfectly possible, but totally irrelevant, that the members of the French parent company's Board did not understand the actual extent of this obligation. . . . [D]efendant French parent company may not rely on [Mr X's] lack of power to sign: Mr X is one of the company's directors, whose name, we must stress, appears as member of the Board and director in the French parent company's annual reports. . . .

[27]   "In Portuguese law (Art. 798 Civil Code), contractual liability presupposes a wrongful failure to perform under an obligation, a damage and a causal relation between the wrongful failure to perform and the damage.

[28]   "The Arbitral Tribunal deems that the participation of S in the tender for the exploitation of Plant I is a violation of paragraph 1 of the non-competition provision of the 1989 Agreement. Defendant French parent company did not prove that this breach of the obligation to abstain from competition cannot be ascribed to it, although it has the burden of such proof under Art. 799 no. 1 of the Portuguese Civil Code. It is unnecessary to decide whether the French parent company's breach was intentional, which does not appear from the evidence supplied by the parties. The provisions of Portuguese law on contractual liability do not require intention for the debtor to be liable.

[29]   "The French parent company's wrongful breach does presuppose that the French parent company was aware of the 1989 Agreement. . . . [E]ven if Mr X did not have the power, within the French parent company, to enter into an obligation for the company, he was nonetheless qualified, as a director, to receive communications. Hence, it is sufficiently established that defendant French parent company was aware of the obligation which it undertook under paragraph 1 of the non-competition provision of the 1989 Agreement. The French parent company should then have taken the necessary measures to ensure that the various companies of its group respected this obligation to

abstain from competition. It appears from the hearing of witness Y . . . that S knew of the agreement binding the French parent company and signed by Mr X. Although it is unnecessary to decide on this issue for the above-mentioned reasons, it is highly likely that S . . . asked for information from French parent company as to the existence and the validity of this agreement.

[30]   "It is much more complex, however, to decide on the other two issues concerning contractual liability, that is, the existence of a damage and of a causal relation. For the French parent company to pay damages, claimant must have suffered a damage and this damage must be a consequence of defendant's wrongful breach.

[31]   "Correctly, all parties refer to the adequate cause theory accepted in Portuguese law.[6] The Arbitral Tribunal shall rely on the criterion of objective expectation: only the damage shall be taken into account, of which it can legitimately be expected that it would not have occurred if there had been no damaging event.

[32]   "In the case at issue, the Arbitral Tribunal deems that the claimant was not damaged by the French parent company's participation in the tender.

[33]   "The Tribunal notes that Portuguese group neither claims nor proves that C would have participated in the tender at issue. That is understandable, as the tender concerned both the construction and the exploitation of a plant, whereas C's corporate object, unlike French Company's, did not cover construction. The Tribunal holds that C did not fail to participate in the tender because of [S's] submission, but because it did not want to, possibly considering that it did not have the necessary technical knowledge. The Tribunal further notes that C could not know the names of the participants until the closure of the tender: this too shows that it was not because of S's participation that C did not submit an offer. Since C failed to participate in the tender, C's alleged loss of profit . . . would have occurred also if S had not participated in the tender at issue and if it had not obtained the contract.

[34]   "Also, claimant may not claim that the French parent company failed to make S co-operate with C on the tender, since the French parent company . . . only had an obligation to abstain from competition. Further, the Tribunal deems that, even if C had participated in the tender, which it did not, one may reasonably think that, in the normal course of affairs and according to general experience, it would certainly not have been granted the contract since, as mentioned before, the construction of plants was not part of its

---

6. "See Andunes Varela, Dos obrigaõ es mem geral, vol. I, 6th ed p. 869."

corporate object and since C was undoubtedly unable to submit a truly competitive offer.

[35]   "Because of the absence of a damage and of a causal relation, the Tribunal dismisses the claim for damages made against defendant, French parent company. For the sake of completeness, the Tribunal notes that, even if it held that there was a damage and a causal relation, the Portuguese group's claims would be mostly rejected as the Portuguese group failed to provide sufficient evidence of the extent of the alleged damage. If the Tribunal had not ruled out the existence of a damage and of a causal relation, it should have had, in all likeliness, to decide in equity on the extent of the compensation. In the Tribunal's opinion, the evidence submitted by the claimant on this point is largely insufficient."

(. . . .)

2. Plant II

[36]   The Arbitral Tribunal reached the same conclusion as in the case of Plant I when examining the tender for the construction and exploitation of another plant in Portugal, where the contract was granted to a consortium including a subsidiary of the French parent company.

[37]   "Here again, . . . the Tribunal necessarily concludes that a damage and a causal relation between this damage and the French parent company's breach of contract are not proven. Even if defendant, French parent company, through one of its subsidiaries, had not participated in the tender, C would not have been granted the contract as it did not submit an offer and, therefore, would not have had the profit for which it now claims compensation. The Tribunal further notes that defendant, French parent company, had no obligation to communicate its technology to C, so that, even if the French parent company's subsidiary had not participated in the tender, C would have been obliged to find associates, since neither C nor the Portuguese group nor the French subsidiary had sufficient technical knowledge to participate in the tender.

[38]   "It is likely that C, whose corporate object did not concern the construction of plants, would not submit a competitive offer on both the construction and the exploitation of the plant. This is certainly the reason why it did not participate on its own in the tender. If C could have found other associates to form a consortium allowing it to submit a competitive offer, it certainly would have done so. The Tribunal deems therefore that, according to the principle of objective foreseeability as required by the adequate causality theory, it is likely, in the ordinary course of things, that C would not have been granted the contract for the construction and exploitation of Plant II even if the defendant had

not participated in the tender. Hence, C did not suffer any damage for which claimant can claim compensation."
(. . . .)

3. Plant III

[39]   In this third case, it was the French parent company-Portugal that participated in a tender. Although it found that the French parent company had violated the obligation of non-competition under paragraph 1 of the non-competition provision of the 1989 Agreement, the Tribunal considered that there had been no damage to C and thus to the Portuguese group as the contract had not yet been granted at the time of the award.

4. Plant IV

[40]   Other than in the previous cases, both C, in a consortium with French subsidiary, and French parent company-Portugal submitted an offer in a tender for the exploitation of Plant IV, yet another plant in Portugal.

[41]   "[B]y allowing one of its subsidiaries to participate in the tender for the exploitation of Plant IV, French parent company violated the non-competition obligation in paragraph 1 of the non-competition provision of the 1989 Agreement. The tender concerned the exploitation of a type of plant explicitly mentioned in this provision of the 1989 Agreement.
(. . . .)

[42]   "Other than in the case of Plant I and Plant II, examined above, C participated in the tender for Plant IV by submitting an offer in collaboration with French company. The Tribunal does not therefore find that there is no damage and that the causal relation is not sufficiently proven, as it did in the two above cases. The Tribunal must examine whether French parent company's breach caused a damage to claimant Portuguese group that is an effect of this breach.

[43]   "In the first place, claimant Portuguese group neither alleges nor proves that C incurred any special expenses in participating in the tender for Plant IV. Hence, defendant French parent company shall not be directed to compensate *damnum emergens*.

[44]   "The issue of loss of profit is more complex. The Tribunal must first note that it is not clearly established that C would have been granted the contract at issue if French parent company had not participated in the tender. If French parent company and the French Company – C consortium had been the only participants in the tender, the Tribunal could hold without doubt that the Portuguese group suffered a loss of profit because of French parent company's participation in the tender through one of its subsidiaries. As it were, six

other participants participated in the tender, so that this issue must be examined more in detail.

[45] "The Tribunal deems that in the present case it must base its evaluation of both the damage suffered by C and the damage suffered by the Portuguese group on the theory of loss of opportunity, which is accepted in Portuguese law.[7] ... In the case at issue, the Tribunal deems that by submitting an offer for this tender, defendant French parent company notably reduced the chances for the consortium formed by C and French company to be granted the contract at issue. The Tribunal strongly regrets that claimant Portuguese group did not offer information as to the results reached by the municipality of Plant IV concerning the offers of the other participants. The document it filed ... , at least in the translated parts, does not allow an assessment of the respective merits of the participants. Also, this document is incomplete. The Tribunal is surprised that the Portuguese group did not file this document in its entirety, in particular the part concerning the third selection criterion, that is, the price of the offers.

[46] "In any case, since the tender concerned the exploitation of a plant in a field in which French Company excelled, the Tribunal deems that, on the basis of the body of evidence submitted, C was undoubtedly able to submit an interesting offer in cooperation with French subsidiary. We cannot affirm with certainty that C would have obtained the contract if defendant French parent company had not submitted an offer. However, French parent company's competitive offer 'and it must have been a competitive offer, since after all French parent company obtained the contract' was such as to diminish, according to the ordinary course of things and general business experience, the chances of success of the submission filed by C and by French subsidiary. In order to determine the extent of the compensation to be paid by French parent company, we must first evaluate the chances lost by C because of the submission by French parent company's subsidiary. Secondly, we must quantify this damage in pecuniary terms. ...

[47] "The Tribunal first notes that it is difficult to assess C's loss of opportunity due to French parent company's breach of contract. Also, C's damage does not automatically affect the Portuguese group. On the elements in its possession and taking into account, in particular, the number of participants which

---

7. "The Arbitral Tribunal referred to: Court of Appeal of Evora, 6 February 1992, in Recueil de jurisprudence 1992 I p. 279; Supreme Court, 28 October 1992, Recueil de jurisprudence du STJ 1992 IV p. 31; Supreme Court, 11 October 1994, Recueil de jurisprudence du STJ III 1994 p. 84; Supreme Court, 23 May 1978, Bulletin of the Ministry of Justice no. 277 p. 264; Court of Appeal of Porto, 16 March 1995, Recueil de jurisprudence 1995 II p. 204; and Supreme Court, 4 February 1993 Recueil de jurisprudence I p. 130."

submitted an offer, the Tribunal estimates that the Portuguese group's loss of a possible profit is 12.5% of C's benefit."

[48]   The Arbitral Tribunal noted that the Portuguese group failed to submit sufficient evidence on this profit and concluded: "The Arbitral Tribunal refers to Art. 566 of the Portuguese Civil Code which, according to a widely accepted liability principle, allows [an arbitral tribunal] to decide in equity (see Art. 42(2) Swiss CC, Art. 1226 Italian CC, Sect. 287 German ZPO). In the present case, on the elements in its possession and considering the Portuguese group's loss of the opportunity to receive, as profit, part of C's profit the Tribunal directs defendant French parent company to pay the Portuguese group . . . in damages."

Final award in case no. 8445 of 1996

Parties:	Claimant: Manufacturer (India)
	Defendant: Manufacturer (Germany)
Place of arbitration:	Zurich, Switzerland
Published in:	Unpublished
Subject matters:	– breach of contract
	– requirement of amicable settlement
	– premature litigation in local court
	– liability for loss: application of the Indian Contract Act (1872)
	– calculation of loss of profits

Facts

Claimant and defendant entered into a know-how/technology licensing contract in which defendant granted claimant a non-exclusive license to produce
and sell six "contract products" in return for a series of payments. As licensor,
defendant was obliged to provide claimant with specific documentation within
three months of entering into the agreement. Claimant paid the initial sum.
A disagreement arose concerning whether the documentation specified in the
agreement was provided for. Claimant maintained that specific data sheets were
necessary for production while defendant offered other alternatives. Claimant
rejected defendant's offer insisting on the right to produce products locally
under defendant's brand name.

The agreement provided for ICC arbitration and the application of Indian
law. Arbitration was initiated in Zurich, Switzerland. The legal action initiated
by claimant in a local court in India was dismissed pending the outcome of this
arbitration.

Claimant contended that defendant breached the contract by failure to
deliver documentation and sought compensation for payment of the initial
sum and lost profits, loss of anticipated profits and loss of image and reputation.
Considering the behavior of parties, the arbitrators rejected defendant's claims
that there was an obligation for the claimant to find an amicable solution and
that the commencement of arbitration proceedings was premature. Turning to

the substantive issues in dispute, the tribunal concluded that defendant breached the contract by not providing the required documentation on time. Claimant had an unconditional right to use defendant's name in connection with "contract products" and was entitled to recover damages. Applying relevant articles of the Indian Contract Act (1872) and Indian jurisprudence the arbitrators held that damages for lost profits minus expenses which would have been paid had performance taken place were allowable while the claim for punitive damages was dismissed.

Excerpt

I.   WERE ARBITRAL PROCEEDINGS BROUGHT PREMATURELY
     BECAUSE CLAIMANT FAILED TO TRY AND SETTLE THE DISPUTE
     AMICABLY?

[1]   "As a preliminary matter, the arbitrators must address the contention made by defendant that claimant has not made any effort to settle the dispute amicably, as called for in . . . the Agreement, and that this arbitration has therefore been brought prematurely.
[2]   "In this connection, the arbitrators have considered the history of the relations between the parties, since the signature of the Agreement and the exchanges of correspondence, including claimant's letter . . . expressing its dissatisfaction, and suggesting termination with compensation to be paid by defendant. This letter was presumably sent before receipt of defendant's letter . . . restricting the use of the brand name, but after successive delays in getting a reply to earlier letters. After receiving defendant's letter . . . , the claimant immediately replied to defendant, rejecting defendant's proposal, and reiterating its desire to terminate with compensation. There were several further letters, with each party maintaining its position. Those positions were far apart, with little prospect of a compromise, and the defendant did not respond to claimant's last proposal for a meeting in India.
[3]   "Against this background, claimant brought an action before the Indian Court, ostensibly to preclude defendant from entering into arrangements for the same products with third parties. Thereafter, litigation having been commenced, the possibility of any amicable settlement was even more remote. This is particularly true in view of the length of time which had elapsed since the signature of the Agreement, the increasingly acrimonious exchanges of letters between the parties, and the large sums eventually demanded by claimant.
[4]   "The arbitrators are of the opinion that a clause calling for attempts to settle a dispute amicably are primarily expression of intention, and must be

viewed in the light of the circumstances. They should not be applied to oblige the parties to engage in fruitless negotiations or to delay an orderly resolution of the dispute.

[5]　"Accordingly, the arbitrators have determined that there was no obligation on the claimant to carry out further efforts to find an amicable solution, and that the commencement of these arbitration proceedings was neither premature nor improper."

II.　BREACH OF CONTRACT

1.　Did Defendant Breach the Contract by Failing to Deliver All of the Documentation?

[6]　"Turning to the substantive issues in dispute, the arbitrators must determine, first, what were the rights and obligations of the parties under the Agreement and, then, whether there has been a breach of those obligations.

[7]　"The Agreement is basically an agreement for the transmission of design and technical production information and know-how, primarily by the furnishing of Documentation, as defined, and for a non-exclusive license from defendant to claimant to use such technical information/know-how in the production and sale of the Contract Products in the defined Territory. The Agreement defines the Documentation to be furnished by defendant . . . as follows:

> '"Documentation" shall mean design, manufacturing and test information as available at and used by LICENSER in its own commercial production or testing of Contract Products, as far as they are necessary for the manufacture or testing by LICENSEE and as described in Annexure 2.
>
> 　"Documentation" does not include any information on raw materials and standard materials which are commercially available.'

[8]　"The Agreement further provides that such Documentation 'which is in [defendant's] possession on the effective date of this Agreement' is to be furnished by defendant to claimant 'within three months', presumably after the 'effective date'. Annexures I and II to the Agreement list the Contract Products to which the Agreement applies, and certain details of the Documentation.

(. . . .)

[9]　"The evidence shows, and there seems to be no dispute, that the Documentation was not in fact furnished by defendant during the initial three-month period called for by the Agreement. . . .

[10] ".... The main block of Documentation was finally sent by defendant ... some two and one-half years after the time foreseen in the Agreement. Even then the Documentation was not complete; defendant appears to recognize this, although the parties disagree strongly as to whether the last missing items of Documentation were contractually required, and if so under what conditions.

[11] "Based on the above, much of which is uncontested, it appears that the defendant is clearly in default of its obligation to deliver the Documentation within the time period specified, and indeed within any reasonable time. The defendant thus appears, prima facie, to have been in breach of the Agreement. The defendant has argued, in defense or possibly in mitigation, that some of the delay was caused by claimant's own delay in sending samples, and, more importantly, that claimant condoned or waived any such breach, by its continued dealings with defendant. ... "

(. . . .)

2. Was the Documentation Defendant Delivered Enough to Fulfill Contractual Obligations?

[12] "It is uncontested between the parties that certain specifications/productions date (frequently referred to in the correspondence as 'receptures') for five special so-called 'catalysts', needed in the production of the Contract Products, were never furnished to claimant by defendant. ... The conditions were not acceptable to claimant, and such receptures were in fact never delivered.

[13] "The claimant maintains that the specifications/data for such so-called 'catalysts' were an essential part of the Documentation required under the terms of the Agreement, and necessary to allow production of the Contract Products locally. In fact, claimant contends that such materials are not 'catalysts' at all, but are principal ingredients or raw materials needed to produce the end products. Claimant asserts that defendant's offer finally to deliver the 'catalyst receptures' but only on condition that the claimant undertake not to use the brand name, was not a valid offer at all. Claimant's position is that it had a clear right to use the brand name in connection with the Contract Products, and that defendant had no right to prescribe new conditions for the delivery of such 'catalyst receptures'. Quite apart from the delays, the claimant alleges that the defendant was never willing to deliver the lacking Documentation, except under unjustified and unacceptable conditions, and was therefore in fundamental breach.

[14] "The defendant, to the contrary, denies that the specifications/data for the 'catalysts' were part of the required Documentation under the Agreement. The

defendant argues that it purchased the materials for such 'catalysts' from third party-suppliers, and that the relevant information was neither ' . . . available at and used by Licensee' in its own commercial production or testing of Contract Products, as referred to in the Agreement nor 'Documentation which is in Licenser's possession on the effective date . . . '. Instead, the defendant, argues, the information concerning such 'catalysts' constituted ' . . . information on raw materials and standard materials which are commercially available', as expressly excluded from the Documentation. . . . Nonetheless, defendant asserts that it made considerable efforts to obtain such data for the claimant, actually providing cost and source data from suppliers, and then offering to furnish the actual 'receptures', albeit under justifiable conditions. Furthermore, the defendant denies that claimant was ever granted the right to use the brand name unconditionally, and that defendant, with legitimate concerns as to quality, was entitled to prevent use of the brand name if claimant was to produce all the ingredients, including the 'catalysts' locally. Thus, the defendant argues that even if it was not obliged to do so, it did eventually offer the last pieces of information, whether they constituted Documentation or not, but that claimant was not willing to receive them or to proceed.

[15] "Taking the above points in turn, and after considering the documentary evidence submitted by both parties, the testimony of the witnesses (no witnesses having been presented by the defendant) and the submissions of the parties, the arbitrators conclude that the specifications and data concerning the so-called 'catalysts' (whether referred to as data sheets, or receptures or otherwise) did constitute part of the required Documentation as defined in the Agreement, and should have been delivered to claimant by defendant.

[16] "The arbitrators note, to begin with, that under the terms of the Agreement defendant was to provide information ' . . . as far as they are necessary for the manufacture or testing by Licensee (claimant) . . . ' and to allow claimant ' . . . to reproduce Contract Products in its own manufacturing facilities in India by using Documentation'. Moreover, Annexure 2 to the Agreement, listing the 'Documentation' to be provided, refers to '*All* technical information relating to Contract Products mentioned in Annexure 1, including but not limited to . . . ' (emphasis added). Defendant itself, in a letter to claimant confirmed that defendant was obliged to send the 'total know-how of the main products of defendant' including 'complete documentation . . . '.

[17] "The arbitrators further note that there is no mention anywhere in the Agreement of 'catalysts' as such, nor of any requirement for claimant to purchase any ingredients from German sources or from defendant specifically. . . .

[18]   ". . . . What is significant is that the so-called 'catalysts' were indisputably essential to allow production of the end-products, and in fact represented very substantial parts by weight and by cost of such end-products.

[19]   "Of perhaps greater significance is the argument advanced by defendant, that the five so-called 'catalysts' are 'raw materials and standard materials which are commercially available', and thus are explicitly excluded from the required Documentation. . . .

[20]   "Against this shifting background, defendant now maintains that the so-called 'catalysts' were 'raw materials and standard materials which are commercially available' and for which no information was required. The 'catalysts', according to defendant, were commercially available from defendant, and defendant in fact offered to sell them, with price quotations, to claimant.

[21]   "The arbitrators, with respect, do not agree. The phrase 'commercially available' as used in the Agreement cannot logically have been intended to mean commercially available from defendant itself. Taken to its extreme, this argument would release defendant from any obligation, since all materials, including the end-products, were available from defendant, and would negate the whole object of the Agreement. 'Commercially available' must be interpreted as referring to common, off-the-shelf commodities readily available on the open market. That the so-called 'catalysts' were not 'commercially available' in this sense is evident from defendant's own letters, which refer to them, e.g., as 'defendant specific', subject to defendant's own testing, etc.

[22]   "Accordingly, the arbitrators conclude that the so-called 'catalysts' were not excluded from the Documentation to be furnished under the Agreement, and that defendant was contractually obligated to provide such information to claimant. Its failure to do so, or its offer to do so only under new extracontractual conditions, if such was the case, constituted a fundamental breach of the Agreement."

3.   Did Claimant Have an Unconditional Right to Use Defendant's Brand Name in Connection with Contract Products?

[23]   "When defendant did finally offer to deliver the information for local production of the 'catalysts' to claimant, it did so on condition that claimant not use the brand name on any such locally produced products. The parties are in sharp disagreement as to whether or not claimant had a contractual right to use the brand name, and whether defendant could subject such use to special conditions.

[24]   "The arbitrators note, to begin with, that there is no provision in the Agreement for the use of the brand name. In fact the brand name is not mentioned.

(. . . .)

[25]   "The Arbitral Tribunal is perplexed by the fact that such a crucial element as the use of the brand name was not addressed in the Agreement, as was also the case for the 'catalysts', another crucial element. Nonetheless, having considered the evidence and the arguments of the parties, the arbitrators conclude that the parties did intend from the outset that claimant have the right to use the brand name. The arbitrators place considerable weight in this respect on the testimony of Mr. [X] and Mr. [Y], which testimony was never controverted, and on the recurrent references to such brand name in the government application. In any event, the situation was made abundantly clear by defendant's own letter . . . - which explicitly confirmed such right. The question of whether Mr. [A], the signatory of such letter, had the legal authority to bind defendant on his sole signature, cannot be used at this stage to nullify its effect; Mr. [A] was the principal interface with claimant during this period, and the defendants never sought to challenge his authority until these proceedings were brought. Even if Mr. [A] did not have actual authority, which was not proven, the Arbitral Tribunal holds that he had apparent authority on which the claimant was entitled to rely. Moreover, the commitment made by Mr. [A] in the letter . . . was ratified, by defendant's letter . . . signed by two representatives of defendant. Such ratification, coupled with numerous letters by claimant asserting its right to use the brand name, was sufficient to constitute either a clarification of the Agreement, or an 'alteration of or addition to' the Agreement. . . . Indeed, after sending its letter . . . defendant did not directly contest such right until late in the relationship. . . .

[26]   "Accordingly, the Arbitral Tribunal concludes that claimant did have an unconditional right to use the brand name in connection with the Contract Products, and that defendant had no right to limit such use in advance to products manufactured in Germany, or to oblige claimant to desist from using the name, in order to receive the remaining Documentation.

(. . . .)

[27]   "On the basis of the foregoing, the Arbitral Tribunal concludes that defendant was in breach of its obligations under the Agreement, by refusing to deliver all of the required Documentation, including critical information on the so-called 'catalysts'. Its offer to deliver such Documentation, but only on the newly-added condition that claimant refrain from using the brand name on products manufactured in India (or, alternatively, that claimant purchase the 'catalysts' from Germany) did not constitute a valid offer of delivery under

Indian law. See, e.g., Indian Contract Act (1872) Sect. 38; *Sabapathi v. Vanmahlinge*, AIR (1915) MAD 210, 216."

(. . . .)

III. DETERMINATION OF RELIEF: APPLICATION OF THE INDIAN CONTRACT ACT (1872)

1. Claims for Relief Related to Loss of Reputation, Loss of Business Opportunities

[28] "Having considered the arguments of the parties, the arbitrators conclude that the Exclusion of Liability Clause of the Agreement[1] cannot be interpreted to limit the loss or damage of the claimant, and certainly not the direct damages, caused by a fundamental breach of the Agreement, such as a failure to deliver a significant portion of the Documentation. A restrictive reading of this clause as is required under Indian law, and a logical one, would limit its effect to liability arising from either faulty products or possibly defective documentation but not for a willful failure to deliver the documentation at all. Any other reading could lead, at its extreme, to a negation of the Agreement itself. Under applicable Indian law (see, e.g., *Lilywhite v. Munuswami*, AIR (1966) Madras 13; *R.S. Deboo v. Dr. M.V. Hindlekar*, AIR (1995) Bombay 68), such a result would be against public policy and unenforceable.

[29] "Accordingly, the claimant is entitled to recover damages caused by the defendant's breach, to the extent they are proved.

[30] "The claimant has presented substantial claims for loss and damages divided among a number of headings. Among these are claims for (i) lost profits (initially called loss of market position, but later explained as meaning profits which would have been earned by claimant had it been able to manufacture the products), (ii) loss of profits which claimant would have made from its participation in a joint venture marketing entity formed to market and apply the products, and (iii) loss of image and reputation affecting claimant's existing business.

(. . . .)

[31] "The arbitrators take note of Sect. 73 of the Indian Contract Act (1872) which provides that, in order to recover damages from a breach of contract, the aggrieved party must show that such damage arose naturally in the usual course

---

1. The Exclusion of Liability Clause of the Agreement reads:

"Any further liability of Licenser for direct or consequential damages is excluded."

of things from such breach, or was damage which the parties knew when they made the contract would be likely to result. The arbitrators hold, as a finding of fact in the present circumstances, that the principal category of damage claimed by claimant, namely a loss of profit from the manufacture and sale of the licensed products, would and did result naturally from the failure to provide the Documentation, and, moreover, that both parties knew or should have known that such loss was likely. The claimant unquestionably expected to make a profit from the local manufacture and sale of the products, and its inability to do so naturally led to a loss of profits, a result which both parties must have known at the time they entered into the Agreement.

[32] "Notwithstanding the foregoing, the defendant maintains that the claimant has not made any adequate proof of the amount of such loss. In this respect, the arbitrators note that under consistent Indian jurisprudence, an injured claimant is not required to prove the amount of damage with absolute certainty, where such certainty is not possible, as is the case with lost profits. Instead, what is required, under Indian law, is a reasonable estimate of the loss, based on such elements as are available. (See, e.g., *State of Kerala v. K. Bhaskaran*, AIR (1985) Kerala 55).

[33] "The arbitrators believe on balance that the claimant has met this test, and, in presenting its evidence, has provided reasonable proof of its lost profits. The reasoned and detailed estimates of the costs of manufacturing the products, of the prices at which the products could be sold and of the ensuing profit do not appear unreasonable. In estimating the costs, the claimant has used the far higher German export prices for certain of the materials; this is contrary to claimant's interest, but results in a conservative estimate, favorable to defendant. In estimating the sales price, claimant has used a price below that of some competing products, again a conservative approach. The claimant has also produced its annual reports, showing historical profits, and while the projected profits are higher than those in some years, claimant has persuasively argued that higher profits can be expected from specialty products, benefiting from a high quality image.

[34] "The estimates as to the overall market in India, claimant's prospective share of such market, and the projected sales growth are necessarily more speculative. However, claimant has submitted detailed studies (from independent sources) of the industry . . . and future anticipated growth. Claimant's estimate that it would achieve 30 percent of such market, with a superior product and allowing for a lower share at the outset, does not seem unreasonable.

[35] "Claimant supported its submissions by the written statements and oral testimony of . . . consultant[s], each of whom were subjected to lengthy and expert cross-examination. No contrary evidence or witnesses were produced by defendant.

[36] "Applying the above-described procedures, the claimant has estimated its lost profits for a period of ten years from anticipated start up. . . .

[37] "The arbitrators accept the argument of defendant that, any lost profits can only be calculated on a basis of seven, and not ten, years. The duration of the Agreement . . . is for seven years to run from the start of production. . . . While it is true, as argued by claimant, that it might have been able to benefit from its leading market position even after termination, it is also true that, over a period of seven years other competitors might have upgraded their product, and defendant itself might have entered the market or licensed others (the Agreement being non-exclusive). Therefore, seven years appears to be a reasonable period. Moreover, the arbitrators believe that it is appropriate to use the average exchange rate . . . existing [at] the time of the Award, rather than the earlier rate used by claimant. . . .

[38] "The arbitrators further believe that, in making a present award of future profits, a present-value factor must be applied to the amount awarded. Applying a present-value adjustment with the appropriate rupee interest/discount rate, the total amount of . . . representing lost profits over the seven years . . . is reduced to a present-value amount of. . . .

[39] "The arbitrators recognize that the claimed lost-profits would have been earned primarily in Indian currency (and have therefore applied an Indian Rupee interest/discount rate). However, the claim was expressed in Deutsch Marks, the defendant is a German entity, and there was no argument about the currency of the claim. Accordingly, the arbitrators conclude that it is appropriate to make the Award in amounts converted into Deutsch Marks, applying the current DM:Rupee exchange rate. . . .

[40] "Finally, recognizing the uncertain nature of the calculations referred to above, as so forcefully argued by defendant, the arbitrators believe it is reasonable and appropriate to apply an additional discount of fifteen percent to the total calculated. . . . "

(. . . .)

2. Damages for Loss of Reputation

[41] "The claimant has also claimed a substantial amount representing alleged loss of reputation/image, and a related loss of profits from its existing lines of business. . . .

[42] "The arbitrators have sympathy for claimant's arguments in this respect, and recognize that claimant may well have suffered some injury to its reputation and image. The arbitrators believe that the claimant was fully justified in contacting prospective customers, after the Agreement was signed but before production was ready, in order to 'prepare' the market, and that its inability to

perform may well have created negative impressions. The arbitrators have also taken note of the various pieces of correspondence with potential customers or third parties submitted as exhibits by claimant, which show disappointment and criticism. . . .

[43]   "However, upon careful consideration, the arbitrators conclude that claimant's proof of such loss, and especially the quantum of any such loss, is too speculative and too uncertain to serve as a basis for an award of damages.

[44]   "The arbitrators also note that, as shown by claimant's audited annual reports, its profits in the year following termination were higher than the previous year, a fact which suggests that any loss in reputation did not have lasting negative impact. Accordingly, this claim must be disallowed.

[45]   "The claimant has in addition claimed reimbursement for certain expenses which it allegedly incurred in connection with the Agreement, including (i) the initial payment made by claimant to defendant, and (ii) expenses representing management time which was spent – in vain, as it turned out – in negotiation and follow-up with defendant, and in preparation for actual production in India (including the hiring of a specialist engineer and the construction of a building).

(. . . .)

[46]   "Because of the decision already taken by the arbitrators with respect to lost profits (see above) the arbitrators do not have to decide on the adequacy of such evidence. For, had the Agreement been performed by both parties in accordance with its terms, and had the claimant earned the profits which are now being restituted, the claimant would have had to bear these expenses in the normal course. In other words, the claimant cannot now recuperate both the profits it would have earned (assuming full performance – sometimes referred to as a 'positive interest') and at the same time the expenses it has incurred (assuming non-performance, or a 'negative interest'). To do so would in effect give the claimant a double recovery. This is true, both for the initial payment, and for the other expenses claimed.

[47]   "The arbitrators hold that claimant, which will recover its lost profits, is not entitled to recuperate also the expenses claimed under these headings."

3.   Exemplary and Punitive Damages

[48]   "Finally, the claimants have made a claim for exemplary and punitive damages, in an amount to be determined by the Tribunal, because of the allegedly conscious and pre-planned breach of the Agreement by the defendants.

[49]   "The arbitrators have some sympathy for the claimant's position. The evidence indicates a troubling failure on the part of defendant to take its contractual obligations seriously, beginning with the long initial delay in providing

any Documentation, and in even responding to claimant's numerous inquiries; followed by a further long delay in furnishing the bulk of Documentation; and culminating in the constantly changing excuses for not delivering, and eventual refusal to deliver, the so-called 'catalysts' information. This behavior may to some degree be explained, although not excused, by defendant's reference to 'top management changes'. A more likely explanation can be inferred from defendant's letter ..., where defendant makes it very clear that it considers the transaction price to be 'out of all proportion' and not financially interesting to defendant. The alternatives subsequently suggested by defendant at various times, would all have resulted in substantially more income for the defendant (and higher cost to the claimant). Thus, the claimant's allegations of conscious and willful behavior are not without some foundation.

[50]   "[T]he arbitrators find that they are not here empowered to award either exemplary or punitive damages. As a matter of Indian law, while the issue was not briefed in detail, the arbitrators find that a court, and thereby by extension an arbitral tribunal, will normally give 'damages for breach of contract only by way of compensation for loss suffered, and not by way of punishment'. See, e.g., *Namayya v. The Union of India*, AIR (1958) AP 533, 541. Moreover, in the present proceedings, no claim for exemplary or punitive damages was set out in the Terms of Reference, or in claimant's initial Request for Arbitration; as a matter of arbitration practice, and in view of [Art.] 16 of the ICC Rules,[2] the arbitrators therefore cannot now entertain such a claim. Accordingly, the arbitrators must disallow claimant's claim for exemplary or punitive damages. (. . . .)

[51]   "The arbitrators have found that the defendant failed to perform its obligations under the Agreement. However, the claimant has claimed, and is being awarded, lost profits calculated as is the Agreement had been performed. For the same reasons as set out in paras. [45]-[47] above, the claimant cannot now claim the benefits of such lost profits, without attributing the related expenses which would have been incurred. Had there been performance, the claimant would have had to pay the balance. . . . Therefore, the arbitrators determine that such amount . . . must be deducted from the amount of lost profits awarded . . . , leaving a net amount . . . to be paid by the defendant to the claimant in damages."

---

2. Art. 16 of the 1998 ICC Rules of Conciliation and Arbitration reads:

"The parties may make new claims or counter-claims before the arbitrator on condition that these remain within the limits fixed by the Terms of Reference provided for in Article 13 or that they are specified in a rider to that document, signed by the parties and communicated to the Court."

IV. COSTS AND FEES ALSO IN RESPECT OF COURT-RELATED
     COSTS

[52] "With respect to the lawsuit commenced by the claimant before the local
court in [India], such lawsuit was ostensibly for conservatory relief only. Such
application for conservatory relief is specifically authorized under the ICC
Rules (see ICC Rules, Art. 8.5),[3] and cannot be considered, in and of itself, a
breach of the Agreement. The local court in [India] initially granted the injunction requested. Upon appeal, the Appellate Court vacated such decision, and
dismissed the application. The Appellate Court, presumably in accordance with
that court's discretion and local rules of procedure, determined that no costs be
assessed. It is not within the purview of this Arbitral Tribunal's authority to
reconsider, or take other decisions with respect to, such court-related costs.
(. . . .)
[53] "Given the finding by the arbitrators that the defendant breached the
Agreement, and the granting of an Award in claimant's favor, the Tribunal
determines that a large part of such costs and fees should be assessed against
defendant. However, not all of claimant's claims were allowed, and the final
amount awarded by the Tribunal is considerably less than the total amounts
claimed. Therefore, it is not appropriate to assess all such costs against the
defendant.
[54] "Taking the above into consideration, the Tribunal determines that
seventy-five percent of the costs of arbitration be assessed against the
defendant. . . .
[55] "The Tribunal similarly determines that the defendant shall reimburse to
the claimant seventy-five percent of claimant's legal costs."
(. . . .)

V. AWARD AND ORDER

[56] "In consideration of the foregoing, the Arbitral Tribunal hereby orders
and awards as follows:

---

3. Art. 8.5 of the ICC Rules of Conciliation and Arbitration reads:

"Before the file is transmitted to the arbitrator, and in exceptional circumstances even thereafter,
the parties shall be at liberty to apply to any competent judicial authority for interim conservatory
measures, and they shall not by so doing be held to infringe the agreement to arbitrate or to affect
the relevant powers reserved to the arbitrator.
(. . . .)"

1. The defendant's submission that this Arbitration has been brought prematurely is rejected;

    (. . . .)

3. The claimant's further claims for damages related to loss of reputation or goodwill, and loss of other business opportunities, are disallowed;

4. The claimant's further claims for exemplary or punitive damages are similarly disallowed;

5. The defendant's counterclaims, other than the above-mentioned offset . . . , are disallowed;"

    (. . . .)

Interim award in case no. 7893 of 1994

Parties:	Claimant: Licensor (US)
	Defendant: Licensee (Japan)
Place of arbitration:	Paris, France
Published in:	Unpublished
Subject matters:	– scope of arbitration agreement
	– arbitrability of antitrust issues under New York State law? (no)
	– violation of public policy
	– parallel arbitration proceedings

Facts

Licensor (US licensor) is a US corporation engaged in the design and manufacture of certain electrical equipment whose equipment includes technology A and an earlier version, technology B. US licensor is a wholly-owned subsidiary of a US company which in turn is a wholly-owned subsidiary of a Swiss company (Swiss parent).

In 1982, the US licensor concluded a License and Technical Assistance Agreement (LTA Agreement) with a Japanese corporation (Japanese licensee) specialized in the manufacture of similar electrical equipment. The LTA Agreement was concluded for a period of ten years. Differences arose between the parties at the end of the ten-year period and they extended the Agreement for one year to allow themselves time to resolve their problems. The LTA Agreement was terminated in 1993. The US licensor and the Japanese licensee concluded a further agreement in November 1992 (the 1992 Agreement).

In the meantime, the Swiss parent concluded an agreement with another Swiss company (Swiss licensor) under which the Swiss licensor granted the Swiss parent the right to continue its activities including a license agreement which it had concluded with the Japanese licensee (Swiss-Japanese license agreement). The Swiss-Japanese license agreement was terminated on the same date in 1993 as the LTA Agreement.

The US licensor initiated ICC arbitration, claiming that the Japanese licensee continued to use its licensed technology after the termination of the LTA Agreement unlawfully and in breach of the contract. The arbitration clause in the LTA Agreement read in relevant part: "If any dispute shall arise concerning the interpretation and/or performance of this Agreement as to which the parties cannot agree, such dispute shall be submitted to and settled by arbitration." The applicable law to the Agreement was New York State law.

At the time the ICC arbitration was initiated, the US licensor and the Swiss licensor had already initiated an ad hoc arbitration in Switzerland against the Japanese licensee under the terms of the arbitration clause in the Swiss-Japanese license agreement.

The US licensor challenged the ICC arbitral tribunal's jurisdiction over two of the Japanese licensee's counterclaims and the latter challenged the arbitral tribunal's jurisdiction over the principal claim. Those issues were settled in the interim award excerpted below. The arbitral tribunal first examined the challenge of its jurisdiction over the principal claim and rejected the Japanese licensee's argument that only claims based on technology B were admissible.

The arbitral tribunal accepted the objection to its jurisdiction over the Japanese licensee's counterclaim finding, inter alia, that the arbitration clause did not contemplate the adjudication of a claim under US antitrust laws, in particular, because the LTA agreement was governed by New York State law and New York State case law held that "it is against the public policy of New York for arbitrators to adjudicate antitrust claims". The Japanese licensor's second counterclaim based on the 1992 Agreement did not fall within the scope of the arbitration clause in the LTA Agreement.

Excerpt

(....)

I. CLAIMS AND COUNTERCLAIMS

[1] "In this arbitration, the US licensor claims that the Japanese licensee continued to use its licensed technology after termination of the LTA Agreement, unlawfully and in breach of contract.

[2] "The Japanese licensee denies this charge; and the Japanese licensee asserts, by way of counterclaim, that the License Agreement upon which the US licensor's claims are based (a) is unenforceable on the grounds that the equipment constructed by the Japanese licensee do[es] not employ, and the License Agreement is not supported by, any legally protectable patents, trade-secrets

or know-how of the US licensor and (b) is contrary to the antitrust laws of the State of New York and of the United States and to the Treaty of Rome.

[3]   "The Japanese licensee also counterclaims 'on the grounds of fraud in the inducement, breach of contract and breach of the US licensor's obligation under New York Law of good faith and fair dealing' with respect to a further 1992 Agreement between the US licensor and the Japanese licensee and referred to by the US licensor in the present arbitration."

(. . . .)

II.   JURISDICTION OVER CLAIM

[4]   "The US licensor has put forward a series of claims against the Japanese licensee. These are summarized in the Terms of Reference, but the gravamen of the US licensor's complaint is that, after the termination of the LTA Agreement, the Japanese licensee wrongfully and in breach of contract and of the applicable law, continued to use information and licensed material which the US licensor had licensed to the Japanese licensee under that Agreement. The Japanese licensee strenuously denies this charge. The Japanese licensee asserts that there is no basis for it either in fact or in law; and the Japanese licensee goes on to raise the first jurisdictional issue considered here, by contending that the arbitral tribunal should dismiss, at this stage, any claims asserted by the US licensor 'to the extent that they are based upon alleged use by the Japanese licensee of technology other than process B technology.

[5]   "It might be asked, why should the Japanese licensee seek to limit the US licensor's claim in this way? Part of the answer to this question lies in the way in which the US licensor itself initially put its case. The US licensor said that it was bringing the arbitration 'to prevent the Japanese licensee from using the US licensor's process B technology on process A equipment'. This statement was repeated often in the Statement of Case. It was not until the meetings in Paris in March of this year, that the US licensor made it clear that it did *not* intend to limit its claim in this way.

(. . . .)

[6]   "The Japanese licensee contends that initially the US licensor intended to press its claims in respect of the alleged mis-use of *process B technology* in this arbitration and to deal with *process A technology* in the Berne arbitration. Ms. Y for the Japanese licensee put the position very plainly:

'The Japanese licensee submits at the outset – and we have articulated this in our briefs – that the US licensor's failure to raise these claims earlier in this tribunal and its very precise statement of claim, which contains a carefully crafted delineation of what is being arbitrated here versus what is being arbitrated in Berne, process B technology versus process A technology, establishes that the US licensor understood that there were two separate licenses here, with two separate licensors, covering, in the end, separate technologies for resolution in different tribunals, pursuant to different rules of law interpreting different contracts.'

[7]   "This analysis appears to be correct. At the Hearing in Washington, Mr X for the US Licensor said:

'In our opening pleading we said, "We want to claim our rights to information." That would give you no clue at all as to what that information was, so we used the phrase "process B technology". And that is more limited than the entirety of the information that we gave to the Japanese licensee. And it was drafted, frankly, in anticipation that we would be able to consolidate the two arbitrations for reasons of economy and expense.

But that proposal – and that point was in our cover letter to the ICC, which requested consolidation. It is quite clear – we were rather surprised, but it's quite clear that the Japanese licensee has refused consolidation. We are bound to accept that.

And we are now forced into the situation of pursuing the claim of: all of the claims of the US licensor under the LTA Agreement in this arbitration. And all of the claims of the Swiss parent will be pursued under their separate 1985 contract.'

[8]   "There is an attractive symmetry to the proposal that this tribunal should deal with claims based on process B technology, leaving the Berne tribunal to deal with claims based on process A technology. This would simplify the work of each tribunal and avoid the risk of duplicated work and – possibly – conflicting decisions. But would it be appropriate to proceed in this way?

[9]   "To answer this question, it is necessary to consider carefully the written and oral arguments which have been advanced by counsel for the contesting parties.

[10]   "The US licensor asserts that its license to the Japanese licensee in the LTA Agreement, was *not* confined to process B. To follow the US licensor's argument, it is necessary to look at certain clauses of the LTA Agreement and at Exhibit A to that Agreement. The LTA Agreement licensed the Japanese licensee to make use of technology which the US licensor claimed as its property, this technology being divided into three classes – Information, Unusual Developments and New Products.

[11]   " 'Information', as can be seen from Art. III of the LTA Agreement, was defined to include 'any or all' of seven types of information with respect to

licensed material, including design, manufacturing and operational information. Art. III, subject to some exceptions, imposed a strict duty of confidentiality on the Japanese licensee with respect to information; and Art. X provided that all information communicated to the Japanese licensee by or on behalf of the US licensor (to the extent that it was not common knowledge in the industry) should remain the legal and absolute property of the US licensor. The scope of the Japanese licensee's license to use information in the design and manufacture of licensed material was defined in Art. II.

[12] "The information which was stated to be licensed to the Japanese licensee, and to be protected as confidential, was information 'with respect to licensed material'. What, then, was 'licensed material'? Exhibit A to the LTA Agreement describes this as ... equipment, employing the US licensor's design and/or manufacturing concepts and characteristics' ... which would include, but not be limited to, two types of equipment and then as Item 3 on the list:

'US licensor/Swiss licensor process A equipment (Subject to Art. III).'

(....)

[13] "The reference in Item 3 to 'US licensor/Swiss licensor process A equipment' would seem, at first impression to indicate that the US licensor, either alone or in conjunction with the Swiss licensor, possessed, or claimed to possess, proprietary information with respect to process A equipment. This impression is supported by the stipulation of Art. IV of the LTA Agreement (governing the use of the US licensor's name) that the term 'Japanese Licensee/US licensor/Swiss Licensor process A equipment' is to be used in connection with 'the manufacture, use and sale by the Japanese licensee of licensed materials of Item (3) of Exhibit A'.

[14] "However, in considering Item 3, account must be taken of the qualification in brackets, which reads: 'Subject to Art. III'. Both the US licensor and the Japanese licensee agree that this is a reference to one particular paragraph in Art. III which, with the sentences numbered for ease of reference, reads:

'(1) The US licensor has entered into an agreement with the original Swiss licensor pertaining to process A equipment.

(2) The Japanese licensee also has an agreement with the Swiss licensor pertaining to process A equipment.

(3) The Agreement between the US licensor and the original Swiss licensor provides, among other things, that the Swiss licensor shall extend to the Japanese licensee the right to maintain direct contact with the US licensor for the purpose of obtaining and exchanging know-how relating to process A equipment.

(4) The US licensor will, therefore, on request of the Japanese licensee, provide the Japanese licensee directly with information and technical assistance of the US licensor and the Swiss licensor in respect of process A equipment to which the Japanese licensee is entitled by reason of its agreement with the Swiss licensor.

(5) It should be understood, however, that royalties which accrue on the process A equipment shall be paid, as in the past, to the Swiss licensor under the License Agreement between the Japanese licensee and the Swiss licensor.'

[15] "What qualification does this paragraph make of the licensed material included in the phrase 'US licensor/Swiss licensor process A equipment'? The US licensor contends that the qualification, or limitation, is to be found in the third sentence of the paragraph which, in essence, reads: 'the US licensor will ... provide the Japanese licensee directly with information and technical assistance of the US licensor and the Swiss licensor *in respect of process A equipment to which the Japanese licensee is entitled by reason of its agreement with the Swiss licensor*' (emphasis added). In other words, any information relating to process A equipment which the US licensor has obtained from the original Swiss licensor may only be passed on by the US licensor to the Japanese licensee if the Japanese licensee is entitled to such information by reason of its agreement with the Swiss licensor.

[16] "This argument appears reasonable, although, of course, it reserves for later consideration the question of whether or not all the information relating to process A equipment came from the Swiss licensor – in which case, there may be considerable force in the Japanese licensee's contention that Item 3 of Art. III 'did not give the Japanese licensee something new'.

[17] "The Japanese licensee submits that the qualifying, or limiting, provision in the relevant paragraph is the final/fourth sentence which stipulates that royalties which accrue on the process A equipment should be paid to the Swiss licensor. The Japanese licensee argues that this in effect confirms 'the Swiss licensor's status as the Japanese licensee's sole licensor of process A technology'.

[18] "The Japanese licensee further submits that the restrictions relating to information which are set out in the LTA Agreement do not apply to process A technology, since such information, if any, comes from the Swiss licensor and accordingly 'is made available to the Japanese licensee by a third party authorized to disclose the same to the Japanese licensee', within the provisions of Art. X.

[19] "The arbitral tribunal has given careful consideration to the cogent arguments advanced on behalf of the parties, both in written submissions and at the hearings in Washington. The first jurisdictional issues is not an easy one to

resolve. However, the arbitral tribunal takes the view that effect must be given to the LTA Agreement and to the description of licensed material set out in Exhibit A to that Agreement.

[20] "The description of licensed material is a wide one and includes, at Item 3, 'US licensor/Swiss licensor process A equipment (Subject to Art. III).' This suggests that the US licensor, either alone or in conjunction with the Swiss licensor, possessed proprietary rights for the design and/or manufacture of process A equipment which it was prepared to licence, and did licence, to the Japanese licensee; and, as already noted, the Japanese licensee was to use the term 'Japanese licensee/US licensor/Swiss licensor process A equipment' in connection with the manufacture, use or sale by the Japanese licensee of such generators.

[21] "As to the restriction on Item 3 contained in the stipulation 'Subject to Art. III', the arbitral tribunal is presently of the view that this refers to the stipulation that any information relating to process A equipment which comes from the Swiss licensor will only be passed on to the Japanese licensee by the US licensor if the Japanese licensee is entitled to receive such information by reason of its agreement with the Swiss licensor.

[22] "It may be, that when it comes to an argument on the merits, the Japanese licensee will be able to sustain the contention which it has made, forcefully and frequently, to the effect that the information, if any, which it has received from the US licensor relates only to process B technology. However, it would appear that the LTA Agreement goes wider than this. Accordingly, the US licensor should be given the opportunity of making good the claims it asserts against the Japanese licensee without being limited jurisdictionally to those claims which are based on process B technology.

[23] "It is true that the focus of the US licensor's Statement of Case was on process B technology, but the opening sentence gave an indication of a wider claim, when it said:

> 'This arbitration is brought to prevent a licensee from continuing to use proprietary information obtained under a license agreement after it has terminated the agreement.'

[24] "In any event, the US licensor's position was made plain at the meeting in Paris and in the Terms of Reference, so that the Japanese licensee should not be put at any unfair disadvantage as a result of this decision. In particular, when the merits of the case come to be considered, the Japanese licensee will be able to put forward arguments as to the limits on the LTA Agreement, which the Japanese licensee has already to some extent foreshadowed in its consideration of the first jurisdictional issue."

III. ARBITRABILITY OF CLAIMS OF ANTITRUST VIOLATIONS

[25] "The Japanese licensee maintains that its first counterclaim, alleging antitrust violations, is arbitrable under the arbitration clause contained in the LTA Agreement. The clause provides as follows:

'If any dispute shall arise concerning the interpretation and/or performance of any provision of this Agreement as to which the parties cannot agree, such dispute shall be submitted to and settled by arbitration.'

[26] "The Japanese licensee agrees that the counterclaim raises no dispute concerning the interpretation of any provision of the agreement. Rather, the Japanese licensee contends that its antitrust counterclaim concerns the performance of provisions of the Agreement, and thus falls within the arbitration clause.

[27] "The basis of the Japanese licensee's antitrust counterclaim is that when the US licensor enforces the license agreement with the US licensor and others, such enforcement constitutes anti-competitive conduct under the antitrust law. This, in turn, is grounded on the allegation by the Japanese licensee that the US licensor has no proprietary technology to support the territorial and other restrictions in its license agreements. Thus, the conduct which the Japanese licensee seeks to remedy, the argument proceeds, concerns 'performance' under the LTA Agreement.

[28] "The Japanese licensee relies heavily on *Mitsubishi Motors v. Soler Chrysler-Plymouth*, 473 US 614 (1985),[1] where the Supreme Court held that antitrust claims were arbitrable under a clause regarding arbitration of 'all disputes, controversies or differences which may arise between Mitsubishi and Soler out of or in relation to Arts. 1-B through V of the Agreement. Until *Soler* there was a serious question as to whether or not statutory claims were arbitrable under the Federal Arbitration Act. The Japanese licensee also relies on *PPG Industries Inc. v. Pilkington PLC* 825 F.Supp. 1465, 1473 (D.Ariz. 1993),[2] where the arbitration clause covered '[a]ny disputes involving the meaning, interpretation, application or violation of the provisions of this agreement'. The district court in *Pilkington* held that the clause did *not* limit arbitral claims simply to claims involving breaches of the agreement; rather the *Pilkington* court said that the arbitration clause was sufficiently broad to cover disputes *relating* to the effect of the agreement.

---

1. Reported in Yearbook XI (1986) pp. 555-566 (US no. 59).
2. Reported in Yearbook XX (1995) pp. 885-890 (US no. 172).

[29]   "The Japanese licensee, citing *Moses H. Cone Memorial Hospital*, 460 US 1 (1983), maintains that the federal policy in favor of the liberal interpretation of arbitration clauses further supports its contention, and adds that any doubts concerning the scope of arbitrable issues should be resolved in favor of arbitration. The Japanese licensee relies on *Fletcher, Kidder Peabody & Co.* 81 NY 2d 623, 601, NYS 686, cert. denied. 114 S.Ct. 554 (1993). New York had a long line of cases holding that anticipatory agreements to arbitrate disputes involving unlawful discrimination claims were arbitrable, such as the antitrust claim in *Soler*. Then the US Supreme Court held in *Gilmer v. Interstate/Johnson*, 500 US 20 (1991) that employment discrimination claims were arbitrable, such as the antitrust claim in *Soler*. In light of *Gilmer*, the New York Court of Appeals compelled a plaintiff to arbitrate a discrimination case brought under New York law. The Japanese licensee argues that since *Soler* held that antitrust claims are arbitrable, New York law would now hold that Donnelly Act antitrust claims are also arbitrable.

[30]   "The US licensor's response to the Japanese licensee's argument is two-pronged: first, the Japanese licensee's antitrust counterclaim does not fall under the arbitration clause since the antitrust claim, as alleged, is 'extrinsic' or not covered by the provisions of the LTA Agreement; and secondly, that in any event, an arbitration clause in a contract to be interpreted under New York law, is not to be construed as covering antitrust violations.

[31]   "As to the first point, the US licensor argues that the Japanese licensee's antitrust counterclaim does not concern 'the interpretation or performance of any provision of the Agreement', that the counterclaim does not allege a dispute over the performance of any provision of the Agreement; that the words 'as to which the parties cannot agree' do not relate to antitrust claims; and that when the parties chose New York law to govern the Agreement, that choice was further evidence of their intent not to arbitrate antitrust claims.

[32]   "It is not disputed, says the US licensor, that the parties performed their obligations with respect to the territorial and other limits on the license. In this regard the US licensor cites *Macy*, 383 NYS 2d (1976) which declared that performance is defined as the fulfillment or accomplishment of a provision, contract or other obligation. The US licensor contends that nothing in the definition of performance concerns the *effect* of performance. And, the US licensor adds, the clause deals with arbitration solely of contractual claims.

[33]   "The US licensor claims that the Japanese licensee confuses disputes concerning the parties' performance of their obligations, with disputes concerning the *effect* of their performance. The US licensor points out that the arbitration clause in the agreement with the Japanese licensee is different from the arbitration clause interpreted in the Berne arbitration, where the

arbitrators *are* asserting jurisdiction over antitrust claims. Art. IX in the Swiss-Japanese license Agreement provides:

'In case of any difference or dispute arising between the parties . . . hereto or in their respective successors . . . touching the construction, meaning or effect of this Agreement or any clause hereof or the rights or liabilities of the parties hereto . . . or their respective successors . . . or otherwise in relation to the premises, any such difference or dispute shall be settled by arbitration in Berne.'

The US licensor specifically calls attention to the word 'effect' in this Agreement.

[34] "It is significant that the arbitration clause in the LTA Agreement refers specifically to disputes 'as to which the parties cannot agree'. It is doubtful whether the parties alone can agree to resolve a dispute involving an antitrust violation, where the public is deeply concerned.

[35] "The US licensor also asserts that to adjudicate antitrust claims would require the arbitrators to consider the US licensor's contracts with other equipment manufacturers, and that there are at least eighteen such contracts.

[36] "The US licensor insists that *Soler* does not help the Japanese licensee. In *Soler* the parties conceded that the arbitration clause covered antitrust claims: it embraced 'all disputes, controversies or differences which may arise between Mitsubishi and Soler out of or in relation to Art. 1B through V [sic] of the agreement'. The critical issue in *Soler*, emphasizes the US licensor, was whether the clause, although broad enough to cover antitrust claims, conferred jurisdiction on the arbitrators to deal with antitrust violations. The majority in *Soler* held that there was no bar to an arbitral tribunal, under the Federal Arbitration Act, entertaining antitrust claims.

[37] "The US licensor argues that *Pilkington* also is inapplicable. *Pilkington*, asserts the US licensor, merely compelled the parties to go to arbitration. In the present situation, the parties are already in arbitration, and the issue is which of the claims asserted is arbitrable. To the same effect, states the US licensor, is *Pepsi Cola Metropolitan Bottling Co. v. Columbia-Oxford Beverage, Inc.*, 474 NYS (2) 127 (App. Div. 1984), which concerned a court's decision to compel the parties to resolve their dispute before an arbitration panel, not an arbitration tribunal's decision whether it had jurisdiction over a particular claim. The US licensor asserts that the 'strong presumption in favor of the arbitrability of disputes in the commercial sector' refers to a court's determination to compel the parties to arbitrate, not the arbitral tribunal's construction of the scope of a particular arbitration clause.

[38] "The US licensor points out that the parties here specifically agreed that New York law would govern the agreement (Art. 15), and under New York law, antitrust claims are not arbitrable: *In the matter of the Arbitration Between Aimcee Wholesale Corp. and Tomar Products, Inc.* 21 NY2d 621, 237 NE2d 223 (1968). This would strongly indicate, the US licensor argues, that the parties did not intend to arbitrate antitrust claims.

[39] "The US licensor asserts that, although the US Supreme Court in *Soler* construed the Federal Arbitration Act (FAA) to permit the arbitration of an antitrust claim, New York courts continue to re-affirm the holding in *Aimcee* that New York does not sanction the arbitration of antitrust claims on the ground that such a procedure would be against public policy: see *Matter of Tomar*, 157 Misc.2nd 703, 707 (1993), where the Court elaborated why using arbitrators to resolve disputes involving antitrust claims is against New York public policy:

> 'Illustrative of the matters which have been held to be beyond the arbitra-tor's jurisdiction are those involving the enforcement of this State's anti-trust laws, which have been recognized as representing "public policy of the first magnitude"' (*Matter of Aimcee Wholesale Corp.* [Tomar Prods.] 21 NY2d 621, 625).

[40] "Consistent with this analysis, the US licensor cites *Armco Steel Co. v. CSX Corporation*, 790 F.Supp. 311 (D.D.C./1991), which holds that if parties to a contract agree to arbitrate their disputes and choose to have their contract construed under a particular state law, and the state law forbids arbitration of antitrust claims, the arbitration clause incorporates any limits on arbitration embodied in the state law referred to. The *Armco* court declared (790 F.Supp. at 319):

> 'The Court today holds that the FAA [Federal Arbitration Act] does not compel parties to arbitrate when the parties have chosen to be governed by state law and the state law relieves the parties of the responsibility to arbi-trate when there is an allegation that the contract itself is a product of a violation of the antitrust laws.'

[41] "It is the opinion of the arbitral tribunal that the arbitration clause here did not contemplate the adjudication by the arbitrators of a claim or claims under the antitrust laws. The only words in the arbitration clause that arguably could be interpreted as covering antitrust claims are 'concerning the perfor-mance of any provision of this Agreement'. We do not believe that the antitrust

claims alleged here concern the *performance* of any provision of the Japanese licensee/US licensor Agreement.

[42]   "Although there is a body of precedent that favors resolving disputes under the arbitration clauses, such presumption is overcome when the language in the arbitration clause does not appear to cover the arbitration of disputes under the antitrust laws and, in addition, the parties specifically provide that the agreement be construed under New York law. The cases decided by New York courts hold that it is against the public policy of New York for arbitrators to adjudicate antitrust claims: *Aimcee Wholesale Corp.* supra. Although it may be argued that *Soler* holds to the contrary in cases under the Federal Arbitration Act, the New York cases decided after *Soler* still adhere to *Aimcee: Matter of Tomar*, 157 Misc.2d 703, 707 (1993).

[43]   "As Judge Hogan held in *Armco*, supra, decided six years after *Soler*, the FAA does not compel parties to arbitrate a particular claim when the parties have chosen to be governed by the law of a particular state and the law of the designated state prohibits the parties from arbitrating a claim or claims under the antitrust laws."

IV.   ADMISSIBILITY OF THE 1992 AGREEMENT AS EVIDENCE

[44]   "The Japanese licensee's second counterclaim is based on the US licensor's assertion in its 'Statement of the Claimant's Case', that the Japanese licensee's execution of the further 1992 Agreement 'is a devastating admission of the worth of the US licensor's process B technology', and 'virtually conclusive proof of the Japanese licensee's liability in this proceeding'.

[45]   "The Japanese licensee alleges that those assertions violate Art. III(3)(b) of the 1992 agreement, which states,

'. . . . nothing in this agreement shall be construed as an admission by the Japanese licensee that the US licensor or any other person has proprietary rights in process A units'.

[46]   "The Japanese licensee recognizes that this arbitration is convened and is to be conducted pursuant to the arbitration clause of the LTA Agreement, not the arbitration clause of the 1992 Agreement. It asserts, however, that its second counterclaim 'concern[s] the interpretation and/or performance of [the LTA Agreement] because it requires the tribunal to determine whether the US licensor was entitled to use the 1992 Agreement as evidence in a dispute under the Japanese licensee/US licensor agreement'. A need to rule on the admissibility of the 1992 Agreement as evidence does not, however, convert the dispute before us into one 'concern[ing] the interpretation and/or performance' of the 1992 Agreement.

In making the challenged assertion, the US licensor is addressing the interpretation or performance of the LTA Agreement, to which Art. III(3)(b) of the 1992 Agreement does not refer.

[47]   "The Japanese licensee also argues that the second counterclaim is arbitrable in this proceeding because the 1982 and 1992 Agreements 'are related and contain similar provisions requiring arbitration under ICC rules' and 'related agreements are arbitrable together ... even if one of the agreements lacks an arbitration clause'.

[48]   "In our opinion, the cases cited by the Japanese licensee are not applicable here, in which the LTA Agreement and the 1992 Agreement each has its own arbitration clause defining the issues that are arbitrable under that clause. The authority of arbitrators under a proceeding convened under the LTA Agreement, as this arbitration is, must be derived from the arbitration clause of that Agreement, which limits their authority to disputes under that Agreement. Accordingly, only disputes concerning the interpretation and/or performance of provisions of the LTA Agreement are arbitrable in this proceeding.

[49]   "This conclusion is not altered by the fact that, if a provision of the 1992 Agreement is offered in evidence here, we will need to determine whether that provision is relevant to the interpretation or performance of the LTA Agreement, and if so, whether offering it is forbidden by Art. III(b)(3) of the 1992 Agreement. If, when the US licensor's argument is fleshed out, we conclude that our considering it is precluded, we will not consider it, and the Japanese licensee will have suffered no injury.

[50]   "In short, the Japanese licensee's second counterclaim is in effect an objection to an offer of evidence. We are of the opinion that, as a counterclaim, it is outside our jurisdiction. However, this conclusion is without prejudice to the right of the Japanese licensee to object at an appropriate time to the admission of that evidence. We express no opinion at this stage on the merit of any such objection."

Final award in case no. 9427 of 1998

Parties:	Claimant: Credit insurer (European country)
	Defendant: Bank (Baltic country)
Place of arbitration:	Paris, France
Published in:	Unpublished
Subject matters:	– on-demand bank guarantee
	– general principles applied in international banking practice
	– assignment of bank guarantee

Facts

A European supplier (supplier) was approached by a Baltic company (the buyer) in connection with the purchase and delivery of supplies for the conversion of a super fishing trawler into a passenger ship. In order to finance the production of the supplies to be delivered, the supplier obtained loans from its Bank (supplier's Bank) as well as an export credit insurance from a government credit insurer (claimant) for 90 per cent of the price of the goods to be supplied, less the 15 per cent down payment.

The buyer's Bank, which was financing the buyer, issued a first Guarantee, the terms of which were not accepted by the supplier, nor its credit insurer or bank. The buyer's Bank subsequently issued a Guarantee referred to as Guarantee No. 1 which was accepted as an unconditional on-demand guarantee by supplier's credit insurer and Bank. Shortly thereafter, supplier signed an Instrument of Assignment assigning the Guarantee to its Bank. The Instrument of Assignment was notified to buyer's Bank and signed and returned to supplier's Bank.

More materials and equipment than originally ordered were needed for the conversion and Guarantee No. 2 was issued for the adjusted amount. Supplier once again signed an Instrument of Assignment to its Bank which in turn sent the assignment for notification to buyer's Bank by registered mail. Buyer's Bank, despite reminders, did not react to this notification.

The Export Credit Guarantee which had been issued by the credit insurer provided, inter alia, that the "Insured shall undertake the recovery of any doubtful debts" and that the "insured shall assign the doubtful debt . . . to the insurer".

The goods were delivered but in spite of several reminders, the buyer failed to make the first instalment payment. The supplier's Bank made a claim under Guarantee No. 2 to buyer's Bank for the first instalment. After numerous exchanges of correspondence, buyer's Bank informed supplier's Bank that buyer was bankrupt. Buyer's Bank agreed to pay the first instalment and requested supplier to stop any further deliveries. However, at the time, all the goods had already been delivered.

Buyer's bank refused to pay the full amount alleging that the conditions of the guarantee – which it considered was not an on-demand guarantee, but rather a conditional guarantee – had not been met. Moreover, in its view, there had been no valid assignment of Guarantee No. 2 by the supplier to its Bank.

Following the dispute over payment, the buyer's Bank instituted court proceedings in the Baltic country seeking to have the Guarantee declared invalid. The Baltic State court held the Guarantee invalid and supplier appealed that decision to the Civil Chamber of the Supreme Court which dismissed the claim. Buyer's bank appealed to the Civil Department of the Senate of the Baltic State Supreme Court. In the meantime, the parties concluded an arbitration agreement submitting the dispute to ICC arbitration. The Terms of Reference required the arbitral tribunal to decide the following issues:

"1. What are the proper laws or rules of law to be applied in this case?
2. Is the Guarantee No. 2 valid and is it an On-Demand Guarantee or a Conditional Guarantee?
3. Is the right of the Beneficiary to make a claim under the Guarantee assignable?
4. Does the claimant have the right to claim payment under the Guarantee?
5. Has a demand under the Guarantee been validly presented?
6. Is the claimant's Claim for Relief justified?
7. Is the [defendant's] Claim for Relief justified?
8. What party should bear the costs of this arbitration and in what proportion?"

The arbitral tribunal in a unanimous award first found that it would decide the case on the basis of the legal principles relating to on-demand guarantees which are generally applied in international banking practice, inter alia, because the Baltic country did not have specific legislation on on-demand guarantees. The Guarantee was found to be an on-demand Guarantee and the right to claim under the Guarantee was found to have been validly assigned to claimant whose claim was granted in full.

Excerpt

I. APPLICABLE LAW

[1] "The claimant contends, with reference to Art. 13(3) of the ICC Arbitration Rules, that if the parties have not determined the law to be applied in the case, the arbitrators should apply the law designated by the rule of conflict of laws which the parties have deemed appropriate. In the opinion of the claimant, in a case concerning an on-demand guarantee, the validity or interpretation of the guarantee should not depend upon the particular provisions of a national law. In addition to this, the claimant is of the opinion that there are no Baltic State rules relating to on-demand guarantees. Therefore, the arbitral tribunal should apply general principles of commercial law. Furthermore, the claimant interprets the Baltic State conflict of laws rules to the effect that it is European law which should apply.

[2] "The defendant contends, referring to Art. 19 of the Baltic State Civil Law[1] that, as there is no contrary agreement between the parties, it is to be assumed that the parties have agreed on the application of the law of the country of performance. Should it not be possible to determine that place, the arbitral tribunal should apply the law of the place where the contract was made. . . . [T]he defendant contends that the claimant has accepted the Agreement of January 1997 between the defendant and the Central Bank of the Baltic Country on the security deposit buyer's Bank made at the Central Bank of the Baltic Country. Art. 18 of the Agreement included a provision to the effect that matters which are not covered by the contract shall be resolved in accordance with the laws of the Baltic country. The defendant points out that the claimant has thus expressly consented to the application of Baltic State laws. To defend this opinion, the defendant also refers to Art. 1821 of the Baltic State Civil Law[2] and to Art. 11 of the Rules on Issue and Registration of Guarantees

---

1. Art. 19 of the Baltic State Civil Law reads:

   "With regard to rights of things and liabilities arising from contracts, it shall first be considered whether or not the parties have agreed according to what laws their mutual relations shall be considered. Such agreement shall have effect to the extent it is not in conflict with the norms by orders or prohibitions of the law of the Baltic country.

   In the event there is no agreement, it shall be assumed that the parties have subjected their commitments as to content and consequences of the law of the country of performance."

2. Art. 1821 of the Baltic Civil Law reads:

   'If the creditor had to make a demand, performance must be given at the place the demand was made.'

by Credit Institutions approved by the Central Bank of the Baltic Country, which rule that the laws of the Baltic country are applicable to guarantees issued by Baltic State banks. Additional arguments made by the defendant include a mention of the fact that the head office of the defendant is in X and the Baltic country is therefore to be considered the place of characteristic performance. In support of this position, the defendant referred also to Art. 27 of the ICC Uniform Rules for Demand Guarantees and Stand-by Letters of Credit.

[3]   "When the different arguments are being considered, the arbitral tribunal notes that, according to the ICC Rules of Arbitration in force as from 1 January 1998, Art. 17(1), in a situation where the parties have not agreed upon the rules of law to be applied to the dispute, the arbitral tribunal shall apply the rules of law which it determines to be appropriate. Art. 17(2) contains, however, an important principle providing that 'In all cases the arbitral tribunal shall take account of the provisions of the contract and the relevant trade usages.' The new ICC Rules of Arbitration, however, do not apply to the present case.

[4]   "In using its discretion in the present case, the arbitral tribunal notes that the first version of Guarantee No. 1 had included a provision to the effect that the Guarantee was governed by Baltic State law. Further, it was added that any disputes should be settled in an amicable way. If this, however, were not possible, the dispute has to be submitted to the Arbitration Court of the Baltic Country in X. When the draft was rejected by supplier, which then proposed an amended draft, there was no longer any mention of the applicability of the Baltic State law nor of the possibility of turning to the Arbitration Court of the Baltic Country. The final Guarantee No. 1, which was dated by the Central Bank of the Baltic Country, February 1994, corresponded to the wishes of supplier. In February 1994, the Central Bank of the Baltic Country accepted Guarantee No. 1. In June 1994, buyer's Bank issued Guarantee No. 2 to replace the first Guarantee and using similar terminology in so far as there was no mention of the applicability of the Baltic State law nor the Arbitration Court of the Baltic Country in X.

[5]   "In the opinion of the arbitral tribunal, it is evident that when the parties agreed not to mention the law applicable to the guarantees they issued, it was an indication of the reluctance of supplier to accept Baltic State law as the governing law. The arbitral tribunal notes, however, that the exchange of messages between supplier and buyer's Bank does not reveal any proposal by the former party to replace the proposal by buyer's Bank by another formulation.

[6]   "As the defendant has referred to Art. 27 of the ICC Uniform Rules for Demand Guarantees, the arbitral tribunal accepts the reference because the basic rule according to this provision is that, unless the Guarantee or Counter-Guarantee provides otherwise, the governing law shall be that of the place of business of the Guarantor or Instructing Party. Art. 28 confirms the same

principle providing that, unless the Guarantee or Counter-Guarantee provides otherwise, any dispute between the guarantor and the beneficiary relating to the Guarantee shall be settled exclusively by the competent court of the country of the place of business of the Guarantor or the Instructing Party. The same principle is adopted in the United Nations Convention on Independent Guarantees and Stand-by Letters of Credit. According to Art. 21 the undertaking is governed by the law the choice of which is stipulated in the undertaking or demonstrated by its terms and conditions or agreed to elsewhere by the guarantor/issuer and the beneficiary. In case no choice of law has been made, the undertaking is governed by the law of the State where the guarantor/issuer has the place of business where the undertaking was issued. Should these principles be applied to the present dispute, the Guarantee would be governed by the law of the Baltic country.

[7]   "At the hearing the arbitral tribunal asked the counsel for the defendant whether the Baltic country had any special legislation governing on-demand guarantees. The counsel could not name any such legislation nor could he inform the arbitral tribunal of any provisions in the Baltic State law applying to on-demand guarantees which were different from the generally applied norms in international trade. It is for this reason that the arbitral tribunal has decided to apply such legal principles relating to on-demand guarantees which are generally applied in international banking practice.

[8]   "In reaching this decision, the arbitral tribunal notes that it cannot accept the opinion presented by the defendant that, by accepting the Agreement of January 1997 between the defendant and the Central Bank of the Baltic Country on the security deposit made by buyer's Bank the claimant had accepted the choice of Baltic State law as the applicable law to Guarantee No. 2. The facsimile transmission of January 1997 to the Central Bank of the Baltic Country by the European Ambassador to the Baltic country cannot be interpreted either as amounting to an acceptance of [its] law as the choice of law by the claimant.

[9]   "The arbitral tribunal notes, furthermore, that in the present case there are also legal issues which have to be solved by applying European law as these facts relate to transactions which have taken place in Europe. Their validity cannot be estimated by the arbitral tribunal without recourse to European law."

II.   LEGAL NATURE AND VALIDITY OF GUARANTEE NO. 2

[10]   ". . . . In order to discuss the validity of the Guarantee, the arbitral tribunal takes up first the question of the legal nature of the Guarantee. The negotiating history of this Guarantee reveals . . . that when the preceding Guarantee was drafted by buyer's Bank the first draft was rejected by supplier's Bank because it could not accept anything else but an on-demand Guarantee.

The arbitral tribunal refers to the telefax dated January 1994 and sent by supplier to buyer. After thanking buyer for having provided a bank guarantee dated January 1994 from buyer's Bank, supplier wrote that this guarantee is not in conformity with the request for a guarantee given by him two weeks earlier. . . . The text goes on as follows:

> 'The bank guarantee received from buyer's Bank has been presented to our bank and the European finance institution, the credit insurer, and by them found to be "only" a conditional guarantee since it contains certain reservations as to supplier's fulfilment of the contract.
>
> This reservation have [sic] caused problems for us from our bank and A.
>
> We, supplier, understand quite well, that you would like to secure your side in a way as prescribed in the guarantee from buyer's bank.
>
> If you and buyer's Bank however insist that the first guarantee from buyer's Bank shall remain as is, then I am afraid, that our possibilities as to achieve the desired credit from the credit insurer will collapse. This also because the credit insurer is informed that a guarantee from the Baltic State central bank is no longer possible to obtain.'

Having written this, the supplier's representative asked buyer to reconsider the situation and to accept the issuing of a bank guarantee in the wording earlier given by him. With this fax supplier's representative annexed a copy of the wording of the requested bank guarantee. The text read, in part, as follows:

> 'We are also informed that the payment terms are 85% of the contract value with four, half-yearly instalments added interest against a bank guarantee.
>
> In consideration hereof, and at the request and for account of our clients we hereby irrevocably undertake to pay you on first demand, waiving all rights of objection and defense, an amount up to [85% of the contract value] plus interest.
>
> Upon receipt of your request for demand accompanied by your statement certifying that the amount is due to you as buyer has failed to fulfil their above-mentioned obligations.'

These paragraphs appear in the final Guarantee No. 1 issued by buyer's Bank in February 1994. Later that month, supplier's Bank confirmed to buyer's Bank its acceptance of the Guarantee adding that supplier had transferred the Guarantee and the rights to supplier's Bank. The telefax ended with a note saying that the Instrument of Assignment would be mailed to buyer's Bank with a request to sign and return it to supplier's Bank. In June 1994, when buyer's Bank provided supplier's Bank with Guarantee No. 2 to replace Guarantee No. 1, the text read in part as follows:

'In consideration hereof, and at the request and for account of our clients we hereby irrevocably undertake to pay you, on first demand, waiving all rights of objection and defense, an amount up to [85% of contract value] plus interest.'

The following paragraph repeats the text of the corresponding paragraph in Guarantee No. 1.

[11]   "In the opinion of the arbitral tribunal, the text of Guarantee No. 2 is typical of an on-demand guarantee. Furthermore, the exchange of views between the two parties to the transaction, the supplier and the buyer's Bank confirmed the insistent standpoint of supplier's Bank and the credit insurer that the only acceptable form of the guarantee was an on-demand guarantee. The arbitral tribunal cannot accept the argument presented by the defendant that Guarantee No. 2 is a conditional guarantee. The defendant suggests that this conclusion is based on the fact that, according to the text of the Guarantee, the conditional nature of the Guarantee is proven in that the payment was subject to the receipt of a demand by the beneficiary together with the requirement of a statement by the beneficiary that the amount was due and that buyer had failed to pay it. The arbitral tribunal cannot, however, accept this interpretation because the request for payment, together with the statement that buyer had failed to pay, cannot be regarded as conditions changing a typical on-demand guarantee into a conditional guarantee.

[12]   "The defendant has also contended that Guarantee No. 2 is invalid. In September 1997, the defendant informed the arbitral tribunal that the defendant had turned to the Civil Court in the Baltic country asking for invalidation of the Guarantee. The arbitral tribunal underlines that the case against buyer and supplier does not feature the claimant as a party. Therefore, as the claimant has not appeared in the Baltic State courts, the outcome of the case cannot be a binding precedent for the case the arbitral tribunal is expected to decide. The claimant and the defendant, however, have kept the arbitral tribunal informed of the decision by the Civil Court, which declared Guarantee No. 2 invalid, as well as of the decision of the Civil Case Chamber of the Supreme Court, which upon appeal dismissed the claim. Buyer's Bank has appealed to the Civil Department of the Senate of the Baltic State Supreme Court. The arbitral tribunal cannot postpone the handling of the present case until the case between buyer's Bank and supplier has been finally decided as that would damage the claimant which has not been a party to the case still pending.

[13]   "In so far as buyer's Bank has informed the arbitral tribunal of its request to have a criminal investigation of a possible fraud by buyer and supplier the arbitral tribunal has been told that no criminal charges have so far been brought against either suspect. Therefore, the arbitral tribunal does not find any validity in the defendant's contention that Guarantee No. 2 is invalid. Accordingly, the arbitral tribunal declares Guarantee No. 2 valid."

III.   ASSIGNABILITY OF THE GUARANTEE

[14]   "Turning to the issue concerning the assignability of the Guarantee, the arbitral tribunal notes that the claimant and the defendant accept as the starting point the fact that Guarantee No. 2 does not include any provision on the assignability of the Guarantee. While this fact, in the opinion of the defendant, is sufficient to lead to the conclusion that it was not possible to assign the Guarantee, the claimant does not accept the defendant's contention as the claimant underlines the importance of the facts surrounding this particular silence about the Guarantee.

[15]   "While the arbitral tribunal agrees with the parties as to the silence of the Guarantee in this particular respect, the arbitral tribunal finds it necessary to investigate carefully the argument presented by the claimant that at the time the preceding Guarantee No. 1 was signed, the assignment was expressly accepted by the defendant. Nor was any objection made by the defendant originally to the assignment of Guarantee No. 2. The arbitral tribunal notes that by a telefax dated December 1993 supplier wrote to the maritime institute to advise the Director of buyer to contact the Central Bank of the Baltic Country and buyer's Bank in order to apply for a combination of guarantees from both banks in case buyer failed to fulfil its obligations. It was added that 'The technics in the matters concerned are, that the credit insurer will be the governmental body in Europe who should be favoured by the Baltic State guarantee. This allows the Central Bank of the Baltic Country to set financing and issue the loan asked for.' The next day supplier informed the maritime institute, after a telephone conversation, that its representative had again been in contact with the credit insurer. The fax included the following passage:

> '[Buyer] must contact buyer's Bank and tell them, that a guarantee from buyer's Bank should be combined with a guarantee from the Central Bank of the Baltic Country, saying, that the Central Bank of the Baltic Country will guarantee for the payment of the supply if buyer's Bank and the ship owner should not be able to fulfil their obligations.
>
> The guarantees to be issued in the name of supplier but allowing for a possible transfer to supplier's Bank at a later date.'

The arbitral tribunal points out that, although the text of Guarantee No. 1 did not include a reference to the assignability when it was signed in February 1994, in February 1994 supplier and supplier's Bank signed an Instrument of Assignment whereby Guarantee No. 1 was assigned to supplier's Bank. The text read in part as follows:

> 'As a consequence of this Instrument of Assignment the bank shall have an exclusive right to receive and give receipt for the amount assigned hereunder without being obliged to document the guarantee for which this Instrument of Assignment has been issued as a security. On the whole, the Bank shall have the exclusive right to exercise all our rights as creditors in respect of the aforementioned guarantee.'

In February 1994, buyer's Bank signed an acknowledgment of notification of assignment. . . . Later that month, supplier's Bank confirmed the acceptance of the document informing buyer's Bank that supplier had transferred the Guarantee and the rights to supplier's Bank. Buyer's Bank was asked to sign and return the Instrument of Assignment to supplier's Bank. The document was then returned signed to supplier's Bank.

[16] "On the basis of the above, the arbitral tribunal has reached the conclusion that, despite the silence of the text of the Guarantee, supplier's Bank and buyer's Bank did agree on the assignment of the Guarantee to supplier's Bank and the notification of assignment was duly returned to supplier's Bank.

[17] "When Guarantee No. 1 was replaced by Guarantee No. 2 in June 1994, supplier's Bank followed the same procedure as they did in connection with the assignment of Guarantee No. 1. In July 1994, supplier's Bank provided a similar Instrument of Assignment as before to the buyer's Bank. The document was properly signed by supplier. This time, however, the buyer's bank did not return the Instrument of Assignment. A further written request by supplier's Bank signed in September 1994, including a new copy of the Instrument of Assignment, was left unanswered by buyer's Bank. At the hearing, the counsel for the claimant explained that both letters were sent by recommended mail and it was impossible that they were not received by buyer's Bank as the letters were never returned to supplier's Bank.

[18] "The arbitral tribunal decides that Guarantee No. 1 was no doubt assignable. The beneficiary, supplier, did assign the Guarantee to supplier's Bank and buyer's Bank acknowledged the Notification of Assignment. Supplier's Bank was also entitled to believe at the time when Guarantee No. 2 was signed that buyer's Bank would agree to the assignment as buyer's Bank did not inform supplier's Bank of any adverse decision. Although supplier's Bank should have continued to demand the return of the Notice of Assignment, which had twice

been mailed by recommended mail, supplier's Bank was, however, entitled to believe that buyer's Bank was only careless in not returning the document. Should supplier's Bank have had any reason to suspect a rejection of the assignment, it would have been entitled to reject Guarantee No. 2. The assignability had been a *conditio sine qua non* for supplier's Bank to accept Guarantee No. 1 and it should have been understood by buyer's Bank as being an absolute condition also when Guarantee No. 2 was signed. Accordingly, the arbitral tribunal decides that Guarantee No. 2 was assignable."

IV. CLAIMANT'S RIGHT TO CLAIM PAYMENT UNDER THE
     GUARANTEE

[19] "The fourth issue mentioned in the Terms of Reference is the question of whether the claimant does have the right to claim payment under the Guarantee. The arbitral tribunal finds this issue closely linked with the issue concerning the assignability of the Guarantee and notes that, immediately after the agreement for deliveries of supplies was signed by supplier and buyer the former informed buyer that 'the technics in matters concerned are that the credit insurer will be the governmental body in Europe who should be favoured by the Baltic State guarantee. This allows supplier's Bank to set financing and issue the loan asked for.' The arbitral tribunal is of the opinion that, since the very beginning of the guarantee arrangement between supplier and buyer's Bank the latter was fully aware of the guarantee and insurance system applied in Europe on a case where a European corporation was in need of financing in order to enter into an agreement with a foreign party. Buyer's Bank knew that, in light of the exchanges between the parties to the guarantee agreement, supplier's Bank needed an insurance from the claimant and that insurance necessitated a transfer of all the rights of supplier to supplier's Bank. Furthermore, supplier's Bank let buyer's Bank have a copy of the conditions of the insurance including the provision that the credit insurer was entitled to take over all rights belonging to supplier's Bank, including the right to take over the case if buyer's Bank refused to pay supplier's Bank the proceeds of Guarantee No. 2. Accordingly, the arbitral tribunal decides that claimant has the right to claim payment under Guarantee No. 2."

V. VALIDITY OF THE DEMAND UNDER THE GUARANTEE

[20] "The fifth issue listed in the Terms of Reference is the question as to whether a demand under the Guarantee has been validly presented. This issue is also closely related to the last two issues which have been discussed above.

The facts of the case indicate in the opinion of the arbitral tribunal that, once the timetable for the partial payments had been established under the Guarantee and the payment authorization vouchers had been signed by buyer in July 1994, the first voucher was due no later than December 1994. In December 1994, supplier sent to buyer's Bank what was called a 'friendly reminder, to insure a smooth payment transfer' informing it that supplier's Bank in January 1995 sent a reminder requesting information. The Tracer No. 1 was sent to supplier's Bank in January 1995. Later that month, buyer wrote a letter promising the credit insurer that all payments concerning the project would be made before January 1995.

[21]   "The arbitral tribunal notes that in January 1995 supplier received a fax from buyer who asked supplier's Bank to demand payment from the buyer's Bank and not from the buyer 'because buyer's Bank keeps our credit money on the own correspondent account'. In January 1995, supplier again reminded buyer of the fact that 'Despite several addresses (letters, faxes, telephone contacts) from supplier's Bank to buyer's Bank and despite supplier's Bank have followed your instruction in your fax on how to approach buyer, no payment has taken place until today.' It was further pointed out that supplier's Bank was seriously considering reporting to the credit insurer in order to release the guaranteed sum, this less 10% which was supplier's own risk. In January 1995, supplier's Bank sent to buyer's Bank a letter reminding buyer's Bank of the fact that in December 1994 supplier's Bank forwarded to buyer's Bank a draft for the first installment maturing in December 1994. The text went on, after the names and addresses of the customers had been mentioned, as follows:

'until now, we have not received payment, and therefore we hereby claim under your guarantee no. 2 – which was issued for a total amount of 85% of the contract value an amount of the first instalment plus interest of 10% p.a. from January 1995 until payment has taken place.

Please consider this matter as very urgent.

For your information above-mentioned guarantee was signed by your President.'

[22]   "The arbitral tribunal accepts this letter as a correct demand under Guarantee No. 2 as the previous exchanges indicate clearly that buyer's Bank had been informed of the refusal or incapacity of buyer to make the payment due under the Guarantee. Exhibits include requests by buyer's Bank to receive many documents relating to the Guarantee together with a reference to a fire which made it impossible for the Bank to check their files.

[23]   "The following letter by supplier's Bank to buyer's Bank was dated January 1995. Supplier's Bank reminded buyer's Bank that

'According to the wording of your Guarantee no. 2 signed by your President the payment has to take place on first demand, waiving all rights of objection and defence.

We have forwarded your good bank a draft for the first instalment with maturity December 1994. Until now we haven't received any payment, therefore we ask you immediately remit the amount of the first instalment plus interest from January 1995, to be calculated at an interest rate of 10% p.a.

Unless we have received full payment latest by February 1995, we have no other possibilities than contact the Central Bank of the Baltic Country to get this matter settled.'

As a reply buyer's Bank, in January 1995, sent a letter which informed supplier's Bank 'that we do not refuse from our obligations under the Guarantee No. 2 for the full amount of the guarantee'. Again, buyer's Bank asked for additional documents. In the opinion of the arbitral tribunal, this letter includes a legally important message as buyer's Bank expressed a statement to the effect that buyer's Bank did not deny their obligations under Guarantee No. 2. This statement was a reply to a letter which referred expressly to the fact that Guarantee No. 2 was an on-demand guarantee. Put simply, the fact that buyer's Bank did not deny its obligations under the Guarantee means implicitly that buyer's Bank accepted the classification of Guarantee No. 2 as an on-demand guarantee. After another exchange of messages supplier's Bank sent, in February 1995, a final notice to buyer's Bank reminding it again that Guarantee No. 2 was an on-first-demand guarantee, waiving all rights of objection and defence. The letter ended with a demand to pay by February 1995. Should there be no payment, supplier's Bank would report the matter to the Central Bank of the Baltic Country and the European Export Council, which would make it impossible for buyer's Bank to continue doing business in Europe.

[24]   "In March 1995, buyer's Bank informed supplier's Bank of the fact that buyer was bankrupt. This letter included a settlement proposal. Should supplier's Bank not present any further claims, buyer's Bank was prepared to pay the first instalment plus 10% interest from January 1995 until payment took place. In March 1995, supplier's Bank rejected the offer which they would under no circumstances accept. Buyer's Bank was reminded of the fact that there were, in all, four instalments which would become due in June 1995, January 1996 and June 1996.

[25]   "After this letter, supplier received from a ship-engineering office in the Baltic country a letter sent in June 1995. This letter informed supplier that as a result of three meetings held in the Baltic country with representatives of buyer's Bank during the past month, buyer and buyer's Bank had agreed that the latter would assume all rights of buyer to manage the project, including the ship, materials, conversion, etc. As a result of an inspection, all the materials delivered by supplier [had] been found to be perfectly safe.

[26]   "The arbitral tribunal finds that in light of all the circumstances supplier's Bank has made a valid claim under Guarantee No. 2. In addition to this, by a letter of October 1997, the credit insurer turned to supplier's Bank and supplier referring to the General Conditions for Guarantees for Supply of Goods and Capital Goods, post shipment, of June 1993. Reference was made to Art. 5(2), 'to confirm as previously agreed that the credit insurer wishes to undertake the recovery of the claims under the above export credit guarantee and any amounts connected therewith'. The text went on as follows:

> 'We shall, therefore, ask you for your signature on the present document to assign to us any claims which you have or may have under the agreements with buyer of December 1993 and May 1994, or under the guarantees from buyer's Bank of February 1994 (Guarantee No. 1) and of June 1994 (Guarantee No. 2), or under any assignment of the said agreements or guarantees of the proceeds thereunder.
>
> The above-mentioned assignments are made and accepted without prejudice to any rights in the said agreements, guarantees or proceeds which we have already acquired as result of our payments to you under our above-mentioned export credit guarantee.'

In January 1998, the credit insurer sent to buyer's Bank a letter on the assignment of rights. In this letter, the credit insurer officially informed buyer's Bank that supplier and supplier's Bank had signed their rights under Guarantee No. 2 to the credit insurer. A copy of the assignment letter from supplier and from supplier's Bank dated October 1997, was attached to the letter. The letter included also a statement to the effect that the notification was without prejudice to the fact that by payment to the assignors under the export credit insurance the credit insurer became subrogated with regard to the rights of the assignors against buyer's Bank under the Guarantee.

[27]   "The arbitral tribunal decides, in conclusion, that in so far as the present issue is concerned, there has been a valid claim presented by the beneficiary supplier's Bank under Guarantee No. 2. Art. 4(1) of the ICC Uniform Rules for Demand Guarantees provides that 'a demand under a guarantee is not assignable unless expressly stated in the Guarantee or in amendment thereto',

paragraph 2 provides that this Article 'shall not, however, affect the Beneficiary's right to assign any proceeds to which he may be, or may become, entitled under the Guarantee'. In the present case, both supplier and supplier's Bank have assigned any proceeds under Guarantee No. 2 to the credit insurer. The credit insurer has as the claimant made a valid demand for payment."

VI. JUSTIFICATION OF THE CLAIMS FOR RELIEF

[28] "The last three issues mentioned in the Terms of Reference need to be decided together as both the justification of the claim made by the claimant and by the defendant depend on the answer given by the arbitral tribunal to the corresponding issues. Likewise, the decision of the arbitral tribunal on the question of which party should bear the costs of this arbitration and in what proportion can only be solved once the claims of both parties are decided.

[29] "Having considered the claims in the light of the evidence presented by both parties, the arbitral tribunal decides that the facts of the case indicate that supplier has fulfilled the terms of the agreement concerning the delivery of the supplies to buyer. All the prices charged for the supplies have been agreed on by the parties involved and there is no evidence to support the defendant's contention that the prices charged by supplier had been higher than had been habitual in their particular field of activity. All the deliveries have been inspected by the representatives of those concerned, too, and there is sufficient evidence to indicate that the supplies were safely stored at least until the time when buyer's Bank decided to take over the conversion work and all supplies delivered by supplier.

[30] "In so far as the demand for Guarantee No. 2 is concerned, the ICC Uniform Rules of Demand Guarantees provide in Art. 10(b) that, 'If the Guarantor decides to refuse a demand, he shall immediately give notice thereof to the Beneficiary by teletransmission, or, if that is not possible, by other expeditious means. Any documents presented under the Guarantee shall be held at the disposal of the Beneficiary.'

[31] "In this case, buyer's Bank has not acted in accordance with the last-mentioned provision, which has been followed generally in international banking practice. On the contrary, in this case buyer's Bank, once the demand for payment was made by the Beneficiary, in January 1995, eventually replied that the Bank did not deny 'our obligations' under Guarantee No. 2 for its total amount. In March 1995, when buyer's Bank made its settlement offer, it did not base its offer on the ground that the Guarantee was considered invalid for some reason. In the opinion of the arbitral tribunal, buyer's Bank neglected its duty to inform immediately the Beneficiary of its decision to reject the demand. Should buyer's Bank have fulfilled its duty in this respect, the claimant could have considerably diminished its losses by taking immediate action against

buyer and buyer's Bank to save the supplies which were stored in the Baltic country. Instead, there is sufficient evidence to prove that buyer's Bank decided to take over the contract between supplier and buyer in order to fulfil the conversion work.

[32] "Based on the above reasoning, the arbitral tribunal decides that the claim for relief submitted by the claimant is justified and that the claim submitted by the defendant is not justified.

[33] "Accordingly, the arbitral tribunal decides that buyer's Bank is ordered to pay the credit insurer the full amount of the Guarantee together with interest at the rate of 10 per cent per annum for each instalment, not compounded, from the original due dates of the instalments . . . until the actual date of payment. The arbitral tribunal decides that the interest rate is 10 per cent per annum, which is the rate the claimant has claimed. In March 1995, buyer's Bank has admitted this interest rate in so far as the first instalment, which was due in December 1994, was concerned.

[34] "In so far as the costs of the arbitration are concerned, the arbitral tribunal points out that, regardless of the above conclusion concerning the justification of the claimant's claim, there have been certain errors in the way the claimant has taken care of its claim, including an involuntary error by supplier's Bank demanding payment for Guarantee No. 1 instead of Guarantee No. 2. This error, however, must have been understood to be an involuntary error by the defendant. . . . Buyer's Bank shall stand for its own legal fees and costs and it is also ordered to pay the legal fees and costs of the credit insurer. The fees and expenses of the arbitrators and the administrative costs fixed by the court shall be shared between the parties on the basis of 30 per cent being paid by the credit insurer and 70 per cent by buyer's Bank."

VII. AWARD

[35] "In light of the conclusions reached above, the arbitral tribunal issues the following Award:
1. Buyer's Bank is ordered to pay the credit insurer [the full amount of the guarantee] together with interest at the rate of 10 per cent per annum for each instalment not compounded, from the original due dates of the instalments . . . in December 1994, June 1995, December 1995 and June 1996 until the actual date of payment. The payment shall be made immediately after the deposit and the interest thereon under the following paragraph 2 have been paid to the claimant.
2. The credit insurer is entitled in accordance with the contract signed in January 1997 by the Central Bank of the Baltic Country and buyer's Bank on the security deposit of buyer's Bank at the Central Bank of the Baltic Country to receive the agreed deposit . . . together with the interest on the deposit according to the

conditions of the contract. The provisions of the contract on the calculation of the interest read as follows:

> '8. The rate of interest on the deposit shall be variable and shall correspond to the Bank's stipulated exchange rate for commercial banks' fixed deposits at the Central Bank of the Baltic Country.
>
> 9. The calculation of the interest on the deposit shall commence on the day when the deposit is included in the special deposit account until the day the deposit is paid out (the day of paying out not being included).
>
> 10. When calculating interest, the actual number of days in the month shall be calculated on the basis of 365 days in a year.
>
> 11. The interest on the deposit shall accumulate in a separate account and shall not be paid out to the depositor nor any third party until the commencement of the conditions for the deposit payment.
>
> 12. The accumulated interest sum shall not be added to the base deposit sum and the Bank shall not have to pay interest on the whole.'

The deposit shall be paid upon the presentation of the Award as specified in paragraph 13 of the Contract between the Central Bank of the Baltic Country and buyer's Bank. The interest thereon will be used as part-payment of the amount mentioned above in paragraph 1. The official rate of exchange on the date of payment to the credit insurer shall be applied.

3. Buyer's Bank shall stand for its own legal fees and costs and it is also ordered to pay the legal fees and costs of the credit insurer. . . . The fees and expenses of the arbitrators and the administrative costs fixed by the court shall be shared between the parties on the basis of 30 per cent being paid by the credit insurer and 70 per cent by buyer's Bank.

4. . . . . . In light of the payment by each party of one half of the advance on costs, no reimbursement will be made. . . ."

Final award in case no. 9466 of 1999

Parties:	Claimant: Charterer (Liberia)
	Defendant: Owner (Russian Federation)

Place of arbitration:	Paris, France

Published in:	Unpublished

Subject matters:	– force majeure
	– breach of contract
	– arrest of ships
	– loss of profits as damages for breach of contract
	– set off (compensation) of arrears against damages

Facts

The claimant, a Liberian company, entered into a contract in March 1995 with the defendant, a Russian Joint Stock Company, whereby the claimant (charterer) chartered seven fishing vessels from the Russian "owner" (owner) with the authorization of the real owner. The charterer sub-chartered the seven vessels to a Chinese company (sub-charterer). Unbeknown to the charterer, the vessels were mortgaged as a guarantee for the repayment of loans granted by a Russian bank to the real owner. Due to default on the loans, under the terms of the mortgage, the vessels were impounded by the creditor in the period running from February 1996 to March 1997.

In July of 1996, the owner notified the charterer by letter that it was terminating the charter contract due to force majeure, i.e., the arrest of the ships. The charterer rejected the termination and in March 1997 notified the owner by letter that it was terminating the charter contract due to breach of contract by the owner.

The charterer initiated ICC arbitration in March 1997, relying on the arbitration clause in the charter contract and seeking a declaration that the termination by owner due to force majeure was invalid and damages. The owner participated in drawing up the Terms of Reference, making a preliminary contention that the arbitration had been initiated without the due authority of the charterer and counterclaiming for various arrears.

The arbitral tribunal was to make a partial award on the question of the authority of the charterer to commence the arbitration. However, before the final deadline for written submissions, the counsel for the owner informed the arbitral tribunal that he was no longer representing the owner in this case. As the owner did not make any further written submissions or appoint any alternative counsel, the arbitral tribunal ultimately decided to rule on the issue of the authority of the charterer to initiate arbitration together with the merits as part of the final award. In November 1998, the owner wrote to the Secretariat of the ICC International Court of Arbitration informing the Court that it had been declared bankrupt by the Russian court in July 1998, but did not submit any further proof of the declaration of bankruptcy.

The arbitral tribunal first examined the very complicated facts revolving around the corporate structure of the charterer and the authority of the charterer to commence the arbitration and held that the arbitration had been commenced and had been continued with the due authority of the charterer. It then found that, based on the specific terms of the contract, the owner was in breach of the contract. Moreover, the termination of the contract on the allegation of force majeure was found to be invalid. The charterer had validly terminated the contract and was entitled to damages. On the other hand, the owner was entitled to arrears for overdue charter fees (but not crew salaries) and that amount was to be set off against the amount awarded for damages.

Excerpt

(. . . .)

I. WAS OWNER IN BREACH OF CONTRACT?

[1] "The claimant entered into the charter contract (the contract) with the defendant in March 1995. The contract does not mention that the seven vessel[s] being the subject of the charter were mortgaged as guarantee for the repayment of loans granted by the Russian Bank and the defendant says he was not aware of the mortgages. It was possibly a negligence on the part of the claimant not to check that before entering into the contract, same as it was certainly contrary to the principle of a fair negotiation, on the part of the defendant, not to disclose such a potentially risky situation. However, the contract was concluded, and we should only consider the legal consequence of the respective contractual undertakings. Possible mistakes or liabilities during the negotiating phase are irrelevant. The parties did know each other pretty well by the time they entered into the contract, and they were certainly trusting each other.

[2]   "In any case, what is important in the present dispute is that, apart from the role the individuals are playing, it is sure that, on the legal ground, a charter contract implies, on the part of the charterer, the obligation to make available the goods which are the subject of the contract to the party to whom the charter is granted, with full guarantee that they can be freely used for the purpose and for the time they have been chartered. This, in fact, is the substance of the concept of the charter itself, and we don't even need to refer to any specific set of rules, since there is no conflict of rules in this respect whatever national rules we should apply.

[3]   "The claimant, when elaborating on the issue of the applicable law, points out that the silence of the parties as to the law that should be applied to their contractual relationship may be construed as a significant indication of their will that their relationship be simply governed by the terms of the contract and/or, whenever necessary, by the general principles of international commercial contracts and trade usages.

[4]   "This is very likely true, and quite understandable in a situation where we are facing a combination of elements attributable to various different nationalities: the contract is between the charterer and the owner. The charterer is a Liberian offshore company, whose management was always located in Spain, and in which Spanish and Russian interests are represented. The owner is a Russian company. The contract was signed in London. The vessels being the subject of the charter contract were apparently flying a Liberian flag and were the property of the 'real' owner, which is very likely another offshore Liberian company controlled by Russians. The mortgages that triggered the impoundment of the vessels were in favour of a Russian bank. The impoundments took place in Singapore and in the Seychelles. The claimed damages, for the time being, are restricted to the loss of profit that the charterer was expecting to earn from a sub-charter contract concluded with a Chinese company.

[5]   "Under the above circumstances, the tribunal is of the opinion that making reference to a specific national law may not be necessary in the present case. First of all, as we did already mention here above, the nature of the contract itself, under any legislation, entails the obligation of the lessor ... to ensure that the lessee retains uninterrupted and free possession of the leased assets until the expiry of the contractually agreed term. Secondly, the contract specifically provides that during the period of its validity (i.e., five years), 'the charterer will operate the fishing vessels according to their best judgment, including the sub-charter of the vessels if this option is considered convenient', and 'will dispose freely of the totality of the catches of the vessels'.

[6]   "Therefore, the tribunal unanimously concludes that the owner is in breach of the contract because of the fact that the owner was deprived of the possession and could no longer dispose of the vessels for the whole period of

time they were chartered. .... However, it may be added here that if the defendant invokes force majeure as a reason of exemption from liability, this constitutes by itself an implicit acknowledgement of the fact that a breach of a contractual obligation did actually occur, whether or not justified for reason of force majeure."

II. WAS TERMINATION BASED ON FORCE MAJEURE EFFECTIVE?

[7] "By fax dated July 1996 (when four vessels were already impounded), the defendant sent to the claimant a 'Notice of Termination' of the charter contract, invoking force majeure. The notice is so worded: 'This is to inform you that due to the force-majeure circumstances (the arrest of vessels) the charter party for the vessels dated March 1995 is terminated from July 1996.' By letter of July 1996, the charterer categorically rejected the termination of the contract on alleged reasons of force majeure, pointing out that it was the owner's duty under the contract to avoid that the vessels be arrested and to procure that the arrest be revoked. By fax of July 1996 the owner of the vessels, the 'real' owner, through their lawyers, requested the charterer to urgently return the vessels, because their charter contract with the owner had been terminated 'inter alia, for non-payment of hire', and so therefore, the owner having no longer any title to the vessels, any other rights granted by the owner to third parties 'including the sub-charter to the charterer' were no longer valid and in force. The charterer both directly and through their lawyers, replied and strongly refuted the above allegations.

[8]   "The force majeure clause of the contract is worded as follows:

> 'The parties will be free from the obligations of the present contract, including the payment of the charter fee, in the event of loss of ship or for any other force majeure circumstances, duly documented, including the breakdown of the basis mechanisms of the vessel, the equipment, and fishing gear. The party which cannot comply with its obligations due to said circumstances should inform the other party immediately about said circumstances, its [sic] beginning and termination, and will afterwards send the corresponding documentation.'

There cannot be any doubt that the 'loss of ship' to which reference is made in this clause, is to be understood as the material loss of the vessel (such as, for instance, because of the vessel's sinking), and does not extend to the very different case of the 'loss of availability' of the ship for any reason other than the material loss (such as, in our case, because of the vessel's impoundment). Moreover, it appears from the wording of the clause '*in the event of loss of ship or for any other "force majeure circumstances"* ' (emphasis added) that it was the parties' intention to consider the loss of ship itself in the frame of the 'force majeure' concept, which means that it would have only [been] relevant in case it was attributable to an event beyond the parties' control.

[9]   "As unanimously recognized by the doctrine, as well as by the jurisprudence, including arbitration awards in international disputes, no matter whether in the frame of a civil law or of a common law system, the essential elements of a 'force majeure' situation are the unforeseeability and the irresistibility of the event. By the time the contract was signed, the seven chartered vessels were all mortgaged as a guarantee for the repayment of loans apparently granted to the shipowner by a Russian Bank. Even if this circumstance is not mentioned in the contract, and whether or not the charterer was aware of it, this is a fact that was certainly known to the owner whose legal representative (Mr. Z) is the same person acting as legal representative of the 'real' owner. Therefore, a possible default of the shipowner, and the consequent possible impoundment of the mortgaged vessels by the creditor were events easily foreseeable by the owner. They cannot be invoked by the owner as 'force majeure' events.

[10]   "It was the owner's duty and responsibility under the contract to make sure that the charterer retains uninterrupted and free possession of the chartered vessels until the expiry of the agreed-upon term. It was also very likely possible for the owner to take in due time appropriate measures in order to avoid such events occurring. Therefore, the element of 'irresistibility' that should characterize a 'force majeure' situation is also missing.

[11]   "The fact that the payment guaranteed by the mortgages was due by a third party (the real owner) does not relieve the owner of their liability vis-á-vis the charterer. A similar situation is very common in the so-called back-to-back contracts, whereby the party in the middle (i.e., the buyer-reseller of the goods) is exposed to the risk that his supplier fails to perform. The foreseeability of the supplier's default excludes that this may be considered as a 'force majeure' event, unless the default is expressly stipulated in the contract as a discharging event.

[12]   "If one considers that, as mentioned here above, Mr. Z was representing both the owner and the 'real' owner, it might also be questionable whether this second company is actually (and not only formally) a third party, totally separated from the owner. Moreover, that the 'real' owner did expressly approve the charter contract.

[13]   "Should we regard the owner and the 'real' owner as a group of companies having joint liability, then the 'real' owner's default would not only be a foreseeable and resistible event, but it would not even be an event 'extraneous' to the party invoking it.

[14]   ". . . [T]he parties, whatever may be the reason, were rather reluctant to provide precise information about the various and changing structures of their

very complex relationship. However, it is sufficiently clear that a Spanish party and a Russian party did join their forces for the management of a fishing fleet that was belonging to the Russian party, even if flying [the] Liberian flag. Whilst the Spanish party is clearly identifiable in the company of Mr. X, the Russian party is acting from time to time through various companies, but it is certainly not by chance that, with the only exception of one company all other above-mentioned companies are represented by the same person, Mr. Z. In such a situation, the minimum one can say is that Mr. Z in his double and parallel capacity of the legal representative of both the owner and the 'real' owner was certainly in the best position to know about the risk that the vessels [would] be impounded, and to take adequate measures, in due time, to [prevent this from happening].

[15]   "As mentioned here above, whilst the owner [was] invoking force majeure, the 'real' owner in its lawyers' fax of July 1996, does not seem to rely on a 'force majeure' situation. Its contention is that its own charter contract with the owner has been terminated, inter alia, due to the default of the owner in paying the relevant hire fee, and so therefore any sub-charter is nullified because the owner no longer has title to dispose of the vessels. Should this be the case, the owner's liability towards the charterer, because of the non-payment of the hire fee due to the 'real' owner, would be even more evident, and certainly its default in the contract with the 'real' owner would not be put forward to the charterer as a 'force majeure' situation.

[16]   "On the other hand, the termination of the original charter contract does not automatically entail the termination of the sub-charter, unless stipulated by the parties. Such a stipulation, which is incorporated in the second sub-charter contract, between the charterer and the sub-charterer, is absent in the first sub-charter contract between the owner and the charterer very likely because this sub-charter was specifically approved by the shipowner itself (the 'real' owner).

[17]   "In any case, even if the termination of the original charter contract should entail the termination of the sub-charters, this would not have any consequence. . . . The owner being liable for the termination of the main charter contract (due to the non-payment of the hire fee) would therefore be certainly liable to the charterer for the consequential termination of the sub-charter. The arbitral tribunal unanimously decides that the termination of the contract by the defendant on the allegation of force majeure is to be declared ineffective."

III.   WAS CANCELLATION BASED ON DEFAULT VALID?

[18]   "It is by letter of March 1997 that the claimant notified the defendant [of] the termination of the contract due to the defendant's failure to fulfil its own contractual obligations. As a matter of fact, the last vessel still available to the

claimant, the vessel no. 7, was impounded in March 1997. This means that no vessels, out of the seven chartered under the contract, were any longer available to the claimant as of this date. Since the tribunal has unanimously decided that the defendant was in breach of the contract and that the previous termination of the contract by the defendant on the allegation of force majeure is to be declared ineffective, the tribunal unanimously decides that the termination of the contract by the claimant due to defendant's default is declared justified and valid."

IV.   ENTITLEMENT TO DAMAGES

[19]   "When a contract is terminated because of the default of one party to fulfil its obligations, the defaulting party is due to refund the other party the damages this last has possibly suffered as a consequence of such a default. It is up to the party claiming compensation of damages to prove their existence as well as their amount. The claimant is only claiming, under this arbitration, the compensation of the damages that constitute its own 'loss of profit'. A reservation has been made by the claimant as to additional damages he might be facing, in case he should be bound to refund damages to the sub-charterer.

[20]   "Since the seven vessels that the defendant had chartered to the claimant had been sub-chartered by the claimant to the sub-charterer, the claimed loss of profit consists of the difference between the sub-charter fee that the claimant was entitled to earn from the sub-charterer and the charter fee that it was bound to pay to the defendant. As to the existence of the damage, the tribunal is satisfied with the documentary evidence provided by the claimant, i.e., the charter contract, on the one hand, and the sub-charter contract on the other hand. (. . . .)

[21]   "The tribunal is of the opinion that the claimed 'loss of profit', to be compensated by the defaulting defendant, can only be reckoned for each vessel separately, counting from the day of its relevant impoundment. The charter fee as well as the sub-charter fee are agreed upon in the respective contracts 'per vessel' and 'per year'. Even if the interest of the claimant might have been to dispose of the totality of the seven chartered vessels, it is clear from the contract that each vessel is to be considered as a separate asset in respect of which, on the one hand, the contractual charter fee is due and, on the other hand, the profit is expected that will result from the earning of a higher sub-charter fee.

[22]   "The separability of the contractual relationship is confirmed by the behaviour of the claimant itself. As a matter of fact, six out of the seven vessels having been impounded one after the other at different dates, the claimant did only terminate the contract after the seventh and last vessel was equally impounded in March 1997.

[23]   "The profit factor, same as the charter and sub-charter fees, is to be considered for each of the chartered vessels separately. For the period of time over which any of the vessels remains available to the claimant, and is actually exploited by the claimant's sub-charterer, the two contractual relationships, between claimant and defendant and between claimant and sub-charterer respectively, are in force as far as such a vessel is concerned, and there is no 'loss of profit'. As a consequence, over that period of time, the claimant is bound to pay the relevant charter fee and is entitled to cash the relevant sub-charter fee, which means that it is in a position to earn the expected profit.

[24]   "The 'loss of profit', for each of the vessels, can only be claimed from the date the vessel in question is impounded, and so therefore no longer available to the claimant, and consequently to its sub-charterer. From that date the claimant shall have no longer the duty to pay the charter fee, on the one hand, and shall no longer be entitled to cash the sub-charter fee, on the other hand."

(. . . .)

V.   ENTITLEMENT TO COUNTERCLAIM FOR ARREARS

[25]   "A counterclaim was made by the defendant first by fax letter of October 1997, and then at the hearing of November 1997, on the occasion of the establishment of the Terms of Reference, requesting that the claimant be ordered to pay alleged arrears of charter hire fees, as well as alleged arrears of crew salaries. The counterclaim was included among the issues to be determined in the Terms of Reference. Even if the defendant did not further elaborate on its requests, after its counsels withdrew and no alternative counsels were appointed, still it is the tribunal's duty to decide on the counterclaim. Therefore, we will consider hereafter separately the two above alleged credits (arrears of charter fees and arrears of crew salaries respectively).

[26]   "*As to the claimed arrears of charter fees*, it is admitted by the claimant that the charter fees for the seven vessels which are the subject of the contract were paid up to April 1996. It is the claimant's first contention that it is 'not liable for any pending charter leasing fees, given that the vessels have already been impounded'. As to the factual situation, this statement is not correct, because in April 1996 one only vessel was impounded.

[27]   "As to the legal aspect of the problem, this tribunal has already indicated here above that a charter contract covering the leasing of several vessels gives rise to a relationship which is separable in respect of each of the leased vessels, which is confirmed in our case by the fact that the charter fee is agreed upon 'per vessel', as well as by the behaviour of the claimant, who did terminate the contract only after the last vessel was impounded. As a consequence, the claimant is bound to

pay the charter fee in respect of each of the chartered vessels until [sic] the relevant vessel remains at its free disposal.

[28]   "The additional claimant's contention that 'the petition must be dismissed' because 'the defendant has not indicated to which specific charter leasing fees and/or periods and to which specific vessels [it] refers to' is also to be rejected. Since it is the claimant's admission that charter fees were only paid up to April 1996, and the claimant's exhibits provide evidence of the dates on which the individual vessels were impounded, the calculation of the overdue charter fees is only a question of mathematics.

(. . . .)

[29]   "As an 'ancillary request' the claimant holds that [the] amount of overdue charter fees, if any, should be compensated 'given the greater losses' it suffered. This request is to be accepted. Since the tribunal has granted the compensation of damages . . . which is greater than the above-reckoned amount of overdue charter fees, this last is to be set-off against the losses.

[30]   "*As to the claimed arrears of crew salaries*, it has never be[en] stated by the defendant which would be the legal basis of its request. In principle, should there be arrears of crew salaries, the legitimation to introduce legal proceedings for the relevant payment would belong to each member of the crew against his employer. A claim on the part of the defendant might only be justified in case the charter contract between the owner and the charterer would have provided that the payment of the crew salaries is made by the owner on behalf and for the account of the charterer which last would then be bound to refund the relevant amounts to the owner.

[31]   "Nothing of this kind is stipulated in the contract, from which, on the contrary, it appears that the charterer was free to dispose of the vessels 'according to their best judgment . . . including the sub-charter', that it was the charterer's direct responsibility to pay the crew salaries, and that even in the case that the charterer would have hired for the chartered vessels crew members from Russia, the owner would have only be[en] responsible to provide certain services, such as the selection of 'experienced crew members . . . and qualified for the functions they will perform according to the requests of the charterer', the organization of 'the necessary crew changes', or the substitution of crew members 'upon request of the charterer'. The above services did not include the payment of the salaries by the owner on behalf and for the account of the charterer.

[32]   "As a matter of fact, when the charterer sub-chartered the vessels to the sub-charterer, it was stipulated in the relevant contract that the sub-charterer was committed:

– to employ Russian crew members in accordance with the labour contracts signed by the charterer;

– to ratify these contracts, and
– to perform all obligations therein, including the payment of wages.

In any case, and in addition to the above (if need should be), the tribunal notice that the defendant has not provided any evidence of the fact that it would have, at any time, paid crew salaries on behalf and for the account of the claimant. Therefore the tribunal unanimously decides that the defendant's request for arrears of crew salaries is dismissed."

VI.   INTEREST

[33]   "It is a general principle of law, as well as of international trade practice, that the harm normally sustained as a consequence of delay in payment of a sum of money be compensated by interest. In accordance with the deliberations of the tribunal, the claimant is entitled to damages for non-performance by the claimant of its non-monetary obligations under the charter contract, and the defendant is entitled to receive payment of certain arrears of the charter fee. It has also be[en] decided that the claimant's debit for overdue charter fees be set-off against its major credit for damages.

[34]   "The claimant requests that the interest on damages accrues from March 1997, which is the date on which the impoundment of the last of the chartered vessels took place. Since the liquidation of damages by the tribunal as well as the above settlement are the result of the legitimate cancellation of the charter contract by the claimant in March 1997, and of its further Request for Arbitration of March 1997, in which the compensation of damages and the payment of the relevant interest was [sic] requested, it seems appropriate that interest on the balance due by the defendant accrues from this last date.

[35]   "As to the rate of interest, the claimant's request that the LIBOR on US$ be applied is justified. Since the request does not specify which LIBOR should apply, the tribunal considers appropriate that the rate be the one of the 'one year' LIBOR. . . ."

VII.   COSTS

[36]   "Taking into account that damages have been granted to the claimant in a smaller amount than requested, and that defendant's counterclaim for the payment of arrears of charter fees was justified, the tribunal unanimously decides that the costs of the arbitration be borne by the parties in equal proportions (50/50) and that each party shall bear its own legal costs."

(. . . .)

Partial award in case no. 9787 of 1998

Parties:	Claimant: Buyer (China)
	Defendant: Seller (US)
Place of arbitration:	Stockholm, Sweden
Published in:	Unpublished
Subject matter:	– waiver of right to arbitrate

Facts

Buyer, a Chinese manufacturer, entered into a series of contracts (the Project contracts) with seller, a US company, to purchase technology as well as equipment and personnel training which would result in the handing over of a complete manufacturing plant for the production of a high technology electronic component. Disputes arose regarding the deliveries, quality and payment and buyer initiated ICC arbitration claiming damages. Seller counterclaimed for payment.

After signing the Terms of Reference and various submissions, seller submitted a motion to dismiss buyer's claim for lack of jurisdiction. Seller alleged that by joining a lawsuit initiated in a United States court by buyer's counsel against seller's counsel, buyer had waived its right to arbitrate as the action related directly to the claims and counterclaims filed in the arbitration.

In its partial award, the arbitral tribunal held that the arbitral tribunal had jurisdiction. Although Art. 1(2) of the Swedish Arbitration Act (the applicable procedural law) prohibited the initiation of an arbitration if a court action regarding the same issue was pending at that time, the arbitration had been initiated prior to the court proceedings. Nor did the United States action divest the arbitral tribunal of its jurisdiction as the parties were not the same and it was not certain that the suit would result in a substantive ruling or that it would address the same issues as the arbitral tribunal. Moreover, neither the ICC Rules nor the Swedish Arbitration Act contained provisions on the waiver of the arbitration agreement. Accordingly, the arbitral tribunal had jurisdiction.

Excerpt

I. TIMELY REQUEST FOR DISMISSAL

[1] "Buyer [claimant] has argued that seller's [defendant's] request that the arbitral tribunal dismiss buyer's claims for lack of jurisdiction has been presented too late, and that seller therefore has waived its right to present this request.

[2] "In this respect, the arbitral tribunal notes the following. Seller's response to and defences against buyer's claims have been laid down in the Terms of Reference . . . as follows:

> 'In June 1998, buyer's attorney, Mr. Y, filed an action against seller's counsel of record, Mr. Z, in a court in Denver, USA. Mr. Y informed the arbitral tribunal that the lawsuit was filed for the purported purposes of protecting the interests of buyer and Mr. Y. The Denver court action seeks a declaratory judgment that buyer's factual contentions in its Reply and Amended Claims are the most reasonable inferences from the facts set forth in this arbitration. By letter dated July 1998, buyer's attorney Mr. X informed the arbitral tribunal that an amended complaint will be filed, adding Mr. X as plaintiff. Seller contends that the initiation of this lawsuit constitutes a breach of the arbitration clause in each of the Project Contracts, and has caused severe damage and prejudice to seller.'

The US Action is also referred to in the Terms of Reference in relation to the issues to be determined by the arbitral tribunal:

> 'In light of the filing of a court action by buyers's counsel in Denver, Colorado, USA, against seller's counsel in relation to pleadings filed in this arbitration, can the arbitral tribunal continue to assume jurisdiction over this arbitration.'

[3] "Furthermore, seller raised the issue of the arbitral tribunal's jurisdiction in Mr. Z's fax of August 1998 to the arbitral tribunal. This issue is mentioned in the context of seller's request for a preliminary hearing:

> 'Such a hearing is needed in order to hear the parties' position on these [procedural] issues and to determine the procedure for future proceedings, as well as any threshold issues, such as the Tribunal's jurisdiction, or any applicable statute of limitation issue.'

[4]   "On the basis of the above, the arbitral tribunal concludes that seller cannot be considered to have waived its right to refer to the US action as a legal ground for its request for the dismissal of buyer's claims for lack of jurisdiction."

II.   APPLICABLE LAW

[5]   "The arbitral tribunal is of the opinion that the issue of jurisdiction should be determined pursuant to its ruling of September 1998 regarding procedural rules. The arbitral tribunal deems that the New York Convention of 1958 is not applicable as such, as the Convention concerns the recognition and enforcement of an arbitral award under certain circumstances, which is not the case in the situation at hand.

[6]   "Even though the arbitral tribunal deems the New York Convention of 1958 to be not applicable to the issue of jurisdiction at hand, the arbitral tribunal is obliged to observe the Convention, as set forth in Art. 35 of the ICC Rules. Lacking any agreement between claimant and defendant to the contrary, the parties' agreement to arbitrate (which provides that the arbitration shall take place in Stockholm, Sweden) leads to the conclusion that Swedish law shall govern the agreement to arbitrate. In Swedish arbitration law it is a well-established principle that an agreement to arbitrate and the 'main agreement' constitute two separate agreements (the doctrine of separability). A corollary to this doctrine is the doctrine of *compétence de la compétence*. Under the latter doctrine, which is also accepted in Sweden (as in many other jurisdictions), the fact that the agreement to arbitrate is allegedly invalid – implying lack of jurisdiction of the arbitrators – does not prevent the arbitrators from deciding the issue of validity.

[7]   "In the present matter, no circumstances have been presented or otherwise appeared that would render the parties' agreement invalid from the beginning (cf. Art. II(3) ('null and void') and Art. V(I)(*a*) of the New York Convention of 1958). The issue of whether the parties' agreement may have ceased to have effect is addressed in Sect. IV below concerning seller's argument relating to buyer's waiver of its right to arbitrate (cf. Art. II(3) ('inoperative') of the New York Convention of 1958). The arbitral tribunal notes in this regard that reported court cases relating to the word 'inoperative' are few.[1] It should also be noted that in the same context it is remarked that the possibility of conflicting court decisions or arbitral awards in related cases 'is, in principle, not a reason to hold the arbitration agreement "inoperative" or "incapable of being performed" '.[2] Finally, no circumstances have been presented, that could render the parties'

---

1. "See van den Berg, *The New York Convention of 1958*, p. 158."
2. "See van den Berg, *The New York Convention of 1958*, p. 159."

agreement to arbitrate 'incapable of being performed' (cf. Art. II(3) of the New York Convention of 1958)."

III.   THE US ACTION

[8]   "As mentioned above, in September 1998, the arbitral tribunal reached certain decisions with regard to, i.a., the rules that shall apply to the procedural issues of this arbitration. The arbitral tribunal found that the proceedings in this arbitration are to be governed by the ICC Rules. Furthermore, the proceedings are to be governed by such decisions as the arbitral tribunal may, from time to time, take, guided by the ICC Rules and the Swedish law governing arbitrations in Sweden.

[9]   "The heading of Art. 6 of the ICC Rules is 'Effect of the Arbitration Agreement'. However, neither this article nor any other article of the ICC Rules, contains any provision regarding the possible effect that a court action may have on an arbitration proceeding regarding the same or related issues.

[10]   "Therefore, when analysing the possible impact of the US action on these arbitration proceedings, the arbitral tribunal will, pursuant to its above-mentioned procedural ruling, mainly consider the provisions of the Arbitration Act.

[11]   "According to Art. I(2) first sentence of the Arbitration Act, '[a]rbitrators may not assume jurisdiction in respect of any question which is the subject of a pending court action'. Any award rendered where the arbitration proceedings were inadmissible will, according to Art. 20(1)(3) of the Arbitration Act, be void.

[12]   "According to well-established Swedish legal doctrine, Art. 1(2) of the Arbitration Act prevents the *initiation* of an arbitration proceeding if a court action regarding the same issue is pending at that time.[3] When the Arbitration Committee presented its proposal for a revised Arbitration Act in 1994, the Arbitration Committee confirmed this interpretation of Art. 1(2) of the Arbitration Act.[4] In this respect, no changes were made when the Government, on 1 October 1998, submitted its proposal to the law committee of the Supreme Court for its consideration.[5]

[13]   "In the case at hand, buyer filed its request for arbitration against seller in December 1997 with the International Court of Arbitration of the ICC. In a letter of March 1998, the Secretariat of the International Court of Arbitration of

---

3. "Cf., for example, Hassler and Cars, *Skiljeförfarande*, 2nd ed., 1989, p. 23."
4. "SOU 1994:81 p. 136."
5. " 'Lagrådsremiss', dated 1 October 1998."

the ICC forwarded the file to the arbitral tribunal. The US action was initiated in June 1998 by Mr. Y against Mr. Z, respectively buyer's and seller's counsel in the present arbitration. Ms. X, buyer's Chinese counsel in the present arbitration was subsequently included as plaintiff to the US action. The arbitral tribunal has been informed during the preliminary hearing that the plaintiffs in the US action, Mr. Y and Ms. X in a submission dated October 1998 have requested that the District Court in Denver County Colorado 'dismiss the US action with prejudice', pursuant to the C.R.C.P. Rule 41(a)(1)(B), each party to bear its own costs and attorney fees. This information is supported by the mentioned submission of October 1998, which has been submitted in this arbitration. The arbitral tribunal has further been informed during the preliminary hearing that the defendant in the US action, Mr. Z, has declined to agree on the dismissal of the US action in the manner proposed by the plaintiffs in the US action.

[14]   "The arbitral tribunal starts from the premise that the parties have expressly agreed to arbitrate all disputes arising out of their various contractual relationships. As far as the arbitral tribunal is aware, there would be no disagreement as to this arbitral tribunal's jurisdiction were it not for the filing of the US action by buyer's counsel. The arbitral tribunal determines, therefore, as a preliminary matter and which has been indicated already in Sect. II above, that this arbitral tribunal has jurisdiction over the claims of the parties.

[15]   "The issue presented by seller's motion to dismiss buyer's claims is whether the US action has somehow divested this arbitral tribunal of that jurisdiction.

[16]   "Seller's motion essentially rests on the contention that the proceedings before this arbitral tribunal and those in the US action are congruent, i.e., that both the District Court in Denver County and the arbitral tribunal will be required to rule upon the same issues of fact and law, and that, as a consequence, there is a risk of inconsistent determinations and inconsistent legal obligations for the parties. The arbitral tribunal disagrees.

[17]   "In the first place, and perhaps most importantly, the parties to the US action and this arbitration are not the same. As long as neither buyer [n]or seller is a party to the US action, it appears highly doubtful to the arbitral tribunal that either would be bound by any legal ruling of the District Court in Denver County. Indeed, the arbitral tribunal notes that neither buyer nor seller has attempted to become a party to the US action, and it is unclear to us whether either could be brought involuntarily within the jurisdiction of the District Court of Denver County. Seller, despite its arguments in the arbitration, has made no attempt itself to join the US action or to have buyer joined.

[18]   "It is, moreover, by no means clear that the US action will result in a substantive ruling. Many lawsuits are dismissed or substantially altered at a preliminary procedural stage. The proceedings in Denver are in a very

preliminary stage, and no one can say at this point if the lawsuit will proceed and, if so, in what fashion. While the arbitral tribunal does not know what course the District Court in Denver County will take, the possibility of a preliminary procedural resolution is clearly present here, since buyer has moved, as noted above, the District Court in Denver County to dismiss its claims with prejudice.

[19] "Further, even if the US action does go to the merits, it is by no means certain that it will address the same issues as this arbitral tribunal. The claims before this arbitral tribunal are, in essence, mutual claims for breach of contract by buyer and seller. The claims in the US action are for fraud, defamation, misuse of legal process, and the like between buyer's and seller's counsels. These claims are very different by their nature. Although there might be some overlap of the factual issues to be considered by the District Court in Denver County and this arbitral tribunal, it seems much more probable that, if both said court and the arbitral tribunal eventually rule on the merits of the claims before them, their rulings will, to a significant extent, address quite different legal and factual issues. Thus, the arbitral tribunal believes that it is highly unlikely that the District Court in Denver County, by adjudicating the matter before it, would resolve the issues before the arbitral tribunal. The arbitral tribunal finds that these circumstances as such would be sufficient to deny seller's motion to dismiss buyer's claims for lack of jurisdiction.

[20] "In addition, the arbitral tribunal notes that the US action was initiated in June 1998, after the transfer of the file to the arbitral tribunal which occurred in March 1998. The arbitral tribunal further notes that the plaintiffs in the US action moved in October 1998 that the US action be dismissed with prejudice and that the defendant in the US action has declined to agree to the dismissal. This is, of course, the defendant's right, and the consequences of its exercise of that right can be determined by the District Court in Denver County. The fact that the defendant in the US action is not prepared to agree on the dismissal as set forth above, should not, however, in the arbitral tribunal's opinion, be allowed to affect the arbitral tribunal's jurisdiction.

[21] "A dismissal of buyer's claims under these circumstances would in the arbitral tribunal's opinion be contrary to the parties' contractual agreement to resolve all disputes arising out of their contractual relationships through arbitration. It would also present the serious risk that the disputes between buyer and seller would not be resolved at all for lack of an agreed forum.

[22] "Taking the above into consideration, and especially that the parties in the US action are not identical with the parties in this arbitration and the uncertainty with respect to the issues to be determined in the US action, and also since the US action was initiated after this arbitration, the arbitral tribunal holds that the US action does not affect the jurisdiction under the parties' arbitration agreement, already assumed by the arbitral tribunal."

IV.   WAIVER OF THE ARBITRATION AGREEMENT

[23]   "Seller has also argued that buyer, as a result of its counsel's initiating the US action, has waived its right to arbitrate.

[24]   "Seller has argued that even though the US action was filed by buyer's counsel against seller's counsel, the action was filed for, and on behalf of, buyer. The arbitral tribunal notes, however, that seller has apparently made no effort itself to become a party to the US action or to add buyer as a party to the US action. As matters now stand, only the counsels themselves are parties to the US action.

[25]   "The arbitral tribunal makes the following general remarks in this respect.

[26]   "By way of introduction, the arbitral tribunal notes that also in this regard, it shall, pursuant to its above-mentioned procedural ruling, mainly seek guidance in the ICC Rules and the Arbitration Act.

[27]   "The concept of waiver of an arbitration agreement is mentioned in Art. 23(2) of the ICC Rules. The provisions of this article relate to a situation where a party, before the file has been transmitted to an arbitral tribunal, applies to a judicial authority for conservatory or interim measures. Such an application shall not be considered as a waiver of the arbitration agreement and shall not affect the relevant powers reserved to the arbitral tribunal.

[28]   "Following the above, the arbitral tribunal finds that the provisions of Art. 23(2) of the ICC Rules are not applicable in this case.

[29]   "The arbitral tribunal notes that the Arbitration Act does not contain any provisions with respect to the issue of waiver of an arbitration agreement.

[30]   "The issue of waiver of an arbitration agreement occurs rarely in legal doctrine. It has, however, been discussed whether a claimant, by his conduct, can be said to have abandoned, or waived, his right to proceed with arbitration against the respondent. Some are of the opinion that there ought to be a means of preventing an arbitration agreement being enforced, where delay by the claimant has prejudiced the respondent's ability to prepare his case and to present it to the arbitral tribunal.[6]

[31]   "The arbitral tribunal notes what seller has stated with respect to US arbitration law and the possibility in that jurisdiction to consider an arbitration agreement to have been waived by a party.

[32]   "On the basis of the above, the arbitral tribunal concludes as follows.

[33]   "Neither the ICC Rules nor the Arbitration Act contains any provision regarding waiver of the arbitration agreement that may apply to the issue at hand. On the basis thereof, and also considering the general discussions in the

---

6. "Redfern and Hunter, *International Commercial Arbitration*, 2nd ed. 1991, pp. 180-181."

legal doctrine referred to above (' ... there *ought* to be a means'), the arbitral tribunal holds that buyer by virtue of the fact that the US action was filed by buyer's counsel, can not be considered to have waived its right to arbitrate.

[34]   "The arbitral tribunal notes that seller claims that the US action has caused it prejudice. The arbitral tribunal understands, however, that as the defendant in the US action, seller's counsel would be able to pursue in the District Court in Denver County remedies for any prejudice it may have incurred in that litigation, and further that this issue should be resolved in said court. The arbitral tribunal believes that seller has not been prejudiced in this arbitration as a result of buyer's counsel's filing of the US action.

[35]   "Since the arbitral tribunal has found that buyer has not waived its right to arbitrate, it is not necessary for the arbitral tribunal to analyse the parties' arguments as to whether the issues raised in the US action are moot.

[36]   "As regards seller's alternative request to suspend the arbitration, the arbitral tribunal finds no reason to suspend the arbitration because of a possible future action in a related matter, that may be initiated by seller in a US court."

V.   CONCLUSION

[37]   "Seller's request that buyer's claims be dismissed for lack of jurisdiction shall be denied. The arbitral tribunal shall so award. Seller's request that the arbitration be suspended shall likewise be denied."

Final award in case no. 8547 of 1999

Parties: Claimant: Seller (Bulgaria)
                     Defendant: Buyer (Greece)

Place of
arbitration: Paris, France

Published in: Unpublished

Subject matters: – arbitration agreement by exchange of telexes
                     – separability of arbitration agreement
                     – applicable law to contract
                     – formation of contract
                     – non-conformity of goods
                     – settlement of debt

Facts

In November 1991, claimant (seller) and defendant (buyer) began business relations and established "terms and conditions" for this relationship. In December
1991, claimant, which was the wholly-owned sales division of the supplier, sold
defendant several thousand tons of goods. Claimant sent a telex to defendant on
3 December setting out the terms of the sales contract with respect to the quantity, delivery terms, price, means of payment, inspection, claims, applicable law
and arbitration. The telex provided, inter alia:

> (. . . .)
> "5. Delivery Terms
> Delivered Duty Unpaid (DDU)
> (. . . .)
> 8. Price
> The goods under this Contract shall be supplied under the FIXED price of
> US$ . . . per tonn. . . . This price to be valid for the deliveries which will
> take place latest 30.03.1992. After that the price to be renegotiate [sic] for
> each next quarter or fixed between the Buyer and the Seller till the end of
> 1992.
> (. . . .)

12. Inspection
Inspection at loading place to be performed by the producer, which is mutually accepted to both Buyer and Seller, whose finding to quality to be final and binding for both parties concerned.
(. . . .)
15. Claims
Claims with regard to quantity and quality, if any, to be communicated promptly within 15 days after the date of arrival and to be considered only against presentation of supporting claim documents issued by neutral surveyor presented within 30 days from the date of arrival.
(. . . .)
20. Applicable Law
The present Contract shall be governed by, constructed and interpreted in accordance with the Uniform Law for the international sale of corporal movables (Hague convention 1/7/64).
21. Arbitration
Any dispute arising in connection with the present Contract shall be finally settled under the Rules of Arbitration of the International Chamber of Commerce – Paris, by three arbitrators appointed according to the said Rules. The decision of the arbitrators shall be final and binding for the parties hereto. The place for arbitration shall be Paris. The language to be used in the arbitral proceedings shall be the English language.
(. . . .)"

On 4 December, defendant replied by telex as follows:

"We confirm this contract, but psl try to correct the following points:

1. ITEM 7
Free of charge time to be three (3) working days instead of 48 hours for discharging and customs clearance.
2. ITEM 8
Price to be valid for the entire 1992 deliveries.
3. ITEM 14
The goods should be covered by the seller by insurance up to the delivery to the end user. . . ."

The transactions between the parties went smoothly until May 1992 when the defendant alleged that bad quality goods had been delivered. Defendant informed claimant immediately and claimant sent Mrs. M, the Managing Specialist of the Quality Control Division of the supplier, to inspect the goods. Although the specialist admitted that the goods were of bad quality, no action was undertaken by claimant to remedy the lack of conformity. Defendant suspended payment for later deliveries in August 1992. In response, claimant suspended the further delivery of goods.

In February 1995, claimant initiated arbitration with the International Chamber of Commerce claiming payment for the goods. Claimant, defendant and a representative of the supplier attended a meeting in B, Bulgaria in May 1995. Defendant alleged in the arbitration that it was agreed at that meeting that damages it had paid to its purchaser of the goods were to be deducted from the amount it owed and that the remainder of its debt would be settled by delivery to supplier of goods of an equal value. Defendant claimed that it fulfilled its obligations as agreed in May 1995, but claimant continued to demand payment.

The arbitral tribunal first upheld its jurisdiction, reasoning that the exchange of telexes constituted a valid arbitration agreement which satisfied the requirements of Art. II(2) of the 1958 New York Convention. Applying the principle of separability, the arbitral tribunal stated that the validity of the arbitration agreement did not depend on the validity of the contract. Moreover, the arbitration agreement was not among the terms objected to in the second telex.

The applicable law to the contract was that stipulated in the contract, the Uniform Law on the International Sale of Goods (ULIS) and the Uniform Law on the Formation of Contracts for the International Sale of Goods (ULF) which in the view of the arbitral tribunal, were to be supplemented by the UNIDROIT Principles. Applying these instruments, the arbitral tribunal held that the contract was not concluded by the exchange of telexes because the answering telex contained material alterations. However, it was concluded by subsequent performance. The arbitral tribunal established that the goods had been delivered and that claimant was aware of the bad quality. On examining the evidence, the arbitral tribunal also determined that a meeting had taken place in May 1995 at which the claimant, its supplier and defendant reached an agreement reducing the remaining price to be paid by the defendant by the amount the defendant had lost on reselling the bad-quality goods. The remainder of the debt was settled by deliveries by the defendant to the supplier. Although claimant had refused to acknowledge that the debt had been settled in full, subsequent admissions and the evidence showed that its claim was unjustified.

Excerpt

I. JURISDICTION

[1] "An agreement to arbitrate was validly reached between the parties. The arbitration agreement was included in claimant's telex of 3 December 1991.

Defendant never objected to this provision of the contract. The defense of the defendant, which states that the arbitral tribunal does not have jurisdiction because no such agreement was put forward, is without success. Therefore the arbitral tribunal upholds the validity of the arbitration agreement.

[2]   "According to Art. 4(3)(d) ICC Rules, a party must include the arbitration agreement when submitted its Request for Arbitration. In its Response to the Statement of Defense claimant included the answering telex to its telex of 3 December 1991 sent by defendant on 4 December 1991. In this telex defendant agrees to the terms of the contract with several exceptions. Provision No. 21 concerning the arbitration agreement is not named in the exceptions. Therefore defendant agreed to the arbitration provision.

[3]   "Art. II(2) of the New York Convention on the Recognition and Enforcement of Foreign Arbitral Awards – New York Convention – states that the arbitral agreement must be in writing, but that an exchange of letters is sufficient.[1] The New York Convention is applicable to the present case, as both Bulgaria and Greece are parties to the Convention.

[4]   "In this case the parties simply exchanged unsigned telexes. Especially in international relations parties hardly meet to conclude a contract, but choose the speedy method of telexes to conduct their business relations. This must be taken into account when interpreting the New York Convention. The exchange of telexes to conclude an arbitration agreement is enough to validate an arbitral clause between the parties.[2]

[5]   "This holds true regardless of whether or not the rest of the contract is deemed to be valid. The defendant itself refers to the generally recognized principle of separability of the arbitration clause. This principle is reflected in Art. 6(4) ICC Rules."[3]

---

1. Art. II(2) of the 1958 New York Convention on the Recognition and Enforcement of Foreign Arbitral Awards reads:

   "The term 'agreement in writing' shall include an arbitral clause in a contract or an arbitration agreement signed by the parties or contained in an exchange of letters or telegrams."

2. "See A.J. van den Berg, *The New York Arbitration Convention of 1958* (The Hague 1981) p. 204 et seq."

3. Art. 6(4) of the 1998 ICC Rules of Arbitration reads:

   "Unless otherwise agreed, the Arbitral Tribunal shall not cease to have jurisdiction by reason of any claim that the contract is null and void or allegation that it is non-existent provided that the Arbitral Tribunal upholds the validity of the arbitration agreement. The Arbitral Tribunal shall continue to have jurisdiction to determine the respective rights of the parties and to adjudicate their claims and pleas even though the contract itself may be non-existent or null and void."

II. VALIDITY OF THE CLAIM

1. Applicable Law

[6] "The applicable law on the substance of the case is The Hague Convention of 1 July 1964 as the law chosen by the parties and the UNIDROIT Principles as supplementary rules which the arbitral tribunal deems appropriate to apply where necessary in accordance with Art. 17(1) ICC Rules.[4]

[7] "As stated in provision No. 20 of claimant's telex of 3 December 1991, the contract shall be governed by 'the Uniform Law for the international sale of corporal movables (Hague convention 1/7/64)'. This clause has evidently been accepted by defendant. Its telex of 4 December 1991 shows no objection concerning the applicable law proposed by claimant. The arbitral tribunal is therefore of the opinion that the relationship of the parties is governed by the substantive law chosen in No. 20 of claimant's telex. This includes the Convention relating to a Uniform Law on the International Sale of Goods (ULIS) and the Convention relating to a Uniform Law on the Formation of Contracts for the International Sale of Goods (ULF).

[8] "According to Art. 4 ULIS, the Conventions shall apply where they have been chosen as the law of the contract by the parties, regardless of whether or not the States of their places of business are parties to the Convention. This is in accordance with the principle of party autonomy, which states that parties are free to choose the law to govern their contract.

[9] "In so far as the Conventions ULIS and ULF did not cover all questions and refering to Art. 17 of the ICC Arbitration Rules, the arbitral tribunal felt it appropriate to turn to the UNIDROIT Principles which provide [a] useful complement to fill the lacuna and allow to find proper solutions."

2. Formation of the Contract

[10] "The contract was not concluded by exchange of telexes, because the defendant proposed certain new conditions in its answering telex of 4 December 1991, which materially altered the terms of the contract according

---

4. Art. 17(1) of the 1998 ICC Rules of Arbitration reads:

"The parties shall be free to agree upon the rules of law to be applied by the Arbitral Tribunal to the merits of the dispute. In the absence of any such agreement, the Arbitral Tribunal shall apply the rules of law which it determines to be appropriate."

to Art. 7 ULF.[5] Defendant asked for different conditions concerning the free of charge time regarding delivery, the guaranteed price for all of 1992, and insurance of the goods by seller up to delivery to the end user. The different terms requested by defendant concern mainly, the price of the goods and the insurance risk of the seller.

[11] "Such demands for changes in the contract by the other parties are considered by jurisprudence to be material alterations which must be specifically accepted by the party having made the initial proposal. To cite just one example, the German Court of Appeal Hamm[6] deemed a demand for payment in advance to be a material alteration. Because the price of the goods is an *essentiale negotii*, anything concerning the price must be considered as a material alteration. The insurance and delivery risk of the seller or buyer are also important terms of the contract, as each party must be able to calculate its possible costs beforehand.

[12] "Therefore the telex sent by defendant on 4 December 1991 constitutes a counter-offer and should have been answered by claimant – either containing a confirmation of the different terms or a new offer. Silence itself cannot have the effect of acceptance, see Art. 2(2) ULF.[7]

[13] "However, the contract was formed by claimant commencing with performance of the contract. The provisions of the contract as proposed in claimant's telex of 3 December 1991 and not disputed between the parties at any time are valid. The rest of the provisions were renegotiated with each delivery.

[14] "Claimant began to deliver goods on 6 December 1991 and continued to do so until August 1992. Defendant accepted delivery of the goods. The contract was formed between the parties the latest with the first delivery by claimant. According to Art. 6(2) ULF 'acceptance may also consist of the dispatch of the goods'.

---

5. Art. 7 of the Uniform Law on the Formation of Contracts for the International Sale of Goods (ULF) reads:

   "1. An acceptance containing additions, limitations or other modifications shall be a rejection of the offer and shall constitute a counter-offer.
   2. However, a reply to an offer which purports to be an acceptance but which contains additional or different terms which do not materially alter the terms of the offer shall constitute an acceptance unless the offeror promptly objects to the discrepancy; if he does not so object, the terms of the contract shall be the terms of the offer with the modifications contained in the acceptance."

6. "Decision of 21 March 1979 cited in; Schlechtriem/Magnus, *International case law on ULIS and ULF*, Baden-Baden (1987) Art. 7 [ULF] No. 4 (on 'price and payment') [140 n. 20]."

7. Art. 2 ULF reads:

   "1. The provisions of the following Articles shall apply except to the extent that it appears from the preliminary negotiations, the offer, the reply, the practices which the parties have established between themselves or usage, that other rules apply.
   2. However, a term of the offer stipulating that silence shall amount to acceptance is invalid."

[15] "The contract was not – as suggested by defendant – renegotiated wholly for each delivery. It continued to exist as the legal framework of the parties to which specific alterations or amendments may have been made from time to time. Those alterations or amendments have no bearing on the present dispute.

[16] "Neither claimant nor defendant ever objected to the terms of performance of the contract during the time period of delivery of the goods. According to the theory of punctation this is to be interpreted as agreement on the undisputed terms of the contract as presented in the telex of 3 December 1991, unless the parties specifically agreed on other terms during its performance. Therefore, the provisions of the contract are primarily applicable, supplemented by the rules of ULF and ULIS.

[17] "When taking into consideration the internationality of the relations between the parties, the UNIDROIT Principles become relevant. Art. 4.5 UNIDROIT Principles states that contract terms should be interpreted as to give effect to as many of them as possible. Therefore, if the parties at one point agreed on certain provisions, this needs to be taken into account when trying to resolve a dispute.

[18] "In the present case, the defendant in its answering telex mainly wanted to alter the matters of price and insurance. Since these matters were put in writing for each and every delivery (as shown by the telexes), they can be said to have been renegotiated and agreed upon every time within the existing framework of the contract."

3. Quality of the Goods

[19] "Delivery of the goods under the contract was never disputed between the parties, but the delivered goods were partially not in accordance with the contract. Defendant claims that goods delivered in May 1992 were of bad quality. This is contested by claimant. It is uncontested that defendant did not protest in accordance with provision No. 15 of the contract. The arbitral tribunal is convinced of the non-conformity of the goods. . . . The strict adherence to the requirement of provision No. 15 now by claimant amounts to an abuse of rights. . . . If claimant could rely on this provision, defendant would have lost any rights in regard to the non-conformity. It is relevant that according to defendant claimant did have the opportunity to examine the goods. Defendant states that claimant sent the Managing Specialist of the Quality Control Division of supplier, Mrs. M, to examine the goods. This witness was not brought forward by claimant – although this was requested by the arbitral tribunal in its Order No. 1.

[20] "Conclusions can be drawn from the fact that claimant refused to produce the witness as asked by the arbitral tribunal. Had the witness been made

available it could have been further investigated whether or not claimant had knowledge of a non-conformity. Claimant justified its refusal in its brief of 30 October 1998 by stating that the person in question has retired and furthermore is not an employee of claimant but of supplier. Therefore any statements made by such a witness could not be binding for claimant.

[21]   "These arguments are not in the least conclusive. It is certainly not a rule of evidence that a statement made by a witness, not an employee of the party in question, cannot be binding for that party. The best witness is an objective witness – without relations to any of the parties. Thus the reasons brought forward by claimant cannot justify the refusal to produce the witness.

[22]   "Claimant, therefore, cannot rely on the non-adherence to the requirement of provision No. 15 of the contract. It remains unclear as to how the claimant was informed of a non-conformity and how claimant reacted to this information. Claimant cannot refuse to produce witnesses who could clear up certain allegations of defendant regarding the non-conformity of the goods."

4.   Payment

[23]   "It was the defendant's right to stop payment because of the non-conformity of the goods. It is undisputed that the bills which have not been paid by defendant sum up to. . . . Although the degree of non-conformity of goods has not been proven, it was the defendant's right to suspend payment after raising the *exceptio non adimpleti contractus*.

[24]   "The contract was to be performed step by step, i.e., payment was to follow the delivery of goods. If the goods are not of the quality agreed upon in the contract, the buyer must give notice of the non-conformity. Until an agreement is reached between the parties as to the degree of the lack of conformity and as to how to proceed in regard to the non-conformity, the buyer does not have to pay the price. The further development of the contract at that point is unclear. It would amount to a curtailment of the rights of the buyer if he had to continue payment of the goods without knowing what will happen in regard to the non-conformity.

[25]   "This is not expressly stated in ULIS, but follows from the general principles of law referred to in Art. 17 ULIS.[8] According to Art. 7.1.3 UNIDROIT

---

8. Art. 17 of the Uniform Law on the International Sale of Goods (ULIS) reads:

"Questions concerning matters governed by the present Law which are not expressly settled therein shall be settled in conformity with the general principles on which the present Law is based."

Principles[9] a party may withhold its performance until performance has been affected by the other party. Thus the above reasoning is in accordance with these principles of law.

[26]   "Once the seller knows of a possible non-conformity it is his duty to act upon this knowledge to clear up the degree of the non-conformity. Since the oral hearing . . . it is undisputed that a meeting took place in V, the place of business of the end user of the purchased products, concerning the quality of the goods. This is proof of the fact that claimant knew of the possible non-conformity of the goods. The degree of non-conformity is therefore irrelevant in regard to the right of the defendant to suspend payment. It is sufficient that defendant informed claimant of the non-conformity and then suspended payment until an agreement concerning the lack of conformity was reached. Defendant suspended payment after the meeting in V took place. This is not a violation of defendant's contractual duties."

5.   Amount Owed

[27]   "The defendant does not owe the sum . . . because all claims between the parties were taken care of during the meeting in B in May 1995 and defendant had performed its obligations resulting from the agreement between the parties and supplier reached in B.

(. . . .)

[28]   "The content and results of the meeting remain contested between the parties. Defendant alleges that it was agreed that the sum still owed had been reduced by DM. . . . This would leave a sum of DM . . . still to be paid by defendant. Payment of DM . . . was to be affected [sic] by deliveries free of charge from defendant to supplier. Claimant contests this allegation.

[29]   "The burden of proof concerning the trilateral agreement lies with the defendant. Any facts that are favorable towards the position of the defendant must be proven by it. Defendant provided two witnesses, one of them – Mr. C, as President of the defendant – stating that he was present at the meeting in B in May 1995 and verifying the results of the meeting. Defendant's second witness, Mrs. P, stated during the hearing that she was not present during the meeting at B. Her testimony is therefore disregarded as far as the agreement reached at B is concerned.

---

9. Art. 7.1.3 UNIDROIT Principles of International Commercial Contracts reads:

"(1) Where the parties are to perform simultaneously, either party may withhold performance until the other party tenders its performance.
(2) Where the parties are to perform consecutively, the party that is to perform later may withhold its performance until the first party has performed."

[30]   "In addition, defendant provides documentary evidence in the form of telexes to and from claimant and supplier. . . . The telexes show that goods for the value of DM . . . were delivered from defendant to supplier and that both claimant and supplier acknowledge this transaction.

[31]   "The acknowledgment of this transaction also forms the basis of the last brief of the claimant of 30 October 1998. In this brief claimant reduces its claim. . . . Thus claimant admits that an agreement was reached in regard to this sum.

[32]   "Claimant still denies the outcome of the meeting in B in May 1995, but does not show proof of its own. Claimant had been asked by the arbitral tribunal to present as witnesses those persons defendant alleges were present at the meeting. According to defendant two representative of supplier and one representative of claimant were present. Claimant refuses to produce these witnesses again on the grounds that one has retired, one has left the company, and that statements made by persons not employed by claimant could not be binding for it.

[33]   "In its brief of 30 October 1998 claimant claims that its representative – Mr. Y – named by defendant was not present at the meeting and would therefore be of no use as witness, since he could only support what had already been put forward in writing. As stated above, this reasoning is not satisfactory. A witness can be heard regardless of which 'side' the witness comes from.

[34]   "The arbitral tribunal had asked claimant to produce these witnesses in order to clear up the issue of the meeting in B. Claimant now admits that such a meeting took place, and should therefore have offered its representative as a witness. If it was not the person named by defendant, claimant should have made the arbitral tribunal aware of this and offered its own witness, who could make a statement as to the content of the meeting. Claimant failed to do this. Instead it continues to simply deny the outcome of the meeting as stated by defendant. With these actions claimant frustrates the attempts of the arbitral tribunal to establish the facts of the case by all appropriate means, Art. 20(1) ICC Rules.[10] This is to be held against claimant.

[35]   "In light of all of these arguments the arbitral tribunal is satisfied that the defendant has proven its line of defense to be true. Therefore any claim that may have existed in favor of the claimant was taken care of in the meeting in B in May 1995. This agreement is binding to all participants: claimant, supplier and defendant. The claim of claimant is therefore already settled."

---

10. Art. 20(1) 1998 ICC Rules of Arbitration reads:

"1. The Arbitral Tribunal shall proceed within as short a time as possible to establish the facts of the case by all appropriate means."

III. COSTS AND FEES

[36] "This arbitral tribunal applies the general rule, that costs should follow the event. The party losing an arbitration is therefore burdened with its costs. Since it is the defendant who is winning this arbitration because the claim of claimant was either withdrawn during the oral hearing or is dismissed by this final award, it is the claimant who is to carry its costs.

[37] "Part of the claim was withdrawn by the claimant at the last moment of the oral hearing. Therefore it must carry all costs of the claim withdrawn. All costs of the claim dismissed go to the claimant, including the lawyer's costs for the defendant and travel expenses for him, the President of the defendant and the witness, Mrs. P."

(...)

Partial award in case no. 8782 of 1997

| Parties: | Claimant: Fish sorting company (Belgium) |
| | Defendant: Manufacturer (Denmark) |

Place of arbitration: Amsterdam, The Netherlands

Published in: Unpublished

Subject matters:
- applicable law in standard conditions
- division of contractual risk
- cancellation of contract due to breach
- limitation of damages
- damages ripe for decision (no)

Facts

A Belgian company whose principal business was to receive, sort and auction fish (claimant) ordered an automated fish-sorting machine from a Danish manufacturer (defendant). Under the provisions of the contract (the Basic Contract), the defendant was to deliver by a contractually agreed-upon date a machine capable of sorting a determined quantity of fish. The Basic Contract also incorporated the General Conditions for the Supply and Execution of Plant and Machinery for Import and Export No. 188 A of March 1957 of the United Nations Economic Commission for Europe (UNECE-Conditions) which provided in Clause 28(1) for ICC arbitration. Clause 28(2) of the UNECE-Conditions provided the contract was governed by the law of the contractor's country, i.e., Denmark.

The defendant was not able to meet the delivery date and the parties agreed to two amendments to the Basic Contract. Under the terms of the amendments, the machine was scheduled for delivery in two phases, a first phase and a second phase, and the total sales price was adjusted.

The machine did not perform properly in either of the phases. After several years of attempting to remedy the problems, the claimant initiated ICC arbitration claiming that he was entitled to cancel the Basic Contract due to the defendant's fundamental breach of contract, and to be refunded the amount paid for the machine.

The defendant responded that he had become aware of problems in meeting the requirements of the Basic Contract and had entered into separate agreements with regard to specific parts of the automated system which had not been developed at the time parties had entered into the Basic Contract. He also argued that the claimant "actually accepted delivery of the automatic feeding system knowing of the problems of operation thereof". Further, the defendant submitted that the relevant provisions of the applicable UNECE-Conditions and the United Nations Convention on Contracts for the International Sale of Goods (CISG) barred the claimant from cancelling the contract after having accepted the machine. The defendant argued that the only remedy open to the claimant was a price reduction for the defective machine under Art. 50 CISG.

The sole arbitrator, in a partial award, established that the defendant's failure to deliver a machine in accordance with the Basic Contract constituted a fundamental breach of contract under Art. 25 CISG. Accordingly, the arbitrator held that under the applicable law, claimant was entitled to cancel the Basic Contract.

Turning to the claimant's request for a refund of the purchase price, the arbitrator observed that although the defendant was obligated to perform according to the Basic Contract and its two amendments, the claimant had been forewarned by the defendant concerning its problems in developing the automated system and could have limited the damages it suffered by terminating the contract at an earlier stage.

Having determined that the Basic Contract had been rightfully terminated, the arbitrator concluded the partial award with the suggestion that the parties attempt to settle the remaining issues such as whether the machine was to be replaced by a new system or if the machine would be used despite its defects, and/or the quantum of damages. At this stage neither damages nor interest could be awarded before the claimant's intentions were clarified.

Excerpt

(. . . .)

I.   ARBITRATION AND APPLICABLE LAW

[1]   "It follows from a fax of claimant to (and agreed upon by) defendant, that the General Conditions for the Supply and Erection of Plant and Machinery for import and export No. 188A of March 1957 of the United Nations Economic Commission for Europe (the UNECE-Conditions) were incorporated into the Contract. This was confirmed by the First Amendment to the Contract. Clause 28.1 of the UNECE-Conditions reads as follows:

'Any dispute arising out of the Contract shall be finally settled in accordance with the Rules of Conciliation and Arbitration of the International

Chamber of Commerce, by one or more arbitrators designated in conformity with those Rules.'

The parties agree that the UNECE-Conditions are incorporated in the Contract and the competence of the arbitrator to deal with the present dispute was not challenged by either party.

[2]　"Clause 28.2 of the UNECE-Conditions reads as follows:

'Unless otherwise agreed, the Contract shall, so far as is permissible under the law of the country where the Works are carried out, be governed by the law of the Contractor's country.'

The parties agree that, pursuant to this clause, Danish Law is applicable to the Contract. The parties also agree that the United Nations Convention on Contracts for the International Sale of Goods (CISG) is applicable."

II.　THE CONTRACT AND THE OBLIGATIONS OF THE DEFENDANT
　　THEREUNDER

[3]　"The arbitrator finds that the machine, both functionally and mechanically, was riddled with problems, serious problems, right from the beginning. The question is: how should these problems be viewed under the Contract, also taking into account the applicable law and other applicable rules? What consequences should they have?

[4]　"It is not denied by the defendant that the machine has caused many problems, functional and mechanical, right from the beginning. The defendant also admits that, shortly after signing the Basic Contract, it became evident that the performance rate stated therein would not be reached. It has also been established that, in the course of time, the problems remained and that also the defendant was losing its initial confidence about its ability to deliver a machine that would work entirely properly, notably in view of the functional problems."

(. . . .)

[5]　The defendant based its defence on Danish law. "The claimant has not denied that Danish law is the law applicable to the Contract. It has not denied either that, under Danish law, the aim is to deduce the true intention shared by the parties to the Contract and that, in determining the true common intention, all documents and the full conduct of the parties must be considered.

[6]　"Therefore, one should look into the said elements relevant under Danish law. First of all, as defendant has submitted, to the Contract."

(. . . .)

[7]   After noting, inter alia, that under the First Amendment to the Basic Contract, the automatic line feeder system agreed upon in the Basic Contract was to be delivered in two parts on two separate dates, the purchase price was revised and payment conditions were modified, the sole arbitrator continued: "It would appear from this First Amendment that the claimant acknowledged that the defendant was encountering difficulties in fulfilling its obligations under the Basic Contract, notably with respect to the automatic Line Feeder System, and that the claimant accepted therefore a certain deviation from these obligations. However not in the sense that it waived delivery of the automatic system in absolute terms. The First Amendment cannot be read in another way than that the claimant accepted a manual feeder system on a temporary basis, the automatic system to be delivered later, with a penalty for late delivery.

[8]   "The Second Amendment does not substantially deviate from the Basic Contract either – nor from the First Amendment. The Second Amendment is to the effect that the delivery time for [a certain part], the contract price, certain costs, payment conditions and the penalty just referred to were amended. The Basic Contract and its execution were explicitly confirmed. In other words: on [the date of the Second Amendment], the claimant certainly did not renounce its right to have delivered and installed a machine as per the Basic Contract.

[9]   "Do any of the other documents to which the defendant has referred as forming the total Contract cast a different light hereon? The answer has to be in the negative.

[10]   "It is true that it appears from the defendant's letters written [before the First Amendment] that the defendant is experiencing some problems in its production of the machine and is expecting some problems also after its installation. It is also true that, in these letters, reference is made to the facts that the machine was a new concept, that claimant was aware thereof and that claimant accepted this to a certain extent: i.e., notably with respect to the delivery time of the machine. But, nevertheless, the defendant accepted its obligations as these essentially were under the Basic Contract, in the First and Second Amendment signed after the correspondence just referred to. In those Amendments, no reservations are made any more with respect to a possible cancellation of the Contract. And, on the other hand, it appears clearly from the letters written by the claimant during that same period that the claimant did not want to renounce or waive its rights as they were, in essence, under the Basic Contract. Notably, the claimant did not wish to accept the possibility for either party to cancel the order and this possibility was apparently not submitted by the defendant thereafter again. At any rate, this possibility was not incorporated in either of the two amendments.

[11]   "In other words, at the time when the Second Amendment was signed, the obligations of the defendant with respect to the machine as such were substantially the same as under the Basic Contract. This does not mean that the

correspondence exchanged between the parties meanwhile is without any meaning or effect. The arbitrator will revert thereto hereafter. But, substantially, the delivery and installation of an automatic ... sorting system for fish ... remained as described in the Basic Contract. Only – in summary – the price and other financial terms and the delivery conditions were amended.

[12]   "The next question is if the defendant's correspondence after the time of the Second Amendment cast a different light on this conclusion. This is not the case either. The correspondence shows that, in the construction of the machine and notably of the automatic feeder, the defendant continued to experience difficulties."

(. . . .)

[13]   The arbitrator reviewed the correspondence between parties and ascertained that the claimant did not accept the defendant's offer to accept a restricted version of an undelivered part. Claimant's letters showed that it had accepted a late delivery and installation of the remaining automatic feeders and had accepted changes in penalties and costs. The arbitrator concluded: "In other words, also at the time when the three remaining automatic feeders were going to be delivered and installed, the claimant again did not accept a substantial deviation from the Contract with respect to the character and operation of the machine. In that respect, none of the documents which, in defendant's view, constitute the entire Contract, change the substance of the Basic Contract.

[14]   "It also follows from what has been said herebefore that with regard to the Basic Contract and the two Amendments there was no question of separate contracts on the substance. On the contrary, the Second Amendment starts by saying that both parties reconfirm the complete contract and shall execute it as mentioned in the Basic Contract. There is no evidence that such separation was agreed upon later either."

III.   THE PERFORMANCE OF THE MACHINE IN THE LIGHT
       OF THE CONTRACT

[15]   " . . . . In the light of the available evidence and of the Contract, the arbitrator comes to the conclusion that the machine, as delivered and installed, did not perform on essential points as the claimant could reasonably expect under the Contract. To such an extent, and to such detriment, that the claimant can be considered to be substantially deprived of what it was entitled to expect under the Contract.

(. . . .)

[16]   "The defendant has argued that the claimant knew that the machine was a new concept which had to be further developed. This is true. But it is equally

true that for a long time ... both parties, including the defendant, were confident that this new concept would succeed.

[17]   "In the relation between the parties, the risk that this would not be the case, that the parties were too optimistic from the beginning, is more for the defendant than for the claimant. The defendant knew, as a concept, exactly what the claimant wanted. The defendant, with its technical background and expertise, was in a better position to judge if this concept could be successful than the claimant. The claimant may be closest to know its own requirements with respect to the handling and grading of flatfish as the defendant has said, but the defendant is, in the arbitrator's opinion, the closest to judge if such requirements can be properly translated into the fully automatic machine which the parties discussed and, eventually, agreed upon. It would have been prudent for the defendant to make more reservations in the Contract – already in the Basic Contract – on the chance of success or failure than it did.

(....)

[18]   "Finally, the arbitrator is not convinced that it was the formula as such – as expressed in the Basic Contract ... that is wrong and the cause of the functional problems that have arisen. The arbitrator is of the opinion that it appeared technically impossible to construct a machine which could work with this formula. That should be considered in principle to be for the risk of the defendant.

(....)

[19]   "The defendant has argued that the machine, even today, is still in operation. That is not relevant. What is relevant is whether the machine is operating in a way that is acceptable under the terms of the Contract.

[20]   "All this does not mean that the claimant did not accept certain risks as well. The arbitrator will revert thereto hereafter. But the principal risk is with the defendant."

IV.   CONSEQUENCES OF BREACH OF CONTRACT

[21]   "If, thus, the facts in this case constitute a fundamental breach of the Contract, the question is what the consequences are.

[22]   "In that respect, the parties agree that Danish law is applicable. There is a dispute between the parties however, first of all, on the implications of the UNECE-Conditions and of the CISG. There is no dispute between the parties that these rules apply. There is also agreement that the text of the Contract takes precedence over both the said rules and that the UNECE-Conditions take precedence over the provisions of the CISG. The arbitrator can very well accept this approach. Has the claimant, in light thereof, the right to cancel the Contract (or avoid it, in the wording of Art. 49 CISG)?

[23]   "The Contract itself has no explicit provision with regard to cancellation, termination or dissolution of the Contract. The parties have not referred to any specific rule of Danish law on this point.

[24]   "The UNECE-Conditions mention the possibility of termination for a specific reason in Clauses 25.3 (termination in case of non-timely performance of a contract for reasons beyond the control of the parties),[1] 10.2 (termination in case of non-acceptance of delivery),[2] 11.7 (termination in case of non-payment)[3] and 20.5 (termination in case of non-completion).[4]

---

1. Clause 25.3 of the UNECE-Conditions reads:

"The effects of the said circumstances, so far as they affect the timely performance of their obligations by the parties, are defined in Clauses 10, 11, 20 and 22. Save as provided in paragraphs 10.2, 11.7 and 20.5, if, by reason of any of the said circumstances, the performance of the Contract within a reasonable time becomes impossible, either party shall be entitled to terminate the Contract by notice in writing to the other party without requiring the consent of any Court."

2. Clause 10.2 of the UNECE-Conditions reads:

"Unless the failure of the Purchaser is due to any of the circumstances mentioned in Clause 25, the Contractor may require the Purchaser by notice in writing to accept delivery within a reasonable time.

        If the Purchaser fails for any reason whatever to do so within such time the Contractor shall be entitled by notice in writing to the Purchaser, and without requiring the consent of any Court, to terminate the Contract in respect of such portion of the Plant as is by reason of the failure of the Purchaser aforesaid not delivered and thereupon to recover from the Purchaser any loss suffered by reason of such failure up to an amount not exceeding the sum named in paragraph A of the Appendix or, if no sum be named, that part of the price payable under the Contract which is properly attributable to such portion of the Plant."

3. Clause 11.7 of the UNECE-Conditions reads:

"Save as aforesaid, if the Purchaser delays in making any payment, the Contractor shall on giving to the Purchaser within a reasonable time notice in writing be entitled to the payment of interest on the sum due at the rate fixed in paragraph B of the Appendix from the date on which such sum became due. If at the end of the period fixed in paragraph C of the Appendix, the Purchaser shall still have failed to pay the sum due, the Contractor shall be entitled by notice in writing to the Purchaser, and without requiring the consent of any Court, to terminate the Contract and thereupon to recover from the Purchaser the amount of his loss up to the sum mentioned in paragraph A of the Appendix."

4. Clause 20.5 of the UNECE-Conditions reads:

"If any portion of the Works in respect of which the Purchaser has become entitled to the maximum reduction provided for by paragraph 3 hereof, or in respect of which he would have been so entitled had he given the notice referred to therein, remains uncompleted, the Purchaser may by notice in writing to the Contractor require him to complete and by such last mentioned notice fix a final time for completion which shall be reasonable taking into account such delay as has already occurred. If for any cause other than one for which the Purchaser or some other Contractor employed by him is responsible, the Contractor fails to complete within such time, the Purchaser shall be entitled by notice in writing to the Contractor, and without requiring the

[25] "In the view of the arbitrator, this does not mean that the UNECE-Conditions should be deemed to exclude cancellation or avoidance of a contract for such essential reasons as a fundamental breach of contract. This is not excluded at all in the UNECE-Conditions and that would, and should, undoubtedly have been the case, explicitly, if it had been the intention to do so.
[26] "Apparently, the principles of Danish law either incorporate the relevant provisions of the CISG with respect to this question or Danish law is essentially the same as these provisions, without having incorporated them explicitly or officially. This would also seem to follow from the defendant's statement that CISG *Part II* on the formation of the Contract is *not* (emphasis added) part of Danish law.
[27] "The CISG has, in Part I, certain provisions on cancellation of contracts in case of fundamental breach. Art. 45 CISG reads:

> '1. If the seller fails to perform any of his obligations under the contract or this Convention, the buyer may:
> a. exercise the rights provided in Articles. 46 to 52;
> b. claim damages as provided in Articles. 74 to 77.
> 2. The buyer is not deprived of any right he may have to claim damages by exercising his right to other remedies.
> 3. No period of grace may be granted to the seller by a court or arbitral tribunal when the buyer resorts to a remedy for breach of contract.'

[28] "The claimant has stated that it wishes to exercise the right provided in Art. 49 under 1a, which thus it is entitled to do under Art. 45. Art 49 1a reads as follows:

> '1. The buyer may declare the contract avoided:
> a. if the failure by the seller to perform any of his obligations under the contract or this Convention amounts to a fundamental breach of contract; or
> (. . . .)'

[29] "In addition, the claimant has asked for damages. Under Art. 45 it is, in principle, equally entitled to do that in addition to its declaration of avoidance. The questions as to how far this is possible, and if Danish law would explicitly deviate in this respect, will be dealt with later.

---

consent of any Court, to terminate the Contract in respect of such portion of the Works and thereupon to recover from the Contractor any loss suffered by the Purchaser by reason of the failure of the Contractor as aforesaid up to an amount not exceeding the sum named in paragraph F of the Appendix, or, if no sum be named, that part of the price payable under the Contract which is properly attributable to such portion of the Works as could not in consequence of the Contractor's failure be put to the use intended."

[30]   "Art. 25 CISG defines a fundamental breach as follows:

'A breach of contract committed by one of the parties is fundamental if it results in such detriment to the other party as substantially to deprive him of what he is entitled to expect under the contract, unless the party in breach did not foresee and a reasonable person of the same kind in the same circumstances would not have foreseen such a result.'

[31]   "... [T]he arbitrator finds that the claimant was substantially deprived of what it was entitled to expect under the Contract. The defendant has not argued that it did not foresee such result. It follows from the defendant's letters ... and from its statements ... that the defendant did foresee such detrimental results: the defendant, after its initial confidence that it could meet the wishes of the claimant, had to conclude that, most likely, it would not be possible to satisfy the terms of the Contract. The defendant could therefore foresee that the delivery of the machine could have detrimental results for the claimant.

[32]   "It has not been argued by the defendant that the exceptions of Art. 49.2 CISG would apply.[5] Rightly so, in the arbitrator's view.

[33]   "Therefore, the claimant's request for a ruling that its notification of cancellation of the Contract was rightful, should be awarded."

V.   MITIGATION OF DAMAGES

[34]   "Basically, there are two consequences to be considered:

– Should the cancellation of the Contract have effect ab initio (ex tunc) or not?
– What damages should be awarded?

---

5. Art. 49.2 of the CISG reads:

   "However, in cases where the seller has delivered the goods, the buyer loses the right to declare the contract avoided unless he does so:

   (a) in respect of late delivery, within a reasonable time after he has become aware that delivery has been made;
   (b) in respect of any breach other than late delivery within a reasonable time:
      (i) after he ought to have known of the breach;
      (ii) after the expiration of any additional period of time fixed by the buyer in accordance with paragraph (1) of article 47, or after the seller has declared that he will not perform his obligations within such an additional period; or
      (iii) after the expiration of any additional period of time indicated by the seller in accordance with paragraph (2) of article 48, or after the buyer has declared that he will not accept performance."

[35] "It has been considered herebefore – in summary:

– that the risk of contracting for and delivering the machine was in principle more for the defendant than for the claimant;
– that the claimant has never formally waived its rights under the Contract.

[36] "It has also been considered herebefore however that the claimant knew:

– at the time of the Basic Contract, that the machine was a new concept;
– at the time of the First and of the Second Amendment, that the defendant was encountering problems in developing and constructing the machine in accordance with the terms of the Contract;
– at the time of the delivery of the First Phase and of the Second Phase of the machine, that these problems were far from being solved.

[37] "It has been considered herebefore that all this did not formally relieve the defendant from its duty to deliver the machine in accordance with the terms of the Contract. Certainly not after the Second Amendment had been accepted by the defendant, in which the Basic Contract was reconfirmed. Without the consent of the purchaser, the defendant could not unilaterally step out of its obligations under the Contract. Such consent – apart from what was explicitly agreed upon in the area of delivery time, price, penalties and the like, as considered herebefore – was not given by the claimant.

[38] "But that should not form the end of the considerations. The question can arise as to whether, at some stage, the purchaser has refused to give such consent on grounds which could – and should – be considered unreasonable. Also, it could be questioned if the claimant could – and should – not have mitigated its damages by relieving the defendant from its obligation to deliver the machine in accordance with the terms of the Contract. Surely, the claimant was in a way invited to do so, explicitly and implicitly: before the signing of the two Amendments, when the defendant raised the issue of cancellation of the Contract in so many words, and before the delivery of the Second Phase of the machine when, notably through its letter of . . . the defendant made clear once more that it might not be able to deliver a machine in accordance with the terms of the Contract.

[39] "In the opinion of the arbitrator, the claimant certainly at that stage took a risk, a serious risk, that indeed the machine might not for a long time – may be even never – work in accordance with the terms of the Contract. It can thus not leave all the consequences thereof for the risk of the defendant.

[40] "In general, there is an obligation for a creditor who is suffering damages or is confronted with the possibility that he might suffer damages to limit or prevent same. There is also the rule of reason: is it reasonable that a party in a

position as the claimant withholds its consent to a voluntary termination of the Contract at certain relevant moments? And finally, if it is true that the defendant, at the time when it delivered the machine, could foresee its detrimental results, the same is true for the claimant.

[41] "There may be other rules and principles under Danish law leading to – basically – the same result. These questions have not been discussed fully by the parties so far. It is not clear either to what extent these – or similar – principles or rules as just referred to can be invoked under Danish law. At any rate, the rules which are applicable to the Contract would form a basis for further considering what the consequences should be, such as:

– Clause 26 on limitation of damages in the UNECE-Conditions;[6]
– Art. 74 CISG;[7]
– Art. 76 CISG.[8]

[42] "In other words, the arbitrator is under the impression that the claimant could have limited the damages which it allegedly suffered. The discussion on that issue, both on the qualitative and on the quantitative aspects, has not been in

---

6. Art. 26 of the UNECE-Conditions reads:

"*Limitation of damages*
1. Where either party is liable in damages to the other, these shall not exceed the damage which the party in default could reasonably have foreseen at the time of the formation of the Contract.
2. The party who sets up a breach of Contract shall be under a duty to take all necessary measures to mitigate the loss which has occurred provided that he can do so without unreasonable inconvenience or cost. Should he fail to do so, the party guilty of the breach may claim a reduction in the damages."

7. Art. 74 of the CISG reads:

"Damages for breach of contract by one party consist of a sum equal to the loss, including loss of profit, suffered by the other party as a consequence of the breach. Such damages may not exceed the loss which the party in breach foresaw or ought to have foreseen at the time of the conclusion of the contract, in the light of the facts and matters of which he then knew or ought to have known, as a possible consequence of the breach of contract."

8. Art. 76 of the CISG reads:

"(1) If the contract is avoided and there is a current price for the goods, the party claiming damages may, if he has not made a purchase or resale under article 75, recover the difference between the price fixed by the contract and the current price at the time of avoidance as well as any further damages recoverable under article 74. If, however, the party claiming damages has avoided the contract after taking over the goods, the current price at the time of such taking over shall be applied instead of the current price at the time of avoidance.
(2) For the purposes of the preceding paragraph, the current price is the price prevailing at the place where delivery of the goods should have been made or, if there is no current price at that place, the price at such other place as serves as a reasonable substitute, making due allowance for differences in the cost of transporting the goods."

depth enough to lead to final conclusions at this stage. The debate thereon should therefore be continued. In the course thereof, it should also be considered at what time the claimant had sufficient knowledge of the risks it was facing in pressing for delivery of the machine under the terms of the Contract. . . ."

VI. DAMAGES

[43]   The arbitrator noted that claimant's specification of its claim for damages and interest gave rise to a number of questions, including whether claimant was entitled to a refund of the purchase price as well as future damages. The arbitrator continued: "[I do] not find this debate very conclusive, probably because it is conducted on a rather abstract level and does not always take into account the facts at hand. In general, the arbitrator would say the following.

[44]   "Indeed, in various systems of law, a distinction is made between 'positive contract interest' and 'negative contract interest'. Indeed it has to be sorted out. (a) Firstly, how these elements are construed under Danish law; and (b) secondly, how they – in principle – should be applied in the case at hand. In this connection, the following is of relevance.

[45]   "The claimant has expressed at various occasions its wish to get rid of the machine. In view of the arbitrator's considerations . . . herebefore, the claimant is in principle entitled to do so. In that case, it would not seem illogical that the purchase price, in so far as paid, be refunded (possibly with a discount if there is some compensation for the abandonment of the machine) – apart from other damages to which claimant may be entitled.

[46]   "However, the claimant, in its Post Hearing Brief, claims future damages as it intends to keep the machine [for fifteen years]. . . . This approach seems inconsistent with an approach whereby the machine is abandoned at this stage.

[47]   "To the arbitrator, it seems that the damages should be calculated:

– either on the basis that the machine is abandoned and a new system has to be acquired;
– or on the basis that the claimant continues to use the machine in spite of its problems and the damages caused thereby.

Both approaches could encompass future damages – but of a different character.

[48]   "The parties should also give their further views on this. During those exchanges of views, also other questions and problems can be discussed and settled, such as the meaning of Clause 27.1 of the UNECE-Conditions.[9] The

---

9. Clause 27.1 of the UNECE-Conditions reads:

"Termination of the Contract, from whatever cause arising, shall be without prejudice to the rights of the parties accrued under the Contract up to the time of termination."

debate thereon may become moot if the claimant would decide to retain the machine. The reference, by the defendant in this context, to Art. 49 (2)(b)(i) CISG is not clear.

[49]   "The defendant has argued that Clause 23.14 of the UNECE-Conditions[10] would prevent claimant from claiming certain damages. The arbitrator does not think that this view is correct. Clause 23.14 is part of the paragraph on the guarantee period. This period, according to Clause 22.1, starts to run as from the time of take-over as described in that paragraph – i.e., after taking-over tests as described in Clause 21.1. As has been observed herebefore, such tests have never taken place in this case and no taking-over certificate was ever issued. The provisions of Clause 23 of the UNECE-Conditions were written for a different situation than for fundamental breach of contract.

[50]   "The defendant has also disputed the extent of the damages claimed by the claimant, among others by denying that the decline in the boarding of fish at Z was caused by the not-proper operation of the machine. Also this aspect can be dealt with in the course of the further debate.

(. . . .)

[51]   "It would seem to the arbitrator that the parties should first of all be given an opportunity to discuss these various questions and sort out answers between themselves. They know now the arbitrator's findings and views on a number of essential issues. It cannot be excluded that, in the light thereof, the parties would be able to agree on a friendly settlement on the outstanding issues regarding the damages to be paid. The arbitrator will give the parties the opportunity thereto. . . . Thereafter, the parties are invited to advise the arbitrator on the position (if agreement has been reached, if the parties want an extension, if no agreement has been reached or if they – or one of them – wish to proceed further)."

VII.   CONCLUSIONS AND AWARD

[52]   ". . . The arbitrator comes to the following conclusions.

(1)   The defendant has failed to deliver a machine in accordance with the terms of the Contract between the parties.

---

10. Clause 23.14 of the UNECE-Conditions reads:

"After taking over and save as in this Clause expressed, the Contractor shall be under no liability even in respect of defects due to causes existing before taking over. It is expressly agreed that the Purchaser shall have no claim in respect of personal injury or of damage to property not the subject-matter of the Contract arising after taking over nor for loss of profit unless it is shown from the circumstances of the case that the Contractor has been guilty of gross misconduct."

(2)   This failure can be considered as a fundamental breach of contract as defined in Art. 25 CISG.

(3)   Therefore, the claimant is in principle entitled to avoid the Contract, to return the machine and to claim damages.

(4)   There is no evidence that the claimant has substantially waived any of the rights referred to under (3); substantially, the claimant has waived certain ancillary rights, such as the right to claim penalties for late delivery. But such claims are not raised by the claimant in this arbitration.

(5)   There is evidence to the effect that also the claimant should have realised, before taking final factual delivery of the machine, that the machine might or would not function in accordance with the terms of the Contract. It is not unlikely that the claimant could – and should – have limited the damages allegedly suffered by it if it had cooperated in terminating the Contract at that stage. This has to be sorted out in a further debate between the parties. It should then also be considered which date would be relevant in this context.

(6)   It follows from the arbitrator's considerations that the defendant would in principle not be entitled to its counterclaim. However, in a situation where the claimant would conclude to keep the machine despite of its right to cancel the Contract, not only the question of a refund of amounts already paid by the claimant would have to be considered, but also the question as to whether the defendant is entitled to further payments (apart from a possible right of set-off against the claimant's claim in that situation).

(7)   Therefore, a final decision on those points cannot be taken at this stage. The parties are invited to initiate a discussion between themselves on the basis and on the questions as set out [in previous paragraphs], taking into account the considerations as laid down in this award.

(8)   The parties are asked to report to the arbitrator . . . about the status of their discussions.

(9)   Any further decision is postponed, including a decision on costs."

Final award in case no. 9302 of 1998

Parties: Claimant: Manufacturer D (Germany)
                    Defendant: Agent S (Colombia)

Place of
arbitration: Paris, France

Published in: Unpublished

Subject matters: – agency contract
                   – timeliness of jurisdictional defense
                   – applicable law to arbitration agreement
                   – effect of corporate changes on jurisdiction
                   – jurisdiction linked to merits

Facts

A German manufacturer D entered into an agency contract (the 1954 Contract) with a Colombian company S.E. (S.E.) which was part of a German group of companies incorporated under the name, S Colombiana, Limitada (S). Under the 1954 Contract, S.E. agreed to promote and distribute D's products and would receive a commission for services rendered and D agreed to support S.E. in these activities. The contract contained a dispute resolution clause providing for arbitration under the ICC Rules of Conciliation and Arbitration and provided that the law applicable to the contract was German law.

In 1964, S Colombiana changed its corporate form from a limited company (*Limitada*) to limited liability company (*Sociedad Anomima*). In the fall of 1971 S. changed its name from S Colombiana S.A. to S S.A. Earlier that summer, S.E. was liquidated. Following the liquidation, S continued to act as D's agent in Colombia. In 1971 a further contract was concluded between D and S (the 1972 contract), followed by another in 1982 (the 1982 contract). Neither of these contracts contained an arbitration clause.

The parties later disputed the nature and extent of their contractual relationships following the liquidation of S.E. D alleged that S.E. was merged into S Colombiana S.A. S argued that S.E. ceased to exist as a result of the liquidation and that there was no merger between S.E. and S.

In June of 1995, D sent S a letter stating its intent to terminate the 1954 Contract as of the end of that year. In August of 1995 S wrote that it accepted the termination and invoked mandatory Colombian law applicable to all agency contracts performed in Colombia, irrespective of contrary choice-of-law clauses. S claimed that under this law it was entitled to compensation to be computed over 41 years (1954-1995). In November 1995, S ordered goods from D. S refused to pay for the delivered goods, "as long as the compensation claims were not settled". Relying on the arbitration clause in the 1954 contract, D initiated ICC arbitration in October 1996 seeking payment and interest for the 1995 order. S objected that the arbitral tribunal did not have jurisdiction because it was not bound by the 1954 contract.

In its Procedural Order no. 1, the arbitral tribunal determined that the issue of jurisdiction and the merits were closely linked. Accordingly, it would deal with jurisdiction and the merits at the same time and not render an interim award on jurisdiction. It its award, the arbitral tribunal first dismissed D's argument that S's challenge to the arbitral tribunal's jurisdiction was time-barred because it had not been raised when submitting his defense. Although commentators on the French law of arbitration have pointed out that a challenge should be raised before raising substantive arguments, the tribunal accepted the view that a party should be free "to raise a defense until the time the Terms of Reference have been established".

With regard to applicable law, the arbitral tribunal held that the arbitration agreement in the 1954 Contract was severable from the contract, thus the choice of German law did not apply to the arbitration clause. The arbitral tribunal found that in order to review whether the parties were bound by the arbitration agreement, it had to determine the intention of the parties. To support this view, the tribunal cited ICC Rules and French case law giving arbitrators the power to decide on their own jurisdiction without referring to specific national laws.

Turning to the issue of whether the 1954 Contract was binding on parties as a result of the corporate changes which occurred in 1971, the arbitral tribunal, applying Colombian law, concluded that S was not the "universal successor" to S.E. Thus S was not bound by the 1954 Contract and its arbitration clause. Further, the arbitral tribunal determined that there was no common intent between parties to continue the 1954 Contract following the 1971 changes in corporate structure. The 1971 Contract which contained no arbitration clause had replaced the 1954 Contract, thus the arbitral tribunal had no jurisdiction over the dispute.

Excerpt

I. JURISDICTION

1. *Timeliness of Defense*

[1] "D's argumentation in this respect can be subdivided into two components. First, D argues that, by participating in the constitution of the arbitral

tribunal, S has accepted that the dispute be settled by arbitration and is estopped from challenging jurisdiction. The fact that a party participates in the constitution of the arbitral tribunal cannot preclude it from challenging jurisdiction, if only because the arbitral tribunal has the power to decide over its own jurisdiction and must be formed in order to do so.

[2]   "D further argues that S must be deemed to have accepted jurisdiction also because it filed its answer under Art. 4(1) ICC Rules without raising lack of jurisdiction at that time.[1] It is accurate that S failed to oppose jurisdiction [in its first submission]. It did not do so before [submitting an unsolicited rejoinder to D's second submission].

[3]   "Should S therefore be deemed to have waived its jurisdictional defense? Under French law of arbitration, there exists no compulsory time limit for a respondent to challenge the arbitrator's jurisdiction. A commentator has pointed out that the challenge to the arbitrators' jurisdiction must be done '*in limine litis*', i.e., before raising any substantive arguments.[2] In an ICC arbitration, one can argue that a respondent is required to raise any jurisdictional defense in the answer filed in accordance with Art. 4(1) of the ICC Rules. Such view may be supported by the relationship between Arts. 4 and 7 of the ICC Rules.[3]

[4]   "However, it is also true that in an ICC arbitration, a party is free to raise any means of defense until the time the Terms of Reference have been established. Thus, one may reasonably hold the view that, unless a party has *expressly* accepted the arbitrators' jurisdiction prior thereto, the arbitrators should not

---

1. Art. 4(1) of the 1988 ICC Rules reads:

   "The Defendant shall within 30 days from the receipt of the documents referred to in paragraph 3 of Art. 3 comment on the proposals made concerning the number of arbitrators and their choice and, where appropriate, nominate an arbitrator. He shall at the same time set out his defence and supply relevant documents. In exceptional circumstances the Defendant may apply to the Secretariat for an extension of time for the filing of his defence and his documents. The application must, however, include the Defendant's comments on the proposals made with regard to the number of arbitrators and their choice and also, where appropriate, the nomination of an arbitrator. If the Defendant fails to do so, the Secretariat shall report to the Court, which shall proceed with the arbitration in accordance with these Rules."

2. "*International Handbook on Commercial Arbitration* France: Y. Derains, R. Goodman-Everard, update February 1998, p. 39."

3. Art. 7 of the 1988 ICC Rules reads:

   "Where there is no *prima facie* agreement between the parties to arbitrate or where there is an agreement but it does not specify the International Chamber of Commerce, and if the Defendant does not file an Answer within the period of 30 days provided by paragraph 1 of Art. 4 or refuses arbitration by the International Chamber of Commerce, the Claimant shall be informed that the arbitration cannot proceed."

reject the jurisdictional defense on the sole ground that it was filed late, as long as it was made prior to the signing of the Terms of Reference.

[5]   "The arbitral tribunal is sympathetic to the latter view, in particular for the following reasons: time limits set by the ICC Rules or by the arbitrators are not an end in themselves. Their purpose is to ensure fairness, equality between the parties, and orderly conduct of the proceedings.[4] In the present case, S's late submission of its jurisdictional defense did not affect any of these purposes;

- the unsolicited rejoinder was filed in February 1997 in parallel to the formation of the arbitral tribunal, which was not completed before May of the same year. Thus the formation of the tribunal was not affected by the late challenge.
- no issue arose under Art. 7 ICC Rules in this arbitration because the prima facie existence of the arbitration agreement was beyond doubt. Thus the late challenge has caused no disruption or delay in this respect.
- by the time the file was forwarded to the arbitrators, S had raised its jurisdictional defense and D had responded. Hence, all the necessary elements for drafting the Terms of Reference were immediately available to the arbitrators.

[6]   "In other words, the timing of S's defense did not disrupt or delay the proceedings, nor did it harm D. To consider that S has waived its challenge of the jurisdiction of the arbitral tribunal by not having submitted it with its first answer to the request for arbitration would be a fictitious assumption which in the circumstances of this case could not be sufficient to establish the arbitrators' jurisdiction. Therefore, the arbitral tribunal does not consider justified to dismiss the jurisdictional defense as untimely and will now review the merits thereof."

2.   Law Applicable to the Arbitration Agreement

[7]   "Which law governs the arbitration agreement? First, as a result of the severability of the arbitration agreement, the choice of German law incorporated in the 1954 Contract does not extend to the arbitration clause, but relates only to the merits of the dispute.

[8]   "Second, Arts. 8(3) and 8(4) of the ICC Rules do not require the application of any specific national law.[5] These provisions leave the question of the

---

4. "W. Laurence Craig, William W. Park, Jan Paulsson, *International Chamber of Commerce Arbitration*, 2nd ed., (New York 1990) pp. 392-393."

5. Art. 8(3) and (4) of the ICC Rules reads:

"(3) Should one of the parties raise one or more pleas concerning the existence or validity of the agreement to arbitrate, and should the Court be satisfied of the *prima facie* existence of such an agreement, the Court may, without prejudice to the admissibility or merits of the plea or pleas,

applicable law open and have been interpreted as conferring upon the arbitrators the power to decide on their own jurisdiction without reference to any specific national law.

[9] "This power is no novelty. So, for instance, the 1982 *Dow Chemical* interim award on jurisdiction referred to it in the following terms:

' . . . in referring to the ICC Rules, the parties incorporated its provisions concerning the arbitral tribunal's authority to decide as to its own jurisdiction, which provisions do not refer to the application of any national law. The reference to French law [chosen by the parties for the main contract] could therefore concern only the merits of the dispute . . . ;
. . . the sources of law applicable to the scope and the effects of an arbitration clause providing for international arbitration do not necessarily coincide with the law applicable to the merits of the dispute submitted to such arbitration. Although this law or these rules of law may in certain cases concern the merits of the dispute as well as the arbitration agreement, it is perfectly possible that in other cases, the latter, because of its autonomy, is governed . . . by its own specific sources of law, distinct from those that govern the merits of the dispute:
. . . this is particularly the case – unless the parties have expressly agreed otherwise – with respect to an arbitration clause referring to the ICC Rules.'[6]

Other ICC awards confirm this approach.[7]

[10] "Third, the arbitral tribunal takes into consideration that the place of arbitration is Paris, and that the French courts would ultimately have jurisdiction to review this award in the context of an annulment action. Under French

---

decide that the arbitration shall proceed. In such a case any decision as to the arbitrator's jurisdiction shall be taken by the arbitrator himself.

(4) Unless otherwise provided, the arbitrator shall not cease to have jurisdiction by reason of any claim that the contract is null and void or allegation that it is inexistent provided that he upholds the validity of the agreement to arbitrate. He shall continue to have jurisdiction, even though the contract itself may be inexistent or null and void, to determine the respective rights of the parties and to adjudicate upon their claims and pleas."

6. "ICC case no. 4131, arbitral tribunal composed of Messrs. Pieter Sanders, Berthold Goldman and Michel Vasseur, *Collection of ICC Arbitral Awards 1974-1985* (Deventer 1990) pp. 146-153."
7. "E.g., ICC case no. 3572, *Yearbook Commercial Arbitration XIV* (1989) pp. 111-116; ICC case no. 4381, *Collection of ICC Arbitral Awards 1974-1985*, pp. 263-265, ICC case no. 5065, *Collection of ICC Arbitral Awards 1986-1990* (1994) pp. 330-333, see also, Craig, Park, Paulsson, op.cit., fn. 2, pp. 72-74, Sect. 5.05; Fouchard, Gaillard, Goldman, *Traité de l'arbitrage commercial international* (Paris, 1996) pp. 245-247, Sects. 436-437."

law, the enforceability of an arbitration agreement depends on the common intent of the parties and there is no need either to refer to any national law. In *Dalico*, the *Cour de cassation* set this rule in the following terms:

' . . . pursuant to a substantive rule of international arbitration law, an arbitral clause is independent from the main contract which contains it either directly or by reference and . . . its existence and efficacy are evaluated, without prejudice to mandatory provisions of French law and international public policy, on the basis of the common intent of the parties, whereby it is not necessary to refer to the law of a State.'[8] (original in French)

[11]   "Therefore, in reliance on the ICC Rules and French law, the arbitrators will review the issue of the enforceability or binding character of the arbitration agreement by reference to the parties' common intent. This being so, they will, however, appreciate the corporate changes and their possible impact on the parties' relationship under Colombian law, being the law with the closest connection, because the standing of companies incorporated under Colombian law is at issue."

3.   Enforceability of the Arbitration Agreement

a.   Issues

[12]   "The 1954 Contract is the only one that provides for arbitration. Hence, it is only if the 1954 arbitration agreement has remained binding on the parties that this tribunal has jurisdiction. Whether the 1954 arbitration agreement is binding depends on two issues: first, whether, as a result of the corporate changes which occurred in 1971, S was bound by the 1954 Contract entered into by S.E.; second, if this is not so, whether S and D have agreed nevertheless to continue to be bound by the 1954 Contract, or at least by the arbitration agreement, following the 1971 changes."

b.   The parties' positions

[13]   "According to S, the documents on record show that S.E. was not merged into S. Therefore, S is not the successor of S.E. and it is not bound by the 1954 Contract and the arbitration clause. The 1954 Contract has not been assigned to

---

8. "Rev.arb. (1994) p. 117, note H. Guademet-Tallon; Supreme Court, 1st Civil Chamber, 20 December 1993, J.D.I. 121 (1994) pp. 432 et seq., note E. Gaillard and pp. 690 et seq., note E. Loquin; see also Fouchard, Gaillard, Goldman, op. cit., pp. 245-247."

S either. To the contrary, the parties have entered into a new contract in 1971, and then again in 1982, which contained all elements required for a valid contract, and the [December 1995] transaction was carried out under the 1982 Contract. [14] "In reply, D asserts that S.E. was merged into S and that, as a result, S became the universal successor to all of S.E.'s rights and liabilities, including the 1954 Contract and arbitration agreement. Hence, the 1954 Contract has continued in force until the end of 1995. The 1971 and 1982 Contracts are mere certificates intended for registration with the Colombian authorities and presentation to third parties. They do not give rise to any contract rights and obligations."

c. 1971 changes in corporate structure

[15] "A careful review of the evidence on records leads this tribunal to the conclusion that S is not the universal successor of S.E. by virtue of any corporate changes. Specifically, the arbitrators make the following observations:

(a)   the certificates issued by the Bogota Chamber of Commerce – which S claims are the only admissible evidence failing which corporate changes are without effect vis à vis third parties – record no merger, only a dissolution and liquidation of S.E., specifically
     – the certificate of 9 March 1998 with respect of S.E. contains the following pertinent wording:

     'Certifies:
     Name: S.E. Limited
     Seat: Bogota D.E.
     (. . . .)
     Certifies:
     that, by public deed no. . . . of . . . 1971 of the Fifth Notary Public District of Bogota D.E., registered in this Chamber of Commerce on . . . 1971 in the relevant Book, *the company was declared to have been dissolved and liquidated.*
     Certifies:
     that by order no. . . . 1972 of the Superintendent of Companies, registered in this Chamber of Commerce on . . . 1972 under number . . . of Book IX, *the liquidation of the company was approved and the cancellation of its register number and license was ordered.*
     Certifies:
     that there is among the documents registered in this Chamber of Commerce *no document relating to the merger of company S.E. with other companies.*" (emphasis added) [original in Spanish]

- the certificate issued by the Chamber of Commerce of Bogota on 28 August 1997 in connection with S S.A. does not record any merger with respect to 1971, it merely mentions the change of name from S Colombiana S.A. to S Soceidad Anonima in the Following terms:

'S Public Limited Company [*Sociedad Anonima*]
(. . . .)
Certifies:
that by public deed no. . . . Notary Public District of Bogota of . . . 1964, registered in this Chamber of Commerce on . . . 1964 under no. . . . of the relevant Book, the company was transformed from limited [*limitada*] to public limited company under the name "S Colombiana S.A".'
(original in Spanish)

(b)   But, even if the arbitrators look to the documents on record other than the certificates of the Chamber of Commerce, the same conclusion arises. Indeed, the minutes of the shareholders' meeting of S.E. held on 7 July 1971 shows the following:
- S.E. has ceased all its operations (pursuant to the minutes as of 30 June 1970);
- S.E. has paid off all its liabilities;
- S.E. has transferred all its assets (not its liabilities) to S Colombiana, i.e., S;
- the only assets of S.E. remaining are shares in S Colombiana, which shares are distributed to S.E.'s shareholders.

It is true that these minutes refer to S.E. having been absorbed by S Colombiana and to a merger agreement (*convenio de fusión*). However, in view of the facts just referred to, these mentions can only refer to a transfer of S.E.'s *assets*, and not liabilities, to S Colombiana. The certificate of the Chamber of Commerce . . . is in conformity with this interpretation, as it refers to an absorption only in connection with the approval of an *inventory of assets (bienes)*, which S.E. transfers to S Colombiana. . . .
[16]   "On the basis of this evidence, the arbitral tribunal considers there has been no merger with universal succession, but a mere transfer of assets. Therefore, there can be no question of an assumption of liabilities (contrary to the statement by D . . .).
[17]   "May one argue that the 1954 Contract is an asset that was encompassed in the transfer of assets from S.E. to S (so, but in the context of a merger, D's argument . . .)? There is no evidence of record identifying any assets encompassed in the transfer. Be this as it may, a distribution/agency agreement cannot

be deemed an asset. Under usual accounting standards, such contracts are not accounted for assets in a corporations's balance sheet. The fact that the accounting and other documentation was delivered to S, a fact on which D relies in this context makes no difference. The mere physical delivery of the corporate records, including contracts, cannot imply any assumption of rights and obligations.

[18]   "In reaching its conclusion according to which the 1954 Contract was not taken over by S.E. by virtue of the changes in corporate structure, the arbitral tribunal has paid close attention to the claimant's allegations and, especially, to the legal opinion. . . . That opinion quotes a passage from a scholarly publication on corporations dealing with universal succession or succession *in universum ius*. At the same time, the opinion observes that the activities of S.E. have ended, that debts have been paid off and assets transferred to S Colombiana, later S. These two statements cannot be reconciled. If, on the one hand, there was, as the legal opinion suggests, a succession *in universum ius*, then there was no need to transfer any 'assets'. In such a case, the shares of S.E. would have been transferred, which D did not allege. If, on the other hand, there was a transfer of 'assets', then there was no succession in *universum ius* and, unless there is specific evidence to this effect, which is not the case, the obligations under the 1954 Contract have not been transferred to S.

[19]   "The arbitral tribunal has further taken into account D's allegation that S took over all obligations of S.E. None of the relevant documents so indicate. To the contrary, the record shows the cessation of all commercial operations, the settlement of all liabilities, and an absorption followed by a liquidation, and a transfer of assets.

[20]   "The arbitral tribunal understands that, without giving any reasons, D has requested that the hearing be reopened, if the tribunal did not follow its argumentation about the existence of a universal succession. Although the tribunal does indeed not follow this line of argumentation, it denies this request as it is now fully informed of all relevant facts and has granted D an opportunity to be heard on all such facts."

d.   No agreement of the parties for the continuation of the 1954 Contract

[21]   "As we have just seen, the 1954 Contract did not continue in force by operation of law after the liquidation of S.E. The next question is thus whether it continued as a result of the parties' intent, which must be a common intent involving a meeting of the minds. The arbitrators find that the evidence shows no such meeting of the minds.

[22]   "There are no contemporaneous express statements on this issue. Consequently, the tribunal must review whether the parties' conduct demonstrates a joint intent.

[23] "The tribunal notes first that, in 1971, the contract was already 17 years old. Upon liquidation of S.E., all employees had been laid off, some of them being hired under new employment contracts by S. It may very well be that S personnel in charge of the distribution of D's products was unaware of the 1954 Contract.

[24] "Second, the arbitral tribunal believes that the wording of the 1971 Contract is of little help for its investigation. On the one hand, the words '*revocamos*'" [we revoke], and '*nuevo agente*' [new agent] point to a new start. On the other hand, the title '*certificado*' [certificate] and the words '*para presentar en Colombia*' [to present in Colombia] could be regarded as a contrary indication.

[25] "In the tribunal's view, beyond the wording, the very fact that the parties have executed a new document following the change of corporation carries some weight. The record does not show who took the initiative of this new document. Whoever it may be, one of the parties, or maybe even both parties, considered it necessary at that time to formalize their relationship anew.

[26] "If the intent was to take over the 1954 Contract, then it would have been sufficient for one party to confirm that such contract continued in existence with S. The other party could then have accepted this statement. But this obvious, natural course was not chosen by either party.

[27] "Indeed, if a document such as the 1971 Contract was really required for purposes of registration and presentation in Colombia only, and the 1954 Contract was to remain in force, then the parties, especially D, could have clarified the position with respect to the continuation of the 1954 Contract in a letter. D did so in 1982, specifically by way of a letter of November 1982. However, it failed to do so in 1971.

[28] "D relies on this November 1982 letter to argue that the 1954 Contract was still in force. For such letter to constitute proper evidence of the parties' intent to be bound by the 1954 Contract and the arbitration agreement, its meaning to this effect must have been (i) understood and (ii) accepted by S. Neither of these requirements is met. First, the letter does not name the 1954 Contract. It simply refers to "*die bestehenden vertraglichen Beziehungen*" [the existing contractual relationship]. Whatever that phrase meant to D, S may very well have understood it as referring to the contractual relationship as it existed since 1971.

[29] "Furthermore, there is no indication on record that S accepted the continuation of the 1954 Contract, assuming arguendo that this was the actual meaning of D's letter. Upon receipt of the letter, S kept silent, which silence cannot be deemed an acceptance in any manner whatsoever considering the circumstances.

[30]   "The tribunal has further considered D's objection that the 1971 Contract is too succinct to provide the basis of a contractual relationship. It is succinct indeed. However, it contains all necessary elements (parties, products, territory, type of contract), but for the consideration. Interestingly enough, the 1954 Contract, with the contents of which D takes no issue, does not specify for the agent's compensation either.

[31]   "The tribunal's attention is also drawn to the fact that, except for the letters surrounding the termination in 1995 and 1996, to which we will revert, there is not one single instance of a reference to the 1954 Contract in the documents from 1971 on. The tribunal appreciates that the parties have not produced contemporaneous documentary evidence for the period between 1971 and 1982. They have, however, produced documentation on the performance of the contract after 1982. From such documentation, it is obvious that the parties operated as if the 1954 Contract did not exist.

[32]   "The fact that D's operational department submitted each year to the legal department a list of contracts in force, including the 1954 Contract, does not refute this observation. It may well be that D was under the impression that the 1954 Contract was still in force. However, this impression was not conveyed to S, which, for its part, appears to have been under the impression that the 1971/1972 Contracts governed its contractual relationship with D.

[33]   "It appears to the arbitral tribunal that there was a genuine bona fide dissent between the parties. This may be due to a different understanding and practice of commercial contracts, the Colombian party emphasizing the formalities and "*Aussenverhältnis*" [external relationship], while the German party attached more importance to the definition of the contract terms in the "*Innenverhältnis*" [internal relationship]. The lack of interest of the Colombian party for specific contract terms can be explained by the fact that Colombian law provides sufficiently detailed rules for agency/distribution relationships on which the agent/distributor relies. Besides, the lack of further and more specific terms in the 1971 and/or 1982 Contracts does not seem to have ever hindered good performance of the parties' contractual relationship in the years up to the termination as of December 1995.

[34]   "Whatever the reasons for the dissent, or more simply the misunderstanding between the parties may be, it prevents any finding of joint intent aiming at the continuation of the 1954 Contract.

[35]   "This being said, the arbitral tribunal was admittedly disturbed by S's own references to the 1954 Contract in several documents *following* the termination. It has seriously asked itself whether these references were sufficient indication that S had accepted the continuation of the 1954 Contract *in 1971*. It has also wondered why, if S truly discovered the 1954 Contract upon receipt of the termination letter, it did not voice any protest in its answer. It is true that

S has explained that the caption and the first paragraph of this answer were mere references to the termination letter. But this is only a partial explanation. In the tribunal's mind, the true explanation is more likely that, in 1995, S has seized the opportunity to support a claim for financial compensation spanning from 1954 to 1995. Whatever the merits of such claim, this cannot mean that S accepted the continuation in 1971, i.e., 24 years earlier."

II. CONCLUSION

[36] "On the basis of the foregoing considerations, the arbitral tribunal holds that S has not taken over the 1954 Contract by operation of corporate law, and that the parties have not jointly agreed to the continuation of the 1954 Contract despite the change of corporation. In other words, from 1971 on, the parties' relationship was governed by terms other than those of the 1954 Contract, including the arbitration clause, which terms were manifested in the 1971 and later the 1982 Contract.

[37] "The parties concur that, if the 1971 Contract replaced the previous one, the arbitral tribunal has no jurisdiction over the dispute. The arbitral tribunal shares this view and will thus not discuss the possibility of a survival of the arbitration clause despite the replacement of the contract. Suffice it to state that, for factual and legal reasons, such a possibility, which no party puts forward, would have to be dismissed.

[38] "When reaching the conclusion that it lacked jurisdiction, the arbitrators were fully aware of the difficulties which this decision will impose on D, especially in a dispute where the claim is not disputed on the merits (except of course for the retention and set off rights, which S claims to have under Colombian law). In this context, the tribunal wishes to remind the parties, and especially the Claimant, that, in the course of the January 1998 hearing held in Paris, it had drawn their attention to this potential risk and, for this and other reasons, attempted to bring about a settlement. Despite its efforts, this attempt remained unsuccessful, the settlement proposal made by the tribunal having been rejected by one of the parties.

[39] "In their deliberations, the arbitrators have also considered the fact that it may be unsatisfactory to reach a decision of lack of jurisdiction after having tried the merits. This may be true in some cases, but not in these proceedings. The arbitral tribunal has set forth its reasons for consolidating the issues of jurisdiction and merits in Procedural Order No. 1, which, in pertinent part, reads as follows:

'Upon reviewing the record as it now stands, the arbitrators are of the preliminary view that the issue of jurisdiction and the merits of the dispute are closely linked, that they depend to a substantial part on the same facts, that the aspects of the merits which are independent from such facts are quite limited, and that the same witnesses are likely to testify on facts material to both jurisdiction and merits. Considering these links and the amount at stake in conjunction with its duty to proceed in a cost effective and expeditious manner, the arbitral tribunal has decided that the further proceedings shall deal with jurisdiction and with the merits at the same time and that it will not render an interim award on jurisdiction.'

[40] "The further course of these proceedings [has] fully confirmed the arbitrators' initial assessment. The witnesses all testified on facts pertinent to both jurisdiction and merits. A substantial, if not dominant, part of these proceedings has been devoted to jurisdiction. This resulted from the complexity of the jurisdictional question and from the limited scope of the substantive issues, the claim being admitted with respect to liability as well as quantum. Moreover, the documents about the liquidation of S.E., which were decisive for the arbitrators' fact findings in relation to jurisdiction, were filed only *after* the witness hearings."

III. COSTS

(. . . .)

[41] "For the reasons set out below, the arbitral tribunal holds that the ICC costs of arbitration shall be shared equally by the parties and that each party shall bear its own legal fees and costs. Although S has prevailed in its defense on lack of jurisdiction and, hence, in this arbitration overall, equal sharing of costs is the most appropriate solution under the circumstances.

[42] "The issue of jurisdiction was a complex one, the outcome of which was difficult to predict. When engaging in this arbitration, both parties, but especially D, which, for reasons of the tribunal's lack of jurisdiction, has not prevailed, can be said to have had legitimate expectations of success. This balanced situation is also reflected if one looks at the positions during contract performance. Apparently, both parties operated in good faith in the genuine belief that different rules governed their relationship. Furthermore, S, which was in control of the facts and the documents surrounding the changes which occurred within its group in 1971, failed to provide conclusive evidence of the lack of jurisdiction early in the proceedings. This being said, the arbitral tribunal wishes to acknowledge that both parties have fully cooperated in the arbitration, and acted, through their counsel, in a highly professional manner, which the tribunal appreciated."

Final award in case no. 8790 of 2000

Parties:	Claimant: Seller (Central Europe)
	Defendant: Buyer (Western Europe)
Place of arbitration:	Paris, France
Published in:	Unpublished
Subject matters:	– inconsistent versions of contract
	– exclusion of common courts
	– 1980 UN Sales Convention (CISG)
	– Incoterms
	– force majeure
	– breach of contract

Facts

Seller, claimant in these proceedings, concluded a contract in the Russian language with buyer, defendant in these proceedings, for the purchase of a processed food product. Under the contract, the buyer was to supply the seller with equipment, fuel, products and technological materials, and the seller was to deliver to buyer 440 tons of the product in periodic shipments. The price was established for the first four months of the contract, and was to be agreed upon for the rest of the year.

Two versions of the contract were signed. One version of the contract was in the Russian language; it was dated and signed on behalf of both parties and bore the stamps of both companies. Another version of the contract, in both Russian and English, was also signed and stamped, but not dated. The bilingual contract was a summarized version of the Russian language contract and contained some variations from the Russian language contract. Art. 8 of the Russian language version of the contract provided for settlement of disputes (as translated by the ICC Secretariat):

"... any dispute or controversy which may arise out of the present contract or in connection with it should be settled as possible in an amicable way. If the parties fail to reach a settlement, any dispute or controversy without recourse to common courts shall be settled by the International Court of

Arbitration of the International Chamber of Commerce in accordance with the Rules of Procedure thereof, awards of which shall be final and binding upon both parties."

The bilingual version did not contain an arbitration clause.

Following four deliveries amounting to 90 tons in August of the contract year, seller informed buyer by fax of 15 August that it was compelled to suspend its deliveries for approximately a month due to a reduction in its supply of raw materials and modification in the assortments of the products of its plants. Moreover, it announced that the price had increased by 10%. Buyer responded, inter alia, that some of the lots had been received in bad condition requiring re-packing and informed seller that it had withheld the payment for the last 90 tons of the product that had been delivered.

The parties made several attempts to settle their differences, during the course of which seller offered to accept to bear 50% of the losses due to the re-packing. The settlement negotiations did not succeed and seller initiated ICC arbitration in which a sole arbitrator was appointed. The Terms of Reference were signed by the seller, but not by the buyer. Buyer did not take part in the arbitration proceedings after filing its Answer, until the eve of the first hearing when it informed the sole arbitrator that it could not and would not cooperate in the arbitration. The buyer, however, eventually submitted a Statement of Defence and attended the second hearing.

In the arbitration, the seller submitted a copy of the Russian language contract and a copy of the bilingual contract. The buyer contested the jurisdiction of the arbitral tribunal, arguing that there was not sufficient evidence of an arbitration agreement because there was no original contract upon which a legally valid arbitration agreement could be based. Moreover, in its view, the dispute settlement clause was to be interpreted as providing that the parties intended to submit their disputes to common tribunals, and only if this were not possible, then to ICC arbitration. Buyer stated that it did not remember having signed a contract including an arbitration clause, but it did not exclude that such a contract might exist. The sole arbitrator considered that there was sufficient evidence to show that the copy of the Russian language contract was a true copy of the original signed by the parties. There was no evidence that it was a forgery, each page was initialed by the parties' representatives, and the contract was signed and stamped. In the view of the sole arbitrator, the bilingual version of the contract was merely a summarized record of the parties' intentions as to the economic conditions of their agreement and did not supersede the Russian language version which contained an arbitration clause. After comparing various translations of the arbitration clause, the sole arbitrator concluded that the Russian text clearly excluded the competence of the common courts. A contract produced by the buyer to illustrate the usual terms on which it concluded its contracts contained an arbitration clause in Russian and English including the words "without recourse to the courts of law". This, in the view of the sole arbitrator, clearly illustrated the parties' intention to exclude the competence of the courts.

Applying the 1980 United Nations Convention on Contracts for the International Sale of Goods (CISG) and the relevant Incoterms, the sole arbitrator found that the seller was entitled to the payment which had been withheld. The drought which the seller had given as the reason for suspending deliveries constituted force majeure, entitling the seller to suspend delivery. Buyer was not justified in withholding payment for the last deliveries as it had not documented or proved its quality complaints. The sole arbitrator awarded the full amount of the withheld payment minus 50% of the re-packing costs which seller had previously agreed to bear.

Excerpt

(. . . .)

I. EVIDENCE OF CONTRACT CONTAINING ARBITRATION AGREEMENT

1. *Russian Language Contract*

[1] "The existence of a contract for the sale by claimant and purchase by defendant of one hundred tons of the product is a fact of this case which is undisputed by both parties. Both claimant and defendant refer to the existence of such a contract and each blames the other party for having failed to perform its obligations under such a contract.

[2] "However, since there are two versions of the contract, and since only one version includes an ICC arbitration clause, the question to be decided is whether the arbitration can proceed on the basis of the ICC arbitration clause included in only one version of the contract.

[3] "On this issue, the arbitral tribunal holds as follows: The arbitral tribunal has not been provided with the original of any version of the contract. The file contains only copies of both versions. There is no evidence that the copy of the Russian language contract including the ICC arbitration clause would be a forgery; each page is initialed by Mr. X, representative of defendant, and the last page bears his signature as well as Mr. A's signature, representative of claimant; one can see the stamps of the two companies; both signatures and stamps are the same as those appearing on the other version of the contract.

[4]   "While in its letter to the ICC defendant declared that it did not remember having signed a contract including an arbitration clause, it did not exclude that such contract might exist. In its aforementioned letter to the ICC, defendant declared that it did not even have a copy of the contract including an ICC arbitration clause. However, during the course of the arbitration, defendant was provided with a copy of this contract and, although it continuously denied the existence of a valid arbitration agreement, defendant never claimed that this copy was a forgery or that the signature of its representative, Mr. X, had been counterfeited.

[5]   "While, in its Answer [to the Request for Arbitration], defendant wrote that its transactions are closed under its own terms, 'excluding any foreign governmental (or other instituts' [sic]) law/contract rules', defendant has produced, as an annex to its Statement of Defence a copy of a contract which it signed with another Central European company [in the same period], bearing the signature of Mr. X, which includes an arbitration clause (Art. 8) similar to the one included in the contract at issue in the present case, except that it does not refer to the ICC but to the Court of Stockholm.[1] This arbitration clause is written in both the Russian and English languages.

[6]   "For the above reasons, the arbitral tribunal considers that there is sufficient evidence to show that the copy of the contract in the Russian language including an ICC arbitration clause is a true copy of the original signed by both parties.

[7]   "Concerning the copy of the undated bilingual version of the contract, the arbitral tribunal agrees with claimant that it should be considered as a summarized record of the parties' intentions as to the economic conditions of their agreement (specifications relating to the product, packing, quantity, price, method of payment, documents, delivery, etc.), in which the legal technicalities, such as the arbitration clause and the clause relating to force majeure have not been reproduced. Significantly, defendant itself, when discussing the issue of force majeure, relies on the definition of force majeure given in Art. 7 of the version of the contract in the Russian language. The arbitral tribunal therefore considers that the undated bilingual summarized version of the contract does not supersede the other version in the Russian language, and does not deprive the arbitration clause contained therein of its validity."

2. Interpretation of Reference to Common Courts

[8]   "The parties disagree on the interpretation of the arbitration clause contained in Art. 8 of the contract. While claimant argues that the parties

---

1. *Note General Editor*. See [10] where reference is made to "Arbitration in Stockholm".

have agreed that any dispute shall be settled through ICC arbitration, defendant claims that the parties have agreed to submit to ordinary courts, and that ICC arbitration would be possible only in the event that the ordinary courts are not competent. In support of such interpretation, defendant relies on the English translation of Art. 8 proposed by claimant, which reads:

'. . . all disputes, except those for which common tribunals are competent, have to be solved by an Arbitration Court of the ICC . . .'.

The Russian text of the said clause reads as follows:

'*c izkloutcheniem podsoudnosti obchim soudam podlejat razrecheniou Arbitrajnom soudié pri Mejdourapodnoi Torgovo-Promychlennoi Palate*'.

The English translation made by the ICC Secretariat reads as follows:

'any dispute or controversy *without recourse to common courts* shall be settled by the International Court of Arbitration of the ICC . . .'.

The arbitral tribunal is of the opinion that the Russian text clearly excludes the competence of the common courts.

[9]   "In support of this opinion, beyond a correct reading of the Russian text, one may observe that the title of Art. 8 which includes the arbitration clauses is 'Arbitration'. The intention of the parties to have recourse to arbitration would be totally undermined if, at the same time, they had wished to exclude from arbitration all disputes over which common courts would accept jurisdiction (i.e., any possible dispute).

[10]   "Moreover, it should be noted that in the contract produced by defendant and referred to above (see [5]), the Russian version of the arbitration clause is strictly identical to the one included in the contract at issue in the present case (except that it does not refer to ICC arbitration, but to 'arbitration in Stockholm'). The English translation of the said arbitration clause reads as follows '*all the disputes and differences are to be submitted, without recourse to the courts of law, to Arbitration in Stockholm*'. The insertion of the words 'without recourse to the courts of law' between two commas leaves no doubt as to the intention of the parties to exclude the competence of the courts. Defendant can therefore not seriously claim that the same Russian wording of the arbitration clause included in the contract at issue in the present case should be interpreted differently.

[11]   "The arbitral tribunal therefore considers that the ICC arbitration clause included in Art. 8 of the Russian language contract is unequivocal and clearly excludes the competence of ordinary courts.

[12]   "Moreover, in view of the fact that the parties have validly and unequivocally agreed to submit the dispute to arbitration under the ICC Rules of Arbitration, the arbitral tribunal cannot accept defendant's argument, that recourse to ICC arbitration in the present case would be in violation of Art. 6 of the European Convention for the Protection of Human Rights and Fundamental Freedoms (4 November 1950).

[13]   "On the basis of the above, the arbitral tribunal decides that there is sufficient evidence of the existence of the Russian language contract, which includes an ICC arbitration agreement binding on both parties. Consequently, the arbitral tribunal considers that it has jurisdiction over the claim brought by claimant."

II.   APPLICABLE LAW TO THE MERITS

[14]   "Both parties agree that the dispute should be settled in accordance with the UN Convention on Contracts for the International Sale of Goods signed in Vienna on 11 April 1980, ratified and in force in the countries of the seller and the buyer. The subject matter of the dispute relates to the performance of a contract for international sale of goods between parties whose places of business are in different Contracting States. The Vienna Convention is therefore applicable to the present case, in accordance with the provisions of Art. 1 of the said Convention.

[15]   "Moreover, since the contract refers to the term 'FOT . . .', the arbitral tribunal will apply the relevant provisions of the Incoterms 1990, i.e., the FCA terms ('Free carrier'), which, in the 1990 version of Incoterms, replaced the terms dealing with some particular modes of transport (FOR/FOT/FOB).

[16]   "The arbitral tribunal has further examined whether it might be necessary to refer to the provisions of law of the country of the seller. But it has not seen any reason to do so. All the points at issue can be decided in accordance with the Vienna Convention supplemented by the relevant provisions of the Incoterms."

III.   ENTITLEMENT TO RELIEF

1.   Claimant's Obligations

[17]   "In order to determine whether claimant is entitled to any or all of the relief it seeks the arbitral tribunal has examined how claimant has fulfilled its obligations under the contract.

[18]   "The contract provided that claimant would sell during the course of the contract year, 1,000 tons of the product at a fixed price, for a period of four months from April to July. For the remainder of the year, the prices would be

agreed in June of the contract year. The deliveries would take place on FOT terms . . . in equal lots packed and marked.

[19]   "It is an established and undisputed fact of the case that, following previous deliveries which are not the subject of the dispute, claimant delivered a quantity of 90 tons of the product, in four equal lots of 22.5 tons each, during the month of August, at the agreed price. Defendant had sent its instructions for a prepayment of the delivery of these 90 tons of the product on 10 August. There is no dispute between the parties regarding the fact that the price for the product thus delivered in August was the agreed price, whereas the contract provided that such price was valid only for the period from April to July 1994.

[20]   "Claimant had no obligation concerning the carriage. The agreed delivery terms under the contract were 'FOT . . .'. Moreover, the contract expressly stipulated that the carriage was defendant's responsibility and at its own costs. In accordance with Art. 67(1) of the Vienna Convention[2] and Clause B.5 of the FCA Incoterm,[3] all risks of the goods were transferred to defendant at the time of delivery of the goods by claimant to the carrier designated by defendant. Claimant has produced as required the waybills, customs declaration CMR (Convention on the Contract for the International Carriage of Goods by Road) delivered by the authorities of seller's country.

---

2. Art. 67(1) of the 1980 United Nations Convention on Contracts for the International Sale of Goods (CISG) reads:

"(1) If the contract of sale involves carriage of the goods and the seller is not bound to hand them over at a particular place, the risk passes to the buyer when the goods are handed over to the first carrier for transmission to the buyer in accordance with the contract of sale. If the seller is bound to hand the goods over to a carrier at a particular place, the risk does not pass to the buyer until the goods are handed over to the carrier at that place. The fact that the seller is authorized to retain documents controlling the disposition of the goods does not affect the passage of the risk."

3. Incoterm 1990 FCA B.5 reads in relevant part:

"The buyer must bear all risks of loss of or damage to the goods from the time they have been delivered in accordance with A.4.
(. . . .)"

Incoterm 1990 FCA A.4 reads in relevant part:

"The seller must deliver the goods into the custody of the carrier or another person . . . at the named place or point on the date or within the period agreed for delivery and in the manner agreed or customary at such point. . . . Delivery to the carrier is completed:
(. . . .)
ii) In the case of *road transport* when loading takes place at the seller's premises, delivery is completed when the goods have been loaded on the vehicle provided by the buyer. When the goods are delivered to the carrier's premises, delivery is completed when they have been handed over to the road carrier or to another person acting on his behalf.
(. . . .)"

[21] "The contract stipulated the claimant also had to present to defendant after loading the goods a certificate of radioactivity, a health certificate, a certificate of quality, and a certificate of origin of the product. These certificates have not been produced in the arbitration. However, it is not disputed by defendant that these documents were actually issued in due time. Moreover, as noted by claimant, failing such certificates, the export of the goods would not have been authorized by the customs officials.

[22] "Claimant argues that the suspension of further deliveries, which it announced by fax of 15 August to defendant, was justified by a case of force majeure. Claimant has produced a certificate issued by the competent local Chamber of Commerce, which states that climatic conditions during the period led to a reduction of raw material yield and that these circumstances, which are beyond human control prevented claimant from fulfilling its contractual obligations towards defendant.

[23] "The arbitral tribunal sees no reason to question the truthfulness of this official statement. Moreover, under Art. 7(3) of the contract, the parties agreed that evidence of circumstances of force majeure shall be brought through 'certificates issued by the Chamber of Commerce for each of the parties'. Defendant argues that drought was not specifically mentioned as a case of force majeure in Art. 7(1) of the contract. But though it is true that drought is not specifically mentioned, Art. 7(1) refers to 'natural catastrophes' and also to 'other circumstances outside control', terms under which one is entitled to include drought.

[24] "Defendant also argues that it has been able during the same period to sign a contract for the supply of the product with another company in the same country as seller, which it considers as a proof that the existence of a drought can be put into doubt. But it can be observed that this other company is located in a city . . . more than 300 kilometers [distant] from [claimant's seat], which does leave the possibility of the existence of a drought in the territory of [claimant's seat].

[25] "Defendant further argues that in its fax of 15 August, announcing the suspension of its deliveries, claimant also mentioned a modification of its assortments, which, in defendant's view, is not a sufficient reason to suspend the deliveries. Taken at its face value this argument may have some weight, but one should also consider:

(i)   that the modification in the assortments could be a consequence of the reduction in the production of the raw material due to the drought;
(ii) that at any rate it is only a subsidiary reason for the suspension of deliveries, the main one being the drought.

[26] "The allegation by defendant that claimant is liable for an anticipatory breach of contract cannot be accepted. The facts of the case demonstrate that,

prior to the occurrence of a case of force majeure, claimant fulfilled its obligations and that, when the case of force majeure materialized, claimant notified defendant, not an impossibility to fulfil the remaining portion of the contract, but only a suspension of the deliveries for a period of one month. Defendant was therefore not entitled to suspend the payment of the purchase price for 90 tons on the grounds of an alleged anticipatory breach.

[27] "As far as the payment of costs is concerned, there is no indication that claimant did not fulfil its obligations in accordance with the contract and the FCA Incoterm (Clauses A.6 and A.9)."[4]

2. Defendant's Obligations

[28] "The arbitral tribunal has also examined defendant's fulfilment of its obligations under the contract. Defendant's main obligation was to pay the price for the goods delivered (Art. 53 of the Vienna Convention,[5] Clause B-1 of the FCA Incoterm). The facts of the case establish, and defendant itself confirms, that after having given instructions for the transfer of an amount . . . for payment of 90 m. tons of the product delivered by claimant, defendant has withheld the effective transfer of this amount to claimant.

---

4. A.6 and A.9 of Incoterm 1990 FCA read:

"A.6 Division of costs
The seller must subject to the provisions of B.6

    – pay all costs relating to the goods until such time as they have been delivered to the carrier in accordance with A.4;
    – pay the costs of customs formalities as well as all duties, taxes, and other official charges payable upon exportation."

"A.9 Checking – packaging – marking
The seller much pay the costs of those checking operations (such as checking quality, measuring, weighing, counting) which are necessary for the purpose of delivering the goods to the carrier.

    The seller must provide at his own expense packaging (unless it is usual for the particular trade to send the goods of the contract description unpacked) which is required for the transport of the goods, to the extent that the circumstances relating to the transport (e.g., modalities, destination) are made known to the seller before the contract of sale is concluded. Packaging is to be marked appropriately."

5. Art. 53 of the CISG reads:

"The buyer must pay the price for the goods and take delivery of them as required by the contract and this Convention."

Incoterm 1990 FCA B.1 reads:

"The buyer must pay the price as provided in the contract of sale."

[29] "In order to justify such a decision, defendant, apart from rebutting the case of force majeure (see above, [22]), claims that it has found dust and cockroaches in some bags of the product, so that it had to clean and repack the product. Defendant also claims that it had to resell previous deliveries at a lower price because the product was downgraded. It says that a Danish laboratory has inspected the product and confirmed its bad quality. However, on the one hand, defendant has not produced any certificate emanating from this Danish laboratory, on the other hand, defendant does not seem to have inspected the goods before their delivery (Pre-shipment Inspection – PSI) as usually recommended by trade practice (see Clause B.9 of the FCA Incoterm 1990).[6] Furthermore, at the time of the reception of the deliveries at its own place of business, defendant did not ask for a contradictory inspection of the goods."

3. Conclusion

[30] "On the basis of these facts and arguments, the arbitral tribunal decides the following: Claimant was entitled to announce a suspension of the deliveries due to the occurrence of a case of force majeure. Therefore, the withholding by defendant of the payment to claimant of the agreed purchase price for the effective delivery of 90 tons of the product is not justified insofar as it was based on the announced suspension of deliveries.

[31] "Concerning defendant's claim relating to the quality of the goods and of the packaging, the relevant facts are the following:

- Although claimant has not produced in the arbitration copies of some of the certificates (health, radioactivity, quality, origin), which claimant had to present to defendant, defendant never claimed that these documents were not actually presented in accordance with the contract.
- Moreover, at the time of delivery of the goods by claimant to the carrier, defendant did not conduct any Pre-shipment Inspection (PSI), as usually recommended when the sale is on FOT (FCA) terms, thus taking a serious risk and making it difficult to prove when the alleged deterioration of the goods occurred. Defendant further failed to produce evidence to show that an independent inspection of the goods was conducted when the goods were received in its country.

---

6. Incoterm 1990 FCA B.9 reads

"The buyer must pay, unless otherwise agreed, the costs of pre-shipment inspection except when mandated by the authorities of the country of exportation."

[32]   "For the above reasons, defendant was not entitled to withhold the payment of the price of the goods on the grounds of alleged quality problems regarding the goods and/or the packaging. For the same reasons, defendant is not entitled to claim that the alleged losses incurred as a result of these alleged quality problems should be set off against claimant's claim for payment of the purchase price for 90 tons. However, after receipt of defendant's fax dated 22 September, in which defendant claimed, inter alia, that it had to incur re-packing costs . . . claimant agreed, in its fax dated 4 November, to bear half of these specific costs alleged by defendant. . . .

[33]   "In view of the above, the arbitral tribunal decides that claimant is entitled to receive payment of the purchase price for 90 tons . . . of the product, less half of the re-packing costs claimed by defendant, which claimant agreed to bear. . . .''

IV.   INTEREST AND COSTS

[34]   "Claimant requests the payment of delay interest in compensation for the non-payment of the sum . . . which remained unpaid by defendant, from 27 August. Claimant bases its request on the interest rates in force in seller's country at the corresponding time and produces a certificate issued by the Bank concerning the applicable interest rates during the relevant period.

[35]   "The following questions must be answered by the arbitral tribunal:

   i.   Is claimant entitled to receive delay interest as a compensation for the non-payment of the purchase price of 90 tons of the product?
  ii.   In the affirmative is interest to be paid on the basic sum . . . or on this sum diminished as calculated above . . .?
 iii.   Is the date selected by claimant as starting point of the delay interest appropriate?
  iv.   Must the interest rates be calculated, as requested by claimant, on the basis of its local interest rates?
   v.   In the negative, on which other basis should the interest be calculated and what is consequently the amount of interest to be award to claimant?

[36]   "[Ad i,] according to the Vienna Convention (Art. 78): 'If a party fails to pay the price or any other sum that is in arrears, the other party is entitled to interest on it, without prejudice to any claim for damages, recoverable under Article 74.' Therefore, since the arbitral tribunal has recognized that defendant has wrongfully withheld the price due for the delivery of 90 tons of the product . . . claimant is entitled to receive delay interest.

[37]   "[Ad ii], since the arbitral tribunal decided that claimant was entitled to claim the payment by defendant of the principal amount of the purchase price of

90 tons minus 50% of the repacking costs, delay interest must be calculated on the basis of this sum.

[38]   "[Ad iii], it was justified on the part of the claimant to select the period starting from the date where it got confirmation that defendant had withheld the payment . . . i.e., 27 August, as the date when delay interest should start running. Claimant is entitled to request the payment of delay interest till it receives full payment of the principal amount awarded. . . .

[39]   "[Ad iv], since the currency of the contract is the US dollar, there is no reason to base the calculation of delay interest rates on the rates applied by the Bank during this period of time. Moreover, the contract stipulated (Art. 1(2)) that in exchange of delivery of the product, defendant would buy certain specific goods listed in Annex 1 to the contract. These goods were not to be bought in seller's country and had to be paid in US$.

[40]   "For these reasons the arbitral tribunal rejects claimant's request that the interest rate should be based on the rates of seller's country and decides that interest should be calculated on the basis of the average rate of the LIBOR 3 months over the period from 27 August of the year in which the default occurred until 1 November 2000, i.e., on the basis of an annual interest rate of 3.887%.

[41]   "Claimant argues that defendant is responsible for the dispute and should therefore bear all costs arising from the arbitration. Defendant argues that, since there is no evidence of a valid arbitration agreement, all costs must be paid by claimant. Defendant's conduct as noted above left claimant no choice but to initiate these proceedings in order to assert its legitimate claim. Moreover, defendant's long abstention from any significant participation in the arbitration led to costly and time-consuming difficulties. For these reasons, the arbitral tribunal considers it appropriate to order that the costs be borne by defendant.

[42]   "Claimant has however never specified the amount and nature of the legal costs it incurred in relation to is party representation in the arbitration. This leaves the arbitration fees and administrative expenses fixed by the ICC. . . . All of this amount has been paid by claimant. The arbitral tribunal considered that this amount is to be borne by defendant."

Final award in case no. 9762 of 2001

Parties:	Claimant: Contractor A (Luxembourg)
	Respondents: (1) Ministry of Agriculture and Water Management of Z (Republic of Z);
	(2) State Fund for Development of Agriculture of Z (Republic of Z);
	(3) Government of Republic of Z
Place of arbitration:	Paris, France
Published in:	Unpublished
Subject matters:	– transfer of credit
	– standing claimant to claim against respondents
	– third party beneficiary to contract containing arbitration agreement
	– jurisdiction over respondents
	– State as party to arbitration
	– acknowledgment of jurisdiction
	– distinction "Government" and "State"
	– sovereign immunity from jurisdiction
	– "Verification Act"

Facts

Two companies in the A group, Ax and Ay, had contracted to carry out several civil and industrial projects in the Republic of Z on the request of the Ministry of Agriculture and Food of Z. The debit and credit situation resulting from the carrying out of the above transactions was checked by the parties in 1996 and a document, later referred to as the "Verification Act", was signed by Ax and the Ministry of Agriculture and Food of Z on 1 July. This document established and accepted the total debt of the Ministry in 'favour' of the companies of the A group. Shortly after the issuing of the Verification Act, Ax transferred all the credits of the A group mentioned in the Verification Act to A.

Meanwhile in Z, the Ministry of Agriculture and Food was liquidated by Presidential Decree (the Presidential Decree) and at the same time a new

Ministry of Agriculture of Z was created. The following day, a new body, the State Fund for Development of Agriculture of Z, was established, also by Presidential Decree (the State Fund Presidential Decree). The Fund was charged with the payment of the debts of the liquidated Ministry. Two years later, the Ministry of Agriculture along with the Ministry for Amelioration and Water Management were abolished and merged into a new Ministry of Agriculture and Water Management.

Difficulties ensued regarding the completion of the contracted projects and the payment of the amounts mentioned in the Verification Act and A initiated ICC arbitration relying on the arbitration clauses contained in contracts concluded between Ax and Ay and the Ministry of Agriculture and Food of Z from which the asserted credits originated. In the arbitration, A claimed against the Ministry of Agriculture and Water Management of Z, as the successor of the former Ministry of Agriculture and Food of Z (first respondent), the State Fund for Development of Agriculture of Z (second respondent) and the Government of Z (third respondent). The second and third respondents did not participate in the proceedings. A based its claim for payment on the Verification Act, claiming the amount mentioned therein. It argued that the Verification Act should be considered a debt acknowledgment under French law and that all three respondents were jointly and severally liable.

At an oral hearing, the Ministry of Agriculture and Water Management of Z declared to have no objections to the jurisdiction of the ICC International Court of Arbitration and this was confirmed in a subsequent Order of the arbitral tribunal which identified it as the legal successor of the former Ministry of Agriculture of Z. The Ministry of Agriculture and Water Management of Z submitted a counterclaim for damages caused by breach of contract by Ax and Ay.

In its award the arbitral tribunal first held that A was a legitimate assignee of the alleged credits transferred to it. In doing so it rejected, inter alia, the argument of the Ministry of Agriculture and Water Management of Z that the transfer of credit did not comply with the formalities required by Art. 1690 of the French Civil Code, which requires that the transfer be made known to or accepted by the debtor. In the view of the arbitral tribunal, the evidence showed that the Ministry was aware of and had acknowledged the transfer. The arbitral tribunal further held that A was not a proper counter-respondent to the counterclaim, as that claim was based on the contracts, not on the alleged credit which had been transferred.

After confirming that the Ministry of Agriculture and Water Management of Z was the legitimate successor of the former Ministry of Agriculture and Food of Z, the arbitral tribunal examined its jurisdiction over the second respondent, the Fund for Development of Agriculture. It held that the Fund had not "fully inherited" the obligations of the former Ministry of Agriculture and Food of Z and was not to be considered as its legitimate successor. Its role was merely to dispose of the money for the payment of the debts toward foreign companies that the Ministry of Agriculture of Z inherited from the former Ministry of Agriculture and Food of Z. Accordingly, the arbitral tribunal concluded that it did not have jurisdiction over the second respondent.

The arbitral tribunal then examined its jurisdiction over the third respondent, the Government of Z, noting that it is not unusual to use "government" to designate "state" as A had done. In the opinion of the arbitral tribunal, the Ministry represented the State and the State was bound by its acts. The Ministry of Agriculture and Water Management of Z had accepted the jurisdiction of the arbitral tribunal at the oral hearing and in doing so, it "implicitly and necessarily also appeared as the representative of the State of Z in a matter pertaining to its department". Thus, the arbitral tribunal held that it had jurisdiction over the State of Z as third respondent, as validly represented by first respondent, the Ministry and no distinction was to be made between their liability.

Looking at the actual circumstances under which the Verification Act was drawn up, the arbitral tribunal concluded that it was nothing more than a "progress report" which represented the situation at a certain date of what had been invoiced and what been paid on a series of transactions. Accordingly, A's claim was dismissed as the Verification Act did not give A sufficient title to payment of the alleged debt.

Excerpt

I. CLAIMANT'S TITLE TO CLAIM

[1]   "The title to claim, as asserted by the claimant, consists in and is proved by the letter that Ax addressed to A on 27 August. This letter, whose subject is 'Transference of credit', is worded as follows:

> 'Please, take duly note that the credit in front of our group from the Ministry of Agriculture of Z or the substituted juridical institution for [amount] at the date of 1 July, as per attached documents subscribed by the creditor and the debitor [sic] is transferred to you. We ask you to send this document back for acceptance duly signed. . . .'

The signatures, preceded by the seal of Ax are those of Mr. P and Mr. O. The authority of these two gentlemen to represent Ax has not been questioned.

The letter, which is addressed to A Luxembourg is also addressed in copy to the: 'Ministry of Agriculture and Food Products of Z. On the bottom of the letter, on the left side, the words in Italian *per accettazione* (i.e., 'for acceptance') are handwritten followed by the seal of A and by the signature of Mr. O. The authority of Mr. O to represent A has not been questioned.

[2]   "On the bottom right corner of the letter, there are: an unidentifiable and unidentified monogram, the handwritten date of '04.09', and a circular office stamp with writing in the Z language and Russian which is only partially legible. Translated into English, the legible part on the circumference of the stamp says 'Ministry of Agriculture and Food Products of Z, Association for . . .' and in the centre: 'Chancellery'.

[3]   "The above letter has been exhibited by the claimant without the 'attached documents' to which it refers. However, it is justified to assume (and it was not contested by the respondent) that reference is made here to the 'Verification Act' of 1 July, which has been separately exhibited by the claimant. It is certainly from this Act that the credit's amount mentioned in the letter has been derived.

[4]   "The fact that the claimant, as it has repeatedly stated, is the 'assignee of a credit', and not the assignee of the contracts from which the credit (if any) originates, does not constitute a reason that might deprive the claimant of the title to claim the payment of its alleged credit. The arguments of the respondent when it says that

'The original signatories to the underlying contracts devised this sham transfer of "credits" to A in order to engage the arbitration with a shell company with no assets, thereby avoiding the risk of having to pay the adverse judgment of the counterclaim'

are based on assumptions that are not supported by any evidence in facts, and that have no ground in law.

[5]   "On the one hand, there is no legal preclusion for a party to a contract to transfer its rights under the contract to a third party without transferring the relevant obligations as well. On the other hand, as the consequence of the assignment of credits, the debtor does not lose the right to raise against the assignee who is claiming the payment the same exceptions he would be entitled to raise against the assignor. He also does not lose the right to sue the party who did sign the contract for whatever reasons, including breach of contract and consequential damages.

[6]   "Similarly groundless is the respondent's objection that the claimant would not have title to claim because he did not sign with the respondent any arbitration agreement, and he could not enforce the arbitration clauses included in the underlying contracts because, in accordance with his own

assertion, these contracts were not transferred to him. As a matter of fact, this plea concerning the existence of an arbitration agreement between the parties does not constitute an objection to the title to claim. It is an objection to our jurisdiction. As such, the plea is precluded to the respondent because he has explicitly accepted our jurisdiction on the occasion of the hearing, as confirmed in the tribunal's Order.

[7]   "The respondent's further plea that the alleged 'transfer of credit' would not be enforceable because, contrary to the provisions of Art. 1690 of the French Civil Code, it was neither duly notified to the debtor, nor duly accepted by it, shall also be rejected by the tribunal. It is true that, in accordance with Art. 1690 of the French Civil Code (whose application follows the acceptance by the parties of the French Law as the governing law of their relationship), the transfer of credit is not enforceable against third parties, or cannot be enforced by third parties, unless it is made known to the debtor or accepted by it in the form of an authentic act. It is also true that the 'third parties' to which Art. 1690 of the French Civil Code refers, are all those who are not parties to the transfer agreement, including but not limited to the initial debtor.

[8]   "As stated by the French *Cour de Cassation*:

> '*Jusqu'à sa signification au débiteur cédé ou son acceptation par celui-ci, la cession de créance n'a d'effet qu'entre les parties. Les tiers, et notamment le débiteur cédé, ne peuvent se la voir opposer ni s'en prévaloir.' (Cass.Civ.III. 12 Juin 1985, Bull.Civ.III, no. 95)*[1]

However it is also true, and recognized by French jurisprudence, that the interest protected by this provision of law is the one of those third parties to whom the transfer may be of prejudice. As stated by the French *Cour de Cassation*:

> '*Il résulte de l'art. 1690 que ne sont des tiers, au sens de ce texte, que ceux qui, n'ayant pas été partie à l'acte de cession, ont intérêt à ce que le cédant soit encore créancier' (Cass.Civ.I, 4 Déc. 1985, Bull.Civ.I, no. 336).*[2]

---

1. "Free translation: 'Until the transfer of credit is either made known to or accepted by the assigned debtor, it is only effective between the parties. Therefore, neither can it be enforced against third parties, nor can third parties enforce it.' "

2. "Free translation: 'In accordance with Art. 1690 may only be considered third parties those parties who, not being parties to the transfer transaction, are interested to further keep the transferor as creditor.' "

And again:

> *'Si la signification de la cession de créance ou l'acceptation authentique de la cession par le débiteur cédé est un principe nécessaire pour que le cession-naaire puisse opposer au tiers le droit acquis par celui-ci, le défaut d'accom-plissement de ces formalités ne rend pas le cessionnaire irrecevable à réclamer au débiteur cédé l'exécution de son obligation quand cette exécu-tion n'est pas susceptible de faire grief à aucun droit advenu depuis la nais-sance de la créance, soit audit débiteur cédé, soit à une autre personne étrangère à la cession.'*[3]

[9] "Of course, this does not exclude the debtor from being a 'third party', as he certainly is. However, the risk that the transfer of the credit may give rise to an actual or potential prejudice to the third party's rights (and so therefore to the debtor's rights whenever the debtor is the third party in question), appears to be the main concern of the Legislator when setting the provisions of Art. 1690. On the basis of the above jurisprudence it might be justified to argue, as the claimant did, that the transfer of credits by the companies of the A Group (or solely by Ax) to A does not actually cause any prejudice to the respondents. All the more so because the transfer occurs between companies of the same group and, as we have already noted here-above, the respondents do not lose any of their rights either to oppose the claimant's claim on the basis of exceptions they might have been entitled to raise against the original contractors, or to introduce claims against the original contractors directly. These remarks however, even if very likely correct, are of no relevance in the instant case where, as we will see under the following point hereafter, the tribunal has come to the conclusion that there is sufficient evidence that the debtor has acknowledged the transfer.

[10] "The requirement under Art. 1690 that the transfer of credit be made known to the debtor does not involve any peculiar formalities. Particularly in a dispute on matters of international trade, international arbitrators are not bound to follow a strict and formalistic interpretation of the rule in question. What is essential under this rule is that the debtor be aware of the transfer.

[11] "In the opinion of the tribunal, this flexible and realistic approach is even more necessary in the instant case, in consideration of the fact that the original debtor, the Ministry of Agriculture and Food of Z, had been liquidated by

---

3. "Free translation: 'Even if the notice of the transfer of credit to or its acceptance by the assigned debtor are essential conditions for the transferee to enforce it against third parties, the non-accomplishment of these formalities does not prevent the transferee from claiming against the assigned debtor the fulfilment of its obligation whenever such a fulfilment does not prejudice the rights acquired either by the debtor or by a party alien to the transfer after the credit originated.' "

Presidential Decree ... and a substantial reform of the agricultural sector had been undertaken, new entities had been established, the partition of the respective competences had been restructured, and it might have been difficult for a foreign company (even if so deeply involved in the Z market, as apparently the claimant was) to identify the proper body to whom the transfer of credit should be formally notified.

[12] "The tribunal is persuaded that a notification was made, and it reached its aim. There is sufficient evidence of the fact that the transfer was acknowledged by the Z party. Among the documents submitted by the claimant, there is a letter that was addressed by the Association for the Construction of Agricultural Objects to Ax, on a date which appears to be '14 April'. This date is certainly wrong because the letter informs of the liquidation of the Z Ministry of Agriculture and Food by Presidential Decree of 24 April, which is a correct date. However, it is by this letter that the Verification Act was sent to the addressee for consideration and signature 'within the term of 10 June'. This means that the correct date of this letter certainly falls between 24 April and 10 Jun, i.e., a date prior to the date on which the transfer of credit took place (28 August). Further to the transfer, two letters have been produced by the claimant that come from the State Fund for the Agriculture of Z. Their respective dates are '24 September' and '16 January', and both are addressed to A.

[13] "We know that the contracts from which the claimed credit originates were entered into by the Ministry of Agriculture and Food of Z in part with Ax and in part with Ay. As to the 'Verification Act', it was established 'On the progress of construction contracts concluded between the Ministry of Agriculture and Food of Z and the company Ax.' No contract was signed by A and in the voluminous documentation exhibited by both parties there is no indication of any direct involvement of A in the business activity of the A group of companies in Z up to the time it became the assignee of the alleged credits from Ax.

[14] "When the respondent asserts that the transfer of credit was 'trickery ... in order to engage the arbitration with a shell company with no assets' (whether or not this is true), such a statement appears as further evidence of the fact that A was unknown to the Z party until credits were transferred to it. Therefore, if the above letters of 24 September and 16 January were addressed (as they are addressed) to A, this can only be explained by the fact that the Z administration was by that time aware of the transfer of credits that had occurred in August.

[15] "For the purpose of establishing that the transfer was known to the Z party, the status of the Fund for Development of Agriculture of Z, in the frame of the Z administration, is irrelevant. We will come back to this point when moving to the issue of whether or not we have jurisdiction in respect of the Fund (second respondent). In any case, even if we should come to the conclusion

(as will be the case) that the Fund is not the successor of the liquidated Ministry of Agriculture and Food and so therefore it is not the debtor, there is no doubt that the Fund is a public body which was set up, among others, in view of providing money for the payment of the debts of the liquidated Ministry. It is part of the Z administration, under the direct control of the President of Z. If the Fund was aware of the transfer, this means that the Z administration was aware of it, including the formal debtor, i.e., the entity that became the legal successor of the former Ministry of Agriculture and Food of Z.

[16]   "By the way, the transfer letter was not communicated to the Fund by Ax. It was addressed in copy to the liquidated Ministry of Agriculture and Food of Z, and handed over to some organization being part of that Ministry and still in operation. As a consequence, we are forced to admit that the Fund came to know of A as assignee of the alleged credits, from some other branch of the public administration, and very likely from the legitimate successor of the liquidated Ministry.

[17]   "Having reached the conclusion that the Z administration was aware of the transfer of the alleged credits, we don't need to consider the respondent's plea according to which the seal and signature at the bottom right-hand corner of the transfer letter exhibited by the claimant would be a forgery.

[18]   "As to the fact that the transferor appears to be Ax, i.e., one only of the two companies that were parties to the contracts, this is a circumstance that does not affect the title of the transferee to claim. It is in the relationship between transferor and transferee that the former is liable to the latter in respect of the existence of the transferred rights (Art. 1693 of the French Civil Code).

[19]   "As far as the debtor is concerned, it might certainly object that the transferor could not transfer more rights than those belonging to him, if and when we should enter into the discussion of the substance of the claim. However, such an objection would possibly affect the quantum claimed. It would not affect the title to claim.

[20]   "Finally, the respondent's plea that the transfer would be a donation because the transfer letter does not indicate any price, and that as a donation it would be null and void because in violation of the provisions of Arts. 931 and 943 of the French Civil Code, is to be dismissed as well.

[21]   "There are certainly many ways in which the transfer of rights from one company to another may be remunerated, particularly when the transfer takes place between companies of the same group, and this doesn't need to be specified in the act of transfer itself. The absence of the indication of a price in the context of the transfer letter is not sufficient to qualify the transaction as a donation. The will of the parties, as it appears from the letter, is clearly one of transferring certain rights from one company to another. There is nothing in the way the letter is worded that might imply the will to donate.

[22]   "In any case, reference to Arts. 931 and 943 of the French Civil Code is misplaced. French law governs the contracts between the transferor of the alleged credits (Ax) and the alleged debtor (Ministry of Agriculture and Food of Z and its successor in title). It does not apply to the different and separate contract under which the credits in question (if any) were transferred by Ax to A. In the absence of a choice by the contracting parties, the proper law of this contract cannot be French law because the transfer has no connection at all with France: nationality, residence of the parties, subject matter of the contract, place of signature, place of execution of the main obligation are connected with countries which in any event are foreign to France.

[23]   "Furthermore, a transfer of credits can not be qualified as a transfer of 'future assets' (which is prohibited by Art. 943 of the French Civil Code). And the applicability of Art. 931 which deals with the form of the act likewise remains excluded in force of the rule *locus regit actum* as well.

[24]   "As a conclusion, the tribunal's decision on this first issue is that the claimant is entitled to claim as legitimate assignee of alleged credits transferred to it by the company Ax."

II. CLAIMANT'S TITLE TO RESIST THE COUNTERCLAIM

[25]   "It is the counterclaimant's allegation that it has suffered substantial damages as a consequence of Ax and Ay having breached the contracts they had respectively entered into with the Ministry of Agriculture and Food of Z. It is the claimant's firm and clear position, as stated right from the introductory act of this arbitration and repeated in all submissions thereafter, that it is the assignee of credits, but it is not the successor to Ax and Ay in the underlying contracts.

[26]   "Both parties agree that the credits (if any) originate from the contracts, and they also agree that our own jurisdiction emerges from an arbitration agreement concerning disputes arising out of or in connection with the contracts. The claimant does not even deny the respondent's right to resist the claim by asserting (for instance) that no payment is due because of the claimant's default in fulfilling its contractual obligations. However, on the one side, the claimant's claim is not directly grounded on the contracts. It is grounded on a few documents (the Verification Act and some further letters from the Z administration) that, in the claimant's view, are deeds constituting acknowledgment of debt. On the other side, the claimant's objection to the counterclaim for damages is that this is based on the alleged non-fulfilment of the contracts by Ax and Ay respectively, and so therefore only these two companies could be sued for damages arising out of the contracts because the credits originating therefrom were transferred to A, but not the contracts with the obligations therein vis-à-vis the respondent.

[27] "Whether or not the above position and views of the claimant with respect to documents on which it relies to prove its claim are correct (which will be considered by the tribunal when discussing the nature, validity and effects of the 'Verification Act' and other submitted documents), there is no doubt that its objection to the counterclaim is correct. An assignee of credits, who is not a successor in the underlying contracts, has no title to resist a counterclaim for damages in an amount that largely exceeds the amount of the claims and which would require a detailed discussion, contract by contract, of the 'if and how' the respective obligations of the parties have been fulfilled.

[28] "The tribunal cannot share the respondent's opinion according to which both the claim and the counterclaim are based on the same contracts and, as a consequence, the title to claim can not be separated from the title to resist the counterclaim. Even if both the credits (if any) and the damages (if any) originate from the same contracts, the claimant's title depends on a transfer agreement which is clearly restricted to the credits only. It does not extend to the contracts as a whole, and so therefore it does not give the claimant the title necessary to resist a counterclaim for damages which depends necessarily and only on the alleged non-fulfilment of the contractual obligations by the companies signatories of the contracts.

[29] "As a conclusion, the tribunal's decision on this second issue is that the claimant is not the proper counter-respondent to the counterclaim, and consequently the counterclaim is dismissed."

III.   TITLE OF FIRST RESPONDENT TO STAY IN THIS ARBITRATION
       AS THE SUCCESSOR OF THE FORMER MINISTRY OF
       AGRICULTURE AND FOOD OF Z

[30] "The respondent is right when it states that this issue is actually superseded by the fact that, at the hearing, the claimant formally accepted the Ministry of Agriculture and Water Management of Z as the proper first respondent, i.e., as the successor of the abolished Ministry of Agriculture and Food of Z, and such an agreement has been confirmed by the tribunal's Order.

[31] "The claimant does not deny this. However, it keeps on maintaining that the Ministry of Agriculture and Water Management of Z 'is not the successor of the former Ministry of Agriculture and Food of Z', and that it has accepted this Ministry be first respondent in this procedure only because, by declaring to assume the liabilities of the former Ministry for the contracts with the companies of the A group, the Ministry of Agriculture and Water Management of Z has become an additional entity that the tribunal will have to hold responsible jointly and severally with second respondent and third respondent.

[32]   "The tribunal might be satisfied with the statement made by the claimant at the hearing (as confirmed in the Order). From the point of view of the proceedings, this is sufficient to qualify the Ministry of Agriculture and Water Management of Z as the proper first respondent.

[33]   "However, it is possibly useful for the tribunal to investigate here whether the Ministry of Agriculture and Water Management of Z is to be considered as the successor of the former Ministry of Agriculture and Food of Z not only formally in these proceedings, but also substantially. As a matter of fact, this investigation will make it easier to discuss, under IV hereafter, the question of whether we have jurisdiction in respect of the Fund for Development of Agriculture of Z (second respondent) that the claimant considers as the entity that would have 'fully inherited' the obligations of the former Ministry of Agriculture and Food of Z.

[34]   "The claimant's position is wrong. By Presidential Decree ... the Ministry of Agriculture and Food of Z was put into liquidation, creating at the same time a new Ministry under the name of 'Ministry of Agriculture of Z'. The Association for Production of Technical Services and the Academy of Agricultural Sciences were subordinated to the new Ministry. Some other Associations ... were directly subordinated to the Cabinet of Ministers. By [subsequent] Presidential Decree the Ministry of Agriculture and the Ministry for Amelioration and Water Management were abolished and actually merged into a new Ministry established under the name of 'Ministry of Agriculture and Water Management of Z'.

[35]   "Based on the presented evidence, it is therefore the tribunal's opinion that the bulk of competence and activity of the former Ministry of Agriculture and Food of Z with some marginal decrease and/or increase, was transferred to the Ministry of Agriculture first and further to the Ministry of Agriculture and Water Management of Z. The respondent has exhibited a declaration from the Cabinet of Ministers, whereby it is confirmed that the Ministry of Agriculture and Water Management of Z is responsible for eight of the contracts signed with the companies of the A group by the former Ministry of Agriculture and Food of Z. ...

[36]   "As a conclusion, the tribunal's decision on this third issue is that the Ministry of Agriculture and Water Management of Z is the legitimate successor of the former Ministry of Agriculture and Food of Z."

IV.   JURISDICTION VIS-À-VIS SECOND AND THIRD
      RESPONDENTS

1. Second Respondent

[37]   "The Fund for Development of Agriculture of Z (hereinafter referred to either as the Fund, or as second respondent) was established by the State Fund

Presidential Decree. The constitution of the Fund is certainly part of the substantial reorganization of the agricultural sector of the country in which the President of Z had engaged. As we have already mentioned, by Presidential Decree, the Ministry of Agriculture and Food of Z was suppressed and a new 'Ministry of Agriculture' set up. The aim of this Decree, as stated in its preamble, was 'to improve the efficiency of the management of agricultural production in Z to increase the autonomy of agricultural producers, and to strengthen their liability for the development of production'. By the same Decree, some entities involved in activities connected with agriculture were attached to the new Ministry. Some others, particularly in the field of food production, which apparently was in the sphere of activity of the previous Ministry ('Ministry of Agriculture and Food') and no longer within the competence of the new one ('Ministry of Agriculture'), were made directly dependant on the Cabinet of Ministers.

[38] "The main purpose of the State Fund Presidential Decree, by which the Fund was created, is 'to provide economic support to the development of agriculture and to the industrial sector involved in processing agricultural products'. It clearly appears from the denomination itself that the Fund is nothing other than a financial institution. It is an autonomous public entity, administered by a Council, whose composition is confirmed by the President of Z (Art. 2 of the Fund's Statutes). Its financial resources are mainly made up of compulsory contributions due to the Fund by other subjects who are carrying out agro-industrial activities under State control (Art. 3 of the Fund's Statutes). The allotment of such resources is decided by the Council, subject to approval by the President of Z (Art. 5 of the Fund's Statutes), and should be in accordance with the series of objects, which are listed in the Fund's Statutes (Art. 4).

[39] "Most of the financial resources of the Fund are obviously assigned to implementation of the reform of the agriculture and water system of the country. However, it is true that among the objects listed in the above-mentioned Art. 4 of the Fund's Statutes, the 'payment of the debts of the Ministry of Agriculture and Associations of the agro-industrial complex deriving from previously stipulated contracts with foreign firms' is included.

[40] "The claimant's mistake is to think that having been entrusted with the above task, the Fund has 'fully inherited' the obligations of the former Ministry of Agriculture and Food of Z, and is to be considered as its legitimate successor. The wording of the Fund's Statutes on the issue in question, proves the contrary. The Fund is entrusted with the payment of debts of 'the *Ministry of Agriculture of Z*' (emphasis added). This is the newly established Ministry and not the suppressed one ('Ministry of Agriculture and Food of Z'). However, the debts to be paid are those deriving from contracts with foreign firms 'previously stipulated', and this necessarily means: contracts that were stipulated with

foreign firms by the former Ministry of Agriculture and Food of Z. Therefore, we have here crystal clear confirmation that:

- the contracts stipulated by the former Ministry of Agriculture and Food of Z, following its suppression and the establishment of the new Ministry of Agriculture of Z are transferred to the latter;
- in case of debts deriving from these contracts, the new debtor (replacing the Ministry of Agriculture and Food of Z) is the new Ministry of Agriculture of Z;
- the Fund is nothing more than the financial institution to which the Ministry of Agriculture can apply for authorizing the payment of the debts in question.

[41]   "In other words: the Fund has no direct liability toward the creditors of the Ministry. It only operates as an institution which disposes (or better said, is supposed to dispose) of the money for the payment of the debts toward foreign companies that the Ministry of Agriculture of Z inherited from the former Ministry of Agriculture and Food of Z. The Fund has never signed any arbitration agreement with the claimant or with any of the companies of the A Group. It does not at all have any contractual relationship with either the claimant or with any of the companies of the A Group.
[42]   "As a conclusion, the tribunal decides that it has no jurisdiction vis-à-vis second respondent."

2. Third Respondent

[43]   "The situation is different with respect to third respondent (the Government of Z). It is not quite clear to the tribunal what exactly the claimant means by 'Government of Z'. In the opinion of the tribunal 'government' and 'state' are not identical. A state is a legal entity, a government is not. The word 'government' is sometimes used purely as a concept to designate a certain system of power. This is the case, for instance, in the Z Constitution . . . where it is said that 'The government is based on the principle of separation of powers into legislative, executive, and judicial powers . . . etc.'
[44]   "The word 'government' might also be used to designate a complex of organs in charge of the exercise of State power. This is the case, for instance, in the same Z Constitution . . . where, under the Chapter 'System of organs of government', it is said that 'The highest governmental power in Z is exercised by the President, Parliament, the Supreme Court, the Supreme Commercial Court, and the Cabinet of Ministers of Z.'
[45]   "Finally, the word 'government' is very frequently used to designate a constitutional collective organ in charge of state affairs at the executive level

whenever the Constitution of the state, apart from the attributions of the individual Ministries, provides for the exercise of executive power through decisions collectively debated and adopted within the 'government' (generally named in this case the 'Council of Ministers' or equivalent).

[46]   "None of the above interpretations of the word 'government' (not even the strictest identification of the 'government' with the 'Council of Ministers') would allow to clearly single out an entity as being a legal person capable of rights and liabilities. The tribunal is of the opinion that the claimant has used the expression 'Government of Z' to designate what it might have better designated as 'State of Z'. This, by the way, appears to be the opinion of the first respondent as well. As a matter of fact, both the claimant and the first respondent have developed their arguments, respectively directed to affirm or to deny our juris-diction with regard to third respondent, by discussing theories and jurispru-dence on the subject of 'sovereign immunity' and on the issue of the extension of arbitration agreements to parties (including States) who did not sign it.

[47]   "It can also be mentioned that even in the language currently used by distinguished arbitrators, it is not uncommon that the word 'government' be used to designate the 'state'. For instance, in the award of Case no. 1803/1972,[4] the People's Republic of Bangladesh is currently designated as 'the Government of Bangladesh', and in the award of Case no. 3493/1983[5] the Arab Republic of Egypt is frequently referred to as 'the Government of Egypt'.

[48]   "The above having been said, as to the identification of third respondent, we should now move to the following two problems:

– if and why the Government of Z might be bound by an arbitration agreement it did not sign;
– whether or not the principle of 'sovereign immunity' should apply.

[49]   "The binding effect of the arbitration agreement against parties who did not sign it is a question widely discussed both in doctrine and in jurisprudence. It is generally accepted that if a third party is bound by the same obligations stipulated by a party to a contract and this contract contains an arbitration clause or, in relation to it, an arbitration agreement exists, such a third party is also bound by the arbitration clause, or arbitration agreement, even if it did not sign it. In other words, the mandatory force of the arbitration clause (or arbitration agreement) cannot be dissociated from that of the substantive contractual commitments.

[50]   "This may be the case of companies belonging to the same 'group of companies', whenever there is a sufficient evidence of the global liability of

---

4. "*Collection of ICC Arbitral Awards 1974-1985*, pp. 40-48."
5. "Ibid., pp. 124-138."

the 'group'. This may be the case of an individual partner being bound by an arbitration clause signed by a general partnership. This may also be the case of States when engaging in transactions of an economic nature through one of their administrative bodies, or even through a separate legal entity provided, in this last case, that the State has full control over it and is bound by the acts of it.

[51]   "What is important in our case is that the contracts with Ax and Ay were not signed by an entity separate from the State of Z, but by a Ministry, i.e., by an organ of the State, whose acts are undoubtedly performed on behalf and in the interest of the State.

[52]   "Even if the Ministry is a legal person, as it certainly is (Art. 1 1 of the 'Provisions' approved by decision of the President of Z . . .), it is defined as 'the body of the state management of the agrarian sector' (Art. 1 of the same 'Provisions'), and it is in charge, among other things, of the 'realization of the agrarian reform' (Art. 5 of the same 'Provisions'). In a few words and as is obvious for any Ministry, particularly in a country where the power is highly centralized in the hand, under the directions, and under the control of the President, first respondent was and is in charge of carrying out the agrarian policy of the government of Z. It represents the State, within its competence, and the State is bound by its acts.

[53]   "The direct involvement of the highest authority of the Government of Z in the fulfilment of the Ministry's obligations under the contracts in question is confirmed (if need should be) by the Presidential Decree that, in establishing the Fund for Development of Agriculture of Z after the contracts with foreign companies had been transferred from the liquidated Ministry of Agriculture and Food of Z to the new Ministry of Agriculture of Z, included among the task of the Fund the one of providing the money for the payment of the Ministry's debts deriving from these contracts. Therefore, when the Ministry of Agriculture and Water Management of Z (first respondent) did accept the jurisdiction of this arbitral tribunal at the hearing, it not only took the position of the successor in title of the former Ministry of Agriculture and Food of Z but, implicitly and necessarily, also appeared as the representative of the State (i.e., the government) of Z in a matter pertaining to its department.

[54]   "No need to say that as far as the 'state immunity' is concerned, if we would retain the theory of restricted immunity based on the distinction between acts of a State as a trader (acts jure gestionis) and acts of a State in its sovereign capacity (acts jure imperii), there should be no doubt that the contracts in question are to be classified in the first category. In any case, the acceptance of our jurisdiction by the Ministry, as representative of the State, does also imply the waiver of immunity from jurisdiction.

[55]   "There is no ground in the respondent's objection according to which, since the Ministry of Agriculture and Water Management of Z took full

responsibility for the contracts, the claimant would not be entitled 'to attempt to find some other respondents to share responsibility for the underlying contracts'. The right of a claimant to act against all possible responsible subjects cannot be denied. The respondent's objection would only be correct if interpreted in the sense that there is no substantial difference between the Ministry and the State. In fact, we might say that we have in this arbitration one only respondent in two: the Government of Z (to be better designated as the State of Z), represented by the Ministry of Agriculture and Water Management of Z.
[56]   "As a conclusion, the tribunal decides that it has jurisdiction vis-à-vis first respondent as validly representing third respondent and as far as need be vis-à-vis third respondent as validly represented by first respondent."

3. Joint and Several Liability of Respondents

[57]   "Following our decision that this tribunal has no jurisdiction vis-à-vis second respondent, this issue now concerns only first respondent and second respondent. As we have already mentioned, first respondent is in fact validly representing third respondent, and alternatively third respondent is validly represented by first respondent. Therefore the liability of first respondent and third respondent (if any) necessarily coincide.
[58]   "As a conclusion, the tribunal decides that no distinction can be made between the liability of first respondent and third respondent (if any)."

V.   LEGAL NATURE AND EFFECTS OF THE "VERIFICATION ACT"

[59]   "The 'Verification Act' is the main document on which the claimant relies in order to prove its title to the claimed payment. In his opinion, this document is a deed that constitutes 'acknowledgment of debt in the light of the French Law'. The above statement would be certainly wrong, even if French law should apply. In accordance with the provisions of Art. 1326 of the French Civil Code, a document containing an acknowledgment of debt should be handwritten in full by the debtor or, as a minimum, in addition to the signature, at least the word 'approved' or similar should be handwritten, as well as the amount due. This is certainly not the case with the 'Verification Act'.
[60]   "However, this tribunal is of the opinion that French law does not apply to this issue concerning the legal nature and legal effects of the 'Verification Act'. In consideration of the fact that the 'Verification Act' was issued in Z and in accordance with the already mentioned rule *locus regit actum*, the tribunal considers that it is necessary to discuss the nature and effects of the Act in question either with reference to Z legislation (should there be any provision in this respect in Z law)

or with reference to the actual circumstances under which the Act was worked out and signed, as well as to the actual purpose for which it was established.

[61] "Neither party has made reference to any specific provision of Z law concerning the acknowledgment of debts. Both parties have submitted legal opinions on the nature and effects of the document. . . . As might have been expected, these legal opinions contradict each other.

(. . . .)

[62] "Apart from the legal opinions and legal cases submitted by the parties, the tribunal itself, after careful consideration of the Verification Act and of the circumstances under which it was established, is of the opinion that this document is nothing more than a 'progress report' (as written on its title) which provides the situation at a certain date of what has been invoiced and what has been paid on a series of transactions that are said to have occurred 'between the Ministry of Agriculture and Food of Z and the company Ax'. The document covers eighteen different 'construction contracts' (much more than the ones for which excerpts have been submitted by the parties in this arbitration), plus nine other transactions that are defined as 'Various works and payments'.

[63] "We know that by that date . . . the Ministry of Agriculture and Food of Z had already been suppressed and the contracts and eventual debts of this Ministry had passed to the new Ministry of Agriculture of Z, its legitimate successor. It is worth noting that the Ministry of Agriculture of Z has not signed this document. As to the suppressed Ministry of Agriculture and Food of Z, the Chief of the Accounting Department has signed the Verification Act, but only 'in relation to the payments made in freely convertible currency'. . . .

[64] "The 'Verification Act' was sent to Ax by the Association for the Construction of Agricultural Objects. This Association is neither a party to the contracts, nor the successor to the Ministry of Agriculture and Food of Z. The covering letter (dated 14 April which is certainly a wrong date) informs that the Ministry of Agriculture and Food of Z has been suppressed by Presidential Decree, that a Liquidation Commission has been set up with the task of 'collecting all data of mutual accounting with foreign companies', and submits to Ax the Verification Act for consideration and signature.

[65] "This means that we are in the preliminary phase of 'collecting data', and the Verification Act is nothing more than a part of this process. Amount of the contract prices, amount of invoices, amount of cash payments, amount of barter payments. Nothing more than figures and mathematical calculations. Whether or not the invoices correspond to actual deliveries, whether or not they are to be paid, whether or not the implementation of the contracts has been completed and the guarantees met, whether or not there are disputes and claims pending between the contracting parties, all these problems are still open. There has been no actual control of the implementation of each individual contract, and this

obviously should not be done by the organizations that have signed the Verification Act, but by the contracting parties, contract by contract, and in accordance with the terms and conditions agreed upon therein for the delivery, assembly, commissioning, testing, and final acceptance of each installation.

[66] "Finally, the 'Verification Act' is certainly not a settlement contract among the parties who have signed this document and it does not constitute a novation in respect of the pre-existing contractual relationship. Even if the respondent, in its briefs, has made reference to these two situations in order to exclude that the Act in question may be construed either as a settlement or as a novation, this in fact has never been the claimant's case. As we have already mentioned in another section of this award (see [26]), the claimant does not deny that the credit he asserts originates from the contracts and that our jurisdiction (accepted by the respondent) depends on the arbitration agreement established in relation to the contracts.

[67] "The claimant's case is that the 'Verification Act', taken by itself or together with other documents we will consider hereafter, constitutes an acknowledgment of debt which entitles the creditor to claim for payment. For the reasons set forth here above, the tribunal does not share this opinion as to the legal nature, purpose, and effects of the Act in question. As a conclusion, the tribunal decides that the Verification Act does not itself give the transferee A (no more than the transferor Ax indeed) sufficient title to payment of the alleged debt by the debtor."

(. . . .)

[68] The arbitral tribunal also examined certain letters relied on by the claimant but came to the conclusion that none of these letters gave sufficient title to payment of the alleged debt. The arbitral tribunal found: "The Verification Act, as well as other documents submitted by the claimant, might possibly constitute pieces of evidence (even if not of a conclusive nature) concerning its alleged credit. However this would require a claim based on the underlying contracts, and not only on the Verification Act and other submitted documents. The claimant has repeatedly stated that it is not a successor to Ax and Ay in the underlying contracts, and that its claim is exclusively based on the acknowledgment of debt resulting from the Verification Act and other submitted documents. As a conclusion and for the above reasons, the tribunal decides that the claimant's claim is dismissed."

(. . . .)

VI.   COSTS

[69] "In consideration of the fact that some of the issues have been decided in favour of the claimant and others in favour of the respondents, the tribunal

considers reasonable that the costs of the arbitration be borne by the claimant on the one side and by first respondent and third respondent on the other side in equal proportion (50/50), and that each party bear its own legal costs. The decision on costs does not apply to second respondent, because the tribunal's decision not to have jurisdiction vis-à-vis this respondent has been taken as a result of a debate between claimant and first respondent, in the absence of second respondent who did not participate in the proceedings, and consequently did not incur any costs in this arbitration."

Final award in case no. 9771 of 2001

Parties:	Claimant: Commodities trading company (Italy) Defendants: (1) Shipping company D (Cyprus); (2) Shipping company A (Cyprus)
Place of arbitration:	Stockholm, Sweden
Published in:	Unpublished
Subject matters:	– assignment of contract – identity of parties to contract – jurisdiction of arbitral tribunal – applicable law to contract – conflict of law rules – non-conformity of goods

Facts

A commodities trading company, claimant in these proceedings, negotiated a contract with shipping company A, second defendant in these proceedings, for the supply of 3,000 tons of a raw material. The commodities trading company faxed the contract bearing its signature to the Moscow office of shipping company A which signed the contract and faxed it back to the commodities trading company. The following day, the same document bearing the same contract number and date was faxed again to the commodities trading company, but with the signature of shipping company D, first defendant in these proceedings. The contents of the contract were unchanged except that shipping company A's name and address had been substituted by that of shipping company D. In addition, a change had been made in the article of the contract regulating the consequences of exceeding one of the quality specifications increasing the allowable content of a component from 14.20% to 14.70%. The signature on behalf of the shipping company on both documents was the same. The commodities trading company only signed the version of the contract faxed to it by shipping company A.

The contract contained an arbitration clause which read:

"Any contingency or claim arising out of or relating to this Contract or any alleged breach thereof shall be settled by arbitration in Stockholm, Sweden, in accordance with the rules of International Chamber of Commerce.

> If the validity of the arbitration clauses or the jurisdiction of the arbitration court is contested by one or the other Party, the arbitration court shall be competent to make a final decision on said issue."

Pursuant to the contract, on 7 June the commodities trading company paid 90% of the purchase price in advance, as invoiced by shipping company D. On the same day, shipping company D invoiced the commodities trading company for the remaining 10% of the purchase price. Both invoices were based on a cargo of 2,828.09 metric tons of the goods which shipping company D delivered to the agreed-upon port on 17 June. Tests were carried out by the commodities trading company and by a surveyor S, which found that the goods contained a higher content of the component than the contractually agreed specifications. The commodities trading company refused to accept delivery of the goods and informed both shipping company D and A of the defect. On 11 July, the commodities trading company confirmed its rejection of the goods by a telefax to shipping company D. The commodities trading company informed the shipping companies that it considered the non-compliance of the goods with the quality specifications to be a breach of contract and claimed reimbursement of the advance payment as well as compensation for all other costs and damages. The commodities trading company resold the goods at a lower price in order to limit the damage.

Various attempts were made to reach an agreement on compensation, but when these proved unsuccessful, the commodities trading company instituted arbitration against both shipping companies and a sole arbitrator was appointed. The arbitration was conducted on documents only and no hearings were held.

The sole arbitrator first examined his jurisdiction with respect to the two defendants. First and second defendant argued that only shipping company D, which had performed the obligations of the seller under the contract, should be a party to the contract. The sole arbitrator found that there was no indication of an express assignment of the contract, as argued by defendants. Although the commodities trading company accepted shipping company D also as a contractual party, this did not mean that it released shipping company A from its obligations. The contract had been signed by shipping company D and confirmed by shipping company A; thus they were both bound by the arbitration clause in the contract.

After finding that the conflict of law rules of the place of arbitration, Sweden, applied to the determination of the applicable law to the substance of the dispute, the sole arbitrator applied the 1955 Hague Convention which is embodied in the Swedish 1964 Act on the Applicable Law on the International Sale of Movables. The 1955 Hague Convention states that the contract will be governed by the law of the place where the seller was domiciled at the time of receiving the order, or if the order is received at a permanent establishment which belongs to the seller, the law of that place. The sole arbitrator found that the order had been received at the representative office of the defendant which was located in Moscow and that Russian law should apply.

The sole arbitrator found that the shipping company D and shipping company A were jointly and severally liable under the contract and that the delivery was not in conformity with the contractual terms and specifications. The commodities trading company, which had already paid 90% of the amount due was awarded the full amount of its claim with deductions for amounts already refunded or not yet paid. Because the claimant essentially succeeded entirely in its claims, the sole arbitrator held that the defendants should bear all costs.

Excerpt

(. . . .)

I. JURISDICTION

[1]　"Before the sole arbitrator may resolve any of the issues to be determined under the Terms of Reference, the issue of the sole arbitrator's jurisdiction has to be resolved. The question of whether both or only one of the shipping companies are parties to this arbitration is determined as follows by the sole arbitrator.

[2]　"The claimant has instituted arbitration proceedings against both shipping company A and shipping company D as defendants arguing that both are parties to the contract and thus to the arbitration or, in the alternative, either of them. The claimant has maintained that the right to chose with whom to contract . . . is a fundamental and basic aspect of the freedom to contract. The claimant maintains that the choice is based on different considerations and that negotiations are conducted in order to define various aspects of a contract while taking into account the characteristics and qualities of the counter party. In particular it is maintained that in international agreements such aspects as the nationality of a party is [sic] taken into consideration as it may influence which law may be applicable to the contract. The clamant maintains that it contracted with both the defendants or at least one of them.

[3]　"The defendants have maintained that not both, but only shipping company D, the party that performed the obligations of the seller under the contract, should be a party to these proceedings. The sole arbitrator notes that the defendants have not contested the fact that the contract exists but only which parties there are to the contract.

[4] "During the time period following the signature of the contract, the correspondence, which has been presented to the sole arbitrator, was at least in part, addressed to both shipping company A and shipping company D together or to shipping company D only at the same fax number. Both defendants have acted in the transaction and replied to correspondence from the claimant. Notably, shipping company A responded to issues concerning the alleged defects and agreed to settle a certain amount in specific manners. From the letterheads of both companies it appears that both have the same address and telephone and fax numbers in Moscow as well as in Cyprus and that the same persons act as it appears from the correspondence on behalf of both of the defendants. The claimant, however, effected payment of the advance payment to shipping company D on the basis of an invoice issued by shipping company D and the delivery was performed by shipping company D. In the invoice for the remaining 10% reference was made to shipping company D as the forwarding agent thus indicating the direct involvement of shipping company A in the transaction. The claimant did not object to shipping company D signing the contract.
(. . . .)

[5] "This arbitration is conducted in accordance with the old 1929 Swedish Act on Arbitrators. This Act does not contain any rules concerning party substitution. As is determined below, there is only one contract to which there are two parties acting as sellers, i.e., the defendants. The contract, signed by shipping company D, contains an arbitration clause, and therefore the sole arbitrator has jurisdiction to hear and determine the issues raised in this case. The question is whether the claimant also can make its claim against shipping company A.

[6] "By first signing the document entitled "Contract . . ." and signed by the claimant, shipping company A expressed a will to contract. What then happened seemed to indicate the substitution of shipping company A with shipping company D.

[7] "It is in this context noted that according to general principles of contract law, including Russian, in particular a debtor may not assign a debt without the approval of the creditor. From this follows that the assignment of a contract containing rights and obligations, such as an arbitration clause, would require the consent of the other party. There is no evidence of any express assignment of the contract having occurred nor may it be inferred from the circumstances and the evidence in this case. In any event, even if there would have been, there is no evidence of the consent having been given by the claimant. This has not even been alleged by the defendants. The sole arbitrator therefore finds that there has not been an assignment of the contract from shipping company A to shipping company D.

[8] "At the same time the claimant did not object to shipping company D signing the contract and acting as seller thereunder and also paid shipping

company D and acted as if it had contracted with shipping company D. Thus the claimant must be considered to have accepted shipping company D also as a contractual party. This does not mean that the claimant intended to release shipping company A from its obligations under the contract to which it had initially subscribed by signing the first document which subsequently was replaced with the contract. Nor is there evidence of any waiver from the claimant to such effect nor has this been confirmed in any other manner by the claimant although alleged by the defendants. On the contrary, the claimant, as evidenced by the correspondence presented in this case, seemed still to consider shipping company A a party to the contract as such correspondence – subsequent as well as prior to the delivery – is addressed to both defendants. This is also evidenced by the active involvement of shipping company A in the issues concerning the defect, repayment, and discussion of the consequences of the defective delivery. Shipping company A therefore must still, in the opinion of the sole arbitrator, be considered a party to and bound by the contract.

[9]   "In the preparation of the new 1999 Swedish Arbitration Act (New Act), there was a proposition to introduce a provision according to which a party, who assigned its rights and obligations under a contract, still should be bound by the arbitration provision and it would only be binding between the successor and the remaining party if the parties specifically and clearly agreed hereto. This rule was motivated by the consideration of the remaining party and that it was not considered reasonable that the assignor should be allowed to avoid its liability under the arbitration clause and thereby, in practice also to choose between either court proceedings or arbitration.

[10]   "Even though, no such rule was included in the new law, recent case law supports this proposition.[1] According hereto the rule has been stated that the arbitration provision shall remain in force between the assignor and the remaining party unless any particular reasons should indicate the contrary. A compelling argument is that the fact that the parties entered into an arbitration agreement from the outset was in due consideration of, among other things, the assignor's ability to pay the costs of an arbitration (fees to the arbitrators etc.) whereas the assignees' possible lack of the ability to do so, may free the remaining party from the obligations under the arbitration agreement.

[11]   "The fact that claimant did not raise any objection against shipping company D signing the contract, nor raised any objection to the minor change made to the text of the contract and did effect the advance payment to shipping company D, demonstrates that the claimant accepted the fact that shipping company D had assumed the obligations as seller under the contract. However, this does not necessarily imply that the claimant also accepted to

---

1. "NJA 1997 p. 866."

release shipping company A from its obligations thereunder. As the claimant rightfully points out it is a fundamental right of a party to choose its contractual party in particular in terms of financial position and with regard to a future arbitration.

[12] "An arbitration clause does contain mutual rights and obligations, which may not be unilaterally assigned or transferred. In order for a party to be released thereunder the party's will must clearly be expressed. It may therefore not, against the objection of the claimant and failing any evidence to such effect, be considered that the claimant accepted that shipping company A freed itself from its obligations under the contract or the arbitration clause it first had signed when shipping company D subsequently signed the contract. In fact its continued involvement in the performance of the contract, in particular concerning the issues relating to the defects and the consequences thereof, constitutes a confirmation of shipping company A's position as a party to the contract.

[13] "Thus, in the opinion of the sole arbitrator, both defendants are bound by the arbitration clause in the contract and may be claimed as parties to these proceedings by the claimant. Consequently, the sole arbitrator finds that he has jurisdiction over the dispute brought before him for the reasons stated above and as summarized below:

- The arbitration clause clearly indicates that the arbitration is an ICC arbitration.
- The sole arbitrator has been appointed correctly in accordance with such rules and the sole arbitrator and the parties to the dispute have accepted such appointment.
- According to the arbitration agreement itself the sole arbitrator may determine his own jurisdiction.
- The dispute concerns an issue of defective delivery and an alleged breach of the contract and the issue is therefore covered by the arbitration clause.
- The contract has been signed by the claimant and shipping company D and confirmed by shipping company A, thus the parties to the dispute and is binding for them."

II. APPLICABLE LAW

[14] "According to Art. 13(3) of the Rules the sole arbitrator shall, in the absence of a choice by the parties, apply the law designated by the rule of conflict, which he deems appropriate. It is clear and undisputed that the contract does not contain any explicit stipulation concerning the choice of law.

[15] "The claimant has made some vague reference to the general UNIDROIT Principles of International Commercial Contracts but without making any

specific argument as to such principles necessarily being agreed to apply as applicable law or to be applied as or instead of the applicable law. The defendants have not made any argument at all on the issue of applicable law. Neither party even contends that there was an agreement as to the applicable law.

[16]　"A general principle of private international law is that the intention of the parties to a contract with regard to the law governing the contract – when the intention is not expressed in words and agreed – is to be inferred from the terms and nature of the contract and from the general circumstances of the case.

[17]　"In this context it may be observed that it is considered that the insertion of an arbitration clause in a contract may be considered to permit the inference that the parties have submitted their contract to the law of the country in which the arbitration is to take place. If one bases the reasoning on this hypothesis, it does still not clarify whether the parties meant the substantive law or the conflict of law of such place.

[18]　"It seems likely that the parties in this case – had they contemplated the matter – would not have been inclined to accept the case being treated with the application of the substantive law (or in the courts) of the other party's country. This may also be the reason why the parties agreed to have their dispute resolved in arbitration governed by the rules of an international arbitral institution. In fact nothing speaks in favour of the intention of either of the parties having been the application of either Cypriotic or Italian substantive law. The indication of Stockholm as the place of arbitration could be interpreted as an indication of the will of the parties to let the law of the place of arbitration govern their contract. In this case nothing seems to warrant such a conclusion. It does, however, support the conclusion that Swedish conflict of law rules should apply in determining the applicable law.

[19]　"According to the sole arbitrator the conflict of law rules of the place of arbitration, i.e., Swedish conflict of law rules, shall apply. This is in accordance with legal writings and practice in international arbitration.[2]

[20]　"This principle is further manifested in Art. III of the 1961 European Convention on International Commercial Arbitration[3] as well as in various

---

2. "See Prof. Julian Lew in his report 'Relevance of Conflict of Law Rules in the Practice of Arbitration' in International Council for Commercial Arbitration Congress Series No. 7, *Planning Efficient Arbitration Proceedings – The Law Applicable in International Arbitration*, Gen. ed. A. Jan van den Berg, (Kluwer Law International 1996) p. 447."

3. *Note General Editor.* The sole arbitrator was apparently referring to Art. VII of the 1961 European Convention on International Commercial Arbitration which reads:

"1. The parties shall be free to determine, by agreement, the law to be applied by the arbitrators to the substance of the dispute. Failing any indication by the parties as to the applicable law, the arbitrators shall apply the proper law under the rule of conflict that the arbitrators deem applicable. In both cases the arbitrators shall take account of the terms of the contract and trade usages.

subsequent arbitration rules and instruments which adopted the same principle (e.g., Art. 33(1) of the UNCITRAL Arbitration Rules[4] as well as Art. 28(2) of the UNCITRAL Model Law).[5] This practice is also confirmed by the review of ICC arbitration practice referred to in Craig, Park and Paulsson, *International Chamber of Commerce Arbitration* (1990).[6]

[21]   In this case the parties have chosen Stockholm as the situs of the arbitration and therefore the sole arbitrator determines that the Swedish conflict of law rules shall apply for the determination of the applicable [law]. The overriding principle of Swedish conflict of law rules is based upon the idea that the law should apply which demonstrates the closest connection to the contract. The contract in this case, as described above, concerns the international sale of goods from Russia entered into between the sellers (the defendants) domiciled in Cyprus at the time of the conclusion of the contract acting out of a representative office in Moscow and the buyer (the claimant) domiciled in Italy.

[22]   "In the case of an international sale of goods, the Swedish conflict of law rules are to be found in the 1964 Act on the Applicable Law on International Sale of Movables (hereafter the 1964 Act), which is the incorporation of the 1955 Hague Convention on the Law Applicable to International Sale of Goods (hereafter the 1995 Hague Convention) into Swedish law or the 1980 UN Convention on Contracts for the International Sale of Goods (hereafter the 1980 Vienna Convention), as well as in the 1980 Rome Convention on the Law Applicable to Contractual Obligations (hereafter the 1980 Rome Convention) which follows and expands the 1955 Hague Convention. Even though the 1980 Rome Convention is not directly applicable in the present

---

2. The arbitrators shall act as *amiables compositeurs* if the parties so decide and if they may do so under the law applicable to the arbitration."

4. Art. 33(1) of the UNCITRAL Arbitration Rules reads:

"1. The arbitral tribunal shall apply the law designated by the parties as applicable to the substance of the dispute. Failing such designation by the parties, the arbitral tribunal shall apply the law determined by the conflict of laws rules which it considers applicable."

5. Art. 28(2) of the UNCITRAL Model Law on International Commercial Arbitration reads:

"(2) Failing any designation by the parties, the arbitral tribunal shall apply the law determined by the conflict of laws rules which it considers applicable."

6. "For Sweden reference is made to Lars Heuman, *Skiljemannarätt* (1999) p. 695; *Arbitration in Sweden*, 2nd edition (1984) pp. 46-47 and Kaj Hobér, 'Das anzuwendene Recht beim Internationalen Schiedsverfahren in Schweden' in Recht der Internationalen Wirtschaft (September 1986, no. 9) p. 688."

case it provides a basis for ascertaining the content of the Swedish conflict of law rules.[7]

[23]   "Further, the 1964 Act is of general application, i.e., it is applied even with respect to States which have not ratified the 1955 Hague Convention. The main principle of the 1955 Hague Convention as of the 1964 Act, is that when parties to an international contract of sale have not agreed on a choice of law, the contract will be governed by the law of the jurisdiction where the seller was domiciled at the time when he received the order *or, if the order is received at a permanent establishment which belongs to the seller, the law in which this is located.*

[24]   "The law of the country of the *buyer* shall prevail only in the event where the seller receives the order from the buyer at the time when he (or his representative or agent) is present in the jurisdiction of the buyer. This has not been the case and this rule is therefore not applicable.

[25]   "In regard to the interpretation of the expression 'permanent establishment', the Swedish preparatory works state that it is where there is a specific structure (establishment) or other permanent facility such as an *office*, plant workshop, trading office or *other trading place*.[8] The Moscow office of the defendants appears to have been actively and decisively engaged in the negotiations, signing and administration and performance of the contract. This leads to the conclusion that the representative office of the defendants was an important and permanent office demonstrating, in the view of the sole arbitrator, that the representative office, from where the signed contract was sent by fax to the claimant, qualifies as a permanent establishment in the sense of the 1964 Act.

[26]   "As to the definition of the expression 'order', it has been indicated to be understood as 'the expression of will of the buyer either . . . in the form of an offer, which later is accepted by the seller; or [in the form] of an acceptance of an offer by the seller'.[9] Swedish jurisprudence also confirms that the signing and conclusion of a contract corresponds to the expression 'order' under the 1964 Act for purposes of applying the Act.[10]

[27]   "Even though the defendants in the present case no doubt are domiciled in Cyprus – where their registered seats are located at the same addresses, the evidence in this case shows that they, as sellers, received the order or draft contract

---

7. "See report by Prof. Emmanuel Gaillard entitled: 'Thirty Years of *Lex Mercatoria*' in the International Council for Commercial Arbitration, Congress Series No. 7, *Planning Efficient Arbitration Proceedings – The Law Applicable in International Arbitration* (Kluwer Law International 1996) p. 585."
8. "See NJA (Swedish Law Reports) II 1965 pp. 454-455."
9. "Ibid."
10. "Kaj Hobér in *Swedish and International Arbitration*, 'In Search for the Centre of Gravity – Applicable Law in International Arbitrations in Sweden' (1994) pp. 32-33."

from the claimant at their representative office in Moscow, not in Cyprus. The acceptance of [the] order or the contract was signed or confirmed . . . from such representative office and then returned to the claimant's office in Italy. It appears that the representative office of shipping company A is the same office and staffed with the same persons as for shipping company D.

[28] "In addition hereto, the parties expressly agreed, by specifying the legend 'Moscow' on the contract, that Moscow should be the place of concluding the contract. Further, the evidence produced in this case shows that the negotiations of the contract took place in part in Moscow, where both the claimant and the defendants have representative offices and through the exchange of telefax messages primarily between the claimant and the defendants at such representative office.

[29] "For the above reasons and in the absence of any evidence to the contrary, the contract is to be considered concluded at the representative office of the defendants in Moscow, Russia. Furthermore, the first exception to the main rule (that the law of the seller's domicile shall apply), of the 1964 Act is to be applied, i.e., '. . . if the order is received at a permanent establishment which belongs to the seller, the law (will apply) in which this is located' – the law of the country where the representative office of the defendants is located, i.e., Russian law, should be applied.

[30] "In addition, also the other evidence of the case shows that the transaction has the closest connection with Russia, which confirms that Russian law should be applied. The 1980 UN Convention on Contracts for the International Sale of Goods is in force in Russia since 1 September 1991 as a consequence of Russia being a legal successor for the USSR. According to Art. 1 of the Convention, it applies to contracts of sale of goods between parties whose places of business are in different states, e.g., when the rules of private international law lead to the application of the law of a Contracting State. The claimant, as the buyer, being domiciled in Italy is also bound by the 1980 UN Convention to which Italy acceded on 1 January 1988. Thus the 1980 UN Convention is to be applied.

[31] "Under Art. 7 of the Convention questions concerning matters governed by the Convention, which are not expressly regulated therein, are to be determined in conformity with the law applicable by virtue of the rules of private international law.[11] From this follows that the appropriate substantive rules of Russian law shall apply subsidiarily in this arbitration.

---

11. Art. 7 of the 1980 United Nations Convention on Contracts for the International Sale of Goods (CISG) reads in relevant part:

"(. . . .)

(2) Questions concerning matters governed by this Convention which are not expressly settled in it are to be settled in conformity with the general principles on which it is based or, in the absence

[32] "Hence, the sole arbitrator finds that the substantive law in force at the defendants' representative office – its permanent business establishment – i.e., Russian law, including the 1980 UN Convention on Contracts for the International Sale of Goods, shall apply to the substantive issues to be adjudicated in this arbitration. The sole arbitrator has also taken into account the provisions of the contract and the relevant trade usages, as applicable, in determining this case."

(. . . .)

III. DISPOSITION OF ISSUES

(. . . .)

1. Number of Contracts and Parties

(. . . .)

[33] "It may be noted that the sequence of events as to the negotiation and performance of the contractual obligations under the contract and as evidenced by the parties' arguments and evidence submitted in these proceedings, are undisputed. In the opinion of the sole arbitrator there is clearly only one contract, i.e., the contract, as defined above. It has been established that the claimant first signed the document entitled 'contract' and sent it to shipping company A at their representative office in Moscow. The contract was then signed by shipping company A and re-faxed to the claimant. The following day the same document was faxed again from the representative office of the defendants. The only difference being that the seller's name had been substituted for the name of shipping company A and a small change to Art. 3 specifying the consequences of certain defects in the goods in the case of which the advance payment had to be repaid where the level of content of a specific component was changed from 14.20% to 14.70%. The quality specifications in Art. 2 of the contract as well as all other terms and conditions remained unaltered. In fact the correspondence between the parties submitted in these proceedings shows that the claimant considered shipping company A still liable under and bound to the contract even though shipping company D effectively acted as the performing seller. The change to the contract is not material in the opinion of the sole arbitrator so as to constitute a new and different contract.

---

of such principles, in conformity with the law applicable by virtue of the rules of private international law."

[34] "The sole arbitrator interprets this to mean that the sellers wanted to share the burden with another party. There is no evidence, which would support the assumption that an assignment has taken place or even was intended. Nor would it have been possible to assign a contract with both rights and liabilities without the consent of the other party. The claimant has never made nor may be considered to have given, such consent. Both parties on the side of the seller, shipping companies A and D appear in the correspondence as both recipients as well as senders of messages.

[35] "Therefore, in these arbitration proceedings, there are in the opinion of the sole arbitrator, two parties on the side of the sellers, those being shipping company A and shipping company D, and one on the side of the buyer, the commodities trading company. This is so even though only one party performed most of the obligations of the seller under the contract. This does not, in the opinion of the sole arbitrator, however, change the fact that the liabilities, in particular under the arbitration clause, towards the buyer, the claimant are still shared by both shipping company A and shipping company D."

2. Joint and Several Liability of Defendants

[36] "The claimant has stated that both shipping company A and shipping company D are liable under the contract. The defendants have maintained that there only could be one contract and therefore only one seller as clearly there was only one performance.

[37] "As confirmed above, the defendants are correct in there only being one contract but the liabilities thereunder are shared jointly and severally between both of the defendants. As the contract and the arbitration clause contains both rights and obligations of the seller, such assignment may not be done unilaterally but also requires the consent of the creditor, i.e., the claimant. There is no evidence that the claimant gave such consent, either implicitly or expressly. In fact, the claimant in these proceedings has stated that it denies that such assignment has occurred. The fact that the claimant did not object immediately to the new party and that it performed its obligations such as the payment, to shipping company D, does not in the opinion of the sole arbitrator constitute evidence that the claimant accepted to exonerate A from its obligations under the contract. In fact the correspondence subsequently between the parties indicate[s] that the claimant made no difference between shipping company A and shipping company D and considered them as one and the same party, and thus, to the contract and to which none of these parties objected to either. Nor does it appear as if shipping company A or shipping company D made any difference between themselves. It seems that they have acted in cooperation and jointly vis-à-vis the claimant in the course of the performance of the contract.

[38]   "For the above reasons the sole arbitrator finds that there is only one contract, the contract, and that the liability of the defendants as sellers under the contract is joint and several."

3.   Delivery in Conformity with Contract?

[39]   "According to the contract, goods of a certain quantity and with a specified quality were to be delivered by the defendants to the claimant. The contract specifically states and specifies the quality in Art. 2, which sets forth the various properties, which the delivered goods must have. . . . According to these specifications the maximum or minimum content of certain properties are expressly stated in the contract. Art. 3 [of] the contract further clearly provides what is to happen in the event the goods do not conform to the specific and agreed quality specifications.
[40]   "In this case the claimant maintains that the goods had a content of a specified component, which exceeded the quantity allowed for and specified under the contract. In such case the buyer is entitled to reject, i.e., not accept, the goods. (In other cases the consequences would be the payment of a penalty). Finally, the contract also in Arts. 6 and 7 states how the determination of quantity and quality is to be made. As to quality, Art. 7 provides that it should be determined by S which is a well recognized and well-established surveillance institute with offices world-wide. Such determination is to be made in the port of destination. In the event the delivered goods do not conform with the agreed specifications the delivery is to be considered non-contractual and the buyer can request the repayment or reimbursement of the advance payment made.
[41]   "The claimant has shown that the surveyor, S, was appointed in accordance with the terms of the contract and that the analysis by S to be made at the delivery port was to be conclusive evidence as to whether the cargo was contractual or not. The defendant has not objected or denied this argument but referred to the analysis performed by Z of the . . . Chamber of Commerce and Industry in the port of [loading in] Russia. A copy of such report has been submitted by the defendants in these proceedings. The defendants have maintained that this analysis demonstrates that the goods delivered were of the quality specified in the contract.
[42]   "According to such report the sampling was clearly performed in the port of loading . . . and not in the port of destination, as prescribed and required under the contract in Art. 3. The claimant has rejected this analysis as not relevant for the determination of the quality under the provisions of the contract, which specifically calls for an analysis by S. The claimant also questions the authenticity of the analysis and whether it refers to the goods actually delivered.
[43]   "The sole arbitrator notes that the contract specifically states that the quality of cargo should be [determined] by S and at the port of delivery. The parties thereby must be considered having agreed at the time of the contract

to jointly nominate a specific surveyor and it must be assumed that this was done in order to avoid future discussions. This would, however, not necessarily be an exclusive method of proving the quality of the goods nor has this been expressly stated in the agreement. However, there is no evidence that either the S report was flawed or any other reason should not be considered conclusive as set forth in the agreement between the parties.

[44] "As set forth in the contract, the inspection and proof of the quality according to the contract should clearly be made and established in the port of destination and not before dispatch. Therefore the evidence of a quality certificate by Z can not be considered conclusive as to the quality of the goods delivered.

[45] "Furthermore, the defendants have not presented any other evidence or arguments why the S survey should not be valid or determinative for the quality of the goods. In the opinion of the sole arbitrator there [is] no such additional evidence and one can therefore not deviate from the express wording of the contract, which specifically indicates S as the jointly appointed surveyor.

[46] "The sole arbitrator, for the reasons stated above and on the basis of the S analysis as compared to the quality specifications of the contract, finds that the delivered goods did not conform to the contractual and agreed terms and specifications."

4. No Breach of Contract for Non-Payment

(. . . .)

[47] "According to the contract the buyer had to make an advance payment corresponding to 90% of the purchase price prior to any goods being shipped and delivered. The defendants therefore sent the claimant an invoice dated 4 June for the total amount due for the goods being delivered. The contract in Art. 9 also specified that the remaining amount, corresponding to 10% of the balance cargo value, was to be paid 'at thirty (30) days from B/L date, after Buyer's original shipping documents and analyse [sic] results at discharging port'. The defendants sent a corresponding invoice dated 7 June to the claimant.

[48] "It is undisputed in these proceedings that the claimant also effected such payment to shipping company D as requested by the defendants, on the same day as it received the invoice, dated 4 June with a value date of 7 June. This is also evidenced in the invoice sent by the defendants for the remaining 10% balance where the amount paid by the claimant is deducted. The claimant therefore did not breach its obligation to pay the amount due as advance payment.

[49] "As the goods were found to be defective, however, no further payment was due for the goods. Instead the claimant was entitled to claim the reimbursement of the advance payment made. In addition, the defendants in a fax letter dated 2 August, expressly relieved the claimant from paying the remaining

outstanding balance for 10% of the price for the goods. The claimant therefore has not either breached the contract by not paying the remaining 10% of the original contract value as invoiced by the defendants through D."

5. *Breach of Contract Due to Failure to Deliver Goods in Conformity with Contract*

[50] "As established above, the delivery of the goods under the contract was not conforming to the contractual terms and specifications. The sole arbitrator therefore finds that the defendants have breached their contractual obligations by not delivering goods of the agreed quality. The parties also had agreed that the weight (Art. 6) and quality (Art. 7) should be determined at the port of destination by S, a well-recognized surveying company acting world-wide. The defendants have not disputed the authenticity of the S's report but have confined themselves to submitting an analysis made by Z dated 7 June, which does not state the day on which the sampling was made but certainly is dated prior to the time of arrival in the port of destination, which was on 17 June. This report does therefore not fall within the scope of the language of the contract which specifies not only that the test should be made by S, but also that such a test should be made at the port of destination. . . .

[51] "The sole arbitrator concludes that the wording of the contract is clear and explicit on this point. The contract clearly states the precise properties which the goods were to have when delivered. The parties also expressly agreed that the analysis by S should be conclusive and should decide whether the goods were in conformity with the contractual specification or not. On the basis of the copy of the analysis by S submitted in these proceedings one notes that in fact the [contents] contrast with the specification of the allowed maxima and minima, respectively, of such properties provided for in the contract. The S report also states the testing method used, the analysis made and the date of the analysis. It also makes reference to the name of the ship delivering the goods. The defendant has neither disputed the quality nor the correctness of the report by S.

[52] "There is therefore no doubt in the mind of the sole arbitrator that the S report properly reflects the results of its analysis of the goods delivered by the defendant and that such an analysis actually was performed. The report is precise and specific and clearly indicates the cargo to which it relates, the ship, the port of shipment and the destination, etc. It may therefore safely be determined that the delivered goods did not comply with the contractual specifications. As a consequence, the claimant in accordance with Art. 7 of the contract was entitled to reject the goods delivered. In such case the defendants should have repaid the advance payment received but did not. Therefore, the sole arbitrator also finds that the defendants have breached the agreement between the parties also in this respect.

[53] "The defendant has not made any argument, which would even give the slightest suspicion that there was any acceptable excuse herefor, such as, e.g., force majeure. Nor did the defendant object to the claim of the claimant immediately subsequent to the delivery. This has only been done in these proceedings. On the contrary, the defendant agreed to repay (and in fact it did) as much as approximately one-third of the advance payment before the present arbitration proceedings were initiated. It is noted that according to the evidence in the case the defendants have not objected to the defective delivery as such nor to being obligated to repay the amount it received from the claimant other than referring to its discussion with the supplier, and its impossibility to repay as it had forwarded the payment of the claimant to supplier.

[54] "In fact, the defendants did not object to their liability at the time of the claimant's rejection. In effect the defendants may be considered, at least indirectly, to have accepted responsibility for the lack of quality of the goods as it only referred to their discussions with its supplier when the claimant raised its claim concerning the defective delivery and by repaying a certain amount and being prepared to compensate the claimant with a non-specified amount on future deliveries.

[55] "According to the claimant, shipping company D undertook to pay the balance also during verbal contacts between the parties. This has not been commented on by the defendants in these proceedings. The sole arbitrator, against the denial of the defendants of any liability, does therefore not give any particular weight to such statements; also in the view that there has been no oral hearing and testimony in this case and no such oral undertaking is therefore considered proven."

6. Entitlement to Damages

[56] "As has been concluded . . . above, the goods delivered were not in conformity with the contractual specification and the sole arbitrator therefore finds that defendants thereby did breach their obligation under the contract to deliver goods of a specific quality. Under such circumstances the claimant is entitled to compensation for the damages suffered. . . . The sole arbitrator holds . . . that Russian law is applicable."

7. Termination of Contract

[57] "It has been established that the delivery did not correspond to the specifications of the contract. Therefore the claimant would have been entitled to terminate the contract and request the reimbursement of the advance payment of 90% of the price in accordance with Art. 3 of the contract. Initially that is also what the claimant did as it rejected the goods. However, as evidenced from

the documentation, the claimant during the course of the negotiations and exchange of faxes during the period following the delivery of the defective goods gave various offers to the defendants of how to resolve the situation. The claimant did not return the goods but instead sold the goods at a different and lesser price than originally sold for. It has claimed that it did so on behalf of the defendants. There is, however, no evidence that the defendants had accepted to return the advance payment, rather on the contrary evidence shows that this was impossible. Nor is there any evidence that the defendants requested the claimant to sell the goods on their behalf. The sole arbitrator therefore interprets this, together with the fact that the claimant in these proceedings has not claimed as if it terminated the contract but rather for damages, to mean that the claimant changed position and conclusively accepted the delivery and instead satisfied itself to claim damages. For the above stated reasons, the sole arbitrator finds that the contract has not been terminated."

8.   Quantum of Damages

[58]   The sole arbitrator awarded claimant the amount that it had effectively claimed, including interest taking into account that defendants had already settled approximately one third of the purchase price and that they should be credited for the additional payment of the remaining 10%. . . . Regarding claimants claim for "other damages", the sole arbitrator held as follows:

[59]   "Finally, the claimant has claimed 'other damages' for the loss of reputation to be determined in these proceedings. The claimant has requested the sole arbitrator to resolve this issue on the basis of *ex aequo et bono*.

[60]   "According to the ICC Rules an arbitrator may not base any decision on the principle of *ex aequo et bono* unless expressly authorized. This is furthermore repeated in the Terms of Reference agreed and signed between the parties in these proceedings. No such agreement has been made. In addition, no other damages or the loss of reputation have been presented or evidenced in these proceedings either to the amount or otherwise. In any arbitration it is a fundamental principle that each party shall have the possibility to present its case and to respond to any claim made against it. Should the sole arbitrator award other damages then the defendant would clearly not have been given such opportunity. The sole arbitrator therefore has no basis on which to determine, or even less award, any damages under this heading. The claim for 'other damages' is therefore denied."

9.   Liability of Defendant or Defendants

[61]   "The claimant has submitted some documentation from shipping company D and shipping company A which it maintains supports the argument

that the defendants have assumed joint and several liability for the defective goods delivered. In the opinion of the sole arbitrator this documentation does, however, not warrant such a conclusion, other than indirectly.

[62] "The defendants, through shipping company D, did in fact pay ... to compensate some of the damages, which the claimant had stated it had suffered, and, through shipping company A, was prepared to settle ... through additional discounts on future deliveries. This indicates that the defendants were prepared to accept, at least some, liability resulting from the defective delivery. Even though there is no explicit evidence that the defendants have denied any liability in the course of the negotiations following the delivery, such liability has been denied in these proceedings alleging that the goods were in conformity with the contractual specifications with reference to a quality analysis performed by Z.

[63] "As set forth above, the claimant diligently performed its obligations under the contract and immediately made the advance payment when notified thereof by the defendants. The defendants, however, as has been established in these proceedings, delivered defective goods and admittedly did not return the advance payment as provided for under the terms of the contract.

[64] "The sole arbitrator also notes that the claimant instead of insisting on the reimbursement of the advance payment which it initially had claimed and taking into account the defendants' alleged impossibility to fulfil such obligation in fact did mitigate the initially claimed damages by reselling the goods at a lower price. It has also been foreseeable by the defendants that the claimant would suffer damages if defective goods were delivered as the goods were commodities and the claimant a trading company intending to resell the goods. The sole arbitrator therefore finds that the evidence in the case warrants the conclusion that the defendants have breached the contract by delivering defective goods and consequently are liable, jointly and severally, to compensate the claimant for damages suffered as a consequence thereof."

10. Law Applicable to Interest

[65] "Art. 78 of the 1980 Vienna Convention (as applicable in this case) stipulates that if a party fails to pay the price or any other sum that is in arrears, such as damages in this case, the other party is entitled to interest on it. As a consequence, the claimant is also entitled to interest on the damages, which is part of the compensation for the breach of contract. The 1980 Vienna Convention does not specify the interest rate to be used. The general view in Sweden (as elsewhere) is that the matter of interest is an issue of substance and thus is governed by the applicable substantive law. The latter is thus to be

determined under the appropriate provisions of the internal Russian legislation, the position of which the sole arbitrator summarizes in the following way:

[66]   "With regard to monetary obligations in the context of which there is continuous situation of default, which arose on 1 January 1995 or later, Art. 395 of the new Russian Civil Code ('Liability for Non-Performance of Monetary Obligations') shall apply. Art. 395 does not set up a fixed legal rate of interest but provides as the main rule rather that the creditor is entitled to a rate corresponding to the discount bank interest rate prevailing at its domicile at the date of performance of obligation. However, it is within the court's discretion to uphold the creditor's demand relying on a rate existing on the date of bringing the action or rendering the judgment. Art. 395 also provides that interest is due up to the date of payment of the debt.

[67]   "The proper construction of Russian law with regard to interest – as accounted for above – shall therefore in the opinion of the sole arbitrator lead to the application of the official discount rate as applicable from time to time in the claimant's domicile, i.e., Italy. The moment from which default interest starts to run is not determined in the applicable Russian legislation but is left to the discretion of the sole arbitrator to determine. According to the relevant Russian Civil Code, Art. 395, the sole arbitrator may award interest from the date the action was brought or from the date of rendering the judgment.

[68]   "In discretionary regard of relevant parameters, the sole arbitrator will award an interest rate corresponding to the official Italian discount rate as applicable from time to time . . . payable to the claimant in this arbitration until full payment. In this case the sole arbitrator finds it reasonable that the default interest starts to run from the time when the request for arbitration was submitted. . . . Consequently, from such date interest shall accrue with a rate of 6.25% p.a corresponding to the official discount rate as decreed by the Bank of Italy. After 10 October 2000 the applicable interest rate shall be 4.75% p.a. as decreed by the Bank of Italy until payment of the debt.

[69]   "The claimant's claim for interest on the advance payment is denied as the claimant has not claimed the reimbursement of such amount in these proceedings and thus is not awarded."

(. . . .)

Final award in case no. 9839 of 1999

Parties:	Claimants: (1) Mergers and acquisitions firm Q, Inc. (US); (2) Mergers and acquisitions firm Q-Spain, S.L. (Spain) Respondent: Mergers and acquisitions firm Q-Z Ltd. (US)
Place of arbitration:	New York, USA
Published in:	Unpublished
Subject matters:	– third-party beneficiary to contract – material breach of contract – good faith – non-solicitation clause – liquidated damages – tortious interference – fraudulent inducement

Facts

Q, Inc., an international mergers and acquisitions firm, specializing in cross-border transactions comprised a network of affiliates, all bearing the Q name. Q Spain, S.L. (Q-Spain) was Q's affiliate in Spain. Q-Z, Ltd. (Q-Z) was Q's affiliate in the United States.

After terminating the managing director of the existing Q office in the United States (Q-Z) due to substandard performances, S, the president of Q, recruited YY as a new US representative. In the lead-up to concluding a contract of representation (the Agreement), YY was informed by S and S's representatives that the office could be started with a modest investment and that it was necessary to recruit an experienced mergers and acquisitions (M&A) consultant to head the team and to set up the necessary computer equipment. YY was also informed of the "File Summary", a list which set forth the status of all Q deals involving the United States, (known as "pipeline deals") as a summary of possible transactions that could generate future income for Q-Z.

Following negotiations between Q and YY, during which Q-Z was represented by counsel, Q and Q-Z entered in the Agreement. Pursuant to the

Agreement, Q-Z became the exclusive representative of Q in the United States for an initial trial period of twenty-four months.

Clause 8(1) of the Agreement provided that either party could terminate the Agreement for any reason upon one month's notice. Clause 8(3)(1) stated that the Agreement could be terminated in the event of "a breach by the other party of any material term of the Agreement, which remains unremedied for 21 days after receiving written notice thereof". Finally, clause 9(2)(1) of the Agreement provided that Q would not be entitled to a portion of any future gross fee income to which it would otherwise be entitled if the Agreement was terminated for any of the reasons set forth in clause 8(3). The Agreement also provided for ICC arbitration.

From the inception of the Agreement, Q and Q-Z had differences with respect to the hiring of an experienced dealmaker and an experienced secretary as well as the failure to update the computers. In response to S's demands to hire a dealmaker, YY identified JJ as a candidate for a dealmaker position with Q-Z on the condition he would be paid a salary. Contrary to Q's general practice of dealmakers only working on commission, Q agreed to pay 40% of JJ's salary and Q-Z hired JJ as a dealmaker. Although two experienced dealmakers were eventually hired, several of Q's European offices had voiced concerns about the performance of the New York office. The initial trial period of the Agreement was extended for another year on the recommendation of Q-Italy, but shortly thereafter Q concluded that it would end its relationship with Q-Z. S verbally informed YY that Q was going to terminate the Agreement. Shortly thereafter, Q notified Q-Z in writing of the termination of the Agreement, with one month's notice.

Several months earlier, Q-Z was involved in the acquisition of U, S.A. a Spanish company by MM Group, a US company (the MM/U transaction) and received a success fee for the transaction from the US company. Pursuant to the fee sharing arrangement in Clause 6(1) of the Agreement, Q-Z was obligated to pay Q a percentage of the success fee. Q in turn was obligated to pay a portion of this amount to Q-Spain, the "selling country". Q-Z failed to remit the fee to Q and after failing to reach an acceptable arrangement for the payment, several days after having notified Q-Z that the contract was terminated, Q also notified Q-Z that it considered Q-Z's action a material breach of the Agreement. The Agreement terminated twenty-one days after the notice of termination and several months later, Q and Q-Spain commenced ICC arbitration against Q-Z.

In the arbitration, Q-Z objected to Q-Spain as a party to the arbitration. Applying New York law which was the applicable law under the contract, the sole arbitrator found that the Agreement did not evidence the parties' intent to confer a right to enforce performance on Q-Spain. Q-Spain was not a signatory to the Agreement nor an intended beneficiary Therefore Q-Spain was not a proper party to the arbitration.

The sole arbitrator held that Q-Z had materially breached the Agreement under Clause 8(3). The contract was first terminated due to Q-Z's "poor performance". Q had then notified Q-Z of a material breach due to its failure to pay the contractual percentage from the MM/U transaction. According to the Agreement, termination due to material breach meant that Q-Z was no longer entitled to a proportion of any Gross Fee Income to which it would otherwise have been entitled. The sole arbitrator, finding that Q-Z's assertions were not sufficiently supported by the evidence, rejected Q-Z's argument that despite its breach of the Agreement it should still be able to recover the fees owed on pipeline deals because Q had breached the implied covenant of good faith and fair dealing which applies to all contracts governed by New York law.

Q also sought liquidated damages from Q-Z because Q-Z had violated the non-solicitation clause in the Agreement by soliciting the services of former and present Q employees. The sole arbitrator, examining the non-solicitation clause under New York law, observed that such clauses must be reasonable in time and scope and were intended to protect the employer's legitimate interests. The sole arbitrator held that the clause was of finite duration (two years) and did not prevent Q-Z from acting as an international M&A advisory firm or from competing with Q. The geographic scope of the non-solicitation clause was worldwide, but it did not restrict Q-Z from soliciting Q's clients or competing with Q anywhere in the world, nor did it prohibit Q's past or present employees from pursuing their vocations anywhere in the world. It only prevented Q-Z from soliciting for a finite time period those person who had acquired knowledge of Q's business and transactions being pursued by Q. Therefore, the non-solicitation clause was a reasonable restriction. The sole arbitrator concluded that the totality of evidence demonstrated that Q-Z had undertaken a pattern of conduct that constituted solicitation of former and present employees of Q. In particular, Q-Z had sent out memos on Q-Z's letterhead soliciting present and former employees of Q. Applying Clause 9(3)(2) of the Agreement which provided for liquidated damages in the event of a breach of the non-solicitation clause, the sole arbitrator found that the sum stipulated in the Agreement for such breach was a reasonable estimate of the expected loss from a violation of the clause.

Q-Z had counter-claimed that Q was liable for tortious interference with Q-Z's contracts. The sole arbitrator agreed with Q's argument that the contracts in question had been voluntarily terminated and that the clients would have done so regardless of Q's contacts with them. The sole arbitrator also did not accept Q-Z's claim that YY had been fraudulently induced into entering into the Agreement. Under New York law, in order to establish a claim for fraud, a plaintiff must show that: '(1) a representation was made, (2) as to a material fact, (3) which was false when made and, (4) was known by the maker at the time to be false, (5) which was made with a present intent to deceive and induce reliance by plaintiff and, (6) upon which the plaintiff did justifiably rely, (7) without notice of its falseness, (8) to his injury'. In the view of the sole arbitrator, Q-Z failed to prove the elements of fraudulent inducement, in particular, the element of reliance. YY was an experienced business man and had an attorney who assisted him in the negotiation of the Agreement but had not examined Q's financial statements before entering into the Agreement. Moreover YY chose not to terminate the Agreement after becoming aware of what he perceived as the falsity of Q's representations. Thus Q-Z was bound by the Agreement.

Q-Z was condemned to pay compensatory damages with interest, liquidated damages and the costs of the proceedings.

Excerpt

(. . . .)

I.   Q-SPAIN A PROPER PARTY TO THIS ARBITRATION

[1]   "Q-Z claims that Q-Spain is not a proper party to the arbitration because Q-Spain is not a signatory to the contract at issue in this case. It contends that because the entitlement of any affiliate to fees on a Q transaction arises only from that affiliate's own Agreement of Representation with Q there is no basis on which Q-Spain can assert a claim against Q-Z.

[2]   "In response, claimants argue that Q-Spain is a proper party to this arbitration because: (1) Q-Spain is a third-party beneficiary of the Agreement; and (2) Q-Z waived any objection to Q-Spain's standing as a proper party under CPLR Sect. 7503(c) by failing to object timely to Q-Spain's claim.

[3]   "The arbitral tribunal concludes that Q-Spain is not a proper party to this arbitration proceeding because there is no existing agreement between Q-Spain and Q-Z that provides for arbitration, and Q-Spain is not an intended third-party beneficiary of the Agreement. Moreover, under the ICC Rules, Q-Z properly asserted its objection to the arbitral tribunal's jurisdiction as to any claims asserted by Q-Spain."

1.   New York Law

[4]   "New York contract law principles determine the scope of the arbitration agreement in this case.[1] New York has adopted the *Restatement (Second) of*

---

1. "The arbitration agreement in this case is governed by Chapter Two of the Federal Arbitration Act, 9 U.S.C. Sect. 202 (FAA) because: (1) the Agreement is in writing; (2) the Agreement

Contracts Sect.302, with respect to the law of intended third-party beneficiaries. Sect. 302 states:

'(1) Unless otherwise agreed between promisor and promisee, a beneficiary of a promise is an intended beneficiary if recognition of a right to performance in the beneficiary is appropriate to effectuate the intention of the parties and either (a) the performance of the promise will satisfy an obligation of the promisee to pay money to the beneficiary; or (b) the circumstances indicate that the promisee intends to give the beneficiary the benefit of the promised performance. (2) An incidental beneficiary is a beneficiary who is not an intended beneficiary.'

Whether a party is an intended third-party beneficiary depends on the intent of the parties to the contract. See *Hylte Brucks Aktiebolag v. Babcock & Wilcox Co.*, 399 F.2d 289, 292 (2d Cir. 1968) citing *Beveridge v. New York Elevated R. Co.*, 112 N.Y. 1, 26, 19 N.E. 489, 496 (1889) ('[T]he language of the contract [needs to] show that it was entered into for the benefit of a third party. . . . ') See, e.g., *Crawford v. Feldman*, 199 A.D.2d 265, 266, 604 N.Y.S.2d 585, 586 (2d Dep't 1993). Therefore, the arbitral tribunal must look to the language of the Agreement to determine whether the signatories intended to make Q-Spain a third-party beneficiary of the Agreement."

2. Intent of the Parties

[5]   "The Agreement evidences no such intent. First, Q-Spain is not referred to anywhere in the Agreement. Second, Clause 6 of the Agreement that provides

---

arisesout of a commercial relationship and . . . (3) the commercial relationship has some connection with one or more foreign states. See *Cheshire Place Assoc. v. West of England Ship Owners Mutual Insurance Assoc.*, 815 F.Supp. 593, 595 (E.D.N.Y. 1993) (describing the three prerequisites for application of Chapter Two of the FAA).

The scope of an arbitration agreement subject to the FAA is governed by federal law. *McPheeters v. McGinn, Smith & Co., Inc.*, 953 F.2d 771 (2d Cir. 1992) ('The Agreement falls within the ambit of the Federal Arbitration Act. . . . Federal law, therefore, governs the current dispute as to the scope of the Agreement.'). Federal law requires a court to look to the contract law of a particular jurisdiction and not to general principles of contract law to determine the scope of an arbitration agreement. *First Options of Chicago, Inc. v. Kaplan*, 514 U.S. 938, 944 (1995) (holding that, under the FAA, in deciding 'whether the parties agreed to arbitrate a certain matter courts generally . . . should apply ordinary state-law principles that govern the formation of contracts'.). In this case, where the parties specified that New York law would govern their agreement, the arbitral tribunal should look to New York law. The New York Court of Appeals has adopted Sect. 302 of the *Restatement (Second) of Contracts* as the law of New York on intended third-party beneficiaries. *Fourth Ocean Putnam Co. v. Interstate Wrecking Co., Inc.*, 66 N.Y.2d 38, 44-45, 485 N.E.2d 208, 495 N.Y.S.2d I, 5 (1985)."

for the apportionment of fees does not confer a benefit on Q-Spain. Specifically, Clause 6.3 states as follows:

> 'As soon as the Representative receives the Gross Fee Income in relation to any particular transaction it shall without delay transmit the balance remaining after its own entitlement has been deducted to Q which shall then be responsible for making the apportionment pursuant to Clause 6.1 above and shall indemnify the Representative in regards thereto.'

With respect to the MM/U transaction, Clause 6(1) of the Agreement recognized that a portion of the gross fee received by Q-Z, was to be paid to another Q office. Pursuant to Clause 6(2), Q-Z was only obligated to pay the gross fee less its share to Q which in turn was responsible for paying any other Q affiliate. Indeed, the requirement that Q indemnify Q-Z with respect to Q's obligation to pay any other affiliates confirms that the primary obligation of paying other affiliates was on Q, not Q-Z. Therefore, the Agreement does not reflect an intent of the parties [to] confer a right to enforce performance on Q-Spain.

[6] "The Agreement created rights and obligations on Q-Z and Q, but did not reflect any intent to confer a right of performance on Q-Spain. Because Q-Spain is not a signatory to the Agreement and is not an intended beneficiary of the Agreement, Q-Spain is not a proper party to this arbitration."

II.   BREACH OF THE AGREEMENT DUE TO FAILURE
TO PAY SUCCESS FEE

[7]   "Q claims that Q-Z materially breached the Agreement by failing to pay Q and Q-Spain their respective portions of the success fee based on the MM/U transaction. Q-Z responds that because of Q's failure to terminate the Agreement according to the Agreement's procedures and Q's violation of the implied covenant of good faith and fair dealing, Q-Z is released from any contractual obligation to pay Q. Addressing the issue of whether Q-Z materially breached the Agreement, the tribunal finds that Q-Z materially breached the Agreement by failing to pay the contractual percentage from the fee received on the MM/U transaction.

[8]   "Clause 6(1)(a) of the Agreement addresses the allocation of fees. The gross fee income on a successful transaction was to be apportioned as follows: 36% to the Q Office covering the buying country; 44% to the Q Office covering the selling country; and 20% to Q. Pursuant to Clause 6(3) of the Agreement, Q-Z

was required to transmit to Q 'without delay' the contractual percentage of this success fee for the MM/U transaction. Instead of complying with the terms of the Agreement, however, Q-Z withheld Q's portion of the MM/U fee for a variety of purported reasons after Q's initial notice of termination of the Agreement.

[9]   "In response, Q by letter [to Q-Z (the material breach letter)], stated that Q-Z's failure to remit the MM/U fee constituted a material breach of the Agreement. Under Clause 8(3)(1) of the Agreement, Q-Z had twenty-one days after receiving this letter to cure the breach. Q-Z failed to do so within the time period under the Agreement. Accordingly, the arbitral tribunal finds that Q-Z's failure to remit the portion of the MM/U fee owing to Q constitutes a material breach of the Agreement."

(. . . .)

III.   MATERIAL BREACH BARS PAYMENT

[10]   "Q claims that Q-Z's material breach of the Agreement precludes it under Clause 8(3) from sharing in any gross fee income generated by Q and its affiliates for transactions initiated during the term of the Agreement but concluded after its termination. Q-Z counters that, since Q did not follow the proper procedures for terminating the Agreement and violated the implied covenant of good faith and fair dealing, Q-Z is entitled to various 'pipeline deals'.

(. . . .)

[11]   "The arbitral tribunal finds that Q-Z is barred from recovering any fees it may otherwise have been entitled to under the Agreement because: (1) Q-Z materially breached the Agreement under Clause 8(3) and (2) Q did not violate the implied covenant of good faith and fair dealing in terminating the Agreement."

1.   *Contractual Provisions*

[12]   "The relevant clauses of the Agreement state:

'8(1) This Agreement maybe terminated during the Initial Trial Period . . . by either party with one month notice.
. . . .
8(3)(1) This Agreement may be terminated by either Q or the Representative in the event of:
. . .

(1) a breach by the other party of any material term of this Agreement, which remains unremedied for 21 days after receiving written notice thereof; 9(2)(1) Unless termination has been for any of the reasons stated in Clause 8(3)above (in which case no entitlement shall arise), the Representative shall have a right to receive a proportion of any Gross Fee Income to which it would otherwise have been entitled pursuant to Clause 6 for all transactions initiated during the term of this Agreement but concluded after its termination.'

Under the above-stated provisions, either party could terminate the Agreement for any reason with one month's notice during the initial two-year term of the Agreement (as subsequently amended). Either party could also terminate the Agreement after giving written notice of a material breach and affording the other party an opportunity to cure the breach.

[13]   "In this case, Q terminated the Agreement under Clause 8(1) due to Q-Z's 'poor performance'. YY admitted that Q's dissatisfaction with Q-Z's performance is well documented in a series of memoranda between Q and Q-Z regarding Q-Z's need to hire dealmakers and a qualified secretary and Q-Z's failure to follow Q procedures. Following Q-Z's failure to remit Q's portion of the MM/U fee, Q notified Q-Z that Q-Z had committed a 'material breach' under Clause 8(3)(1). Q-Z failed to cure this material breach within twenty-one days."

2.   Covenant of Good Faith and Fair Dealing

[14]   "Q-Z argues that despite its breach of the Agreement, it should still be able to recover the fees owed on pipeline deals because Q breached the implied covenant of good faith and fair dealing. The implied covenant of good faith and fair dealing applies to all contracts governed by New York law. *Kader v. Paper Software, Inc.*, 111 F.3d 337, 342 (2d Cir. 1997) ('The covenant of good faith and fair dealing [is] implied in every contract under New York law. . . .') Good faith and fair dealing mean that 'neither party [. . .] shall do anything which has the effect of destroying or injuring the right of the other party to receive the fruits of the contract. . . .' *M/A-Com Sec. Corp. v. Galesi*, 904 F.2d 134, 136 (2d Cir. 1990) (per curiam). See also *Walther v. Bank of New York*, 772 F.Supp. 754, 763 (S.D.N.Y. 1991). The implied covenant of good faith and fair dealing does not, however, 'extend so far as to undermine a party's general right to act on its own interests in a way that may incidentally lessen the other party's anticipated fruits from the contract'. *M/A-Com Sec. Com.*, 904 F.2d at 136.

[15]   "Q-Z asserts that Q violated the implied covenant of good faith and fair dealing under the Agreement by terminating the Agreement for reasons other than the justifications proffered by Q such as Q-Z's failure to hire dealmakers

and a secretary. Q-Z asserts that S induced YY to extend the trial period for another year so that he could steal Q-Z's clients and employees by availing himself of the most advantageous termination method available under the Agreement. Moreover, Q-Z alleges that S prevented YY from developing a lucrative business because he simply wanted YY to stabilize the US business rather than complete transactions before terminating the Agreement. Q-Z alleges that, in so doing, S withheld support from Q-Z, denigrated YY to the Q network, and circumvented the non-solicitation clause of the Agreement by agreeing that Q would pay 40% of JJ's salary in exchange for excluding JJ from the non-solicitation clause in the Agreement.

[16] "Q-Z's assertions are not supported by a preponderance of the evidence. During the initial trial period of the Agreement, Q did not need to offer any reason for terminating the Agreement. Q did provide ample evidence that it terminated the Agreement due to what it perceived was Q-Z's poor performance rather than in a bad faith effort to prevent Q-Z, from developing business. For example, employees testified that during the two years that Q-Z was affiliated with Q, Q's foreign offices were not given adequate support by the US office and that Q-Z's employees lacked the 'business acumen' needed for succeeding in the M&A business. Witnesses also testified that Q-Z failed to recruit and hire dealmakers fast enough, that Q-Z lacked proper secretarial and computer support and that Q-Z failed to implement certain Q rules and procedures as set forth in the procedure manual. Q was legally entitled to protect its business interest by terminating the Agreement during the 'Initial Trial Period'. Accordingly, the termination of the Agreement in accordance with contract terms does not render Q's conduct a breach of the covenant of good faith and fair dealing under New York law.

[17] "Q followed the procedure under the Agreement when it notified Q-Z of a material breach. . . . Q-Z failed to cure the breach within twenty-one days of notice from Q. As a result, Q-Z forfeited its right to any pipeline deals that it otherwise would have been entitled to under the Agreement. . . . Therefore, the arbitral tribunal concludes that Q-Z is not entitled to any of the fees that were or may have been generated by the foregoing transactions according to the terms of Clause 9(2)(1) of the Agreement."

(. . . .)

IV. UNFAIR BUSINESS PRACTICES IN VIOLATION OF
NEW YORK LAW

[18] "Q claims that Q-Z engaged in an ongoing scheme to solicit employees in violation of the non-solicitation clause of the Agreement. It alleges that Q-Z's actions amount to improper interference with Q's present and former

representatives. Specifically, Q seeks liquidated damages for each violation of the non-solicitation clause with respect to AA, BB and CC, all former dealmakers.
[19]   "Q-Z counters that Q violated Art. 18 of the ICC Rules because it did not set forth any relief with respect to respondent's alleged solicitation activities and did not amend the Terms of Reference to incorporate specific claims of violation of the non-solicitation clause. Moreover, Q-Z argues that it did not 'solicit' employees, but that these former Q employees 'voluntarily' approached Q-Z and VV to discuss possible future working relationships.
[20]   "At the evidentiary hearing, counsel for Q-Z conceded that Q-Z had been aware that Q was asserting this issue in the arbitration and that both parties had a full and fair opportunity to brief the issue during the proceeding. This claim was also expressly referred to in para. 3(13) of the Amended Terms of Reference, which states: 'Claimants amended their Request to allege that Q-Z improperly interfered with Q's present and former representatives.' Consequently, the arbitral tribunal considers this issue properly presented for determination in this proceeding."

1. Solicitation

[21]   "Clause 9(3)(1) of the Agreement prevents solicitation of present employees and persons who had been Q employees in the two years prior to termination and for a two-year period following termination. The non-solicitation clause states:

> 'In the event of termination of this Agreement for any reason whatsoever, neither the Representative nor any company controlled by the Chief Executive Officer shall for a period of two years solicit the services of any person employed by Q or by any of the Q Offices at any time within two years prior to the said termination without the express prior permission of Q.'

This means that neither Q-Z nor any company controlled by YY could solicit for a two-year period current employees or persons who had been employees from the commencement of the Agreement. Q alleges that Q-Z violated Clause 9(3)(1) with respect to former and present Q employees AA, BB, and CC. .... All three of these former Q employees are covered by terms of the non-solicitation clause."

2. VV

[22]   "After Q terminated the Agreement with Q-Z, YY continued to engage in the M&A advisory business in both domestic and international markets through

Q-Z and VV. Q-Z 'primarily deals with companies on the domestic side', and VV, a VV-D corporation, [formed several months after the Agreement had been terminated], concentrates on the international mergers and acquisition markets. VV is owned by YY's wife and YY is the chairman of VV. The offices of Q-Z and of VV are the same for all practical purposes. YY claimed that because his wife is the sole shareholder of VV, VV is not covered by the non-solicitation clause because it is not 'a company controlled by the Chief Executive Officer of Q-Z'. The fact that YY's wife nominally 'owns' VV does not alter the fact that YY has effective 'control' of the company. As its chairman, YY is in control of the day-to-day operations of VV. Furthermore, YY admitted that his wife did not actively manage or run Q-Z or VV and that VV has no other officers or directors besides himself. Hence, YY 'controls' VV for purposes of the non-solicitation clause."

3. Contacts with Former Q Employees

[23]   "It is undisputed that YY and KK of Q-Z traveled to London in the Fall of 1997 in order to meet with EE, AA, BB and CC, all former employees covered by the terms of the non-solicitation clause. During this meeting, the attendees, KK, DD, CC, AA and BB discussed in YY's words, 'forming an affiliation with a new company' and meeting with the owners of an English company. Both BB and CC were affiliated at this time with the English company. At this time, YY also planned to meet Q-Spain's former representative FF, who was also covered by the non-solicitation clause. However, this meeting did not occur. Q-Z also attempted to set up a meeting with Q's Swiss Representative. Lastly, AA helped YY make contacts in the Scandinavian M&A market.

[24]   "Despite the foregoing evidence demonstrating Q-Z's contact with these former Q employees, Q-Z denies having 'solicited' any Q employees to become involved in Q-Z. YY testified that although Q-Z had communications with EE, CC, AA and FF, these former Q dealmakers volunteered their services to Q-Z and 'asked to join [Q-Z] at some point'. YY further testified that: (1) Q-Z never discussed working with Q's Swiss affiliate 'other than his [Q's Swiss affiliate] expressing possible interest in cooperation between our consulting businesses . . . '; VV had no contractual relationship with AA; and (3) YY had never discussed working with EE.

[25]   "Lastly, YY testified that upon termination of the Agreement . . . Q-Z actually held an employee meeting at which Q-Z's attorney warned employees to avoid violating the non-solicitation clause. However, even though he denies that Q-Z ever solicited any Q employee covered by the clause, YY also testified that Q-Z's attorney told the Q-Z personnel in attendance that he did not believe that New York law would sustain a 'global non-solicitation clause'

such as Clause 9(3)(1) because it did not contain, in his opinion, reasonable geographic or temporal restrictions.

[26] "Q argues that, despite YY's protestations to the contrary, the evidence of the foregoing meetings and affiliations with former Q employees covered by the non-solicitation clause, taken in its totality, demonstrates that: Q-Z, at the very least, 'solicited' BB, CC and AA in violation of the non-solicitation clause.

[27] "In determining whether Q-Z violated the non-solicitation clause, it is first necessary to examine whether the clause itself is valid under New York law. Then it is necessary to determine whether Q-Z violated Clause 9(3)(1) by 'soliciting' Q present or former employees. Only if the tribunal finds that Q-Z 'solicited' Q employees in violation of Clause 9(3)(1) of the Agreement, will it be necessary to consider whether the liquidated damages provided in Clause 9(4) are reasonable."

4. Enforceability of the Non-Solicitation Clause

[28] "Under New York law, non-solicitation clauses, such as the one embodied in Clause 9(3)(1), must be reasonable in time and scope and intended to protect the employer's legitimate interests. See *Reed, Roberts Assoc., Inc. v. Strauman*, 40 N.Y.2d 303, 307, 353 N.E.2d 590, 593, 386 N.Y.S.2d 677, 679 (1976) ('[A] restrictive covenant will only be subject to specific enforcement to the extent that it is reasonable in time and area, necessary to protect the employer's legitimate interests, not harmful to the general public and not unreasonably burdensome to the employee.') The reasonableness of a restrictive clause's duration is 'determined in large part by the specific circumstances of the case'. *Bijan Designer for Men, Inc. v. Katzman*, 1997 WL 65717, *5 (S.D.N.Y. 1997); see also *Reed, Roberts Assoc., Inc. v. Strauman*, 40 N.Y.2d at 307.[2] Therefore, it is necessary to determine whether the non-solicitation clause at issue is reasonable in duration and geographical scope within the circumstances and context in which enforcement is sought.

[29] "Q-Z was represented by New York counsel in the negotiation of the Agreement. Furthermore, Q-Z's counsel specifically negotiated the language that appears in Clause 9(3)(1). Q-Z never disputed the geographic and temporal limits of the non-solicitation clause during the negotiation of the clause by its own counsel.

---

2. "The New York cases cited by respondent relate to non-competition clauses where employees were being restrained from pursuing their chosen vocation and soliciting their prior employer's customers. These cases do not address the kind of non-solicitation clause at issue here, which prohibits the solicitation of Q employees *not* customers."

[30]   "Under Clause 9(3)(1), Q-Z is prohibited for two years after termination of the Agreement from soliciting present Q employees or former Q employees who were employed during the period beginning two years prior to the termination. This clause is of finite duration. It does not prevent Q-Z from acting as an international M&A advisory firm or from competing with Q. Moreover, the conduct at issue occurred within months of termination. Therefore, a clause of such duration is not facially unreasonable nor is it unreasonable as applied in these circumstances. See, e.g., *Gelder v. Webber*, 41 N.Y.2d 680, 394 N.Y.S.2d 867, 363 N.E.2d 573 (1997) (a restrictive covenant not to compete for a period of five years found reasonable in covenant restricting professionals from competing with a former employer); *Seidman v. Hirshberg*, _ N.Y.2d_, 1999 WL 319086 (13 May 1999) (holding a 'reimbursement clause' valid under New York law in an agreement between the parties requiring defendant to compensate the plaintiff for serving any client within eighteen months after the termination of his employment); *Karpinski v. Ingrasci*, 28 N.Y.2d 45, 320 N.Y.S.2d 1, 268 N.E.2d 751 (1971) (enforcing restraint in competition agreement with no time limit in the context of limited, rural locales). See generally *Smith Barney v. Robinson*, 12 F.3d 575, 520 (5th Cir. 1994) (applying Louisiana law) (finding that a covenant to not solicit employees for a one-year period after leaving employment was lawful under Louisiana law).

[31]   "The geographic scope of the non-solicitation clause is worldwide, just as is the international business in which Q engages. However, the clause does not restrict Q-Z from soliciting Q's clients or competing with Q anywhere in the world, nor does it prohibit Q's past or present employees from pursuing their vocations anywhere in the world.[3] The clause only prevents Q-Z from soliciting for a finite time period those persons who have acquired knowledge of how Q does business and of the particular transactions being pursued by Q. This is a reasonable restriction. Accordingly, the tribunal finds that Clause 9(3)(1) is reasonable under the circumstances and is therefore enforceable under New York law."

---

3. "Thus, the arbitral tribunal need not consider whether the clause interferes with Q employees' 'ability to pursue a vocation', or Q employees' ability to carry on a certain type of business after termination of the employment arrangement. See, e.g., *American Broadcasting Co., Inc. v. Wolf*, 52 N.Y.2d 394, 404, 420 N.E.2d 363, 368, 438 N.Y.S.2d 482, 486-487 (1981); *Independent Metal Strap Co., Inc. v. Cohen*, 96 A.D.2d 830, 830, 465 N.Y.S.2d 579, 580 (2d Dep't 1983) ('In the absence of a showing that an employee has used or disclosed trade secrets or confidential customer lists, or that his services are special, unique or extraordinary, a covenant which prohibits an employee from pursuing a similar vocation after termination of employment is unenforceable') (citations omitted). Both Q-Z and Q employees are free to pursue their vocations."

5. Definition of Non-Solicitation

[32]   "Whether Q-Z actually violated the non-solicitation clause by conducting meetings or corresponding with former and present Q employees depends on the definition of the word 'solicit'.[4] The plain meaning of the word 'solicit' is 'to ask or seek earnestly or pleadingly', and 'to appeal for something', 'to ask for the purpose of receiving', and 'to endeavor to obtain by asking'. See *United States v. Friedenthal*, 1997 WL 786371, *3 (S.D.N.Y. 1997) quoting *Webster's New World Dictionary* 1276 (3d ed. 1988) and *Webster's Third New Int'l Dictionary* 2169 (1993). Respondent relied on the *Webster['s] Third New International Dictionary* definition of 'solicit' in its papers submitted in this proceeding.

[33]   "In a recent case involving the definition of 'solicitation' in a criminal statute, the court rejected defendant's argument that sought to limit the meaning of the term 'solicit' to 'the initial contact with a potential buyer or customer, that is unilaterally undertaken by the seller', opting instead for a broader reading of the meaning of the word. *United States v. Friedenthal*, 1997 WL 786371, *3 (S.D.N.Y. 1997). In so doing, the court found that: 'Solicitation is a process by which the solicitor asks, requests or attempts to persuade an individual to act in a certain manner.' Id. Therefore, to 'solicit' is not limited to making initial contact, but also includes contacts where the solicitor asks or 'lures' a person to act in a certain manner, such as to render particular services. Id.

[34]   "The arbitral tribunal concludes, based on the totality of the evidence, that Q-Z undertook a pattern of conduct that constituted solicitation of former and present employees in violation of Clause 9(3)(1). The evidence presented by Q regarding Q-Z's contacts, affiliations and communications with BB, CC, AA and other former employees covered by the non-solicitation clause indicates that Q-Z either asked or enticed these employees to render services to Q-Z.

[35]   "Shortly after the Agreement was terminated Q-Italy wrote GG of Q-Z that a Q-Italy employee, 'would no longer work with him or Q-Z staff on anything nor would [he] have any communication with them'. Upon receiving this letter GG left a message on the Q-Italy employee's answering machine stating: 'you are going to have to decide whether to keep working with Q or to work with us on this side. The legal situation is getting too complicated. If you don't come with us you'll end up "gettin' nothing".'

[36]   "Q-Z created documentation shortly after termination of the Agreement stating that its principal source for identifying 'potential partners' was 'Q Alumni'. Q-Z's announcement of its new operations following termination

---

4. "The language in the non-solicitation clause was specifically changed from 'secure the service' to 'solicit' at the request of Q-Z's counsel."

stated that its international offices would include 'highly regarded alumni of the Q International organization'.

[37] "Q-Z's documents not only demonstrate an intent to solicit past and present employees, but the results of doing so. In a memo on Q-Z letterhead to BB, copies of which were sent to YY, AA, FF and GG, Q-Z identified a schedule of meetings, including a meeting where '[t]he 4 founders meet to review the documents and discuss affairs of state'. This was followed by a Q-Z memorandum to BB, AA, FF, and YY (that referred to 'our meeting last week in Paris' and additional names for 'our new corporation'. The letter asked the four recipients to 'vote' on their top two choices of names for their new corporation. It is apparent that the '4 founders' include former Q employees BB, AA and FF.

[38] "The foregoing, and particularly the documents sent out by Q-Z on Q-Z stationery, demonstrate that Q-Z engaged in the process of 'soliciting' present and former employees. As a result, the tribunal concludes that Q-Z violated Clause 9(3)(1) of the Agreement by soliciting present or former employees of Q in the weeks and months immediately following the termination of the Agreement."

6. Liquidated Damage Clause

[39] "Clause 9(3)(2) of the Agreement provides for liquidated damages in the event of a breach of the non-solicitation clause. This clause states:

'In the event of any breach of the obligations contained in Clause 9(3)(1) above the party or parties responsible shall be liable to pay to Q by way of liquidated damages and not as a penalty the sum of. ... '

Liquidated damages are compensatory damages that parties have agreed to pay to satisfy a breach of contract. 'In effect, a liquidated damage provision is an estimate made by the parties, at the time they enter into an agreement, of the extent of the injury that would be sustained as a result of breach of agreement.' See Truck Rent-a-Center, Inc. v. Puritan Farms 2nd Inc., 41 N.Y.2d 420, 424, 361 N.E.2d 1015, 1018, 393 N.Y.S.2d 365, 368 (1977) (citation omitted). In determining whether a liquidated provision clause is enforceable, it is necessary to determine whether it is a reasonable attempt to estimate the measure of compensation, in which case it is enforceable, or whether it is a penalty, in which case it is unenforceable. Id. at 369. Courts look to the intent of the parties at the time of the formation of the contract, the surrounding circumstances and the nature of the transaction to determine whether a stipulation for damages constitutes a penalty or liquidated damages. See id. at 361. If the sum stipulated to bears no reasonable proportion to the actual loss sustained by a breach, it will be deemed a penalty. See *Wirth & Hamid Fair Booking, Inc. v. Wirth*, 265 N.Y. 214, 223, 192 N.E. 297, 301 (1934) (Liquidated damages 'must bear reasonable proportion to the actual loss'.)

[40]   "As a general rule when the actual damages are uncertain and difficult to prove and the contract does not give any data for their ascertainment, a stipulation to an amount which is not unreasonable will be held to be liquidated damages. See *City of Rye v. Public Service Mut. Ins. Co.*, 34 N.Y.2d 470, 473, 358 N.Y.S.2d 391, 393 (1974) ('Where, however, damages flowing from a breach are difficult to ascertain, a provision fixing the damages in advance will be upheld if the amount is a reasonable measure of the anticipated probable harm.') (citations omitted). If a court finds that the liquidated damages constitute an invalid penalty, however, the amount awarded will be limited to actual damages. See *Borek Stockel & Co. v. Slevica*, 203 A.D.2d 314, 314-315, 609 N.Y.S.2d 679, 679-680 (2d Dep't 1994).

[41]   "Applying these principles to this case, the arbitral tribunal finds that the sum stipulated to in Clause 9(4) for breach of the non-solicitation clause is a reasonable estimate of the expected loss from a violation of the clause. At the time the Agreement was negotiated, Q-Z's counsel thoroughly went over the contract and, in so doing, never questioned the sum specified in the liquidated damages clause. In addition, the stipulated sum bears a reasonable relationship to the probable loss suffered by Q-Z's violation of the clause. There was testimony that [the amount] has a rational relation to the amount invested in establishing the network divided by the number of Q offices.

[42]   "Although Q contends that the liquidated damages sum applies to each individual violation, the arbitral tribunal rejects that argument and interprets the clause as providing for liquidated damages for the totality of conduct that occurred following termination of the Agreement. Thus, the arbitral tribunal finds that an award of liquidated damages in the total amount is appropriate under the Agreement for Q-Z's violation of Clause 9(3)(1). Accordingly, since Q violated the non-solicitation clause in the months following the termination of the Agreement, Q-Z is entitled to the [contractually stipulated amount] in liquidated damage. . . ."

(. . . .)

V.   FAILURE TO PAY FEE UNDER AGREEMENT

[43]   "Q has not breached the Agreement by failing to pay Q-Z a fee for a transaction [which was in the 'pipeline'] because Q-Z materially breached the Agreement. Q-Z is thereby precluded from receiving any gross fee income, including the fee with respect to the [pipeline] transaction (see III above)."

VI. TORTIOUS INTERFERENCE

[44] "Q-Z claims that Q is liable for tortious interference with Q-Z's contracts with X Holdings Ltd. and Y Enterprises. Q counters that it did not tortiously interfere with these two contracts and that X Holdings and Y Enterprises voluntarily and independently terminated their contracts with Q-Z and would have done so regardless of Q's contacts with either company.

[45] "In the case of X Holdings, Q-Z had entered into a retainer agreement with X Holdings on 15 September 1997, to secure a joint venture partner for X Holdings's retail operations in the United Kingdom. At the time of the execution of the contract, X Holdings was unaware that Q had terminated the Agreement with Q-Z and thereby believed that by signing a contract with Q-Z, it would also receive the assistance of Q's UK office that was part of the Q network. However, Q-UK informed X Holdings that Q-Z was no longer affiliated with Q. Subsequently, X Holdings terminated its relationship with Q-Z and entered into a contract with Q's UK office. At the time of the termination of the contract with Q, X Holdings had paid Q-Z a retainer fee. Q-UK's efforts on behalf of X Holdings however, never resulted in a successful transaction. Similar to the fee retainer agreement with X Holdings, Q-Z also signed a contract with Y Enterprises shortly thereafter that called for monthly retainer payments for six months and a success fee. After Q informed Y Enterprises that it was no longer affiliated with Q-Z, Y Enterprises cancelled its contract with Q-Z after paying Q-Z an amount in retainer fees and additional expenses. S testified, however, that he did not ask anyone at Y Enterprises to stop dealing with Q-Z and that no transaction ever occurred with Y Enterprises that resulted in a success fee being paid to I.

[46] "Q-Z alleges that the above-stated actions on the part of Q with respect to X Holdings and Y Enterprises amount to tortious interference. A claim of tortious interference 'requires proof of (1) the existence of a valid contract between plaintiff and a third party; (2) the defendant's knowledge of that contract; (3) the defendant's intentional procuring of the breach; and (4) damages'. *Foster v. Churchill*, 87 N.Y.2d 744, 749-750, 665 N.E.2d 153, 156, 642 N.Y.S.2d 583, 586 (1996) (citation omitted). 'Intentional procurement of a breach is an essential element of the tort of interference with contractual relations.' *Sharma v. Skaarup Ship Mgmt. Co.*, 916 F.2d 820, 828 (2d Or. 1990), cert. denied, 409 U.S. 907 (1991) (In a tortious interference claim '[a] plaintiff must allege that "there would not have been a breach but for the activities of defendants".') (citations omitted).

[47] "The tribunal concludes that Q did not tortiously interfere with the retainer agreements signed by Q-Z with X Holdings and Y Enterprises. First X Holdings and Y Enterprises both were free to sign a contract with

any other M&A firm at the same time they had their retainer agreements with Q-Z and were free to terminate their fee agreements with Q-Z on notice. Second, the evidence demonstrates that both Y Enterprises and X Holdings would have terminated their contracts with Q-Z regardless of Q's actions with regard to these two companies.

[48] "A representative of X Holdings testified that '[s]ince virtually all of the work was to be done in the United Kingdom, [it] wanted an advisor who was present in and familiar with [the UK] market'. In addition, X Holdings testified that during the three months between the signing of the retainer with Q-Z and its termination, it 'saw no evidence of any work being done by Q-Z other than to bill us for their retainer payments'. S also testified that he perceived that Y Enterprises in large part terminated its contract with Q-Z due to its general unhappiness with Q-Z's lack of performance and not due to any alleged interference by Q. There was no evidence to the contrary.

[49] "Accordingly, the tribunal finds that Q did not tortiously interfere with Q-Z's contracts and denies this claim."

VII. FRAUDULENT INDUCEMENT

[50] "Q-Z claims that YY was fraudulently induced into entering into the Agreement with Q based on a number of alleged misrepresentations about the revenues, staffing and investment involved in establishing Q-Z. Q counters that not only did YY have all the material information available to him when he entered and performed the Agreement, but that as a sophisticated businessman YY was responsible for verifying the accuracy of the alleged misrepresentations.

[51] "Q-Z argues that S and the Chairman of Q-Italy fraudulently induced YY to join the network by misrepresenting the network's size, strength, success and history and concealing Q's reputation and financial affairs in the United States in order to revive the business and then to 'steal it back' from YY. The basis for Q-Z's fraudulent inducement claim centers on an introductory letter from S to YY stating that in [the previous year] Q-Z ' . . . was profitable (although not very)'; '[a]part from rent and secretarial assistance [. . .] a likely annual budget would be . . . '; 'we would bring in our two current Dealmakers, together with the current pipeline of deals'; and '[o]ur current Dealmakers all work on a no-salary basis [. . .] [w]e would probably need one of two additional Dealmakers to assist in the handling and developing of our business and we foresee no problems recruiting them on our customary terms'.

[52] "YY testified that he was misled by the above-stated representations by S and Z, for the following reasons: (1) [in the year prior to concluding the Agreement] the US operation had actually grossed approximately three-quarters of the stated amount; (2) S failed to add payroll fees, costs and taxes, databases,

computers and equipment in his estimate of a 'modest investment', (3) HH acted in a secretarial capacity, not as a junior dealmaker; and (4) KK, a Q Dealmaker in the US office, never met with YY to disclose the financial problems that occurred under the prior management of the US office.

[53] "In addition, YY stated that Q concealed from him that the pipeline deals listed in Q's File Summary were in fact 'a sham'; that the US office 'had encountered severe difficulties in meeting operating expenses'; that Q-Z should only be expected to 'close about 2 deals a year on the average'; that the US office had posted losses [for the previous five years]; and that a functional M&A firm should have already had computers and databases in place. In YY's words, '[i]n short had I known the truth and not been misled and misinformed, I would not have affiliated with Q nor rented new office space, hired new people, and bought new equipment'.

[54] "Q counters these assertions by offering evidence that Q-Z had all material information it needed when entering into the Agreement and that Q provided a 'true' description of the state of US operations to YY prior to the execution of the Agreement. First, S testified that Q never denied YY access to any of Q-Z's financial documents. Second, in a memorandum from the Chairman of Q-Italy to S regarding his meetings with YY, the Chairman of Q-Italy stated: 'I met for an hour with YY. . . . Q explained our methodology, structure and track record. Q also explained that although we have been in the United States for a long time . . . the NY office was substandard compared to the rest of the offices in Europe.' Furthermore, Q argues that S's representations to YY in his letter were not 'concrete representations of absolute terms of facts' that could be reasonably relied on by YY. Moreover, the evidence suggests that Q did in fact have two dealmakers at the time of S's letter, that the vast majority of Q files never close and that over a two-year period, Q-Z expenditures, excluding salaries, averaged [less than the amount stated in the letter].

[55] "Under New York law, 'a person who induces another to enter into a contract by misrepresenting a material fact or making a promise that he has no intention of keeping may be held liable for damages in fraud'. *Heineman v. S&S Machinery Co.*, 750 F.Supp. 1179, 1183 (E.D.N.Y. 1990). In order to establish a claim for fraud, a plaintiff must show that: '(1) a representation was made, (2) as to a material fact, (3) which was false when made and, (4) was known by the maker at the time to be false, (5) which was made with a present intent to deceive and induce reliance by plaintiff and, (6) upon which the plaintiff did justifiably rely, (7) without notice of its falseness, (8) to his injury'. Id. See also *New York University v. Continental Ins. Co.*, 87 N.Y.2d 308, 318, 662 N.E.2d 763, 769, 639 N.Y.S.2d 283, 289 (1995). Each of the above elements must be proved by 'clear and convincing evidence'. *Simcuski v. Saeli*, 44 N.Y.2d 442, 453, 377 N.E.2d 713, 719, 406 N.Y.S.2d 259, 265 (1978).

[56] "In order to establish fraud it is not necessary to show that a party knew a statement was false. Rather, it is sufficient if the representation was made with reckless disregard for the truth. See, e.g., *Merrill Lynch, Pierce, Fenner & Smith v. Chipetine*, 221 A.D.2d 284, 285, 634 N.Y.S.2d 469, 470 (1st Dep't 1995). Allegations of fraud, however, cannot be 'based upon a statement of future intentions, promises or expectations which were speculative or an expression of hope at the time when made'. *Heineman*, 750 F.Supp. at 1183 citing *Roney v. Janis*, 77 A.D.2d 555, 430 N.Y.S.2d 333, 335 (1st Dep't 1980).

[57] "A fraudulent inducement claim cannot be based on the absence of information that could have been obtained through diligent inquiry. See *Klamberg v. Roth*, 473 F.Supp. 544, 552 (S.D.N.Y. 1979) ('It is therefore not deceptive to fail to disclose information that was "easily enough available by duly diligent inquiry".') (citation omitted). Where the facts could have been discovered through the exercise of due diligence, reliance will not be deemed justified or reasonable. See, e.g., *Superior Reality Co. v. Cardiff Realty, Inc.*, 126 A.D.2d 633, 634, 511 N.Y.S.2d 70, 71 (2d Dep't 1987). New York courts are disinclined to find justifiable reliance '[w]here sophisticated businessmen engage in major transactions' and enjoy access to critical information but 'fail to take advantage of that access'. *Keywell Corp. v. Weinstein*, 33 F.3d 159, 164 (2d Cir. 1994) citing *Grumman Allied Industries v. Rohr Industries, Inc.*, 748 F.2d 729, 737 (2d Cir. 1984); see also *Most v. Monti*, 91 A.D.2d 606, 607, 456 N.Y.S.2d 427, 428 (2d Dep't 1982).

[58] "Q-Z has failed to prove by clear and convincing evidence the elements of fraudulent inducement. This failure is most apparent in connection with the element of reliance. *See Rotanelli v. Madden*, 172 A.D.2d 815, 816, 569 N.Y.S.2d 187, 188 (2d Dep't 1991) (holding reliance is a required element for fraudulent misrepresentation). Even though YY was not an expert in M&A transactions, he was a sophisticated businessman – the CEO of a multimillion dollar firm. He could readily discover the truth of the representations made by S in his letter, but chose not to examine Q's financial statements before entering into the Agreement. YY had an attorney who negotiated the specific terms of Agreement before YY signed the Agreement, but that attorney did not ask for any financial information regarding Q. YY was certainly aware that certain financial information could be checked, because he had his accountant run a retail credit check on Q before entering into the Agreement. Thus, YY chose to obtain certain information, but apparently was not interested in other information at the time.

[59] "Accordingly, YY did not 'reasonably rely' on any of Q's alleged 'misrepresentations'. Moreover, YY chose not to terminate the Agreement despite his assertions that he was aware, as early as [the first year of the Agreement], of what he perceived as the falsity of Q's financial representations prior to signing the Agreement. Having failed to terminate the Agreement and having admitted

that he 'wanted to stay part of the [Q] organization', YY can hardly expect to recoup damages for his two-year investment in Q-Z that he knowingly continued despite his awareness of what he now alleges was fraud on the part of Q. Respondent's argument that Q fraudulently induced YY to enter into the Agreement appears to be an afterthought on YY's part in an attempt to justify Q-Z's subsequent actions.

[60]   "For the foregoing reasons, the tribunal finds that Q did not fraudulently induce Q-Z into entering and performing the Agreement. Thus, Q-Z is bound by the provisions of the Agreement."

(. . . .)

VIII.   DEALS

[61]   The sole arbitrator examined Q-Z's claims that it was denied fees relating to several transactions, holding that in one instance Q had properly followed the contractual procedure in deciding that no fee was due, and in the others, no fee was due, inter alia, because Q-Z had materially breached the Agreement.

IX.   DAMAGES

[62]   "Q seeks compensatory damages for the MM/U success fee from the date of the material breach of the contract. Q's claim for compensatory damages is granted for the reasons set forth above in [7]-[9]. In addition, Q seeks liquidated damages for Q-Z's breach of the non-solicitation clause. Q's claim for liquidated damages is granted to the extent and for the reasons set forth above in [18]-[42]. In turn, Q-Z's claims for compensatory damages are denied in their entirety for the reasons set forth above." In addition, the sole arbitrator denied Q-Z's claim for punitive damages because of Q-Z's material breach of the Agreement and the denial of Q-Z's claims for fraudulent inducement and tortious interference with Q-Z's contacts.

X.   INTEREST

[63]   "Under New York CPLR 5001(a)(b), Q is owed 9% interest from 'the earliest ascertainable date the cause of action existed' for failure to pay the fee based on the MM/U transaction. The interest in this case begins to run from the date when Q's cause of action accrued. . . . Q's cause of action accrued on [the date the termination was effective], and the 9% interest on the award runs from [that date] until Q receives full payment of the sum awarded.

[64]   "With respect to the claim for breach of the non-solicitation clause for which liquidated damages have been awarded, the tribunal concludes that

interest should not be awarded on this sum since both the parties agreed to the fixed sum as the full measure of liquidated damages."

XI.   COSTS

[65]   "Clause 10(2)(b) of the Agreement states that 'the arbitrator shall divide costs incurred in conducting the arbitration in his final award in accordance with what he deems just and equitable under the circumstances'. In light of Q-Z's wrongful conduct in withholding the MM/U fee from Q, the tribunal finds that Q-Z should bear the entire costs of the proceeding. By withholding the MM/U fee from Q, Q-Z unnecessarily prolonged resolution of this dispute and generating a host of claims against Q, thereby forcing Q to engage in lengthy arbitration proceedings to recover a fee to which it was clearly entitled under the Agreement. Therefore, it is just and equitable that Q-Z pays the full costs of this arbitration proceeding in their entirety."

Final award in case no. 10274 of 1999

Parties:	Claimant: Dairy and agricultural company D (Denmark) Respondent: Poultry producer B (Egypt)
Place of arbitration:	Copenhagen, Denmark
Published in:	Unpublished
Subject matters:	– applicable law to substance – 1955 Hague Convention on the Law Applicable to International Sales of Goods – *Kompetenz-Kompetenz* – formation of contract – 1980 UN Sales Convention (CISG) – installment contract – breach of contract – calculation of damages – applicable law to interest

Facts

A dairy and agricultural product dealer, D, regularly sold feed products to a poultry company, B. Their usual practice was that D would telefax the complete contract to B which would stamp and sign the last page and telefax that page to D. D would then forward pro forma invoices to B and B would open corresponding letters of credit. In the case at issue, D allegedly concluded two contracts with B, one for the supply of 400 metric tons (mts) of feed product A and the other for 2000 mts of feed product B. In each case, the delivery was to be made in four installments. The parties subsequently disagreed as to whether the contracts were actually signed and accepted. D sent pro forma invoices to B for the first installments, one set, dated 2 December, referred to feed product A; the other set of invoices dated 7 January of the following year, referred to feed product B. B opened letters of credit covering the shipment of 100 metric tons (mts) of feed product A and 500 mts of feed product B. D accepted the letters of credit.

On 14 January, D concluded two contracts with a feed producer, one for 400 mts of feed product A and the other for 2,000 mts of feed product B.

Both contracts named B as the designated importer, indicated four different dates for various shipments and referred to the letters of credit that been opened by B. On 26 January, D telefaxed B informing B that due to problems with its supplier, the shipment of 100 mts of feed product A and 500 mts of feed product B would be shipped on 28 February, and that the following shipment would be ready on 2 April. The invoices for the February shipment were sent on 16 and 28 February respectively.

After arrival of the goods, B telefaxed D on 13 April, complaining that the shipment of feed product B comprised 499 instead of 500 mts. Furthermore, there had been problems related to the delayed transmittal of a veterinary certificate and the carrier had discharged the goods at the wrong location in the port. D responded on the same day that it would issue a credit note for the value of the missing amount, but would not compensate B for the other alleged losses which it did not consider to be its responsibility. D also informed B that the April shipment had been rebooked for 24 April and asked B to confirm the opening of letters of credit for that shipment by 14 April. Otherwise, D would consider the contracts to be "null and void". On 14 April, B telefaxed D that it was astonished by D's reluctance to reimburse them for the other losses. This was followed by a second telefax reading:

> "Due to the problem and losses we bear in every deal we work together and due to the shipment has not been released due to your delay in sending the certificate and your insist (sic) not to pay your fault, we are obliged to inform you that any further shipment will not [sic] before July."

D responded the same day writing that the contract at issue was cancelled and that it would not continue to do business with B. However, on 30 April, D telefaxed B a settlement offer, stating that if the offer was not accepted, it would sell the goods elsewhere. No settlement was reached and D agreed with its supplier K that it would only take delivery of 1,500 mts of feed product B and that 300 mts of feed product A would be kept by K at no charge to D. On 29 July, D concluded a contract with trade company O for the delivery of 1,500 mts of feed product B at a lower price than the price it would have received from B.

D claimed damages from B for loss of profit. When B did not respond, D initiated ICC arbitration. The arbitration clause in the contracts provided for arbitration in Copenhagen, to be conducted in English. A sole arbitrator was appointed. At the oral hearing, the claim against a second respondent, Dr. W, was withdrawn by D.

The sole arbitrator first determined the applicable substantive law to be applied. Each party argued, respectively, for the application of its national law. Relying on Art. 17 of the ICC Rules which, absent a choice of law by the parties, allows the arbitral tribunal to apply the rules of law which it deems appropriate, the sole arbitrator looked to Art. 4(1) of the Rome Convention and Art. 3 of the 1955 Hague Convention on the Law Applicable to International Sales of Goods, both of which led to the domestic law of the country of the seller, i.e., Danish law. Denmark was a party to the 1980 United Nations Convention on Contracts for the International Sale of Goods (CISG), but had made a reservation with regard to Part II of the CISG. Thus the obligations under the contracts and the contractual remedies were governed by the CISG but Danish law (without the incorporation of the CISG) applied to the formation of the alleged contracts.

The respondent challenged the jurisdiction of the arbitral tribunal, alleging that the contracts containing the arbitration clauses had never been concluded. The sole arbitrator, relying on the doctrine of *Kompetenz-Kompetenz*, examined if the contracts had actually been concluded in order to determine if the parties had agreed to arbitration. After examining the documentary materials submitted by the parties, and the conduct of the parties, the sole arbitrator concluded that the parties had concluded the contracts, including the arbitration clauses although "one could have imagined a more professional way to document the conclusion of the delivery contract on the part of the claimant as supplier".

D claimed damages for lost profits with respect to the contract for feed product A and the difference in the sale price for feed product B which had been sold later at a lower price. The sole arbitrator, applying Art. 25 CISG, found that the contracts had been breached when B failed to open the required letter of credit for the second installment and refused to accept any further shipment before July. According to Art. 73 CISG, D was entitled to avoid the contracts. Applying Arts. 74 and 75 CISG, the sole arbitrator awarded damages to D for lost profit with respect to feed product A contract and for the price differential arising from the later sale of feed product B. Interest was calculated under the law of the forum state, the Danish *Rentelover*, at the rate of 5% per annum over the applicable discount rate of the Danish Bank, from the date of the request for arbitration.

Excerpt

I.   APPLICABLE LAW

[1]   "The parties are of conflicting opinions as to which substantive law should be applied by the tribunal in general and namely with regard to the issue of formation of contracts. Claimant is of the opinion that contracts of sale should be governed by the law of the seller's country. In the case at hand this would be Danish law since claimant is a Danish party. Respondent refers to Art. 4 of the EC Convention on the Law Applicable to Contractual Obligations (Rome Convention). While this Convention is not directly applicable in the case at hand, as respondent concedes, respondent nevertheless sees the Rome Convention as a statement of generally applicable conflict rules.

[2]   "Art. 4(1) Rome Convention states that to the extent that the law applicable to the contract has not been explicitly chosen, the contract shall be governed by the law of the country with which it is most closely connected. Furthermore, it shall be presumed that the contract is most closely connected with the country where the party effecting the performance characteristic of the contract has, at the time of conclusion of the contract, its central administration. Respondent argues that these factors point to Egypt and thus, Egyptian substantive law should apply.

[3]   "The ICC Rules of Arbitration (ICC Rules) provide in Art. 17(1) with respect to the substantive law to be applied by the arbitrators that the parties shall be free to agree upon the rules of law to be applied by the arbitral tribunal to the merits of the dispute. In the absence of any such agreement, the arbitral tribunal shall apply the rules of law which it determines to be appropriate. In the case at hand the parties have not agreed upon the rules of law to be applied by the tribunal. Even if the alleged contracts including the arbitration clauses were concluded by the parties, they do not contain a choice of law provision.

[4]   "Thus, the tribunal must determine which rules of law are appropriate for the settlement of the dispute in the case at hand. Art. 17(1) ICC Rules, which states that the tribunal shall apply the rules of law which it determines to be appropriate, gives the tribunal broad discretion for its decision. The provision of Art. 17(1) ICC Rules does not provide for specific rules for the choice of law that the tribunal should apply. However, the freedom of the tribunal in the choice of law process does not liberate it from applying some system of law to govern the substance of the contract.[1]

---

1. "Reisman/Craig/Park/Paulsson, *International Commercial Arbitration* (New York 1997) p. 708."

[5]   "The tribunal hereby confirms the opinion expressed in its Procedural Order No. 2 relating to the applicable law. Thus, the CISG contains the generally applicable law. However, with respect to the contract formation, Danish law applies.

[6]   "Generally, the United Nations Convention on Contracts for the International Sale of Goods (CISG) is applicable since both Denmark and Egypt are parties to the Convention and have thus, both incorporated the CISG in their domestic law.[2] Denmark, however, has made a reservation with regard to Part II (Formation of the Contract) of the Convention.[3] Thus, with respect to the issue of the formation of the contracts here in dispute (and only with respect to this issue), the CISG (as part of Egyptian domestic law) is only applicable if Egyptian law applies. The CISG would not be applicable if Danish law applies since Denmark has, as stated above, made a reservation excluding the application of the CISG for issues relating to the formation of contracts.

[7]   "Both parties refer to principles that are well known in the choice of law discussion. Claimant's position is contained in the Convention on the Law Applicable to International Sales of Goods, agreed at The Hague, on 15 June 1955. Art. 3 of this Convention provides that in default of a law which was declared applicable by the parties a sale shall be governed by the domestic law of the country in which the vendor has his habitual residence at the time when he receives the order. As mentioned above, respondent's position is contained in the Rome Convention.

[8]   "It can be left open, however, which principle applies in the case at hand since both principles agree that Danish law applies with respect to the issue of formation of contracts. This is the clear result if the tribunal would follow claimant's position, because claimant as the seller is a Danish party. Should the tribunal follow respondent's position, the result would also be the application of Danish law, because (contrary to respondent's contention) Denmark (and not Egypt) is the country most closely connected with the contracts here in question.

[9]   "The goods to be sold are produced in Denmark, claimant as the seller is a Danish party and respondent has to fulfill its main obligation (which is payment of the purchase price) in Denmark. Even though the Rome Convention is not applicable in the case at hand, it underlines the tribunal's result because Art. 4(2) of the Rome Convention refers to the country where the party who is to effect the performance characteristic of the contract has its central administration.

---

2. "Schlechtriem, *Commentary on the UN Convention on the International Sale of Goods (CISG)*, 2nd ed. (Munich 1998) p. 707."

3. "Ibid."

Since the contract at hand is a sales contract, *the characteristic performance is effected by the claimant as the seller who is residing in Denmark*. Thus,

– the obligations under the alleged contracts and the contractual remedies are generally governed by the CISG.
– However, with regard to the issue of the formation of the alleged contracts (and only with regard to this issue), Danish law (without incorporation of the CISG) applies."

II.   JURISDICTION AND FORMATION OF CONTRACTS

[10]   "Even though respondent challenges the jurisdiction of the tribunal by alleging that the arbitration clauses here in dispute have never been concluded, the tribunal has jurisdiction to decide about the issue of jurisdiction based on the *Kompetenz-Kompetenz* doctrine. There is substantial agreement that in international commercial arbitration the arbitrator should, in ordinary circumstances, have the power to determine his or her own jurisdiction without prior recourse to the courts.[4] The *Kompetenz-Kompetenz* doctrine holds that arbitrators are competent, at least as an initial matter, to rule on their own competence to hear the dispute.[5]

[11]   "The tribunal has jurisdiction if the parties concluded an agreement to arbitrate, which gives the tribunal the power to settle the dispute here in question. Since the arbitration clause invoked by claimant is contained in the same document as that on which claimant relies as proof for the conclusion of the delivery contracts, the issue of jurisdiction is identical to the issue of whether or not the parties have concluded such alleged contracts. Thus, the issues of the conclusion of an agreement to arbitrate and the conclusion of the contracts here in question, will be dealt with together.

[12]   "Claimant alleges that it entered into two delivery contracts relating to feed product A and feed product B on 2 and 22 December with respondent, and such contracts at the same time contained the alleged arbitration clause. According to the claimant, the contracts were concluded in the way that the contractual document was sent via telefax to respondent, who sent it back via telefax stamped and signed to document its acceptance.

[13]   "Respondent alleges that it did not sign the contractual documents and that, as a result, the arbitration clause contained in such documents does not confer jurisdiction. Respondent furthermore alleges that the Exhibits provided by the claimant relating to the contracts are forgeries since respondent neither

---

4. "Reisman/Craig/Park/Paulsson, op. cit., p. 646."
5. "Reisman/Craig/Park/Paulsson, op. cit., p. 540."

had them in hand nor stamped or signed them. In the event that the tribunal assumes the alleged contracts to have been concluded amongst the parties, respondent argues that the content of the contracts was subsequently changed, because claimant accepted letters of credit that were not conforming with the alleged contracts.

[14] "Under Danish law the pertinent rules with regard to the conclusion of contracts are contained in Sects. 1 to 9 of the Law of Agreements and Other Legal Transactions in the Field of Property Law (*Aftaleloven*). According to these provisions, contracts are concluded by offer and acceptance. The burden of proof for the conclusion of a contract is on the party claiming rights out of the contract. Since the arbitration clause is also a contract, the same rules are applicable for the arbitration clause. Thus, in the case at hand the claimant must establish the conclusion of the alleged contracts and of an arbitration clause for each alleged contract.

[15] "As proof for the conclusion of the alleged contracts, including arbitration clauses, claimant offered copies of the pages that it alleges to have sent to respondent and the original telefax receipt pages of signature pages (allegedly resent by respondent). These documentary materials, together with the conduct of the parties, are sufficient for the tribunal to find that the parties concluded the contracts at hand, including arbitration clauses conferring jurisdiction on the tribunal. The tribunal comes to this conclusion even though one could have imagined a more professional way to document the conclusion of delivery contracts on the part of the claimant as supplier. With such an improved practice the current dispute might even have been avoided. Nevertheless, the tribunal finds that claimant has met its burden of proof.

[16] "Claimant was ordered by the tribunal to deliver original documents regarding the conclusion of the contracts."

1. The First Contract (Feed Product A)

[17] "In the Oral Hearing in Copenhagen, claimant provided for the *sale of 400 mts of feed product A* an original telefax page (Exhibit 2a). This page contains the stamp of respondent together with a signature, as well as the telefax address of respondent on the top of the page. Claimant has further provided a copy of a contractual document (Exhibit 1) and a copy of the last page of a contractual document (Exhibit 2, which appears to be a copy of the original telefax page later submitted as Exhibit 2a). The last page of Exhibit 1 bears the stamp of the claimant together with a signature. Exhibit 2 and 2a show the stamp of respondent together with a signature. Contents and format of the last page of Exhibit 1 appear to be identical with Exhibit 2 respectively Exhibit 2a.

[18]   "After reviewing the provided evidence, the tribunal comes to the conclusion that there are two possible courses of events with regard to the alleged contract for the sale of 400 mts of feed product A. The first possibility is that claimant sent via telefax a *signed* version of the contractual document to respondent (Exhibit 1). Respondent received the document but lost it somehow or, telefax transmission problems occurred so that it was necessary for claimant to send respondent another *unsigned* copy on which respondent could express its consent. Respondent stamped and signed the last page of such copy and sent it back to claimant (Exhibit 2 and original in Exhibit 2a). The signed version of the contract sent to respondent by the claimant would under such assumption qualify as an offer. This offer was accepted by respondent by signing and stamping the copy of the last page of the document.

[19]   "The second possibility is that claimant sent an *unsigned* copy (unsigned by claimant) of the contractual document to respondent who, after stamping and signing it, sent the last page back to claimant (Exhibits 2 and 2a). Claimant, after having received the stamped and signed page from respondent, stamped and signed another copy of the last page of the contractual document. In this case the sending of the unsigned copy of the contractual document qualifies as an invitation to make an offer. Respondent made this offer by sending back the stamped and signed last page of the contractual document (Exhibits 2 and 2a). Claimant accepted this offer by stamping and signing another copy of the contractual document (Exhibit 1).

[20]   "Thus, even if the facts are allowing two possibilities as to how a contract regarding the sale of 400 mts was concluded between the parties, the tribunal finds that the respective contract was concluded between the parties since both possibilities lead to the conclusion of the formation of the contract."

2.   The Second Contract (Feed Product B)

[21]   "With regard to the *2,000 mts of feed product B contract* the situation is more complicated. Claimant also provided a copy of a contract document with a signature page showing its stamp and signature (Exhibit 3 last page), a copy of the last page of the contractual document showing stamps and signatures of both claimant and respondent (Exhibit 4), and finally an original telefax page showing the telefax address of respondent at the top and stamps and signatures of respondent and claimant on the bottom (Exhibit 4a). The content and format of Exhibit 4a (and Exhibit 4) are identical with Exhibit 2a. Respondent's telefax address appears on the top of Exhibits 4 and 4a as well as the receiving time which shows that Exhibit 4a was received two minutes after Exhibit 2a. Both Exhibit 4a and Exhibit 2a are stamped and signed by respondent. The position of the appearing signature shows, however, that Exhibits 4a and 4 are not copies of Exhibit 2a. The signature on Exhibits 4a and 4 is situated inside the stamp of

respondent. On Exhibit 2a it is situated at the upper part of the stamp. Consequently, the representative of respondent stamped and signed Exhibit 2a as well as Exhibit 4a, and thus *two* different signature pages.

[22]   "Exhibit 3 last page shows two different dates under the provided signature lines for buyer and seller. . . . Exhibit 3 last page, however, is not identical with Exhibits 4 and 4a in that claimant's stamp on the copy is in another position than on the telefax page. Furthermore, the content is different. Under the heading 'Force major' the Exhibits 4 and 4a (unlike the last page of Exhibit 3) have the additional provision that 'the shipper shall not be responsible for any changing matters in connection with this contract'.

[23]   "Again, there appear to be, in the tribunal's finding, also in the case of the second contract two possible courses of events. The first possibility is that claimant sent via telefax a *signed* version of the contractual document. Respondent lost this copy somehow, or, other reasons caused claimant to send another copy to respondent. This time, claimant, for whatever reason, did not send the last page of the original contractual document but sent another copy of the last page of a contract form used by claimant in other cases such as for the sale of 400 mts of feed product A. Respondent stamped and signed this copy and sent it back via telefax to claimant. Claimant, even though it had already signed the first copy of the contractual document, which was sent to respondent, (again) stamped and signed the received page from respondent.

[24]   "Here, the stamped and signed copy of the contractual document, which was sent via telefax from claimant to respondent, qualifies as an offer (Exhibit 3). Respondent accepted this offer by stamping and signing the second copy of the contractual document (Exhibits 4 and 4a). The fact that the second transmitted copy was a last page of another contract form (for instance the sale of 400 mts of feed product A) is not detrimental for the contract formation as long as *the signature* of this page had to be viewed from the vantage point of the claimant as recipient as the acceptance of the second contract (2000 mts of feed product B).

[25]   "In this context it is important that on 22 December *two* contracts were under consideration for both of which claimant had submitted to respondent either an offer or an invitation to make an offer. Respondent clearly returned *two* different signature pages. The location of the signature in the stamp suggests that the pages were individually signed. Consequently, the claimant as recipient was urged to assume that respondent as sender of the two different pages wanted to accept two different contracts (and not send twice the acceptance of only one contract). Thus, the tribunal concludes that a contract regarding the sale of 2,000 mts of feed product B was concluded between claimant and respondent.

[26]   "The second possibility is, again, that claimant sent an *unsigned* copy of the contractual document to respondent. For reasons that are unknown to the tribunal, it was necessary to send respondent via telefax another copy of the last

page of the contractual document for which claimant used the last page of another contract form (for instance for the sale of 400 mts of feed product A). If the events happened like this, the sending of the unsigned copy of the contractual document qualifies as an invitation to make an offer to conclude a contract for the sale of 2,000 mts of feed product B addressed to respondent. Respondent made this offer, even though it signed a page that was originally a last page of another contract form. Claimant accepted this offer by stamping and signing Exhibit 4a. Both possibilities lead to the conclusion that a contract for the sale of 2,000 mts of feed product B was concluded between the parties. Thus, the tribunal finds that a contract for the sale of 2,000 mts of feed product B was concluded between the parties in addition to the contract for the sale of 400 mts of feed product A.

[27]   "The defenses made by respondent do not convince the tribunal.

[28]   "(i) As far as respondent alleges never to have seen the contracts in question, respondent could not provide a reasonable explanation why the Exhibits 2a and 4a *bear the telefax address of respondent.* The usual way telefax machines are working is that they print the address of the sender on the received telefax sheets. Thus, the telefax address on the Exhibits 2a and 4a are a strong sign for the fact that they were dispatched from a telefax machine controlled by respondent.

[29]   "Thus, the tribunal assumes (absent any explanation by respondent to the contrary) that respondent has seen the contracts at hand and sent two individually signed signature pages at two different times (02.34 p.m. and 02.36 p.m.), however, on the same day from its telefax machine to claimant.

[30]   "(ii) As far as respondent alleges that the parties usually concluded contracts in a way that claimant sent pro forma invoices and respondent opened letters of credit if it wanted to contract with the claimant, the allegations by respondent are contradictory. In its Post Hearing Submission, respondent explains the fact that its telefax address appears on Exhibits 2a and 4a by alleging that these Exhibits relate to other contracts that were already executed. Thus, there must have been contracts between the parties that were concluded in the same way as the contracts here in dispute.

[31]   "(iii) Furthermore, respondent alleges that the stamped contract pages are mere forgeries and are not signed by respondent. The tribunal could not determine that the Exhibits 2a and 4a are forgeries. Besides the allegation that the documents in question are forgeries, respondent provided in addition to the mere denial of the document's authenticity, no evidence that could lead to the conclusion that the documents are forged.

[32]   "Respondent could have provided a copy of its original stamp so that the tribunal could have compared the original stamp with the stamp appearing on the Exhibits 2a and 4a. Furthermore, both Exhibits show a signature (however in

different places) in the stamp of respondent. Regarding this signature, respondent also provided no original signatures of its representatives for the purpose of comparison. Thus, the provided information and evidence by respondent is not sufficient to establish that the Exhibits 2a and 4a are forgeries. It is the tribunal's finding that they are authentic telefax receipts, evidencing respondent's acceptance of the two contracts here in question (first possibility) or offers for the conclusion of the contracts here in question (second possibility).

[33] "(iv) Moreover, the allegations by respondent that it has not seen the contracts and the signed contract pages to be forgeries, *are not consistent with the conduct of respondent.* During the discussion between the parties prior to the arbitration respondent received several times documents by the claimant that refer to the shipment of 400 mts of feed product A and 2,000 mts of feed product B. The list of such documents starts with the pro forma invoices for the shipment of the installments (Exhibits 7 to 16). Even though the pro forma invoices do not refer to the concluded contracts, they refer exactly to the goods for which the contracts were concluded. In addition, the majority of the provided pro forma invoices (Exhibits 8-11, 13, 15, 16) clearly order opening the respective letter of credit 'in full *for all 4 consignments*' (emphasis added).

[34] "In Exhibit 23, claimant refers to a lot that 'was due for you on shipment on 14 April . . . '. In his telefax dated 14 April claimant expressly refers to 'Contract 2,000 mt danish mbm 55% as well as 400 mt danish feed product A'.

[35] "In all his responses, *respondent did not object once in a way that only the shipment of 100 mts of feed product A and 500 mts of feed product B was agreed.* Respondent did not only fail to object, it refers to future shipments in his telefax dated 14 April (Exhibit 25). Even though respondent had no legal duty to object in order to protect its rights, the conduct of respondent nevertheless shows in the tribunal's evaluation that it knew of the contracts and assumed them to be valid. Consequently, the conduct of respondent confirms the tribunal's finding that respondent entered into the contracts here in dispute with claimant.

[36] "(v) The fact that the last page of Exhibit 3 shows two different dates under the provided signature lines for buyer and seller . . . has no legal consequences. It appears to the tribunal that this discrepancy is based on a simple typing error. According to the content of Exhibit 3 all four installments had to be delivered by July. Thus, it appears that the correct date is 2 December of the previous year and as for as the year appearing on the buyer's side it should be the [previous] year.

[37] "(vi) Finally, the argumentation of respondent with respect to the content of the contracts is not convincing to the tribunal. It cannot be concluded that the content of the contracts remained open from the fact that respondent only signed and returned the last page of the contracts. For an acceptance, it is required that the accepting party expresses its consent in an unequivocal

form. However, in the case at hand it was not necessary that respondent expressed its consent by sending *all pages* of the contract signed and stamped to claimant. Sending the last page of each contract was sufficient to express the consent and thereby to accept the contracts. This is also in accordance with accepted practices and customs in international trade.

[38] "(vii) Lastly, the content of the contracts was, in the evaluation of the tribunal, not changed by the claimant accepting two letters of credit that cover only one installment of each contract. Respondent issued two letters of credit that were not conforming to the contracts because they did not cover the full amount of the contracts, but rather only one installment of each contract. However, by accepting a performance that is nonconforming, the accepting party does not necessarily express its consent to change the whole contract. In the absence of further statements to this effect, a party who accepts a lesser security for a delivery contract than was originally contracted does not express its intention to reduce the volume of the contract to the amount of the security. Consequently, the tribunal finds that claimant did not express his consent to change the contracts into sales contracts for 100 mts of feed product A and 500 mts of feed product B by accepting the nonconforming letters of credit.

[39] "(viii) Thus, the tribunal holds that claimant and respondent entered into two contracts one for the sale of 400 mts of feed product A and the other for the sale of 2,000 mts of feed product B. Both contracts contain *an arbitration clause conferring jurisdiction to the tribunal for the dispute at hand.*"

III.   AVOIDANCE AND DAMAGES

[40] "With regard to the issues of avoidance and damages as well as the quantum of claimant's claim, the two contracts must be taken individually in account, since the claimed damages follow different rules."

1.   Feed Product A

[41] "It is uncontested that claimant reached an agreement with the producer K according to which K would keep the remaining 300 mts of feed product A at no cost to claimant. Thus, claimant demands payment of lost profits under the contract. Respondent is of the opinion that its conduct with regards to the remaining 300 mts of feed product A does not constitute a fundamental breach under Art. 25 CISG.

[42] "With regard to damages, the applicable law is the CISG (see above [1]-[9].). Since the parties in the case at hand concluded an installment contract, the legal consequences for the installment announced for April and the installments following this shipment must be separately distinguished."

a. Installment Announced for April

[43] "The provision of Art. 73(1) CISG states that in the case of a contract for delivery of goods by installments, if the failure of one party to perform any of its obligation with respect to any installment constitutes a fundamental breach of contract with respect to that installment, the other party may declare the contract avoided with respect to that installment.[6]

[44] "According to Art. 25 CISG, a breach of contract committed by one of the parties is fundamental if it results in such detriment to the other party as to substantially deprive him of what he is entitled to expect under the contract, unless the party in breach did not foresee and a reasonable person of the same kind in the same circumstances would not have foreseen such a result.[7]

[45] "After the shipment of the first installment, claimant announced the shipment of the next installment in his telefax dated 26 January and requested respondent to open the necessary letter of credit. Respondent did not open the required letter of credit causing claimant to rebook the shipment. By telefax dated 13 April, claimant again demanded the letter of credit. According to the contract, respondent was obligated to deliver the letter of credit and to accept the installment.

[46] "Respondent refused to deliver the letter of credit. In addition, respondent declared in its telefax dated 14 April that it will not accept any further shipment before July [of that year]. The conduct of respondent constitutes a fundamental breach according to Art. 25 CISG in two ways. First, respondent delayed and finally refused the delivery of the required letter of credit, thus causing claimant to rebook the shipment which resulted in more costs for the claimant. This conduct alone constitutes a fundamental breach because it deprived the claimant of what it could expect under the sales contract.

[47] "Second, respondent refused to accept any installment before July. According to the contract concluded between the parties, the last installment was to be shipped in July/August. Thus, the statement of respondent in its telefax dated 14 April can be seen as a final refusal to perform because the installment following the April installment was already due for May/June. Consequently, respondent declared that it will not accept the April installment. A final refusal of performance constitutes a fundamental breach in the sense of Art. 25 CISG.[8]

[48] "Under the contract, claimant was entitled to expect that respondent accepts the shipment of the different installments. By his final refusal to

6. "Schlechtriem, op. cit., p. 542."
7. "Ibid., p. 173."
8. "Ibid., Art. 25, note 17."

accept the April installment, respondent deprived claimant of what claimant was entitled to expect under the contract. Furthermore, respondent did foresee this result as well as any reasonable person of the same kind would have foreseen this result. Thus, the tribunal finds that the conduct of respondent with respect to the April installment of 100 mts of feed product A constitutes a fundamental breach according to Art. 25 CISG. Under Art. 73(1) CISG[9] claimant was entitled to declare the contract avoided with respect to the April installment of feed product A. Claimant declared the avoidance in his telefax dated 14 April.

[49]   "The avoidance of the April installment results in the applicability of Art. 81 CISG which states that the avoidance of the contract releases both parties from their obligations under it, subject to any damage which may be due."

b.   Installments due for May/June and July/August

[50]   "With regard to the last two installments under the contract Art. 73(2) CISG is the applicable provision. Under Art. 73(2) CISG one party may declare the installment contract avoided for the future if the other party's failure to perform any of its obligations in respect of any installment gives good grounds to conclude that a fundamental breach of contract will occur with respect to future installments.[10]

[51]   "The pertinent conduct of respondent is the telefax dated 14 April. Respondent declared that it will not accept any further installment before July, although respondent must have known that it was obligated under the contract to accept at least the March/April installment and May/June installment. In this context respondent also refused to deliver letters of credit for the March/April installment.

[52]   "This conduct with respect to the March/April installment gave claimant good grounds to conclude that a fundamental breach of contract will also occur with respect to the May/June installment and the July/August installment. By declaring not to accept any further installment before July, respondent made clear that it will neither deliver letters of credit for the May/June installment nor

---

9. Art. 73(1) of the 1980 United Nations Convention on Contracts for the International Sale of Goods (CISG) reads:

   "(1) In the case of a contract for delivery of goods by instalments, if the failure of one party to perform any of his obligations in respect of any instalment constitutes a fundamental breach of contract with respect to that instalment, the other party may declare the contract avoided with respect to that instalment."

10. "Schlechtriem, op. cit., p. 542."

accept this installment which would have constituted a fundamental breach according to Art. 25 CISG.

[53] "Thus, the tribunal finds that claimant was entitled to declare the contract avoided also for the future. Claimant declared the avoidance in his telefax dated April 14. The avoidance results again, as in the case of the April delivery, in the applicability of Art. 81 CISG."

c. Damages

[54] "According to Art. 81 CISG, the claimant is entitled to damages. The pertinent provisions with regard to damages are Arts. 74 [et seq.] CISG. Art. 74 CISG provides that damages for breach of contract consist of a sum equal to the loss, including loss of profit, suffered as a consequence of the breach."

[55] The sole arbitrator noted that the claimant was able to reach an agreement with the producer K that K would keep the remaining 300 mts of feed product A at no cost for claimant. Claimant had claimed the lost profit under the contract, which amounted to the difference between the price at which it had purchased feed product A and its anticipated sales price to respondent and the sole arbitrator awarded this amount.

2. Feed Product B

[56] "With respect to the remaining 1,500 mts of feed product B, claimant alleges to have resold them to O. . . . [C]laimant demands the difference between the contract price and the price obtained in the cover sale.

[57] "Respondent alleges that even if claimant may have entered into a contract with O, this contract has never been performed, i.e., the contract has been concluded for the purpose of fabrication of a damage for the present arbitration. Furthermore, respondent alleges that the goods sold to O are different from the goods that should have been sold to respondent."

a. April Installments

[58] "Since the contract regarding the shipment of 2,000 mts of feed product B is an installment contract, Art. 73(1) CISG is again the applicable provision. The conduct of respondent with respect to the April installment of feed product B is identical to the April installment of feed product A. Thus, respondent refused to deliver the required letter of credit and finally refused to accept the shipment by refusing any further shipment before July. Consequently, the conduct of respondent with respect to the April installment of feed product B constitutes a fundamental breach according to Art. 25 CISG.

[59]   "Thus, the tribunal finds that claimant was entitled to declare the contract avoided with respect to the April installment of feed product B under Art. 73(1) CISG. Claimant declared the avoidance in his telefax dated 14 April. Thus, Art. 81 CISG is applicable."

b.   May/June and June/July Installments

[60]   "The applicable provision is Art. 73(2) CISG. The conduct of respondent with respect to the April installment gave claimant good grounds to conclude that a fundamental breach of contract will occur with respect to future installments, since respondent refused to deliver the required letter of credit and refused to accept any shipment before July. Thus, the tribunal finds that claimant was entitled to declare the contract avoided for the future under Art. 73(2) CISG. Claimant declared the contract avoided for the future in his telefax dated 14 April. Consequently, Art. 81 CISG is applicable."

c.   Damages

[61]   "With respect to the claimed damages, the situation for feed product B is different from the situation of feed product A because claimant could not reach an agreement with the producer K. The applicable provisions are again Arts. 74 et seq. CISG.

[62]   "Based on the provided documents, the tribunal finds that claimant concluded a contract with O for the sale of 1,500 mts of feed product B. This finding is based on the contract dated 29 July, and the undated statement by O. The tribunal could not find signs of these documents to be forgeries. Thus, it is the tribunal's finding that the documents are authentic.

[63]   "According to the contract, O purchased 1,500 mts of feed product B. . . . Due to the statement of O the tribunal is convinced that these 1,500 mts of feed product B are the goods ordered by the claimant to fulfill its obligation under the contract with respondent. O confirms that it bought 1,500 mts of feed product B from the claimant. The document is stamped and signed by O and even though it bears no date the tribunal sees no signs for the document to be forged in any way.

[64]   "According to Art. 75 CISG, the party claiming damages may recover the difference between the contract price and the price in the substitute transaction as well as any further damages recoverable under Art. 74 CISG if the contract is avoided and if, in a reasonable manner and within a reasonable time after avoidance the seller has resold the goods. In the case at hand, claimant as the seller declared the avoidance in April and resold the goods in July. In this context it is important to note that Art. 75 CISG, only requires that a contract has been

concluded. The contract does not have to have been performed yet.[11] Thus, it was sufficient in the case at hand that plaintiff proved the conclusion of the contract with O. Furthermore, it is important to note that under Art. 75 CISG a notice to the contract partner in breach prior to the resale is not required, notwithstanding the fact that claimant gave notice to respondent in his telefax dated 30 April.

[65]   "The goods are resold in a reasonable manner if the seller acted like a prudent and reasonable seller would have acted.[12] Claimant tried to resell the goods for more than two months before selling them to O for a price which was nearly 20% per mt less than the price agreed with respondent. Thus, claimant acted like a prudent and reasonable seller when selling the goods to O because it is not unreasonable to resell goods with a discount of nearly 20% after unsuccessfully trying to resell them at a higher price.

[66]   "Thus, the tribunal finds that, with regards to the 1,500 mts of feed product B, claimant is entitled to claim the difference between the price agreed with respondent and the price agreed with O. . . ."

III.   INTEREST

[67]   "According to Art. 78 CISG, one party to the contract is entitled to interest on the price or any other amount due, if the other party fails to pay. Thus, claimant in the case at hand is entitled to interest on the amounts claimant can demand from respondent. The applicable interest rate is not regulated by the CISG. Thus, this gap in the CISG has to be filled by the tribunal. Two approaches to this question have been suggested: first, an attempt could be made to refer to general principles of the CISG in order to determine the interest rate and so reach an international, uniform rule.[13] However, the (probably) majority view is that the interest rate should be determined by the domestic law applicable in accordance with the conflicts rules of the forum state.[14]

[68]   "The tribunal is of the opinion that the first mentioned approach is too broad to lead to satisfying results. It is not clear which general principles of the CISG relate to the issue of interest. Thus, the goal of the approach, to find a common interest rate, will never be reached. Consequently, the tribunal follows the second mentioned approach and determines the interest rate in the case at hand according to the applicable national law of the forum state.

---

11. "Ibid., Art. 75, note 3."
12. "Ibid., Art. 75, note 7."
13. "Ibid., Art. 78, note 21."
14. "Ibid."

[69]   "The interest rate is to be determined by the domestic law applicable in accordance with the conflicts rules of the forum state.[15] The forum state is Denmark since the place of arbitration in the case at hand is Copenhagen. In this context the tribunal follows claimant's argument that in the case of a sales contract the law of the seller's state should be applied. Denmark is a signatory to the Convention on the Law Applicable to International Sale of Goods agreed at The Hague in 1955. As mentioned above, Art. 3 of this Convention states that in default of a law declared applicable by the parties, a sale shall be governed by the domestic law of the country in which the vendor has his habitual residence at the time when he receives the order. Thus, the tribunal finds that, with regard to the issue of interest, Danish law is to apply.

[70]   "The applicable Danish law is the Law of Interest (hereinafter referred to as *Renteloven*). According to Sects. 3 and 5(2) *Renteloven* the applicable interest rate in the case at hand is 5% p.a. over the applicable discount rate of the Danish Bank. According to Sect. 3 *Renteloven*, the party in default is obligated to pay interest one month after the day a reminder was sent to the obliged party which contains the statement that the default will lead to the payment of interest. Besides, in case an action was started the obliged party may, however, claim interest from the day the suit was filed. By letter of its former counsel, claimant demanded payment from respondent on 16 September. This letter does not contain a statement with regards to interest. Thus, claimant can claim interest from the day the arbitration was requested. Thus, the tribunal finds that respondent is to pay interest in the amount of 5% over the discount rate of the Danish Bank from [the date the arbitration was initiated]."

IV.   COSTS

(. . . .)

[71]   "The provision of Art. 31(3) ICC Rules gives the tribunal broad discretion for the allocation of the costs. In its decision over the allocation of the costs the tribunal is guided by the win/loss proportion in the case at hand. The tribunal holds that claimant is entitled to the full amount of his request including interest. Thus, respondent lost to the full extent. For the tribunal it is therefore reasonable that generally respondent must bear the costs of the arbitration. Thus, respondent must bear the costs and expenses of the arbitrator and the ICC administrative expenses. . . .

[72]   "Respondent must also bear the legal costs of the claimant. However, in this context it is important to note that claimant changed counsel during the arbitration. Even though this act produced more costs since the new counsel of the claimant had

---

15. "Ibid."

to spen[d] time to get to know the case, claimant did not claim the costs for its former counsel. It is therefore reasonable for the tribunal to find that claimant can claim its submitted legal costs to the full amount. . . . Respondent has to bear its own legal costs.

[73]　"With respect to Dr. W, claimant withdrew the claim with consent of Dr. W and respondent. A claimant can withdraw a claim with consent of the respondent at any stage of the procedure. The legal consequence is, however, that generally the claimant must bear the legal costs of the respondent.[16] Dr. W has not specified his legal costs. In addition, Dr. W was represented by the same counsel as respondent. Thus, at least some part (however small) of the legal costs claimed by respondent was also caused by Dr. W. The tribunal estimates that part at roughly 10% of the counsel fees claimed by respondent. Thus, it is reasonable for the tribunal to make a deduction from claimant's legal costs in order to take the withdrawal into consideration. . . ."

---

16. "Reiner, *ICC-Schiedsgerichtsbarkeit* (Wien 1989) p. 240."

Final award in case no. 10329 of 2000

Parties:	Claimant: Seller D (Switzerland)
	Respondent: Buyer S (Italy)
Place of arbitration:	Geneva, Switzerland
Published in:	Unpublished
Subject matters:	– applicable law to formation of contract
	– formation of contract
	– formal validity of contract
	– power to represent company
	– enforceable arbitration award
	– arbitration agreement "in writing"
	– 1958 New York Convention, Art. II(2)
	– relationship 1980 UN Sales Convention (CISG) and national law
	– material mistake in entering contract due to negligence

Facts

S, as buyer, approached D, as seller for the purchase of a quantity of a industrial product. On 18 August, D confirmed by fax to S, the sale of a quantity of the product, according to the specifications and conditions mentioned in the fax. The stipulated condition of payment was "by irrevocable L/C at 90 days B/L date". Mr. M, on behalf of D, also stated in the fax that "our official order confirmation will follow shortly". Mr. A, president of S, wrote by hand on the fax, under the payment conditions "*E. O. remissa diretta*" [sic] (translation: "and/or directly payment 90 days"), countersigned the fax and sent it back to D on 18 August or shortly after that date. On 21 August, Mr. M of seller D faxed S a contract in the form of an "Order Confirmation" for the specified quantity of the product, asking S to send it back "duly countersigned for acceptance". The Order Confirmation provided for a letter of credit as a condition of payment as follows:

"by irrevocable letter of credit payable at 90 days from B/L date to be advised on [the bank] opened in favour of: D. . . . L/C to be opened by

14 September and to be payable against presentation of the following documents. . . ."

The Order Confirmation (also sometimes referred to by the parties as the contract) was dated 20 August and signed for D by Mr. K. The Order Confirmation was returned on or after 21 August, countersigned by the president of S, Mr. A, who had signed above the words "for acceptance". His signature was also on the other pages of the contract, together with the corporate stamp.

On 9 September, Mr. P, on behalf of D, sent by courier two originals of the contract that had been previously faxed, inviting S to "revert with one duly countersigned original for our reference". On 13 October, S's legal counsel wrote to D stating that the offer for the supply of the goods had been modified in respect of the condition of payment which, therefore, under Italian law, was to be considered as a new offer to which his client had not agreed. On 14 October, D informed S by fax that the goods were ready at the port of loading and were to be shipped the second half of October and on 16 October, D's legal counsel wrote to S, asking S to confirm that it was ready to perform its obligations under the contract. On 26 October, D's lawyers informed S that D was taking measures to mitigate its loss as a result of S having failed to take delivery of the goods and on 18 November, D sold the goods to a Filipino client at a reduced price.

Early the following year, D filed a request with the ICC for arbitration, relying on the arbitration clause in the contract which provided for ICC arbitration in Geneva. S contested the validity of the contract containing the arbitration clause and requested that the sole arbitrator render a preliminary award holding, inter alia, "that there was no binding arbitration agreement. The sole arbitrator in his Procedural Order No. 2, decided that the further examination of the case would not be limited to the preliminary issues.

The sole arbitrator dealt first with the question of the existence of a valid arbitration agreement. S had argued that it had never entered into a contract with D. The sole arbitrator applied the conflict rules of Art. 178(2) of the Swiss Private International Law Act (PILA) and found that in this case it would suffice for the substantive validity of the arbitration agreement that it conformed to Swiss law. However, S's only argument relating to the substantive validity of the arbitration agreement was that the parties had not agreed on the method of payment. This question, in the view of the arbitrator, did not affect the validity of the arbitration agreement and only should be examined with the merits of the case. According to Art. 178(1) PILA which sets out the formal requirements for an arbitration agreement, a valid arbitration agreement resulted, on the one hand, from the fax sent on 21 August by D to S, to which the "Order Confirmation" containing an arbitration clause was attached as confirmation of a buying order made by S on 18 August and, on the other hand, from the fact that the 21 August fax was returned signed by S. S had also argued that Mr. K did not have the power to bind D. According to the applicable law, which was Swiss law since D had its seat in Switzerland, even if an unauthorized agent had signed the contract, D had at least implicitly ratified the contract, in particular, by seeking its performance. The sole arbitrator also rejected S's argument that the award would be unenforceable under the 1958 New York Convention following the reasoning of "the majority of legal scholars and the Swiss Supreme Court" that Art. II(2) of the Convention must be interpreted in relation to Art. 7(2) of the UNCITRAL Model Law on International Commercial Arbitration and that "the formal requirements of the [1958 New York Convention] match up" with Art. 178(1) PILA which was inspired by the UNCITRAL Model Law.

The contract provided that it was governed by the laws of Switzerland which resulted in the application of the 1980 United Nations Convention on Contracts for the International Sale of Goods (CISG) and the application of the Swiss Code of Obligations for all matters not covered by the CISG. Applying the CISG, the sole arbitrator rejected S's argument that there was no binding contract between the parties because S had not signed and returned the original contract. This was because the contract's validity was not contingent on the use of the written form. The sole arbitrator accepted S's argument that initially no contract had been made between the parties because they had not agreed on a material term, the method of payment. However, by then signing above the words "for acceptance", and sending the contract back to D, S had accepted the terms of the contract. S also argued that A had signed without reading the contents in the belief that the contract had been altered to comply with his payment requirements. The sole arbitrator accepted that A had signed the contract in error and that S would not be bound by the contract which it had entered into under a "material mistake". However, since the error was due to A's negligence, S was bound to compensate for the resulting damage. Damages were awarded to D for the price difference resulting from the sale of the goods to the Filipino buyer.

Excerpt

(. . . .)

I. PRELIMINARY ISSUES

1. Arbitration Proceedings to be Limited to the Preliminary Issues?

[1] "Respondent had requested at the outset of this arbitration that the proceedings be limited to the examination of preliminary issues that should be

disposed by way of a partial award. In Procedural Order No. 2 the arbitrator dealt with these procedural questions and answered negatively for the first part thereof, while reserving his decision as for the second part."[1]
(. . . .)

2. Existence and Validity of the Arbitration Agreement

[2] "Respondent's submissions in this respect are threefold: first of all, respondent submits that a contract has never been entered into between the parties; secondly, it argues that claimant's representatives who intervened in this matter and eventually sent documents to respondent had no valid powers to bind their principal, i.e., claimant; thirdly, respondent submits that in case the arbitrator would retain jurisdiction over the matter, an arbitral award would not be enforceable due to the lack of a valid arbitration clause by application of the Convention on the Recognition and Enforcement of Foreign Arbitral Awards signed in New York (USA) on 10 June 1958 (hereinafter referred to as the New York Convention)."
(. . . .)

a. Existence of a Contract Between the Parties

[3] "Respondent explains that, as a matter of fact, it returned by fax claimant's fax of 18 August whereby it had expressed the will to have the '*E/O remissa diretta*' payment clause inserted in the Contract and, also by fax, the 20 August 'order confirmation' without understanding it but with its signature.

---

1. In Procedural Order No. 2, it was decided, inter alia, that:

"– the further examination of the case would not be limited to the preliminary issues; . . .
– the possiblity of rendering a partial (interim) arbitral award on preliminary issues after the Oral Hearing was reserved".

The sole arbitrator's reason were as follows:

"In so deciding, the arbitrator had considered Art. 20(1) of the ICC Rules, the very nature of the arbitral process that must be speedy and cost efficient, as well as the safe and fair administration of justice that is required for any arbitration. In addition, the arbitrator took into account the relatively low amount in contention and lack of real complexity of the issues to be determined. In addition, he considered that limiting the examination of the case to preliminary issues would manifestly be contrary to the principles referred to above. He had also paid due consideration to his right to decide any relevant issue or issues by way of partial (interim) award as provided for by the Terms of Reference and to the parties' observations made during the 4 October Procedural Hearing, as well as the arbitrator's duty to render an award within six months from the signature of the Terms of Reference, as prescribed by Art. 24(1) of the ICC Rules."

[4]   "Respondent also points out that no letter of credit has ever been opened by 14 September according to the terms of the Contract, which did not prompt any reaction from claimant thereon. Respondent concludes on the basis of these factual elements, together with the additional fact that it did not return duly signed the original Contract received from claimant by courier of 9 September, that no contract has ever been entered into between the parties and, as a result, no arbitration agreement was ever agreed upon.

[5]   "As a matter of law, respondent submits that no agreement was reached on the essential elements of the Contract according to Art. 1 of the Swiss Code of Obligations (hereinafter referred to as CO),[2] in particular as regards payment of the goods to be delivered. Claimant opposes to respondent the contents of Art. 178(3) of the Swiss Federal . . . Private International Law Act (hereinafter referred to as the PILA) which provides, inter alia, that the validity of an arbi-tration agreement cannot be contested on the ground that the main contract may not be valid. Pointing out that such provision establishes the well-known principle of severability of the arbitration agreement, claimant submits that respondent has not any of the possible exceptions to such principle such as a party's incapacity or the fact that the agreement has been signed under duress.

[6]   "On the merits, claimant acknowledges that respondent did not return the Contract received by courier duly countersigned, but stresses that this very same document was previously forwarded by fax from respondent to claimant. Claimant also adds that after the receipt of the Contract in original, respondent did not express any disagreement as to its contents until it was informed by claimant, on 14 October, that the goods were ready for shipment.

[7]   "As a matter of law, claimant, relying on the United Nations Convention on Contracts for the International Sale of Goods signed in Vienna (Austria) on 11 April 1980 (hereinafter referred to as the Vienna Convention or CISG) which it considers being applicable in the instant case, argues that its own fax of 18 August was a 'proposal for concluding' within the meaning of Art. 14 CISG.[3]

---

2. Art. 1 of the Swiss Code of Obligations (CO) reads:

"1. For a contract to be concluded, a manifestation of the parties' mutual assent is required.
2. Such manifestation may be either express or implied."

3. Art. 14 of the 1980 United Nations Convention on Contracts for the International Sale of Goods (CISG) reads in relevant part:

"(1) A proposal for concluding a contract addressed to one or more specific persons constitutes an offer if it is sufficiently definite and indicates the intention of the offeror to be bound in case of acceptance. A proposal is sufficiently definite if it indicates the goods and expressly or implicitly fixes or makes provision for determining the quantity and the price.
(. . . .)"

Such an offer was not altered by the handwritten note (*E/O remissa diretta*) of Mr. A because it contained the alternative 'and/or', thus falling under Art. 19(2) CISG.[4] Claimant adds that in any event the 'order confirmation' may be considered as a new offer subsequent to previous telephone conversations and correspondence between the parties that confirmed their agreement on all essential points of the transaction.

[8] "It also states that the Contract was returned – at least by fax – by respondent, signed on all pages and concludes that such agreement was final and binding upon the parties when received by claimant, pursuant to Arts. 18 and 23 CISG.[5]

[9] "On the issue of whether respondent had real intent to be bound by the Contract – as it did not return the originals – claimant, relying on Arts. 1 and 2 CO[6] and related case law, submits that, to the contrary, the parties had indeed reached mutual assent on all essential terms of the transaction and, in particular,

---

4. Art. 19 of the CISG reads:

"(1) A reply to an offer which purports to be an acceptance but contains additions, limitations or other modifications is a rejection of the offer and constitutes a counteroffer.

(2) However, a reply to an offer which purports to be an acceptance but contains additional or different terms which do not materially alter the terms of the offer constitutes an acceptance, unless the offeror, without undue delay, objects orally to the discrepancy or dispatches a notice to that effect. If he does not so object, the terms of the contract are the terms of the offer with the modifications contained in the acceptance.

3. Additional or different terms relating, among other things, to the price, payment, quality and quantity of the goods, place and time of delivery, extent of one party's liability to the other or the settlement of disputes are considered to alter the terms of the offer materially."

5. Art. 18 of the CISG reads in relevant part:

"(1) A statement made by or other conduct of the offeree indicating assent to an offer is an acceptance. Silence or inactivity does not in itself amount to acceptance.

(2) An acceptance of an offer becomes effective at the moment the indication of assent reaches the offeror. An acceptance is not effective if the indication of assent does not reach the offeror within the time he has fixed or, if no time is fixed, within a reasonable time, due account being taken of the circumstances of the transaction, including the rapidity of the means of communication employed by the offeror. An oral offer must be accepted immediately unless the circumstances indicate otherwise.

(. . . .)"

Art. 23 of the CISG reads:

"A contract is concluded at the moment when an acceptance of an offer becomes effective in accordance with the provisions of this Convention."

6. Art. 2 CO reads:

"1. When the parties have agreed with regard to all essential points, it is presumed that a reservation of ancillary points is not meant to affect the binding nature of the contract.

it was the parties' discernible intent to be legally bound by the exchange of faxes which took place on or around 18 August.

[10]   "Prior to the examination of the issue of the existence of an arbitration agreement binding on the parties, the arbitrator shall determine the law applicable to said agreement. In August, at the time of the drafting of the arbitration clause contained in the 'order confirmation', respondent had its domicile outside Switzerland. Moreover, the place of the arbitration is Geneva. The prerequisites of Art. 176(1) of the PILA are therefore met.[7] As a result, the provisions of Chapter 12 of said statute do apply in the instant case. It is also to be noted that the parties had agreed in the Terms of Reference to refer the matter to those of the provisions of the PILA that are mandatory.

[11]   "Art. 178(2) of the PILA provides that an arbitration agreement is valid, as regards its substance, if it conforms either to the law chosen by the parties, or to the law governing the subject-matter of the dispute, in particular the law governing the main contract, or if it conforms to Swiss law. Such a provision sets out connecting factors between which [there] does not exist any hierarchy; it suffices that the arbitration agreement be valid, in respect of its substance, under one of these three laws.[8] The conflict of law rule stated in Art. 178(2) of the PILA aims at ensuring the validity of the arbitration agreement (*in favorem validitatis*) and avoiding to the extent possible disputes that may arise in this respect.[9] [Here] it suffices therefore for the arbitration agreement to be valid on the substance that it conform to Swiss law.

[12]   "The issue of the existence of the arbitration agreement, as raised by respondent, pertains to the substantive validity (*validité matérielle*) of the arbitration agreement pursuant to Art.178(2) of the PILA.[10]

---

2. Where agreement with regard to such ancillary points so reserved is not reached, the judge shall determine them in accordance with the nature of the transaction.

3. The forgoing shall not affect the provisions regarding the form of contracts (Arts. 11-16)."

7. Art. 176(1) of the PILA reads:

"1. The provisions of this chapter shall apply to all arbitrations if the seat of the arbitral tribunal is situated in Switzerland and if, at the time when the arbitration agreement was concluded, at least one of the parties had neither its domicile nor its habitual residence in Switzerland."

8. "Bernard Dutoit, *Commentaires de la loi fédérale du 18 decembre 1987*, 2nd Edition (Helbing & Lichtenhahn, Basle 1997) *ad* Art. 178, No. 7, pp. 498-499."

9. "See decision of the Swiss Supreme Court of 16 May 1996 in the matter *G. S.p.A. v. M.Z.* published in the Bulletin of the Swiss Arbitration Association (hereinafter ASA Bulletin) 1996, No. 4, pp. 667 et seq., espec. section 4; see also the Swiss Supreme Court's decision published in ATF (official record of the decisions rendered by the Swiss Supreme Court) 119 II 380, espec. section 4a with references."

10. "Marc Blessing, *Introduction to Arbitration – Swiss and International Perspectives*, Swiss Commercial Law Series, Volume 10 (Helbing & Lichtenhahn, Basle 1999) No. 488, p. 185."

[13] "However, Art. 178(2) does not list matters that are governed by the substantive law.[11] The substantive law questions relating to an arbitration agreement include for example issues relating to the valid conclusion of the arbitration agreement,[12] in particular the mechanism of conclusion of contract: offer and acceptance, time and moment for a contract to be perfected as well as all what may affect the parties' mutual assent (error, fraud, duress, etc.) and the consequences thereof.[13]

[14] "In the present case, respondent does not argue that the arbitration agreement, in respect of its essential elements, was subject to any lack of mutual assent from the parties. It simply says that it was not discussed between them. Respondent only submits that the parties did not reach an agreement as to the payment of the goods to be supplied. The arbitrator considers therefore that this particular issue does not affect the validity of the arbitration agreement and only needs to be examined with the merits of the case.[14]

[15] "Anyhow should the arbitrator declare, on the merits, that there is no contract binding on the parties this would not necessarily cause the invalidity of the arbitration agreement by virtue of Art. 178(3) of the PILA which affirms the well internationally established principle of 'severability' or 'separability' of the arbitration agreement;[15] this would be particularly true in this matter should the arbitrator state, as example, a lack of the parties' mutual assent limited to the payment clause of the Contract.

[16] "Respondent still submits that the Contract was signed by error. However like above, respondent does not claim that such error was affecting one of the essential elements constituting the arbitration clause. Finally, it is worth noting that respondent does not argue that the arbitration agreement would have been made under duress pursuant to Art. 29 CO[16] which, the case may be, might have affected its validity if proven.[17]

[17] "Furthermore, respondent submits that the 'order confirmation' contained a specific provision (Sect. 17) providing for the agreement to be

---

11. "Pierre Lalive, Jean-François Poudret, Claude Reymond, *Le droit de l'arbitrage interne et international en Suisse* (Payot, Lausanne 1989) *ad* Art. 178, No. 14, pp. 321 et seq."
12. "Blessing, op. cit., No. 489; Dutoit, op. cit., No. 8."
13. Lalive/Poudret/Reymond, op. cit., idem, No. 15; Dutoit, op cit., idem."
14. "See infra [51] et seq."
15. "ATF 119 II 1380/384 with references."
16. Art. 29 CO reads in relevant part:

    "1. Where a contracting party has been unlawfully forced to conclude a contract while under material duress, whether originating from the other party or a third person, the party who acted under duress is not bound by the contract.
    (. . . .)"

17. "ATF 119 II 380 idem; ATF 88 I 100."

made in 'two originals'. According to respondent, since the agreement sent by DHL was not returned duly countersigned there had been no agreement between the parties and, as a result, no arbitration agreement was validly existing between them. According to respondent not only no original document was returned by respondent to claimant but also no original signatures were ever affixed by respondent on those documents.

[18]   "As a matter of law, respondent relies on Art. 16(1) CO which provides that where the parties have decided to use a special form there is a presumption that they shall not be bound until such special form is complied with. Respondent raises therefore the issue of formal validity (*validité formelle*) of the arbitration agreement. The seat of this Arbitral Tribunal being in Switzerland and at least one of the parties having been domiciled [at the time of the transaction] outside Switzerland, the PILA is applicable pursuant to its Art. 176(1).

[19]   "Such validity is governed by Art. 178(1) of the PILA which provides that an arbitration agreement is valid if made in writing, by telegram, telex, telecopier or any other means of communication which permits it to be evidenced by a text. Art. 178(1) sets forth one of the five prerequisites for an arbitration agreement to be valid.[18] Art. 178(1) of the PILA does not appear very restricting as to the requirements of form: not only such provision of law does not require the written form as meaning a document signed by all parties concerned (Art. 13 CO),[19] but it is also satisfied with a commitment, even not signed, set out on a medium that may be reproduced in writing and which states the mutual assent of the parties on its contents.[20] This may be, for example, an exchange of facsimiles or by any other means which provide a record of such mutual assent.[21]

---

18. "Dutoit, op. cit., No. 1, p. 497."
19. Art. 13 CO reads:

> "1. A contract which by law must be in written form (Art. 12) must bear the signatures of all persons who are to be bound by it.
> 2. Where the law contains no provision to the contrary, a letter or a telegram is deemed to be in writing, provided that the letter or the telegram form bears the signatures of the persons binding themselves."

20. "Dutoit, op. cit., No. 5, p. 498; see Lalive, Poudret, Reymond, op. cit., idem, No. 10, p. 318 and Blessing, op. cit., No. 482, p. 184; see also Marc Blessing, *The Arbitration Agreement – Its Multifold Critical Aspects* – Preface and Introductory Report, in ASA Special Series No. 8, pp. 12-13, and Jean-François Poudret, 'Le droit applicable à la convention d'arbitrage', in ASA Special Series No. 8: *The Arbitration Agreement – Its Multifold Critical Aspects*, p. 25, bottom."

21. "Lalive/Poudret/Reymond, op. cit., No. 9; see also Werner Wenger in *International Arbitration in Switzerland – An Introduction to and a Commentary on Articles 176-194 of the*

[20]   "In the instant case one can easily state that an arbitration agreement results (i) from the fax sent out by claimant to respondent on 21 August to which the 'order confirmation' was attached and which reproduced the text of said arbitration agreement, as confirmation of a buying order made by respondent on 18 August 1998, and (ii) from the fact that said fax was then returned by respondent to claimant, bearing its signature above the terms 'for acceptance'. In so far as respondent did not allege that there was a lack of mutual assent on the arbitration clause, the requirements of Art. 178(1) of the PILA are met. The agreement of the parties results therefore from this exchange of facsimiles and related text and signature. It does not matter that respondent did not return duly countersigned the 'original' contract attached to claimant's letter of 9 September couriered to respondent which, in any case, was nothing but the 'order confirmation' referred to above, to be forwarded again to claimant for its 'reference' only.

[21]   "In view of the considerations made above, the arbitrator considers that there exists a valid arbitration agreement between the parties."

b.   Signatory Powers of Claimant's Representatives

[22]   "Respondent submits that Mr. K who had signed the 'order confirmation' dated 20 August had no power to bind claimant – at least alone – since, at the time, he was neither member of the Board of Directors nor was duly authorized to represent the company, whether collectively or not. Likewise, respondent submits that Mr. M, who had signed the fax sent on behalf of claimant on 18 August confirming the transaction between the parties, had no authority to represent this company. Respondent concludes therefore that the Contract was not validly signed by claimant. Respondent also dismisses the ratification of Mr. K's signature by claimant which had submitted in the present arbitration a decision of the Board of Directors stating that its representative was duly authorized to sign the 'order confirmation' and ratifying, if need be, this document. Claimant's ratification of the Contract more than one year after is not acceptable under these circumstances according to respondent who concludes that no contract and, in particular, no arbitration clause was validly signed.

[23]   "Respondent raises here again the formal validity of the Contract which directly affects the validity of the arbitration agreement and, thus, needs to be examined now.[22] The preliminary question is to determine the law applicable to that issue. Chapter XII of the PILA does not expressly provide the issue of the

---

Swiss Private International Law Statute (Helbing & Lichtenhahn/Kluwer Law International, Basle-Geneva-Munich, 2000) *ad* Art. 178, Nos. 10 et seq., pp. 333 et seq."

22. "Lalive/Poudret/Reymond, op. cit., *ad* Art. 178, No. 23, p. 326."

law applicable to the representation powers necessary to enter into an arbitration agreement. According to case law and the majority doctrine cited by one of the leading legal scholars,[23] the powers to represent a moral person are governed by the law applicable to such person, namely the law of its seat according to the general rule set forth by Art. 155 lit. i of the PILA.[24] Consequently, such issue is governed by Swiss law as claimant has its seat in Switzerland. It is worth mentioning in passing that the parties, in their respective pleadings, have argued this issue in application to that law.

[24]   "Claimant argues that Mr. K was 'internally' authorized to sign alone the 'order confirmation' and responds to respondent's argument that the latter fails to appreciate the law of agency which protects bona fide third parties against the refusal by the represented entity to be bound by the contract and not to allow said third parties to withdraw from the contract. Claimant also explains that Arts. 718 et seq. CO protect third parties because whenever a person registered in the Trade Register signs on behalf of a company that company may not claim that such person was not empowered to do so; a company may empower any other persons not registered in the Trade Registry to sign on its behalf pursuant to Arts. 32 et seq. CO as this is a common practice, claimant explains.

[25]   "According to respondent Messrs. K and M have not been empowered by the Board of Directors to represent the company – at least alone – within the meaning of Art. 720 CO[25] according to the records of the Trade Registry submitted by claimant. Moreover respondent is of the view that claimant may not be left with the choice to decide at its sole option whether or not, in the particular case, it was bound by the sole signature of Mr. K.

[26]   "As a matter of fact it flows, indeed, from the extract of the Trade Registry submitted by claimant that Mr. K, as company manager (*direttore*) – and not 'director' within the meaning of Swiss law – had the power to represent claimant under his signature, but only together with the signature of the Chairman (*presidente*) or a substitute (*delegato*), whilst regarding Mr. M the

---

23. "Poudret, op. cit., p. 28 and references cited."

24. Art. 155 lit. i of the Swiss Private International Law Act (PILA) reads:

"Except for Articles 156-161 PILA, the law applicable to the company governs in particular:

. . .

(i) the power of representation of persons acting on its behalf on the basis of its organization."

25. Art. 720 CO reads:

"The board of directors shall notify the office of the commercial register for the purpose of the registration in the commercial register of the persons authorized to act for the corporation (Art. 718), together with a certified copy of the resolution by which such authority is granted. The persons to be registered shall sign at the office of the commercial register or file their certified signatures."

latter had no authority at all to represent the company if one considers the records of the Trade Registry in this respect. Mr. K explained during his testimony that this is claimant's internal policy for one representative to sign alone if the other is prevented to do so, for instance when traveling, as regards collective signatories.

[27]   "On this second factual element internal arrangements between claimant and its employees have no effect vis-à-vis bona fide third parties unless such arrangements are brought to the attention of these third parties, pursuant to the analogical application of Art. 933(2) CO.[26,27] It does not seem that such arrangement, if made in this case, was communicated to respondent.

[28]   "It is to be considered from the evidence submitted, that Mr. K had no powers to sign alone, but instead, collectively. Limitation was therefore made as to his mode of representation of the company, although, from the reading of the Trade Registry, Mr. K's authority to do in the company's name all acts which the company's object may entail was not altered pursuant to Art. 718a CO.[28, 29] The mode of representation as determined by the contract, the By-laws or the Trade Registry does not exclude the agency within the meaning of Arts. 32 et seq.[30] It is necessary to take into account the circumstances of the case and to put emphasis on the safety of the business transactions (principle of *sécurité des transactions*).[31] Furthermore when signing a contract, a company may also give a power of attorney to a third party; it is not obliged to be represented by individuals registered at the Trade Registry to this effect.[32]

---

26. "Pascal Montavon, *Droit suisse de la SA*, Tome III (Editions Juridiques AMC, Lausanne 1997) No. 5.1, p. 126."
27. Art. 933(2) CO reads:

   "2. When a matter which requires registration is not registered, it can only be invoked against third parties if it is shown that the third persons were aware of it."

28. "See ATF 121 III 368/375, *Semaine Judiciaire* (SJ) 1996 177/180 cited by respondent."
29. Art. 718a CO reads:

   "1. The persons authorized to act for the corporation may perform all legal acts on behalf of the corporation which the purpose of the corporation (Art. 626(2)) may entail.
   2. Restrictions of these powers may not be enforced vis-à-vis bona fide third parties; provisions restricting the authority to act for the principal office or for a branch office (Art. 642) or requiring joint representation of the corporation shall be exempted therefrom if such provisions are registered in the commercial register."

30. "ATF 104 II 197 section 3b."
31. "See Pierre Engel, *L'apparence efficace en droit privé*, in SJ 1989 p. 73 et seq., espec. p. 82; see also Pierre Tercier, *Le droit des obligations*, 2nd Edition (Schulthess, Zurich 1999) No. 415, pp. 78-79."
32. "Montavon, op. cit., No. 4, p. 126 with references."

[29]   "Given the nature of the business transaction in this matter, namely a straightforward international sale of goods transaction, and the need to secure business transactions for the safe functioning of the trade against too stringent formalities, the arbitrator is of the opinion to apply the principle mentioned above. This issue shall therefore be examined in accordance with Arts. 32 et seq. CO. In order to bind the principal, the agent must have been authorized by the latter to act on its behalf pursuant to Art. 32(1).[33] In this case it is beyond doubt that claimant had the intent to be bound by Mr. K; however formally speaking, the latter had no . . . single formal power of attorney to that effect. Respondent may be entitled in law to consider that it was not bound by contract. However it is necessary to examine the possible ratification of the contract as alleged by claimant but disputed by respondent.

[30]   "As a matter of law Art. 38(1) CO[34] provides that where an unauthorized person has entered into a contract purporting to act as agent, the alleged principal acquires no rights nor incurs obligations until he ratifies the contract. Such ratification is not submitted to any specific form; it may be implicit or result from conclusive acts (*actes concluants*) or may even result from the passivity or the silence of the third person on behalf of which a contract was made; from this viewpoint, the behaviour of that person shall be examined, as if a bona fide man would have been entitled to do it.[35] The contract is deemed ratified for instance when such third person has, later on, performed itself the contract.[36]

[31]   "In the instant matter, the arbitrator is of the view that claimant has – at least – implicitly, if not by conclusive acts, ratified the Contract. In effect, it may be considered that, by 16 October at the very latest, claimant had ratified the Contract when, through its lawyers whose authority is not questioned, it had sought performance of the contract in granting respondent a certain time-limit to perform its own obligations.

---

33. Art. 32(1) CO reads:

"If one who is authorized to represent another party enters into a contract in the other party's name, then the party represented, but not the agent, shall have the rights and shall be bound by the obligations resulting therefrom."

34. Art. 38 CO reads:

"1. If one, without having been authorized, has entered into a contract acting as an agent, the person represented shall become an obligor or an obligee only if he ratified the contract.
2. The other party is entitled to require the principal to elect within a reasonable time whether to ratify the contract, and shall no longer be bound if the principal fails to ratify within such time period."

35. "ATF 93 II 302/307, SJ 1968 p. 542/547-548; see also Pierre Engel, *Traité des obligations en droit Suisse*, 2nd Edition, pp. 404-405."

36. "ATF 43 II 293, Journal des Tribunaux (JdT) 1917 I 642."

[32] "Anyhow under the circumstances claimant had no real reason to expressly ratify such contract as respondent had not, at that time, put into question the validity of the signature of claimant's representatives. It is worth noting that such issue was raised only during this arbitration and that respondent did not request earlier from claimant whether it was ratifying the contract pursuant to Art. 38(2) CO. Finally, formal ratification of the Contract by claimant that occurred on 15 October [of the following year] can also be considered as valid, notwithstanding respondent's opinion to contrary, since the right of ratification is not contingent upon any time-limit.[37] Accordingly, respondent's argument that it had not been bound by contract with claimant for the ground discussed above is rejected."

c. Enforceable Arbitral Award

[33] "Respondent still submits that should . . . the arbitrator retain jurisdiction over the matter, the ensuing award would not be capable of enforcement pursuant to the New York Convention. Whilst exchange of facsimiles containing an arbitration agreement constitutes a valid arbitration clause pursuant to the PILA, the New York Convention has other prerequisites that are more strict, in respondent's view. Respondent explains that the application of the New York Convention to this matter should lead to conclude that no arbitration agreement has been validly made considering the absence of original signature on any document.

[34] "As a matter of law, respondent opposes the requirements for the formal validity of the arbitration agreement of Art. II of the New York Convention to those provided for by Art. 187(1) of the PILA.[38] This raises the issue of the relationship between these two provisions and whether one prevails over the other. For the majority of legal scholars and the Swiss Supreme Court,[39] Art. II (2) of the New York Convention[40] must be interpreted in relation to the Model Law of the United Nations Commission on International Trade Law

---

37. "ATF 101 II 222, JdT 1976 I 141."

38. *Note General Editor*: The sole arbitrator was apparently referring to Art. 178(1) PILA which reads:

   "1. As regards its form, the arbitration agreement shall be valid if made in writing by telegram, telex, telecopier or any other means of communication which permits it to be evidenced by a text."

39. "See ATF 121 III 38 section 2c, pp. 43-44, JdT 1995 I 377/379-380 cited by respondent; see also Dutoit, op. cit., No. 4, pp. 497-498."

40. Art. II(2) of the 1958 New York Convention reads:

   "2. The term 'agreement in writing' shall include an arbitral clause in a contract or an arbitration agreement signed by the parties or contained in an exchange of letters or telegrams."

(UNCITRAL) on International Commercial Arbitration (hereinafter referred to as the UNCITRAL Model Law) which provides in its Art. 7(2) *in initio* that the arbitration agreement shall be in writing and that an agreement is in writing if it is contained in a document signed by the parties or in an exchange of letters, telex, telegrams or other means of telecommunication which provide a record of the agreement. For the Swiss Supreme Court and the majority doctrine, Art. 178(1) of the PILA is clearly inspired from such formula that took into account the development of modern means of telecommunication and which should also assist in the interpretation of Art. II(2) of the New York Convention; on this basis, these authors and the Swiss Supreme Court express the view that the formal requirements of this Convention match up with those of the PILA.[41] Given the circumstance of the case, the arbitrator considers that there is not reason to depart from this legal view in this matter.

[35] "Those formal requirements having been already examined above within the framework of Art. 178(1) of the PILA, there is therefore no need to examine them again under the light of Art. II(2) of the New York Convention. In any case, should this issue be examined under Art. II(2) of the New York Convention the same conclusion would be reached. This legal provision distinguishes two hypotheses: the first where an agreement was made in writing and signed by the parties, the second, that results from an exchange of letters or telegrams to which similar means of communications may be associated which, by essence, do not necessarily imply the parties' signatures.[42] In this matter, the facts of the case correspond to the second hypothesis: an 'exchange' of documents – in fact the same document – took place, respondent having returned 'accepted' claimant's fax that evidenced, at least, the agreement of the parties on the arbitration agreement and its contents. In view of the above, respondent's last objection is rejected and the arbitrator declares having jurisdiction to settle the present dispute."

III.   PARTIAL ARBITRAL AWARD ON THE
       PRELIMINARY ISSUES

[36]   "Apart from having requested that the examination of this matter be limited to preliminary issues, respondent also requested the rendering of a decision under the form of a partial/interim award limited to said issues. The arbitrator does not see any need to render a partial award in so far as the disposal of the case on the merits does not justify further delay, given the substantive

---

41. "ATF 121 III idem p. 44; see also Wenger, op. cit., No. 18, p. 337."
42. "ATF 121 III ibidem p. 45; see also Poudret, '*A propos de la validité d'une clause arbitrale – Un arrêt pouvant prêter à confusion*', in JdT 1995 pp. 354 et seq/357-358."

issues that appear to be straightforward and ready for decision. Furthermore, the arbitrator's reasons set out in Procedural Order No. 2 shall also apply here mutatis mutandis. Consequently, the arbitrator shall now examine the matter on the substance. Prior to decid[ing] on whether there has been a contract between the parties, the arbitrator shall preliminarily examine which law shall govern this issue."

1.   Substantive Issues

a.   Applicable Law

[37]   "Respondent argues that no agreement was reached by the parties as the essential elements of the Contract were not agreed upon by application of Swiss law (Art. 1 CO). Claimant, referring to Sect. 15 of the Contract, submits that the formation, validity, construction and performance of the contract are governed by Swiss law. But it also adds that the United Nations Convention on Contracts for International Sale of Goods signed in Vienna on 11 April 1980 (hereinafter referred to as the Vienna Convention or CISG) is applicable in this instant matter given the nature of the business transaction, the origin of the parties and according to the well-established principle pursuant to which an international treaty such as the CISG is applicable to all disputes governed by Swiss law in so far as the parties have not explicitly opted it out.

[38]   "The Vienna Convention applies, inter alia, to contracts of sale of goods between parties whose place[s] of business are in different States that are Contracting States pursuant to Art. 1(a) CISG. With the entry into force of the Vienna Convention in Switzerland, international sale of goods regulations have been modified in that country: the Vienna Convention has become the main legal reference, the Swiss Code of Obligations having only kept a limited role in this context; hence, when a contract is entered into between a party established in Switzerland and the other in another Contracting State, the Vienna Convention applies as international convention.[43] However, Art. 6 CISG provides, inter alia, that the parties may exclude the application of the Vienna Convention; such exclusion may be made either expressly or implicitly.[44]

[39]   "In this matter, the parties have their respective place of business in the Contracting States, i.e., Switzerland for claimant and Italy for respondent. It is

---

43.   "Jean-Paul Vulliéty, *Le transfert des risques dans la vente internationale – Comparaison entre le Code suisse des obligations et la Convention de Vienne des Nations Unies du 11 avril 1980* (Helbing & Lichtenhahn, Basle-Geneva-Munich 1998) p. 47."

44.   "See Karl Neumayer, Catherine Ming, *Convention de Vienne sur les contrats de vente internationale de marchandises – Commentaire* (CEDIDAC, Lausanne 1993) pp. 84-85."

also not disputed that the business transaction involved may be characterized as a sale of goods contract; in addition, this matter does not fall within the categories that are excluded from the scope of the Vienna Convention (Art. 2 CISG).[45]

[40]   "However, it must be stated that Sect. 15 of the Contract – for which respondent has not submitted that it may have been subject to any lack of parties' mutual assent – provides that 'the formation, validity, construction and performance of this contract are governed by the laws of Switzerland'.

[41]   "The issue is to determine therefore whether such contractual provision providing for the application of the law of one of the Contracting State[s] may be considered, within the meaning of Art. 6 CISG mentioned above, as referring the matter to the domestic law of that State, namely the Swiss Code of Obligations or the specific legal prescriptions governing international sales, i.e., the CISG that is part of Swiss law.[46] In order to determine the meaning of this choice of law clause, it is necessary to ascertain the intent of the parties according to the provisions of Art. 8 CISG,[47, 48] in so far as such intent may be found.

[42]   "In the instant case, such intent is hardly ascertainable. However, the arbitrator is of the view that it is appropriate to apply the presumption formulated by

---

45. Art. 2 of the CISG reads:

   "This Convention does not apply to sales:
   (a) of goods bought for personal, family or household use, unless the seller, at any time before or at the conclusion of the contract, neither knew nor ought to have known that the goods were bought for any such use;
   (b) by auction;
   (c) on execution or otherwise by authority of law;
   (d) of stocks, shares, investment securities, negotiable instruments or money;
   (e) of ships, vessels, hovercraft or aircraft;
   (f) of electricity."

46. "Neumayer/Ming, op. cit., No. 5, p. 87."
47. "Idem."
48. Art. 8 of the CISG reads:

   "1. For the purposes of this Convention statements made by and other conduct of a party are to be interpreted according to his intent where the other party knew or could not have been unaware what that intent was.
   2. If the preceding paragraph is not applicable, statements made by and other conduct of a party are to be interpreted according to the understanding that a reasonable person of the same kind as the other party would have had in the same circumstances.
   3. In determining the intent of a party or the understanding a reasonable person would have had, due consideration is to be given to all relevant circumstances of the case including the negotiations, any practices which the parties have established between themselves, usages and any subsequent conduct of the parties."

one of the leading legal scholars: when the parties have designated Swiss law because one of them or their contractual relationships have a link with Switzerland, it may be assumed that the parties have made such a choice because they have considered that such link with Swiss law should prevail; if such is the case, Swiss substantive law on international sales contracts, i.e., the CISG, must apply.[49] Such solution is in accordance with the well-spread opinion according to which the reference to the law of a contracting State implies the application of the CISG.[50] Indeed, claimant has its place of business in Switzerland and, therefore, a link with that country. It is therefore presumed in this case that such a link should prevail.

[43]   "The arbitrator shall therefore apply the Vienna Convention and, for all aspects of the matter not covered by such convention the Swiss Code of Obligations."

b.   Non-performance of the Contract by Respondent

[44]   "Respondent justifies the non performance of the Contract because:

– the contract was not binding in view of the absence of an original contract signed by respondent;
– claimant's representatives did not have any authority to sign the Contract;
– the parties' agreement on essential terms of the Contract was lacking;
– respondent signed the Contract by error.

[45]   "Respondent points out the contents of Sect. 17 of the Contract which provides, among others, that 'this contract has been drawn in English language in two originals'. Since it did not return to claimant the original contract duly signed, respondent considers that there is no contract binding between the parties. The arbitrator considers that respondent interprets Sect. 17 of the Contract as making its validity contingent upon the use of the written form.

[46]   "Art. 11 CISG provides that a contract of sale need not be concluded in or evidenced by writing and is not subject to any other requirement as to form. Hence, the Vienna Convention does not submit sale of goods contracts to any particular form; such a provision only governs the offer and the acceptance, according to the aim of the Convention as defined in Art. 4 CISG, first sentence.[51, 52]

---

49. "Walter Stoffel, 'Le droit applicable aux contrats de vente internationale de marchandises', in *Les contrats de vente internationale de marchandises* (CEDIDAC, Lausanne 1991) p. 32."
50. "Neumayer/Ming, op. cit., No. 5, p. 88."
51. "Neumayer/Ming, op. cit., pp. 127-128."
52. Art. 4 first sentence of the CISG reads:

[47]   "According to Art. 16(1) CO where the parties to a contract for which the law requires no special form have stipulated to use a special form, there is a presumption that they shall not be bound until the special form is complied with. Such a reservation is valid only if made prior to the entering into the contract.[53] No such reservation may be found in the instant matter. From claimant's witnesses' deposition, it results – to the contrary – that claimant which drafted the Contract wanted to be bound by contract as soon as an agreement was to be reached by fax, without waiting for respondent's signature and the receipt of the original documents that, according to claimant are in practice often not returned by counterparts.

[48]   "Such statements are consistent with the fact that claimant's courier of 9 September 1998 – to which the original contracts were attached for signature and return – was sent 'for [its] reference' only. Moreover, respondent has never alleged having made the reservation referred to above.

[49]   "Accordingly, respondent has not demonstrated that the validity of the contract at stake was dependent upon the compliance of the written form. The related objection is therefore rejected.

[50]   "The issue of the alleged lack of authority of claimant's representatives to bind their principal has been examined at length in respect of the validity of the arbitration agreement. The disposal of said issue applies mutatis mutandis for the contract as regards its substantive part. Further developments are therefore not necessary. To sum up, it suffices to say that all communications sent by claimant's representatives to respondent should be considered as having been ratified by claimant.

[51]   "As already seen, respondent argues that no contract has been made between the parties because an agreement on essential terms of the Contract was lacking. As a matter of fact, such a disagreement is limited to payment. Respondent does not claim that other elements of the Contract were subject to disagreement between the parties. It is therefore necessary to analyse now in detail how, and if ever, a contract was entered into between them by application of the Vienna Convention.

[52]   "Claimant's fax of 18 August to respondent can be considered as an offer within the meaning of Art. 14(1) CISG, namely a proposal indicating the goods and making provisions for determining the quantity and the price. Such fax was returned back by respondent duly countersigned with the mention 'E/O R.D. 90 DS' (and/or direct payment 90 days) next to the

---

"This Convention governs only the formation of the contract of sale and the rights and obligations of the seller and the buyer arising from such a contract. . . ."

53. "ATF 54 II 300, JdT 1929 I 66; see also Tercier, op. cit., No. 530, p. 96."

term 'Payment' without it being precisely clear when it was exactly returned to claimant.

[53] "Contrary to claimant's view, the arbitrator considers that the payment element was not an 'ancillary point', when considering the following. Art. 19(1) CISG provides that a reply to an offer which purports to be an acceptance but contains additions, limitations or other modifications is a rejection of the offer and constitutes a counter-offer. Art. 19(2) CISG, however, sets forth that a reply to an offer which purports to be an acceptance but contains 'additional or different terms which do not materially alter the terms of the offer' constitutes an acceptance unless objection of the offeror to the discrepancy. Additional or different terms relating among other things to 'payment' are considered 'to alter the terms of the offer materially' according to Art. 19(3) CISG.

[54] "In the arbitrator's view, the terms 'E/O R.D. 90 DS' added by respondent under the payment condition on claimant's fax of 18 August did alter the offer because it is understood from respondent's President's oral statement, that he made it clear, at least initially, that it did not want to have the letter of credit as sole means of payment. Therefore, respondent's reply to claimant's fax of 18 August cannot be considered as an acceptance within the meaning of the above-mentioned provisions.

[55] "Later on claimant, 'following [its] previous fax dated 18 Aug. and [its] previous phone-conv', sent the Contract by fax of 21 August to respondent, asking the latter to 'sign it and send back to [respondent] duly countersigned for acceptance'. The contract attached to that fax – and dated 20 August – did not reproduce respondent's alteration. To the contrary, payment by letter of credit was maintained.

[56] "Asked by counsel for respondent why such a different term had not been taken into account in the Contract, the witness M explained during the Oral Hearing that he had advised respondent that it was not possible for claimant to accept payment without a letter of credit for guarantee's reasons, but that he would nevertheless see with claimant's insurance department whether other payment arrangements would be possible for future transactions.

[57] "Asked by counsel for claimant what were the contents of the telephone conversation referred to in claimant's fax of 21 August, Mr. M testified that he had explained to respondent that it was not possible to have payment without a letter of credit and respondent acknowledged that fact. Such a testimony is consistent with the contents of claimant's fax of 21 August and the fact that respondent did return the Contract duly countersigned, without any new material alteration.

[58] "As a matter of law the arbitrator considers, under those circumstances, that claimant renewed its offer pursuant to Art. 14(1) CISG. The sending back of the Contract by fax by respondent to claimant – whatever the date may

be – bearing the respondent's signature above the terms 'for acceptance' must be considered as an acceptance within the meaning of Art. 18(1) CISG. Such acceptance became effective at the moment it reached claimant pursuant to Art. 18(2) CISG, that is on or shortly after 21 August. Immaterial is the fact that, later, claimant did not react to the non-opening of the letter of credit. The arbitrator reaches therefore the conclusion that the parties were bound by the Contract dated 20 August.

[59]　"Credit must be granted to the oral statement of respondent's President, Mr. A, who explained during the Oral Hearing that he had signed the 21 August Contract without reading its contents, but on the firm belief that the alteration he had made on the 18 August offer had been actually accepted by claimant. It may well be that Mr. A misinterpreted the contents of the telephone conversations held with claimant's representatives.

[60]　"In view of the above, the arbitrator understands that respondent signed the Contract by error: its President actually thought that claimant had finally agreed not to have payment by letter of credit only, whilst this was the sole means of payment finally retained in the Contract. As a matter of law, the arbitrator is bound to conclude that the parties were indeed lacking mutual assent as regards payment of the goods to be sold.

[61]　"Since the Vienna Convention does not regulate legal issues pertaining to the lack of mutual assent,[54] Arts. 23 et seq. CO must be examined. Art. 23 CO provides that a party is not bound by contract if it entered into the contract under a 'material mistake'. The mistake is 'material' when, inter alia, the mistaken party undertook an essentially greater consideration or accepted an essentially smaller one than was its intention pursuant to Art. 24(1)(iv) CO[55] which

---

54. "See Art. 4 CISG; see also Neumayer/Ming, op. cit., No. 6, p. 71; François Dessemontet, 'La Convention des Nations Unies du 11 avril 1980 sur les contrats de vente internationale de marchandises' in Les contrats de vente internationale de marchandises (CEDIDAC, Lausanne 1991) p. 64."

55. Art. 24(1) CO reads:

"1. An error is, in particular, deemed to be material in the following cases:

1. if the party in error intended to enter into a contract different from that to which he gave his assent;

2. if the party in error had another thing in mind than the one which is the object expressed in the contract, or another person, provided that the contract was concluded with a particular person in mind;

3. if the party in error promised a consideration considerably greater in extent, or accepted a consideration considerably smaller in extent than he had intended;

4. if the error related to certain facts which the party in error, in accordance with the rules of good faith in the course of business, considered to be a necessary basis of the contract."

sets out a non-exclusive list of instances where the mistake is to be considered 'material'.[56]

[62]   "This is the arbitrator's opinion that respondent's mistake is material within the meaning of those provisions of law: Respondent wanted a payment that would not require to set up any form of guarantee whilst payment by letter of credit required to the contrary such sort of guarantee at the costs of respondent. There was therefore a difference on one of the elements of the Contract pursuant to Art. 24(1) CO and such difference was significant.

[63]   "According to Art. 23 CO cited above, a party under a material mistake is not bound by contract. However Art. 26 CO provides that where the mistake is due to the negligence of the rescinding party, the latter is bound to compensate for the damage resulting from the cancellation of the contract unless the other party knew or should have known the mistake. According to Swiss case law someone who signs a contract without having read it is negligent within the meaning of Art. 26 CO.[57]

[64]   "Respondent has actually admitted that he did not read the Contract or that he did it but only after he had signed it upon receipt of a hard copy thereof. The arbitrator considers under these circumstances that respondent was negligent and should have taken the necessary and appropriate measures in such a case, by asking his daughter to translate the document – as he usually did – before signing it. Consequently, respondent is not discharged of its obligations under the Contract and must compensate claimant for the damages suffered pursuant to Art. 26(1) CO.

c.   Claimant's Claim for Damages; Amount of Damages

[65]   "Claimant's damages may be calculated according to Art. 75 CISG which provides that if the seller has resold the goods within a reasonable time from contract avoidance, the party claiming damages may recover the difference between the contract price and the price in the substitution transaction. In this case claimant, after having requested respondent to perform its obligations under the Contract by letter of 16 October, advised then respondent on 26 October that it was taking measures to mitigate its loss. Claimant finally sold the goods on 18 November to a Filipino customer. Such behaviour is consistent with Art. 77 CISG which provides that a party who relies on a breach of contract must take such measures as are reasonable in the circumstances to mitigate the loss.

[66]   "Claimant calculates its damages as corresponding to the price difference per metric ton for the goods to be sold to respondent and those actually sold to the Filipino customer, in adding the storage costs; those costs are not disputed by respondent. Respondent alleges that the [price at which the goods were sold

---

56. "ATF 34 II 523."
57. "ATF 69 II 234, JdT 1944 I 22."

to the Filipino customer] does not represent the market price at the time of the substitute transaction. . . .

[67] "From the evidence submitted in this regard, the arbitrator is satisfied that [the price at which the goods were sold to the Filipino customer] was a fair market price. Such amount was justified by the fact that claimant had tried to sell the goods an two occasions to other customers but that it did not succeed due the latter's failing to confirm the order; the price per metric ton discussed with those customers . . . may also evidence the fact that the market price of the product was decreasing continuously as from August. Finally, claimant demonstrated that the transaction with the Filipino client materialized as early as 18 November and that the price for said goods was actually paid by the client.

[68] "As a matter of law, the arbitrator considers that claimant took the necessary and appropriate measures in time and place to mitigate its damages. Its claim for damages . . . is therefore admitted.

d. Interest

[69] "The [amount awarded] shall bear an interest of 5% per annum from the date of the filing of the Request for Arbitration until full payment, in accordance with the provisions laid down in Arts. 78 CISG and 104 CO."

4. Costs of the Arbitration and Legal Costs

[70] "Art. 31(3) of the ICC Arbitration Rules provides that the final Award shall fix the costs of arbitration and decide which of the parties shall bear them or in what proportion those costs shall be borne by the parties. Decision shall also be made on the 'reasonable legal and other costs incurred by the parties for the arbitration', pursuant to Art. 31(1) of the said Rules. It is generally recognized that ICC arbitrators have a wide discretionary power in the apportionment of arbitration costs. Furthermore, 'legal costs' do not encompass only attorneys' fees but also the costs of a party itself provided that they are reasonable and incurred in connection with the preparation and presentation of the arbitration case.

[71] "Claimant having obtained in full what it has been claiming for in these proceedings, respondent shall, therefore, be condemned to bear the costs of the arbitration, fixed by the ICC International Court of Arbitration in their entirety.

[72] "In the instant matter each Party's counsel submitted a statement of the legal costs incurred by his client in this arbitration. . . . The arbitrator finds also legitimate under the present circumstances to condemn respondent to support claimant's legal costs for the amount indicated above, said amount being reasonable and equivalent to the fees charged by the Swiss and Italian counsel of respondent. Respondent shall bear its own legal costs."

(. . . .)

Interim award in case no. 9781 of 2000

Parties:	Claimant: Buyer (Italy)
	Defendant: Seller (Germany)
Place of arbitration:	Geneva, Switzerland
Published in:	Unpublished
Subject matters:	– jurisdiction
	– 1980 UN Sales Convention
	– applicable law to form and substance of arbitration clause
	– applicable law to contract
	– qualification as sale contract

Facts

In March of 1996, the German company D concluded a sales agreement with the Italian company C for the delivery of a waste recyling plant (the March sales agreement). The March sales agreement specified the type of plant and the guaranteed capacity. The agreement was executed in Italian and German. Both versions provided in Art. 6 that in case of a dispute arising out of the agreement, German law was applicable and, further provided for the jurisdiction of the competent courts in Germany. An offer for the recyling plant (the offer) was also drawn up by D.

The Italian financing company F intervened at C's request and with D's consent. As a consequence, in April 1006 F submitted to D its Order (the April order) for the recyling plant. In May 1996, D confirmed this order by letter (D's confirmation letter) directly to F. By a letter of the following day (referred to as the May sales agreement or May letter) F, referring expressly to the April order, provided that "in derogation to our April order and in partial modification of the same, we communicate to you the variations to bring thereto, as agreed upon with the lessee" and introduced several amendments. It also contained the following dispute settlement and applicable law clauses:

"This agreement shall be submitted in all its aspects to Italian law and it is deemed to have been concluded in Italy. All questions which might be raised relating to the construction and/or implementation of the present agreement shall be submitted to the International Chamber of Commerce of Paris."

The letter was signed *"Per accettazione specifica delle presenti variazioni"* by both C and D. F's signature was labeled as *fornitore* (supplier) and C's was labeled as *conduttore* (lessee).

Problems arose with respect to the recyling plant and in December of the following year, C initiated ICC arbitration against D, alleging breach of contract. D had started an arbitration against F (the D-F arbitration). D and F had agreed upon a sole arbitrator and F had asked the ICC International Court of Arbitration (ICC Court) to extend the D-F arbitration to C, since both disputes concerned the same legal relationship. C suggested to join the two arbitrations.

D in its response, contested the existence of a valid arbitration agreement between itself and C. Subsequently D agreed to conclude an arbitration agreement with C provided, inter alia, that the arbitration be consolidated with the D-F arbitration and that the same arbitrator be appointed. The parties initially agreed to this, but subsequently withdrew their agreement. The ICC Court decided that the arbitration between C and D should proceed separately, designated Geneva as the seat of the arbitration and appointed a different sole arbitrator.

In their Terms of Reference, the parties agreed that the ICC Rules applied and where these rules were silent, the arbitration would be governed by Chapter 12 of the Swiss Private International Law Act (PILA). The Terms of Reference also provided that the arbitrator would first decide in an interim award on jurisdiction and the applicable law to the merits of the case.

The sole arbitrator held that the arbitration agreement was valid as to form and substance and superseded the jurisdiction clause contained in the March sales agreement. He concluded that he did have jurisdiction and that the United Nations Sales Convention 1980 applied to the parties' agreement. With respect to the validity of the arbitration agreement, the arbitrator first determined that Art. 178 of the Swiss Private International Law Act applied to this question. The arbitration agreement was concluded in a valid form as both D and C had signed F's May letter "for specific acceptance". The substantive validity was examined under Italian law, as the law governing the object of the dispute. The sole arbitrator rejected D's argument that C did not have capacity to enter into the arbitration agreement as it had only signed the May letter in its sole capacity as lessee. The sole arbitrator examined this question from the point of view of whether C had acted as an agent for F or had signed in its own capacity, finding that C had signed in its own name and on its own behalf. The sole arbitrator further held that the May sales agreement entirely replaced the March sales agreement and that the arbitration clause in the May sales agreement was the only existing jurisdiction clause binding the parties.

Claimant argued that Italian law, rather than the CISG, applied to the agreement, as the contract was a procurement contract (a *contratto d'appalto*) as characterized under Italian law, rather than a sales contract, as argued by the defendant. The sole arbitrator reasoned that Germany and Italy were both parties to the CISG and that the contract was to be characterised under the Convention which provided a uniform substantive rule for the characterisation of the contract. Moreover, the place of business of the parties were in different States which satisfied the basic criterion of Art. 1(1) of the Convention. Because only five to seven per cent of the contract price related to services, rather than the supply of goods, this was not sufficient to bring the contract outside the scope of the Convention. Nor had the parties opted out of the application of the Convention as the clause in the contract stating that the agreement was deemed to be made in Italy could not be construed as an exclusion clause.

Excerpt

I. JURISDICTION

[1] "The first observation of the Tribunal with respect to the issue of jurisdiction is the following: the only question to be resolved at this stage is the validity of the arbitration clause contained in the May sales agreement as regards C as such. The only questions to be dealt with at this stage are indeed the following:

(i) Is the arbitration clause contained in the May sales agreement valid as to form as regards C and

(ii) Is the arbitration clause contained in the May sales agreement valid as to substance as regards D and C? In particular, did C sign the arbitration clause in its capacity as agent to F or in its own name and on its own behalf?

(iii) Does the arbitration clause contained in the May sales agreement supersede, as the case may be, the jurisdiction clause contained in the March sales agreement?

[2] "Before entering into the discussion of the questions at stake, the issue has to be addressed of the law applicable to the validity as to form and as to substance of the arbitration clause. It being recalled that the Terms of Reference expressly provide for the application of the ICC Rules and, where the rules are silent, of Chapter 12 of the Swiss Private International Law [Act] (PILA), one notes:

(i) that the ICC Rules are silent on the issue of validity of the arbitration clause;

(ii) that Art. 178 PILA provides that:

'1. As to form, the arbitration agreement shall be valid if it is made in writing, by telegram, telex, telecopier or any other means of communication that establishes the terms of the agreement by a text.

2. As to substance, the arbitration agreement shall be valid if it complies with the requirements of the law chosen by the parties or by the law governing the object of the dispute and, in particular, the law applicable to the principal contract, or with Swiss law.

3. The validity of an arbitration agreement may not be contested on the grounds that the principal contract is invalid or that the arbitration agreement concerns a dispute which has not yet arisen.'

[3] "Thus, Art. 178(3) PILA clearly states that the issue of the main contract, its validity, its binding effect, is foreign to the question of the validity of the arbitration clause. As set out by the legal writers:

'When the parties to an agreement containing an arbitration clause enter into that agreement, they concluded not one but two agreements, the arbitral twin of which survives any birth defect or acquired disability of the principal agreement.'[1]

As a consequence thereof

'*L'arbitre est compétent pour juger sur tout grief portant sur l' existence ou la validité du contrat principal, pourvu que la convention d'arbitrage per se ne soit pas entachée d'une clause [rectius: cause] de nullité.*'[2] (Translation: 'The arbitrator is competent to decide on any claim regarding the existence or the validty of the main contract, provided that the arbitration agreement [is] not vitiated by a [reason for] nullity . . . ').

[4] "The conclusion to be drawn from the above is crystal clear: the question as to whether C is entitled to the claims brought in these proceedings against D or not is foreign to the question of jurisdiction at stake.

---

1. "S. Schwebel, *The Severability of the Arbitration Agreement, International Arbitration: Three salient problems* (Grotius 1987) pp. 1-60."

2. "A. Dimolitsa, '*Autonornie et "Kompetenz - Kompetenz"*', Revue de l'Arbitrage (1998) pp. 305 et seq. p. 309."

[5] "This being said, the question remains of the validity as to form and to substance of the arbitration clause contained in the May sales agreement.

[6] "*As to form*, Art. 178(1) PILA sets a substantive rule of direct application.[3] The arbitration clause shall therefore be deemed as valid if it complies with the requirements provided for in this article. There is little to discuss in this respect. The arbitration clause contained in the May sales agreement undoubtedly complies with Art. 178(1) PILA, inasmuch as the proposed clause results from F's May letter to D and has been executed by both C and D with the same wording, i.e., '*Per accettazione specifica delle presenti variazioni*' (Translation: 'For specific acceptance of the present variations'). . . . [T]he fact that C is identified as *Il Conduttore* (the lessee) relates to C's rights (contested by D) to the claims brought in these proceedings, and not to the validity of the arbitration agreement as such.

[7] "*As to substance*, Art. 178(2) PILA sets a rule of conflict of law *in favorem validitatis* which constitutes an alternative connection.[4] The validity as to substance of the arbitration clause will be admitted in the first place if the clause complies with the law chosen by the parties for this specific clause or for the agreement as a whole.[5] As a matter of fact, the May sales agreement does only refer as a whole to Italian law. In the absence of any specific choice of law applicable to the arbitration clause only, the validity of the latter shall therefore be examined under Italian law.

[8] "Art. 808(3) of the Italian Code of Civil Procedure[6] provides that:

'The validity of the arbitration clause must be examined autonomously with respect to the contract to which it refers; however, the power to stipulate the contract includes the power to enter into the arbitration clause.'

As recalled by legal writers, the lack of capacity is held as a cause of nullity of the arbitration clause.[7]

[9] "D's reasoning with respect to the issue of C's capacity to enter into the May sales agreement does not specifically address the issue. In a nutshell, D contends that C is not a party to the agreement mentioned, inasmuch as this

---

3. "P. Lalive, J. F. Poudret, *Le Droit de l'Arbitrage interne et international en Suisse* (Payot, Lausanne 1989) ad Art. 178 at 8, p. 317; at 14, p. 321."
4. "P. Lalive, J.F. Poudret, *op. cit.*, ad Art. 178, at 14, p. 321."
5. "P. Lalive, J.F. Poudret, *op. cit.*, ad Art. 178, at 15, p. 322."
6. "In its version as per Art. 3 of the Italian International Private Law of 5 January 1994, n. 25."
7. "Giuseppe Mirabelli, '*La capacità a compromettere in arbitri*', Rivista dell'arbitrato (Giuffrè, Milano 1994, no. 2) pp. 215 etseq., p. 223, and references."

agreement only concerns two parties, D on the one side (the seller) and F on the other side (the buyer), C having simply signed the agreement in its capacity as lessee and its purpose being limited to evidencing its approval and consent to the variations of F's April Order. D adds that for C to be a party to the May sales agreement, it would have been necessary that F expressly assign its rights as buyer to C, which it did not.

[10] "In the opinion of the Tribunal, the issue at stake is actually foreign to the reasoning recalled above. In the present discussion on the validity of the arbitration clause, the only question to examine is clearly to know whether C signed the agreement and the arbitration clause contained therein in its own name and on its own behalf, or conversely, in F's name and on the latter's behalf. In this case indeed (and in this case only), C would clearly not be bound to the May sales agreement or to the arbitration clause. As set out in Art. 1388 of the Italian Civil Code (CCIt) indeed:

> '*Il contratto concluso dal rappresentante in nome e nell'interesse del rappresentato, nei limiti delle facoltà conferitegli, produce direttamente effetto nei confronti del rappresentato.*'

Translation: 'The agreement concluded by the agent in the name and on behalf of the principal, within the limits of the powers conferred to it, produces effects directly to the principal.'

Pursuant to Italian case law:

> '*La contemplatio domini, necessaria perché il contratto concluso dal mandatario produca effetti nei confronti del mandante, non richiede formule solenni, nè deve risultare espressamente dal contratto, essendo sufficiente, perché si realizzi, che il rappresentante abbia reso noto all'altro contraente, in modo esplicito e non equivoco, che egli intende agire, oltre che nell'interesse, anche nel nome di altro soggetto.*'[8]

Translation: 'The *contemplatio domini*, necessary for the contract concluded by the agent to produce effect towards the principal, [requires] neither ... formal declarations, nor must result expressly from the contract, it being sufficient, for it to be achieved, that the agent ha[s] brought to the other contracting party's knowledge in explicit and unambiguous terms that it intends to act in the interest as well as in the name of the other individual.'

---

8. "Cass, 7 December 1994, No. 10523; 24 February 1986, No. 1125; 5 September 1985, No. 4614; 20 February 1982, No. 1071; 4 December 1980, No. 6320."

In other words, Italian law admits that an agency relationship may be inferred from any circumstances showing that the agent has made known to the contracting party expressly and unequivocally that the contract it executed was not binding upon itself but upon other persons.

[11] "Now, not only does D not raise such an argument, but moreover it clearly states that C signed the agreement in its capacity as lessee, and lessee only. Thus D does not allege that it ever considered that C signed the agreement in the name and on behalf of F. C does not allege it either.

[12] "The conclusion to be drawn from the above is simple: C signed the May sales agreement in its own name and on its own behalf, and thus the arbitration clause contained therein is valid and binding upon the parties, D on the one side, and C on the other side.

[13] "The last question to be solved with respect to the jurisdiction issue is as to whether the arbitration clause contained in the May sales agreement replaced the jurisdiction clause contained in the March sales agreement.

[14] "Relying in particular on the so-called *collegamento funzionale*, C contends that the May sales agreement modified and integrated the March sales agreement, and that the jurisdiction clause contained in the latter in favour of the ordinary courts at [Germany] was superseded by the arbitration clause contained in the former. D holds on its side that the May sales agreement was in substitution of each previous agreement on the same matter, and in particular of the March sales agreement, that it actually replaced.

[15] "The Tribunal notes in the first place that both claimant's and defendant's reasoning . . . lead to the same result: the sole existence of the arbitration clause contained in the May sales agreement, either because this agreement modified the jurisdiction clause contained in the March sales agreement (claimant's thesis) or because the May sales agreement entirely replaced the March sales agreement (defendant's thesis). Both parties are therefore substantially in agreement on this point.

[16] "Moreover, the Tribunal notes that the only question to resolve at this stage is to know whether the arbitration clause contained in the May sales agreement actually replaced the ordinary jurisdiction present in the March sales agreement. This question does not relate, in the opinion of the Tribunal, to the so-called theory of the *collegamento funzionale* (which actually relates to the May and March sales agreements as well as to other agreements at stake, such as the Leasing agreement . . . and/or the agreement between C and P [the purchaser of the output of the plant] which regards the substance of the claims, but merely to the construction of the May sales agreement.

[17] "In this respect, the Italian applicable law provides that the first rule to be complied with is the *literal* method.[9] As set forth by legal writers:

---

9. "Cass. 96/2372; 80/4864; 75/1314."

'Il giudice si dovrà limitare all'esame del senso letterale delle parole in quanto la comune volontà delle parti emerga in modo certo e immediato dalle espressioni adoperate, di modo che l'elemento letterale assorba ed esaurisca ogni altro criterio di interpretazione.'[10]

Translation: 'The judge must limit himself to the examination of the literal meaning of the words inasmuch as the common intent of the parties results from the wording used in a certain and immediate way so that the literal element integrates and exhausts any other criterion of interpretation.'

Only where there is some ambiguity or doubt left, Art. 1362 CCIt will apply, pursuant to which:

'Nell'interpretare il contratto si deve indagare quale sia stata la comune intenzione delle parti e non limitarsi al senso letterale delle parole.

Per determinare la comune intenzione delle parti, si deve valutare il loro comportamento complessivo anche posteriore alla conclusione del contratto.'

Translation: 'In interpreting the contract, one ha[s] to enquire on the common intent of the parties and not limit oneself to the literal sense of the words.

For determining the common intent of the parties, one must estimate their behaviour as a whole also after the execution of the contract.'

When examining the wording of the May sales agreement, one notes:

(i)   that it expressly integrates F's April order, in partial modification thereof and in express agreement with the lessee, C;

(ii) that it expressly refers to the description of the goods (*descrizione dei beni*) as set out in the March offer.

[18]   "There is therefore, in the opinion of the Tribunal, little room left for interpretation: the parties to the May sales agreement, i.e., as set out above, F, D and C whatever the rights of which of them can be as a result therefrom, intended to:

(i)   integrate, hence hold as contractually binding upon all the three parties concerned the description of goods as per D's March offer;

---

10. "Cian Trabucchi, *Commentario breve al Codice Civile* (CEDAM, Milano 1997) Art. 1362, Note III with reference to stable case law."

(ii)   integrate, hence hold as contractually binding upon all three parties concerned the F's April order;

(iii) modify these orders, as the case might be, in the clear and unambiguous wording of the May sales agreement.

[19]   "*Ex abundanti cautela*, if we proceed to a comparison between the provisions contained in the March sales agreement and the contractual documents set forth above ([18]), one notes that the provisions of the parties contained in the latter are contained anew, albeit modified as the case may be, in the former. Thus, and in particular:

(i)   the (general) description of the goods to be manufactured and delivered ex Arts. 1 and 2 of the March sales agreement as well as the consideration therefor result anew from (i) F's April order, (ii) D's confirmation letter, and (iii) D's March offer;

(ii)   the guarantee clause ex Art. 3 of the March sales agreement result anew from (i) D's March offer, (ii) D's confirmation letter of F's April order;

(iii) the payment's rates ex Art. 4 of the March sales agreement result anew in the May sales agreement;

(iv)   the jurisdiction clause ex Art. 6 of the March sales agreement is contained anew, albeit modified, in the May sales agreement.

[20]   "The conclusion reached by the tribunal at this stage of these proceedings, and without prejudice of the existence or absence of the rights claimed therein, is that the May sales agreement, together with the documents expressly mentioned therein, namely (i) D's March offer, (ii) F's April order together with D's confirmation letter of this order, all as amended, as the case may be, by the May sales agreement itself, entirely replaced the March sales agreement. Therefore, the arbitration clause contained in the May sales agreement constitutes the only existing jurisdiction clause binding upon the parties."

II.   THE LAW APPLICABLE TO THE DISPUTE

1.   Position of the Parties

[21]   "In its Request for Arbitration, the claimant refers to Art. 6 (b) of the May sales agreement which provides for the application of Italian law to the agreement. The defendant contends on its side that both 'the terminated March sales agreement and the May sales agreement are governed by the UN-Convention on Contracts for the International sales of Goods of April 1980 (CISG), Italy and Germany being contracting states to the CISG.

[22]   "The defendant holds indeed that the preconditions of Art. 3(1) CISG are fulfilled. Defendant had to supply goods, which were to be manufactured. The defendant further contends that as per Art. 3(2) of the CISG, the predominant part of the obligations assumed by D did not consist in the supply of labour and other services. Although defendant had to erect and commission the recycling plant, the value of these services was approximately 5 to 7% of the total Order amount. The defendant still notes that there is no agreement between the parties to exclude the application of the CISG according to Art. 6 CISG,[11] the reference to German law in the March sales agreement or to Italian law in the May sales agreementnot constituting such an exclusion. Defendantalso relies on Art. 13(5) of the ICC Rules[12] relating to relevant trade usages reflected in international conventions, thus the CISG. The defendant finally relies on the arbitral tribunal's Order No. 4 in the F-D arbitration, whereby the tribunal held that the May sales agreement is governed by the CISG.

[23]   "The claimant replicates in confirming that the CISG has been ratified in Italy by Law No. 765 of 11 December 1986 (recte: 1985) and hence became Italian law. The claimant admits that the CISG applies to the sale of goods (including contracts for the supply of goods to be manufactured ex Art. 3 CISG). However, C holds that the agreement under scrutiny is to be characterised as a *contratto d'appalto* as per Art. 1655 CCIt, and not as a sale contract as per the characterisation given to it by Art. 1470 CCIt. The difference between the two as identified by the claimant is that while in the sales contract, the main feature is the transfer of the ownership of a good against a consideration (Art. 1470 CCIt), in the *contratto d'appalto*, the performance of the works prevails on the materials. Claimant indeed contends that the main feature is to produce a given result arising from the performance of the work rather than to transfer the ownership of the good. In the case of *contratto d'appalto*, the plant must not be a standardised one. The *appaltatore* undertakes to design, plan and manufacture the plant as per the customer's requirements. In the claimant's views, the criteria cited are all met in the case at stake.

[24]   "In its final brief, D notes that even if under Italian law, the May sales agreement had to be characterised as a *contratto d'appalto* (which is contested

---

11. Art. 6 of the United Nations Convention on Contracts for the International Sale of Goods (1980) (CISG) reads:

    "The parties may exclude the application of this Convention or subject to article 12, derogate from or vary the effect of any of its provisions."

12. Art. 13(5) of the ICC Rules of Conciliation and Arbitration 1988 reads:

    "In all cases the arbitrator shall take account of the provisions of the contract and the relevant trade usages."

by D), the contractual relationship at stake would remain governed by the CISG, since the latter is a multilateral treaty providing for uniform substantive rules relating to international sales of goods. The defendant contends that, in line with Art. 7(1) CISG[13] and the prevailing doctrine, it is a matter for the CISG, and not for the Italian Civil Code, to characterise the contract. The defendant confirms that in its view the May sales agreement is exclusively governed by the CISG.

[25]   "In its final brief, C contends that the May sales agreement is a purely domestic contract since it is expressly 'deemed to have been made in Italy'. As a consequence thereof, Italian domestic law is applicable to the exclusion of the CISG, which relates to international relationships. The claimant repeats that the plant ordered [from] D is not a standardised one, and therefore, the performance of the work prevails over the supply of the material. That was the very reason for C to apply to a foreign company, notoriously specialised in the design, planning and manufacturing of the required plant.

[26]   "C further refutes D's argument as per Art. 7 CISG, in that this provision applies to contracts precisely governed by the Convention, which is not the case of the *contratto d'appalto*, excluded by Art. 3(2) of the CISG.

[27]   "Finally, C rejects D's argument resulting from the arbitral tribunal's Order No. 4 in the F-D arbitration, inasmuch as the tribunal's conclusion that the CISG is applicable to the May sales agreement is contradicted by the same tribunal's grounds that:

(i)   the agreement at stake has to be characterised as a *contratto d'appalto;*
(ii)   the choice of Italian law in the May sales agreement is binding upon the parties so that Italian law is applicable;
(iii)   the expression 'the contract shall be deemed to have been made in Italy' is recognised as classifying the contract as a pure domestic agreement.

C emphasised D's contradiction in arguing, on the one hand, that C is not a party to the May sales agreement, and, on the other hand, that the present tribunal is bound to the conclusion reached by the sole arbitrator in the F-D arbitration that the law applicable to the May sales agreement is the CISG."

---

13. Art. 7 CISG reads:

"(1) In the interpretation of this Convention, regard is to be had to its international character and to the need to promote uniformity in its application and the observance of good faith in international trade.
(2) Questions concerning matters governed by this Convention which are not expressly settled in it are to be settled in conformity with the general principles on which it is based or, in the absence of such principles, in conformity with the law applicable by virtue of the rules of private international law."

2. CISG Applies

[28]   "The tribunal emphasises at the outset . . . that it is surely not its task to scrutinise and discuss the arbitral tribunal's Order No. 4 in the F-D arbitration, incorporated verbatim in the partial award of the same tribunal. C was not and still is not a party to these proceedings. The conclusion reached by the tribunal in the F-D arbitration could therefore in no possible way bind as such the parties to the present arbitration proceedings.

[29]   "Be it as it may, the tribunal entirely shares the conclusion reached by the sole arbitrator in the F-D arbitration that the CISG is applicable to the May sales agreement for the reasons set out hereafter.

[30]   "Being undisputed, and indeed indisputable, that both Italy and Germany are State Parties to the CISG,[14] the first question to be dealt with is the characterisation of the May sales agreement as an international or a domestic contract, as argued by the claimant. It is undisputed and indeed indisputable, that since now like at the time the May sales agreement was entered into, C was and still is a company with its registered offices in Italy, and that D was and still is a company with its registered offices in Germany, Italian Private International Law (IPIL)[15] applies. This law indeed:

> 'rappresenta . . . una codificazione organica del diritto internazionale privato, riunendo in un unico testo normativo la disciplina delle situazioni che presentano elementi di estraneità rispetto all'ordinamento italiano . . . '.[16]

Translation: 'represents . . . an organic codification of private international law, putting together in a single normative text the discipline of the situations which present foreign elements as compared to the Italian legal order . . . '.

[31]   "Art. 1 IPIL provides that the law is applicable to the issues of jurisdiction, *applicable law*, enforcement of foreign decisions. Art. 2 IPIL read as follows:

> '1. Le disposizioni della presente legge non pregiudicano 1'applicazione delle convenzioni internazionali in vigore per l'Italia.
> 2.Nell'interpretazione di tali convenzioni si terrà conto del loro carattere internazionale e dell'esigenza della loro applicazione un forme.'

---

14. "The CISG entered into force in Italy on 15 January 1988 and in the Federal Republic of Germany on 15 January 1991."
15. "No. 218 of 31 May 1995, entered into force on 1 September 1995, with the exception of Sect. IV relating to the enforcement of foreign decisions."
16. "F. Pocar, *Il nuovo diritto internazionale privato italiano* (Giuffrè, Milano 1997) pp. 4 and 5."

Translation: '1. The provisions of the present law do not prejudice the application of the international conventions in force for Italy.
2. For the interpretation of these conventions, one shall take into account their international character and the need for their uniform application.'

Pursuant to the Report to the law presented to the Senate:

'Il comma 2 dell'art. 2 ribadisce i principali criteri di interpretazione delle convenzioni in vigore, prescrivendo che si tenga conto del loro carattere internazionale e dell'esigenza della loro applicazione uniforme. Ciò tende ad evitare che, in sede interpretativa, le considerazioni desumibili dall'unità del sistema giuridico italiano prevalgano sulla natura internazionale della disciplina convenzionale; questa invero va applicata da tutti i contraenti in modo uniforme. A tal fine, dovranno essere valorizzati i criteri interpretativi ispirati dalla prassi degli altri Stati contraenti ....'[17]

Translation: 'Art. 2(2) reaffirms the main criteria of interpretation of the conventions in force, prescribing that their international character and the need for their uniform interpretation must be taken into account. This tends to avoid, in matter of interpretation, that considerations drawn from the unity of the Italian legal system prevail over the international nature of the international discipline; the latter must be applied by all contracting parties in a uniform manner. With this aim in view, the criteria of interpretation inspired by the praxis of the other Member States ... must be [fully appreciated].'

[32] "Hence, the rule is clear: the criterion to be used for the characterisation of the May sales agreement as an international contract in the meaning of the CISG (and without prejudice of the characterisation of the agreement as such as a contract of sale in the meaning [o]f this Convention or not) or conversely, a domestic contract not governed by the CISG is to be taken in the CISG itself.
[33] "Pursuant to Art. 1 of the CISG:

'(1) This Convention applies to contracts of sale of goods between parties whose places of business are in different States:
(a) when the States are Contracting States; or
(b) when the rules of private international law lead to the application of the law of a Contracting State.

---

17. *"Relazione al Disegno di Legge N1192 'Riforma del sistema italiano di diritto internazionale privato' presentati nel corso della XI legislatura al Senato della Repubblica ... il 29 aprile 1 993."*

(2) The fact that the parties have their places of business in different States is to be disregarded whenever this fact does not appear either from the contract or from any dealings between or from information disclosed by, the parties at any time before or at the conclusion of the contract.
(3) ....'

Thus, the basic criterion of Art. 1 for the application of the Convention is 'that the places of business of the parties are in different States'.[18] As set out by the legal authorities:

'The mere place of contracting does not constitute a place of business (see Honnold, *Uniform Law*, 80-81); neither does the locality where the negotiations have taken place. Reference is made to a permanent and stable business organisation and not the place where only preparations for the conclusion of a single contract have been made.'[19]

The conclusion to be drawn from this principle is that the criterion of the place of conclusion of the agreement as set out in the May sales agreement *'questo contratto ... si considera stipulato in Italia'* is of no relevance to the effect of the (general) application of the CISG.
[34]   "Regarding the exception set out in Art. 1 (2) of the CISG ... the tribunal notes that the fact that D's place of business was situated in Italy *[rectius:* Germany] was perfectly known by C at the time of the negotiations and conclusion of the agreement in dispute. Indeed, C explains:

'If the plant was a standardised one, supplied also by the Italian market, it is not understandable why claimant should have applied to a foreign company (respondent), notoriously specialised in the design, planning and manufacturing of the required kind of plant.'

One is bound to conclude from this very admission of the claimant that the exception of Art. 1 (2) CISG is not applicable in the present case: the claimant was perfectly aware of D's foreign place of business at the time of the negotiations and conclusion of the agreement.
[35]   "The second issue to examine is whether the May sales agreement is 'a contract of sale' in the meaning of the CISG (D's contention) or conversely, is to be held as a procurement contract *(contratto d'appalto)* not comprised in this

---

18. "Secretariat's Commentary, Official Records, I, 15."
19. "C.M. Bianca, M.J. Bonell, *Commentary on the International Sales Law, the 1980 Vienna Sales Convention* (Giuffrè, Milan 1987) at Art. 1, at 2.3., p. 30."

international convention (C's contention). The first observation to be made here is that the question of the legal characterisation of the May sales agreement has to be made autonomously (i.e., independently of any domestic law and in particular in the present case, of Italian domestic law) with respect to the CISG. This principle results beyond any possible ambiguity from the very Report to the IPIL as quoted above ([31]). Therefore, the question as to whether the May sales agreement is to be identified as a *contratto d'appalto* pursuant to Art. 1655 CCIt or a '*sales contract*' pursuant to Art. 1470 CCIt is relevant only to the extent that the CISG is deemed not to be applicable to this agreement.

[36] "Pursuant to Art. 3 CISG:

'(1) Contracts for the supply of goods to be manufactured or produced are to be considered sales unless the party who orders the goods undertakes to supply a substantial part of the materials necessary for such manufacture or production.

(2) This Convention does not apply to contracts in which the preponderant part of the obligations of the party who furnishes the goods consists in the supply of labour or other services.'

[37] "The interpretation of Art. 3 CISG is given in the first place by the CISG itself. Thus, Art. 42 of the same provides, with respect to the obligation of the seller to deliver goods which are free from any right or claim of a third party, the case where:

'The right or claim results from the seller's compliance with technical drawings, designs, formulae or other such specifications furnished by the buyer.'[20]

It stands to reason therefore that the fact that the goods are manufactured on the basis of technical specifications given by the buyer does not preclude as a matter of principle the application of the CISG

[38] "Moreover, legal writers and case law unanimously set forth specific criteria as to whether, and in the affirmative, to which extent, a contract providing for both work and materials falls within the scope of the CISG. Thus:

(i)   A contract for work and materials (Art. 3(1)) is basically treated as a contract of sale.[21] 'It is otherwise only where the party ordering the

---

20. "Claude Witz, *Les premières applications jurisprudentielles du droit de la vente internationale, Convention des Nations Unies du 11 avril 1980 (L.G.D.J.* 1995) at 16, p. 35."
21. "OLG Frankfurt, RIW (1991) p. 850 with a note by Schlechtriem, EWiR Sect. 25 CISG 1/91, 1081."

goods has to supply a "substantial part" of the necessary raw materials or semi-finished goods.'[22]

(ii) A contract for supply and installation (Art. 3 (2)) is clearly outside the scope of the CISG 'if the obligation to supply or obtain labour or other services alongside the obligation to deliver goods . . . constitutes the preponderant part of the obligations. . . . In view of the uncertainty associated, in most cases, with the need to estimate those values, it will be necessary for the share of services to be clearly in excess of 50%.'[23]

[39] "By comparing the above mentioned principles to the May sales agreement as presented and argued by the parties, one is bound to conclude that this agreement clearly falls within the scope of the CISG. Indeed:

(i) the fact that the seller or *appaltatore* as per the claimant's definition undertakes to design, plan and manufacture the plant as per the customer's requirement (above, at [23]) not only does not preclude the application of the CISG, but moreover is expressly provided by Art. 3(1) of the same (above, at [36]);

(ii) None of the parties ever alleged in the present proceedings that the party ordering the goods (or in the present case, the lessee) had to supply *any part* of the necessary raw materials or semi-finished goods. The May sales agreement as identified above (at [35]), i.e., together with D's March offer and F's April order, does not provide anything of the kind. On the contrary, it results from the very same order and D's confirmation letter thereto that the entire raw materials and 'semi-finished' goods had to be supplied by C;

(iii) C never contested D's contention that although the defendant had to erect and commission the recycling plant, the value of these services was approximately 5 to 7% of the total order amount (above, at [22]). This figure has therefore to be held as correct. However, and as confirmed by legal writers and international case law, the figure required for the exclusion as per Art. 3(2) of the CISG is of 50% at least.

[40] "The tribunal is bound to conclude from the above analysis that, as a matter of principle, the May sales agreement is actually governed by the CISG. However,

---

22. "Peter Schlechtriem, *Commentary on the UN Convention on the International Sale of Goods (ClSG)* (Clarendon Press, Oxford 1998) Art.3, at 1, p. 39."
23. "Peter Schlechtriem, *op. cit.*, Art. 3, at 2, p. 39, with reference to Honnold, para 60.1; Enderlein/ Maskow/Strohbach, Art. 3, note 5; ICC Case No. 7153/93, JDI (1992) 1005, 1006 on the supply and assembly of plant for a building project (predominant value of the goods supplied leads to the application of the CISG)."

the question remains as to whether the parties to the May sales agreement excluded the application of the CISG as per Art. 6 of the same, or not. It has to be emphasised in this respect that the claimant does not discuss the defendant's argument that there was no such an exclusion in the case under scrutiny.

[41]　"Be it as it may, the tribunal notes that pursuant to doctrine and case law:

> *'Si l'exclusion peut se faire de manière implicite, encore faut-il que la volonté des parties soit certaine. En cas de doute sur cette volonté, c'est le principe de l'applicabilité de la Convention qui doit l 'emporter: l'application de la Convention n'est en effet pas subordonnée à la volonté des parties. C'est le système du "opting out" et non du "opting in"qui a été retenu par les rédacteurs de la convention.'[24]*

> Translation: 'If the exclusion can be implicit, still the will of the parties must be certain. In case of doubt, the principle of applicability of the Convention must prevail: indeed, the application of the Convention is not subject to the parties' will. It is the principle of the "opting out" and not of the "opting in" which had been held by the Convention's authors.'

Thus, in an ICC Arbitration referred to by legal writers, the tribunal held that the contractual provision [stating] that the tribunal shall apply 'the substantive laws of France' does not constitute a valid 'opting out'.[25]

[42]　"The application of these principles to the case under scrutiny aims at putting aside any voluntary exclusion of the parties in the meaning of Art. 6 CISG. It is true that the May sales agreement expressly states that 'the agreement is deemed to be made in Italy' (above, at [24]). However, this contractual provision – already discussed above (at [33]) – cannot be construed – in the tribunal's view – as an exclusion clause. This is not argued by the claimant either. The tribunal is bound to conclude from the above analysis that the May sales agreement is actually governed by the CISG.

[43]　"It has to be emphasised at this point that the said characterisation does not entirely exclude the application of Italian domestic law to the resolution of the present dispute. As set forth by Art. 4 of the CISG:

> 'This Convention governs only the formation of the contract of sale and the rights and obligations of the seller and the buyer arising from such a contract.'

---

24. "Claude Witz, *op. cit.*, p. 44., confirmed by OLG Dusseldorf, 8 January 1993, NJW-RR (1993) pp. 999 etseq.; OLG Koln, 22 February 1994, RIW (1994) pp. 972 et seq."
25. "ICC Case No. 6653, 1993, JDI (1993) p. 1040, obs. JJA."

Art. 5 then sets forth a *non exhaustive* list of subject matters not concerned by the Convention such as:

'(a) the validity of the contract or of any of its provisions or of any usage; (b) the effect which the contract may have on the property in the goods sold.'

[44] "Amongst the various questions remained outside the scope of the Convention, one may quote for example the issue of representation[26] or question of the identity of the parties to the contract.[27] Thus, it is the clear opinion of the tribunal that the question as to whether the claimant – in its capacity as lessee – is entitled to exercise part or all of the buyer's rights is a question submitted to Italian law."

III.   CONCLUSION

[45] "On the basis of its analysis of the facts and the law and the conclusions with respect thereto as expressed above, the tribunal makes the following Interim Award:

A.   As to jurisdiction: The tribunal is competent to decide on the dispute pending between, C on the one side, and D, on the other side, resulting from the May sales agreement between the parties;
B.   As to the applicable law:

1.   The May sales agreement is governed by the United Nations Convention on Contracts for the International Sale of Goods (CISG);
2.   For contractual matters not governed by the United Nations Convention on Contracts for the International Sale of Goods (CISG), Italian Law is applicable.

C.   Costs: The tribunal makes no order as to the costs of the arbitration in this Interim Award, and reserves the same for a subsequent Award."

---

26. "ICC Case No. 7197, 1992, JDI (1993) p. 1029."
27. "LG Hamburg, 26 Sept. 1990, RIW 1990, p. 1015 etseq.; IPRax 1991, p. 400 et seq.; CLOUT, 17 May 1993, p. 3."

Final award in case no. 10060 of 1999

Parties:	Claimants: Director of Finance and Administration K (Sweden)
	Respondent: International Organization A (Kenya)

Place of arbitration:	Nairobi, Kenya

Published in:	Unpublished

Subject matters:	– termination of employment contract
	– rules of natural justice
	– procedural errors in termination
	– calculation of damages

Facts

Mr. K, a Swedish national, worked in industry for sixteen years and for an international organization for five years prior to being employed by the international organization A as the Director of Finance and Administration. A is an autonomous non-profit international organization with operations in a variety of countries. Its Charter provides for it to have legal status, a Board of Trustees (BoT), and a Director General (DG) who acts as chief executive. The BoT is at the top of the organizational structure, with the Director General and the Deputy Director General (DDG) immediately under it. Next in the hierarchy are the Director of Research, the Director of Training and Information and the Director of Finance and Administration (FINAD), with the latter being responsible for four units: finance, human resources, operations and information systems. A's employment policies were incorporated in the Personnel Policy Manual (PPM).

Mr. K was employed by A and following a probationary period was informed three years later by letter that his employment would run for ten years. Several years later, following several incidents, including the failure at an international donors conference to procure certain funds for the organization, which apparently irritated or frustrated the DG, Mr. K was asked to comment at a Management Committee meeting on the behaviour of a member of the staff, Mr. B, regarding some possible financial irregularities. Mr. K declined to do so. The DG met with him the following day and once again asked for his opinion on this question, and Mr. K again declined to comment.

The DG considered this to be insubordination and, after conferring with the Chairman of the BoT, convened a Disciplinary Panel, a step provided for in the PPM. The Disciplinary Panel recommended that Mr. K's contract be terminated because of insubordination. Mr. K appealed to a Grievance Panel, a step also provided for in the PPM. The Grievance Panel concluded that the termination was justified.

Mr. K initiated arbitral proceedings against A, claiming that his employment was unlawfully terminated relying on a violation of the rules of natural justice and irregularities in the constitution of the Disciplinary Panel which he claimed had "not been constituted"; that its members were witnesses to the events complained of; that it was chaired by the DG, the main protagonist in the termination; that one of its members may have been biased against him; and that the DG had compromised the Disciplinary Panel's ability to form a fair and unbiased opinion because he informed the members that the Chairman of the BoT had suggested termination.

The sole arbitrator found that the termination of Mr. K's employment was justified on the ground of insubordination but wrongful and unjustified because the procedures adopted did not comply with the Personnel Policy Manual. Moreover they were a breach of the rules of natural justice which applied in this case because Mr. K had the possibility of appearing before a kind of tribunal and the expectation of a fair hearing. The Disciplinary Panel lacked independence. In the proceedings before the Disciplinary Panel and the Grievance Panel Mr. K was not allowed to copy documents which had been submitted in the proceedings, nor was he given an opportunity to change as prescribed under the PPM. The findings of the Grievance Panel would have been correct only if the Disciplinary Panel has been properly appointed and unbiased and had followed the rules of natural justice.

In deciding on Mr. K's monetary entitlement, the sole arbitrator calculated the amount of time which would have had to be allowed for if all the procedures had been followed. This included two consecutive annual performance evaluations ranked as "fair" and the staff member having been made aware of the situation, put on an improvement plan and given a six-month opportunity to change.

Excerpt

I. BACKGROUND

[1] "A's organizational structure is very simple at the level with which this arbitration is concerned: the Board of Trustees (BoT) is at the top of the tree with

the [Director General] DG and the Deputy Director General (DDG) immediately under them. Then the hierarchy splits three ways:

1. Director of Research under whom come all the Scientific Programmes and Regions each answerable directly to the Director of Research.
2. The Director of Training and Information – again with individual Programmes directly referable to the Director and finally
3. The Director of Finance and Administration (FINAD) responsible for four units namely: Finance, Human Resources, Operations and Information Systems. The claimant of course was the Director of FINAD . . . .

[2] "Because of its international organization connection, its recent creation, its donor funding, its non-profit motivation, A aims to be a modern, progressive, fair employer adopting the best of modern human resource policies and practices with salaries and benefits designed to attract and hold highly competent international staff from the competitive international market. All this it has endeavoured to incorporate in its Personnel Policy Manual (PPM)."

1. The Personnel Policy Manual

[3] "The first thing to notice about the PPM is that it is a Guide only (Clause 1(3)). It is a long document running to 44 pages of small print which reflects not only that it attempts to cover every eventuality in respect of both international and local employees but was presumably drafted with the thought in mind that A could be employing a national from any one of the [member states of the international organization] and could equally well have a presence in any one of those countries although its main focus is in the tropics. The document states (Clause 1(2))

> 'It is the desire of A to establish conditions of employment that are recognized clearly as being fair to the interest of those concerned and (to) encourage staff to take a sincere interest and pride in A and its programme of work and to exert their best talents and efforts in the discharge of their responsibilities.'

The emphasis on fairness is repeated again (Clause 1 (5)) and also the wish to encourage self-development opportunities and to discourage discrimination in all its forms. High standards of work and ethics are demanded (Clause 1(6) and 8(4)) with particular cautions about outside interests and conflict of interest but care is taken to provide for health, transport, career advancement, staff and professional associations in addition to the more mundane provisions for leave, training, remuneration, allowances and so forth. In a few words A employees are expected to be highly competent, honest, dedicated and hard working while on its part A sets out to be a model employer providing good salaries and benefits to what it hopes will be long-term staff.

[4]   "All appointments are by the DG but in practice he does not act dictatorially. The interview process for senior staff can last a week: candidates meet in differing ways and both socially and in the work environment virtually all those with whom they would have a work relationship. Senior appointments are not done lightly and while the ultimate responsibility lies with the DG, he will have considered the view of many subordinates before making decisions: then he refers to the BoT on a non-objection basis (Clause 2(3)).

[5]   "The restriction on the employment by A of relatives is at Clause 2(4) and Probation and Duration of Employment are at Clause 2 (6). It is under this clause that Mr. K having served his probationary period, claims under the letter dated three years after his employment that his employment would run for 10 years from the initial appointment subject to 'termination in the case of redundancy, unsatisfactory performance or other cases as stipulated in the termination policy'.

[6]   "For the purpose of this dispute the important part of the PPM is the Disciplinary Code which appears at Clause 8. Paragraph 8(1) in its second paragraph reads:

> 'The need to invoke disciplinary measures is rare and should remain so. The objective of A disciplinary provisions is primarily prevention or correction rather than punishment.'

Paragraph 8(2) deals with termination and under the heading 'Disciplinary Termination' states:

> 'If in the judgment of a panel composed of the Director General or another as delegated plus at least two other directors, a staff member is not fulfilling the terms of their appointments or responsibilities after being made aware of the situation and being given opportunity to change or becomes involved in situations detrimental to A's status, such an appointment may be terminated. The staff member will be entitled to the normal period of notice and termination benefits.'

[7]   "This is the provision for the Disciplinary Panel of which more later; it is the first step in the dismissal procedure but any staff member who feels seriously unfairly treated or cannot resolve the issue after a fair hearing by his immediate superior and within his next 2 levels of management has the right under

paragraph 8(4) to a hearing before the Grievance Panel: the first three paragraphs read:

'8(4) It is of primary concern to A that staff members should feel that they have been treated fairly and equitably. All employees should be given a fair hearing by the immediate supervisor or manager concerning any grievance that they may wish to raise. There is also a grievance procedure which is outlined in the next paragraph.

All staff members who feel they are being subjected to seriously unfair(ly) treatment and who have not solved the matter within the 2 next levels of management have the right of appeal to an ad hoc grievance panel. A staff member who wishes to lodge an appeal must present a written statement of the grounds of appeal to the Human Resources Unit within 10 working days of notice of the disciplinary action that is contested.

An appeal against the imposition of a disciplinary action is allowed provided that the grounds of appeal are related to the procedural correctness of the disciplinary process or there is a claim that the disciplinary action is unjust, because of suspicion of prejudice; unreasonable, because of disproportionate punishment in relation to the offence; or unwarranted, because the offence did not take place.'

[8]   "However right at the end of this section there appears this paragraph:

'The DG may reject or accept the recommendations of the panel and this will be final and binding.'

It follows that the DG has the ultimate power to hire and fire. It is clear from the PPM and the actual practice that he does not act alone: he acts on the advice of others but is not compelled to do so. It follows that, that if acting fairly, he would only disregard advice for good reason and probably state those reasons but he is exposed to the risk when dealing with senior staff that he is witness, judge, jury and executioner. The average managing director in a company in the private sector is in no different position but A has gone to the trouble to spell out the need for a fair hearing, an investigation and appeal procedure: having done that A has to comply with it.

[9]   "Another way of looking at the PPM is to say that senior staff in A in a sense is subject to self-discipline. If one of the team misbehaves or fails to perform then subject to the overriding power of the DG, other members of the team will be involved in scrutinizing and sitting in judgment on the misbehaviour or failure to perform. It is well recognized that self-discipline is often difficult, sometimes embarrassing and almost always painful; that is particularly so where those

subject to self-discipline form a small group which is expected in normal circumstances to work as a team. It is for consideration whether in looking again at the PPM after this decision A might not involve some external input into the disciplinary process either from a sister agency or external professional advisers."

2. Mr. K's Case in a Nutshell

[10] "Mr. K says his employment was unlawfully terminated. His performance evaluations for the first four years were basically 'very good': he was strong in finance; not so strong in administration; not so strong in working relationships with latterly reluctance on financial grounds to embrace every new system the gimmicky information technology industry could offer. It needs to be remembered also that A is a young organization and Mr. K found himself dealing with all sorts of problems – such as building contracts – not always the province of a Director of FINAD in addition to a variety of obstacles thrown at A by the main host government . . . .

[11] "I will deal with the events leading to the dismissal of Mr. K later. At this stage it is pertinent to note two important aspects of Mr. K's case:

[12] "Of the Disciplinary Panel he says by way of preliminary objection:

– It was not constituted at all: the PPM is silent as to who appoints it.
– All its members were witnesses to the events complained of.
– The DG took the chair even though he was the main protagonist against the claimant even though he is specifically given power to delegate.
– One of its members Mrs. M may have been biased against him for reasons extraneous to his termination.
– Its ability to make a fair and unbiased opinion was also compromised by the DG who, A admits, spoke to the chairman [of the BoT] on the Mr. K problem. The Chairman [of the] BoT suggested disciplinary termination for insubordination and this information was given by the DG to the members of the Disciplinary Panel before the Disciplinary Panel made its decisions.

[13] "And by way of substantive objection:

– That he had no opportunity or no proper opportunity of being heard by the Disciplinary Panel.
– The Grievance Panel considered matters extraneous to his letter of termination in its deliberations.

[14] "The Disciplinary Panel having found against him, Mr. K claims that the Grievance Panel, the next stage in the process, which was properly constituted,

had material before it damaging to his case which he did not have and indeed of which he was denied copies (although he was permitted to read it) and that therefore once again he was denied a proper opportunity to present his case.

[15]   "The rules of natural justice he claims were not complied with by either panel."

3.   The Rules of Natural Justice

[16]   "There are a great many cases on this subject. What is essential is that both sides should be heard or have the opportunity of being heard by an unbiased tribunal. Counsel for the claimant has cited to me the case of *Cinnamond v. British Airports Authority* 1980 2 All ER p. 368. This was a case of rogue taxi drivers at London Airport who were excluded from the airport premises under a byelaw. Essentially they had all been jumping the queue of authorized taxis to pick up unsuspecting foreigners whom they then overcharged for the journey into London. They had all been prosecuted many times but were not only persistent offenders but had left a series of fines unpaid. They complained that the rules of natural justice had not been complied in that they had not had the opportunity of being heard before the decision was taken by the Authority to exclude them from the Airport. Lord Denning MR had no difficulty in deciding that there had been no breach of the rules of natural justice because in view of their conduct the taxi drivers could not have had a legitimate expectation of being heard.

[17]   "He has also referred me to a number of English and one East African case. The English cases to which I have been able to refer to the full report are *Malloch v. Aberdeen Corporation* 1971 2 All ER 1278, *Gunton v. London Borough of Richmond upon Thames* 1980 3 All ER 577 and *Stevenson v. United Road Transport Union* 1977 2 All ER 941. The East African case is *De Souza v. Tanga Town Council* 1961 EA 377 which in some respects bears remarkable similarity to the present case.

[18]   "I should mention in parenthesis that the common law of contract of England as modified by equity (and by some but by no means all English statutes) applies to Kenya. The upshot of those cases is that a court needs to look at the terms of the contract with the employee to see what that specifies in relation to the disciplinary process. If those terms indicate that the employee for example has the advantage of appearing before a tribunal of some kind then the rules of natural justice apply. Counsel for A on the other hand cited to me cases from the Court of Appeal in Kenya to the effect that the rules of natural justice do not apply to a simple contract of employment.

(. . . .)

[19]   "His first case is *Rift Valley Textile Limited v. E O Oganda*, Nakuru Civil Appeal 27 of 1992 which held that 'the rules of natural justice have no application to a simple contract of employment unless the parties themselves have specifically provided in their contract that such rules shall apply'. This decision was supported in Nairobi Civil Appeal No. 194 of 1991 *A J Githinji v. Mumias Sugar Co Ltd* and Civil Appeal No. 120 of 1997 *Kenya Ports Authority v. E Otieno*. I have also been referred to *Oloo v. Kenya Posts & Telecommunications* I KAR 655 where an employee who retired early in the public interest with a gratuity and an immediate reduced pension was recalled to service under a statutory power enabling the KPT to recall persons who had retired early but were medically fit and under 50: the real reason for his recall was that he had taken a profitable job in the private sector. He was asked to confirm his willingness to return to service failing which his pension would be deferred until he would be 50.

[20]   "It was held citing *DeSouza v. Tanga Town Council* 1961 EA 377 with approval . . .

> 'the regulation there being considered did not in terms say that an opportunity of showing cause should be given. In my judgment, the requirement of natural justice that the appellant should be given a fair opportunity of giving an explanation or of showing cause, whichever way it is put, continued after the appellant had been retired in the public interest. . . . But in my judgment, neither of the letters to which I have referred can fairly be construed as inviting the appellant to give an explanation for his acceptance of the new appointment or of showing cause why he should not be required to accept further office with the consequence of losing his pension, at least until 1989, if he did not do so.'

[21]   "I find no inconsistency in the cases cited by learned counsel. If the claimant in this case (or in any of the cases cited for that matter) had a legitimate expectation of being heard, then the rules of natural justice apply. It is clear that PPM is no simple contract and an A employee has an expectation both of a fair hearing and a judgment. The rules of natural justice apply thereto and I so hold."

4.   A's Case in a Nutshell

[22]   "A's case is very simple. Mr. K was employed as Director of FINAD: his early annual evaluations were 'Very Good' and he received the appropriate merit increases in the first four years of employment. There was an increasing unease between the DG and Mr. K which came to the surface at the fourth year Performance Evaluation. In parenthesis, this Evaluation is carried out under PPM Clauses 6(1)(1) and 6(1)(2) and is common to all employees. It involved

at any rate at the director level a one-to-one discussion between Mr. K and the DG about the achievements of the past year: the plans for the coming year and the areas of work which have been less well carried out by the employee during the year just past. The Evaluation is wide ranging.

(. . . .)

[23] "The object of the exercise is to do a bit of soul searching especially into the weaker areas of performance and to give in this case both the DG and Mr. K the opportunity to communicate their hopes and also their fears, their satisfactions and also their dissatisfactions. There is provision for both parties to sign their agreement to the Evaluation at the end . . . but this by no means always happened. At all events Mr. K, when he went to see his fourth-year Evaluation in the Human Resources Unit office, found that some comments made by the DG with which Mr. K did not agree had been added after the evaluation meeting and crossed them out and returned the document to the Human Resources Unit file. This incident unimportant in itself was nevertheless symptomatic of growing tension between the DG and Mr. K.

[24] "The DG noticed a decline in his view of Mr. K's performance from about February of the fifth year and more so from the middle of the year. It seems that there were no major incidents but a number of minor ones which caused the DG irritation or frustration. That seems to have deteriorated markedly at an international donor meeting in the autumn of the fifth year. This is a week in October each year . . . where donor agencies meet with the representatives of international organization agencies who rely on donor funds for their finance. It is clearly a hectic week . . . meeting many different nationalities, agencies, foundations and governments each doubtless with its own agenda and restrictions or strings attached and each with more or less generous budgets. It often involves breakfast lunch and dinner engagements in addition to the working day so it is hardly surprising that minor incidents can swell out of proportion under the stress of all the activity.

[25] "There was a question about Mr. K's dress on one occasion but probably more important to the DG was the failure of Mr. K, as the DG saw it, to pursue a potential donation of US$ 100,000 for a programme run by A from the Government of X. I suspect there was a genuine misunderstanding by Mr. K who thought that the Government of X had given as much as it could without a further vote of approval from the Parliament of X which he had been informed would not approve more – when in fact this was money already approved for another project which could not use it and which the DG's contact thought he could divert to A for the programme run by A without further parliamentary approval. The failure to secure the additional $100,000 added to the DG's irritation and frustration with Mr. K which at this point seems to have turned to active dissatisfaction. The programme in question, be it noted, is the DG's primary scientific programme of which he is the Co-ordinator.

[26]   "On return to Nairobi in considering the case of Mr. B involving a senior employee 'borrowing' funds from A without authority for personal purposes (of which more later) at a Management Committee meeting comprising the DG, the Deputy Director General (DDG), Mrs. M, Mr. K and Mr. E [the Director of Training and Information]. Mr. K, despite being asked three times for his comments on what disciplinary action to take against Mr. B not only declined to comment but failed to explain his lack of comment. It is probably true to say that from this point onwards the DG had so lost confidence in Mr. K, that Mr. K was going to have an uphill struggle to restore it.

[27]   "The DG very rightly did not push Mr. K again at that point but arranged a one to one meeting with Mr. K the next day. There is a divergence of evidence as to what exactly transpired but whichever version one accepts it matters little. In essence the DG again asked for Mr. K's comments on the Mr. B matter to be met once again with no comment and no explanation why there was no comment. A says that the failure of the Director of FINAD to comment on a financial defalcation by a senior staff member when asked to do so by the DG at the Management Committee meeting was insubordination. From that time the process for disciplinary termination under the PPM was put in train and resulted in the disciplinary termination of Mr. K's employment. A says that was entirely lawful. It is important to emphasize that throughout the whole Mr. K affair there was never any criticism of Mr. K's financial skills nor any question as to his financial integrity."

5.   Discipline of Other Senior Staff

[28]   "Now I have to go back in time to look at four cases where employees had been guilty of financial impropriety of varying degrees. They were not dealt with consistently and to some extent Mr. K's failure to comment on the Mr. B case at the Management Committee meeting and the meeting with the DG may have been because he was concerned or confused by the inconsistent treatment of defaulting staff in other cases.

[29]   "Mr. O was an accounts clerk. One of this duties was to buy Airport Tax Stamps in bulk. A has staff and visitors travelling out of Kenya almost every day. Under the system then in force it saved time and hassle at the Airport to be able to buy your airport tax stamps in the office rather than at the Airport.

[30]   "Mr. O bought $5000 worth of stamps: he was unable to account for them or the cash in lieu to a material extent. This was not his first default. He was referred to a Disciplinary Panel but as someone is alleged to have said 'The dices were loaded.' I never did discover and it does not matter – whether this was a misquote, or misspoken or misheard. The quaint plural has some how stuck in everyone's memory and the phrase has become a 'leitmotif' in these proceedings

in relation to disciplinary proceedings. The meaning was clear. Mr. O's employ-ment was going to be terminated whatever he said to any panel. He was given an 'opportunity to change' under the PPM but with a time limit. When he missed the time limit by a day or two, he was dismissed.

[31] "Mr. M is a scientific officer . . . on the international staff. He is valuable to A. He misled A about his rent and where he was living so that he was paid a housing allowance far in excess of what would have been paid had the truth been known. Eventually the truth emerged. He was given an opportunity to repay and to change. He was disciplined by a Disciplinary Panel but only to the extent of being suspended for three months.

[32] "Mr. B was a senior A staff member. He had marital problems. His wife went wild with his Gold Card. He had a daughter undergoing overseas college education. Without permission he 'borrowed' several thousand dollars from A to pay for this daughter's education with the full intention of paying it back over a period. Mr. B admitted franking the 'borrowing' and offered to repay. It was in the course of considering what to do about him that the Mr. K incident leading to Mr. K's termination occurred.

[33] "Mrs. I: In addition to being Director of Research at A, Mrs. I had a respon-sibility in an allied French organization, D, which required her to travel to France. A paid initially for a number of air tickets but the cost of some of the sectors was refunded to Mrs. I direct by D. Her bank statements were sent to her rural home in France. Mrs. I was very slow (up to 4 years) to account for the refunds to A. Mr. K had raised this issue with Mrs. I in February of the year in question and it had arisen in FIN AD meetings under the heading of 'monies due from A' several times. The facts were confused initially but it finally transpired that Mrs. I had been refunded by D but had not passed all the refunds on to A. Her lack of transparency in this financial matter made Mr. K somewhat reluctant to approve her appointment as Director of Research. Subsequent to Mr. K's termination, Mrs. I was subject to a Disciplinary Panel inquiry and given a first and last written warning. She was given an opportunity to change and repaid what was due.

[34] "I bear in mind that at the time of the Management Committee meeting only Mr. O and Mr. M had been dealt with. Both had taken money from A: having failed to take the opportunity to change, one was dismissed: one it seems took the opportunity and was merely suspended."

6. Management Committee Meeting

[35] "This was the beginning of the end for Mr. K. The Management Committee on this occasion consisted of the DG, the DDG, Mrs. I, EZ [Director of Training and Information], Mr. K, F as Secretary and Mr. L [of the Human Resources Unit] for part of the meeting.

[36]   ". . . [T]he main events in so far as they concern Mr. K are not seriously in dispute. They arose when the misappropriation by Mr. B came for discussions as to what to do. There is a minor issue as to whether Mr. B's memo was referred to the Management Committee by Mr. K as instructed by the DG or whether the DG was the one to raise it at the Management Committee. The minutes say that Mr. K had refused so to refer it but I do not think that is likely although he may have delayed doing so partly as the result of the extra work caused to everyone by the international donor meeting. Mr. B was obviously in an emotional state possibly as a result of the delay in dealing with his problem: the DDG thought he was 'very fragile'; counseling was thought desirable but the DDG, Mrs. I, and EZ and I assume the DG (although the Minutes do not say so) all thought that his employment should be terminated but that he should be given the opportunity to resign preferably with effect in approximately eight weeks. The DG had previously used the tactic of offering staff thought or found unsatisfactory the opportunity to resign: it was until Mr. K's case universally accepted.

[37]   "Mr. K according to the DG declined to comment or to express an opinion: according to Mr. K he said he had nothing to add. It does seem that Mr. K thought he had a right to remain silent. That of course is not so: the law does give a right to silence but only in very specific cases: for example, in answer to a caution by a police officer to a criminal charge. Whichever it was, the DG sensed there might be something on Mr. K's mind that he was not prepared to discuss in a management meeting and very quickly and very rightly did not push the confrontation with Mr. K there and then. He did ask to see Mr. K the next day on this issue."

7. Meeting of DG and Mr. K on the Following Day

[38]   "Not surprisingly this was a tense meeting and did not last long. Memories differ as to what was said. The DG was clearly irritated that Mr. K would not comment on the case of Mr. B and further would not give his reasons for not commenting. When Mr. K repeated his stance, the DG asked for Mr. K's resignation. This was refused so the DG said he would initiate steps for termination. After further exchanges about the bank test codes and Mr. K's contribution to the visit to the international donor meeting, the meeting ended."

8. The Disciplinary Panel

[39]   "In the absence of 2 levels of management above Mr. K, what should have happened next is that a disciplinary panel should have been convened by the DG under Clause 8(2) of the PPM. There is a fundamental disagreement as to what did happen. Mr. K alleges that there was no proper appointment, hearing or

sitting: that he had no opportunity to address it and to present his case and goes on to say that he was given no or no adequate opportunity to change having been made aware of his situation.

[40]   "Clause 8(2) seems to make it a condition precedent to disciplinary termination that a 'staff member is not fulfilling the term of their appointment or responsibilities after being made aware of the situation and being given opportunity to change . . . '. I have to consider whether this Disciplinary Panel was properly constituted. Clause 8(2) of the PPM under Disciplinary Termination is silent as to who appoints it as it is evident from the passage I have already quoted. If anyone serves on it in lieu of the DG he has to be 'delegated'. The members of this Disciplinary Panel were not aware they were part of a Disciplinary Panel until they were sitting around the table and maybe not even then. There is no suggestion that this Disciplinary Panel was appointed in writing: at the best it was an ad hoc Disciplinary Panel convened verbally and only informed of the purpose of its inquiry as it sat. In terms of the PPM, the Disciplinary Panel has to give a 'fair hearing' and exercise its 'judgment'. Given those formalities, I hold that the appointment of all Disciplinary Panel members should at least be in writing and accordingly, I hold that the DG was not properly appointed or convened. It follows its proceedings and decision were invalid.

[41]   "The DG says there was a de facto Disciplinary Panel; something which had not infrequently happened before; that he consulted with EZ [Director of Training and Information] and Mrs. I – who I note were witnesses to some of the conduct complained of and also with the DDG on the phone abroad. There was no delegation. He had also consulted on the phone with the Chairman of the BoT who in fact had suggested disciplinary termination for insubordination. The DG passed this information to the Disciplinary Panel members before they made any decision.

[42]   "A was admittedly in a hurry to get this Disciplinary Panel procedure out of the way in view of a meeting of the BoT scheduled for a week later. It is being in such a hurry that I consider A made an error of judgment entirely understandable: entirely bona fide but an error of judgment nevertheless. Summary justice is all very well: it is usually summary but seldom justice. Indeed there was no intent to mete out summary justice; but A gave itself only the inside of a week for Mr. K's Disciplinary Panel to be appointed, to meet; to hear; to deliberate; to give an opportunity to change and to decide. I have only to set out those steps for it to be self-evident that the process could not possibly be completed within 5 working days and do justice.

[43]   "Of course I am viewing these events with the huge advantage of hindsight and without the various extraneous pressures that affected those making decisions at the time. Contrast this hasty impromptu procedure with that illustrated in the Disciplinary Panel proceedings into the allegation against Mrs. I

which occurred in early in the following year. For a start the panel members were not witnesses to Mrs. I's defaults. The whole procedure was more measured; certainly the facts were more complex; a preliminary meeting; a hearing of Mrs. I and a final meeting to make the decision and report. None of that happened in the case of Mr. K.

[44]   "Clause 8(1) of the PPM emphasizes fairness and order in the treatment of individuals. In order to be fair, the panel surely has to be free of bias and independent at least in the sense that no panel member is a witness or is possibly prejudiced by having been told that the Chairman of the BoT thought this or that relative to the behaviour complained of.

[45]   "It was a pity that neither Mrs. I nor EZ (who were members of the de facto Disciplinary Panel) were not called as witnesses. EZ has left A employment but Mrs. I could have been made available. I therefore have only the evidence of the DG from the A side of the Disciplinary Panel proceedings and as already noted Mr. K was not present. Having heard and read the evidence so far as it goes of the de facto Disciplinary Panel's proceedings I have no hesitation concluding that the rules of natural justice were not complied with and I hear at the end of it an echo, faint but clear: 'The dices were loaded' and I so find. The proceedings of the Disciplinary Panel resulted in the Mr. K receiving his letter of disciplinary termination six days after the Disciplinary Panel meeting."

9.   *Mr. K's Actions Immediately Subsequent to His Termination*

[46]   "Mr. K did five things:

i.   He appealed to the BoT for a review. This was summarily rejected.
ii. He wrote to the BoT alleging a conflict of interest in the employment of the DG's wife C and Mrs. I's husband by A through a programme run by A to do scientific research for which A's own scientists could equally well have done.
iii. He wrote to the BoT raising the question of Mrs. I's integrity a propos the airtickets and the D's refunds.
iv. He appealed, following the BoT's rejection, to the Grievance Panel: this I deal with later in this Award.
v.   He wrote to the Swedish Ambassador: Mr. K being a Swedish national and Sweden being a major financial supporter of A. . . ."

10.   *Conflict of Interest and Mrs. I's Integrity*

[47]   "These two matters are important in the sense that they form the foundation of the allegations by Mr. K [in his Request for Arbitration] that his

termination was mala fides mainly activated by ill-will on the part of the DG towards Mr. K. Mala fides in Kenya requires a high standard of proof similar to that for fraud or duress. The DG would have been particularly sensitive to the conflict of interest matter as it involved his wife and to some degree his integrity. Mr. K says he first raised both issues with the DG by letter dated five months earlier: the DG says he never saw the letter. I have no doubt that Mr. K typed the letter and presented it or he may even have taken it to the DG's office: I am equally in no doubt that the DG never read it: I note that the letter in evidence is probably a copy of the original which might indicate the original was never delivered. If the DG had received it, I would have expected a very strong reaction of which there is no evidence. If the DG never read the letter then there would have been no reason for him to bear any ill-will towards Mr. K and I so hold.

[48]   "I also hold that Mr. K was in order to bring to his superiors' attention the possibility of a conflict of interest situation developing and the doubts he harboured about Mrs. I's integrity. In the events which happened, the conflict of interest issue was the subject of an external review which found no wrongdoing: Mrs. I's integrity was scrutinized by a Disciplinary Panel: she was given a last and final warning and any monies due from her were paid."

11.   The Grievance Panel

[49]   "The Grievance Panel is provided for under Clause 8(4) of the PPM. This is the first Grievance Panel ever convened by A. The appeal has to be lodged within 10 days of notice of the disciplinary action complained of and is limited to

'the procedural correctness of the disciplinary process or that there is a claim that the action is unjust because of suspicion of prejudice: unreasonable, because of disproportionate punishment in relation to the offence or unwarranted because the offence did not take place'.

The Grievance Panel's composition is clearly set out as is the disqualification from membership of the Grievance Panel for anyone substantively involved in the case under investigation. No complaint is made as to the appointment or composition of the Grievance Panel . . . .

[50]   "At the beginning of the Grievance Panel, Mr. K was not allowed to have his advocate present. I think that was a correct decision. The Grievance Panel is a purely domestic tribunal: properly conducted there is no reason why a Grievance Panel should not resolve internal employment issues satisfactorily. Paradoxically had the lawyer been admitted, the Grievance Panel might well have not fallen into the error that it did, and the errors of the Disciplinary Panel might well have been exposed earlier than they were.

[51]   "In many ways, the Grievance Panel dealt with the case against Mr. K very much more fairly and properly than did the Disciplinary Panel. Even so, it erred in three important respects:

i.   It did not permit Mr. K to make copies of some documents although he was allowed to read them. The reason given was that they were confidential: with respect, a ridiculous reason. An employee accused is entitled to see and hear and receive copies of the whole case against him: that is a fundamental part of each party having the opportunity to state its case: you cannot state your case on documents you do not have in your possession.

ii.   The session of the Grievance Panel in so far as investigating facts was without Mr. K's presence – again a breach of the basic rules of natural justice. Notwithstanding these errors the Grievance Panel did a reasonable job in sifting through what had happened and for example in finding that Mr. K should have been given the opportunity to address the Disciplinary Panel. Where it failed, was not to recognize the essential invalidity in the appointment and membership of the Disciplinary Panel and how imperative that loss of opportunity was to the validity of the whole Disciplinary Panel procedure.

iii.   It listened to and came to some conclusion on matters prejudicial to Mr. K which were not strictly within the purview of the conduct complained in the Letter of Termination.

[52]   "It also failed to assess correctly the 'opportunity to change': In a climate of increasing tension between the DG and Mr. K a truly independent tribunal acting without haste would surely have wanted to see a cooling off period on both sides and an attempt at reconciliation. Once each party had taken a position, and bear in mind these are exceptionally able and strong men, neither was going to back off or compromise without a substantial and very careful rethink not possible in under a few days. The Grievance Panel members recognized this but except for one member's minority report did not have the courage of their convictions. Of course by the time the Grievance Panel came to sit, it would have been difficult for it to have considered reinstatement without there being a major reconciliation between the DG and Mr. K. In such a small team and after the meeting of the DG with Mr. K and the manner of the Disciplinary Panel proceedings, such would have been very difficult to achieve, without willingness and a major effort from both men.

[53]   "In one respect however, I agree with the Grievance Panel. The failure by Mr. K to comment one way or the other on Mr. B's misappropriation of funds when requested by the DG to do so was insubordination. The question was fully

within Mr. K's area of responsibility whether this was pointed out to him by the DG or not; the very least that the DG was entitled to expect of his Director of FINAD would be a comment one way or the other. If for personal reasons Mr. K preferred not to comment, the least the DG was entitled to was some indication of the reason for abstention. In fact all Mr. K needed to say was that he did not agree with the decision to terminate Mr. B but that he could live with it. Mr. K has not explained satisfactorily why he did not reply nor explain his silence: the inconsistency in the previous staff problems may have contributed as may have Mr. K's belief in the right to silence but I cannot believe they were the whole reason: maybe there was a repressed crisis in his relations with the DG to which Mr. K's defensive reaction was to say nothing.

[54]   "I would also comment that for Mr. K to criticize previous inconsistencies in the handling of staff problems is a two edged sword. If the Human Resources Unit had been inconsistent, it was for Mr. K as Director of FINAD to direct the Human Resources Unit into a consistent line as that unit came directly within Mr. K's area of responsibility."

II.   THE SOLE ARBITRATOR'S FINDINGS

[55]   Relying on the above findings, the sole arbitrator concluded that the termination of RK's employment with A was justified on the grounds of insubordination, but the procedure adopted was breach of the Disciplinary Code and therefore wrongful and unjustified. The express provisions of the PPM were not properly followed and the termination was not within the spirit and objectives of the PPM. The rules of natural justice applied to the termination and it was carried out in breach of these rules. There was no evidence of mala fides especially given that a higher standard of proof is required. A had tried bona fine to follow the proper procedure but had failed to do so in all respects.

[56]   A did try to appoint a de facto Disciplinary Panel, but a de facto appointment was not in accordance with the PPM and was invalid. In the view of the sole arbitrator: "A Disciplinary Panel should be totally independent and be formally appointed in writing and its members should if at all possible, not be liable to be biased nor be witness(es) of the incident(s) complained of." Even if the Disciplinary Panel had been properly appointed, "it did not conduct itself properly under the PPM or under the law". The rules of natural justice applied to the proceedings of the Disciplinary Panel and it acted in breach of them.

[57]   The sole arbitrator continued: "The DG had expressed reservations about some aspects of the claimant's work performance prior to the Management Committee meeting but such reservations were more in the nature of genuine differences of opinion for example about the speed of adopting new technology or frustration or irritation of the DG that the claimant had not done precisely

what the DG wanted him to do. The only active dissatisfaction was the failure to secure an allocation of $ 100,00 for the A programme, which I hold to have been due to a misunderstanding."

[58]   Claimant had been asked by the DG to table the Mr. B memorandum and did not do so. His non-participation in the Mr. B discussion was better characterized as "abstention than refusal". The claimant did circulate the Mr. B memorandum to all the Directors, although the DG said he never received it.

[59]   The Grievance Panel investigated what happened at the meeting between the DG and the claimant but were unable to establish what happened. The sole arbitrator stated that he had "no doubt the claimant was asked at least once for his comments on the Mr. B memorandum and three times for his reasons for making no comment". He held "the claimant was not asked for his professional assessment on that occasion, but whether he was so asked or not, makes no difference. It was his duty as Director of FIN AD to comment."

[60]   The sole arbitrator concluded that the truth lay somewhere between the two accounts of what transpired at the meeting between the DG and Mr. K. There was some tension, irritation and frustration between the DG and Mr. K in the period leading up to the termination, but no ill will.

[61]   Mr. K was shown, but denied copies of memorandum prepared by Mr. L for the Grievance Panel and all the documents appended to the Grievance Panel's report. The Grievance Panel was properly appointed but did not conduct itself and its proceedings strictly in accordance with the PPM or the rules of natural justice. The Grievance Panel found that Mr. K was given an opportunity to change, but in the view of the sole arbitrator, he was only given a "momentary opportunity to change". He was not given an adequate opportunity to change under the PPM and thus the finding of the Grievance Panel was untenable.

[62]   In considering if the Report of the Grievance Panel complied with the provisions of the Personnel Policy and whether its holdings and findings were correct, valid, justified and tenable, the sole arbitrator held: "The Report of the Grievance Panel was a carefully considered document and as such is in accordance with the PPM. However, I hold as regards its findings:

> 'Clause 2(1) It is the opinion of the panel that the arrangement for disciplinary termination, with three months notice and suspension of duties, is justified.'
> *Answer:* These findings would have been correct only if a properly appointed unbiased Disciplinary Panel had followed the rules of natural justice: it follows that this finding was invalid and unjustified.
> 'Clause 2(2) The panel agrees with the degree of punishment, resulting in disciplinary termination.'

Answer: I agree that disciplinary termination properly implemented under the PPM would have been a proper degree of punishment for insubordination. As disciplinary termination was improperly implemented, no punishment can be imposed.

'Clause 2 (2) It is the opinion of the grievance panel that proper procedures were followed, and that Mr. K was given an opportunity to change (in the meeting with the DG).'

Answer: I agree that while an attempt was made to follow proper procedures, proper procedures under the PPM were not followed nor was Mr. K given an adequate or reasonable opportunity to change.

'Clause 2(3) The panel concluded that Mr. K's actions during the Management Committee meeting and during a discussion with [the DG] the next day are correctly characterized as insubordination.'

Answer: I hold that the abstention from comment by the Director of FINAD on the Mr. B affair both at the Management Committee meeting and in the meeting with the DG amounted to insubordination in the absence of an explanation for such abstention.

'Clause 2(4) It is the grievance panel's opinion that the decision in the disciplinary termination matter was not made based on presumption, was not personal, and was not biased or disproportionate.'

Answer: I hold that the Disciplinary Panel members all knew the DG and the BoT Chair were in favour of disciplinary termination prior to giving its decision. While its decision was not personal, it was based on presumption and bias and was disproportionate in all the circumstances. In addition:

i.   The DG should not, as one of the principal protagonists, have been a member of the Disciplinary Panel due to the risk of bias.
ii. Mrs. I, one of the members of the de facto Disciplinary Panel should have been disqualified from sitting on the Disciplinary Panel because of the risk that she was biased against Mr. K because Mr. K to her knowledge had queried her integrity.

'Clause 2(5) It is the grievance panel's opinion that Mr. K's statement about the "Open-ended contract with A of continuous employment with a maximum tenure of 10 years" is negated by stipulations regarding termination in the Personnel Policy Manual.'

Answer: I agree with the Grievance Panel that Mr. K's employment for 10 years is subject to the 'termination in the case of redundancy, unsatisfactory performance, or other cases as stipulated in the termination policy'.

'Clause 2(5) It is also the panel's opinion that sufficient evidence exists of increasingly unsatisfactory performance of Mr. K to justify disciplinary termination.'

Answer: While there is evidence of incidents of unsatisfactory performance particularly in the previous six months and while there had been verbal expressions of dissatisfaction by the DG there had been no verbal or written warning(s) or express opportunity to change since the fourth year Performance Evaluation and I hold such unsatisfactory performance in those circumstances did not warrant disciplinary termination: in any event these incidents were not the subject of the Letter of Termination and should not have been considered by the de facto Disciplinary Panel nor by the Grievance Panel."

[63]   The sole arbitrator further found that the Grievance Panel erred in its finding that "sufficient evidence existed of unsatisfactory performance by the claimant to justify disciplinary termination and overlooked the fact that this was neither formally brought to the claimant's attention nor the subject of the Letter of Termination: further the claimant was not given an opportunity to change as per the PPM.

[64]   In addition, the sole arbitrator held that "the reference by the DG to the Chair of the BoT of the claimant's refusal to give his opinion on the Mr. B affair was highly improper and disqualified the BoT from giving its opinion on the claimant's termination and on the procedures."

III.   QUANTUM

[65]   "Having decided on the issue of liability that A is liable, I have to quantify the amount of Mr. K's claim taking into account the provisions of the appointment letter to Mr. K from the DG which states in part

'I am pleased to inform you that your current contract . . . is hereby renewed as per the revised [PPM]. Therefore you are hereby offered continuing employment. Your appointment has a maximum of 10 years and is subject to termination in case of redundancy, unsatisfactory performance or other cases as stipulated in the termination policy.'

This offer was accepted. It is under this letter that Mr. K claims his total emoluments from the date of his dismissal giving credit of course for what he was paid for in the three months following the letter of termination. The total is 4 years, 8 months = 56 months of which 3 months was paid at the rate of the last year of employment.

[66] "Mr. K obtained alternative employment in an Asian country and there is no argument that he has in his claim to give credit for the amounts earned from other sources in mitigation less deductions for the higher cost of living in the Asian country. Mr. K's calculation of hisnet entitlement is to be found following his advocate's submissions . . . .

[67] "No question of redundancy was raised or argued or seems likely. However, there is a question of satisfactory performance. Under Kenyan law, what I have to do is to place the employee, so far as money can do so, in the same position as if the contract had been performed to its end, whenever that might be. Where there is a fixed term contract that means the remuneration for the remainder of the fixed term less mitigation. This is the figure as calculated by Mr. K in the final submissions.

[68] "Where there is a provision in the contract for termination by notice, then prima facie the employee is only entitled to remuneration for the notice period. I have to determine whether and if so when notice would have been given remembering A's generous employment policy.

[69] "I hold that circumstances giving rise to summary dismissal given the seniority of Mr. K would have been inherently unlikely to arise again. The worst case scenario following that holding is that Mr. K's employment could have been terminated under Clause 211(1)(5) of the PPM. This involved either:

i.   Two consecutive 'fair' performance evaluations if the staff member has been made aware of the situation, put on an improvement plan – developed in this case by the DG with assistance from the Human Resources Unit and given a chance to correct the situation,

ii.   Failure to improve following a 6 month improvement plan.

[70] "Dealing with this in order:

i.   the next performance evaluation would have been due early in the following year. Two consecutive performance evaluations would take us to February-March of the subsequent year. Although the PPM does not say so specifically it seems to me that the staff member would be entitled to six months' notice under this provision. That would take us to September of the subsequent year as the earliest date Mr. K's employment could be terminated following two consecutive 'Fair' evaluations.

ii.   If given a specific improvement plan, looking at the totality of the evidence, I think it very unlikely that Mr. K would not have made significant improvement in his performance although whether enough to satisfy the DG is an open question.

For those reasons, I do not propose to calculate exactly the earliest date for the termination of Mr. K's employment under this head.

[71] "So I now have the earliest date for lawful termination on certain assumptions 22 months from the date of dismissal of which 3 months were paid at the rates prior to termination. I also have the latest date for leaving A's employment at the expiry of the 10 years namely, 56 months less the 3 months already paid as above. I have to decide whether Mr. K would have continued in A employment to the end of his contract.

[72] "What are the factors for and against him doing so:

For:

i. Strong on finance: undoubted integrity.

ii. Resignation unlikely even when under pressure to do so – vide the one-to-one meeting with the DG.

iii. Age; disability on medical grounds; death; redundancy: all either not applicable or unlikely.

iv. Probably amenable to change but whether enough so to restore the DG's lost confidence in him open to question.

Against:

v. Not so strong in administration – nor in inter-personal relationships.

vi. Readily replaceable.

vii. Some decline in performance in the final year of employment.

viii. Had lost the confidence of the DG which would be difficult or very difficult to restore.

ix. Tendency to delay dealing with acute personnel problems, e.g. – Mrs. I and Mr. B.

x. Unexplained inability to deal with the Mr. B problem which was essentially very simple. Possibly indicative of deeper malaise which remains unexplained and could recur.

xi. The very strong position of the DG in the organizational structure and under the PPM which makes the DG lawfully judge, jury and executioner regardless of Disciplinary Panels and Grievance Panels. See the last sentence of PPM 8(4).

xii. The BoT would have been unhappy with a situation in which the DG and Director of FIN AD were in conflict. While having no direct part in management, I think it likely the BoT would put strong pressure on the DG to cure the problem.

[73] "Taking all these matters into account, I hold that Mr. K would not have remained in the service of A beyond the end of two years: that would make

25 months from the termination of which 3 were paid at the pre-termination rates . . . .

[74]   "Under Kenyan law and practice interest on general damages is awarded from the date of judgment. In the case of a Kenya Shilling judgment, the current practice in the absence of a contractual rate would be to award interest at between 12% and 15% per annum on the judgment debt. Such a rate would be considered by the courts inappropriate to a US dollar judgment where interest would be awarded at a rate appropriate to that currency. While there is no law on the subject, there is widespread reference in practice to dollar LIBOR rates both in the courts and in private contracts rather than to rates quoted in New York probably more as a result of geography and history than for any other reason. The dollar LIBOR rate would only be looked at as a guide and not followed slavishly. This award being in US dollars and in the nature of general damages, I award interest at 5½% compounded monthly from the date of the award until payment in full."

[75]   The sole arbitrator also directed that A pay the costs of arbitration and Mr. K's legal costs because in his view "costs follow the event".

Interlocutory award in case no. 10596 of 2000

Parties:	Claimant: Distributor A (nationality not indicated)
	Respondent: Manufacturer B (nationality not indicated)
Place of arbitration:	Paris, France
Published in:	Unpublished
Subject matters:	– jurisdiction to order interim relief
	– requirements for interim relief
	– interim relief in form of award

Facts

The manufacturer B concluded two distribution agreements with distributor A for certain pharmaceutical products, including product X. One agreement covered the territory of Hong Kong, and the other (the Distribution Agreement) covered the People's Republic of China (PRC). A dispute arose between the parties regarding the termination of the two agreements and A initiated ICC arbitration proceedings. Shortly after filing its Answer and Amended Claim, B also filed an Application for Interim and Conservatory Measures (the Application) requesting that A deliver documentary materials to it issued by the authorities in the PRC (including the PRC Registration Certificate and Pricing Approval, hereinafter the documents) and Hong Kong. A responded with a Counter application requesting the arbitral tribunal to make a declaration that A had no obligation whatsoever towards B with respect to the Hong Kong certificates and that the relief requested by B could not be granted by the tribunal. Further, A also requested that B be ordered to take appropriate measures to mitigate its losses, in particular to take any steps likely to enable B to be in possession of the PRC certificate. If an order were to be made against it, A further requested security of US$ 1 million. B subsequently withdrew its application with respect to the Hong Kong certificates.

B argued that it could not commercialise the products formerly distributed by A without the documents and that it was urgent that A return the documents as it was incurring losses which increased daily. A responded that the Pricing Approval did not exist as a separate document and that, implicitly, its delivery was impossible; in addition A stated that it had been trying to obtain the Registration Certificate from its distributor, but the distributor would not comply unless the stock was repurchased which B was unwilling to do. A also objected that the relief sought was not an interim or conservatory measure in the meaning of Art. 23(1) of the ICC Rules and that the outcome of the request was too closely linked to the merits to be dealt with by way of interim relief. Moreover, A argued that B's conduct was in breach of the duty to mitigate losses as it should have either obtained duplicate originals, or repurchased the stock, and finally, that the relief sought lacked urgency.

The arbitral tribunal first established that the relief sought fell under the category of "interim and conservatory measures", holding that it was ICC practice not only to prohibit actions which would aggravate the dispute, but also to order a party to perform certain contractual duties to avoid further losses. The arbitral tribunal then established that there was a likelihood of success on the merits since there was prima facie a right to obtain the relief sought. Under the terms of the Distribution Agreement, A was prima facie under an obligation to return the documents at issue. It was irrelevant that the documents were held by a third party. Nor was A's reliance on B's duty to mitigate its losses of any avail, as B could not reasonably be expected to step into A's relationship with the Chinese distributor. The arbitral tribunal also did not accept A's argument that the order could only be granted after a close review of the merits, as the Distribution Agreement provided for the return of the documents in the event of any termination.

The arbitral tribunal found that although, strictly speaking, B's monetary loss would not be irreparable harm, it would be unreasonable to refuse the relief because "any non marginal risk of aggravation of the dispute is sufficient to warrant an order for interim relief" as the purpose was to prevent the loss in the first place. Urgency was also to be broadly interpreted and the fact that the loss was likely to increase with the mere passing of time made it unreasonable to require a party to wait for the final award. Thus A was ordered to deliver the documents to B.

The arbitral tribunal granted the relief in the form of an award rather than an order, because, at least under French law, a decision does not need to resolve an issue definitively in order to qualify as an award and because this possibility was envisioned in Art. 23(1) of the ICC Rules. A's request for security was rejected.

Excerpt

I. PRIMA FACIE STANDARD OF REVIEW

[1] "This decision rules on an application for interim relief. Consequently, it applies a prima facie standard of review. It makes no final findings of fact or law.

In other words, no findings made herein prejudice the merits of the dispute. In particular, the present decision is rendered without consideration of the lawfulness of the termination, an issue which will be litigated on the merits. The provisional nature of the present dispute further means that all issues addressed in this decision may be reargued by the parties in the later course of the arbitration and revisited by the arbitral tribunal in the final award."

II.   APPLICABLE RULES

[2]   "Pursuant to Art. 1494(1) of the *Nouveau Code de Procédure Civile*, the present arbitral proceedings are governed by the rules chosen by the parties, i.e., by the ICC Rules of Arbitration supplemented by any procedural rules to be agreed upon by the parties or determined by the tribunal."

III.   JURISDICTION

[3]   "Art. 23(1) of the ICC Rules expressly grants the tribunal jurisdiction to order 'any interim or conservatory measure it considers appropriate'. The tribunal does not accept A's argument that the relief sought by B does not fall under the category of 'interim and conservatory measures'. Under longstanding practice in ICC arbitration (since well before the entry into force of Art. 23 of the 1998 version of the ICC Rules), the parties must refrain from taking any action which may aggravate the dispute. Arbitrators sitting under the ICC Rules have the power to issue decisions prohibiting such actions; this power flows from their jurisdiction to order interim relief.[1] Conversely, these principles apply to any inaction which may aggravate the dispute; there are several instances in which arbitrators have ordered a party to continue to perform

---

1. "See award rendered in 1982 in lCC case no. 3896, *Journal du droit international* (1983) p. 914, 918; interim award rendered in 1984 in ICC case no. 4126, *Journal du droit international* (1984) p. 934, 935; Donovan, D.,' *Le pouvoir des arbitres de rendre des ordonnances de procedure, notamment des mesures conservatoires, et leur force obligatoire à l'égard des parties*', 10 *Bulletin de la Cour internationale d'arbitrage*, no. 1, pp. 59-74, *67-68*; Goldman, C., '*Mesures provisaires et arbitrage international*', *Revue de droit des affaires internationales* (1993) pp. 3-26, *15* and *18-20*; Schwartz, E., 'The Practices and Experience of the lCC Court' in *Conservatory and Provisional Measures in International Arbitration*, ICC no. 159 (Paris 1993) pp. 45-69, *69*; see also decision rendered under ICSID Rules on 9 December 1983, XI *Yearbook Commercial Arbitration* (1986) p. 159, 161. This general principle of international commercial arbitration also underpins the 1998 version of the ICC Rules; see Reiner, A., '*Le reglement d'arbitrage de la CCI, version 1998*', Rev. arb. (1 998) pp. 25-82, *39-40*."

certain contract duties, precisely in order to avoid further losses and an increase of the amounts in dispute.[2]

[4] "Therefore, assuming that the relief sought by B is likely to avoid the aggravation of the dispute, which will be seen below, it can be characterised as an 'interim measure' within the meaning of Art. 23(1) of the Rules and the arbitral tribunal has jurisdiction and the power to grant such relief."

IV. REQUIREMENTS FOR INTERIM RELIEF

1. Likelihood of Success on the Merits

[5] "The first requirement for interim relief is that the applicant render plausible that it has a prima facie contractual or legal right to obtain the relief it seeks.[3] Art. XV(7)(1) of the Distribution Agreement reads as follows:

'7. Upon expiration or termination of this Agreement for any reason, A shall:
7(1) Promptly and unconditionally cease any use of the Registration and put such Registration at B's disposal . . . .'

The term Registration is defined . . . as 'any official approval, or licensing by the competent bodies of the territory regarding the Products, including, if applicable, their selling prices and social security approvals, allowing the lawful marketing of the Products within the territory'.[4]

[6] "Accordingly, A is prima facie under an obligation to return the *Registration Certificate* and the *Pricing Approval* to B. We will deal bellow with A's objection that the latter is not a separate document.

[7] A did not dispute that it is under a contractual duty to return the documents. This is particularly obvious from the fact that it requested a declaration that it complied with such duty with respect to Hong Kong. Similarly, when B asked it to return the documents, it never challenged its obligation to do so. Quite to the contrary, it allegedly attempted to recover the documents, but was unsuccessful.

---

2. "Reiner, *op. cit., loc. cit.*; Schwartz, *op. cit*, pp. 61-62; see also examples given by Cremades, B., 'The Need for Conservatory and Preliminary Measures', Paper for IBA conference of 13 November 1998 on *Dispute Resolution in International Long-term Construction and Infrastructure Projects.*

3. "This requirement is found both in judicial and in arbitral practice. See, for instance, interim award rendered on 12 December 1996 in case no. 1694 of the Netherlands Arbitration Institute, XXII *Yearbook Commercial Arbitration* (1998) p. 97, *105.*"

4. "The term 'Registration' is defined at Art. 1(5) and undoubtedly applies to the Registration Certificate sought by B."

[8]   "A rather objects that it is in no position to return the documents because they are held by its Chinese distributor. A also stated that the situation in the PRC was created by B because B's management of the termination was heavy-handed and contrary to local business practice.

[9]   "The arbitral tribunal considers that these objections are irrelevant in the present context. Under Art. III(1) of the Distribution Agreement, A is deemed to be an independent trader, operating for its own profit and at its own risk. Art. III(2) provides that A bears the costs of performing its contractual duties. Moreover, the broad wording of Art. XV(7)(1) implies that, if the documents to be returned are held by a third party, A has a duty to recover them. Indeed, the parties probably contemplated that A would have to remit certain documents to third parties, at least temporarily. Yet, the Distribution Agreement makes no reservation regarding A's duty to return the documents in that event.

[10]   "Therefore, any difficulties which A may have with its sub-distributors must be solved at that level and do not concern B. If A becomes liable to B for a sub-distributor's refusal to return certain documents, then A may consider seeking compensation from that sub-distributor. In any event, on a prima facie basis, the tribunal does not see which contractual provision or legal principle would compel B to take an action vis-à-vis the Chinese distributor, which action should normally be taken by A.

[11]   "In this context, A relies on B's duty to mitigate its losses. Such duty is of no avail here. In accordance with Art. 44 of the Swiss Code of Obligations, which governs as a result of a contractual choice of law, that duty is limited to actions which can be reasonably expected from a party.[5] Stepping into A's relationship with its Chinese distributor cannot be reasonably expected of B.

[12]   "Still in relation to mitigation, A argues that, contrary to a submission made by B, 'obtaining a duplicate original [of the Registration Certificate] is not only possible but ordinary proceedings' and that obtaining this type of document is best done through someone used to dealing with Chinese officials adding that it has this experience and implying that B does not. If that is the case, then the arbitral tribunal does not understand why A itself has not sought or even offered to seek a duplicate original. Whatever the reason, this fact also leads the arbitral tribunal to disagree with A on the issue of mitigation.

[13]   "The tribunal does not either accept A's submission that the relief sought by B can only be granted after a close review of the merits. Indeed, A does not

---

5. "Brehm, R., Berner Kommentar, *Das Obligationenrecht, Die Entstehung durch unerlaubte Handlungen, Kommentar zu Art. 41-69 OR* (Bern 1998) note 50 re Art. 44 CO; Engel, P., *Traité des obligations en droit suisse, Dispositions générales du CO*, 2d ed. (Bern 1997) p. 721; Oftinger, K., Stark, E., *Schweizerisches Haftpflichtrecht, 1. Bd., Allgemeiner Teil* (Zurich 1995) pp. 261-264, paras. 40-47 and references, in particular p. 262, para. 41."

dispute the termination as such. In particular, it does not seek specific performance of the Distribution Agreement. The parties' dispute hinges, not upon the
principle of the termination, but upon its cause and consequences. Thus, there is
no issue that the contract will not continue to be performed. Hence, there is no
need to review the merits to decide on the return of the certificates, as the
Distribution Agreement provides for such return in the event of any termination, whatever its cause and consequences.

[14]   "A objects that the Pricing Approval is not a separate document and, by
implication, that it cannot be returned for this reason. Prima facie at least, the
document appearing as B's Exhibit 2 in the English translation . . . seems to be a
self standing and separate document, not just an excerpt of a register.
Admittedly, on its face, it is unclear whether it was issued to A or is simply
intended for internal use between administrative bodies in China.

[15]   "Despite this uncertainty, the Document appears to fall within the definition of a 'Registration' of Art. 1(5) of the Distribution Agreement, which in
particular includes 'any official approval . . . by the competent bodies . . .
regarding the Products, including, if applicable, their selling prices . . . allowing
the lawful marketing of the Products within the territory'. Indeed, the contents
of the document suggests that it is an approval of the selling prices. It annexes a
'Table of prices for 48 types of imported medicines, including product X' and
orders that these prices be implemented:

> 'Under the "Provision Measures for Managing Prices of Medicines" and
> other supplementary regulations, a table of the present applicable tax inclu-
> sive at port prices; wholesale prices and retail prices for 48 types of exam-
> ined and approved imported medicines, including product X, has been
> printed and is distributed to you herewith. Please implement these prices
> accordingly.'

Therefore, the arbitral tribunal considers B's entitlement to the return of the
Pricing Approval sufficiently evidenced under prima facie standards of review."

2. *Risk of Imminent and Irreparable Harm / Aggravation of the Dispute*

[16]   "A further requirement for interim relief is the risk of imminent and
irreparable harm, or of aggravation of the dispute.[6] B has argued that, as long
as it does not dispose of the documents, it is incurring significant harm, for it
cannot commercialise the products with a different distributor. This situation
impairs the shelf life of products already packaged for the PRC market, and is

---

6. "See, for instance, Schwartz, *op. cit.*, pp. 60-61 and references."

detrimental to the product market profile and future sales opportunities are lost. On this basis, B contends that it cannot wait for the final award.

[17]   "As stated above, A admits that B needs the documents to be able to commercialise its products, but it has argued that monetary loss is not irreparable harm, as, assuming that A were to be held liable for such loss, B would be able to recover it in the form of damages. Although, strictly speaking, this view may be correct, the arbitral tribunal considers that it would be unreasonable to refuse the relief sought on those grounds. The tribunal has already explained that the parties must refrain from any conduct (whether action or inaction) which may aggravate the dispute, and that arbitrators sitting under the ICC Rules have the power to issue decisions prohibiting such conduct.

[18]   "Therefore, any non marginal risk of aggravation of the dispute is sufficient to warrant an order for interim relief. Indeed, it would be foolish for the tribunal to wait for a foreseeable, or at least plausibly foreseeable, loss to occur, to then provide for its compensation in the form of damages (assuming that B is entitled to such damages, which is not the issue here), rather than to prevent the loss from occurring in the first place. Therefore, the fact that B may recover losses in the form of damages is no valid objection and does not preclude it from seeking provisional relief."

3. Urgency

[19]   "A final requirement for interim relief under ICC practice is that the request relates to a matter of urgency, it being understood that 'urgency' is broadly interpreted; the fact that a party's potential losses are likely to increase with the mere passing of time and that it would be unreasonable to expect that party to wait for the final award suffices.[7] The considerations relating to the risk of irreparable harm apply equally to the requirement of urgency. B has made a plausible case that it is exposed to further economic harm if it does not recover the documents and that such harm may increase with the passing of time. Because the tribunal considers that this possible result should be avoided rather than remedied, the sooner action is taken the better.

[20]   "The tribunal cannot follow A's argument that B had failed to take any appropriate action prior to filing the Application and that, therefore, the urgency is not met. From a factual and chronological standpoint, the argument is wrong. B had made requests to A regarding the documents before and after A filed its Request for Arbitration and filed its Answer and Counterclaim. The time elapsed

---

7. "Schwartz, op. cit., p. 60; Bond, S., 'The Nature of Conservatory and Provisional Measures' in Conservatory and Provisional Measures in International Arbitration, ICC no. 159 (Paris 1993) pp. 8-20, 18-19."

between the latest correspondence on this issue between the parties and B's Application is a matter of a few weeks at most. In fact, the last letter from counsel for B is dated . . . three days prior to the filing of the Application. B can hardly be deemed to have forfeited its right to seek interim relief merely for having sought to resolve the issue directly with A.

[21]   "As a consequence, B's request meets the requirements for interim relief under Art. 23(1) of the ICC Rules and the arbitral) tribunal will grant such relief."

V.   COUNTERAPPLICATION

(. . . .)

1.   Declaration Relating to Mitigation of Damages

[22]   "The arbitral tribunal does not, on a prima facie basis and at this stage, agree with A's reasons in support of its statement that B has failed to mitigate its damages. That being said, pursuant to the law governing the substance of the dispute and to generally recognised principles of international trade law, *both* parties are in any event under a duty to mitigate damages. A declaration to that effect by the arbitral tribunal would thus have no impact beyond a mere restatement of a statutory duty. For these reasons, the tribunal denies this particular prayer for relief."

2.   Declaration That the Relief Sought Cannot Be Granted

[23]   "For the reasons given above at III and IV, the arbitral tribunal cannot follow A's position and denies this particular prayer for relief."

VI.   FORM OF THE DECISION

[24]   "B has requested a decision in the form of an award, mainly for the purpose of enhancing the prospects for enforcement in the PRC. Alternatively, it has requested an order. A argues that the tribunal cannot render a decision in the form of an award without an in depth review of the merits. Should the tribunal nevertheless do so, it would prejudice the case and exceed the powers vested in it by Art. 23(1) ICC Rules. Furthermore, A alleges that an award could not be enforced as a matter of practice and that Art. 35 of the lCC Rules[8] compels the arbitral tribunal to take this fact into consideration.

---

8. Art. 35 of the International Chamber of Commerce Rules of Arbitration 1998 reads:

[25] "Art. 23(1) ICC Rules empowers the tribunal to grant interim relief in the form of an award, without specifying under which circumstances an award is to be preferred over an order. Commentators of the ICC Rules provide little guidance. The consideration most often referred to in favour of an award is that invoked by B, namely the prospects of enforcement.[9] As for legal authorities, an *award* is usually defined as a decision by which the tribunal disposes of issues in dispute. In other words, under this view, an interim or partial award is characterised by the fact that it resolves the questions it addresses and cannot later be revisited by the tribunal.[10] Specifically, in the recent *Brasoil* case cited by B, the *Cour d'appel de Paris* held that the decision by which an arbitral tribunal declares a request for revision of an award inadmissible resolves part of the dispute submitted to arbitration and thus constitutes an award.[11]

[26] "It has, however, also been advocated that decisions by which the tribunal orders that certain measures be implemented for the duration of the arbitration proceedings can be considered as awards, provided that they cannot be changed

---

"In all matters not expressly provided for in these Rules, the Court and the Arbitral Tribunal shall act in the spirit of these Rules and shall make every effort to make sure that the Award is enforceable at law."

9. "See 'Final Report on Interim and Partial Awards by a Working Party to the Commission on International Arbitration', reprinted in Craig, W.L, Park, W., Paulsson, J., *International Chamber of Commerce Arbitration*, loose-leaf binder, vol. 2, Appendix V, pp. 3-4 (hereinafter 'Final Report'). The Working Party has recommended that interim relief be granted in the form of an order and that an award should be issued only if 'appropriate'; however, other than prospects for enforcement, the 'Final Report' cites few decisive factors; see 'Final Report, pp. 8, 10. See also Craig, W.L., Park, W., Paulsson, *J., Annotated Guide to the 1998 1CC Arbitration Rules* (1998) p. 138 (hereinafter 1998); Derains, Y., Schwartz, E., *A Guide to the New ICC Rules of Arbitration* (1998) pp. 36-37, 275; Schwartz, *op. cit.*, p. 64."

10. "*Resort Condominiums International Inc. v. Bolwell*, Supreme Court of Queensland, 29 October 1993, quoted and commented by Pryles, M., 'Interlocutory Orders and Convention Awards: the Case of Resort Condominiums v. Bolwell', 10 Arbitration Int'l (1994) pp. 385-394, *391-392;* Craig, Park, Paulsson (1998) p. 33; Craig, W.L., Park, W., Paulsson, J., *International Chamber of Commerce Arbitration*, 2d ed. (1990) p. 322 (hereinafter 1988); Fouchard, Gaillard, Goldman, *[Traité de l'arbitrage commercial international* (Paris, Litec 1996)] pp. 751-752, para. 1355-1 357; see further definitions supplied by Wirth, M., 'Enforceability of a Foreign Security Award in Switzerland' in *The New York Convention of 1958, ASA Special Series no. 9*, pp. 245-256. *252-255.*"

11. "*Braspetro Oil Services Company ('Brasoil') c / The Management and Implementation of the Great Man-made River Project ('GMRA')*, Cour d'appel de Paris, 1 July 1999, 14 Int'l Arb. Report (Aug. 1999, no. 8); the *Cour d'appel* also took into account the fact that the decision contained reasons and that it was rendered in adversarial proceedings after careful examination of the parties' arguments."

at any time.[12] Certain authors consider that finality is not a characteristic of an award;[13] such is the case for awards *'avant dire droit'*, known under French law, which decide an issue on a provisional basis and which can later be rescinded or amended.[14] Thus, at least under French law, a decision does not need to resolve an issue definitively in order to qualify as an award.

[27] "This conclusion is also evident from Art. 23(1) ICC Rules. That provision could not contemplate the issuance of decisions on *interim relief*, which is by essence temporary,[15] in the form of an award, if the award was necessarily a *final*[16] decision. Under the 1975 and 1988 versions of the ICC Rules, several decisions granting interim and provisional relief were rendered in the form of awards.

[28] "On the basis of the foregoing considerations, the arbitral tribunal comes to the conclusion that the decision will be issued in the form of an award. The form so chosen does not mean that this decision is final. It is not, and the arbitrators may revisit it in the final award, if appropriate."

VII. SECURITY

[29] "A requests security in the amount of US\$ 1,000,000. However, it fails to substantiate any risk of loss which may arise out of the interim relief. The possibility of a loss is all the more so unlikely, considering that A does not own the documents and that they have no intrinsic value, which is not dispute. Under these circumstances, the tribunal dismisses A's request."

(...)

VIII. AWARD

"On the basis of the foregoing, the arbitral tribunal:

---

12. "Besson, S., *Arbitrage international et mesures provisoires, étude de droit comparé* (Zurich 1998) pp. 139-140; see also authorities quoted by Wirth, *op. cit.*, pp. 251-252 (on an order to issue a security for the amount under dispute)."

13. "See, for instance, Craig, Park, Paulsson (1988) pp. 418-419; Fouchard, Gaillard, Goldman, *op. cit.*, p. 730, para. 1318; Schwartz, *op. cit.*, p. 63; van den Berg, A.J., 'The Application of the New York Convention by the Courts' in: *Improving the Efficiency of Arbitration Agreements and Awards: 40 Years of Application of the New York Convention*, ICCA Congress Series no. 9 (1999) pp. 25-34 29."

14. "M. de Boisséson, *[Le droit français de l'arbitrage interne et international* (1990)] p. 287."

15. "Final Report, p. 8; Bond, *op. cit.*, p. 9."

16. "A decision may qualify as an 'award' within the meaning of the ICC Rules, but not under the New York Convention, under the law of the seat of the arbitration, or under the law of the place where it is to be enforced. It is thus the applicant's ultimate responsibility and risk to seek and obtain enforcement of an award granting interim relief."

1. orders A to immediately deliver and/or procure delivery to B the Registration Certificate for product X issued by the Bureau of Drug Administration and Policy, Ministry of Public Health, the People's Republic of China and the Pricing Approval issued by the National Development Planning Committee, the People's Republic of China;
2. dismisses A's request for security;
3. dismisses A's Counterapplication;
4. reserves its order on costs for adjudication with the final award;
5. dismisses any further prayers for interim relief."

Interim award in case no. 10973 of 2001

Parties:	Claimants: (1) Trust C (Isle of Sark);
	(2) US Corporation (US);
	(3) Mr. W (US)
	Respondents: (1) Latvian Group (Latvia);
	(2) Latvian Finance Company (Latvia);
	(3) Trust L (Latvia)
Place of arbitration:	Paris, France
Published in:	Unpublished
Subject matters:	– power to order interim relief before signing of Terms of Reference
	– requirements for interim relief

Facts

In April 1999, Mr. W contacted the Latvian Group about a possible banking relationship with a view to establishing a secured line of credit and setting up a security trading account. At the Latvian Group's suggestion, Trust C and the US Corporation (together with Mr. W, the claimants) were established for this purpose. Two accounts were established, Accounts I and II, to be used for investments and stock trading. Problems arose with respect to a loan agreement, signed in August 1999, providing for a US$ 20 million credit line granted to Mr. W by the Latvian Group. In February 2000 the Latvian Group foreclosed on assets which Mr. W had transferred to it because of an alleged deficit of approximately US$ 250,000. In doing so, the Latvian Group relied on the Customer Agreement which provided that in case of a "failure to pay any and all debit balances within 5 days after statements as posted", the Latvian Group had a right of liquidation of any property, including securities and other property held in any of the accounts carried or serviced by the Latvian Group. Mr. W disputed the existence of the deficit or that it had constituted grounds for a margin call on Account I.

The claimants instituted arbitral proceedings relying on the Loan Agreement which provided for ICC arbitration in Paris in the event "of any dispute of any kind arising under the laws of any country in contract, tort or otherwise". They requested the arbitral tribunal to issue a procedural order, to be followed by an interim and conservatory award instructing the respondents to immediately place, in an escrow or similar account or safekeeping arrangement, under the control of the arbitral tribunal or a neutral third party selected by the arbitral tribunal, at a major French bank, selected by the arbitral tribunal the amount claimed in damages and the shares or depositary receipts evidencing shares of Trust C and all shares or depositary receipts evidencing shares of the US Corporation acquired by Trust C or any L entity.

The arbitral tribunal issued an Order for Interim and Conservatory Relief reading:

"The arbitral tribunal finds that the claimants have established a prima facie case that Mr. W is the beneficial owner of Trust C and that the claimants' trading profits amount to [the amount claimed]. However, this order is not a decision by the arbitral tribunal as to the merits of the case.

Art. 23 of the ICC Rules provides that the arbitral tribunal may make the granting of an interim measure subject to appropriate security being furnished by the requesting party. The arbitral tribunal notes that, according to a statement made by the respondents' counsel . . . the mutual assets are already 'frozen' by the respondents. The arbitral tribunal does not find that a security is appropriate in this situation.

ORDER

A. The arbitral tribunal, by virtue of Art. 23 of the ICC Rules, in view of the risk that irreparable damage may be caused to the claimant if no assets are available to enforce an award in their favour – if an award were to be rendered in their favour – now orders Trust L . . . to immediately place in the following escrow account opened by the Paris Bar Association (Ordre des Avocats à la Cour de Paris - service CARPA), managed by the Chairman of the arbitral tribunal . . .

1. Either assets in the form of the mutual funds indicated in the respondents' statement, namely W, X, Y, Z held for the account of the US Corporation and/or Trust C or [the amount claimed].
2. All shares, receipts and/or certificate representing the shares of Trust C and the US Corporation.

B. This order shall be immediately enforceable.
C. This order will also be issued in the form of an Arbitral Award.
D. The parties' further requests are rejected."

Trust L informed the arbitral tribunal that they had fully complied with the Order as the relevant documents were sent by Latvian postal service which was the normal Latvian procedure for such transfers. Three weeks later, the arbitral tribunal established that no amounts had been registered on the relevant escrow accounts or any document received in the post. Counsel for Trust L informed the arbitral tribunal that no funds had been transferred, that the documents had been sent by registered mail and received by the bank ten days earlier.

The claimants responded that irrespective of which documents might eventually be received by the bank, the respondents had failed to comply with part 1 of the Order which specifically required the respondents to turn over either assets in the form of the mutual funds or the sum of the amount claimed. Transferring "documents of ownership" in their view was not sufficient. Accordingly, the claimants requested the arbitral tribunal to reissue its Interim and Conservatory Order in the form of an Interim and Conservatory Award so that they could immediately begin enforcement proceedings.

Shortly thereafter, the arbitral tribunal acknowledged that share certificates in the US corporation and Trust C had arrived at the Bank, thus complying with section 2 of the Order. However, because the respondents had not relinquished control of the mutual funds or paid the cash sum, the arbitral tribunal issued an Interim Award ordering the respondents to transfer the mutual funds or the disputed amount.

In making its award, the arbitral tribunal first determined that, based on the arbitration agreement and Art. 23(1) of the ICC Rules, it had prima facie jurisdiction to order interim and conservatory measures and to do so before the Terms of Reference had been drawn up. The requirement under French law, that there be urgency in the matter was fulfilled as there was a substantial risk of significant prejudice if the measure were not granted. To do so would not be a violation of French international public policy. There was a probability that the claimants would succeed in their claim as they had established a prima facie case that Mr. W was the beneficial owner of Trust C and that the claimant's trading profits were in the order of the amount claimed. The assets which the respondents had placed in a "frozen" account were ordered to be placed in a neutral escrow account, i.e., a "neutral zone" and not in a zone controlled by one of the parties.

Excerpt

I.   POWER TO GRANT INTERIM AND CONSERVATORY MEASURES

[1]   "The issue is whether the arbitral tribunal has the power to grant interim and conservatory relief in a case such as the present one, i.e., where the place of arbitration is in France. Moreover, should this be the case, it has to be decided

what measures could be taken and the exact form and nature of these measures. We are here concerned with the question of placement of assets in an escrow account or similar account or safekeeping arrangement under the control of the arbitral tribunal or a neutral party selected by the tribunal (there to remain until this arbitration is finally concluded). Furthermore, the tribunal notices that claimants request that the tribunal provide for the provisional enforcement of any award or order granting the relief requested.

[2] "The Terms of Reference have not yet been agreed and signed in the case. A first draft established by the arbitral tribunal late March 2001, was commented on by the claimants and the respondents during April and May 2001. Currently, the arbitral tribunal is drafting a second revised draft taking into account the parties' comments."

1. Jurisdiction

[3] ". . . [T]he ICC Court decided that the matter should proceed in accordance with Art. 6(2) of its Rules. In other words, the ICC Court was prima facie satisfied that an arbitration agreement under the ICC Rules may exist. The issue of jurisdiction as to the merits of the case will be subject to a separate decision by the arbitral tribunal after having heard the parties' submissions on this issue.

[4] "The ICC Rules Art. 23(1) provides:

'Unless the parties have otherwise agreed, as soon as the file has been transmitted to it, the arbitral tribunal may, at the request of a party, order any interim or conservatory measure it deems appropriate. . . . Any such measures shall take the form of an order, giving reasons, or of an Award, as the arbitral tribunal considers appropriate.'

Thus, it is clear that a general power is conferred by the Rules to the arbitrators to order interim and conservatory measures. One could also note that such a power has been recognized in arbitral case law, e.g., ICC Award No. 4126 (1984),[1] ICC Award No. 7489 (1992).[2] These measures can well be granted by the arbitrators in the form of an award, e.g., ICC Award No. 3540 (1980);[3] obviously, in the present case, this follows directly from the ICC Rules Art. 23, presently in force.

---

1. "*Collection of ICC Arbitral Awards 1974-1985*, p. 511."
2. "*Collection of Procedural Decisions in ICC Arbitration, 1993-1996.*"
3. "*Collection of ICC Arbitral Awards 1974-1985, p.105.*"

[5]   "The arbitral tribunal finds, by virtue of the arbitration agreement included in the governing operative loan documents and Art. 23(1) of the Rules, that it has jurisdiction to make an interim and conservatory award."

2.   Interim and Conservatory Relief Prior to Terms of Reference

[6]   "There is no requirement in the Rules that Terms of Reference have been drawn up before an interim measure is granted. Art. 23(1) provides that 'as soon as the file has been transmitted to it' the arbitral tribunal may entertain a request of a party for interim or conservatory measures. In this connection, Art. 13 of the Rules provides that the ICC Secretariat shall transmit the 'file' to the arbitral tribunal as soon as it has been constituted and provided the claimant has paid the advance on costs. As from the date of receipt of the file, the arbitral tribunal is effectively operational. Thus, it is now (since the amendment of the ICC Rules in 1998) clear under the ICC Rules that an arbitral tribunal may grant interim and conservatory relief before the Terms of Reference provided for in Art. 18 are signed or become operative. Under the 1975/1988 Rules, it has not been clear that the arbitral tribunal could do so although this right could be implied. At all events, an arbitral tribunal should be ready to act promptly in relation to requests for orders of this kind."

3.   Requirements for Interim and Conservatory Relief

[7]   "In the present case, the arbitral tribunal must be convinced, in issuing an interim award, that there is a substantial risk of significant prejudice to the claimants if the relief sought is not granted. In French domestic procedural law, it must notably be proven that there is 'urgency' (*péril en la demeure*) in the matter[4] (which concerned the escrow of disputed shares). However, in an ICC case it was held that 'the arbitrator may lawfully grant the measure applied for, provided he is satisfied that justice will be served that way' (terms used by sole arbitrator in ICC case No. 7489 (1992),[5] given that French domestic procedural law was not applicable.

[8]   "We are convinced that there is, in the present case, a substantial risk of significant prejudice to claimants if we do not grant the measure. Moreover, there is urgency.

[9]   "Art. 15 of the ICC Rules presently in force[6] authorizes the parties and the arbitrators to conduct the arbitral proceedings outside any specific national

---

4. "See CA Paris, 12 Dec. 1990, *Terex v. Banexi* 1991 Bull. Joly 595."
5. *"Collection of Procedural Decisions in ICC Arbitration 1993-1996."*
6. Art. 15 of the 1998 ICC Rules of Arbitration reads in relevant part:

procedural law. However, any mandatory provision of such law is applicable, see, e.g., Philippe Ouakrat: *'L' arbitrage commercial international et les mesures provisoires: Etude générale'*[7]

> *'le juge n'a ... aucun pouvoir decontrôle del' opportunité de la solution retenue par l'arbitre. Plus encore, sous la seule réserve de l'exception d'ordre public, il ne peut normalement contrôler le bien-fondé de cette solution.'*

[the court is not empowered to verify the appropriateness of the arbitrator's solution. Moreover, with the exception of the objection of public policy, the court cannot check the adequacy of the grounds for this solution.]

[10]   "Art. 1498 of the French New Code of Civil Procedure provides:

> *'Les sentences arbitrales sont reconnues en France si leur existence est établie par celui qui s'en prévaut et si cette reconnaissance n'est pas manifestement contraire à l'ordre public international.*
>
> *Sous les mêmes conditions, elles sont déclarées exécutoires en France par le juge de Vexecution.'*

[Arbitral awards shall be recognized in France if the party relying on them establishes their existence and if this is not manifestly contrary to international public policy.

Under the same conditions arbitral awards shall be declared enforceable in France.]

Moreover, Art. 1504 of the same Code, taken together with Art. 1502, no. 5,[8] provides that this international public policy (*ordre public international*) is also applicable to international arbitration awards. According to a judgment rendered by the *Cour de cassation* on 19 November 1991,[9] the violation against

---

"1. The proceedings before the Arbitral Tribunal shall be governed by these Rules, and, where these Rules are silent, by any rules which the parties or, failing them, the Arbitral Tribunal may settle on, whether or not reference is thereby made to the rules of procedure of a national law to be applied to the arbitration."

7. "14DPCI (1988, no. 2) pp. 239-273, no. 39."
8. Art. 1502, no. 5 of the French New Code of Civil Procedure provides:

"Appeals of a court decision granting recognition or enforcement is only available on the following grounds:

. . .

5. if recognition or enforcement is contrary to international public policy."

9. "Revue de l'arbitrage (1992, no. 1) p. 76."

public policy has to be *'flagrante et effective'* [glaring and effective] and *'concrète'* [concrete]. Furthermore, the French public policy applicable to international relations should be appreciated *'de manière moins rigoureuse'* [less strictly] than public policy in purely internal, that is national, relations.

[11]   "The arbitral tribunal establishes that there is no evidence suggesting that French international public policy will be violated if the tribunal grant an award on interim and conservatory measures in the present case.

[12]   "It is a general rule in international arbitration that a claimant must prove the *fumus boni juris*, i.e., that there exists a probability that his claims, regarding the question(s) as to the merits of the case, will be successful. In other words, he must be able to justify a likelihood that he will subsequently obtain a favourable award from the arbitral tribunal in the matter. The arbitral tribunal finds that the claimants have established a prima facie case that Mr. W is the beneficial owner of Trust C and that the claimants' trading profits amount to the amount claimed. However, this is not a decision by the arbitral tribunal as to the merits of the case.

[13]   "The requested measure should not frustrate the outcome of the arbitration or prejudge it. The respondents stated during the hearing that they have already placed the assets in a 'frozen' account. In ordering that the assets are to be placed in an escrow account, the arbitral tribunal does not really change the positions of the parties. The tribunal merely applies the fair principle that the assets be placed in a 'neutral zone', pending the arbitration, and not in a zone being controlled by one of the parties. The arbitral tribunal does not find that it is necessary in these circumstances, that a security is furnished by the claimants.

[14]   "It follows from the above discussion that the arbitral tribunal has the powers to grant an interim and conservatory relief. In the present case, the claimants have requested the placement of already 'frozen' accounts in a neutral escrow account (or similar arrangement). We have concluded that it lies within the powers of the arbitral tribunal to grant an award on such a placement in a situation like the one considered in the present case. As a consequence, the claimants' application for interim and conservatory relief, if granted, would be lawful.

[15]   "Finally, the claimants request that 'the tribunal provide for the provisional enforcement of any award or order granting the relief requested'. This request will be granted in view of the urgency of the matter."

II.   THE INTERIM AWARD

[16]   "We now make the following award:
The respondents shall immediately and unconditionally place in the following escrow account opened by the Paris Bar Association (*Ordre des Avocats à la*

Cour de Paris – service CARPA), managed by the Chairman of the arbitral tribunal . . .

– Either assets in the form of the mutual funds indicated in the respondents' statement namely W, X, Y and Z, held for the account of the US corporation and/or Trust C
– or [the amount claimed],

thereby relinquishing control over the assets or the sum.
This Award shall be immediately enforceable.
This Award replaces the arbitral tribunal's Order [for Interim and Conservatory Relief].
This Award is not final. It is subject to changes that the arbitral tribunal may decide in the process of the arbitral procedure."

Award by Consent in case no. 11443 of 2001

Parties: Claimant: Energy company (Belgium)
                          Respondents: Steel company A (India), et al.

Place of
arbitration: London, England

Published in: Unpublished

Subject matters: – interim measures
                          – award by consent

Facts

Following the Government of India's announcement of a new power policy opening up the electricity sector to foreign companies, a Belgian energy company entered into a joint venture agreement with a group consisting of several Indian companies and industrialists, all of whom were involved with the Indian companies. The purpose of the joint venture was to setup and operate a thermal power plant in an Indian city. Among the agreements concluded in the period from 1995 through 1997 in this context were a Power Purchase Agreement (PPA), a Fuel Supply Agreement (FSA), a Substation Agreement, a Shareholders' Agreement and a Subscription Agreement.

The Shareholders' Agreement contained an arbitration clause in Clause 16 reading

> "... In the event of any dispute in connection with this Agreement, both parties and all Energy Company Affiliates and Indian Affiliates will seek an amicable settlement during a sixty-day period, failing which the matter under dispute will be referred to an arbitration tribunal as per ICC rules and the arbitration will be conducted in London, England.
>
> The award of the arbitrator shall be final and conclusive and binding upon the parties and Energy Company and Indian Affiliates and the parties and the Energy Company and Indian Affiliates shall be entitled (but not obliged) to enter the judgement thereon in any one or more of the highest courts having jurisdiction. The New York Convention shall apply to the award resulting from an arbitration pursuant to this Clause and any such award shall for the purposes of the New York Convention, the laws of any

other country in which recognition and enforcement is sought, be treated as relating to a dispute or disputes arising out of a commercial legal relationship. In relation to the enforcement of an award in India, the parties and the Energy Company and the Indian Affiliates agree that such an award is not a domestic award but is for all purposes, and shall be deemed to be, a foreign award. The parties and the Energy Company and the Indian Affiliates further agree (to the maximum extent possible and allowed to them) that such enforcement shall be subject to the provisions of the Indian Arbitration and Conciliation Act 1996 relating to the enforcement of foreign awards and neither party nor any Energy Company and Indian Affiliate shall seek to resist the enforcement of any award in India on the basis that that award is not subject to such provisions. . . . "

Disputes arose among the parties to the joint venture and the Belgian energy company initiated arbitration in March 2001 claiming that the Indian group had breached its obligations under the Shareholders' Agreement, the PPA (by failing to respect the tariff provisions set out therein) the FSA and the Substation Agreement. The Indian Group denied that it had breached any of the agreements and claimed that the Shareholders' Agreement, the PPA, the FAS and the Substation Agreement had been repudiated and/or rescinded.

The Belgian Energy Company applied to the arbitral tribunal to issue an interim measure preserving the contractual status quo in the form of an order and an award which could be enforced in India with the assistance of the national courts if necessary. The arbitral tribunal granted the interim measure in the form of an Award on Consent as the parties had agreed on the terms under which it would be granted. Accordingly, the respondents were ordered to refrain from contending that the various agreements were repudiated or rescinded and the agreements were declared to remain in force.

Excerpt

[1]   "The stated purpose of the claimant's Application for Interim Measures of Protection was to preserve the contractual status quo until such time as the tribunal ruled upon the merits of the parties' disputes. The award sought by the claimant, it alleges, would prevent the respondents from changing the status quo in a way that would cause irreparable harm to the claimant and/or aggravate the existing disputes.

[2]   "The claimant considers that the respondents have already acted in such a way as to deny its rights under the Shareholders' Agreement and other agreements relevant to this arbitration. According to the claimant, the respondents

took the position that these agreements were repudiated and/or rescinded for the first time in their Answer and Counterclaims.

[3] "The claimant denies that it has acted in such a way as to breach the relevant agreements, or that any of the agreements have been repudiated and/or rescinded. It contends that the respondents, on the one hand, have argued that their rights under the Shareholders' Agreement should be respected and enforced, and on the other hand, that this Agreement has been repudiated. The claimant concludes that by such conduct, the respondents are estopped from claiming that the Agreement has been repudiated.

[4] "The Application seeks an Order on interim measures of protection, and an Award to ensure compliance with the tribunal's Order which, if necessary, could be enforced in India with the assistance of the national courts

[5] "Pursuantto Clause 16(1) of the Shareholders' Agreement, the laws of the Republic of India (excluding Indian international private law) are the governing law of the Agreement and the arbitration. Pursuant to Clause 16(2) of the Shareholders' Agreement, the procedural law, to the extent not governed by the ICC Rules, is English law. London being the venue of this arbitration, the applicable lex arbitri is the 1996 English Arbitration Act. Sect. 39(1) of the 1996 English Arbitration Act expressly authorizes arbitrators to grant interim or conservatory measures.

[6] "The ICC Rules of Arbitration in force as from 1 January 1998, and particularly the provisions of Art. 23, grant a direct and positive power to arbitrators to order interim or conservatory measures. Art. 23 explicitly authorizes arbitral tribunals to order interim or conservatory relief. This competence is recognized by the authors.[1] Art. 23(1) of the ICC Rules of Arbitration, provides as follows:

'Unless the parties have otherwise agreed, as soon as the file has been transmitted to it, the Arbitral Tribunal may, at the request of a party, order any interim or conservatory measure it deems appropriate. . . . '

And 'in fine':

'Any such measure shall take the form of an order, giving reasons, or of an award, as the Arbitral Tribunal considers appropriate.'

---

1. "See generally, Derains and Schwartz, *A Guide to the New ICC Rules of Arbitration* (Kluwer Law International 1998) p. 272 et seq.; *Fouchard, Gaillard and Goldman on International Commercial Arbitration* (Kluwer Law International 1999) p. 710 et seq.; Craig, Park and Paulsson, *International Chamber of Commerce Arbitration*, 3rd Edition (Oceana Publications Inc. 2000) p. 460 et seq."

[7]   "This power granted to ICC arbitrators may be exercised to secure assets, to preserve the subject matter of the dispute, to avoid prejudice to the rights of the parties during the pendency of the proceedings, to preserve the status quo or to enjoin certain conduct pending the outcome of the proceedings themselves.[2]

[8]   "As noted above, Art. 23(1) gives discretion to the arbitral tribunal to decide whether its decision on interim or conservatory measures should be in the form of an order or of an award. The authors express the view that the matter will often depend upon the nature of the measure and the laws of the place of arbitration or the country where the measure is to be carried out.[3]

[9]   "The nature of the measures sought by the claimant is to maintain the contractual status quo between the parties and to prevent irreparable harm to the claimant. Following an exchange of correspondence between the parties and the tribunal prior to the preliminary hearing, the parties agreed on the terms under which the claimant's Application for Interim Measures of Protection would be granted. They also agreed that the tribunal would issue an Interim Award in the same terms as those agreed in Procedural Order No. 2. The Order specifically notes this agreement. The tribunal notes that the respondents did not object to the substantive points of law developed in the claimant's Application for Interim Measures of Protection.

[10]   "The claimant, in its Application for Interim Measures of Protection, submitted that an Award on interim measures was necessary in addition to a procedural Order, to ensure the chances of enforcement of the arbitrators' decisionin the country of the respondents, i.e., India, ifnecessary. By virtue of the parties' agreement to embody the agreed terms of Procedural Order No. 2 into an Interim Award, and considering the discretionary powers conferred to it by Art. 23 of the ICC Rules of Arbitration, the arbitral tribunal considers it appropriate to issue the following decision:

[11]   "The arbitral tribunal issues the present Interim Award, and hereby decides unanimously as follows: Pending determination in the Final Award of the arbitral tribunal on the issues of repudiation and rescission pleaded in the respondents' Answer and Counterclaim:

1.   The respondents are ordered to refrain from contending that the Shareholders' Agreement, the PPA, the FSA and the Substation Agreement have been repudiated or rescinded and they shall conduct themselves in

---

2. "See Derains and Schwartz, *op. cit.*, pp. 272-276; Craig, Park and Paulsson, *op. cit.*, p. 460 et seq.; Redfern and Hunter, *Law and Practice of International Commercial Arbitration*, 3rd Edition (Sweet & Maxwell 1999) p. 345 et seq."

3. "See Derains and Schwartz, *op. cit.* particularly, p. 275, and Craig, Park and Paulsson, *op. cit.*, pp. 464-465."

relation to those agreements as though no claim for repudiation or rescission has been made.

2. It is declared that the Shareholders' Agreement, the PPA, the FSA and Substation Agreement remain in force as though no claim had been made that these agreements had been repudiated or rescinded. For the avoidance of doubt, nothing in this paragraph is intended to affect the respondents' contention that certain clauses of the PPA and the FSA have not come into effect by reason of non-fulfillment of conditions precedent.

3. A's letter . . . is ordered to be withdrawn insofar as it claims that the Shareholders' Agreement has been repudiated.

4. Costs of this proceedings are reserved for determination in the tribunal's Final Award."

Final award in case no. 10377 of 2002

Parties:	Claimant: Buyer (Portugal)
	Respondent: Seller (Finland)
Place of arbitration:	Amsterdam, The Netherlands
Published in:	Unpublished
Subject matters:	– standard conditions
	– 1980 UN Sales Convention (CISG)
	– timely notification of defects
	– substantiality of defects
	– termination of contract (no)
	– restitution of goods (no)
	– reduction of purchase price
	– costs of arbitration

Facts

In 1996, the Finnish seller of a machine for the production of a household textile product submitted an "Offer" to the Portuguese buyer for the purchase of the machine, including assembly of the machine. The Offer referred to the General Conditions for the Supply of Mechanical, Electrical and Associated Electronic Products (the ORGALIME). The Offer specified that the machine would produce four to six units per minute and could be operated by one person. The machine was delivered several months later and ninety percent of the purchase price was paid.

The machine was assembled and the seller's technicians conducted trial runs and prepared protocols about the trial runs. Shortly thereafter, the buyer complained to the seller about the production capacity of the machine and the seller sent technicians to improve the situation. As a result of further complaints, the seller informed the buyer that there were problems with two motors and that it was necessary to send technicians. Based on the reports of the technicians, the seller informed the buyer that the buyer had caused the problem by using poor quality raw material, a wrong component and that the buyer's employees were not willing to be sufficiently instructed in the operation of the machine.

The seller faxed the buyer recommending the use of a component produced by a particular supplier and stated in the same telefax that according to the seller's technician (Mr. T) the machine was capable of producing four to six units per minute. In that telefax, the seller also demanded the remaining ten percent of the purchase price.

During the course of the following year, the seller and buyer exchanged several letters dealing with complaints regarding the production capacity of the machine and the frequent interruptions in the production process. In 1998 the buyer demanded that the seller replace the machine and declared that it would rescind the contract if it were not satisfied. Several months later, the buyer rescinded the contract and subsequently initiated ICC arbitration as provided for in the ORGALIME Conditions.

In the arbitration, the buyer asserted that the machine never produced the capacities set forth in the purchase agreement and that there were other defects. The buyer also asserted that it had validly rescinded the purchase agreement. Consequently, the buyer claimed the return of the portion of the purchase price already paid as well as compensation for economic losses incurred equal to fifteen percent of the purchase price, plus interest on both sums. . . . The buyer also requested twelve percent post-award interest.

The seller maintained that the machine conformed to the purchase agreement and that the problems were caused by the buyer. Moreover, the seller maintained that the buyer did not notify it of the defects within the prescribed time limit. Consequently, the seller claimed the remainder of the sales price plus interest. In the event that the tribunal were to hold that the purchase agreement had been rescinded, the seller alternatively claimed compensation for damages based on the depreciation of the machine.

The sole arbitrator appointed an expert who concluded that both parties had not complied with the agreements made and that it would be equitable to reduce the price of the machine by twenty-five percent.

The sole arbitrator noted that the dispute was governed by the ORGALIME supplemented by the 1980 Convention on the International Sale of Goods (CISG). Under the ORGALIME terms, the purchase agreement could be terminated if the machine was defective when delivered, the buyer notified the seller of the defect, the seller did not rectify the defect, the defect was so substantial as to deprive the buyer of the benefit of the contract and the termination right was not excluded by any other applicable rule. The defects alleged by the buyer were either not established, were not timely notified or were not substantial enough to be considered as depriving the buyer of the benefit of the contract.

The sole arbitrator then looked to the CISG. Under Art. 82(1) CISG the buyer loses the right to terminate the contract or the right to substitute goods if it is impossible to make restitution of the goods substantially in the condition in which they were received. Under Art. 82(2) CISG, however, the contract could be terminated if the impossibility was not due to an act or omission of the buyer. The sole arbitrator determined that the buyer had used the machine after the defect had been discovered and also after having declared the termination of the purchase agreement thus causing the impossibility. This led to the conclusion that even though the machine was defective, the termination right was excluded since it was impossible to return the machine in the condition in which it was received and the claim for repayment of the ninety percent of the purchase price was unfounded. Furthermore, since under ORGALIME, the claim for compensation for loss suffered is dependent on the right to termination, the buyer could not claim compensation for losses suffered.

The sole arbitrator rejected the seller's counterclaim to the remaining ten percent of the purchase price as the machine had been defective at the time of delivery. Thus, the seller was only entitled to ninety percent of the purchase price.

As the buyer's claims were substantially denied and the seller's counterclaims were totally unsuccessful, the sole arbitrator concluded that it was reasonable for the parties equally to bear the costs of the arbitration and the expert. In awarding the legal fees, the sole arbitrator took into account that the buyer had instituted the arbitration, the buyer's claims were substantially unsuccessful, the respondent's counterclaims were totally unsuccessful and the amount of the claims greatly exceeded the amount of the counterclaims. Accordingly, the seller was awarded a portion of its legal fees.

Excerpt

I.   APPLICABLE RULES

[1]   "In the Terms of Reference, the Parties have agreed that the dispute shall be governed by the ORGALIME supplemented by the Convention on the International Sale of Goods (CISG). Even without this agreement the CISG would supplement the ORGALIME since the ORGALIME provide in No. 45 that any dispute 'shall be governed by the substantive law of the country of the Supplier's place of business most closely connected with the contract'. Since Respondent as the supplier is a Finnish company, Finnish law applies. Finland signed the CISG on 26 May 1981 and ratified the CISG on 1 January 1989.[1]

---

1. "Schlechtriem, *Commentary on the UN Convention on the International Sale of Goods (CISG)* (Munich 1998) page 707."

[2]   "According to Art. 1(1)(b) CISG, the CISG applies to contracts of sale of goods between parties whose place of business is in different states when the rules of private international law lead to the application of the law of the contracting state. According to the Finnish rules of private international law, parties may enter into choice of law clauses. The parties in the case at hand have chosen to apply Finnish law. Finland is a contracting state and thus the CISG would apply even without an express agreement of the parties."

II.   ANALYSIS

[3]   "ORGALIME No. 33 b) provides:

'Where the defect has not been successfully remedied as stipulated under Clause 32, where the defect is so substantial as to significantly deprive the Purchaser of the benefit of the contract, the Purchaser may terminate the contract by notice in writing to the supplier. The Purchaser is then entitled to compensation for the loss he has suffered up to a maximum of 15 per cent of the purchase price.'

Thus, claimant would have a right to terminate the purchase agreement, according to No. 33 b) ORGALIME, if

(a) the Machine had a defect at the time of the delivery,
(b) claimant timely notified respondent of the defect,
(c) respondent did not remedy the defect,
(d) the defect is so substantial as to significantly deprive the purchase of the benefit of the contract and
(e) the termination right of claimant is not excluded by any other applicable rule (such as the CISG)."

1. Alleged Defects

[4]   "From claimant's allegation for purposes of analysis under No. 33 b) ORGALIME, six types of defects must be distinguished:

(*a*)   the insufficient production capacity of the Machine,
(*b*)   the excessive use of the component,
(*c*)   the stain damages on the product,
(*d*)   the significant deviation of weight of the product produced,
(*e*)   the lack of the safety measure for the operating staff and
(*f*)   the frequent interruptions in the production process.

As will be substantiated below in more detail, the problems described above under (a) to (c) have, in the opinion of the Arbitral Tribunal, not been established by claimant to be defects. Regarding the problems described under (d) and (e), defects have been established, but the Arbitral Tribunal finds that claimant did not timely notify respondent.

[5]　"Lastly, the problem referred to under (f) has been proven to be a defect which has also been timely notified by claimant. However, it appears doubtful whether it constitutes a defect so substantial as to deprive claimant of the benefits of the purchase agreement. This issue, however, can be left open since the Arbitral Tribunal holds in any event a termination right of the contract to be excluded under the applicable CISG rules."

a.　Production capacity

[6]　"The Arbitral Tribunal is convinced that the Machine meets the contractually agreed production capacity. The first question to be answered is which production capacity was actually agreed upon. In this respect, the Arbitral Tribunal interprets the meaning of the contractual stipulations in accordance with the opinion of the Expert, i.e. that the production capacity mentioned in respondent's Offer (... *rendement de la ligne* ...) refers to the net operating time of the machine without taking into account breaks in the production process. A specification of the production capacity of a machine regularly states the number of units a machine is capable of producing during the net time of its operation. In this context, the parties to a purchase agreement generally have the opportunity to stipulate either a maximum or a minimum production capacity. The maximum production capacity reflects the number of units the machine is capable of producing under optimum conditions whereas the minimum production capacity states the number of units the machine must be capable of producing in any event.

[7]　"The Parties entered into the purchase agreement based on the specifications in respondent's Offer (the Offer). The pertinent specification in the Offer reads as follows:

'*Le rendement de la ligne est jusqu'à 4-6 ... par minute. ...* '

Because of the word '*jusqu'à*' this specification must be understood as a description of the *maximum* and not the minimum production capacity of the Machine. Hence, the Offer solely states the number of the units the Machine is capable of producing under optimum conditions. It follows that a minimum capacity was not expressly stipulated. This is not to say that claimant could not reasonably expect some minimum production capacity based on implied terms. This capacity, however, is not identical with the stipulated maximum number and would allow some downward deviation from this number, as long as such deviation is not so significant as to frustrate claimant's reasonable expectations.

[8]   "It is undisputed (and confirmed by the findings of the Expert) that the Machine is capable of producing at least 3.4 units per minute during its net operating time. This is conceded by claimant itself and during the test runs conducted in the presence of the Expert even a level of 'slightly above 4 units per minute' was achieved. The Arbitral Tribunal concludes that this deviation from the stipulated maximum production capacity range is not outside the reasonable expectations claimant could have under the circumstances. This conclusion is also based on a comparison with the results of the Expert's inspection of the similar machine in Germany, which claimant inspected before ordering the Machine in question. Even though the (German) machine is fitted with two filling boxes, it produced 3 units per minute i.e. less than the Machine. Thus, the production capacity is in conformity with the purchase agreement as has also been confirmed by the Expert.

[9]   "According to the Expert, the maximum production capacity is influenced by numerous factors, particularly the nature of the raw material, the amount of the component used and the expertise of the operating staff. Under the given circumstances, namely in the absence of a clear minimum capacity requirement in the Order, claimant could not expect that the Machine would produce more than 3.4 units per minute. Furthermore, it has to be taken into account that, based on the Expert's findings claimant's workers are not trained appropriately, which inevitably must have a negative impact on the production capacity.

[10]   "Thus, the Arbitral Tribunal finds that the Machine meets the contractually agreed upon production capacity. If claimant wanted to stipulate a minimum production capacity it should have insisted on an unequivocal stipulation in the order, for instance by replacing the term 'up to' by the term 'at least' or, according to the French language of the purchase agreement to replace 'jusqu'à' by 'au moins'. Thus, the Arbitral Tribunal holds that, with regard to the production capacity, the Machine is not defective."

b.   Use of component

[11]   "As far as claimant alleges that the Machine requires a certain amount of component which leads to an increase in the production costs, also no defect can be found. The Arbitral Tribunal's conclusion in this respect is based on the observations of the Expert expressed in his oral testimony and the Expert Opinion.

[12]　"The Expert's observations with regard to this point, are particularly log-ical and free from any contradictions. His examination of the Machine mainly comprised of three test runs and a drying test. His on-site inspection was preceded by an inspection of a comparable machine in Germany. Thus, the Expert dili-gently carried out his task. Moreover, the Expert outlined his observations in a convincing way during the Oral Hearing. These aspects together with the personal impression of the Arbitral Tribunal of the Expert and his expertise led the Arbitral Tribunal to come to the conclusion that the Expert's observations can be used for the present arbitration without qualification.

[13]　"As the Expert states in his Expert Opinion, the production capacity of the Machine depends on the component treatment of the raw material. In other words, the production capacity is also directly linked to the amount of component used. Based on this observation of the Expert, the Arbitral Tribunal comes to the conclusion that the fact that during the inspection of the Machine, a production capacity of slightly over 4 units was achieved, might also be the consequence of increasing the amount of the component.

[14]　"In any event, since the Machine is capable of producing 3.4 units per minute, even without increasing the amount of the component, the fact that an excessive amount of such component was used during the test runs is not rel-evant. The increase in the amount of component used is thus not required since the Machine would still produce an amount of units sufficient to remain within the contractually agreed parameter. Thus, the Arbitral Tribunal concludes that, due to the fact that the Machine already meets the agreed production capacity without excessive use of the component, the excessive amount of the component used during the test runs carried out by the Expert and increased production costs incurred thereby also does not constitute a defect."

c.　Stain damage on product

[15]　"The same is true for claimant's allegation that the Machine produces stain-damaged products by using an excessive amount of the component. The production of the product damaged by stains is to be distinguished from the increase in the production costs. Even though both are caused by the excessive use of the component, they do not necessarily need to occur together. However, as it has been set out above, the increase in the amount of the component used is not required for the Machine to produce an amount of units sufficient to remain within the contractually agreed parameter. Thus, the fact that when using an excessive amount of the component in an effort to even further increase the production the Machine produced units damaged by stains is not relevant in the case at hand and cannot be qualified as a defect."

d. Weight deviation

[16]   "The inability of the Machine to produce products of equal weight does constitute a defect but claimant did not timely notify respondent of such defect. As a general rule, a defect according to No. 22 ORGALIME occurs when the product delivered deviates from what the parties have agreed upon.[2] In other words, the question of whether there is a defect in the contract object depends primarily on the contract itself.[3] When detailed contract specifications are lacking, the existence of a defect will depend on an ordinary interpretation of the contract according to the provisions of the background law."[4]

[17]   The sole arbitrator quoted the weight specification in the Offer and continued: ". . . When the Expert assesses that, in this respect, the Machine does not conform since the distribution of weight is higher than stated in the equipment data sheets, he refers to the . . . stipulation [in the Offer]. However, this specification only refers to raw material S. Claimant only uses raw material P in its production and only raw material P was used during the test runs. According to the Expert, the raw material element S has to be distinguished from the raw material P. Thus, the . . . specification regarding the weight distribution which refers to raw material S cannot be transferred to raw material P. Since the Parties have not made any other stipulations concerning the production capacity, the purchase agreement does not contain a specific provision which relates to the ability to produce products of equal weight when raw material P is used.

[18]   "Thus, the existence of a defect has to be determined based on an ordinary interpretation of the contract according to the provisions of the CISG which provides the applicable statutory law in the case at hand. Art. 35(1) CISG provides:

'The seller must deliver goods which are of the quantity, quality and description required by the contract.'

Art. 35(2)(a) CISG states:

'Except where the parties have agreed otherwise, the goods do not conform with the contract unless they:
(a) are fit for the purpose for which goods of the same description would ordinarily be used;'

---

2. "Orgalime Publication: *General Conditions S 2000: Guide on Their Use and Interpretation* (Brussels 2000) page 100."
3. "Ibid."
4. "Ibid."

[19] "The Arbitral Tribunal finds that with respect to the deviation in the weight of the units produced, the Machine is not fit for the purposes for which machines of the same description would ordinarily be used. The uniform weight of products of one kind is obviously an essential quality. Sellers of the product require a uniform weight in order to base the price on the weight and to provide products of the same quality.

[20] "According to the Expert, the average weight deviation concerning the units produced is 15% . It is not relevant in this respect that the Expert refers to the . . . provision in the purchase agreement which is not applicable since this misunderstanding of the contractual stipulation by the Expert has no impact on the observation with regard to the weight deviation.

[21] "An average weight deviation of 15% cannot be regarded as conforming since this number has a material impact on the production costs, transportation costs and on claims of buyers of the product which are not equal in weight. Since the Machine is not capable of producing units of equal weight it does not conform with the purchase agreement. Thus, it is defective in this respect."

e. Lack of safety measures

[22] "The same is true for the lack of safety measures which has been established based on the findings of the Expert. The purchase agreement does not contain a stipulation concerning the safety measures for workers operating the Machine. Thus, it is decisive whether the Machine is fit for the purposes for which machines of the same description would ordinarily be used. The Expert observed, that due to the lack of safety measures, it is possible that the hands of workers operating the Machine can be injured by the cutting cylinder. Machines of the same description like the one in question are regularly fit to produce the product without injuring or endangering workers. As the Expert states, due to the lack of safety measures, the Machine does not meet this standard. The Machine is not fit for the purposes for which machines of the same description would ordinarily be used and, therefore defective since it is not fitted with the required safety measures in order to protect the workers who operate the Machine. Thus, the Machine does not conform with the purchase agreement."

f. Faulty design which led to frequent interruptions

[23] "The Machine is also truly defective with regard to its faulty design leading to frequent interruptions in the production process which requires a high level of maintenance and cleaning. In the view of the Arbitral Tribunal, the issue of interruptions in the production process has to be distinguished from the production capacity, as analyzed above under *a*. The specification of the

production capacity of a machine does not necessarily indicate for which period the specified production capacity can be upheld. As set forth above, it only indicates the performance of a machine during the net time of its operation, regardless of any breaks and interruptions. The fluency of the production process is a separate issue. Even though this aspect has, like the production capacity, an impact on the total output of a machine, it should be distinguished therefrom since it includes other specifications of a machine, in particular the level of maintenance required. The Arbitral Tribunal concurs also in this regard with the analysis of the Expert.

[24]   "As regards the necessity of frequent interruptions of the production process for purposes of cleaning, readjustment and maintenance, the Machine does not conform with the purchase agreement. As the test runs of the Expert revealed, the Machine requires cleaning and maintenance works at the latest one hour after the production had commenced. During test runs 2 and 3, the Machine even stopped production only 30 minutes after it had commenced. During the inspection of the similar machine delivered by respondent in Germany, the Expert observed only 15 minutes of cleaning and maintenance works during an eight hour production period. This shows that the Machine is not fit for the purposes for which machines of the same description would ordinarily be used.

[25]   "The Expert comes to the conclusion that the frequent interruptions of the production process due to maintenance and cleaning works are the result of faults in the conception and of the realization but also the incorrect use of the line by the staff. To what extent these two causes are responsible for the defect is not relevant at this point, since it is sufficient that one of the causes observed by the Expert has been caused by respondent. Thus, the Arbitral Tribunal finds that the Machine was defective since its faulty design leads to frequent interruptions in the production process.

[26]   "Consequently, defects of the Machine have been established with respect to:

d.   the inability to produce products of equal weight,
e.   the lack of adequate safety measures and
f.   faulty design which leads to frequent interruptions."

2. Timely Notification of the Defects

[27]   "The three groups of defects must again be distinguished with regard to the requirement of timely notification by claimant to respondent."

a. Unequal weight and defective safety measures

[28] "With regard to the inability to produce units with equal weight and the lack of adequate safety measures, according to Nos. 23 and 25 ORGALIME, claimant is no longer entitled to have the defects remedied since it did not timely notify respondent of the defects.

[29] "No. 25 ORGALIME provides:

'The purchaser shall without undue delay notify the supplier of any defect which appears. Such notice shall under no circumstances be given later than two weeks after the expiry of the period given in Clause 23. Where the defect is such that it may cause damage, the notice shall be given immediately. The notice shall contain a description of the defect. If the Purchaser does not notify the Supplier of a defect within the time-limits set forth in this Clause, he shall lose the right to have the defect remedied.'

No. 23 ORGALIME states:

'The Supplier's liability is limited to defects which appear within a period of one year from delivery. If the daily use of the Product exceeds that which is agreed, this period shall be reduced proportionately.'

[30] "Since the delivery was carried out in November 1996, the relevant period for the notification in the case at hand runs from December 1996 to November 1997. Throughout this period, claimant communicated numerous complaints *but did not notify respondent of the two types of defects here in question.* The following excerpts from the documents submitted to the Arbitral Tribunal show that claimant notified respondent of the (non-existing) defect of insufficient production capacity and the defect of frequent interruptions in the production process but did not submit evidence of complaints, during the relevant time period, concerning weight deviation and safety measures."

(. . . .)

[31] The sole arbitrator reviewed the correspondence between the parties and concluded "the broadest interpretation of the above cited correspondence could not lead to the conclusion that claimant had timely notified respondent of the defects in question. In contrast, it appears that these defects were only deter- mined by the Expert during his test runs and then made part of claimant's complaint. The weight of the product produced and lack of safety measures required are aspects to be clearly distinguished from the production capacity and the production process. Thus, even taking into account that the purchaser does not have to specify the defect in detail, claimant's notifications did not

include complaints about the weight of the units produced and the lack of safety measures.

[32] "Thus, during the relevant time period from December 1996 to November 1997 (and even until June 1998), claimant did not notify respondent of the defects that the Machine does not produce units of equal weight and lacks safety measures. In order to comply with the procedure foreseen in No. 25 ORGALIME, claimant would have been required ... to notify respondent of the facts that would have brought respondent into a position to determine that the Machine lacks the ability to produce units of equal weight and devices to protect the operating workers. Thus, the Arbitral Tribunal concludes that according to No. 25 ORGALIME, claimant lost the right to have the above mentioned defects remedied."

b. Design defect

[33] "However, with respect to the design defect which led to frequent interruptions of production, claimant has complied with the procedure foreseen in No. 25 ORGALIME."

(. . . .)

[34] After reviewing the correspondence, the sole arbitrator concluded that the correspondence "constitute[s] sufficient notification according to No. 25 ORGALIME. It has to be taken into consideration in this context that the required description of the defect need not be very detailed or contain a diagnosis of the cause of the defect.[5] Thus, it was sufficient that claimant notified respondent ... of frequent interruptions in the production process and that (in claimant's view) these interruptions are due to jammed rollers. From this notification, respondent, as the producer of the Machine, could assess the nature of the defect and the consequences resulting therefrom.

[35] "In this context, it is not relevant that claimant primarily focused on the production capacity, which in its view, constituted the main defect: As it has been set out above, the fluency of the production also has an impact on the production output even though it should be distinguished from the production capacity. Thus, it is not significant, that claimant focused on this aspect while complaining about frequent interruptions in the production process. Furthermore, the notification was made without undue delay after the defect had appeared. The delivery and assembly of the Machine commenced in November 1996. Taking into consideration a period for adjusting and preparing the machine for production, the first notification on 25 November 1996, in connection with the specification made on 14 February 1997 must be regarded as sufficient.

---

5. "Ibid., page 110."

[36]　"Thus, the Arbitral Tribunal concludes that the Machine is defective since its production process is frequently interrupted by maintenance and cleaning works due to faults in the conception and assembling and that claimant timely notified respondent of the defect."

3.　*Failure to Remedy the Notified Defect*

[37]　"Respondent has not remedied the frequent interruptions in the production process. Despite the fact that respondent sent technicians several times to claimant, the Machine, as the Expert observed, is still not capable of producing the product without frequent interruptions in the production process."

4.　*Substantiality of Defect*

[38]　"No 33 b) ORGALIME provides:

'Where the defect has not been successfully remedied as stipulated under Clause 32, where the defect is so substantial as to significantly deprive the Purchaser of the benefit of the contract, the Purchaser may terminate the contract by notice in writing to the supplier. The Purchaser is then entitled to compensation for the loss he has suffered up to a maximum of 15 per cent of the purchase price.'

As the Expert observed, the frequent interruptions in the production process are the results (i) of the faulty design of the Machine as well as (ii) of the improper handling of the Machine. Claimant has to establish the substantiality of the defect of frequent interruptions in the production process but, during the taking of evidence, it could not be clarified which of these two causes is dominant. The fact that it remained open whether the design of the Machine is the dominant cause for the frequent interruptions in the production process would thus result in claimant's failure to prove the substantiality of the defect. However, a decision with regard to the substantiality is not required since a right of termination is excluded in any event by the applicable CISG rules."

5.　*Exclusion of Termination Right*

[39]　"Art. 82(1) and (2) CISG provide:

'(1) The buyer loses the right to declare the contract avoided or to require the seller to deliver substitute goods if it is impossible for him to make restitution of the goods substantially in the condition in which he received them.

(2) The preceding paragraph does not apply:

(a) if the impossibility of making restitution of the goods or of making restitution substantially in the condition in which the buyer received them is not due to his act or omission;

(b) if the goods or part of the goods have perished or deteriorated as a result of the examination provided for in Art. 38; or

(c) if the goods or part of the goods have been sold in the normal course of business or have been consumed or transformed by the buyer in the normal use before he discovered or ought to have discovered the lack of conformity.'

A termination right of claimant is excluded by Art. 82(1) CISG since it is impossible for claimant to make restitution of the Machine substantially in the condition in which it received the Machine.

[40]   "Art. 82(1) CISG is applicable. As stated above the Parties have agreed in the Terms of Reference, that the dispute shall be governed by the ORGALIME supplemented by the Convention on the International Sale of Goods (CISG). The ORGALIME do not provide an all-encompassing regulation of the contractual relationship governed by them since they are incomplete with regard to certain circumstances namely those which can arise in connection with the exercise of a termination right. The legal consequence foreseen by No. 33 b) ORGALIME is that the purchaser returns the product to the supplier in exchange for the payment made to the supplier.[6]

[41]   "However, cases like the one at hand show that sometimes the purchaser is not in a position to return the product in the condition in which it has received it. To argue that the ORGALIME are complete in this respect and that the purchaser may return the goods in any condition would lead to unjust results. The purchaser would receive the full purchase price paid but the supplier would not receive back the product sold in the condition in which it was delivered. Thus, the purchaser could exploit the product sold without being obligated to any kind of reimbursement.

[42]   "The Arbitral Tribunal observes that it is already a principle in Roman law that restitution may be claimed only if the buyer can return the goods in the condition in which it received them.[7] This principle has not been incorporated in the ORGALIME. In the light of the unjust results which would arise if damages

---

6. "Ibid., page 139."

7. "Schlechtriem, *Commentary on the UN Convention on the International Sale Of Goods (CISG)* (Munich 1998) Art. 82, note 6."

of the goods are not to be taken into account, the Arbitral Tribunal comes to the conclusion that the ORGALIME are incomplete in this respect and have to be supplemented by the CISG.

[43]　"A balanced system of legal consequences if the goods cannot be returned in the condition in which they had been received is contained in Arts. 82-84 CISG. These rules provide the legal consequence in order to provide for fair restitution of the performances of both parties to a purchase agreement. Art. 82(1) blocks the buyer's right to avoid the contract if it is impossible for him to make restitution of the goods in an unimpaired condition.[8] The term 'Impossibility' refers to an actual objective impediment to restitution.[9] It is regarded as an actual impediment if the goods have been damaged, lost, destroyed, or stolen.[10] In the case at hand, it is clearly impossible for claimant to return the Machine substantially in the condition in which claimant had received the Machine.

[44]　". . . [T]he Expert states:

'The whole machine shows areas of oxidisation, with excessive movement in the access door to the feeder, with useless pearcings (sic!) in the metal and leaks, both of liquid and raw material. It is obvious that the machinery has been running production (sic!) for a long time, as it shows marks where the paint is worn away on the lower part of the filing unit; there is also wear on the sealing joints.'

. . . [T]he Expert furthermore explains:

'I observed that the machine was really used in production (it is, however, extremely difficult to judge exactly in terms of quantity of units produced).'

During the Oral Hearing . . . the Expert moreover explained that after being in use for several years the Machine 'is not substantially in the same state in which it was when it was delivered'. The Expert assumed that for each year the Machine was used in production, a decrease in the original value of 25% occurred.

[45]　"Based on these observations of the Expert, the Arbitral Tribunal has no doubt that claimant used the Machine over the last years. The respective marks are obvious from the pictures annexed to the Expert Opinion and let the

---

8. "*Ibid.*, note 8."
9. "*Ibid.*, note 9."
10. "*Ibid.*"

Machine appear substantially worn. Claimant received the Machine from respondent in a mint condition. As the Expert has explained convincingly, the Machine in its present condition fails to meet the condition in which it has been delivered by far. Thus, the Arbitral Tribunal comes to the conclusion that it is impossible for claimant to return the Machine substantially in the condition in which claimant had received the Machine. Thus, no termination right exists.

[46] "Art. 82(1) CISG is not excluded by Art. 82(2) CISG which states that the consequence of Art. 82(1) CISG does not apply if the impossibility of making full restitution of the goods substantially in the condition in which the buyer received them is not due to an act or omission of the buyer. From the observations of the Expert, it is obvious that claimant used the Machine for a substantial period of time even after it had discovered the defect and also after having declared the termination of the purchase agreement. Consequently, the impossibility is caused by an act of claimant.

[47] "Furthermore, Art. 82(1) CISG is not excluded by Art. 82(2)(c) CISG which states that Art. 82(1) does not apply if the goods have been consumed or transformed in the course of normal use before the buyer discovered or ought to have discovered the lack of conformity. As it has been set out above, claimant used the Machine before and after it discovered the defects here in question. Art. 82(2)(c) CISG is therefore not applicable. Hence, Art. 82(1) CISG is not excluded by Art. 82(2) CISG."

III.   CONCLUSION

[48] "Thus, the Arbitral Tribunal concludes that even though the Machine is defective, a termination right of claimant is excluded by Art. 82(1) CISG, since it is impossible for claimant to return the Machine substantially in the condition in which claimant had received it. Regarding respondent's letter of June 1998, in which it threatens to terminate the purchase agreement based on the nonpayment of the outstanding 10% of the purchase price, it has not been submitted by either Party that respondent has actually declared the termination. Thus, the purchase agreement is still in force. The Arbitral Tribunal therefore concludes that claimant's claim for repayment of 90% of the purchase price is unfounded."

IV.   THE ISSUE OF COMPENSATION FOR LOSS SUFFERED

[49] "As it has been set out above, a termination right of claimant is excluded. Since according to No. 33 b) ORGALIME the claim for compensation for loss suffered is dependent upon the termination right, claimant cannot claim any such compensation for losses suffered."

V. THE COUNTERCLAIMS

[50]   "Respondent is of the opinion that the purchase agreement is still in force and that, as a result, it is entitled to the outstanding 10% of the purchase price. According to respondent, claimant has no right to refuse payment. Claimant alleges that respondent is not entitled to the remaining 10% of the purchase price since the purchase agreement has been terminated. If the Arbitral Tribunal concludes that the purchase agreement has not been terminated, claimant is of the opinion that respondent has at least not fully performed its obligations arising from the purchase agreement.

[51]   "The purchase agreement between the Parties provides for a purchase price from which 10% remains outstanding. However, claimant has the defence of being entitled to a purchase price reduction of 10% according to No. 33 a) ORGALIME. Respondent's claim for the outstanding 10% of the purchase price is therefore unfounded. As it has been set out above under Section III, the purchase agreement between the Parties is still in force. Thus, if claimant would have no defences respondent would be entitled to the outstanding 10% of the purchase price. However, claimant has the defence that the Machine was defective which results in a right for claimant to reduce the purchase price based on No. 33 a) ORGALIME. No. 33 a) ORGALIME provides:

> 'Where the defect has not been successfully remedied, the Purchaser is entitled to a reduction of the purchase price in proportion to the reduced value of the Product, provided that under no circumstance shall such reduction exceed 15 per cent of the purchase price.'

[52]   "In its pleadings, claimant has not expressly referred to a defence based on No. 33 a) ORGALIME. The Arbitral Tribunal holds, however, that claimant impliedly raised this defence since it argued that based on the defects of the Machine respondent cannot be entitled to the outstanding part of the purchase price. Thus, even without mentioning the pertinent ORGALIME provision claimant raised the defence that it is entitled to a purchase price reduction.

[53]   ". . . [T]he Machine was defective at the time of its delivery and the defect has not been successfully remedied by respondent with regard to the defect of frequent interruptions. Thus, claimant is entitled to a reduction of the purchase price according to No. 33 a) ORGALIME. However, in the view of the Arbitral Tribunal, the defect in the case at hand reduces the value of the Machine by an amount of no more than 10% of the purchase price.

[54]   "As the Expert states, the value of the Machine is reduced by 25% of the purchase price taking into account all defects found by the Expert. . . .

[T]he Expert states that the defect of the excessive use of the component in his view leads to a reduction of the value by 5% of the purchase price. This defect, however, was not timely notified to respondent. From the remaining 20% of value reduction, the Arbitral Tribunal concludes to attribute 10% to the defect of frequent interruptions in the production process and 10% to the other defects found. In the view of the Arbitral Tribunal, this appears to be justified since the ability to produce units of equal weight and the lack of safety measures constitutes defects which reduces the value of the Machine by the same amount as the defect of frequent interruptions in the production process does. Thus, claimant is entitled to a purchase price reduction of 10%.

[55] "Since claimant has the right to reduce the purchase price by 10% respondent is only entitled to receive a payment of 90% of the purchase price under the purchase agreement. Because respondent already received such amount from claimant, respondent's counterclaim is unfounded. In this context, it should be observed that after taking into account the purchase price reduction to which claimant is entitled, the purchase price is deemed to be paid in full and the title to the Machine has passed on to claimant. Thus, the Arbitral Tribunal concludes that respondent is not entitled to be paid the outstanding 10% of the purchase price since claimant is entitled to a purchase price reduction of 10%. This counterclaim is therefore unfounded.

[56] "Respondent further claims compensation for [certain] expenses. . . . In the view of the Arbitral Tribunal it has to be distinguished between the expenses incurred by respondent prior to the arbitral proceedings and those incurred in connection with the arbitral proceedings. Expenses incurred prior to the arbitration proceedings may be subject to a separate claim while expenses in connection with the arbitration proceedings, after such proceedings have commenced, are adjudicated within the decision on the costs of the arbitral proceedings. [Certain] expenses have been incurred by respondent prior to the arbitral proceedings. However, they have to be qualified as costs related to the attempts to remedy defects since they have all been incurred in the course of the dispute between the Parties regarding the conformity of the Machine prior to the institution of the present arbitration proceedings. Since the expenses have been incurred in connection with the attempts to remedy defects, respondent is not entitled to reimbursement for the[se] expenses.

[57] "No. 26 ORGALIME provides:

'On receipt of the notice in writing under Clause 24 the Supplier shall remedy the defect without undue delay and at his own cost as stipulated in Clauses 22-37 inclusive.'

No. 27 ORGALIME states:

'If the Purchaser has given such notice as mentioned in Clause 25, and no defect is found for which the Supplier is liable, the Supplier shall be entitled to compensation for the costs he has incurred as a result of the notice.'

The Tribunal concludes that respondent cannot claim the[se] expenses according No. 27 ORGALIME. . . . [C]laimant has notified respondent of the frequent interruptions in the production process. As far as respondent has incurred expenses in connection with the attempts to remedy this defect it has to bear these costs itself according to No. 26 ORGALIME. [These] expenses have been incurred in connection with the attempts to remedy the frequent interruptions in the production process.

[58]   "The fact that claimant also notified respondent of the non-existing defect of the (nonexistent) insufficient production capacity is irrelevant in this respect since respondent would have incurred expenses claimed in any event due to the existing defect of frequent interruptions in the production process. Moreover, the[se] expenses are not covered by the Terms of Reference and are thus excluded according to Art. 19 ICC-Rules.[11]

[59]   "As regards the [remaining] expenses, these are costs directly related to the present arbitration proceedings. As such, they become part of the decision on costs and cannot be subject to a separate claim. Hence, the [remaining] expenses will be subject to the decision on costs.

(. . . .)

[60]   "The Alternative Counterclaims 1 and 2 are raised only if the Arbitral Tribunal finds that the purchase agreement is terminated. Since this is not the case (see above Part Three) the Alternative Counterclaims 1 and 2 need not be considered further. . . ."

VI.   COSTS OF THE ARBITRATION

[61]   "According to Art. 31(3) ICC-Rules, the final Award shall fix the costs of the arbitration and decide which of the parties shall bear them or in what proportion they shall be borne by the parties. The costs of the arbitration

---

11. Art. 19 of the ICC International Court of Arbitration Rules of Arbitration (ICC-Rules) reads:

"After the Terms of Reference have been signed or approved by the Court, no party shall make new claims or counterclaims which fall outside the limits of the Terms of Reference unless it has been authorized to do so by the Arbitral Tribunal, which shall consider the nature of such new claims or counterclaims, the stage of the arbitration and other relevant circumstances."

shall, according to Art. 31(1) ICC-Rules, include the fees and expenses of the arbitrators and the ICC administrative expenses fixed by the Court, as well as the fees and expenses of any experts appointed and the reasonable legal and other costs incurred by the parties for the arbitration.

[62]   "The determination of the proportion of total costs to be borne by each party is a matter for the discretion of the arbitral tribunal.[12] Furthermore, arbitrators are completely free to determine, at their own discretion, which of the legal and other costs of the parties they consider as reasonable.[13]

[63]   "The Court fixed the ICC administrative expenses and the fees and expenses of the Arbitral Tribunal (together the ICC costs of arbitration). . . . The fees and expenses of the Expert are fixed by the Arbitral Tribunal . . . according to Sect. 1(11) of Appendix III to the ICC Rules. The ICC costs of arbitration and the fees and expenses of the Expert have already been paid by the Parties in equal parts. It appears reasonable to the Arbitral Tribunal that the Parties bear the ICC costs of arbitration and the Expert's fees and expenses in equal shares. This reflects that claimant's claims substantially and respondent's counterclaims totally remain unsuccessful and that both claims and counterclaims involve the same issues. The fact that claimant instituted the present arbitration proceedings will be taken into account below.

[64]   "The Parties have submitted to the Arbitral Tribunal their legal and other costs accompanied by invoices of their counsel. . . . In the light of the length and the complexity of the arbitration proceeding at hand, the Arbitral Tribunal considers the legal costs claimed by the Parties generally as reasonable. The hourly rates of both counsel appear not to be excessive and the amount of time spent appears appropriate. The same is true for the expenses. In the light of the course of the proceedings, they appear to be reasonable.

(. . . .)

[65]   "However, the fact that the legal fees and expenses incurred are reasonable does not automatically lead to the conclusion that they are fully recoverable. It is in the discretion of the arbitral tribunal to determine the amount of costs recoverable and to allocate these costs between the parties.[14] One method of allocating costs is to determine the win-loss ratio and to base the decision on costs thereon. This method, however, does not always lead to reasonable and fair results in cases where both a claim and a counterclaim have been raised which

---

12. "Craig/Park/Paulsson, *International Chamber of Commerce Arbitration*, 2nd ed. (Paris 1990) page 339; Redfern/Hunter, *Law and Practice of International Commercial Arbitration*, 3rd ed. (London 1999) note 8-88."
13. "Craig/Park/Paulsson, *op. cit.*, page 338. Kreindler, *Transnational Litigation: A Basic Primer* (New York 1998) page 295."
14. "Craig/Parkl Paulsson, *op. cit.*, pages 338, 339."

involve substantially the same factual and legal issues. In such cases it appears to be not determinable which costs have been caused by the claim and which by the counterclaim. Furthermore in such cases, a cost decision which is only based on the win-loss ratio does not reflect the course of the proceedings that can have a substantial impact on the costs incurred.

[66] "Against this background, it appears fair and reasonable to the Arbitral Tribunal to hold that claimant is to reimburse respondent from the total legal fees and expenses incurred in a partial amount. This amount reflects the fact that claimant instituted the present arbitration proceedings. While claimant's claims substantially and respondent's counterclaims totally remained unsuccessful the amount of the claims exceeded by far the amount of the counterclaims but both claims and counterclaims involve substantially the same issues. Thus, the Arbitral Tribunal holds that claimant shall reimburse respondent from its total legal fees and expenses incurred in a partial amount. Additional cost reimbursement claims of the Parties are denied.

[67] "Respondent is entitled to be paid interest in the amount of 10% on its arbitration costs beginning four weeks after this final award has been rendered. The interest rate contained in No. 20 ORGALIME does not apply to the costs and expenses of arbitral proceedings. Thus, it cannot be referred to in the case at hand. The ICC-Rules do not contain any provisions with regard to interest on the costs and expenses of arbitral proceedings. The provisions concerning arbitral proceedings contained in the Sixth Book of the Dutch Book of Civil Procedure, which are applicable in the case at hand according to the Terms of Reference, do also not provide for interest on the costs and expenses of arbitral proceedings. As far as the Dutch Book of Civil Procedure contains provisions regarding the costs of procedures before the Dutch state courts, these provisions are tailored to procedures before the Dutch state courts and cannot be transferred to the present arbitration.

[68] "Thus, the determination on the interest rate should be made in the light of the current interest rates on the European market. The Arbitral Tribunal finds it therefore reasonable to fix the interest rate at 10% which compensates respondent sufficiently in the event that claimant does not pay. Moreover, the Arbitral Tribunal grants a grace period of 4 weeks after the date of this Award. As far as respondent claims further interest, this claim is denied."

(. . . .)

VII. THE AWARD

[69] "Claimant's claims are dismissed as far as they regard a repayment of 90 % of the purchase price and damages in the amount of 15 % of the purchase price. But claimant is entitled to a purchase price reduction of ten percent in

conformity with No. 33 a) ORGALIME. In view of the defects of the Machine, respondent is not entitled to the outstanding ten percent of the purchase price. Therefore, respondent's counterclaims are dismissed in full.

[70]   "The ICC costs of arbitration have been fixed at USD . . . which were paid by the Parties in equal shares. The Parties shall bear these costs in equal shares. From respondent's legal fees and expenses claimant is to reimburse respondent an amount of EURO . . . plus interest in the amount of 10% per annum thereon beginning 4 weeks after the date of this Award. All other cost reimbursement claims of respondent and claimant are dismissed. This decision takes into account that claimant instituted this arbitration, the win-loss ratio but also the fact that the claims and the counterclaims involve substantially the same issues.

[71]   ". . . The Parties shall bear the fees and expenses of the Expert in equal shares."

Final award on jurisdiction in case no. 10904 of 2002

Parties:	Claimant: Contractor (Germany)
	Respondent: Employer (Jordan)

Place of arbitration:	Paris, France

Published in:	Unpublished

Subject matters:	– jurisdiction
	– court-ordered interim measures
	– claim on the merits of the dispute
	– waiver of right to arbitration

Facts

Claimant, as contractor, concluded a turnkey contract with the respondent, as employer, for a plant in Jordan. The contract was subject to the FIDIC Conditions of Contract (International) for Electrical and Mechanical Works, Second Edition (1980) (the Conditions) as modified by the parties. Sect. 49.3 of the Conditions provides for arbitration of disputes between the employer and the contractor to be settled by arbitration under the Rules of Conciliation and Arbitration of the International Chamber of Commerce. The contract was governed by the law of the Hashemite Kingdom of Jordan and the parties agreed that this law also governed the arbitration clause.

The respondent refused to issue a Taking-Over Certificate, inter alia, for the plant as a whole, claiming that the plants were not performing as specified in the contract. When negotiations failed, the respondent cashed the performance guarantees that had been issued by claimant in connection with the project.

The claimant requested an interim injunction in Jordan from the Judge of Urgent Matters "to prevent the liquidation of Bank Guarantees" issued by the Bank to the benefit of the respondent. The interim injunction was granted the same day. Claimant then requested a judgment from the Court of First Instance preventing respondent from claiming the amount of the bank guarantees. Respondent filed a counterclaim to prevent the claimant from claiming the value of the four bank guarantees. Claimant applied to the Court of First Instance requesting that it suspend the legal proceedings due to the arbitration clause. Respondent argued that claimant had waived the right to arbitration. The

Court of First Instance discontinued the proceedings until the arbitral award would be made.

Respondent appealed this decision to suspend the proceedings to the Jordanian Court of Appeal which held that the claimant had waived its right to arbitration. Claimant, in turn, appealed this decision to the Jordanian Court of Cassation which upheld the decision of the Court of Appeal. The Court of Cassation reasoned that claimant had resorted to Jordanian courts to resolve its dispute with the respondent and submitted the original claim. Respondent had submitted a defense on the merits. The application to suspend the counterclaim was made after entering into the merits and was not raised by claimant at the first available opportunity.

In the meantime, claimant had initiated arbitration. The arbitral tribunal had already drafted its award when the decision of the Court of Cassation was received by the arbitral tribunal. The arbitral tribunal noted that the decision of the Court of Cassation did not influence its determinations and the conclusions that it had already reached that it did not have jurisdiction.

The arbitral tribunal first examined the parties' arguments and the relevant Jordanian legislation and jurisprudence as to whether claimant's request for a permanent injunction from the Court of First Instance constituted a claim for final relief.

Art. 152 of the Jordanian Code of Civil Procedure (CCP) requires that a party must file a lawsuit within eight days after the granting of an attachment in order to prove its right. The arbitral tribunal rejected claimant's argument that Art. 152 CCP did not require filing a lawsuit that included its substantial rights, but simply one that addressed the problem from the angle of procedural law. Proving the right regarding the bank guarantees could only be done by determining whether the claimant had performed the underlying contract.

The arbitral tribunal noted, however, that Art. 152 CCP only applied to precautionary attachments, and did not refer to the other types of interim injunctions. Such other types of interim injunctions would not be subject to the eight-day time limit for filing the court action. To grant a precautionary attachment, the court must ensure that the property sought to be attached is owned by the defendant. The performance guarantees were not part of the respondent's assets as long as they were not liquidated and thus such a proceeding did not fall within the concept of precautionary attachment. Accordingly, the claimant was wrong in believing that it had to file an action before the Court of First Instance in order to prolong the life span of the Order. The Order was an interim injunction, and as such, remained valid until it was confirmed or vacated upon the final determination of the rights of the parties, or otherwise revoked. Thus, the lawsuit filed by claimant was not necessary and did not expand the life span of the interim injunction ordered by the Judge of Urgent Matters.

The bank guarantees had been paid by the bank one day before the application to the Judge of Urgent Matters. Thus, it was neither useful nor necessary for the claimant to have requested the injunction or to have filed the lawsuit.

The arbitral tribunal then examined whether the claimant had waived the arbitration agreement. Art. 6 of the Jordanian Arbitration Act 1953 contained a strict waiver rule, that is, the mere fact of filing a lawsuit by a party to an arbitration agreement constituted an irrefutable presumption that it waived its right to arbitration, regardless of its actual intent. This was confirmed by a number of cases cited by the respondent, the subsequent Jordanian Arbitration Act 2001, Art. II(3) of the 1958 New York Convention and Art. 8 of the UNCITRAL Model Law. By filing a lawsuit which was found to be a claim on the merits, the claimant waived its right to arbitrate. Moreover, by not resisting the case filed by claimant, the respondent accepted claimant's waiver of the arbitration agreement. Nor did the reservation made by the claimant of its right to commence arbitration constitute a countervailing factor negating the waiver by the claimant.

Referring again to the requirement under Art. 152 CCP to file a lawsuit, the arbitral tribunal held that if Art. 152 were applicable, the claimant could have satisfied the requirement by filing a request for arbitration.

The arbitral tribunal concluded that the claimant had waived the arbitration agreement and that the arbitral tribunal had lost jurisdiction.

Excerpt

I. CLAIM FOR FINAL RELIEF

1. Claimant's Allegations

[1] "Claimant made an interlocutory application to the Judge of Urgent Matters, claiming an interim injunction to seize the encashment of the Performance Guarantees. The Court granted claimant's application. The life span of such an injunction being very short, claimant had to comply with Art. 152 CCP[1] and apply to the Court of First Instance [within eight days] to expand it. Later, the claimant filed a Request for Arbitration with the ICC for the substance of the claims related to the Contract.

---

1. Art. 152 of Jordanian Code of Civil Procedure (CCP) reads:

"If an attachment is ordered prior to the filing of the lawsuit, the party that requested it has to file the lawsuit within eight days from the date of the order to prove his right. If the lawsuit is not filed within the prescribed period, the attachment is cancelled."

[2] "Art. 152 requires that a substantive claim be initiated in the court within the 8 days following the interim relief 'to prove its right for asking for the interim judgment' and extend the life span of the interim order. Accordingly, the application filed with the Court was not an application for final relief. According to claimant, Art. 152 does not require to file a lawsuit that includes the substantial issues of the dispute but simply one that addresses the problem from the angle of procedural law.

[3] "Claimant was seeking a relief which leads to a provisional blocking of the bank guarantees. It insists that the request dealt exclusively with the prevention of the calling of the guarantees which is by nature a non-final relief. In its statement of claim . . . it applied for 'prevention' – and thus hindrance of future events – not for the return or restitution of money cashed in the past. Therefore it was decisive to prolong the life span of the interim court order.

[4] "Claimant believes furthermore that its action was authorized by the jurisdiction clause in the guarantees that stipulates: 'This letter of guarantee is governed by the Jordanian laws and is subject to the non-exclusive Jordanian courts' jurisdiction.'"

2. Respondent's Allegations

[5] "Respondent alleges that, in its statement of claim claimant claims final relief in the form of a permanent injunction in relation to the encashment of the Guarantees, yet a claim for final relief necessarily requires a decision to be made on the merits. As a matter of fact, claimant asserts that respondent was not entitled to cash the Guarantees because it had correctly performed the Contract. The question of performance is thus at the heart of the dispute between the parties. Therefore claimant's claim before the Jordanian court requires by necessity a determination of the merits of the dispute which it is seeking to submit to arbitration.

[6] "Art. 152 requires the commencement of a 'lawsuit' (Da'awa), which means that a party granted interim relief is obliged thereafter to establish the necessity for preserving that decision by proceeding on the merits before a judicial authority. Under Jordanian law, the interim application then becomes part of the record of the ensuing lawsuit. (Civ. Cass. Dec. 364/67 (Ex. R52) and Civ. Cass. Dec. 75/77 (Ex. R53)). As explained by the Jordanian Court of Cassation in Cass. 257/67, 'the purpose of the legislator in . . . [Art. 152] is not to keep the attached properties under attachment for an unspecified period of time before filing the lawsuit proving the claimed right . . . '.

[7] "Respondent maintains that although Art. 152 CCP requires that a substantive claim be initiated within 8 days following the interim relief, claimant could have fulfilled the requirement by initiating the arbitration."

II. DETERMINATION OF THE ISSUE

1. *Major Differences Between Interim Relief and Final Relief*

[8] "In Jordan as anywhere else, an application for interim relief is fundamentally different from a claim for final relief. The most significant differences according to the Jordanian Code of Civil Procedure are as follows. The original jurisdiction to hear and decide applications for interim relief is for the Judge of Urgent Matters. (CCP, Art. 32)[2] Other courts can only hear and decide such application if filed with it as ancillaries and in connection with a claim on the merits already filed with the same court. (CCP, Art. 30(3))[3] By contrast, a claim for final relief is within the exclusive jurisdiction of the Court of Substance. The Judge of Urgent Matters cannot hear or decide such claims. (Civ. Cass. Dec. 1778/98 Jordan Bar Rev., p. 1235(1998)) Since jurisdiction of the subject matter is of Public Order (CCP, Art. 111), an application for interim relief filed independently with a Court of Substance will be dismissed for lack of jurisdiction. The same is also true if a claim for final relief is filed with the Judge of Urgent Matters. (C.A. 892/94, published in H. Alsmadi, *Decisions of the Amman Court of Appeal*, 1996 (in Arabic), hereinafter *Alsmadi*) If the Court of Substance or the Judge of Urgent Matters does not dismiss the claim or the application, as the case may be, its decision will be null and void. (Civ. Cass. Dec. 1778/98 Jordan Bar Rev., p. 1235 (1998)).

[9] "An interim relief is, by definition, temporary and does not determine the rights of the parties to the dispute. (CCP, Arts.32, 33(3); C.A. 1033/92, *Alsmadi*,

---

2. Art. 32 of the Jordanian CCP reads:

"The judge of Urgent Matters may order provisional measures without determining the merits of the claim in the following cases, but this does not affect the jurisdiction of the Court of substance if the matter is ancillary to a claim on the merits:

1. Urgent matters that may be impaired by the lapse of time.

2. Requests for the appointment of an agent, receiver, custodian, precautionary attachment or prevention from traveling.

3. Urgent inspection of any property to establish the status quo.

4. Proceedings to hear a witness on a matter that is not yet submitted to a court but that is likely to be submitted if the testimony might not be available then but the party requesting the testimony shall bear all the expenses."

3. Art. 30 of the Jordanian CCP reads in relevant part:

"1. Unless otherwise provided, the Court of First Instance has jurisdiction to hear all suits (civil and commercial) not assigned to the Magistrate Court.

(...)

3. The Court of First Instance] also has jurisdiction to hear urgent and all other requests related to the original claim regardless of their value or type."

p. 16) Therefore, it has been held that since an interim relief is not final and does not affect the substantive rights of the parties to the dispute, it may be revoked or modified if there is a change of the material facts or the legal positions of the parties or one of them. (C.A. 660/95, *Alsmadi*, p. 237; see also Alquddah, M. *Civil Procedures and Judicial System in Jordan*, 2nd ed. 1999, pp. 142-144 (in Arabic); Antaki, R. *Principles of Procedures in Civil and Commercial Matters*, 5th ed. 1962, pp. 258-259 (in Arabic); Abu Alwafa, A. *Principles of Civil Procedures*, 4th ed. 1989, pp. 282-283 (in Arabic)) A court of substance cannot revoke or modify its decision on the merits of the dispute.

[10]   "The terminology used in the proceedings of an application for an interim relief differs from the one used in the case of a claim for final relief. In the case of a final relief the proceedings are called a 'lawsuit' (*Da'wa*) and the lawsuit is initiated by a written statement called 'statement of claim' (*La'ahat Da'wa)*, while in the case of interim relief the proceedings are called an 'application' (*Talab*) and are initiated by a written statement called 'application or motion'. The party filing an application for an interim relief is called the 'applicant' (*Almustad'i*); in contrast, the party filing a claim for final relief is called the 'plaintiff' (*Almudda'i*)

[11]   "Decisions on urgent matters may not be appealed to the Court of Cassation without permission or leave to appeal. (CCP, Art. 176). In most cases the interim relief is accorded without the benefit of a contradictory procedure and ex parte, which would be completely unacceptable in a lawsuit."

2. Nature of Relief Sought by Claimant

[12]   "Art. 152 CCP provides that in case an attachment is ordered by the Judge of Urgent Matters prior to the filing of the lawsuit, the plaintiff has to file a lawsuit within 8 days to prove his right; otherwise, the attachment is cancelled. Claimant admits that a lawsuit filed under Art. 152 CCP is a lawsuit for substantive claims but justifies its action by saying it was compelled to initiate such a lawsuit 'to prove its right for asking for the interim judgment' and extend the life span of the interim order. As such, it claims, Art. 152 does not require to file a lawsuit that includes the substantial issues of the dispute but simply addresses the problem from the angle of procedural law. The Tribunal does not agree.

[13]   "Proving the right on the bank guarantees can only be done by determining whether the plaintiff has performed the underlying contract according to its terms with the consequence that if, in the case of a suit to prevent claiming the value of the guarantees, the court finds that the plaintiff did not breach the contract, it will make a final judgment preventing the defendant from claiming its value. If, on the other hand, the court finds that the plaintiff has breached the

contract it will dismiss the case and uphold the defendant's right to claim the value of the guarantees. (Civ. Cass. Dec. 411187 Jordan Bar Rev., p. 864 (1990)). Such a consequence is consistent only with a claim for final relief.

[14]   "According to the Jordanian Court of Cassation, 'It is not permissible to interpret a provision of a statute without taking into account the rest of the provisions of the statute. An interpretation must be done on the basis that a statute is an undividable whole.' (Civ. Cass. Dec. 389/75 Jordan Bar Rev., p. 1274 (1976); see also Civ. Cass. Dec. 711/85 Jordan Bar Rev., p. 769 (1986); Civ. Cass. Dec. 158/90 Jordan Bar Rev., p. 1656 (1991)). Therefore, any interpretation of Art. 152 must take into account the provisions of Arts. 30-33. Under these articles a claim filed initially with a Court of substance pursuant to Art. 152 must be a claim for final relief. Art. 152 contains an elaboration of the procedural rules relating to the Urgent Matters governed by Arts. 30-33. The preamble to Art. 32 provides that the decisions of the Judge of Urgent Matters on the matters enumerated in the article are of a temporary nature and do not determine the original rights of the parties. Art. 33(3) adds that an interim injunction issued in accordance with these provisions is of a temporary nature pending determination of the dispute on the merits. Construing Art. 152 as allowing a claim for interim relief would mean that there could be no dispute on the merits, which makes Arts. 32 and 33(3) meaningless.

[15]   "The underlying purpose of Art. 152 is not only to prolong the life span of the interim injunction but also and mainly to protect the other party who may be seriously prejudiced if the injunction remains in force for an indefinite period of time. Therefore, Art. 152 requires the party who obtained an interim injunction to file a claim on the merits to prove its right so that the court will determine whether to vacate the interim injunction or to make it permanent. The sanction for not complying with the requirement of this article is the loss of the temporary protection only. The right to file a claim for final relief with the competent court or with an arbitral tribunal is not lost. The Arbitral Tribunal holds that: By filing a lawsuit in the Court of First Instance, claimant did apply for final relief."

III.   NECESSITY OF LAWSUIT TO EXPAND LIFE SPAN OF INTERIM INJUNCTIONS

[16]   "In its application to the Judge of Urgent Matters, claimant requested an interim injunction to prevent the liquidation of the bank guarantees, and in the statement of claim submitted it requested the Court to 'join the urgent order to the filed case' against defendant to prevent it from calling upon the guarantees. The request was made allegedly pursuant to Art.152 of the CCP, thus indicating

that the order obtained by the Judge of Urgent Matters fell within the provision of Art. 141 of the CCP, 1988.[4]

[17]   "According to Jordanian law, interim injunctions are accorded, in principle, until the adjudication of the case (Art. 32(1) CCP) and are not subject to Art. 152 CCP. This legal fact stems from the express wording of Art. 152, which tackles only the precautionary attachments leaving the other interim injunctions without any reference. In other words, all interim orders of the Judge of Urgent Matters remain in force until the case is determined by the court of substance. Indeed, the plaintiff remains free to choose the time for filing the court action against the defendant. There is only one exception to this principle: when the urgent application is for a precautionary attachment order. In such a case, the applicant shall file a court action within a period not exceeding 8 days from the date of the precautionary attachment order otherwise the attachment can be cancelled. (Art. 152 CCP).

[18]   "The admissibility of the precautionary attachment order and the conditions, which must be fulfilled before such an order is issued, are determined by Arts. 141-152 of the CCP. In deciding whether to grant this particular interim relief the Judge of Urgent Matters has to ensure that the property sought to be attached is owned by the defendant. The precautionary attachment is denied if the property belongs to a third party.

[19]   "In the case at hand plaintiff requested an order addressed to the bank enjoining it from paying the guarantees to defendant. The aim of plaintiff was to preserve the status quo pending a final determination by the Arbitral Tribunal. However, the performance guarantees were furnished by plaintiff to provide defendant with security and they are thus not part of defendant's assets as long as they are not liquidated. Clearly such a proceeding does not fall within the concept of precautionary attachment contemplated in Arts. 141 and 152 of the CCP, which aim to bring defendant's property under the custody of the court until a judgment is rendered on the substance.

[20]   "In light of the foregoing, it can be asserted that claimant was wrong in believing that it had to file an action before the Court of First Instance in order to prolong the life span of the Order granted by the Judge of Urgent Matters against defendant restraining it from cashing the guarantees. In the same vein, respondent was not obliged to file a counterclaim in order to defend its position

---

4. Art. 141 of the Jordanian CCP 1988 reads:

"The creditor may address a request to the Judge of Urgent Matters or the Court before a lawsuit is filed, when it is being filed or during the procedures for a precautionary attachment, until the adjudication of the claim, of the debtor's movable and immovable properties whether they are in the hands of the debtor or of a third party, by presenting documents or evidence he may have."

nor to submit a statement of defense or raise issues concerning the merits of the dispute. Instead, respondent could have submitted an application in limine for the dismissal of the principal court action in accordance with the Arbitration Act in force at that time.

[21]   "Claimant's application to the Judge of Urgent Matters for an interim injunction to prevent the liquidation of the guarantees was for an urgent matter but could not be for a precautionary attachment. Accordingly, Art. 152 is not applicable to the case at hand and claimant was not required to file its lawsuit in order to extend the life span of the interim injunction.

[22]   "The interim injunction ordered by the Judge of Urgent Matters did not have a limited life span under CCP 1988. In principle, such an injunction remains valid until it is confirmed or vacated upon the final determination of the rights of the parties or revoked by the Court of Appeal upon the application of respondent or by the Judge of Urgent Matters if respondent could prove a change of the material facts or the legal positions of the parties (C.A., 660195, *Alsmadi*, p. 237)

[23]   "The CCP of 1988 was amended by Law No. 14 of 2001. The amendments do not apply to the case at hand but the new version of Art. 152 confirms the Tribunal's interpretation. It explicitly extends the obligation to file a lawsuit within 8 days of the date of issuing of the interim order to precautionary attachment, prevention from traveling and any other preventive measures. This was not the situation before the amendment.

[24]   "In conclusion, the interim injunction sought by claimant cannot, in any way, be construed as a precautionary attachment order. It is an interim injunction within the meaning of Arts. 32(1) and 33 which does not ultimately require filing a lawsuit within a prescribed period to expand the life span of such an injunction.

[25]   "The Arbitral Tribunal holds that: The lawsuit filed by claimant in the Court of First Instance was not necessary and did not expand the life span of the interim injunction ordered by the Judge of Urgent Matters to prevent respondent from liquidating the guarantees."

IV.   USEFULNESS OF LAWSUIT IN JORDANIAN COURTS

(. . . .)

[26]   The arbitral tribunal charted the chronology of the relevant events relating to the request by the respondent to the bank for the payment of the guarantees and the proceedings in the Court of First Instance for Urgent Matters and the Court of First Instance and continued as follows: "Payment under the guarantees was made one day prior to claimant's application for the interim injunction and one week prior to the filing of the lawsuit. Therefore, it was neither necessary nor useful for claimant to file its lawsuit [when it did] in order to

extend the life span of the interim injunction that did not have a subject matter at that date and its extension would have been meaningless.

[27]   "Claimant contended that it did not know or was not officially informed that payment under the guarantees was made when it filed its lawsuit. This argument by claimant should be disregarded. Claimant knew that payment was made prior to [the filing of the lawsuit].

[28]   "Claimant was informed by its bank [earlier] that a request for payment was received. This is furthermore evident from its letter to the bank the day before it filed the lawsuit, in which it stated:

> "Through our contact ... *we recently learnt* that you affected payments under the above mentioned guarantees. ... We repeatedly requested to specify the date and time on which payments were made."

[29]   "A copy of this letter was sent to claimant's attorney. Furthermore, a letter from the bank to the court informing it that payment under the guarantees was effected was placed on file. Claimant's attorney could have consulted the court file before filing the lawsuit.

[30]   "The Arbitral Tribunal holds that: The injunction requested from the Judge of Urgent Matters had no subject matter. Claimant knew when it filed its lawsuit at the Court of First Instance that the extension of the life span of the injunction was not useful."

VI.   IMPLIED WAIVER OR RENUNCIATION OF THE ARBITRATION AGREEMENT

1.   *The Parties' Allegations*

[31]   "The parties do not agree on whether claimant waived its right to arbitration. Respondent says that it definitely did when it addressed a competent court of justice to determine the core of the dispute of the construction contract underlying the bank guarantees. Claimant disagrees and says that it certainly did not waive its right to arbitration when it requested the Court to block the bank guarantees until it could obtain an arbitral award. Claimant further insists that according to applicable Jordanian statutes, waiver of an arbitration agreement has to be explicit."

a.   *Respondent's allegations*

[32]   "According to Jordanian law, the arbitration agreement is binding but can be waived if the parties agree to waive it (Art. 4 Jordanian Arbitration Law,

Law 18 of 1953 (JAL 1953)). Furthermore, waiver can be implicit or result from an act that clearly indicates the party's intention not to be bound anymore by the agreement. Such an intention is clear if a party applies to a national court for a decision on the merits of a dispute that ought to be arbitrated.

[33]   "Claimant clearly indicated its intention not to be bound by the arbitration agreement when it applied to the Jordanian court for a final relief. At that moment respondent could have requested the Court to suspend the proceedings and send the matter to arbitration according to the arbitration agreement. (Art. 6 JAL 1953) However, respondent chose not to object to the change of forum and sealed the agreement to waive the arbitration to the civil court by filing a counterclaim for damages rather than requesting the stay of the proceedings. The Arbitral Tribunal lost its jurisdiction because both parties applied to the courts for decisions on the merits of the dispute.

[34]   "Respondent also contends that the continuous affirmation by claimant in its briefs that it intended to continue to be bound by the arbitration agreement is contradicted by its acts when in Jordan the acts should prevail. (Art. 238 CC)

[35]   "Respondent claims that its reasoning is supported by a number of decisions by the Jordanian Court of Cassation, respondent's Expert Dr. S, and the Arbitration Act of 2001 as well as by the international arbitration practice, and an ICC Award confirmed by the Paris Court of Appeal."

b.   Claimant's allegations

[36]   "Claimant is at issue with all of respondent's allegations. Claimant argues that it filed its application with a Jordanian court as the jurisdiction of the Jordanian courts was stipulated in the bank guarantees and stated that the request dealt exclusively with the prevention of the calling of the guarantees and had nothing to do with the construction Contract and the claims arising from it.

[37]   "Claimant also insists that any waiver would require – among other elements – in some form, a declaration of intent that the waiving party does not want anymore to be bound by the agreement in question. Claimant alleges, not only that it did not intend to waive the agreement but that, to the contrary, it repeatedly insisted that it wanted the arbitration to proceed. Such clear explicit statement cannot be construed as an implicit waiver of rights. Moreover, it was respondent, not claimant who touched the core of the construction dispute in the Jordanian court. Thus it was to claimant, not to respondent, to accept the change of forum or to refuse it by objecting to the jurisdiction of the Jordanian courts. This is precisely what claimant did in due time. The parties did not agree to waive the arbitration agreement and the Arbitral Tribunal is still competent.

[38]   "Claimant claims that its reasoning is supported by Arts. 215 and 216 of the Civil Code and is further confirmed by Art. 12 of the Arbitration Act 2001."

2.   The Determination of the Issue

[39]   "As claimant's claim was a claim on the merits of the dispute, the Tribunal has to determine whether it waived the arbitration agreement.

[40]   "Art. 4 of the Arbitration Act 1953 provides:

'Unless otherwise expressly provided therein, an arbitration agreement may not be revoked without the consent of the parties thereto, or the approval of the Court, and it shall have the same force in all respects as a court judgment.'

[41]   "According to this article, an arbitration agreement is binding unless it is renounced or waived by the parties. The article does not determine the legal conditions of waiver and in particular whether the intention of a party to waive the agreement has to be explicit, as claimant asserts, or if it could be inferred from the behavior of the parties, as is suggested by respondent. In the absence of a specific rule, these questions are to be answered in light of the general rules of interpretation and the Jordanian judicial decisions and authorities.

[42]   "Art. 93 CC stipulates:

'The expression of the will shall be by word, writing, the customary sign even from a person who is not dumb, the actual exchange denoting consent and by any other behavior which in the circumstances leaves no doubt of the indication of consent.'

[43]   "It is obvious from this article that an offer, an acceptance or any other declaration of intention may be implied from the conduct of the parties. Further on, Art. 27(2) CCP stipulates:

'Jordanian Courts have jurisdiction to determine a lawsuit even if it is not within their jurisdiction if their jurisdiction is accepted by a party [defendant] expressly or impliedly.'

[44]   "Art. 6 of the Arbitration Act 1953 stipulates:

'If either of the parties to arbitration initiate against the other party legal proceedings before any court with regard to any matter which was agreed to be referred to arbitration, the other party may, (before pleading the

374   Reprinted from the Yearbook Commercial Arbitration

subject matter of the case,) request that the court gives a ruling to suspend such proceedings. If the court is satisfied that the petitioner who requested suspension of the proceedings was prepared and is still desirous to take the necessary measures to proceed properly with the arbitration and there is no reason to prevent referring the matter to arbitration in accordance with the agreement, then the court shall give a ruling to suspend such proceedings.'

[45] "This article states the conditions of waiver when legal proceedings are initiated by a party. The question was discussed at length in the briefs despite the fact that its meaning is clear and accepted universally. The article is no more than a straightforward application of the general principles adopted by Art. 93 CC and Art. 27(2) CCP. Thus, according to Art. 4, a party (usually, the claimant in the judicial case) who initiates judicial instead of arbitral proceedings indicates, without any possible doubt, its decision not to he bound by the arbitration agreement. In such a case, the other party (usually the defendant in the judicial proceedings) may either accept the change of forum or request the court to implement the arbitration agreement. The other party's decision to enter into the merits of the judicial case is again the irrefutable indication that the offer to waive the arbitration agreement has been accepted. This is simply the basic scenario of an offer accepted by the offeree. For efficiency reasons, the Court is invited to verify the parties' seriousness.

[46] "Arts. 4 and 6 deal with an important 'negative' effect of an arbitration agreement. The agreement to submit a certain matter to arbitration means that this matter shall not be heard and decided upon by any court, irrespective of whether this exclusion is expressed in the agreement. If, nevertheless, a party starts litigation, the court shall refer the parties to arbitration unless it finds the agreement has been waived. The wording of Art. 6 does not make any reference to the intent of the party who files the court action or the intent of the defendant who fails to raise the defense before entering into the merits of the dispute. This means that the article adopts a strict waiver or estoppel rule. That is, the mere fact of filing a lawsuit by a party to an arbitration agreement constitutes an irrefutable presumption that it waived its right to arbitrate regardless of its actual intent. The same also applies to failure by the defendant to raise the defense before entering into the merits of the dispute.

[47] "This strict waiver rule is necessary due to the type of the defense and the time at which it must be raised. The aim of the defense is to suspend the court proceedings and it must be raised before entering into the merits of the dispute. This makes it akin to defenses referred to in Art. 110 CCP that stipulates:

'1. The motion for invalidation which is unrelated to public policy and all motions related to the procedures which are unrelated to the public policy and motion for the absence of local jurisdiction must all be raised before any other procedural motion, request or defence in the lawsuit otherwise the right to raise them is lost.

Also the right of the petitioner in these motions is lost if the reasons are not mentioned in the motions writ.'

[48]   "Art. 110 CCP justifies subjecting the defense in case of waiver to the same rule applicable to other defenses envisaged in the same article. Art. 110(1) adopts a strict waiver rule: according to this article, if the defences referred to therein are not raised before entering into the merits of the case, the right to raise them at a later stage is permanently lost regardless of the actual intent of the party concerned. In fact it has been held that the defense of the existence of an arbitration agreement is within the ambit of Art. 16 of CCP 1952, which is the predecessor of Arts. 109 and 110 of CCP 1988. (Civ. Cass. Dec. 4331/76, p. 514, 1977, produced in A. Al Momani, *Arbitration in Jordan and Comparative Legislation*, 1982, p. 184 (in Arabic)

[49]   "Claimant insists that waiver has to be explicit but did not cite – nor could the tribunal find – a single Jordanian authority that supports its affirmation. To the contrary a number of decisions and authorities confirm respondent's inter-pretation of Jordanian law on this matter.

[50]   "The more relevant decisions are the following:

Court of Cassation (Civ. Cass. Dec. No. 23/93 Jordan Bar Rev., p. 2250) (Ex. R19):
Referral to arbitration for settlement of disputes is an exceptional method that is not part of the public order, and it may be waived expressly or impliedly, and the right to refer to arbitration will be repudiated after entering into the merits of the case.
Court of Cassation (Civ. Cass. Dec. 1223/98 Jordan Bar Rev., p. 305 (1999) (Ex. R56)):
... the plaintiff's filing of the lawsuit before the court represents an implied reversal [waiver] of the arbitration agreement and the fact that the defendant entered into the merits of the case means that he has waived the defence of the existence of the arbitration condition.
Court of Cassation (Civ. Cass. Dec. 106/53 Jordan Bar Rev., p. 603 (1953)):
If the defendant objected to the jurisdiction of the court because of the existence of an arbitration agreement and the plaintiff showed that he was willing to settle the dispute by arbitration but the defendant did not insist on the defense and entered into the merits of the case, this conduct on the part of the defendant is considered waiver of the defense of the existence of an arbitration agreement.

Court of Cassation (Civ. Cass. Dec. 80/67 Jordan Bar Rev., p. 514 (1967)): If the defendant pleaded the subject of the case in his answer to the statement of claim before requesting the court to suspend the proceedings because of the existence of an arbitration agreement, his request to suspend the proceeding made after that is not acceptable.

Court of Cassation (Civ. Cass. Dec. 770/85 Jordan Bar Rev., p. 232 (1988)): According to the wording of Art. 6 of the Law of Arbitration No. 18 of 1953, the defense of the existence of an arbitration agreement ... must be raised before entering into the merits of the case. ...

Court of Cassation (Civ. Cass. Dec. 1455/96 Jordan Bar Rev., p. 1536 (1994)): The defendant who refused to respond to the plaintiff's notification to settle the dispute in accordance with the arbitration clause is estopped from raising the defense of the existence of the arbitration clause which it refused to apply consensually, and did not seriously insist on it before the Court of First Instance.

[51]   "This interpretation of Arts. 4 and 6 of the Arbitration Act is further confirmed by Dr. Ahmad Al Momani, in *Arbitration in Jordanian and Comparative Legislation* (Part 1, 1982). Under the heading 'When the Defense [of the Existence of an Arbitration Agreement] Should Be Raised', the author states:

'The Law of arbitration stipulated in article 6, referred to above, that the defendant should raise his defense to suspend the proceedings of the lawsuit before entering into its merits, which is a stage of the proceeding that begins after the service of the statement of claim on the defendant and before his answer to it. If, however, the defendant entered into the merits of the case and argued it, he is deemed to have waived this defense, as explained earlier, and lost the opportunity to force the defendant (sic) to return to arbitration and the dispute will be heard by the court. The filing of the lawsuit by the plaintiff and the entering into the merits of the dispute by the defendant is deemed to be an implied (revocation) renunciation of the Arbitration Agreement.' (p.180)

[52]   "The Jordanian Arbitration Act has been updated in 2001 and claimant emphasized that the new version supported its approach. Art. 12 of the new Act stipulates:

'a. The court of law which finds a lawsuit filed that includes a dispute covered with an arbitration agreement, must dismiss that lawsuit if the defendant raised that issue before entering into the core of the dispute.

b. Filing the above mentioned lawsuit shall not stop or prevent initializing arbitration, proceeding with any arbitration and/or ruling upon the merits in any arbitration, unless the parties have agreed to the contrary.'

[53]   "This article confirms the previous legal situation. As a matter of fact, the legal principles underlying the present case are generally and universally accepted. They were already expressed in Art. II(3) of the 1958 New York Convention on the Recognition and Enforcement of Foreign Arbitral Awards:

'The court of a Contracting State, when seized of an action in a matter in respect of which the parties have made an agreement within the meaning of this article, shall, at the request of one of the parties, refer the parties to arbitration, unless it finds that the said agreement is null and void, inoperative or incapable of being performed.'

The same principle is also embodied in Art. 8 of the UNCITRAL Model Act:

'A court before which an action is brought in a matter which is the subject of an arbitration agreement shall, if a party so requests not later than when submitting his first statement on the substance of the dispute, refer the parties to arbitration unless it finds that the agreement is null and void, inoperative or incapable of being performed.'

[54]   "The Tribunal is aware that the dispute is to be decided according to Jordanian law. However, as the contractual place of arbitration is Paris, reference can be made to the *Uzinexportimport* case in which the Paris Court of Appeal confirmed that the waiver of an arbitration agreement 'can be inferred from the fact that [the party] has applied to a court, provided that the claim in question concerns the merits of the dispute and thus ought to have been submitted to arbitration'. (*Uzinexportimport Romanian Co. v. Attock Cement Co.* 1995 Rev. Arb. 107, Note Sigvard Jarvin, Ex. R20)

[55]   "The Arbitral Tribunal holds that: According to Jordanian law, waiver of an arbitration agreement can be implicit and result from the behavior of the parties. The filing by claimant of its lawsuit which was found to be a claim on the merits with respect to issues covered by the arbitration agreement, constitutes a waiver of its right to arbitrate. By not resisting the case filed by claimant, respondent accepted claimant's waiver of the arbitration agreement. The arbitration agreement was waived by the parties."

VII.   ARBITRATION INSTEAD OF FILING A LAWSUIT

[56]   "Clause 49.3 of the Contract, which dealt with arbitration, contained the following:

'If at any time any question, dispute or difference shall arise between the Employer and the Contractor in connection with or arising out of the Contract or the carrying out of the Works (whether during the progress of the Works or after their completion, and whether before or after the termination, abandonment or breach of the Contract) which cannot be settled amicably either party shall, as soon as reasonably practicable, but not earlier than three months after a request made to settle the dispute amicably has been made to the other party, give to the other notice in writing of the existence of such question, dispute or difference specifying the nature and the point at issue, and the same shall be finally settled by Arbitration under the Rules of Conciliation and Arbitration of the International Chamber of Commerce by one or more Arbitrators appointed in accordance with those Rules.'

The parties do not agree on the implications of this clause A."
(. . . .)
[57] The arbitral tribunal noted that on the one hand, the respondent stated that Art. 152 left claimant free to choose between the court and arbitration and that on the other hand, claimant stated that Art. 152 left it with no other choice than filing a lawsuit because the conciliation clause contained in the arbitration agreement did not allow arbitration before three months after an attempt for an amicable solution failed. Moreover the respondent maintained that the three-month period began when the request to settle the dispute amicably was made and not when such an effort had failed. The arbitral tribunal agreed with the respondent that the three-month period started running from the date of the request made to settle the dispute amicably. The arbitral tribunal then examined the actions of the parties and concluded that "by November 1999 and considering respondent's reactions, it became obvious that no bona fide negotiations were still possible and any technical delay would have been prejudicial to claimant. It is our opinion that claimant was released from the three-month obligation and could have requested arbitration by November 1999.
[58] "The possibility for parties to apply to a competent judicial authority for conservatory relief is admitted and confirmed by Art. 23(2) of the ICC Arbitration Rules:

'Before the file is transmitted to the Arbitral Tribunal, and in appropriate circumstances even thereafter, the parties may apply to any competent judicial authority for interim or conservatory measures. The application of a party to a judicial authority for such measures or for the implementation of any such Measures ordered by an Arbitral Tribunal shall not be deemed to be an infringement or a waiver of the arbitration agreement and shall not affect the relevant powers reserved to the Arbitral Tribunal. . . . '

[59] "Art. 152 CCP would have been satisfied if a Request for Arbitration had been filed with the ICC (CCP, Art. 57(5)). Claimant did not have to wait for an Arbitral Tribunal to be constituted. This is confirmed by Art. 4(2) of the ICC Rules that states:

> 'The date on which the Request is received by the Secretariat shall, for all purposes, be deemed to be the date of the commencement of the arbitral proceedings.'

[60] "The Arbitral Tribunal holds that: Art. 152 of the Jordanian Code of Civil Procedure, if applicable, would have been satisfied if a Request for Arbitration had been filed by claimant instead of a lawsuit in Jordanian Courts. Claimant could have begun arbitration proceedings despite the conciliation clause."

VIII. RESERVATION OF RIGHT TO COMMENCE ARBITRATION

[61] "In its statement of claim claimant expressly reserved its right to commence arbitration proceedings under the construction contract. Paragraph Eighthly of the statement of claim provided:

> 'In accordance with the conditions of the contract and its articles, the conflicts regarding the contract or its execution or its interpretations is the jurisdiction of the International Court of Arbitration at the International Chamber of Commerce in Paris (ICC) and the plaintiff reserves this right and will initiate proceedings in that respect urgently since it sustained damages and incurred major losses as the result of the practices of the defendant during the construction period.'

The parties did not agree on the effect of this reservation."

1. The Parties' Allegations

[62] "On one side, claimant argues that its position was crystal clear as it repeated in each and every brief filed in the Jordanian Courts explicitly that it intended to respect and be bound by the arbitration agreement. Claimant also relies on Art. 215 CC, which stipulates: 'Invigorating the words is better than disregarding them.'

[63] "On the other side, respondent stated:

> ' . . . by filing the same statement of claim, which it has moreover continued to pursue, claimant waived precisely the right it purported to reserve. The situation is therefore that claimant's words are in direct contradiction to its

actions. Such a situation is provided for by Sect. 238 of Jordanian Civil Code No. 43 of 1976, which states: "If any person seeks to disavow any act performed by himself, such attempt is entirely disregarded.'"

[64]   "The effect of this provision is to prevent claimant from denying the effects that follow from its actions. By initiating proceedings for final relief before the Jordanian courts, claimant has waived its right to arbitrate, and respondent accepted claimant's waiver. This cannot now be avoided by claimant's statement to the contrary."

2.   Determination of the Issue

[65]   "Claimant contends that the scope of the lawsuit is limited to the bank guarantees and does not touch the core of the contractual dispute. The Tribunal has determined however that claimant's lawsuit was a claim on the merits of the construction contract. Moreover, the reservation made by claimant in its statement of claim does not constitute a countervailing factor that may negate waiver of the arbitration agreement on its part for the following reasons.

[66]   "The reservation made by claimant in its statement of claim of January 2000 is inconsistent with the reasons of the claim and the request made therein. In paragraphs four to seven claimant stated that it had performed the construction contract in accordance with its conditions of the contract. It then requested the court, upon proof of the above facts, to issue its ruling to prevent respondent from claiming the value of the guarantees. Whether claimant has fulfilled its contractual obligations or not is the most important issue to be determined by the Arbitral Tribunal according to the Arbitration Clause. Therefore, by placing this issue before the court for final determination and at the same time reserving its right to have it determined by arbitration, claimant created a contradiction between the express terms of its statement of claim. Since claimant is the drafter of the statement of claim, this contradiction should be resolved against its interest by disregarding its reservation. Furthermore, the main object of the statement of claim is to have the court determine the issues raised therein. Therefore, if the paragraph embodying the reservation contradicts with the other paragraphs embodying the main object of the statement of claim and it is not possible to reconcile them, the paragraph embodying the reservation should be disregarded because it is less important.

[67]   "The mere act of filing a statement of claim in respect of a dispute which is the subject of an arbitration agreement constitutes waiver of the arbitration agreement by the party who filed the statement of claim. Claimant, however, attempted to avoid this eventuality by making the reservation in the same statement of claim and relied on it, at a later stage, in order to suspend the court proceedings and force respondent to return to arbitration. This conduct by

claimant brings into play Art. 238 CC, which provides: 'Whoever attempts to undo what he has done shall not benefit from his attempt.'

[68]   "The Arbitral Tribunal holds that: The reservation made by claimant does not constitute a countervailing factor negating waiver on its part.

[69]   "The only question the Arbitral Tribunal has to answer in this Final Award is whether claimant has waived the arbitration agreement with the consequence that the Tribunal has lost its jurisdiction to decide the claim on the merits of the dispute. The answer is yes. The Arbitral Tribunal holds that: The Arbitral Tribunal lacks jurisdiction to decide the merits of the dispute between claimant and respondent."

IX.   COSTS

[70]   "The Tribunal reached the conclusion that claimant had waived the arbitration agreement and the Tribunal lost its jurisdiction. The Tribunal now has to determine the costs of arbitration according to Art. 31 of the ICC Rules. . . . [5]

[71]   "The case at hand was not frivolous. It raised very serious questions of law under Jordanian law and international arbitration practice in general. While the Tribunal was handling the case, parallel proceedings were in progress at the Jordanian Court of First Instance and the Court of Appeal and these two Courts reached opposite conclusions. Counsel presented serious and structured opinions and relevant exhibits and no one tried to take advantage of the process, or unduly extend or delay the proceedings. To the contrary, the Tribunal was privileged to work with highly professional Counsel. Due to these circumstances and because the question is related to the jurisdiction of the Tribunal and to the very essence of due process, the Tribunal decides that each party shall bear its own legal fees and expenses and share equally the ICC administrative fees and the Arbitrators' fees and expenses.

[72]   "The Arbitral Tribunal holds that: Each party shall bear its expenses including the fees and expenses paid to its lawyers and experts. Each party shall bear half of the ICC administrative expenses and the Arbitrators' fees and expenses fixed by the ICC Court of Arbitration."

---

5. Art. 31 of the ICC Rules reads:

"1. The costs of the arbitration shall include the fees and expenses of the arbitrators and the ICC administrative expenses fixed by the Court, in accordance with the scale in force at the time of the commencement of the arbitral proceedings, as well as the fees and expenses of any experts appointed by the Arbitral Tribunal and the reasonable legal and other costs incurred by the parties for the arbitration.

2. The final Award shall fix the costs of the arbitration and decide which of the parties shall bear them or in what proportion they shall be borne by the parties."

Interim award in case no. 11333 of 2002

Parties:	Claimant: Insurer (US) Respondent: Manufacturer (Italy)
Place of arbitration:	Paris, France
Published in:	Unpublished
Subject matters:	– 1980 UN Sales Convention (CISG) – applicable law to substance – relationship 1980 UN Sales Convention (CISG) and choice of law – applicable law to limitation period

Facts

In 1991, a Canadian company entered into an Equipment Purchase Agreement (the Agreement) whereby the Canadian buyer agreed to purchase two machines from the Italian manufacturer. The Agreement also provided that the manufacturer would supply engineering and supervision as well as additional accessories. In addition the manufacturer agreed to warrant the delivered equipment against defects in material and workmanship for a period of twelve months from the final date of commissioning, but in no event exceeding eighteen months from the date of delivery.

Any dispute which could not be settled amicably was to be settled by ICC arbitration, in Paris, and the applicable law to the sales conditions would be French law.

The machines were delivered in 1992. In October 1998, the buyer and the insurer entered into a machinery insurance policy (the Policy) for the period 30 June 1998 to 30 June 1999. According to the Policy, the buyer's rights of recovery against any person or organization in the event of any payment made under the Policy were subrogated to the insurer. According to the insurer, in January 1999, one of the machines ruptured and the insurer indemnified the buyer for the damage. The insurer subsequently instituted arbitration against the manufacturer.

The proceedings were bifurcated and it was agreed that the arbitral tribunal would in the first stage determine the matters of applicable law and limitation periods.

The arbitral tribunal first determined the applicable law. Because the 1980 Convention on the International Sale Goods (CISG) entered into force in Canada after the conclusion of the contract, the CISG did not apply by the sole virtue of Art. 1(1)(a) which provides that the Convention applies when both contracting parties have their place of business on contracting States. However, according to Art. 1(1)(b) the Convention would also be applicable if the rules of private international law led to the application of the law of a Contracting State. The relevant private international law is that of the forum state which in this case was France. Because arbitrators are, however, not bound by the conflict of laws rules of the forum, the principle of party autonomy prevails. Unless the parties had agreed to exclude the CISG, the reference to French law would mean that the Convention applied. After examining relevant doctrine and case law, the arbitral tribunal held that the reference to French law did not suffice to exclude the application of the CISG. Nor did the fact that the parties had agreed on a limitation period different from that in the CISG suffice to exclude the application of the Convention.

Regarding the statute of limitations, the CISG provides in Art. 39 that the buyer must notify the seller of a lack of conformity within a reasonable time after he discovered it, or ought to have discovered it. If the lack of conformity is not apparent, there is an absolute time limit of two years for notification. The notification was not made within two years, but Art. 40 CISG provides that Art. 39 does not apply in case of hidden defects. The arbitral tribunal noted that the time limitation of the CISG should not be confused with the statute of limitations which are determined by domestic law, namely, French law. It was in their view appropriate to apply the general ten-year limitation period provided by Art. 189*bis* of the French Code of Civil Procedure, and thus the claim was not time barred as less than ten years had elapsed between the conclusion of the Agreement in 1991 and the filing of the request for arbitration in 2000. This finding was without prejudice to the determination of whether the buyer knew or could not have been unaware of the alleged lack of conformity as this issue was not part of the issues which had been bifurcated.

Excerpt

(. . . .)

I. THE APPLICABLE LAW

1. Preliminary Remark

[1] "The buyer and the respondent agreed in the Agreement that '[t]he law to be applied to the sales conditions is the French law', without any precision as to whether this reference includes the CISG or whether reference is made to domestic French law.

[2] "In their written submissions, the parties advanced conflicting opinions on this issue. While claimant has contended that the Agreement should be interpreted as meaning that domestic French law, particularly the French Civil Code, applies, respondent has advocated the application of the CISG."

2. The CISG Is the French Law of International Sales of Goods Since 1 January 1988

[3] "The CISG entered into force in France on 1 January 1988. Since then, it is the French law of international sales of goods.[1] In other words, the CISG will govern all international contracts for the sale of goods within the meaning of Art. 1 CISG, provided that they satisfy the conditions laid down in Art. 1 [(1) (a) and (1) (b)], that the sale is not one of a kind excluded (Art. 2 or Art. 3) and that the parties have not excluded the application of the CISG (Art. 6)."

3. The Conditions of Art. 1(1)(a) CISG Are Not Met

[4] "According to Art. 1(1)(a), the CISG 'applies to contracts of sale of goods between parties whose places of business are in different States when the States are contracting States'. The relevant time for the examination of this condition is the date of the conclusion of the contract. Thus, Art. 100(2) provides that the CISG

'applies only to contracts concluded on or after the date when the Convention enters into force in respect of the Contracting States referred to in

---

1. "See M. Fallon, *'Le domaine d'application de la Convention de Vienne'*, in Ann. Dr. Louvain, 1998, p. 268."

subparagraph (1)(a) or the Contracting State referred to in subparagraph (1)(b) of article 1'.

[5]   "In the case at hand, the CISG entered into force in Italy on 1 January 1988, i.e. before the conclusion of the Agreement in 1991. However, the CISG entered into force in Canada on 1 May 1992 only, i.e. after the conclusion of the Agreement.[2] Consequently, the CISG does not apply to the present instance by (the sole) virtue of Art. 1(1)(a)."

4.   *The Conditions of Article 1(1)(b) CISG Are Met*

[6]   "Pursuant to Art. 1(1)(b), the CISG also applies to

'contracts of sale of goods between parties whose places of business are in different States when the rules of private international law lead to the application of the law of a Contracting State'.

It is commonly acknowledged that 'the rules of private international law' referred to in Art. 1(1)(b) of the CISG are the conflict of law rules of the forum.[3] However, an arbitrator, unlike a national judge, has no forum.[4] It follows from this premise that arbitrators are not bound by the conflict of laws rules of a forum to choose the law applicable to the substance of the dispute.

[7]   "The principle of party autonomy, according to which the parties may freely choose the law governing their relationship, is without doubt part of 'the rules of private international law' referred to in Art. 1(1)(b) of the CISG (cf. Art. 17(1) of the ICC Rules of Arbitration[5] and Art. 1496 of the New French

---

2. "See '*Geltungsbereich des Ubereinkommens*' in H. Honsell (ed.), *Kommentar zum UN-Kaufrecht* (Berlin and Heidelberg 1997) p. 1092."

3. "K. Siehr, in H. Honsell (ed.), *Kommentar zum UN-Kaufrecht* (Berlin and Heidelberg 1997) no. 17, p. 51; B. Audit, *La vente internationale de marchandises* (L.G.D.J., Paris 1990) p. 22."

4. "H. van Houtte, 'The Vienna Sales Convention in ICC Arbitral Practice', in ICC International Court of Arbitration Bulletin Vol. 11/No. 2, p. 22; *Fouchard, Gaillard, Goldman, International Commercial Arbitration*, edited by Emmanuel Gaillard and John Savage (Kluwer Law International 1999) no. 1181, p. 637."

5. "Art. 17(1) of the ICC Rules of Arbitration reads:

"The parties shall be free to agree upon the rules of law to be applied by the Arbitral Tribunal to the merits of the dispute. In the absence of any such agreement, the Arbitral Tribunal shall apply the rules of law which it determines to be appropriate."

Code of Civil Procedure).[6] Accordingly, unless the parties agreed to exclude the application of the CISG, the reference made to 'French law' in the Agreement leads to the application of the CISG, which is, since 1 January 1988, the French law of international sales of goods. Thus, the issue is whether by referring to French law the Parties intended to exclude the CISG and agreed on the application of the French Civil Code."

5. *A Reference to a National Law Does Not Suffice to Exclude the Application of the CISG*

[8]   "According to Art. 6 CISG

'[t]he parties may exclude the application of this Convention or, subject to article 12, derogate from or vary the effect of any of its provisions'.

Rightly, none of the parties has contended that the application of the CISG has been expressly excluded. However, even though Art. 6 of the CISG does not specifically state it, such exclusion can also be tacit.[7]

[9]   "In this context, it has been suggested that a choice of law clause in favour of a national law constituted a presumption that the parties intended to exclude the application of the CISG.[8] However, the opinion advocated by these authorities, disputed by a large majority of commentators, is of no use in the present case. It concerns principally a different hypothesis, namely where the conditions of Art. 1(1)(a) of the CISG are met and the CISG would thus apply, but the parties nevertheless include in their contract a choice of law clause in favour of a

---

6. Art. 1496 of the New French Code of Civil Procedure reads:

    "The arbitrator shall decide the dispute in accordance with the rules of the law chosen by the parties or, in the absence of such choice, in accordance with the rules of the law he considers appropriate. In all cases he shall take the usages of the trade into consideration."

7. "R. Herber, in v. Caemmerer/Schlechtriem, *Kommentar zum Einheitlichen UN-Kaufrecht* (Verlag C.H. Beck, München 1995) no. 6, p. 84; K. Siehr, in *op. cit.*, no. 6, p. 81; K.H. Neumayer/ C. Ming, *Convention de Vienne sur les contrats de vente internationale de marchandises, Commentaire* (CEDIDAC, Lausanne 1993) no. 3, p. 85; C. Witz, *Les premieres applications jurisprudentielles du droit uniforme de la vente internationale*)L.G.D.J., Paris 1995) p. 44; V. Heuzé, *La vente internationale de marchandises* (L.G.D.J., Paris 2000) no. 95, p. 91."

8. "K.H. Neumayer/C. Ming, in *op. cit.*, p. 89; W. Stoffel, '*Le droit applicable aux contrats de vente internationale de marchandises*', in *Les contrats de vente internationale de marchandises* (CEDIDAC, Lausanne 1991) p. 33; *Cour d'Appel de Colmar* (France), 26 September 1995, in Case Law on UNCITRAL Texts (CLOUT), case no. 326; *Tribunale Civile di Monza* (Italy), 14 January 1993, in CLOUT, case no. 54; Ad hoc Arbitral Tribunal, Florence (Italy), 19 April 1993, in CLOUT, case no. 49."

national law. Yet, it has been demonstrated above that the CISG is not applicable in the present case by the (sole) virtue of its Art. 1(1)(a).

[10] "Moreover, this opinion is far from being dominant and has been clearly rejected in several recent cases. In November 1998, the *Bundesgerichtshof* (German Supreme Court) has held that a choice of law clause such as 'German law applies' does not contradict the finding that the CISG governs a legal relationship between a German party and an Austrian party even though the CISG is applicable through its Art. 1(1)(a) as both Germany and Austria are contracting States.[9]

[11] "The same determination has to be made where the parties, notwithstanding the *de plano* application of the CISG by virtue of Art. 1(1)(a), refer to the law of a third-party State (a State in which neither party has its place of business), very likely for the reason that such law is seen as a neutral law. Leading authors confirm the principle that, even in this case, a general reference to a particular national law should not be interpreted as a tacit exclusion of the CISG, unless the intention of the parties calls for a different conclusion.[10] A similar trend can be observed in case law.[11]

[12] "In the case at hand, it is not possible to infer such an intention to exclude (tacitly) the application of the CISG from the Agreement. In addition, the parties have not shown any element enabling this Tribunal to ascertain a common intention to exclude the application of the CISG."

6. The Contractual Modification of a Particular Provision of the CISG Does Not Suffice to Exclude the Application of the CISG

[13] "Claimant contends that the agreed limitation of respondent's warranty obligation to a duration of 12 months from the final date of commissioning is incompatible with the CISG and should be interpreted as meaning that the parties intended to exclude its application in favour of French domestic law.

[14] "When a contractual clause governing a particular matter is in contradiction with the CISG, the presumption is that the parties intended to derogate from the CISG on that particular question. It does not affect the applicability of

---

9. "*Bundesgerichtshof* (Germany), 25 November 1998, in CLOUT, case no. 270."

10. "K. Siehr, in *op. cit.*, no. 7, p. 82; B. Audit, in *op. cit.*, no. 43, p. 38; R. Herber, in v. Caemmerer/ Schlechtriem, *Kommentar zum Einheitlichen UN-Kaufrecht*, no. 16, p. 86; C. Witz, *Les premières applications jurisprudentielles du droit uniforme de la vente internationale* (L.G.D.J., Paris 1995) p. 44; F. Ferrari, *Contrat de vente international* (Helbing & Lichtenhahn, Bâle 1999) p. 142; V. Heuzé, in *op. cit.*, no. 96, p. 93."

11. "ICC Award no. 9448, in ICC International Court of Arbitration Bulletin, Vol. 11/No. 2, p. 105; ICC Award no. 9187, in ICC International Court of Arbitration Bulletin, Vol. 11/No. 2, p. 95; ICC Award no. 6653, in JDI 1993, p. 1040."

the CISG in general.[12] The parties' specific agreement to reduce, to 12 months, the two-year time limit provided for in Art. 39 CISG does not lead the Arbitral Tribunal to another finding. As stated in a recent award rendered under the auspices of the Stockholm Chamber of Commerce, Art. 40 CISG applies equally, whether the parties contractually modified the two-year time limit of Art. 39 CISG or not.[13] Taking the above into consideration, the Arbitral Tribunal finds that the CISG is the law governing the merits of the present dispute."

II. THE STATUTE OF LIMITATIONS

1. Preliminary Remark

[15] "As far as the statute of limitations issue is concerned, both parties have argued their case under the CISG, be it as a subsidiary argumentation for claimant or as a principal one for respondent. Claimant argues that Art. 39 CISG is not applicable to the present instance, which should be addressed in the light of Art. 40. Respondent contends principally that Art. 40 CISG does not apply unless claimant shows that respondent was aware or could not have been unaware of the alleged lack of conformity and that the whole case should be decided in the light of Art. 39."

2. The Seller's Warranty Obligation under Arts. 39 and 40 CISG

[16] "The CISG affords the buyer several remedies if the sold goods are not in conformity with the contract (Arts. 35 et seq.) However, the buyer loses the right to a remedy on a lack of conformity if he does not give notice to the seller specifying the nature of such lack of conformity within a reasonable time after he has discovered it or ought to have discovered it (Art. 39(1)). When it comes to a lack of conformity which is not apparent and which the buyer is thus not in a position to notify to the seller, Art. 39(2) CISG sets an absolute time limit of two years from the date on which the goods were actually handed over to the buyer within which the buyer has to give notice to the seller. The buyer who fails to comply with these requirements cannot rely on the alleged lack of conformity and is deprived of the remedies which the CISG affords in case of lack of conformity.

---

12. "K. Siehr, in *op. cit.*, no. 9, p. 83; V. Heuze, in *op. cit.*, no. 95, p. 92; F. Ferrari, in *op. cit.*, p. 147."
13. "Stockholm Chamber of Commerce, Award of 5 June 1998, *Beijing Light Automobile Company, Ltd. v. Connell Limited Partnership*, <www.cisg.law.pace.edu/cisg/wais/db/cases2/980605s5.html>."

[17]   "In the present instance, it is uncontested that claimant did not notify to respondent any lack of conformity of the machines within the two-year time limit. However, the CISG offers a lifeline to the buyer who has not complied with the requirements of Art. 39. Art. 40 provides that

> '[t]he seller is not entitled to rely on the provisions of articles 38 and 39 if the lack of conformity relates to facts of which he knew or could not have been unaware and which he did not disclose to the buyer.'

In other words, if the conditions of Art. 40 CISG are met, the buyer is released from the requirements of Arts. 38 and 39.

[18]   "By way of example, the seller who knows, from complaints received from other customers in the context of previous sales of similar goods, that the goods lack conformity cannot rely on the fact that the buyer did not give notice within the time limit of Art. 39 CISG.[14] This Arbitral Tribunal is obliged to ascertain whether the seller knew or could not have been unaware of the lack of conformity, which claimant specifically preferred. This issue could be shunned only if, as respondent pleads, claimant's action can be declared time-barred without any fact-finding. This is not the case, as we will now show."

3.   The CISG Left the Time Limitation Issue to National Laws

[19]   "The time-limit set by Art. 39 CISG exclusively pertains to the notice of lack of conformity to be given by the buyer and should not be confused with statute of limitations deadlines. The CISG does not deal with the limitation periods.[15] Issues of limitation period are to be determined in conformity with the domestic law applicable by virtue of the rules of private international law."[16]

---

14. "See B. Hanotiau, 'L'exécution du contrat selon la Convention de Vienne', in Ann. Dr. Louvain, 1998, p. 291)."
15. "C. Witz, 'L'application de la Convention de Vienne en France', in Les ventes internationales, Journée d'étude en l'honneur du professeur Karl H. Neumayer (CEDIDAC, Lausanne 1998) p. 18; F. Ferrari, in op. cit., p. 158; V. Heuzé, in op. cit., no. 313, p. 276."
16. U. Magnus, in Honsell (ed.), Kommentar zum UN-Kaufrecht (Pringer Verlag, Berlin and Heidelberg 1997) no. 11, p. 440; C. Witz, 'L'application de la Convention de Vienne en France', in Les ventes internationales, Journée d'étude en l'honneur du professeur Karl H. Neumayer (CEDIDAC, Lausanne 1998) p. 18; F. Ferrari, 'Contrat de vente internationale', Helbing & Lichtenhahn, Bâle 1999) p. 158."

4. *The CISG Calls for the Application of a Sole Limitation Period*

[20] "The application of national time-limitations in the context of the CISG is not straightforward. It is often difficult to identify, among various statute of limitations rules provided for by the applicable national law, the applicable rule in a particular instance. In the present instance, the law applicable by virtue of the rules of private international law is French law. Accordingly, it is under French domestic law that the validity of the defence raised by respondent under the statute of limitations has to be determined.

[21] "French law does provide various limitation periods the application of which could be contemplated. The parties have considered different limitation periods in their respective submissions. Among these various limitation periods, one may highlight the generally-applicable 10-year time limit from the conclusion of the agreement provided for in Art. 189*bis* of the French Code of Commerce and the five-year time limit of Art. 1304 of the French Civil Code. With respect to hidden defects, Art. 1648 of the French Civil Code requires the buyer to lodge its action 'within a brief period' ('*dans un bref delai*') which runs from the time he has discovered the defects.

[22] "However, the application of different limitation periods to the rights provided for by the CISG amounts to artificially re-creating distinctions existing under the applicable national law and from which the CISG was detached with a view to international uniformity. This objective of uniformity would be defeated if each national law were to supply the judge or arbitrators with numerous time limits.[17] Limitation periods provided for by the national laws have been adopted to apply specifically to particular actions of the national laws, and not to actions provided for a heterogeneous source of law such as the CISG.

[23] "The Arbitral Tribunal is of the view that it is thus fit to apply the general 10-year limitation period, provided for by Art. 189*bis* of the French Code of Commerce, independently of the specific cause of action.[18]

[24] "Consequently, the Arbitral Tribunal finds that claimant's claim is not time-barred by the 10-year statute of limitation applicable to it as less than 10 years have elapsed between the conclusion of the Agreement in 1991 and claimant's filing of its *Demande d'Arbitrage* with the ICC in December 2000.

---

17. "See V. Heuzé, in *op. cit.*, no. 313, p. 277; S. Marchand, *Les limites de l'uniformisation matérielle du droit de la vente internationale* (Helbing & Lichtenhahn, Basle and Frankfurt-on-the-Main 1994) no. 293, p. 286."

18. "V. Heuzé, in *op. cit.*, no. 313, p. 278; C. Witz, '*L'application de la Convention de Vienne en France*', in *Les ventes internationales, Journée d'étude en l'honneur du professeur Karl H. Neumayer* (CEDIDAC, Lausanne 1998) p. 19."

[25]   "This finding is without prejudice to the obligation on claimant (in Art. 40 CISG) to demonstrate that respondent knew or could not have been unaware of the alleged lack of conformity. This issue has not been 'bifurcated', and neither the Parties' submissions nor this award did address it."

III.   AWARD

[26]   "Taking the above into consideration, the Arbitral Tribunal renders the following Award on preliminary issues:

1. The CISG applies to the merits of the dispute, including the issue whether claimant's right to rely on a lack of conformity of the goods sold is lost under Arts. 39 and 40 CISG.
2. Claimant's claim is not barred by the 10-year statute of limitation applicable to it.
(. . . .)
3. All remaining issues shall be determined in a subsequent award.
4. The arbitration costs, legal fees and other expenses in connection with this preliminary award shall be addressed in the Final Award."

Final award in case no. 11440 of 2003

Parties:	Claimant: Buyer (Italy)
	Respondent: Seller (Germany)
Place of arbitration:	Zurich, Switzerland
Published in:	Unpublished
Subject matters:	– scope of settlement agreement
	– Merger and Acquisition contract
	– interpretation of contract
	– purchase price adjustment
	– duty of information
	– year 2000 (Y2K) computer problems

Facts

In 1998, the parties entered into a Master Agreement (MA) by which the respondent sold its business to claimant. For the determination of the final purchase price the MA provided a purchase price adjustment mechanism based on a Consolidated Financial Statement (CFS). Because of discrepancies between the auditors' reports with regard to the CFS, the parties entered into negotiations which resulted in 1999 in a Settlement Agreement (SA).

Notwithstanding the SA, the buyer alleged that the seller had violated representations, warranties and other obligations arising out of the MA and initiated ICC arbitration, claiming compensation from the seller. The seller asserted several counterclaims.

Because the seller argued that most of the claims were covered by the SA, the arbitral tribunal first established its scope, using a systematic approach to determine the intention of the parties. The first paragraph of the SA dealt with the adaptation of the purchase price. The second paragraph dealt with compensation for the negative issues. There was no direct or indirect reference to claims based on the "Representations and Warranties" as stipulated in Sect. 7 of the MA. The arbitral tribunal noted that: "If experienced business people advised by high-profile lawyers conclude a Settlement Agreement that comprises a whole bundle of claims based on Representations and Warranties – the core element of the MA and any such transaction – it is hardly conceivable that this is not reflected in the text of the SA." Hence, the settlement clause of the SA comprised only claims within the framework of the price adjustment procedure and claimant was not precluded from founding its claims of breach of Representations and/or Warranties pursuant to Sects. 7 and 8 of the MA.

The buyer argued that it was entitled to compensation from the seller for the renewal of non-transferable software licences (the Licences). In the view of the buyer, the Licences were assets and should be transferred as part of the business. Moreover, the seller had not included them on the list of Licences specified in the MA. The seller argued that the Licences could not be qualified as assets and that it only was required by the MA to give the buyer "reasonable assistance" regarding the licences. The arbitral tribunal noted that the MA provided that a list should be supplied of licences for intellectual property rights which would not be able to be used by buyer. The seller had not provided such a list and had violated its information duties and thus breached the guarantee. The buyer was to be put in the same position it would have been if it had been supplied with the correct and complete information. The arbitral tribunal rejected the seller's argument that the buyer had not suffered any damage, but did find that the buyer had been negligent as it had been aware that there might be a problem. Therefore, the damage was to be reduced by one third.

The buyer also claimed compensation for expenses incurred as a result of computer problems related to the change from 1999 to 2000 (the Y2K-problem or -phenomenon). The arbitral tribunal held that also this claim did not fall under the SA, but was a claim for a breach of representations and warranties. It examined the buyer's actions from the ex ante point of view of what steps a "carefully acting businessman" should take, rather than using ex post judgment, i.e., with hindsight. The concept applied by the seller for dealing with this matter was in the view of the arbitral tribunal consistent and adequate. After determining which of the buyer's claims had been proven and their value, the arbitral tribunal reduced the total amount by one third because most of the buyer's replacements led to a higher standard of software and the buyer's policy was a broad approach including follow-up problems. Seller sought to reduce the compensation under the concept of "new for old". The arbitral tribunal found that the damages could be mitigated if the reduction did not constitute an unbearable burden for the buyer and that this determination should be made using judicial discretion. The buyer had been under a duty to inform the seller of facts which could be the basis for claims, but had not done so, although this did not appear to be intentional. However, the seller was aware of the problems and the failure to notify was without financial consequences. Any added value had, however, been taken into account by the deduction of one third.

A number of other smaller claims decided by the arbitral tribunal are not included in this excerpt.

Excerpt

I.　JURISDICTION AND APPLICABLE PROCEDURAL RULES

[1]　"This arbitration is an 'International Arbitration' in the sense of Chapter 12 of the Swiss Private International Law Statute of 18 December 1987 (PILS) and therefore subject to the relevant rules of the PILS.

[2]　"In its para. 19 the Master Agreement contains the following Arbitration Clause:

> . . . .
> '19.1 Any differences or disputes arising from this Agreement, its Annexes, the Local Sales Agreements or any agreements regarding the performance of this Agreement shall be settled by an amicable effort on the part of the parties. . . .
> 19.2 If an attempt at settlement has failed, the dispute shall be finally settled under the Rules of Arbitration of the International Chamber of Commerce ICC in Paris (the "Rules") by three arbitrators in accordance with the Rules.
> (. . . .)
> 19.4 The place of arbitration shall be Zurich, Switzerland. The procedural laws of this place shall apply where the Rules are silent.
> 19.5 The language of arbitration shall be English.'

[3]　"Based on that agreement of the parties, pursuant Art. 182 PILS[1] this arbitration is conducted under the Rules of Arbitration of the International Chamber of Commerce (in force as of 1998) and subsidiarily the procedural

---

1. Art. 182 of the Swiss Private International Law Statute reads:

"1. The parties may, directly or by reference to arbitration rules, determine the arbitral procedure; they may also submit it to a procedural law of their choice.

2. Where the parties have not determined the procedure, the arbitral tribunal shall determine it to the extent necessary, either directly or by reference to a law or to arbitration rules.

3. Whatever procedure is chosen, the arbitral tribunal shall assure equal treatment of the parties and the right of the parties to be heard in an adversarial procedure."

laws of the Canton Zurich. In addition, the rules agreed upon by the parties and the Arbitral Tribunal apply.

[4]   "Pursuant to said Arbitration Clause the Arbitral Tribunal has jurisdiction in the case at issue."

II.   APPLICABLE LAW

[5]   "Regarding the applicable substantive law the Master Agreement contains the following clause:

'This Agreement shall be governed by German substantive law without reference to other laws. The application of the United Nations Convention on Contracts for the International Sales of Good of 11 April 1980 shall be excluded.'

The Arbitral Tribunal has to apply the German Civil Code without the changes that have been made by the recent major revision."[2]

III.   SCOPE OF SETTLEMENT AGREEMENT

[6]   "Respondent from the outset of the proceeding argued that most of claimant's claims were covered by the Settlement Agreement and therefore without merit. To the contrary, the claimant holds that the claims raised do not fall in the scope of the Settlement Agreement. It is for that reason that Arbitral Tribunal deals with the scope and applicability of the Settlement Agreement as a preliminary matter.
(. . . .)
[7]   "The interpretation of a contract is a duty of the Arbitral Tribunal. Based on the relevant provisions of the Civil Code (Sects. 133, 157 BGB)[3] German courts and doctrine have developed a canon of means and a set of rules for the interpretation of contracts that has to be applied ex officio. Therefore, the parties have no obligation to offer or produce evidence regarding the interpretation

---

2. "The German Civil Code (BGB) will be applied in it's version before 1 January 2002; cf. Art. 229(5)."
3. Sects. 133 and 157 of the German Civil Code (*Bürgerliches Gesetzbuch* – BGB) read:
   "Section 133
   In interpreting a declaration of intention, the true intention shall be sought without regard to the declaration's literal meanings.
   Section 157
   Contracts shall be interpreted as good faith requires, taking trade usages into account."

itself. With regard to the factual basis of the contract, however, and in particular to the intentions they had when they entered into the contract, the parties have to establish the facts. Insofar the rules on allegation of facts and on the burden of proof apply."[4]

1. Real Intentions of the Parties

[8] "Based on these rules, as a first step and the predominant aim of any interpretation, the Arbitral Tribunal must try to find out what the common 'real intentions' of the parties were when they concluded the contract. There is no room or need for any further interpretation if those intentions are established. They are of factual nature and, therefore, must be alleged and in the case of dispute proved by the party who wishes to rely on it.

[9] "Though in the case at hand the scope of application of the SA was in dispute from the very first exchange of Briefs, no evidence was offered with respect to the parties' intentions. This is rightly stated by respondent regarding Claimant's Briefs but it is in the same way true for respondent's own submissions. The reason for that seems to be that claimant and respondent have the view that there is no need for any proof since the wording of the contract was clear and would correctly reflect the parties' intentions. Both parties' arguments illustrate, however, that they substantially disagree on the meaning of the text. Therefore either of the parties should have proved its thesis of the real intentions. Since such proof has not been furnished it is for the Arbitral Tribunal to assess by the above mentioned means and rules the will the parties presumably[5] had and based thereupon to determine the content of the SA."

2. Tribunal's Interpretation of the SA

[10] "It is the wording of the contract any interpretation has to start with, followed by a systematic approach, i.e. putting the single word in the context of the phrase and the single provision into the framework of the contract as a unit. In addition, the history of the contract, the parties' interest and their behaviour after the conclusion are generally accepted means for the assessment of the meaning of the contract.

[11] "The paramount elements of the text of the SA are the 'purchase price adjustment' and the numerous references to the MA.

[12] "(1) In the ingress of the SA the parties, after referring to Sects. 4/5 of the MA and the therein provided purchase price adjustment mechanism and the

---

4. "BGHZ 20, 109 et seq."
5. "For this so called normative interpretation cf. *Palandt*/Heinrichs, Sect. 133 margin nos. 9, 12."

reports delivered by Consulting Society 1 and Consulting Society 2, '*in connection with this adjustment procedure*' state that

- claimant has raised claims based on the Consulting Society 2 Report *in connection with the price adjustment procedure*', and that
- the parties have come to an agreement regarding their differences in the determination of the amounts *payable under the purchase price adjustment* and the claims raised by the claimant, referring to the before quoted claims also related to the price adjustment procedure.

[13]   "(2) Consequently, the SA in its para. 1 deals with the adaptation of the purchase price.

[14]   "(3) Para. 2 of the SA concerns 'compensation for negative issues affecting 1999 as ascertained in the Consulting Society 2 Report'. Although the negative issues are not specified, the reference to the Consulting Society 2 Report in light of the above quoted sequence of the ingress,[6] indicates that the compensation is understood as part of the price adjustment mechanism. Furthermore, there is no direct or indirect reference to claims based on the Representations and Warranties as stipulated in Sect. 7 of the MA. Taking in consideration the permanent references made to the MA in the other parts of the SA one would expect that a respective reference had been made to Sect. 7 of the MA if the compensation was a payment based on that provision.

[15]   "(4) At a first glance an indirect relation to Representations and Warranties might be seen in the second sentence of para. 2 of the SA that reads:

'The amount as per Sect. 8.2 last sentence of the Master Agreement[7] (total amount of claims that can be made under the representations and warranties) shall be limited to . . . '.

Having a closer look at the function of Sect. 8.2 MA it turns out that the provision contains nothing else than a formula for the calculation of the 'total amount of claims that can be made' under that title (so called 'cap'). Thus, the second sentence of para. 2 of the SA only states the cap calculated on the basis of the new price pursuant paras. 1 and 2 of the SA. Therefore, from the sentence itself no conclusions can be drawn with respect to the question whether claims for Representations and Warranties are comprised. It is different from a systematic view: If the payments taken into account for the calculation of the cap

---

6. " 'The claimant has raised claims based on the Consulting Society 2 Report *in connection with the price adjustment procedure.*' "
7. "Sect. 8 of the MA deals with 'Remedies for Representations and Warranties'."

had been those for breach of Representations and Warranties one could certainly expect that this was mentioned exactly at this point of the contract. Again, the missing reference to Sect. 7 of the MA indicates that there was no link.

[16]   "(5) With regard to said second sentence of para. 2 both parties use the tool of systematic interpretation: Whereas claimant holds the view that 'the calculation of the cap itself establishes that no claims for Representations and Warranties were covered by the Settlement Agreement', respondent argues that if those claims were covered the calculation of the cap makes sense for claims arising in the future under the Representations and Warranties stipulated in para. 7 MA. It is true that claims under that title may arise after the SA had been concluded. On the other hand it is rather strange that – in respondent's hypothesis – a whole bundle of claims for Representations and Warranties was covered and the cap was not reduced but fixed at a higher amount. Be that as it may, decisive for the Arbitral Tribunal is – as already mentioned – that no reference to the claims under Sect. 7 of the MA was made. If experienced business people advised by high-profile lawyers conclude a Settlement Agreement that comprises a whole bundle of claims based on Representations and Warranties – the core element of the MA and any such transaction – it is hardly conceivable that this is not reflected in the text of the SA.

[17]   "(6) Para. 3 of the SA, in respondent's view, clearly indicates that the parties wanted to settle 'all mutual claims'. In support for this interpretation reference is made to a decision of the Appellate Court of Cologne.[8] The Court held that the clause 'all mutual claims between the parties are settled'[9] covers claims not known to the parties at that time without additional clarification in that respect. First of all, any interpretation of a contract clause is individual and not transferable to another contract, in particular not to a very specific contract as the SA. Secondly, the published excerpt contains only the quoted phrase and, thus, leaves the context open which is of eminent impact for any interpretation. But even assuming that the Court wanted to state that its interpretation reflects a common understanding of such clause and that such common accepted language has to be taken in consideration in the normative interpretation the Arbitral Tribunal has to apply,[10] the statement of the Court is not relevant for the case at hand.

[18]   "The reason for that is twofold: The issue here is not whether the parties wanted unknown claims to be comprised, but to find out what kind or sort of claims they intended to settle. Because of that aim of interpretation it is

---

8. "Decision of 25 August 1999, partly published in MDR (*Monatsschrift für Deutsches Recht*)) 2000, 140."

9. "*Sämtliche wechselseitigen Ansprüche zwischen den Parteien erledigt sind.*"

10. "See above [9]. . . ."

necessary to read the first sentence as a whole, in its context and as part of a unit. Again, the clause is conceived with reference to the 'purchase price adjustment procedure' which is the dominating element of the SA. There is no indication that all possible claims for Representations and Warranty should be settled effecting claimant's renouncement of possible claims in a volume of ... million DM. Neither the language nor the structure of the SA give reason for the conclusion that this was implicitly done. In fact, it is not very plausible that parties of the standing of the claimant and respondent would make such renouncement without having it included in the wording of the contract. This view is supported by the reference that is made twice (para. 3 first and second sentences) to the Consulting Society 2 Report on which claimant's claims were – as expressly stated in the ingress – based 'in connection with the price adjustment procedure'.[11]

[19]   "(7) For all these reasons the Arbitral Tribunal is of the opinion that the settlement clause in para. 3 of the SA comprises only claims within the framework of the price adjustment procedure. [There] is therefore no need to discuss the meaning of the disputed formula 'a party ... could have raised' insofar as Representation and Warranties claims are concerned. If some of the facts claimant relies on now for its claims could have been taken into account in the price adjustment procedure claimant is not precluded by the SA from founding its claims on breach of Representations and/or Warranties pursuant Sects. 7/8 MA."

3.   The Arbitral Tribunal's Conclusion

[20]   "Regarding the disputed scope of SA the Arbitral Tribunal comes to the conclusion that the claims for representations and warranties as raised by claimants are not covered by the SA. The SA rather comprises all claims in connection with the price adjustment procedure."

IV.   LICENCES

[21]   "It is claimant's case that respondent has to pay to compensate the claimant for the costs it had to pay for the renewal of not transferable Software Licences (the Licences) in Germany, Turkey and South Africa." ... The claimant argued that in its view they were assets and to be transferred as part of the business. By not including them on the list of licences required by Sect. 7.13.1 lit. (b), respondent did not disclose their non-transferability and had violated its specific duty of information. Respondent argued, inter alia, that the Licences could not be qualified as assets. Pursuant to Sect. 7.13.1 MA respondent would under all circumstances

---

11. "Cf. [11]."

only have to 'give reasonable (*zumutbare*) assistance . . . to Buyer'. Further the claimant was aware of the non-transferability of the Licences.
(. . . .)

1. The Tribunal's Deliberations and Conclusions

[22]   "There are some basic and undisputed facts: claimant could use all Licences until 30 September 2000. From an operational view, no visible change occurred since the computer operations were performed by respondent. (footnote omitted) Thus, one could say that on a factual level the Licences were transferred as part of the business.

[23]   "For that reason both parties may have been not fully aware of the legal impact: On one hand the Licences were not included in the list attached as Annex 7.13.1 to Sect. 7.13.1 MA. This 'List of license agreements' comprises only licences that were granted respondent. (footnote omitted) Therefore, this was not the list for the Licences to be included. On the other hand, there is no second list, in particular no list pursuant to lit.(b) of [Sect. 7.13.1] which reads:

'all licences for Intellectual Property Rights, including cross licences, which Seller or any of the Controlled Companies uses, or intends to use in the Business by virtue of a license granted to Seller or any Seller's Group Company and which, in the future, the Buyer or the Controlled Companies, as the case may be, *will not be able to use in the manner as at present or as at presently intended, as a result of the transaction contemplated hereby*'. (emphasis added)

[24]   "The Licences match exactly the criteria as set in the text of lit. (b): Based on one hand on the wording of lit. (b) and its context as well as the position and function of Sect. 7.13.1 MA in the framework of the whole contract and on the other hand on the undisputed fact that the Licences were not transferable and, therefore, could not be used by claimant in its own right, the Licences had to be named under the lit. (b) and the respective list. Not producing such list must be interpreted as seller's statement: There are no licences of that category. Not putting the Licences in the list pursuant lit. (b) – which actually was not established at all – in any case results in a violation of the duty of information. As usual in M&A transactions the duty of disclosure and of correct information is expressed several times and conceptualized as a guarantee. Thus, the ingress of Sect. 7 explicitly states:

'In entering into this Agreement, Buyer relies on the correctness of the representations and warranties made by Seller herein. Seller represents and warrants to Buyer in the form of an independent promise of guarantee the representations and warranties contained hereinafter are, and as of the Effective Date will be, true, complete and correct.'

Moreover under the title 'Correctness of Information' such duty is explicitly provided in Sect. 7.20 MA which reads:

'All information disclosed to the Buyer up to the date of this Agreement or included in the Disclosure Letter or to be given to the Buyer in the course of Buyer's due diligence investigation is or, when given, will be complete and accurate in all respect.'

Based on these provisions and the concept of the MA as a whole, the Arbitral Tribunal has to discuss the issue of the transferability of the Licences under the aspect of correct and complete information.

[25]   "The crucial question is whether respondent has provided claimant with the 'correct and complete information' regarding the Licences. This is not the case. Firstly, there is no written document by which respondent informed claimant that the Licences were not transferable and could not be used after [the] transition period. In particular, the list (b) in which the Licences had to be included was not established. Secondly, and equally important, is the testimony of the two persons who handled the IT issue for the companies. (footnote omitted) When the witnesses were examined both modified their witness statements which had been rather straight-forward and contrary. Although some differences remained the development of the negotiations and the result became quite clear: The problem of transferability was an issue in the discussions, but Mr. P [witness called by respondent] could give no clear statement on that matter since he had no personal knowledge and no access to the relevant information. Mr. P therefore never expressly informed Mr. A [witness called by claimant] that the Licences were not transferable to claimant.

[26]   "It might very well be that he believed that 'Mr. A was well aware of the fact that the transferability of Licences was neither guaranteed nor approved by the Licensor' but he 'thought that, since I had clearly identified this problem, this problem would be discussed among the attorneys during the closing phase'. As a result however 'the respondent due diligence team never filed formal confirmation that the rights were not transferable'. Since the non-transferability was apparently neither solved by the attorneys nor 'addressed in the closing negotiations' (Mr. P) it remained unsolved. As a first consequence respondent's argument that claimant is precluded from the claim by its knowledge of the non-transferability has no factual basis. It can, therefore, be left open whether

the alleged Sects. 460, 464 BGB (old version) could apply at all with regard to representations and warranties.

[27]   "Hence, the violation of the duty of information is apparent. Respondent did not provide claimant with the necessary information regarding the Licences: Neither was the list (b) as required under Sect. 7.13.1 MA established, nor was the information given to the buyer 'complete and accurate in all respects' in the sense of Sect. 7.20 MA.

[28]   "In principle, violations of information-duties are cured by a specific mechanism: The person that has the right to be correctly informed has to be put in the position it would have if it had received the correct information in time. Thus, if damage results from the incorrect or incomplete information that damage must be compensated.[12] The MA provides a different solution that stems from the practice of M&A contracts. In these contracts information-duties are conceptualized as guarantees. Consequently, they have been included in the MA – as already mentioned above – in the category of 'Representations and Warranties'. It follows that a breach of an information-duty which is understood as guarantee must have consequences that correspond to that legal qualification.

[29]   "Based thereupon the 'Remedies for Representations and Warranties' as set forth in Sect. 8 MA have to be applied. The here relevant part of Sect. 8.1 reads:

> 'In the case of a breach of the representation or warranties contained in Sect. 7 of this Agreement, the damage resulting therefrom shall be the amount which is necessary in order to procure, at the choice of Buyer to be made for each individual breach of warranty, either for the Buyer or Local Buyer concerned or for the Controlled Company concerned (but only for one of them) the financial position which would have existed if the representation and warranty had been true. . . . '

[30]   "It is clear from this text that the parties primarily had in mind representations/warranties on assets, goods and alike. Then the buyer should be entitled to claim damages calculated on the hypothesis that the respective representation/warranty is considered true. But it is obvious that the same pattern must apply if seller warrants correct and complete information. Then the buyer must be put into a position he would have if the given information was true.

[31]   "On the factual basis developed above claimant had reason to believe that no such licences existed as provided in lit. (b) of 7.13.3 MA. Instead, it could trust that the Licences because of their necessary use 'to run the business' would

---

12. "Most recently OLG Düsseldorf, WM (*Wertpapiermitteilungen*) 2003, 1263."

be transferred as part of the business.[13] In addition, if the information given to claimant was considered as complete in the sense of Sect. 7.20 MA it had no reason to doubt that the Licences were transferable. Consequently, claimant claims based on the wording of Sect. 8.1 MA as 'the amount which is necessary in order to procure [. . .] the financial position which would have existed if the representation and warranty would have been true' the amount that it had to pay to the Licensor to acquire the licences.

[32]   "With regard to Sect. 7.13.1 respondent is of the opinion that the buyer has no damage claim at all. Instead, seller *only* has to 'give reasonable assistance'. This interpretation of Sect. 7.13.1 MA has no basis in the text. It is rather clear from the wording of the section and the context as well as from the concept of the MA that the duty to assist is an additional obligation of seller. There is no indication – expressly or indirectly – that the assistance should replace other remedies if the Licences could not be used by buyer. In fact, it would be quite unusual that the buyer should have no remedy if the seller fails to assist and the warranted License can not be used. Therefore, the Arbitral Tribunal takes the view that Sect. 8.1 MA applies in the case of Sect. 7.13.1 MA. Even if one did not share the Tribunal's interpretation of that provision, Sect. 8.1 would apply based on the violation of the warranted completeness of information pursuant Sect. 7.20 MA.

[33]   "Respondent further argues that claimant suffered no damage by the non-transferability of the Licences since they were correctly displayed in the balance sheet. This argument fails since it is not in congruence with the concept of the MA and the regime provided therein for breach of representations and warranties. The question is not whether claimant paid an adequate price for Licences that could be used for two more years. Rather respondent has – as provided by Sect. 8.1 MA and described above – to put claimant into a position as if the representations and warranties were complete and true.

[34]   "Further respondent maintains that in any case claimant's claim must be reduced due to contributory negligence (Sect. 254 BGB).[14] Claimant argues that

---

13. "The list attached as Annex 7.13.1 does only comprise licences granted *by* respondent not those granted *to* resondent (cf. above [27]). The licences granted to respondent and used in the sold businesses were seemingly not listed at all."

14. Sect. 254 BGB reads:

"1. Where the occurrence of the damage is co-caused by the damaged party, the obligation of compensation as well as the amount of that compensation shall depend on the circumstances, in particular on to what extent the damage was mainly caused by one or the other party.

2. This shall also apply when the damaged party's fault only consists in failing to draw the debtor's attention to the danger of an exceptionally high damage of which the debtor neither was nor could be aware, or in failing to prevent or mitigate the damage. The provision of Sect. 278 shall apply."

Sect. 254 BGB is not applicable to warranty claims.[15] With regard to the technique of an M&A transaction and to its typical mechanism of representations and warranties it may generally be true that there is no room for the application of a contributory negligence rule as Sect. 254 BGB. However, in the case at hand the parties have explicitly agreed upon the applicability of Sect. 254 BGB in Sect. 8.6 MA.[16] Therefore, the Arbitral Tribunal has to take into consideration any contributory negligence of the buyer.

[35]   "In light of the testimonies given by Mr. A and Mr. P and based on the description they gave on their exchanges and communications,[17] there can be no doubt that Mr. A was aware that the Licences might cause a problem. Mr. A testified that he had reported that the problem 'was an open issue and that nothing was filed in the due diligence data room'. Since the problem was not taken care of on both sides it resulted in a violation of the warranty as discussed above. If on claimant's side Mr. A's advice had been followed up the damage caused could have partially been avoided, e.g. by reduction of the purchase price.

[36]   "It is a generally accepted principle of contract law that the parties already have mutual obligations in their pre-contractual relationship. They include the duty of fair dealing and avoiding of damages for both future partners.[18] Claimant by its negligence with regard to the advice given by Mr. A violated this duty.

[37]   "Claimant's claim pursuant Sect. 8.1 MA is a damage claim.[19] Hence, the Arbitral Tribunal has to take in account this negligence on the basis of Sect. 254 BGB. Weighing all aspects discussed and taking into consideration the factual situation it assesses the contributory negligence of claimant with one third. . . . No additional deduction as requested by respondent can be granted with regard to the undisputed fact that in Turkey and South Africa only parts of the business have been acquired. The Arbitral Tribunal insofar follows claimant's interpretation that Sect. 8.1(b) MA does not apply in this matter."

2. The Arbitral Tribunal's Decision

[38]   "Based on the evidence submitted, the Arbitral Tribunal holds that respondent has violated its information-duties and thereby breached the guarantee given in Sect. 7 of the MA, in particular Sect. 7.13.1 and 7.20.

---

15. "[H]owever in its Reply and expressly in its Brief, claimant states that the parties 'intended to define their obligations according to Sect. 254 BGB'."
16. " 'Sect. 254 BGB shall apply to all claims under indemnities, representations and warranties.' "
17. "Cf. above [29] with [Sect. 7.13.1 lit (b) MA]."
18. "Precontractual Relationship (*Vorvertragliches Verhandlungsverhältnis*), now codified in the revised German Civil Code Sect. 241(2) and Sect. 311 (culpa in contrahendo)."
19. "Cf. Sect. 8.1 lit. (a) 'equal to the damage if the damage is calculated as the damage of the Buyer concerned'."

Therefore the remedy of Sect. 8.1 applies. Hence, claimant is entitled to claim the amount it spent for the renewal of the Licences in Germany, Turkey and South Africa. Assessing claimant's contributory negligence the amount claimed is reduced by one third."

V.   YEAR 2000 (Y2K) COSTS

(. . . .)

[39]   The arbitral tribunal next examined claimant's claim for compensation for expenses allegedly incurred as a result of computer problems related to the change from 1999 to 2000 (Y2K-problem or -phenomenon). The respondent denied the legal and factual basis for the claims and maintained that claimant had violated its duty of information established in Sect. 8.6 MA by not promptly informing it of a possible claim under the Representations and Warranties.

[40]   The arbitral tribunal continued: "The Arbitral Tribunal first has to decide the two interrelated questions whether Sect. 7.18.3 MA applies and, if so, whether the measures taken by claimant were necessary in the sense of that provision. Sect. 7.18.3 MA reads:

> 'All action has to be taken (or, to the extent this is not the case, the full cost of all action yet to be taken after the Effective Date will be reserved against in the Consolidated Closing Financial Statements) which are [sic] necessary in order to avoid any disruption, disturbance, confusion or other detriment resulting from the change of the calendar from the year 1999 to the year 2000 or by the change of the currency of member states of the European Union to the Euro.'

[41]   "It is respondent's view that claimant cannot found its claim on Sect. 7.18.3 MA since it is covered by the SA. In light of the interpretation of the SA by the Arbitral Tribunal ([10]-[19]) claims for breach of representations and warranties are not excluded. Respondent has not maintained that the costs have been 'reserved against in the Consolidated Closing Financial Statement'. Hence, the provision of Sect. 7.18.3 MA is applicable.

[42]   "Respondent has assured that its electronic equipment was modern and state of the art so that no further steps were necessary to be prepared for Y2K. This raises two questions: Were the measures taken by claimant related to the Y2K issue and were they 'necessary'. As to the necessity the parties have different approaches: In respondent's view only such measures were necessary that were unavoidable to keep the systems working. If that was the case [it] should be viewed by an expert but in an ex post judgement. Claimant holds that one has to look at the problem ex ante. Necessary are measures that a prudent and reasonable businessman would have taken in that situation.

[43]　"Which steps are 'necessary' in the sense of Sect. 7.18.3 MA must be established by the way of interpretation. When respondent guarantees that it has taken all necessary action it must be understood as: All measures that might be taken as precaution based on the available knowledge. Hence, the Arbitral Tribunal is of the opinion that the necessity of measures has to be judged on an ex ante view. Therefore it has to decide whether the steps taken by claimant can be considered as necessary from view of a carefully acting businessman confronted with the Y2K problem. The Arbitral Tribunal, therefore, has to check the positions listed by claimant from that point of view taking in consideration respondent's corresponding list with comments on each position.

[44]　"Before going into the detailed discussion the general approach of claimant has to be taken into account. [Witness for claimant,] Mr. F, in his testimony, explained that claimant in 1998 had developed a concept for the whole group to deal with the Y2K problem. This concept was implemented in Germany where it was applied with some modifications due to the late start in January 1999. Then, in his testimony [witness for claimant,] Mr. J who was at that time and still is in charge of the IT infrastructure at [a company belonging to the claimant group] described the method of determining 'the year 2000 deficits' and the costs [of] 'prospective measures'. Asked [as] to the degree of Y2K safety required he described the claimant policy as follows:

> 'The definition was that no manual actions were allowed to be undertaken and no additional software could be made use of. That means that all systems had to make the date change automatically and that all succeeding critical dates were automatically changed as well.'

In addition Mr. J explained that not only the change from 1999 to 2000 but also and related to that change the multitude of dates and the succeeding dates caused problems that had to be solved, i.e. made a replacement of a product necessary.

[45]　Confronted with the possibility to change the dates by manual measures Mr. J stated

> 'In co-ordination with respondent, we defined some systems where these actions had to be undertaken. The problem was that the manufacturer of these systems did not guarantee that the succeeding date problems would be resolved as well.
>
> 　One further point was that the manufacturer also did not guarantee that all other system disturbances related to the Y2K problem would be resolved.'

Finally, Mr. J confirmed that free upgrades . . . were used.

[46]   "Assessing the weight of the evidence submitted by claimant with respect to its policy implemented in Germany regarding the Y2K problem, and in particular in light of the testimony of Mr. J, the Arbitral Tribunal comes to the conclusion that the concept claimant applied is consistent and adequate for a group like claimant. Therefore, the approach as such could be qualified as the attitude of a reasonable businessman required for the 'necessity' of the measures to be taken ([44]). Based on this general judgement the Arbitral Tribunal has to check the single positions.

[47]   "Before doing so the Arbitral Tribunal has taken into consideration the appointment of an expert. It came to the conclusion that – based on its just explained view on claimant's policy – an expertise is not necessary. It must not be decided whether the method of the claimant used to make its electronic devices Y2K safe was the cheapest or easiest way from an [ex post] view of an expert. Instead the Arbitral Tribunal has to decide whether the measures taken were Y2K caused and whether the costs claimed have actually been spent in connection with that problem and for its solution. With regard to the costs and said purpose claimant has the burden of proof."

(. . . .)

[48]   Using this standard the arbitral tribunal determined which of the claims had been proven and established the amount of the expenses that had been made with respect to the technical matter of the Y2K issue. It then proceeded to decide to which degree the costs occurred were owed by respondent as compensation for the breach of Sect. 7.18.3 MA.

[49]   "Respondent, under the title 'new for old', requests a reduction of the compensation. Claimant argues that such deduction in the case at hand should not be granted since it 'is not reasonable (*zumutbar*) for the damaged party'. Although the German Civil Code contains no specific provision dealing with it, the principle 'new for old' is generally accepted and constantly confirmed by case law.[20] The rule is part of the broader concept of compensation of damages by benefits received (*compensatio lucri cum damno – Vorteilsanrechnung, - ausgleichung*). The court must apply the rule but the decision whether the reduction is justified is an act of discretional judgement.[21] This decision comprises two steps: First, a decision whether such compensation is justified including the question whether it is bearable for the damaged person. Second, a decision on the degree of mitigation has to be made.

---

20. "BGHZ 30, 29 et seq.; 102, 322 et seq.; *Palandt*/Heinrichs, Introductory Remark 146 Sect. 249 BGB; *Staudinger*/Schiemann, BGB (1998) Sect. 249 Note 175 with further references to case law."
21. "*Palandt* Introductory Remark 122 Sect. 249; *Staudinger*/Schiemann Sect. 249 Note 137 et seq."

[50] "First, the application of the doctrine requires a causal link between the violation from which damage results and the received benefits. In the case at hand claimant itself maintains that the replacements were a consequence of respondent's violation of Sect. 7.18.3 MA. However, a mitigation of damages by received benefits can only be taken into account if such reduction of the damage claim does not amount to an unbearable burden for the damaged person.[22] In light of the reported cases[23] and taking into consideration the character of the transaction and financial power of claimant the Arbitral Tribunal holds the view that mitigation for received benefits does not amount to an unbearable burden for claimant.

[51] "As to the degree of such mitigation neither doctrine nor case law have developed generally applicable criteria.[24] In the case at hand one way would be to appoint an expert. In light of the documents in the file and taking into consideration the testimonies in the hearing the Arbitral Tribunal doubts that an expert would be able to establish the factual basis for the decision it has to make. It deems, therefore, more appropriate not to decide on the basis of an item by item evaluation but by using the judicial discretion[25] which is the core element of the mitigation of damages by benefits and the 'new for old' principle as well.

[52] "Insofar the application of the principle 'new for' old is a special kind of the free assessment of damages which is codified in the German ZPO Sect. 287.[26] This principle is also generally accepted in international arbitration, but applied even more extensively than in German law. Furthermore, Swiss Procedural Law and Swiss Arbitration Law provide the judge with ample discretion in assessing and estimating damages.[27]

[53] "The Arbitral Tribunal takes into consideration that most of the replacements lead to a higher standard of the electronic equipment. In addition, many exchanged devices were rather old and had to be replaced sooner or later. Further,

---

22. "In general BGHZ 10, 107 et seq. and regarding 'new for old' BGHZ 30, 29 et seq."
23. "*Palandt*, Introductory Remark 146 Sect. 249 Note 146."
24. "*Staudinger*/Schiemann Sect. 249 Note 176 with overview of case law."
25. "Clearly expressed by the Federal Court in BGHZ 30, 29, at page 33: '*bei der Entscheidung über die Anrechenbarkeit eines vorteils als einer Rechtsfrage eine Gesamtschau über die Interessenlage vorzunehmen ist*'."
26. Sect. 287(1) of the German Code of Civil Procedure (*Zivilprozessordnung* – ZPO) reads in relevant part:

   "1. Where the parties disagree as to the existence of a damage and the amount of that damage or interest to be compensated, the court shall freely decide hereon taking into account all circumstances. It is left to the court's discretion whether and to what extent to grant a request for taking of evidence or order an expert report ex officio. . . . ."

27. "Ruede/Hadenfeldt, *Schweizerisches Schiedsgerichtsrecht* (Swiss Arbitration Law), 2nd edition (1993) page 275."

the Arbitral Tribunal has to take into account that 'claimant policy' to handle the Y2K matter was a broad approach including follow up problems. Under these premises the Arbitral Tribunal deems a deduction of one third of the claimed damages for breach of Sect. 7.18.3 MA as reasonable and appropriate.

(. . . .)

[54]   "Finally, respondent denies any liability due to claimant's failure to inform respondent. This argument is twofold: Firstly, respondent relies on Sect. 377 German Commercial Code (HGB)[28] and, secondly, on an alleged violation of Sect. 8.6 MA. Claimant maintains that Sect. 377 HGB does not apply in the case at hand. Further, claimant denies a violation of Sect. 8.6 MA.

[55]   "The Arbitral Tribunal is of the opinion that Sect. 377 HGB by its wording and also by its rationale cannot be applied to this transaction. For the sale of an enterprise a specific contract-type has been developed. One of the special features of such a contract are the Representations and Warranties which exclude by their nature and purpose the application of legal remedies for defective goods delivered. Therefore, it is not necessary to expressly exclude Sect. 377 HGB. According to that pattern the MA has been drafted.

[56]   "Sect. 8.6 MA – already discussed above (cf. [34]) – constitutes a duty to inform: 'If Buyer becomes aware of any facts that may be a basis for claims under representations and warranties, it shall inform seller thereof without undue delay.' Such information had to be given in writing (Sect. 22.3 MA) to be valid. In addition, both parties had nominated the person to be notified (Sect. 22.4 MA). It is not disputed that claimant has not informed respondent as set forth in the MA.

(. . . .)

[57]   "Having heard the claimant's witnesses, the Arbitral Tribunal does not have the impression that the non-information was planned or that claimant intentionally did not comply with the duty to inform respondent. On the other hand, it seems rather strange that experienced business people should

---

28. Sect. 377 of the German Commercial Code (*Handelsgesetzbuch* – HGB) reads:

"1. Where the purchase is a commercial transaction for both parties, the buyer shall inspect the goods immediately after delivery by the seller, insofar as this is possible according to the normal course of business; where there is a defect, he shall communicate it to the seller immediately.

2. If the purchaser fails to make such communication, the goods shall be deemed accepted, unless the defect was not detectable upon inspection.

3. If such defect subsequently appears, it shall be communicated immediately after discovery; otherwise the goods shall be deemed accepted also in respect of this defect.

4. The timely dispatch of the communication suffices to preserve the buyer's rights.

5. The seller who deceitfully concealed the defect may not rely on these provisions."

not have been able to find the person to inform at respondent, even if he was not formally notified. Nevertheless the Arbitral Tribunal is of the opinion that a formal approach will not lead to any result since both parties have though to a different degree not fully complied with the duties set forth in Sect. 8.6 MA in connection with Sect. 22.3 and 4 MA. Respondent did not notify claimant that Mr. K no longer was the addressee for notices and that he had left the company. Claimant sent information to Mr. K which, however, was not accepted under the fax number indicated by respondent. No further attempts were then made by claimant in this respect.

[58]   "In the Arbitral Tribunal's view these violations are not decisive for the following reasons: It is established that with regard to the Y2K issue, claimant was in contact with respondent on different levels. Even more important is the fact that the adaptation of the electronic equipment was done either by or in cooperation with a unit of the respondent group. Given these circumstances, respondent must be considered as 'informed' of the Y2K problem. If respondent insists on the position that it should have been formally notified, the Arbitral Tribunal considers this as formalistic and, therefore, would ignore it based on the principle of good faith, especially in light of the fact that respondent did not fully comply with Sect. 8.6 MA.

[59]   "But even if one shared respondent's point of view it would not change the outcome. The violation namely was without financial consequences. If respondent had been notified it could not have given other support than it actually gave. In particular, respondent had no right to force claimant to apply 'cheaper' solutions. If and insofar claimant has chosen higher standards or newer technology the added value has been taken into account by the deduction of one third. It is for that reason that the Tribunal does not consider an additional deduction under the title of Sect. 254 BGB.

[60]   "It is only for the sake of completeness that the Arbitral Tribunal states that it also does not share respondent's interpretation of Sect. 8.6 MA as a substitute for Sect. 377 HGB. If there is a sanction for the violation of Sect. 8.6 MA it would be a deduction based on Sect. 254 BGB which the Tribunal denied."

(. . . .)

VI.   COSTS

1.   Allocation of Costs

[61]   The arbitral tribunal compared the awards awarded respectively to the claimant and respondent and concluded: "the ratio for allocating the costs between claimant and respondent is 71.48% and 28.52%. Based on that ratio,

the costs of arbitration and the parties' costs have to be allocated as follows:[29] In principle, therefore, claimant is to carry 71.48% and respondent 28.52% of the total costs of this arbitration."

2. Parties' Costs

(. . . .)

[62]   "In the view of the Arbitral Tribunal, the fees for legal services are disproportionate. The Arbitral Tribunal therefore decided to reduce the fees to the same level. To reach a just equilibrium, the Arbitral Tribunal exceptionally accepts the In-house Council fees submitted by respondent as legal service fees. Consequently, the legal fees considered as justified by the Arbitral Tribunal are fixed at [an equal amount] for each party.

[63]   "With regard to the travelling costs, claimant's much higher expenses can reasonably be explained by the greater number of witnesses and the longer travelling distances. . . . Based thereupon, claimant has to pay to respondent 71.48% of respondent's costs. Respondent has to pay to claimant 28.52% of claimant's costs."

(. . . .)

---

29. "Cf. Craig/Park/Paulsson, *International Chamber of Commerce Arbitration*, Third Edition (2000) Chapter 21."

Final award in case no. 11849 of 2003

Parties:	Claimant: Distributor (US) Respondent: Manufacturer (Italy)
Place of arbitration:	Paris, France
Published in:	Unpublished
Subject matters:	– distributorship agreement – 1980 UN Sales Convention (CISG) – notification of additional time for performance – termination of contract due to failure to pay – valid termination of contract – payment by letter of credit – consequences of failure to perform

Facts

Claimant and respondent concluded an exclusive distributorship agreement (the Agreement) whereby claimant was granted exclusive distributorship rights to a brand of respondent's fashion products. The Agreement provided that respondent would deliver the products in one or more instalments for the Fall/Winter and Spring/Summer seasons, respectively. Payment was by means of a letter of credit (L/C). Difficulties arose in the course of the Agreement but the parties continued to do business and to negotiate regarding the various problems.

A new dispute arose between the parties when respondent in January sent claimant its price list for that year's Fall/Winter season, indicating that such list was subject to "little changes". This list was subsequently substituted by a second one which included higher prices. In June, respondent sent claimant the order confirmations for that year's Fall/Winter season, asking that a letter of credit be opened by claimant "as soon as possible". The order confirmation was based on the second price list and claimant requested that it be changed to reflect the first price list. Respondent rejected this request and a dispute arose as to the price of the Fall/Winter season goods. After some attempts to settle this difference, respondent wrote to claimant on 2 August demanding the opening of the letter of credit for the Fall/Winter season within twenty days of receipt and stating that if claimant failed to do so, the Agreement would be terminated. Following a meeting of the parties to attempt to settle their differences, claimant E-mailed respondent on 10 August urging respondent to refrain from terminating the Agreement pending the negotiations. Respondent replied asking claimant to send its proposal for settlement. Claimant replied on 10 August stating that "we should follow strictly the letter and intent of the distributorship agreement. In this spirit, please send me the particulars necessary to open a letter of credit for the pending shipments". Claimant sent several requests to respondent asking for information regarding the letter of credit, but did not receive any reply. On 12 September, claimant informed respondent that it had opened a letter of credit. On 19 September, respondent terminated the Agreement.

Claimant initiated ICC arbitration according to the arbitration clause in the Agreement claiming direct losses, lost profits and harm to its reputation. Respondent counterclaimed for payment of overdue invoices and other matters.

The sole arbitrator first determined that the Agreement was governed by the 1980 United Nations Convention on the International Sale of Goods (CISG), as agreed by the parties in the Agreement. In doing so, he rejected the claimant's argument that the termination should be assessed according to Italian law because the CISG did not apply to a long-term contract for distribution of goods. In the view of the arbitrator, the parties had clearly shown that they intended to avoid their respective internal laws and to resort to neutral solutions. The whole agreement was subject to the CISG and its application was not limited to single sales of products as claimant argued.

The sole arbitrator then determined that the applicable provisions of the CISG were Art. 63(1) which allows the seller to fix an additional period for performance by the buyer and Art. 64(1)(b) which allows the seller to terminate the contract if the buyer does not pay within the additional period fixed by the seller. The failure to open the letter of credit was such a failure to pay.

Claimant argued that the Agreement had derogated from the CISG because it provided for termination if the claimant failed to meet agreed seasonal goals in three successive seasons or in case of bankruptcy. In the view of the arbitrator this had not been evidenced. Moreover, construing these articles in the Agreement as a renunciation of resort to the remedies in the CISG would be tantamount to a total waiver during the first two years if the seasonal goals were not reached. This would allow a remedy to one party, but none to the other.

The sole arbitrator tested the validity of the termination against the conditions set in Art. 64(1)(b) CISG. Although respondent had earlier accepted a wire transfer as payment, this did not mean that the Agreement had been amended in respect of means of payment as claimant argued. Hence claimant was not released from its obligation to pay by letter of credit. Also, the disagreement over the price lists did not entitle the claimant to refuse to open the letter of credit. Refusal to open a letter of credit was tantamount to a total refusal to pay, which was a disproportionate reaction in respect of a disagreement. The obligation to open the letter of credit was a fundamental obligation of the Agreement and in the circumstances the claimant could not rely on the exceptio non adimpleti contractus (Art. 71 CISG) as there was no apparent risk of a future breach by the respondent of its obligations.

The sole arbitrator then considered whether the claimant had been properly notified. The Agreement provided that all notices be sent to the President or Managing Member of the respective party written in English if to the claimant, and in Italian if to the seller. Although the notice was sent in Italian to the New York office of the claimant, not expressly addressed to the President or managing director, the sole arbitrator felt that these circumstances did not deprive the notification of its effectiveness. Further, in the opinion of the sole arbitrator, the twenty additional days was a reasonable period. A letter of credit could be opened in a matter of hours and the Agreement provided that the letter of credit had to be opened within fifteen business days following acceptance of the confirmation orders.

The letter of 2 August allowing an additional twenty days for payment did not, however, constitute notice of termination which would have to be done separately according to Art. 26 CISG. After receiving the letter of 2 August on 10 August, the claimant informed the respondent that it intended to pay and requested the necessary information. Respondent did not respond until 23-24 August. In the view of the sole arbitrator, the respondent could not be allowed to take advantage of the elapsing of the additional time granted to the claimant when the claimant was prevented from performing by respondent's late response. The claimant had opened the letter of credit on 12 September. Thus, the twenty-day period did not start to run until then. Because the notice of termination was sent on 19 September, the respondent was no longer entitled to terminate the Agreement.

Moreover, a general principle of good faith prevents a party from taking undue advantage of the remedies provided in case of breach of the other parties' obligations. It appeared that the respondent pretended not to be aware that claimant had opened the letter of credit and that respondent had already decided to terminate the Agreement before the expiration of the additional time period. Hence the Agreement had been wrongfully terminated by respondent.

The sole arbitrator calculated the damages due to claimant for direct losses, lucrum cessans and damage to its reputation, as well as the amounts owed to respondent for unpaid invoices and other expenses. Interest was awarded to claimant at the contractually agreed rate. As no contractually agreed rate of interest applied to the respondent, the sole arbitrator applied the LIBOR rate as the generally accepted rate in international financial markets. As it appeared that the respondent "was seriously considering closing down and transferring its business to a newly formed company" the sole arbitrator granted the claimant's request to declare the award provisionally enforceable.

Excerpt

I. TERMINATION OF THE AGREEMENT

1. Summary of the Parties' Positions

[1] "... [C]laimant has taken the view that a distribution agreement should not be considered as a mere sale of goods, and that the Vienna Convention on International Sale of Goods (hereinafter CISG) would consequently be inappropriate to govern the termination of such a complex and long-term contract. Claimant has therefore submitted that the termination of the Agreement by respondent should be assessed according to Italian law, and in particular to Art. 1564 of the Italian Civil Code,[1] rather than by the CISG.

[2] "... Claimant has further stated that

'the Vienna Convention applies to sales contracts concluded pursuant to a distributorship agreement but not to a contract for distribution of goods over a period of years'

and that

'pursuant to international private law rules on contracts, it is necessary to determine the law having the closest links with the contract. Regarding the Agreement signed between claimant and respondent, as the goods were produced and delivered in Italy by an Italian company, Italian law shall be deemed appropriate to govern issues not provided for the the Vienna Convention.'

---

1. Art. 1564 of the Italian Civil Code reads:

"Where one of the parties fails to perform (Art. 1218) in respect of individual performances, the other party may request termination of the contract if the nonperformance is noticeably important (Art. 1455) and is such as to lessen [that party's] trust in the correctness of successive performances."

[3]   "Respondent has taken the view that

'the parties intention was to have their relationships governed by the clauses of the contract . . . and that the arbitrator should use the Vienna Convention (Art. 11.2) for everything not expressed or implied in the contract. . . . At no time the contract refers to other statutes or legal principles in addition to the contract, to the Vienna Convention and to the uniform customs and practices for documentary credits. Consequently, it appears that in dealing with all disputes submitted, the arbitrator should only rely on the contract, on the Vienna Convention and on the uniform customs and practices for documentary credits as these documents allow the arbitrator to solve all the issues.'

[4]   "Respondent also submitted that

'the Vienna Convention provides answers to the points in debate, as the termination of the agreement and the issue of damages'.

More specifically, respondent considers that

'with respect to the termination terms and breach of contractual obligations, the CISG regulates these matters and the Convention provides the answers sought for the dispute between claimant and respondent. . . . In fact, the Chapter III, Sect. III of the CISG regulates the seller's remedies in case of breach of the contract by the buyer, and its Arts. 61 and 64, as well as Chapter V of the CISG, should be applied to the contract.'

[5]   "According to respondent , the application of the CISG to the assessment of the correctness of the Agreement's termination derives from the parties' will, and 'a different approach would violate the contract and the parties' original intention, which the arbitrator is required to enforce'."

2.   *Rules of Law Applicable to the Agreement's Termination*

(. . . .)

a.   *Is the CISG applicable to the assessment of the agreement termination?*

[6]   "Claimant has submitted that Italian law, rather than the CISG, should be applied to the assessment of the correctness of the Agreement's termination. In this regard, Art. 17(1) of the Rules should, first of all, be recalled:

'The parties shall be free to agree upon the rules of law to be applied by the Arbitral Tribunal to the merits of the dispute. In the absence of any such agreement, the Arbitral Tribunal shall apply the rules of law which it determines to be appropriate.'

[7] "In the instant case, the parties have agreed that the CISG would apply to the Agreement. As a matter of fact, Art. 11.2 of the Agreement provides that:

'The Arbitrator shall apply the 1980 UN Convention on the International Sale of Goods for what is not expressly or implicitly provided for under the contract. Letters of Credit shall be governed by the Uniform Customs and Practices for Documentary Credits (1993 Revision), International Chamber of Commerce Publication no. 500.'

[8] "Claimant's submission that the CISG should be disregarded is based on the assumption that such instrument does not materially regulate the assessment of the correctness of a long-term distribution contract termination. More precisely, claimant's assumption is that the reference to the CISG in the Agreement should be construed as governing only the single sales taking place between the parties (e.g. possible disputes relating to defaults of the goods), and not to the general framework of the parties' relationship.

[9] "The Arbitrator does not share this view. First of all, by submitting the Agreement to the CISG (when such instrument does not, in principle apply to a long term distribution contract), and also by referring to the ICC Uniform Customs and Practices for Documentary Credits, the parties have clearly indicated their intention to avoid their respective internal law rules, and to resort to neutral solutions. Secondly, the way Art. 11.2 of the Agreement has been drafted shows that the parties did not intend to limit the application of the CISG to possible disputes related to single sales of products, but did rather submit the whole Agreement to its rules, with the only exception of what 'is not expressly or implicitly provided' by it. The intention of the parties to apply the CISG rules to their possible disputes has therefore been clearly expressed.

[10] "This does not mean that the application of other rules of law should necessarily be ruled out. As a matter of fact, the CISG does not regulate all possible questions arising from a sales contract. In case of gaps, Art. 7(2) CISG provides that

'questions concerning matters governed by this convention which are not expressly settled in it are to be settled in conformity with the general principles on which it is based or, in the absence of such principles, in conformity with the law applicable by virtue of the rules of international private law'.

In this case, according to Art. 17(1) of the Rules, Art. 7(2) of the CISG would in case of gaps lead to the subsidiary application of the appropriate rules of law. The same reasoning should apply whether a given CISG rule could practically not be applied to a particular disputed issue, due to the nature of a contract not falling within the material scope of the uniform law (such as a long-term distribution agreement), but to which it would nonetheless have been submitted by the parties.

[11] "The pertinent question is therefore, in the present case, whether it is practically possible to apply the CISG to the assessment of the Agreement's termination by respondent. The answer to that question should be positive, as the CISG provide rules which can easily be applied to the termination of a distribution agreement. Pursuant to Art. 17(1) of the Rules, the parties' will to apply the CISG to their dispute should therefore be obeyed. It remains to be seen, still, which of the CISG rules should be applied in the present case."

b. *Selection of the applicable CISG rule*

[12] "Respondent has relied upon Sect. III, Chapter III of the CISG ('Remedies in case of breach of the contract by buyer'). Sect. III, Chapter III provides for two different rules in case of termination of the contract by the seller in case of breach of the purchaser's obligations.

[13] "The first of these rules has a general scope: Art. 64(1)(a) of the CISG provides that

'The seller may declare the contract avoided if the failure by the buyer to perform any of his obligations under the contract or this Convention amounts to a fundamental breach of contract.'

[14] "The second of these rules applies specifically in case of breach of the purchaser's obligation to pay the price or to take delivery of the goods: Art. 64(1)(b) of the CISG provides that

'The seller may declare the contract avoided if the buyer does not, within the additional period of time fixed by the seller in accordance with paragraph 1 of article 63, perform his obligation to pay the price or take delivery of the goods, or if he declares that he will not do so within the period so fixed.'

Art. 63(1) of the CISG, which Art. 64(1)(b) refers to, provides that:

'The seller may fix an additional period of time or reasonable length for performance by the buyer of his obligations.'

[15]   "In its submission no. 1, respondent relied upon Art. 64(1) but referred to both paragraphs (a) and (b) of such article. Respondent has not been more specific in its submission no. 2. In its additional notes, it referred generically to 'Arts. 61 to 64' of the uniform law. During the oral pleadings, respondent responded to a question from the Arbitrator, and stated that the rule to be relied upon would be Art. 64(1)(a) and not Art. 64(1)(b). It clearly appears, however, that respondent has always considered the alleged breach of claimant's obligation to open a letter of credit as a breach of its obligation to pay the price of the goods.

[16]   "Reference can be made, in this regard, to the respondent's Answer to the Request for arbitration:

> 'the distribution agreement requires claimant to pay the price for ordered goods by means of a letter of credit within 15 days of the order. . . . Since the distribution agreement contains no provision limiting respondent's remedies in the event claimant fails to make payment as required under the agreement, the remedies provided by the UN Convention were available to respondent when claimant failed to provide a letter of credit in payment for its order for the Autumn/Winter season, during an additional period of time of reasonable length for performance by the buyer of its obligations.'

[17]   "It is, in fact, logical to consider that the purported breach of obligation to open the letter of credit (failure to open the letter of credit is the alleged breached obligation of claimant mentioned both in the 2 August letter and in the termination letter dated 19 September) is tantamount to a breach of its obligation to pay the price. As a matter of fact, the opening of the letter of credit was provided in the Agreement as a means of payment of the price of the goods (Art. 3.6.3: 'payment shall be made in the currency indicated on the price list, by means of a letter of credit to be issued within 15 business days following acceptance of the comprehensive seasonal confirmation'). It can also be noted, in this regard, that Art. 54 of the CISG provides that the buyer's obligation to pay the price

> 'includes taking such steps and complying with such formalities as may be required under the contract or any laws and regulations to enable payment to be made'.

Such proviso refers, in particular, to the opening of a letter of credit when the contract provides for such an obligation.

[18] "It can therefore be concluded that the purported breached obligation, upon which termination was justified, is the obligation to pay the price of the goods. The rule applicable to the assessment of the correctness of the termination is therefore the one which is specifically meant to sanction a breach of such obligation (i.e. Art. 64(1)(b)).

[19] "This conclusion is reinforced by the fact that respondent in its 2 August letter, granted claimant an additional period of time to perform its obligation to open the letter of credit. The granting of such an additional period of time, in the CISG system, falls under Art. 63(1). Such 2 August notification can therefore not be construed as a termination declaration pursuant to Art. 64(1)(a), which would be incompatible with granting an additional period of time for performance, but as the notification provided by Art. 63(1). This circumstance also leads to identify Art. 64(1)(b) as the applicable rule, as such rule specifically provides for termination after the elapsing of the additional period of time granted under Art. 63(1).

[20] "It is therefore clear that, while correctly referring to Chapter III, Sect. III of the CISG as being applicable to the assessment of the Agreement's termination, respondent in fact made reference to Art. 64(1)(b) of the CISG (and not Art. 64(1)(a), in combination with Art. 63(1)."

c. Article 64(1)(b) of the CISG derogated by the agreement?

[21] "Finally, we must determine whether it is correct that the reference in the Agreement to certain conditions of termination should be construed as an implicit exclusion of the rule provided by Art. 64(1)(b) CISG. Art. 6 of the CISG provides that:

> 'The parties may exclude the application of this Convention or, subject to article 12, derogate from or vary the effect of any of its provisions.'

In the instant case, Art. 3.4.3 of the Agreement provides that respondent may terminate the Agreement in case of failure of claimant's obligation to achieve the agreed seasonal goals in three successive seasons. Art. 10 of the Agreement also provides that:

> 'Either party may terminate the present contract with immediate effect, without being liable for any indemnity to the other party, by means of registered letter with return receipt, should the other party become subject to a winding up, bankruptcy or any kind of reorganisation between the bankrupt and the creditors not dismissed within 60 days. Upon contract termination due to Importer, respondent shall be entitled to terminate any and all supply contracts for Products still to deliver.'

[22] "The claimant has submitted that such clauses derogate from the applicable CISG rules relating to termination. Claimant states that

> 'the Agreement only provides for two grounds for termination of the Agreement: failure to reach a sales quota (Art. 3.4.3), and bankruptcy of either party (Art. 10). Albeit the letter of credit is mentioned under Art. 3.6.3 as the preferred method for payment, the Agreement provides for no sanction or penalty for failure to issue the document. The only remedy provided for in the contract for failure to open a letter of credit, where it amounts to failure to pay the price for delivered goods, is interest, not termination of the Agreement.'

[23] "The Arbitrator does not share this view. As a matter of fact, although parties may implicitly derogate CISG, some evidence should be provided of their will to do so. In the instant case, there is no such evidence.

[24] "Furthermore, leaving aside the question of the validity of Art. 10 of the Agreement under the profile of mandatory bankruptcy rules (which is not an issue in this arbitration), it cannot be considered that such proviso, along with Art. 3.4.3 of the Agreement, expresses any intention to waive the remedies provided by the applicable rule of law in case of breach of the Agreement.

[25] "It should, in this regard, be highlighted that the scope of Art. 10 is limited to one single cause of termination (bankruptcy of a party), while Art. 3.4.3 is not applicable during the first two years of the Agreement (period during which no seasonal goals were provided).

[26] "Construing such articles as a renunciation to resort to the remedies provided by the CISG would be tantamount to a total waiver (albeit for the first two years only if the breach is related to the seasonal goals) of the right to terminate the Agreement for breach of the other party's obligations. Such a renunciation would lock a party in the contract while the other party would have totally ceased to perform, which is an unreasonable situation the parties have certainly not looked for, in particular regarding a breach consisting in a default of payment.

[27] "It should therefore be considered that Arts. 3.4.3 and 10 of the Agreement were meant to supplement the remedies provided by the CISG, to which the parties did not renounce."

II. TERMINATION OF THE AGREEMENT (ARTICLE 64(1)(B) CISG)

[28] "Respondent's position is that, in refusing to open a letter of credit as required by the Agreement, claimant has violated its obligation to pay the price, which justified the termination of the contract. Art. 64(1)(b) of the CISG sets several conditions on a valid termination of a contract. First of all, claimant

needs to have been in breach of its obligation to pay the price when the additional period of time was granted (1). Second, the additional period of time granted for performance of the debtor's obligation must have been of reasonable length (2). Finally, respondent must have properly terminated the Agreement after the expiration of such additional period (3)."

1. *Was Claimant in Breach of its Obligation to Pay the Price When the Additional Period of Time Was Granted?*

(. ...)

a. *Respective positions of the parties*

[29]   Claimant has, inter alia, submitted that respondent had no right to terminate the Agreement in view of the fact that:

– 'the parties agreed, in the course of their relationship, to abandon the letter of credit and use the wire transfer, under different terms, as a standard mean of payment',
– 'the letter of credit was neither the only mean of payment according to the Agreement (it was used just one time) nor a fundamental provision to sign such contract',
– respondent's request that claimant open a letter of credit for the Fall/Winter collection was voided by a disagreement between the parties on the prices of the goods for such collection,
– respondent would have breached its own obligations by its 'continuous and material delay in carrying out the delivery of goods under the terms of the Agreement'.

[30]   "Respondent has, inter alia, replied that:

– 'the fact that respondent was forced by claimant's behaviour to accept payment methods other than L/C cannot be construed as depriving respondent of its right to insist on payments to be made by L/C',
– no amendment to the Agreement was ever agreed upon in writing by the parties ... reference can also be made to the additional notes, in the note on 'the importance of the letter of credit and the trade practice to waive the discrepancies',
– the payment of the goods by means of a letter of credit was of fundamental importance to respondent as such letter of credit was 'a fundamental factor in respondent's relationships with its distributors and, incidentally, in the contract executed with claimant',

– the confirmation orders for the Fall/Winter collection have been accepted by claimant on the basis of the second price list; reference can also be made to the additional notes, in the note 'highlighting claimant's indefensible position with respect to the A/W season's price list',

– any delay in the delivery of goods by respondent has been caused by claimant's own delays in purchasing the samples and in processing the orders."

b. Did the parties accept to amend the agreement in respect of the means of payment?

[31]   "The Arbitrator does not share claimant's view that respondent has accepted to vary Art. 3.6.3 of the Agreement in respect of the requirement that the payments be made by means of a letter of credit. In this respect, it should first be noted that the Agreement provides, in its Art. 12.4, that 'no addition or modification to this agreement shall be valid unless made in writing'. This clause reflects the parties' will to make sure that their behaviour in the course of their relationship may not be construed as a waiver of any of their rights.

[32]   "Such clause has to be enforced. In this regard, reference can be made to a general principle of international trade, illustrated by Art. 2.18 of the [1994] Unidroit principles:

> 'A contract in writing which contains a clause requiring any modification or termination by agreement to be in writing may not be otherwise modified or terminated. However, a party may be precluded by its conduct from asserting such a clause to the extent that the other party has acted in reliance on that conduct.'

[33]   "In this case, it cannot be considered that respondent's behaviour led claimant to believe that the letter of credit requirement would be irrevocably abandoned. On the contrary, it seems quite clear that the demand by respondent to claimant, made in July of the previous year that the payment be made by wire transfer rather than by letter of credit, was determined by the exceptional circumstances prevailing at that time, and in particular by its difficulties with its manufacturer M with Mr. N.

[34]   "It should, furthermore, be noted that Art. 8(3) of the CISG provides that, in drawing legal consequences from the conduct of a party, due consideration should be given to their pre-contractual negotiations. In this regard, it has to be noted that respondent heavily insisted, while negotiating the Agreement, on the importance of the opening of letters of credit. As a matter of fact, the

parties have exchanged a number of different drafts, and each time the letter of credit was not provided as the sole means of payment, respondent insisted that it be so

[35]   "It should therefore be considered that claimant has not been released by respondent from its obligation to pay the goods by means of a letter of credit."

c.   Was claimant entitled to refuse the opening of the letter of credit?

[36]   "Art. 3.6.3 of the Agreement provides that the letter of credit was to be issued within 15 business days following acceptance by claimant of the comprehensive seasonal confirmation. The order confirmations for the Fall/Winter season were sent by claimant to respondent for approval in mid-June. However, claimant refused to approve them, because they were based upon the second price list rather than the first price list. Claimant consequently sent respondent a request for rectification based on the first price list, which respondent refused.

[37]   "The question is therefore whether this disagreement released claimant from its duty to open the letter of credit. The Arbitrator does not believe so. It is true that the Agreement did not allow respondent to modify its price list after it was sent to claimant according to Art. 3.6.1 of the Agreement. In this regard, the Arbitrator does not share the view, expressed by respondent that by advising that the [first] price list was subject to 'little changes', it reserved its right to issue a different price list. As a matter of fact, an increase in the range of 10-15% can certainly not be considered as ' little changes' in prices.

[38]   "It is also true that claimant immediately protested after receiving the second price list. . . . Nevertheless, the disagreement on the prices did not prevent claimant from opening the letter of credit. Claimant could, as a matter of fact, perfectly have opened a letter of credit on the basis of the first price list.

[39]   "A refusal to open any letter of credit is, pursuant to Art. 54 of the CISG, tantamount to a total refusal to pay the price, which was an excessive and disproportionate reaction in respect of a disagreement related to 10 or 15% only of the prices."

d.   Was the obligation to open a letter of credit a fundamental obligation of the Agreement?

[40]   "The Arbitrator believes that the question of whether the opening of letters of credit by claimant was fundamental or not in the parties' intention is totally irrelevant for the assessment of the correctness of the contract's termination. As a matter of fact, it has been determined that the correctness of the termination of the Agreement by respondent should be assessed according to Arts. 63(1) and 64(1)(b) of the CISG, and not to Art. 64(1)(a).

[41] "In Art. 64(1)(b) of the CISG, there is no requirement related to the fundamental nature of the breach. Such article allows the seller to terminate the contract, in case of breach of the other party's obligation to pay the price, under the sole condition that an additional period of time of reasonable length has been granted to the debtor. In this case, as it has been said, the obligation to open the letters of credit is tantamount to the obligation to pay the price (Art. 54 of the CISG).

[42] "Respondent was therefore entitled to resort to the remedy provided by Art. 63(1) of the CISG in the perspective of a termination as provided by Art. 64(1)(b) of the CISG, regardless of the fundamental nature of such obligation. Besides, it can hardly be sustained that the obligation to pay the price by the means indicated in the contract would not be a fundamental requirement in a distribution agreement."

e. The possible application of Article 71 CISG

[43] "Claimant has submitted that it was entitled not to perform its own obligations, due to the failure of respondent to perform its own. In the CISG system, the exceptio non adimpleti contractus is regulated by Art. 71, which provides that

'A party may suspend the performance of his obligations if, after the conclusion of the contract, it becomes apparent that the other party will not perform a substantial part of his obligations as a result of (a) a serious deficiency in his ability to perform or in his credit-worthiness; or (b) his conduct in preparing to perform or in performing the contract.'

[44] "Art. 71 of the CISG might be applied only in respect of the risk of a future breach of a party's obligations, in the light of the conduct of such party, or of its ascertained inability to comply with its obligations. It should therefore be seen whether claimant had serious reasons to believe, at the time when the opening of the letter of credit for the Fall/Winter collection was requested that respondent would not perform its future obligations. It should also be assessed whether the formal requirements set by Art. 71 have been met by claimant.

[45] "In this regard, it should first of all be stressed that the circumstance that claimant disagreed on the prices for the collection does not in itself justify the application of Art. 71 of the CISG. As a matter of fact, such disagreement does not relate to the performance of one of respondent's obligations, but to the performance of claimant's own obligation to pay the price.

[46] "Leaving that issue aside, it appears that claimant had no particular reason to believe, in June, that respondent would fail to comply with its obligation of

timely delivery of the orders. . . . In any event, claimant has failed to justify compliance with Art. 71(3) of the CISG, which provides that 'A party suspending performance, whether before or after dispatch of the goods, must immediately give notice of the suspension to the other party . . . '.

[47]   "Claimant's submission that it was entitled to resort to the exceptio non adimpleti contractus to justify its refusal to open the requested letter of credit shall therefore be rejected."

f.   The possible application of Art. 80 CISG

[48]   "It appears from the above developments that respondent was entitled, in August, to resort to the remedy provided by Art. 63(1) of the CISG in the perspective of a termination of the Agreement pursuant to Art. 64(1)(b) of the CISG. Claimant, however, has submitted that its failure – at the time the 2 August notification was sent – to open the letter of credit was caused by respondent's own failure to comply with the Agreement. Consequently, according to claimant, Art. 80 of the CISG prevented respondent from summoning claimant to open the letter of credit within 20 days, as it did on 2 August.

[49]   "Art. 80 of the CISG provides that

'party may not rely on a failure of the other party to perform, to the extent that such failure was caused by the first party's act or omission.'

To be successful in its submission, claimant must provide evidence that its failure to open a letter of credit for the Fall/Winter season collection was – at the time the 2 August notification was sent – determined by an act or omission of respondent.

[50]   "In other words, claimant must prove that respondent's behaviour has, at that time, made the opening of the required letter of credit impossible or almost impossible. The Arbitrator does not find in the file any such evidence. On the contrary, as it has been said, the parties' disagreement on the Fall/Winter season price list did not prevent claimant from opening a letter of credit on the basis of the first price list. Given that claimant does not bring evidence that its failure to open the letter of credit was at that time due to an impediment caused by respondent, its submission based upon Art. 80 of the CISG shall be rejected."

2.   Additional Period of Time of Reasonable Length

[51]   "It has been ascertained that, at the beginning of August, claimant found itself in breach of the obligation, provided by Art. 3.6.3, to pay for the Fall/Winter season collection by means of a letter of credit. Respondent was

therefore entitled to resort to the remedy provided by Art. 63(1) of the CISG, in the perspective of termination pursuant to Art. 64(1)(b) of the CISG. . . ."

a. The regularity of the 2 August 2001 notification

[52] "On 2 August, respondent sent claimant the following registered letter:

> 'In relation with the above-captioned contract, we hereby ask you to proceed, within 20 days from receipt of the present letter, to the opening of the letter of credit as provided in Art. 3.6 of said contract. Such letter has now been requested to you repeatedly. It is understood that if you don't comply as above requested in the indicated period of time, the contract shall be considered terminated.' (Arbitrator's translation of Italian original)

According to such letter, respondent granted to claimant 20 additional days to comply with its obligation to open the letter of credit, and advised claimant that, failing to do so within such period of time, the Agreement would be terminated. By doing so, respondent resorted to the remedy provided by Art. 63(1) of the CISG, according to which 'the seller may fix an additional period of time of reasonable length for performance by the buyer of his obligation'.

[53] "Claimant, however, has submitted that such letter did not comply with the requirements set forth by Art. 12.5 of the Agreement, because it was drafted in Italian, and not sent to the President or to a managing director of claimant. According to said Art. 12.5,

> 'all notices and requests in connection with this agreement shall be given in writing . . . to the President or Managing Member of the party to receive notice. . . . All notices, requests and other documents delivered pursuant to this section shall be given in the English language if to Importer, and in the Italian language if to respondent.'

[54] "As to the argument related to the fact that the notification was not sent to the President or to a managing director of the company, the Arbitrator notes that the letter was sent to the New York office of claimant at the address indicated in the Agreement. The circumstance that the notification was not expressly addressed to the President or managing director of claimant is irrelevant as long as the letter was sent to the proper address indicated in the Agreement for this kind of communication. The letter was therefore, under this profile, compliant with Art. 12.5 of the Agreement.

[55]   "There is, conversely, no doubt that, in sending to claimant a notification drafted in Italian language, respondent did not comply with Art. 12.5 of the Agreement. The Arbitrator, however, does not believe that such circumstance should deprive the notification of its effectiveness.

[56]   "The Arbitrator believes . . . that the letter was properly understood by the managers of claimant. In this regard, it should be recalled that Mr. C speaks Italian. It should also be added that, even if the letter was not immediately understood by the person who received it, it was certainly not difficult to immediately translate it, which was certainly done (or, in any event, should have been done by a diligent party) given the highly contentious context of the relationship between the parties at that time. Besides, we must stress that Mr. CC [another manager] was informed of the notification by an email received the same day when the registered letter was received at claimant's New York offices.

[57]   "In rejecting claimant's submission as to the irregularity of the 2 August notification, the Arbitrator believes that due consideration should be given to Art. 27 of the CISG, which provides that

'Unless otherwise expressly provided . . . if any notice, request or other communication is given or made by a party . . . by means appropriate in the circumstances, a delay or error in the transmission of the communication or its failure to arrive does not deprive that party of the right to rely on the communication.'

Such article sets a general principle of effectiveness of notifications, which prevents claimant from prevailing itself of a mishap in the communication of the summons such as its drafting in the Italian language."

b.   Additional period granted of reasonable length?

[58]   "Claimant has submitted that the 20 days additional period granted in respondent's letter dated 2 August to open the letter of credit was not reasonable in light of the circumstances. The Arbitrator does not share that view.

[59]   "Once again, claimant could perfectly, given the disagreement on the second price list, have opened a letter of credit on the basis of the first price list. In the normal course of business, a letter of credit can be opened within a few hours from request. In granting an additional period of 20 days, when Art. 3.6.3 of the Agreement provides that letters of credit have to be opened within 15 business days following acceptance of the confirmation orders, respondent complied with the requirement set forth by Art. 63(1) of the CISG that the additional delay be of reasonable length."

3. Is Agreement Properly Terminated?

a. When was the Agreement terminated?

[60] "In the CISG system, termination of a contract is only triggered by a notice to the other party. In this regard, Art. 26 of the CISG provides that '[a] declaration of avoidance of the contract is effective only if made by notice to the other party'.

[61] "In this case, respondent sent two notifications to claimant in relation to the Agreement's termination. The first one, dated 2 August, summoned claimant to open the letter of credit within 20 days, advising that, failing to do so, the contract would be terminated. The second, dated 19 September, declared the Agreement terminated. . . .

[62] "The 2 August letter cannot be regarded as having terminated the Agreement. As a matter of fact, such letter granted claimant an additional period of time to comply with its obligation, as provided by Art. 63(1) of the CISG, which is not compatible with immediate termination. Nor can it be considered that the 2 August letter terminated the Agreement automatically after the expiration of such additional period of time. As a matter of fact, according to Art. 26 of the CISG, termination needs a specific notification to the other party.

[63] "Therefore, when an additional period of time has been granted for performance of the other party's obligation, termination needs a second, specific, notification to be sent after the elapsing of such additional period of time. In this case, such second notification was sent by respondent to claimant on 19 September. It is consequently at such date that the Agreement was terminated by respondent. We must therefore verify whether, on 19 September, respondent was still entitled to terminate the Agreement."

b. Was respondent still entitled to terminate the Agreement?

[64] "Art. 64(2)(a) of the CISG provides that

'in cases where the buyer has paid the price, the seller loses the right to declare the contract avoided unless he does so (a) in respect of late performance by the buyer, before the seller has become aware that performance has been rendered'.

The combined system of Arts. 63(1), 64(1)(b) and 64(2)(a) of the CISG is therefore that, when seller has granted purchaser an additional period of time for payment of the price (Art. 63(1)), and when purchaser has not complied within such indicated additional period, seller has the right to declare the Agreement terminated (Art. 64(1)(b)), provided that he does so before becoming aware that purchaser has performed late (Art. 64(2)(a)). This means that the CISG allows purchaser to avoid termination by complying before seller has notified the contract's termination, even if compliance is late in respect of the additional period of time granted pursuant to Art. 63(1). In other words, contrary to the situation prevailing in Italian law (Art. 1454 of the Civil Code), and contrary to respondent's view ... the expiration of the additional period of time granted to purchaser (Art. 63(1) of the CISG) does not in itself trigger an ipso facto termination, but only allows seller to notify termination, provided that compliance did not take place before he does so (Art. 64(1)(b)) of the CISG). In such a case, termination is triggered by such second notification, and not by the elapsing of the additional period of time fixed by the first notification (Art. 26 of the CISG).

[65]   "This system is justified both by the necessity to oblige seller to notify termination as soon as possible after the additional period of time granted to purchaser has unsuccessfully elapsed, and by the need to avoid termination when such a remedy is no longer necessary to protect the interests of seller (i.e. when purchaser has already performed)."

(....)

[66]   The sole arbitrator reviewed the contacts between the parties following the granting of the additional period of time, noting that claimant had opened a letter of credit and that respondent was aware of it before sending the termination letter. He concluded that: "[p]ursuant to Art. 64(2)(a) of the CISG, respondent had therefore lost the right to terminate the Agreement. We shall therefore rule that the Agreement was wrongfully terminated by respondent. Such conclusion is reinforced by three further considerations.

[67]   "First of all, it should be reminded that, according to Art. 63(2) of the CISG, the seller cannot avoid the contract before the additional period of time granted pursuant to Art. 63(1) has elapsed.

[68]   "In this case, the parties disagree on the date when the 2 August letter was received. Claimant has also submitted that the additional period of time fixed by such letter was suspended."

(....)

[69]   The sole arbitrator determined that the 2 August letter was received on 10 August and continued: "Nevertheless, it cannot be ignored that, on the very same day, Mr. C [of claimant] informed Mr. J [of respondent] that he intended to comply, and required to be sent 'the particulars necessary to open a letter of credit for the pending shipments'. Such information was provided by respondent.

[70]   "The Arbitrator does not share respondent's view that such information was unnecessary to claimant. Is was certainly not improper, in the litigious context of the parties' relationship at that time, to make sure that the letter of

credit would be compliant with respondent's requirements. Furthermore, if the required information was so easily available, respondent could have provided it immediately, instead of waiting until 23 and 24 August. Claimant therefore found itself in the situation of having to wait for the requested information before complying.

[71]   "It would certainly be contrary to a general principle of good faith (and to Art. 80 of the CISG) to allow respondent to take advantage of the elapsing of the additional time granted to claimant while claimant was prevented to perform because of respondent's late response to a request for information necessary for performance. It should therefore be considered that the twenty days period of time granted in the 2 August letter received on 10 August, did not run from the latter date, but from the date when respondent responded to the request for information sent by claimant on 10 August.

(. . . .)

[72]   "This means that, in any event, termination could not have been validly notified on 19 September, as the letter of credit had already been opened at such date. Termination was therefore irregular both under Art. 64(1)(b) and (assuming such rule would be applicable) Art. 64(1)(a) of the CISG.

[73]   "Secondly, termination could not, either, be justified under Art. 73(2) of the CISG, which provides, in contracts for delivery of goods by instalments, that

> 'If one party's failure to perform any of his obligations in respect of any instalment gives the other party good grounds to conclude that a fundamental breach of contract will occur in respect to future instalments, he may declare the contract avoided for the future, provided that he does so within a reasonable period of time.'

As a matter of fact, when the Agreement was terminated on 19 September, claimant had performed its obligation by opening the requested letter of credit, and it had declared, in its email dated 11 August, that it intended to 'follow strictly the letter and intent of the distributorship agreement'. Respondent had therefore no reason to believe that claimant would breach its future obligations.

(. . . .)

[74]   "Finally, a general principle of good faith (also recalled in Art. 7 of the CISG) prevents a party from taking undue advantage of the remedies provided in case of breach of the other party's obligations. In this case, there are a number of indications that respondent did not act in good faith when it decided to terminate the Agreement. The delay in responding to claimant's request for information (see above) is one of these indications. Reference can also be made to the fact that, in the 19 September termination letter, respondent

pretended not to be aware of the opening of any letter of credit, while this information had been provided by claimant twice. An email from Mr. R . . . also shows that respondent had decided to terminate the Agreement even before the expiration of the additional period of time granted to for performance, and that its real scope was to use termination to renegotiate new contract terms, which is contrary to the principle of good faith and fair dealing in international trade.

[75] "The Agreement having been wrongfully terminated by respondent, such company is liable for damages to claimant."

III. LUCRUM CESSANS

(. . . .)

[76] The sole arbitrator first rejected the claim for direct losses as the claimant's fixed and variable costs were a direct consequence of the performance of the Agreement, not of its wrongful termination. He then continued with the question of lucrum cessans: "Art. 74 of the CISG provides that

> 'Damages for breach of contract by one party consist of a sum equal to the loss, including loss of profit, suffered by the other party as a consequence of the breach.'

Art. 7.4.2 of the Unidroit principles also provides, as an expression of a generally accepted principle of law, that the harm suffered by the aggrieved party includes any gain of which such party has been deprived.

[77] "Loss of profit, to be indemnifiable, needs to have been foreseeable by the party in breach at the time of the conclusion of the contract (Art. 74 of the CISG). In this case, it was perfectly foreseeable to respondent, at the time the Agreement was signed, that its premature termination would cause a loss of profit. Claimant is consequently grounded in principle to claim the loss of profit suffered as a consequence of the Agreement's termination."

(. . . .)

IV. INTEREST

[78] Having quantified the sums due to each party, the sole arbitrator ruled on the issue of interest as follows: "The CISG does not provide for any indication as to the interest to be applied to sums due by a party to another. The Agreement provides, in Art. 3.6.4, that in case of delay of payment of the price due to respondent, the interest rate applicable shall be the Italian Prime Rate increased by two points. . . ."

1. Interest on Amounts Due by Claimant

[79] "Art. 3.6.4 of the Agreement is applicable only to the payment of the price of the goods to respondent. It shall therefore be applied to respondent's credit against claimant. The Italian Prime Rate is provided by the Associazione Bancaria Italiana (A.B.I) once every two weeks. At the date of the present award, the latest published rate was 7.375%. . . . Interest will therefore accrue, at the rate of 9.375% (i.e the latest Italian Prime Rate known at the date of the present award plus two points), from 9 August until payment."

2. Interest on Amounts Due by Respondent

[80] "The Agreement does not contain any indication as to the interest rate applicable to the sums due by respondent to claimant. Claimant has submitted that the legal rate applicable in the State of Washington should apply because this is the place where it is registered. The Arbitrator does not believe such solution to be appropriate. As a matter of fact, by submitting the Agreement to the CISG, the parties have clearly indicated their intention to avoid their respective internal law rules, and to resort to neutral solutions. This will should be respected also regarding interest.
[81] "In international arbitration, arbitrators have the broadest powers to determine interest on the basis of the most appropriate rate, without resorting to any rule of conflict. As indicated above, the interest rate to be applied should correspond to a generally accepted rate, applied on the international financial markets to the currency in which the damages shall be paid. In this regard, the London Inter Bank Offered Rate (LIBOR) on the US$ at 12 months (around 1.5%), increased of a spread of two points, constitutes a correct reference. An interest of 3.5% per year shall therefore be applied to all amounts due by respondent to claimant from the date of the present award until payment."

V. AWARD PROVISIONALLY ENFORCEABLE

[82] "Claimant has asked the Arbitrator to declare the Award provisionally enforceable. Such a request falls within the powers of an international arbitrator sitting in France. As a matter of fact, Art. 1479 of the French *Nouveau Code de Procedure Civile* expressly grants to arbitral tribunals the power to declare their awards provisionally enforceable.
[83] "In the instant case, there is evidence that respondent is seriously considering closing down and transferring its business to a newly formed company. . . . The declared intention of respondent to close down shortly is,

in itself, a circumstance which justifies that the present award be declared provisionally enforceable.

[84]   "Besides, it can also be noted that, according to respondent's own declarations, [it] has very limited assets, which all the more justifies that the award be declared provisionally enforceable."

VI.   ARBITRATION AND LEGAL COSTS

[85]   "Regarding legal costs and the costs of the arbitration, reference should be made to Art. 11.1 of the Agreement, which provides that 'Fees and expenses of the arbitration shall be allocated by the arbitrator in favour of the substantially prevailing party'. As claimant is the substantially prevailing party, respondent shall bear its own legal costs for the arbitration proceedings, for other proceedings before State courts in Italy and in the United States, and for the costs of the arbitration.

[86]   "Respondent shall indemnify claimant for its share of the advance on the costs of the arbitration, as well as for the legal costs it sustained in the present arbitration. Claimant, however, shall bear the legal costs sustained in other proceedings before State courts in Italy and in the United States."

(. . . .)

Final award in case no. 7722 of 1999

Parties: Claimant: Contractor (France)
                                Respondent: Client (country X)

Place of
arbitration: Capital city, country X

Published in: Unpublished

Subject matters: – construction contract
                        – applicable law to contract
                        – applicable law to arbitral proceedings
                        – interpretation of contract
                        – extension of contractual time limits
                        – liability for default
                        – assignment of construction activities
                        – applicable law to assignment
                        – standing in arbitration of claimant

Facts

A French contractor S, S.A. and company Q, as client, entered into a contract in July 1990 for a construction project (the project). Company Q is a subsidiary of company P, a company controlled by a government ministry of the Middle Eastern country X. The parties' agreement comprised a Form of Agreement (the Agreement) and numerous other documents including General Conditions of Contract and a Bid Form. Under Clause 3 of the Agreement, the documents were to be interpreted as complementary to one another. However, to the extent that there was a conflict, ambiguity or discrepancy, the document having a later date would prevail over the earlier one.

The Financial Bid attached to the Bid Form provided for a performance guarantee and liquidated damages and stipulated the maximum time permitted for the various sections of the project. The General Conditions of Contract (GENCOCO), broadly based on the FIDIC Form, provided that the applicable law to the contract was the law of country X and further provided for ICC arbitration in the event that an amicable settlement could not be reached.

Various difficulties and disputes occurred during the course of the project and in 1993 the contractor (claimant) initiated ICC arbitration proceedings at the capital city of country X, the contractually specified place of arbitration. During the course of the arbitral proceedings, company Q (respondent) initiated court proceedings in country X asking the court to revoke the authority of the arbitral tribunal and to issue an ad-interim and temporary injunction restraining the parties from proceeding further with the arbitration until the court had decided on the request to revoke the authority of the arbitral tribunal. The request for a temporary injunction was denied by the lower court, but granted on appeal until the hearing on the request to revoke the authority of the arbitral tribunal. The latter request was not granted and the stay order was vacated, allowing the arbitral tribunal to proceed with the case.

In 1995, claimant transferred the whole of a certain type of construction activities to a new company which was also part of the same group of companies as the claimant. The transfer was registered in the local French court and the claimant continued in existence after the transfer.

During the three years while the case was pending in the courts, the parties attempted to settle the dispute amicably. In June 1997, the arbitral tribunal was informed that a settlement had been reached but that it required Government approval. The arbitral tribunal was never informed of such approval, but claimant nonetheless indicated that it would respect the terms of the settlement and would not seek payment of more than the agreed sum even if the claimant were awarded a higher amount by the arbitral tribunal.

In the arbitration, the arbitral tribunal dealt with two preliminary issues – the interpretation of allegedly contradictory contractual clauses and the standing of the claimant as a result of the transfer of activities – before deciding on the substantive claims arising out of the project. Only the preliminary issues are reported here.

Parties agreed that the Contract was governed by the laws of country X, but disagreed on the interpretation to be given to certain clauses of the Contract, in particular, Clause 12.8.2 (Execution of the Works) (see below footnote 2) which regulated the granting of an extension of time and compensation by the client for delays beyond the control of the contractor. Claimant argued that this clause should be applied broadly and would affect the meaning of other clauses, whereas respondent argued that the clause did not override other specific provisions in the Contract dealing with related issues. The arbitral tribunal found that Clause 12.8.2 could not be interpreted, as claimant argued, as a kind of "super-clause" voiding other clear clauses of the Contract, but that it could be given a broader interpretation and a higher priority than that suggested by respondent, namely, that claimant could only ask for compensation under Clause 12.8.2 in situations where claimant was entitled to an extension of time under the other clauses of the Contract. After reviewing the relevant contractual clauses, the arbitral tribunal held that the Contract contained a number of clauses assigning clear liability for defaults by one or the other party. However, in addition, in every instance of delays not caused by the contractor, the contractor was entitled to an extension of time under Clause 12.8.2 and could claim compensation as certified by the client to be "fair". The arbitral tribunal added that the client did not have an "unfettered discretion to act capriciously or abusively". Rather the arbitral tribunal expected the respondent "to exercise his discretion reasonably and in good faith". In determining the substantive claims, the arbitral tribunal took account of respondent having generally refused to grant time extensions or when it did, having made it a condition that the claimant would have to abandon its claims for compensation which in the opinion of the arbitral tribunal did not meet the standards of reasonableness and good faith expected between parties in a commercial contract.

The respondent questioned the standing of the claimant in the arbitral proceedings as a result of the transfer by claimant (referred to as Old Company) of the construction activities to another company (New Company) within its group of companies. With respect to the lex arbitri, the arbitral tribunal first found that the Contract was governed by the law of country X, as specified in the Contract and that the law of country X was "the law most closely connected with the hearing". However, the arbitral proceedings were governed by the ICC Rules and there had been no need to resort to any other procedural rules.

Respondent asked the arbitral tribunal to determine if the transfer from the Old Company to the New Company constituted an assignment as prohibited in Clause 3.1 of the Contract. Applying the law of country X and the definition of "Assignment" in *Black's Law Dictionary*, rather than French law as argued by claimant, the arbitral tribunal held that because it constituted a transfer of property, the conveyance of rights was prohibited as an assignment under Clause 3.1 of the Contract.

The arbitral tribunal then examined the standing of the New Company and the Old Company. The arbitral tribunal relied on the United Kingdom House of Lords decision in *Linden Gardens* (see below) to determine that under the law of country X the transfer was ineffective to vest contractual rights in the New Company as against the respondent and consequently the New Company had no standing to sue the respondent in this arbitration. The arbitral tribunal next examined whether the Old Company, by virtue of the transfer, had lost its right to sue the respondent under the terms of the Contract, relying on the House of Lords decision in the *St. Martins* case (see below) which had been decided on appeal together with *Linden Gardens*. If neither the New Company nor the Old Company had standing to sue, the claim to damages would disappear into a "legal black hole". Thus as an exception to the general rule that a plaintiff can only recover damages for his own loss, the arbitral tribunal found that the claimant still had a right to assert the rights and obligations under the Contract vis-à-vis the respondent. This was particularly the case, as unlike the *St. Martins* case, the contractual breach occurred prior to the transfer of rights.

The arbitral tribunal awarded the majority of the claimant's substantive claims and several of the respondent's counterclaims. As to the costs, the arbitral tribunal held that the claimant was to pay thirty percent of the costs and legal fees and the respondent was to pay seventy percent.

Excerpt

I. LEGAL BACKGROUND OF THE PRESENT PROCEEDINGS

1. *Applicable Law to Contract*

[1] "Both parties agreed that under Clause 15.2 of GENCOCO the Contract shall be governed by, and construed and interpreted in accordance with, the laws of country X. And there is also no dispute that contracts in country X are governed by the Contract Act. An exhaustive law as it is, it covers almost all aspects of contracts and has been in operation . . . for over a century without any major change.

[2] "In interpreting a law in country X, the Courts give importance and priority to the written texts of the law itself. If anything clear and unambiguous is found in the law, it shall invariably be followed. Where in any case any provision of the law is not clear or admits of different interpretations, the Court will rule on it giving authoritative interpretation. The Courts of country X would refer to foreign rulings or case law, mostly of common law jurisdictions, only when there is no clear or relevant ruling of the domestic courts on any subject or point.

[3] "Because of the above legal position, the tribunal has mostly concentrated its attention on the different provisions of the Contract Act and the rulings and commentaries thereon and applied them in the interpretation of different clauses and terms of the Contract and claims and counterclaims of the parties.

[4] "Another point which needs mentioning here is that though the Evidence Act expressly provides that it is not applicable to proceedings before an arbitrator, the procedure the tribunal has followed is generally consistent with the principles of that Act. In other words, the tribunal did not take a rigid stand on evidence, and in deciding an issue the entire Contract and its relevant provisions, the sequence of the clauses, the works programme, the purpose of the Contract, the circumstances, the mutual understandings and agreements at various stages of the contractual period and the loss and damages suffered by each party due to the occurrence of different events have been looked into, examined and given due weight.

[5] "It should further be noted that both parties have referred to the applicability of certain sections of the Contract Act. . . ."

2. Interpretation of Contract

[6] "The parties are in disagreement on the interpretation that should be given to certain clauses of the Contract that binds them. While the General Conditions of the Contract are broadly based on the FIDIC form of contract, there are notable differences in important clauses (such as the clause dealing with *force majeure*). The amendments and additions made to GENCOCO, particularly those made through the Minutes of Understanding signed in June 1990, gave rise to different interpretations to the Contract. In at least one instance, the amendment to Clause 12.8.2, an important modification was made without clarifying its relationship with certain other clauses of the Contract that related to the same or a similar subject.

[7] "The result of those modifications was less than felicitous and lead to continuing disagreement between the parties as to their proper interpretation during the execution of the Contract. Counsel for each party before the tribunal took great pains to try and reconcile those various clauses, without completely succeeding, in the opinion of the tribunal.

[8] "Finally, throughout the implementation of the Contract, some specific provisions of GENCOCO or of its subsidiary agreements were either completely ignored or were not observed in full by one or the other party, on various occasions, during the execution of the works. The most obvious and consequential example in that regard is the failure of the respondent to appoint an Engineer as required by GENCOCO. Under a FIDIC type of contract, the Engineer, although designated by the client, is to be a semi-independent authority who will ensure that the works to be undertaken under the contract are going to be executed according to the provisions of that contract and who will exercise a professional, impartial judgement in awarding relief to the contractor, either in terms of time extension or in terms of compensation or in both terms, when such relief is allowed under the contract. Sect. 2.4 of the FIDIC contract provides specifically that the Engineer 'shall exercise such discretion impartially within the terms of the Contract and having regard to all the circumstances'. In the present case, right from the start, the Project Manager for the respondent assumed the functions of the Engineer. When one sees the functions attributed to the Engineer, it becomes clear that the semi-independent function of the Engineer completely disappeared and serious distortions were introduced in the relationship envisaged between the parties under the Contract. . . .

[9] "The tribunal was told by a witness for the claimant that it would have been futile to object to the decision by the respondent to have its own project manager acting as the *de facto* Engineer. The claimant proceeded with the performance of the works under those conditions, even though the failure by the respondent to appoint an Engineer created a serious disequilibrium between the parties, contrary to what was envisaged under the Contract. In light of the subsequent acquiescence of the claimant, at least by its silence, such a failure to

appoint an Engineer does not void the Contract and the claimant has made no specific claim in that regard. In such circumstances, an arbitral tribunal must interpret the Contract in a reasonable way which takes into account both the intention of the parties and their actual behavior in their mutual relationship. The Contract Act and the case law support that conclusion. Thus, referring to previous case law, [the authors of a commentary on the Contract Act] state:

> 'A contract is to be construed in harmonious manner and each part is to be construed in harmony with other parts so that a rational meaning is given to all the parts of the contract.'

and

> 'the intention of the parties has to be gathered not only from the words used in the contract by the parties but also from the circumstances, their belief, knowledge and intention as expressed in their correspondence'.[1]

[10]   "The main sections of the Contract [Act] to be applied in the present case are the sections dealing with performance of a contract and the sections concerning the consequences of a breach of contract.
(. . . .)
[11]   "As to the Contract, the main clauses to be considered and about which there is the strongest disagreement between the parties are the following ones in GENCOCO: Clause 9.9 (Extension of Time), Clause 12.8.2 (Execution of the Works), Clause 14 (14.1, 14.2, 14.3, 14.4) (Special Risks) and Clause 15.1 *(Force Majeure)*.
(. . . .)
[12]   "The difficulty in reconciling those provisions of the Contract arises, in part, out of the fact that Clause 12.8.2 is an amendment to GENCOCO agreed to by the parties in June 1990, through a Memorandum of Understanding covering a number of amendments.[2] The first text of GENCOCO of July 1989 read:

> '12.8.2. Should, for any reason beyond the control of the Contractor such works or payments be delayed, an extension of time will be granted by the Client to the Contractor by mutual agreement.'

---

1. *"The Contract Act* . . . at 5-6."
2. The June 1990 text of Clause 12.8.2 read:

   "Should, for any reason beyond the control of the Contractor, such works be delayed, an extension of time will be granted to the Contractor by the Client who shall certify such sum as, in his opinion, shall be fair to cover the expense incurred, which sum shall be paid by the Clients to the Contractor."

[13]   "The difference between the two Sub-Sections is therefore the removal of the words 'or payments', 'by the Client to the Contractor' and 'by mutual agreement' and the replacement of those last words by 'to the Contractor by the Client who shall also certify such sum as, in his opinion, shall be fair to cover the expense incurred, which sum shall be paid by the Client to the Contractor'.

[14]   The inclusion of that amendment to GENCOCO was the subject of intensive negotiations during a three-day meeting, in June 1990, between the parties. In fact, the Business Development Manager of the claimant at the time of the negotiations, testified that, due to what he stated were the well-known difficulties and uncertainties of executing a construction contract in country X, the claimant would not have been willing to sign the Contract, at the price submitted in its bid, without an amendment which provided for financial compensation for delays resulting from any reason beyond the control of the Contractor, whether or not the Client was responsible for the delays.

[15]   "At the beginning of the discussions between the parties, the claimant had also requested amendments to Clause 8.2 (Possession of Site) and Clause 9.9 (Extension of Time for Completion). In light of the fact that Clause 9.9 stipulated that

> 'the Contractor shall have no other claim against the Client in respect of delay and disorganization of work arising from the occurrences herein mentioned, except where such is elsewhere expressly provided for in the Contract'

the claimant felt that the last line of that Sub-Section rendered unnecessary the negotiation of an amendment to Sub-sect. 9.9. It is to be noted that Sub-sect. 8.2 contains no similar reservation to the one found in Sub-sect. 9.9. It merely states at the end:

> 'If the contractor suffers delay or incurs expense from failure on the part of the Client to give possession in accordance with the terms of this clause, the Engineer shall grant an extension of time for the completion of the Works.'

In that regard, claimant's Business Development Manager testified that Clause 12.8.2 was adopted in order to cover situations like the one mentioned in that last sentence and ensure that, whenever the Contractor was not responsible for a delay, he would be entitled to compensation.

[16]   "As to the respondent, it argues that the claimant is putting too much emphasis on Clause 12.8.2 and is presenting it as a kind of 'super-clause' which would affect the meaning of a great number of other clauses which were never intended to be affected. In the opinion of the respondent, Clause 12.8.2 has to be read in the context of the whole Contract and it cannot override other provisions

of the Contract dealing with related issues and replace all other liability clauses of the Contract. According to the respondent, the Contract covers a number of eventualities and adopts different solutions; these solutions cannot be erased by the simple adoption of Clause 12.8.2. In addition, the respondent notes that Clause 12.8.2 appears in the Payments and Certificates clause under the heading of 'Execution of Works' and it refers to an Interim Submission on Additional Costs of September 1991, in which an unspecified representative of the claimant, referring to Clause 12.8.2, stated:

> 'Generally, the consequences of breach of contract are covered, in the Contract Act. . . . [T]he Contractor is entitled, each time the Clients fails to fulfil a contractual obligation (breaches of contract) to claim damages in the Courts of country X. However, to avoid this problem of having to seek recourse to the Courts to obtain compensation each time that the Client is in breach of a particular obligation, the Parties agreed to include the provision of Clause 12.8.2 (as amended . . .) in the contract.
>
> This, basically, means that the Client will certainly be responsible for compensation and to award an extension of time, wherever applicable, each time there is a breach of an obligation which it clearly has undertaken.'

[17] "Finally, the respondent argues that, if Clause 12.8.2 meant that it was to be obligated to pay any additional costs for any delay that occurred due to any cause beyond the control of the claimant even if they did not result from any breach of a contractual obligation by the respondent, this would fail to give any weight to other clauses of the Contract. The respondent refers in particular to Clauses 6.12 (Insurance), 8.2 (Possession of Site/Right of Way), 8.6 (Rate of Progress), 9.9. (Extension of Time for Completion), 9.10 (Delay in Mobilization and/or Completion), 11 (Valuation of Variations).

[18] "The respondent concludes . . . that 'It is only in a situation where Contractor would have failed to meet a completion date for reasons beyond its control calling for an extension of time then that Clause 12.8.2 is attracted.'

[19] The tribunal agrees with the respondent that Clause 12.8.2 cannot be interpreted as a kind of 'super-clause' voiding other clear clauses of the Contract. On the other hand, the tribunal is of the view that Clause 12.8.2 can be given a broader interpretation and a higher priority, than the one proposed by the respondent, without contradicting the other related provisions of the Contract.

[20] "Let us start with Clause 12.8.2 itself. As mentioned above, this Clause was the subject of separate and intensive negotiations between the parties and resulted in an amendment to the Contract. It should be noted in that respect that

Clause 3 of the Agreement, signed by the parties in July 1990, and which describes all the documents that are to be part of the Contract, states:

'The aforesaid documents shall be taken as complementary and mutually explanatory of one another, but in the case of conflicts, ambiguities or discrepancies the latter in issue shall prevail over the earlier.'

In this case, Clause 12.8.2 was amended in June 1990, while other clauses of the Contract remained as they appeared in the text issued by the respondent in July 1989. By agreeing to this amendment, the parties clearly wanted to change something to the proposed Contract and at least one of them wanted something more than what was already provided for under the Contract Act and under the proposed Contract.

[21]   "The Contract Act already provides that the party to a contract who is at fault is liable to pay compensation to the other party for any loss occasioned by him by his fault and there is nothing in the Contract which changes that particular potential liability.

[22]   "On the other hand, the tribunal is of the view that to limit the right of the claimant to ask for compensation under Clause 12.8.2 to situations where the claimant is entitled to an extension of time under the other clauses of the Contract, as is suggested by the respondent, would be an excessively restrictive interpretation of that Clause, taking into account the text of that Clause as well as that of other related Clauses in the Contract.

[23]   "Clause 12.8.2 is very clear and it states in unequivocal terms that, if the works are delayed 'for any reason beyond the control of the Contractor' two things will happen: (1) an extension of time will be granted; (2) the Client shall certify what compensation shall, in his opinion, be fair in the circumstances and paid to the Contractor. It is clear that this Clause is not limited to cases where the Client is at fault. It covers all instances where a delay has occurred in the works, whatever the cause, provided it is not the Contractor's own fault. In those instances the respondent has a duty to grant an extension of time.

[24]   "Such an interpretation need not be inconsistent with the other Clauses referred to by the respondent. For instance, Clause 6.12 refers to Insurance of Materials, Works etc. and was amended, through the Memorandum of Understanding of June 1990, to exclude the requirement for insurance to cover 'risks such as, but not limited to, riots, strikes, civil commotion including malicious damage, terrorism, explosion and operation of nature'. Far from con-tradicting Clause 12.8.2, that Clause, as amended, strengthens the interpretation given to it by the tribunal. The fact that there was a specific insurance clause in the Contract meant that, in considering whether compensation should be paid by the respondent to the claimant in a particular instance, the respondent would

take into account whether that particular delay was covered by insurance or not; similarly, the claimant was expected to claim under its insurance contract, if the event was covered, rather than to turn to the respondent. In addition, the exclusion provided for under the amendment confirms the view of the claimant that, in order to keep the price of insurance and, thereby, of the Contract at a reasonable level, the excluded events would be covered through some other means, i.e. Clause 14 which clearly spells out the liability of the respondent in the case of Special Risks similar to those excluded by the amendment to Clause 6.12, and Clause 12.8.2 which is of a more general nature.

[25] "As to Clause 8.2, it refers to Possession of Site/Right of Way and the relevant part for this discussion is the last sentence which states:

> 'if the Contractor suffers delay or incurs expense from failure on the part of the Client to give possession in accordance with the terms of this clause, the Engineer shall grant an extension of time for the completion of the Works'.

Leaving aside the fact that this Clause requires the Engineer to grant an extension of time while Clause 12.8.2 puts this obligation on the shoulders of the respondent, it does not by any means prevent the claimant from claiming compensation under the latter Clause.

[26] "The respondent also refers to Clause 8.6 concerning Rate of Progress. That Clause confers substantial powers to the Engineer to order work acceleration '(s)hould the rate of progress of the Works or any part thereof be at any time in the opinion of the Engineer too slow ... ' and, in the case of such acceleration or of extension of time granted by the Engineer in such circumstances, the claimant was not to be entitled to any additional compensation. Again, this Clause can be interpreted consistently with Clause 12.8.2. In light of that latter Clause, Clause 8.6 should be interpreted as referring to cases where the delay in the Works is due to the claimant's fault and not to another cause; apart from the actual text of the two Clauses, it would be illogical to conclude that Clause 8.6 eliminates the possibility of any compensation to the claimant, even in cases when the respondent would have been responsible for the slowness of the Works. The Contract does not eliminate the liability of a party at fault under [the relevant sections] of the Contract Act.

[27] "As to Clause 9.9, concerning Extension of Time for Completion, it raises more difficulties. It provides that the Engineer shall grant extension of time 'as may be justified' in cases where delay is resulting from 'extra or additional work or any cause beyond the reasonable control of the Contractor ... '. It also provides that 'The Contractor shall have no other claim against the Client in respect of delay and disorganization of work arising from the occurrences herein mentioned, except where such is elsewhere

expressly provided for in the Contract'. By virtue of Clause 3 of the Agreement, Clause 12.8.2, being the later in issue, does prevail over Clause 9.9, 'in the case of conflicts, ambiguities or discrepancies ... '. Clause 12.8.2 transfers from the Engineer to the Client the obligation to grant an extension of time for delays beyond the control of the Contractor and it also provides for the possibility of compensation. In addition, Clause 9.9 specifically provides for the possibility of such compensation where it 'is expressly provided for in the Contract'; Clause 12.8.2 expressly so provides. In fact, this is one of the more patent cases of discrepancy between two Clauses of the Contract and Clause 3 of the Agreement takes care of it.

[28] "Then comes Clause 9.10, referred to by the respondent, which deals with Delay in Mobilization and/or Completion. That Clause, in the opinion of the tribunal, has nothing to do with Clause 12.8.2. It deals with situations where the Contractor is at fault in failing to mobilize and/or complete the Works in accordance with the Contract and it provides for liquidated damages in favor of the Client. That Clause can be given full application without affecting the interpretation given by the tribunal to Clause 12.8.2.

[29] "The next clause mentioned by the respondent is Clause 11.1 concerning Valuation of Variations. It states that the Engineer can order variations to the Contract but that such variations cannot, without the consent of the Client, exceed 10% of the value of the Contract. That Clause also provides for a mechanism whereby the Engineer and the Contractor will agree on an acceptable compensation. Again, the tribunal fails to see how this particular Clause would be prevented from having its full application by its broad interpretation of Clause 12.8.2.

[30] "Then comes Clause 14 which deals with Special Risks. The tribunal believes that there is no contradiction between that Clause and Clause 12.8.2. Clause 14.1 provides that

'The Client shall indemnify and save harmless the Contractor against and from the same (the Special Risks) and save harmless the Contractor against and from all claims, demands, proceedings, damages, costs, charges and expenses whatsoever arising thereof or in connection therewith.'

Clause 14.3 adds that the Client is only obligated to repay the costs which are 'directly and entirely attributable to the said special risks. . . . The obligations mentioned in Clause 14 explain the amendment made to Clause 6.12 on insurance and in no way do they contradict Clause 12.8.2. In fact, Clause 14 adds a stricter obligation to compensation by the respondent.

[31] "The last Clause to examine is Clause 15.1 concerning force majeure, some elements of which contained in its definition under the Contract repeat

some of the events covered under the Special Risks Clause. Strangely enough, contrary to what is stated in Clause 14, Clause 15.1.3 provides that

> 'Neither party shall be liable to the other party for loss or damage sustained by such other party arising from any *Force majeure* event referred to above or for any delays arising from any such event.'

Once again, the tribunal has to try and reconcile the differences between the relevant articles. It is clear to the tribunal that Clause 14 has to be given priority since it begins with the words: 'Notwithstanding anything contained in the Contract the following shall obtain. . . . ' [T]herefore, any contradiction between that Clause and the force majeure Clause has to be resolved in favor of the first Clause.

[32] "Finally, the claimant's document of September 1991 quoted above by the respondent is of no authority in this case; in fact, the tribunal is of the view that its legal analysis is wrong. The alleged removal of the obligation to go before the Courts of country X to claim damages is not at all the result of Clause 12.8.2, but of Clause 15.3 on arbitration. In addition, there was no need for Clause 12.8.2 if it was merely to cover situations where the respondent would have been at fault. This was already clearly covered by the Contract Act. Finally, that statement was attached to an Interim Submission on Additional Costs and no evidence has been adduced before the tribunal as to whether those additional costs were only referring to incidents where the respondent was at fault, which could explain the conclusion of that statement.

[33] "In conclusion, there are in the Contract a number of Clauses assigning clear liability for defaults by one or the other party; however, in addition, in every instance of delays not caused by the Contractor, he is entitled to an extension of time under Clause 12.8.2. Moreover, he can claim from the Client such compensation as the Client 'shall also certify . . . in his opinion, shall be fair to cover the expense incurred . . . '.

[34] "If the Contractor has an absolute right to extension of time in such circumstances, his entitlement to compensation is not so firm. The amount is here left to be determined by the Client and that amount has, in his opinion, to be fair to cover the expense incurred. Such a provision however does not give the Client an unfettered discretion to act capriciously or abusively, rather it expects him to exercise his discretion reasonably and in good faith. In the present instance, the respondent has generally refused to grant time extensions or, when it did, it made it a condition that the claimant would have to abandon its claims for compensation. The tribunal concludes therefore that the respondent has not met the standards of reasonableness and good faith expected between parties in a commercial contract. The tribunal will, therefore, when

necessary, rely upon Clause 12.8.2 and determine when an extension of time should have been granted, but refused though claimed, and the amount of compensation which should have been paid in all fairness.

[35]   "It will be seen, however, that, although the interpretation of Clause 12.8.2 gave rise to strong debate between the parties, it will not be necessary for the tribunal to resort to that Clause in order to reach its conclusions on many of the claims made by the claimant. Other provisions of the Contract and the relevant provisions of the Contract Act will frequently suffice in that regard."
(. . . .)

II.   LEX ARBITRI, STANDING OF CLAIMANT AND JURISDICTION

1. Background

[36]   "These issues arose out of certain developments in Paris in respect of the claimant S, S.A. (the Old Company). As stated earlier, at the end of 1995, a restructuring of the A Group of Companies, to which the claimant belonged took place. A decision was taken to transfer the whole of certain construction activities of the group to a new company known as S (the New Company) shares of which were 100% held by its parent company, S, S.A., itself a 100% subsidiary of A. An agreement was signed concerning Conveyance-Scission of a Complete and Autonomous Business Branch (*Traite d'apport-scission d'une branche enti-ère et autonome d'activité*) dated November 1995, but effective January 1995. An 'Engagement' was submitted in November 1995 to the Registrar of the local Tribunal de Commerce through which the Old Company transferred to the New Company the whole of certain construction activities, including the rights, assets and liabilities pertaining thereto. That transaction took place under the regime for partial contribution of assets for complete and autonomous branches of activities governed by Arts. 371 et seq. of the French law of 24 July 1966. The Old Company nonetheless was continued in existence. The New Company was organized to henceforth carry out all of the particular construction activities formerly undertaken by the Old Company. In consideration for the spin-off, the Old Company received 10 registered shares of the New Company.

[37]   "The information regarding the said restructuring led to a serious debate. . . . The respondent has submitted . . . the following questions to be considered by the tribunal:

    1. Is not the *Lex Arbitri* the law of country X, it being the national law of the country in which the arbitration is taking place, country X being the agreed place of arbitration?

    2. Whether the Old Company, which is the only party in the present proceedings before the tribunal, having been divested of 'the whole of its rights and

obligations' under the Contract, has standing to continue and maintain the arbitration proceedings?

3. Whether the tribunal has jurisdiction to proceed with this arbitration proceedings in which only the Old Company is a party before it, and where the New Company has not been added or substituted and is not entitled to be added or substituted for the Old Company as a party since the New Company is not a party of the Contract, is not the universal successor of the Old Company, nor [is] there ... a valid assignment under country X's law of rights under the Contract from the Old Company to the New Company?

4. Whether the New Company, which is not a party to the Contract containing the arbitration clause, not having been in existence when the Contract was executed in July 1990 nor when the arbitration clause was invoked in 1993 to institute the arbitration proceedings, can claim to be added or substituted for the Old Company as a party on the basis of a 'succession' or assignment which is not valid or recognized under the law of country X?"

(....)

2. Lex Arbitri

[38]   "The respondent relies on the following propositions set out in Alan Redfern and Martin Hunter, *Law and Practice of International Commercial Arbitration*, London 1991 (2nd ed.) at page 299, to support its claim that *Lex Arbitri* should be the law of country X:

'An international commercial arbitration is governed by the national law of the country in which it takes place. ... '

The claimant disputes this contention stating that even the authors of the quoted text are far from suggesting that this short sentence represents the necessary and exclusive rule on which *lex arbitrati* is to be determined. It is argued that in reality one should always determine and refer to the actual intention of the parties. It is further stated by the claimant that reference to the ICC Rules of International Arbitration at Clause 15.3 of the Contract showed that it was the parties' intention that, despite agreeing to the venue of the arbitration at the capital of country X, the rules governing the proceedings would not necessarily be those of country X.

[39]   "Clause 15.3 of the Contract reads as follows:

'15.3 Arbitration
If any dispute between the parties arises from the works or from this Contract, the Engineer, the Client and the Contractor shall use their best

efforts to settle the dispute amicably by negotiation. If the dispute is not settled by such negotiations said dispute shall exclusively and finally be settled by arbitration. Arbitration shall be carried out under rules of conciliation and arbitration of the international chamber of commerce by one or more arbitrators selected in accordance with such rules. The award of the arbitrator shall be final and binding on the parties and shall be in lieu of any other remedy. The venue of the arbitration shall be the capital of country X.'

[40] "Finally, the claimant states that:

'So, it shall be decided in the instant case that country X law is not applicable to the arbitration agreement and proceedings. Accordingly, the arbitration tribunal is free to judge, as regards the respondent's preliminary questions here discussed, according to such rule it deems proper and favorable to arbitration, in disregard of the municipal law of the "venue" of this arbitration. . . . '

[41] "The respondent, in turn, submits that:

'There are no factors in the present case which point to any system of law other than law of country X which can be treated as the law which should govern the arbitration agreement and the arbitration proceedings.'

[42] "While we do accept that, in accordance with the so-called 'delocalization theory' regarding the separability of the arbitration clause from the rest of a contract, the law governing the arbitration clause might not necessarily be the law governing the rest of the Contract, many circumstances in this case lead us to find attachment to country X and its law as most closely connected with the present hearing. As Redfern and Hunter state:

'Accordingly, and with some notable exceptions discussed below in the context of the delocalisation theory, it is essential to have regard to the law of the place in which the arbitration takes place, since this law will regulate (if only in outline) many aspects of the arbitral process. It is also essential, although this is less easily identifiable, to have regard to the usual rules and practice in the place in which the arbitration is held – which is likely to include such matters as disclosure of documents, rules of evidence, freedom of the parties to be represented by counsel of their own choice and so on.'[3]

---

3. "Page 77."

[43]   "In the present case, we note that the country X law was specifically chosen as the proper law of the Contract. Besides the chosen place of hearing is the capital city of country X, the place where the works were to have been executed is country X, country X is domicile of the respondent, and it is country X where the Contract was signed.

[44]   "At the same time, so far as the proceedings are concerned, Clause 15.3 of the Contract states clearly that the Arbitration shall be carried out under the Rules of Conciliation and Arbitration of the International Chamber of Commerce. And those Rules provide at Art. 11 that:

> 'The rules governing the proceedings before the arbitrator shall be those resulting from these Rules and, where the rules are silent, any rules which the parties (or, failing them, the arbitrator) may settle, and whether or not reference is thereby made to a municipal procedural law to be applied to the arbitration.'

The arbitration was conducted under the 1988 version of the ICC Rules.

[45]   "In the instant case, while the parties have provided for the substantive law governing the Contract, they have not provided for the law governing the arbitral proceedings themselves.

[46]   "According to the Contract itself, as already mentioned above, it shall be governed by the laws of country X. There is, therefore no doubt as to the contents and substance of the Contract. As to rules governing the proceedings, the tribunal has applied Art. 11 of the Rules of Conciliation and Arbitration of the International Chamber of Commerce; it has not needed to resort to any other rules. Had there been mandatory procedural rules to be applied under country X law, the tribunal would have abided by them; no party has indicated that such mandatory rules existed or that, if they existed, the tribunal has infringed them."

3.   *Standing of the Old Company and Jurisdiction of the Arbitration Tribunal and Other Related Issues*

[47]   "The other main issues raised by the respondent are:

1.   Does the transfer from the Old Company to the New Company constitute an assignment as prohibited by Clause 3.1 of the Contract?
2.   Even if the transfer constitutes a prohibited assignment, was it effective to vest a cause of action in the New Company as assignee?
3.   If such assignment was ineffective to vest the cause of action in the new Company, can the Old Company, as the original contracting party, maintain these proceedings and recover damages?

[48] "Clause 3.1 of the Contract states that:

'The Contractor shall not assign the Contract or any part thereof or any benefit or interest therein or thereunder (otherwise than by a charge in favor of the Contractor's Bankers of any monies due or become due under this Contract) without the prior written consent of the Client.'"

a. Does transfer constitute a prohibited assignment?

[49] "The first question is whether the transfer from the Old Company to the New Company constitutes an assignment as prohibited by the said Clause 3.1 of the Contract. The claimant contends that the transfer of rights does not constitute an assignment as prohibited under Clause 3.1 of the Contract, but rather, is legally a 'corporate succession' not falling within the contractual prohibition. Indeed, the claimant has gone to great lengths to demonstrate how the restructuring of the claimant company was legal under French corporate law and how under the French law of corporate succession the New Company would acquire the rights formerly held by the Old Company.

[50] "This may well be the case. . . . However, it seems that the question of the validity of the transfer under French corporate law is besides the point, for the real question to be answered is whether the transfer constitutes an assignment as prohibited by Clause 3.1 of the Contract. The transfer may well have been valid or legal in many other respects, while still falling under the mutually agreed upon prohibition against assignments.

[51] "Clause 15.2 of the Contract clearly states that the governing law of the Contract shall be country X law. It reads as follows:

'15.2 Applicable law
This Contract shall be governed by and construed and interpreted in accordance with the laws of country X.'

So, it is clear that it was within the parties' contemplation that the substantive or governing law, as stipulated at Clause 15.1 – the 'proper law of the Contract', as it is known, would be country X law. Therefore, we must determine whether the transfer constituted an assignment under country X law, and not under French regime.

[52] "The main source of the law in that regard will be the Contract Act. Reference will also be made to country X judicial decisions, as well as to those of India, Pakistan, the United Kingdom and other common law jurisdiction[s] when the law is identical or is silent on a particular matter. As explained earlier, the common law may be invoked when local law is silent on any legal

issue and its proper interpretation is available in common law. This is the practice usually followed by country X courts in the matter of interpretation of any law on identical or near, similar issues. But it should be noted that foreign rulings have no binding effect and are consulted only for enlightenment and guidance in arriving at their own conclusion by the local courts.

[53] "The Contract Act does not contain a specific definition of the word 'assignment', but it contains ... a general provision concerning the obligation of parties to contracts. It says:

> 'The parties to [a] contract must either perform, or offer to perform, their respective promises, unless such performance is dispensed with or excused under the provisions of this Act, or of any other law.'

[54] "In their commentary on the Contract Act, the authors, referring to case law state:

> 'A party to a contract can, by agreement with the other party, drop out of the contract and assign his interest in it to a third party. An assignment of contract might result in a transfer either of the rights or of the obligations thereunder. But there is well-recognized distinction between these two classes of assignments. As a result, obligation under a contract can not be assigned except with the consent of the promisee, and when such consent is given, it is really a novation resulting in substitution of liabilities. On the other hand, rights under a contract are assignable unless the Contract is personal in its nature or the rights are incapable of assignment, either under the law or under an agreement between the parties.' (footnote omitted)

[55] "*Black's Law Dictionary* defines assignment as follows:

> 'Assignment. A transfer or making over to another of the whole of any property, real or personal, in possession or in action, or of any estate or right therein. It includes transfers of all kinds of property, including negotiable instruments. The transfer by a party of all of its rights to some kind of property, usually intangible property such as rights in a lease, mortgage, agreement of sale or a partnership. Tangible property is more often transferred by possession and by instruments conveying title such as a deed or a bill of sale.'[4]

[56] "It can not be more clear that, by its very essence, the 'transfer' from Old Company to New Company falls within the definition of assignments under the

---

4. "*Higgins v. Monckton*, 28 Cal. App. (2d) 723, 83 P. 2d 516 at 519."

common law. In its submissions, the claimant itself employs the language of 'transfer' of rights in describing the conveyance to the New Company, as does the French law under which the conveyance was made, as cited in the claimant's submission. (footnote omitted)

[57]   "The claimant has cited the decision of the House of Lords in the case of *National Bank of Greece and Athens S.A. v. Metliss*,[5] as authority that English Courts look to the law of the transferor as the proper law to decide questions of an assignment's validity. While this may ordinarily be so, the *National Bank of Greece* case is not relevant for our purposes because in the Contract at issue here, a non-assignment clause is present, where none was evidenced in *National Bank of Greece*. Thus, while the principle in *National Bank of Greece* may well apply where no non-assignment clause is present, the tribunal does not believe that case is of much use in the context of the present arbitration. For similar reasons (the absence of a non-assignment clause) the other authorities cited by the claimant . . . are also irrelevant.

[58]   "From the above we conclude that, because it constituted a transfer of property, the conveyance of rights was prohibited as an assignment under Clause 3.1 of the Contract."

b.   Cause of action

[59]   "The next question is whether, even if the transfer constitutes a prohibited assignment under the Contract, it was effective to vest a cause of action in the New Company as assignee? The respondent has argued that (1) the New Company has no standing to continue or to maintain the present arbitration proceedings since it is not a party to the Contract containing the arbitration clause in question, it has not and cannot become a party to this arbitration, it cannot be regarded as the universal successor of the Old Company, and it is not an assignee of the Old Company since, under country X law, the assignment is invalid without the consent of the other party and (2) in any event no assignment is permitted under country X law of a claim for damages.

[60]   "Then, what are the effects of Clause 3.1? In the decision of *Linden Gardens Trust Ltd. v. Sludge Ltd.*, it was decided by the House of Lords that an assignment of contractual rights in breach of a prohibition against such assignment is ineffective to vest the contractual rights in the assignee.[6] While the parties have referred to a number of older and lower British court decisions, neither party has cited this decision, which is the leading case on the question of transfers of rights made in violation of a contractual prohibition against assignments.

---

5. "(1958) A.C. 509."
6. "[1993] 3 All ER 417 (HL)."

[61]   "In *Linden Gardens*, the House of Lords adjudicated on two separate appeals in which questions arose as to the effect of a contractual provision prohibiting a party from assigning the benefits of a contract, and whether the original owner of a property could recover substantial damages for breach of a building contract if he had parted with the property and had no proprietary interest in the works at the time when the breach occurred. Noteworthy are the facts of the second case under appeal in the *Linden Gardens* decision – *St. Martins Property Corp. Ltd. and anor. v. Sir Robert McAlpine & Sons Ltd.* – as the facts in that case are strikingly similar to those with which we are faced in the present arbitration. In *St. Martins*, the first plaintiff, St. Martin Property Corp. Ltd. (Corporation) entered into a building contract with the respondent (McAlpines), which contract contained a stipulation prohibiting assignments of rights as between the Corporation and McAlpines.

[62]   "Corporation was a wholly-owned subsidiary of St. Martins Holdings Ltd., which was itself wholly owned by the State of Kuwait. In the mid-1970s, a scheme was implemented for tax reasons whereunder all the property interests of the State of Kuwait were to be vested in another wholly-owned subsidiary of St. Martins Holdings Ltd., St. Martins Property Investments Ltd. (Investments), the second plaintiff. Pursuant to that scheme, a deed of assignment was executed under which Corporation for full value assigned to Investments all Corporation's interests in the property. It further purported to assign to Investments 'the full benefit of all contracts and engagements whatsoever entered into by the assignor and existing at the date hereof for the construction of and completion of the Development'.[7]

[63]   "The consent of McAlpines to the assignment of the benefit of the building contract was neither sought nor given. No notice of the assignment was given to McAlpines until 10 years later. When, five years after the assignment of the property to Investments, the construction works were found to contain defects, an action was taken by Corporation and Investments against McAlpines for breach of contract. In its judgement, the House of Lords first held that the Contractual stipulation prohibited the assignment of the benefit of the Contract, as well as any accrued rights of actions under the Contract. It was also held that no policy reason existed to hold such a contractual prohibition on assignment of contractual rights contrary to public policy. On the question of whether the assignment (although prohibited) was effective to transfer the causes of action to the assignee, Lord Browne-Wilkinson held that such assignment was ineffective to vest the contractual rights in the assignee.

[64]   "On the latter point, Lord Browne-Wilkinson, giving the leading judgement, states his reasoning clearly and succinctly. He also comments on several

---

7. "*Linden Gardens* at 426."

cases cited by the parties to that arbitration, notably *Shaw & Co. v. Moss Empires Ltd.*[8] (relied upon by the claimant) and *Helstan Securities Ltd. v. Hertfordshire Country Council*[9] (relied upon by the respondent.). For this reason, the tribunal feels it worthwhile to cite the following passage from his judgement at length:

'It was submitted that, even though the assignments were in breach of [the non-assignment clause], they were effective to vest the causes of action in the assignees. . . . This argument was founded on two bases: first, the decision in *Shaw & Co v. Moss Empires Ltd.* (1908) 25 TLR 190; second, the fact that an assignment of a leasehold term in breach of a covenant against assignment is effective to vest the term in the assignee.

In the *Shaw* case an actor, B, was engaged by Moss Empires under a contract which prohibited the assignment [of] his salary. B assigned 10% of his salary to his agent, Tom Shaw. Tom Shaw sued Moss Empires in 10% of the salary joining B as second defendant. Moss Empires agreed to pay the 10% of the salary to Tom Shaw or B as the court might decide, i.e. in effect it interpleaded. Darling J held (at 191) that the prohibition on assignment was ineffective: "it could no more operate to invalidate the assignment than it could interfere with the laws of gravitation". He gave judgement for the plaintiffs against both B and Moss Empires, ordering B to pay the costs but making no order for costs against Moss Empires.

The case is inadequately reported and it is hard to discover exactly what it decides. Given that both B and Moss Empires were parties and Moss Empires was in effect interpleading, it may be that the words I have quoted merely indicate that as between the assignor, B, and the assignee Tom Shaw, the prohibition contained in the Contract between B and Moss Empires could not invalidate B's liability to account to Tom Shaw for the moneys when received and that, since B was a party, payment direct to Tom Shaw was ordered. This view is supported by the fact that no order for costs was made against Moss Empires. If this is the right view of the case, it is unexceptionable; a prohibition on assignment normally only invalidates the assignment as against the other party to the Contract so as to prevent a transfer of the chose in action; in the absence of the clearest words it cannot operate to invalidate the Contract as between the assignor and the assignee and even then it may be ineffective on the grounds of public policy. If on the other hand Darling J purported to hold that the Contractual prohibition was ineffective to prevent B's contractual rights against Moss Empires being transferred to Tom Shaw, it is inconsistent with authority and was wrongly decided.

---

8. "(1908) 25 TLR 190."
9. "[1978] 3 All ER 262."

In the *Helstan Securities* case Croom-Johnson J did not follow the *Shaw* case and held that the purported assignment in breach of the Contractual provision was ineffective to vest the cause of action in the assignee. That decision was followed and applied by the Court of Appeal in the *Reed Publishing Holdings* case: see also *Re Turcan* 40 Ch D 5.

Therefore the existing authorities establish that an attempted assignment of contractual rights in breach of a contractual prohibition is ineffective to transfer such contractual rights. I regard the law as being satisfactory settled in that sense. If the law were otherwise, it would defeat the legitimate commercial reason for inserting the Contractual prohibition, viz., to ensure that the original parties to the Contract[] are not brought into direct contractual relations with third parties.'[10]

Subsequent decisions of English Courts have followed the House of Lords decision in the *Linden Gardens* case.[11]

[65] "The passage quoted above settles, in our opinion, the state of the law on this issue. We therefore conclude that based on the principle set out in *Linden Gardens*, under country X Law, the transfer was ineffective to vest contractual rights in the New Company as against the respondent. It follows that the New Company has no standing on which to sue the respondent in the present arbitration."

c. Standing to continue and maintain proceedings

[66] "The final question is, if the assignment was ineffective, can the original contracting party (the Old Company) maintain these proceedings and recover damages? The respondent contends that the Old Company has lost standing to continue and maintain the present proceedings. The respondent bases its argument on the fact that the Old Company 'admittedly' divested itself at the end of 1996 of the whole of the rights and obligations arising from the agreements entered into by the Old Company before operation of the re-structuring pursuant to the 'engagement' submitted to the local court in November 1995. The term 'whole of the rights and obligations', it is alleged, is manifestly comprehensive and must include the right under the Contract of the claimant to prosecute its claims and to continue and maintain the present arbitration proceedings. Therefore, it is claimed, if the Old Company admittedly stands

---

10. "*Linden Gardens* at 431-432. . . ."
11. "See, in particular, *Hendry v. Chartsearch Ltd.*, Court of Appeal (Civil [Division]), 23 July 1998, unreported as yet; *David Charles Flood v. Shand Construction*, Court of Appeal, 81 BLR 31; and *Yeandle v. Wynn Realisations Limited*, Court of Appeal (Civil Division), 47 Con. L.R. 1."

divested of all of its rights under the Contract, clearly it no longer has the right to continue with the arbitration.

[67]   "The issue here is whether the Old Company, by virtue of the transfer of its rights and liabilities to the New Company, has lost its right to sue the respondent under the terms of the Contract. In *Linden Gardens*, this question arose in a somewhat different manner as the defendant in that case merely accepted that, since the attempted assignment by the purported assignor of its rights under the Contract to the purported assignee was ineffective, the assignor had retained those rights and was entitled to judgement against the defendant for any breach of contract.[12] It was argued, however, that since Corporation had parted with its interest in the property for adequate consideration [] before any breach of the building contract had occurred, it had suffered no loss.

[68]   "Here is what Lord Browne-Wilkinson had to say about the arguments of the defendant in the *St. Martins* case:

'Therefore, it is said, neither of the plaintiffs has any right to substantial damages: Investments (the purported assignee) has incurred damage (being the cost of rectifying the faulty work) but has no cause of action, Corporation (the purported assignor) has a cause of action but has suffered no loss. If this is right, in the words of Lord Keith of Kinked in *GUS Property Management Ltd. v. Littlewoods Mail Order Stores Ltd.* 1982 SC (HL) 157 at 177, the claim to damages would disappear ... into some legal black hole, so that the wrongdoer escaped scot-free.'[13]

[69]   "In the case at hand were we to agree with the respondent's arguments as against both the Old Company and the New Company, it would seem inescapable that we would fall into Lord Keith's 'black hole' as well.

[70]   "Lord Browne-Wilkinson continues his reasoning:

'in my judgement the present case falls within the rationale of the exceptions to the general rule that a plaintiff can only recover damages for his own loss. The Contract was for a large development of property which, to the knowledge of both Corporation and McAlpines, was going to be occupied, and possibly purchased, by third parties and not by Corporation itself. Therefore it could be foreseen that damage caused by a breach would cause loss to a later owner and not merely to the original contracting party, Corporation. As in contracts for the carriage of goods by land, there

---

12. "The issue in *Linden Gardens* was the measure of damages allowable pursuant to the Contractual breach."
13. "*Linden Gardens* at p. 432."

would be no automatic vesting in the occupier or owners of the property for the time being who sustained the loss of any right of suit against McAlpines. On the contrary, McAlpines had specifically contracted that the rights of action under the building contract could not without McAlpines' consent be transferred to third parties who became owners or occupiers and might suffer loss. In such a case, it seems to me proper, as in the case of carriage of goods by land, to treat the parties as having entered into the Contract on the footing that Corporation would be entitled to enforce contractual rights for the benefit of those who suffered from defective performance but who, under the terms of Contract, could not acquire any right to hold McAlpines liable for breach. It is truly a case in which the rule provides a remedy where no other would be available to a person sustaining loss which under a rational legal system ought to be compensated by the person who has caused it.

I would therefore hold that Corporation is entitled to substantial damages for any breach by McAlpines of the building contract.'[14]

[71] "It has been argued that Lord Browne-Wilkinson's holding constitutes a limited principle, such that it only applies in the case where it is foreseeable that the damages caused by the breach would cause loss to a later owner. Indeed, the House of Lords was not unanimous in accepting the reasoning of Lord Griffiths, which seems to imply that the duty to pay the original contracting party remains on the breaching party, regardless whether the original party still owned the property concerned, and whether or not transfer of the property was contemplated.[15]

[72] "At least one commentator, Andrew Tettenborn, has come out in favor of Lord Griffiths' expansive view:

'If one may so with respect, Lord Griffiths' view seems the more sensible and certain. The other members of the House did not openly support it; but then they did not dissent from it either, merely feeling that it was better to leave a final decision until later.'[16]

[73] "In any event, it remains that in the arbitration at hand, if the Contract was breached by respondent, such a breach would have occurred, prior to the transfer of rights from the Old Company to the New Company. In the *St. Martins* case, unlike our own, the Contractual breach took place after the date of assignment,

---

14. "*Linden Garden* at 436-437."
15. "See Andrew Tettenborn, 'Loss, Damage and the Meaning of Assignment', [1994] Comb. L.J. 25."
16. "Tettenborn at 26."

that is to say at a time when Corporation (the assignor) no longer had an interest in the property. Thus, based on Lord Browne-Wilkinson's sound reasoning, it would seem that if an assignor can sue to recover damages which had not yet accrued when the assignment was purported to have been made, a fortiori, the assignor can sue for damages that were already accrued at the time of transfer.

[74] "To answer the respondent's argument (in support of which, we note, the respondent has cited no authority), while the Old Company may have purported to divest itself of its rights under the present Contract such that the New Company would henceforth benefit from those rights, such an undertaking, in the circumstances of the present matter, has no effect vis-à-vis respondent, given that, (as the respondent has itself argued) those rights did not pass to the New Company, insofar as respondent is concerned.

[75] "The claimant was, therefore, correct in asserting that the rights and obligations of the Contract, including the right to arbitration, still exist. These rights have not 'disappeared', as might be the curious result had the Old Company been dissolved or had otherwise ceased to exist as a legal person.[17] However, in the present case, the Old Company, as a legal entity which was a party to the Contract and which initiated the present arbitration, is still very much in existence and it remains a valid party to the present proceedings. Therefore, in our opinion, it remains vested with all the rights and obligations under the Contract which it concluded with respondent."

4. Conclusions

[76] "In the light of the above analysis, we answer as follows the questions raised by the respondent in its Memorial on Jurisdiction and which it requested the tribunal to determine:

[77] "In answer to [the] question:

'Is not the *Lex Arbitri* the law of country X, it being the national law of the country in which the arbitration is taking place, country X being the agreed place of arbitration?'

The tribunal says: yes. But in the present case, the tribunal has not yet had to rely upon the procedural law of country X, Art. 11 of the Rules of Conciliation and Arbitration of the International Chamber of Commerce having proven sufficient for the purpose of this arbitration. Had it been necessary to resort to

---

17. "On this point, see *Baytur SA v. Finagro Holding SA*, [1991] All ER, 129 (CA) at 133: 'An arbitration requires two or more parties. There cannot be a valid arbitration when one of the parties has ceased to exist.' (Lloyd LJ)"

additional procedural law, the tribunal would have applied the country X procedural law.

[78]   "In answer to the question:

'Whether the Old Company, which is the only party in the present proceedings before the tribunal, having been divested of "the whole of its rights and obligations" under the Contract, has standing to continue and maintain these arbitration proceedings?'

The tribunal says: yes.

[79]   "In answer to the question:

'Whether the tribunal has jurisdiction to proceed with these arbitration proceedings in which only the Old Company is a party before it, and where the New Company has not been added or substituted and is not entitled to be added or substituted for the Old Company as a party since the New Company is not a party of the Contract, is not the universal successor of the Old Company, nor is there a valid assignment under the country X law of rights under the Contract from the Old Company to the New Company?'

The tribunal says: yes.

[80]   "In answer to the question:

'Whether the New Company, which is not a party to the Contract containing the arbitration clause, not having been in existence when the Contract was executed in July 1990, nor when the arbitration clause was invoked in 1993 to institute the arbitration proceedings, can claim to be added or substituted for the Old Company as a party on the basis of a "succession" or assignment which is not valid or recognized under country X Law?'

The tribunal says: no."

(. . . .)

[81]   The arbitral tribunal's findings on the claimant's submissions relating to specific aspects of the works are not reported here. In conclusion the arbitral tribunal noted: "[C]ounsel for the claimant indicated that its client would respect the terms of a settlement agreed to by the parties but subject to the approval of the government of country X – which approval was never confirmed – and that it would not seek payment of more than the agreed sum, if the claimant was awarded a higher amount by the tribunal."

Final award in case no. 9613 of 1999

Parties:	Claimant: Investment company (nationality not indicated)
	Respondent: Mining company (nationality not indicated)
Place of arbitration:	Geneva, Switzerland
Published in:	Unpublished; original in English
Subject matters:	– binding nature of agreement
	– duty to negotiate in good faith
	– Art. 1337 Italian Civil Code
	– costs of arbitration shared proportionally
	– parties bear own legal costs

Facts

In April 1993, a Regional Government (the Region) in country A decided to privatize a mineral processing plant, Company Z, which had been shut down and was under administered receivership. The claimant, an investment company, was requested to solicit offers from and conduct negotiations with investors.

Negotiations were initially held with Company N, with which Company Z also executed an Exclusive Sales Agreement. This agreement was terminated on 24 June 1995 because Company N allegedly did not meet its commitment to distribute Company Z's products on a large scale.

In January 1995, after Company N failed to submit a "buying plan" before the agreed deadline, 31 December 1994, the claimant commenced negotiations with the respondent, a mining and mineral processing company of the Y group. A draft agreement was concluded in February 1995. On 7 July 1995, the claimant informed the respondent, through merchant bank E, that Company Z's general assembly of shareholders was willing to proceed to the sale of shares on the basis of the draft agreement.

On 5 August 1995, the claimant and the respondent concluded Heads of Agreement in respect of the sale of Company Z's shares (the HOA). The HOA noted the parties' interest in selling and purchasing the shares and stated that the parties would conclude a Final Purchase Agreement in respect of the sale. They also contained a guarantee that Company Z was fully operational and provided, inter alia, that the respondent would carry out due diligence reviews; that the sale price would be subject to adjustment based on the outcome of those reviews and that payment would be guaranteed in part by a Corporate Guarantee "preferably issued by an EU corporate", to be agreed upon by the parties in the Final Purchase Agreement. Art. 17 of the HOA provided for the application of Italian law; Art. 19 referred disputes to ICC arbitration.

On 21 September 1995, the parties also executed a Management of Transition Agreement to enable the respondent to monitor certain decisions with respect to the management of Company Z.

The due diligence reviews were completed in September 1995. They evidenced, inter alia, the existence of a large claim against Company Z for pollution and the fact that the Exclusive Sales Agreement with Company N might still be binding. Negotiations between the parties resumed in October 1995. They concerned, inter alia, certain issues in respect of the agreement reached with Company Z's creditors ("composition with creditors") and measures to counteract Company Z's financial difficulties. A decision was also taken to sell a certain amount of products to Y International Ltd, a company in the Y group to which respondent also belonged. This delivery was later objected to because of alleged defects.

Negotiations also concerned the fresh water supply that was essential for the plant's operation. In periods of drought, the plant had to use bore wells which were polluted and therefore unsuitable, but had been allowed on one occasion to draw water from a nearby dam. The respondent sought a commitment in this respect from the claimant. When it became clear that the fresh water supply was a political issue that went beyond the claimant's authority, the respondent sought a commitment from the Region.

Further negotiations ensued, but the parties could not reach a final agreement in respect of several issues, including, inter alia, the respondent's request for certain additional funding and for guarantees in respect of certain subsidized financing and the fresh water supply, as well as its request to prevent Company Z from selling its products to third parties. On 5 April 1996, a draft Final Purchase Agreement was made along these lines.

On 13 May 2006, the respondent, through merchant bank E, sought to lay down the agreement it believed had been reached on all pending issues by sending two letters to the claimant and the Region, respectively. The claimant countersigned the letter it had received; the Region did not reply to its letter, which concerned mainly the fresh water supply.

On 12 August 1996, the respondent sought attachment of Company Z's shares before a court in country A on the basis of the HOA complemented by the two letters of 13 May 1996. On 6 April 1997, the court denied the request, holding that there was no binding agreement to sell and purchase between the parties.

In April 1997, the claimant resumed negotiations with Company N.

On 21 July 1997, the claimant filed a request for ICC arbitration against the respondent, seeking damages because of the respondent's alleged failure to act in good faith when negotiating the Final Purchase Agreement. The respondent filed counterclaims for damages and specific performance, that is, the sale of Company Z's shares. At a hearing on 16 December 1998, the respondent withdrew this latter counterclaim upon being informed that Company Z had been sold in the meantime to Company N on 26 May 1998. On 10 March 1999, the respondent's other counterclaims were dismissed for failure to pay the advance on costs.

By the present award, the ICC arbitrators unanimously denied the claimant's claim, holding that although the HOA were not a binding contract and the claimant was therefore entitled to rely on the provision in the applicable Italian law that provides for pre-contractual liability, the respondent did not act in violation of good faith.

The arbitrators first noted that Art. 1337 of the Italian Civil Code (CC) provides that parties shall act according to good faith when negotiating and concluding a contract. There can be no such pre-contractual liability, however, if the parties conclude a binding agreement. This was not the case here.

In the arbitrators' opinion, "a mere reading" of the HOA showed that the parties had no intention to be contractually bound. The HOA stated, inter alia, that the parties were "interested" in selling and purchasing the capital share of Company Z, respectively, and left unaddressed essential issues such as the adjustment of the sale price based on the outcome of the due diligence reviews and on the (un)availability of certain subsidized financing. The sale price was thus in fact undetermined and undeterminable.

The subsequent behavior of the parties, as evidenced by their correspondence, confirmed this conclusion. Nor did the two letters of 13 May 1996 support the respondent's contention. While the claimant countersigned the letter and thus accepted the respondent's requests in respect of the issues still pending, the Region left its letter unanswered. Hence, it did not enter into any commitment in respect of the fresh water supply. The arbitrators noted that the respondent could not contend that it would have entered into the Final Purchase Agreement even without such commitment since it explicitly stated in a July 1996 letter that it would not finalize the agreement unless the Region accepted its request.

Hence, the HOA, even if complemented with the 13 May 1996 letters, were not a binding contract and the claimant was not precluded from seeking remedy under Art. 1337 Italian CC.

The arbitral tribunal held, however, that the claimant's argument that the respondent did not act in good faith by making unreasonable additional demands that were not contemplated by the HOA, failing to submit a viable and complete industrial plan for Company Z and refusing to pay a substantial part of the price of the products sold to its affiliate Y International Ltd., thereby bringing the negotiations to a stop, was unfounded. On the contrary, in the tribunal's opinion, all the requests made by the respondent in the final stages of the negotiation "substantially remained within the framework of the HOA".

The arbitrators first reasoned that while Italian case law tends to limit the scope of Art. 1337 CC to cases of unjustified withdrawal from negotiations, this restrictive interpretation is disputed by Italian doctrine, which considers that a party who did not withdraw from the negotiations may nevertheless be liable under Art. 1337 CC if it acts in violation of the principle of good faith. The arbitral tribunal followed this broader approach.

The arbitrators then examined the claimant's arguments in detail. They first held that the respondent's requests for additional funding was justified by the finding, in the due diligence reviews, that there was a large claim pending against Company Z for pollution, whereas the HOA stated that there was no "undisclosed litigation or the threats thereof". Also, the net value of the company had substantially decreased since it was determined and warranted in the HOA and similarly justified a request for additional funding.

The respondent's request, in the 13 May 1996 letter to the Region, that subsidized financing be provided was also not a violation of good faith. The respondent had initially only asked that the claimant use its best efforts to obtain such financing. However, the HOA provided that if subsidized financing could not be obtained and the price adjustment also foreseen in the HOA would be insufficient to compensate the respondent, then the parties would have to agree upon an alternative form of compensation. Thus, it could not be said that the respondent made mala fide additional requests to the initial provisions contained in the HOA.

The respondent also requested that Company Z be prevented from selling its products to third parties, arguing that the sale policy of Company Z deviated from the principles laid down in the Management of Transition Agreement and impaired the company's financial situation, as evidenced by a large number of unpaid invoices. The tribunal found that this request did not impose unbearable restrictions on Company Z, as alleged by the claimant. Rather, the respondent, as the future controlling shareholder, had a direct interest in protecting its market position by preventing sales made to competitors.

As to the respondent's demands in respect of a fresh water supply, the arbitrators noted that the HOA guaranteed that Company Z was fully operational. As fresh water was a raw material for the production cycle, in whose absence the plant could not be operational, it was neither unreasonable nor against good faith for the respondent to subordinate its entering into the

Final Purchase Agreement to a commitment by the Region in that respect. The arbitrators added that the respondent first negotiated with the claimant and only commenced direct discussions with the Region later on, when it became clear that settlement of this issue was beyond the claimant's reach.

Nor was the proceeding commenced in the court in country A by the respondent, seeking attachment of Company Z's shares, in violation of good faith. The respondent had advised the claimant that it would seek appropriate remedies in case the claimant and the Region would refuse to proceed with the implementation of the deal under the terms and conditions allegedly agreed upon. Thus, the respondent could not be blamed for having filed an action which in its opinion might have pulled the negotiations out of a deadlock.

The arbitral tribunal apportioned the costs of the arbitration. It reasoned that, on the one hand, the claimant's claim was rejected but its contention that the HOA did not have a binding character, which constituted a substantial part of the discussion and award, was upheld. On the other hand, the respondent's counterclaims required a "considerable amount of time and attention" by the tribunal and the claimant as these counterclaims were only withdrawn at a late stage in the arbitration. The arbitrators therefore held that the costs should be shared in the proportion of two thirds for the claimant and one third for the respondent.

The arbitral then exercised its discretionary power to reach the "equitable" decision that each party should bear its expenses, including lawyers' fees.

Excerpt

[1]   "The legal ground upon which claimant rests its claim against respondent is Art. 1337 of the Italian Civil Code (CC) which provides:

> "*Trattative e responsabilità precontrattuale. Le parti, nello svolgimento delle trattative e nella formazione del contratto, devono comportarsi secondo buona fede*. [Negotiations and pre-contractual liability. The parties shall act according to good faith in the contract's negotiation and formation.]"

[2]   "Indeed, according to claimant, during the negotiations of the Final Purchase Agreement contemplated by the Heads of Agreement [HOA], respondent behaved with plain bad faith, causing thus damages which claimant seeks to recover in the present litigation. In short, claimant contends that, during the negotiations, respondent made additional requests not contemplated by the HOA and which overcame the limit of reasonableness such as: (i) request for additional funding, (ii) guarantees with respect to the subsidised financing,

(iii) guarantees from the Region with respect to the allocation of fresh water, (iv) imposition on Company Z of a sale policy deviating from the Management of Transition Agreement which prevented the company from selling its products to third parties. Besides, respondent never fulfilled its obligation to submit a viable and complete industrial plan for Company Z nor undertook concrete technical commitments as concerns the plant. Furthermore, respondent gave only a generic assurance about the approval of the transaction by its Government. Lastly, respondent did refuse, on fallacious grounds, to pay a substantial part of the sale price of the finished products ordered and shipped to its affiliated company, i.e., Y International Ltd, and to deliver a bank guarantee for future consignments; respondent refused also to procure a bank guarantee for the payment of the deferred price of Company Z's shares, when requested to do so by claimant which, at this time, entertained legitimate doubts as to the respondent's solvability. Respondent's request for the seizure of Company Z's shares filed with the court in country A is also a clear indication of respondent's bad faith during the whole negotiations.

[3] "According to claimant, respondent's conduct should lead the arbitral tribunal to find that respondent conducted the negotiations in a manner contrary to the principle of good faith as set out by Art. 1337 CC; therefore, based on this finding, the arbitral tribunal should condemn respondent to indemnify claimant for all the losses incurred as a consequence of such a behavior.

[4] "Prior to discussing the issue of respondent's responsibility as per Art. 1337 CC, a preliminary question is to be examined by the arbitral tribunal. Indeed, since the above-mentioned Article sets out a pre-contractual liability, i.e., a liability in tort, the execution of a binding agreement must necessarily exclude any remedy founded on Art. 1337 CC. As decided by the Italian *Corte di Cassazione* [Supreme Court]:

> '*Il fatto che l'accordo si formi a condizioni diverse da quelle che si sarebbero avute se una delle parti non avesse tenuto verso l'altra un comportamento contrario a buona fede non rileva come ipotesi di responsabilità precontrattuale ex Art. 1337 CC perchè la configurabilità di questa è preclusa dalla intervenuta conclusione del contratto.* [The fact that the agreement is concluded on different terms than those which would have been agreed if one party had not acted against good faith vis-á-vis the other party does not give rise to pre-contractual liability under Art. 1337 CC because [pre-contractual liability] is precluded by the conclusion of the contract.] (see Cass. 16 April 1994, no. 3621).'

[5] "It should here be recalled that respondent based its counterclaims, in particular the one dealing with specific performance, on the ground that the

HOA together with the letters of 13 May 1996 were to be considered as a preliminary agreement obliging the parties to execute the Final Purchase Agreement. True, in the course of the proceedings, respondent waived its counterclaim related to the specific performance of the sale of Company Z's shares, but did not give up this legal construction to counter-claimant's requests.

[6] "Should respondent's contention succeed, then no remedy based on Art. 1337 CC would be available to claimant, since the application of this legal provision is precluded by the execution of a binding contract (cf. Cass. no. 3621, quoted above). On the other hand, to award damages to claimant on another legal basis than the one which is stated in claimant's prayers for relief would amount to an 'ultra petita' or 'extra petita' award which could be set aside in application of Art. 190(c) of the Swiss PIL Act (see the decision of the Swiss Federal Tribunal of 30 April 1992, commented by F. Perret, *Les conclusions et leurs causes juridiques au regard de la règle: ne eat judex ultra petita partium*, in *Etudes de droit international en l'honneur de Pierre Lalive*, Bâle, 1993, p. 595 et seq.).

[7] "Therefore, claimant's claims can only succeed if the arbitral tribunal decides that the HOA are to be qualified as a mere letter of intent or as a so-called 'punctuactio' or list of points drafted solely for the purpose of expressing or formalising the intent to negotiate and which are merely interlocutory or preliminary to the execution of a binding agreement, which is claimant's contention."

I. HOA ARE NOT BINDING CONTRACT?

[8] "Whether the HOA integrated with the letters of 13 May 1996 are to be considered as a preliminary agreement or as a 'punctuactio' is thus a preliminary issue which is decisive for the decision to be rendered by the arbitral tribunal, since there is no room for an application of Art. 1337 CC when a binding contract has already been executed by the parties.

[9] "To decide on this preliminary issue, the arbitral tribunal must test the common intention of the parties, which is a rule set out by Art. 1362 CC, and, for that purpose, the arbitral tribunal shall rely on several criteria such as the wording of the document at stake and the parties' conduct during and after the signature of the said document (see BIANCA, Il contratto, Milan, 1998, p. 390).

[10] "In the opinion of the arbitral tribunal, a mere reading of the HOA shows that an intention to be contractually bound was negatived. Firstly, its Preamble recites that 'the seller is interested' and that 'the buyer is interested', respectively to sell and to purchase 100 % of the capital share of Company Z. .... The parties expressed thus an interest to conclude the transaction but did not commit themselves to execute a future agreement.

[11] "Furthermore, two essential issues are left unaddressed in the HOA. Indeed, the purchase price is subject to adjustment deriving on the one hand from the results of the due diligence reviews (see Art. 4) and, on the other hand, from the possible unavailability of the subsidised financing guaranteed by Art. 11.1(o) (see Art. 5). However, the above-mentioned contractual provisions do not set up the terms and conditions of this possible adjustment which was to be defined in the Final Purchase Agreement (see Art. 5 *in fine*). This leads the arbitral tribunal to find that the purchase price has not been determined in the HOA and that it is not determinable, although this element is an essential one in a sale contract.

[12] "In addition, with respect to the seller's representations and warranties, Art. 12 of the HOA leaves completely open the issue of the indemnification which is to be dealt with in the Final Purchase Agreement. True, with respect to that issue, the parties could have relied on the legal remedies provided by Italian law, i.e., recess from the contract or reduction of the sale price and payment of damages. However, this was not their intent, since they agreed that specific contractual remedies were to be defined in the Final Purchase Agreement.

[13] "Art. 3 of the HOA is another clause which leads the arbitral tribunal to consider that the document did not oblige the parties to execute the Final Purchase Agreement. In the said clause, the parties merely envisaged that the Final Purchase Agreement should be executed within two weeks from completion of the due diligence reviews but did not set a fixed term within which the said Agreement should be signed.

[14] "It should here be underscored that Art. 3 is to be read in correlation with Art. 16 of the HOA which provides that the seller shall refrain from negotiating with any third party for the sale of the capital stock of Company Z 'from the date of these HOA until three weeks after completion of due diligence reviews'. In the opinion of the arbitral tribunal, this provision might mean that the execution of the Final Purchase Agreement was depending upon the result of the due diligence reviews. In case this result would cause a downward adjustment of the purchase price unacceptable for claimant, then claimant, once the deadline set forth in Art. 16 expired, was free to initiate negotiations with third parties. This is another decisive element which leads the arbitral tribunal to consider that any contractual intention, i.e., any intention of the parties to be bound to execute the Final Purchase Agreement, was negatived by the terms of the HOA.

[15] "That the HOA are to be considered as a pre-contractual document is supported by the subsequent behaviour of the parties, in particular of respondent. This results from the various meetings between the parties and from the several exchanges of letters occurring between them from 5 August 1995 until 13 May 1996. During this whole period, respondent attempted to solve the issues which were left unaddressed in the HOA or which emerged thereafter. . . .

[16] "The language used by the parties, in particular by respondent in the exchanges of letters and memoranda which followed the execution of the HOA, reflects the parties' negotiations with respect to specific points to be inserted in the Final Purchase Agreement. For instance, in the letter of 21 December 1995 addressed by respondent's merchant bank E to respondent and claimant, the solution of the several pending issues were defined as 'conditions to be fulfilled for the signing of the contract'; and the same memorandum ended with the sentence: 'Commence contractual negotiations on 22 January 1996'. Besides, the HOA are identified in the said document by the acronym 'LOI 5 August' which undoubtedly means 'letter of intent'. Thus, the drafter of the above-cited letter considered that the document of 5 August 1995 was tantamount to a mere 'punctuactio' recalling the points upon which an agreement had already been reached. . . .

[17] "Furthermore, by its letter of 10 April 1996 addressed to respondent, merchant bank E set out the basis upon which respondent would be prepared to complete the acquisition of the share capital of Company Z and advised claimant that 'both parties must determine their position finally and immediately' and that 'the letter remains open for acceptance, to be communicated in writing, until close of business on Friday 12 April 1996'. . . .

[18] "Such a language shows beyond any doubts that the parties were still in the process of negotiating what should be the Final Purchase Agreement. Indeed, claimant was invited by the said letter to accept respondent's position on certain issues which were considered by respondent as a condition 'sine qua non' for its entering into the Final Purchase Agreement. In other words, at this stage, had claimant refused to commit itself with respect to these issues, the negotiations would have failed and no binding contract would have been executed by the parties, although later on respondent softened its position on certain of the said issues.

[19] "The draft of the Final Purchase Agreement, although not submitted to claimant, constitutes another piece of evidence as to the pre-contractual nature of the HOA. Indeed, the said draft not only did address the issues left open in the HOA, such as the mechanism of the downward adjustment of the purchase price, but also added certain clauses, such as the one dealing with claimant's obligation not to compete with respondent, which the parties did not contemplate in the HOA.

[20] "It should here be underscored that E's letter addressed to claimant on 13 May 1996 does not support respondent's contention as to the binding effect of the HOA with the subsequent integration of the said letter. True, Witness 16 countersigned the abovementioned letter and therefore accepted, on behalf of claimant, all respondent's requests regarding the still pending issues, except that of the fresh water supply which were dealt directly with the Region; however, the letter addressed to this public authority on the same date was left

unanswered, which means that the Region did not want to commit itself with respect to that issue.

[21]   "In this connection, respondent cannot contend that it would have executed the Final Purchase Agreement without any guarantee from the Region on the fresh water supply issue . . . because this contention is in contradiction with Witness 16's own statements . . . and with respondent's letter addressed to claimant on 10 July 1996, which clearly indicated that respondent was prepared to finalise the share purchase agreement only after receiving 'the acceptance by the Region of the conditions set out in the letter which E sent to the Region on 13 May 1996'. . . .

[22]   "Therefore, a binding final agreement could only be achieved had the Region agreed upon the terms and conditions expressed in E's letter of 13 May 1996 addressed to the Region and approved the engagements subscribed by claimant. This did not occur. Failing such an agreement. Respondent did not intend to enter into a binding agreement with claimant and clearly expressed this intent to claimant.

[23]   "Based on these considerations, the arbitral tribunal decides that the HOA with the subsequent integration through the letters of 13 May 1996 do not constitute an agreement obliging the parties to execute the Final Purchase Agreement, which means that claimant is not precluded to seek legal remedies based on Art. 1337 CC.

[24]   "These considerations are totally in line with Italian case law. In particular, in a recent case, the *Corte di Cassazione* decided as follows:

'*affinchè possa ritenersi sussistente l'accordo in materia di vendita (o prelimi-nare di vendita), non è sufficiente che nel documento sottoscritto dalle parti siano stati individuati l'oggetto della vendita, il prezzo e le modalità di paga-mento, ma occorre che lo scritto esprima la volontà negoziale, consistente nella disposizione immediatamente operativa sulla situazione giuridica esistente, ovvero il comando cioè la regola obbligatoria del comportamento dei sotto-scriventi.*' [for a sale agreement or preliminary sale agreement to be deemed to exist, it is not sufficient that the document signed by the parties specify the object of the sale, the price and the manner of payment. The written docu-ment must also state the intention to conclude an agreement, that is, to directly affect the existing legal situation, i.e., an order or mandatory regulation of the signatories' behavior] (Cass. 17 March 1994, no. 2548)"

II.   GOOD FAITH NEGOTIATIONS (ART. 1337 ITALIAN CC)

[25]   "Having decided that no binding contract could have resulted from the execution of the HOA together with the letters of 13 May 1996, the arbitral

tribunal must now discuss the issue of whether or not respondent did conduct the negotiations with claimant in a manner in contrast with good faith.

[26]   "It should here be recalled that the party which fails to meet the requisite of Art. 1337 CC commits a 'culpa in contrahendo' and therefore is obliged to indemnify the other party for any damages incurred as a result of the breach of its pre-contractual duty to act during the course of the negotiations in conformity with the principle of good faith.

[27]   "Italian case law tends to limit the scope of Art. 1337 CC to cases of unjustified withdrawal from negotiations (see Cass. 18 October 1980, no. 5610 in Riv. Dir. Comm., 1982, II, 167; Cass. 13 March 1990, no. 2623; Cass. 25 February 1992, no. 2335; and Cass. 1 February 1995, no. 1163). If the arbitral tribunal were to follow such a restrictive approach, then claimant's claim would certainly fail since it results from the circumstances of the present case that respondent did not interrupt the negotiations but, on the contrary, insisted on the finalisation of the deal, however on certain conditions which were not accepted by claimant and by the Region. In particular, respondent filed a petition for the judicial sequestration of Company Z's shares showing by this legal action its intention to implement the deal.

[28]   "However, the restrictive interpretation of Art. 1337 CC has been disputed by Italian doctrine which considers that a party which has not withdrawn from the negotiations may nevertheless incur an extra-contractual liability if it adopts a conduct contrary to the principle of good faith (cf.: SCOGNAMIGLIO, Dei contratti in generale, in Commentario del Codice Civile, Scialoja and Branca, gen. eds., Arts. 1321-1352 CC, Bologna, 1970, p. 203; CARRESI, Il contratto, in Trattato di Diritto Civile e Commerciale, Cicu and Messineo, gen. eds., Vol. XXI, Part 2, Milan, 1987, p. 731; BIANCA, Il contratto, op. cit., p. 171; CUFFARO, Responsabilità precontrattuale, in Enc. dir., XXXIX, Milan, p. 1265).

[29]   "The arbitral tribunal shall follow the trend of the Italian case-law and legal doctrine mentioned above and shall examine hereafter if respondent's conduct during the negotiations was such as to be in contrast with good faith, although respondent was not the party which interrupted the negotiations.

[30]   "As it is stated before, it is claimant's contention that respondent behaved during the negotiations with plain bad faith making unreasonable demands whilst resisting to claimant's legitimate requests. As concerns the alleged mala fide demands of respondent, the following can be said:

[31]   "The arbitral tribunal finds that all respondent's requests submitted to claimant during the negotiations substantially remained within the framework of the HOA, to the exception of the guarantee regarding the composition with creditors which anyhow was waived by respondent. . . . In this respect, it should here be noted that a certain claim which surfaced as a result of the due diligence

reviews was directly connected with the issue of the composition with creditors. On this item, claimant could by no means object to respondent's request to be compensated, had the party making that certain claim succeeded since the seller represented and warranted that, at the time of the execution of the HOA, there was no 'undisclosed litigation or the threats thereof' (see Art. 11.1(e)).

[32] "The same comments can be made with respect to the other issues which emerged after the completion of the due diligence reviews. For instance, according to Art. 11. 1(n) of the HOA, claimant warranted that the net asset value of the Company, as at the Closing Date, shall not be lower than a certain amount 'which was the net value of the company as per its balance sheet of 31 December 1994'. However, as of 31 December 1995, the net asset value of Company Z substantially decreased. Respondent was thus entitled to be financially compensated by claimant, reason for which it requested the injection of additional funds by claimant. . . .

[33] "The subsidised financing is another issue, in respect to which claimant considers that the final request made by respondent before the breaking of the negotiations was excessive and in mala fide. Indeed, in the letter of 13 May 1996 addressed to claimant, respondent simply requested to claimant to use its best efforts in view of obtaining the subsidised financing; however, in the interconnected letter to the Region of the same date, respondent requested . . . that subsidised financing be actually provided on or before 30 September 1996 and that, in case of delay, claimant and/or the Region insured the coverage of its financial needs.

[34] "The arbitral tribunal does not consider that the requests by respondent resulting from the two interconnected letters of 13 May 1996 were in violation of its duty of good faith in conducting the negotiations. In fact, the HOA contain two provisions at Arts. 5 and 11.1(o) according to which if the subsidised financing contemplated at Art. 11 were not received notwithstanding the bona fide efforts of seller and purchaser, the purchase price had to be adjusted consequently (Art. 5). Moreover, Art. 11.1(o).3 stated that, should the adjustment of price foreseen in Art. 5 be insufficient to compensate the purchaser for the non-availability of such financing, then the parties would have to agree upon alternative forms of compensation.

[35] "In consideration of the above, the arbitral tribunal finds that the requests by respondent as incorporated in the two letters of 13 May 1996, and especially those addressed to the Region, do not constitute mala fide additional requests to the initial provisions contained in the HOA.

[36] "The issue of the fresh water supply is encompassed by Art. 11.1(k) of the HOA. According to the said clause, the seller guaranteed that 'the Company is fully operational, with plant and facilities in good working order and with all the

necessary infrastructure in place'. As confirmed by certain witnesses ... fresh water was to be considered as a raw material for the production of the product in the absence of which the plant could not be operational. ... Besides, the dramatic impact of the lack of fresh water on the operation of the plant has been emphasised by Company Z in its letter dated 22 December 1995 to the Region. ... Respondent, as a responsible and diligent contractor, could only but show serious concerns with respect to this issue, even more as the water, available in limited quantities from the bore wells, was polluted and was thus inappropriate for the production cycle.

[37] "When respondent became aware that the allocation of fresh water from a nearby dam depended upon a decision of a political nature which was beyond claimant's authority, it resolved itself to involve the Region which was empowered to make allowance of fresh water in an emergency situation. Besides, respondent was led by claimant to take such a step since claimant, when confronted with this issue, did limit itself to pass to respondent information received from the Regional Authority. ...

[38] "In this connection, it should here be noted that the fresh water supply requested to the Region as per letter of 13 May 1996 did not deviate in quantity and quality from the information given by the Region and communicated to respondent by claimant's letter of 30 April 1996 ... except for the quantity to be supplied until the end of the year 1996, which had to come exclusively from the dam. It should be further noted that the Region was prepared to commit itself to supply fresh water in the quantities and quality required by respondent, even more as funds ... were available for the implementation of a project of a waste water purifying plant to be installed in the vicinity. However, the Region did not intend to assume any financial commitment in case the quantities and the quality guaranteed could not be obtained. ...

[39] "As the Region did not intend or could not accept the financial consequences of a possible disregard of the guarantees given in respect to the fresh water issue, it did not sign the letter of 13 May 1996 addressed to it, and did not give its consent to claimant's engagement of the same date.

[40] "Considering the utmost importance for the plant of a continuous supply of fresh water in quantities and quality which would permit the plant to operate profitably, it appears not unreasonable or against good faith for respondent to subordinate its entering into the Final Purchase Agreement to engagements concerning the supply of fresh water needed by the plant and, in case of lack or deficiencies in the required supply, to the fixing of the ensuing compensation. The arbitral tribunal finds that, having the seller started the negotiations guaranteeing with the HOA, at Art. 11.1(k), a certain status of the plant, i.e. that the 'plant and facilities (are) in good working order and with all the necessary infrastructure in place', it was not unreasonable for the prospective

purchaser to request compensation in case of discrepancy between the warranted situation and the actual one.

[41]   "The other criticisms addressed by claimant to respondent's conduct during the negotiations deserve only few additional comments. As concerns the sale policy of Company Z resulting from the Management of Transition Agreement, the arbitral tribunal finds that such policy did not impose on Company Z unbearable restrictions. It was indeed the direct interest of the company not to flood the market with huge quantities of finished products. On the other hand, respondent was to become the controlling shareholder of the company and therefore had to protect its future position which could be jeopardised by sales made to aggressive competitors. Furthermore, the sales made by Company Z during the interim period, did indeed impair the financial situation of the company and this is evidenced by the unpaid invoices amounting by the end of the year 1995 to a certain amount. . . . Respondent had therefore good reasons to complain with the company's actual sale policy which deviated from the principles that laid behind the Management of Transition Agreement.

[42]   "Claimant cannot possibly contend that the problem which arose with respect to the delivery of a certain quantity of finished products to Y International Ltd constituted another example of the bad faith with which respondent conducted the negotiations. First of all, the sale to a respondent's affiliated company was a separate deal which should have had no impact on the negotiations of the Final Purchase Agreement. Furthermore, as concerns the bad quality of the products alleged by Y, it is true that the material was inspected . . . prior to its shipment; but it is also true that Company Z production during the second half of the year 1995 might have been defective since the fresh water used in the production cycle was coming from the bore wells which contained a polluting substance. . . . Under these circumstances, it is conceivable that the shipment consigned by Y International Ltd to the ultimate purchaser did not meet the required specifications. This commercial dispute between Company Z and Y is at present pending before the court of W. . . .

[43]   "The arbitral tribunal believes that the commercial incident referred to above contributed to the deteriorating of the negotiating atmosphere between the parties. Evidence of such relevance of the issue is also provided by the letters exchanged by the parties after May 1996, where the issue was examined in conjunction with those more strictly linked to the acquisition of Company Z's shares. . . . Notwithstanding this contribution to the deteriorating of the relations among the Parties, the tribunal finds that this incident, having possible objective grounds and being typical of a common commercial transaction, cannot be considered as evidence of a bad faith behaviour of respondent in conducting the negotiations for the acquisition of Company Z's shares.

[44]   "Likewise, claimant cannot blame respondent for having refused to provide a bank guarantee for the deferred payment of Company Z's shares; this was indeed a new request of claimant since the parties in the HOA had foreseen a corporate guarantee to be given by an affiliated company of the Y Group, preferably an EU company (see Art. 7 of the HOA). Such a new request is not considered by the arbitral tribunal as directly linked to and imposed by the difficulties experienced by the two parties in their commercial transaction; consequently, the refusal by respondent to provide a bank guarantee cannot be considered evidence of bad faith in negotiating the terms of the contract.

[45]   "Claimant's accusations addressed to respondent for having failed to timely proceed with the procedure to obtain the necessary approvals or to submit a complete industrial plan are also without merits. Irrespective of the vagueness of such contention, which by itself is a sufficient ground for its dismissal, the arbitral tribunal notes that it did not make sense for respondent to formally request approvals ... or to prepare a complete and concrete industrial plan as long as such an important issue as that of the fresh water supply was still pending.

[46]   "Lastly, the arbitral tribunal does not see in the filing by respondent with the court in country A of a request for the seizure of Company Z's shares an act in contrast with good faith. It should here be underscored that respondent duly advised claimant that it will seek appropriate remedies in case claimant and the Region would refuse to proceed with the implementation of the deal under the terms and conditions allegedly agreed upon. ... Therefore, the action brought before the court in country A could not come as a surprise, even more as the letter of 13 May 1996 addressed by merchant bank E to the Region was never answered. Moreover, Witness 12 had informed respondent by letter dated 18 July 1996 that from now on no positive outcome could be expected from the Region. ...

[47]   "Under these circumstances, respondent cannot be blamed for having initiated a legal procedure which might, in respondent's opinion, have had the effect to pull the negotiations out of the deadlock, but that did not occur.

[48]   "On the other side, in March/April 1997 claimant, without advising respondent, initiated with Company N discussions for the sale of the plant whilst respondent was making a last attempt with the Regional Authority to re-start the negotiations. ... Eventually, respondent learnt by press article published in *Il Sole 24 Ore* of 3 February 1998 that the N transaction was achieved. ... Claimant was certainly entitled to start negotiations with a third party as provided by Art. 16 of the HOA.

[49]   "Based on the foregoing considerations, the arbitral tribunal concludes that respondent, when negotiating with claimant the acquisition of Company Z's shares, did not act in contrast with good faith; considering all the circumstances of the case, respondent's requests were neither unreasonable nor against

good faith. Consequently, claimant's claims based on Art. 1337 CC are to be dismissed."

III.   COSTS

[50]   "Pursuant to Art. 31 of the applicable ICC Rules, the arbitral tribunal must decide on the costs of the proceedings. In the practice of international arbitration, institutional (such as ICC) or ad hoc, arbitral tribunals have full discretion in this matter. As to the costs of the arbitration proper, (i.e. the administrative costs of the ICC, expenses and arbitrators fees), it is generally accepted that the winning party should be compensated to some extent with regard to its advances. However, there is no such general principle as concerns the contribution to the expenses and lawyers' fees of the winning party where considerable differences do exist among arbitrators (see ICC case no. 6401/ ... p. 125 et seq.).
[51]   "In the present case, the arbitral tribunal has rejected the claim by claimant that respondent behaved in bad faith during the negotiations for the acquisition of Company Z's shares. However, the arbitral tribunal has upheld the basic contention of claimant that the HOA executed in 1995 had no binding character, rejecting thus the contrary contention sustained by respondent. The arbitral tribunal underscores that a substantive part of the litigation, as well as of the present Award ... had to deal with this issue.
[52]   "The arbitral tribunal notes, in addition, that respondent waived its counterclaim relating to the specific performance of the sale of Company Z's shares at the arbitral session of 16 December 1998 when it was officially informed by the Chairman of the arbitral tribunal that Company Z's plant had been actually sold to a third party; moreover, all other counterclaims by respondent were maintained almost till the end of the procedure and were considered withdrawn only in March 1999 for the failure to effect the payment of the requested advances. ... Therefore, a considerable amount of time and attention had to be devoted to these issues by the arbitral tribunal and by claimant.
[53]   "In consideration of the above, the arbitral tribunal decides that the arbitration costs, fixed by the ICC Court at US$ 500,000, have to be shared in the proportion of two thirds for claimant and one third for respondent.
[54]   "As to the costs and expenses incurred by the parties for their legal representation and defence in the procedure, the arbitral tribunal, taking into account the absence of generally accepted legal principles and the variety of arbitral decisions in this regard, and considering the characteristics of the present litigation and its outcome, decides that the parties shall each support the expenses incurred by it, including lawyers' fees. The arbitral tribunal is of the opinion that this solution is an equitable one which remains within the discretionary powers recognized to it in this respect."

Final award on jurisdiction in case no. 11663 of 2003

Parties:	Claimants: (1) Company A (nationality not indicated); (2) Company B (nationality not indicated) Respondent: Company C (nationality not indicated)
Place of arbitration:	Paris, France
Published in:	Unpublished
Subject matters:	– penalty (contractual) – conditions for relief from forfeiture – calculation of damages – costs (legal)

Facts

On 26 October 1999, company EFD, owned by Mr. RB, entered into a Memorandum of Understanding with the Ministry of Oil and Mineral Resources of Country W (the Ministry) by which they agreed to start negotiating a crude oil production sharing agreement in respect of an area in Country W. EFD subsequently became a subsidiary of C International.

On 31 March 2000, company C, also a subsidiary of C International, concluded a Shared Management Agreement (SMA) with two other companies, A and B, in order to define their respective rights and obligations with respect to the conduct of future petroleum operations under the production sharing agreement being negotiated with the Ministry. The SMA established a Management Committee and a joint account for the project and set forth the Participating Interests of the parties – that is, the percentage interest of each party in the rights and obligations, privileges and liabilities derived from the SMA – as being fifty percent for A, thirty percent for C and twenty percent for B. The SMA also provided, inter alia, for the sharing of costs and expenses of the operations, for the procedures to be followed if a party failed to make a required payment and for the consequences of any default in payment. In particular, its Art. 8.7(a) provided that if a defaulting party remained in default for more than sixty days after receipt of a default notice it was obliged upon request of a non-defaulting party to forfeit and assign its Participating Interest to that party. Art. 8.7(b) provided that, notwithstanding the forfeiture and assignment of its Participating

Interest, the defaulting party remained liable for its proportionate share of costs, expenses and penalties and remained obliged to perform certain defined acts. Arts. 4.1(c) and 4.2 provided that in the event of a material breach of the SMA, the PSA or any other agreement to which A and C were parties relating to the Operations, that C could be removed as Operator. The SMA also provided for the application of the laws of England and contained a clause for ICC arbitration of disputes in Paris.

On 31 March 2000, A, B and C also concluded a Participation Agreement in which they made a number of financial commitments relating to the project. In particular, A and C were to provide irrevocable letters of credit to the Ministry after signing the production sharing agreement; C and B were also to provide back-up letters of credit to A within thirty days of the production sharing agreement becoming effective.

On 2 April 2000, A, B and C concluded the Production Sharing Agreement (PSA) with the Ministry and with W Company for Investment in Oil and Minerals (WICOM). The PSA became effective on 2 September 2000, upon ratification by the Parliament of Country W. The PSA, whose provisions were supplemented by the provisions in the SMA, granted to A, B, C and WICOM (collectively, the Contractor) certain rights for the exploration, development and production of oil in the defined area. In return the Contractor agreed to, among other things, undertake minimum work and expenditure obligations for two successive exploration periods. The PSA provided that the Contractor would deliver to the Ministry within thirty days from the date on which the PSA became effective an irrevocable letter of credit in the amount of the minimum financial commitment. It also provided that C would be the Operator during the exploration period. The PSA contained a clause referring disputes to ICC arbitration.

On 2 April 2000, A, B, C and WICOM also concluded a Joint Operating Agreement (JOA) establishing the parties' respective rights and obligations with regard to operations under the PSA. The JOA provided that it was governed by the laws of England and for arbitration of disputes by ICC arbitration in Paris.

A dispute arose between the parties when C allegedly breached its obligations under the SMA and the Participation Agreement by failing, inter alia, to deliver in a timely manner the letters of credit and to make timely payments of cash calls under the agreements. Also, C allegedly failed to comply with the "SMA Determination" issued by the Management Committee on 28 April 2001, removing C as Operator following its failure to meet its financial obligations under the agreements and appointing A in its place.

On 9 July 2001, A and B filed a joint request for ICC arbitration against C based on the arbitration agreements found in the SMA and JOA. C objected to the arbitrators' jurisdiction. On 31 July 2002, the arbitral tribunal issued a Partial

Award on Jurisdiction, holding that the tribunal was properly constituted and had jurisdiction over the parties' claims and counterclaims. This was referred to in the final award as the jurisdiction phase.

In September 2002, C's position in respect of the dispute changed following a change in the control of C International. The new Board of Directors appointed Mr. RB, the acting president of C, to represent C in the proceedings. Mr. RB on behalf of C no longer denied C's past violations of the agreements, argued that the prior management was dishonest and stated that he wished to settle the dispute in order to preserve C's Participating Interest in the project. In November 2002, C withdrew its counterclaim.

By the present Final Award, the arbitral tribunal denied C's request for relief from forfeiture and granted A and B's claims.

The arbitral tribunal noted at the outset – and later repeated in the award – that although both sides were requesting equitable relief in addition to other forms of relief in the arbitration, such requests did not amount to a request to the tribunal to act as an amiable compositeur or ex aequo et bono.

Though no longer contesting that it violated its contractual obligations, C argued that Art. 8 of the SMA was a "draconian" provision amounting to a penalty and as such was not enforceable under the applicable English law. In the alternative, the tribunal should exercise its discretion to grant C temporary relief from forfeiture to allow it sufficient time to arrange for financing to pay its past debts and to ensure its future financial commitments to the project.

Based on the relevant English jurisprudence, the tribunal held that it should determine whether the forfeiture of C's Participating Interest under Art. 8 was a penalty upon the terms of the SMA and the relevant circumstances at the time that the agreement was made. It reasoned that the SMA was one of a number of agreements relating to the same project. In particular, the PSA provided for the sharing of costs and expenses because the operations were expected to be costly and each party was expected to contribute according to its respective Participating Interest. One party's default would be the whole project at risk unless the other parties took over the defaulting party's burden. The arbitral tribunal concluded that the forfeiture obligation in Art. 8 was not oppressive but on the contrary provided "a fair and business-like arrangement designed to preserve a project". It also noted that the forfeiture provision reflects an international practice and was explicitly accepted by C at the time of negotiating the SMA.

The tribunal then considered whether it should grant equitable relief to C against forfeiture. It first reasoned that it was allowed to grant such relief under both the dispute resolution clause in the SMA, which expressly provided that a tribunal had the authority to award any remedy or relief proposed by the claimants or the respondent(s), and the applicable English law. It could also exercise this power in the case at issue because the requirements therefor under English law were met, that is, the forfeiture was of a possessory or proprietary interest and the primary purpose of the forfeiture provision in the contract was to secure a stated result (e.g., the payment of money) which can be attained when the matter comes before the court.

However, the arbitrators held that they should not grant C's request for relief. They expressed "considerable sympathy" for Mr. RB's efforts to reform C but concluded that the corporate entity with which A and B contracted remained the same and the change of management did not remove corporate responsibility for its past conduct. C had a long history of default which persisted to the time of the arbitration and in fact it had not yet tendered performance of its outstanding financial obligations but merely indicated that if relief against forfeiture were to be granted, it was confident of being able to procure the necessary finance to satisfy its past and future financial obligations. Equitable relief is typically granted, sparingly, in cases "where the party in default has been guilty of a single breach, which may have resulted from inadvertence, and in respect of which a prompt tender of performance is made". This was not the case here.

The arbitral tribunal dismissed C's argument that the claimants had waived any right to forfeiture by retaining one of C's defective letters of credit rather than returning it to C. The tribunal noted that a waiver in this case would have required an election on the part of the claimants not to require forfeiture of C's interest. The claimants did not make such election nor did they represent in any manner that they did not intend to rely on their legal rights.

The arbitrators then examined and granted all declaratory relief sought by the claimants in respect of both the project's operations and the forfeiture. They granted, inter alia, a declaration that C was in breach of the SMA, that the Management Committee properly determined that C was removed as Operator and replaced by A, that C forfeited its Participating Interest under the SMA due to its default and material breach and was obliged to assign its Participating Interest to A and B.

The tribunal also granted the claimant's request for specific performance, that is, that C be ordered to assign its Participating Interest to A and B and resign as Operator.

Finally, the arbitral tribunal granted damages and interest to A and B and held that C should bear the costs of the arbitration, including the jurisdiction phase, considering that the claimants had prevailed on all points. The tribunal did, however, reduce the amount of the claimants' legal, witness and other costs for the merits phase of the arbitration, finding them "somewhat high". The tribunal noted in particular that those costs included the costs of seven lawyers and one paralegal for claimants' legal team. It reasoned that while claimants' counsel "have every right to organize their work as they wish ... respondent should not be required to pay for it all".

Excerpt

[1]   "... [T]he essential facts in this case are not in dispute between claimants and respondent. Where there were differences with regard to the facts or their interpretation, respondent no longer relies on such differences as the basis of its case. ... In effect, C says to the tribunal: we admit that we defaulted on our obligations and caused harm to the claimants. That occurred under the former management; we are sorry; new management will right all the past wrongs and make claimants whole; we will assure you that we will meet our financial obligations in the future. Please give us another chance by exercising your powers of equity.

[2]   "Indeed both sides in this arbitration have requested the tribunal to grant them equitable relief in addition to other forms of relief. Claimants have requested a number of orders from the tribunal for specific performance by C of its contractual obligations. Respondent has requested relief from forfeiture of its Participating Interest, which is also an equitable remedy.

[3]   "The parties' requests for equitable relief are examined fully below. It should be said at this point only that, in requesting equitable remedies, the parties are not asking the tribunal to act as an *amiable compositeur* or *ex aequo et bono* (see Art. 17.3 of the ICC Rules[1] and [at [17]]).

[4]   "Since C no longer contests that its actions ... are violations of its contractual obligations, the tribunal must examine the two arguments which it presently relies upon in its defense and in requesting equitable relief. Its first argument is that the sanction of forfeiture under the SMA, Art. 8,[2] amounts to a penalty. As such, it is not enforceable as a matter of English law. Its second argument is that in the circumstances of this case, the provision for forfeiture should not be applied. Respondent requests the tribunal, in the exercise of its powers of equity, to grant temporary relief from forfeiture to allow respondent

---

1. Art. 17.3 of the ICC Rules reads:

   "3. The arbitral tribunal shall assume the powers of an *amiable compositeur* or decide *ex aequo et bono* only if the parties have agreed to grant it such powers."

2. Art. 8.7(a) of the SMA provided that if a defaulting party remains in default for more than sixty days after receipt of the default notice it shall upon request of a non-defaulting party forfeit and assign its Participating Interest to that party. Art. 8.7(b) provided that, notwithstanding the forfeiture and assignment, the defaulting party remained liable for its proportionate share of all costs, expenses and penalties and remained obliged to perform certain defined acts.

sufficient time to arrange for financing to pay its past debts and to ensure its future financial commitments to the project. The tribunal will now examine each of these arguments.

[5]   "C contends that the provisions of Art. 8.7(a) of the SMA (which Art. 5.4 Participation Agreement incorporates) contain draconian powers intended to ensure that each party made payment promptly, that on their face the powers would apply even to an extremely small failure to pay, and that the consequences of non-payment could (and would in this case) be wholly disproportionate to the breach. . . .

[6]   "According to C, there are two related doctrines in English law relevant to these provisions: the doctrine of penalties and that of relief against forfeiture. . . . Claimants rely on Art. 8 of the SMA in respect principally of two separate claims: C's failure to provide a conforming letter of credit as required by Art. 5.2.2 of the Participation Agreement, and C's failure to make certain cash calls. In respect of both defaults, the claimants sought forfeiture and assignment pursuant to Art. 8.7(a) of the SMA. In respect of the cash calls, they also relied on Art. 8.7(b) of the SMA. . . ."

I.   FORFEITURE OF PARTICIPATING INTEREST

1.   Forfeiture Provision in Agreements Amounts to Penalty (No)

[7]   The arbitral tribunal noted the English jurisprudence setting out the doctrine of penalties and the cases referred to by C, in particular the case decided by the Court of Appeal in *Nutting v. Baldwin* in 1995.

[8]   "In *Nutting v. Baldwin* [1995] 1 WLR 201, the Court had to consider rules of an association formed for the purpose of coordinating and financing the prosecution of claims by several Lloyds Names in respect of the activities of the managing agents of two Lloyds syndicates and other agents. The rules empowered a committee to levy subscriptions from members of the association. Some of the members failed to pay the subscriptions and the committee sought a declaration that the defaulting members were not entitled to a share in the amount recovered by way of settlement. The Court concluded:

'True it is that the rules of the association constitute a contract between the members, and true it is that by failing to pay their additional subscriptions in accordance with the rules the defendants are in breach of that contract. However, I accept the plaintiff's submission that it would be wrong to regard rule 6.6 as a penalty for breach of contract. In my judgement the essence of the contract between the members of the association is that the burden and benefit of enforcement of the members' claims against the agents should be shared between all members. There is a pooling of all such claims and a pooling of contributions in the form of subscriptions for the purpose of financing the enforcement of such claims. It is an essential part of the arrangement that if a member ceases to contribute to the pool of financial contributions to the costs of pursuing the claims there should be power for the committee on behalf of all the members to determine that he shall cease to share in the pool of benefit represented by the proceeds of such claims. In other words, a member who fails to shoulder his share of the burden of this essentially multilateral arrangement runs the risk of being excluded from his share of the benefit of the arrangement. This is not a penalty for breach of contract. It is an essential part of the pooling arrangement thereby effected.' (208B-D)

[9]　"It is apparent from the judgments referred to above that this tribunal should decide the question whether or not Art. 8.7(a) is a penalty upon the terms of the SMA and the relevant circumstances judged at the time that the agreement was made. As already mentioned, it was one of a number of agreements, and Art. 5.4 of the Participation Agreement expressly incorporated Art. 8 of the SMA, including Art. 8.7(a).

[10]　"Under the PSA, C and the claimants, as Contractor, were jointly liable to conduct the Operations. . . . Nevertheless, among themselves they made arrangements for the sharing of costs and expenses in carrying out those operations. They did so because the operations were expected to be costly, and, although there might be a good return, there was a risk that the expenditure would not be recovered. Each party was expected to contribute according to its respective Participating Interest. If one defaulted, the whole project would be put at risk unless the others (or one of them) took over the burden of the defaulting party. Although not referred to as joint venturers, they treated the project as if it were a joint venture.

[11]　"The SMA and the Participation Agreement set out the terms of the arrangements made between C and the claimants . . . including Art. 8.7 of the SMA, which provided what would happen in the event of a default as to any payment provided for in that agreement. Art. 5.4 of the Participation Agreement also provided that any failure by a party to provide a required letter of credit within the specified time period would constitute a default under Art. 8 of the SMA, unless and until the defaulting party cured the default.

[12]　"In considering whether or not the default provisions were penal, the tribunal has considered the purpose of the provisions as well as their consequences. We have done so as at the time the SMA and other agreements were made. At that time, C was appointed Operator because, according to the evidence . . . C insisted upon that role. Although its Participating Interest was

smaller than that of A, C was in no sense in an inferior bargaining position whereby it would be dominated by A.

[13]   "Mr. RB was part of the team that negotiated the agreements. In reviewing the SMA, B's representative asked Mr. RB if the forfeiture provision which became Art. 8.7(a) was too harsh. Mr. RB replied that it was acceptable, and B was advised that it was standard practice in the oil and gas industry. . . . This advice was borne out by the AIPN [Association of International Petroleum Negotiators] model form international operating agreement, 1995 . . . which includes an alternative clause on lines similar to Art. 8.7(a).

[14]   "The SMA is a commercial agreement concluded between three corporations, each of which had an interest in a joint project. Art. 8.6(e) stated in clear terms that it was a 'fundamental principle' of the SMA that each Party paid its Participating Interest share of all amounts due under that agreement as and when required. The Participation Agreement incorporated this provision in respect of a failure to provide a required letter of credit within the specified time limit (Art. 5.4). This statement of principle reflected part of the scheme of the transaction dealing with joint rights and the balancing of risks and rewards. At the same time, it made clear from the outset the consequences of a default because a default by one party unless remedied by one or other of the parties could jeopardize the whole project. No one party was singled out for special treatment; the consequences of a default by any party would be the same. . . .

[15]   "Having considered the terms of the agreements, including the remedies for default, and all the relevant circumstances, the tribunal is convinced that Art. 8.7(a) of the SMA is not oppressive. On the contrary, it provides a fair and business-like arrangement designed to preserve a project in a case of a specified default. Accordingly, the tribunal finds that neither Art. 8.7(a) of the SMA nor Art. 5.4 of the Participation Agreement are penal and that both are enforceable according to their terms."

2. Relief Against Forfeiture

[16]   "If, as the tribunal has concluded, the 'forfeiture' provisions of Art. 8.7(a) of the SMA are not unenforceable as a penalty, the respondent seeks to invoke the equitable jurisdiction of the tribunal to grant relief against forfeiture. It is common ground that the tribunal has jurisdiction to grant such relief in an appropriate case – not only by reason of Art. 15.1(b) of the SMA . . . but also since the power of a tribunal to grant such relief forms part of English law, which the parties have expressly chosen to govern their relationship.

[17]   "As we have observed [at [3]] above, the power and, indeed, the obligation of the tribunal to apply principles of equity as developed in the English courts as well as principles of common law, is not to be confused with a power to

decide *ex aequo et bono* or to act as *amiables compositeurs*, which the tribunal, having been given no such power under the contract, is not entitled to do.

[18] "The equitable doctrine of relief against forfeiture forms part of English law – albeit originally deriving from the practices of the former courts of equity, which were merged with those of the common law courts in the late 19th century. One significant difference between the application by a tribunal of the principles of equitable relief against forfeiture, as opposed to the application of English common law principles concerning penalties, is that, whereas, in the case of the latter, if a contractual provision is held to be a penalty, it is unenforceable as a matter of law, the power of a tribunal to grant equitable relief against forfeiture is a discretionary remedy, albeit such discretion must be exercised judicially according to established principles rather than some vague notion of what the tribunal considers in all circumstances to be fair.

[19] "The definitive statement of the principles upon which, in a modern context, a tribunal, whether court or arbitral, should exercise its powers is found in the speech of Lord Wilberforce in the case of *Shiloh Spinners Ltd v. Harding* [1973] AC 691, at pp. 723-724, in the following terms:

> 'It remains true today that equity expects men to carry out their bargains and will not let them buy their way out by uncovenanted payment. But it is consistent with these principles that we should reaffirm the right of courts of equity in appropriate and limited cases to relieve against forfeiture for breach of covenant or condition where the primary object of the bargain is to secure a stated result which can effectively be attained when the matter comes before the court, and where the forfeiture provision is added by way of security for the production of that result. The word "appropriate" involves consideration of the conduct of the applicant for relief, in particular whether his default was wilful, of the gravity of the breaches, and of the disparity between the value of the property of which forfeiture is claimed as compared with the damage caused by the breach.'

[20] "Just as in relation to the possible application of the common law relating to penalties, it has also been emphasized by the English courts in relation to the possible grant of relief against forfeiture, that the primary task of the courts (and arbitral tribunals applying English law) is to give effect to the mutual intention of the parties as expressed in the terms of the contract between them, and not to re-make the parties' bargain in a manner which the tribunal may consider more fair. Just as the courts should be slow to 'descry' a penalty clause . . . so equitable relief against a contractual provision giving a right to require a forfeiture of another party's rights under the contract should only be granted in rare cases – particularly in a commercial contract between commercial parties

with comparable bargaining power, which has been negotiated in detail through legal teams on both sides.

[21] "A second difference, which may be of some relevance in the present case, is that, whereas in relation to the question whether a contractual provision is penal, that question must be judged as at the date of the contract, whether or not equitable relief against forfeiture should be granted may be judged by reference to subsequent events, whether as they exist at the date of the relevant default or the purported exercise of the right, or when the matter finally comes before the tribunal, is a question to be considered hereafter.

[22] "The issues which arise in relation to the respondent's purported reliance on the doctrine of equitable relief against forfeiture in this case can be discussed under two heads, namely: (i) Does the tribunal have jurisdiction to grant such relief in this case? (ii) If so, should it do so in the circumstances?"

a. Jurisdiction to grant relief

[23] "In this context, the tribunal is not concerned with the question whether it has jurisdiction in a technical sense to grant equitable relief in an appropriate case. As we have already stated, the parties acknowledge that such jurisdiction exists. Rather, the tribunal is concerned with the 'threshold' question whether this is the type of case in which the tribunal is entitled to move to the second stage of considering whether in all the circumstances it is right for relief to be granted. The English jurisprudence, as reflected in the passage from the *Shiloh Spinners* case to which we have referred ... makes it clear that it is only in certain types of case that the jurisdiction can be invoked. Thus, where the tribunal is considering the possible application of the doctrine there are essentially two questions: (i) *May* the tribunal grant relief? (ii) *Should* the tribunal grant relief? It is the former question to which we refer in the context as one of 'jurisdiction'.

[24] "It is common ground between the parties that equitable relief against forfeiture cannot be granted in every contractual situation where a possible forfeiture arises. It can only be granted: (i) if the forfeiture is of a possessory or proprietary interest;[3] and (ii) if it is concluded that the primary purpose of the forfeiture provision in the contract is to secure a stated result (e.g., the payment of money) which can be attained when the matter comes before the court. (....)

[25] "... [A]lthough we are aware of no authority specifically in point which can provide us with assistance on the facts of this case (and neither party was able to produce any such authority despite a request at the hearing for further

---

3. "Snell's Equity, Thirtieth Edition, paragraph 36-14 and *BICC Plc. v. Burndy Corp* [1985] Ch 232 at p. 252."

assistance), we would, if necessary, be prepared to conclude that the respondent's contingent right to share in the petroleum produced from the concession in the event of its proving to be commercially viable is a proprietary or possessory right, in respect of which it is or may be appropriate to grant relief against forfeiture.

[26] "Despite respondent's counsel's considerable efforts, the tribunal was not persuaded that Art. 8.7(a) of the SMA did have as its primary objective the provision of security to achieve a stated result, namely prompt payment by the parties of their contractual indebtedness. As Oliver LJ put it in the case of *Sport International Bussum BV v. Inter-Footwear Limited* [1984] 1 WLR 776 at p. 789, 'No doubt one object was to provide a stimulus for performing the defendants' obligations on time'; but we find the primary objective of Art. 8.7(a) was to ensure that the Operator had the necessary means (a) to explore, develop and exploit the concession, and (b) to satisfy the obligations of the joint venture partners vis-a-vis the Government of W and, to that end, to ensure that each participant in the joint venture provided its share of the funds required to be invested.

[27] "If any one (or more) of the joint venture partners failed to put up its share of the funds required, then the whole project and the concession itself would be put in jeopardy, unless the defaulting party were removed and one (or more) of the other partners were prepared and able to increase its investment above and beyond its agreed share in return for increasing its participation in the hoped-for benefits [footnote omitted]. As the parties expressly acknowledged in Art. 8.6(e) of the SMA, the prompt satisfaction by each contracting party of its financial obligations was of fundamental importance.

[28] "The position is not dissimilar to that considered by the courts in *The SCAPTRADE* [1983] AC 694, where, in the context of the obligation of time charterers of a vessel to make prompt and regular payments of hire under the charterparty, Lord Diplock said, at page 702:

> 'In the case of a time charter it is not possible to state that the object of the insertion of a withdrawal clause, let alone the transaction itself, is essentially to secure the payment of money. Hire is payable in advance in order to provide a fund from which the shipowner can meet those expenses of rendering the promised services to the charterer that he has undertaken to bear himself under the charterparty: in particular the wages and the victualing of master and crew, the insurance of the vessel and the maintenance in such a state as will enable her to continue to comply with the warranty of performance.'([1983] AC 694)

[29] "Indeed, in our view, the position is even stronger in this case, since not only did the Operator need the agreed contributions from its joint venture

partners in order to satisfy its obligations, but this was a true joint venture relationship, in which it is clearly of fundamental importance that the parties should be able to trust and depend, each upon the others, to do their share to enable the project to progress to its ultimate and hopefully profitable conclusion. In such a relationship, if one party fails to pay its share, one can well understand that the other parties may wish it to be excluded from he joint venture for the future – as both A and B wish the exclusion of C in this case. Putting it another way, Clause 8.7(a) of the SMA reflected the broad commercial basis of the agreements between A, B and C, namely that they should each put up an agreed share of the investment needed in return for a like share of the rewards: if one party were not willing to put up his share of the outgoings, it should no longer be entitled to share in the reward.

[30]   "It is very much like the case of *Nutting v. Baldwin*, already discussed [at [8]], in which the court upheld the relevant provisions of the agreement and declined to grant relief against forfeiture. . . . While the situation in the present case is not identical to that in *Nutting v. Baldwin*, in that here the exploration for oil has not been successfully concluded, nevertheless the risks and costs of the exploration have for over 18 months been borne by A and B and not at all by C.

[31]   "For these reasons, we do not consider this is the sort of case in which the tribunal may grant relief against forfeiture, and it is therefore not necessary to move to consider whether, in all the circumstances, it would be right to do so. However, lest we be wrong in this conclusion, we do consider the second question briefly.

b.   Granting of relief in case at issue (no)

[32]   "As Lord Wilberforce explained in the *Shiloh Spinners* case, equitable relief, which deprives a party to a conflict of the benefit of part of the contractual bargain, should only be granted in rare cases, especially in a commercial context.

[33]   "Although the tribunal feels considerable sympathy for Mr. RB who has clearly made great efforts to get the respondent back on an even keel after the apparently disastrous period during the [prior] management and who is held in high esteem by all parties concerned, it is neither right nor fair to A or B to allow the slate to be wiped clean. The corporate entity with which A and B contracted remains the same, and the change of management does not remove corporate responsibility for its conduct in the past. Were it otherwise, the stability of modern commercial transactions would be undermined.

[34]   "There are two particular features of this case which we consider militate against the grant of the relief against forfeiture: first, the long history of default on the part of C, and second, the fact that, even now, C has not tendered performance of its outstanding financial obligations, but has merely indicated that

if relief against forfeiture were to be granted, it is confident of being able to procure the necessary finance to be able to satisfy its financial obligations as to the past as well as the future.

[35]   "One interesting question which arises in this case and which we have already touched upon is whether, in relation to the respondent's plea for equitable relief against forfeiture, the tribunal should look at the matter:

  (i)   as at the date when the claimants first purported to exercise their contractual right to call for a forfeiture;
 (ii)   as at the date when the arbitration was commenced by the filing of the claimants' Request; or
(iii)   when the matter finally came before the tribunal on the main hearing on the merits.

[36]   "Whilst we acknowledge that in a case, for example, of a claim for damages where, looked at as at the date of the Request, it would be necessary to speculate as to future events such as changes in market prices, a tribunal can take account of what has actually occurred up to the time of the making of its award, generally speaking the tribunal is charged with the task of considering whether or not a claimant had a good cause of action at the time when the relevant proceedings were commenced. In this case, the claimants sought (inter alia) a declaration that they were entitled to require the forfeiture of C's contractual right under Art. 8.7(a) of the SMA. In these circumstances, there is much to be said for the view that it is at the date the claimants filed their Request for Arbitration that we should examine whether or not the prima facie entitlement of the claimants should be defeated by the grant of equitable relief.

[37]   "However, we acknowledge that the passage from the speech of Lord Wilberforce in *Shiloh Spinners* ([at [19]]) would suggest that the tribunal can take into account developments up to the time when it falls to the tribunal to make its decision. In any event, it is not in our view necessary to decide the point, since the respondent's claim for relief could only possibly be justified by the recent development whereby Mr. RB took over management of the company, acknowledged its previous defaults, and sought to make efforts to make A and B 'whole'. But, this being the case, the respondent cannot invite the tribunal to ignore C's behavior up to the time when this *volte face* took place.

[38]   "This is not the typical case for the grant of equitable relief, where the party in default has been guilty of a single breach, which may have resulted from inadvertence, and in respect of which a prompt tender of performance is made. This is a case in which C has been in breach of its financial obligations for a very long time. A and B not only waited for the 60-day default period provided in Art. 8.7(a) before purporting to exercise their right to call for forfeiture, but also

gave substantial further time to C before launching these arbitration proceedings. Furthermore, this is not a case of one breach (C's failure to put up a conforming letter of credit to back up the letter of credit which A had been required to supply to the Ministry in respect of completion of the minimum contractual work programme) which has continued for over 2 years without being remedied, but of continuing failures by C to respond to contractual cash calls, each of which was followed by the relevant contractual default notice and, subsequently, a 'without prejudice' notice of forfeiture.

[39]   "For a long period before Mr. RB took over its management, C had been in flagrant and repeated breach of contract, which it failed and refused to acknowledge, and which continued after this arbitration was commenced. Furthermore, the conduct of the arbitration was itself subject to delay, partly at least as a result of C's wholly unmeritorious attempt to challenge the jurisdiction of the tribunal. It is not the sort of case in which tribunals have exercised a jurisdiction which authority dictates should be exercised sparingly.

[40]   "Finally, as we have already noted, even at this late stage, C has not tendered contractual performance. It has not offered to pay its outstanding indebtedness, but has merely indicated that, if equitable relief were to be granted, it is confident that it would be in a position to pay, and would for this reason be prepared to submit to a conditional order – in terms that if C fails to come up with the money within, say, 14 days from the date of our award, which itself would inevitably not be published until several weeks or months after the hearing, specific performance should be granted.

[41]   "This seems to us to be 'putting the cart before the horse'. We cannot conclude that C has satisfied that part of the test adumbrated by Lord Wilberforce, namely that the objective which C contends the forfeiture provision was designed to secure (payment by C of its contractual contributions to the joint venture funds), or that we have found [at [19]-[20]] (ensuring that the Operator has the necessary funds from the joint venture participants, including C) to fulfil its obligations), can be attained 'when the matter comes before the court' – or in this case before the arbitral tribunal.

[42]   "We accept that this is not because at this stage C remains unwilling to perform its contractual obligations. We accept that Mr. RB intends to do his utmost to satisfy any obligation necessary to allow C to come back into the fold, but it is plainly unable to do so without the assistance of a third party as a result of its parlous financial state. Not only has payment not been tendered, but C has offered no guarantee or letter of credit in respect of further performance. Despite Mr. RB's considerable efforts, all he has been able to come up with is a letter, annexed to his second witness statement, from another commercial entity, XYZ, which is said to be financially sound, and which is willing to undertake an obligation to C (rather than to the claimants) to put it in funds

to pay its indebtedness and satisfy its future financial obligations to A and B if equitable relief is granted, and subject to 'due diligence'. There is an additional uncertainty arising from the federal and local investigations of the previous managers and from various lawsuits pending against the C companies which could have a destabilizing effect on C.

[43]   "Despite our sympathy for Mr. RB and our sincere desire to help him if we could, this is simply not a sufficient basis upon which this tribunal could grant equitable relief in accordance with the principles laid down in the authorities, so as to deprive A and B of their prima facie contractual rights. We can well understand the reluctance of both claimants to accept the letter from XYZ as being in any way sufficient to allay their fears that, if C's interest were to be allowed to be maintained, the pattern in the future may simply repeat that of the past.

[44]   "Accordingly, and for the above reasons, we decline to grant relief against forfeiture."

3. Waiver

[45]   "It was further submitted on behalf of the respondent (without much apparent enthusiasm) that the claimants had waived any right to forfeiture by retaining [one of the 'defective' letters of credit], rather than returning it to C.

[46]   "We reject this argument. First, to constitute a waiver in these circumstances, it would be necessary for there to be an 'election' on the part of the claimants not to require forfeiture of C's interest, or some representation that they did not intend to rely on their strict legal rights. Not only is there no evidential basis for such a conclusion, but, on the contrary, the claimants made it clear that they were exercising their contractual rights by operating the contractual machinery. The letter of credit was not operated, and it was for C, if it wished, to ask for it to be returned, although this would have been inconsistent with the stance it was adopting at the time of denying any breach. Furthermore, as we have pointed out, C continued to be in default of its obligations by failing to respond to A's cash calls, in respect of which in each case a precautionary notice of default and without prejudice request for forfeiture was served."

II. CLAIMANTS' CLAIMS

[47]   "Having examined respondent's defense based on 'penalty' and its request for equitable relief against forfeiture and having declined to grant relief on those grounds, the arbitral tribunal now turns to the requests for relief made by claimants. These requests for relief were modified in claimants' post-hearing brief by comparison with the requests made previously: some of the original

claims have been deleted; others have been modified or expressed in a new way. The tribunal deals hereafter only with the requests for relief as made in the post-hearing brief. The arbitral tribunal does not consider these modified claims to be new claims within the meaning of Art. 19 of the ICC Rules of Arbitration because they are encompassed within the claims set forth in the Terms of Reference, albeit worded differently. Each of claimants' requests for relief in their post-hearing brief are set out below, followed, in each case, by the tribunal's decision."

1. Claims in Relation to the Operatorship

[48]   "The claimants request the following declaratory relief[4] in relation to the Operatorship.
[49]   "(1) A declaration that C has materially breached the SMA and its default provisions by failing to provide a conforming letter of credit for US$ 1,290,000 within the times specified in the Participation Agreement and SMA.
[50]   "The arbitral tribunal has found as an established fact that C failed to provide a conforming letter of credit for US$ 1,290,000 within the required time. . . . Respondent does not contest this. Art. 5.4 of the Participation Agreement states that failure to provide a L/C within the specified time is a default under the SMA to the same extent as a failure to make a payment [footnote omitted]. The SMA, Art. 8.6(e), states as a fundamental principle of the Agreement the payment by each party of its share of all amounts due. So there can be no doubt that failure to provide a timely and conforming L/C is a material contractual breach. Claimants' request for this declaration is, therefore, granted.
[51]   "(2) A declaration pursuant to SMA Art. 4.1(c) that A properly elected to become Operator.
[52]   "Art. 4.1(c) of the SMA provides that A may elect to become Operator immediately if there is a material breach of the agreements to which it and C are parties relating to operations as the result of any action or inaction by C [footnote omitted]. Since the tribunal has found that C materially breached its obligations under the agreements ([at [50]]), it is clear that A had the right under Art. 4.1(c) of the SMA to elect to become Operator, a right which it exercised pursuant to the relevant contractual provisions. . . . This request is, therefore, granted.
[53]   "(3) A declaration pursuant to SMA Art. V that the Management Committee properly determined that C was removed as Operator and replaced by A.

---

4. "Art. 15.1(b) of the SMA gives the arbitral tribunal authority (which it undoubtedly has anyway) to make declaratory judgments."

[54] "The tribunal has recounted . . . that the Management Committee met and made a 'SMA Determination' dated 28 April 2001 in which it decided that C was removed as Operator and A appointed in its place. In so doing, the Management Committee was exercising the powers granted to it by Art. 5.2(b) and 5.2(h) of the SMA, following C's contractual breaches. The arbitral tribunal, therefore, finds that the Management Committee properly determined that C was removed as Operator and replaced by A and grants claimants' request.

[55] "(4) A declaration that G breached SMA Art. 21.3 by failing to resign as Operator under the JOA.

[56] "C was obligated by Art. 21.3 of the SMA . . . to resign under the JOA if, as was the case, it was removed or was to be replaced as Operator. It did not do so. C was, consequently, in breach of its contractual obligation. The arbitral tribunal, therefore, grants this request."

2. Claims in Relation to Forfeiture

a. Declaratory relief

[57] "The claimants request the following declaratory relief in relation to forfeiture.

[58] "(1) A declaration pursuant to SMA Art. 8.7(a) that C has forfeited its Participating Interest under the SMA due to its default and material breach.

[59] "Under Art. 8.7(a) of the SMA, the consequence of having failed to provide a timely and conforming letter of credit and to pay cash calls is that the non-Defaulting Parties (A and B) have the right to have forfeited to them and to have the Defaulting Party (C) assign to each of them C's entire Participating Interest. Claimants exercised this right in accordance with the procedures stipulated in the SMA by first sending a Default Notice to C and then by waiting the stipulated time period for C to cure its default. . . . When the default remained uncured, they exercised their right to have C's Participating Interest forfeited to them. . . . The tribunal has decided that such forfeiture is not a penalty ([at [5] et seq.]) and has denied respondent's request for relief against this forfeiture ([at [16] et seq.]). Consequently, this request for a declaration is granted.

[60] "(2) A declaration pursuant to the SMA Art. 8.7(a) that C is obliged to assign its Participating Interest to A and B.

[61] "Art. 8.7(a) of the SMA obligates the Defaulting Party, if it has not timely cured its default, to assign its entire Participating Interest to the non-Defaulting Parties. Consequently, C, as a Defaulting Party, which had not cured its default within the contractual time period, is required to assign its Participating Interest to A and B in accordance with the provisions of Art. 8.7(a). This request for a declaration is, therefore, granted.

[62]   "(3) A declaration pursuant to SMA Art. 8.7(c) that C holds its Participating Interest in trust in favor of A and B until such assignment is completed and approved under the SMA, JOA and PSA.

[63]   "As A's counsel explained in his letter of 18 February 2003, the parties to the SMA anticipated that a Defaulting Party's assignment of its Participating Interest pursuant to Art. 8.7(a) of the SMA would require the approval of the Ministry and other W Government authorities (see also PSA, Art. 20.2). The parties provided in Art. 8.7(c) of the SMA that, until such approval was granted, the Defaulting Party would hold its Participating Interest in trust for the non-Defaulting Parties.

[64]   "It follows from the tribunal's decision that C must assign its Participating Interest to claimants that, pending the necessary W governmental approvals for such assignment and the completion of the assignment, C must, as it agreed in Art. 8.7(c) of the SMA, hold its Participating Interest in trust in favor of claimants. This request is, therefore, granted.

[65]   "(4) A declaration that, notwithstanding the forfeiture and assignment of its Participating Interest, C remains liable for, and shall pay to the Project's Joint Account, its proportionate share of all costs, expenses and penalties, and it remains obliged to perform certain acts, as stipulated by SMA Art. 8.7(b).

[66]   "[Under] Art. 8.7(b) of the SMA . . . C is obligated to continue certain payments and to perform certain acts described therein following the forfeiture of its Participating Interest. Among the payments which C is required to continue making under this provision are the cash calls. C does not contest that since October 2001 these cash calls remain unpaid. C does not contest the validity of Art. 8.7(b) of the SMA (as it does Art. 8.7(a) . . .). In light of the foregoing, the tribunal grants the declaration requested by claimants.

[67]   "(5) A declaration pursuant to SMA Art. 8.7(a) that C has no rights or benefits under the SMA.

[68]   "Art. 8.7(a) of the SMA states that a Defaulting Party shall cease to be a party to the SMA and shall have no rights or benefits thereunder. C being a Defaulting Party, this request for a declaration is granted."

b.   *Specific performance*

[69]   "The claimants request that C be ordered to specifically perform its obligations under SMA Art. 8.7 by taking all steps necessary to assign its Participating Interest to A and B. Such steps to include, without limitation, those required by the JOA Art. 10 for the assignment of C's Participating Interest.

[70]   "This is a request for equitable relief. As with respondent's request for relief in equity, this is not a request for the tribunal to act as an *amiable compositeur* or *ex aequo et bono* (see [at [17]]). One test for granting specific performance of a contractual obligation is whether damages are an adequate

remedy.[5] Here they are not, because an award of damages alone would leave respondent as a partner in what is essentially a joint venture in which all the parties must be able to work harmoniously together, which, from claimants' standpoint, is obviously not the case.

[71]　"In this case, we have a situation in which, to use Lord Wilberforce's language in *Shiloh Spinners v. Harding* (see [at [19]]) at p. 725, claimants 'should not be compelled to remain in a relation of neighborhood with a person in deliberate breach of his obligations'. C has, in the past, consistently failed to fulfill its obligations under the agreements, and its ability to do so in the future is uncertain. C's defaults have imposed additional burdens on the claimants to maintain the project. The arbitral tribunal, consequently, is prepared to exercise its discretion in granting specific performance.

[72]　"It follows from the tribunal's decision that respondent's Participating Interest in the Project has been forfeited pursuant to Art. 8.7(a) of the SMA that respondent is obligated by the provisions of that same article to assign its Interest to the claimants. In doing so, it must follow the requirements of the JOA concerning assignments. Therefore, this request for specific performance is granted."

3. Damages

[73]　"The claimants request that the respondent be ordered to pay the claimants[6] the following amounts, in compensation for their damages arising from respondent's breaches of contract:

1. Cash calls from October 2001 through March 2003	US$ 2,841,108
2. Default interest on late-paid and unpaid cash calls (from 8 June 2001 through 15 March 2003)	US$ 78,445
3. Additional damages	US$ 111,255
Total:	US$ 3,030,808

. . . .

---

5. "See Snell's Equity, thirtieth edition, paragraph 40-05."
6. "Claimants did not specify to which claimant or in what proportion to each of them amounts awarded should be paid; so the tribunal has ordered payments generally to 'claimants', leaving it up to them to determine how to allocate the amounts between them."

a. Cash calls

[74] "Claimants have provided as an annex to Witness X's second witness statement a table of unpaid and late paid cash calls through 31 December 2002; and this table was brought up to date through March 2003 in claimants' post-hearing brief. It shows cash calls in an amount of US$ 2,841,108 unpaid by C.

[75] "In its closing submissions, respondent stated that it does not dispute its liability to pay its share of the cash calls plus interest thereon. However, it raised certain questions about the quantum of the cash calls. In particular, it questioned whether it had been 'over-cash-called' and whether it had been cash-called for part or all of a third well which exceeded Contractor's minimum work obligation and which was drilled after C was excluded by claimants from the project. Claimant responded to these questions in their comments on respondent's closing submissions, dated 28 March 2003.

[76] "The arbitral tribunal is satisfied by the evidence that costs for drilling the third well have not been included in cash calls addressed to respondent. . . . The tribunal also is satisfied by claimants' explanation . . . that respondent had not been over-cash-called. Since no final accounting has been made at this point in time of the expenditures made from the amounts of the cash calls, respondent remains liable under the agreements for its share of the 'cash calls' whether above or below the amount actually expended.

[77] "In . . . its closing submissions dated 14 March 2003, respondent raised the question whether claims for cash calls made after the commencement of the arbitration may be technically regarded as outside the Terms of Reference. . . . It indicated that if so, it was willing to consent to the necessary modification of the Terms of Reference. The arbitral tribunal believes that all the claimants' claims respecting cash calls, whether due before or after the arbitration began, fall within . . . the Terms of Reference.

[78] "In conclusion, the arbitral tribunal awards to claimants US$ 2,841,108 in unpaid cash calls from October 2001 through March 2003 provided that, should a final accounting of cash calls and expenditures show an excess of the amount of the cash calls paid by respondent by comparison with the actual expenditures made, claimant will reimburse to respondent such excess."

b. Default interest

[79] "Claimants claim interest on the amount of the late-paid or unpaid cash calls, which the tribunal has now awarded to them. They have submitted a calculation of the interest due . . . from the due date of each cash call until paid (in the case of the late-paid cash calls) or through 15 March 2003 (in the

case of the unpaid cash calls) at the Default Interest Rate stipulated in the SMA (see Arts. 8.4 and 1 of the SMA . . .). Respondent has not contested its liability for interest or the calculation by claimants. . . .

[80] "Consequently, the tribunal awards interest on the late and unpaid cash calls of US$ 78,445 through 15 March 2003."

c. Additional damages

[81] "Claimants' claims for additional damages were summarized and quantified in Witness X's first witness statement . . . as follows:

1. Value of project assets improperly retained by the respondent (office furniture and equipment, and the Operator's vehicle)	US$ 98,072
2. Cost of renting an automobile to replace the Operator's vehicle (from 13 June to 1 August 2001)	US$ 1,500
3. Missing funds in Project Joint Account at W Commercial Bank	US$ 11,683
Total:	US$111,255

[82] "Respondent requested and received from claimants certain documentation in support of these claims for additional damages, which arise from C's failure to cooperate in the transfer of the Operatorship to A. In its closing submissions, respondent stated it did not dispute these claims or the amounts claimed which total US$ 111,255, except that it offered to transfer ownership of the Operator's automobile, which the parties agreed has a value of US$ 34,825. . . . Respondent, therefore, requested that these damages be reduced to US$ 76,430.64. On the other hand, claimants requested that the tribunal award the full amount and undertook not to pursue enforcement of the portion of such award corresponding to the value of the vehicle once it had been transferred to A with the respondent's cooperation.

[83] "The tribunal is satisfied that, in the circumstances described in this Award, compensation is justified and that the amount of this claim has been adequately justified and is reasonable.

[84] "The arbitral tribunal decides that respondent should pay to claimants the amount of US$ 111,255 as damages for expenses incurred by them as a result of respondent's failure to cooperate in the transfer of the Operatorship, provided that claimants shall not pursue enforcement of this award of damages in an amount of US$ 34,825 if the Operator's automobile is transferred to A with respondent's cooperation."

4. Interest

[85]   "The claimants request that the tribunal award interest at the Default Interest Rate, as of 1 March 2003, namely 3.338%, on all principal amounts awarded to them as compensation for damages (viz., cash calls and additional damages), running from 15 March 2003 until the date of full payment by the respondent.

[86]   "Art. 8.4 of the SMA provides that all unpaid amounts of 'payments provided for in this Agreement' shall bear interest at the Default Interest Rate until paid. It is, consequently, clear that such interest is due on unpaid cash calls until paid. Interest on these unpaid cash calls through 15 March 2003 has been calculated and awarded [at [79]-[80]].

[87]   "Looking forward from 15 March 2003, claimants claim interest on the principal amount of the unpaid cash calls and on the amount of the 'additional damages' awarded [at [84]] running from 15 March until the date of full payment by respondent. This interest is claimed at the Default Interest Rate as of 1 March 2003, i.e., 3.338%, which, by definition . . . is compounded on a monthly basis. Respondent has not contested the principle of such interest or the rate claimed.

[88]   "The arbitral tribunal finds that payment of such interest is warranted. Under Sect. 49(3)-(4) of the English Arbitration Act 1996, the tribunal may award simple or compound interest from such dates, at such rates and with such rests as it considers meets the justice of the case. While the Default Interest Rate does not, by the terms of Art. 8.4 of the SMA, apply to the 'additional damages' because these are not amounts 'provided for in this Agreement', the tribunal finds that the rate claimed, 3.338%, is a reasonable rate commercially, and, noting that respondent has not contested this rate, is prepared to apply it. Applying this rate of interest to the additional damages from the date of 16 March 2003, not 15 March as requested by claimants since interest has been awarded separately through 15 March 2003 (see [at [80]]), is eminently reasonable, since in English practice interest normally would be applicable from the date when the damage occurred.

[89]   "Claimants, therefore, are entitled to interest on the amount of unpaid cash calls (US$ 2,841,108) and on amounts awarded to them for 'additional damages' at the Default Interest Rate as of 1 March 2003, namely 3.338%, beginning on 16 March 2003 and running until paid (or in the case of the value of the automobile referred to [at [82]-[84]], until the automobile is transferred with the respondent's cooperation). Such interest shall be compounded on a monthly basis, as is the Default Interest."

III.   RESPONDENT'S COUNTERCLAIM

[90]   "The claimants request that the respondent's counterclaim be dismissed with prejudice.

[91] "... Respondent has agreed to withdraw its counterclaim and has assented to the tribunal's dismissing it with prejudice. The tribunal so decides."

IV. COSTS

[92] "Both sides have claimed costs in this arbitration. Costs claimed include the fees and expenses of the arbitrators and the ICC administrative expenses fixed by the ICC Court as well as the legal costs and certain travel and other expenses incurred by the parties for the arbitration.
[93] "It is a generally accepted principle in ICC arbitrations that under Art. 31 of the ICC Rules, the arbitral tribunal has complete discretion to allocate the costs of the arbitration as it sees fit (see Derains & Schwartz, *A Guide to the New ICC Rules of Arbitration*, at p. 341).
(. . . .)
[94] "Given the outcome of this arbitration, in which the claimants have prevailed on all points, and taking into account that respondent has, since new management has been in place, essentially admitted that its actions ... constitute violations of its contractual obligations, the arbitral tribunal finds that the costs of the arbitration should be borne by respondents.
[95] "This decision applies to the costs and expenses of the jurisdiction phase of the case, where respondent's objections were entirely rejected, as well as to those incurred in the merits phase of the arbitration.
[96] "The tribunal finds that the amount of claimants' claim for costs and expenses in the jurisdictional phase is entirely reasonable, especially when compared with the amount of respondent's legal costs and, therefore, awards the full amount, US$ 174,845.35, to claimants.
[97] "As for the claimants' legal, witness and other costs for the merits phase of the arbitration, however, the tribunal finds that the amounts claimed are somewhat high. They include the costs of participants at the January 2003 hearing, whom claimants had every right to have present, but which respondent should not be required to pay. They also include the costs of seven lawyers and one paralegal for claimants' legal team; and, again, while claimants' counsel have every right to organize their work as they wish – and the tribunal appreciated the high quality of the work of all counsel – respondent should not be required to pay for it all. The tribunal, consequently, reduces claimants' claims for these costs, which total US$ 1,386,086, to US$ 1,000,000. Respondent is ordered to pay this amount to claimants.
[98] "Respondent is also ordered to pay to claimants the amounts of advance deposit which they have made to the ICC, that is, US$ 250,000, to cover arbitrators' fees and expenses and ICC administrative expenses."
(. . . .)

Final award in case no. 12172 of 2003

Parties:	Claimant: Software development company (UK)
	Respondent: Software company (US)
Place of arbitration:	Toronto, Canada
Published in:	Unpublished; original in English
Subject matters:	– acceleration of payment
	– payment due and owing
	– costs of arbitration
	– legal costs

Facts

On 17 April 2001, the parties concluded a Software Licence Agreement granting the respondent the right to use the claimant's software in one of its own software products. The Agreement provided for the application of English law and ICC arbitration of disputes "[e]xcept in connection with an action by either party for an injunction or to compel specific performance (or for other equitable relief)". The arbitration clause further provided that the parties agreed to "share equally the fees and expenses of the arbitrators".

Under the Agreement, the respondent was to pay to the claimant royalties on each sale. The Agreement also provided for advance royalty payments (or prepaid royalties) to be made at the signing of the contract, on 31 July 2001, 31 December 2001 and 31 August 2002, as well as for an annual sum for maintenance service to be paid for the first time on 1 January 2002 and then on the first day of each year. The respondent was allowed to terminate the Agreement for convenience; if it did so before 31 December 2001, it would not have to make the advance royalty payments due on 31 December 2001 and 31 August 2002; if it terminated the Agreement before 31 August 2002, it would not have to make the payment due on that date. The Agreement further provided that interest could be charged on overdue invoices at a rate of 1.5 percent per month (18 percent per annum).

The respondent made the first two advance royalty payments. On 17 December 2001, however, the parties rescheduled the payments by entering into an Addendum because the respondent was experiencing financial difficulties. According to the revised schedule, the advance royalty payment due on 31 December 2001 would become contractually committed on that date but would be paid in instalments on 30 April, 30 June and 31 August 2002; the advance royalty payment due on 31 August 2002 would become contractually committed on that date but would be paid in instalments on 31 March, 30 June and 31 August 2003. Further, the maintenance service payment for 2002 originally due on 1 January 2002 would be paid in instalments on 31 March, 30 June, 31 July and 31 August 2002.

The Addendum also provided that if a committed payment was not received, the claimant reserved its right to accelerate all sums due and demand full payment of all committed payments.

A dispute arose between the parties when the respondent failed to meet the first payments due under the revised schedule, that is, the maintenance service instalment due on 31 March 2002 and the advance royalty payment due on 30 April 2002. The claimant exercised its right to accelerate all sums due and submitted two invoices to the respondent for the entire amount of the advanced royalty payment due on 31 December 2001 and the maintenance service payment for 2002. On 16 August 2002, the respondent terminated the Agreement for convenience as provided for in the Agreement.

On 10 June 2002, the claimant filed a request for ICC arbitration, seeking payment of the outstanding sums.

On 29 July 2002, the respondent in turn filed an action in country X, seeking equitable relief regarding the rights of the parties under the Agreement. In particular, it sought a declaration that the Agreement provided that royalties should only be paid to the claimant when there was a sale or the reasonable certainty of future sales of the relevant software. The court in country X dismissed the claimant's motion to compel arbitration.

In the arbitration, the respondent requested the ICC Court to dismiss or stay arbitration pending the outcome of the court proceedings in country X. The ICC Court denied the request. It determined that arbitration should proceed in accordance with Art. 6(2) ICC Rules, under which the Court allows arbitration to proceed, where there are pleas concerning the existence, validity or scope of the arbitration agreement, if it is prima facie satisfied that an arbitration agreement under the Rules may exist.

By a Partial Award on jurisdiction of 17 February 2003, the sole arbitrator held that he had jurisdiction because the claim fell within the scope of the Agreement. He therefore denied the respondent's request that the arbitration be dismissed or stayed pending court proceedings in country X.

By the present Final Award, the sole arbitrator found on the merits that both the advance royalty payment that became contractually committed on 31 December 2001 and the maintenance service payment that became contractually committed on 1 January 2002 were due and owing by the respondent to the claimant.

The arbitrator dismissed the respondent's contention that the royalty payments were only payable to the claimant when and if the respondent made a sale of its software product that contained the claimant's software. He relied on the testimony of a witness – who had participated in the negotiations on behalf of the claimant and stated that the advance royalty payments were minimum guaranteed payments which were to be paid regardless of the respondent's actual sales and were fundamental to the business arrangement – as well as on statements by the respondent and the "clear and unambiguous text" of the Agreement itself, which confirmed this position.

The arbitrator also dismissed the respondent's argument that it had no obligation to make the maintenance service payments because it did not utilize the services. He found that it was clear from the wording of the Agreement that those payments were to be made whether or not the respondent actually made use of the services and added that it appeared in fact from the evidence that the respondent did utilize the services provided by the claimant.

Hence, the respondent owed to the claimant both the advance royalty payment originally due on 31 December 2001 and the maintenance service payment for 2002.

The sole arbitrator held that the claimant had the right under the Addendum to request immediate payment of these sums because the respondent had defaulted on committed payments. However, the advance royalty payment originally due on 31 August 2002 had not become contractually committed on that date because the respondent had terminated the Agreement on 16 August 2002. As a consequence, the claimant could not accelerate this payment.

The sole arbitrator then noted that the claimant requested interest on the outstanding sums in accordance with the terms of the Agreement at 1.5 percent per month (eighteen percent per annum). He obtained from counsel for the claimant confirmation that the applicable English law recognizes pre-award and post-award interest, Specifically, the rate agreed upon by the parties applies to pre-award interest, the general practice being to give judgment for the amount of principal and interest outstanding as of the date of the award. English law then provides for post-award interest at the rate of eight percent. The arbitrator awarded interest accordingly.

He then held that the claimant should be reimbursed for the sum it had advanced on behalf of the respondent toward the costs of the arbitration and should bear its own part of those costs, in accordance with the provision in the Agreement that the parties were to share equally the costs and expenses of the arbitration.

The arbitrator finally considered the legal costs. Counsel for the claimant had submitted a summary of its legal expenses billed to a date before the hearing in the amount of US$ 31,520.49 and estimated that the legal expenses in respect of the preparation for and attendance at the hearing would represent an additional amount of approximately US$ 9,000. The arbitrator noted that no bill had been submitted in respect of these additional costs, but held this estimate to be reasonable and awarded US$ 40,000 as the reasonable legal and other costs incurred by the claimant.

Excerpt

I. DISCUSSION

[1] "In its pre-hearing briefs in response to the claimant's claim, the respondent has maintained that the royalty payments were only payable to the claimant when and if the respondent made a sale of its software product that contained the claimant's software. In these briefs ... the respondent stated that in the negotiations leading to the Agreement, it projected the volume of sales it could make of its software package containing the claimant's software and that the payment of royalties was linked to the respondent's sale of its products. A witness stated that the reason for the structured payments was an accounting issue, i.e. the respondent did not want to be invoiced and to have to pay for each transaction as they occurred. Instead, he maintained that they negotiated the advance royalty payment schedule as a form of accounting convenience.

[2] "The claimant's witness at the hearing was directly responsible for negotiating the contract with the respondent. His evidence was that ... it was very clear in the course of those negotiations that the Advance Royalty Payments were minimum guaranteed payments which were to be paid regardless of the respondent's actual sales. He stated that the minimum payment guarantee was fundamental to the business arrangement and he would not have entered into the agreement absent such a provision. In the course of the evidence at the hearing, he also pointed to several communications between him and representatives of the respondent leading to the formalization of the Agreement in which it is clear that there were to be guaranteed prepaid royalties. In one email, a representative of the respondent stated 'we do not have an issue with prepaid royalty commitments, only the payment schedule'.

[3] "The Clamant's witness gave his evidence in a forthright and straightforward manner. He was a credible witness and I accept his evidence.

[4] "Apart from the above evidence, the Agreement itself is quite clear that the Advance Royalty Payments were payable as minimum payments regardless of

the actual units sold by the respondent. The words of the Agreement are clear and unambiguous. There is no basis for giving the words any meaning other than their clear and ordinary meaning; namely, that the Advance Royalty Payments are due and payable regardless of the respondent's actual sales.

[5] "With respect to the Maintenance Service Payments, the respondent's position is that it has no obligation to pay the sum in respect of the Maintenance Service Payments because it did not utilize the services. It is clear from the wording of the Agreement that the Maintenance Service Payments were payable whether or not the respondent actually made use of such services. The payment obligation is for having such services available if and when the respondent elects to utilize those services. It is also clear from the documents submitted at the hearing that, in fact, the respondent did utilize the services provided by the claimant.

[6] "Accordingly, the Advance Royalty Payment originally payable on 31 December 2001 and the Maintenance Service Payment originally payable on 1 January 2002 are both due and owing by the respondent to the claimant.

[7] "However, the Advance Royalty Payment originally payable on 31 August 2002 is not due and owing. The Addendum extended the payment terms for the Advance Royalty Payment due on 31 December 2001. It stated that 'this Advance Royalty Payment becomes contractually committed on 31 December 2001'. This means that if the respondent did not terminate the Agreement prior to 31 December 2001 it was contractually committed to pay the total amount in accordance with the extended payment schedule.

[8] "A similar provision is contained in the Addendum in relation to the payment due on 31 August 2002. It provides that 'this Advance Royalty Payment becomes contractually committed on 31 December 2002'. In my view, this means that the respondent had the right to exercise the right to terminate for convenience up to 31 December 2002 with respect to the Advance Royalty Payment originally due on 31 August 2002.

[9] "Upon the respondent's default, the claimant had the right to and did in fact exercise its right to accelerate all sums due and immediately demand full payment of all 'committed payments'. This meant that it had the right to demand full payment of the Advance Royalty Payment that was committed on 31 December 2001. However, this did not accelerate the payment originally due on 31 August 2002 because it only became contractually committed on 31 December 2002. The claimant's best position is that if the respondent defaulted, the terms of the original contract applied. This would mean that the second payment was due and payable on 31 August 2002. However, the respondent would still have the right to terminate the Agreement for convenience prior to 31 August 2002. It did so on 16 August 2002.

[10] "Counsel for the claimant took the position that because the respondent was in default under the terms of the Addendum, it did not have the right to

exercise the right of termination for convenience. I do not accept that argument. There is nothing in the Agreement that provides that the right to terminate for convenience depends on a party not being in default under the Agreement.

[11] "Counsel for the claimant also maintained that the termination for convenience was not effective because the respondent did not intend it to be effective. He pointed to the fact that subsequent to the notice of termination, the respondent continued to attempt to sell the respondent's product containing the claimant's software product. There was one transaction in which the respondent sold a product containing the claimant's software. In this case, the claimant was paid a royalty, but the royalty payment was made expressly without prejudice to the parties' rights. That transaction does not have any impact on the effectiveness of the notice of termination provided by the respondent on 16 August 2002.

[12] "I find that the Agreement was validly terminated by the respondent on 16 August 2002 and the respondent was thereby relieved of its payment obligation of the sum due and owing on 31 August 2002."

II.   INTEREST AND COSTS

[13] "The claimant has also requested interest in accordance with the terms of the Agreement at 1.5% per month (18% per annum). In the course of the hearing I asked counsel for the claimant to provide a post-hearing brief confirming that pre-award and post-award interest is payable under the law of England (which is the agreed upon law in the Agreement). The claimant submitted a post-hearing brief. In the post-hearing brief, counsel for the claimant confirmed that English law does recognize pre-award and post-award interest. Specifically, the law of England is that, where the rate is agreed upon in the contract, that rate of interest would apply to pre-award interest. The general practice is to give judgement for the amount of principal and interest outstanding as of the date of the Award. English law also provides post-award interest at the rate of 8%.

[14] "A copy of the claimant's post-hearing brief was sent to counsel for the respondent. By letter . . . the respondent was invited to respond by a certain date to the claimant's hearing brief, on which date I proposed to declare the proceedings closed. The respondent did not to respond.

[15] "Although the Agreement would appear to provide for compound interest, counsel for the claimant indicated that the claimant was prepared to accept simple interest. Accordingly, I award pre-award interest at the rate of 18% per annum and post-award interest on the total principal and interest owing as of the date of the award at the rate of 8%.

[16] "The claimant has also asked for costs of the arbitration including the advance of costs submitted to the ICC Court. The claimant submitted a sum as

its share of the advance an costs and the same sum as the respondent's share of the advance on costs as a result of the respondent's failure to fulfil its payment obligation.

[17] "The Rules (Art. 31) provide that the ICC Court can fix the costs of the arbitration which include the fees and expenses of the arbitrator and the ICC Court's administrative expenses. These were fixed by the ICC Court at a certain amount. The arbitration clause in the Agreement provides that the parties are to share equally the costs and expenses of the arbitrators. Accordingly, the claimant is not entitled full reimbursement for the costs and expenses of the arbitration as fixed by the ICC Court. In my view, the proper disposition is that the claimant should be reimbursed for the sum advanced by it on behalf of the respondent, but it should not be reimbursed for the sum advanced on its own behalf.

[18] "Art. 31 of the Rules also permits the arbitrator to award the reasonable legal and other costs incurred by the parties for the arbitration. Counsel for the claimant submitted a summary of its legal expenses billed to a date before the hearing in the amount of US\$ 31,520.49. He estimated that the legal expenses and disbursements in respect of the preparation for and attendance at the hearing would represent an additional amount of approximately US\$ 9,000. A bill has not been submitted in respect of these additional costs, but this estimate appears reasonable. I am prepared to award US\$ 40,000 as the reasonable legal and other costs incurred by the claimant.

[19] "The claimant has requested post-award interest on the award of costs of the arbitration and the legal and other costs at the rate of 8% per annum. I would so award."

Sentences Arbitrales de la CCI

initialement publiées au *Journal du Droit International* (Clunet)

2001–2007

Sentence partielle rendue dans l'affaire n° 7710 en 1995 (original en anglais).

I. — Droit applicable. — Absence de choix exprès des parties. — Attente légitime des parties. — Facteurs objectifs et choix implicite.

II. — Droit applicable. — Absence de choix des parties. — Choix négatif. — Rejet de tout droit national.

III. — Droit applicable. — Justice naturelle. — Droit de procédure. — Règles de conflit. — Droit matériel.

IV. — Droit applicable. — Contrats d'Etat. — Equilibre entre les parties. — Délocalisation.

V. — Droit applicable. — Principes UNIDROIT. — Principes jouissant d'un large consensus international.

VI. — Droit applicable. — Absence de choix exprès ou implicite. — Voie directe. — Voie indirecte. — Principes Unidroit.

VII. — Contrats. — Interprétation. — Langue — Elément non pertinent.

Un Tribunal arbitral siégeant à La Haye était saisi d'un litige opposant un Etat X, demandeur, à une entreprise britannique Y, concernant neuf contrats (ci-après les « Contrats ») relatifs à la vente, la fourniture, la modification, la maintenance et le fonctionnement de matériels ainsi qu'aux services auxiliaires s'y rapportant. Ces Contrats ayant été résiliés à la suite d'événements politiques intervenus dans l'Etat X, les parties se réclamaient respectivement le règlement de diverses sommes.

Tous les Contrats ne contenaient pas des dispositions identiques en matière de résolution des litiges:

— Contrat 1: arbitrage CCI à La Haye, Pays-Bas;

— Contrat 2: résolution amiable par les parties;

— Contrat 3: litiges définitivement résolus « *according to natural justice* » par arbitrage CCI à Paris, France;

— Contrat 4: litiges définitivement résolus « *according to natural justice* » par arbitrage CCI à Paris, France;

— Contrat 5: litiges définitivement résolus « *according to natural justice* » par arbitrage CCI à Paris, France;

— Contrat 6: litiges définitivement résolus « *according to the laws of natural justice* » par arbitrage;

— Contrat 7: les litiges non résolus à l'amiable seront réglés définitivement « *in accordance with natural justice* » par arbitrage;

— Contrat 8: les litiges non résolus à l'amiable seront réglés définitivement par arbitrage à (dans l'Etat X);

— Contrat 9: les litiges non résolus à l'amiable seront réglés par arbitrage à (dans l'Etat X), comme indiqué à la clause 16 et à l'Annexe V, article 4 et 15 du contrat, prévoyant respectivement que (a) quand les règles applicables à la procédure contenues dans ladite annexe sont silencieuses, la procédure sera régie par toutes les règles que les parties, ou, à défaut les arbitres, peuvent déterminer « *in accordance with the rules of natural justice* » et (b) dans tous les cas non expressément réglés dans ladite annexe les arbitres agiront dans l'esprit des règles prévues à l'Annexe et de la « *natural justice* » et feront leur possible pour s'assurer que la sentence soit susceptible d'exécution forcée.

Fort heureusement, les parties décidèrent ultérieurement que tous les litiges résultant des contrats seraient tranchés selon le Règlement d'Arbitrage de la CCI, par un tribunal arbitral unique siégeant à La Haye. Le problème, en vérité insoluble autrement, de la consolidation de procédures d'arbitrage connexes, certaines dans différents pays, ne se posait donc plus. Le tribunal arbitral devait en revanche se prononcer sur le droit applicable au fond du litige, les parties exprimant des positions opposées sur ce point.

Selon l'Etat X, il convenait d'abord d'examiner tous les Contrats pour déterminer, selon l'article 13 (3) du Règlement d'Arbitrage de la CCI (dans sa version de 1988) s'il y avait des indications de la volonté des parties quant au droit applicable. L'Etat X estimait que les circonstances ci-après reflétaient ou indiquaient l'intention implicite des parties de soumettre les Contrats aux principes généraux du droit :

— l'existence d'éléments inter-gouvernementaux dans les transactions;

— l'expression « natural justice », figurant dans plusieurs des contrats, et à laquelle ne saurait être donnée la signification étroite qu'elle a en droit anglais, où elle vise certains principes d'équité procédurale, déjà reflétés dans le Règlement de la CCI;

— l'histoire des négociations contractuelles, révélant qu'aucune des parties n'avait accepté le droit de l'autre, ni le droit d'un Etat tiers.

Au cas où le tribunal arbitral ne l'aurait pas suivi dans son analyse de la volonté implicite des parties, l'Etat X estimait que la règle de conflit la plus appropriée pour déterminer le droit applicable selon l'article 13 (3) du Règlement d'arbitrage de la CCI était, soit les principes généraux du droit international privé, soit le droit international privé de l'Etat X. Dans le premier cas, la nature de contrats d'Etat ou de contrats entre Etats, d'au moins sept des Contrats faisait qu'en vertu des principes généraux du droit international privé, les principes généraux du droit ou la *lex mercatoria* étaient applicables. L'Etat X ajoutait que l'application du droit du pays de l'exécution de la prestation caractéristique du contrat n'était pas un principe général du droit international privé et que la Convention de Rome de 1980 n'était pas applicable parce qu'il n'y était pas partie et qu'elle avait été ratifiée par le Royaume-Uni après la date de conclusion du contrat. Dans le second cas, le droit de l'Etat X était applicable en raison de l'intervention d'une partie étatique, du lieu de conclusion des Contrats dans l'Etat X et du fait que certain des Contrats avaient ou devaient être exécutés dans cet Etat.

L'entreprise Y considérait que le tribunal arbitral devait recourir à la « *voie indirecte* » (en français dans le texte), c'est-à-dire choisir la règle de conflit qu'il retenait comme appropriée. A cet égard, aucune règle de conflit nationale ne devait être appliquée exclusivement ou cumulativement avec une autre. Cependant, si un choix devait être fait entre la règle de conflit anglaise ou celle de l'Etat X, la première devait être préférée.

A défaut de choix entre le système de conflits de lois anglais et celui de l'Etat X, Y prétendait à l'application des principes généraux du droit international privé concernant la fourniture internationale de biens et de services. En vertu de ces principes, chaque contrat était séparément régi par la loi de l'Etat avec lequel il avait la relation la plus étroite, cet Etat étant celui de la résidence habituelle ou du centre administratif de la partie dont la prestation est caractéristique du contrat.

Par application de ces principes, huit contrats sur neuf étaient soumis au droit anglais. L'entreprise Y soulignait qu'il en irait de même si les règles de conflit néerlandaises ou anglaises étaient déclarées applicables. Elle ajoutait que les références contractuelles à la « *natural justice* », aux « *laws of natural justice* » et aux « *rules of natural justice* » avaient toutes la même signification et visaient simplement des principes d'équité procédurale, sans conséquence sur le droit applicable aux contrats.

Statuant à la majorité, le Tribunal arbitral interpréta l' article 13 (3) du Règlement d'arbitrage de la CCI (version de 1988) comme suit :

« Selon le tribunal, l'article 13 (3) du Règlement d'arbitrage de la CCI doit être interprété comme visant le choix exprès, implicite ou présumé, par les parties du droit applicable aux contrats. Cette interprétation rejoint celle d'autres textes créés sur la base d'un large consensus international, tel que l'article 33 (1) des Règles d'arbitrage de la CNUDCI (voir VII UNCITRAL Yearbook, 178-179 (1977); voir également I. Dore, Arbitration and Conciliation under the Uncitral Rules: a textual analysis, M. Nijhoff, 65 (1986) et l'article 28 de la Loi Modèle de la CNUDCI, qui a pris comme "modèle" l'article 33 des Règles d'arbitrage de la CNUDCI et pour lequel la délégation allemande participant aux discussions concernant cette clause a indiqué, sans soulever d'opposition, qu'elle inclut également le choix "implicite" ou "présumé" du droit applicable par les parties (voir H. Holtzmann & J. Neuhaus, A guide to UNCITRAL Model Law on International Commercial Arbitration, Kluwer, 778, 784 (1989). C'est également la solution qu'indique la pratique de l'arbitrage international, y compris les arbitrages CCI (voir E. Gaillard, Arbitrage Commercial International, Droit applicable au fond du litige: Juris-Classeurs, Fasc. 586-9 (Droit International); Fasc. 1070-1 (Procédure civile), n° 7, 3, 4 (1991)). L'autonomie des parties dans le choix de la loi régissant les obligations contractuelles qui peut être aussi bien exprès, présumé ou implicite est, à vrai dire, un principe généralement accepté par "les systèmes juridiques contemporains" (H. Batiffol, P. Lagarde, 2 Droit International Privé: LGDJ n° 565, 257 (1983); voir également pour l'Angleterre, Dicey & Morris (L. Collins General Editor) 2 Conflict of Laws, Stevens, 11th Ed. 1162/1163 (1987) et que doivent observer les tribunaux arbitraux internationaux sur la base du principe de la bonne foi dans le cadre des transactions commerciales internationales avec des Etats (Sentence du 10 juin 1955 par R. Cassin dans l'"Affaire des cargaisons déroutées" 45 Revue Critique de Droit International Privé 278 (1956) Note Batiffol).

En l'absence de stipulations expresses quant au droit applicable aux Contrats, le tribunal devra déterminer si les parties ont implicitement décidé du choix du ou des droits régissant les Contrats. A cet effet, le tribunal ne considérera pas chaque contrat isolément mais comme des expressions entrelacées d'une longue relation entre les parties couvrant plus de dix années [. . .]. Cependant, ceci n'implique pas qu'il convienne de se passer d'un jugement ni sur le degré d'influence réciproque ou d'interdépendance entre les différents Contrats ni sur l'impact que l'exécution totale ou partielle ou l'inexécution de ces Contrats peut avoir sur un autre d'entre eux ou sur tous les autres.

Le tribunal estime également que les indications des parties concernant le droit applicable visées à l'article 13 (3) du Règlement d'arbitrage de la CCI doivent être interprétées [. . .] sur la base d'un test objectif révélant ce qu'aurait dû être l'intention et l'attente raisonnable des parties concernant le droit applicable, comme en témoigne aussi bien toutes les circonstances entourant la négociation des Contrats que les dispositions contractuelles susceptibles de révéler le droit applicable, c'est-à-dire une approche "contextuelle" (voir Sentence Arbitrale Ruler of Qatar v. International Marine Oil Company, ILR 534, 544 (1957); P. S. Atiyah, An Introduction to the Law of Contract, Oxford, 154 (1986); E. Allan Farnsworth, Contracts, Little Brown 478, 492-493 (1982); N. Nassar, Sanctity of Contracts Revisited, Martinus Nijhoff, 27, 28, 54-55 (1995)).

A cet égard, la question du droit applicable était clairement une question importante au cours de la négociation des Contrats et qui a fait l'objet d'une considération attentive de la part de chaque partie dans ses efforts pour promouvoir l'application de son droit national respectif. Des domaines aussi étroitement liés que la neutralité du droit applicable et le mécanisme de la solution des litiges étaient au premier plan des intérêts et des discussions des parties, et il est évident que la manière dont elles furent finalement traitées s'est trouvée au centre des compromis négociés avec soin persuadant les parties de contracter.

Au cœur des considérations de chacune des parties au cours des négociations contractuelles était la ferme résolution de ne pas accepter l'application du droit national du cocontractant, ainsi que le montre, par exemple, l'absence dans les Contrats de stipulations concernant l'application d'un de ces droits ou d'une combinaison d'entre eux [. . .].

Six des neuf contrats contiennent les expressions "natural justice", "rules of natural justice" ou "laws of natural justice" en relation avec la résolution des litiges par l'arbitrage commercial [. . .].

Il est donc clair que la présence d'expressions telles que "natural justice", "laws of natural justice" et "rules of natural justice", qui étaient indubitablement le sujet d'une considération et d'une négociation attentive, ne peut être ignorée afin d'estimer si et dans quelle mesure les parties ont indiqué les droits ou principes régissant les Contrats. Toutefois, afin de comprendre leurs significations, il serait inapproprié de recourir exclusivement, aux concepts juridiques de l'un des systèmes de droit national dont l'application est en jeu. Le fait que les Contrats soient rédigés en anglais n'est pas décisif car cette langue est devenue un instrument international utilisé afin d'exprimer les conditions de transactions sophistiquées, même entre parties n'étant pas ressortissantes de pays anglophones ou s'engageant dans des transactions sans aucun rapport avec l'un de ces pays. Recourir à l'anglais lorsqu'il s'agit d'exposer noir sur blanc la substance même d'une affaire n'implique pas nécessairement adopter la signification technique qu'une juridiction spécifique de "common law" attribuerait aux termes utilisés, particulièrement alors que l'anglais est également la langue d'autres juridictions de "common law" qui ne connaissent pas l'expression "natural justice" ou ne lui donnent pas le sens qui lui est attribué en droit anglais (par exemple, cette expression, et d'autres telles que "rules of natural justice" ou "laws of natural justice" sont dépourvues de toute signification technique aux Etats Unis, ne sont pas utilisées couramment par des tribunaux et ne figurent même pas dans le Black's Law Dictionnary (5ᵉ édition 1979)). Ces expressions sont donc particulièrement ambiguës lorsqu'on les trouve dans des contrats internationaux qui ne sont pas expressément soumis au droit anglais et plus spécifiquement par rapport à la partie non anglaise et dont le système juridique ne fait pas partie de la "common law".

La détermination des connotations procédurales ou matérielles de l'expression "natural justice" ainsi que d'autres termes similaires, a un impact sur le droit ou les droits applicables aux Contrats et fait partie du processus de choix ayant pour objet la détermination de ce droit ou ces droits. D'autre part, cinq des six contrats dans lesquels le terme "natural justice" ou des expressions similaires sont utilisées, furent, depuis le début, soumis par les parties à l'arbitrage commercial international. Le sixième contrat fut soumis à une forme d'arbitrage commercial hautement délocalisée et indépendante comparable à l'arbitrage commercial international, un trait confirmé par la conduite ultérieure des parties puisqu'elles soumirent ce neuvième contrat avec les autres à une forme unifiée d'arbitrage commercial international. En conséquence, il convient, sur la base des dispositions des Contrats et de toutes les circonstances environnantes, d'établir la signification et la portée du terme "natural justice" et des expressions similaires, de la perspective autonome tant du droit international que de l'arbitrage commercial international.

C'est un principe général d'interprétation largement accepté par les systèmes juridiques nationaux et par la pratique des tribunaux arbitraux internationaux, y compris les tribunaux CCI, qu'en cas de doute ou d'ambiguïté, les dispositions, termes ou clauses contractuelles doivent être interprétés à l'encontre de la partie qui les a rédigés ("contra proferentem") (E. Gaillard : Juris Classeurs, Arbitrage Commerical International, Droit Applicable au fond du litige, Droit International, Fasc. 586-9-1; Procédure civile, Fasc.

1070-1, n° 56, 16-17, 1991; Anson's Law of Contract (A.G. Guest Ed.), 26th Ed. Oxford, 137, 1984). D'autre part, la signification devant être attribuée aux expressions contenues dans des transactions internationales soumises, ab initio, à l'arbitrage commercial international, doit être cohérente avec la nature et le rôle attendu de la méthode choisie par les parties afin de résoudre le litige et l'impact concomitant de ce choix non seulement par rapport aux aspects procéduraux mais également par rapport à la loi régissant le fond du litige. Enfin, c'est également une pratique généralement acceptée par les tribunaux arbitraux internationaux, fondée sur des notions élémentaires de cohérence et de rationalité, que d'assumer que les mêmes mots ou expressions doivent avoir la même signification dans tous les documents qui les contiennent (E. Gaillard, op. cit., n° 55). Le tribunal estime, sans trop étendre la portée de ces principes, que cela s'applique à des situations telles que celle auquel il est confronté, et dans laquelle les expressions identiques ou similaires sont répétées dans différents contrats entre les mêmes parties, montrant une inter-relation fonctionnelle notable, et qui, de plus, doivent être considérées comme un ensemble afin de déterminer le droit applicable au fond du litige.

Le mot commun à ces expressions contenues dans six des neuf contrats ("natural justice", "laws of natural justice", "rules of natural justice"), est précisément le mot "justice" qui, indubitablement, est l'élément prédominant qui doit être pris en considération afin d'estimer leur signification et leur portée. Dans l'arbitrage commercial international, bien qu'il soit imaginable que le terme "justice" soit utilisé uniquement dans le sens de justice procédurale, c'est-à-dire respect du droit d'être entendu et à un procès juste, il est communément interprété comme se référant à la justice arbitrale dans un sens large, et comprenant non seulement la justice procédurale arbitrale mais également un type de solution du fond du litige — pas nécessairement le même que celle qui serait obtenue des tribunaux nationaux — qui est escompté par les parties lorsqu'elles choisissent l'arbitrage commercial international en vue de résoudre leurs litiges. En conséquence, il n'est pas rare que soit mentionné le fait que les parties ont souvent recours à l'arbitrage afin d'avoir accès à une "justice" autre que celle qu'elles auraient obtenues par l'application d'un "droit national", particulièrement lorsqu'en raison des circonstances inhérentes à l'affaire, un droit national ne serait pas adapté à la solution du litige (R. David, Arbitrage et Droit comparé, 11 : Revue Internationale de Droit comparé, 11-14, 1959; B. Goldman, La Lex Mercatoria dans les contrats et les arbitrages internationaux, 106 : JDI (Clunet) 1979, p. 475, 481). Une évidente confirmation que les notions de justice dans l'arbitrage commercial international ne sont pas uniquement procédurales mais également matérielles, est que la majorité des lois nationales traitant de l'arbitrage international, des conventions internationales d'arbitrage non seulement concernées par la reconnaissance et l'exécution des clauses et des sentences arbitrales et des règlements d'arbitrage internationaux, contiennent des dispositions procédurales et des dispositions sur le droit applicable, c'est-à-dire, des dispositions prévoyant des solutions de droit applicable ne devenant pertinentes que lorsque le litige a été soumis à l'arbitrage commercial international et qui peuvent tout aussi bien différer de celles qui auraient été adoptées si la décision avait été laissée à des tribunaux étatiques et à leur droit international privé.

Le tribunal, étant confronté, selon le mandat des parties, à un exercice de choix de droit pour déterminer la loi applicable aux Contrats, doit également examiner la signification du mot justice dans le cadre des conflits de lois. Selon un des textes classiques anglais de droit international privé, la notion de justice a un sens clairement matériel et pas seulement procédural, et, en effet, la justice dans son sens matériel constituerait une pierre angulaire de la discipline, étant donné que "le principe motivant dominant" d'un système de droit international privé comme le système anglais est "le désir de rendre la justice dans des affaires impliquant un élément étranger". Plus précisément, "en ce qui concerne le droit anglais, le principe se trouve a priori selon la loi dans les termes du serment que chaque juge doit prononcer avant d'entrer dans ses fonctions judiciaires; et, deuxièmement, la justice apparaît dans les résultats comme dans les prémisses. La décision du juge, qui, elle-même, établit ou applique une règle, convertit le postulat de justice en une réalité". Il est clair également qu'on n'entend pas simplement la justice comme une justice de conflits fondée sur une désignation aveugle, mécanique et "neutre" de la loi applicable au travers d'une règle de conflits qui opère sur la base d'une localisation géographique de la transaction, mais qu'elle touche aux conséquences de l'équité résultant de l'application de telle ou telle règle matérielle au point litigieux en cause (R. H. Graveson, Conflict of Laws, Private International Law : Sweet & Maxwell, 7th ed., 7-8 (1974)).

Cette essence matérielle de la justice de droit international privé est par ailleurs illustrée par une référence à des décisions de différentes cours ou autorités anglaises [. . .] L'équilibre et l'opportunité de la solution matérielle des litiges ont largement été considérés comme participant de la justice naturelle et du principe du raisonnable inhérent à cette notion [. . .] La tendance favorisant les méthodes de choix de loi qui ne seraient pas indifférentes à assurer l'application de lois ou normes matérielles offrant la "meilleure" solution pour le cas spécifique en fonction des considérations d'équité, de justice substantive, d'attentes raisonnables des parties et du fait que la règle applicable avancée est la mieux adaptée aux circonstances de l'affaire, est loin d'être limitée à des systèmes nationaux isolés de droit international privé [. . .].

Il y a, donc, une correspondance claire entre, d'un côté, le mandat d'arbitres internationaux de rendre une décision équitable et juste, adaptée à la controverse spécifique qui est en cause sans être liés par des précédents ou des considérations abstraites et, comme c'est le cas en l'espèce, sans stipulations contractuelles des parties amenant les arbitres à appliquer une loi nationale ou un système juridique particulier, et, d'un autre côté, des méthodes de conflit de lois visant à atteindre des solutions équitables et justes en appliquant des règles juridiques et des principes matériels qui sont mieux adaptés aux circonstances de l'affaire [. . .] Du point de vue des principes de conflit de lois dans l'arbitrage commercial international, la notion de justice dépasse l'équité procédurale et joue un rôle important dans la détermination de la loi matérielle applicable.

En particulier, associée à l'arbitrage commercial international, la justice du choix de la loi est fondée sur l'idée que les affaires internationales sont imparfaitement régies par des lois d'une seule juridiction nationale, vu que par leur nature, elles constituent un "ensemble social et économique", pour lequel, en ce qu'il dépasse les frontières nationales, il n'existe pas "d'unité de droit" équivalente complète et faite sur mesure, suffisamment adaptée aux circonstances d'affaires internationales et aux attentes des parties, qui lui donnerait une solution matérielle équitable et juste [. . .] Des méthodes de conflits de lois proposant l'application de ce type de règles matérielles aux affaires internationales sont alors les mieux adaptées pour résoudre les affaires commerciales internationales sur la base de la justice matérielle, des attentes équitables des parties et des circonstances de l'affaire [. . .].

S'agissant de transactions comme les Contrats, dans lesquelles (i) il n'y a pas de stipulation expresse de choix de loi désignant la loi d'une quelconque des parties ou d'un pays tiers et où la neutralité quant au droit applicable constituait un élément essentiel révélé par le rejet par les parties de leur loi respective et l'absence de référence explicite ou implicite au droit d'un pays tiers; et où (ii) les parties ont garanti la neutralité quant à la loi applicable par l'acceptation de soumettre leurs litiges contractuels à l'arbitrage commercial international, encore que sans donner pouvoir au tribunal d'agir ex æquo et bono ou comme amiable compositeur, on ne peut que conclure qu'aucune loi nationale n'a été jugée adéquate ou adaptée pour régir de telles transactions, sous peine de rompre l'équilibre de neutralité entre les parties. En conséquence, quand les parties ont négocié et finalement conclu les Contrats, elles n'ont laissé la place qu'à l'application de règles de droit général et de principes suffisamment adéquats pour régir les Contrats, mais non originaires d'un système spécifique de droit national. Un tel équilibre de neutralité, qui comprend la neutralité du droit matériel applicable, constitue une part essentielle de la justice matérielle attendue des parties relativement aux Contrats. Un tel choix "négatif" par les parties appelle autant de respect qu'un quelconque choix de loi exprès aurait mérité si les parties avaient inséré dans les Contrats des dispositions quant au choix de la loi; aussi, afin de ne pas troubler la commune intention des parties à cet égard, ce tribunal doit s'abstenir de choisir une quelconque loi nationale comme loi applicable. Au travers de références à la "justice naturelle" ou expressions similaires, les parties ont indiqué leur intention que les Contrats soient gouvernés par des règles matérielles n'appartenant à aucun système juridique particulier et répondant de manière appropriée à leurs préoccupations de neutralité du droit applicable.

Bien que les parties aient exclu l'application d'une quelconque loi nationale aux Contrats, il ne s'en suit pas qu'elles n'ont pas pu supposer l'application d'autres règles ou principes matériels et ainsi laisser la décision quant à la désignation de la loi applicable aux Contrats aux hasards des méthodes de conflits de lois [sur] lesquelles elles n'ont aucun contrôle, particulièrement quant à leur neutralité pour déterminer la loi applicable. A cet égard, le postulat que "[. . .] les principes de conflits de lois pleinement neutres sont une illusion" (A. Lowenfeld, "Lex Mercatoria : an arbitrator's view" in Lex Mercatoria and Arbitration (Carbonneau Ed.) Transnational Juris Publications, Inc. 37, 45 (1990)) est certainement pertinent et prend ici une signification particulière.

Une telle interprétation est particulièrement opportune si la seule alternative offerte en l'absence de dispositions expresses ou implicites quant au choix de la loi était de s'en remettre à des critères de conflits de lois supposés neutres et objectifs, telle que la notion talismanique de la localisation de l'obligation caractéristique, un groupement informe de points de contact ou le rattachement le plus étroit, connus de certains systèmes juridiques nationaux qui, en tirant au sort, et sans prendre en compte les intérêts et attentes des parties quant à la justice matérielle, y compris la neutralité du droit applicable, impose la loi de l'une des parties ou d'un état tiers qui peut aller à l'encontre des intentions des parties.

"[. . .] cinq contrats sur neuf comprenaient des clauses d'arbitrage international prévoyant des tribunaux excluant les nationaux du pays de l'une quelconque des parties. Les autres contrats, bien qu'ils ne soient pas expressément soumis à l'arbitrage international institutionnel, à la fois à cause de l'introduction d'expressions telles que justice naturelle ou lois ou règles de justice naturelle eu égard au processus de résolution du litige (comme indiqué précédemment, de tels termes ont à la fois des connotations procédurales> et matérielles>) et l'omission de la désignation d'une lex arbitrii nationale ou de loi procédurale, renvoyaient à une sorte d'arbitrage commercial extrêmement délocalisé sans tenir compte du siège du tribunal arbitral [. . .] Le comportement ultérieur des parties, c'est-à-dire leur décision de soumettre globalement leurs litiges résultant des Contrats à l'arbitrage international sous l'égide des règles CCI, est une preuve claire et la confirmation que les parties ont préféré la délocalisation du système de résolution des litiges eu égard à tous les Contrats en conformité avec leurs fortes préoccupations quant à la neutralité du cadre légal matériel et procédural dans leurs relations à long terme concrétisées par les Contrats".

De telles considérations prennent une importance particulière quand les transactions en cause, en plus d'être commerciales et internationales, sont aussi colorées — comme en l'espèce — par un certain degré de participation étatique ou publique des deux côtés. Le tribunal considère qu'aucune preuve concluante ne lui a été présentée démontrant que les Contrats pouvaient être regardés comme des contrats entre Etats vu qu'il n'a pas été prouvé que le Défendeur est organiquement lié à l'Etat britannique, investi d'une quelconque de ses fonctions ou sinon assimilé à l'Etat britannique de manière à acquérir une position considérablement différente de celle d'une partie privée. Néanmoins, les Contrats, bien que commerciaux par nature, ont une partie étatique, ont été négociés, exécutés, et les obligations des parties se sont insérées dans un contexte dans lequel les intérêts et la politique de l'Etat sont très étroitement concernés des deux côtés [. . .] Les Contrats, appartiennent alors indiscutablement à la catégorie des contrats du commerce international (qui pour les besoins de cette sentence seront ci-après dénommés "contrats d'Etat") qui ont fait l'objet d'une résolution de l'Institut de Droit International sur "L'Arbitrage entre Etats, Entreprises Publiques, Entités Publiques et Entreprises Etrangères" adoptée le 12 septembre 1989 au cours de la session Saint Jacques de Compostelle de l'Institut. Une telle Résolution visait à servir de guide aux arbitres du commerce international pour, entre autres, déterminer les lois, règles et principes applicables à la substance de ce type de transaction [. . .].

Les contrats d'Etat comportent un certain nombre de caractéristiques paradigmatiques que ce tribunal considère d'importance eu égard aux Contrats. Parmi ceux-ci les suivants sont pertinents : (i) l'Etat partie ne devrait pas être autorisé à utiliser ses pouvoirs législatifs non dans l'intérêt général mais pour améliorer sa position juridique ou échapper à sa responsabilité contractuelle [. . .] (ii) les parties peuvent expressément ou implicitement délocaliser les contrats d'Etat pour les soustraire aux systèmes juridiques nationaux et les soumettre à des règles légales transnationales [. . .] (iii) la loi applicable devrait respecter le principe que "l'équilibre contractuel" matériel entre les parties tel qu'entendu au moment de contracter ne soit pas rompu [. . .] (iv) détachement du processus arbitral et de la lex fori arbitrale en général (y compris les méthodes de conflits de lois pour déterminer la loi applicable au fond) de la loi du siège de l'arbitrage [. . .] (v) le choix de l'arbitrage international commercial en matière de contrats d'Etat a un impact sur le droit matériel applicable à la substance du litige.

Eu égard à ce dernier aspect, il est pertinent de souligner que les parties et les arbitres jouissent d'une plus grande autonomie pour délocaliser le contrat et déterminer les lois ou règles applicables quand les litiges naissant en matière de contrats d'Etat sont soumis à l'arbitrage international qu'autrement, et, ainsi, que de choisir l'arbitrage commercial international a des effets délocalisant quant à la loi applicable : ceci peut être démontré par exemple quand on compare (i) le Préambule et les dispositions de la Résolution adoptée par l'Institut de Droit International lors de sa session d'Athènes sur le Droit Applicable au Contrat dans les Conventions entre un Etat et une Personne Privée Etrangère, traitant en général de thèmes intéressant le droit applicable à un contrat d'Etat qui en principe n'est pas nécessairement soumis à l'arbitrage commercial international [. . .] avec (ii) la Résolution de Saint Jacques de Compostelle mentionnée ci-dessus, en particulier ses art. 4 et 6, qui concernent exclusivement la loi applicable aux contrats d'Etat par les arbitres du commerce international. Le détachement des méthodes de choix de loi et du droit substantiel applicable grâce à ces méthodes des systèmes juridiques nationaux afin de préserver l'équilibre recherché par l'Etat et la partie privée est alors un caractère commun à l'arbitrage en matière de contrat d'Etat qui doit être pris en compte au moment d'interpréter de tels contrats et les circonstances les entourant pour déterminer la loi les régissant.

En l'espèce, un tel équilibre était une partie intégrante du cadre matériel et de justice de résolution des litiges que les parties avaient en vue quand elles ont conclu les contrats d'Etat qui les lient. Aussi, les références à la "justice naturelle" et "lois" ou "règles" de "justice naturelle" que l'on trouve dans la majorité des Contrats devraient être interprétées avec logique et uniformément comme se référant non seulement à la justice procédurale mais également au type particulier de justice matérielle que les parties avaient en vue, basé sur la neutralité de la loi applicable au fond et les mécanismes de résolution des litiges choisis par les parties pour rendre effective la neutralité matérielle, ce dernier aspect étant confirmé par la suite par la soumission ultérieure et complète par les parties de leurs litiges nés des Contrats à l'arbitrage international CCI.

Le choix de l'arbitrage international ou délocalisé pour résoudre des litiges éventuels, lequel est explicite depuis le début dans la plupart des Contrats mais qui a été par la suite étendu à l'ensemble des Contrats, devrait alors être entendu comme un élément complémentaire pour soutenir davantage et maintenir un tel équilibre de justice matérielle. Un tel choix joue un rôle "localisant" en matière de contrats d'Etat internationaux et commerciaux n'ayant pas de stipulation expresse de choix de loi, dès lors que cela révèle l'exclusion des critères de choix de loi normalement applicables par les juridictions nationales, qui devrait conduire à l'application exclusive de droits nationaux, et donc désigne par exclusion un tertium genus ou des principes généraux de droit qui peuvent être seulement définis dans la négative comme telles règles ou principes n'appartenant pas exclusivement à un système juridique national unique [. . .] S'agissant de contrats d'Etat internationaux et commerciaux, la référence dans les Contrats à la justice naturelle ou autres dispositions similaires, de même que l'absence de référence à une loi nationale, peut donc être raisonnablement interprétée comme conduisant à l'application de telles règles ou principes juridiques matériels adaptés aux Contrats et aux faits et circonstances les entourant, qui, pour n'appartenir à aucun système juridique national particulier, répondent aux préoccupations des parties quant à la neutralité de la loi applicable. Les règles et principes matériels remplissant de tels critères peuvent n'être que des règles et principes de droit généraux quant aux obligations contractuelles internationales et jouissant d'un large consensus international.

De plus, le tribunal considère que son mandat [. . .] requiert que, dans la mesure où cela s'avère possible à ce stade, quelques précisions soient données quant à la substance de tels principes et règles juridiques. Il devrait être noté que le Demandeur comme le Défendeur, à différents stades de leurs argumentations successives, ont exprimé leurs préoccupations quant à l'imprécision des principes généraux du droit ou quant à la possibilité (du moins concernant les tribunaux anglais) qu'une sentence rendue sur la base de tels principes pourrait ne pas être susceptible d'exécution forcée devant des tribunaux nationaux.

Prenant en compte de telles circonstances, les discussions à ce sujet avec les parties [. . .] et aussi l'exigence que les arbitres "[. . .] ne fassent pas moins que ce qui est nécessaire pour exercer pleinement leur autorité [. . .]" (Institut du Droit International Privé, Saint Jacques de Compostelle, Résolution citée ci-dessus, Art. 1, 63 II International Law Institue Yearbook 326 (1990)), ce tribunal considère que les règles et principes généraux jouissant d'un large consensus international, applicables aux obligations contractuelles internationales et applicables aux Contrats, sont principalement reflétés par les Principes relatifs aux Contrats de Commerce International adoptés par UNIDROIT (les "Principes Unidroit") en 1994 [. . .]. En conséquence, sous réserve de la prise en compte des dispositions des Contrats et des usages du commerce applicables, le tribunal considère que les Contrats sont régis par, et doivent être interprétés conformément [aux] Principes Unidroit eu égard à toutes les questions entrant dans le champ d'application de ces Principes, et pour toutes les autres questions, par les autres règles et principes juridiques généraux applicables aux obligations contractuelles internationales jouissant d'un large consensus international, qui seraient considérés comme applicables pour trancher des questions controversées dans le cadre du présent arbitrage.

Les raisons pour lesquelles le tribunal considère que les Principes Unidroit sont la composante principale des règles et principes généraux concernant les obligations contractuelles internationales jouissant d'un large consensus international, lesquelles constituent la loi même des Contrats, sont variées : (1) les Principes Unidroit sont la reformulation de principes juridiques internationaux applicables aux contrats du commerce international fait par un groupe distingué d'experts internationaux venant de tous les systèmes juridiques dominants dans le monde, sans l'intervention d'Etats ou de gouvernements, ces deux circonstances contribuant à la haute qualité et à la neutralité du produit et à sa capacité à refléter le présent état de consensus sur les règles et principes juridiques internationaux régissant les obligations contractuelles internationales dans le monde, principalement en raison de leur équité et du fait qu'ils sont appropriés aux transactions du commerce international entrant dans leur champ d'application; (2) en même temps, les Principes Unidroit sont largement inspirés [par] un texte de droit uniforme international qui jouit déjà d'une large reconnaissance internationale et généralement considéré comme reflétant les usages et pratiques commerciaux internationaux dans le champ de la vente internationale de marchandises, qui a déjà été ratifié par presque 40 pays, la Convention de Vienne de 1980 sur la Vente Internationale de Marchandises; (3) les Principes Unidroit sont spécialement adaptés aux Contrats objets de cet arbitrage, étant donné qu'ils couvrent à la fois la vente internationale de marchandises et la fourniture de services; (4) les Principes Unidroit (voir leur Préambule) ont été particulièrement conçus pour s'appliquer aux contrats internationaux en cours dans lesquels, comme dans la présente procédure, il a été considéré que les parties avaient consenti à ce que leurs transactions soient régies par les règles et principes de droit généraux; et (5) plutôt que des principes vagues ou des directives générales, les Principes Unidroit sont pour la plupart constitués de règles clairement énoncées et spécifiques, organisées de manière cohérente et de façon systématique [. . .].

Les précisions données par le tribunal dans le précédent paragraphe [. . .] devraient suffire à dissiper toutes préoccupations quant au caractère exécutoire d'une sentence rendue dans cette procédure sur la base des règles et principes de droit généraux applicables aux obligations internationales du fait de l'imprécision ou du manque de précision de tels principes [. . .] Des opinions de personnalités éminentes indiquent que la tendance actuelle en Angleterre se dirige vers l'admissibilité et le caractère exécutoire dans ce pays des sentences arbitrales fondées sur la lex mercatoria ou les principes généraux du droit, particulièrement quand la sentence n'a pas été rendue en Angleterre ou n'est pas soumise à la loi anglaise et que les lois du pays où la sentence est rendue ne rendent pas invalides une sentence émise dans de telles conditions [. . .].

Les conclusions susmentionnées n'auraient pas été différentes si le tribunal n'avait pas considéré que les parties avaient fait un choix implicite quant au droit applicable aux Contrats. Tout d'abord, il devrait être noté qu'il est communément accepté dans le droit international privé comparé qu'il n'y a pas de délimitation claire entre les critères pour déterminer le choix de loi implicite fait par les parties quant à la substance des obligations contractuelles et ceux à observer en l'absence de choix et en fait les frontières entre de tels critères sont souvent imprécises [. . .] Les mêmes circonstances objectives, telles qu'en l'espèce, l'intention des parties de ne pas soumettre les Contrats à leur droit respectif ou au droit d'un pays tiers et donc leur volonté de voir leur litige tranché conformément aux règles de droit et non ex æquo et bono, la nature de la relation entre les parties (contrats d'Etat) et leurs préoccupations quant à la neutralité eu égard au droit applicable révélé, par exemple, par les négociations contractuelles, l'insertion de termes tels que "justice naturelle" ou "lois de justice naturelle" ou "règles de justice naturelle" et la soumission de tous litiges à l'arbitrage commercial international militent également en faveur de la conclusion que les règles et principes généraux du droit quant aux obligations contractuelles internationales jouissant d'un large consensus international auraient été considérés comme le droit régissant les Contrats même en l'absence d'une stipulation contractuelle implicite à cette fin.

Le tribunal en serait venu à cette conclusion que ce soit en recourant à la voie directe (en français dans le texte) ou à la voie indirecte (en français dans le texte). La pratique des tribunaux arbitraux de la CCI, acceptée par une doctrine qui fait autorité, a montré que l'article 13 (3) du Règlement de la CCI ou des dispositions semblables, n'interdit pas aux arbitres de recourir à la voie directe (voir note J. J. Arnaldez, JDI 1992, 1017; B. Goldman, "Les conflits de lois dans l'arbitrage international de droit privé", 109, Recueil de La Haye 1963, 390/391; Y. Derains, "Attente légitime des parties et Droit applicable au fond en matière d'arbitrage commercial international", Travaux du Comité Français de Droit International Privé, 1984-1985, 81, 85 (1987)). Les circonstances identifiées dans [. . .]

522

la présente sentence auraient conduit à la conclusion, par application de la voie directe, sans l'interposition d'une règle de conflits de lois, que les contrats sont régis par les règles et les principes généraux applicables aux obligations contractuelles, telles que définies plus haut.

[. . .] la détermination du droit applicable est un exercise qui ne peut ignorer le résultat matériel du processus du choix de loi. Si on s'attache au domaine de l'arbitrage commercial international et à l'interprétation de la partie pertinente de l'article 13 (3) du Règlement d'arbitrage CCI, la conclusion nécessaire est que la distinction même entre voie indirecte et voie directe devient imprécise et est sur le point de disparaître, car les deux poursuivent les mêmes finalités avec essentiellement les mêmes moyens, soit, l'application du "meilleur droit", c'est-à-dire les règles, lois et principes matériels les mieux adaptés à une solution juste et équitable du litige, sur la base des circonstances de l'affaire et des attentes des parties, par la prise en compte directe, à cet effet, du contenu des règles et principes matériels à appliquer. En vertu des considérations exposées dans [. . .] la présente sentence à l'égard des Contrats, ce "meilleur droit" se trouve dans les règles et principes généraux concernant les obligations contractuelles jouissant d'un large consensus international. Comme ces règles et principes sont censés être directement applicables, en l'absence de choix, aux transactions définies comme des contrats d'Etats commerciaux internationaux, leur application peut aussi être expliquée selon la méthode de la voie indirecte car cette définition est précisément une règle de conflit, quoique différente des règles traditionnelles, en ce que sa mise en œuvre ne dépend pas de la localisation géographique d'un facteur de rattachement (B. Goldman, JDI, 1990, 430, 440; du même auteur, Nouvelles réflexions sur la lex mercatoria, Etude de Droit International Privé en l'honneur de Pierre Lalive (Dominice, Patry & Reymond, Eds), Helbing & Lichtenham, 241, 253 (1993)). Comme l'a souligné F. A. Mann, « . . . la référence à un système juridique qui n'est pas territorialement défini est tout à fait conciliable avec la doctrine traditionnelle des conflits de lois » (F. A. Mann, Studies in International Law (Oxford) 226 (1973)).

"[. . .] L'article 13 (3) du Règlement d'Arbitrage de la CCI n'impose pas aux arbitres d'appliquer les règles de conflit de lois généralement acceptées ou, dans ce cas précis, une règle particulière de conflit de lois nationale ou anationale. [. . .] Dans cette procédure on a suffisamment débattu de façon convaincante que la méthode cumulative, c'est-à-dire l'application des systèmes de conflit de lois des Etats des parties au litige, n'aurait pas été utile car les règles de droit international privé anglaise et de l'Etat X auraient conduit à des solutions incompatibles plutôt que convergentes quant au choix du droit en ce qui concerne la plupart des contrats. D'autre part, étant donné la diversité des systèmes de droit international privé dans le monde, une recherche de droit comparé ne permettrait pas d'identifier les grands principes de droit international privé qui jouissent d'une reconnaissance internationale pour la détermination du droit applicable aux contrats internationaux en l'absence de choix explicite ou implicite des parties. [. . .]"

Néanmoins, on peut prétendre que, lorsqu'il s'agit de déterminer la substance de telles règles et principes généraux applicables en l'absence d'une stipulation implicite par les parties, l'application des principes UNIDROIT est impossible car le préambule à ces principes indique qu'ils peuvent être appliqués "lorsque les parties sont convenu que leur contrat sera régi par les principes généraux du droit, de la lex mercatoria ou équivalent". La version du projet original des principes UNIDROIT, qui, en fin de compte, ne fut pas approuvée à cet égard par le Conseil UNIDROIT, prévoyait (Art. 1.2 (b)) que ces principes seraient également applicables "lorsque les parties n'ont pas choisi de droit pour régir leur contrat" [. . .]. Cette condition fut exclue du texte des Principes UNIDROIT finalement approuvé et ne fait pas partie du Préambule car le Conseil UNIDROIT estimait qu'en l'absence de choix par les parties, cela reviendrait à exclure l'application de la loi interne du système juridique national rendu applicable parles règles de droit international privé [. . .].

Toutefois, en se basant sur au moins deux facteurs, il n'aurait pas été impossible au tribunal de se référer aux Principes UNIDROIT comme à une partie du droit applicable aux contrats en l'absence de stipulation expresse ou implicite d'un choix de droit : (i) [. . .] les contrats sont régis, ainsi qu'il résulte d'une décision préliminaire, par des règles et principes généraux concernant les obligations contractuelles internationales, qui jouissent d'un large consensus international, c'est-à-dire qu'ils ne sont pas régis par un droit national particulier. En conséquence, et dans le cas présent, aucun conflit entre une quelconque loi nationale et les Principes UNIDROIT n'est possible; et (ii) l'application des Principes UNIDROIT ne dépend pas de leur propre critère d'application, mais des pouvoirs reçus par le tribunal en vertu de l'article 13 (3) du Règlement d'Arbitrage de la CCI, lesquels ne sont pas limités à la voie indirecte et l'autorisent à déterminer directement le droit applicable qu'il juge le plus approprié pour régir le fond du litige, c'est-à-dire, dans ce cas, les règles et principes juridiques généraux concernant les obligations con-tractuelles internationales qui jouissent d'un large consensus y compris, sans exclusion, les Principes UNIDROIT comme une reformulation adéquate et une expression de ces règles juridiques et principes généraux. L'application de ces Principes en cas d'absence de choix repose donc sur l'article 13 (3) du Règlement d'Arbitrage de la CCI et sur le mandat conféré au tribunal pour trouver et déterminer le droit applicable aux Contrats.

[. . .] Le tribunal conclut alors, à la majorité, [. . .] que, sous réserve de la prise en compte des dispositions des Contrats et des usages de commerce pertinents, les Contrats seront régis et interprétés en accord avec les règles juridiques et principes généraux concernant les obligations contractuelles internationales qui jouissent d'un large consen-sus international, y compris les Principes UNIDROIT, eu égard à toutes les situations qui entrent dans le champ d'application de ces principes. »

OBSERVATIONS. — I. — Cette sentence, avec un souci pédagogique trop rare maintenant que l'arbitrage commercial international se banalise de plus en plus en raison de son succès comme mode de solution des litiges du commerce international, fait le point sur la situation de l'arbitre lorsqu'en l'absence de choix exprès des parties, il lui appartient de déterminer le droit applicable au fond du litige. Il est vrai que le litige se présentait sous un jour particulier, s'agissant de contrats d'Etats dans lesquels les parties avaient fait diverses références à la « *justice naturelle* », sans dire expressément qu'elles y voyaient le droit applicable. Cependant, dans un style dense, parfois un peu touffu, au point qu'une traduc-tion ne peut qu'être imparfaite, le Tribunal arbitral affirme avec vigueur le caractère artificiel de l'application des règles traditionnelles de conflit de lois en matière d'arbitrage commercial international, dont le résultat répond rarement à l'attente légitime des parties.

Selon le Tribunal arbitral, le choix des parties quant au droit applicable peut être aussi bien implicite qu'exprès. Interprétant l'article 13 (3) du Règlement d'arbitrage de la CCI, dans sa version de 1988, il en déduit que ce n'est donc qu'en l'absence d'un choix même implicite qu'un arbitre doit appliquer la loi désignée par la règle de conflit qu'il jugera appropriée en l'espèce. L'intérêt de cette approche dépasse celui de l'interprétation d'un texte aujourd'hui périmé. En effet, comme le rappelle le Tribunal arbitral, la solution de l'article 13 (3) du Règlement d'arbitrage de la CCI de 1988 (. . . « *A défaut d'indications par les parties du droit applicable, l'arbitre appliquera la loi désignée par la règle de conflit qu'il jugera appropriée en l'espèce* ») se retrouve à l'article 33 (1) du Règlement d'arbitrage de la CNUDCI et également à l'article 28 (2) de la Loi Modèle de la CNUDCI. De plus, la notion de choix par les parties du droit applicable doit également être précisée lorsqu'il s'agit de mettre en œuvre le texte actuellement en vigueur du règlement d'arbitrage de la CCI dont l'article 17 dispose : « . . . *A défaut du choix par les parties des règles du droit applicable, l'arbitre appliquera les règles de droit qu'il juge appropriées* ». L'absence d'un choix exprès n'équivaut pas à un défaut de choix si les arbitres peuvent établir un choix implicite.

Pour découvrir le choix implicite des parties quant au droit applicable, le Tribunal arbitral recherche à partir de facteurs objectifs ce qu'auraient été leurs « *intentions et attentes raisonnables* » ce qui a pu paraître plus simple de définir comme « *l'attente légitime des parties* » (cf. *Y. Derains, Attente légitime des parties et droit applicable au fond du litige en matière d'arbitrage commercial international : Travaux Comité fr. DIP, 1984-1985, p.81*). Il a été suggéré que l'attente légitime des parties s'apparente « *étrangement à la fiction que constitue la volonté implicite des parties à laquelle le juge étatique a parfois recours* » *(C. Seraglini, Lois de police et justice arbitrale internationale, n° 509, p. 242)*. La présente sentence montre au contraire que la recherche de l'attente légitime des parties permet de faire perdre à la volonté implicite son caractère de fiction en la soumettant à des tests objectifs et concrets fondés sur une analyse des circonstances entourant les négociations contractuelles et des dispositions du contrat.

II. — Parmi les facteurs objectifs sur lesquels se fonde le Tribunal arbitral pour déterminer la volonté implicite des parties, le refus de chacune d'entre elles de soumettre les Contrats au droit du pays de l'autre joue un rôle prépondérant. Soulignant que pendant la négociation des Contrats, les parties ne se sont pas non plus entendues sur le droit d'un Etat tiers, les arbitres estiment qu'elles ont exprimé un choix négatif, excluant l'application de tout droit étatique. Cette démarche est tout à fait légitime. Comme l'a justement souligné E. Gaillard « . . . *Lorsque les parties n'ont pas choisi elles-mêmes la loi applicable à leurs relations, il est souvent moins conforme aux impératifs de prévisibilité et de sécurité juridique de contraindre les arbitres à choisir entre les droits étatiques en présence que de leur permettre de faire application de principes généraux puisés dans la jurisprudence arbitrale internationale et le droit comparé* » *(E. Gaillard, Trente ans de lex mercatoria. Pour une application relative de la méthode des principes généraux du droit : JDI 1995, p. 5)*. Là encore le souci de répondre à l'attente légitime des parties est sous-jacent puisque pour E. Gaillard, il s'agit essentiellement de ne pas surprendre les parties par l'application d'un droit étatique sur lequel n'avait pas porté leur choix. Mais la présente sentence va plus loin. Elle ne se contente pas de considérer que l'application d'un droit étatique serait inappropriée en l'espèce. Elle déduit de l'opposition des parties sur le choix d'un droit étatique la volonté implicite de voir appliquer des normes transnationales, à savoir des principes généraux jouissant d'un large consensus international.

III. — La référence à la « justice naturelle » dans six des neuf contrats joue évidemment un rôle prépondérant dans la découverte de cette volonté implicite. Les arbitres y voient une préoccupation des parties non seulement de soustraire leurs litiges éventuels aux règles procédurales de la justice étatique, déjà exprimée par le recours à l'arbitrage international qui implique l'intervention de règles de conflit non étatiques, mais surtout la crainte que l'application d'un droit étatique, dont l'objet est de régler des transactions internes, soit incompatible avec leur souci de neutralité juridique de la solution substantielle qui sera retenue. Ils considèrent aussi que la notion de justice naturelle s'oppose à la méthode conflictualiste classique. On ne peut s'empêcher de songer aux convictions de René David selon qui les parties recourraient à l'arbitrage pour y trouver une autre justice *(R. David, L'arbitrage dans le commerce international, n° 13, p. 20*; pour une analyse approfondie mais critique de cette thèse, voir *T. Clay, L'arbitre, p. 222 s.)*. Mais la similitude n'est que partielle. René David pensait d'une part que l'arbitrage ouvre une voie vers une justice extérieure au droit mais d'autre part, que les commerçants peuvent, par l'arbitrage « *chercher à élaborer et appliquer dans les rapports du commerce international, un droit commercial nouveau, autonome par rapport aux différents systèmes de droits nationaux, dont les théoriciens des conflits de lois, dans les différents pays, préconisent l'application* » *(R. David, op. cit., n° 16, p. 21)*. Telle est l'approche des auteurs de la présente sentence. Ils n'estiment pas que les parties ont souhaité des solutions de fond extérieures au droit, et soulignent d'ailleurs qu'ils ne sont pas amiables compositeurs. Pour eux, la référence à la « justice naturelle » est un facteur objectif supplémentaire de ce que le silence des parties quant à l'application d'un droit étatique est l'expression d'une volonté de soumettre leurs transactions à des normes transnationales. Cette démarche a l'avantage d'être réaliste et de respecter la volonté des parties. Ce serait en effet lui donner bien peu d'importance que d'appliquer au contrat, rétroactivement, en cas de litige, une loi nationale qu'une des parties au moins a expressément écartée et n'a, par conséquent, pas pris en compte pendant l'exécution du contrat. L'intervention à ce stade des solutions d'un droit étatique par le jeu d'une règle de conflit de lois choisie par l'arbitre parce qu'il l'estimait appropriée, constitue un élément de surprise, source d'une insécurité juridique beaucoup plus grande que celle susceptible de découler de l'application de normes transnationales. Comme l'avait justement souligné la sentence rendue en 1995 dans l'affaire n° 8385 *(JDI 1997, p. 1061, obs. Y. Derains) : « l'application de principes internationaux offre beaucoup d'avantages. Ils s'appliquent uniformément et sont indépendants des particularités de chaque droit national. Ils prennent en compte les besoins des relations internationales et permettent un échange fructueux entre les systèmes parfois exagérément liés à des distinctions conceptuelles et ceux qui cherchent une solution juste et pragmatique des cas particuliers ».*

IV. — La présence de l'Etat comme partie à chacun des contrats est aux yeux des arbitres un autre indice de la volonté des cocontractants de se soumettre à des normes transnationales. La question a été largement controversée et l'application de la loi de l'Etat contractant, du droit international public et de normes transnationales a été successivement préconisé en la matière. La formule de la Cour Permanente de Justice Internationale dans l'affaire des Emprunts Serbes *(CPJI, série A, Emprunts Serbes, n° 20/21, p. 41-42)* selon laquelle « *un Etat souverain . . . ne peut être présumé avoir soumis la substance de sa dette et la validité des engagements pris par lui à une loi autre que sa loi propre»* a perdu beaucoup de sa portée, surtout dans les relations avec une personne privée étrangère (cf. *J.-M. Jacquet, L'Etat opérateur du commerce international : JDI 1989, p. 621,* notamment *p. 623-626).* Sans doute parce que, comme l'a justement relevé P. Mayer, « *un contrat d'Etat ne peut comporter engagement de l'Etat souverain que s'il est soustrait, soit par une clause expresse, soit par une interprétation de la volonté des parties, au droit de l'Etat » (P. Mayer, Contrats d'Etat et pouvoir normatif de l'Etat : JDI, 1986, p. 33).* La présente sentence s'en explique fort bien en soulignant qu'il ne serait pas concevable que la partie étatique puisse utiliser son pouvoir normatif pour se dégager de ses obligations. Cela signifierait qu'en réalité elle n'est pas obligée. De même, le recours au droit international public a fait l'objet de vives réticences car la personne privée n'est pas sujet du droit international, même si l'Institut de Droit International, en 1979, à sa session d'Athènes, a adopté une résolution qui prévoit, à son article 2 que, dans les contrats d'Etat, « *les parties peuvent notamment choisir comme loi du contrat . . . le droit international » (Rev. crit. DIP 1980, p. 427),* en l'absence d'un choix explicite des parties *(F.A. Mann, The law governing states contracts, Studies in International law, p. 179).* C'est pourquoi, l'Institut du Droit International, en 1989, lors de sa session de Saint-Jacques de Compostelle *(Rev. crit. DIP 1990, p. 191)* a adopté une résolution prévoyant que lorsque les parties n'ont pas choisi le droit applicable à un contrat d'Etat, les arbitres doivent rechercher « *les règles et principes nécessaires* » parmi ceux énumérés à l'article 4 de cette résolution, où l'on trouve, entre autres, « *les principes généraux du droit international privé ou public* » et les « *principes généraux de l'arbitrage international* ». Il s'agit là de la délocalisation du contrat d'Etat que la présente sentence considère indispensable au respect de l'équilibre contractuel. Telle était déjà la solution affirmée avec vigueur par la sentence rendue en 1992 dans l'affaire n° 1992 *(JDI 1993, p. 1004, obs. Y.D.) :* « *A défaut de loi étatique applicable, le système de droit objectif gouvernant au contrat d'Etat international est formé par les principes généraux du droit des contrats internationaux* ».

V. — Pour le Tribunal arbitral, les Principes UNIDROIT fournissent aux principes généraux du droit des contrats internationaux un contenu qui en fait le « *meilleur droit* ». Son argumentation est claire et éloquente. Elle n'appelle pas de commentaires particuliers, sinon que l'on peut la rattacher, sur ce point, à l'approche de la sentence rendue en 1994 dans l'affaire n° 7331 *(JDI, 1995, p. 1001, obs. D. H.)*, dont la conclusion n'était qu'en partie différente. Cette sentence estimait en effet que les « *principes généraux du droit commercial* » et les « *usages acceptés dans la pratique commerciale internationale* » sont contenus *"de la manière la plus complète dans la Convention des Nations Unies sur la Vente Internationale des Marchandises", résultat d'un accord inter-étatique, fruit d'une collab-oration sur plus d'une décennie* ». En 1994, année de l'adoption des Principes UNIDROIT, leur texte était peu connu. Mais surtout, il est significatif que la sentence ici rapportée relève, pour justifier leur application, que les Principes UNIDROIT sont largement inspirés par la Convention de Vienne de 1980 sur la Vente Internationale de Marchandises. On peut donc voir une certaine filiation entre les deux décisions, même si contrairement à celle de 1994, celle de 1995 voit un avantage certain à ce que les Principes UNIDROIT aient été élaborés « *sans l'intervention d'Etats ou de gouvernements* ».

Il n'est pas inutile de rappeler que la notion de « *meilleur droit* » conduit également les arbitres du commerce international à appliquer les Principes UNIDROIT pour confirmer le bien fondé d'une solution puisée dans un droit national, en montrant que cette solution a été confirmée par les Principes UNIDROIT *(sentence rendue en 1996 dans l'affaire n° 5835 : Bull. Cour Internationale d'Arbitrage de la CCI, 1999, vol. 10/2, p. 34, p. 33; sentence rendue en 1996 dans l'affaire n° 8486, Bull. Cour Internationale d'Arbitrage de la CCI, 1989, vol. 10/2, n° 71; JDI 1998, p. 1047, obs. Y. D.)*. Dans ces affaires, le droit applicable avait été déterminé par les arbitres et leur souci de donner une justification complémentaire à leur décision n'est pas surprenante. Mais il arrive aussi qu'ils recherchent l'appui des Principes UNIDROIT pour justifier une solution du droit national choisi par les parties. Ainsi, dans la sentence rendue dans l'affaire n° 8233 en 1998 *(Bull. Cour Internationale d'Arbitrage de la CCI, 1999, vol. 10/2, p. 59)* où les parties avaient prévu l'application du droit français, l'arbitre jugea nécessaire de renforcer sa décision fondée sur le droit français en indiquant : « *l'analyse du tribunal arbitral a cet égard se trouve confortée par l'article 2.19 des Principes UNIDROIT applicables en matière de contrats commerciaux. . . .* ».

VI — Le Tribunal arbitral s'attache à démontrer qu'à défaut d'un choix implicite par les parties de normes transnationales, il aurait néanmoins décidé d'appliquer de telles normes, que ce soit par application ou non d'une règle de conflits de lois. Ceci lui permet d'opposer ce qu'il appelle la voie indirecte à la voie directe (sur cette notion, cf. *P. Lalive, Les règles de conflits de lois appliquées au fond du litige par l'arbitre international siégeant en Suisse : Rev. arb. 1976, p. 155*). Mais il souligne immédiatement qu'une telle distinction est largement artificielle, tout au moins en matière d'arbitrage international. En effet, à partir du moment où l'arbitre est autorisé à ce dégager des systèmes de conflits nationaux ou conventionnels pour appliquer la règle de conflits qu'il estime appropriée en l'espèce, la notion de règle de conflits perd la plus grande partie de son contenu. Une règle est censée s'appliquer de façon générale et non pas seulement si elle paraît appropriée en l'espèce à celui qui est chargé de l'appliquer. Comme le rappelle la sentence ici rapportée, les arbitres statuant dans le cadre des versions de 1975 et 1988 du Règlement de la CCI, ne se sont pas privés de recourir à la voie directe bien que le Règlement exigeait alors l'application de la « *loi désignée par la règle de conflits* » qu'ils jugeraient « *appropriée en l'espèce* ». Pour beaucoup d'entre eux, la voie directe était une « *règle de conflits appropriée* », puisqu'elle consistait à appliquer un système juridique national ou transnational, présentant des titres à régir le contrat. Mais il est bien évident qu'il s'agissait là, sinon d'un artifice, d'un procédé destiné à montrer aux parties le caractère légitime de la solution adoptée qui ne pouvait qu'être conforme à leur attente. C'est pourquoi le Règlement de la CCI, dans sa version de 1998, dans son article 17 (1), a prévu, suivant l'exemple donné par l'article 1496 du Nouveau Code de Procédure Civile Français, qu'à défaut de choix par les parties du droit applicable « *l'arbitre appliquera les règles de droit qu'il juge appropriées* . . . ».

VII — A côté du rappel de principes d'interprétation classiques comme celui de cohérence ou la règle « *contra proferentem* », le Tribunal arbitral s'interroge sur le rôle à donner à la langue du contrat lorsqu'il s'agit d'interpréter certains de ses termes.

La langue a cessé depuis bien longtemps d'être un indice significatif du droit applicable au contrat (cf. *P. Mayer, Droit international privé, n° 721, p. 469*). La sentence ici rapportée souligne qu'en matière internationale il convient d'être très prudent lorsque l'on cherche à en faire un instrument d'interprétation des dispositions contractuelles. Ainsi, les arbitres ont raison de se refuser à donner aux termes « *natural justice* » le sens étroit qu'ils ont en droit anglais. Dans une transaction internationale, la langue de communication des parties est utilisée en dehors d'un contexte juridique national déterminé et donner aux mots le sens précis qu'ils ont dans ce contexte isolé serait une erreur grave. La langue du contrat est celle qui exprime la pensée des parties au contrat et non pas celle du ou des pays où cette langue est majoritairement parlée. Cette observation joue essentiellement pour l'anglais qui est la langue de communication la plus pratiquée dans le commerce international. Le nombre de contrats internationaux en langue anglaise conclus par de non anglophones est très important. Les auteurs de ces contrats ont rarement conscience de la portée juridique en droit anglais ou américain de termes qu'ils insèrent dans leur convention. Mais ceci ne joue pas seulement pour l'anglais. Les mots « *force majeure* » en fournissent un excellent exemple. De nombreux contrats rédigés en anglais contiennent une clause intitulée « *force majeure* » en français. Pas plus le droit français que le droit anglais n'est a *priori* applicable. Dans un tel contrat, rechercher la portée de la clause d'exonération de responsabilité intitulée « *force majeure* » à la lumière du droit français trahirait l'intention réelle des parties qui se sont appropriées, parfois sans le savoir, un terme juridique français mais n'ont pas intégré dans leur contrat des solutions de droit français dont il est le support.

Y.D.

Sentence rendue dans l'affaire n° 8501 (original en langue anglaise).

I — Contrat. — Droit applicable. — Absence de stipulations contractuelles. — Usages du commerce international. — Incoterms. — RUU. — Convention de Vienne sur la vente internationale de marchandises. — Principes Unidroit relatifs aux contrats du commerce international.

II — Contrat. — Inexécution. — Force majeure.

Quatre contrats et un *addendum* avaient été signés par les demandeurs, acheteurs européens, et le défendeur, vendeur extrême oriental. L'opération contractuelle envisagée consistait en la fourniture de riz long blanc provenant du pays du vendeur. Devant les difficultés d'exécution rencontrées par le défendeur, les demandeurs avait accepté de renégocier à plusieurs reprises ces contrats. L'échéancier des dates de livraison avait ainsi été revu afin de donner plus de temps au défendeur pour remplir ses obligations. Le prix de la marchandise avait été notablement et plusieurs fois réévalué. La qualité de la marchandise et les quantités avaient également été modifiées afin de permettre au défendeur de satisfaire plus aisément à ses obligations. En cours de procédure arbitrale, les parties avaient aussi entrepris des négociations en vue d'arriver à un règlement amiable de leur différend. La procédure arbitrale, provisoirement suspendue lors des négociations des parties, avait repris suite à l'échec de ces négociations.

Les parties n'avaient pas soumis l'opération contractuelle à un droit particulier. Le Tribunal arbitral, appelé à se prononcer sur la question de la détermination du droit applicable, renvoie d'abord au règlement d'arbitrage de la CCI de 1988.

« *L'article 13 du Règlement CCI dispose que :*

« *(3) Les parties sont libres de déterminer le droit que l'arbitre devra appliquer au fond du litige. A défaut d'indication par les parties du droit applicable, l'arbitre appliquera la loi désignée par la règle de conflit qu'il jugera appropriée en l'espèce.*

(. . .)

« *(5) Dans tous les cas l'arbitre tiendra compte des stipulations du contrat et des usages du commerce.* »

Le Tribunal poursuit:

« *Les contrats conclus entre les parties et sur lesquels est fondée la présente procédure sont muets en ce qui concerne la loi qui doit s'appliquer au fond. Il n'existe ainsi aucune clause désignant expressément la loi applicable. De même, en ce qui concerne la correspondance échangée entre les parties, le tribunal arbitral estime qu'un choix implicite de la loi applicable ne peut être déduit de la relation entre les parties.*

Les contrats, ainsi que le présent arbitrage, impliquent d'une part un vendeur [d'un pays d'extrême Orient] *et d'autre part un acquéreur* [européen] *agissant par l'intermédiaire de sa société française. Le lieu de l'arbitrage est Paris, France.*

Le litige a des liens avec plusieurs lois nationales, toutes pouvant jouer un rôle pertinent. Conformément à l'article 13 (3) du Règlement de la CCI, le Tribunal arbitral appliquera la loi désignée par la règle de conflit de lois « *qu'il jugera appropriée en l'espèce* ».

Le Tribunal arbitral remarque que la défenderesse ne s'est pas prononcée sur la loi applicable. [La défenderesse] *n'a jamais avancé, dans le cadre du présent arbitrage ni dans les échanges de correspondance entre les parties que* [la loi du pays de la défenderesse] *devrait s'appliquer. Le Tribunal arbitral est d'avis qu'il ne lui incombe pas ex officio d'identifier les questions éventuelles qui pourraient se poser dans le cadre de la* [loi du pays de la défenderesse].

Bien que les contrats ne contiennent pas de clause désignant la loi applicable, ils font référence aux usages du commerce international.

[Un] *article de chacun des contrats, relatif au prix que l'acquéreur doit verser, dispose que les INCOTERMS de 1990 s'appliqueront.*

De même, [un] *article des contrats dispose, pour ce qui est des cas de force majeure, que la clause des RUU 500 sera applicable.*

Il apparaît donc que les parties ont, dans une large mesure, convenu de soumettre leur relation aux usages du commerce reconnus, tels que les INCOTERMS ou les Règles et usances uniformes relatives aux crédits documentaires (RUU) publiées par la CCI. Le Tribunal arbitral considère qu'en faisant référence à la fois aux INCOTERMS et aux RUU 500, les parties ont montré leur volonté que leurs contrats soient régis par les coutumes et usages du commerce international.

L'application des usages du commerce pertinents est compatible avec l'article 13 (5) du Règlement de la CCI et la pratique arbitrale :

« *Dans un nombre croissant de litiges internationaux, les arbitres décident que les obligations des parties doivent être déterminées conformément aux usages et coutumes du commerce international ou aux principes généraux du droit sans référence à une loi nationale particulière. Dans de nombreuses affaires, ces sentences peuvent traduire plus exactement la véritable intention des parties que ne le ferait l'application d'une approche conflictualiste qui cherche à imposer le choix d'une seule loi nationale* »

(W. Laurence Craig, William W. Park, Jan Paulsson : International Chamber of Commerce Arbitration, 2ᵉ éd., p. 295).

Pour ces raisons, le Tribunal arbitral conclut qu'il tranchera la présente affaire en faisant application aux contrats conclus entre les parties des usages du commerce et des principes du commerce international généralement acceptés. En particulier, le Tribunal arbitral se référera, lorsque les circonstances le requerront, aux dispositions de la Convention de Vienne de 1980 sur les contrats de vente internationale de marchandises (Convention de Vienne) ou aux principes relatifs aux contrats du commerce international édictés par Unidroit, en ce qu'ils révèlent les pratiques admises dans le droit du commerce international. »

Le Tribunal répond ensuite à l'argument de la défenderesse selon lequel les livraisons n'ont pas pu avoir lieu du fait de problèmes de congestion du port d'embarquement de la marchandise dans le pays de la défenderesse et d'une décision du Ministre du commerce de diminuer les quotas d'exportation. Le Tribunal retient une absence de justification à la non-exécution contractuelle.

« *Le Tribunal arbitral remarque que la défenderesse n'a jamais attiré l'attention des arbitres sur aucun fait qui puisse constituer un cas de force majeure ou donné aucune explication à cet effet. Compte tenu du défaut de la défenderesse d'invoquer et de prouver l'existence de faits constituant un cas de force majeure, le Tribunal arbitral considère qu'il aurait pu s'abstenir de considérer plus avant cette question.*

Toutefois, les demanderesses sollicitent du Tribunal arbitral dans leur demande de réparation que celui-ci conclut que [la défenderesse] *a violé le contrat* « *et ne peut s'appuyer sur la force majeure* ». *Les demanderesses, dans laurs mémoires, abordent également la question de savoir si la défenderesse a le droit de se prévaloir de la force majeure pour justifier son défaut d'exécution.*

Compte tenu du fait que les demanderesses, dans leur demande de réparation, ont sollicité des arbitres qu'ils disent que [la défenderesse] *ne pouvait s'appuyer sur la force majeure, le Tribunal arbitral examinera ci-après cette question.*

Le dossier contient plusieurs lettres de la défenderesse aux demanderesses dans lesquelles [la défenderesse] *explique qu'elle ne pouvait effectuer les livraisons envisagées en raison de la réglementation relative aux exportations de riz mise en place par le gouvernement* [de son pays]. *La question juridique est celle de savoir si ces mesures gouvernementales équivalent à un cas de force majeure justifiant le défaut d'exécution de ses obligations par la défenderesse.*

[Un] *article, commun aux quatre contrats, stipule que la clause de force majeure des RUU 500 de la Chambre de commerce internationale est incorporée dans le contrat. L'article 17 de ce règlement dispose :*

« *Force majeure*

Les banques n'assument aucun engagement ni responsabilité quant aux conséquences pouvant résulter de l'interruption de leurs activités provoquée par tout cas de force majeure, émeutes, troubles civils, insurrections, guerres et/ou toute autre cause indépendante de leur volonté, ainsi que par des grèves ou "lockout". »

Bien que les RUU ne définissent pas précisément ce que l'on entend par cas de force majeure, il résulte des principes régissant le droit du commerce international que seules des circonstances exceptionnelles peuvent être qualifiées d'événements de force majeure. En particulier, les juges et les arbitres considèrent qu'un événement de force majeure ne peut être invoqué que si ledit événement était indépendant de la volonté de la partie défaillante et que cet événement a rendu l'exécution des obligations du contrat impossible.

La perspective des RUU 500 est proche de celle de l'article 79 de la Convention de Vienne. Cette disposition prévoit qu'une partie n'est pas responsable de la non-exécution si : « *elle prouve que cette inexécution est due à un empêchement indépendant de sa volonté et que l'on ne pouvait raisonnablement attendre d'elle qu'elle le prenne en considération au moment de la conclusion du contrat, qu'elle le prévienne ou le surmonte ou qu'elle en prévienne ou surmonte les conséquences* ».

Dans le cas présent, comme nous l'avons déjà indiqué, il a été fait allusion, dans plusieurs lettres adressées par la défenderesse aux demanderesses, à l'existence de difficultés en raison de décisions gouvernementales.

(. . .)

Les éléments du dossier indiquent clairement que, même si [la défenderesse] *rencontrait des difficultés pour obtenir les autorisations nécessaires, elle n'était pas dans l'impossibilité de se conformer aux exigences des contrats. Plusieurs éléments vont dans le sens de cette conclusion.*

Tout d'abord, le vocabulaire employé par [la défenderesse] *dans ses lettres montre qu'elle ne considérait pas comme impossible l'exécution de ses obligations mais simplement plus lourde, onéreuse ou retardée.*

Un autre facteur important, qui va à l'encontre de la reconnaissance d'un événement de force majeure, est le fait que pendant la période concernée, la défenderesse était en mesure de vendre du riz à d'autres acquéreurs.

Dans un courrier [date], [une des demanderesses] *a indiqué à* [la défenderesse] *qu'elle ne pouvait pas accepter l'explication de la défenderesse selon laquelle les autorisations d'exportation ne pouvaient être obtenues, puisque, en fait, la défenderesse avait, dans un passé récent, un programme de riz très important. Les demanderesses ont joint à leur courrier un tableau indiquant le programme global d'exportation conduit par* [la défenderesse] *à cette époque.*

Dans ses courriers ultérieurs, la défenderesse n'a pas démenti les affirmations des demanderesses et a en effet confirmé qu'elle était en mesure de et disposée à procéder à des livraisons de riz supplémentaires.

Dans ces circonstances, le Tribunal arbitral considère que la défenderesse n'était pas dans l'impossibilité de remplir ses obligations au titre des contrats. Par conséquent, le Tribunal arbitral n'a pas besoin de considérer le fait de savoir si les événements avancés étaient ou non indépendants de la volonté de la défenderesse. »

Considérant que la défenderesse a manqué à ses obligations contractuelles sans justification et après avoir déterminé les quantités de marchandises non livrées, le Tribunal évalue la réparation due aux demanderesses.

« En ce qui concerne la loi applicable à la question de la réparation, le tribunal arbitral, comme mentionné précédemment, considère que les parties ont exprimé leur volonté commune de voir leurs relations régies par les principes généraux du commerce international.

Les INCOTERMS de 1990 ou les RUU 500, auxquels il est fait référence dans les contrats, ne contiennent aucune disposition concernant l'effet de la non-exécution par l'une des parties de ses obligations au titre d'un contrat.

Le Tribunal arbitral considère que cette question devrait être étudiée à la lumière des principes du commerce international généralement admis tels que contenus par exemple dans les traités internationaux. Pour cette raison, le Tribunal arbitral est de l'opinion que les principes consacrés par la Convention de Vienne correspondent aux règles et usages du commerce largement admis. Bien que la Convention de Vienne ne soit pas en tant que telle applicable aux contrats ([l'Etat de la défenderesse] n'ayant pas ratifié cette convention), le Tribunal arbitral estime qu'il peut faire référence à ses dispositions comme l'expression des usages du monde du commerce international (V. P. Fouchard, Les usages, l'arbitre et le juge : Droit des relations économiques internationales, 1982, p. 67).

Le Tribunal arbitral fait référence à l'article 76 (1) et (2) de la Convention de Vienne et observe:

« La méthode de calcul des dommages-intérêts dans la Convention de Vienne est similaire à celle envisagée par les différentes lois nationales ».

Le tribunal conforte la solution dégagée par la Convention de Vienne en citant l'article 51 (3) de la loi sur la vente de marchandises *(Sale of Goods Act)* en droit anglais, le paragraphe 2-713 du Code de commerce uniforme américain *(Uniform Commercial Code)*, l'article 191 (3) du Code suisse des obligations et l'article 7.4.6 des principes d'Unidroit relatifs aux contrats du commerce international.

OBSERVATIONS. — I. — A défaut de stipulations contractuelles désignant le droit applicable au fond du litige, quelles solutions s'offrent aux arbitres du commerce international pour déterminer le droit appelé à régir l'opération juridique litigieuse ? La présente sentence finale s'inscrit dans la lignée d'une jurisprudence arbitrale établie mais n'en présente pas moins des particularités intéressantes en matière de sources du droit commercial international.

Le raisonnement suivi par le Tribunal arbitral s'articule autour de deux axes. Tout d'abord, après avoir rappelé que cette manière de procéder lui était imposée par l'article 13 (3) du règlement d'arbitrage de la CCI alors en vigueur, le tribunal se livre à une recherche du droit étatique applicable en l'espèce selon la méthode conflictualiste. Le Tribunal justifie cette approche en faisant remarquer qu'il est impossible de déduire du comportement des parties un quelconque choix implicite du droit applicable. Le Tribunal n'identifie pas les critères de rattachement susceptibles d'être retenus mais insiste implicitement sur la pluralité de ces critères en relevant la différence de nationalité des parties et le lieu de l'arbitrage. Le Tribunal en déduit que plusieurs lois nationales ont une vocation égale à s'appliquer et qu'il n'est pas possible d'identifier un droit étatique auquel l'opération juridique serait plus étroitement rattachée. La méthode conflictualiste fondée sur le recours aux systèmes de conflits de lois intéressés au litige est écartée, après quoi le tribunal énonce que, sur le fondement du règlement d'arbitrage CCI, le pouvoir lui est donné de déterminer le droit applicable selon « *la règle de conflit de lois qu'il jugera appropriée en l'espèce* ».

Ensuite, conformément à l'obligation qui est mise à sa charge par l'article 13 (5) du règlement d'arbitrage applicable, le Tribunal examine les stipulations contractuelles et y découvre une mention des Incoterms 1990 et des Règles et usances uniformes de la CCI relatives aux crédits documentaires, publication CCI n° 500 (RUU 500), qu'il analyse comme étant une référence aux usages du commerce international. De la référence à ces deux corps de règles élaborées par la CCI, le Tribunal déduit que les parties ont plus généralement entendu soumettre l'opération juridique aux « *coutumes et usages du commerce international* ». Cette approche semble être admise par une certaine doctrine citée par le Tribunal arbitral. Le Tribunal conclut qu'il est donc autorisé à trancher le litige « *en faisant application (. . .) des usages du commerce et des principes du commerce international généralement acceptés* » et notamment des dispositions de la Convention de Vienne de 1980 sur la vente internationale de marchandise et les principes Unidroit.

Au regard des éléments fournis par la sentence, la référence aux Incoterms 1990 prête à discussion. La condition d'application des Incoterms rappelée avec le plus d'insistance par la CCI depuis la création de ces termes commerciaux, en 1936, est la nécessité d'une incorporation expresse dans les contrats de vente internationaux. L'incorporation consiste alors en l'indication de l'Incoterm choisi, c'est-à-dire du « mot-code » de trois lettres et d'un lieu, et du millésime; en l'espèce « Incoterms 1990 ». Cette condition d'application est également rappelée avec insistance par la doctrine qui, bien qu'admettant d'autres moyens d'incorporation des Incoterms dans les contrats, par exemple par référence aux usages ou à la volonté implicite des parties, considère que l'incorporation expresse par référence est le moyen juridique le plus sûr pour en permettre l'application *(J. Ramberg, Guide des Incoterms 1990 : Publication CCI n° 461/90, 1991, p. 13)*. Dans la présente affaire, la sentence finale et l'acte de mission, insistaient sur le fait que les contrats contenaient le terme commercial FOB ST (port du pays du défendeur), mais l'emploi du mot « Incoterm » n'était pas rapporté et aucun millésime n'était indiqué. Le terme commercial FOB *(Free on Board/Franco bord)* est généralement considéré comme le terme commercial le plus ancien *(D. M. Sassoon, CIF and FOB contracts, coll. British Shipping Laws, 4ᵉ éd. : Sweet & Maxwell, 1995, p. 347)*, et celui qui a le plus d'interprétations divergentes entre les droits nationaux et même au sein de ceux-ci (voir notamment l'étude de la CCI à ce sujet, *Trade Terms, Document CCI n. 16, 1955)* et de variantes. FOB ST *(Free on Board Stowed and Trimmed)* est justement l'une de ces variantes posant un grand nombre de difficultés pratiques *(A. Räty, Variants on Incoterms (part. 2), Incoterms in Practice : Publication CCI, n° 505, 1995, p. 155)*. Il apparaît difficile, à défaut d'éléments supplémentaires venant confirmer cette analyse, d'affirmer que la simple mention de ce terme commercial renvoie incontestablement à la variante de l'Incoterm 1990 FOB (. . . port d'embarquement convenu). La présente sentence vient s'ajouter à la liste des décisions, tant arbitrales que judiciaires, qui, en l'absence de précisions suffisantes quant à la satisfaction des conditions d'application des Incoterms, ne permettent pas de déterminer avec certitude si les parties au litige avaient réellement fait référence aux Incoterms dans leur contrat *(E. Jolivet, Les Incoterms, étude d'une norme du commerce international : thèse Montpellier, 1999, n° 355 s. et n° 434)*.

A supposer que les contrats contenaient effectivement une référence aux Incoterms 1990, s'agissait-il incontestablement d'une référence aux usages du commerce international ? La question a déjà été posée à l'occasion de la mention du terme commercial C&F dans un contrat de vente international *(obs. J.-J. A. sous la sentence n° 6653 de 1993, reproduite dans J.-J. Arnaldez, Y. Derains, D. Hascher, Recueil des sentences arbitrales 1991-1995 : Kluwer/CCI, Publication CCI n° 553, p. 520)*. Le caractère international de l'Incoterm est avéré mais sa qualification d'usage est plus douteuse. La doctrine majoritaire considère les Incoterms comme des usages, voire des coutumes, or cette analyse méconnaît profondément le rôle de la CCI dans l'élaboration de ces termes commerciaux. L'Incoterm FOB (. . . port d'embarquement convenu), pour n'envisager que le terme évoqué en l'espèce, ne correspond exactement à aucun autre terme commercial FOB. La combinaison du champ d'application de l'Incoterm, de l'étendue et de la diversité des obligations qu'il met à la charge des parties à une vente internationale, en font un terme novateur, même s'il constitue une reformulation de règles préexistantes. Terme « neuf », créé par la CCI, l'Incoterm n'est pas un usage. L'usage n'est pas le terme *per se*, mais la pratique des acteurs du commerce international consistant à faire référence à la proposition contractuelle que constitue l'Incoterm *(E. Jolivet, op. cit, n° 367 s. et 460)*.

Même si les RUU sont bien des usages du commerce international, comme il l'a été affirmé par d'éminents auteurs *(F. Osman, Les principes généraux de la lex mercatoria : LGDJ, 1992, p. 276-278)*, la sentence énonce que c'est l'existence d'une double référence aux Incoterms 1990 et aux RUU 500 qui permet d'affirmer que les parties ont entendu soumettre leurs contrats aux coutumes et usages du commerce international. Le raisonnement aurait-il été le même en présence d'un renvoi aux seuls RUU?

Le Tribunal renvoie aux notions de coutumes, d'usages et de « *principes du commerce international généralement acceptés* » sans préciser les distinctions entre ces trois notions (sur ce point voir *E. Gaillard, La distinction des principes généraux du droit et des usages du commerce international, Etudes Bellet : Litec, 1991, p. 203)*. Qualifier les Incoterms d'usages peut être discuté, mais les qualifier de coutumes, et ainsi distinguer cette notion de l'usage, requiert au minimum de définir précisément le concept juridique de coutume. Le Tribunal n'attachait-il que peu d'importance à cette précision terminologique et conceptuelle et considérait-il les termes d'usages et de coutume comme synonymes, ou le Tribunal, en mentionnant la coutume, envisageait-il l'une des deux principales théories de cette notion, à savoir la théorie traditionnelle ou romano-canonique, ou à l'inverse la théorie jurisprudentielle de la coutume ? D'une part, l'insistance avec laquelle la CCI rappelle constamment le caractère facultatif du recours aux Incoterms et RUU pour les parties à une vente internationale et la Recommandation numéro 5 du Centre des Nations Unies pour la facilitation du commerce et les transactions électroniques *(ECE/TRADE/259, 4ᵉ éd., mai 2000)* incitant à l'emploi des Incoterms semblent incompatibles avec l'*opinio juris seu necessitatis*, élément psychologique de la coutume dans la théorie traditionnelle telle que formulée par le Doyen Gény (pour une présentation générale de la coutume voir *A. Lebrun, Rép. civ., 1971, Vᵒ Coutume)*. D'autre part, attribuer force de coutume à ces termes sur le fondement de la théorie jurisprudentielle exigerait de ces règles qu'elles aient connu une sanction juridictionnelle. Exiger une telle sanction aboutirait à favoriser l'émergence d'interprétations différentes de ces règles selon les pays et les juridictions, et ferait éclater le statut de règles uniformes des Incoterms, certains ayant fait l'objet de décisions judiciaires ou arbitrales, d'autres pas. Les Incoterms et les RUU ne sont pas des coutumes. Ils ne sont pas non plus des principes du commerce international. Ils sont des normes contractuelles dont l'application est librement décidée par les parties. Dès lors, il est possible de s'interroger sur l'extrapolation opérée par le Tribunal arbitral. La référence à ces règles traduisait-elle une volonté plus générale des parties de soumettre les contrats aux usages et coutumes du commerce ? Le Tribunal répond par l'affirmative et considère que le renvoi aux Incoterms et RUU s'analyse en une volonté implicite des parties de se soumettre à des usages, des coutumes, d'ailleurs non-identifiées, et des principes généraux au rang desquels le tribunal arbitral fait figurer les solutions posées par la Convention de Vienne — non-applicable en tant qu'instrument conventionnel uniforme, l'Etat de la défenderesse n'ayant pas ratifié la convention — et les principes Unidroit.

Il convient de relever que la démarche suivie par le Tribunal arbitral correspond à une pratique établie des arbitres du commerce international : l'utilisation des Incoterms comme critère de détermination de la règle de droit applicable. L'Incoterm stipulé au contrat, ou réputé stipulé au contrat, peut être interprété comme désignant le droit national applicable (sentences CCI n° 2734 et 2840 de 1977 citées par *F. Eisemann et Y. Derains, La pratique des incoterms, usages de la vente internationale, coll. Exporter, 3ᵉ éd. : EJA Jupiter, 1988, p. 29 ;* sentence CCI n° 5713 de 1989, in *S. Jarvin, Y. Derains, J.-J. Arnaldez, Recueil des sentences arbitrales 1986-1990 : Kluwer/CCI, Publication CCI n° 514, p. 224*). Dans la présente affaire, le Tribunal arbitral suit un raisonnement qui avait déjà été suggéré par la doctrine (voir notamment *E. Loquin, L'application de règles anationales dans l'arbitrage international, in CCI, L'arbitrage commercial international : L'apport de la jurisprudence arbitrale, coll. Dossiers de l'Institut du droit et des pratiques des affaires internationales, publication CCI n° 440/1, 1986, p. 87*). De l'absence de désignation du droit étatique applicable par les contrats, et de l'absence de revendication d'application d'un droit étatique particulier en cours d'instance arbitrale, le Tribunal déduit que les parties n'ont pas entendu soumettre l'opération juridique à un droit étatique mais au contraire à des règles « reconnues » ou encore « généralement acceptées ». Le renvoi opéré aux Incoterms 1990 et aux RUU 500 dans les contrats est envisagé comme une manifestation de la volonté des parties de se référer directement aux usages et aux principes du commerce international.

Suivant une tendance des tribunaux arbitraux, les arbitres dans la présente affaire, lorsqu'ils font application des usages du commerce, prennent le soin de justifier leur décision par des références à des lois nationales retenant des solutions similaires. Le but recherché est manifestement de conforter la solution adoptée mais dès lors que le Tribunal avait expressément déclaré qu'il trancherait « *la présente affaire en faisant application aux contrats conclus entre les parties des usages du commerce et des principes du commerce international généralement acceptés* », cette surabondance de motivation ne serait-elle pas de nature à introduire un doute sur le bien fondé de cette dernière ?

II. — Dans cette sentence, le Tribunal arbitral examine l'existence d'un fait de nature à justifier la non-exécution de ses obligations de livraison par le vendeur. Le Tribunal relève à juste titre que les parties ont incorporé par référence dans leurs contrats de vente une clause de force majeure, à savoir l'article 17 des RUU 500. D'un point de vue de technique contractuelle, il est intéressant de relever que les parties ont préféré incorporer dans des contrats de vente une clause de force majeure destinée à régir des crédits documentaires, et donc des rapports contractuels entre parties différentes, plutôt que la clause-type de force majeure élaborée notamment pour l'incorporation dans les contrats de vente *(Publication CCI n° 421, 1985)*. Cette dernière clause-type est nettement plus élaborée que la clause figurant dans les RUU, mais peut être le fait que les paiements correspondant au prix des marchandises vendues doivent être effectués par crédits documentaires a-t-il incité les parties à incorporer la clause de force majeure des RUU 500 dans leurs contrats de vente. Le Tribunal relève d'ailleurs le caractère incomplet de la clause des RUU qui ne définit « *pas précisément ce que l'on entend par cas de force majeure* ». En effet, la rédaction de la clause est maladroite : parmi les événements constitutifs de la force majeure, la clause mentionne . . . la force majeure ! Le Tribunal ne précise cependant pas comment une clause exonérant les banques de responsabilité en cas d'interruption de leurs activités pourrait s'appliquer à un vendeur n'ayant pas satisfait à son obligation de livraison. A défaut d'indications données par la clause, le Tribunal énonce les conditions que présentent les événements constitutifs de la force majeure : le caractère exceptionnel des circonstances, leur indépendance de la partie défaillante et l'impossibilité d'exécution de ses obligations par la partie défaillante. Constatant que cette dernière condition fait défaut, le Tribunal ne poursuit pas plus avant son examen de la situation et rejette la qualification d'événements de force majeure des événements ayant rendu l'exécution du contrat plus onéreuse et difficile.

E. J.

Sentence rendue dans l'affaire 10758 en 2000 (original en langue anglaise).

I. — Groupe de sociétés. — Clause compromissoire. — Opposabilité aux sociétés du groupe (non). — Levée du voile social. — Conditions.

II. — Clause compromissoire. — Consentement. — Droit suisse. — Article 178 (1) de la Loi de droit international privé. — Exigence d'un document.

A la suite d'un appel d'offres lancé par une société publique égyptienne B pour la conception, la fourniture et la construction en Egypte d'une usine d'ammoniaque, un contrat a été conclu par une société française A avec une société égyptienne C, filiale de B. Ce contrat prévoyait l'application au fond du droit égyptien.

Après la réalisation de l'ouvrage en 1993, les parties contractantes ont rencontré un certain nombre de difficultés provoquant de la part de la société C l'engagement d'une procédure arbitrale contre son cocontractant, la société française A. Dans le cadre de cette procédure, la société A introduisait une demande reconventionnelle.

Peu après et parallèlement à cette procédure, la société française A engageait à son tour une procédure d'arbitrage à l'encontre de la seule société B, nonsignataire du contrat en cause, au motif que cette dernière, seule actionnaire de sa filiale C, avait décidé d'exclure du capital de sa filiale certains actifs ce qui réduisait ainsi ses chances de récupérer le montant des dommages qu'elle réclame. Elle invoquait en outre que la société B qui avait lancé l'appel d'offres, avait également participé à la négociation, la conclusion et l'exécution du contrat à travers sa filiale C, signataire du contrat.

Dans cette deuxième procédure, le défendeur, la société égyptienne B, ayant soulevé une exception d'incompétence, le Tribunal arbitral siégeant à Genève devait se prononcer sur sa compétence celle-ci devant, suivant l'acte de mission, être tranchée conformément à l'article 186 de la Loi de droit international privé suisse (LDIP). Les arbitres examinent tout d'abord l'argument du demandeur tiré de l'existence d'un groupe de sociétés pour tenter d'opposer au défendeur B les effets de la clause compromissoire signée par sa filiale C:

« Le demandeur soutient que:

« Il ne fait absolument aucun doute que [la filiale du défendeur] *fait partie d'un groupe de sociétés sur lequel* [le défendeur] *exerce un contrôle absolu,* [la filiale du défendeur] *n'ayant pour sa part aucun pouvoir de décision ... ».*

De plus, le demandeur soutient que [le défendeur] *et ses filiales forment un:*

« ... groupe de sociétés qui se caractérise par le plus haut degré possible de centralisation du pouvoir et d'unité dans l'objectif économique ... ».

Les sentences arbitrales dans lesquelles une convention d'arbitrage signée par certains membres d'un groupe de sociétés se sont avérées lier les autres membres du groupe sont bien connues; le demandeur en particulier fait référence à l'affaire CCI 4131/1982 (Dow Chemical c/ Isover Saint Gobain).

L'extension de la convention d'arbitrage à une partie qui n'est pas signataire de cette convention est une question qui doit être abordée avec prudence.

L'autonomie des parties est la base du droit de l'arbitrage et le pouvoir d'un tribunal arbitral est tiré d'une référence consensuelle. Le corollaire de l'autonomie des parties est l'effet relatif des contrats. La doctrine de l'effet relatif des contrats est partagée par la plupart des systèmes juridiques, et est explicitement reconnue à l'article 152 du Code civil égyptien qui dispose qu'un contrat ne crée pas d'obligations liant les tiers. Il convient

également de reconnaître que dans certains Etats, y compris en Egypte, l'accès aux jur-
idictions étatiques pour la détermination des droits est reconnu et protégé par leurs con-
stitutions respectives. De plus, le concept de la personnalité juridique distincte des sociétés
est établi depuis longtemps dans le commerce international et la légitimité de la répartition
par un groupe de sociétés des droits et des obligations contractuels entre différentes
personnes morales doit également être respectée.

Les concepts de « groupe de sociétés » ou de « réalité économique unique » sont apparus
dans de nombreuses sentences et ont été débattus dans des articles de doctrine mais leur
utilité analytique peut être mise en cause. Ces concepts encouragent la preuve et l'argu-
mentation, comme dans la présente espèce, surce qui définit un groupe de sociétés ou une
réalité économique unique. L'extension d'une convention d'arbitrage à un non-signataire
n'est pas une simple question de structure ou de contrôle entre sociétés mais plutôt une
question de participation du non-signataire aux négociations, à la conclusion ou à l'exécu-
tion du contrat ou de son attitude (y compris des déclarations expresses ou implicities ou la
mauvaise foi) envers la partie qui cherche à introduire le non-signataire dans l'arbitrage
(ou à l'en exclure). C'est de cette participation au contrat ou de son attitude enverse l'autre
partie que le Tribunal arbitral peut déduire « la commune intention des parties . . . » *qui a*
été reconnue dans de nombreuses sentences (y compris l'affaire Dow Chemical) *comme*
justifiant l'extension de la clause compromissoire à un non-signataire.

Le Tribunal est conforté dans cette opinion par la décision de l'affaire Westland
Helicopters, *dans laquelle le Tribunal fédéral suisse a déclaré que le strict contrôle*
d'une entité juridique par une autre ou la relation étroite entre deux entités « n'est pas
un élément suffisant pour rencerser la présomption résultant de l'absence de signature de la
clause compromissoire par [une entité] selon laquelle seule la société qui a signé la clause
est partie à l'arbitrage . . . ».

Le Tribunal arbitral dans l'affaire CCI n° 5721/1990 a déclaré:

« . . . l'appartenance de deux sociétés à un même groupe ou la domination d'un
actionnaire ne sont jamais, à elles seules, des raisons suffisants justifiant de plein droit
la levée du voile social. Cependant, lorsqu'une société ou une personne individuelle
apparaît comme étant le pivot des rapports contractuels intervenus dans une affaire particulière, il convient d'examiner avec soin si l'indépendance juridique des parties ne doit pas,
exceptionnellement, être écartée au profit d'un jugement global. On acceptera une telle
exception lorsque apparaît une confusion entretenue par le groupe ou l'actionnaire majoritaire . . . » *(JDI 1990, p. 1024).*

Par conséquent, lorsqu'une structure sociale est utilisée de mauvaise foi comme un
instrument de confusion ou de dissimulation, ou pour faire échec à une éventuelle sentence
contre la partie nommée à une convention d'arbitrage, alors le tribunal arbitral pourrait
être justifié à lever le voile social. Le demandeur a soutenu que tel était le cas en l'espèce.
En particulier, il soutient que la personnalité juridique distincte de [la filiale du défendeur]
est une « . . . fiction . . . » *et qu'en conséquence des actions du* [défendeur] [la filiale du
défendeur] *est ou a été liquidée, a transféré une partie de son actif à un autre membre du*
groupe et que « il est clair qu'il existe un risque véritable que les demandes du [demandeur]
à l'encontre de [la filiale du défendeur] constituent [. . .] un recours illusoire . . . ».

Il n'est pas contesté que conformément à la loi [égyptienne] *n° 203/1991, le défendeur et*
[la filiale du défendeur] *ont des personnalités juridiques distinctes et indépendantes. Le*
Tribunal reconnaît également qu'elles disposent de partrimoines financiers distincts et
indépendants.

Le demandeur a apporté un certain nombre de preuves attestant l'exercice du contrôle
par le défendeur sur [sa filiale].

L'assemblée générale de [la filiale du défendeur] *est composée principalement de repré-*
sentants du [défendeur]; *le président et la plupart des membres du conseil d'administration*

de la filiale du défendeur sont nommés, conformément à la loi (L. n° 203/1991, art. 21), *par* [le défendeur] *de même que le directeur général. De plus, le demandeur s'est appuyé sur les résolutions des actionnaires de* [la filiale du défendeur] *préparées par* [le défendeur] *et également sur* « ... l'orientation générale ... » *commune du* [défendeur] *et de ses filiales. De l'avis du Tribunal, les actionnaires possèdent normalement ces pouvoirs de nomination et proposent et font des résolutions aux assemblées générales et il n'y a rien d'anormal dans le type ou le niveau de contrôle exercé par le défendeur sur ses filiales.*

Ces preuves ne vont pas jusqu'à établir que la personnalité juridique distincte de [la filiale du défendeur] *est une* « ... fiction ... » *ou que le défendeur* « ... exerce un contrôle absolu sur toutes les décisions ... » *de* [la filiale du défendeur].

Le demandeur, se référant à la « doctrine sur la levée du voile social » *soutient ensuite que l'extension au défendeur de la clause compromissoire contenue à l'article 17 du contrat est justifiée par la situation financière du signataire (à savoir* [la filiale du défendeur]) *et le* « ... très sérieux risque ... » *que ses demandes à l'encontre de* [la filiale du défendeur] *s'avèrent un recours illusoire que* [le défendeur] *aurait provoqué au détriment du demandeur. Il a mentionné une transaction par laquelle* [la filiale du défendeur] *aurait transféré une partie substantielle de son actif (et, selon le demandeur, la partie la plus rentable) à une autre filiale du* [défendeur], *qui aurait laissé quelques doutes sur le statut juridique et la viabilité de* [la filiale du défendeur], *selon le demandeur, cette autre filiale n'étant pas partie à l'arbitrage.*

Le défendeur, dans ses conclusions, a qualifié les préoccupations du demandeur, en ce qui concerne la solvabilité de [la filiale du défendeur] *de* « ... imaginaires ... » *et de* « ... fictives ... ».

Le contrat produit comme preuve par le demandeur ne soutient pas ses allégations.

Ce « Contrat concernant les conséquences juridiques découlant de la division de [la filiale du défendeur] » *(ci-après désigné annexe x) effectue, il est vrai, un transfert d'éléments d'actif par* [la filiale du défendeur] *à une filiale mais se présente également comme une restructuration de bonne foi de sociétés. En particulier, on note :*

1. *L'annexe [x] prévoit un transfert non seulement d'éléments d'actif mais aussi des éléments du passif y afférents;*

2. *L'actif net transféré ne représente que 12% de l'actif net préexistant de [la filiale du défendeur];*

3. *Il ressort des documents déposés que le transfert a été effectué dans le respect des formalités juridiques et de la personnalité juridique de toutes les parties. Le transfert a eu lieu après une enquête et un rapport d'un comité constitué conformément à une résolution d'un administrateur du défendeur; les recommandations du comité ont été approuvées à la fois par les administrateurs du défendeur et par une assemblée générale extraordinaire de* [la filiale du défendeur]; *les éléments de l'actif et du passif ont été évalués selon leur catégorie, apparemment par un comité constitué à cette fin et sur la base des comptes audités et il y a des indications selon lesquelles les évaluations auraient reçu un accord ministériel; et*

4. *Une telle restructuration de filiales constitue l'un des objectifs énoncés dans les statuts du défendeur.*

Sur la base de la preuve qui nous est présentée, l'annexe [x] constitue une opération sociale légitime. Il n'y a aucune preuve de dissimulation ou d'intention délibérée d'éviter l'exécution d'une éventuelle sentence contre [la filiale du défendeur] *qui puisse justifier la levée du voile social.*

Par conséquent, le Tribunal ne trouve aucune justification dans la structure sociale ou les opérations du défendeur et de ses filiales pour soutenir que le défendeur doit être considéré comme une partie au contrat. De même, le Tribunal ne trouve aucune justification pour lever le voile social afin de rendre le défendeur responsable au titre du contrat. »

Ayant refusé de considérer l'existence d'un groupe de sociétés comme suffisant pour lier l'ensemble de ses entités à la convention d'arbitrage signée par l'une d'entre elles et écarté tout comportement illicite de la part de la maison mère, le tribunal arbitral procède ensuite à l'analyse de l'existence éventuelle d'une convention d'arbitrage liant les parties à la procédure arbitrale :

« Dans un arbitrage commercial international, la convention d'arbitrage remplit plusieurs rôles importants dont le principal, dans le présent contexte, est de montrer que les parties ont consenti à résoudre leurs litiges par la voie de l'arbitrage. Cet élément du consentement est essentiel, car ce sont les parties qui confient au Tribunal arbitral le pouvoir de rendre une décision qui les liera.

De plus, la convention d'arbitrage doit respecter les règles impératives relatives à sa forme de la loi du siège de l'arbitrage ou de celle du pays dans lequel la sentence doit être rendue. Dans la présente espèce, la Suisse est à la fois le siège de l'arbitrage et le pays dans lequel cette sentence doit être rendue. Les dispositions de la loi fédérale sur le droit international privé (LDIP) sont par conséquent applicables.

La doctrine et la jurisprudence suisses concluent que la validité formelle d'une convention d'arbitrage doit être analysée au regard de l'article 178 (1) de la LDIP; une disposition impérative selon laquelle :

« 1. Quant à la forme, la convention d'arbitrage est valable si elle est passée par écrit, télégramme, télex, télécopieur ou tout autre moyen de communication qui permet d'en établir la preuve par un texte ».

A la lumière de cette disposition, la clause compromissoire invoquée par le demandeur pour introduire sa demande — l'article 17 du contrat — est formellement valide, puisqu'elle est conforme à la fois aux dispositions impératives de l'article 178 (1) de la LDIP et aux exigences généralement observées dans l'arbitrage commercial international. En particulier, elle a été établie par écrit, elle fait partie du contrat et elle a été signée par les parties au contrat, c'est-à-dire, le demandeur et [la filiale du défendeur].

Cependant, en l'espèce, les signataires de la clause compromissoire figurant à l'article 17 du contrat (le demandeur et la filiale du défendeur) diffèrent des parties au présent arbitrage (le demandeur et le défendeur).

Néanmoins, le demandeur soutient que le défendeur est lié par cette clause compromissoire en raison de sa participation à la négociation, à la conclusion et à l'exécution du contrat, tandis que le défendeur nie expressément sa participation au contrat et/ou être lié par la clause compromissoire.

Par conséquent, ce Tribunal considère maintenant le rôle du défendeur dans la négociation et l'exécution du contrat, afin de déterminer si les actions du défendeur suggèrent une intention d'être partie au contrat et/ou d'être lié par la clause compromissoire qu'il contient. Nous remarquons que lorsqu'il est avancé, comme en l'espèce, qu'un non-signataire avait l'intention d'être une partie à la convention d'arbitrage et y a consenti, alors cette intention ou ce consentement doivent être prouvés par écrit.

Cette exigence d'un écrit peut être satisfaite de diverses manières, chacune étant maintenant analysée.

Le demandeur a fait référence à une importante correspondance et à d'autres documents (annexes [. . .]) qui, selon lui, établissent que le défendeur a joué un rôle essentiel dans la négociation et la conclusion du contrat et dans son exécution. Le demandeur soutient qu'au moment de la négociation du contrat, les intérêts du défendeur [. . .] et les intérêts de la filiale du défendeur étaient « . . . totalement entremêlés . . . ».

Il ressort des documents produits que le défendeur s'est impliqué dans la négociation du contrat; des offres ont été soumises aux bureaux du défendeur, des réunions concernant les détails contractuels se sont tenues en présence de représentants du défendeur et le défendeur a informé le demandeur du succès de son offre. Cette correspondance indique que le défendeur a assisté, et peut-être même contrôlé les étapes finales des négociations du contrat. Toutefois, à aucun endroit dans les communications sur lesquelles se fonde le demandeur, il n'est suggéré que le défendeur ait accepté la clause compromissoire qui y figurait. De plus, et plus important, le contrat lui-même signé peu après ces communications pré-contractuelles l'a été par la seule [filiale du défendeur]. *Comme le soutient le défendeur dans ses dernières conclusions, le demandeur a signé ce contrat avec* [la filiale du défendeur] *sans aucune réserve. Si le demandeur avait souhaité que le défendeur soit partie au contrat ou à la clause compromissoire, il aurait pu insister à ce moment-là.*

Les demandeurs font remarquer qu'il est une pratique courante dans le secteur public en Egypte que la négociation et la signature d'un contrat soit réalisée par des organisations générales pour l'industrialisation [. . .] et sa mise en œuvre par une société d'exploitation; conformément à cette pratique, l'organisation et la société signeraient le contrat toutes deux avec l'organisation transférant ensuite ses droits et obligations à la société d'exploitation. Même si cet argument — développé par le demandeur dans le contexte de la question du transfert — s'avérait fondé, il indique néanmoins qu'en ne signant pas le contrat, le défendeur entendait respecter l'indépendance juridique de la personnalité morale de [la filiale du défendeur] *et être en harmonie avec le principe de l'effet relatif des contrats, c'est-à-dire précisément ne pas devenir partie au contrat pas plus qu'à la clause compromissoire qu'il contenait.*

Lorsque l'on se tourne vers l'exécution du contrat, il est important de conserver à l'esprit qu'il s'agit d'un contrat pour la conception, la fourniture et la construction d'une usine industrielle. Son exécution impliquait une relation complexe sur un grand nombre d'années. Il s'agissait d'un contrat dans lequel le demandeur avait des obligations de conception, de supervision de la construction et de formation du personnel. [La filiale du défendeur] *était responsable de la construction même et, bien entendu, son personnel était formé pour faire fonctionner l'usine.*

La relation est tout à fait différente des affaires concernant la fourniture de marchandises dans lesquelles l'identité d'une société particulière dans un groupe qui fournit effectivement le produit peut ne pas avoir d'importance pour le vendeur et l'acquéreur. En revanche, un haut niveau de coopération et de communication entre les parties était nécessaire pour exécuter le contrat. Cependant, le demandeur n'a apporté aucune preuve de l'implication du défendeur dans l'exécution ou la mise en œuvre du contrat entre la signature de celui-ci en décembre 1988 et septembre 1996. Nous estimons qu'il ne pouvait y avoir de plus claire indication de ce que [le défendeur] *n'était pas partie au contrat.*

Le demandeur produit d'autres preuves de l'implication du [défendeur] dans le contrat après la naissance du litige.

Le Tribunal considère que cette implication, commençant huit ans après la signature du contrat ne révèle pas une quelconque intention d'accepter quelque responsabilité que ce soit au titre du contrat ou de sa clause compromissoire. Une société mère peut assister une filiale à 100 % pour résoudre un litige concernant un projet important dans lequel cette dernière est impliquée, en particulier lorsque la loi la charge de superviser ses filiales comme dans la présente espèce, sans pour autant assumer la responsabilité du projet; autrement, elle pourrait rétrospectivement assumer des responsabilités qu'elle n'avait pas souscrites à l'origine ou devenir elle-même partie au litige ou à l'arbitrage qui s'ensuit.

Nous remarquons, à ce stade, que la Cour d'appel de la province de Bâle [Obergericht, Basel-Land, 5 juill. 1994, DIETF Ltd (nationalité non précisée) c/RF AG (nationalité non précisée) dans 5 (1995) Basler Juristische Mitteilungen 254] *a déclaré que :*

« . . . En exigeant un écrit, l'article II de la Convention de New York entend exclure des conventions d'arbitrage conclues oralement ou tacitement . . . ».

Compte tenu du pouvoir d'appréciation de la preuve par les arbitres (Loi Modèle de 1985, art. 19.2), *le Tribunal arbitral conclut qu'aucun document n'a été produit établissant :*

1. *L'existence d'une proposition écrite de recourir à l'arbitrage de la part d'une partie et une acceptation écrite communiquée par l'autre partie; ou*

2. *L'acceptation expresse par le défendeur de la clause compromissoire figurant à l'article [x] du contrat; ou*

3. *Une convention d'arbitrage signée par le demandeur et le défendeur ou contenue dans un échange de lettres ou télégrammes entre le demandeur et le défendeur ou autre moyen de communication écrite,*

conformément aux exigences formelles prévues par l'article 178.1 de la LDIP.

Cette conclusion suffit pour que ce tribunal décline sa compétence. Néanmoins, nous remarquerons, eu égard aux arguments présentés par les parties fondés sur la loi égyptienne, que la question de la compétence doit être exclusivement tranchée selon la loi suisse. Qui plus est, puisque les parties à la présente procédure ont expressément exclu toute référence à la loi égyptienne comme lex arbitrii *au § 12 de l'acte de mission [qui précise que «* ... le Tribunal arbitral décidera de sa propre compétence conformément à l'article 186 de la loi fédérale suisse sur le droit international privé (1987) ... *»], leurs arguments fondés sur la loi égyptienne dans leurs mémoires ultérieurs doivent être considérés comme des demandes additionnelles, non autorisées par ce tribunal et, par conséquent, elles doivent être ignorées conformément à l'article 19 du Règlement de la CCI. »*

OBSERVATIONS. — I. — La présente sentence offre de nouveau un exemple du refus des arbitres d'étendre les effets obligatoires de la convention d'arbitrage à une entité d'un groupe de sociétés, non-signataire du contrat en cause. En affirmant qu'une telle extension à une société d'un groupe qui n'a pas signé la convention d'arbitrage « *n'est pas une simple question de structure ou de contrôle entre sociétés mais plutôt une question de participation du non-signataire aux négociations, à la conclusion et à l'exécution du contrat ou de son attitude envers la partie qui cherche à introduire le non-signataire dans l'arbitrage* », le Tribunal arbitral n'apparaît pas s'écarter d'une jurisprudence fermement établie. De fait, comme la présente chronique s'en est fait l'écho, les arbitres du commerce international se prononcent en tenant principalement compte de la volonté ou de l'attitude des parties, l'existence d'un groupe de sociétés ne se révélant être qu'un commencement de preuve qui ne se trouve confirmée que par la participation effective des entités du groupe aux opérations contractuelles *(Cf.* : sentence rendue dans l'affaire n° 4131 en 1982 : *JDI 1983, p. 899, obs. Y. Derains.* — V. également les références les plus récentes citées sous la sentence rendue dans l'affaire n° 8385 en 1995 : *JDI 1997, p. 1072, obs. Y. Derains).* A l'évidence, le principe de l'effet relatif des contrats et la personnalité juridique distincte des sociétés membres d'un groupe exigent que seules la participation à la négociation, la conclusion et l'exécution du contrat ou encore le comportement entre les membres du groupe ou l'attitude envers l'autre partie justifient l'extension de la clause compromissoire à une entité d'un groupe non-signataire du contrat en cause.

Dans la présente espèce, il est intéressant de relever que les arbitres, en application du droit suisse auquel les parties se sont référées pour toute question relative à la compétence du tribunal arbitral, refusent de retenir les concepts de groupe de sociétés ou de réalité économique unique pour étendre les effets obligatoires d'une convention d'arbitrage à une société du groupe. De fait, le droit suisse ignore la notion de groupe de sociétés et ne retient que la personnalité morale et l'indépendance juridique de chacune de ses entités par rapport, en particulier, à la maison mère. Seul le fait pour une maison mère de recourir à une filiale pour se soustraire à ses propres obligations constituerait une fraude à la loi ou un abus de droit justifiant la levée du voile social (Cf. *Jean-François Poudret, L'extension de la clause compromissoire : approches française et suisse : JDI 1995, p. 893 s.*). A l'évidence, l'abus de droit dans le contrôle d'une société peut justifier que celui qui l'exerce soit considéré comme responsable des obligations de ladite société. Ce sont donc à l'examen et à l'analyse de la structure sociale, des relations entre les entités d'un groupe, maison mère et filiale par exemple, que doivent procéder les arbitres pour pouvoir justifier la levée du voile social *(Cf.* la sentence rendue en 1990 dans l'affaire n° 5721 : *JDI 1990, p. 1020, obs. J.-J. A.).* Comme dans la sentence ici rapportée, le degré d'intervention de la maison mère sur sa filiale, le contrôle effectif exercé et les effets d'une restructuration entre certaines sociétés du groupe apparaissent être autant de critères pouvant être retenus pour éventuellement décider de percer le voile social dès lors que ces critères conduiraient à établir l'existence d'un comportement abusif à l'égard de tiers. Ce n'est donc pas l'existence d'un groupe en tant que tel mais plutôt la constatation de l'absence d'indépendance juridique des sociétés qui le compose, l'immixtion de l'une dans la gestion et le fonctionnement de l'autre ou la confusion entretenue entre elles qui sont pris en considération. Comme l'a relevé Yves Derains dans ses observations sous la sentence rendue dans l'affaire n° 8385 précitée, « *[c]e qu'il convient avant tout d'éviter, c'est que [. . .] la personnalité morale ne soit utilisée pour protéger des comportements illégitimes au détriment de parties extérieures au groupe des sociétés* ».

II. — Dans l'affaire qui fait l'objet de la sentence ici rapportée, le contrat fixait le lieu de l'arbitrage à Genève et retenait l'application au fond du droit égyptien, les parties ayant ultérieurement convenu dans l'acte de mission de l'application de la Loi de droit international privé suisse (LDIP) à toute question relative à la compétence du tribunal arbitral.

A la différence du droit français de l'arbitrage international, le droit suisse pose une règle matérielle restrictive en n'exigeant certes plus la signature de la convention d'arbitrage *(Concordat Intercantional d'Arbitrage, art. 6)* mais en requérant l'existence d'un texte ou document qui établit la preuve du consentement des parties à l'arbitrage. C'est ce qui résulte de l'alinéa 1 de l'article 178 de la LDIP aux termes duquel s'agissant de la forme, « *la convention d'arbitrage est valable si elle est passée par écrit, télégramme, télex, télécopieur ou tout autre moyen de communication qui permet d'en établir la preuve par un texte* ». Si, en l'espèce, l'existence formelle d'une convention d'arbitrage n'était pas en cause, il en était différemment de l'identité des parties l'ayant acceptée et de celles présentes à la procédure arbitrale. Dès lors, il appartenait aux arbitres de rechercher parmi les documents produits l'indication d'une volonté expresse du non-signataire de se soumettre à l'arbitrage. Tel n'était pas le cas en raison non seulement de l'absence d'implication du non-signataire dans la mise en œuvre et l'exécution du contrat, lequel exigeait un haut niveau de coopération et de communication entre les parties signataires du contrat, mais surtout de l'inexistence d'une preuve écrite manifestant une volonté de se soumettre à la convention d'arbitrage. Cette exigence de forme posée par l'alinéa 1 de l'article 178 de la LDIP suisse a pour résultat de limiter considérablement la mise en cause de tiers (cf. *P. Lalive, J.-F. Poudret, C. Reymond, Le droit de l'arbitrage interne et international en Suisse, Lausanne, 1989, p. 322).*

Il doit être relevé que le rejet par les arbitres de toute argumentation fondée sur le droit égyptien résulte du choix opéré par les parties dans l'acte de mission en faveur du droit suisse. De fait, s'agissant de la validité de la convention d'arbitrage et donc de sa portée, l'alinéa 2 de l'article 178 de la LDIP pose une règle de conflit à rattachement alternatif désignant « soit le droit choisi par les parties, soit le droit régissant l'objet du litige et notamment le droit applicable au contrat principal, soit encore le droit suisse ». Les parties ayant expressément choisi le droit suisse pour toute question relative à la compétence du tribunal arbitral, l'application d'un autre droit était exclue.

J.-J. A.

Sentence partielle rendue dans l'affaire n° 10526 en 2000.

I. — Procédure. — Pluralité de contrats. — Soumission à une seule procédure des demandes relatives à deux contrats différents. — Moment de la constitution du Tribunal arbitral.

II. — Provision pour frais. — Condamnation de la partie défenderesse à rembourser à la partie demanderesse la moitié de l'avance des frais que la demanderesse a versée à la CCI. — Une demande de condamner la défenderesse à rembourser la provision payée par la demanderesse n'est pas une mesure conservatoire ou provisoire. — L'obligation pour chaque partie de payer une provision est une obligation contractuelle. — Les arbitres sont compétents pour condamner la défenderesse à verser sa part de la provision.

Affaire soumise au Règlement 1998. Lieu d'arbitrage : Paris.

La demanderesse, établissement public à caractère industriel et commercial d'un pays africain, avait introduit en juin 1999 une demande d'arbitrage à l'encontre de la défenderesse, une société italienne. A l'origine du litige sont deux marchés portant sur l'électrification en deux temps de la défenderesse de deux tronçons ferroviaires. La demanderesse fondait sa demande sur les clauses compromissoires contenues dans chaque marché. Ces deux clauses, rédigées en termes identiques, étaient ainsi libellées : « *Tout différend découlant du présent contrat sera tranché définitivement suivant le Règlement de conciliation et d'arbitrage de la Chambre de Commerce internationale (Paris) par un ou plusieurs arbitres nommés conformément à ce Règlement.* »

La défenderesse avait ensuite, en décembre 1999, demandé au Tribunal arbitral que celui-ci se prononce, par une sentence partielle, sur « l'exception d'incompétence » que constitue l'impossibilité de soumettre au même tribunal arbitral des demandes relatives à deux contrats différents. La défenderesse contestait donc, à ce stade, la jonction des deux demandes en une même procédure.

Dans sa décision, le Tribunal commence par procéder à une qualification des contestations soulevées :

« *Il apparaît que le problème soulevé par la défenderesse n'est pas, même si le terme a été utilisé par les deux parties, un problème de compétence. Il est certain que le Tribunal arbitral, tel qu'il est constitué, est compétent à l'égard du premier marché comme il l'est à l'égard du second. Cette compétence résulte simplement du fait que (a) la clause compromissoire contenue dans chaque marché prévoit un arbitrage selon le Règlement de la CCI, (b) les demandes présentées par la demanderesse sont bien relatives, les unes à l'exécution du premier marché, les autres à l'exécution du second marché, et (c) le Tribunal arbitral a été constitué en application du Règlement d'arbitrage de la CCI. La défenderesse se reconnaît d'ailleurs incapable de dire à l'égard de quel marché le tribunal serait compétent et à l'égard duquel il serait incompétent. S'il l'est à l'égard du premier marché, il l'est également, par identité de raisons, à l'égard du second. Et dès lors qu'il a compétence à l'égard de l'un (quelconque) de ces marchés, on ne voit pas comment le fait d'être saisi de questions relatives à l'autre pourrait le priver de cette compétence.*

En réalité, ce que conteste la défenderesse, c'est la possibilité de réunir en une seule procédure, devant un unique tribunal, *des demandes relatives à des marchés différents, comportant chacun une clause compromissoire, même rédigée en termes identiques. La thèse de la défenderesse est que les demandes de la demanderesse relatives au premier marché devraient être soumises à un tribunal arbitral, et celles relatives au second marché à un autre tribunal arbitral. »*

Pourtant, la défenderesse avait préalablement, dans sa première réponse à la demande de la demanderesse, déclaré être d'accord avec la demanderesse sur « *la recevabilité de la demande d'arbitrage introduite selon le règlement de conciliation et d'arbitrage de la CCI, ce recours étant prévu aux dispositions des articles 36 et 39 des marchés qui ont donné lieu au présent litige* ».

De plus, la défenderesse avait présenté sa défense sur les deux marchés, formulé une demande reconventionelle et désigné un arbitre. Le Tribunal arbitral a donc pu constater :

« *le présent Tribunal a bien été constitué en vue de la résolution d'un litige portant sur deux marchés différents. (. . .) Il a donc bien été constitué, avec la participation des deux parties et de la Cour internationale d'arbitrage, un Tribunal arbitral (le présent Tribunal) pour connaître des demandes relatives aux deux marchés. Le dossier de la procédure a été transmis à ce Tribunal par le Secrétariat de la Cour le 27 octobre 1999, et il en est donc saisi depuis cette date.* »

Etant donné que la défenderesse avait dans un premier temps reconnu la recevabilité des deux demandes en tant que pouvant faire l'objet d'une seule procédure et avait, dans un deuxième temps, contesté cette recevabilité, il appartenait au tribunal arbitral de trancher la question de savoir si la défenderesse pouvait valablement revenir sur son attitude antérieure par ses contestations soulevées postérieurement à la nomination des arbitres et à la transmission du dossier, mais antérieurement à la signature de l'acte de mission. Cette question soulève le problème de la détermination du moment de la constitution du Tribunal arbitral et de sa mission. Le Tribunal constate :

« *Il ne saurait être soutenu que la constitution d'un Tribunal unique pour connaître des deux marchés restait en suspens jusqu'à la signature de l'acte de mission (. . .) Une fois le troisième arbitre nommé, le Tribunal arbitral est définitivement constitué, sous réserve des cas de récusation (. . .) et de remplacement (. . .). L'article 13 [du Règlement d'arbitrage] mentionne en effet que le dossier est remis au tribunal arbitral « dès que celui-ci est constitué », et l'article 18 confie au tribunal arbitral la tâche d'établir un acte précisant sa mission. Ce n'est donc pas cet acte (acte de mission) qui constitue le Tribunal arbitral; au contraire, son établissement suppose que le Tribunal arbitral était déjà constitué pour connaître du litige tel que défini par les échanges préalables d'écritures entre les parties (. . .)*

Le présent Tribunal était saisi d'un litige au moins provisoirement défini, et [qu']il n'appartenait pas à une partie de l'amputer ensuite unilatéralement d'une fraction des demandes formulées par son adversaire. »

Le Tribunal arbitral en tire la conséquence que la jonction des demandes ne saurait être remise en cause que si deux conditions étaient réunies, à savoir :

« *d'une part que la demanderesse n'avait pas la possibilité d'imposer la constitution d'un seul tribunal arbitral pour les deux marchés; d'autre part qu'il était encore possible pour la défenderesse de remettre en cause cette constitution après que la Cour internationale d'arbitrage y eut procédé.* »

Ainsi, pour que la demande de la demanderesse de joindre les deux demandes soit recevable, il suffirait qu'une desdites conditions ne soit pas remplie. Le Tribunal continue :

« *La difficulté est incontestablement sérieuse. S'il est en effet conforme à une bonne administration de la justice, tant sur le terrain de la découverte de la vérité, que de l'économie de temps et de coûts, et de la cohérence des décisions prises, que deux litiges étroitement connexes soient examinés dans une procédure unique par un tribunal unique, et si l'on peut s'étonner que l'une des parties veuille imposer une division de la procédure aussi manifestement contraire à son déroulement efficace, il est loin d'être certain, au vu des arguments soulevés par la défenderesse, que la demanderesse eût pu imposer la constitution d'un Tribunal arbitral unique si la défenderesse s'y était opposée.*

Toutefois, le Tribunal n'aura pas à trancher cette difficulté, dans la mesure où — et c'est la seconde question annoncée — la défenderesse, non seulement ne s'est pas opposée à cette constitution, mais y a volontairement et consciemment participé. (. . .)

Il est tout d'abord évident que le Tribunal arbitral n'a pas le pouvoir de se dessaisir volontairement d'une partie du litige qui lui a été soumis, sur la simple dénonciation unilatérale par l'une des parties de demandes soumises par l'autre. Si une partie peut se désister de tout ou partie de ses propres demandes (la question étant par ailleurs discutée de savoir si l'autre partie peut s'opposer à ce désistement), il est certain que chaque partie est en droit de maintenir les demandes qu'elle a formulées même si l'autre partie lui demande de les retirer.

Par conséquent, seule une irrégularité de la constitution ou de la saisine, *que le Tribunal constaterait, pourrait le conduire à se déclarer non saisi de tout ou partie des demandes formulées, ou irrégulièrement constitué. »*

Le Tribunal arbitral constate ensuite l'absence d'irrégularité dans la constitution du Tribunal et dans la saisine, puisque la défenderesse avait clairement exprimé son accord à cette constitution. Il termine par rappeler :

« Dès lors que la constitution et la saisine étaient régulières, et que le processus les réalisant était achevé, aucune partie ne pouvait les remettre unilatéralement en cause. Ce n'est pas parce qu'une partie aurait eu le droit de s'opposer à la constitution d'un Tribunal unique (à supposer qu'il en soit bien ainsi), qu'elle a le droit, lorsqu'elle ne s'y est en fait pas opposée et qu'elle a au contraire participé à la constitution, de détruire unilatéralement l'acte juridique complexe (résultant des déclarations de volonté des parties, des arbitres pressentis et de l'institution d'arbitrage) qu'elle a contribué à élaborer. »

. . .

La demanderesse ayant payé la part de provision de la défenderesse pour le compte de celle-ci, la première demandait au tribunal arbitral que la défenderesse soit condamnée à rembourser le montant ainsi payé. La demanderesse rappelait que le tribunal arbitral était compétent pour prononcer une telle condamnation en l'espèce, en application de l'article 23 du Règlement d'arbitrage de la CCI relatif aux mesures conservatoires et provisoires. La défenderesse répondait (entre autres objections) que les frais, à ce stade antérieur à la sentence, sont réclamés par la Cour et ne peuvent l'être par une partie. De plus, la demande ne pouvait être considérée comme provisionnelle car d'une part le Tribunal aurait dû au préalable se prononcer sur l'apparence virtuelle d'une responsabilité au fond, ce qui aurait été impossible en l'état, d'autre part aucune urgence ne pouvait être invoquée en l'espèce.

Le Tribunal rejette l'argumentation de la défenderesse dans les termes suivants :

« La demande de la demanderesse, objet de la présente sentence, est relative à la provision et non pas à la répartition définitive des frais.

Cette demande, précisément parce qu'elle a un objet distinct de la demande relative à la répartition des frais, n'est pas une demande de mesure provisoire : d'une part elle ne se fonde pas sur une simple apparence, d'autre part la décision à intervenir à son sujet n'est pas susceptible d'être remise en cause par une sentence ultérieure. »

Le Tribunal arbitral constate ensuite que sa compétence repose en l'espèce sur la clause compromissoire figurant dans chacun des deux marchés. Il procède par définir l'obligation de chaque partie de la procédure arbitrale de payer sa part de la provision.

« *Dans la mesure où le Règlement est ainsi incorporé par référence dans le contrat, l'obligation de payer la moitié de la provision, prévue par ce Règlement, doit être considérée comme une obligation contractuelle, et tout différend à son sujet est un « différend découlant du présent contrat » au sens de la cause compromissoire.*

La compétence du Tribunal arbitral ne serait exclue que dans la mesure où le Règlement lui-même attribuerait compétence à un autre organe, par exemple à la Cour qui fixe le montant de la provision, et non les arbitres. On pourrait également douter que le Tribunal arbitral puisse ordonner à une partie de payer à la CCI sa part de provision, d'autant que le Secrétariat peut inviter le Tribunal arbitral à suspendre ses activités tant qu'une demande de provision n'est pas satisfaite. Mais en l'espèce la demande tend à voir condamner la défenderesse à rembourser à la demanderesse la part que celle-ci a versée pour elle, ce qui ne met pas en cause le fonctionnement de la Cour internationale d'arbitrage en tant qu'institution.

La demande de la demanderesse paraît également fondée en droit. En ne payant pas sa part de la provision, la défenderesse à méconnu son obligation contractuelle. Elle a par là obligé la demanderesse à effectuer un paiement à sa place, ce à quoi elle ne pouvait se soustraire sans perdre la possibilité de voir le Tribunal arbitral statuer sur ses demandes. La responsabilité contractuelle de la défenderesse est donc engagée, et le préjudice qu'elle a causé à la demanderesse en l'obligeant à effectuer un paiement qui ne lui incombait pas ne saurait être mieux réparé qu'en condamnant la défenderesse à verser à la demanderesse un montant identique à celui déboursé par celle-ci (autrement dit à la « rembourser »), étant précisé que cette condamnation est totalement indépendante de ce qui sera décidé par la suite par le Tribunal arbitral relativement à la répartition des frais de l'arbitrage. »

C'est ainsi que le Tribunal arbitral, dans une sentence partielle, a condamné la défenderesse à rembourser à la demanderesse la somme de USD 95 000, représentant la moitié de la provision fixée par la Cour internationale d'arbitrage, que la demanderesse avait dû verser pour son compte.

OBSERVATIONS. — I. — Le Règlement CCI ne précise rien en ce qui concerne le nombre de contrats qui peuvent faire l'objet d'une seule et même demande d'arbitrage. Son article 4 (1) prévoit simplement qu'une partie, désirant avoir recours à l'arbitrage selon le Règlement CCI adresse sa demande d'arbitrage au secrétariat et, plus loin, dans son paragraphe (3), que la demande contient un exposé de la nature et des circonstances du litige à l'origine de la demande ainsi que les conventions intervenues et notamment la convention d'arbitrage. Par conséquent, rien n'empêche un demandeur d'introduire contre une même défenderesse une demande d'arbitrage relative à plusieurs marchés tant que la clause compromissoire contenue dans chacun des marchés est une clause CCI et que les clauses sont identiques, ou au moins ne sont pas différentes quant à la procédure de nomination des arbitres et leur nombre ainsi que le lieu d'arbitrage. Ceci est l'une des avantages incontestables d'être demandeur dans un arbitrage CCI puisque c'est le demandeur qui décide quelle partie il va entraîner dans sa procédure d'arbitrage et quels contrats seront à la base de cet arbitrage.

Il n'est pas dans le pouvoir de la défenderesse dans une situation comme dans le case d'espèce de séparer les deux contrats avec l'effet d'obliger la demanderesse ou la CCI de traiter la demande unique présentée par la demanderesse comme visant deux arbitrages distincts. Dans ces circonstances, la défenderesse n'a donc aucune possibilité de proposer deux arbitres différents, un pour chacun des contrats faisant l'objet du litige.

Pour un cas semblable dans lequel existaient deux contrats liés contenant des clauses CCI non identiques mais compatibles entre elles, prévoyant un même lieu d'arbitrage (Genève), voir l'affaire CCI n° 5989 rendue en 1989 (*JDI 1997, n° 4*).

La situation aurait été différente si la demanderesse avait introduit successivement contre la défenderesse deux demandes d'arbitrage relatives à chacun des contrats. Cette situation est prévue à l'article 4 (6) du Règlement de la CCI. Ce paragraphe dispose pour un tel cas que si la nouvelle demande est relative à une relation juridique faisant déjà l'objet d'une procédure d'arbitrage entre les mêmes parties, la Cour de la CCI peut décider de joindre les deux affaires à condition que l'acte de mission n'ait pas été signé ou approuvé par la Cour. Une telle jonction aurait pour conséquence que le Tribunal arbitral constitué dans la première affaire serait compétent pour juger aussi la deuxième demande d'arbitrage.

II. — Le problème du défaut de paiement par l'une des parties de sa part de la provision n'est pas nouveau dans l'arbitrage CCI, ni d'ailleurs dans les arbitrages ad hoc. C'est un des plus vieux problèmes, et une cause répétée de retard, dans l'arbitrage CCI. Dans le passé, les parties ont essayé différentes solutions à ce problème selon le lieu de l'arbitrage et/ou le droit applicable, le plus souvent en soumettant une requête à une juridiction étatique. Ainsi, dans l'affaire CCI n° 7734 (non publiée), la partie demanderesse allemande avait commencé une procédure contre la défenderesse américaine devant les tribunaux américains. A la suite d'une objection d'incompétence présentée par la défenderesse basée sur l'existence d'une clause CCI, le tribunal étatique américain avait renvoyé les parties devant la CCI. La défenderesse ne versait pas la provision fixée par la Cour de la CCI et la demanderesse saisit alors le tribunal étatique américain d'une demande de voir condamner la défenderesse à payer sa part de la provision à la Cour d'Arbitrage de la CCI. Le tribunal (*Superior Court of New Jersey, Law Division, Middlesex county docket n° L 4310-90*) décida par ordre le 4 mars 1994, que la défenderesse devait payer à la CCI sa part de la provision d'un montant de USD 4 000.

Il faut rappeler les principales caractéristiques du système régi par l'article 30 du Règlement de 1998 de la CCI. En vertu de cet article, le versement de la provision pour frais se fait en en trois étapes. Chaque demande d'arbitrage soumise à la CCI doit être accompagnée d'une avance de USD 2 500. Dès réception de la demande d'arbitrage, et c'est la deuxième étape, le Secrétaire général « peut » fixer une avance sur la provision pour frais, due par le demandeur seulement. Son paiement conditionne la remise du dossier au Tribunal, articles 13 et 30 (1). L'article 30 (2) du Règlement dispose que la provision totale est fixée « dès que possible » et c'est la troisième étape. Une fois que la provision totale a été fixée « dès que possible » et c'est la troisième étape. Une fois que la provision totale a été fixée par la Cour de la CCI, elle est due à 50% par le demandeur, moins l'avance éventuellement versée sur la provision, et à 50% par le défendeur. Le principe du partage à parts égales entre les deux parties est inchangé par rapport au Règlement de 1988 de la CCI.

Qu'advient-il en cas de défaut de paiement de la provision totale ? Le nouveau Règlement maintient la possibilité de la substitution d'une partie à une autre, article 30 (3). Normalement, le demandeur règle la part du défendeur récalcitrant, et il peut toujours s'en acquitter en fournissant une garantie bancaire (*Appendice III, art. 1 (6))*. En cas de défaut de paiement, une fois que le dossier a été remis aux arbitres, le Secrétariat, qui est expressément autorisé à les inviter à suspendre leurs activités, les consultera sur la marche à suivre. Le Secrétariat peut impartir à la partie défaillante un délai de paiement de 15 jours au minimum. Si, passé ce délai, la somme demandée n'a pas été versée, ou si aucun délai n'a été accordé, la demande sera considérée comme retirée, sauf objection de la partie concernée. Dans ce dernier cas, une démarche sera suivie, mais en l'absence de paiement à son issue, la demande sera réputée retirée *(art. 30 (4))*.

L'obligation pour la défenderesse de verser la moitié de la provision n'est pas une nouveauté selon le Règlement 1998; cette obligation existait aussi selon la version antérieure du Règlement, la version 1975/1988, voir *Jarvin, Wenn die beklagte Partei ihren*

Anteil des Kostenvorschusses nicht bezahlt; Folgen der Nichtzahlung, in Festschrift für Ottoarnd Glossner : Heidelberg, 1994, p. 155 s. Il est significatif, à cet égard, de rappeler la note du Secrétariat de la Cour en date du 1er janvier 1993 (voir *Guide de l'arbitrage de la CCI, publication CCI n° 448 (F), 1994, p. 112*) qui précisait (*p. 114*) :

> « *En cas de défaillance d'une partie à s'acquitter du premier versement de 25 %, l'autre partie doit payer comptant la part de la partie défaillante pour que le tribunal arbitral puisse être saisi de l'affaire. Si la partie défaillante persiste à ne pas s'acquitter de sa part de provision après communication ou approbation de l'acte de mission, l'autre partie peut soit payer comptant les 50 % restants, soit fournir une garantie bancaire.*
>
> *Toutefois, il convient de noter que dans les arbitrages CCI, le fait qu'une partie refuse de payer tout ou partie de la provision pour frais mise à sa charge et laisse le soin à l'autre partie de s'en acquitter à sa place n'en est pas une pratique normale. Si la CCI autorise une partie à se substituer à l'autre pour le paiement de la provision, ceci ne doit en aucun cas être considéré comme un aval ou une acceptation de la part de la CCI du non-paiement par une partie de la part des frais lui incombant.* »

La décision prise par le Tribunal arbitral, de condamner la défenderesse à verser sa part, est conforme à la solution préconisée par *Fouchard-Gaillard-Goldman, dans leur Traité de l'arbitrage commercial international (Litec, Paris, 1996, § 1254, p. 700)*, par *Derains-Schwartz, A Guide to the New ICC Rules of Arbitration (1998, p. 321)* et par *Craig-Park-Paulsson, International Chamber of Commerce Arbitration (3rd ed., 2000, p. 268)*. Le Tribunal arbitral a situé le problème comme étant un problème contractuel et non une question de mesure provisoire. C'est dans son analyse de la question de sa compétence que la sentence partielle présente un intérêt particulier. Selon les arbitres, le Règlement de la CCI est incorporé par référence dans le contrat. L'obligation de verser la moitié de la provision est une obligation expresse du Règlement CCI et en adoptant l'arbitrage CCI pour résoudre leurs litiges, les parties ont accepté de se soumettre aux contraintes dudit Règlement. Toutefois, nous observons que cette obligation ne figure pas dans le contrat lui-même. Il faut donc bien remarquer qu'un différend portant sur l'obligation de verser une partie de la provision fixée par la Cour de la CCI n'est qu'indirecte-ment un différend « découlant du présent contrat ». Selon la sentence, la source de la compétence des arbitres réside dans l'obligation de payer une provision stipulée dans le Règlement de la CCI, ce Règlement étant convenu contractuellement entre les parties, le différend découle donc de l'application du contrat. Or, on peut ne pas être accord avec cette analyse et adopter une attitude différente sur la compétence de l'arbitre dans ce cas. M. Mitrovic, cité par Me Favre-Bulle dans l'article ci-dessous mentionné, est d'avis que « *les dispositions du Règlement sur la provision représentent les conditions générales des prestations des services arbitraux de la Cour et qu'il s'agit de rapports de la Cour avec les parties, c'est-à-dire avec chacune d'elles et non de rapports mutuels entre les parties* ».

Il faut signaler qu'un autre Tribunal arbitral, siégeant en Suisse, vient de rendre une décision identique à celle dans l'affaire 10526 dans une autre affaire CCI, citée dans le *Bulletin ASA n° 2 de 2001, p. 285 (X Company, Panama c/Y.S.A., Suisse)*. Cette dernière affaire et les problèmes de principe que le défaut de paiement de la provision par une des parties soulèvent, ont fait l'objet d'un article dans le même numéro du *Bulletin ASA par Me Xavier Favre-Bulle, p. 227 s.* Dans son article Me Favre-Bulle exprime l'avis que la question de la provision est de nature administrative et par conséquent de la seule com-pétence de la CCI, et non de celle des arbitres *(p. 238)*. Si les arbitres sont saisis de cette question, ils ne peuvent, à son avis, rendre une décision de droit matériel par une sentence partielle parce qu'ils ne sont pas compétents pour statuer à la place de la CCI sur une question administrative. Il pense par contre que les arbitres sont compétents pour prendre une mesure provisionnelle ou conservatoire afin d'obtenir la participation d'une partie au paiement de la provision.

Mis à part quelques doutes de principe sur la compétence des arbitres, nous pensons que la solution adoptée par les arbitres dans l'affaire en cause est satisfaisante dans une perspective plus générale : les questions de procédure qui se présentent dans l'arbitrage CCI doivent, dans la mesure du possible, trouver une réponse à l'intérieur du système d'arbitrage CCI, sans recours inutile à un organe extérieur.

S. J.

Sentence rendue dans l'affaire n° 7986 en 1999

I. — Arbitrage international. — Procédure arbitrale. — Procédure pénale parallèle. — Sursis à statuer (non).

II. — Procédure arbitrale. — Pluralité de débiteurs. — Détermination des parties défenderesses. — Privilège du demandeur.

III. — Droit applicable. — Amiable composition — *Ex æquo et bono.* — Equité. — Pouvoirs de l'arbitre.

IV. — Intérêts moratoires. — Taux. — Point de départ.

V. — Frais de l'arbitrage. — Répartition. — Amiable composition.

Un groupe français, agissant par une société française X et une société luxembourgeoise XL, demanderesses, avaient conclu avec une société d'un groupe belge, Y, défenderesse, plusieurs protocoles d'accord par lesquels cette dernière s'engageait, pour elle-même et les membres de son groupe en vue d'une participation commune et égalitaire dans le capital d'une autre société belge, Z. L'exécution de cet accord a donné lieu à de nombreuses difficultés dont certaines furent soumises à un tribunal arbitral de trois membres, siégeant à Luxembourg.

Les arbitres durent examiner diverses demandes de sursis à statuer, dont l'une était fondée sur l'existence de procédures pénales à Bruxelles et au Luxembourg. La défenderesse se prévalait de l'adage « *le criminel tient le civil en l'état* ».

Le tribunal arbitral rejeta la demande de sursis à statuer dans les termes suivants:

« *En cours d'instance, Y a fait valoir une nouvelle demande de surséance à statuer, fondée sur l'ouverture d'une instruction pénale à Bruxelles consécutive à un jugement prononcé le . . . par la sixième chambre de commerce de Bruxelles dans le cadre du litige. Le Tribunal de commerce avait, en effet, décidé de ne pas statuer avant que « l'aspect pénal de la cause soit éclairci ». A cet égard, cette autorité judiciaire se référait à une note écrite de monsieur le Procureur du Roi requérant la communication du jugement, ce qui incita le Tribunal de commerce à communiquer le dossier au Procureur du Roi avant même qu'une décision ne soit rendue.*

C'est en se fondant sur cette démarche du Tribunal de commerce que la partie défenderesse a soutenu que l'instruction pénale en cours pourrait aboutir à l'annulation du Protocole d'Accord du . . . et du . . . et que dès lors la question de leur validité aurait une incidence certaine sur l'issue de la présente procédure. Le principe « le criminel tient le civil en l'état » est ainsi invoqué par la partie défenderesse à l'appui de sa demande de sursis à statuer.

Les parties demanderesses s'opposent à cette demande tout en précisant qu'elles ont déposé une plainte pénale au Luxembourg le . . . et qu'elles se sont constituées parties civiles contre MM. . . . et contre les responsables et bénéficiaires économiques de la société . . . pour abus de confiance au préjudice de la société . . . Cela étant, les demanderesses font valoir que l'action pénale en Belgique n'en est qu'au stade de l'information, l'action publique n'étant pas encore intentée. Dans ces conditions, le principe « le criminel tient le civil en l'état » ne saurait faire obstacle à la poursuite de la procédure arbitrale dès lors qu'en vertu de l'article 4 du Code Belge d'Instruction Criminelle, il faut, pour qu'un tel adage puisse s'appliquer, que l'action publique ait été initiée. En outre, les parties demanderesses soulignent que les actions pénales ne devraient avoir aucune influence sur la procédure arbitrale et que Y ne fait valoir aucune cause de nullité s'agissant du protocole du ...

Il ne fait aucun doute et les parties sont d'accord sur ce point, que le tribunal arbitral est compétent pour se prononcer sur l'application de l'adage « le criminel tient le civil en l'état ».

S'agissant de la procédure belge, le tribunal arbitral relève que les effets territoriaux de l'adage « le criminel tient le civil en l'état » méritent une analyse circonstanciée. De l'avis de la doctrine qui fait autorité en matière d'arbitrage international, cet adage relèverait du seul ordre public interne. Ainsi J. Robert souligne dans « Arbitrage, Droit interne — Droit international privé », 1983 que « l'incident criminel n'est fondé en droit interne que sur la nécessité d'éviter la possible contrariété de la chose jugée au criminel et au civil, comme sur la précédence de la juridiction criminelle sur le civil, causes dont la conjonction conduit au sursis à statuer sur le civil dès lors que le criminel est saisi. Cette disposition est d'ordre civil interne. Dès lors que l'arbitrage intervient en matière internationale, l'ordre public interne reste sans effet ».

Le tribunal arbitral fera sienne l'opinion de J. Robert tout en soulignant qu'une action pénale en cours dans un pays autre que celui du lieu de l'arbitrage pourrait avoir une certaine incidence sur la procédure arbitrale elle-même. Toutefois, considérant que l'adage « le criminel tient le civil en l'état » n'est pas d'application automatique lorsque l'action pénale est pendante dans un Etat autre que celui où est situé le siège de l'arbitrage, la question du sursis à statuer relève du seul pouvoir d'appréciation du tribunal arbitral et ne doit donc être ordonnée que si des motifs d'opportunité le commandent. Or, tel n'est manifestement pas le cas en l'espèce.

En premier lieu, la procédure pénale belge en est au stade de l'information de sorte que l'issue de cette procédure sera très éloignée dans le temps. Dans ces conditions, suspendre la procédure arbitrale équivaudrait à un déni de justice formel. En second lieu, la suspension ne devrait être ordonnée que si la cause qui motive cette suspension, soit la procédure pénale belge, revêt un caractère préjudiciel ou dont le sort est de nature à influencer de manière déterminante celui de la présente procédure. Cette condition n'est pas non plus remplie. En effet, à supposer que la signature du protocole d'accord du ... puisse constituer une infraction pénale, auquel cas sa validité pourrait être sérieusement mise en cause, il n'en demeure pas moins qu'une éventuelle nullité dudit protocole n'aurait aucune incidence sur la validité [des autres accords conclus par les parties].

En conséquence, force est d'admettre que le risque de contrariété de décisions lié à l'existence d'une autre procédure connexe, soit la procédure pénale belge, est inexistant, ce qui est un motif suffisant pour ne pas ordonner le sursis à statuer dans la présente procédure en raison de ladite procédure pénale.

En ce qui est de l'action pénale introduite par ... au Luxembourg, celle-ci a été intentée contre MM. ... et contre les responsables et bénéficiaires économiques dans le cadre de l'affaire ... Bien évidemment, cette affaire fait partie des opérations ayant été décrites par les parties dans leurs mémoires, mais elle est certainement étrangère à l'objet de cet arbitrage. Le prétendu abus de confiance au préjudice de ... intéresse les actionnaires de cette société qui sont aussi les parties au présent litige, sans que la procédure pénale au Luxembourg ait pour autant des liens qui sont de nature à conditionner les décisions à prendre dans le cadre de cet arbitrage.

Pour ces motifs, la requête de sursis à statuer de la défenderesse est rejetée ».

Y s'était par ailleurs opposée à être désignée comme unique partie défenderesse alors que deux des protocoles d'accord indiquaient:

« Y agissant tant en son nom personnel qu'au nom et pour le compte des sociétés du groupe indiquées dans les opérations visées par le présent protocole notamment ... — d'une part — et

X . . . d'autre part ».

Le tribunal arbitral rejeta l'objection de la défenderesse comme suit:

« Y conclut qu'elle ne pourrait être condamnée seule à exécuter les engagements sur lesquels les demandes de X et de XL se fondent, considérant que ces engagements auraient été souscrits en réalité par l'ensemble des sociétés de son groupe . . .

Selon les demanderesses, Y est tenue de l'intégralité de ces engagements eu égard à la solidarité qui est de droit entre plusieurs commerçants tenus d'une même obligation contractuelle.

Selon les principes généraux de procédure, applicables également à une procédure arbitrale, il appartient à la partie demanderesse et à elle seule de désigner la partie contre laquelle elle entend plaider. Si la cause est indivisible, soit lorsqu'il y a une consorité nécessaire, la demande dirigée contre un seul des consorts échouera, faute de légitimation passive de celui-ci, l'action devant être diligentée contre tous les consorts nécessaires. En revanche, si la cause est divisible, ce qui sera le cas dans l'hypothèse d'une solidarité passive, le demandeur peut décider d'agir contre une seul débiteur solidaire, lequel, le case échéant, pourrait appeler en cause ses co-débiteurs pour faire valoir contre eux une action récursoire. Dans cette seconde hypothèse, se posent alors les questions délicates telle celle concernant les procédures multi-parties qui peuvent être ou ne pas être consolidées en fonction du règlement d'arbitrage applicable.

En l'espèce, il ne fait aucun doute que les obligations que la défenderesse a souscrites à teneur des protocoles des . . . , tant en son nom personnel qu'au nom et pour le compte des sociétés du groupe sont des obligations solidaires. Dans ces conditions, les parties demanderesses pouvaient choisir d'attraire dans la procédure arbitrale la seule société Y et non les autres membres du groupe, dont on peut se demander — question qui n'a pas à être résolue ici — si ceux-ci sont également liés par la clause compromissoire. Le moyen soulevé par la Défenderesse doit donc être rejeté, étant précisé que l'autorité de la chose jugée de la présente sentence ne déploiera d'effet qu'à l'égard de la défenderesse, soit Y ».

La convention d'arbitrage conclue entre les parties contenait la disposition suivante:

« L'arbitre unique, ou les trois arbitres, jouira des pouvoirs d'amiable compositeur statuant ex æquo et bono *sans être astreint à se conformer aux délais et aux règles ordinaires de procédure ».*

Les parties avaient de l'étendue des pouvoirs de l'arbitre amiable compositeur des conceptions différentes, ce qui amena le tribunal arbitral à fournir les précisions suivantes:

« Pour Y les pouvoirs d'amiable composition obligent les arbitres à trancher le litige en équité. L'amiable composition confère aux arbitres le pouvoir, sinon de s'écarter, dans la mesure que commande l'équité, des dispositions légales ou contractuelles en principe applicable au litige, à tout le moins, d'atténuer les conséquences trop rigoureuses auxquelles ces dispositions pourraient conduire. Y met en avant les limites de l'amiable composition au regard de l'ordre public.

X pour sa part met l'accent sur le fait que ses demandes ne sont pas inéquitables. Par ailleurs, elle reconnaît que le sujet de l'étendue des pouvoirs des amiables compositeurs n'est traité que succinctement dans la littérature juridique au Luxembourg. Par conséquent, elle conclut que les pouvoirs des amiables compositeurs sont ceux définis dans l'ouvrage International Commercial Arbitration de Craig, Park et Paulsson (Ed. Oceana, t. 1, § 18.02). Les arbitres devront donc apprécier les faits de la cause en se fondant sur une vision d'ensemble des relations entre les parties tant d'un point de vue économique que dans la perspective d'une solution équitable.

Ce nonobstant, les parties ont toutefois discuté dans leurs écritures, de la question du droit applicable au fond du litige.

En particulier, la partie défenderesse se fondant sur certains critères de rattachement, estime que le droit applicable serait le droit belge, mais la solution résultant d'une application de ce droit devra être tempérée par les principes de l'équité.

Jusqu'à très récemment, la question de l'étendue des pouvoirs des arbitres autorisés à statuer en tant qu'amiables compositeurs était controversée. Ainsi, une certaine doctrine s'était efforcée de distinguer l'amiable composition de l'arbitrage en équité. La doctrine la plus récente a considéré une telle distinction comme artificielle, car dans un cas comme dans l'autre, les « arbitres pourront faire prévaloir sur toute autre considération leur sentiment de ce que requiert la justice au cas d'espèce » (cf. P. Fouchard, E. Gaillard, P. Goldman: Traité de l'arbitrage commercial international, Paris 1996, n° 1502, p.849).

Selon cette même doctrine:

« L'amiable composition se définit donc essentiellement de manière négative comme le pouvoir des arbitres de ne pas s'en tenir à l'application des règles de droit, ce qui leur permet aussi bien de les ignorer complètement que de s'en écarter en tant que leur sentiment de l'équité l'exige » (cf. Fouchard, Gaillard, Goldman, op. cit. ad, § 1502, p. 849).

Sur la base des enseignements de la doctrine la plus moderne, le Tribunal arbitral déterminera l'étendue de ses pouvoirs d'amiable compositeur de la manière suivante:

Dès lors que les parties se sont contentées de stipuler une clause d'amiable composition sans autre précision, les arbitres ne feront pas application d'une loi étatique déterminée ou de règles transnationales (cf. Fouchard, Gaillard, Goldman, op. cit. ad, § 1505, p. 850).

Les arbitres, sans être tenus de respecter les dispositions strictes du contrat, ne les appliqueront pas moins, sauf si elles conduisent à des résultats inéquitables (cf. Fouchard, Gaillard, Goldman, op. cit. ad § 1507, p. 852). *En d'autres termes, les arbitres prendront en compte les objectifs poursuivis par les parties dans le cadre de leurs stipulations contractuelles et veilleront à ce que l'esprit du contrat soit sauvegardé. Ainsi, dans leur recherche d'une solution équitable, les arbitres s'efforceront de dégager la volonté des parties telle qu'elle a été exprimée dans leur accord au jour de sa signature et s'abstiendront de modifier l'équilibre contractuel en résultant.*

Enfin, les arbitres veilleront à ce que les règles d'ordre public international tel le principe « pacta sunt servanda » soient respectées (cf. Fouchard, Gaillard, Goldman, op. cit. ad § 1508, p. 853; voir aussi P. Lalive, J. F. Poudret, C. Reymond, Le droit de l'arbitrage interne et international en Suisse, Lausanne 1989, p. 400 s.) ».

Le tribunal arbitral se prononça sur le taux et le point de départ des intérêts moratoires:

« X et XL réclament les intérêts calculés au taux légal à partir de la mise en demeure de Y par X le 30 décembre 1992.

Le tribunal après analyse de chacun des chefs de la demande, et considérant qu'il existe davantage de liens de rattachement avec la loi française (du fait de la signature du protocole d'accord à Paris et de la nationalité française de l'une des parties) décide de condamner la défenderesse au paiement des intérêts au taux légal en France et ce à compter de la date de la requête d'arbitrage, conformément à la demande d'arbitrage. A ce sujet, le tribunal arbitral relève par analogie que les demanderesses, si elles avaient placé les montants dont question est ici auprès d'une banque commerciale française en francs français, auraient perçu un intérêt au taux légal. Cette solution relève des pouvoirs des arbitres agissant en qualité d'amiables compositeurs ».

La sentence donna gain de cause aux demanderesses. Cependant, le tribunal arbitral ne mit à la charge de la défenderesse que la moitié des frais de l'arbitrage, chaque partie supportant ses propres frais et honoraires d'avocat:

« Sur cette question, le tribunal arbitral possède un large pouvoir d'appréciation. En règle générale, la partie qui succombe, en l'espèce la défenderesse, doit supporter la

totalité ou une grande partie des frais d'arbitrage. Toutefois, considérant d'une part que les arbitres sont dotés d'un pouvoir d'amiable compositeur, d'autre part que les demanderesses n'ont et de loin pas obtenu le plein de leurs conclusions, il y a lieu de compenser les frais d'arbitrage et de condamner chacune des parties à supporter par parts égales lesdits frais . . .

Toujours en vertu de ses pouvoirs d'amiable compositeur, le tribunal arbitral décide que chacune des parties supportera les frais qu'elle a exposés pour sa défense y compris les frais et honoraires des avocats ».

Observations. — I. — Le principe selon lequel « *le criminel tient le civil en l'état* » est-il d'ordre public international? Il y a, semble-t-il, des doutes à cet égard en droit français (cf. *T. Clay, L'arbitre, n° 200, note 8, p. 164; Fouchard, Gaillard, Goldman on International commercial Arbitration, n° 1660, p. 960*). Telle n'est pas la solution du droit suisse qui estime que ce principe n'est pas d'ordre public, ainsi que le souligne le Tribunal Fédéral dans un arrêt du 7 septembre 1993 *(Bull. assoc. Suisse arb. 1994, p. 248).* Dans une résolution adoptée à Helsinki en 1996, l'Association de Droit International a considéré que le fait qu'une procédure judiciaire, civile ou pénale, présente des relations avec une procédure arbitrale ne suffisait pas, en soi, à justifier l'arrêt ou la suspension de la procédure arbitrale *(Rev. arb. 1996, p. 563, obs. E. Gaillard).*

C'est à ce dernier point de vue que semblent se rallier les arbitres dans la présente affaire. Ils retiennent que l'application du principe n'est pas automatique et que le sursis à statuer relève du seul pouvoir d'appréciation des arbitres et ne doit être ordonné que si des motifs d'opportunité le commandent. Ceci revient à priver les effets du principe « *le criminel tient le civil en état* » de toute spécificité en matière d'arbitrage par rapport aux autres situations où se pose le problème de l'opportunité de la suspension d'une procédure arbitrale en raison de l'existence d'une procédure parallèle, qu'elle soit arbitrale ou judiciaire, civile, commerciale ou pénale. Comme le soulignait la sentence rendue en 1991 dans l'affaire n° 6610 « *un tribunal arbitral a ordinairement la compétence ou le pouvoir de suspendre un arbitrage lorsqu'il semble juste et opportun de le faire dans les circonstances particulières de l'affaire* » *(Recueil des sentences arbitrales de la CCI — 1991-1995, J.-J. Arnaldez, Y. Derains et D. Hascher, p. 280).* Le principe « *le criminel tient le civil en l'état* » se trouve donc ramené au niveau de l'ordinaire, et ce n'est que justice. Comme l'a souligné Jean Robert, ainsi que le rappellent les arbitres dans la sentence ici rapportée, le principe ne vise qu'à « *éviter la possible contrariété de la chose jugée au criminel et au civil* » et sur « *la précédence de la juridiction criminelle sur le civil* » *(J. Robert, Arbitrage, droit interne — droit internationl privé* », *1983, n° 344, p. 296).* Il s'agit finalement, au sein d'un système judiciaire particulier, d'une solution particulière aux problèmes de la litispendance et de la connexité dont la spécificité s'explique par la prééminence conférée à la juridiction pénale. Cependant, la litispendance entre juridiction étatique et juridiction arbitrale n'existe pas. Une sentence rendue en 1988 dans l'affaire n° 5103 *(JDI 1988, p. 1207, obs. G. Aguilar Alvarez)* s'en explique très clairement:

« *La litispendance, à proprement parler, ne peut surgir qu'entre deux juridictions d'un même Etat ou de deux Etats différents, lorsque les règles de compétence de leur for les autorisent l'une et l'autre à connaître d'un même litige (sur l'admission récente de la litispendance internationale par la jurisprudence française qui la subordonne cependant à la double compétence du juge français et du juge étranger, cf. Cass. 1re civ., 26 nov. 1974: JDI 1975, p. 108, note A. Ponsard; Rev. crit. DIP 1975, p. 19, note D. Holleaux; cf. A. Huet, J. Cl. droit international, fasc. 581-D, n° 110 s.). Cette situation de compétence concurrente ne peut surgir entre une juridiction arbitrale et une juridiction étatique, pour la raison que leur compétence respective ne dépend que d'un seul facteur: l'existence, la validité et l'étendue de la convention d'arbitrage ».*

La solution est constante (cf. *sentence rendue en 1975 dans l'affaire n° 2637: Rec. sentences arbitrales CCI 1974-1985, Y. Derains et S. Jarvin, p. 12; sentence rendue dans l'affaire n° 7153 en 1992: JDI 1992, p. 1005, obs. D. Hascher*). Elle vaut également pour la connexité *(D. Hascher, obs. sous la sentence n° 7153 préc.).* On ne voit donc pas pourquoi le seul fait qu'une juridiction pénale soit saisie devrait inspirer une solution différente et contraindre les arbitres à se dessaisir ou surseoir à statuer, pour autant, bien entendu, que les questions soumises aux arbitres entrent dans le champ d'application de la convention d'arbitrage et soient objectivement arbitrables. Mais c'est là un autre débat. Comme on l'a justement fait remarquer, admettre la fin du principe selon lequel « *le criminel tient le civil en l'état* » en matière d'arbitrage revient à fournir le moyen à une partie désireuse de se soustraire à l'arbitrage de parvenir à ses fins en suscitant une procédure pénale (cf. *P. Fouchard, E. Gaillard, P. Goldman*, op. cit., loc. cit.). Cela reviendrait également à interdire en pratique à la partie qui engage une procédure d'arbitrage de recourir à une procédure pénale connexe. Or, comme l'avait indiqué la sentence précitée rendue dans l'affaire n° 5103 en 1998, « *les actions pénales . . . ne peuvent être considérées comme . . . contraires aux conventions d'arbitrage* ». Elles peuvent même être complémentaires dans l'hypothèse où une partie souhaite légitimement établir certains faits grâce à une procédure pénale, pour bénéficier de moyens d'investigation qui échappent aux arbitres. C'est l'un des cas où l'arbitre peut décider qu'il est opportun de surseoir à statuer. Mais il en est seul juge.

II. — Le tribunal arbitral rappelle qu'il appartient à la partie demanderesse, et à elle seule, de désigner la partie contre laquelle elle agit. Il se fonde pour cela sur des principes généraux de procédure qu'il estime également applicables à l'arbitrage. Cette transposition est sans doute exacte si on se limite au choix initial du défendeur par le demandeur. Elle ne l'est plus au-delà. Les procédures judiciaires connaissent l'appel en garantie et surtout l'intervention, forcée ou volontaire (par example *art. 327 NCPC)* qui ne trouve pas aisément sa place en matière d'arbitrage, sauf à mettre en place des mécanismes contractuels dont l'efficacité a rarement été démontrée. A cet égard, le tribunal arbitral invoque les questions délicates concernant les procédures multi-parties qui peuvent ou non « *être consolidées en fonction du règlement d'arbitrage applicable* ». Mais ce n'est là qu'un aspect particulier et, somme toute, bénin, de la difficulté. Le règlement d'arbitrage CCI, tel que révisé en 1988, a pu apporter une solution au problème de la constitution des tribunaux arbitraux en cas de pluralité de parties. Son article 10 prévoit que, dans certaines circonstances, la Cour Internationale d'Arbitrage peut directement nommer les trois membres du Tribunal Arbitral. Mais il n'en demeure pas moins que c'est le demandeur qui, dès l'introduction de la procédure, décide du caractère multi-parties ou non de la procédure en désignant le ou les défendeurs. S'il en désigne plus d'un, il court alors le risque d'être privé du droit de choisir un arbitre dans l'hypothèse où les défendeurs multiples ne pourraient ou ne voudraient s'entendre sur le nom d'un seul arbitre. En cas de solidarité passive, un débiteur solidaire contre lequel le demandeur n'a pas estimé opportun d'agir, ne peut intervenir. De même, le défendeur ne peut appeler une autre partie en garantie ni agir à titre reconventionnel contre une partie autre que le demandeur s'il se trouve avec ce dernier dans des liens de solidarité passive ou de consorité. La sentence rendue en 1987 dans l'affaire n° 5625, sous l'empire du Règlement d'Arbitrage CCI de 1975 affirmait clairement: « *Il y a une seule façon pour être partie à un arbitrage selon le règlement de la CCI: c'est au moyen de l'article 3, en vertu d'une demande par laquelle une partie se constitue comme demanderesse ou est identifiée par la demanderesse comme défenderesse* » *(Recueil des sentences arbitrales de la CCI, 1986-1990 par S. Jarvin, Y. Derains et J. J. Arnaldez — traduction libre). Le Règlement de 1998 n'a rien changé à cette situation* (cf. *Y. Derains et E. Schwartz, A guide to the new ICC Rules of Arbitration, p. 74).* On est donc loin d'une transposition à l'arbitrage des principes généraux de procédure et c'est sans doute là, à côté de nombreux avantages, une faiblesse de la procédure arbitrale.

III. — On a pu écrire que lorsque l'arbitre jouit des pouvoirs d'amiable compositeur « *la liberté de l'arbitre est poussée à son paroxysme* » *(T. Clay, op. cit., n° 811, p. 623)*. Dans la présente sentence, les arbitres définissent cependant des limites à cette liberté: celles-ci se trouvent d'une part dans le contrat, d'autre part dans les règles d'ordre public international. S'agissant du contrat, les arbitres estiment être tenus d'en appliquer les dispositions pour autant qu'elles n'aboutissent pas à des résultats inéquitables, en privilégiant l'aspect du contrat et ses objectifs, et en s'abstenant d'en modifier l'équilibre; s'agissant de l'ordre public international ils se réfèrent de toute évidence à l'order public véritablement international, et non pas à l'ordre public international d'un Etat déterminé (sur ce point cf. *Pierre Lalive, L'ordre public international (ou véritablement international) et l'arbitrage international: Rev. arb. 1986, p.329*). La mention du principe « *pacta sunt servanda* » en témoigne. Il est particulièrement intéressant de noter qu'ils déduisent de ce que les parties leur ont donné les pouvoirs d'amiable composition, sans autre précision, qu'elles n'ont pas mainfesté le souhait qu'ils appliquent des régles transnationales. La confusion selon laquelle il y aurait une relation entre le pouvoir d'amiable compositeur et celui d'appliquer la lex mercatoria paraît donc bien dépassée (cf. *sentence rendue en 1979 dans l'affaire n° 3267: JDI 1980, p. 967, obs. Y. Derains; sentence rendue en 1980 dans l'affaire n° 3380: Rec Sentences arbitrales CCI, 1974-1985, op. cit, p. 90)*.

IV. — On est plus surpris par la démarche des arbitres en ce qui concerne la détermination du taux des intérêts moratoires qu'il rattache à leurs pouvoirs d'amiables compositeurs. Il est généralement admis que les arbitres internationaux, amiables compositeurs ou non, jouissent de la plus grande liberté dans ce domaine. Ainsi, la sentence rendue en 1990 dans l'affaire n° 6219 *(JDI 1990, p. 1047, obs. Y. Derains)* rappelait:

« *Dans le cadre d'un arbitrage international, cette détermination n'est pas gouvernée par des règles rigoureuses et précises.*

La tendance générale qui se dégage, en doctrine et dans la pratique arbitrale internationale, est de laisser à l'arbitre une grande liberté dans la fixation de ce taux (V. notamment *J. Gillis Wetter, Interest for an element of damages in the arbitral process: International Financial Law Review, dec. 1986, p. 20-25. — S. Boyd, Interest for the late payment of money: Arbitration International, July 1985, p. 153; sentence ad hoc Liamco c/Lybie, Genève, 12 juill. 1977: Rev. arb. 1980, p. 132, spécialement p. 187 s.; sentence CIRDI AGIP c/ Gouvernement de la RP du Congo, 30 nov. 1979: Rev. crit. DIP 1982, p. 92, spécialement p. 104; Yearbook Commercial Arbitration, 1933, p. 133, spécialement p. 142; sentence CIRDI Benvenutti et Bonfante c/ Gouvernement de la RP du Congo, 8 août 1980, Yearbook Commercial Arbiration, 1983, p. 144, spécialement p. 151; sentence CCI 17 févr. 1984 n° 4237, Yearbook Commercial Arbitration, 1985, p. 52, spécialement p. 59; sentence du Tribunal irano-américain, Mc Cullough & Company, Inc., 22 avr. 1986, citée par T. G.: Bull. assoc. Suisse arb. 1987, p. 55, spécialement p. 57). Celui-ci n'est pas tenu de se référer au taux légal d'un système juridique national, qu'il s'agisse de celui de la loi contractuelle ou de celui du lieu de l'arbitrage* ».

Dans la sentence ici rapportée, les arbitres n'avaient donc nul besoin de se référer à leur pouvoir d'amiable compositeur pour fixer le taux d'intérêt par une démarche en réalité conflictualiste qui se fonde sur des facteurs de rattachement à un système juridique national. En effet, les arbitres appliquent le droit français au motif que le protocole d'accord a été conclu à Paris et qu'une des parties est française. Quant à l'observation selon laquelle le créancier aurait perçu le taux légal français s'il avait placé les montants dus auprès d'une banque commerciale français, elle laisse pour le moins perplexe.

V. — La décision des arbitres quant à la répartition de la charge de la procédure arbitrale se fonde en premier lieu sur le principe selon lequel la partie qui succombe doit supporter les frais de l'arbitrage, y compris les frais de défense que celle qui obtient gain de cause a exposés pour sa défense. Cependant, les arbitres font usage de leur pouvoir d'amiables compositeurs pour modérer les effets du principe qu'ils invoquent: ils répartissent par moitié la charge des frais de procédure.

Là encore, le recours aux pouvoirs d'amiables compositeurs paraît inutile. Les arbitres sont toujours libres de fixer la charge des frais de la procédure arbitrale comme ils l'entendent, pourvu qu'ils motivent leur décision. Ils ne se privent pas dans la pratique de faire usage de cette liberté, mettant souvent à la charge de la partie qui obtient gain de cause une part des frais de l'arbitrage, soit que la solution des problèmes posés était suffisamment ardue pour que la résistance de la partie condamnée ne soit pase considérée comme abusive, soit que le vainqueur ait eu un comportement procédural ayant contribué à une complication inutile du dossier.

Y. D.

Sentence rendue dans l'affaire n° 8423 en 1998

I. — Concurrence. — Arbitrabilité. — Exception de nullité d'une clause contractuelle de non-concurrence.

II. — Concurrence. — Droit portugais. — Droit européen de la concurrence. — Examen d'office.

Le tribunal arbitral, siégeant à Bruxelles, était appelé à trancher un litige né d'un accord soumis au droit portugais et conclu en 1989 par lequel deux sociétés portugaises (le Groupe portugais), dont la demanderesse, et une société française B, deuxième défenderesse agissant tant en son nom personnel qu'au nom de toute personne morale de son groupe (le Groupe français), se sont associées au sein d'une société portugaise X pour l'exploitation d'usines de traitement d'eaux usées, d'eau potable et d'ordures ménagères. La société française A, première défenderesse et maison mère de la société B, était intervenue dans le cadre de cet accord agissant tant en son nom personnel qu'au nom des sociétés de son groupe (le groupe de la société A) sans toutefois prendre de participation au capital de la société X.

Dans une sentence partielle prononcée en 1996, le Tribunal arbitral s'est déclaré compétent à l'égard de la société française A, première défenderesse, estimant que l'accord litigieux la liait.

L'objet de la sentence finale porte pour l'essentiel sur le grief fait par la partie demanderesse aux deux sociétés défenderesses d'avoir violé l'obligation de non concurrence de l'article 5.1 de l'accord qui leur interdisait d'exercer leurs activités au Portugal dans le domaine de l'accord autrement que dans le cadre de la société X. Parmi les questions à résoudre par le Tribunal Arbitral *(pt VII de l'acte de mission)*, figure la question de savoir si les engagements pris à l'article 5.1 du contrat sont compatibles avec l'article 85 du Traité CE.

« L'on rappellera que selon l'article 5.1 de la convention litigieuse:

« *Le Groupe Portugais, le Groupe Français [deuxième défendeur] et le Groupe de la Sociéé à [premier défendeur] intervenant aux présentes, s'engagent à ce que leurs activités au Portugal dans le domaine de l'exploitation d'usines de traitement d'eaux usées, d'eau potable et d'ordures ménagères, l'activité faisant partie de l'objet social actuel de [la société commune X], soient exercées exclusivement au travers de leur participation dans le capital et dans la gestion de la société X et des éventuelles sociétés régionales ci-dessus* ».

Dans son mémoire du 10 décembre 1996, la société A, deuxième défendeur, a demandé au Tribunal arbitral, après s'en être expliquée, de dire que la convention du 21 juin 1989 était nulle comme contraire aux dispositions de l'article 85 du Traité de Rome.

Dans son ordonnance de procédure n° 6 du [date], rendue après l'audience d'audition des témoins des [dates], le Tribunal arbitral a invité les parties à déposer le [date] au plus tard une note complémentaire sur diverses questions et notamment:

« *La prétendue nullité du contrat au regard des exigences posées par l'article 85 du Traité de Rome, notamment la nullité partielle ou totale, l'exemption possible (85/3) et les conséquences de cette réglementation sur le présent arbitrage* ».

Ces notes ont été déposées et les parties ont ensuite plaidé sur la question le [date]; après quoi le Tribunal Arbitral, dans une ordonnance de procédure n° 9 du [date], leur a demandé de fournir au plus tard le [date] toutes informations relatives à la notion de « marché » nécessaires au Tribunal pour déterminer la compatibilité de l'accord du 21 juin 1989 avec les exigences de l'article 85 du Traité CE.

Des mémoires sur la question ont été effectivement déposés par les parties en exécution de l'ordonnance de procédure . . .

C'est à la lumière de l'ensemble de ces [. . .] commentaires que le Tribunal a examiné la compatibilité de l'article 5.1 du contrat avec le Traité de Rome.

L'on rappellera en premier lieu que la clause de non concurrence de l'article 5.1 est strictement limitée à certains domaines d'activité spécifiques de la société commune X:

— l'exploitation d'usines de traitement d'eaux usées;

— l'exploitation d'usines de traitement d'eau potable;

— l'exploitation d'usines de traitement d'ordures ménagères.

Les autres domaines d'activité restent dès lors ouverts à la concurrence, ce qui est également confirmé par l'article 6.2 de l'accord.

Il était également prévu que le Groupe Français [deuxième défendeur] mette son *know how* à la disposition de la société commune AGS à titre exclusif dans les domaines d'activité repris dans l'article 5.1, en contrepartie de quoi la société X devait lui verser des royalties *(art. 8.1 et 8.1.1 de la Convention)*.

La première question qui se pose au Tribunal est celle de l'arbitrabilité des litiges portant sur l'application du droit communautaire de la concurrence. Le droit communautaire étant considéré d'ordre public international, il appartient au Tribunal de se saisir d'office de la question, même en l'absence de toute contestation de la part des parties.

L'arbitrabilité des litiges mettant en cause l'application du droit de la concurrence et concernant notamment la validité ou la nullité de l'accord au regard desdites règles est pleinement admise aujourd'hui par les juridictions (pour la France, voir *CA Paris, 19 mai 1993, Labinal: Rev. arb. 1993, p. 645. — 14 oct. 1993, Velcro: Rev. arb. 1994, p. 164;* pour l'Italie, *CA Bologne, 21 déc. 1991, Yearbook 1993 p. 422;* pour l'arbitrabilité du droit américain de la concurrence, voir notamment *C. suprême, 2 juill. 1985, Mitsubishi Motors Corp. v/ Soler Chrysler-Plymouth Inc.: Yearbook 1986, p. 555; Rev. arb. 1986 p. 273;* pour la Suisse, voir *Trib. fédéral, 28 avr. 1992, ATF 118 II 193: Bull. ASA 1992 p. 368; RSDIE 1994, p. 198; Rev. arb. 1993, p. 124;* sur cette question en doctrine, voir notamment *Fouchard, Gaillard, Goldman, Traité de l'arbitrage commercial international, Paris 1996, n° 575 et les nombreuses références; Redfem/Hunter, International Commercial Arbitration, 2ᵉ éd., Londres, 1991 p. 139 s. — Bernard Hanotiau, L'arbitrage et le droit européen de la concurrence, in L'arbitrage et le droit européen, Actes du Colloque international du CEPANI du 25 avril 1997, Bruxelles 1997, p. 33-64 [pour la Belgique, p. 44-45]; sentence CCI n° 1397/1966: JDI 1974, p. 878; sentence CCI n° 2811/1979, ml 1978 p. 984; sentence CCI n° 6106/1990 citée par Fouchard, Gaillard, Goldman en note 432 p. 364).* Le Tribunal constate que les parties sont d'ailleurs en accord sur ce point.

La deuxième question à résoudre par le Tribunal a trait au point de savoir si la société X est une entreprise commune concentrative ou coopérative, et par voie de conséquence, si le problème de compatibilité de l'article 5.1 de l'accord avec le droit communautaire de la concurrence doit être résolu aux termes du règlement CEE n° 4064/89 *(Règlement du Conseil du 21 juin 1989 relatif au contrôle des opérations de concentration: JOCE, 1990, n° L 257/14)* ou aux termes de l'article 85 du Traité, sachant que le règlement n° 4064/89 s'applique aux entreprises communes concentratives tandis que l'article 85 du Traité s'applique aux entreprises communes coopératives.

La Commission a publié une communication relative à la distinction entre entreprises communes concentratives et entreprises communes coopératives, établie par l'article 3, paragraphe 2 du règlement n° 4064/89 relatif au contrôle des opérations de concentration entre entreprises *(JOCE 1994, n° C 385/1).* Suivant l'article 3, paragraphe 2 du règlement n° 4064/89 et la communication précitée, peuvent être considérées comme entreprises communes concentratives les entreprises qui de manière cumulative:

a. sont capables d'exercer de manière durable toutes les fonctions d'une entité écono-mique autonome *(art. 3, § 2 du règlement)*. Cela signifie que l'entreprise commune « *doit opérer sur un marché, en y accomplissant les fonctions qui sont normalement exercées par les autres entreprises sur ce marché. Pour ce faire, l'entreprise commune doit disposer de toutes les ressources nécessaires, en termes de financement, de personnel et d'actifs (cor-porels et incorporels) pour exercer une activité économique de manière durable* » *(pt 13 de la communication)*. La Commission précise qu'en matière de droits intellectuels, la condition est remplie si ces droits font l'objet d'une licence octroyée à l'entreprise com-mune pendant sa durée d'existence *(pt 13 de la communication)*.

b. ont pour objet de fonctionner de manière durable *(pt 16 de la communication)*.

c. n'ont pas pour effet de coordonner le comportement concurrentiel des sociétés qui demeurent indépendantes *(art. 3, § 2 du règlement et pt 8 de la communication)*.

Le Tribunal est d'avis que les conditions d'une entreprise commune concentrative ne sont pas remplies en l'espèce et que l'accord litigieux constitue dès lors une entreprise commune coopérative dont la compatibilité avec le droit communautaire de la concurrence doit être appréciée au regard de l'article 85 du Traité.

La troisième question que doit résoudre le Tribunal concerne la compatibilité effective de la clause de l'article 5.1 de l'accord avec l'article 85 du Traité. Sur cette question, les parties, par la voie de leurs experts respectifs, arrivent à des conclusions diamétralement opposées. Le demandeur conclut à la compatibilité de l'article 5.1 de l'accord avec l'article 85, paragraphe 1er. La deuxième défenderesse quant à elle est d'avis que cette clause est nulle de plein droit en application de l'article 85, paragraphe 2 en tant qu'elle contrevient aux dispositions de l'article 85, paragraphe 1.

Le Tribunal a analysé attentivement l'ensemble des éléments qui lui ont été commu-niqués par les parties tant au cours des plaidoiries que dans leurs écrits antérieurs et postér-ieurs à celles-ci, accompagnés par ailleurs de l'avis d'experts. Sur base de cette analyse, le Tribunal est arrivé à la conclusion, pour les raisons énoncées ci-après que les éléments en sa possession ne permettent aucunement d'établir que les engagements pris à l'article 5.1 de l'accord du 21 juin 1989 seraient incompatibles avec l'article 85 du Traité de Rome.

D'après l'article 85 (1), « *sont incompatibles avec le Marché Commun et interdits tous accords entre entreprises, toutes décisions d'association d'entreprises et toutes pratiques concertées qui sont susceptibles d'affecter le commerce entre les Etats Membres et qui ont pour objet ou pour effet d'empêcher, de restreindre ou de fausser le jeu de la concurrence à l'intérieur du Marché Commun . . .* ».

Dans le cadre de l'appréciation de la compatibilité de l'article 5.1 de l'accord avec l'article 85, il appartient en premier lieu de délimiter le marché affecté par ledit accord.

Il ressort des statuts de la société commune X que l'object de cette société est « *la prestation de services de gestion, maintien et exploitation de systèmes de captation, traite-ment, dépôt et distribution d'eau ou de gaz, de systèmes de drainage et de traitement d'effluents, et de ramassage, traitement et recyclage de déchets solides, ainsi que toute activité connexe* ».

Le marché de la prestation de ces services est donc le marché du produit affecté par l'accord. Au plan géographique, le marché à retenir est le territoire communautaire. Il est relativement fréquent que d'autres entreprises d'autres Etats Membres se présentent à des appels d'offre lancés par les autorités portugaises.

Par ailleurs, l'application de l'article 85, paragraphe 1 du Traité CE est subordonnée à la vérification cumulative de deux conditions: l'affectation du commerce entre les Etats Membres et l'atteinte à la concurrence.

En ce qui concerne l'affectation du commerce entre les Etats Membres, la communi-cation de la Commission sur les accords d'importance mineure *(JOCE 12 sept. 1986, n° C*

231, p. 2) précise que « *l'interdiction des ententes édictée à l'article 85* (1) *du Traité instituant la communauté Economique Européenne ne vise pas les accords qui n'affectent que d'une manière insignifiante le commerce entre Etats Membres ou la concurrence. Seuls sont interdits les accords qui ont des effets sensibles sur les conditions du marché, en d'autres termes, qui modifient de façon sensible la position sur le marché des entreprises étrangères tierces et des utilisateurs, c'est-à-dire leurs débouchés ou leurs sources d'approvisionnement* « (§ 2).

Il ressort du dossier que les deux sociétés portugaises [constituant le Groupe portugais] sont deux entreprises sans expérience dans le domaine d'activité de la société commune X et que leur dimension est absolument négligeable à l'échelle communautaire. Par ailleurs, le groupe de la société A n'est qu'un des groupes opérant sur le marché du produit en cause en France. Il est certes vrai que le groupe dispose d'une solide expérience internationale et d'une forte capacité technique et financière, il n'en est pas moins vrai qu'un nombre important d'entreprises tant françaises que dans d'autres Etats Membres sont à même de le concurrencer.

En outre, aux termes du paragraphe 3 de la communication pré-rappelée, « *la définition du caractère sensible donnée par la Commission* (§ 7), *n'a (. . .) pas une valeur absolue; il est tout à fait possible que, dans les cas d'espèce, des accords conclus entre des entreprises qui dépassent les seuils indiqués n'affectent le commerce entre Etats Membres ou la concurrence que dans une mesure insignifiante et, par voie de conséquence, ne tombent pas sous le coup des dispositions de l'article 85 (1)* ».

Au regard des éléments en sa possession, le Tribunal estime qu'il est difficilement soutenable que la clause litigieuse affecte sensiblement le commerce entre Etats Membres au sens de l'article 85 (1).

L'accord porte-t-il par ailleurs atteinte à la concurrence au sens de cette même disposition ?

D'une part, le Tribunal constate que l'accord n'a pas pour objet de restreindre la concurrence mais de « *développer au Portugal les activités relevant de l'object social (de la société commune X)* ».

D'autre part, la Commission ne se satisfait pas, lorsqu'il s'agit de déclarer qu'un accord a pour effet de restreindre la concurrence, d'une restriction quelconque. Elle exige que la restriction ait des effets sensibles sur la concurrence. La question se pose dès lors de savoir si l'article 5.1 de l'accord est de nature à restreindre sensiblement la concurrence.

Selon les dispositions de l'article 5.1 de l'accord, les Groupes portugais et français et le Groupe de la société A se sont engagés à ce que leurs activités faisant partie de l'objet social de la société commune X soient exercées, au Portugal, exclusivement au travers de leur participation dans le capital et dans la gestion de ladite société X.

Si, à première vue, un tel comportement semble susceptible d'entraîner une restriction de concurrence dans le marché dans lequel la société commune X opère, dès lors que quatre entreprises s'abstiennent d'entrer en concurrence, il reste qu'il importe de déterminer si ledit comportement restreint effectivement la concurrence et dans l'affirmative, si cette restriction a des effets sensibles.

La jurisprudence de la Commission sur la question fait ressortir ce qui suit:

— d'une part, afin de considérer que la création d'une filiale commune constitue en soi une restriction de concurrence, les entreprises qui s'associent doivent être des concurrents réels ou potentiels sur le marché du produit et sur le marché géographique en question avant cette association *(Déc. 21 déc. 1994, n° IV/M.535, § 4, Mannesmann Demag/Delaval Stork: JOCE 1995, n° C 023/4 et Déc. 17 déc. 1986, n° IV/31340, § 19, Mitchell Cotts/Sofiltra: JOCE 1987, n° L 041/31).*

— d'autre part, il n'est pas possible de considérer que la création d'une filiale commune restreint la concurrence lorsque les entreprises associées ne développaient pas les mêmes activités auparavant ou lorsqu'aucune d'elles ne serait capable de fournir la prestation qui est l'objet de l'activité de la filiale de façon indépendante *(Déc. 14 juill. 1986, n° IV/30320, § 46, Fibres Optiques: JOCE 1986, n° L 236/30 et Déc. 24 oct. 1988, n° IV/32437/8, § 17, Eurotunnel: JOCE 1988, n° L 311/36).*

— enfin, lorsque le nombre de concurrents sur le marché est élevé, la création de la fIliale commune peut ne pas entraîner de restriction de concurrence *(Déc. Mitchell Cotts/Sofiltra, § 19 préc.).*

Cette interprétation est renforcée par la Commission dans sa « Communication sur le traitement des entreprises communes à caractère coopératif en application de l'article 85 du Traité CE » *(n° 93/C 43/02: JOCE n° C 43, 16 févr. 1993, p. 2)* dans laquelle la Commission affirme *qu'« un rapport de concurrents potentiels ne peut exister que si chacun des fondateurs est en mesure de remplir seul les missions confiées à l'entreprise commune et qu'il n'a pas perdu cette capacité avec la création de l'entreprise commune ».*

Il ressort des éléments et dossiers communiqués par les parties et des témoignages [. . .], qu'aucune des parties à l'accord, et spécialement la partie portugaise, n'était à l'époque de la conclusion de l'accord litigieux, en bonne position pour opérer dans le marché naissant. Le Groupe portugais ne disposait manifestement pas de la technologie nécessaire pour aborder seul le marché avec des chances de succès raisonnable. D'autre part, les Groupes français et de la société A, bien que dotés d'une solide expérience internationale, ne connaissaient pas les particularités du marché portugais. Les parties ne pouvaient être considérées à l'époque de la signature de l'accord comme des concurrents réels ou même potentiels. L'on remarque d'ailleurs que la société commune X n'a pas été en mesure de se présenter aux appels d'offre pour la construction de [deux différentes usines] par manque du know how et de la technologie nécessaire.

L'article 5.1 de l'accord n'était donc manifestement pas de nature à restreindre sensiblement la concurrence.

Même si la conclusion du Tribunal avait été différente, ce dernier considérant que l'accord avait pour effet de restreindre la concurrence entre ses signataires, il n'en resterait pas moins que son effet sur la structure de la concurrence sur le marché concerné devrait être considéré comme amplement positif, avec la conséquence qu'il faudrait en tout état de cause le considérer comme non restrictif de concurrence. Tel est le point de vue prôné par la Commission dans sa Communication sur le traitement des entreprises communes à caractère coopératif, précitée, dans laquelle il est précisé que l'article 85, paragraphe 1 n'est pas applicable à une entreprise commune, même entre concurrents, *« lorsque la coopération (. . .) peut être objectivement considérée comme étant pour les fondateurs la seule possibilité de pénétrer sur un nouveau marché (. . .) et que leur présence renforce la concurrence ou en empêche l'affaiblissement ».*

Le Tribunal conclut dès lors que l'ensemble des données et éléments en sa possession ne permettent aucunement d'établir que l'article 5.1 du contrat du 21 juin 1989 serait incompatible avec l'article 85 (1) du Traité CE. »

Observations. — I. — Comme le rappelle la présente sentence, la question de l'arbitrabilité des litiges portant sur l'application du droit européen de la concurrence est dorénavant pleinement admise. Des chroniques précédentes ont déjà eu l'occasion de le souligner *(sentence n° 6932 de 1992: JDI 1994, p. 1065 ou Recueil des sentences arbitrales de la CCI 1991-1995, p. 560, obs. Y. D.; sentence n° 7539 de 1995, JDI 1996, p. 1030, obs. Y. D.; sentence 8626 de 1996, JDI 1999, p. 1074, obs. J. -J. A.).* Dans la présente espèce, les arbitres ne manquent d'ailleurs pas de constater que les parties sont en accord sur ce point.

Le principe de l'arbitrabilité d'un litige relatif au droit européen de la concurrence a été progressivement affirmé par la Cour d'appel de Paris qui a finalement reconnu qu'en matière internationale, l'arbitre peut apprécier sa propre compétence quant à l'arbitrabilité du litige au regard de l'ordre public international et dispose du pouvoir d'appliquer les principes et les règles qui en relèvent ainsi que d'en sanctionner la méconnaissance éventuelle, sous le contrôle du juge de l'annulation *(Paris, 16 févr. 1989, Almira Films: Rev. arb. 1989, p. 711, note L. Idot. — 29 mars 1991, Ganz: Rev. arb. 1991, p. 478, note L. Idot. — 19 mai 1993, Labinal: Rev. arb. 1993, p. 645, note Ch. Jarosson et JDI 1993, p. 957, note L. Idot. — 14 oct. 1993, Aplix c/Velcro: Rev. arb., 1994, p. 164, note Ch. Jarosson).* En Suisse, le Tribunal fédéral a de même reconnu la compétence d'un arbitre siégeant à Genève pour examiner au regard du droit communautaire de la concurrence la licéité d'une entente découlant d'un contrat entre sociétés belge et italienne *(T. Féd. Suisse, 28 avr. 1992, G.S.A. c/V.S.p.A.: Rev. arb. 1993, p. 124, note L. Idot).* Ce mouvement avait été précédé d'un arrêt de la Cour Suprême des Etats-Unis, rendu en 1985, dans lequel l'arbitrabilité des questions d'atteinte à la concurrence avait été affirmée en droit américain *(Sherman Act)*, à propos d'un contrat soumis au droit suisse, signé entre des parties américaine, suisse et japonaise, et arbitré au Japon *(Mitsubishi Motors Corp. v. Soler Chrysler-Plymouth, Inc.: Rev. arb. 1986, p. 273).* L'arbitre du commerce international dispose donc du pouvoir d'appliquer le droit européen de la concurrence.

II. — Au motif que le droit communautaire est d'ordre public, les arbitres estiment dans la présente sentence devoir se saisir d'office, même en l'absence de toute contestation de la part des parties. L'applicabilité de la réglementation communautaire en matière de concurrence ne faisait aucun doute en la présente espèce: le droit portugais avait été choisi par les parties et le litige qui impliquait diverses sociétés européennes, portait sur l'exécution d'un contrat dans l'espace communautaire. A l'évidence, lorsque le droit applicable à la convention est le droit d'un Etat membre de l'Union européenne, les arbitres ont le devoir d'appliquer les règles d'ordre public du droit communautaire de la concurrence en vertu de leur effet direct en droit interne (cf. *B. Hanotiau, L'arbitrage et le droit européen de la concurrence, p. 31-64,* et *Y. Derains, L'application du droit européen par les arbitres — Analyse de la jurisprudence, p. 65-80 in: L'arbitrage et le droit européen, Actes du Colloque International du CEPANI du 25 avril 1997: Bruylant, Bruxelles, 1997).* En indiquant devoir se saisir d'office, les arbitres estiment que les règles d'ordre public de la *lex contractus* les obligent à en assurer le respect, même dans le cas où aucune des parties n'en demande expressément l'application. Dans un tel cas, comme dans la sentence ici rapportée, les arbitres « *doivent appeler les parties à en débattre, de façon à ce que le principe de contradiction soit respecté.* » (V. *obs. Y. D., sous sentence n° 7339 de 1995: JDI 1996, p. 1030).*

J. -J. A.

Sentence partielle rendue dans l'affaire n° 7983 en 1996.

I. — Cession de créance. — Transmission de la clause compromissoire. — Cession de contrat. — Nécessité d'un consentement tacite ou exprès.

II. — Droit applicable au contrat de cession.

III. — Clause de confidentialité. — Caractère *intuitu personae.* — Incessibilité du contrat et de la clause arbitrale.

Un tribunal arbitral siégeant en Europe occidentale était saisi d'un litige opposant une société d'Afrique sub-saharienne « X », demanderesse, à une autre société africaine « Y », défenderesse, concernant la cession d'un contrat, y compris sa clause compromissoire.

Par un contrat de fourniture de 1988, la société d'Europe centrale, « P », non partie à l'arbitrage, s'était engagée à fournir à la défenderesse, dont la majorité du capital est propriété de l'Etat et autres organismes publics de cet État, divers équipements et prestations d'ingénierie pour une usine de broyage. Le contrat prévoyait que le paiement s'effectuerait pour partie par souscription d'actions au capital de la défenderesse, Y, pour partie par deux virements bancaires et par huit billets à ordre avalisés par l'État de la société défenderesse.

L'ensemble des équipements ayant été livré, seuls les deux virements avaient été effectués par Y qui, face à des difficultés financières, avait demandé une révision des conditions contractuelles.

A la demande expresse de cette dernière et de son gouvernement, la demanderesse X s'était rapprochée de P et avait finalement racheté ses créances sur Y par un contrat en date du 6 mai 1992.

Mandat était donné par P à X et à un bureau d'études dans le cadre de leurs compétences respectives à l'effet de déterminer, discuter, négocier avec Y, ses actionnaires et tous les autorités et organismes concernés, les conditions nécessaires à l'exploitation rentable de l'usine sur le plan technique, financier, juridique et fiscal, les conditions de participation de P ou de toute société se substituant à elle, au capital de Y ou de toute autre nouvelle société détenant la propriété de l'usine et/ou l'exploitant. Mandat était enfin donné de conclure tous accords relatifs aux objets ci-dessus, de faire toutes démarches et signer tous documents ou actes.

Par un télex du 21 mai 1992, Y demanda à P les éléments d'information sur leurs relations contractuelles.

X, par lettre du 29 mai 1992, et P, par télex du 4 juin 1992, informèrent respectivement le Gouvernement de l'État de la défenderesse et Y de la cession de créance intervenue entre elles.

Des discussions furent menées de juin à septembre 1992 avec le Ministre du Commerce en vue du rachat de gré à gré de ces actions sous réserve de la notification officielle par P du mandat donné à X.

Ayant endossé les billets à ordre, X, la demanderesse, a présenté à l'encaissement l'effet venant à échéance le 20 novembre 1992. La banque présentatrice refusa le paiement en raison d'un contentieux qui serait en cours entre P et Y.

A la date du 11 janvier 1993, X signifia alors à Y l'acte de cession de créance qui avait été faite entre P et elle-même.

X prétendait dans son courrier qu'en tout état de cause, conformément aux principes fondamentaux du droit cambiaire un différend entre Y et P ne pouvait être opposé à X tiers endossataire des effets.

En réponse à un télex du 17 février 1993 de P, Y indiqua par lettre du 1er mars 1993, qu'elle avait émis des réserves sur l'opposabilité de l'acte de cession de créances entre P et X, accord conclu sans qu'elle ait été préalablement informée. Elle avisait en conséquence P qu'elle entendait suspendre le paiement de sa dette vis-à-vis d'elle jusqu'à l'évaluation de leurs prestations réciproques et de l'étendue des droits et obligations de chacune.

Par lettre du 19 juillet 1993, le Président du conseil d'Administration de Y notifia au liquidateur de P la résiliation du contrat du 28 mars liant les deux sociétés à compter du 30 avril 1991, date de la mise en liquidation de cette dernière.

C'est dans ce contexte que X a introduit une requête en vue d'obtenir le paiement de sa créance.

L'article 32 du contrat de fourniture de 1988 signé par P et Y stipulait:

« *Tous les différends découlant de l'accomplissement du présent contrat seront réglés conformément aux stipulations des conditions générales. Si cette manière de procéder échoue, les litiges liés au présent contrat seront réglés par la Cour d'arbitrage, conformément aux règles de la Chambre de Commerce internationale à Paris. Le comité d'arbitrage sera composé de trois membres, l'un d'eux étant élu par l'Acheteur, le deuxième par le Vendeur et le troisième par deux juges, nommés par les parties. Le troisième membre sera le juge supérieur.*

(« . . . »)

Les sentences du tribunal d'arbitrage seront régies par les lois suisses. »

La clause d'arbitrage contenue dans le contrat de « cession de créances et autres droits » du 6 mai 1992, signé par P et X stipulait:

« *Tout litige survenant entre les parties à l'occasion du présent Accord sera exclusivement soumis à un ou plusieurs arbitres nommé(s) conformément au Règlement d'Arbitrage de la Chambre de Commerce internationale.*

Le lieu de l'arbitrage sera à . . . [ville d'un pays d'Europe occidentale].

La langue de l'arbitrage sera le français.

La décision des arbitres sera définitive et exécutoire.

Le présent Accord sera interprété conformément aux règles de droit qui sont les mieux susceptibles de donner à ses dispositions le sens qui s'accorde avec les règles et usages du Commerce international. »

X indique dans sa requête en arbitrage:

— « *Qu'en concluant l'acte de cession de créance, P a agi conformément aux objectifs fixés dans le compte rendu de la réunion du 7 juin 1992, avec son partenaire ainsi que lors des entretiens entre X, Y et les autorités de l'État Y au cours des missions effectuées en 1991 sur invitation du Gouvernement de l'État Y.*

— *Que c'est également en conformité avec ce compte rendu que Y et les autorités de l'État ont invité X à effectuer les études préalables nécessaires à la reprise de Y, tant en novembre 1991, qu'au mois de juillet 1992, et lui ont communiqué les informations utiles à la réalisation desdites études.*

— *Que la totalité prévue des fournitures et prestations de montage a été réalisée.*

— *Que par contre, Y n'a pas rempli ses obligations relatives au démarrage de l'usine, qu'elle doit en supporter toutes responsabilités et conséquences en droit.*

— *(« . . . »)*

— Qu'en raison de son engagement permanent dans les affaires de Y, l'État soit considéré comme le véritable cocontractant du contrat conclu avec P et comme le débiteur de la créance cédée à la demanderesse.

— (« . . . »)

— La transmissibilité de la clause d'Arbitrage et l'Arbitrabilité du litige entre elle et Y.

« Pour X, en sa qualité de cessionnaire et de porteur de bonne foi, aucune exception tirée des rapports entre P et Y ne peut lui être opposée.

Y soutient que:

— « la demande devant un Tribunal Arbitral est irrecevable.

— X n'a pas de qualité pour invoquer une clause d'arbitrage contenue dans un contrat auquel elle n'a jamais été partie en l'absence d'un lien juridique existant à ce moment-là entre X et P et du fait que par la suite, elle n'a jamais accepté les obligations nées du contrat conclu entre P et Y.

— Y s'est toujours opposée à la novation opérée par cette cession.

— le contrat dont se prévaut X comme cessionnaire de créance a été résilié de plein droit du fait de la mise en liquidation de P le 30 avril 1991.

— cette Société n'a jamais rempli ses obligations au titre du contrat.

— la cession de créance a été consentie à X en violation de l'article 23 du contrat conclu entre les parties. Aux termes dudit article: « Pendant une période de 8 ans à compter de la mise en vigueur du contrat, les dispositions du contrat ne doivent pas être révélées à des tiers, à l'exception de ceux qui devront nécessairement en prendre connaissance en vue de son exécution. Au cas où une des parties désirerait communiquer tout ou une partie du contrat à des tiers autres que ceux ci-dessus, elle devra obtenir par écrit l'accord préalable de l'autre partie.

Y décline en conséquence la compétence de la Cour internationale d'Arbitrage, la clause d'arbitrage contenue dans le contrat litigieux ayant un caractère intuitu personae *dont ne peut se prévaloir X qui n'était pas partie à la convention. Elle estime de ce fait que le Tribunal Arbitral ne peut être valablement saisi, elle se dit bien fondée à refuser l'arbitrage, la situation litigieuse n'ayant pas été prévue par les contractants eux-mêmes. Elle en conclut que le Tribunal Arbitral est mal venu pour se prononcer sur la demande de X tendant à la condamnation de Y et de l'État de Y, par ailleurs non partie à l'arbitrage. »*

Dans l'Acte de Mission l'objet du litige fut ainsi défini:

« *La contestation porte*

1) Sur la question de savoir si le bénéfice de la clause compromissoire stipulée à l'article 32 du contrat signé en 1988 entre Y et P, son partenaire industriel, a été transférée à la demanderesse du fait d'une cession de créances intervenue entre celle-ci et P et si dès lors le Tribunal Arbitral est compétent pour recevoir par requête un arbitrage introduit par X fondé sur cette cession de créances alors que selon la défenderesse, la validité de la cession de créance est contestable, que ce type de litige n'a pas été prévu à l'article 32 relatif à la clause d'arbitrage et que la clause d'arbitrage par son caractère intuitu per-sonae *est incessible.*

2) Sur la question de savoir si, eu égard à son immixtion dans la gestion des affaires de Y, l'État peut être considéré comme le véritable cocontractant de P et débiteur de la créance cédée, Y et l'État ne constituant qu'une seule et même partie audit contrat. »

Toujours dans l'Acte de Mission, les points litigieux à résoudre étaient ainsi définis:

« *a) Pour se prononcer sur sa compétence, le Tribunal devra dire si la cession de créance est valable, si la clause d'arbitrage a un caractère personnalisé, si la validité éventuelle de la cession a pour effet de transférer la clause d'arbitrage au tiers concessionnaire même dans l'hypothèse où la clause d'arbitrage serait de ce fait incessible, et si dans cette hypothèse la cause litigieuse est arbitrable.*

(« . . . »)

b) Statuer en même temps sur le point de savoir si l' État encourt les responsabilités de véritable titulaire du contrat signé entre Y et P et doit de ce fait être considéré comme débiteur de la créance cédée à la demanderesse. En cas de réponse positive, le Tribunal devra déterminer les conséquences éventuelles de cette décision sur la composition du Tribunal et la procédure arbitrale. »

Pour examiner sa compétence, le Tribunal Arbitral a commencé par déterminer le droit applicable au fond. Il le fit dans les termes suivants:

« *En effet, dans la mesure où les parties n'ont pas contesté que la loi (. . .)* [d'un pays d'Europe occidentale] *est applicable à la procédure, l'interprétation raisonnable à donner à la clause sur le droit applicable à l'article 32, est que le droit suisse régit le contrat de base.*

En ce qui concerne le contrat de cession, il obéit également au principe d'autonomie qui permet aux parties de choisir la loi applicable. En l'espèce, le contrat de cession stipule à son article 4, dernier alinéa, que:

'Le présent accord sera interprété conformément aux règles de droit qui sont les mieux susceptibles de donner à ses dispositions le sens qui s'accorde avec les règles et usages du commerce international.'

Il ne résulte pas de cette disposition, au demeurant laconique, que les parties aient choisi une loi autre que le droit suisse pour régir leur opération. Or en l'absence de choix, il est permis de présumer que la cession de contrat ou de créance obéit au même régime que le contrat de base. Par conséquent, le droit suisse est également applicable au fond à cette opération avec laquelle il existe un rattachement suffisamment fort.

En effet, le contrat de cession qui est un contrat accessoire a été conclu par rapport à une relation contractuelle préexistante, le contrat de base, lequel est soumis ainsi que jugé plus haut au droit suisse. »

Le Tribunal Arbitral a ensuite procédé à l'examen de la validité de la transmission du contrat de base comme suit:

« *La clause arbitrale ne peut se transmettre seule. Sa transmission suppose que le contrat ou les droits qui en dérivent aient été préalablement transmis. La cession doit donc être valable.*

Pour contester la validité de la transmission de la clause arbitrale à X, la défenderesse invoque l'existence d'une clause de confidentialité conférant au contrat un caractère intuitu personae *le rendant incessible.*

Sur le point de savoir si la cession est valablement intervenue, on peut retenrque:

1°) L'opération intervenue entre P et X est plus qu'une simple cession de créance: c'est une cession de contrat dans la mesure où elle comporte des droits et des obligations à la charge de X, notamment le mandat de:

Déterminer, discuter, négocier . . . les conditions nécessaires à l'exploitation rentable de l'usine aux plans technique, financier, juridique et fiscal.

Du reste, l'adoption de la qualification de cession de créance ne compromet pas la suite du raisonnement.

2°) Le contrat de base est intuitu personae *en raison de l'existence de la clause de confidentialité. Celle-ci perd sa substance si le contrat peut, sans l'accord d'une des parties, faire l'objet d'une cession à un tiers. De ce fait, la validité de la cession du contrat nécessite l'accord de l'autre partie, en l'occurrence Y; il est vrai que le Code suisse des obligations, applicable en l'espèce, prévoit que 'le créancier peut céder son droit à un tiers sans le consentement du débiteur' (art. 164). Mais il réserve le cas où la cession est interdite par 'la loi, la convention ou la nature de l'affaire' (art. 164, al. 1ᵉʳ in fine). On peut considérer que tel est le cas en présence d'une clause de confidentialité.*

3°) Mais l'accord peut être donné à tout moment, même avant la conclusion de l'opération et il peut être déduit des relations des parties en présence. On peut ainsi considérer que tel est le cas en l'espèce dès lors que Y a autorisé, voire encouragé, X à entrer en pourparlers avec P dans le cadre de la privatisation des entreprises publiques, dont celle de Y elle-même.

(« . . . »)

Pour la défenderesse, le contrat de base a été résilié de plein droit par la mise en liquidation de P avant même la cession qui n'aurait ainsi jamais pu se produire. Cette argumentation est contestée. En effet, la date d'effet de la mise en liquidation est discutée. De plus, la résiliation n'implique pas l'inexistence de relations de droits et d'obligations entre les parties. Enfin, il faut insister sur l'autonomie de la clause compromissoire par rapport au contrat, de sorte que tous les litiges relatifs à la liquidation d'un contrat résilié ou nul relèvent de la compétence du Tribunal Arbitral. Dans ce sens, le Règlement CCI dispose que:

'Sauf stipulation contraire, la prétendue nullité ou inexistence alléguée du contrat n'entraîne pas l'incompétence de l'arbitre s'il retient la validité de la convention d'arbitrage. Il reste compétent, même en cas d'inexistence ou de nullité du contrat, pour déterminer les droits respectifs des parties et statuer sur leurs demandes et conclusions (art. 8, al. 4).'

(« . . . »)

La défenderesse soutient que toute clause a un caractère intuitu personae *et conventionnel interdisant sa cession. Cet argument apparemment pertinent est contredit par une jurisprudence suisse (notamment les arrêts du T. fédéral suisse: ATF 101 II 168 et ATF 103 II 75), relative à la cession de la clause compromissoire en même temps que la cession de contrat ou de créance.*

(« . . . »)

De ce qui précède, il résulte que les arguments de la défenderesse sur l'incompétence du Tribunal Arbitral ne sont pas décisifs..

C'est donc en vertu de l'article 32 du contrat litigieux et de l'article 8, alinéa 4, du règlement de la Chambre de Commerce internationale que le tribunal arbitral retient sa compétence pour connaître le fond du présent litige sur lequel il réserve sa décision. »

Observations. — I. — Il est fréquent que les parties à une procédure d'arbitrage ne soient pas celles qui ont conclu à l'origine la clause compromissoire. En effet, il arrive qu'une partie, au cours d'une relation d'affaires, transmette ses droits et obligations à un tiers dans le cadre d'un transfert général (fusion, contribution partielle au capital social ou succession) ou spécial (transmission d'un contrat, d'une créance ou d'une dette, ou novation résultant d'un changement du créancier ou du débiteur). Dans une telle situation, les parties au litige doivent examiner les accords de base ainsi que le droit applicable pour déterminer si c'est le cédant ou le cessionnaire qui devrait être partie à la procédure arbitrale.

Dans la présente sentence, le problème posé aux arbitres était de savoir si la cession de créance faite par P en faveur de X emportait transfert de la clause compromissoire en faveur du cessionnaire. Le Défendeur Y ou cédé avait en effet contesté la compétence des arbitres au motif que la validité de la cession était contestable, que le litige n'avait pas été prévu dans la clause d'arbitrage, qui par son caractère *intuitu personae* était incessible. Le Tribunal Arbitral devait donc examiner le droit du cessionnaire d'invoquer la clause compromissoire à l'encontre du cédé.

Le Tribunal Arbitral a fait droit à cette demande et a rejeté l'objection soulevée par le cédé, défendeur à l'action, au vu des faits portés à sa connaissance.

Il a tout d'abord indiqué que la clause compromissoire ne pouvait pas se transmettre seule. Elle suppose que le contrat ou les droits qui en dérivent aient été préalablement transmis. Le Tribunal Arbitral a pris soin à cet effet de préciser que l'opération entre P et X était plus qu'une simple cession de créance. Celleci s'analysait en une cession de contrat compte tenu des droits et obligations mis à la charge de X, dont le mandat de discuter et de négocier les conditions nécessaires à l'exploitation de l'usine. Le Tribunal Arbitral semble ainsi justifier la transmission de la clause compromissoire à X par la cession du contrat qui la contient. Si tel est le cas, on comprend difficilement comment le cédant peut unilatéralement transférer le contrat à une tierce partie sans le consentement du cédé. Celui-ci ne pourrait-il pas alors décliner la compétence du Tribunal Arbitral au motif que la cession du contrat lui est inopposable? Pour éviter une telle critique, le Tribunal Arbitral aurait pu justifier la transmission de la clause par la cession de créance. Il est en effet admis que le créancier puisse transférer unilatéralement sa créance sans l'accord du débiteur. Cette possibilité s'explique par le fait que la personnalité du débiteur est plus importante que le créancier. Le débiteur peut être insolvable tandis que le créancier, quel qu'il soit, doit être simplement payé.

Le Tribunal Arbitral a indiqué ensuite que « *l'adoption de la qualification de cession de créance ne compromet pas la suite du raisonnement* ». On peut alors penser — mais la motivation est trop succincte pour le confirmer — que le Tribunal Arbitral a justifié indistinctement le droit d'action du cessionnaire contre le cédé par la cession de contrat ou de créance bien que leur transmission n'obéisse pas nécessairement aux mêmes règles. Selon le Professeur Loquin (*E. Loquin, Différences et convergences dans le régime de la transmission et de l'extension de la clause compromissoire devant les juridictions françaises: Gaz. Pal. 5 et 6 juin 2002, p. 7-25,* voir en particulier *§ 18 à 20.* — V. dans un même sens, *obs. C. Legros* à propos d'un arrêt rendu par la Cour de cassation française, en matière d'arbitrage interne, *Cass. 2e civ., 20 déc. 2001, Société Quille le Trident c/ Société CEE Euro Isolation: Rev. arb., 2002, p. 379-389*), l'acceptation de la cession emporte acceptation de la clause compromissoire qui est transférée à la partie qui vient aux droits de l'un des contractants, en raison de la nature procédurale et de l'autonomie de la clause compromissoire par rapport au contrat. Elle permet de ce fait aux arbitres de ne pas se référer à la volonté expresse ou tacite du bénéficiaire de l'action transmise et du contractant cédé: « *La clause compromissoire est bien une convention différente du contrat qui la contient. La clause compromissoire est une convention de procédure qui, produisant une restriction du droit d'action, laquelle ne pourra être exercée que devant la jurisprudence* (sic) *arbitrale, est une modalité du droit d'action . . . C'est le droit d'action qui est l'objet de la convention d'arbitrage et non les droits substantiels. Or le droit d'action est autonome par rapport au droit substantiel . . . La convention d'arbitrage est l'accessoire du droit d'action, lui-même accessoire du droit substantiel. Cette structure explique que la convention d'arbitrage soit autonome du contrat litigieux . . . Elle existe tant que le droit d'action existe . . . La transmission de la clause compromissoire est la conséquence d'un double rapport d'accessoire à principal. La clause compromissoire suit le droit d'action qui lui-même suit le droit substantiel . . . ».*

De l'avis du Professeur Loquin, la transmission de la clause s'opère donc en cascade: elle est l'accessoire du droit d'action qui est lui-même un accessoire de la créance. Le droit du cessionnaire de recourir à l'arbitrage en cas de différend est préservé car le cédant ne peut lui transmettre moins ou plus de droits qu'il ne dispose au moment de la transmission (Sur les conséquences de l'adage *Nemo plus juri,* voir notamment *Cass. Ire civ., 12 juill. 1950: JDI 1950, p. 1206, note B. Goldman. — Paris, 22 janv. 1986: Rev. arb., 1988, p. 565 et JDI 1986, p. 1021, note E. Loquin*). Les intérêts du cédé sont également préservés puisque le cédant ne peut modifier unilatéralement la situation contractuelle du cédé en excluant la clause insérée dans le contrat de base (V. *Cass. 1re civ., 5 janv. 1999, arrêt Worms: Rev. arb. 2000, p. 85-95, note D. Cohen: La clause d'arbitrage international, valable par le seul effet de la volonté des contractants, est transmise au cessionnaire avec la créance, telle que cette créance existe dans les rapports entre le cédant et le débiteur cédé*). La seule limite à une telle transmission tient à la nullité manifeste de la clause.

Un examen de la jurisprudence étrangère tend à confirmer cette approche. On peut ainsi citer l'arrêt du Tribunal fédéral suisse du 16 octobre 2001 qui a admis sur la base de l'article 170 CO qu' « *en cas de cession de créance ou de reprise d'une relation contractuelle, la clause compromissoire, en tant que clause accessoire de nature procédurale, est transférée au cessionnaire ou au repreneur, sauf convention contraire* » (V. C. Legros, op. cit. sous note n°2, p. 388. — *M. Scherer, Three Recent Decisions of the Swiss Federal Tribunal Regarding Assignments and Transfer of Arbitration Agreements: Bull. ASA, n° 1, mars 2002, p. 109-119*).

On peut également mentionner la sentence italienne du 6 avril 2001, rendue en matière d'arbitrage interne, qui admet que « *par l'effet de la cession, la créance est transférée au cessionnaire avec les privilèges, les garanties personnelles et réelles et avec les autres accessoires* » (V. C. Legros, op. cit. sous note n° 2, p. 388: *Riv. dell'arb., 2001, p. 519, note L. Salvaneschi*).

Rappelons toutefois qu'il ne s'agit pas d'une solution unanime. La nature accessoire de la clause compromissoire ne suffit pas, à elle seule, à justifier sa transmission avec celle du contrat de base. L'arrêt *Emja* de la Cour suprême de Suède du 15 octobre 1997 exige le consentement ou tout du moins la connaissance de la clause compromissoire par le cessionnaire, pour que celle-ci produise effet à son égard *(C. suprême Suède, 15 oct. 1997, MS Emja Braach Shiffahrts KG c/ Wärtsilä Diesel Aktiebolag: Rev. arb., 1998, p.431-438, note A.-C. Hansson Lecoanet et S. Jarvin.* V. également *S. Jarvin, Assignment of Rights under a Contract containing an Arbitration Clause — Assignee bound to Arbitrate. Decision by Sweden's Supreme Court in the « Emja » case »: Swedish and International Arbitration, 1997, p. 65-72).* Cette exigence s'explique par le fait que la clause compromissoire contient des droits (le droit de chaque partie au contrat principal de recourir à l'arbitrage) et des obligations (l'obligation de chaque partie de se soumettre à l'arbitrage et de payer les frais de l'arbitrage). On pourrait arguer que, face au risque financier, tel que le non-paiement des frais de l'arbitrage par le cessionnaire, la partie restante au contrat — la partie cédée — doit pouvoir choisir entre une procédure devant un tribunal étatique ou arbitral. La Cour suprême n'a pas accepté cette idée de laisser la partie cédée spéculer sur le choix de la forme de la procédure. Elle a décidé en conséquence que la partie cédée doit être liée par la clause d'arbitrage, sauf circonstances particulières.

On peut signaler également le projet de loi norvégien sur l'arbitrage qui a été rédigé en 2001 par le comité d'étude du Ministère de la Justice norvégien (V. *Voldgift — Lov om voldgift (voldgiftsloven), NOU, Norges offentlige utredninger, 2001:33*, en particulier *p. 121-135 Draft statute — The Arbitration Act; Brief summary and overview of the report).* Le projet, qui est largement inspiré de la loi-type de la CNUDCI sur l'arbitrage commercial international de 1985, prévoit un transfert automatique de la convention d'arbitrage avec le transfert de la relation juridique à laquelle elle s'applique, sauf accord contraire des parties (*§ 2-2 (2)) § 2-2 (2):* « Sauf accord contraire des parties dans la convention d'arbitrage, la convention d'arbitrage est réputée être transférée avec le transfert de la relation juridique à laquelle elle s'applique. »; [Traduction libre de l'auteur de la version originale anglaise: « *(2) Unless otherwise agreed between the parties in the arbitration agreement, the arbitration agreement shall be deemed to be transferred together with any transfer of the legal relationship to which the arbitration agreement applies.* »]). La rédaction de cet article est particulièrement libérale car elle permet le transfert de convention d'arbitrage dans le cadre d'un transfert général ou spécial de la relation juridique des parties. Il suffit à l'une d'entre elles de justifier le rattachement de la convention à la relation juridique en cause pour qu'elle produise ses effets. Le consentement des parties n'est plus nécessaire *a priori*, de même que la considération du droit applicable au transfert. Le transfert de la convention semble opérer en tant qu'acte matériel du transfert de la relation juridique. Il sera intéressant de suivre les commentaires des milieux concernés sur ce projet, et en particulier l'issue qui sera réservée à l'article § 2-2 (2) mentionné ci-dessus.

II. — Le Défendeur ayant contesté la validité de la cession, le Tribunal Arbitral a commencé par déterminer le droit applicable au contrat de cession. Il a estimé, dans le silence des parties, qu'elles ont probablement voulu soumettre la cession de créance au même droit qui est applicable au contrat de base, soit le droit suisse. L'identité du régime légal est justifié d'autant plus que, selon le Tribunal Arbitral, le contrat de cession est un contrat de cession est un contrat accessoire, qui a été conclu par rapport à un contrat de base.

Le raisonnement du Tribunal Arbitral est cohérent car en l'absence d'une indication claire en sens contraire des parties, la loi qui régit la créance cédée est la loi du contrat d'où elle puise son origine (V. *Fouchard/Gaillard/Goldman, Traité de l'arbitrage commercial international: Litec, 1996, p. 434, n° 696*). C'est donc par application du droit suisse, droit qui régit la créance cédée que les arbitres ont déterminé la validité de la cession, les rapports entre cessionnaire et débiteur, les conditions d'opposabilité de la cession au débiteur et le caractère libératoire de la prestation faite par le débiteur. Le Tribunal Arbitral a évité ainsi l'application des principes généraux du droit et usages du commerce international que les parties ont pourtant, semble-t-il, choisi dans le contrat de cession *(art. 4)*.

III. — Par application de l'article 164 CO, les arbitres constatent que le droit suisse n'exige pas le consentement du débiteur en cas de cession d'un droit par le créancier. Cette solution se retrouve dans la plupart des droits et n'appelle pas de commentaires particuliers en tant que principe général du droit (V. notamment *E. A. Farnsworth, Farnsworth on Contracts, Little: Brown and Company, 1990, § 11.10. — J. Ghestin, Traité de Droit Civil — les effets du contrat, 1994, § 378. — D. Veaux, Juris-Classeur Civil, 1996, fasc. 10, § 46. — V. également D. Girsberger et C. Hausmaninger, Assignment of rights and agreement to arbitrate: Arbitration International, vol. 8, n° 2, p. 121 s.*).

La seule limite à la liberté du créancier tient à l'interdiction de la cession par la loi, la convention ou la nature de l'affaire. Les arbitres se sont attachés à examiner la clause de confidentialité qui a été conclue *intuitu personae* entre Pet Y dans le contrat de base. La cession étant interdite, la clause compromissoire n'a pas pu être normalement transmise, sauf un accord contraire, qui peut être donné à tout moment ou encore déduit des relations des parties en présence. Tel est le cas en l'espèce puisque Y a autorisé, voire encouragé, X à entrer en contact avec P dans le cadre de la privatisation des entreprises publiques, dont celle de Y elle-même.

Le Tribunal Arbitral se déclare compétent pour examiner le fond du litige. Il rappelle à cette occasion le principe de « compétence-compétence »;, qui lui permet d'examiner et de statuer sur les demandes respectives des parties, dès lors qu'il a retenu la validité de la clause compromissoire. La prétendue nullité du contrat ou de la cession des droits alléguée par le cédé n'entraîne pas l'incompétence du Tribunal Arbitral.

Précisons que cette sentence a fait l'objet d'un recours en annulation et d'un pourvoi devant la juridiction suprême de l'État du lieu de l'arbitrage. Il sera intéressant de suivre la décision de la juridiction suprême sur la question, somme toute classique, de la transmission et de l'autonomie de la clause compromissoire, dans le cadre de la cession d'un contrat ou d'une créance.

S. J.

Sentence rendue dans l'affaire n° 9333 en 1998

I. — Contrat de courtage. — Commission illicite (non). — Contrat contraire aux mœurs (non). — Corruption (non). — Code suisse des obligations.

II. — Charge de la preuve.

III. — Loi américaine sur la lutte contre la corruption *(Foreign Corrupt Practices Act).* — Applicabilité (non). — Convention de l'OCDE sur la lutte contre la corruption d'agents publics étrangers dans les transactions commerciales internationales du 17 décembre 1997. — Applicabilité (non).

IV. — Intérêts moratoires. — Recevabilité. — Réclamation tardive et/ou en dehors des limites de l'Acte de Mission. — Article 104 du Code suisse des obligations. — Usages du commerce international (CISG et Principes UNIDROIT).

Un arbitre unique siégeant à Genève était saisi d'un litige opposant un particulier nord-africain X, demanderesse, à une société française Y, défenderesse, concernant le versement d'une commission.

Début 1995, les parties signaient un contrat aux termes duquel X devait conseiller et assister la défenderesse en vue de l'obtention et de l'exécution d'un contrat relatif à un projet de pipe-line dans un pays nord-africain.

La commission était fixée à FFrs 1 900 000 hors taxes, si la valeur du marché obtenue par la défenderesse n'était pas inférieure à FFrs 7 000 000.

Le demandeur allègue que la défenderesse a obtenu le marché prévu mais qu'elle ne lui a pas versé l'intégralité des sommes dues. Il indique que la défenderesse aurait cessé ses paiements après être passée sous le contrôle d'une société américaine.

La défenderesse invoque la nullité du contrat en raison du caractère illicite ayant pour objet le paiement de pots-de-vin, et prétend que les paiements sont contraires à la loi américaine sur la lutte contre la corruption *(US Foreign Corrupt Practices Act)* et à la Convention de l'OCDE à ce sujet.

Le demandeur réfute l'argumentation de la défenderesse, dans la mesure où il estime que (i) la convention liant les parties n'a en aucun cas un objet illicite et n'est nullement contraire aux bonnes mœurs et que (ii) le demandeur justifie parfaitement son droit à commission par l'attribution du marché à la défenderesse et son entrée en vigueur, ce qui atteste de la réalité et de l'efficacité des prestations fournies par le demandeur.

En exécution de la convention, la défenderesse a effectué un premier versement de FFrs 415 000 le 27 mars 1995 suite à une facture émise par la société International S.A. à Lausanne. Le versement a été fait sur le compte de cette société auprès d'une banque en Suisse.

Au mois de juillet 1995, la défenderesse fut rachetée par la société américaine R Inc. Suite à cette acquisition, la défenderesse affirme avoir notifié à ses agents et représentants commerciaux que la rémunération des services qu'ils ont fournis à la société serait faite exclusivement dans le pays dans lequel ils étaient situés et les services rendus. La défenderesse aurait introduit ces directives sur la base de la loi américaine sur la lutte contre la corruption *(Foreign Corrupt Practices Act,* ci-après « FCPA ») que la maison mère américaine et les sociétés membres du groupe R devaient respecter.

Cependant, la défenderesse a versé, en date du 22 janvier 1996, un montant de FFrs 310 000 facturé par International S.A. le 19 décembre 1995. L'argent fut versé sur le même compte bancaire que le précédent transfert, auprès d'un établissement bancaire à Lausanne.

Le 26 mars 1996, International S.A. a envoyé à la défenderesse une troisième facture de FFrs 435 000, laquelle était restée impayée.

Suite à l'absence de paiement, le demandeur a contacté Monsieur A, qui lui a alors suggéré de s'adresser à Monsieur B, directeur des marchés de la défenderesse.

Une rencontre entre Monsieur B et le demandeur eut lieu le 3 juillet 1996. Les versions des parties sur le contenu exact de cette entrevue divergent. Monsieur B affirme avoir expliqué au demandeur la nouvelle politique de la défenderesse qui interdisait des paiements en dehors du pays de l'agent. Par conséquent, Monsieur B a refusé de continuer le paiement de la commission du demandeur sur un compte en dehors du pays nord-africain. Le demandeur se serait alors fâché et aurait expliqué qu'il devait partager sa rémunération avec certains employés de la société nord-africaine qui ne voulaient pas recevoir le paiement dans ce pays. Monsieur B considérait cette déclaration comme un aveu de la part du demandeur que la rémunération était affectée en partie à des versements de pots-de-vin. Par conséquent, Monsieur B suspendit tout paiement destiné au demandeur.

La procédure arbitrale a été introduite par le demandeur sur la base de l'article 8 de la convention conclue entre les parties en 1995 qui stipule:

« *Tout différend naissant éventuellement de l'application du présent contratsera dans toute la mesure du possible réglé à l'amiable.*

Si un accord amiable ne pouvait être trouvé, le différend sera tranché définitivement suivant le règlement de Conciliation et d'Arbitrage de la Chambre de commerce internationale par un Arbitre unique nommé conformément à ce règlement.

Le lieu de l'arbitrage sera fixé par l'arbitre;

Le Code suisse des Obligations s'appliquera.

La décision arbitrale sera exécutoire par les parties. »

Dans l'Acte de Mission, le demandeur a pris notamment les conclusions suivantes:

« *— Condamner la Société Y à payer à Monsieur X une somme de 1 175 000 francs français;*

— Dire et juger que le lieu de paiement des commissions dues à Monsieur X, est situé en Suisse. »

La défenderesse a demandé au Tribunal arbitral de:

« *— dire et juger que le contrat de 1995 a un objet illicite et contraire aux mœurs; en conséquence, prononcer la nullité du contrat;*

— constater que la Société Y a effectué le règlement des sommes de 310 000 Francs et 415 000 Francs français à Monsieur X, au titre du contrat;

en conséquence, réduire le montant des demandes de Monsieur X, de la somme de 725 000 Francs français réglée par la société Y. »

L'arbitre a d'abord examiné la nature de la convention de 1995. Il le fit dans les termes suivants:

« *Les rapports instaurés par la convention entre les parties relèvent du contrat de courtage (art. 412 et s. CO). Les obligations des parties en vertu de la convention sont en effet caractéristiques du courtage tel qu'il est défini par l'article 412, alinéa 1 CO:*

'*1. Le courtage est un contrat par lequel le courtier est chargé, moyennant un salaire, soit d'indiquer à l'autre partie l'occasion de conclure une convention, soit de lui servir d'intermédiaire pour la négociation d'un contrat.*'

Quant à la convention, selon son article premier, 'les services de Monsieur X consisteront en l'apport d'informations, de conseils et d'assistance pour permettre à la société Y d'obtenir et d'exécuter le contrat relatif au projet'. *Le droit à la commission du demandeur est cependant acquis dès que* 'par l'intermédiaire de Monsieur X, le contrat est attribué à la société Y et est entré en vigueur' *(Art. 2), donc dès l'obtention du marché par la défenderesse. Ce mécanisme est caractéristique du courtage. Ainsi l'article 413 CO stipule à son alinéa I que* 'Le courtier a droit à son salaire dès que l'indication qu'il a donnée ou la négociation qu'il a conduite aboutit à la conclusion du contrat.'

La modalité de paiement échelonné, évoquée à l'article 4 de la convention, permet à la défenderesse de ne pas avoir à avancer des fonds pour payer le courtier, mais d'utiliser le revenu généré par le projet. Le principe énoncé à l'article 2, selon lequel le droit du courtier à la rémunération est créé par l'obtention du marché, n'est pas remis en cause par ce mécanisme.

Le fait que la convention prévoit des services allant au-delà de la simple obtention du marché, et dont l'article 2 montre l'importance secondaire aux yeux des parties, n'en fait pas un mandat simple. Du reste, le Tribunal estime au vu du dossier que le demandeur a rendu tous les services qui lui ont été demandés. »

Ensuite, l'arbitre a examiné la question de savoir dans quelles conditions la convention peut être nulle. Il le fit comme suit :

« *L'article 20 CO dispose:*

'Le contrat est nul s'il a pour objet une chose impossible, illicite ou contraire aux mœurs'.

Le caractère illicite et contraire aux mœurs de la convention réside, selon la défenderesse, dans le fait qu'elle a pour objet des paiements de pots-de-vin à des responsables de la société nord-africaine. La défenderesse fonde son argumentation sur le témoignage de Monsieur B tel qu'il ressort de son attestation, témoignage confirmé par Monsieur B lors de l'audience. Monsieur B est le « Contracts Manager » de la défenderesse. Il est en fonction depuis novembre 1995 suite au rachat de la défenderesse par R en juillet 1995. Monsieur B a déclaré que le demandeur aurait avoué lors d'une entrevue le 3 juillet 1996 que les paiements qu'il recevait de la part de la défenderesse n'étaient pas uniquement destinés à lui seul.

Le demandeur conteste avoir fait une telle déclaration.

Un contrat peut être illicite, selon les catégories proposées par un auteur autorisé, si la conclusion du contrat est interdite ou si la prestation prévue par le contrat est interdite ou bien si le but poursuivi par les deux contractants est contraire au droit (P. Engel, Traité des obligations en droit suisse: Dispositions générales du CO, Berne 1997, p. 275 s. — V.a. A. Koller, Schweizerisches Obligationenrecht: Allgemeiner Teil, Band I, Bern 1996, p. 215 s. — E. Bucher, Schweizerisches Obligationenrecht, Allgemeiner Teil, Zurich 1988, p. 250 s. — Sent. arb. 23 févr. 1988: Bull. ASA 1988, p. 136, 138). En l'occurrence, toutefois, le contrat entre les parties ne peut être illicite selon l'article 20 CO dès lors que la défenderesse soutient que le demandeur aurait agi à son insu.

Le contrat de pots-de-vin, qui a donc pour objet de payer le corrompu pour accomplir son devoir ou pour ne pas l'accomplir, serait en droit suisse, considéré non pas comme illicite mais comme étant contraire aux mœurs (Engel, p. 289. — A. Heritier, Les post-de-vin, Genève 1981, p. 105 s. — J.-B. Zufferey-Werro, Le contrat contraire aux bonnes mœurs, Fribourg 1988, 282 s. — Koller, loc. cit., p. 237). Or, pour la raison évoquée ci-dessus, l'absence d'un but commun visant la corruption d'un tiers, la convention ne peut pas non plus être contraire aux mœurs selon l'article 20 CO (voir Sent. arb. CCI n° 4145: Rec. sent. arb. CCI, 1986-1990, p. 53, 58. — Sent. arb. CCI n° 7047, publiée dans Bull. ASA 1995, p. 301, 334).

Dans l'hypothèse, qu'aucune partie n'a développée dans cette procédure, que la défenderesse connaissait ou aurait dû connaître la prétendue intention du demandeur de verser des pots-de-vin, la question aurait alors pu se poser de déterminer si la défenderesse ne devrait pas se voir opposer le principe 'Nemo auditur turpitudinem propriam allegans'.

Dans la logique de la défenderesse, il conviendrait donc non pas de déclarer nulle la convention selon l'article 20 CO, comme elle le demande, mais d'examiner quelles étaient les sanctions de l'infidélité prétendue de son concontractant. Ce sont des conclusions de cette nature, que la défenderesse aurait dû prendre. Quoi qu'il en soit, si la défenderesse n'apporte pas la preuve d'un versement de pots-de-vin par le demandeur, ou d'un engagement pris à ce sujet avec un tiers, il n'y aura pas lieu d'établir d'éventuelles sanctions.

Même si elle ne vise pas la corruption d'employés de la société nord-africaine, la convention pourrait éventuellement être contraire aux mœurs s'il était constaté qu'elle enfreigne de manière particulièrement choquante des droits fiduciaires d'un tiers (Sent. arb. CCI n° 6248: Rec. sent. arb. CCI, vol. III, p. 239, 243 et les références y citées). Le Tribunal examinera donc si les faits plaidés devant lui sont constitutifs d'une violation des droits fiduciaires de tiers. »

L'arbitre a donc examiné l'allégation de corruption:

« *Le Tribunal arbitral a entendu tant Monsieur B que le demandeur lors de l'audience du 30 octobre 1997. Tous les deux ont persisté dans leur version des faits. Il est impossible au Tribunal, confronté à ces versions des faits diamétralement opposées, de savoir ce qui s'est vraiment passé lors de l'entretien entre Monsieur B et le demandeur. Le Tribunal arbitral n'a aucune raison objective de privilégier l'un de ces témoignages par rapport à l'autre.*

Il sied donc d'analyser certains indices qui pourraient forger la conviction du Tribunal quant aux faits allégués de part et d'autre (A. S. El Kosheri et Ph. Leboulanger, L'arbitrage face à la corruption et aux trafics d'influence: Rev. arb. 1984, p. 3 s. et 7).

Il est inutile de s'arrêter à un examen approfondi du contrat ou de la commune intention des parties à la convention. Aucune des parties n'affirme en effet que celle-ci cacherait, derrière des termes anodins, une entente réelle des parties au sujet d'agissements illicites.

Un indice important, qui peut donner naissance à des soupçons, est le montant de la commission stipulé à l'article 3 de la convention. Cette disposition prévoit une commission de FFrs 1 900 000 pour l'obtention d'un marché qui n'est pas inférieur à FFrs 7 000 000, soit un pourcentage de presque 30 % de la valeur du marché. Une commission tellement élevée et sans commune mesure avec les profits escomptés par l'attribution du marché, peut en effet paraître exorbitante. Un montant disproportionné par rapport aux usages peut légitimement éveiller des soupçons quant à savoir si là 'une commission n'en cache pas une autre', *car on pourra supposer qu'elle sert partiellement de post-de-vin (Jeffrey P. Bialos, Gregory Husisian, The Foreign Corrupt Practises act: Oceana, 1997, Appendix, p. 4. — El Kosheri et Leboulanger, loc. cit., p. 7).*

Cependant, il faut bien se garder de considérer le montant de la rémunération, sans examiner également le contexte dans lequel le contrat a été négocié et conclu. D'abord, il se peut que l'intermédiaire soit simplement avide (comme Bialos et Husisian, loc. cit., Appendix, p. 4, observent à juste titre: 'your agent may just be greedy') *et que l'employeur ait mal négocié son contrat (tel qu'illustré dans la Sent. arb. CCI n° 7047: Bull. ASA 1995, p. 301 335 où des agents faisaient remarquer, au sujet du montant de leurs commissions,* 'there were no 'standard-commissions'; [I took] 'whatever I could get').

Quelle que soit la réponse à cette question, le Tribunal estime que les circonstances particulières de l'espèce justifiaient le versement d'une commission supérieure (au moins en pourcentage) à la norme. Ainsi il ressort de l'attestation de Monsieur A:

— que la défenderesse n'aurait pas pu décrocher le marché envisagé sans l'intervention du demandeur, dès lors

— que la défenderesse n'était pas connue de la société nord-africaine

— que Monsieur C, Président de la société nord-africaine avait été aidé dans sa carrière par le père du demandeur, un conseiller intime du Chef de l'Etat du pays nord-africain

— que le demandeur avait fourni tous les services qui lui incombaient selon la convention

— que la commission initialement réclamée par le demandeur était de FFrs 4 000 000 et qu'elle fut unilatéralement réduite à FFrs 2 puis à FFrs 1 900 000 par la défenderesse.

Le PDG de la défenderesse et signataire de la convention, a déclaré en outre:

— que le marché concerné ne tombait pas dans le champ d'activités habituel de la défenderesse;

— que celle-ci voulait grâce à ce marché 'stratégique' accéder à un domaine neuf.

Quant au demandeur, celui-ci a maintenu lors de l'audience:

— que le marché finalement attribué à la défenderesse avait déjà été alloué à une autre société.

Cette affirmation n'est pas contestée par la défenderesse. En tout cas, Monsieur A confirme dans son attestation qu'un concurrent était déjà bien placé avant l'arrivée de la défenderesse.

Monsieur A est la seule personne qui avait des rapports directs à la fois avec le demandeur et avec la société nord-africaine. Le PDG était PDG de la défenderesse à l'époque de la conclusion de la convention. Le Tribunal attribue donc une importance particulière à ces témoins pour la période concernée.

Tous les éléments évoqués par Monsieur A et le PDG montrent qu'il était particulièrement difficile pour la défenderesse de décrocher ce marché, dans un domaine neuf, voire même impossible sans l'intervention du demandeur. Eu égard, en plus, à la nature stratégique du marché, une commission plus élevée que la norme était justifiée et raisonnable. Tout porte à croire que la défenderesse était prête — et obligée —, pour se placer dans un marché neuf, de payer un montant de FFrs 1 900 000 au demandeur.

En résumé, bien qu'une rémunération de presque 30% sur un marché puisse paraître à première vue excessive, elle est justifiée dans les circonstances particulières de l'espèce. La défenderesse devait la considérer, non pas en pourcentages mais en montant absolu, comme un 'investissement' nécessaire. »

L'arbitre a ensuite discuté de l'absence de preuves documentaires et d'indices permettant de retenir un cas de corruption. Il constate l'absence de preuves documentaires de la défenderesse. Selon l'arbitre, « *on aurait en effet pu s'attendre à ce que la défenderesse ait pris la précaution de constituer un dossier à toute épreuve pour ne pas encourir le risque, dans une procédure ultérieure, de ne pas pouvoir démontrer sa version des faits devant un Tribunal Arbitral. La défenderesse ne pouvait en effet avoir des doutes quant à la probabilité qu'un tribunal soit saisi du litige. Au moment où la défenderesse avait pris la décision de ne pas verser des commissions à ses agents en dehors de l'état dans lequel ils rendaient leurs services, il aurait donc fallu prêter une attention particulière aux questions de preuves, par exemple en expliquant la nouvelle politique aux agents par écrit. De même, il aurait été prudent de confirmer immédiatement et par écrit la teneur d'un entretien au cours duquel un agent aurait avoué devoir verser des pots-de-vin. On aurait en outre pu songer à la préparation immédiate d'un 'witness statement' signé par Monsieur B et des conseils extérieurs que la défenderesse affirme avoir consultés.* »

L'arbitre a constaté « *que la défenderesse n'a pas produit des preuves de l'époque. La déclaration de Monsieur B date de 6 mois après son entretien avec le demandeur. Lors de l'audience, Monsieur B a affirmé que sa déclaration était basée sur une note interne datant de l'époque. Cependant, la défenderesse a refusé de verser celle-ci dans la procédure. La défenderesse n'était pas non plus prête à produire des preuves démontrant la mise en œuvre de sa politique basée sur la loi FCPA ou des suspensions de paiements dans d'autres cas. Le Tribunal n'a pu que prendre acte de son refus lors de l'audience. Il a toutefois explicitement rappelé que chaque partie est libre de produire toute pièce qu'elle juge utile pour soutenir son cas et qu'elle assume les risques au niveau de l'insuffisance des preuves.* »

Ensuite l'arbitre a constaté « *que la prétendue notification de la suspension de paiements en dehors du pays de l'agent est également restée sans preuves. Plus particulièrement, quant à la notification du demandeur, il ne semble pas qu'il y ait eu une correspondance préalable à celle du 3 juillet 1996 dans laquelle le demandeur aurait été informé du changement de politique de la défenderesse: Aucune des parties n'a été en mesure de produire cette pièce demandée par le Tribunal dans son Ordonnance de procédure. La défenderesse savait très bien que les paiements allaient s'effectuer en Suisse. Elle avait donné son accord et avait procédé par deux fois au paiement des commissions en Suisse. Elle ne l'a pas découvert après coup. Et elle n'a pas non plus estimé que ceci était illicite ou contraire aux mœurs. Sinon, comment expliquerait-elle ses deux paiements en Suisse et surtout le paiement en janvier 1996, après la mise en place de sa nouvelle politique qui suspendait, selon elle, tous ces versements?* ».

La défenderesse avait produit aussi un « *Statement and opinion* » d'un avocat américain que l'arbitre avait rejeté dans les termes suivants:

« *L'avocat américain exerçant à Chicago et associé dans le cabinet dont sont également membres les conseils parisiens de la défenderesse. Outre son affiliation, l'avocat affirme compter des sociétés du groupe parmi ses clients. Il ne s'agit donc pas d'un avis de droit 'neutre'. Partant, c'est comme déclaration d'une partie que le Tribunal doit apprécier cette déclaration.*

L'avocat soutient avoir été consulté par les supérieurs de Monsieur B suite à l'entretien du 3 juillet 1996. Il affirme avoir considéré la prétendue déclaration du demandeur comme critique à l'égard de la loi FCPA. Il aurait dès lors conseillé à ses clients de ne plus effectuer des paiements au demandeur.

Le témoignage de l'avocat n'est pas celui d'un témoin direct mais est basé sur un double ouï-dire: il relate ce qu'il affirme avoir entendu de la part des supérieurs de Monsieur B qui à leur tour avaient appris par Monsieur B ce qu'ils communiquaient à l'avocat. Le Tribunal n'a pas de raison de penser que la déclaration de l'avocat ne corresponde pas à la version des faits qui lui avait été relatée par ses clients. Cependant, en l'absence d'autres preuves et notamment de tout document datant de l'époque, le Tribunal ne peut pas considérer cette version comme mieux fondée du fait de l'attestation de l'avocat. Ceci d'autant moins que celle-ci ne fut produite par la défenderesse qu'au stade du mémoire final et après l'audience du 30 octobre 1997 qui devait servir à l'audition des parties et de tous les témoins pouvant faire la lumière sur les faits contestés.

L'inexistence de pièces produites étonne d'autant plus que la défenderesse affirme être soumise à la loi FCPA qui oblige en fait les sociétés concernées à tenir des livres très complets (Jeffrey P. Bialos, Gregory Husisian, The Foreign Corrupt Practices Act: Oceana, 1997, p. 61). Ces documents doivent être tenus à la disposition des autorités, la confidentialité et le secret des affaires étant limités par la loi FCPA. Leur existence supposée, on ne voit donc pas' pour quelles raisons la défenderesse n'aurait pas pu produire, dans cet arbitrage, des documents appropriés pour soutenir sa thèse (le cas échéant selon des modalités garantissant une confidentialité encore accrue par rapport à la confidentialité habituelle caractérisant l'arbitrage). »

Mais l'arbitre a encore constaté d'autres éléments qui permettaient de retenir l'absence d'actes de corruption. Selon l'arbitre, on aurait pu « *s'attendre d'un intermédiaire qui partage ses commissions avec des fonctionnaires indélicats, qu'il objecte vigoureusement contre toute réduction de sa commission dès lors que celle-ci aurait une incidence non seulement sur sa propre marge de profit mais aussi sur celle du fonctionnaire corrompu. Monsieur A avait en fait déclaré que la défenderesse avait réduit la commission du demandeur consécutivement de 4 à 2 millions et finalement à FFrs 1 900 000. Cependant, il ne paraît pas que le demandeur ait réagi à cette démarche unilatérale de la défenderesse.*

De même, si les personnes habilitées à engager la société nord-africaine avaient eu un intérêt pécunier (sic) *à ce que le marché soit attribué à la défenderesse, on voit mal pour quelle raison la société aurait négocié une baisse substantielle de l'offre de la défenderesse, et, arguendo, du montant des pots-de-vin dont elle aurait pu bénéficier* (cf. *Sent. arb. CCI n° 4145: Rec. sent. arb. CCI, 1986-1990, p. 53, 59*). »

L'arbitre a donc conclu que « *Selon l'article 8 du Code civil suisse, chaque partie doit prouver les faits qu'elle allègue pour en déduire un droit. La charge de la preuve pour le fait de corruption allégué incombait donc à la défenderesse (Sent. arb. CCI, n° 7047: Bull. ASA 1995, p. 301, 343). Cette dernière a échoué dans cette preuve. Seule la déclaration de Monsieur B reste pour étayer cette version des faits. Le manque de preuves circonstancielles, défaut volontaire ou non, et d'un faisceau d'indices indiquant un cas de corruption, n'est pas à même de renforcer la valeur probante de l'attestation de Monsieur B.* »

L'arbitre a ensuite examiné l'incidence de la loi FCPA et de la Convention de l'OCDE sur le litige qui était soumis au droit suisse.

« *Un contrat qui est contraire non pas au droit suisse, mais à un droit étranger, n'est en principe pas illicite selon l'article 20 CO, cette disposition ne protégeant que le respect de la loi suisse. Dans des circonstances exceptionnelles, une violation d'un droit étranger peut néanmoins être considérée comme contraire aux mœurs selon l'article 20 CO si elle est irréconciliable avec les mœurs suisses (Bucher, loc. cit., p. 258. — Koller, loc. cit., p. 223. — Sent. arb. CCIG: Bull. ASA 1988, p. 136, 140). Tel n'est pas le cas en l'occurrence.*

Le Tribunal est arrivé à la conclusion que le grief de corruption n'était pas établi par des preuves. Une atteinte aux valeurs fondamentales suisses faisant défaut, l'éventuelle violation du droit étranger ne pourra pas être sanctionnée selon l'article 20 CO.

Une loi étrangère ayant la qualité de loi de police pourrait éventuellement trouver application à un contrat, autrement soumis au droit suisse, par le biais de l'article 19 LDIP. Une violation d'une telle loi de police, à supposer réunies les conditions d'application de l'article 19, pourrait entraîner l'illicéité du contrat (Koller, loc. cit., p. 223). La question de savoir si l'article 19 LDIP s'applique à un arbitre international ainsi que les conditions d'application de cette disposition est controversée. Le Tribunal fédéral a laissé la question ouverte dans un arrêt du 30 décembre 1994 (Bull. ASA 1995, p. 217, 225). Pour un tour d'horizon de l'état du débat, voir D. Hochstrasser, Choise of law and 'foreign' mandatory rules in international commercial arbitration: American Review of International Arbitration, vol. 7, n° 3-4/1996, 319-357. — S. Lazareff, Mandatory extraterritorial application of national law: Arbitration International 1995, p. 137).

La question peut toutefois être laissée ouverte dès lors que le Tribunal arbitral est de l'avis que (i) l'application de la FCPA à titre de loi de police étrangère ne se justifie pas, et que (ii) en toute hypothèse, les conditions d'application de la FCPA ne sont pas réunies.

La présente procédure met en cause la défenderesse, filiale française de la société américaine R, et le demandeur, un ressortissant d'un pays nord-africain. La société américaine R n'est pas partie à la procédure. Il n'y a aucun rattachement avec le droit américain hormis le fait que la société américaine. Ce rattachement serait en tout état de cause insuffisant pour appliquer la loi FCPA à titre de l'article 19 LDIP.

Il n'est cependant pas nécessaire de chercher un rattachement, car la loi FCPA ne s'applique pas aux filiales de sociétés américaines à l'étranger (J. P. Bialos, G. Husisian, The Foreign Corrupt Practises Act: Oceana, 1997, p. 31. — O. Th. Johnson, Les lois américaines applicables aux commissions illicites, in Les commissions illicites: Publication CCI 480/2, 1992, p. 11s. — K. C. Little, D. R. Johnson, The foreign Corrupt Practise Act, p. 11 ainsi que U.S. Department of Commerce / U.S. Department of Justice, Antibribery Provisions, in International Practitioners' Workshop Series, vol. V, ABA Section of International Law and Practise, 1994, p.4). En revanche, selon la loi FCPA, la société mère basée aux Etats-Unis est responsable pour les agissements des sociétés appartenant au groupe qu'elle chapeaute. C'est dans cette optique, afin de limiter le risque lié à leur propre responsabilité, que les multinationales américaines ont instauré des programmes dans toutes les sociétés du groupe qui devraient permettre d'assurer le respect de la loi FCPA (J.-P. Bialos, G. Husisian, préc., p. 89). »

Ainsi l'arbitre a conclu en ce qui concerne l'application de la FCPA, que « *dès lors que la société américaine n'est pas partie au présent arbitrage, ce Tribunal est totalement incompétent pour en juger.* »

L'arbitre a écarté l'applicabilité de la « *Convention de l'Organisation de Coopération et de Développement Economique (OCDE) sur la lutte contre la corruption d'agents publics étrangers dans les transactions commerciales internationales du 17 décembre 1997* », dès lors que la procédure n'avait pas permis de déceler un cas de corruption. L'arbitre décida qu'il était alors inutile d'examiner dans le détail l'argument de la défenderesse. « *Il est toutefois à noter que la Convention n'est pas encore en vigueur.* »

L'arbitre a condamné la défenderesse à payer un montant de FFrs 1 175 000 au titre de sa commission (FFrs 1 900 000 moins les deux versements de FFrs 310 000 et FFrs 415 000 déjà effectués par la défenderesse).

La demanderesse avait réclamé l'obtention d'intérêts moratoires, calculés au taux de 5% conformément aux dispositions de l'article 104 du Code suisse des Obligations (et non au taux légal français) et ceci à compter du dépôt de la requête d'arbitrage. Dans son mémoire final, la défenderesse avait contesté la réclamation du demandeur comme étant tardive. Elle aurait été avancée après la signature de l'Acte de mission. De plus, la convention ne prévoyait pas de droit au paiement d'intérêts.

L'arbitre a rejeté les arguments de la défenderesse dans les termes suivants.

« *Le demandeur a réclamé le paiement d'intérêts dans sa Requête d'arbitrage déjà. Aurait-il persisté à fonder sa demande sur le droit français, il aurait incombé au Tribunal, non pas de déclarer irrecevable la demande, mais d'appliquer le Code suisse des obligations.*

On peut d'ailleurs s'interroger sur la question de savoir si les intérêts ne font pas de toute façon partie de la demande principale. Ainsi, un auteur a récemment écrit ce qui suit:

'From a functional perspective, the interest claim in Art. 78 CISG just as the one incorporated in Art. 7.4.9 of the Principles and any statutory interest claim constitutes the minimum lump sum compensation for damages in areas where the creditor need not prove the actual damages incurred. It is a long standing practice of international arbitrators as well as of the Iran-U.S. Claims Tribunal to consider the interest claim as part of the general claim for damages.'

(K. Peter Berger, International Arbitral Practice and the UNIDROIT Principles of International Commercial Contracts: The Americain Journal of Comparative Law, vol. 46, 1998, p. 135 s.).

Enfin, la 'modification' reste dans les limites de l'Acte de mission en vertu duquel (8.2) le Tribunal arbitral doit examiner les obligations des parties découlant de la convention.

Selon l'article 104 CO, auquel la convention est soumise, tout débiteur qui est en demeure pour le paiement d'une somme d'argent doit l'intérêt moratoire de 5% l'an. Rien dans la convention ne permet d'admettre que les parties avaient l'intention d'exclure le droit au paiement d'intérêts en cas de demeure. Une telle exclusion aurait du reste été difficile à réconcilier avec les usages du commerce international dont se font l'écho, entre autres, la Convention des Nations Unies sur les contrats de vente internationale de marchandises (Convention de Vienne), ou encore les Principes UNIDROIT pour les contrats commerciaux internationaux, évoqués par l'auteur précité.

Au vu de l'article 104 CO et des conclusions du demandeur, il convient donc d'assortir toute condamnation de la défenderesse au paiement de commissions d'une condamnation au paiement d'intérêts au taux de 5% dès le dépôt de la Requête d'arbitrage. »

OBSERVATIONS. — I. — Il est banal de constater que le commerce international incite à la corruption du fait de l'importance des enjeux financiers, de la concurrence acharnée entre les acteurs sur un marché devenu aujourd'hui vraiment global et des inégalités économiques entre les opérateurs participant à un investissement transnational: agents commerciaux, groupes multinationaux et fonctionnaires d'État ou autres organismes de droit public.

La presse (économique spécialisée) fait régulièrement état d'importants versements de sommes d'argent à des personnes exerçant une influence déterminante sur la conclusion d'un marché. L'organisation non-gouvernementale Transparency International a constaté *(Le Figaro économique, 30 août 2002, p. II)* une corrélation entre prospérité et pratiques commerciales: les pays les plus vertueux sont aussi les plus prospères. Le président de cette ONG, Monsieur Peter Eigen, ancien haut fonctionnaire de la Banque Mondiale, se déclare convaincu que la corruption est un des facteurs essentiels du sous-développement et de la pauvreté. *« Ce sont les pots-de-vin, les bakchichs qui gangrènent les sociétés, les maintiennent dans la pauvreté. Dans les pays en développement, des élites politiques corrompues travaillent de concert avec des hommes et des femmes d'affaires avides de gain ainsi que des investisseurs sans scrupules. »* Les résultats obtenus par Transparency International se révèlent assez comparables aux classements de compétitivité ou de richesse économique par pays que produit le World Economic Forum de Davos ou l'IMD de Lausanne. En tête des deux classements (pays vertueux et pays prospères), on retrouve à peu près les mêmes pays.

De plus en plus souvent les cas de corruption, les affaires de pots-de-vin sont aujourd'-hui portées devant les tribunaux étatiques pour en faire toute la lumière et où ils sont exposés aux yeux critiques du public des pays concernés. Par contre, les affaires de corruption portées devant la juridiction privée et confidentielle qu'est l'arbitrage sont encore assez rares. Les exemples ne manquent pourtant pas et le sujet suscite un vif intérêt dans les milieux du commerce international et de l'arbitrage international comme en témoignent les colloques, séminaires et livres *(Arbitration and Unlawful Transactions,* séminaire organisé par le comité national suédois de la CCI en avril 1994; *Les conventions illicites, ICC Dossiers, publication n° 480/2,* qui était l'aboutissement d'un séminaire de l'Institut du droit et des pratiques des affaires internationales de la CCI, tenu en 1992).

Les affaires de corruption ont systématiquement donné lieu à des condamnations par les arbitres internationaux, dont les méthodes employées ont été très différentes.

On se souvient d'abord de la sentence arbitrale CCI dans l'affaire n° 1110, rendue en 1963 par Monsieur Le Juge Gunnar Lagergren. Après avoir relevé que la plupart des commissions réclamées par le demandeur avaient pour destination probable le versement de pots-de-vin, l'arbitre déclina la compétence du tribunal arbitral au nom, non pas de règles nationales sur l'arbitrabilité, mais d' *« un principe général de droit, reconnu par les nations civilisées, que des contrats qui violent sérieusement les bonnes mœurs ou l'ordre public international sont non valables, ou à tout le moins insusceptibles d'exécution forcée et qu'ils ne peuvent recevoir la sanction des tribunaux ou des arbitres . . . : les parties qui s'allient dans une telle entreprise doivent réaliser qu'elles ont perdu tout droit de s'adresser à la justice (qu'il s'agisse de juridictions nationales ou des tribunaux) pour faire trancher leur différend »* (Sent. CCI, aff. n° 1110 partiellement, publiée: *Julian Lew, Applicable Law: International Commercial Arbitration: New York, 1978, p. 553 s.*). Cette sentence a été revue et complétée par Maître Gillis Wetter qui a considéré que l'arbitre avait bien appliqué le principe de compétence-compétence et celui de l'autonomie de la clause compromissoire — précisons qu'il s'agissait d'un compromis dans le cas d'espèce; v. *Arbitration International, vol. 10, n° 3 (1994) p. 277 s.: « Issues of corruption before International Arbitral Tribunals: The Authentic Text and True Meaning of Judge Lagergren's 1963 Award in ICC Case n° 1110 »*).

La décision de Monsieur Lagergren a été largement critiquée par la doctrine: l'arbitre devait examiner le fond du litige et s'il trouvait le contrat illicite ou une autre violation du principe de bonnes mœurs, il devait en prononcer la nullité.

Les arbitres ont, depuis l'affaire n° 1110, adopté une autre approche des litiges en matière de corruption. Ils ne refusent plus de connaître le fond du litige parce qu'une partie allègue l'existence de la corruption, une autre violation de l'ordre public ou le principe de bonnes mœurs (voir les affaires CCI n° 3916 et n° 4145; la décision du Tribunal fédéral suisse confirmant une sentence partielle dans l'affaire CCI n° 6401 citée dans l'article de Monsieur Wetter constatant qu'on « *doit actuellement considérer [la sentence de Monsieur Lagergren] comme dépassée; par ailleurs, elle se révèle inconciliable, de prime abord, avec les dispositions de l'article 178, al. 3 LDIP.* »).

La sentence dans l'affaire n° 9333 ici commentée est un exemple significatif. La tendance actuelle montre également que les arbitres n'hésitent pas à rejeter des demandes en paiement de commissions au nom de la nullité des engagements pour illicéité ou violation du principe des bonnes mœurs. La sentence CCI n° 3913, reproduite dans *ce Journal en 1985 aux p. 988-990*, en est un bon exemple. La sentence dans l'affaire CCI n° 5622, reproduite dans le *Rec. Sent. arb. CCI, 1991-1995, p. 220* et dans la *Rev. arb. 1993, p. 327*, en est un autre. Dans l'affaire CCI n° 8891 *(JDI 2000, p. 1076)*, le Tribunal Arbitral avait déclaré que le caractère illicite des contrats portant sur le versement de pots-de-vin était bien établi dans la jurisprudence arbitrale.

La plupart des sentences arbitrales condamnant les pratiques de pots-de-vin invoquent la violation d'une norme d'ordre public. Ce dernier peut être national ou international; certains parlent même d'un ordre public « *réellement* » international, à savoir un principe général reconnu par les nations civilisées.

Comme l'a démontré le Professeur Oppetit *(Le paradoxe de la corruption à l'épreuve du droit du commerce international: JDI 1987, p. 5)*, quand la loi nationale est appliquée, le résultat dépendra de l'attitude du pays en question; certains droits nationaux sont rigoureux sur le plan de la condamnation des pratiques de corruption, alors que d'autres manifestent peu d'intérêt ou même de l'indifférence face au problème pourvu que les pots-de-vin permettent la conquête de marchés extérieurs. L'ordre public « réellement » international offrirait-il une norme universellement acceptée, une *lex mercatoria* globale, vu que les arbitres ne se limitent généralement pas à fonder leur décision sur un droit étatique, mais font encore appel à un principe général du droit, à l'ordre public international ou transnational ?

A notre avis, son existence mais surtout son contenu exact reste encore à démontrer. Notons toutefois que la Convention de New York permet de refuser l'exécution d'une sentence contraire à l'ordre public du pays en question et qu'un corps de décisions arbitrales existe depuis un bon nombre d'années à l'appui de la théorie de l'existence d'un ordre public transnational. Examinons les arguments des parties et les conclusions de l'arbitre sur ces points de vue.

Dans le cas d'espèce, l'arbitre unique a pris comme point de départ pour son examen le droit suisse, droit prévu dans l'Acte de mission et dans la convention conclue entre les parties. Ce choix du droit applicable est important, puisque c'est le droit suisse qui déterminera si les actes prétendus de corruption sont illégaux ou non.

On note qu'il n'y a aucun attachement avec le droit suisse hormis le choix des parties du droit suisse dans leur convention. L'agent était ressortissant d'un pays nord-africain où il résidait, l'investissement a eu lieu dans un pays nord-africain, la défenderesse était une société française, devenue membre d'un groupe américain. Le seul rattachement avec la Suisse était le compte bancaire de l'agent qui ne voulait pas recevoir ses commissions dans son pays de résidence.

Il ne faut pas perdre de vue que les agissements des personnes prétendument impliquées dans une affaire de pots-de-vin sont presque toujours localisés dans un autre pays, en dehors du pays dont le droit applicable a été choisi par les parties. Les marchés internationaux sont en général obtenus après de nombreuses discussions et rencontres dans des lieux divers entre les représentants des parties et leurs intermédiaires qui sont d'origine diverse. On peut alors se demander dans ce cas, si le droit national convenu entre les parties doit être uniquement appliqué — étant donné que cette loi peut être moins sévère que la loi du pays du lieu d'investissement et où les transactions résultant des pots-de-vin produisent leurs effets.

II. — Selon les règles ordinaires concernant la charge de la preuve, il appartient à la partie qui allègue l'illicéité de la prouver. C'est aussi le principe préconisé par l'arbitre unique dans la présente affaire. Comme l'avait justement remarqué un autre tribunal arbitral *(dans l'affaire CCI n° 8891: JDI 2000, p. 1079)* « *une telle preuve s'avère souvent difficile. L'objet illicite est généralement dissimulé derrière des dispositions contractuelles d'apparence anodine.* »

Les arbitres n'ont souvent d'autre choix que de se fonder sur des indices. C'est précisément ce qu'a fait l'arbitre unique dans la présente affaire en l'absence de preuves documentaires. Il arrive à la conclusion que la corruption n'était pas prouvée; sa décision est en ce sens contraire à l'issue dans l'affaire CCI n° 8891 (citée plus haut).

L'arbitre unique a utilisé plusieurs indices pour rejeter l'existence des pots-de-vin.

(i) *Le montant de la commission*

L'arbitre trouve une commission de presque 30 % de la valeur du marché tellement élevée qu'elle peut paraître exorbitante. En cela, il partage l'avis d'autres arbitres et notamment ceux qui avaient tranché le litige dans l'affaire CCI n° 8891, qui avaient trouvé qu'un taux de commission de 8 % constituait « *une présomption de ce que l'intermédiaire devait reverser certaines sommes. En effet, il est rare dans la pratique qu'un simple agent reçoive des commissions supérieures à 1 ou 2 %.* »

L'arbitre dans l'affaire d'espèce a estimé que des circonstances particulières justifiaient le versement d'une commission supérieure à la norme.

(ii) *Inexistence des pièces malgré l'obligation faite par la loi FCPA de tenir des livres complets*

L'arbitre a critiqué la défenderesse de ne pas avoir produit des documents qu'elle était tenue, selon cette loi, de maintenir à la disposition des autorités.

(iii) *Réduction du montant de la commission*

L'arbitre a trouvé que l'absence de protestation de l'agent contre la démarche unilatérale de la défenderesse de réduire la commission constituait un indice qui permettait de retenir l'absence d'actes de corruption.

(iv) *La défenderesse avait de bons arguments pour obtenir le marché sans payer des pots-de-vin*

Un argument important retenu par l'arbitre est que le marché avait déjà été attribué à une autre société, à un prix supérieur au prix offert par la défenderesse. La défenderesse avait donc de bons arguments pour arracher le marché puisque le prix des prestations de la défenderesse — commission comprise — était plus intéressant pour la société nord-africaine.

(v) *Rapports familiaux entre les parties*

Un autre argument plaidant contre l'existence de pots-de-vin était la relation entre l'agent et la personne responsable pour l'attribution du marché auprès de la société nord-africaine. Le dirigeant de la société avait été pistonné par le père de l'agent dans sa carrière. Il serait invraisemblable que cette personne demande des pots-de-vin au fils de son mentor.

(vi) *L'activité de l'agent*

Il était incontesté que l'agent avait agi activement pour résoudre toutes les difficultés qui avaient surgi au long du projet. Il avait donc eu une activité réelle.

III. — La loi FCPA incrimine la corruption tentée ou consommée des fonctionnaires étrangers dès lors que l'infraction a été commise par toute personne relevant du contrôle de la *Securities and Exchange Commission* (« SEC »). La loi permet de poursuivre des citoyens américains ou des sociétés américaines à l'étranger mais non — selon l'arbitre — les filiales des sociétés américaines à l'étranger. En d'autres termes, si la société mère américaine est responsable pour les agissements des sociétés appartenant au groupe qu'elle contrôle, la loi ne s'applique pas directement à la filiale française dans le cas d'espèce. Il semble donc que la filiale française ne soit pas soumise à la juridiction de la SEC.

L'arbitre a tout de même examiné l'hypothèse où la loi FCPA aurait été applicable à la défenderesse, société française. L'arbitre a conclu qu'un Tribunal arbitral international n'était pas tenu de l'appliquer:

« *Même à supposer (i) qu'il s'agit d'une loi de police et (ii) que l'arbitre admet qu'une telle loi peut être appliquée nonobstant l'élection d'une autre loi matérielle encore faudrait-il démontrer des intérêts puissants et légitimes des Etats-Unis à l'application de cette loi. De sérieux doutes à ce sujet pourront en effet résulter du fait que la loi FCPA ne vise pas en premier lieu à protéger l'ordre public fondamental des Etats-Unis mais qu'elle a pour but de restaurer la confiance du public dans l'intégrité des entreprises américaines dont la réputation a été ternie par une série de scandales retentissants.* »

L'arbitre a retenu « *que la lutte contre la corruption, but certes louable, ne justifie pas nécessairement l'exportation des méthodes ou du code de conduite singulier de la loi FCPA pour atteindre ce but, méthodes qui ont d'ailleurs suscité de nombreuses critiques, aux Etats-Unis comme à l'étranger.* »

Le raisonnement de l'arbitre est intéressant. Il retient le droit d'appliquer ou non les lois de police (étrangères dans le sens qu'elles n'ont pas été choisies par les parties ou qu'elles ne présentent aucun rattachement direct avec les parties au litige) qu'il trouve applicables. L'arbitre fait son choix en fonction des méthodes utilisées par la loi étrangère pour combattre un but universellement approuvé et se place ainsi en position de juge à partir des critères que lui détermine souhaitables ou pas.

IV. — La question posée à l'arbitre par la défenderesse était de savoir si la réclamation du demandeur tendant à obtenir des intérêts moratoires au taux légal suisse (et non au taux légal français) était recevable dans la mesure où elle avait été présentée tardivement, après la signature de l'acte de mission. En d'autres termes, la demande était-elle dans « les limites fixées par l'acte de mission » ?

Rappelons que l'acte de mission a pour objectif de fixer l'objet du litige soumis à l'arbitrage. Il contient en effet les demandes qui doivent être tranchées par le tribunal arbitral. Dès lors, la question est de savoir si les parties peuvent formuler de nouvelles prétentions ou de nouvelles demandes après la signature de l'acte de mission. Le problème ne se pose pas en cas d'accord des parties. Dans l'hypothèse inverse, il incombe au tribunal arbitral de décider sur la question après avoir entendu les parties. En l'espèce, l'arbitre a rejeté l'argument de la défenderesse sur ce point en considérant que le demandeur avait réclamé le paiement des intérêts dès le début de l'arbitrage, soit dans la requête d'arbitrage (Dans un même sens, v. *Sent. finale CCI n° 5029 (1991): Bull, CCI, vol. 3, n° 2, p. 49-51*). Le taux des intérêts moratoires étant déterminé par le droit national applicable, l'arbitre a appliqué le taux de 5 % conformément à l'article 104 CO *(H. Schönle, Intérêts moratoires, intérêts compensatoires et dommages-intérêts de retard en matière d'arbitrage international in Études de Droit international en l'honneur de Pierre Lalive: Helbing & Lichtenhahn, 1993, p. 649-670)*. L'arbitre est conforté dans sa décision d'autant plus que les parties n'avaient pas exclu expressément le droit au paiement d'intérêts en cas de demeure. Cette solution s'inscrit dans le cadre des usages du commerce international, dont se font l'écho, entre autres, la Convention de Vienne et les principes UNIDROIT.

S. J.

Sentence partielle rendue dans l'affaire n° 9443 en 1998 (original en langue française)

I. — Contrat. — Qualification.

II. — Contrat. — Durée. — Prohibition des engagements perpétuels.

III. — Contrat. — Sanction des engagements perpétuels. — Nullité absolue. — Contrat à durée déterminée. — Contrat à durée indéterminée. — Résiliation. — Délai de préavis.

La demanderesse et la défenderesse avaient signé un contrat de concession de technologie et d'assistance technique, un contrat de licence de marques et quatre avenants aux termes desque la demanderesse fournissait à la défenderesse la technologie nécessaire à la fabrication des produits contractuels et autorisait la défenderesse à apposer sur ces derniers la marque de la demanderesse. Les contrats se substituaient à un « *accord de franchisage de production et de commercialisation* ». Ils étaient soumis au droit français, comprenaient une clause d'arbitrage donnant compétence à la Chambre de commerce internationale pour trancher tout différend éventuel et désignaient Paris comme siège de l'arbitrage. Peu après la signature des contrats, une société regroupant les franchisés de la demanderesse dans le pays X fut constituée pour une durée de cinquante ans. Le troisième avenant aux contrats avait modifié la durée initiale de dix années de ceux-ci. Leur durée était maintenue à dix ans, mais il était prévu que cette durée soit « *prorogeable pour des périodes égales d'une manière obligatoire pour la demanderesse et facultative pour la défenderesse* ».

Dix neuf ans après l'entrée en vigueur des contrats, la demanderesse mit fin unilatéralement à la relation contractuelle en donnant à la défenderesse un préavis de douze mois susceptible d'être écourté si cela présentait un avantage pour la défenderesse. Cette dernière, dans le délai de préavis, s'opposa à la dénonciation du contrat par la demanderesse comme étant nulle et abusive, considéra que la dénonciation, ajoutée à d'autres fautes contractuelles commises par la demanderesse constituait un motif de résiliation des contrats, et résilia ces derniers tout en demandant à la demanderesse réparation du préjudice subi pour un montant correspondant à ce qu'aurait gagné la défenderesse si la demanderesse avait respecté ses engagements contractuels.

La demanderesse alléguait que la relation contractuelle avec la défenderesse « *était d'une durée perpétuelle et donc résiliable ad nutum* », que la dénonciation du contrat était une mesure conservatoire légitime car étant destinée à préserver le futur des produits contractuels et les marques de la demanderesse dans le pays X, que le délai de préavis permettait à la défenderesse de trouver une solution de remplacement, que la défenderesse n'avait pas réparé ses manquements contractuels passés et en avait commis de nouveaux, qu'elle empêchait le bon fonctionnement d'une société commune regroupant les franchisés de la demanderesse dans le pays X, et que la défenderesse s'était rapprochée d'un concurrent de la demanderesse.

La défenderesse soutenait notamment que les parties n'avaient « *point voulu établir un contrat de durée indéterminée qui pouvait être dénoncé ad nutum par la demanderesse* », qu'elles avaient « *fixé de façon implicite la durée minimum de leur relation contractuelle à cinquante ans* », que faute de proposer à la défenderesse de l'indemniser la dénonciation de la relation contractuelle par la demanderesse était fautive et traduisait l'intention de la demanderesse de transformer la défenderesse en filiale dans le cadre de la politique de la demanderesse de filialisation de son réseau de fabrication et de distribution dans le pays X.

Dans cette sentence partielle, le tribunal arbitral examine d'abord la question de la durée des contrats et observe:

« Les contrats [. . .] contenaient des clauses quant à la durée du contrat et quant à sa résiliation.

Article XI du contrat de concession de technologie et d'assistance technique entre [la demanderesse] et [la défenderesse]:

« Article XI — Durée du contrat et clause de résiliation

1. Le présent contrat aura une durée de 10 ans comptés à partir de la notification de son approbation officielle et il prendra effet le [date], tout cela sous la condition de son approbation par les Autorités [du pays X].

2. Chaque partie aura le droit de résilier le présent contrat moyennant un préavis de 6 mois, exprimé par lettre recommandée avec accusé de réception, dans l'un des deux cas suivants:

— faute grave de l'autre partie, considérant comme telle la violation intentionnelle du présent contrat,

— violation d'une clause quelconque du présent contrat après une mise en demeure d'avoir à la respecter, faite par lettre recommandée avec accusé de réception, demeurée sans effet trois mois après son envoi.

3. Tout acte de concurrence déloyale pourra justifier la résiliation du contrat de concession. Toutefois, il demeure convenu qu'un délai de trois mois sera accordé à la partie en faute pour satisfaire aux exigences du présent contrat et si elle ne le fait pas, la partie victime pourra résilier le contrat, moyennant une lettre recommandée avec accusé de réception.

4. Nonobstant les dispositions des paragraphes 2 et 3 du présent article XI, [la demanderesse] pourra, de plein droit, mettre fin au présent contrat, sans préavis, dans les circonstances suivantes:

a) Si la société concessionnaire est dissoute, en faillite ou en cessation de paiement ou toute autre situation similaire selon les lois de son pays.

b) En cas de fusion de la société concessionnaire ou de prise de participation majoritaire dans son capital par des tiers, si ladite fusion ou les personnes physiques ou morales prenant le contrôle de la société concessionnaire, n'ont pas obtenu l'agrément de [la demanderesse] (la même règle est applicable également aux filiales de la société concessionnaire).

c) En cas de modification de la forme juridique de la société concessionnaire sans accord préalable et écrit de [la demanderesse].

d) En cas de non-paiement des redevances, après mise en demeure de le faire exprimée par lettre recommandée demeurée sans effet 30 jours après son envoi.

5) Avant l'expiration de la durée prévue pour le présent contrat, les parties s'obligent à rechercher une nouvelle formule de collaboration par la création d'une structure internationale, dans laquelle s'intégrera la société concessionnaire et dont l'objet sera l'élaboration de la politique internationale et l'adoption de toutes les décisions nécessaires au développement des produits [. . .], objets du présent contrat.

Cependant, compte tenu de la volonté et de l'intérêt des parties à définir ladite structure internationale aussi rapidement que la situation objective le permettra, le délai stipulé pourra être abrégé dans le cas où, avant son expiration, les parties auraient défini et mis en œuvre la nouvelle forme de collaboration et d'intégration dans la structure internationale ».

Article VIII du contrat de licence de marques entre [la demanderesse] et [la défenderesse]:

« Article VIII — Durée et fin de la licence

1. La présente licence est concédée pour tout le temps de validité des marques qui en sont l'objet et de leur renouvellement.

2. La présente licence pourra être résiliée, par l'une ou l'autre des parties, moyennant un préavis de deux mois exprimé par lettre recommandée avec accusé de réception, dans l'un des deux cas suivants:

— faute grave de l'autre partie, considérant comme telle la violation intentionnelle du présent contrat,

— violation d'une clause quelconque du présent contrat après une mise en demeure d'avoir à la respecter, faite par lettre recommandée avec accusé de réception, demeurée sans effet trois mois après son envoi.

3. Tout acte de concurrence déloyale pourra entraîner la résiliation du présent contrat. Cependant, un délai de trois mois est accordé à la partie en faute afin que, dans ce délai, elle mette son comportement en conformité avec le présent contrat. Si elle ne le fait pas, passé le délai de trois mois précité, l'autre partie aura le droit de résilier le présent contrat avec effet immédiat, en informant la partie fautive par lettre recommandée avec accusé de réception.

4. Malgré les dispositions des paragraphes 2 et 3 ci-dessus, [la demanderesse] pourra mettre fin au présent contrat ou le résilier, de plein droit et sans préavis, dans les circonstances suivantes:

a) si la société licenciée est dissoute, est déclarée en faillite, cessation de paiement, procédure collective de règlement de ses dettes ou se trouve dans une situation similaire selon les lois de son pays,

b) en cas de fusion de la société licenciée ou de prise de participation majoritaire dans son capital par des tiers, si ladite fusion ou les personnes physiques ou morales prenant le contrôle de la société licenciée ne sont pas agréés par [la demanderesse] (la même règle est applicable également aux filiales de la société licenciée) ».

Le tribunal arbitral rappelle que le troisième avenant a modifié la durée des contrats en ces termes:

« *QUATRIEMEMENT*

Le contrat de transfert de technologie et d'assistance technique, signé par les parties en date du . . . , <u>sera prorogé automatiquement pour une ou plusieurs périodes de dix ans, comptées à partir de la fin de sa durée actuelle, de façon obligatoire pour [la demanderesse] et facultative pour le licencié. Si le licencié prétend résoudre le contrat, il devra notifier à [la demanderesse], par lettre recommandée avec accusé de réception</u>, son intention de ne pas le renouveler au terme de la période en vigueur, cette notification qui devra être faite avec un préavis de 18 mois avant ce terme. Le présent protocole s'intègre dans les contrats précités, en date du [. . .], c'est pourquoi il aura la même durée que ceux-ci et le même régime de reconductions ». (souligné dans le texte de la sentence).

Le tribunal poursuit:

« *Cet article, tout en étant la base juridique des prétentions des 'parties litigantes', n'excelle pas en clarté. Il appartient dès lors au tribunal arbitral de l'interpréter.*

La seule lecture possible de cette clause serait que seule la partie [défenderesse] pourrait mettre fin à un contrat qui serait automatiquement renouvelé tous les dix ans et qui dès lors aurait une durée indéterminée pour la partie [demanderesse].

Mais une telle lecture doit être écartée pour différentes raisons:

1) Un engagement perpétuel de la part de [la demanderesse] serait à l'encontre des principes du droit français.

En effet, plusieurs textes du Code civil français interdisent la perpétuité des contrats. Ainsi:

— implicitement, l'article 686, relatif aux servitudes, prohibant les services « imposés à la personne ou en faveur de la personne ».

— explicitement:

- *l'article 1709, définissant le louage des choses,*
- *l'article 1780, sur le louage des domestiques et ouvriers,*
- *l'article 1838, limitant à 99 ans la durée des sociétés.*

On peut ajouter, à ces références au Code civil, l'article L. 131-1 du Code de la propriété intellectuelle: « La cession globale des œuvres futures est nulle ».

De ces textes, la jurisprudence a tiré un principe général: la prohibition des engagements perpétuels. Ainsi fait la Cour de cassation, sous le seul visa de l'article 1134 du Code civil, dans son arrêt du 8 juillet 1981 (Gaz. Pal: 1981, I, somm. p. 263).

Il est même à observer que:

— la Cour de cassation a décidé que l'engagement pris pour une durée de 50 ans, en application d'une clause contenue dans les statuts d'une société à capital variable, étant « conclu pour un laps de temps égal ou supérieur à la durée moyenne de la vie professionnelle, ne respecte pas la liberté individuelle de celui qui l'a souscrit » (Cass. civ., 27 avr. 1978: Bull. I, n° 161, p. 128);

— ce n'est pas seulement la liberté des personnes physiques qui est ainsi protégée de la perpétuité des contrats, mais aussi bien celle des personnes morales. Ainsi, Cass. civ., 18 mars 1987: Bull. II, n° 59, p. 35 (« une telle clause, qui met à la charge de la société . . . et de ses ayants droit une obligation personnelle dont la durée ne comporte aucune limite, est nulle »), ou encore Cass. com., 3 janv. 1989: Bull. IV, n° 3, p. 2.

La prohibition des engagements perpétuels protège donc non seulement la liberté individuelle, mais encore les intérêts économiques des contractants. Un engagement perpétuel constituerait en outre « une formidable barrière à l'entrée sur le marché qui empêche les agents économiques qui seraient en mesure de devenir des concurrents de se porter candidats à une relation contractuelle en raison de l'indissolubilité des liens préexistants » (Contrats, conc., consom., août-sept. 1991, p. 1).

Cette justification supplémentaire, tirée du droit de la concurrence, rejoint ainsi l'unanimité doctrinale qui fait de la prohibition de l'engagement perpétuel un principe traditionnel (V. Terré, Simler, Lequette, Les obligations: Dalloz 6ᵉ éd., n° 286, p. 241).

Ces derniers auteurs classent la perpétuité parmi les causes d'illicéité de la prestation. Ils écrivent: « La sanction de la prohibition des engagements perpétuels est, en principe, la nullité de l'engagement et non sa limitation à la durée autorisée. Cette nullité revêt un caractère absolu, l'utilité sociale du contrat s'opposant à ce que celui-ci présente un caractère perpétuel, « sous peine de sclérose des échanges économiques » ».

Il y a donc lieu de considérer comme nul l'engagement de [la demanderesse] contenu dans l'article IV du [troisième avenant].

2) Un tel engagement serait également inconciliable avec les principes généraux du commerce international. Il est par exemple inimaginable que deux sociétés puissent s'obliger à coopérer éternellement sans que l'une ou l'une ou l'autre puisse mettre fin à la coopération.

3) Enfin, faire comme la défenderesse le suggère, c. à d. créer « ex nihilo » une troisième catégorie de contrats, notamment « des contrats à durée déterminée comportant le droit d'une des parties à des reconductions indéfinies » (. . .) reviendrait à une solution qui ne peut être accueillie pour sauver la clause litigieuse, car le droit de l'une des parties à obtenir la reconduction indéfinie reposerait sur l'obligation perpétuelle de l'autre partie de consentir à la reconduction.

Puisque l'engagement de la demanderesse prévu à l'article 4 précité, est nul, il est indiqué de rechercher les conséquences de cette nullité.

La nullité de l'engagement perpétuel transforme l'ensemble contractuel en un contrat à durée indéterminée.

En effet, l'article Cuarta étant nul et non avenu en son paragraphe premier, le deuxième paragraphe reste valide, ce qui signifie que le contrat [date] est confirmé.

D'ailleurs la nullité de l'article Cuarta [du troisième avenant] ne peut affecter les contrats antérieurs à l'avenant (. . .).

Dès lors on se retrouve dans une situation contractuelle régie par les deux contrats [le contrat de concession de technologie et d'assistance technique et le contrat de licence de marques] formant un ensemble contractuel unique et indivisible, tel que reconnu par la lettre de [la demanderesse] (. . .) expressément approuvée par [la défenderesse] (. . .).

Cet ensemble contractuel prévoyait une durée de 10 ans « a partir de la notificación de su aprobación official » (XI-1). Toutefois, aucune des parties n'a pu fournir des éléments pour constater la date exacte de ladite notification et donc la durée exacte dudit contrat.

Une prorogation automatique comme ce fut le cas pour [le troisième avenant] (art. 4, devenu caduque) n'était pas prévue; bien au contraire à l'article XI du contrat de concession, du [date] il est fait état à différentes reprises de l' « expiración » dudit contrat.

Ledit contrat ne prévoit pas de préavis en dehors des cas de faute du cocontractant prévus à l'article XI.2.

Puisque les parties ont toutefois poursuivi leurs relations contractuelles, il faut en conclure que cette relation contractuelle est devenue une relation à durée indéterminée.

Cette relation peut toujours et à tout moment être résiliée par une des parties (Cass. civ., 11 juin 1996: Bull. civ., I, n° 246) moyennant le respect d'un délai de préavis raisonnable (jurisprudence constante de la Cour de cassation). La seule exception est celle d'une faute grave qui justifie une rupture immédiate, faute qui n'a nullement été invoquée par la demanderesse lors du préavis du 3 décembre 1996.

C'est au juge du fond à apprécier souverainement la durée du préavis (Cass. com., 13 juin 1978: Bull. civ., IV, n° 164). Il revient donc au tribunal arbitral de fixer la durée raisonnable du préavis.

L'appréciation du caractère raisonnable du préavis dépend de l'objet de l'activité exercée, en particulier de la durée habituelle des pourparlers précontractuels et des délais de livraison qui s'appliquent aux opérations initiées, et de la spécificité des biens vendus qui peut rendre plus difficile la recherche d'un nouveau concédant ou d'un nouveau concessionnaire; elle dépend aussi de la façon dont le concessionnaire évincé exerce son activité, la reconversion s'avérant plus mal aisée s'il consacre toute son activité à la commercialisation des produits du concédant (CA Paris, 5ᵉ ch. B., 8 déc. 1994: RJDA 3/95, n° 272).

En l'occurrence, il faut également souligner que les parties ont voulu consolider leur relation contractuelle par [le troisième avenant].

On observe en effet en l'espèce que la volonté commune des parties s'est exprimée en faveur d'un allongement de la durée du préavis.

Cette durée était de 6 mois dans le contrat [initial] (article XI, paragraphe 2 du contrat du [date]). Elle est de 18 mois dans la clause « Cuarta » [du troisième avenant]; la nullité de ce texte, pour les raisons développées ci-dessus, ne fait pas obstacle à la constatation de l'intention des parties d'accroître la durée du préavis alors que l'ancienneté des relations contractuelles s'accroissait elle-même.

En outre, précisément du fait de la nullité de l'engagement perpétuel contenu à la clause « Cuarta », le contrat est devenu à durée indéterminée, si bien que la rupture pouvait intervenir à tout instant, mettant ainsi chaque contractant à la merci d'une décision inopinée de son cocontractant, ce qui rend nécessaire un délai de préavis plus long que dans un contrat à durée déterminée, où l'approche d'une échéance permet à chacun de se préparer à la dénonciation que l'autre est en droit de notifier.

Une période de 24 mois apparaît donc nécessaire, dans les circonstances de l'espèce, pour retrouver, après la résiliation, l'équilibre économique antérieur.

C'est dès lors en tenant compte de tous les éléments et aussi des circonstances spécifiques de la cause, que le tribunal arbitral a jugé qu'un délai de deux ans serait un délai raisonnable. Ce délai aurait dû prendre cours au moment de la cessation en fait des rapports contractuels.

Ce délai de deux ans doit être converti en dommages-intérêts, mais uniquement pour le « lucrum cessans », puisque la défenderesse n'a prouvé aucun « damnum emergens ».

Malgré son allégation quant à la nécessité de vendre à un bas prix une partie de ses outillages et de licencier une partie du personnel tout en l'indemnisant, ces événements n'ont pu occasionner des dommages dès l'instant où, comme elle l'a reconnu, [la défenderesse] a décidé de continuer ses activités de livrer des produits [similaires].

Cette solution a d'ailleurs l'avantage de coller à la réalité, puisqu'il est clair que les deux parties contractantes voulaient en finir avec leur contrat de franchisage et se reconvertir vers d'autres concessionnaires ou concédants.

En effet tandis que [la demanderesse] achète la plupart des franchises, [la défenderesse] annonce son intention d'entrer en concurrence et semble avoir pu se réorganiser en quelques jours de temps après la dénonciation ».

Le tribunal examine ensuite successivement les demandes des parties et déclare que le non-respect du délai de préavis par la demanderesse ouvre droit au paiement de dommages et intétêts à la demanderesse au titre du « *lucrum cessans durant un délai de deux ans* », le *quantum* de ces dommages et intérêts devant être évalué contradictoirement. La dénonciation du contrat pouvant « *être considérée comme valable, la résiliation d'un contrat déjà dénoncé est devenue sans objet, sans qu'il soit encore nécessaire d'examiner le bien-fondé de cette résiliation ».*

(. . .) Les deux parties restent toutefois tenues de respecter leurs engagements découlant de l'ensemble contractuel jusqu'à la date de cessation effective de leurs relations contractuelles.

(. . .) Le tribunal arbitral est d'avis que l'examen des violations du contrat par la défenderesse, tel que celui-ci a été demandé par la demanderesse, est sans objet puisque la demanderesse n'a pas jugé utile de baser sa dénonciation sur des manquements par la défenderesse.

La défenderesse est condamnée à payer les redevances « *dues pour la période durant laquelle les parties ont en fait continué leurs relations commerciales ».*

Les parties sont invitées à s'informer mutuellement sur les chiffres et les prestations, faute de quoi un expert sera désigné à cet effet.

OBSERVATIONS. — I. — Dans cette sentence partielle rendue sous l'empire du règlement d'arbitrage de 1988, le tribunal arbitral saisi du litige se prononce sur la validité et les effets de stipulations contractuelles relatives à la durée d'une opération juridique internationale sans jamais qualifier juridiquement ladite opération. Le tribunal reconnaît que l'opération juridique procède d'un « *ensemble contractuel* », parfois désigné par le terme de « *contrat* » dans la sentence, constitué de deux contrats et de quatre avenants. Le tribunal insiste d'ailleurs sur « *le caractère unitaire de cette relation contractuelle* » et rappelle l'accord des parties selon lequel « *les deux contrats forment un ensemble contractuel unique et indivisible* ». Le tribunal identifie donc d'abord le montage contractuel de l'opération juridique puis retient que plusieurs *instrumentum* concourent à la formation d'un *negotium* unique. L'intérêt de la sentence sur ce point réside dans l'absence de qualification juridique de l'ensemble contractuel. Est-on dans le cadre d'une opération juridique complexe (en ce qu'elle implique une multiplicité de consentements des parties) ou dans celui d'une opération mixte (un même contrat étant soumis à plusieurs régimes juridiques) ? Il semble que le tribunal retienne implicitement la première hypothèse. Le tribunal ne semble pas retenir, du moins n'y fait-il aucunement référence expressément, la qualification de contrat *sui generis* pour appliquer un régime juridique spécifique à cet agrégat de documents contractuels. Au contraire, le tribunal emploie tour à tour les qualifications de « *concession* », « *transfert de technologie* », « *licence de marques* » et « *franchise* » pour caractériser l'opération juridique. Le tribunal suit ainsi les qualifications employées par les parties alors qu'il n'y est pas tenu et dispose d'un pouvoir souverain d'appréciation en la matière (voir par exemple *le rappel opéré par le tribunal arbitral dans la sentence finale dans l'affaire n° 8056 rendue en 1996 et rapporté dans le Bull. int. arb. CCI, vol. 12, n° 1, 2001, p. 68: « Il est de principe que la qualification juridique d'une relation ne dépend pas de ce que les parties imaginent avoir créé, ni du titre que ces parties inventeront ou adopteront pour définir ces relations* »; voir aussi obs. sous la sentence rendue dans l'*affaire CCI n° 3243 rendue en 1981, S. Jarvin et Y. Derains: Rec. sent. arb. CCI, 1974-1985, publication CCI n° 433, 1990, p. 432)*. Toutefois, le tribunal ne fait jamais application des différents régimes juridiques auxquels ces qualifications renvoient. Il aurait, par exemple, pu examiner si les renouvellements successifs du contrat par périodes de dix ans ne contrevenaient pas aux dispositions du droit applicable à ces contrats nommés. Le tribunal n'envisage le problème soulevé par la durée de l'engagement contractuel que sur le seul terrain du droit des obligations. Une telle approche ne pourrait-elle pas être susceptible de soulever des interrogations quant à la solution dégagée par le tribunal arbitral? Il ne le semble pas. L'approche retenue, consistant à appliquer le « droit commun » des obligations plutôt que des régimes dérogatoires, si elle n'est pas novatrice, n'en est pas moins empreinte de pragmatisme, et évite au tribunal de susciter interrogations et débats auxquels les parties se sont refusées ou semblent ne pas avoir pensé.

II. — Le tribunal devait d'abord se prononcer sur la nature d'une stipulation contractuelle selon laquelle le contrat était conclu pour une durée déterminée. Si le terme *a quo* du contrat, à savoir la notification de l'approbation de ce dernier par les autorités étatiques compétentes, était clairement identifiable et non contesté par les parties, le terme *ad quem* prêtait à controverse. En effet, le troisième avenant prévoyait d'une part une prorogation automatique du contrat, c'est-à-dire en l'absence de toute réitération de volonté des parties, par périodes de dix ans, et d'autre part que cette prorogation serait obligatoire pour la demanderesse et facultative pour la défenderesse. En application de cette stipulation, toute manifestation de volonté de la demanderesse était dépourvue d'effet. Le tribunal relève le manque de clarté de cette stipulation, ce qui rend nécessaire son interprétation. Le jeu des prorogations successives confère-t-il un caractère perpétuel à l'engagement de la demanderesse ? Pouvait-on au contraire, ainsi que le prétendait la défenderesse, limiter le nombre des prorogations automatiques par la reconnaissance d'un terme *ad quem* implicite ? En l'espèce, le terme implicite correspondait à la durée d'existence de la société regroupant les franchisés de la demanderesse dans le pays X. Rejetant la thèse du terme implicite, le tribunal déclare que la seule interprétation possible de la clause est celle qui lui reconnaît la nature d'engagement perpétuel. Le tribunal refuse de lui donner effet précisément au motif qu'elle lierait l'une des parties au contrat, en l'espèce la demanderesse, de manière perpétuelle. Or, appuyant son raisonnement sur l'analyse des textes du code civil et du code de la propriété intellectuelle, de la jurisprudence et d'une doctrine particulièrement autorisée, le tribunal rappelle la prohibition générale de tels engagements en droit français. Il refuse de considérer qu'outre les contrats à durée indéterminée et ceux à durée déterminée, il existerait une troisième catégorie de contrats, à savoir « *des contrats à durée déterminée comportant le droit d'une des parties à des reconductions indéfinies* ». Le tribunal ne distingue d'ailleurs aucunement entre la prorogation du contrat qui correspond à la continuation de la même relation contractuelle, seul le terme extinctif étant repoussé, et la reconduction du contrat qui consiste à substituer un nouvel accord au contrat initial (pour une étude d'ensemble de ces deux notions voir *J. -M. Mousseron, Technique contractuelle: 2ᵉ éd., Francis Lefebvre, 1999, n° 915 s. et n° 928 s.).* L'absence de qualification de la relation contractuelle par le tribunal arbitral lui permet d'écarter la solution qui serait par exemple retenue en matière de concession commerciale et qui est rappelée par un autre tribunal arbitral dans l'affaire n° 8056: « *C'est en effet un principe général que la tacite reconduction n'emporte pas prorogation du contrat primitif mais donne naissance à un nouveau contrat, de durée indéterminée, dont les clauses reproduisent cependant l'ancien* » (Bull. int. arb. CCI, *op. cit.*, p. 72).

La limite à la validité du renouvellement des contrats à durée déterminée est donc le risque d'enfreindre la prohibition des engagements perpétuels. Le tribunal relève le caractère variable, selon la nature de l'engagement, voire les circonstances de l'espèce, de la durée globale à prendre en considération et au-delà de laquelle un engagement contractuel n'est plus valide. Par la reconnaissance de la contrariété des engagements perpétuels aux principes généraux du commerce international, le tribunal reconnaît à la liberté contractuelle la valeur de principe général du commerce international. On peut s'interroger sur la portée du raisonnement du tribunal au regard de l'acceptation générale de ce principe dans les droits nationaux, et spécialement au regard du droit applicable en l'espèce (voir *G. Marty, P. Raynaud, Droit civil, Les obligations, t. l, les sources, 2ᵉ éd.: Sirey, 1988 n° 72 s.).* Etait-il besoin d'invoquer les principes du commerce international ?

III. — Le tribunal devait ensuite se prononcer sur la sanction de l'engagement perpétuel souscrit par les parties. Le tribunal énonce que cet engagement est frappé de nullité absolue et cherche à déterminer l'étendue de cette nullité. Il considère que la nullité absolue n'est qu'une nullité partielle, puisque n'affectant que la clause contenant l'engagement, c'est-à-dire celle figurant dans le troisième avenant. Le tribunal reconnaît dès lors que la clause nulle ne présente pas un caractère impulsif et déterminant de l'accord des parties et déclare que les clauses de durée stipulées dans les contrats antérieurs à l'avenant, à savoir les contrats de concession de technologie et d'assistance et de licence de marques, doivent se voir reconnaître plein effet. Ces contrats étaient conclus pour une durée déterminée mais la poursuite des relations contractuelles au-delà du terme *ad quem* stipulé a transformé ces contrats à durée déterminée en contrats à durée indéterminée, pouvant être résiliés sous réserve du respect d'un préavis. Si la résiliation du contrat n'ouvre pas droit à indemnisation *per se*, c'est au titre de l'exercice de cette faculté, soit que la délai de préavis ne soit pas respecté soit que la mise en œuvre du délai de préavis soit fautive, qu'une des parties pourrait demander réparation (voir *C. Quyen C. Truong, Les différends liés à la rupture des contrats internationaux de distribution dans les sentences arbitrales CCI, Coll. Bibl. de droit de l'entreprise, t. 56: Litec, 2002, n° 215 et 217).*

Le tribunal affirme sa compétence pour fixer le délai de préavis qui aurait dû être respecté par toute partie cherchant à mettre fin à la relation contractuelle. Il prend en compte les circonstances de l'espèce: objet de l'activité et faculté de reconversion pour la partie subissant la résiliation, et relève que les parties, par la signature du troisième

596

avenant et même si la clause de durée de ce dernier est nulle, ont, d'un commun accord, entendu allonger le délai de préavis. Le tribunal conclut qu'un préavis de vingt quatre mois, excédant la durée mentionnée dans le troisième avenant et *a fortiori* celle stipulée dans les contrats, était nécessaire et devait être respectée. Il est intéressant de noter que le tribunal ne prend pas en compte la durée totale de la relation contractuelle, soit dix neuf ans, pour déterminer le caractère raisonnable du délai de préavis à respecter (voir *C. Quyen C. Truong, loc. cit. et* notamment la référence *à la sentence finale dans l'affaire CCI n° 7146 (inédite) en matière de concession commerciale et n° 264).* Le délai de préavis est considéré comme la durée devant nécessairement être respectée pour permettre aux parties, après la résiliation, de retrouver le *statu quo ante*, celui-ci étant entendu non pas comme la situation des parties avant la signature du contrat mais avant la résiliation. Même si le tribunal n'apporte aucune précision sur ce point, il est manifeste que le délai de préavis ne garantit pas le retour à « *l'équilibre économique antérieur* ». Tout au plus doit-il, en principe, permettre aux parties de revenir à la situation précédant la résolution, que cette situation soit favorable à toutes les parties ou à l'une d'elles uniquement. Le respect du délai de préavis n'a donc aucun effet correctif du contrat résilié. En l'absence de la preuve d'une perte subie rapportée par la défenderesse, le tribunal déclare que le non-respect du délai de préavis ouvre seulement droit à une réparation pour le gain manqué dans la limite de la durée fixée par ce préavis.

E. J.

Sentence rendue dans l'affaire n° 7081 en 1994 (original en langue Française).

I. — Compétence. — Compétence des arbitres (oui). — Fondement. — Troisième Convention de Lomé. — Article 55 du Cahier général des Charges.

II. — Recevabilité — Appréciation de la recevabilité. — Globalité. — Recevabilité des demandes tendant à constater la prétendue illégalité de la décision d'une organisation internationale de droit public, Y, suite à son appel d'offres (oui). — Recevabilité de la demande tendant à ce que le tribunal arbitral enjoigne à Y d'adjuger les marchés à la demanderesse (non).

III. — Mesures conservatoires. — Demande de suspension de l'exécution d'un marché (non). — Mesures conservatoires que le tribunal jugera utiles (non). — Irrecevabilité.

IV. — Marché de droit public — Décision de non attribution prise par le Secrétaire exécutif de Y. — Pot de vin (non). — Discrimination (oui). — Illégalité (oui). — Conséquences. — Dommages et Intérêts (non). — Expertise (non).

V. — Manque à gagner — principes en matière de réparation de la perte d'une chance.

Un tribunal arbitral, siégeant à Paris, était appelé à trancher un litige concernant un appel d'offres restreint lancé en 1989 par une organisation africaine de droit international public, Y, défenderesse en l'espèce. Le marché en cause était financé par le Fond européen de développement des Communautés européennes, et portait sur la fourniture, l'installation et la mise en place d'un service après-vente et d'entretien, d'équipements photovoltaïques dans les pays du Sahel.

Une société de droit italien, X, demanderesse à l'action, a fait une soumission pour les lots n° 2 (Burkina Faso et Mali) et n° 3 (Niger et Tchad). Les plis d'offres qui ont été ouverts en séance publique tenue à la DG VIII de la Commission européenne, en novembre 1989 à Bruxelles, ont montré que les offres de X faites pour les lots n° 2 et n° 3 ont été les plus intéressantes. Le délai de validité des offres a été par la suite prorogé de deux mois.

Par lettre de mai 1990, Y a informé X, ainsi que d'autres soumissionnaires, qu'ils n'ont pas été retenus pour les marchés précités. Le lot n° 2 a été attribué provisoirement à deux sociétés P et TE et le lot n° 3 à P. L'attribution définitive est intervenue en janvier et en avril 1991.

Par lettre de juillet 1990 à Y, X a soutenu que son exclusion a été illégale et a demandé à Y d'annuler sa décision afin de lui permettre de participer à la suite de la procédure jusqu'à l'attribution définitive des marchés. Elle s'est réservée par ailleurs la possibilité de recourir éventuellement à l'arbitrage prévu par l'article 238 de la Convention de Lomé III (ci après Lomé III). Y, par lettre du 14 septembre 1990, a rejeté l'allégation et la demande de X.

X, par requête d'août 1990, a introduit devant la Cour de Justice des Communautés européennes, contre la Commission des Communautés européennes, un recours en annulation et une demande en référé visant à obtenir un sursis à l'exécution ou toutes autres mesures provisoires propres à assurer réadmission dans la procédure. Cette demande en référé a été rejetée par ordonnance du Président de la Cour en octobre 1990.

C'est dans ces circonstances que X a introduit une requête d'arbitrage en décembre 1990.

Dans une sentence partielle prononcée en 1992, le tribunal arbitral s'est prononcé sur différents points.

— En ce qui concerne tout d'abord sa **compétence**, le tribunal arbitral s'est déclaré compétent pour connaître le litige en se basant sur l'article 238 de Lomé III, et sur l'article 55 du Cahier général des Charges.

Y a contesté la compétence du tribunal arbitral au motif que Lomé III ne pouvait s'appliquer en l'espèce car aucune des parties n'était partie à la convention. X ne pouvait pas par ailleurs invoquer la convention car celle-ci ne créait pas de droits pour les particuliers. Y était, quant à elle, investie d'une personnalité propre qui empêchait que les engagements contractés par les Etats qui l'avaient constitué lui soient opposés. La défenderesse avait invoqué également l'absence d'un consentement spécifique qu'elle aurait dû émettre pour soumettre le différend à l'arbitrage. Enfin, les articles 24 de l'appel d'offres et 55 du Cahier général des Charges ne s'appliquaient qu'aux différends portant sur l'exécution des marchés.

Cette argumentation a été rejetée par le tribunal arbitral car l'article 238, § 1 de Lomé III, dispose que « *le règlement des différends entre l'administration d'un Etat d'Afrique, des Caraïbes et du Pacifique (ACP) et un entrepreneur, un fournisseur ou un prestataire de services candidat ou soumissionnaire, à l'occasion de la procédure de passation ou de l'exécution d'un marché financé par le Fonds s'effectue par voie d'arbitrage conformément à un règlement de procédure adopté par le conseil des ministres.* »

Les paragraphes 2 et 3 de ce même article précisent que ce règlement sera ultérieurement adopté par décision du Conseil des ministres CEE/ACP et, qu'à titre transitoire, « *tous les différends seront tranchés définitivement suivant le Règlement de conciliation et d'arbitrage de la Chambre de commerce internationale.*»

Le tribunal arbitral relève que « *l'article 238 est une disposition importante dans l'économie de la Convention de Lomé, ayant pour objectif — conforme à l'ordre juridique communautaire — qu'un recours juridictionnel soit mis à la disposition des soumissionnaires et adjudicataires. Les parties à Lomé III ont convenu — pour diverses raisons juridiques, politiques et pratiques — que ce recours serait l'arbitrage.*

Dans la mesure où l'article 238 de Lomé III dispose que "le règlement des différends entre l'administration d'un Etat ACP et un entrepreneur (. . .) ou soumissionnaire (. . .) s'effectue par voie d'arbitrage" il énonce une obligation claire et précise qui n'est subordonnée dans son exécution ou ses effets à l'intervention d'aucun acte ultérieur. On ne trouve en effet pas dans le texte de l'article 238 une conditionnalité à laquelle serait soumis le recours à la procédure, ou encore un choix qui serait laissé aux Etats ACP entre plusieurs solutions.

Le tribunal arbitral est d'avis que l'article 238 de Lomé III consigne l'accord des Etats ACP de soumettre à l'arbitrage les différends qui les opposeraient ultérieurement à des particuliers dans le cadre de l'attribution ou de l'exécution de marchés financés par le Fonds européen de développement. L'article 238 est en effet formulé d'une manière inconditionnelle qui contraste avec la rédaction des clauses d'arbitrage contenues dans nombre d'actes internationaux et qui ne visent pas à introduire une obligation mais seulement une possibilité de recourir à la procédure arbitrale.

En conclusion, le tribunal arbitral estime que le consentement des Etats ACP au règlement d'arbitrage des litiges qui pourraient les opposer aux soumissionnaires ou adjudicataires des marchés financés par le Fonds européen de développement a été exprimé par ces Etats lors de leur ratification de la Convention de Lomé III et que ce consentement constitue une base conventionnelle suffisante tant en ce qui les concerne que, par assimilation, en ce qui concerne Y ellemême. »

Le tribunal arbitral fonde également sa compétence sur l'article 55.1 du Cahier général des Charges qui disposait que « *tout différend survenant, soit entre l'administration et un soumissionnaire à l'occasion de la procédure de passation d'un marché, soit entre l'administration et l'attributaire, et résultant de l'interprétation ou de l'exécution d'un marché, est résolu par voie d'arbitrage, conformément au règlement d'arbitrage qui est arrêté par le conseil d'association.* »

Selon le tribunal, l'article 55 « *prolonge et confirme le consentement donné par les Etats (ou groupes d'Etats) ACP dans l'article 238 de Lomé III, au règlement arbitral des litiges qui pourraient les opposer aux soumissionnaires ou adjudicataires des marchés financés par le Fonds européen de développement; inclus dans le dossier d'appel d'offres préparé et utilisé par Y, l'article 55 rend en outre ce consentement spécifique à l'appel d'offres litigieux, et cela directement dans le chef d'Y elle-même.* »

Le tribunal en conclut qu' « *il y a bien eu sur l'arbitrage une expression de volonté des deux parties au présent litige, expression suffisante au regard du droit de l'arbitrage en général, tenant compte de l'ordre juridique propre aux Communautés européennes et prolongé dans l'organisation de leurs relations avec les Etats ACP. Cette conclusion est parfaitement conciliable avec la nature réglementaire du Cahier général des Charges, dans les relations entre le pouvoir adjudicateur et un soumissionnaire évincé.* »

— La **recevabilité** de l'action a été ensuite examinée par le tribunal arbitral.

Y a soulevé l'irrecevabilité de l'action de X en soutenant que la régularité de la procédure de passation des marchés et la justification du choix de l'attribution n'avaient pas à être discutées devant le tribunal arbitral, qu'un soumissionnaire ne pouvait contester l'attribution d'un marché et demander au tribunal arbitral de remplacer la décision d'attribution par une autre.

Dans son mémoire du 15 novembre 1991, la défenderesse a réaffirmé que la demanderesse n'avait pas le droit de faire contrôler la décision de conclure un contrat, de faire annuler un contrat passé avec un tiers et de forcer la défenderesse à conclure un contrat avec elle — ce qui constituerait une restriction au droit fondamental de la liberté contractuelle. Par ailleurs, la demanderesse n'a pas établi l'existence d'un droit de contrôle, d'annulation ou de substitution à la décision de Y. C'est la raison pour laquelle l'action de X serait irrecevable.

Le tribunal a énoncé dans un premier temps quelques précisions d'ordre général. Selon lui, la recevabilité « *s'apprécie d'abord en ce qui concerne les conditions préalables exigées pour que le tribunal arbitral saisi puisse passer à l'examen du fond. Ces conditions portent, non pas sur la compétence de la juridiction saisie — question qui doit être réglée préalablement à celle de la recevabilité — mais sur les titres que peut faire valoir un demandeur pour agir (sa capacité, son intérêt et sa qualité d'agir) et sur les formes et formalités procédurales de saisine (délais et mode de saisine en particulier). Si ces conditions ne sont pas satisfaites, l'action est irrecevable dans sa totalité; il n'y a pas lieu de passer à l'examen du fond.*

Lorsque les conditions de recevabilité ci-dessus rappelées sont remplies, une nouvelle question de recevabilité peut se poser à propos des conclusions de la demande, c'est-à-dire des solutions qu'il est demandé au tribunal arbitral d'adopter, des décisions et mesures qu'il lui est demandé de prendre. Alors même qu'un demandeur remplit toutes les conditions pour agir, ses conclusions peuvent être irrecevables comme tendant à faire adopter par le tribunal arbitral des solutions, décisions ou mesures qu'il n'est pas dans son pouvoir d'édicter. Si un demandeur n'adresse que des conclusions se rapportant à des décisions et mesures qu'il peut adopter elles sont entièrement recevables. S'il dépose des conclusions portant sur des décisions et mesures qui échappent totalement au pouvoir du tribunal arbitral, elles sont entièrement irrecevables. Les conclusions peuvent porter sur des décisions et mesures relevant les unes du pouvoir du tribunal arbitral, les autres non. Elles sont alors pour parties recevables, pour parties irrecevables.»

Quant à X, elle a demandé tout d'abord au tribunal arbitral de constater l'illégalité de la décision de Y qui l'a écartée de la procédure d'adjudication. Celui-ci y fait droit car *« une telle conclusion, qui se borne à demander au tribunal de dire le droit pour aboutir à la constatation qu'une décision est illégale ou non, relève de la mission essentielle d'un tribunal arbitral, elle est donc recevable. »*

Par contre, la demande de X tendant à obtenir du tribunal arbitral qu'il ordonne à Y de lui adjuger les marchés pour lesquels elle a soumissionné, a été rejetée *« car une telle conclusion tend à faire adresser par le tribunal un ordre à l'égard d'une des parties, qu'il n'est pas dans son pouvoir d'édicter. Elle est donc irrecevable. »*

La demanderesse a requis enfin du tribunal arbitral qu'il condamne Y à la dédommager du préjudice subi à raison de son exclusion illégale de la procédure. Selon le tribunal, *« une telle conclusion se borne à demander au tribunal de déterminer les droits à réparation qui découleraient pour X de son exclusion illégale de la procédure; elle relève du pouvoir du tribunal arbitral, elle est donc recevable. »*

— Par requête complémentaire du 26 août 1991, X a saisi le tribunal arbitral d'une demande visant au prononcé de **mesures provisoires** à son bénéfice. X a sollicité d'une part, *« la suspension immédiate de l'exécution des marchés litigieux »*, et d'autre part, *« toute autre mesure conservatoire que le tribunal jugera utile, dans l'attente d'une décision sur le fond »*.

Selon X, le tribunal arbitral avait *« le pouvoir d'ordonner de telles mesures conservatoires en vue notamment de préserver le statu quo entre les parties, dès lors que l'absence de telles mesures serait susceptibles de compromettre l'effectivité de la procédure arbitrale »*. La compétence du tribunal arbitral résulterait expressément de l'article 8 (5) du Règlement d'arbitrage de la CCI.

Le tribunal va constater que *« la première mesure conservatoire demandée consiste en "la suspension immédiate de l'exécution des marchés litigieux". Contrairement à ce que semble soutenir X, cette demande ne vise pas simplement à rétablir le "statu quo"; il s'agirait en réalité d'obtenir au provisoire une partie substantielle de ce qui est demandé au fond.*

Cette demande est, en toute hypothèse, irrecevable dès lors que le tribunal arbitral pourra seulement examiner au fond les demandes tendant à la constatation de l'illégalité de la décision de Y d'écarter X et, le cas échéant, à réparer le préjudice subi. La demande qui tend à faire suspendre l'exécution d'un marché dépasse bien entendu pareille constatation et/ou pareille réparation.

Quant à la demande sollicitant "toute autre mesure conservatoire que le tribunal jugera utile, dans l'attente d'une décision sur le fond", le tribunal arbitral la considère également comme irrecevable, cette fois à défaut de précision suffisante. La demanderesse n'a en effet aucunement déterminé quelles mesures elle visait ni a fortiori leur utilité. Le tribunal arbitral ne saurait y suppléer.

Les demandes de mesures conservatoires sont donc toutes irrecevables, quand bien même le tribunal arbitral serait compétent en matière de mesures conservatoires sur base de l'article 8 (5) du Règlement d'arbitrage. »

L'objet de la sentence finale prononcée en 1994 porte pour l'essentiel sur le grief fait par X à l'égard du Secrétaire exécutif de Y qui aurait eu un traitement discriminatoire envers elle.

Le tribunal commence par rappeler que le principe d'égalité ou de traitement non discriminatoire est inscrit dans la Convention de Lomé III (articles 226, 2 et 233) ainsi que dans l'article 5.2 du Cahier général des Charges.

Les griefs formulés par X ont été ensuite examinés par le tribunal sur la base des deux questions suivantes: « *La demanderesse a-t-elle avec certitude été traitée différemment des autres soumissionnaires et cela a-t-il eu des effets significatifs sur la mise en concurrence ? Si oui, ce traitement différencié était-il néanmoins justifié par les données spécifiques des offres de la demanderesse ? »*

Selon le tribunal, « *la thèse de la demanderesse semble être qu'elle aurait été écartée pour avoir refusé ce qui aurait été en réalité une demande de pot-de-vin, transmise par un proche de l'ancien Secrétaire exécutif de Y. En effet ce dernier aurait souhaité obtenir la signature d'un contrat qui aurait eu pour objet une "mission d'appui" afin de faire obtenir par X "par tous les moyens possibles" l'attribution des lots n° 2 et 3; en cas de succès, la commission aurait été de 12,5 % ou 10 % du montant hors taxe des marchés. Les attributaires des lots 2 et 3 auraient peut-être été approchés par le même intermédiaire et auraient accepté ses propositions. Cette thèse serait renforcée par le fait que le Secrétaire exécutif serait arrivé à Bruxelles lors de la phase finale des délibérations de la Commission technique, afin d'exercer de "fortes pressions (. . .) pour influencer les conclusions de cette dernière".*

Le tribunal arbitral considère qu'il ne peut décider avec certitude que la demanderesse aurait été traitée différemment des autres soumissionnaires avec des effets significatifs sur la mise en concurrence. Pour plusieurs griefs toutefois, le doute existait et ce n'est qu'après des hésitations importantes que le tribunal arbitral a conclu négativement sur l'ensemble. »

Quant à la discrimination que le Secrétaire exécutif de Y aurait commis à l'égard de X pour le service après-vente des lots n° 2 et n° 3, « *le tribunal arbitral conclut qu'une discrimination a été commise par le Secrétaire exécutif de Y envers la demanderesse, concernant le service après-vente du lot n° 3. Sur cet aspect et pour le lot, celle-ci n'a pas été traitée comme les autres soumissionnaires, ayant été écartée sur base d'une simple motivation par référence à la fois insuffisante et incorrecte. Cette différence de traitement a eu des effets significatifs sur la mise en concurrence dès lors que, dans l'opinion même du Secrétaire exécutif, le service après vente présentait un caractère déterminant pour les décisions d'attribution et de non-attribution. Par ailleurs, le défendeur n'a pas établi que ce traitement différencié aurait été justifié par les données spécifiques de l'offre du demandeur pour le service après vente du lot n° 3. La discrimination ainsi établie rend illégale la décision de ne pas attribuer le lot n° 3 à la demanderesse; cette discrimination et la faute qu'elle constitue ont été en revanche sans effet sur la décision de ne pas lui attribuer le lot n° 2. »*

La conclusion qui précède appelle l'examen d'une réparation éventuelle de X, qui a décomposé son préjudice allégué en trois éléments principaux: le coût de la participation à l'appel d'offres, le manque à gagner et les préjudices économiques résultant de son exclusion, le coût de la procédure qu'elle a intentée devant la Cour de Justice des Communautés européennes et les frais d'arbitrage.

Y a soutenu, quant au principe même de la responsabilité, que X devait établir la causalité entre la prétendue illégalité et le dommage réclamé; en d'autres termes, elle devait établir qu'en l'absence de la prétendue illégalité, les marchés lui auraient été attribués. X a sur ce point répondu qu'en l'absence de son exclusion illégale, elle aurait obtenu les lots n° 2 et 3 car elle avait fait les offres les plus intéressantes. Le dommage est-il réparable ?

En ce qui concerne la participation de la demanderesse à l'appel d'offres, « *le tribunal va constater que le lien causal entre la faute commise et le préjudice allégué n'a pas été établi par la demanderesse. En effet quel que soit le choix de l'administration, les frais liés à la participation à l'appel d'offres aurait été exposés. De plus, les frais de participation ont été exposés. De plus, les frais de participation ont été exposés en relation à la fois avec l'offre pour le lot n° 2 et avec l'offre pour le lot n° 3. »*

Quant au manque à gagner, le tribunal va énoncer le principe avant de l'appliquer à l'espèce. Selon lui, « *la perte d'une chance est en principe indemnisable, à condition qu'elle soit sérieuse ou réelle. En l'espèce, si P n'avait pas été désigné attributaire pour le lot n° 3, le choix du Secrétaire se serait porté, de manière sinon certaine du moins hautement probable, sur TE et non la société X. Le tribunal va en déduire que ce deuxième préjudice allégué n'est pas réparable à défaut de chance sérieuse qu'aurait eu la demanderesse de se voir attribuer le lot n° 3.*

En ce qui concerne les coûts des procédures intentées par le demandeur, le tribunal va estimer, en considération de l'ensemble des circonstances, que c'est légitimement que la demanderesse avait pris diverses initiatives sur le plan juridictionnel. En ce concerne les procédures dirigées contre la Commission des Communautés européennes, ces recours ont été introduits à ses risques et sans que Y soit à la cause.

Dans ces conditions, un lien causal direct et suffisant n'a pas été établi entre la faute commise et le coût des procédures engagées devant la Cour de justice. Le troisième préjudice allégué n'est donc pas réparable. »

OBSERVATIONS: I. — La politique communautaire de coopération entre l'Union européenne et les pays ACP a été mise en place par les Conventions de Yaoundé (1963 et 1969) et de Lomé (1975, 1979, 1984 et 1989 révisée en 1995). La troisième Convention de Lomé faisait partie, au moment des faits, du droit des Etats ACP (membres ou non de Y), des Communautés européennes et de ses Etats membres. Lomé III a été depuis remplacée par Lomé IV. Le titre III de la troisième partie de Lomé III organisait la coopération financière et technique entre les Communautés européennes et les Etats ACP, dans le cadre duquel s'est déroulé l'appel d'offres lancé par Y.

L'article 238 de la Convention, dont l'applicabilité est contestée par l'une des parties, précisait le mode de règlement des différends relatifs aux marchés négociés ou conclus dans le cadre de cette coopération. Y a souligné qu'elle n'était pas partie à la Convention de Lomé III en tant que telle car elle était dotée d'une personnalité distincte de celle de ses Etats membres. Elle ne saurait en conséquence se voir opposer les obligations contractées par ces derniers à titre individuel.

Le tribunal arbitral répond à juste titre « *que la reconnaissance de la personnalité juridique internationale n'a pas pour effet d'affranchir l'organisation de l'ensemble des obligations juridiques qui auraient été contractées par ses Etats membres. Si l'article 238 de Lomé III prévoit que les Etats ACP recourront à l'arbitrage (. . .) la même obligation pèse sur une organisation qu'ils auraient constituée pour l'accomplissement de tâches communes. »*

Toutefois, on peut se demander si, dans le cas d'espèce, le consentement spécifique des parties à la procédure d'arbitrage ne faisait pas défaut. Le caractère volontaire du recours à l'arbitrage constitue un principe établi du droit de l'arbitrage national et international. Le consentement des parties est la condition *sine qua non* de la compétence du tribunal arbitral. Même si ce consentement peut être exprimé sous des formes diverses, il est essentiel que l'expression de volonté de l'une et de l'autre partie soit certaine.

Dans le cas d'espèce, le terme « parties » est susceptible d'une double interprétation. Il s'agit d'une part, des parties à Lomé III, soit les Etats ACP, les Communautés européennes et leurs Etats membres et, d'autre part, des parties à l'arbitrage, soit les Etats (ou groupes d'Etats) ACP, et les entrepreneurs ou soumissionnaires. L'identification n'était donc pas aussi claire que dans les accords d'arbitrage interétatiques, où les parties à l'accord sont les parties à l'arbitrage. Il existe toutefois un parallèle évident entre le présent cas et celui des accords conclus entre Etats pour la protection des investissements. Les clauses d'arbitrage insérées dans ces derniers accords visent en effet les litiges qui naîtraient non pas entre les Etats parties, mais entre l'Etat sur le territoire duquel l'investissement est opéré et l'investisseur privé qui fait cet investissement *(en matière de compétence du CIRDI, voir à titre d'exemple la décision du 24 décembre 1996, JDI 2000, p. 151).*

La question était ici de savoir si l'engagement des Etats membres et par conséquent celui de Y pouvait être exprimé de manière abstraite et générale (par la Convention de Lomé) sans à être réitéré sous la forme d'une convention d'arbitrage expresse. Faisant un parallèle entre le présent cas et celui des accords conclus entre les Etats pour la protection des investissements, le tribunal arbitral *« va estimer que le consentement des Etats (ou groupes d'Etats) ACP au règlement arbitral des litiges qui pourraient les opposer aux soumissionnaires ou adjudicataires des marchés financés par le Fonds européen de développement a été exprimé par ces Etats lors de leur ratification de la Convention de Lomé III et que ce consentement constitue une base conventionnelle suffisante tant en ce qui les concerne que, par assimilation, en ce qui concerne Y elle-même ».*

Y a en effet adhéré à l'ensemble du système de coopération organisé par Lomé III, dont le règlement arbitral visé à l'article 238. Cette adhésion est par définition un acte de volonté. Quant au consentement de X, celui-ci a été exprimé par sa participation à une procédure d'appel d'offres qui comportait une clause arbitrale et ensuite par sa requête en arbitrage.

Le tribunal arbitral a estimé que quand bien même *« l'article 238 de Lomé III devait être écarté sur le plan du consentement au règlement arbitral du litige: la volonté clairement exprimée par Y en lançant un appel d'offres qui comporte des dispositions expresses relatives au règlement arbitral des litiges liés à l'appel d'offres, suffit à justifier en l'espèce la compétence arbitrale ».*

On doit approuver la conclusion du tribunal arbitral. Bien qu'il n'y ait pas eu un accord express entre Y et le soumissionnaire évincé, les parties ont bien exprimé leur consentement à l'arbitrage.

II — En ce qui concerne la recevabilité de l'action introduite par X, le tribunal arbitral a commencé par des précisions d'ordre général *(voir supra).* Il a distingué ensuite entre la demande de X tendant à faire constater l'illégalité de la décision de Y et celle qui tend à enjoindre à Y de lui adjuger les marchés pour lesquels elle a soumissionnés.

La première, qui s'est bornée à demander au tribunal de dire le droit pour aboutir à la constatation qu'une décision est illégale ou non, relève selon le tribunal de la mission essentielle d'un tribunal arbitral. Elle est donc recevable.

Quant à la seconde, elle porte sur l'étendue du contrôle juridictionnel sur une décision prise par Y. En effet, le tribunal arbitral doit déterminer s'il est en mesure de contrôler et de modifier la décision prise par Y d'adjuger le marché à d'autres soumissionnaires que X. Afin de se prononcer sur l'étendue de son pouvoir juridictionnel, le tribunal arbitral a examiné les règles applicables au litige, à savoir, les règles visées dans l'appel d'offres. Il constate qu'aucun des textes applicables ne précise les pouvoirs des arbitres et en particulier ne leur donne celui d'adresser des injonctions aux parties.

Ne disposant pas des pouvoirs d'amiable compositeur, le tribunal arbitral a défini la mission des arbitres comme consistant *« essentiellement à dire le droit, à constater s'il a été respecté ou non, à en tirer les conséquences quant aux droits subjectifs des parties. Ils ne comportent pas au fond, sauf clause ou disposition contraire, un pouvoir de commandement permettant d'adresser des injonctions aux parties de substituer une décision à une autre ou de faire échec à une exécution en cours. »*

L'approche du tribunal arbitral qui consiste à considérer comme irrecevable la demande faite par X est prudente. Tout en constatant que la décision de Y de ne pas attribuer les lots 2 et 3 à X était illégale, il ne pouvait pas pour autant résilier les marchés attribués aux sociétés P et TE afin de les accorder à X.

Faisant un parallèle avec les juridictions étatiques administratives, le tribunal constate que même si celles-ci étaient investies de la totalité du pouvoir juridictionnel, elles n'étaient pas non plus en mesure et en droit de prendre des décisions qui imposaient aux parties d'adopter un comportement déterminé. Aussi important que soit leur pouvoir, elles ne pouvaient enjoindre aux parties d'adopter une solution donnée sauf texte spécial ou principe constant. Ces limites s'imposent également à un tribunal arbitral.

Sauf disposition contraire des parties, le tribunal arbitre ne peut donc pas adresser des injonctions aux parties quel que soit leur statut.

III — Le rejet par le tribunal arbitral de la demande visant au prononcé des mesures conservatoires est également justifiée. La suspension immédiate de l'exécution des marchés litigieux demandée en l'espèce par la demanderesse ne pouvait aboutir car elle ne visait pas à préserver un « *statu quo* » mais à obtenir une partie de ce qui était demandé au fond, soit l'attribution des marchés.

Par ailleurs, l'attribution des marchés litigieux était déjà réalisée avant la requête complémentaire sur les mesures conservatoires. Par conséquent, une décision de suspendre l'exécution des marchés en cause porterait préjudice aux sociétés P et TE, attributaires des marchés visés et tiers à l'arbitrage. Le tribunal arbitral ne peut donc pas demander à Y de remettre en cause l'exécution des marchés en cours.

Quant à la demande de X sollicitant « *toute autre mesure conservatoire que le tribunal arbitral jugera utile* », celle-ci a été considérée comme irrecevable à défaut de précisions suffisantes. Il lui appartient en effet de déterminer les mesures conservatoires qu'elle vise ainsi que leur utilité.

Il est intéressant de rappeler que les pouvoirs des arbitres de prononcer des mesures conservatoires étaient implicites dans le Règlement CCI de 1975 (1988). La demande faite par X procédait d'une interprétation de l'article 8 (5) qui autorisait « *exceptionnellement*» les parties à « *demander à toute autorité judiciaire des mesures provisoires ou conservatoires (. . .) sans préjudice du pouvoir réservé à l'arbitre à ce titre*». Ceci signifiait que les parties devaient solliciter de telles mesures auprès des arbitres en l'absence de circonstances exceptionnelles. Une telle interprétation ne correspondait pas à la pratique car les arbitres estimaient généralement, sauf dispositions expresses contraires de la loi de procédure, qu'ils étaient autorisés à prendre de telles mesures « *à titre de directives aux parties à l'arbitrage*» même si le Règlement CCI de 1975 (1988) ne contenait pas de dispositions expresses à cet égard. Cette ambiguïté est désormais supprimée avec le nouveau Règlement CCI de 1998 dont l'article 23 (1) prévoit expressément que le tribunal arbitral peut « *ordonner toute mesure conservatoire ou provisoire qu'il considère appropriée*». Le tribunal arbitral peut également subordonner cette décision à la constitution de garanties adéquates par le requérant *(v. notamment S. Jarvin, « Eléments de la procédure d'arbitrage*», *Bull. arb. CCI, Supplément spécial, Le Règlement d'arbitrage de la CCI de 1998 — Actes de la conférence de présentation du nouveau Règlement, p. 37; Y. Derains et E. Schwartz, A Guide to the New ICC Rules of Arbitration, Kluwer 1998, p. 272; Craig, Park & Paulsson's Annotated Guide to the 1998 ICC Arbitration Rules with commentary, Oceana Publications, Inc./ICC 1998, p. 137; Supplément au Bull. arb., Mesures conservatoires et provisoires en matière d'arbitrage international, Publication CCI n° 519, 1993).*

IV — Dans l'affaire ci-dessus rapportée, la procédure relative au marché était déterminée par les règles expressément visées par le dossier d'appel d'offres et le Cahier général des Charges (CGC) des marchés publics de travaux et de fournitures financés par le Fonds européen de développement.

La procédure relative au marché peut être synthétisée, pour l'essentiel, en quatre phases:

— la phase de présélection aboutissant à la désignation des entreprises admises à participer à l'appel d'offres;

— les recommandations de la commission de dépouillement;

— le choix du soumissionnaire par Y;

— l'intervention de la Commission européenne.

La commission de dépouillement établit seulement une proposition car la, décision finale est prise par Y qui envoie la lettre de marché à l'attributaire. La Commission des Communautés européennes, quant à elle, ne fait qu'examiner la proposition en vue de l'attribution du marché.

Dans un premier temps, le tribunal va se prononcer sur l'étendue de son pouvoir de contrôle sur la décision prise par Y. Il a estimé ainsi qu'il pouvait l'exercer pleinement sur le respect des règles et principes applicables en ce qui concerne la procédure à suivre pour l'attribution du marché, l'égalité entre les candidats, la nature des conditions à remplir pour la recevabilité des offres, et la nature des critères à prendre en considération pour l'appréciation et la comparaison des offres.

Il en est de même pour l'exactitude matérielle des faits pris en considération pour l'exclusion des offres et l'attribution du marché.

En revanche, le contrôle du tribunal arbitral devait être plus restreint en ce qui concerne les appréciations techniques, et l'appréciation de l'offre économiquement la plus favorable. Dans ces derniers cas, le tribunal arbitral devait se limiter à l'appréciation de l'erreur manifeste, faisant apparaître l'arbitraire de l'administration.

Le tribunal arbitral constate en l'occurrence que la procédure a été régulière.

Avant d'examiner la question d'une éventuelle discrimination à l'égard de X, le tribunal arbitral a vérifié si une tentative de corruption a bien été exercée comme allégué par X. Sur la base des pièces produites par les parties, il constate qu'un intermédiaire connaissait effectivement le projet, la procédure et le Secrétaire exécutif de l'époque. Il avait ainsi proposé son intervention à la demanderesse moyennant une commission dont le pourcentage n'était pas inhabituel dans certaines pratiques du commerce international. Mais au-delà de cette constatation, il n'y a eu que des suspicions sur lesquelles il ne pouvait pas fonder sa décision.

Le problème du tribunal arbitral dans un tel cas est réel. Le doute ne suffit pas à permettre au tribunal arbitral de prendre une décision tant que la corruption n'a pas été prouvée (*voir en ce sens, sentence CCI n° 9333 JDI 2002, p. 1093, observations Jarvin; M. Scherrer, « International Arbitration and Corruption — Synopsis of Selected Arbitral Awards », Bulletin ASA 2001, vol. 19, n° 4, p. 710*).

Quant à la présence du Secrétaire exécutif de Y, lors de la phase finale des délibérations de la Commission technique, elle n'a pas pu être retenue comme indice par le tribunal arbitral. En effet, à défaut de disposition contraire du dossier d'appel d'offres ou du droit applicable, la présence à Bruxelles du Secrétaire exécutif n'était pas fautive. Elle l'aurait été en cas de véritables immixtions dans les travaux de la Commission technique, ce qui n'a pas été prouvé en l'espèce. Dans tous les cas, elle aurait été très difficile à établir pour X.

En revanche, le tribunal arbitral constate qu'une discrimination a été effectivement commise par le Secrétaire exécutif de Y à l'égard de X, concernant le service après-vente du lot n° 3 et a examiné la réparation éventuelle de son dommage qui doit être certain, établi et en relation causale avec la faute commise. En l'espèce, le préjudice de X se décomposait en plusieurs éléments: le coût de sa participation à l'appel d'offres, le manque à gagner, les préjudices économiques résultant de son exclusion, le coût de la procédure qu'elle a intentée devant la Cour de Justice des Communautés Européennes et les frais d'arbitrage. L'analyse du tribunal arbitral tendant à constater l'inexistence de dommages réparables, est claire et ne nécessite pas de commentaires particuliers.

V. — Le manque à gagner mérite une attention particulière. Le rappel du tribunal arbitral des principes en matière de réparation de la perte d'une chance est essentiel. Le tribunal arbitral indique ainsi que la perte d'une chance est en principe indemnisable. C'est le cas, par exemple en droit français et belge de la responsabilité (*voir les références bibliographiques citées dans la sentence arbitrale: Mazeaud, Traité de la responsabilité civile, 5ᵉ éd., n° 219; Ghestin, Traité de droit civil, La responsabilité, par Viney, 1982, n° 278 et s.*). Elle doit être cependant « sérieuse » (*Viney, op. cit. et n° 283*) ou « réelle» (*Dirix, Het begrip schade, Bruxelles, 1984, p. 83 et s. et réf.*) et ne peut consister en une simple éventualité. Par ailleurs, le caractère sérieux ou non de la chance perdue, ainsi que l'évaluation du préjudice subi, relève de l'appréciation souveraine du juge de fond (*Cass. belge, 4 mars 1975, Pas. 1975 — I — 682 et obs. Dalcq, Rev. crit. Jur. belge 1981, p. 123, n° 111, qui écrit même — en un apparent paradoxe — que la chance indemnisable doit être « certaine »*).

Le tribunal arbitral observe que ces principes sont appliqués en matière de marchés publics et cite un certain nombre de jurisprudences belges et françaises (*v. par exemple en droit belge, Flamme, Commentaire pratique de la réglementation des marchés publics, éd. 1986, n° 64*). Selon l'arrêt du Conseil d'Etat français invoqué par la demanderesse (*CE, 28 mars 1980, Centre Hospitalier de Seclin, JCP 1981, n° 19542, obs, P. L. et réf. — arrêt relatif à un refus illégal de l'administration d'autoriser une entreprise à soumissionner à une adjudication restreinte, hypothèse donc très différente de celle en l'espèce*), le manque à gagner peut être réparé lorsqu'il y avait une « chance sérieuse d'emporter l'adjudication des travaux ». La chance sérieuse est également requise en matière d'appels d'offres (*v. CE, 4 juin 1976, Desforets, Rec. Lebon, p. 301; CE, 13 juin 1979, OLGEMA, Rec. Lebon, p. 403*); Bréchon (*in Bréchon et al., Droit des marchés publics, op. cit., III, 630.3, p.9*) considère qu'il faut « démontrer que l'entreprise aurait eu une chance sérieuse, voire très sérieuse d'emporter le marché ». L'exigence d'une chance sérieuse ou réelle est appréciée au cas par le juge administratif sur la base de tous les éléments utiles des dossiers ou d'un seul élément (*Bréchon, op. cit., p. 10: qualification, nombre candidats, prix . . .*). Elle se justifie d'autant plus en matière d'appels d'offres restreints où un soumissionnaire — fut-il le plus intéressant — n'a pas pour autant un droit automatique à l'attribution du marché. En l'espèce, le tribunal arbitral a estimé que la demanderesse n'avait pas vraiment de chances sérieuses de se voir attribuer les marchés afférents au lot n° 3. Il a rejeté en conséquence la demande en réparation de la demanderesse.

La décision des arbitres s'inscrit dans le courant de la jurisprudence arbitrale internationale qui subordonne logiquement la réparation à la certitude du dommage. Les arbitres apprécient toutefois avec souplesse l'existence du dommage en tenant compte de la prévisibilité du dommage, des aléas qui peuvent l'affecter et plus généralement des circonstances particulières à chaque cas (*v. en ce sens, J. Ortscheidt, « La réparation du dommage dans l'arbitrage commercial international », Dalloz 2001, p. 19 et s.; v. dans un même sens l'article 7.4.3 (1) des principes relatifs aux contrats du commerce international d'Unidroit; v. également l'article 4.501 (2) des principes européens du droit des contrats de la Commission sur le droit européen des contrats*). En l'espèce, le refus des arbitres d'accorder la réparation du manque à gagner sollicitée par X était justifié dans la mesure où X n'a pas réussi à démontrer qu'elle aurait vraisemblablement et raisonnablement obtenu les marchés visés, même si elle avait fait les offres les plus intéressantes.

S. J.

Sentence finale rendue dans l'affaire n° 10422 en 2001 (original en langue française).

I. — Compétence. — Organisation de la procédure. — Examen préalable de la compétence de l'arbitre. — Devoir de l'arbitre de se prononcer sur sa compétence par une sentence partielle.

II. — Compétence. — Clause pathologique. — Clause attributive de juridiction. — Règles de procédure. — Interprétation. — Commune intention des parties. — principes UNIDROIT relatifs aux contrats du commerce international. — Participation à la procédure. — Acceptation de la compétence.

III. — Droit applicable. — Absence de choix des parties. — Lex mercatoria. — principes UNIDROIT relatifs aux contrats du commerce international.

IV. — Contrat. — Négociation. — Formation. — Défaut d'identité de l'offre et de l'acceptation. — Accord partiel. — Validité.

V. — Contrat. — Durée déterminée. — Résiliation. — Modalités. — Bonne foi.

VI. — Contrat. — Résiliation. — Faute. — Effet. — Calcul du préjudice.

La demanderesse et la défenderesse avaient signé deux contrats de distribution exclusive ayant pour objet la revente des produits de la défenderesse par la demanderesse sur deux territoires distincts (A) et (B). Les deux contrats avaient été conclus pour une durée renouvelable, de cinq ans à compter de sa date de signature pour l'un (A) et de trois ans à compter de sa date de signature pour l'autre (B). Treize mois après la signature des contrats, la défenderesse informait la demanderesse qu'elle avait confié à une société tierce (X) « *le management, le suivi et le contrôle* » des produits contractuels pour un territoire englobant les deux territoires définis dans les contrats de distribution exclusive. La demanderesse refusait de traiter avec une autre société que la défenderesse, s'opposait à la modification des conditions de paiement des commandes des produits contractuels du fait d'un transfert de certaines obligations de la défenderesse à (X) et exigeait de la défenderesse qu'elle exécute ses obligations de livraison, notamment en ce qui concerne deux commandes de produits passées par la demanderesse à la défenderesse. S'ensuivit une négociation portant sur la modification des conditions de livraison et de paiement des produits, et la prorogation du contrat conclu pour cinq ans. Ayant sollicité de la demanderesse la communication des chiffres d'affaires relatifs à la vente des produits contractuels pour les deux dernières années et constaté, à la réception de ces derniers, qu'ils étaient inférieurs à ceux prévus contractuellement, la défenderesse résilia les deux contrats de distribution la liant à la demanderesse. Cette dernière engagea alors une procédure d'arbitrage.

Au cours de l'échange de mémoires, la défenderesse limita son argumentation à la contestation de la compétence de l'arbitre unique et demanda à ce dernier de se prononcer exclusivement sur la compétence par une sentence partielle.

Selon l'arbitre, la défenderesse « *a demandé dans son mémoire (du) [date] au Tribunal Arbitral de rendre une sentence intérimaire sur la compétence, avant d'aborder le fond du litige et a réitéré cette demande oralement dans l'audience de plaidoiries.*

Le Tribunal arbitral confirme la position déjà prise pendant la procédure et déclare cette demande tardive et par conséquent irrecevable.

Les parties et l'arbitre ont établi d'un commun accord, lors de l'audience du [date], un calendrier qui faisait référence à la procédure arbitrale dans son ensemble et non pas seulement à la question de la compétence.

Les parties ont échangé leurs mémoires conformément à ce calendrier et, seulement à la fin de cette phase, par un mémoire envoyé après l'échéance du délai pour soumettre les mémoires, [la défenderesse] a demandé à l'arbitre de statuer préalablement, par une sentence partielle, sur sa compétence, et de réserver la décision sur le fond à une phase successive de la procédure arbitrale.

Il est par conséquent évident que cette demande ne peut pas être accueillie.

En tout cas, même si la demande en question avait été présentée à temps, le Tribunal arbitral aurait eu le droit de décider, à sa discrétion, de l'accepter ou de la refuser ».

L'arbitre examine ensuite la question de sa compétence à connaître du litige. Il commence par rappeler que 1'*« article 12 des deux contrats contient la clause suivante: (. . .)*

12. FOR COMPETENT

12.1. Le présent contrat, comme toutes ses dispositions, seront régies par la "CHAMBRE DE COMMERCE INTERNATIONALE" ou à son défaut par une législation neutre définie d'un commun accord entre les parties, mais qui en aucun cas ne pourront être les Tribunaux de justice des pays respectifs des parties contractantes.

12.2. Toutes les interprétations que ce contrat nécessiterait, ainsi que les litiges qui pourraient surgir entre les parties contractantes, seront soumises aux Juges et aux Tribunaux des Cours définies au point 12.1, ceci impliquant que les deux parties renoncent à se prévaloir de tout autre for, dans le cas où ils existeraient ».

Puis, l'arbitre interprète cette clause *« en recherchant la commune intention des parties, sans s'arrêter au sens littéral des termes, selon un principe largement répandu et aussi repris dans les principes Unidroit à l'article 4.1, qui dit:*

"1. Le contrat s'interprète selon la commune intention des parties.

2. Faute de pouvoir déceler la commune intention des parties, le contrat s'interprète selon le sens que lui donnerait une personne raisonnable de même qualité placée dans la même situation".

Dans l'application de ce critère il faut considérer que les personnes qui ont rédigé et négocié la clause n'étaient pas des juristes et n'avaient pas une idée précise de la signification (au point de vue juridique) des notions de for compétent, arbitrage et loi applicable.

(. . .) Pour comprendre la signification de la clause il faut donc se placer dans la condition des parties (ou d'une personne raisonnable de la même qualité [. . .]), qui, n'étant pas des juristes ont tendance à confondre les notions de loi applicable et de juridiction, leur souci principal étant celui de mettre en place une solution la plus neutre possible pour la solution d'éventuels litiges.

Or, si l'on lit l'article 12 dans cette perspective, la référence à la Chambre de Commerce Internationale, contenue dans l'article 12.1 doit être comprise en premier lieu comme visant à établir la juridiction, ce qui du reste est confirmé par la dernière partie de la phrase, lorsqu'on poursuit en disant: "(. . .) qui en aucun cas ne pourront être les Tribunaux de justice des pays respectifs des parties contractantes".

En d'autres termes, lorsque les parties déclarent vouloir soumettre le contrat à une loi applicable (de la CCI) autre que les tribunaux des pays respectifs (en mettant sur le même plan la loi et la juridiction), il apparaît qu'elles voulaient se référer à la juridiction de la CCI et par conséquent à l'arbitrage de la CCI.

Ceci est ultérieurement confirmé par le titre de l'article ("For compétent"), ainsi que par le fait que l'article 12.2 renvoie aux tribunaux définis à l'article 12.1, ce qui confirme

610

que, dans l'esprit des parties, la fonction de l'article 12.1 était de déterminer la juridiction. La défenderesse a fait valoir que la référence à une législation qui n'existe pas (celle de la CCI) ou à une législation neutre qui, toutefois, devait être définie (et n'a pas été définie) par les parties, rendrait l'article 12.2 inopérant. Toutefois, cela reviendrait à attendre des parties une subtilité juridique qu'elles n'avaient certainement pas: il est beaucoup plus raisonnable d'attribuer aux parties la volonté de faire référence à la CCI comme ''juridiction'' et de considérer la référence à la loi applicable comme une imprécision due à leur impréparation juridique.

Pour conclure: si l'on regarde l'article 12 dans son ensemble et si l'on cherche à déterminer sa portée substantielle (au-delà de la signification juridique précise des termes utilisés), on voit que le souci des parties était de régler leurs différends éventuels d'une façon neutre en faisant recours à la Chambre de Commerce Internationale, qu'elles considéraient comme un instrument notoirement approprié à ces fins. Et, si les parties ont voulu attribuer à la CCI la résolution de leurs litiges éventuels, cela ne peut que signifier qu'elles entendaient avoir recours à l'arbitrage, étant donné que la CCI est universellement connue comme institution d'arbitrage et que les parties elles-mêmes avaient prévu, dans un contrat précédent, la compétence arbitrale de la CCI.

Cette interprétation de l'article 12 est en outre conforme au principe de l'effet utile, contenu dans l'article 4.5 des principes Unidroit, selon lequel:

> *''Les clauses d'un contrat s'interprètent dans le sens avec lequel elles peuvent toutes avoir quelque effet, plutôt que dans le sens avec lequel certaines n'en auraient aucun''.*

Or, si on devait interpréter l'article 12 comme ne contenant pas une clause arbitrale CCI, les parties ne pourraient ni recourir à l'arbitrage, ni aux tribunaux étatiques normalement compétents (c'est-à-dire les tribunaux du défendeur ou du lieu d'exécution des obligations contractuelles), étant donné que leur compétence a été expressément exclue par la clause en question. Ceci porterait à priver les parties de toute possibilité d'action en cas de litige, à moins de considérer la clause dans son ensemble comme ne produisant aucun effet.

En ce qui concerne l'argument de la demanderesse que [la défenderesse] aurait accepté l'arbitrage de la CCI en proposant la nomination d'un arbitre, il faut relever que la participation à la procédure arbitrale n'implique pas acceptation de la compétence arbitrale si la partie qui conteste la compétence arbitrale maintient, tout en participant à la procédure, l'exception d'incompétence, comme c'est le cas ici. En outre, la question n'a pas besoin d'être décidée, une fois que l'existence et la validité de la clause arbitrale a été établie.

Par conséquent le Tribunal arbitral affirme sa compétence à décider le litige ».

L'arbitre unique recherche alors le droit applicable au fond du litige et observe que « *l'article 12 des Contrats fait référence à la CCI et à une « législation neutre définie d'un commun accord entre les parties ». Etant donné qu'une législation de la CCI n'existe pas, et que les parties n'ont pas défini d'un commun accord une législation neutre, il faut conclure que les parties n'ont pas fait un choix exprès de la loi applicable.*

Le Tribunal arbitral devra par conséquent déterminer la loi applicable conformément à la seconde phrase de l'article 17(1) du Règlement d'arbitrage de la CCI qui dit que:

> « *A défaut de choix par les parties des règles de droit applicables, l'arbitre appliquera les règles de droit qu'il juge appropriées* ».

Le Tribunal arbitral estime que, pour déterminer les règles de droit les plus appropriées, il faut tenir compte du fait que les parties désiraient une solution neutre.

Or, à défaut d'indication expresse d'un tiers droit national, la solution la plus appropriée dans le cas où il apparaît que les parties désirent une solution neutre est d'appliquer les règles et principes généraux en matière de contrats internationaux ou lex mercatoria.

Dans ce contexte on pourra se référer pour les questions touchant à la réglementation générale des contrats aux « principes relatifs aux contrats de commerce international » de l'Unidroit, qui représentent — exception faite pour quelques règles très particulières (comme par exemple les articles en matière de hardship: v. sentence arbitrale dans l'affaire CCI n° 8873 du 1998, Journal droit int., 1998, 1017) — un « restatement » fidèle des règles que les entreprises opérant dans le commerce international considèrent comme conformes à leurs intérêts et attentes. Ceci est reconnu par de nombreuses sentences arbitrales qui ont appliqué les principes Unidroit comme expression de la lex mercatoria ou des usages du commerce international: v. par exemple, les sentences partielles dans l'affaire CCI n° 7110, Bull. Arb. CCI 1999, p. 40-50; la sentence dans l'affaire CCI n° 7375, Mealeys International Arbitration Report, vol. 11/n° 12 (décembre 1996), p. A1-A69; la sentence dans l'affaire CCI n° 8502, Bull. Arb. CCI 2/1999, p. 74-77.

« Le Tribunal arbitral appliquera par conséquent les règles et principes généralement reconnus dans le commerce international (lex mercatoria) et notamment les principes Unidroit, dans la mesure où ils apparaissent comme une transposition fidèle des règles reconnues comme applicables aux contrats internationaux par les commerçants engagés dans le commerce international ».

L'arbitre aborde ensuite les questions de fond soumises à son appréciation.

La première de ces questions est la violation alléguée des stipulations contractuelles par la défenderesse du fait de son refus de livrer les produits commandés et les conséquences de cette violation.

S'attachant en premier lieu à la période précédant l'ouverture des négociations entre les parties, l'arbitre rappelle que la défenderesse « *a demandé à [la demanderesse] de payer les commandes en cours en avance, nonobstant la clause contractuelle [numéro] qui prévoyait expressément que le paiement devait être fait à 120 jours de la date d'expédition. [la défenderesse] avait justifié cette demande comme suit:*

> *"Etant donné les montants importants dus par [la demanderesse] à [la société X], [la défenderesse] ne peut expédier vos commandes sans recevoir un paiement par avance".*

Cette conduite de [la défenderesse] est en principe contraire à une règle fondamentale du droit des contrats, la règle pacta sunt servanda, reprise aussi dans les principes Unidroit à l'article 1.3, par lequel:

> *"Le contrat valablement formé lie ceux qui l'ont conclu. Les parties ne peuvent le modifier ou y mettre fin que selon ses dispositions, d'un commun accord ou encore pour des causes énoncées dans ces principes".*

Il ne s'agit bien entendu pas d'un principe absolu, et il est concevable, dans des situations particulières, qu'un fournisseur puisse être exonéré du respect strict des conditions de paiement convenues. Ainsi, il serait contraire au principe de bonne foi d'obliger un fournisseur à continuer à livrer ses produits à son distributeur, sans pouvoir au moins prétendre qu'il donne des garanties de paiement, lorsqu'il y a des motifs justifiés de craindre que ce dernier ne paiera pas la marchandise à l'échéance ».

L'arbitre retient que si « *une certaine prudence avant d'accepter les ordres* » était compréhensible au regard de certains éléments, comme notamment l'importance du montant des commandes passées dans les mois précédant la résiliation et les relations d'affaires délicates que la demanderesse entretenait avec une société du groupe (X) qu'elle avait assigné en justice, « *ces éléments n'étaient pas suffisants pour justifier la décision unilatérale de [la défenderesse] de changer les conditions de paiement d'un concessionnaire dont la solvabilité n'était pas en question. Dans ces conditions, le refus pur et simple de [la défenderesse] de livrer aux conditions contractuelles constituait certainement une inexécution du contrat ».*

L'arbitre envisage en deuxième lieu les négociations entre les parties et leur aboutissement. Au sujet de l'obligation de livraison et de paiement du prix des deux commandes, l'arbitre retient que la défenderesse a accepté sans réserves les propositions de la demanderesse, à « *la seule différence, tout-à-fait négligeable, (. . .) que [la défenderesse] a accepté de payer la différence entre le fret aérien et le fret maritime alors que [la demanderesse] lui demandait de prendre en charge le fret aérien tout entier.*

Ceci ne s'oppose toutefois pas à ce que l'accord puisse être considéré comme validement conclu. En effet dans le contexte de la lex mercatoria le principe de la correspondance entre offre et acceptation n'est pas imposé d'une façon rigide et il est accepté (conformément à ce qui est l'opinion courante des commerçants internationaux) qu'une acceptation contenant des modifications ou intégrations donne lieu à un accord si les modifications sont de faible importance. Ainsi, l'article 2.11, alinéa 2, des principes Unidroit, dit que:

> *"(. . .) la réponse qui se veut acceptation mais qui contient des éléments complémentaires ou différents n'altérant pas substantiellement les termes de l'offre, constitue une acceptation, à moins que l'auteur de l'offre, sans retard indu, n'exprime son désaccord sur ces éléments. S'il ne le fait pas, les termes du contrat sont ceux de l'offre avec les modifications énoncées dans l'acceptation."*

Dans le cas d'espèce, [la demanderesse] n'a pas contesté la modification contenue dans l'acceptation de [la défenderesse] et l'accord sur les modalités de paiement et de livraison des deux commandes peut par conséquent être considéré comme conclu aux conditions (non contestées) de l'acceptation de [la défenderesse] ». Dès lors qu'existait un accord entre les parties, toute nouvelle proposition de modification de ce dernier formulée par la demanderesse devait nécessairement être acceptée par la défenderesse pour se voir conférer force obligatoire, la défenderesse étant libre d'accepter ou de refuser une telle proposition.

Au sujet des commandes futures, l'arbitre retient que les parties se sont accordées pour modifier les modalités de paiement. Au paiement différé à 120 jours était substitué un paiement à l'avance moyennant une remise de 5% correspondant au coût de l'argent dans le territoire contractuel. Aucun accord sur « *les critères à utiliser pour fixer le montant de la remise en cas de modification du taux d'escompte* » n'avait cependant été atteint. Répondant à la question de savoir s'il y a eu accord sur les conditions de paiement des commandes futures, l'arbitre énonce qu'« *il faut considérer que nous sommes en présence d'une négociation par étapes, c'est-à-dire d'une négociation qui porte les parties à arriver à un accord par négociations successives. Dans un cadre de ce genre il est possible d'arriver à des accords partiels (qui laissent ouvertes certaines questions), sauf dans le cas où les parties ont voulu subordonner leur consentement à un accord global couvrant tous les détails.*

Ce principe est reconnu par l'article 2.13 des principes Unidroit, selon lequel:

> *"Lorsqu'une partie, au cours des négociations, exige que la conclusion du contrat soit subordonnée à un accord sur certaines questions relatives au fond ou à la forme, le contrat n'est conclu que si les parties parviennent à un accord sur ces questions."*

En effet, cette règle implique, a contrario, que l'accord sur une partie des questions en discussion lie les parties pour ce qui est convenu, à moins qu'il n'y ait la volonté de subordonner la conclusion du contrat à la solution des questions laissées ouvertes. Ceci correspond d'ailleurs aux usages et à la pratique du commerce international, dans laquelle il est fréquent de conclure des contrats "par étapes" et de considérer valable l'accord sur la partie convenue, avec une obligation des parties de se mettre d'accord sur les aspects restés ouverts: v. par exemple la sentence arbitrale dans l'affaire CCI n° 8331, Bull. Arb. CCI 2/1999, p. 67-70.

Or, dans le cas d'espèce, il est certain que les parties étaient d'accord sur le fait que la remise devait être déterminée sur la base du taux d'escompte [en vigueur dans le territoire contractuel] (. . .). On ne peut pas douter que les parties étaient arrivées à un accord (au moins implicitement) sur le fait que la remise devait être rapportée au taux d'escompte [en vigueur dans le territoire contractuel] sur 120 jours. En effet, la référence dans la lettre de [la défenderesse] du [date] au "taux d'escompte de 5%" (sans précisions ultérieures) n'implique pas un refus de ce qui était déjà acquis (c'est-à-dire du principe que 5% était calculé en relation au taux d'escompte [en vigueur dans le territoire contractuel]) mais simplement l'absence d'une réponse à la proposition ultérieure de [la demanderesse] de ne procéder à la modification du taux de 5%, établi provisoirement, que dans le cas où le taux annuel [en vigueur dans le territoire contractuel] aurait varié de plus de 0,5%.

Or, il est évident que l'absence d'accord sur un détail de si faible importance ne peut pas mettre en discussion l'accord global des parties sur les nouvelles conditions de paiement et de livraison.»

Examinant en troisième lieu la réparation du préjudice causé à la demanderesse par le refus de la défenderesse de livrer les produits, l'arbitre rappelle d'une part que la non-livraison par la défenderesse constitue une inexécution contractuelle mais d'autre part que les négociations entre les parties et l'accord sur les nouvelles conditions de paiement et de livraison qui en résultent constitue une transaction ayant notamment pour objet de réparer le préjudice subi par la demanderesse. La demanderesse ne peut donc pas de nouveau réclamer réparation de ce préjudice, ni un dédommagement pour le préjudice occasionné par le refus de la défenderesse de livrer des produits aux conditions originelles, alors que ces conditions avaient été modifiées par une nouvel accord des parties.

La deuxième de ces questions de fond est la résiliation des contrats par la défenderesse. L'arbitre commence par répondre à l'argument de la demanderesse selon lequel « *la résiliation ne pouvait être prononcée sans avoir mis au préalable [la demanderesse] en demeure, en lui donnant la possibilité de remédier à ses prétendus manquements* ». L'arbitre répond que « *cette position serait justifiée s'il y avait (comme il arrive fréquemment dans la pratique contractuelle, surtout anglo-saxonne) une clause par laquelle la partie qui procède à la résiliation du contrat est tenue de donner à l'autre partie un terme pour qu'elle puisse remédier à l'infraction. Toutefois, ceci n'étant pas le cas ici, il faut se référer à la règle générale, retenue aussi par l'article 7.3.2, § 1, des principes Unidroit selon lequel:*

"La résolution du contrat s'opère par notification au débiteur".

Par conséquent, l'absence d'une mise en demeure préalable ne peut pas infirmer la validité de la résiliation ».

L'arbitre examine ensuite l'objection de la demanderesse tenant à la tardiveté de l'invocation par la défenderesse de la non-réalisation du chiffre d'affaires pour l'avant dernière année précédant la résiliation. L'arbitre décide que la contestation pour cette année est tardive.

« *Le principe de bonne foi impose à une partie qui entend résilier le contrat à cause d'un manquement de l'autre partie d'informer l'autre partie de son intention dans un terme raisonnablement bref à partir du moment où il a eu connaissance du manquement. Ce principe est contenu aussi dans les principes Unidroit. Ainsi, l'article 7.3.2, § 2, dit que:*

"Lorsque l'offre d'exécution est tardive ou que l'exécution n'est pas conforme, le créancier perd le droit de résoudre le contrat s'il ne fait parvenir à l'autre partie une notification dans un délai raisonnable à partir du moment où il a eu, ou aurait dû avoir, connaissance de l'offre ou de la non-conformité."

Or, dans le cas d'espèce, [la défenderesse] savait dès le commencement de l'année [au cours de laquelle a eu lieu la résiliation] que [la demanderesse] n'avait pas atteint les chiffres d'affaires prévus pour l'année [précédant celle au cours de laquelle a eu lieu la résiliation] et n'a jamais contesté ce fait, jusqu'à [la date de résiliation].

Par conséquent, seule la contestation relative à l'année [au cours de laquelle a eu lieu la résiliation] sera prise en considération ci-après ».

L'arbitre poursuit en abordant le caractère justifié ou non de la résiliation.

« Le principe qu'un contrat à terme peut être résilié avant son échéance en présence de motifs graves constitue un principe largement reconnu dans le commerce international. Aussi les principes Unidroit reconnaissent, dans des termes généraux, à l'article 7.3.1, § 1, que:

> *"Une partie peut résoudre le contrat s'il y a inexécution essentielle de la part de l'autre partie".*

(. . .) dans le cas examiné ici il n'y a pas besoin de se référer à la règle générale, étant donné qu'une clause contractuelle expresse [numéro d'article] prévoit la possibilité de résilier le contrat avant son échéance en cas d'infraction grave à une de ses clauses.

Il s'agit alors de voir si les manquements de [la demanderesse] invoqués par [la défenderesse] constituent une infraction grave aux Contrats, pouvant justifier leur résiliation avant l'échéance.

Contrairement à une pratique contractuelle répandue, les Contrats ne spécifient pas expressément que la non-réalisation des chiffres d'affaires convenus autorise le concédant à résilier le contrat. L'article [numéro] des Contrats entre [la demanderesse] et [la défenderesse] se limite à prévoir des chiffres annuels d'achat (. . .), sans préciser les conséquences de la non-réalisation éventuelle des achats annuels indiqués. Ceci signifie que la non-réalisation des chiffres d'affaires prévus ne peut justifier la résiliation que dans la mesure où elle constitue une infraction grave à une clause contractuelle.

Etant donné qu'une infraction à une clause implique nécessairement la violation d'une obligation prévue par cette clause, il est essentiel d'établir si l'article [numéro] vise à établir une obligation d'achat, ou au contraire, une simple prévision non obligatoire.

Le terme utilisé ("presupuesto") semble indiquer des objectifs plutôt que des minima. D'autre part, la présence d'une signature des parties à côté de la clause en question, souligne l'importance que les parties attribuaient à cet aspect.

(. . .) [Il] faut aussi relever que la clause, qui se limite à dire que les parties ont convenu certains objectifs de vente, ne contient pas une obligation pour [la demanderesse] de garantir que ce résultat soit atteint: si telle avait été l'intention des parties, elles auraient simplement convenu que [la demanderesse] s'engageait à acheter les quantités annuelles prévues dans la clause.

Dans ces conditions, la non-réalisation des objectifs d'achat ne constitue pas en tant que telle une inexécution contractuelle et ne peut pas être par conséquent considérée en elle-même comme un juste motif de résiliation anticipée.

Or, dans le cas d'espèce il n'y a pas de preuve que la non-réalisation du chiffre d'affaires soit dû à des raisons imputables à [la demanderesse] plutôt qu'à des conditions de marché adverses ou à la longue négociation sur les nouveaux termes de paiement (qui avait été déclenchée par le refus, injustifié, de fourniture de la part de [la défenderesse]). Dans ces conditions la simple référence à la non-réalisation des objectifs de vente ne peut pas être considérée comme un motif suffisant pour la résiliation anticipée d'un contrat qui n'était même pas arrivé à la moitié de son terme ».

Selon l'arbitre, l'attitude de la demanderesse aurait tout au plus pu justifier une mise en demeure et une sommation de s'expliquer sur ses intentions futures. Aucune inexécution contractuelle grave ne pouvait être imputée à la demanderesse. Il s'ensuit que la résiliation est fautive. Dès lors, quels sont les effets d'une telle résiliation? L'arbitre observe que « *la question des effets d'une résiliation abusive d'un contrat à terme est abordé d'une façon différente dans les différents systèmes juridiques: dans quelques pays (surtout de civil law) on considère la résiliation abusive comme nonproductive d'effets, avec la conséquence que le contrat continue à être en vigueur et les parties continuent à être tenues de respecter leurs obligations; dans d'autres législations (particulièrement dans les pays de common law), on attribue à la résiliation l'effet de faire cesser la relation contractuelle, et l'on fait dépendre du caractère abusif de celle-ci uniquement l'obligation pour la partie qui l'a résilié abusivement de dédommager l'autre partie pour le préjudice qui en découle.*

Cette dernière approche, qui a l'avantage de ne pas laisser subsister de situations d'incertitude quant aux effets de la résiliation sur la poursuite de la relation contractuelle, est normalement retenue dans le droit du commerce international. Aussi les principes Unidroit semblent confirmer ce point de vue en prévoyant à l'article 7.3.2, § 1, que:

> *"La résolution du contrat s'opère par notification au débiteur".*

et à l'article 7.3.5, § 1, que:

> *"La résolution du contrat libère pour l'avenir les parties de leurs obligations respectives".*

Le Tribunal arbitral estime que cette dernière solution correspond aux règles et principes applicables dans le commerce international et que, par conséquent, les conséquences du caractère abusif de la résiliation se limitent à l'obligation de la partie qui a effectué la résiliation abusive de réparer le préjudice ainsi causé à l'autre partie ». Les prétentions de la demanderesse tendant à faire exécuter les obligations de livraison et de respect de l'exclusivité stipulés aux contrats sont rejetées.

L'arbitre détermine ensuite le montant du préjudice de la demanderesse. « *Comme il est établi dans l'article 7.4.2 des principes Unidroit:*

> *"Le créancier a droit à la réparation intégrale du préjudice qu'il a subi du fait de l'inexécution. Le préjudice comprend la perte qu'il a subie et le bénéfice dont il a été privé, compte tenu de tout gain résultant pour le créancier d'une dépense ou d'une perte évitée".*

Or, le bénéfice que [la demanderesse] a perdu à cause de l'interruption du contrat, et par conséquent des livraisons de [la défenderesse] n'est pas la marge brute sur le prix de vente, mais le bénéfice net, après déduction de tous les frais encourus.

Ce principe est généralement reconnu dans la jurisprudence arbitrale: v. sentence arbitrale dans l'affaire CCI n° 1250 (in Jarvin, Derains, Recueil des sentences arbitrales de la CCI 1974-1985, p. 30-33) concernant un concessionnaire libanais pour lequel les arbitres ont reconnu un dédommagement basé sur le "average net profit"; sentence arbitrale dans l'affaire CCI n° 5418 (in Jarvin, Derains, Arnaldez, Recueil des sentences arbitrales de la CCI 1986-1990, p. 132), se référant au "net profit"; sentence arbitrale dans l'affaire CCI n° 8362 (in Yearbook Commercial Arbitration, XXII-1997, p. 164-177), qui considère comme dommage les "lost net profits".

Etant donné qu'aucune indication n'a été fournie pour établir la marge nette, le Tribunal arbitral estime devoir utiliser le critère contenu dans l'article 7.4.3, § 3, des principes Unidroit, selon lequel:

> *"Le préjudice dont le montant ne peut être établi avec un degré suffisant de certitude est évalué à la discrétion du tribunal".*

Pour cette évaluation le Tribunal arbitral considérera d'une part la valeur des produits achetés par [la demanderesse] auprès de [la défenderesse] et d'autre part les ventes de produits de [la défenderesse] réalisées par [la demanderesse] (rapportées aux prix d'achat correspondants).

(. . .) N'ayant pas d'éléments pour connaître la marge nette de [la demanderesse], le Tribunal arbitral estime, à sa discrétion, comme raisonnable une marge nette correspondant à 40% du prix d'achat ».

Observations. — I. — Cette sentence présente un intérêt particulier en matière procédurale. Elle illustre de manière claire et concise le traitement par un arbitre d'un incident de procédure qui, bien que ne donnant pas lieu à de nombreux commentaires doctrinaux ni à une jurisprudence arbitrale abondante, n'en constitue pas moins une difficulté à laquelle les arbitres du commerce international sont souvent confrontés. Dès lors que les parties et les arbitres se sont accordés sur la mission du tribunal arbitral et sur la conduite de la procédure, en l'espèce par la signature de l'acte de mission, qui conférait notamment à l'arbitre la liberté *« de décider une ou plusieurs questions par une sentence partielle ou intérimaire »,* et l'établissement du calendrier du déroulement de la procédure, une partie dispose-t-elle d'une quelconque latitude pour imposer au tribunal arbitral certains actes de procédure? La réponse doit être recherchée d'une part dans l'application du droit des obligations et d'autre part dans la nature des documents dont l'interprétation et l'application par le tribunal sont discutées. La signature de l'acte de mission matérialise l'acceptation des dispositions de ce dernier par les parties signataires. La force obligatoire contractuellement conférée à ce document interdit à l'une des parties de s'affranchir unilatéralement des règles qui y sont fixées. Le règlement d'arbitrage de la CCI, en son article 18 (4) ne requiert pas, en revanche, l'accord des parties sur le calendrier du déroulement de la procédure. Celles-ci ne sont que consultées par le tribunal arbitral préalablement à l'établissement de ce dernier document. Ceci s'explique en premier lieu par la finalité pratique de ce document. Il s'agit de permettre aux parties et au tribunal de s'organiser, tout en limitant l'impact de manœuvres dilatoires, comme par exemple le refus d'une partie de produire un mémoire à une date donnée. Conditionner la validité du calendrier à sa signature par les parties reviendrait à permettre à l'une d'elles d'ériger en condition *sine qua non* de son accord l'acceptation par le cocontractant potentiel des dates qu'elle aurait choisies, fussent-elles anormalement étalées dans le temps. La non-exigence de signature s'explique en second lieu par la nature prévisionnelle de ce document. Le calendrier prévisionnel est un document appelé à évoluer et qu'il convient donc de ne pas figer par un accord contractuel afin de préserver la souplesse et l'efficacité de la procédure arbitrale. Si l'une des parties peut demander une modification du calendrier, elle ne peut pas en imposer unilatéralement la modification au tribunal arbitral.

Dans la présente affaire, la demande formulée par la défenderesse auprès de l'arbitre de se prononcer sur sa compétence par une sentence partielle pouvait être interprétée comme étant soit une demande unilatérale de modification de l'acte de mission et du calendrier de déroulement de la procédure, soit une procédant d'une interprétation de ces documents auxquels la défenderesse reprochait une certaine ambiguïté, rien n'étant expressément prévu concernant la forme que l'arbitre devait donner à la décision sur sa propre compétence. L'arbitre unique retient la première hypothèse et rappelle, avec clarté et fermeté, qu'il s'est accordé avec les parties sur un calendrier de procédure ne distinguant pas chronologiquement le traitement des questions de compétence et de fond et qu'en conséquence il n'y avait pas lieu d'opérer une telle distinction à la demande de la seule défenderesse. L'arbitre souligne également le caractère tardif de cette demande au regard du calendrier de procédure dont les différentes échéances ont été respectées par les parties sans objections. Il conclut sur ce point en rappelant le pouvoir discrétionnaire reconnu à tout arbitre de se prononcer sur un point par voie de sentence partielle ou seulement, et avec tout les autres chefs de demande, dans la sentence finale. La solution retenue est ici classique. A défaut d'accord exprès des parties, notamment dans l'acte de mission, sur les éléments du litige devant être tranchés dans une sentence partielle, l'arbitre jouit de toute liberté pour déterminer le type de sentences auquel il entend recourir pour formuler ses décisions *(Cass. 1re civ., 8 mars 1988, Sofidif c/OIAETI, 1988, Bull. civ. I, n° 64, p. 42).*

II. — La présente sentence présente également un intérêt au regard de l'interprétation qui est faite d'une clause attributive de compétence pathologique. Lorsqu'ils désirent recourir à l'arbitrage CCI, les acteurs du commerce international n'incorporent pas systématiquement la clause type d'arbitrage de la CCI dans leurs contrats. Il arrive fréquemment qu'à tort ou à raison, en fonction des caractéristiques de leur opération juridique et commerciale, les parties considèrent cette clause comme incomplète. Elles tendent alors à compléter la clause standard par l'ajout de diverses précisions réputées essentielles. Mal maîtrisée, la rédaction de la clause compromissoire devient un exercice dangereux créateur d'incertitude juridique ou, à tout le moins, de difficultés lors de la conduite de l'instance arbitrale *(Ph. Fouchard, E. Gaillard, B. Goldman, « On International Commercial Arbitration », Kluwer Law International, 1999, p. 262 et s.; B. G. Davis, « Pathological Clauses: Frédéric Eisemann's Still Vital Criteria », Arbitration International, vol. 7, n° 4, 1991, p. 365 et s.; Obs. G. A. Alvarez sous la sentence rendue dans l'affaire n° 5103 en 1988, JDI 1988, p. 1207).* En l'espèce, la pathologie de la clause compromissoire tient à l'absence de référence expresse au règlement d'arbitrage de la CCI et à la méconnaissance de la distinction entre la juridiction compétente et les règles de procédure applicables. Appelé à se prononcer sur sa compétence, l'arbitre devait déterminer si la clause compromissoire insérée dans le contrat lui attribuait le pouvoir de connaître du litige. Se posait ainsi un problème d'interprétation du contrat. L'interprétation littérale des termes de ce dernier ne permettait pas de déceler la commune intention des parties. L'arbitre écarte une telle méthode d'interprétation et recherche l'intention des parties en s'appuyant sur « un *principe largement répandu »,* notamment consacré par l'article 4.1 des principes Unidroit. L'arbitre évite ainsi de rechercher la solution par référence à un droit étatique applicable, les parties n'ayant pas expressément retenu un tel droit. L'arbitre justifie sa démarche par la qualité des rédacteurs du contrat et leur ignorance du sens des concepts juridiques employés.

Analysant les stipulations contractuelles *in abstracto,* par référence au standard juridique d'une « *personne raisonnable de même qualité placée dans la même situation »,* comme l'y invitent l'article 4.1 des principes, l'arbitre considère que la clause attributive de juridiction procède d'une recherche de neutralité du mécanisme juridique mis en place pour le règlement de litiges éventuels. La référence à la CCI et l'exclusion des tribunaux étatiques démontrent, selon l'arbitre, que la clause est une clause attributive de juridiction. Le postulat de ce raisonnement est que seule la CCI peut être considérée comme offrant le mécanisme neutre de résolution des différends envisagé par les parties. L'arbitre poursuit son raisonnement en posant que toute attribution de compétence à la CCI suppose que les parties ont entendu faire application du règlement d'arbitrage de cette institution. Cette affirmation pourrait *a priori* être critiquée. Si la CCI est surtout connue en matière de règlement des différends pour son activité d'arbitrage, elle offrait à l'époque où les parties ont rédigé leur contrat d'autres services, comme la conciliation ou l'expertise, que les parties auraient pu envisager. Le renvoi à l'arbitrage CCI dans un contrat précédent existant entre les parties rend cependant probable la volonté des parties de soumettre leurs différends à l'arbitrage CCI. La référence « *aux juges et aux Tribunaux des Cours »* abonderait d'ailleurs dans le sens de l'analyse retenue par l'arbitre. Les parties recherchaient une solution de nature juridictionnelle à leur dispute. Afin de dissiper tout doute que cette analyse susciterait, l'arbitre confirme le bien fondé de la solution dégagée par un renvoi au principe de l'effet utile formulé dans l'article 4.5 des principes Unidroit. Seule l'interprétation de la clause litigieuse opérée par l'arbitre permet de ne pas aboutir à priver les parties de juges et donc à un déni de justice. La méthode de raisonnement suivie s'inscrit en cela dans une lignée de la jurisprudence arbitrale bien établie *(Voir notamment sentence rendue dans l'affaire n° 8331 en 1996, obs. Y. Derains, JDI 1998, p. 1041 et s.; sentence rendue dans l'affaire n° 3460 en 1980, obs. Y. Derains, JDI 1981, p. 425 et s.; sentence intérimaire rendue dans l'affaire n° 2321 en 1974 et les obs., JDI 1975, p. 938 ets.).* La démarche intellectuelle de l'arbitre procède d'une volonté pédagogique indéniable ainsi que de faire accepter sa décision par les parties.

L'arbitre était également appelé à se prononcer sur la question de l'acceptation de la compétence du tribunal arbitral par une partie du fait de la participation de cette dernière à la procédure. La sentence relève justement que la nomination d'un arbitre par une partie constitue une participation à l'instance arbitrale mais n'équivaut pas à une acceptation de la compétence du tribunal dès lors que cette partie avait soulevé et maintenu une exception d'incompétence. Cette solution, bien que l'arbitre ne le mentionne pas expressément, résulte d'une lecture *a contrario* de l'article 33 du règlement d'arbitrage de la CCI. Soulevant le caractère surabondant de cet argument tiré de la participation à la procédure, l'existence et la validité de la clause ayant été démontrées, l'arbitre ne juge pas nécessaire d'y répondre et affirme sa compétence à connaître du litige.

III. — La recherche du droit applicable par l'arbitre s'appuie sur une prémisse qui suscite une interrogation. Le recours à l'article 17(1) du règlement d'arbitrage de la CCI est justifié par une interprétation de l'article 12.1 du contrat qui tendrait à l'assimiler à une clause d'élection de droit applicable. De la référence à la CCI et à une « *législation neutre définie d'un commun accord entre les parties* » d'une part et de l'absence d' « *une législation de la CCI* » et du défaut d'accord des parties sur une législation neutre d'autre part l'arbitre déduit l'absence de choix exprès de la loi applicable. Cette prémisse peut-elle valablement être retenue dès lors que l'arbitre a précédemment déclaré que l'article 12.1 devait être compris comme une clause attributive de compétence et a rejeté l'interprétation avancée par la partie défenderesse selon laquelle « *la clause 12.1 serait une clause de choix de la loi matérielle applicable* » ? L'arbitre considère en réalité, sans le dire expressément, que l'article 12.1 désigne à la fois la juridiction compétente et le droit applicable. De nombreux contrats soumis à l'arbitrage international contiennent de telles clauses *(voir par exemple l'article 10 du Contrat modèle simplifié CCI d'agence commerciale internationale et l'article 13 du Contrat modèle simplifié CCI de concession internationale, publ. CCI n° 634, 2001).* La rédaction maladroite de l'article 12.1 permettait à l'arbitre d'en faire l'interprétation implicite opérée.

Les parties n'ayant pas déterminé le droit neutre devant régir leur relation contractuelle, l'arbitre, par application de l'article 17(1) du règlement d'arbitrage de la CCI, choisit directement le droit applicable, « *les règles et principes généralement reconnus dans le commerce international (lex mercatoria) et notamment les principes Unidroit* », sans recourir à la méthode des conflits de lois faisant appel à la recherche de critères de rattachement. La démarche de l'arbitre s'inscrit en cela dans un courant de la jurisprudence arbitrale bien établi *(F. Osman, Les principes généraux de la lex mercatoria, Contribution à l'étude d'un ordre juridique anational, Bibl. de droit privé, t. 224, LGDJ, 1992, p. 369 et s.; pour une étude approfondie de la question, voir H. A. Grigera Naón, Choice-of-law problems in international commercial arbitration, Recueil des cours, Académie de droit international de La Haye, t. 289, Martinus Nijhoff, 2001).*

L'apport de la sentence à la jurisprudence arbitrale et au droit du commerce international réside davantage dans le choix des principes Unidroit. Ces principes sont maintenant fermement ancrés dans la pratique internationale, que ce soit celle des rédacteurs de contrats *(voir notamment, CCI, The ICC Model Distributorship Contract, Sole Importer-Distributor, publ. CCI n° 646, 2002, article 24; M. Fontaine, Les principes d'Unidroit: expression de la pratique contractuelle actuelle?, Suppl. Spécial, ICArb. Bull, 2002, p. 101 et s.; H. Raeschke-Kessler, Les principes d'Unidroit dans la pratique contractuelle d'aujourd'hui, op. cit., p. 107 et s.)*

que celle des juges du contrat *(E. A. Farnsworth, Le rôle des principes d'Unidroit dans l'arbitrage commercial international: point de vue américain sur leurs finalités et leur application, p. 27 et 28)*. Retenir ces principes comme droit matériel applicable n'est pas original, bien que leur application d'office, sans choix exprès ou acceptation, même tacite, des parties puisse soulever des interrogations *(P. Lalive, Les principes d'Unidroit en tant que lex contractus, avec ou sans choix explicite ou tacite de la loi: point de vue de l'arbitre, Suppl. Spécial, Bull. arb. CCI 2002, p. 87)*.

L'originalité réside dans l'analyse de ces principes. Selon l'arbitre, ils constituent l'une des composantes de la *lex mercatoria*. Cette dernière est donc envisagée comme un ensemble de *« règles et de principes généraux en matière de contrats internationaux »* ouvert aux instruments d'origine étatique et ne procédant pas directement de la pratique contractuelle internationale *(en ce sens, voir E. A. Farnsworth, op. cit., p. 22)*. La neutralité des principes est affirmée mais ce caractère n'est pas précisé. La neutralité tient-elle à la nature de l'auteur des principes, à savoir Unidroit? Il pourrait être considéré que l'élaboration des principes par cet organisme international permet de s'affranchir de traditions juridiques influençant nécessairement un législateur national. La neutralité tient-elle aussi ou uniquement à leur contenu? Les règles posées correspondraient au droit positif en matière de contrats internationaux et ne feraient donc pas appel à des notions inconnues des acteurs du commerce international. Or, l'arbitre déclare que si les principes sont généralement une formulation *«fidèle des règles que les entreprises opérant dans le commerce international considèrent comme conformes à leurs intérêts et attentes »*, ils posent également des règles qui n'ont pas ce caractère. Les principes en matière d'imprévision, ou *« hardship »*, sont expressément mentionnées comme ne correspondant pas aux *« intérêts et attentes »* des acteurs du commerce international. Le propos pourrait être nuancé, mais il est certain que l'acceptation par des contractants de l'imprévision comme fait générateur d'une adaptation du contrat est exceptionnelle *(voir M. Curvello de Almeida Prado, Le hardship dans le droit du commerce international, thèse Université de Paris X-Nanterre, 2001; contra, M. Fontaine, F. De Ly, Droit des contrats internationaux, Analyse et rédaction de clauses, 2ᵉ éd., FEC, Bruylant, 2003, p. 487 et s.; la CCI a récemment rendu public une clause de hardship, « ICC Force Majeure Clause 2003 and ICC Hardship Clause 2003 », publ. CCI n° 650, 2003)* et que des arbitres ont déjà écarté l'application des principes relatifs à l'imprévision au motif qu'ils ne correspondaient pas aux pratiques courantes du commerce international *(sentence CCI dans l'affaire n° 8873, Bull. arb. CCI., vol. 10, n°2, 1999, p. 81 et s.)*.

La dichotomie entre les différents principes posée par l'arbitre le conduit à ne retenir comme droit applicable que ceux qui *« apparaissent comme une transposition fidèle des règles reconnues comme applicables aux contrats internationaux par les commerçants engagés dans le commerce international »*. La sentence en soulignant l'introduction d'éléments novateurs dans les principes et en tirant de cette création des conséquences pour leur application invite à s'interroger sur la valeur normative des principes *(J.-M. Mousseron, J. Raynard, R. Fabre, J.L. Pierre, Droit du commerce international, Droit international de l'entreprise, coll. Manuel, 3ᵉ éd., Litec, 2003, p. 78)*.

IV. — L'intérêt de cette sentence arbitrale provient aussi de l'analyse minutieuse qui y est faite du mécanisme de formation du contrat. En l'espèce, les volontés des parties ne s'étaient pas rencontrées sur certains éléments. L'acceptation ne correspondait pas à l'offre. L'existence même d'un contrat était *a priori* discutable. L'arbitre affirme la validité du contrat nonobstant l'absence d'accord exprès des parties sur tous les termes du contrat. Le choix de la *lex mercatoria* et des principes Unidroit comme droit matériel applicable par l'arbitre l'autorise à déroger à la règle subordonnant la formation d'un contrat à la nécessaire identité de l'offre et de l'acception. Selon le droit applicable en l'espèce, il existe un tempérament à cette règle qui permet de ne pas automatiquement qualifier de contre-offre toute modification de la pollicitation initiale dans l' « acceptation ». Le contrat est valablement conclu dès lors que les ajouts contenus dans l'acceptation sont des « *éléments complémentaires ou différents n'altérant pas substantiellement les termes de l'offre* » et que ces ajouts ne fassent pas l'objet d'un refus par le pollicitant *(sur ce point, voir J.-M. Mousseron, Technique contractuelle, 2ᵉ éd., Francis Lefebvre, 1999, p. 122 et s.).* Ces deux conditions étant remplies en l'espèce, l'arbitre conclut que le contrat était bien formé. Toute modification n'était possible que par un accord mutuel des parties. Un tel accord est intervenu concernant les conditions de paiement des commandes passées en application du contrat. Toutefois, le caractère lacunaire de l'accord amenait à s'interroger sur la validité de ce dernier. Selon l'arbitre, les parties étaient engagées dans un processus de formation progressive du contrat, ce qui pouvait aboutir à la conclusion d'un accord partiel devant par la suite être complété. L'arbitre cherche à conforter cette solution par une interprétation *a contrario* extensive de l'article 2.13 des principes Unidroit. L'article 2.13 envisage la conclusion du contrat dans sa totalité et subordonne cette conclusion à un accord sur certaines questions de fond ou de forme. L'accord sur les questions secondaires ne saurait suffire à former le contrat. L'accord sur les questions érigées en conditions *sine qua non* de formation du contrat est également nécessaire. Lorsque les parties n'ont pas subordonné la formation du contrat à un accord sur certaines questions, le contrat serait formé dès que les parties s'accordent sur ses termes. Or, l'accord sur tous les termes n'interviendra pas simultanément. L'arbitre en déduit une possibilité de conclure le contrat par accords successifs, sous réserve que les parties n'aient pas eu « *la volonté de subordonner la conclusion du contrat à la solution des questions laissées ouvertes* ». Dans la présente affaire, l'arbitre ne décèle pas une telle volonté. L'accord des parties sur les conditions de paiement est donc valable bien qu'incomplet.

V. — La sentence illustre de manière limpide l'application des principes Unidroit aux conditions de résiliation d'un contrat de distribution. L'arbitre énonce d'abord qu'il n'existe pas dans la pratique internationale, à la différence de certains droits nationaux, de principe général de mise en demeure d'un débiteur défaillant de remédier au défaut d'exécution de ses obligations afin de prononcer une résiliation valable. La règle est que la résiliation opère par simple notification au débiteur, ainsi que l'énoncent les principes Unidroit. La résiliation doit être opérée de bonne foi, ce qui impose au créancier de l'obligation non exécutée d'agir dans un délai raisonnable à compter de la connaissance de l'inexécution ou de la date où celle-ci aurait dû être connue *(en ce sens, Sentence rendue dans l'affaire n° 2520 en 1975, obs. Y. Derains, JD 1976, p. 992 et s.).* Le non-respect de cette exigence de prompte dénonciation de l'inexécution vaut renonciation de la part du créancier de l'obligation à se prévaloir du défaut d'exécution.

En l'espèce, le contrat résilié était un contrat à durée déterminée comprenant une clause permettant expressément au créancier de l'obligation inexécutée « *de résilier le contrat avant son échéance en cas d'infraction grave à une de ses clauses* ». La validité d'une résiliation anticipée d'un contrat à durée déterminée ne posait donc pas de difficulté. Il ne pouvait être avancé que le créancier aurait dû attendre le terme α *quo* du contrat *(sur ce point, voir J. — M. Mousseron, op. cit., p. 350 et, p. 638 et s.).* L'arbitre juge néanmoins opportun de préciser que la possibilité de résilier le contrat pour manquement grave d'une partie à ses obligations est une règle générale du commerce international, notamment consacrée par les principes Unidroit. En l'absence de clause expresse autorisant la résiliation, la règle générale aurait conduit au même résultat. Le recours aux principes par les arbitres en appui d'une solution qu'ils ont dégagée en application d'autres règles de droit applicables correspond à une pratique bien établie dans l'arbitrage international *(voir par exemple, P. Mayer, Le rôle des principes dans la pratique de l'arbitrage de la CCI, Suppl. Spécial, Bull. arb. CCI 2002, p. 117).* Le caractère surabondant de l'observation de l'arbitre la prive de portée pratique mais confirme, si besoin était, une solution déjà consacrée par la jurisprudence arbitrale.

VI. — Au terme d'une analyse détaillée des stipulations contractuelles, l'arbitre qualifie la résiliation de fautive, puis s'interroge sur les'effets d'une telle résiliation. Le droit du commerce international tendrait à admettre que la résiliation fautive mette fin au contrat, le caractère fautif de la résiliation ouvrant droit à réparation du préjudice subi. L'arbitre considère que cette solution présente une sécurité juridique plus grande que celle retenue par certains systèmes juridiques et privant la résiliation fautive de tout effet. Il invoque les principes Unidroit au soutien de son raisonnement. Le renvoi aux principes pourrait être discuté. Les principes Unidroit, ainsi que le relève d'ailleurs implicitement l'arbitre en les mentionnant avec quelque réserve (« *[les] principes Unidroit semblent confirmer »),* ne prévoient pas expressément de règle afférente aux effets d'une résiliation fautive.

Cette sentence fournit un exemple instructif de l'application des principes Uni-droit en matière de calcul du préjudice. Les principes sont d'abord évoqués pour justifier la réparation intégrale du préjudice et la prise en compte dans l'évaluation de celui-ci tant du *damnum emmergans* que du *lucrum cessons.* Conformément à une jurisprudence arbitrale fixée depuis de nombreuses années et rappelée par l'arbitre, le préjudice ne correspond pas à la marge brute sur le prix de vente des produits contractucls mais au « *bénéfice net, après déduction de tous les frais encourus ».* Les principes sont ensuite évoqués pour calculer le « *bénéfice net* » ou « *marge nette* », les parties n'ayant pas fourni d'indication sur la méthode de calcul à utiliser. L'arbitre unique, ainsi que l'y autorisent les principes, fixe discrétionnairement la marge nette raisonnable correspondant au préjudice subi par la demanderesse.

E.J.

Sentence rendue dans l'affaire n° 6317 en 1989 (original en langue Française).

I. — Affacturage international. — Groupe international d'affacturage. — Rapport des membres régi par un langage codifié. — Volonté des parties. — Valeur du langage codifié.

II. — Bonne foi. — Exécution des engagements respectifs avec bonne foi en matière d'affacturage international.

Un arbitre unique, siégeant à Nice, était saisi d'un litige opposant une société française X, demanderesse, à une société espagnole, Y, défenderesse. Les parties, toutes deux membres d'un groupe international d'affacturage, le Groupe W, ont eu des difficultés d'interprétation afférentes à des télexes échangés entre elles.

Dans le cadre du Groupe W, un exportateur qui souhaite obtenir la garantie à 100% des créances commerciales sur ses clients étrangers (importateurs), la gestion de ses comptes clients étrangers et le financement immédiat des factures garanties, peut avoir recours à l'opération d'affacturage qui consiste à obtenir d'une société d'affacturage, un factor, sous certaines conditions, la garantie et les services ci-dessus résumés.

L'exportateur s'adresse au factor de son pays (le Factor Export) qui ensuite entre en rapport avec son correspondant qui se trouve dans le pays vers lequel la marchandise doit être exportée (le Factor Import). Les responsabilités de chaque Factor sont alors réparties au sein du Groupe W.

Le Factor Export s'engage contractuellement à l'égard de l'exportateur à assumer la responsabilité des services ci-dessus décrits. Quant au Factor Import, il s'engage à l'égard du Factor Export et non de l'exportateur à assumer soit la garantie à 100 % des créances commerciales (sous certaines conditions), soit la gestion des comptes clients et le recouvrement amiable ou contentieux des créances.

Dans ces conditions, le Factor Import s'interpose entre le Factor Export et l'importateur, ce dernier devant régler les factures au Factor Import qui, conformément à ce qui a été indiqué ci-dessus, assure la garantie à 100% des créances et la gestion des comptes clients.

Dans le présent différend, la société française X est le Factor Export, demandeur à l'action, et la société espagnole Y, le Factor Import, défendeur.

Pour assurer le bon fonctionnement des rapports entre les membres du Groupe W, de nombreuses règles existent et sont acceptées par chaque factor du Groupe lors de son admission dans le Groupe.

En particulier, les parties ont accepté le *Data Exchange* (DEX), un langage informatique du Groupe qui permet, grâce à une liste d'indicatifs codifiés auxquels correspondent les messages standardisés relatifs aux opérations d'affacturage entre les membres du Groupe, un très rapide déroulement desdites opérations. Ce langage permet ainsi d'éviter les éventuelles incertitudes sur les termes et conditions des transactions. Le DEX a ainsi remplacé l'ancien système de communication du Groupe (échange de lettres, télex ou formulaires standardisés ou non selon le type d'opération), qui a été abandonné pour éviter les incertitudes sur les termes et conditions des transactions, n'a pas ainsi la valeur d'une « tradition » existante entre les parties.

Les rapports entre la société X et la société Y concernent des exportations de ferrailles de France réalisées par la Société V à l'égard de certains importateurs espagnols, parmi lesquels les sociétés E et A.

En ce qui concerne l'importateur E, la société X a reçu l'approbation dans le langage codifié, de la société Y, sans aucune condition de paiement imposée pour FRF 7 000 000 valable jusqu'au 1er mars 1986. Lors de la demande de renouvellement de l'approbation, le 28 février 1986, la société Y a confirmé dans un premier temps, son engagement avec la condition « *term 90 days accepted bill of exchange* ». Quelques heures plus tard, la société Y a envoyé un deuxième télex à la société X dans les termes suivants: « *Please disregard our previous telex (. . .) and by means of present you can consider FRF 7 000 000 — terms 90 days extended up to first March 1987.* »

L'interprétation de ce télex va poser problème.

Pour la société X, le premier télex a été envoyé par erreur et a été tout de suite corrigé par le deuxième télex, dans lequel les conditions normales de garantie sans réserves ont été confirmées. Tout au contraire, la société Y, soutient que la condition « *90 jours lettre de change acceptée* » est une condition requise traditionnellement appliquée, ce qui explique pourquoi la société Y n'a pas estimé nécessaire de la répéter dans son deuxième télex.

De la même manière, en ce qui concerne le deuxième importateur espagnol A, la société X a reçu, dans le langage codifié, l'approbation de la société Y sans aucune condition de paiement imposée pour FRF 2 500 000 jusqu'au 30 avril 1986.

N'ayant pas reçu des importateurs le paiement des factures dans le cadre des exportations en Espagne, la demanderesse a soutenu qu'en vertu de la garantie il incombe au défendeur de payer les factures. Ce dernier conteste son engagement et nie devoir payer les sommes demandées par la demanderesse dans ces deux affaires, d'où la naissance de ce litige.

L'arbitre résume ainsi la position des parties: « *Y conteste avoir assumé à l'égard de X un tel engagement; selon Y, les opérations d'affacturage avaient été exploitées toujours « avec la condition requise de réception de lettre de change acceptée pour prendre part au risque ». Cette thèse serait confirmée par l'examen des factures relatives aux opérations d'affacturages contestées, où se trouve l'indication suivante: « paiement par traite acceptée ». X conteste cette thèse, faisant remarquer que cette indication prévoit l'existence de la traite seulement en tant que moyen de paiement, et pas comme condition à l'octroi d'une garantie. En d'autres termes, dans les factures contestées, l'expression « traite acceptée » se référait au moyen de paiement, et non aux conditions de l'octroi de la garantie. Une telle condition, en effet, aurait dû être formulée selon les règles du langage codifié.* »

La première question que l'arbitre va devoir trancher est celle de savoir « *si la garantie d'Y en ce qui concerne les montants qui font l'objet de cette affaire, est une garantie sans conditions ou bien si elle est conditionnée à la réception par Y d'une lettre de change acceptée.* »

Afin de pouvoir y répondre, l'arbitre s'intéresse dans un premier temps à la question de savoir si les rapports entre les membres du Groupe W peuvent être régis par d'autres formes et d'autres langages que celui qui est codifié.

Selon la défenderesse, le langage codifié ne serait pas un langage « *ad solemnita-tem* », et le seul qui doit être utilisé. Les rapports entre les membres du Groupe « *seraient perfectionnés par le simple consentement, sans que la condition solennelle ou formelle d'un contrat puisse être présumée* ». Le langage DEX aurait seulement une valeur subsidiaire. N'ayant pas reçu la lettre de change acceptée, la société Y nie l'existence de la garantie à l'égard de la société X puisque l'entrée d'Y dans le risque de l'importateur dépendait de la réception de la lettre de change acceptée.

L'arbitre y répond en indiquant que « *le langage (DEX) doit être considéré comme le "langage typique" du Groupe, c'est-à-dire l'instrument qui régit normalement toute opération des factors. Dès qu'une transaction a été stipulée entre les parties moyennant le DEX, il n'est pas possible d'en déroger ou bien d'en ajouter d'autres conditions ou termes sinon par messages qui doivent trouver leur référence dans le langage codifié.* » A titre d'exemple, l'arbitre cite « *le Code K80, qui établit un trait d'union entre le DEX et les autres moyens de communication, à propos des règles en matière d'annulation des garanties, prévoyant qu'il est possible de donner telle annulation par lettre enregistrée, télex, ou câble, mais il faut toutefois transmettre toujours et tout de suite la confirmation de cette annulation dans le langage DEX.* »

L'arbitre remarque que « *les rapports entre X et Y, en ce qui concerne la garantie à l'égard de E et A étaient régis par une garantie qui dans le langage codifié, n'était pas subordonnée à des conditions spécifiques, et en particulier n'était pas subordonnée à la réception par Y d'une lettre de change acceptée. En réalité, si Y avait voulu subordonner son risque et sa garantie à quelque condition particulière, elle aurait dû le faire en le communiquant avec les messages codifiés ou autrement mais d'une façon incontestablement certaine et claire. Cela n'est pas arrivé, et donc on peut bien retenir qu'il n'existait pas de limites à la garantie contrairement à la thèse d'Y, mais simplement une garantie avec "unspecified conditions".*

Par conséquent, le tribunal arbitral va retenir que la garantie d'Y à l'égard de X était existante sans conditions et sans être subordonnée à la réception d'une lettre de change, et que donc Y doit payer à X les montants relatifs aux factures qui ont été remises par V jusqu'au moment où l'annutotion de la garantie a pris effet (voir ci-dessous). »

Le 4 mars 1986, la société Y transmet un télex à la société X où elle lui communique la « suspension » des garanties pour les deux importateurs. Par le biais du langage codifié, la société Y va utiliser la « clef » qui lui permet de sortir du langage DEX pour communiquer selon les moyens traditionnels, avec un renvoi au télex du 4 mars 1986.

Le 6 mars 1986, la société Y envoie un deuxième télex à la société X, dans lequel elle lui confirme sa position du 4 mars et lui communique les codes d'annulation DEX.

La deuxième question à trancher par le tribunal arbitral « *concerne l'interprétation et la portée du télex d'Y du 4 mars 1986, où elle communique la "suspension" des garanties* ».

La demanderesse X conteste qu'une telle communication puisse avoir un sens dans le langage du Groupe, car le message codifié correspondant à la « suspension » d'une garantie n'existe pas dans le DEX. En particulier, elle souligne qu'il ne pouvait y avoir d'annulation en l'absence du code requis et, de surcroît, de toute explication claire.

De son côté, tout en rappelant la non exclusivité du langage codifié, le défendeur Y soutient que le contenu du télex était clair et précis au sens commun et général. Dès lors, même si la « suspension » n'était pas prévue dans le DEX, on ne peut pas lui nier tout effet.

Le tribunal arbitral y répond en indiquant que « *si le langage codifié est le langage "typique" du Groupe, ce n'est pas un langage exclusif. En outre lorsque le langage codifié ne prévoit pas le message qu'un factor veut envoyer à un autre factor, il n'est pas possible d'en tirer comme conclusion que le premier est empêché d'envoyer ledit message par d'autres langages, verbaux ou bien écrits.* »

En l'espèce, le contenu du télex en discussion est apparu clair et précis à l'arbitre.

« *Quant aux messages qui ont été envoyés par Y moyennant le DEX*, l'arbitre va souligner *que la défenderesse a quand même utilisé la "clef" K80 en rappelant à X son télex, ce qui suffisait à donner au* Factor Export *les renseignements nécessaires pour lui permettre d'aviser son exportateur V.* »

En outre, selon l'arbitre, on ne peut oublier que X et Y « *sont membres du même Groupe, et que donc l'obligation fondamentale d'exécuter les engagements respectifs avec bonne foi apparaît encore plus important que dans les autres rapports contractuels. Par conséquent, il était normal d'attendre, de X tout du moins, un comportement en conformité aux indications du télex relatif à la suspension. »*

En conclusion, l'arbitre retient que Y avait dûment communiqué à X le 4 mars 1986 que sa garantie pour les risques de solvabilité des importateurs n'existait plus. Ainsi les marchandises expédiées ainsi que les factures remises après le 5 mars 1986 ne sont couvertes par aucune garantie.

OBSERVATIONS. — I. — Cette sentence illustre la difficulté qu'il peut y avoir à déterminer la portée juridique d'un langage codifié intervenant dans un milieu professionnel donné (*voir aussi à ce sujet la sentence dans l'affaire 3202 en 1978, JDI 1979, p. 1003*). Un tel langage est-il *ad solemnitatem* et le seul à pouvoir être utilisé? Le *Data Exchange (DEX)*, le langage informatique du Groupe W, a été mis en place et accepté par toutes les sociétés de ce groupe aux fins d'assurer le bon fonctionnement des rapports entre elles et de garantir notamment la certitude de leurs transactions réciproques. En particulier, l'arbitre relève que selon les termes du contrat qui régit l'activité du Groupe, « *[DEX] is the [W] Group electronic system handling its cross border transactions* ». Ce langage existe et a été accepté par chaque factor du Groupe lors de son admission. L'arbitre a considéré à juste titre qu'il s'agit du langage « typique » du Groupe, c'est-à-dire l'instrument qui régit normalement toute opération des factors. Par conséquent, il estime qu'on ne peut déroger à cet instrument que par d'autres messages qui doivent être référencés dans le langage codifié, soit par exemple le Code K80. L'arbitre ne fait donc que respecter le fonctionnement du groupe en donnant effet à ce langage.

L'arbitre indique que ce langage DEX n'est pas exclusif. Si le langage codifié ne prévoit pas le message qu'un factor veut envoyer à un autre factor, il est normal d'admettre que d'autres langages, verbaux ou écrits, puissent être utilisés. L'absence d'un mot codifié dans le vocabulaire de le DEX ne peut avoir pour conséquence d'empêcher une partie d'envoyer un message en utilisant ce mot à condition que le message soit clair et précis. Une telle solution doit être approuvée.

II — L'arbitre souligne l'obligation fondamentale des parties, membres d'un même groupe, d'exécuter leurs engagements de bonne foi (*voir P. Kahn, « Les principes généraux du droit devant les arbitres du commerce international ». JDI 1989, p. 305*). Nombreuses sont les sentences qui font peser sur les parties une obligation de coopérer de bonne foi. Il existe, en effet, une tendance de la jurisprudence arbitrale qui privilégie le principe de bonne foi (*voir Y. Derains, « Les tendances de la jurisprudence arbitrale internationale », JDI 1993, p. 829 et S. Jarvin, « L'obligation de coopérer de bonne foi; exemples d'application au plan de l'arbitrage international », dans L'apport de la jurisprudence arbitrale, Les dossiers de l'Institut, CCI, publication no. 440/1, 1986*). Certains auteurs vont jusqu' à dire que « *l' exigence fondamentale de bonne foi (. . .) [se] trouve dans tous les systèmes de droit, qu'il s'agisse des droits nationaux ou du droit international* » (*Sentence AMCO 25 septembre 1983 rendue dans le cadre du CIRDI, Revue de l'arbitrage 1985, p. 252, observations E. Gaillard*). « *Appartenant au fond commun des droits nationaux, l'obligation de se comporter loyalement dans les relations contractuelles constitue naturellement un principe des rapports économiques internationaux* » (*sentence rendue dans l'affaire CCI n° 5030, Recueil des sentences arbitrales de la CCI 1991-1995, p. 482*).

En l'espèce, l'arbitre a fait application du principe de bonne foi sans passer au préalable par la détermination du droit applicable. Le principe de bonne foi est-il alors conçu par l'arbitre comme étant un principe général du droit du commerce international, un usage ou simplement comme un principe inhérent au fonctionnement du groupe? On peut regretter que la sentence ne le précise pas. Par ailleurs, on peut avoir des doutes quant à la portée de ce principe si, comme il nous semble, l'arbitre en fait un principe universel d'application générale, car le principe de bonne foi n'est pas d'application universelle.

En effet, tous les systèmes de droit ne reconnaissent pas le principe de bonne foi. Si ce principe se retrouve dans le droit français (*article 1134 du Code civil*), dans le droit allemand (la doctrine et la jurisprudence le rattachent à, § 242 BGB) ainsi que dans le droit italien (*article 1366 du Code civil italien*), il ne s'impose pas en tant que tel aux parties dont le contrat est soumis à certains autres droits tels que le droit anglais et américain.

Selon Alberto M. Musy, Professeur à l'université économique de Novara, Italie, le principe de bonne foi n'a pas la même portée dans les différents systèmes de droit en Europe. Dans le système romano-germanique, l'approche la plus minimaliste est celle des tribunaux français qui n'appliquent pas le principe de bonne foi dans la même mesure que leurs homologues allemands ou italiens. Une approche encore plus minimaliste est celle du droit de *common law*. En effet, en vertu de ce droit, il n'existe aucune obligation générale des parties à un contrat de se conformer au principe de bonne foi (« *The good faith principle in contract law and the precontractual duty to disclose: comparative analysis of new differences in legal cultures* », ICER (International Centre for Economic Research), Working Papers n° 19-2000, http://ideas.repec.org/p/icr/wpicer).

De nos jours, le droit anglais n'impose plus une obligation générale de bonne foi aux parties à un contrat (*R. Powell, « Good faith in contracts », Current Legal Problems, 38 [1956]*). Le droit du commerce anglais reconnaissait ce principe jusqu'à sa disparition au XVIIIe siècle (*J. H. Baker, « An Introduction to English Legal History », 3rd edition, London, 1990*). Le principe en *common law* est que la gestion des affaires est dominée par la règle du « *rough and tough* », à savoir l'application stricte des termes du contrat. Par conséquent, il revient aux parties de veiller à leurs intérêts. L'application d'une telle règle est toutefois modérée dans certains domaines où on peut retrouver l'application du principe de bonne foi. Il en est ainsi en matière de contrat d'assurance qui nécessite une *uberrima fides*. Quant aux relations fiduciaires en *common law*, elles génèrent plusieurs obligations qui, en droit civil, se rattacheraient au principe de bonne foi. Il arrive même que les tribunaux anglais dégagent des contrats une volonté implicite des parties, adoptant ainsi une approche comparable à celle des tribunaux français ou allemands. Ceci ne permet pas pour autant d'affirmer qu'il existe un principe général de bonne foi en droit anglais (*P. D. V. Marsh, Comparative Contract Law, Gower Publishing, Aldershot, 1994, p. 38-39*). Cette analyse a été confirmée par Roy Goode, professeur à l'université d'Oxford (Grande-Bretagne). Cependant, selon Christian Twigg-Flesner, maître de conférence à l'université de Notthingham (Grande-Bretagne) il convient de noter une évolution du droit anglais des contrats sur ce point, tant au niveau jurisprudentiel que doctrinal (*R. Brownsword, Positive, Negative, Neutral: The Reception of the Good Faith in English Contract Law and J. Wightman, Good Faith and Pluralism in the Law of Contract in Brownsword, Hird, and Howells, Oxford, Clarendon Press, 1997*), notamment depuis l'adoption de la directive européenne sur les clauses abusives (*C. Twigg-Flesner, A « Good Faith » Requirement for English Contract Law?, WLR 1353, CA*).

Le droit américain, fortement influencé par le droit allemand, a inclus dans la section 1-203 de l'*Uniform Commercial Code* un principe général de bonne foi (« *every contract or duty within this Act imposes an obligation of good faith in its performance or enforcement* »). De même la Section 205 du *Restatement Second of Contracts*, inspirée du Code, impose une obligation générale de bonne foi (« *every contract imposes upon each party a duty of good faith and fair dealing in its performance and enforcement* »). Le droit américain s'est ainsi définitivement éloigné des courants doctrinaux et jurisprudentiels de la théorie classique des contrats du droit de *common law*, purement fondée sur la volonté des parties, et s'est rapproché des concepts de droit civil.

Cependant, en opposition au droit civil, cette obligation reste limitée à l'exécution des contrats et ne s'applique pas dans le cadre des négociations et des relations précontractuelles. De plus, selon Allan E. Farnsworth, Professeur à l'université de Columbia (Etats-Unis), il n'existe pas de définition claire et précise de ce principe en droit américain. Le

Code en comprend déjà deux relatives à la vente de marchandises et différents courants doctrinaux s'opposent quant à la définition de ce principe, sa nature (objective ou purement subjective) et son impact sur les tribunaux américains (*A. E. Farnsworth, « The Concept of Good Faith in American Law », Saggi, Conferenze e Seminari; www.uniromal.it*). Malgré tout, par opposition au droit anglais, un principe général de bonne foi semble désormais inclus dans le droit des contrats de tous les Etats américains.

L'Australie, autre grand pays de droit de *common law*, reste aujourd'hui fortement influencée par le droit anglais et ne connaît pas de principe général de bonne foi. Cependant, soumis à l'influence américaine, le droit des contrats australien pourrait évoluer à terme vers l'affirmation d'une telle obligation.

En réalité, l'application du principe de bonne foi en l'espèce semble découler de l'appartenance des parties à un groupe international d'affacturage. L'arbitre, respectueux de leur volonté, fait en premier lieu application du langage DEX auquel les deux parties membres du groupe sont soumises. L'arbitre tire ensuite les conséquences de l'insuffisance du système. Il constate le caractère non exclusif du langage DEX et la possibilité pour les parties d'employer d'autres langages verbaux ou écrits, tel qu'un télex clair et précis. Il est donc normal qu'une partie puisse s'attendre à un comportement en conformité avec un tel télex, surtout de la part d'un autre membre du groupe. Dès lors, on peut penser que l'appartenance à un groupe impose à chacun de ses membres, une obligation de vigilance et de coopération renforcée vis-à-vis des autres membres. C'est le non respect de cette obligation que l'arbitre sanctionne. Une solution d'espèce bien adaptée.

S. J.

Sentence rendue dans l'affaire n° 10264 en 2000

I. — Arbitrage commercial international. — Critères de qualification.

II. — Droit applicable au contrat. — Absence de détermination par l'arbitre. — Choix implicite des parties.

III. — Contrat de mandat d'intérêt. — Contrat d'agence. — Contrat de commission. — Qualification. — Distinction. — Effets.

IV. — Caractère brutal et abusif de la résiliation du contrat. — Absence d'un préavis raisonnable. — Indemnité compensatrice.

L'arbitre unique siégeant à Paris était appelé à se prononcer sur la validité de la résiliation d'un contrat cadre conclu entre les parties en janvier 1981 aux termes desquels les sociétés défenderesses A (France) et B (France) (dénommées les « mandantes ») ont désigné les sociétés X (France) et Y (France) demanderesses (dénommées les «mandataires») pour les représenter pour la vente de leurs produits fruitiers et de les approvisionner en matières premières. Les demanderesses étaient payées sous forme de commissions.

Le contrat a été résilié par la défenderesse A en 1998 suite à une restructuration du groupe.

Les demanderesses ont sollicité en vain auprès des défenderesses une réparation du préjudice subi du fait de la résiliation du contrat, avant de soumettre le différend à la CCI sur la base de la clause compromissoire suivante: « *En cas de contestation sur les présentes, il sera fait appel au Règlement de la Chambre de Commerce Internationale de Paris* ».

Aux termes de l'acte de mission signé par les parties, l'arbitre devait principalement résoudre la question de savoir si les défenderesses devaient être condamnées ou non solidairement à réparer le préjudice subi par les demanderesses du fait de la résiliation brutale et abusive du contrat. L'arbitre a toutefois d'abord procédé à la qualification du contrat qui lie les parties en raison de sa complexité. Les parties n'ayant pas prévu le droit applicable au fond, l'acte de mission a rappelé qu'à défaut d'un tel choix, l'arbitre appliquera les règles de droit qu'il juge appropriées conformément à l'article 17 du Règlement CCI.

La qualification du contrat

Les parties étaient en désaccord sur la qualification du contrat et les conséquences juridiques applicables à la nature de leurs relations contractuelles. De ce fait, l'arbitre a dû entamer un travail de qualification en droit afin de pouvoir en tirer les conséquences juridiques.

> « *Dans la mesure où les demanderesses forment une demande d'indemnité pour rupture brusque et abusive du contrat, il faut d'abord qualifier le contrat qui liait les parties pour s'attacher ensuite aux conséquences d'une rupture unilatérale de ce contrat.*
>
> *En effet, de nombreuses qualifications sont utilisées dans les pièces et écritures soumises (mandat, représentation, courtage, commissionnaire, agent commercial, contrat d'intérêt commun, etc.).*
>
> *À titre principal, les demanderesses considèrent qu'un contrat d'intérêt commun liait les parties, alors que les défenderesses considèrent qu'il s'agit d'un contrat de commissionnaire.*

Trois qualifications peuvent être étudiées en l'espèce pour tenter de rendre compte de l'activité des demanderesses, à savoir celle de commissionnaire, de mandataire d'intérêt commun et d'agent commercial.

La première qualification envisageable est celle de contrat de commission tel que défini à l'article 94 du Code de commerce. Le commissionnaire est celui qui agit en son nom propre pour le compte d'un commettant.

Ensuite, la qualification de mandat d'intérêt commun pourrait être retenue. Le mandataire agit au nom et pour le compte de l'entreprise mandante. En outre, il faut que le mandataire ait un intérêt au développement de la clientèle qu'il démarche, cet intérêt se traduisant notamment sous la forme de commissions qui lui sont versées.

Enfin, le mandataire peut relever du statut des agents commerciaux prévu par la loi du 25 juin 1991. L'agent commercial exerce un mandat d'intérêt commun et justifie en général d'une immatriculation sur un registre spécial tenu au greffe du Tribunal de commerce.

Ainsi, si le mandataire d'intérêt commun (ou l'agent commercial qui n'en constitue qu'une application spécifique) et le commissionnaire agissent tous deux pour le compte d'une autre personne, le commissionnaire agit en son nom propre alors que le mandataire (ou l'agent commercial) agit au nom du mandant. À la différence du mandataire d'intérêt commun ou de l'agent commercial, aucune indemnité de rupture (sauf abus de droit) n'est allouée au commissionnaire.

Tout d'abord, dans la lettre du contrat comme dans l'esprit des parties, il semble que le contrat cadre conclu le 19 janvier 1981 était un véritable mandat et non un simple contrat de commission. En effet, ce contrat est qualifié de mandat, les sociétés A et B sont qualifiées de mandantes et celles de Monsieur S. sont qualifiées de mandataires. La lettre de résiliation du 9 février 1998 mentionne d'ailleurs expressément "la fin du mandat qui ne sera pas renouvelé lors de la prochaine campagne" ou encore "la dénonciation du mandat".

En outre, les pièces versées aux dossiers et les débats qui ont eu lieu lors de l'audience du 15 octobre 1999 ont fait apparaître que les parties avaient des réunions régulières de travail, que les affaires et la clientèle se sont étoffées au fil des ans et que Monsieur S. et ses sociétés, rémunérés sous forme de commissions versées à chaque nouveau contrat signé, avaient un intérêt évident à voir prospérer cette relation d'affaires. Pour toutes ces raisons notamment, le contrat du 19 janvier 1981 devrait être qualifié de mandat d'intérêt commun.

En revanche, en ce qui concerne l'application stricte du statut d'agent commercial selon la loi du 25 juin 1991, on notera que les demanderesses n'ont versé aux débats qu'un certificat d'immatriculation daté du 25 avril 1991, relatif à la seule société X qui, en outre, ne justifie pas de son renouvellement comme le prévoit le décret du 23 décembre 1958. Il est vrai cependant que l'immatriculation ne semble pas constituer une condition nécessaire pour bénéficier du statut d'agent commercial.

Il résulte de ce qui précède qu'une première analyse du mandat qui liait les demanderesses et les défenderesses conduit à une qualification, sinon de contrat d'agent commercial, à tout le moins de mandat d'intérêt commun.

L'analyse des contrats d'application versés au dossier à titre d'exemple confirme partiellement cette conclusion.

Le contrat du 26 avril 1994 fait apparaître que Monsieur S., sur un papier à entête X, a servi d'intermédiaire pour la signature d'un contrat entre B (« le vendeur ») et une société allemande E. (« l'acheteur ») pour un contrat portant sur des pêches au sirop. Dans ce contrat, Monsieur S., représentant légal de la société X, a agi au nom et pour le compte de son mandant, B, puisque c'est bien B qui est désigné comme le vendeur. Monsieur S. a agi en tant qu'intermédiaire à l'exportation des produits B.

De même, dans son activité d'intermédiaire à l'importation des produits frui-tiers, le contrat du 27 mai 1994 prouve à nouveau que Monsieur S. a servi d'inter-médiaire pour la signature d'un contrat entre B (cette fois-ci désignée comme « l'acheteur ») et une société thaïlandaise (« le vendeur ») pour l'importation de papayes. Dans ce contrat, Monsieur S., représentant légal de la société X, a agi au nom et pour le compte de son mandant, A, puisque c'est bien A qui est désigné comme l'acheteur.

Par ces deux contrats d'application, il apparaît clairement que Monsieur S. et ses sociétés agissaient en tant que professionnel indépendant au nom et pour le compte de leurs mandants. Ces deux contrats confirment que les demanderesses et les défenderesses étaient liées par un mandat, lequel, pour les raisons sus-évo-quées, était d'intérêt commun.

En revanche, il apparaît au vu du troisième contrat d'application, du 24 décembre 1986, que l'activité commercial de Monsieur S. et de ses sociétés ne se limitait pas uniquement à des activités relevant du mandat d'intérêt commun.

En effet, aux termes de ce contrat, il apparaît que la société Y (« l'acheteur ») a acheté à la société B (« le vendeur ») des cocktails de fruits pour les revendre à un autre distributeur, la société I, filiale du groupe P. Dans cette espèce, Y a donc agi comme commissionnaire puisque l'opération s'est faite en [s] *son nom propre mais (apparemment) pour le compte du commettant À l'audience, les demanderesses ont expliqué que ce contrat était une exception dans les relations commerciales qui liaient les parties, et concernait les stocks invendus de produits de marque B, qui étaient écoulés, hors marque et à sa demande, vers d'autres distributeurs.*

Il résulte de ce qui précède que la qualification des relations commerciales unissant les demanderesses et les défenderesses n'est pas unique. Ces relations contractuelles sont d'une nature hybride: quelques contrats relèvent du mandat d'intérêt commun et d'autres de la commission. Il semble cependant que la qual-ification dominante soit bien celle de mandat d'intérêt commun, comme cela résulte, notamment, des réunions régulières de travail qui se sont tenues entre les parties . . . ».

La résiliation du contrat

Après avoir qualifié le contrat en cause, l'arbitre a tiré les conséquences juridiques de sa résiliation dans les termes suivants.

« Tout d'abord, il y a lieu de constater que la résiliation du contrat du 19 janvier 1981 n'est fondée sur aucune faute commise par Monsieur S. et est seulement motivée par de « nouvelles dispositions consécutives à la restructuration de la société » comme cela est mentionné dans la lettre de résiliation du 9 février 1998.

À cet égard, il ne fait aucune doute que la réorganisation de l'entreprise man-dante peut éventuellement justifier, suivant les circonstances (au demeurant non précisées par les demanderesses), la résiliation du mandat liant les parties. Pour autant, une telle réorganisation ne saurait justifier une rupture brutale et abusive.

La résiliation unilatérale d'un contrat, pour lequel aucun terme n'a été prévu ni aucun préavis fixé, constitue normalement l'exercice d'un droit par l'une ou l'autre des parties. Pour autant, et en l'absence de faute de la part du mandataire, la résiliation du contrat par le mandant doit respecter un préavis raisonnable faute de quoi une indemnité compensatrice est due.

Le calcul de l'indemnisation d'une résiliation brutale et abusive varie suivant les cas d'espèce. En matière commerciale, l'usage est que le préavis varie entre trois mois et quelques années suivant la nature et l'ancienneté des relations commerciales entre les parties. Ainsi, le préavis prévu pour les agents commerciaux selon la loi du 25 juin 1991 en son article 11 est de trois mois, au-delà de trois années de relations commerciales. En outre, selon l'article 12 de cette même loi, une indemnité compensatrice du préju-dice subi est attribuée et varie, selon la jurisprudence et selon les espèces, entre quelques mois et quelques années de commissions.

En effet, les 22 janvier 1998 et 4 février 1998 — soit avant la lettre de résiliation du 9 février 1998 — puis les 11 février 1998, 16 et 18 mars 1998, B contactait divers fournisseurs de fruits avec lesquels Monsieur S. faisait ses affaires pour leur indiquer que les contrats seraient désormais établis directement, sans passer par l'intermédiaire habituel qu'était Monsieur S.

Il apparaît donc au regard de ces différents documents que le préavis de six mois, résultant de la lettre de résiliation, n'a pas été respecté, puisque avant même le 9 février 1998, des contacts étaient pris avec les fournisseurs de Monsieur S. pour mettre fin au contrat d'intermédiaire. Ces lettres envoyées directement aux fournisseurs de Monsieur S. ne pouvaient que désorganiser son réseau et porter atteinte à sa notoriété et à l'image commercial de ses sociétés. À cet égard, le fait que des courriers et des contacts aient pu être pris avant même la résiliation du contrat de mandat par lettre du 9 février 1998, est constitutif d'un abus de droit caractérisé.

L'arbitre retient des indications chiffrées fournies par les parties (attestations du Cabinet C du 20 novembre 1998 et attestations du Cabinet I du 7 novembre 1999) que les commissions reçues par les demanderesses sur les quatre dernières années et sans prendre en compte l'année 1998 pour laquelle l'activité du commerce des fruits de Monsieur S. a fortement baissé du fait de la résiliation du contrat, se sont élevées, en moyenne, à 933.000 francs par an.

Aussi, compte tenu de l'ancienneté et de l'importance des relations commerciales unissant les parties et du caractère abusif de la rupture, mais considérant cependant que ces relations n'étaient pas uniquement formées de mandats d'intérêt commun, il y a lieu de juger qu'une indemnisation globale correspondant à un préavis effectif de neuf mois doit être versée. En conséquence, l'Arbitre condamne solidairement les sociétés A et B à payer aux sociétés X et Y une indemnité pour rupture brusque et abusive d'un montant globale de 700.000 francs . . . ».

OBSERVATIONS. — I. — En considérant le fait que le contrat a été conclu par des sociétés françaises et que la langue de la procédure est le français, on aurait pu être tenté de conclure qu'il s'agissait d'un arbitrage interne français. Il n'en est rien puisque l'arbitre, sans l'exprimer expressément, a implicitement évoqué le caractère international de l'arbitrage compte tenu de l'activité et du tissu de relations d'affaires des parties qui dépassaient largement le cadre économique français.

Cette approche est intéressante car elle souligne une caractéristique constante de la notion française d'internationalité qui fait abstraction de la nationalité ou de la résidence des parties pour se concentrer sur une définition exclusivement économique de l'arbitrage international. Il suffit pour que le litige soit soumis à l'arbitre qu'il porte sur une opération qui ne se déroule pas économiquement dans un seul État. Le transfert des biens ou des fonds au-delà des frontières suffit à satisfaire ce critère. Une telle définition présente également l'avantage incontestable de limiter le rôle de la volonté des parties en ce domaine. Celles-ci ne peuvent pas librement déterminer elles-mêmes la nature — interne ou internationale — de l'arbitrage qui est tributaire exclusivement d'un critère économique (sur l'ensemble de la question, v. notamment *Fouchard-Gaillard-Goldman, Traité de l'arbitrage commercial international,* Litec 1996, n° 78. — M. Béhar-Touchais et G. Virassamy, *Les contrats de distribution,* LGDJ 1999, n° 666. — D. Ferner, *Droit de la distribution,* 3ᵉ édition, Litec 2002, n° 172. — C. Truong, *Les différends liés à la rupture des contrats internationaux de distribution dans les sentences arbitrales CCI,* Litec 2002, n° 14. — Paris, Iʳᵉ Ch., 17 janv. 2002: Rev. arb. 2002, p. 401, note J.-B. Racine. — Paris, 1ʳᵉ Ch., 29 mars 2001: Rev. arb. 2001, p. 543, note D. Bureau. — Cass. civ. Iʳᵉ, 21 mai 1989, Zanzi: Rev. arb. 1999, p. 260, note Ph. Fouchard. — Cass. civ. 1ʳᵉ, 21 mai 1997, Jaguar: Rev. arb. 1997, p. 537, note E. Gaillard. — art. 1492 du nouveau code de procédure civile français).

II. — Le contrat n'ayant pas prévu le droit applicable au fond, l'arbitre est normalement tenu, conformément à l'article 17 du Règlement CCI, d'appliquer les règles de droit qu'il juge appropriées. En l'occurrence, l'arbitre n'a pas jugé nécessaire de le déterminer car les parties avaient implicitement choisi d'un commun accord le droit applicable, en plaidant conformément au droit français. L'arbitre a donc raisonné vraisemblablement en droit français.

III. — Une des difficultés essentielles à laquelle l'arbitre est confronté est de déterminer la relation juridique qui lie les parties. En effet, celles-ci étaient liées par un « contrat cadre » qui est matérialisé par des contrats d'application de nature différente, à savoir notamment un contrat de représentation et un contrat d'approvisionnement.

Les parties étant en désaccord sur la qualification du contrat, à l'exception du fait qu'il s'agit d'un mandat, il appartient à l'arbitre de qualifier la nature exacte du contrat afin de déterminer les conséquences juridiques. Les demanderesses estiment que c'est un « contrat d'intérêt commun » dont la résiliation brutale et abusive justifie l'allocation d'une indemnisation. Les défenderesses considèrent par contre que c'est un « contrat de commissionnaire » dont la résiliation, qui a été régulièrement faite, n'ouvrait droit à aucune indemnité.

Pour tenter de rendre compte de l'activité des demanderesses et en partant du principe qu'il existe un contrat de mandat entre les parties, l'arbitre a analysé trois types de mandats possibles, à savoir le contrat de commission, de mandataire d'intérêt commun et d'agence commerciale.

L'arbitre a tout d'abord rejeté l'existence d'un contrat de commission car le commissionnaire, par définition, agit en son nom « propre » pour le compte d'un commettant *(art. 94 du Code de commerce français)*. Or, les demanderesses agissaient au nom et pour le compte des défenderesses en l'espèce.

L'arbitre n'a pas non plus retenu l'existence d'un contrat d'agent commercial qui agit au nom et pour le compte du mandant. Cette qualification a été rejetée pour une raison de fait, à savoir le défaut d'immatriculation d'une des demanderesses, bien qu'il ne s'agisse pas, comme l'admet l'arbitre, d'une condition nécessaire pour bénéficier du statut d'agent commercial qui est régi par la loi du 25 juin 1991.

L'arbitre a finalement retenu que la qualification prépondérante du contrat est celui du contrat de mandat d'intérêt commun en considération du fait que les demanderesses ont agi effectivement « *au nom et pour le compte de l'entreprise mandante* », soit les sociétés défenderesses. Les demanderesses ont en outre un intérêt commun avec les mandantes, à savoir le développement de la clientèle qui conditionne leurs droits à toucher une commission pour tout nouveau contrat conclu. Nonobstant cette qualification, l'arbitre admet finalement que les relations contractuelles des parties étaient de nature « hybride », certains contrats conclus relevant du mandat d'intérêt commun et d'autres de la commission.

On peut le regretter compte tenu de la spécificité et de tout l'intérêt du mandat d'intérêt commun. En effet, le mandat d'intérêt commun déroge tout d'abord au principe de la révocabilité *ad nutum* du mandant (*art. 2004 du Code civil français*). Ceci signifie que le mandant ne peut plus révoquer le mandat quand bon lui semble, sans verser de dommages-intérêts sauf faute du mandataire. L'intérêt économique commun des parties justifie qu'il ne puisse pas être révoqué par la volonté d'une seule partie, mais seulement de leur consentement mutuel. Rappelonsque cette catégorie particulière du contrat de mandat est une création jurispruden-tielle dont le but est de protéger le mandataire en cas de résiliation du contrat. Le mandat étant conclu dans l'intérêt commun des parties, à savoir « *l'essor de l'entreprise par création et développement de la clientèle* », la protection du mandataire est justifiée dans ce cadre, à la différence du mandat normal, où le mandataire intervient dans le seul intérêt du mandant et de la vente (V. *D. Ferrier, op. cit., n° 177. — v. également A. Brunei, Clientèle commune et contrat d'intérêt commun, in Mélanges Weill, Dalloz 1983, p. 85. — J. Ghestin, Le mandant d'intérêt commun, in Mélanges Derruppé, Litec 1991, p. 105. — Ph. Grignon, Le concept d'intérêt commun dans le droit de la distribution, Mélanges Cabrillac, Dalloz-Litec 1999, p. 127*).

De cette protection, le mandataire d'intérêt commun a droit à une indemnité compensatrice, sauf en cas de faute prouvée par le mandant (*V. Versailles, 19 juin 1997: D. Aff. 1997, p. 1251, production insuffisante du mandataire. — Cass. com., 6 janv. 1975: Bull. civ. IV n° 1, chiffre d'affaires insuffisant. — Cass. com., 13 nov. 1990: Bull. civ. IV n° 269, clause de quota*) ou qu'elle a été dictée par nécessité pour des raisons économiques, telle que la réorganisation de l'entreprise (*Cass. com., 11 juill. 1963, Bull. III, n°376: « Les laboratoires étaient en droit de préférer réorganiser leurs services en envoyant directement leurs marchandises aux grossistes sans passer par un dépositaire ». — Cass. com., 28 juin 1967: JCP 1967, II, 15290 bis, note P. Level, cessation de la fabrication des produits que le mandataire était chargé d'écouler. — Cass. com., 10 mars 1976: D. 1976, somm. 49*). La charge de la preuve des justes motifs est renversée puisqu'elle incombe désormais au mandant.

IV. — Tout en acceptant le fait que la restructuration de l'entreprise mandante aurait pu justifier la résiliation du contrat, l'arbitre a surtout retenu les circonstances de sa résiliation pour sanctionner les défenderesses selon les termes suivants: « *la résiliation unilatérale d'un contrat, pour lequel aucun terme n'a été prévu ni aucun préavis fixé, constitue normalement l'exercice d'un droit par l'une ou l'autre des parties. Pour autant, et en l'absence de faute de la part du mandataire, la résiliation du contrat par le mandant doit respecter un préavis raisonnable faute de quoi une indemnité compensatrice est due* ».

Le résultat auquel aboutit l'arbitre est correct, sauf à expliciter davantage le raisonnement qu'il a suivi pour justifier sa décision. En effet, si l'arbitre a admis que la relation des parties était « dominée » par l'existence du mandat d'intérêt commun, il aurait été suffisant d'indiquer que la résiliation unilatérale par les défenderesses dans ces conditions était illégale en l'absence d'un consentement mutuel des parties, d'une renonciation expresse de l'une d'entre elles ou de toute faute des mandataires (v. *supra*), et d'en tirer les conséquences.

Comme indiqué par le Professeur Ferrier, « *si un mandat d'intérêt commun est résilié à l'initiative du mandant, sans que la rupture soit justifiée par une cause légitime, ce dernier* [le mandataire] *a une "droit à une indemnité compensatrice du préjudice subi" (. . .) elle "répare le préjudice consécutif à la perte du droit de prospecter une clientèle et d'en tirer bénéfice en percevant des commissions"* » (*op. cit.,* n° 178).

Le principe de l'indemnisation est acquis en l'absence de toute faute des demanderesses mandataires, et l'absence de préavis alléguée par les demanderesses pour justifier la « brutalité » de la résiliation, n'affecte pas le droit à une indemnisation. Seul le montant de l'indemnisation peut varier en fonction des circonstances de la résiliation. En l'espèce, l'arbitre a admis que la résiliation était brutale en l'absence du respect d'un préavis raisonnable. L'arbitre a usé de son pouvoir d'appréciation de cette question de fait en s'appuyant essentiellement sur les attestations fournies par les parties, les usages existants et l'ancienneté des relations contractuelles (*V. sentence partielle CCI n° 7146 de 1994 où le tribunal arbitral a pris en compte la durée de la relation contractuelle et la spécificité des produits distribuées, in C. Truong, op cit. n° 217. — v. également la sentence partielle CCI n° 6725 de 1985 où l'arbitre a utilisé un raisonnement par analogie aux contrats d'agence pour établir le délai de préavis raisonnable en droit suisse, in C. Truong, op. cit. n° 218*).

L'arbitre a également décidé que la résiliation était « abusive » compte tenu du fait que les défenderesses ont commencé, bien avant la résiliation du contrat, à contacter les fournisseurs des demanderesses pour leur indiquer que les contrats seraient désormais établis directement avec elles. Les courriers et les contacts directs auprès de ces fournisseurs ont contribué à désorganiser le réseau des demanderesses et à porter atteinte à leur image de marque, et constituent un abus de droit caractérisé (*V. notamment l'affaire CCI n° 7514 de 1994 où l'abus de droit était constitué par le fait pour une des parties de rompre un contrat avec effet immédiat pour perte de confiance et désorganisation de la société contractante, in C. Truong, op. cit., n° 268).*

Compte tenu du caractère abusif de la résiliation, de l'ancienneté des relations (plus de 15 ans), de la moyenne des commissions perçues par les demanderesses durant les quatre dernières années, l'arbitre leur a accordé une indemnisation compensatrice de 700.000 francs français, en sus d'une indemnisation globale correspondant à un préavis effectif de neuf mois en considération du fait que les relations des parties *«n'étaient pas uniquement formées de mandat d'intérêt commun ».* On peut à nouveau regretter que l'arbitre n'ait pas tiré toutes les conséquences juridiques de la qualification du contrat de mandat d'intérêt commun qu'il a pourtant retenu à titre principal (V. *supra* sur la qualification du contrat). L'arbitre s'est appuyé sur la nature « hybride » de la relation des parties, tantôt dominée par l'activité de commission ou de mandataire général pour justifier l'indemnisation des demanderesses. Il s'agit pourtant de différentes formes de contrats qui sont soumis à des régimes juridiques distincts.

On admet bien volontiers le pouvoir de requalification des arbitres qui n'est pas lié par celle des parties (*V. notamment la sentence CCI n° 8056 (1996) où le tribunal arbitral rappelle qu'« il est de principe que la qualification juridique d'une relation ne dépend pas de ce que les parties imaginent avoir créé, ni du titre que ces parties inventeront ou adopteront pour définir ces relations »: Bull. CCI., Vol. 12, n° 1, 2001 p. 68. — v. également dans une affaire similaire CCI n° 9443 de 1998 où l'opération juridique a été qualifiée de « concession », « franchise », « transfert de technologie », « licence de marque »: JDI 2002, p. 1106, note E. Jolivet. — Fouchard-Gaillard-Goldman, Traité de l'arbitrage commercial international, op. cit., n° 1477*). Toutefois, l'approche adoptée par l'arbitre est susceptible de soulever un certain nombre d'interrogations sur la solution dégagée. Si l'arbitre a décidé de retenir la qualification dominante du contrat de mandat d'intérêt commun, il aurait pu en tirer toutes les conséquences juridiques liées à cette qualification. La résiliation unilatérale est en principe interdite, et le mandant qui a rompu unilatéralement le contrat doit verser à son co-contractant une indemnisation compensatrice. À défaut de disposer de règles précises de calcul, l'arbitre pouvait raisonner par analogie en s'appuyant sur les règles applicables autres types de contrats de distribution. Inversement, si l'arbitre a décidé de retenir plutôt la nature hybride de la relation contractuelle des parties, et rien ne l'y empêchait, il aurait pu appliquer le régime juridique propre à chaque type de contrat retenu, soit le mandat d'intérêt commun ou la commission.

S. J.

Sentence finale rendue dans l'affaire n° 10527 en 2000 (original en langue française)

I. — Sentence. — Forme. — Référence aux pièces du dossier.

II. — Droit français. — Force majeure. — Article 1147 du Code civil. — Eléments constitutifs — Irrésistibilité (non). — Contrôle des changes.

III. — Force majeure. — Mise en œuvre. — Information de la partie créancière de l'obligation non-exécutée.

IV. — Force majeure. — Effet suspensif. — Durée. — Mise en demeure d'exécuter les obligations auparavant suspendues. — Offre d'exécution amiable des obligations.

La demanderesse, société privée française, avait absorbé une autre société française (S) du secteur de l'habillement, liée par un « contrat de licence » à la défenderesse, une entreprise publique algérienne. La société absorbée était titulaire de la marque A et de marques complémentaires exploitées pour désigner un certain type d'articles d'habillement. La défenderesse était productrice de ces articles d'habillement et s'était vue attribuer, par un contrat de licence conclu avec la demanderesse pour une durée de trois ans et concernant un territoire contractuel comportant l'Algérie et étendue à d'autres pays d'Afrique pour les deux premières années, un droit exclusif d'utiliser la marque A et les marques dérivées pour « *fabriquer et faire fabriquer, diffuser et commercialiser* » les produits contractuels. En contrepartie des droits reconnus par la demanderesse à la défenderesse, cette dernière devait verser à la première une redevance annuelle de 6%, calculée sur le chiffre d'affaires hors taxe réalisé sur les ventes de produits contractuels portant la marque A. Le contrat stipulait pour chaque année une redevance minimale, quelles que soient les ventes de produits contractuels. La défenderesse paya uniquement les redevances dues au titre de la première année et du premier semestre de la deuxième. Aucune indication sur le montant des ventes pour la troisième année ne fut même fournie par la défenderesse à la demanderesse.

La demanderesse introduisit une demande d'arbitrage sur la base de la clause compromissoire stipulée au « contrat de licence ».

Dans la seule sentence rendue dans cette affaire, l'arbitre unique nommé par la Cour internationale d'arbitrage, après un rappel de la procédure, une présentation des faits et des prétentions des parties, poursuit:

> « *en se fondant sur l'article* [relatif aux redevances] *du Contrat de Licence,* [la demanderesse] *demande le paiement des redevances minimales dues au titre du deuxième semestre de* [la deuxième année] *et de l'ensemble de* [la troisième] *année.*
> [La défenderesse] *ne conteste pas l'existence du Contrat de Licence mais soutient qu'elle n'a pu exécuter l'obligation de paiement des redevances minimales du fait d'événements politiques et économiques revêtant les caractéristiques de la force majeure, et qu'elle est par conséquent exonérée de son obligation.*
> *En particulier,* [la défenderesse] *soutient que des restrictions apportées par le gouvernement aux importations et aux paiements en devises l'auraient empêchée: (a) d'une part, de produire les* [articles d'habillement portant la marque A] *au cours de* [la troisième année] *et, de l'autre, (b) d'effectuer le versement des sommes dues à la société* [S] *au titre du deuxième semestre de* [la deuxième année].*

Il faut au préalable souligner que la gravité et les conséquences de la crise politique et économique algérienne ne sont pas contestées par [la demanderesse]. *Néanmoins, cette dernière conteste que lesdits événements aient pu réaliser un cas de force majeure qui aurait empêché* [la défenderesse] *d'exécuter ses obligations contractuelles.*

(a) Sur la possibilité par la société [défenderesse] de produire des chaussures
La [défenderesse] *soutient qu'elle devait être exonérée de son obligation de payer les redevances minimales puisqu'elle a été dans l'impossibilité de produire des articles* [d'habillement] *revêtus de la marque* [A] *au cours de* [la troisième année] *du fait de l'absence de matières premières et de machines nécessaires au fonctionnement de ses sites de production.*

Il faut tout d'abord remarquer que l'obligation de paiement des redevances minimales n'était pas subordonnée à la fabrication ou à la vente d'un certain volume de [produits contractuels]. En effet, aux termes de l'article [relatif aux redevances] *du Contrat de Licence,* [la défenderesse] *s'était engagée à payer une redevance minimale "quelles que soient ses ventes de produits sous licence".*

En tout cas, même en admettant que l'empêchement de produire de la société [défenderesse] *ait pu altérer le rapport synallagmatique entre les parties, il n'est pas prouvé que la société* [défenderesse] *ait été dans l'impossibilité de produire des* [articles d'habillement revêtus de la marque A] *du fait d'événements ayant les caractéristiques de la force majeure.*

En ce qui concerne les dispositions législatives relatives à la force majeure, au regard de l'article 1147 du Code civil: "Il n'y a lieu à aucun dommages-intérêts lorsque, par suite d'une force majeure ou d'un cas fortuit, le débiteur a été empêché de donner ou de faire ce à quoi il était obligé, ou a fait ce qui lui était interdit".

La force majeure se définit en droit français comme étant un événement irrésistible, imprévisible et extérieur (Encyclopédie Dalloz, 1997, p. 2; 2ᵉ Chambre Civile, 1ᵉʳ avril 1999, Bull. n. 65). Ces trois conditions doivent être réunies cumulativement pour que l'événement soit considéré comme un cas de force majeure.

Or, l'irrésistibilité exige du débiteur une impossibilité totale et absolue d'exécution; l'exécution rendue plus difficile ou plus onéreuse est sans effet sur l'étendue de l'engagement du débiteur (Ceri, Pratique des contrats internationaux, 1995, p. 23). Donc, la force majeure est un phénomène contre lequel on ne peut rien, il n'y a force majeure que pour autant qu'il n'existe aucun autre moyen d'exécuter; on dit aussi qu'elle est insurmontable (Cass. com. 6 février 1973 (verglas), Bull. civ. IV, n. 62; 31 octobre 1978 (grève), Gaz. Pal. 1979.1 panor.38; Cass. 2ᵉ civ. 17 janvier 1979 (glissement de terrain), Bull. civ. II, n. 21; 21 janvier 1981 (idem), JCP 1982.II. 19814; Paris, 9 juin 1961, D. 1962.297).

Ainsi en matière contractuelle, la force majeure met le débiteur dans l'impossibilité d'agir autrement (J. Radouant, Rep. civ., 1ʳᵉ éd., Voir Force majeure). Il faut donc que la partie qui se déclare empêchée n'ait pu recourir à une solution alternative qui aurait, même à un coût supérieur, permis l'exécution (H. Lesguillons, Contrats internationaux, tome 3, Lamy 1999).

En l'espèce, [la défenderesse] *n'était pas dans l'impossibilité absolue de produire des* [articles d'habillement revêtus de la marque A]. *Cette conclusion ressort des pièces versées aux débats qui établissent les événements suivants:*

Par lettre du [date] (pièce 2 annexée à la demande d'arbitrage (. . .)), [la défenderesse] *a informé la demanderesse des difficultés d'approvisionnement des matières d'importations liées aux restrictions en matière de financement extérieur de l'économie algérienne.*

Par lettres du [date] (pièces 4 et 5 annexées à la demande d'arbitrage (. . .)), la demanderesse a suggéré à la défenderesse de poursuivre la fabrication des [articles d'habillement] *en utilisant « les meilleures matières premières disponibles localement » et qu'ensuite les modèles ainsi réalisés lui soient proposés pour qu'elle puisse les approuver ou les refuser.*

La défenderesse a refusé d'utiliser les matières premières disponibles locale-ment (lettre du [date], pièce 8 annexée à la demande d'arbitrage (. . .)) en se fondant sur l'article [numéro] *du Contrat de Licence. À cet égard, il convient de préciser que la proposition de la demanderesse ne violait pas les dispositions de l'article* [numéro] *du Contrat de Licence. Cet article prévoit, en effet,* [que la défenderesse] *utilise les meilleures matières disponibles pour fabriquer les produits licenciés.*

Il ressort donc des échanges de correspondance rappelés ci-dessus que [la demanderesse] *avait autorisé* [la défenderesse] *à utiliser les matières premières disponibles localement.*

Par conséquent, [la défenderesse] *aurait pu utiliser les matières premières disponibles localement sans encourir une violation du Contrat de Licence. Elle avait donc à sa disposition le recours à une solution alternative qui aurait permis l'exécution de ses obligations.*

En ce qui concerne les dégâts causés par les actes de sabotage enregistrés au sein des Unités de la société [défenderesse], *il ressort des pièces versées aux débats que ces actes de sabotages n'ont pas placé cette dernière dans l'impossibilité totale de fabriquer les* [articles d'habillement portant la marque A].

En effet, la société [défenderesse] *dispose de 8 sites de productions distincts (voir « Actions de sabotage liées au terrorisme (. . .) », pièce annexée aux con-clusions en réplique* [de la défenderesse] *du [date]), parmi lesquels la défenderesse avait réservé « un minimum de 3 usines, et non des moindres, pour la production à 100% des* [articles d'habillement portant la marque A] » *(voir lettre du [date], pièce 8 annexée à la demande d'arbitrage (. . .)).*

Seul l'un des sites de production [de la défenderesse] *a été détruit pendant la période d'exécution du Contrat de Licence le [date], soit 4 mois seulement avant l'expiration du Contrat de Licence. En outre, le matériel épargné par l'incendie a été réparti à travers les autres Unités de production (voir l'article du quotidien* [nom] *du [date], pièce annexée aux conclusions en réplique* [de la défenderesse] *du [date] et « Actions de sabotage liées au terrorisme [date], pièce annexée aux conclusions en réplique* [de la défenderesse] *du [date]). De plus, la défenderesse n'a pas démontré que le site détruit produisait des* [articles d'habillement portant la marque A].

Donc, il est évident que les dégâts subis par les sites de production de la société [défenderesse] *n'ont pas empêché cette dernière de produire des articles* [revêtus de la marque A].

Il ressort de la correspondance [de la défenderesse] *(voir la lettre du [date], pièce 2 annexée à la demande d'arbitrage (. . .)) que « en l'absence de ressources provenant de l'exportation, les niveaux de production projetés pour* [la troisième année] *ne pourraient guère dépasser 50.000* [articles] ». *Il ressort aussi d'une lettre de la société* [défenderesse] *(pièce 8 du dossier de fond complémentaire* [de la défenderesse]*) que celle-ci a « commercialisé » 21.603* [articles] *revêtus de la marque* [A] *pour le seul premier trimestre* [de la troisième année].

La société [défenderesse] *a donc assuré une certaine commercialisation* [des articles d'habillement portant la marque A] *même* [la troisième année]. *Et le fait d'avoir vendu des articles* [revêtus de la marque A] *démontre qu'il a été possible de produire, même si c'est en quantité inférieure à ce qui était prévu.*

À aucun moment la société [défenderesse] *n'a informé la demanderesse de son incapacité totale de produire les articles sous licence, ni n'a invoqué l'existence d'un cas de force majeure, comme elle aurait dû le faire aux termes de l'article* [numéro] *du Contrat de Licence.*

Il résulte donc de l'ensemble des faits et des pièces produites que les événements politiques et économique algériens invoqués par la défenderesse ne constituent pas un empêchement irrésistible ou insurmontable à la production des [articles revêtus de la marque A] *et, par conséquent, ne réalisent pas un cas de force majeure.*

(b) Sur l'obligation et la possibilité de payer les redevances minimales

Le Contrat de Licence, on l'a déjà dit, met à la charge de la société [défenderesse] *une obligation de payer des redevances minimales (article* [numéro] *du Contrat de Licence) quels que soient les volumes* [d'articles revêtus de la marque A] *produits et vendus.*

De l'ensemble des dispositions du Contrat de Licence, il résulte que cette obligation de paiement à la charge [de la défenderesse] *constitue la contrepartie « des droits qui lui sont concédés »* par [S]; *notamment: le droit exclusif d'utiliser la marque* [A] *pour fabriquer, diffuser et commercialiser des articles* [d'habillement] *(article* [numéro] *du Contrat de Licence) sur le territoire comprenant l'Algérie (article* [numéro] *du Contrat de Licence) et 18 autres pays africains pour les deux premières années du Contrat de Licence (article* [numéro] *du Contrat de Licence); le droit à l'assistance technique en ce qui concerne la conception, la fabrication et l'utilisation des produits licenciés (article* [numéro] *du Contrat de Licence).*

Il ne fait pas de doute qu'en principe [la défenderesse] *était tenue de payer les redevances minimales pour toute la durée du Contrat de Licence* [terme a quo et terme ad quem]. *Malgré cela,* [la défenderesse] *a réglé seulement les paiements des redevances dues au titre de* [la première] *année et du premier semestre de* [la deuxième] *année.*

La société [défenderesse] *soutient que des restrictions apportées par le gouvernement algérien aux paiements en devises l'auraient empêchée d'obtenir de sa banque le virement bancaire des sommes dues à la demanderesse. Selon la société* [défenderesse]*, ces événements de force majeure l'exonéreraient de son obligation de paiement des redevances minimales.*

En particulier, [la défenderesse] *affirme que sa banque aurait refusé de procéder au virement des redevances dues pour le deuxième semestre* [de la deuxième année] *en application d'une instruction gouvernementale du 18 août 1992 (pièce 12 du dossier de fond complémentaire* [de la défenderesse]*) recommandant la réduction des importations et des paiements en devise.*

En effet, il résulte des pièces produites par [la défenderesse] *que celle-ci en* [deuxième année] *et* [troisième année] *a relancé sa banque à plusieurs reprises pour que le montant relatif aux redevances minimales du 3e et 4e trimestre* [de la deuxième année] *soit transféré sur le compte de* [S] *(pièces 1 et 2 du dossier de fond complémentaire* [de la défenderesse] *du* [date]*).*

Par contre, [la défenderesse] *n'a pas démontré avoir mise en œuvre de pareilles démarches de relance auprès de sa banque à partir de* [la troisième année]. *De même,* [la défenderesse] *n'a pas démontré qu'à partir de* [la troisième année] *le non-paiement des redevances pouvait être imputable à des restrictions imposées par les autorités bancaires ou à tout autre fait « irrésistible ».*

En outre, on remarque [que la défenderesse] *n'a jamais pris de mesures pour que soit effectué le paiement des redevances minimales dues au titre de* [la troisième année].

En effet, la demanderesse soutient que les restrictions en question sont aujourd'hui levées et la défense [de la défenderesse] *n'a jamais contesté cette affirmation.*

Or, la doctrine admet de façon aujourd'hui indiscutée que « en cas d'impossibilité momentanée d'exécution d'une obligation, le débiteur n'est pas libéré, cette exécution étant seulement suspendue jusqu'au moment où l'impossibilité vient à cesser » (P. -H. Antonmattei, Contribution à l'étude de la force majeure, LGDJ,

1992, p. 207 et ss.; voir également l'arrêt suivant: Cass. civ., 24 février 1981, D. 1982, 479).

Il en découle que, puisque les restrictions imposées par les autorités bancaires ne sont plus en vigueur au jour d'aujourd'hui, [la défenderesse] *est tenue de payer les redevances minimales et est sans conteste en mesure d'effectuer ces paiements.*

À l'appui de ce qui est dit ci-dessus, on remarque qu'il ressort de l'extrait du procès-verbal de la réunion du [date], *regroupant le directoire du holding* [de la défenderesse], *le Directeur Général de la banque et le PDG de la société* [défenderesse] *(pièce 4 du dossier de fond complémentaire* [de la défenderesse]*), la reconnaissance de la part de la défenderesse de son obligation.*

En conclusion, il n'est pas prouvé [que la défenderesse] *était dans l'impossibilité de produire des* [articles revêtus de la marque A], *ainsi que de payer les sommes dues au titre des redevances minimales. Il en découle que l'exception soulevée par la défenderesse de l'existence de cas de force majeure qui l'auraient exonérée de ses obligations est sans fondement.*

Par conséquent, [la défenderesse] *demeure tenue de payer les redevances minimales prévues à l'article* [relatif aux redevances] *du Contrat de Licence pour les* [deuxième] *(relatives au deuxième semestre) et* [troisième] *années.*

(c) Les sommes dues

Aux termes de l'article [relatif aux redevances] *du Contrat de Licence, la redevance minimale à laquelle* [la défenderesse] *est tenue est de* [montant 1] *pour* [la première] *année, de* [montant 2] *pour* [la deuxième] *année et de* [montant 3] *pour* [la troisième] *année. Etant donné que ce sont les redevances minimales pour le deuxième semestre de* [la deuxième année] *et pour* [la troisième] *année qui demeurent impayées, la défenderesse est tenue de payer la somme de* [montant 4 correspondant à 0,5 fois le montant 2 + le montant 3] *au titre des redevances minimales du deuxième semestre de* [la deuxième année] *et de* [la troisième] *année.*

La demanderesse a demandé que les intérêts au taux légal soient comptés à partir de la cessation des restrictions imposées par le gouvernement algérien au transfert de devises, mais elle n'a pas indiqué la date exacte à laquelle les restrictions auraient cessées.

Il est également nécessaire de prendre en compte le fait que la demanderesse ait depuis l'expiration du Contrat de Licence entrepris des démarches amiables pour le règlement de sa créance; démarches qui n'ont pas abouti. La demanderesse n'a donc réellement mis en demeure la société [défenderesse] *de lui régler la somme de* [montant 4] *correspondant aux redevances impayées que le* [date] *(pièce 9 annexée à la demande d'arbitrage (. . .)).*

La demande de la société [demanderesse] *concernant le paiement des intérêts n'est donc recevable qu'à compter de la mise en demeure, conformément à l'article 1153 du Code civil. Dès lors, les intérêts légaux sont dus à partir de la date de la lettre de mise en demeure adressée par la demanderesse à la défenderesse, soit le* [date].

Compte tenu de ce qui est dit ci-dessus et aux termes de l'article 31 du Règlement d'Arbitrage de la CCI, il y a lieu de décider que le paiement des frais de l'arbitrage incombe à la partie défenderesse, tandis que chacune des parties est tenue de supporter ses propres frais de défense ».

OBSERVATIONS. — I. — Le règlement d'arbitrage de la CCI n'impose aucune forme particulière pour la sentence arbitrale, si ce n'est l'obligation de la motiver *(article 25(2) du règlement d'arbitrage de 1998, publication CCI n° 808, 2003)*. Les arbitres structureront la sentence en fonction de divers facteurs tenant notamment à leur tradition juridique, aux caractères du litige, aux prétentions des parties ainsi qu'à la manière dont ces deux derniers éléments auront été présentés par les parties, au déroulement de la procédure et au droit applicable *(D. Byrne, Award writing: a judge's view: Arbitration 2003, vol. 69, n° 4, p. 272 et suiv. — M. Fontaine, La rédaction de la sentence du point de vue d'un juriste de droit continental: Bull. CIArb. CCI 1994, vol. 5, n° 1, p. 30 et suiv. — H. Lloyd, Rédaction des sentences, la conception d'un juriste de common law, op. cit., p. 38 et suiv. et spéc, p. 41).* Dans la présente sentence, l'arbitre prend un soin particulier à mentionner de manière systématique les pièces du dossier sur lesquels il appuie son argumentation. Ces pièces sont toutes définies par leur nature, leur auteur et leur date. Si l'identification précise dans la sentence des pièces étayant le raisonnement juridique développé par les parties ou l'arbitre est nécessaire, elle l'est d'autant plus lorsqu'il s'agit pour l'arbitre de souligner que la procédure n'est pas entachée de vice de nature à permettre à l'une des parties d'en contester la validité *(sur la question connexe de l'obligation pour l'arbitre de rendre une sentence susceptible d'être exécutée voir G. Horvath, The duty of the tribunal to render an enforceable award: Journal of International Arbitration 2001, vol. 18, n° 2, p. 135 et suiv.).* Ainsi, la mention de ces pièces tend à démontrer que les prétentions des parties ont été examinées, que l'égalité de traitement des parties a été scrupuleusement respectée *(sur cette question voir D. Hascher, Principes et pratiques de procédure dans l'arbitrage commercial international, Académie de droit international de La Haye, Recueil des cours de 1999, vol. 279, 2000, p. 126 et suiv.)* et que le principe du contradictoire n'a pas été bafoué. La présente sentence illustre cette préoccupation. La défenderesse ne s'était pas présentée à l'audience de plaidoirie fixée par l'arbitre, bien qu'elle ait été régulièrement convoquée, et avait mentionné qu'elle n'envisageait pas de plaider son dossier *(en général sur la procédure par défaut, voir J. -F. Poudret, S. Besson, Droit comparé de l'arbitrage international, Bruylant, LGDJ, Schulthess, 2002, p. 535 et suiv.).* La demanderesse était la seule à plaider son dossier. Il importait donc à l'arbitre d'une part de prendre en compte les arguments respectifs des parties, les uns exclusivement écrits, les autres oraux et écrits, afin de se former une opinion, et d'autre part de mentionner de manière explicite que tous ces argument avait été considérés.

II. — Confrontée à des difficultés d'exécution de certaines obligations contractuelles, il est fréquent qu'une partie invoque la force majeure. Cette notion est caractéristique de certains droits et, selon les droits qui la connaissent, ne recouvre pas nécessairement les mêmes circonstances factuelles excusant l'inexécution contractuelle *(ce qui explique par exemple la technique de rédaction choisie par la CNUDCI lors de la rédaction de l'article 79 de la Convention des Nations Unies sur les contrats de vente internationale de marchandise de 1980, Nations Unies, Document A/CN.9/562, 9 juin 2004, n° 5, p. 2; sur la mutabilité du concept de force majeure, voir P. -H. Antonmattei, Contribution à l'étude de la force majeure, LGDJ, 1992, p. 10 et suiv.).* La sentence expose avec concision la notion de force majeure et son régime en droit français. Après avoir rappelé les trois composantes traditionnelles d'un événement de force majeure, à savoir son irrésisti-bilité, imprévisibilité et extériorité, qui distingue cette notion de notions voisines telles par exemple, que l'imprévision ou le *hardship (voir en général M. Almeida Prado, Le hardship dans le droit du commerce international, Feduci, FEC, Bruylant, 2003),* l'arbitre examine le caractère irrésistible de certains « *événements politiques et économiques* ».

L'arbitre prend tout d'abord soin de préciser que ces événements sont « *des restrictions apportées par le gouvernement aux importations et aux paiements en devises* ». L'acte de mission précisait que, selon la défenderesse, les « *banques, institutions sous la tutelle de l'État* [ne pouvaient] *accorder (. . .) des autorisations de transfert d'argent pour des produits importés qu'en cas de produits considérés comme vitaux (. . .) abstraction faite de l'aisance financière de l'entreprise* » *(à rapprocher de la sentence rendue dans l'affaire n° 2216 en 1974, S. Jarvin, Y. Derains, Recueil des sentences arbitrales de la CCI 1974-1985, Kluwer, 1990, p. 225 et suiv. et spéc. p. 228-229. — sentence rendue dans l'affaire n. 3093/3100 en 1979, op. cit., p. 365. — sentence rendue dans l'affaire n. 7539 en 1995, obs. Y. Derains, J. -J. Arnaldez, Y. Derains, D. Hascher, in Recueil des sentences arbitrales de la CCI 1996-2000, Kluwer law international, 2003, p. 445 et suiv.).* L'événement devant remplir les trois critères énoncés est donc clairement identifié.

L'arbitre examine ensuite les stipulations contractuelles et retient qu'elles n'interdisaient pas à la défenderesse de s'approvisionner en matières premières locales. Ni l'arbitre ni les parties n'invoquent le courant jurisprudentiel considérant que les choses de genre ne peuvent être affectées par la force majeure en vertu de l'adage *genera non pereunt* (*G. Marty, P. Raynaud, Droit civil, tome 1, les sources, 2ᵉ éd., Sirey, 1988, p. 695*). Le contrôle des changes mis en place par les autorités algériennes et qui semble empêcher l'importation de matières premières conduisait seulement à modifier le schéma de production, les produits contractuels ayant été fabriqués jusqu'à la mise en place de ce contrôle avec de telles matières premières. L'existenced' « *une solution alternative qui aurait permis l'exécution de ses obligations* » par la défenderesse montre que cette dernière n'était pas dans l'impossibilité de produire les articles d'habillement du fait du contrat. La modification du schéma de production aurait toutefois pu rendre l'exécution du contrat plus onéreuse pour la défenderesse et susciter un débat (qui n'a pas eu lieu) sur le changement d'équilibre des prestations contractuelles.

Les actes de sabotage subis par les unités de productions de la défenderesse et invoqués par celle-ci auraient pu présenter un caractère insurmontable. Encore aurait-il fallu, ce qui n'était pas le cas en l'espèce, que l'intégralité des moyens de production fut affectée et mette la défenderesse dans l'impossibilité totale de fabriquer les produits contractuels. À supposer que l'arbitre ait retenu le caractère irrésistible de ces actes, la question de leur extériorité par rapport à la personne de la défenderesse aurait vraisemblablement été délicate *(sur ce point voir P. -H. Antonmattei, op. cit., p. 30 et suiv.).* Il aurait par exemple fallu que la défenderesse rapporte la preuve que ces actes n'avaient pas été commis ou facilités par une personne participant à l'exécution du contrat.

La défenderesse soutenait que son défaut de paiement était dû au régime de contrôle des changes instauré par le gouvernement algérien prohibant les transferts de devises à l'étranger. Selon la défenderesse, il s'agissait d'un événement insurmontable constitutif d'un cas de force majeure. Certaines sentences ont en effet retenu que des mesures prises par des autorités étatiques rendant impossible l'exécution du contrat par une entreprise publique nationale ne faisaient pas obstacle à ce que soit reconnue l'existence d'un cas de force majeure au bénéfice de cette entreprise *(sentence rendue dans l'affaire n° 2478 en 1974, S. Jarvin, Y. Derains, Recueil des sentences arbitrales de la CCI 1974-1985, Kluwer, 1990, p. 233 et suiv. et spéc. p. 236. — Comparer à la sentence rendue dans l'affaire n. 3093/3100 en 1979, loc. cit.).* Ces mêmes sentences montrent que la condition d'extériorité de la force majeure, lorsqu'elle est exigée, est dans la situation envisagée plus délicate à établir.

L'arbitre unique relève justement que la défenderesse n'a pas rapporté la preuve d'avoir engagé toutes les démarches nécessaires pour exécuter ses obligations, même si l'engagement de ces démarches n'était qu'une simple obligation de moyens. Ainsi aucune relance ne fut effectuée par la défenderesse auprès de sa banque pour demander le paiement des redevances à la demanderesse. On peut d'ailleurs s'interroger sur la possibilité qu'aurait eu la demanderesse de consigner les sommes dues auprès d'un tiers afin de démontrer sa bonne foi et sa volonté d'exécuter le contrat.

L'arbitre unique relève également avec pertinence l'absence de lien de causalité entre le défaut de paiement de la défenderesse et les « *restrictions imposées par les autorités bancaires ou [. . .] tout autre fait "irrésistible"* » pour la troisième année du contrat. La précision a son importance. Même si le caractère irrésistible de l'événement avait été établi, la nécessité de prouver la relation causale entre l'événement et l'inexécution de l'obligation aurait persisté.

Aucun des événements invoqués par la défenderesse n'ayant un caractère imprévisible, l'existence d'un cas de force majeure n'est pas avéré. L'arbitre unique considère comme inutile de poursuivre l'examen des deux autres caractères de la force majeure.

III. — Afin de produire ses effets (extinction d'obligations, suspension de leur exécution, ou réduction du contrat), la force majeure doit être portée à la connaissance du créancier de l'obligation non-exécutée par le débiteur de celle-ci *(à rapprocher de l'article 7.1.7 (3) des Principes UNIDROIT relatifs aux contrats du commerce international 2004)*. En l'espèce, et malgré la précision du contrat qui, alors que cela n'est pas systématiquement le cas dans les contrats internationaux *(M. Fontaine, F. De Ly, Droit des contrats internationaux, Analyse et rédaction de clauses, 2ᵉ éd., FEC, Bruylant, 2003, p. 452 et suiv.)*, imposait obligation de notification à la défenderesse, celle-ci n'a invoqué ni une incapacité totale de production, ce qui aurait pu constituer un événement irrésistible, ni même l'existence d'un événement de force majeure. Faute de respect des stipulations contractuelles, à supposer l'événement invoqué par la défenderesse constitutif d'un cas de force majeure, cette dernière n'aurait pas pu produire ses effets en l'espèce.

IV. — Lorsqu'il est reconnu un effet suspensif à la force majeure, cet effet se prolongera, sauf stipulation particulière, jusqu'à la disparition de l'événement constitutif de la force majeure *(voir par exemple, sentence dans l'affaire n. 1703 rendue en 1971, obs. R. Thompson, S. Jarvin, Y. Derains, Recueil des sentences arbitrales de la CCI 1974-1985, Kluwer, 1990, p. 195 et suiv.)*. Certains contrats prévoient que l'achèvement de la période de suspension des obligations et donc l'effet libératoire de l'exécution de ses obligations par le débiteur doit être porté à la connaissance du créancier de ces obligations *(M. Fontaine, F. De Ly, op. cit., p. 463)*.

En l'espèce, le contrat ne prévoyait pas que la disparition d'un événement de force majeure entraînait *ipso facto* l'exigibilité des obligations jusque là suspendues et la responsabilité contractuelle de la défenderesse en cas d'inexécution. De même, aucune stipulation n'imposait au créancier, à savoir la demanderesse, de mettre en demeure le débiteur, à savoir la défenderesse, d'exécuter ses obligations.

L'arbitre n'ayant pas retenu l'existence d'un cas de force majeure, se posaient alors plusieurs questions. La demanderesse avait-elle mis en demeure la défenderesse d'exécuter les obligations préalablement à la survenance de l'événement prétendument constitutif de force majeure? Dans l'affirmative, la demanderesse devait-elle réitérer cette mise en demeure une fois l'événement à l'origine de l'inexécution contractuelle ayant disparu? À défaut de mise en demeure antérieurement à la survenance de cet événement, la demanderesse devait-elle mettre la défenderesse en demeure et selon quelles modalités?

L'arbitre énonce que la disparition de l'événement prétendument constitutif de force majeure ne dispense pas d'une mise en demeure du débiteur. L'arbitre était ainsi amené à déterminer si la demande de paiement des intérêts à compter de « *la cessation des restrictions imposées par le gouvernement algérien au transfert de devises* » mais sans indiquer « *la date exacte à laquelle les restrictions auraient cessées* » ou les tentatives de règlement amiable de la créance constituaient une mise en demeure, ou si cette dernière ne pouvait résulter que de la demande expresse formulée après l'échec des tentatives de règlement amiable. L'arbitre retient la troisième solution admettant ainsi implicitement que la mise en demeure ne puisse, en l'espèce, résulter que d'un acte interpellant expressément le débiteur de l'obligation de paiement et indiquant expressément la date à partir de laquelle les obligations de paiement pouvaient de nouveau être exécutées. Le non-respect de l'une de ces conditions entraîne la nullité absolue de la mise en demeure. Lorsque ces conditions sont satisfaites, la mise en demeure produit effets à compter de sa réception par le débiteur.

Les intérêts moratoires au taux légal demandés par la demanderesse ne courent qu'à partir de la date de mise en demeure. Selon l'arbitre, seule la lettre envoyée par le demandeur constituait une interpellation suffisante au sens de l'article 1153 du Code civil. C'est précisément pour éviter cette dernière solution retardant le point de départ des intérêts moratoires que certaines parties engagent immédiatement une procédure contentieuse, arbitrale ou judiciaire. Il sera intéressant d'observer si le développement des procédures de règlement amiable des différends s'inscrivant dans un cadre d'une institution (par opposition aux procédures *ad hoc*) amène les arbitres du commerce international à considérer que l'initiation d'une telle procédure, ou que certaines étapes d'une telle procédure (par exemple une citation à comparaître lors d'une audience de conciliation), valent mise en demeure du débiteur de l'obligation non exécutée.

E. J.

Sentence rendue dans l'affaire n° 7139 en 1995

I. — Contrat. — Conditions Générales — Conditions Générales de Vente de Machines des Nations Unies — Acceptation.

II. — Contrat. — Crédit documentaire — Contenu — Effet sur les dispositions contractuelles.

III. — Contrat d'entreprise. — Réception — Mise en exploitation par le maître de l'ouvrage — Réception tacite.

IV. — Contrat d'entreprise. — Garantie — Usages du Commerce International.

V. — Contrat d'entreprise. — Responsabilité — Limitation de responsabilité — Gain manqué et dommages indirects — Usages du commerce International — Faute lourde — Définition.

VI. — Contrat. — Droit choisi par les parties — Domaine — Formalisme — Souplesse — Droit de l'État de la partie responsable d'obligations de forme.

Un arbitre unique, siégeant à Genève, était saisi de difficultés d'exécution d'un contrat par lequel une entreprise allemande X, s'était engagée à fournir à une entreprise française Y une chaudière permettant le séchage des fibres de bois ainsi qu'à mettre en route l'installation. La confirmation de commande renvoyait aux conditions générales de vente de machines de la Commission Economique pour l'Europe des Nations Unies, lesquelles déclarent applicable, sauf accord différent des parties, le droit du vendeur, donc, en l'espèce, le droit allemand. Le désaccord des parties portait essentiellement sur les qualités et la productivité de l'installation livrée dont l'entreprise française, demanderesse à l'arbitrage, jugeait les performances insuffisantes et se refusait à payer l'intégralité du prix.

L'arbitre devait tout d'abord décider si les conditions générales visées dans la confirmation de commande étaient opposables à Y. Il le fit dans les termes suivants:

> « La Demanderesse retient que les Conditions Générales ECE-188 ne lui ont jamais été remises, ni au moment de la signature du contrat, ni lors de la phase précontractuelle.
>
> Elle semble être d'avis que les Conditions Générales n° 188 A, qui incluent le montage, sont préférables et que la référence que fait le contrat aux Conditions ECE-188 est manifestement erronée. Subsidiairement, la Demanderesse semble conclure que les dispositions légales doivent être appliquées, à la place des conditions générales nulles ou inapplicables
>
> La Défenderesse, qui est en principe de l'avis que les Conditions Générales n° 188 sont applicables, a néanmoins admis que l'on applique au présent litige les conditions ECE-188 A, dans une interprétation complétive du contrat ("Ergänzende Vertragsauslegung"), si le contrat ou les conditions ECE-188 ne contenaient pas de règle pour juger des faits en question (. . .).
>
> Le tribunal arbitral rappelle que le § 2 du AGB-Gesetz (AGBG), qui concerne la validité de l'incorporation de conditions générales dans un contrat, n'est selon le § 24 al. 1 AGBG pas applicable aux affaires conclues entre commerçants. Cependant, même entre commerçants, une partie au contrat doit, en principe, donner l'occasion à l'autre partie de prendre connaissance des conditions générales

utilisées (BGH Z 102, p. 304). Cette condition est remplie si la partie au contrat a reçu les conditions générales à sa demande; il n'est pas nécessaire que ces conditions générales aient été jointes au contrat ou à la confirmation de commande (BGH NJW 1976, 1880; 1982, 1750). C'est seulement dans le cas où la partie qui les demande ne les reçoit pas que l'autre partie ne peut plus invoquer les conditions générales (Hamm DB 1983, 2619). Par ailleurs, les conditions générales sont valables s'il y a été fait référence dans le contrat ou au moment de la confirmation de commande.

Par conséquent, au plus tard lors de la remise de la confirmation de commande (. . .), la Défenderesse a valablement intégré les conditions générales ECE dans son contrat.

Il est par ailleurs surprenant et inadmissible que la Demanderesse laisse maintenant entendre que les conditions générales ECE-188, qui contiennent la clause arbitrale régissant le présent litige, seraient nulles ou inapplicables alors qu'elle s'y est référée elle-même dans son courrier du 17 juillet 1990 (. . .), dans sa requête d'arbitrage (. . .) et dans l'Acte de mission qu'elle a signé.

La question de savoir si les conditions ECE-188 ou ECE-188 A ont été intégrées est plus délicate. Le Tribunal est cependant de l'avis que la Défenderesse — malgré la dénomination littérale quelque peu imprécise de ces conditions — s'est clairement référée à la variante 188. La Demanderesse, qui invoque aujourd'hui l'application des conditions 188 A, aurait dû rectifier la mention qu'elle juge à présent incorrecte. Au vu de la jurisprudence mentionnée ci-dessus, le fait qu'elle n'ait reçu les conditions générales ne modifie rien à cet égard, puisqu'elle aurait pu les requérir de la Défenderesse ou se les procurer au secrétariat des Nations Unies.

Pour l'interprétation juridique du présent litige, il faut dès lors se baser, en principe, sur le contrat et sur les conditions ECE-188 (. . .). Par conséquent, le tribunal arbitral se fondera prioritairement sur le contrat de base du 8 septembre 1988 et sa concrétisation, soit la confirmation de commande du 5 octobre 1988, et sur les conditions générales ECE-188, ainsi que sur les dispositions du BGB, du HGB (étant donné que les parties sont commerçantes) et de l'ABGB. À titre supplétif, soit en vertu de l'accord intervenu entre les parties, le tribunal arbitral se référera aux conditions ECE-188 A, dans la mesure notamment où le contrat et les conditions ECE-188 ne contiennent pas de règles (cf. l'accord des parties sur ce point) ».

Parmi les conditions de paiement, le contrat prévoyait l'ouverture d'un crédit documentaire irrévocable (accréditif) pour 80% du prix, payable comme suit:

– 50% sur présentation des documents de prise en consigne du matériel par le transporteur,

– 20% à la fin du montage du matériel et contrôle avant mise en route,

– 10% à la mise en route.

Cependant, le crédit documentaire ouvert par une banque en faveur de X à la demande de Y contenait des conditions de réalisation non prévues au contrat de vente et notamment la présentation d'un procès verbal de mise en route signé par les deux parties. L'arbitre estima que, faute d'objection de X à l'époque, il en résultait une modification des conditions contractuelles de paiement:

« *Le crédit documentaire ouvert par la banque de la Demanderesse ne contient dès lors pas seulement des précisions quant aux expressions utilisées dans le contrat, mais également des changements, subordonnant notamment le paiement de l'avant-dernier acompte à la condition d'un procès-verbal de réception définitive et le dernier acompte à la condition d'un procès-verbal de mise en route. (. . .)*

La Défenderesse prétend avoir protesté contre cette modification et ne se sent liée que par les termes du contrat du 5 octobre 1988, deuxième version n° 060/88A.

648

Il convient dès lors d'examiner de plus près le développement des négociations à ce sujet.

Il est exact de considérer que ni les offres (. . .), ni le contrat de base (. . .), ne contiennent comme condition, l'établissement d'un procès-verbal. Après la conclusion de la première version (. . .) du contrat (. . .), le représentant de la société demanderesse (. . .) a, entre autre, proposé dans une lettre (. . .) une modification de la clause concernant le paiement de l'acompte de 20%, en stipulant pour celui-ci la condition de la signature d'un procès-verbal. Cette proposition n'a pas rencontré l'approbation de la Défenderesse étant donné que la version (. . .) du contrat ne la contient pas.

Par courrier du 21 février, la Demanderesse a envoyé à la Défenderesse un téléfax, auquel était joint une proposition pour l'ouverture de l'accréditif. Ce projet reprenait, quant à l'acompte de 20%, la proposition suggérée dans le courrier, à savoir l'établissement d'un procès-verbal, et rajoutait la même condition pour l'acompte de 10%.

La Défenderesse prétend qu'elle aurait, par courrier du 22 février, immédiatement protesté contre ces modifications préconisées par la Demanderesse et les aurait refusées. (. . .)

Le tribunal arbitral ne saurait partager ce point de vue: la lettre du 22 février ne se réfère nulle part aux modifications relatives aux acomptes, mais à des points accessoires, entre autres à la notice technique, au certificat d'origine et au procès-verbal de contrôle technique au départ de la marchandise effectué chez X. Les modifications proposées par la Demanderesse ont ainsi trouvé leur approbation tout au moins tacite de la part de la Défenderesse. (. . .)

Force est donc de constater que la Défenderesse n'a pas remis en cause ou refusé les conditions de paiement telles qu'elles résultent de l'accréditif ouvert par la Demanderesse le 24 mai 1989. Par conséquent, les conditions de paiement prévues dans le contrat ont été modifiées selon les termes de l'accréditif; c'est donc la pièce 243 (. . .) qui fait foi. En outre et selon l'avis du tribunal arbitral, cette manière de voir est plus conforme au concept usuel de paiement dans la construction pour les cas notamment où le montage fait partie des prestations de l'entrepreneur, comme en l'espèce. Il serait en effet exagéré de demander au maître de l'ouvrage de payer des sommes, relatives à la fourniture du matériel à des dates échelonnées sans qu'il ait la possibilité de faire constater officiellement que le montage a véritablement été exécuté. L'exigence de l'établissement d'un procès-verbal est donc, d'un point de vue pratique et juridique (cf. § 640 BGB, par analogie), tout à fait compréhensible ».

Les parties s'opposaient, entre autres, sur la question de savoir si la réception de l'installation était intervenue. L'arbitre décida que tel était le cas parce que, tout en se refusant à prononcer la réception, Y avait néanmoins procédé à la mise en route et commencé la production de panneaux de fibre:

« Les parties divergent sur la question essentielle de savoir si une réception de l'installation a eu lieu. Il résulte du contrat (p. 31) et des termes de l'accréditif que les parties entendaient par cette "réception" que la "mise en route", soit la "prise en charge après essais" selon ECE-188 A ait préalablement eu lieu.

La Demanderesse est de l'opinion qu'une réception n'a en tout cas pas eu lieu avant que la présente procédure arbitrale ait été engagée en février 1991 (. . .)

Le tribunal arbitral ne peut pas suivre la théorie de la Demanderesse selon laquelle une réception n'a jamais eu lieu. En effet, il serait contraire à l'usage, mais aussi à la réalité de soutenir cette thèse.

L'examen par APAVE qui doit être assimilé à la prise en charge du matériel, a eu lieu le [X]. La mise en route, qui avait déjà débuté quelque temps auparavant, doit être considérée comme étant terminée au plus tard début mai 1990, soit quand la Demanderesse a commencé sa production de panneaux de fibre (. . .). Or, cette date équivaut à la prise en charge après les essais au sens des articles 21 et 22 des Conditions générales ECE-188 A. on ne saurait considérer à présent que, dès lors que les parties n'ont pas signé de procès-verbal à cet effet, une réception n'aurait pas eu lieu. Cette manière de voir serait trop formaliste et, par ailleurs, contraire à la pratique en matière de construction, de même qu'au droit allemand.

En effet, la notion de réception tacite est connue en matière d'arbitrage de la construction comme le démontre, par exemple, la sentence de la CCI rendue dans l'affaire n° 3243 en 1981 (Clunet 1982, p. 968 s., observations, p. 971):

"La sentence ici rapportée tranche un irritant problème qui se pose assez fréquemment au plan international. Il s'agit du cas où un acheteur se refuse à procéder à la réception contractuelle d'une marchandise ou d'un ouvrage mais n'hésite pas pour autant à en prendre possession, ni même à en faire un usage commercial. Confrontés à cette situation, les arbitres en tirent la conclusion qui s'impose: l'utilisation commerciale des équipements livrés équivaut à leur réception".

En outre, le droit allemand prévoit une solution analogue: le § 640 BGB, qui est applicable au présent contrat (. . .), ainsi que les §§ 373 ss HGB disposent que le maître de l'ouvrage est obligé de réceptionner l'ouvrage, à moins qu'une réception soit exclue au vu de sa qualité. (. . .)

En bref, la Demanderesse a, en commençant à utiliser commercialement l'installation, tacitement réceptionné celle-ci, étant toutefois consciente de certains défauts de ladite installation, déjà connus de la Défenderesse, notamment par les constatations résultant du rapport de l'APAVE.

La réception entraîne un certain nombre de conséquences qui ne sont pas toutes pertinentes au présent litige (cf. Palandt, BGB, op. cit., ch. 5 ad § 640 BGB). Il sied, cependant, de relever que la réception peut signifier que les paiements dus à l'entrepreneur viennent à échéance et que le maître de l'ouvrage est privé des droits découlant des §§ 633 (Nachbesserung; Mängelbeseitigung) et 634 (Gewährleistung: Wandelung, Minderung) BGB, s'il reçoit l'installation sans réserve, bien qu'il connaisse les défauts. En outre, la réception sans réserve peut rendre une peine contractuelle caduque (§ 341 III BGB), ce qui sera à examiner sous le chef de demande relatif au "dépassement des délais". Enfin, les délais de prescription selon le § 638 BGB commencent à courir, sous réserve d'un délai de garantie (. . .) ».

L'arbitre s'attacha également à définir l'obligation de garantie à la charge du fournisseur de l'installation. Il le fit à la lumière des usages professionnels:

« *Il est rare dans l'industrie et le commerce international que les parties suivent avec la plus grande rigueur les lois et les accords passés entre eux pendant la phase d'exécution du contrat. Ce n'est qu'au moment où survient un litige que les parties se souviennent de la lettre du contrat et évaluent leurs actes à sa lumière. Il n'en est pas autrement dans le présent litige. C'est donc la tâche de l'arbitre de trouver le système de garantie applicable en l'espèce qui reflète au mieux l'intention des parties, et ce à partir des sources auxquelles les parties ont fait référence (contrat, conditions générales, loi).*

Le système de garantie prévu par les conditions générales ECE-188 A est le suivant:

Après le montage, il sera procédé à des essais de prise en charge (par. 21.1). Si, au cours des essais de prise en charge, l'ouvrage est reconnu défectueux ou non conforme au contrat, le constructeur devra remédier en toute diligence et à ses frais au défaut constaté ou faire en sorte que l'ouvrage réponde aux spécifications du contrat (par. 21.2). Dès que l'ouvrage est terminé conformément au contrat et a subi avec succès tous les essais de prise en charge à effectuer en fin du montage, l'acheteur est réputé l'avoir pris en charge et la période de garantie commence à courir.

L'acheteur devra alors remettre au constructeur une attestation, dénommée "procès-verbal de prise en charge" (par. 22.1). Le constructeur s'engage à remédier pendant la période de garantie (dont le point de départ sera la prise en charge) à tout vice de fonctionnement provenant d'un défaut dans la conception, les matières ou l'exécution (par. 23.1, par. 23.2). L'acheteur doit aviser sans retard et par écrit le constructeur des vices qui se sont manifestés. Il doit lui donner toute facilité pour procéder à la constatation de ceux-ci et y porter remède (par. 23.6). Si le constructeur refuse d'exécuter son obligation ou ne fait pas les diligences nécessaires en dépit d'une sommation, l'acheteur est en droit de procéder aux réparations nécessaires aux frais et risques du constructeur pourvu qu'il agisse avec discernement (par. 23.11). L'obligation du constructeur ne s'applique pas aux vices dont la cause est postérieure à la prise en charge et, notamment, dans le cas de modifications sans l'accord écrit du constructeur (par. 23.13). Après la prise en charge, il est de convention expresse que le constructeur ne sera tenu à aucune indemnisation envers l'acheteur pour manque à gagner, à moins qu'il ne résulte des circonstances de l'espèce que le constructeur a commis une faute lourde (par. 23.14, 23.15).

Les conditions générales ECE reflètent l'usage des professionnels tel qu'il se présente dans l'industrie internationale et plus spécifiquement dans le contexte de livraisons d'installations industrielles complètes. Devant leur acceptation générale, le droit applicable n'apparaît qu'en arrière plan (. . .)

Dans son analyse, Schneider arrive à la conclusion que la majorité des contrats d'installation prévoit, après d'éventuelles réceptions partielles, une réception après réussite des essais de prise en charge, documentée par un procès-verbal (certificate of substantial completion).

Selon le même auteur, la plupart des conditions générales font courir la période de garantie à partir de ce procès-verbal et prévoient une deuxième réception (final certificate) après laquelle d'éventuels remèdes ne peuvent plus être demandés. Toutefois, dans le présent litige, les parties ont adopté une solution contractuelle spécifique et n'ont par ailleurs pas prévu une réception finale au sens du "final certificate".

Par conséquent, la situation est la suivante:

Le "procès-verbal de réception définitive" de l'accréditif était prévu pour la fin du montage et équivaut, selon l'avis du tribunal arbitral, au procès-verbal d'APAVE du 18 avril 1990 (réception partielle selon l'analyse exposée ci-dessus). La période suivante aurait dû être la mise en route et aurait dû se terminer, selon l'accréditif, par le "procès-verbal de mise en route" (certificate of substantial completion), ce qui correspond au procès-verbal de prise en charge avec essais réussis au sens du para. 22.1 des conditions générales ECE-188 A.

Toutefois, selon les termes du contrat (. . .), le délai de garantie de 12 mois a commencé à partir de la fourniture du matériel qui peut se comprendre uniquement comme date de la dernière fourniture (cf. aussi l'accord entre les parties concernant l'accréditif). Comme il a été établi ci-dessus, la Défenderesse a encore fourni du matériel en décembre 1989. Lors du contrôle par APAVE, cette dernière a constaté que certaines livraisons faisaient toujours défaut. En plus, la Demanderesse soutient (. . .) que certains éléments prévus par le contrat, n'ont jamais été livrés par la Défenderesse, à savoir le système d'introduction de la boue dans le foyer (. . .), le système d'injection d'eau contrôlé par un détecteur de température qui permet d'éteindre d'éventuels incendies (. . .), les différents barreaux transversaux avec revêtement en plastique spécial pour l'écarquilleur (. . .).

Compte tenu de ce qui précède, ainsi que du fait qu'il ne serait pas judicieux de faire commencer une période de garantie par rapport à chaque élément fourni (puisqu'il peut arriver qu'un seul défaut concerne plusieurs systèmes fournis à des temps différents et dès lors soumis à différentes durées de garantie), le tribunal arbitral est de l'avis qu'il convient de fixer un moment précis et connu comme point de départ de la garantie. Puisque certaines fournitures n'ont jamais été effectuées mais que la Demanderesse a néanmoins mis en route et en opération l'installation complète, le point de départ de garantie doit être le moment où la Demanderesse a commencé à se servir de l'installation, à savoir le moment où l'acception tacite a eu lieu, soit début mai 1990 (. . .) ».

La partie demanderesse contestait la validité au regard du droit allemand des dispositions des conditions générales applicables limitant la responsabilité du fournisseur. L'arbitre rejeta cette argumentation dans les termes suivants:

« *La Demanderesse est de l'avis que tant la clause 9.16 des ECE-188 que la clause 23.14 des ECE-188 A seraient contraires à l'art. 9 al. 2 ch. 1 du AGBG et seraient partant nulles dans la mesure où le tribunal arbitral devrait admettre que cette clause exclut des dommages-intérêts fondés sur l'absence de qualités promises de l'ouvrage (. . .).*

La position de la Demanderesse est erronée. Le chiffre 23.14 (analogue au 9.16 dispose:

"Après la prise en charge, et même pour les défauts dont la cause est antérieure à celle-ci, le constructeur n'assume pas de responsabilité plus étendue que les obligations définies dans le présent article. Il est de convention expresse que le constructeur ne sera tenu à aucune indemnisation envers l'acheteur pour accidents aux personnes ou dommages à des biens distincts de l'objet du contrat intervenus après la prise en charge, ni pour manque à gagner, à moins qu'il ne résulte des circonstances de l'espèce que le constructeur a commis une faute lourde".

Ainsi, le paragraphe 23.14 admet une responsabilité illimitée en cas de faute lourde et limite l'exclusion de la responsabilité pour manque à gagner et les autres dommages consécutifs à un défaut aux cas de fautes ordinaires. Il maintient par conséquent la responsabilité complète du fournisseur pour ce qui est de ses obligations cardinales.

Une clause limitant la responsabilité (Haftungsbegrenzungsklausel) entre commerçants, comme dans le cas de l'art. 23.14, est admise sous le régime de l'AGBG pour autant que l'art. 9 AGBG soit respecté (Palandt, BGB, op. cit. ch. 38 et 45 ad art. 9 AGBG).

Le tribunal arbitral considère le par. 23.14 comme conforme à l'AGBG, dès lors qu'il ne supprime pas, en l'espèce, la responsabilité pour les obligations cardinales, puisqu'il se réfère à une notion de faute lourde (définie au par. 23.15) qui couvre toute défaillance grave du fournisseur (. . .).

En outre, l'exclusion des dommages consécutifs à un défaut et du manque à gagner est tout à fait usuelle dans les conditions générales de ce type et fréquente dans le commerce international; elle est même d'usage dans l'industrie concernée. De ce fait, elle ne peut pas être remise en cause par les évaluations spécifiques préconisées par l'AGBG.

Une autre interprétation ne peut, en l'espèce, entrer en ligne de compte, puisque le paragraphe 26.1 prévoit:

"Dans le cas où l'une des parties est tenue envers l'autre à des dommages-intérêts, ceux-ci ne peuvent excéder la réparation du préjudice que la partie fautive pouvait prévoir lors de la formation du contrat".

Ainsi, la clause excluant les dommages consécutifs et le manque à gagner — hormis la présence d'une faute lourde — entre parfaitement dans le système de base de ces conditions générales exprimé par le paragraphe précité.

Par conséquent, la Demanderesse ne peut demander des dommages-intérêts pour manque à gagner ou un dommage dit "consécutif" (Mangelfolgeschaden) que dans la mesure où il serait établi que la Défenderesse aurait commis une "faute lourde" au sens du paragraphe 23.15 des conditions ECE-188 A qui est d'ailleurs identique au par. 9.17 ECE-188. (. . .)

Le paragraphe 23.15 ECE-188 A (ainsi que le par. 9.17 ECE-188) décrit la "faute lourde" de la manière suivante:

> «*Par "faute lourde" on entend un acte ou omission du constructeur supposant de la part de celui-ci un manque de précaution caractérisé, eu égard à la gravité des conséquences qu'en l'espèce un professionnel diligent aurait normalement prévues, ou laissant supposer un mépris délibéré de ces conséquences et non pas n'importe quel manque de soin ou d'habileté*».

> *Selon l'avis du tribunal arbitral, la "faute lourde" peut s'entendre de deux manières: d'une part, la faute constitue l'expression et la mesure pour les défauts (techniques) dont l'entrepreneur doit répondre; d'autre part, elle englobe tous les actes ou omissions de l'entrepreneur qui aggravent le dommage résultant de tels défauts techniques*».

Enfin, l'arbitre estima que l'acheteur français n'était pas tenu par le formalisme du droit allemand applicable au contrat en matière de notification des vices de l'installation:

> « *La Défenderesse soutient que la Demanderesse n'aurait pas droit à des dommages-intérêts puisqu'elle a omis de suivre la procédure (notamment la mise en demeure) prévue au § 633 al. 3 BGB. Par ailleurs, elle n'aurait jamais soumis la Défenderesse à l'obligation de réparer les vices conformément au § 634 al. BGB (. . .).*

> *La Demanderesse argue apparemment qu'elle n'était pas obligée de fixer un délai pour la réparation des vices puisqu'elle avait perdu toute confiance en la Défenderesse. En outre, elle prétend avoir concrètement avisé la Défenderesse des vices par une mise en demeure en juin 1990 et le 17 juillet 1990 (. . .).*

> *Le tribunal arbitral examinera ces arguments à la lumière des conditions générales ECE-188 A, étant donné que le contrat ne contient pas de disposition à ce sujet.*

> *Selon l'art. 23 des conditions générales, le constructeur s'engage à remédier à tout vice de fonctionnement provenant d'un défaut dans la conception, les matières ou l'exécution pendant la période de garantie dont le point de départ est la prise en charge (avant la prise en charge, la situation est pareille en vertu du paragraphe 21.2 ECE-188 A). L'acheteur doit aviser sans retard et par écrit le constructeur des vices qui se sont manifestés. Il doit lui donner toute facilité pour procéder à la constatation de ceux-ci et y porter remède. Le constructeur ainsi avisé remédie au vice en toute diligence et à ses propres frais.*

> *Ce système est compatible avec le droit allemand, soit en particulier avec le § 377 HGB, applicable au contrat d'entreprise-vente. Cette disposition prévoit également l'obligation de vérifier l'ouvrage et d'aviser des défauts sans retard après la livraison. Le tribunal arbitral est cependant de l'avis qu'il serait exagéré de vérifier dans le présent cas si la Demanderesse a avisé la Défenderesse de chaque défaut en bonne et due forme et sans retard. En effet, étant donné que de nombreuses pannes et défauts ont été constatés déjà avant la mise en route, à savoir avant l'utilisation commerciale de l'installation, et étaient connus et ont même partiellement été reconnus par la Défenderesse qui était représentée sur les lieux, il ne serait pas juste de vérifier maintenant pour chaque défaut si la Demanderesse a bel et bien suivi la procédure prévue par les conditions générales. Par ailleurs, la Demanderesse a produit certaines pièces qui peuvent être assimilées à des avis de défauts et de manquements (. . .).*

> *Les règles du BGB, mentionnées ci-dessus, constituent un formalisme particulier du droit allemand. Il se justifie dès lors, au sens d'une Sonderanknüpfung, de*

*vérifier à ce sujet le point de vue du droit international privé allemand: l'art. 32 al.
II du Einführungsgesetz zum Bürgerlichen Gesetzbuch (EGBGB) prévoit:*
*"In bezug auf die Art und Weise der Erfüllung und die vom Gläubiger im Fall
mangelhafter Erfüllung zu treffenden Massnahmen ist das Recht des Staates, in
dem die Erfüllung erfolgt, zu berücksichtigen".*
*Le commentaire Palandt, BGB, op. cit., ch. 4 ad art. 32 EGBGB, précise que
cette disposition est notamment applicable à la "Untersuchungs — und Rügep-
flicht". Cela signifie que la Demanderesse pouvait de bonne foi s'appuyer sur le
droit français en ce qui concerne l'obligation de vérifier l'ouvrage et d'aviser ses
éventuels défauts. Or, le droit français ne connaît pas le même système de garantie
pour les contrats d'ouvrage. L'art. 1792-6 du Code civil français prévoit que le
maître de l'ouvrage fait constat des défauts lors de la réception. La garantie de
parfait achèvement, à laquelle l'entrepreneur est tenu, est d'une année à partir de
la réception (cf. également Dutilleul/Delebecque, Contrats civils et commerciaux,
Paris, 1991, ch. 737 et 744). De même, les dispositions sur la vente ne connaissent
pas l'obligation de vérifier la chose et de notifier immédiatement les défauts;
toutefois, selon l'art. 1648 CC, l'acquéreur doit intenter son action en garantie
dans un bref délai, ce qui a été précisé par la jurisprudence de cas en cas, avoi-
sinant, dans l'ensemble, un an (Dutilleul / Delebecque, op. cit., ch. 282 ss).*

*On ne saurait dès lors reprocher à la Demanderesse de ne pas avoir immédiate-
ment notifié les vices à la Défenderesse. Vu les circonstances et la situation juridique expliquée ci-dessus, les avis de défauts du 2 février (. . .), 14 juin (. . .) et
17 juillet 1990 (. . .) suffisaient, sans par ailleurs tenir compte des admonesta-
tions et constatations qui ont dû avoir lieu directement sur le chantier.*

*Comme il a été exposé ci-dessus, l'art. 23 des conditions générales ECE-188 A
ouvre d'abord au constructeur la possibilité de remédier aux vices constatés à ses
propres frais. Le paragraphe 23.11 stipule que "si le constructeur refuse d'exécuter son obligation ou ne fait pas les diligences nécessaires en dépit d'une sommation, l'acheteur est en droit de procéder aux réparations nécessaires aux frais et
risques du constructeur pourvu qu'il agisse avec discernement".*

*Le tribunal arbitral constate que ces dispositions sont en parfait accord avec le
droit allemand, notamment les §§ 633 ss BGB. Il convient dès lors de se référer,
pour l'interprétation de l'art. 23, à ces dispositions ainsi qu'à la jurisprudence et
doctrine y relatives.*

*Ce faisant, il convient de rappeler d'abord que le tribunal arbitral a assimilé le
début de la production de panneaux de fibre, début mai 1990, à la réception tacite
de l'installation.*

*Jusqu'au moment de la réception de l'ouvrage, le maître de l'ouvrage dispose
d'un droit à l'accomplissement (Erfüllungsanspruch) de l'œuvre promise sans
défaut. L'entrepreneur a le choix de refaire l'ouvrage (Neuherstellung) ou de
remédier aux défauts (Mängelbeseitigung) au sens du § 633 BGB. Le maître de
l'ouvrage peut faire valoir les droits de garantie (Wandelung, Minderung) sous les
conditions mentionnées au § 634 BGB, mais ne peut pas réclamer des dommages-
intérêts selon le § 635 (Palandt, BGB, op. cit. ch. 5 ad § 635 BGB et Staudinger-
Peters, Kommentar zum Bürgerlichen Gesetzbuch, 1991, ch. 24 ad § 635).*

*La Demanderesse demande cependant des dommages-intérêts pour des vices
survenus déjà avant la réception de l'installation. Il convient dès lors de vérifier si
elle y a droit en vertu du § 633 III BGB, seul fondement d'une telle réclamation en
cas de demeure de l'entrepreneur.*

*Pour mettre l'entrepreneur valablement en demeure, le maître de l'ouvrage doit
lui signaler les défauts et lui impartir un délai raisonnable pour la réparation. Le
maître de l'ouvrage doit en outre indiquer qu'il renoncera à faire effectuer la
réparation par l'entrepreneur au cas où ce dernier ne réagirait pas. Toutefois,*

le tribunal arbitral est de l'avis qu'il serait exagéré de soumettre une société française à cette jurisprudence allemande . . . ».

OBSERVATIONS. — I — La question de savoir si les conditions générales de vente de machines de la Commission Economique pour l'Europe des Nations Unies étaient applicables en l'espèce devait se résoudre simplement. En effet, la partie demanderesse s'y était référée afin d'invoquer la clause d'arbitrage CCI qu'elles contiennent pour introduire sa demande. De ce fait, elle ne pouvait ultérieurement prétendre qu'elle ne les avaient pas acceptées après que la partie défenderesse s'y fût référée dans sa confirmation de commande. Quoique l'arbitre ne l'indique pas expressément, en constatant l'application de ces conditions générales, la demanderesse enfreignait le principe « *venire contra factum propium* », un principe du droit du commerce international *(cf. sentences rendues en 1988 dans les affaires n° 5103: JDI 1988, p. 1207, obs. G.A.A. et n° 5832: JDI 1988, p. 1198, obs. G.A.A. — plus généralement voir E. Gaillard, L'interdiction de se contredire au détriment d'autrui comme principe du droit du commerce international: Rev. arb. 1985, p. 241).*

Cependant, indépendamment de l'acte positif d'acceptation des conditions générales qui découle de la mise en œuvre d'une de leurs clauses, l'arbitre souligne, en évoquant le droit allemand, qu'une partie qui a eu l'occasion de prendre connaissance de conditions générales visées dans un contrat ou dans une confirmation de commande ne peut prétendre les ignorer. Si elle ne les connaissait pas, il lui appartenait de s'en enquérir, en les demandant à l'autre partie ou en se les procurant directement auprès de l'organisation qui les a établies (en l'espèce les Nations Unies). La solution se trouvait déjà dans la sentence rendue en 1991, dans l'affaire n° 6309 *(JDI 1991, p. 1041, obs. J.-J. A.)* qui soulignait:

> « *Si, contrairement à ce que stipulait la confirmation de commande, lesdites conditions n'avaient pas été jointes à celle-ci, il va de soi que la défenderesse aurait dû protester en réclamant à la demanderesse de lui envoyer les conditions qui devaient faire partie intégrante du lien contractuel. Si elle a omis de contester, elle ne peut plus invoquer d'excuses pour cet oubli, ni s'opposer à l'application desdites conditions ».*

Il s'agit là d'un nouvel exemple de la présomption de compétence professionnelle que les arbitres font peser sur les opérateurs du commerce international et qui a été soulignée dans cette chronique dès 1974, dans des observations sur la sentence rendue en 1972 dans l'affaire n° 1990 *(JDI 1974, p. 897, obs. Y. D.)*. Elle apparaissait déjà dans une sentence de 1966 dans l'affaire n° 1397, mentionnée dans les observations figurant au pied de la sentence rendue dans l'affaire n° 1990. Cette présomption a été confirmée par diverses sentences ultérieures *(cf. les sentences rendues en 1975 dans les affaires n° 2438: JDI 1976, p. 969, obs. Y. D. — n° 2291, JDI 1976, p. 989, obs. Y. D. — de même, voir les sentences de 1980 pour les affaires n° 3380: JDI 1981, p. 928, obs. Y. D., et n° 3130: JDI 1981, p. 932, obs. Y. D., ainsi que dans la sentence rendue en 1988, dans l'affaire n° 5346: JDI 1991, p. 1060, obs. Y. D.).*

II — Bien que les Règles et Usances Uniformes relatives aux crédits documentaires de la CCI *(Publication CCI n° 500 de 1994)* s'appliquent à tous les crédits documentaires ouverts dans le monde entier, les sentences arbitrales rendues dans ce domaine sont rares. Dans ses trente ans d'existence, cette chronique ne rapporte que quelques sentences concernant la matière *(sentences rendues en 1969 dans l'affaire n° 1675: JDI 1974, p. 885, obs. Y. D. — en 1977, dans l'affaire n° 3031: JDI, 1978, p. 999, obs. Y. D. — en 1979, dans l'affaire n° 3226: JDI 1989, p. 959,. obs. Y. D. — en 1984, dans l'affaire n° 4338: JDI 1985, p. 982, obs. Y. D.).* On consultera aussi avec intérêt la sentence rendue en 1981 dans l'affaire n° 3820, publiée dans le *Recueil des sentences arbitrales de la CCI 1974-1985* par S. Jarvin et Y. Derains, p. 115. L'une des caractéristiques principales du crédit documentaire est son autonomie par rapport au contrat de base dont il constitue un moyen de paiement, ce que souligne expressément l'article 4 des Règles et Usances de la CCI. La banque émettrice du crédit documentaire ne peut se prévaloir de ses rapports avec le vendeur pour s'opposer à la réalisation du crédit et il lui est pareillement interdit d'invoquer l'inexécution ou la mauvaise exécution du contrat de vente pour se soustraire à ses obligations de paiement si les documents qui lui sont présentés par le bénéficiaire du crédit (le plus souvent l'acheteur) remplissent les conditions posées par celui-ci. Comme on l'a justement souligné, c'est là « *une conséquence du caractère abstrait de l'engagement bancaire, caractère qui est à la fois une condition de la sécurité du bénéficiaire et une conséquence inévitable de la qualité d'étranger au contrat de vente qu'a la banque* » *(J. Stoufflet, Crédit documentaire: J.-Cl. Banque Crédit Bourse, Fase. 1080, ° 119).* Cependant, l'autonomie du crédit documentaire par rapport au contrat de base est purement fonctionnelle et son caractère abstrait ne saurait occulter que contrat de base et crédit documentaire constituent des éléments d'une seule et même opération économique. L'émission du crédit documentaire n'est pas une opération abstraite et n'a de sens qu'en ce qu'elle permet l'exécution d'une obligation de paiement résultant d'un contrat sous-jacent. Il en résulte que s'il est vrai que l'exécution du contrat de base n'affecte les obligations de la banque que lorsqu'elle se traduit par la présentation ou non présentation de documents définis dans le crédit documentaire, cette définition peut avoir des incidences sur le contenu des obligations naissant du contrat de vente. C'est ce qu'illustre la sentence ici rapportée en estimant qu'en incluant dans le crédit documentaire des conditions de paiement non prévues au contrat (en l'espèce la présentation de procès-verbaux), ces conditions nouvelles constituent des amendements aux conditions contractuelles de paiement. Il suffit alors que le bénéficiaire du crédit documentaire (le vendeur) ait accepté le texte de celui-ci sans s'opposer à des exigences qui n'étaient pas prévues au contrat, pour que les conditions contractuelles de paiement se trouvent modifiées. Ceci a évidemment des conséquences directes sur l'obligation de paiement de l'acheteur, mais aussi sur le contenu de l'obligation du vendeur. Tant que le procès-verbal visé au crédit documentaire n'a pas été établi, non seulement l'obligation de paiement de l'acheteur ne naît pas, mais l'obligation contractuelle de livrer du vendeur n'est pas exécutée, à moins bien entendu qu'il lui soit possible, comme en l'espèce, de démontrer que par la mise en exploitation de l'ouvrage, l'acheteur a procédé à une réception tacite.

III — Il faut néanmoins relever que la solution retenue par l'arbitre selon qui une partie ne peut, d'une part prendre possession d'une marchandise ou d'un ouvrage et en faire un usage commercial et d'autre part se refuser à procéder à sa réception, n'est pas unanimement accepté. Ainsi, on a pu estimer que *«faute de stipulation contraire du contrat, en principe (. . .)* [la] *possession ne vaut pas réception tacite* » *(cf. P. Glavinis, Le contrat international de construction, GLN Joly, 1993, n° 195, p. 136).* C'est pourquoi l'arbitre, tout en se fondant à titre principal sur la jurisprudence arbitrale (la sentence CCI rendue dans l'affaire n° 3243, en 1981) mentionne à titre supplémentaire les solutions semblables du droit allemand, applicable en l'espèce. C'est aussi la solution qui prévaut en droit français *(cf. Cass. civ. 3ᵉ, 3 mai 1990: D. 1990, IR, p. 125; JCP G 1990, IV, 245)* pour autant que la prise de possession puisse s'analyser en une volonté manifeste d'accepter la marchandise ou l'ouvrage. C'est là où la mise en exploitation commerciale joue un rôle déterminant. En effet, elle caractérise la prise de possession en confirmant que l'acheteur ou le maître de l'ouvrage considère que, malgré des défauts éventuels, la marchandise ou l'ouvrage remplit pour l'essentiel les conditions fondamentales de qualité qui avaient justifié la commande. La présence de défaut s'oppose à ce qu'il s'agisse d'une réception définitive. C'est à une réception provisoire qu'équivaut alors la prise de possession accompagnée d'un usage commercial.

IV — Cette réception provisoire, selon l'arbitre, fait courir la période de garantie. Le vendeur ou le constructeur reste tenu de réparer les défauts, à moins que l'acheteur ou le maître de l'ouvrage soit autorisé, selon le contrat ou le droit applicable, à y procéder pour le compte ou aux frais de son co-contractant. Malheureusement, comme en l'espèce, les dispositions contractuelles sont souvent confuses et, plus souvent encore, les parties ne les respectent pas dans la pratique et ne s'y réfèrent qu'après la survenance du litige. C'est ce que souligne l'arbitre avec justesse en relevant qu'« *il est rare, dans l'industrie et le commerce que les parties suivent avec la plus grande rigueur les lois et les accords passés entre eux pendant la phase d'exécution du contrat*». Aussi, l'arbitre estime-t-il nécessaire, plutôt que d'appliquer rétroactivement le contrat à la lettre en ignorant la réalité pratique des relations contractuelles, de redéfinir l'obligation de garantie du fournisseur en s'inspirant à la fois du contrat, des usages professionnels et des modalités d'exécution par les parties des prestations auxquelles elles s'étaient engagées. Il impose ainsi une solution *sui generis* pour fixer le point de départ de la garantie du fournisseur.

V — On a relevé à juste titre que la « *réparation intégrale du dommage, par l'allocation à la victime du damnum emergens et du lucrum cessons est un principe commun aux principaux systèmes juridiques, et dès lors, un principe général du droit qui peut être considéré comme une source du droit international* » *(cf. la sentence CIRDI du 20 novembre 1984, Amco Asia et autres c/République d'Indonésie: JDI 1987, p. 145, obs. E. Gaillard. — plus généralement, voir J. Ortscheidt, La réparation du dommage dans l'arbitrage commercial international, Dalloz, p. 61 s.).* Cependant, le principe de réparation intégrale ne s'oppose pas à ce que les parties puissent valablement introduire dans leur contrat une clause limitative de responsabilité. Comme le relève la sentence ici rapportée, une telle pratique est fréquente, les parties excluant alors parfois la réparation du gain manqué et presque toujours celle des dommages-intérêts indirects *(voir la sentence rendue en 1985 dans l'affaire n° 4567: Recueil des sentences arbitrales de la CCI 1986 — 1990, par S. Jarvin, Y. Derains et J.-J, Arnaldez, p. 27).* Ces clauses sont respectées par les arbitres qui n'hésitent pas à affirmer que «*le respect de la volonté contractuelle et le désir de multiplier les transactions militent en faveur d'une réparation limitée* » et que « *fondée sur le respect de la volonté individuelle la limitation de la réparation aux dommages prévisibles apparaît comme une conséquence du principe de l'autonomie de la volonté* » *(sentence rendue dans l'affaire n° 2404 en 1975: JDI 1976, p. 995, obs. Y. D.)* Il n'y a pas là de contradiction avec le principe de réparation intégrale. Dans les deux cas, les arbitres s'attachent avant tout à garantir le respect total de l'accord des parties. Bien entendu, les clauses de limitation de responsabilité sont inopposables en cas de fraude *(dans le même sens, voir la sentence rendue dans l'affaire n° 3031 en 1977: JDI 1978, p. 999, obs. Y. D.)* et, selon les usages, en cas de faute lourde. Celle-ci ne peut pas être définie de façon générale puisque sa mesure dépend de l'obligation contractée. C'est pourquoi les précisions données par l'arbitre en l'espèce sont intéressantes, en ce qu'il considère qu'il peut s'agir de défauts techniques graves ou d'actes du vendeur ou du maître de l'ouvrage qui aggravent de tels défauts.

VI — Le rejet du formalisme en matière de notification des défauts de la marchandise achetée ou de l'ouvrage construit est une constante de l'attitude des arbitres du commerce international. Il s'est manifesté à diverses reprises s'agissant des notifications à l'ingénieur qui, selon les conditions générales de la Fédération Internationale des Ingénieurs Conseils (FIDIC) doivent être faites à l'ingénieur pour que des réclamations puissent être examinées et ensuite éventuellement soumises à l'arbitrage. Ainsi, dans la sentence CCI de 2001, rendue dans l'affaire n° 9951 (inédite), le tribunal arbitral déclare qu'il n'accepte pas «*une approche formaliste* » et que « *ce qui est décisif pour tout droit à réparation ou extension de délai est que l'ingénieur / maître de l'ouvrage ait connu pendant l'exécution du contrat les difficultés d'exécution rencontrées et leur impact allégué sur les délais et/ou les coûts, détruisant la confiance de l'ingénieur / maître de l'ouvrage en ce que tout se passait bien. Le Tribunal Arbitral doit être guidé par le but même des stipulions relatives aux notifications, c'est-à-dire éviter la surprise et les réclamations «en embuscade » et ne doit pas écarter des demandes valables sur la base de fondements purement formalistes* ». Cette formule est reprise dans une sentence de 2002, rendue dans un arbitrage *ad hoc* (inédite).

La sentence ici rapportée, qui écarte le formalisme de la jurisprudence allemande en matière de notification de défauts, bien que le droit allemand était applicable au contrat, se situe dans la même veine. Cependant, l'arbitre se fonde sur le droit international privé allemand qui lui permet de se référer aux dispositions françaises en la matière, considérant que l'on ne peut attendre d'une entreprise française qu'elle respecte le formalisme particulier du droit allemand. En réalité, la solution est celle de la Convention de Rome du 19 juin 1980 sur la loi applicable aux obligations contractuelles dont l'article 10(2) précise que «*pour les modalités d'exécution et les mesures à prendre par le créancier en cas de défaut d'exécution, on aura égard à la loi du pays où l'exécution a eu lieu*». Selon P. Mayer et V. Heuzé, des préoccupations de commodité sont derrière cette règle *(P. Mayer et V. Heuzé, Droit international privé, 7ᵉ éd., n° 744, p. 498)*. C'est surtout un souci de justice qui anime ici l'arbitre. On notera à l'occasion que l'arbitre étend la solution à la mise en demeure, *(contra P. Lagarde, Le nouveau droit international privé des contrat après l'entrée en vigueur de la Convention de Rome du 19 juin 1980: Rev. crit. DIP 1991, p. 333, n° 56)*.

Y. D. - B. D.

Sentence rendue dans l'affaire n° 9800 en 2000

I. — Procédure arbitrale. — Procédure judiciaire parallèle — Demande de sursis à statuer.

II. — Procédure arbitrale. — Procédure judiciaire parallèle — Sentence arbitrale antérieure — Autorité de la chose jugée.

III. — Contrat. — Assurance — Subrogation — Obligation de loyauté.

IV. — Contrat. — Responsabilité — Perte d'une chance.

Un Tribunal arbitral siégeant à Paris était saisi du litige opposant une société A et quatorze compagnies d'assurance dont elle était le mandataire, à une banque B. La banque B avait confirmé plusieurs crédits documentaires et avait souscrit six polices d'assurance-crédit auprès de la société A agissant pour le compte des quatorze compagnies d'assurance. Chacune de ces polices était soumise au droit français et prévoyait qu'une quotité de 5 à 10 % du risque resterait à la charge de l'assuré. La banque émettrice des crédits documentaires consentis n'ayant pas exécuté ses obligations nées des crédits documentaires, la banque B avait payé ses clients exportateurs puis s'était retournée vers ses assureurs auprès desquels elle avait préalablement déclaré le sinistre. À l'expiration du délai d'attente de 480 jours stipulé par les polices d'assurance, les assureurs ont refusé d'indemniser la banque confirmatrice en faisant valoir notamment une violation par la banque B de l'une des conditions essentielles des polices dans la mesure où elle avait reporté sur ses clients exportateurs la quotité non garantie. Il en est résulté une première procédure arbitrale, engagée par la banque B, qui s'est conclue par une sentence finale au terme de laquelle le tribunal arbitral a fait droit aux demandes de la banque et a condamné les assureurs à lui payer les indemnités prévues par les polices, grossies des intérêts au taux légal français à compter de leur exigibilité. Il a également décidé que les intérêts seraient capitalisés. La sentence a été exécutée par les assureurs dans les mois qui ont suivi son prononcé.

Parallèlement au déroulement de la procédure arbitrale, la banque B avait sollicité et obtenu du juge de l'exécution en France l'autorisation de pratiquer une saisie conservatoire sur des comptes bancaires ouverts auprès d'établissements français par la banque émettrice. Elle avait ensuite engagé une procédure au fond contre la banque émettrice devant le tribunal de commerce de Paris qui, par un jugement intervenu avant le prononcé de la sentence, a condamné la banque émettrice au paiement de certaines sommes majorées des intérêts au taux légal. La banque B a alors pratiqué plusieurs saisies conservatoires pour un montant qui s'est révélé être inférieur au montant des intérêts calculés sur la base du jugement, les a converties en saisie-attribution et a dénoncé ces conversions au débiteur, la banque émettrice.

Tant la conversion que la dénonciation sont intervenues après le prononcé de la sentence et alors que les compagnies d'assurance avaient commencé à exécuter cette dernière. Après complète exécution, elles ont exigé de la banque B qu'elle remette les originaux des huit lettres de crédit restées impayées' par la banque émettrice, qu'elle établisse à son bénéfice un acte de subrogation aux fins de pouvoir exercer leur recours à l'encontre de la banque émettrice et qu'elle remette 90 à 95 %, selon les cas, des sommes recouvrées au moyen de la saisie-attribution. La banque B a refusé de se soumettre à ces exigences et a saisi le juge de l'exécution de ce qu'elle considérait être une difficulté d'exécution du jugement du tribunal de commerce. À la suite de diverses péripéties procédurales, la cour d'appel de Paris a statué en des termes ainsi rapportés par la sentence commentée:

« *Sur les difficultés d'exécution du jugement* [(. . .) *la cour*] *a considéré qu 'il lui appartenait "de déterminer la portée de la subrogation des assureurs et des droits qui leur ont été transmis en raison de l'exécution de la sentence arbitrale au regard des règles d'imputation des paiements". Or, sur ce point, elle a développé la motivation suivante:*

"Considérant qu'il n'est pas contesté que selon les polices souscrites, le risque assuré était le non-paiement du seul montant des lettres de crédit, à hauteur des quotités garanties par la [banque B] *(95 % du montant des crédits documentaires pour la société* (. . .), *et 90 % pour la société* (. . .), *hors les intérêts sur ces montants pendant la période correspondant à l'écoulement des délais de carence de 450 jours à compter de la déclaration de sinistre et d'échéance de 30 jours, qui restaient à la charge de la* [banque B];

que la subrogation de l'assureur dans les droits de l'assuré ne peut lui conférer plus de droits que ceux résultant du paiement de l'indemnité pour le risque assuré;

que ni l'article 22 de la loi du 22 juillet 1972, ni les conventions d'assurance en leur article (. . .) *des conditions générales, ne dérogent aux règles légales d'imputation des paiements; que la* [banque émettrice] *n'a fait connaître aucune préférence pour l'imputation de ses paiements; que dès lors, les paiements doivent s'imputer en vertu de l'article 1254 du code civil d'abord sur les intérêts calculés selon les dispositions du jugement (intérêts au taux légal à compter de chacune des demandes de couverture) et ensuite sur le capital;*

Considérant que la société (. . .), *ou les compagnies d'assurances qui l'ont mandatée, ne peuvent donc faire valoir leurs droits au titre de leur subrogation dans les droits de la* [banque B], *que dans la limite du principal de la condamnation prononcée par le jugement;*

Considérant que tant que la [banque B] *ne sera pas totalement payée des intérêts qui lui sont dus en vertu dudit jugement, les paiements effectués au titre de son exécution par la* [banque B] *lui reviennent;*

Qu'il n'est pas contesté que les sommes saisies, d'un montant de [N], *sont insuffisantes pour couvrir les seuls intérêts ainsi dus; que dès lors les sommes saisies-attribuées doivent revenir à la* [banque B], *sans que la* [société A] *ou les assureurs puissent y prétendre* ».

Alors que la procédure était pendante devant la cour d'appel, la société A et les compagnies d'assurance dont elle était mandataire ont introduit une seconde procédure arbitrale qui a donné lieu à la sentence commentée pour demander la condamnation de la banque B à leur restituer le montant de l'indemnité qu'elles lui avaient payée en exécution de la sentence arbitrale. En cours de procédure, elle a demandé au tribunal arbitral de surseoir à statuer dans un premier temps jusqu'au prononcé de l'arrêt de la cour d'appel, ce qui lui a été consenti, puis dans un second temps jusqu' à l'issue du recours en cassation qu'elle avait introduit contre ce même arrêt. La banque B, défenderesse à cette nouvelle procédure arbitrale, s'opposait à ce second sursis à statuer et demandait au tribunal arbitral de « *considérer que la demande en restitution de l'indemnité globale versée par les assureurs a l'autorité de la chose jugée, tant par la sentence arbitrale* (. . .) *que l'arrêt de la cour d'appel de Paris* ». Subsidiairement, elle concluait au débouté de l'intégralité des prétentions des demanderesses comme étant juridiquement mal fondées et dans tous les cas elle demandait reconventionnellement que les demanderesses soient condamnées à lui payer des dommages-intérêts pour procédure abusive. Chaque partie demandait par ailleurs que l'autre soit condamnée à lui rembourser les frais occasionnés par la procédure arbitrale.

Au soutien de leur demande de sursis à statuer, les demanderesses faisaient valoir que la cour d'appel de Paris avait fait application de l'article 1254 du Code civil alors que les règles légales d'imputation des paiements, si elles sont applicables aux relations entre un créancier et son débiteur, ne sauraient l'être aux relations entre un assureur et son assuré lesquelles sont régies par les lois relatives au contrat d'assurance et les éventuelles dispositions particulières ou complémentaires des polices conclues. Elle en déduisait que l'arrêt serait vraisemblablement censuré par la cour de cassation et qu'il serait d'une bonne administration de la justice arbitrale de surseoir à statuer.

La demande est rejetée par le tribunal arbitral au motif que:

> « *l'instance dont il est saisi est destinée, ainsi que sa motivation ultérieure le fera apparaître, à vider le contentieux qui s'est noué entre les parties à la suite de la première sentence arbitrale rendue le (. . .) et à apprécier, à cette fin, le comportement adopté par elles postérieurement à cette sentence. Or, sur ces points, le tribunal arbitral considère que les mémoires échangés par les parties lui ont fourni d'ores et déjà tous les éléments à la prise de sa décision, et que l'instance judiciaire parallèle, uniquement relative à des mesures d'exécution, est nettement distincte du contentieux qui lui est soumis, et ne prête pas la voie à un risque de contrariété de décisions.*
>
> *Le tribunal arbitral observe, en outre, que les demandeurs au sursis à statuer, c'est-à-dire les assureurs, sont ceux-là mêmes qui ont introduit la présente instance arbitrale, et qu'ils ont pris soin dans leurs écritures de conclure subsidiairement au fond; que le pourvoi en cassation qu'ils ont aujourd'hui formé contre l'arrêt de la cour d'appel de Paris n'est pas, par ailleurs, lui-même doté d'un effet suspensif; que d'ores et déjà deux reports de date de sentence ont été accordés par les arbitres et avalisés par la Chambre de commerce internationale et qu'il apparaît donc, dans ces conditions, d'une bonne administration de la justice arbitrale de trancher maintenant, sans plus attendre, un litige dont l'origine se situe il y a une dizaine d'années. »*

Le tribunal arbitral examine ensuite l'affaire au fond. Au soutien de la demande de répétition de l'indemnité payée par les assureurs, ceux-ci soutenait en premier lieu que la défenderesse avait fautivement mis en échec leurs droits de subrogation et cela alors qu'elle leur avait donné acte, dans le cadre de la première procédure arbitrale, qu'elle remettrait les sommes saisies « *au titulaire de la créance, et cela en vertu du rapport de subrogation dont bénéficient les sociétés d'assurance* ». Les demanderesses relevaient que la banque B non seulement avait refusé de signer les actes de subrogation que lui proposait leur mandataire, mais s'était de surcroît précipitée pour convertir en saisie-attribution les saisies conservatoires obtenues à l'encontre de la débitrice puis avait invoqué l'article 1254 du Code civil afin de revendiquer, au profit de ses clients exportateurs, une imputation prioritaire des sommes recouvrées en totale contradiction avec les conditions de la police d'assurance, seules applicables, qui stipulaient qu' « *après le règlement d'un sinistre, toute somme recouvrée ainsi que les frais engagés pour le recouvrement seront partagés entre les assureurs et l'assuré en proportion du pourcentage du sinistre à leur charge respective* ».

En second lieu, les assureurs reprochaient à la défenderesse un refus fautif de leur remettre les lettres de crédit en sa possession qui se seraient révélées utiles pour l'exercice d'un recours subrogatoire.

Ils invoquaient enfin l'article 2037 du Code civil, lequel dispose que la « *caution est déchargée, lorsque la subrogation aux droits, hypothèques et privilèges du créancier ne peut plus, par le fait de ce créancier, s'opérer en faveur de la caution* ».

En défense, la banque B faisait valoir que les assureurs n'avaient jamais pu croire échapper à tout recours avec les exportateurs alors que seuls 90 à 95 % des contrats commerciaux étaient garantis. Elle ajoutait que la subrogation des assureurs était nécessairement une subrogation légale partielle limitée aux seules quotités garanties, à l'exclusion des intérêts sur la totalité de la dette de la banque émettrice. Notamment, selon la défenderesse, les intérêts payés par les assureurs sur les indemnités à compter de leur date d'exigibilité sont des intérêts moratoires qui ne sauraient être identifiés aux intérêts dus par la banque émettrice à la défenderesse en vertu de la décision du tribunal de commerce. Ce sont les assureurs qui auraient eu un comportement fautif en sollicitant la signature d'un acte conventionnel de subrogation plus étendue, intégrant une créance d'intérêt, et la fraction du principal non garanti et violant ainsi les droits légitimes des exportateurs.

La défenderesse faisait également valoir que les lettres de crédit n'étaient pas nécessaires aux assureurs pour poursuivre le recouvrement de la créance. Elle ajoutait quant à l'article 2037 du Code civil qu'il ne bénéficie qu'aux seules cautions et en tout état de cause que les conditions de son application n'étaient pas satisfaites.

Le tribunal arbitral commence par retracer l'évolution des créances nées du non-paiement par la banque émettrice des crédits documentaires. Il constate que la banque B est devenue créancière de la banque émettrice dès lors qu'elle a payé ses clients et que sa créance porte intérêt dès ce paiement. Elle est par ailleurs devenue créancière d'une indemnité vis-à-vis des compagnies d'assurance demanderesses ainsi que des intérêts portés par l'indemnité d'assurance dès l'expiration du délai d'attente. Jusqu'à la date du paiement effectif de l'indemnité d'assurance, la défenderesse disposait donc, à l'encontre de la banque émettrice, d'une créance en principal et d'une créance d'intérêts portés par ce principal. Le paiement de l'indemnité d'assurance a eu pour effet de la désintéresser pour le montant de sa créance en principal et de la part des intérêts qui lui étaient dus à compter de l'exigibilité de l'indemnité d'assurance. Il en résulte, selon le tribunal arbitral, que la défenderesse :

> « *après le paiement reçu des assureurs, ne demeure plus créancière de la* [banque émettrice] *que des seuls intérêts qui ont couru entre le jour du paiement qu'elle a dû effectuer entre les mains des exportateurs et le jour où l'indemnité d'assurance aurait dû lui être versée. En d'autres termes, ce sont là les intérêts produits, pendant 450 jours, par la somme déboursée par la* [défenderesse] *au profit des exportateurs* ».

De surcroît, faisant application de l'article 22 de la loi n° 76-650 du 11 juillet 1972, il constate que :

> « *Par la subrogation issue du paiement de l'indemnité d'assurance, la créance en principal contre la* [banque émettrice] *est passée automatiquement dans la patrimoine des assureurs. (. . .)*
>
> *Peu importe, au demeurant, que le paiement effectué par les assureurs l'ait été en exécution de la sentence arbitrale dans la mesure où celle-ci est simplement venue déclarer l'obligation contractuelle préexistante de règlement pesant sur eux sur le fondement direct des polices d'assurance, et où aucune novation d'obligation ne saurait donc être retenue.*
>
> *Les assureurs ont donc récupéré dans leur propre patrimoine, par subrogation de plein droit, la créance en principal de* [la défenderesse] *contre* [la banque émettrice]. *C'est-à-dire que, à compter de cette subrogation, leur créance contre la* [banque émettrice] *a produit intérêts à leur profit.*
>
> *En conséquence,*
>
> *avant la subrogation* [la défenderesse] *était bien créancière à la fois du capital et des intérêts contre la* [banque émettrice] *(. . .) et l'article 1254 du Code civil, d'après lequel, à défaut d'obtenir le consentement contraire du créancier, le paiement effectué par un débiteur s'impute d'abord sur les intérêts avant de s'imputer sur le capital, avait bien vocation à jouer au profit de* [la défenderesse] *;*
>
> *en revanche après la subrogation des assureurs produite par leur propre paiement,* [la défenderesse] *n'est plus créancière de la* [banque émettrice] *qu'à raison*

d'intérêts, et donc plus en capital. Dès lors, l'article 1254 du Code civil, qui suppose l'existence d'un créancier unique, auquel sont dûs un capital et des intérêts, n'a plus vocation à jouer au profit de [la défenderesse] ».

À la date de la conversion par la défenderesse de sa saisie conservatoire en saisie-attribution, prévalait une situation intermédiaire et la banque émettrice avait deux créanciers:

« [La défenderesse] :
– pour la partie du principal non indemnisé par les assureurs ;
– pour les intérêts portés par le principal pendant 450 jours.
Les assureurs:
– pour la partie du principal qui correspond aux indemnités payées à [la défenderesse], *et ce par l'effet de la subrogation de plein droit;*
– et pour les intérêts portés par cette somme ».

Selon le tribunal, il « *apparaît un nouveau concours, pour lequel les assureurs, qui viennent par hypothèse de payer l'essentiel des sommes auxquelles les a condamnés la sentence arbitrale, peuvent alors légitimement penser qu'il se réglera dans le respect des modalités des polices d'assurance, c'est-à-dire selon la clé de répartition prévue par l'article* (. . .) *des conditions générales aux termes duquel ''après le règlement d'un sinistre'', toute somme recouvrée ainsi que les frais engagés pour le recouvrement seront partagés entre les assureurs et l'assuré en proportion du pourcentage du sinistre à leur charge respective* ».

Or, « *une semaine à peine après avoir obtenu des assureurs l'essentiel des indemnités* » qui lui étaient dues, la banque B a adopté « *une attitude directement contraire à toute idée de répartition des sommes recouvrées* » en convertissant les saisies conservatoires en saisies-attributions et en se plaçant sur le terrain de l'article 1254 du Code civil, plutôt que celui du contrat.

Pour le tribunal,

« [cette] *attitude est assurément significative. Certes, à partir du moment où la* [défenderesse] *n'a pas été encore, au début du mois d'octobre 1995, entièrement payée par les assureurs, elle demeure bien créancière de la banque émettrice tant en principal qu'en intérêts* (. . .), *et son invocation de l'article 1254 n'est donc pas en soi fautive, et peut même être considérée comme juridiquement fondée dans ses résultats, ainsi que l'a récemment admis, dans le cadre du contentieux parallèle de l'exécution, la cour d'appel de Paris dans son arrêt.*

Mais, en revanche, c'est la demande même de conversion en saisie-attribution formulée par la défenderesse qui apparaît, au tribunal arbitral, comme fautive et destinée à mettre en échec le droit de subrogation nouvellement acquis des assureurs ».

Elle lui permet en effet d'invoquer l'article 1254 alors qu'elle ne peut qu'avoir la conviction que bientôt il ne pourra plus jouer en sa faveur et faire obstacle à l'application des stipulations contractuelles favorables aux assureurs. Selon le tribunal arbitral:

« *Cette attitude n'a manifestement plus la justification d'une légitime protection de ses droits qu'elle aurait eue en l'absence de paiement des assureurs; elle apparaît comme une atteinte consciente et fautive au droit de subrogation d'assureurs qui, sans elle, auraient, lors de leurs ultimes paiements, pu prétendre récupérer 90 ou 95 % des sommes saisies* ».

Ces derniers ne peuvent invoquer l'article 2037 qui bénéficie aux seules cautions réelles et personnelles:

« *en revanche, ils sont fondés à obtenir restitution de l'indemnité versée à la défenderesse à la mesure du préjudice que l'attitude fautive de cette dernière leur a causé dans la mise en œuvre de leur droit de subrogation, et ce du moment que les principes de solution gouvernant l'article 2037 du Code civil, et son équivalent en droit des assurances que constitue l'article L. 121-12, alinéa 3, du Code des assurances, ont vocation à être généralisés à travers l'obligation pour tout subrogeant, en application de l'article 1134, alinéa 3, du Code civil et de l'exigence de bonne foi dans l'exécution des conventions, de ne pas compromettre le recours subrogatoire du subrogé. Il découle, en effet, manifestement de l'obligation de loyauté qui doit présider à l'exécution des contrats que le contractant qui a obtenu de son partenaire en situation de garant le paiement de ce qui lui était dû par le fait d'un tiers débiteur définitif ne doit pas, par son comportement, faire échec à l'exercice d'un recours subrogatoire destiné, par essence, à permettre le report sur ce tiers du poids définitif de la dette (cf. déjà, en faveur de cette obligation de bonne foi du subrogeant, Pothier, Traité des obligations, n° 519; adde, Duranton, Cours de droit civil français, t. XVIII, n° 382; P. Guiho, Le recours contre l'auteur d'un dommage ouvrant droit à une indemnité d'assurance, th. Caen, 1948, p. 110; J. Mestre, la subrogation personnelle, LGDJ 1979, pp. 667-691; Req., 2 mai 1900, S. 1901, I, 14; Paris, 8 janvier 1908, D.P. 1908, V, 10). »*

Pour évaluer le préjudice souffert pas les demandeurs, après avoir relevé que la non-remise aux assureurs des lettres de crédit est indifférente dans la mesure où elles ne sont pas nécessaires à l'exercice d'un recours fondé sur une subrogation légale de plein droit, le tribunal arbitral tient compte en sa faveur des efforts initiaux réalisés par la banque B pour recouvrir certaines sommes de la banque émettrice. Il estime que:

« au regard de la mise en échec fautive du droit de subrogation des assureurs par la défenderesse le tribunal arbitral est conduit à dire que celle-ci, par l'exercice des saisies conservatoires, a initialement protégé ce droit à une époque où les assureurs refusaient le principe même de payer et donc toute idée de subrogation ultérieure, mais l'a, en revanche, ultérieurement altéré, en excluant, par la conversion hâtive de ces mesures conservatoires en saisie-attribution, toute participation des assureurs sur les sommes qu'elle avait su préserver et qui, sans elle, n'aurait peut-être pas été aujourd'hui présentes. En d'autres termes, la [banque B] a fait perdre aux assureurs une chance de concourir sur des sommes sur lesquelles elle leur avait initialement, et contre leur volonté de l'époque, donné une chance de concourir. »

Après avoir rappelé que, pour évaluer une perte de chance, *« le tribunal arbitral doit (. . .) tenir compte non seulement de l'existence, mais aussi du degré de l'aléa, c'est-à-dire de la probabilité plus ou moins grande de la réalisation de la chance perdue »*, il constate que l'aléa, compte-tenu des circonstances de l'espèce, était *« loin d'être négligeable »* et alloue aux demanderesses une somme correspondant approximativement à un tiers de celle recouvrée par la défenderesse.

Le tribunal s'explique alors brièvement sur l'exception d'autorité de la chose jugée soulevée par la banque B.

À cet égard, la défenderesse faisait valoir en premier lieu que la première sentence avait conclu à son absence de faute en dépit du fait, notamment, qu'elle n'avait pas conservé à sa charge une partie du risque assuré, *« de sorte que la présente demande des assureurs ne [pouvait] valablement être examinée, même si elle [avait] l'habileté procédurale de solliciter, non plus la déchéance initiale de la [banque B] dans ses droits à indemnité, mais sa déchéance a posteriori, à travers une prétendue obligation pour elle de restituer les indemnités perçues. »*

Elle observait en second lieu qu'en demandant au tribunal arbitral de statuer dans l'attente de l'arrêt de la cour d'appel, la demanderesse avait souhaité lui imposer l'autorité de la chose jugée de l'arrêt à intervenir. En outre, cet arrêt avait *« expressément précisé que ni l'article 22 de la loi du 11 juillet 1972, ni les polices d'assurance en leur article (. . .)*

des conditions générales ne dérogeaient aux règles légales d'imputation des paiements, de sorte que l'article 1254 du code civil avait bien vocation à fonder le droit de la [banque B] *à recueillir toutes les sommes récupérées contre la* [banque émettrice] *aussi longtemps que sa créance d'intérêts contre elle n'était pas définitivement éteinte, et que, dans ces conditions, les assureurs ne justifiaient ni d'une faute de la* [banque B], *ni d'un quelconque préjudice dans l'attribution judiciaire des fonds saisis.* »

Le tribunal arbitral lui répond en ces termes:

« *La motivation ainsi développée sur le fond fait, au demeurant, également apparaître le caractère infondé de l'exception de chose jugée invoquée par la défenderesse dans la présente instance arbitrale. Le litige soumis aux arbitres n'a pas, en effet, le même objet que celui relatif aux suites des mesures d'exécution qui est actuellement pendant devant la cour de cassation, après le pourvoi formé contre l'arrêt de la cour d'appel de Paris du 1ᵉʳ juillet 1999, et il est également nettement distinct de celui tranché par la sentence arbitrale (. . .) puisqu'il trouve sa source dans les comportements adoptés par les parties postérieurement à cette sentence.* »

Les demanderesses étant parvenues à démontrer une atteinte à leurs droits de subrogation, le Tribunal estime que leur demande ne saurait constituer l'exercice fautif du droit d'agir en justice et rejette la demande reconventionnelle formée contre elle pour procédure abusive. Par ailleurs, «*dès lors qu'aucune des deux parties n'est totalement fondée dans ses prétentions* », le tribunal partage entre elles les frais d'arbitrage, et laisse à la charge de chacune d'elles les frais qu'elle a engagés pour assurer sa défense.

OBSERVATIONS. — I. – La suspension des procédures arbitrales dans l'attente de l'issue d'une procédure parallèle a essentiellement été envisagée ces derniers temps en relation avec le principe selon lequel « *le criminel tient le civil en l'état* » dont on s'est demandé s'il était d'ordre public international ou non *(par exemple, voir récemment Y. Derains, obs. sous la sentence 7986 de 1999: JDI 2002, p. 1071. — J.-B. Racine, note sous Cass. civ. 1ʳᵉ, 6 mai 2003, CA Paris 13 févr. 2003 et CA Paris, 10 sept. 2003: Rev. arb. 2004, p. 311)*. On sait que la cour d'appel de Paris a opté pour la seconde solution et a décidé que: « *l'article 4 du Code de procédure pénale qui oblige le juge à surseoir à statuer lorsque, procédant des mêmes faits, l'action civile et l'action publique sont exercées séparément ou que la décision à intervenir au pénal est susceptible d'influer sur celle à rendre par la juridiction civile, est sans application pour l'arbitre statuant en matière internationale en raison de l'autonomie de la procédure arbitrale qui obéit à des règles propres, (. . .) cependant, rien n'interdit à l'arbitre d'estimer qu'une procédure pénale est de nature à influer sur la solution du litige dont il est saisi et d'ordonner pour ce motif un sursis à statuer dont il lui appartient d'apprécier l'opportunité* » *(CA Paris, 13 mai 2002: Rev. arb. 2002, p. 973, note J.-B. Racine)*.

Lorsque la procédure parallèle n'est pas une procédure pénale mais une procédure judiciaire, la solution ne fait aucun doute comme le soulignait la sentence rendue en 1991 dans l'affaire 6610: « *un tribunal arbitral a ordinairement la compétence ou le pouvoir de suspendre un arbitrage lorsqu'il semble juste et opportun de le faire dans les circonstances particulières de l'affaire* » *(Recueil des sentences arbitrales de la CCI 1991-1995, J.-J. Arnaldez, Y. Derains et D. Hascher, p. 280 dans la traduction donnée par Y. Derains, obs. sous la sentence 7986 précitée)*.

Dans la présente espèce, les arbitres ne s'interrogent pas, à juste titre, sur leur pouvoir de prononcer ou de refuser de prononcer la suspension de la procédure. Ils n'y étaient d'ailleurs pas invités par les parties qui ont manifestement considéré leur pouvoir discrétionnaire en la matière comme allant de soi. Ils le tiennent en effet tant de l'article 1494(2) NCPC que de l'article 18(4) du Règlement CCI, lequel donne au seul tribunal arbitral le pouvoir de fixer, « *lors de l'établissement de l'acte de mission, ou aussi rapidement qu'il est possible après celui-ci (. . .) le calendrier provisionnel qu'il entend suivre et le communiquer à la cour et aux parties. Toute modification ultérieure de ce calendrier sera communiquée à la cour et aux parties ».* Certes, une modification du calendrier prévisionnel, ou le refus d'une modification demandée par une partie ne devrait être adoptée qu'après consultation des parties *(Y. Derains et E. Schwartz, A Guide to the New ICC Rules of Arbitration, Kluwer Law International 1998, p. 246-247).* Sauf règle procédurale d'ordre public international s'imposant à eux ou dont l'ignorance risquerait d'entraîner l'annulation ou un refus *d' exequatur* de la sentence, les arbitres ont donc tout pouvoir pour rejeter une demande de sursis à statuer. On peut en revanche se demander si les arbitres, dans le cadre d'un arbitrage CCI, ont tout pouvoir pour ordonner la suspension de la procédure. Ils ont en effet l'obligation, aux termes de l'article 24 du règlement de rendre la sentence dans un délai de six mois à compter de l'établissement de l'acte de mission. Seule la Cour, aux termes de l'article 24.2 *« peut, sur demande motivée du tribunal arbitral ou au besoin d'office, prolonger ce délai, si elle l'estime nécessaire ».* Les arbitres ont-ils dès lors un pouvoir discrétionnaire d'ordonner une suspension de procédure, notamment lorsqu'une des parties s'y oppose qui, sans motif sérieux, entraînerait nécessairement une prolongation du délai dans lequel la sentence pourra être rendue?

On notera à cet égard que le tribunal arbitral tient compte de la longueur de la procédure pour rejeter la demande de sursis à statuer. Il observe que le délai pour rendre la sentence avait déjà été prolongé deux fois et qu'il apparaissait *« donc, dans ces conditions, d'une bonne administration de la justice arbitrale de trancher maintenant, sans plus attendre, un litige dont l'origine »* remontait à plus de dix ans. Les arbitres ont en effet l'obligation de prononcer la sentence dans un délai raisonnable au regard des circonstances de l'espèce. Reste à s'interroger sur les motifs qui légitimeraient une décision de sursis à statuer. Dans un arrêt précité du 23 mai 2002, la cour d'appel de Paris se référait à la possibilité qu'une procédure pénale soit *« de nature à influer sur la solution du litige »* dont le tribunal arbitral est saisi, ce dernier étant seul juge de l'opportunité d'ordonner pour ce motif un sursis à statuer. Dans un même esprit, le tribunal arbitral rejette en l'espèce la demande de sursis à statuer présentée par la demanderesse au motif qu'il *« considère que les mémoires échangés par les parties lui ont fourni d'ores et déjà tous les éléments à la prise de sa décision, et que l'instance judiciaire parallèle, uniquement relative à des mesures d'exécution, est nettement distincte du contentieux qui lui est soumis, et ne prête pas la voie à un risque de contrariété de décisions ».*

II. — La question de l'autorité de la chose jugée et de l'arbitrage international est longtemps restée peu débattue mais fait l'objet depuis peu d'un certain nombre de travaux doctrinaux *(voir D. Hascher, L'autorité de la chose jugée des sentences arbitrales: Travaux Comité fr. DIP 2000-2002, p. 17. — B. Hanotiau, L'autorité de la chose jugée des sentences arbitrales, in L'arbitrage complexe: question de procédure: Bulletin de la Cour internationale d'Arbitrage de la CCI, Supplément 2003, p. 45).* De nombreuses sentences arbitrales ont reconnu cependant que des sentences arbitrales antérieures ou des décisions judiciaires bénéficient de l'autorité de la chose jugée tant il est vrai que son principe semble universellement admis *(voir à cet égard les sentences citées par D. Hascher, op. cit.; pour un exemple de sentence reconnaissant l'autorité d'une décision judiciaire, voir la sentence rendue dans l'affaire n° 2745 en 1977: JDI 1978, p. 990, obs. Y. D.).* L'autorité de la chose jugée assure en effet la sécurité des situations juridiques définitivement acquises, interdisant qu'on les remette en cause. On peut ainsi lire dans la sentence 6233 de 1992, sans plus d'explication *« le défendeur soulève à bon droit, cependant, que la demande soumise au tribunal arbitral ne peut conduire, directement ou indirectement, à modifier les sentences qui ont été rendues. Le tribunal arbitral doit évidemment respecter l'autorité de la chose jugée de ces deux sentences»* (Recueil des sentences arbitrales de la CCI 1991-1995, par J.-J. Arnaldez, Y. Derains et D. Hascher, p. 335). Dès lors qu'il considérait, à tort ou à raison, que le litige qui lui était soumis était différent, par son objet, de ceux tranchés par le premier tribunal arbitral et la juridiction française, le tribunal ne pouvait donc qu'écarter l'exception de chose jugée soulevée par la défenderesse. On peut néanmoins regretter qu'il ne s'interroge pas sur le fondement juridique de l'autorité de la chose jugée des sentences arbitrale qu'il admet sans discussion. Plusieurs fondements on été proposés. Pour les uns, l'autorité de la chose jugée aurait une nature processuelle et devrait être appréciée selon la loi de procédure de l'arbitre qui se prononce sur cette autorité. Pour d'autres, elle relèverait du droit du fond. D'autres enfin suggèrent que l'autorité de la chose jugée des sentences arbitrales relève d'une règle matérielle (*D. Hascher, op. cit.*). Dans une sentence CCI 12226 de 2004, inédite, les arbitres écrivent ainsi que « *le principe* [de l'autorité de la chose jugée] *appartient à l'ordre juridique international. Il s'impose d'abord pour des motifs évidents de sécurité et d'économie. Lorsqu'une autorité compétente, qu'il s'agisse d'un juge ou d'un arbitre, a tranché définitivement une difficulté opposant deux parties, la décision qui est prise a pleine force juridique: "le droit est dit"* ». Il est vrai qu'en l'espèce la question du fondement de l'autorité de la chose jugée, tant de la sentence que de l'arrêt, était théorique puisque tant la loi du siège que la loi du fond étaient la loi française.

III. — Le tribunal arbitral reconnaît que, contrairement à ce que soutenaient les demanderesses, la position soutenue par la défenderesse devant les juridictions françaises était juridiquement fondée et qu'aucune faute ne pouvait leur être reproché à cet égard. Il pouvait difficilement faire autrement sans remettre en cause l'autorité de la chose jugée par la cour d'appel de Paris. Le tribunal recoure donc à la notion de bonne foi dans l'exécution du contrat pour condamner la défenderesse qui a précipitamment mis en œuvre les droits que lui reconnaissait le droit français pour échapper aux conséquences inéluctables de ses obligations contractuelles après le paiement imminent de la totalité de l'indemnité d'assurance. Le recours au principe de bonne foi par le tribunal pouvait ici reposer sur l'article 1134 du Code civil, le droit français étant applicable au fond. Il pourra néanmoins être rappelé que le principe de bonne foi est fréquemment invoqué par les arbitres qui en font parfois un principe du droit international. Une sentence 5030 de 1992 déclarait ainsi que: « *Appartenant au fonds communs des droits nationaux, l'obligation de se comporter loyalement dans les relations contractuelles, constitue naturellement un principe des rapports économiques internationaux* » (*JDI 1993, p. 1004, obs. Y. Derains*).

IV. — Admettant une faute contractuelle de la défenderesse justifiant une indemnisation du préjudice des demanderesses (l'impossibilité de faire jouer leur droit de subrogation), les arbitres ne leur accordent pas, et de loin, le plein de leurs prétentions, estimant que leur préjudice doit être évalué à l'aune de leur chance de concourir sur les sommes pouvant être recouvrées de la banque émettrice. Ce recours à la notion de perte de chance pourrait surprendre dès lors qu'il ne semble pas avoir été discuté par les parties. Le tribunal semble néanmoins ne devoir encourir aucune critique an regard d'une récente jurisprudence de la cour d'appel de Paris (*CA Paris, 27 févr. 2003: Rev. arb. 2003, p. 547*) qui, après avoir rappelé que le principe du contradictoire exige notamment « *qu'aucun moyen de droit ou de fait ne soit soulevé d'office par le tribunal arbitral sans que les parties n'aient été invitées à présenter leurs observations éventuelles* » approuve une sentence au motif suivant:

> « *Il ressort de l'étude détaillée des écritures des parties produites dans le cadre de l'instance arbitrale qu'en retenant la notion de perte de chance, la juridiction arbitrale n'a pas introduit un moyen nouveau dans le débat et a respecté les termes de sa mission.*
> *Sur le calcul du dommage réparable, le tribunal arbitral a déterminé la fraction des différents chefs de préjudices correspondant à la perte de chance de les éviter en se fondant uniquement sur les éléments fournis par les parties et les dépositions des témoins, sans rien y ajouter, étant observé que le demandeur à l'arbitrage a fourni des éléments quantifiés à l'appui de sa demande en réparation, lesquels ont*

été discutés par les autres parties; l'arbitre, qui dispose du pouvoir de dégager des pièces et des débats les constatations sur les chances en cause, a donc apprécié les préjudices à partir d'éléments présents dans les débats.

Il n'existe ni violation du principe de la contradiction ni non-respect de la mission à ne pas soumettre préalablement au prononcé de la sentence sa motivation au débat contradictoire, sauf à empêcher la juridiction arbitrale de statuer s'il fallait toujours provoquer les explications des parties sur le raisonnement à tenir ».

Y. D. - B. D.

Sentences partielle et finale rendues dans l'affaire CCI n° 9608 en 1998 et 1999

I. — Langue de la procédure arbitrale. — Fixation par l'arbitre.

II. — Droit applicable à un contrat de vente. — Détermination de « l'activité commerciale rattachée de la façon la plus étroite au contrat ». — Conditions Générales Orgalime.

III. — Convention de Vienne sur la vente internationale de marchandises. — Applicabilité.

IV. — Expertise. — Désignation de l'expert. — Étendue de la mission. — Appréciation des constatations par l'arbitre.

L'arbitre unique siégeant à Luxembourg était saisi d'un litige relatif à l'exécution d'un contrat de vente d'une installation technique entre une société hollandaise A, demanderesse, et une société française B, défenderesse. La demanderesse allègue que la défenderesse a refusé illégalement de régler le solde des paiements dus aux motifs que l'installation était défectueuse.

Le contrat de vente renvoyait aux conditions générales Orgalime pour la fourniture de produits mécanique, électrique et électroniques associés (S92). Orgalime est une fédération européenne des associations de l'industrie nationale qui représente les différentes parties impliquées dans les contrats de l'industrie mécanique, électrique, électronique et métallique. Elle siège à Bruxelles et rédige notamment des guides et des modèles de contrats destinés à l'usage des entreprises industrielles (www.orgalime.org).

L'article 44 des conditions générales Orgalime inséré dans le contrat prévoyait que « *Tous les différends découlant du présent contrat seront tranchés définitivement selon le Règlement de Conciliation et d'Arbitrage de la Chambre de Commerce Internationale par un ou plusieurs arbitres nommés conformément à ce Règlement, complété, si besoin est, des règles de procédures en vigueur dans le pays où le Fournisseur a son activité rattachée de la façon la plus étroite au contrat* ».

L'introduction de la demande d'arbitrage et l'établissement de l'acte de mission ont eu lieu sous l'empire du Règlement CCI de 1988. Les ordonnances de procédure ainsi que les sentences ont toutefois été rendues par l'arbitre conformément au Règlement CCI de 1998.

Bien que l'arbitre n'ait rien indiqué à ce propos, on peut déduire que l'application du Règlement CCI de 1998 a été faite par celui-ci en accord avec les parties, comme il est permis par la CCI (*V. en ce sens la communication du Secrétaire Général de la Cour Internationale d'Arbitrage de la CCI du 20 novembre 1987 concernant le Règlement de 1988* : « *The amended ICC Rules of Arbitration will govern arbitrations which commence on or after January 1, 1988. Parties may also agree to have the amended Rules govern arbitrations initiated prior thereto.* ». — *v. également Craig, Park, Paulsson, International Chamber of Commerce Arbitration, Oceana Publications, 2000, p. 142-145. — Y. Derains et E. Schwartz, A Guide to the New ICC Rules of Arbitration, Kluwer, 1998, p. 76-78. — M. Bühler et S. Jarvin, The Arbitration Rules of the International Chamber of Commerce, in Practitioner's Handbook on International Arbitration, C. H. Beck et DJØF, 2002, p. 156*).

Préalablement à l'examen au fond du litige, et en raison du désaccord des parties, l'arbitre s'est prononcé tout d'abord sur la langue de la procédure avant de déterminer le droit applicable.

Sur la langue de la procédure

Par une décision préalable à l'établissement de l'acte de mission, l'arbitre a fixé le français comme la langue de l'arbitrage « *en vertu de l'article 15 § 3 du Règlement d'Arbitrage de la CCI (. . .) en tenant compte des circonstances et notamment de la langue du contrat»*. Il a ainsi fait droit à la requête de la défenderesse, qui a sollicité l'utilisation du français contrairement à la demanderesse qui a introduit la requête d'arbitrage en anglais.

Sur le droit applicable au fond

Par une sentence intérimaire rendue en 1998, l'arbitre a déterminé le droit néerlandais comme droit applicable au fond, après avoir examiné les prétentions des parties.

«La Confirmation de Vente signée par la demanderesse ainsi que par la défenderesse avec apposition de son cachet renvoie expressément aux Conditions Orgalime annexées à la Confirmation de Vente;

Comme relevé par la défenderesse dans ses conclusions du 22 décembre 1997, les parties sont d'accord sur le fait que l'article qui doit être appliqué est l'article 45 des Conditions Orgalime, ce qui n'est par ailleurs aucunement contestable;

L'article 45 des Conditions Orgalime stipule:

45. Le contrat est soumis à la loi du pays où le Fournisseur a son activité commerciale rattachée de la façon la plus étroite au contrat.

2° La demanderesse soutient que son activité commerciale rattachée de la façon la plus étroite au contrat est la vente d'une installation de machines livrée CPT Saumur, c'est-à-dire que la vente s'est réalisée à partir du moment que (sic) le vendeur a transmis les choses vendues au premier transporteur, de sorte, qu'en l'occurrence, elle a fourni les choses vendues à la défenderesse à son entreprise à [. . .] (Pays-Bas);

La demanderesse fait valoir qu'elle a donc effectué sa prestation distinctive ou caractéristique — la fabrication et la fourniture des choses vendues — à son entreprise à [. . .] (Pays-Bas);

3° La défenderesse soutient qu'il faut entendre par activité commerciale rattachée de la façon la plus étroite au contrat la négociation du contrat intervenue entre les parties et que toute la question est de savoir si l'activité commerciale de la demanderesse pour parvenir à la conclusion du contrat la liant à la défenderesse est ou non intervenue en France; [. . .]

Il n'est pas contesté ni contestable que la Confirmation de Vente est une convention de vente d'une installation comprenant plusieurs équipements;

La défenderesse ne conteste aucunement que l'installation a été fabriquée à l'entreprise de la demanderesse située à [. . .] aux Pays-Bas;

La Confirmation de Vente, prévoyait (p. 10) que la livraison s'effectue à la condition CPT Saumur, selon Incoterms 1990, valable depuis le 1er juillet 1990, Incl. montage, excl. TVA;

La condition de livraison Carriage Paid To Saumur signifie, conformément aux Incoterms 1990 valable depuis le 1er juillet 1990, que les frais de transport sont pris en charge par le vendeur, mais que le vendeur remplit le contrat dans le pays d'expédition ou d'envoi, c'est-à-dire au moment où le vendeur remet les choses vendues au premier transporteur (voir: ICC Incoterms 1990, Introduction, sub12);

5° Dès lors, l'activité commerciale de la demanderesse consistant à vendre une installation fabriquée par elle à son siège à [. . .], Pays-Bas, et à remplir son contrat de vente s'est effectuée à [. . .] aux Pays-Bas; [. . .]

La défenderesse ne peut être suivie dans son argument que l'activité commerciale rattachée de la façon la plus étroite au contrat est la négociation du contrat intervenu entre les parties;

La négociation d'une ou de conventions est une caractéristique commune à toute sorte de contrat, nommé ou innomé, c'est-à-dire régi par des dispositions légales spécifiques pour ce type du contrat, ou régi par la liberté des parties;

Dans le cas d'espèce il s'agit d'un contrat de vente, intervenu entre parties par la Confirmation de Vente et précédé par des négociations qui pour autant ne constituent pas l'activité commerciale de la demanderesse rattachée de la façon la plus étroite au contrat; [. . .]

Il est constant que dans les contrats commerciaux internationaux interviennent des intermédiaires commerciaux dont le statut juridique peut prendre diverses formes (par exemple: agent commercial, commissionnaire, concessionnaire, courtier ou employé); [. . .]

Il est sans pertinence de savoir si la société O et/ou Monsieur M. a le statut d'employé de la demanderesse, comme le soutient la défenderesse, ou si Monsieur M. est employé de la société O, qui elle-même serait intermédiaire commercial, courtier ou autre qualification juridique, de la demanderesse, ou, même, de la défenderesse;

L'analyse des pièces soumises par les parties démontre sans équivoque que le lien juridique a été établi directement entre la demanderesse et la défenderesse; [. . .]

Le Tribunal Arbitral établit dès lors que le Fournisseur, c'est-à-dire la demanderesse, a son activité commerciale rattachée de la façon la plus étroite au contrat aux Pays-Bas, de sorte que la Confirmation de Vente, c'est-à-dire le contrat intervenu entre parties, est en vertu de l'article 45 des Conditions Orgalime soumis à la loi des Pays-Bas . . . ».

Sur l'expertise

L'installation faite par de la demanderesse ayant été défectueuse, l'arbitre, en accord avec les parties, a nommé l'expert et défini sa mission (v. article 20(4) du Règlement CCI de 1998 et article 14(2) du Règlement CCI de 1988).

« Vu que l'hypothèse où les parties se sont mis [sic] d'accord sur la mission de l'expert mais non sur son identité s'applique, de sorte que le Tribunal Arbitral:

1. nomme comme expert le Prof. Dr. Z;

2. avec comme mission:

> *Se rendre au siège social de la défenderesse, [. . .]:*

> *En présence des parties et leurs conseillers, examiner l'installation, fournie et mise en service par la demanderesse [. . .] selon les spécifications agréées par les parties et jointes à la confirmation de vente . . . ;*

> *Examiner si cette installation est entachée de défauts, le cas échéant définir ces défauts, en tenant compte des spécifications mentionnées dans la confirmation de vente n° 961364 du 17 octobre 1996; indiquer s'il y a des fautes dans la fabrication, l'installation ou la mise en service de la machine mentionnée, le tout en tenant compte du contrat entre les parties, en particulier des spécifications mentionnées dans la confirmation de vente . . . ;*

> *Le cas échéant, indiquer les réparations nécessaires et les travaux d'adaptation à effectuer par [la demanderesse] et, après avoir indiqué le délai d'exécution, contrôler cette exécution et dire si les travaux ont été effectués conformément à ses instructions;*

> *Seulement si les travaux n'ont pas été effectués conformément par [la demanderesse], estimer les frais de réparation éventuels ou les travaux d'adaptation éventuels, ainsi que la durée de ces travaux éventuels; examiner s'il y a en matière une diminution de valeur ou une diminution de jouissance, le cas échéant les estimer . . . ».*

L'expert, après avoir procédé à sa mission, a tiré les conclusions suivantes:

« 12. CONCLUSION DEFINITIVES (. . .)

1. Concernant le poids des balles, la société [demanderesse] a rempli ses obligations contractuelles.

2. Concernant le problème de ligature, la société [demanderesse] est responsable . . .

3. Le problème de fermeture du caisson . . . est un problème de conception. Le contrat ne prévoit rien dans le contexte. La société [demanderesse] ne peut pas nier son intervention, soit par l'intermédiaire d'un délégué, lors de la discussion de l'exclusion des caissons du contrat. Il me semble raisonnable que les deux parties prennent en charge chacune 50 % des frais de réparation, estimés à 36.000 FF par la société L.

4. La société [demanderesse] est responsable pour le non fonctionnement du bras de dévoiement. Le poste 3 dans la lettre de [la défenderesse] à [la demanderesse] du . . . ne spécifie pas un prix détaillé pour ce bras de dévoiement. Ce poste indique le montage d'un convoyeur équipé en extrémité d'un système escamotable de détournement de produits vers une benne posée sur le sol. Après une considération de tous les éléments, nous estimons une moins value de 25.000 Nfl comme une compensation réaliste. [. . .]

6. Il est indéniable que la société V [société tierce à laquelle la défenderesse avait commandé du matériel construit sur les plans de la demanderesse] a subi des préjudices dus aux problèmes 1 à 4 discutés ci-dessus. Après avoir considéré tous les facteurs jouant dans ce problème, et notamment les avantages de la société V par le solde, nous considérons un montant total de 100.000 FF comme réaliste.

7. La discussion de l'application de l'article 43 des conventions Orgalime se situe sur le plan judiciaire et non sur le plan technique . . . ».

L'arbitre a accepté de suivre pour l'essentiel l'avis de l'expert. Il a toutefois refusé l'estimation proposée par ce dernier à propos de la moins value du matériel défectueux, estimant qu'elle était « *disproportionnée de sorte que le tribunal arbitral estime que la moins value à appliquer (. . .) doit être évaluée à (. . .) ».*

L'arbitre a rappelé également, et fort opportunément, que le rapport d'expertise a servi comme un des moyens justifiant ses décisions qui ont été rendues « *entre autre sur base du rapport de l'expert ».*

Observations. — I. — Le Règlement CCI n'impose pas un moment et une forme particulière à l'arbitre qui est libre d'apprécier le moment où il doit déterminer la langue de la procédure. Dans le cas d'espèce, l'arbitre a rendu sa décision préalablement à l'établissement de l'acte de mission. Conformément à l'article 15.3 du Règlement CCI de 1988 alors en vigueur, l'arbitre a fixé la langue de l'arbitrage « *en tenant compte des circonstances et notamment de la langue du contrat ».* En l'occurrence, l'arbitre a choisi le français en considération du fait que le contrat a été rédigé en français.

Le Règlement CCI de 1998 met toujours l'accent sur la volonté des parties car la fixation de la langue par l'arbitre est seulement possible « *à défaut d'accord entre les parties ».* Dans ce dernier cas, l'arbitre prend sa décision en tenant compte de « *toutes circonstances pertinentes, y compris la langue du contrat. » (sur les modifications rédactionnelles de l'article 16 du Règlement CCI de 1998, v. notamment S. Lazareff, La langue de l'arbitrage institutionnel; Bull. CCI, vol. 8/n° 1, mai 1997, p. 18, spéc. p. 20. — Y. Derains et E. Schwartz, A Guide to the New ICC Rules of Arbitration, op. cit., spéc. p. 216. — v. également les ordonnances fixant la langue de la procédure dans les affaires CCI n° 8817 (1996) et 8764 (1996): JDI 1999, p. 1080, obs. D. H.).*

À la différence du Règlement CCI, certains autres règlements d'arbitrage, tels que celui de l'Institut d'arbitrage de la Chambre de Commerce de Stockholm (*art. 23*) et de la CNUDCI (*art. 17*), laissent le choix de la langue d'arbitrage, à défaut d'accord des parties, à l'arbitre sans d'autres précisions ou obligations que celle de les consulter. D'autres règlements d'arbitrage établissent par contre, en l'absence d'un choix exprès des parties, une présomption en faveur de la langue du contrat. C'est le cas notamment du Règlement de l'OMPI (*art. 40*), de l'AAA (*art. 14(a)*) et du Règlement de la LCIA (*art. 17*). Enfin, en l'absence d'une volonté contraire des parties, certains Règlements accordent une priorité à la langue territoriale du centre d'arbitrage (v. le Règlement de la CIETAC [*art. 85*] et de la Cour d'arbitrage de la Chambre de Commerce et d'Industrie de la Fédération de la Russie [*art. 10*]).

II. — Le droit de la vente internationale est complexe du fait de l'existence de multiples conventions internationales dont l'articulation est parfois difficile à appréhender (*V. notamment, M. Carbo, Le droit positif de la vente internationale: Petites Affiches, 11 févr. 1999, p. 4*). L'adhésion des parties aux conditions générales Orgalime a été dans cette affaire une source de difficulté supplémentaire.

L'article 45 des conditions générales Orgalime, annexées à la confirmation de vente, prévoit que le contrat conclu est soumis « *à la loi du pays où le fournisseur a son activité commerciale rattachée de la façon la plus étroite au contrat* ». Cette formulation ambiguë a donné lieu à une divergence d'interprétation entre les parties.

Selon la demanderesse, le droit néerlandais était applicable au fond dans la mesure où la prestation caractéristique a été exécutée aux Pays-Bas, à savoir la fabrication et la fourniture de la chose vendue. Elle s'est basée en outre sur le choix particulier de l'Incoterm CPT Saumur pour renforcer le choix du droit néerlandais.

La défenderesse a sollicité l'application du droit français en s'appuyant notamment sur le fait que les négociations ont eu lieu principalement en France. Ce critère a été rejeté fort justement par l'arbitre car la détermination du droit applicable ne peut être lié aux aléas du lieu de négociations des parties.

L'arbitre a fait droit à l'argumentation de la demanderesse en s'appuyant sur un ensemble d'indices jugés pertinents, à savoir l'Incoterm CPT Saumur, le lieu de fabrication et de fourniture du bien vendu, comme allégué d'ailleurs par la demanderesse.

S'agissant de la référence à l'Incoterm, on peut être réservé si on tient compte de l' objectif des Incoterms qui « *ne sont rien d'autre que des règles pour l'interprétation des dispositions concernant la livraison, et ne s'appliquent à aucune autre stipulation du contrat de vente* » (*V. J. Ramberg, Guide ICC des Incoterms 2000; ICC 200, p. 11. — ICC, Incoterms 2000, p. 129: « . . . les Incoterms visent seulement les droits et obligations des parties à un contrat de vente, en ce qui concerne la livraison de la marchandise vendues (marchandises tangibles, à l'exclusion des intangibles comme la fourniture de logiciels* ». — *plus généralement, v. E. Joli-vet, Les Incoterms — Étude d'une norme du commerce international, Litec 2003*).

Le rattachement du contrat aux Pays-Bas, comme lien de rattachement le plus étroit au contrat est par contre tout à fait convaincant d'autant plus qu'il s'agit d'un contrat de vente d'une installation fabriquée dans ce pays même. L'arbitre a donc respecté les dispositions de l'article 45 des conditions générales Orgalime, applicables par la volonté des parties. On peut toutefois mentionner le fait que l'arbitre aurait pu aboutir à la même conclusion en s'appuyant sur l'article 4 de la Convention de Rome de 1980 qui est applicable en l'espèce compte tenu de la nationalité des parties. La France et les Pays-Bas sont signataires de la Convention de Rome. En réalité, quelque soit le terme utilisé (« liens le plus étroit », ou encore « lieu des prestations caractéristiques du contrat »), il s'agit pour les arbitres de mesurer l'importance économique de chaque indice qu'ils ont répertorié. C'est de cette combinaison qu'ils vont déterminer le droit applicable au fond et convaincre les parties de la pertinence de leur choix (*v. C. Truong, Les différends liés à la rupture des contrats internationaux de distribution dans les sentences CCI, Litec 2002, p. 167*).

On peut indiquer que l'ambiguïté soulevée par l'article 45 est désormais supprimée avec la nouvelle version des Conditions Générales Orgalime 2000. Le nouvel article 45 dispose en effet clairement que « *Le contrat est soumis à la loi du fond du pays du fournisseur* ».

III. — Dans la mesure où le contrat en cause est un contrat de vente internationale, on peut se demander pourquoi les parties, et encore moins l'arbitre, n'ont pas appliqué la Convention de Vienne sur la vente internationale de marchandises de 1980 (« CVIM »).

En effet, la CVIM était au moment des faits en vigueur dans les deux pays concernés, en France depuis le 1er janvier 1988 et aux Pays-Bas depuis le 1er janvier 1992. La CVIM est incorporée de ce fait dans le droit national et a vocation à s'appliquer de plein droit sauf exclusion expresse des parties (*art. 6*) (*V. par exemple sentence CCI n° 6653 (1993): JDI 1993, p. 1040, obs. J.-J. A. — citée par Cl. Witz, « La Convention de Vienne sur la vente internationale des marchandises à l'épreuve de la jurisprudence récente »: D. 1995, chron. 143, spéc. p. 144*).

À défaut pour les parties d'avoir invoqué les dispositions de la CVIM, il appartient à l'arbitre, tout comme un juge, de soulever son application d'office (*V. N. Watté et A. Nuyts, Le champ d'application de la Convention de Vienne sur la vente internationale. La théorie à l'épreuve de la pratique: JDI 2003, p. 365, spéc. p. 421. — Cl. Witz, L'exclusion de la Convention des Nations unies sur les contrats de vente internationale de marchandises par la volonté des parties (Convention de Vienne du 11 avril 1980): D. 1990, chron. p. 107. — v. également Cass. civ. 1re, 23janv. 1996: D. 1996, jurispr. p. 334*). L'application de la CVIM n'est donc aucunement subordonnée à la manifestation de volonté des parties, à moins qu'elles ne souhaitent exclure la convention par l'usage du système de « opting out ».

L'exclusion « tacite » par les parties de la CVIM est possible à condition que leur volonté soit certaine (*V. notamment les arrêts de la Cour Suprême d'Autriche, 12 févr. 1998 et de la Cour Fédérale d'Allemagne, 25 nov. 1998, cités par Cl. Witz, op. cit.: D. 1999, jurispr., p. 356. — v. également sentence CCI n° 8453, (1995): Bull. CCI 2000, vol. 11/n° 2, p. 56. — F. Ferrari, Exclusion et inclusion de la CVIM: RDAI 2001, p. 401 et s.*). En cas de doute, l'application de plein droit de la CVIM doit l'emporter (*V. V. Heuté, La vente internationale des marchandises. Droit uniforme, LGDJ, 1999, p. 93*).

La position adoptée par l'arbitre peut s'expliquer en réalité par le respect du choix des parties d'appliquer au contrat les conditions générales Orgalime, qui renverse la priorité d'application des normes. Les conditions générales acquièrent une force contractuelle et leurs stipulations priment sur les dispositions du droit applicable, dont fait partie éventuellement la CVIM. Dans l'espèce commentée, la CVIM et le droit néerlandais ont vocation à s'appliquer à titre supplétif pour compléter les dispositions ou lacunes des conditions Orgalime. C'est le cas notamment de la question des dommages-intérêts qui doit être réglée par les dispositions du droit national applicable (*pour une analyse détaillée des rapports entre la CVIM et les conditions Orgalime dans leur version de 2000, v. N. Seghers et F. Walschot, Les contrats type en rapport avec la CVIM: RDAI 2001, p. 415*).

On peut regretter que l'arbitre n'ait pas mentionné l'applicabilité de la Convention de Vienne dans la sentence intérimaire sur le droit applicable, quitte à affirmer ensuite la similitude des dispositions, voire des solutions, entre les différentes sources applicables, soit la CVIM et le droit néerlandais (*V. en ce sens les extraits de sentences citées par H. van Houtte, La Convention de Vienne dans la pratique arbitrale de la Chambre de Commerce Internationale: Bull. CCI 2000, vol. 11, n° 2, p. 22 et s.*).

IV. — Dans le cadre de sa mission, l'expert devait examiner l'installation fournie, les défauts techniques et les fautes éventuelles en tenant compte des dispositions contractuelles. Il devait en outre indiquer les réparations nécessaires, contrôler leur exécution et examiner également s'il y a lieu en matière à une diminution de valeur ou de jouissance, et le cas échéant les estimer.

En tant que technicien, l'expert ne se prononce pas normalement sur les questions juridiques dans le cadre de sa mission (*V. Th. Bernard, The Administration of Evidence in Countries of Civil Law, in Evidence in International Arbitration Proceedings, AIJA, 1994, p. 25*). La Cour de cassation française a eu l'occasion de rappeler cette règle en indiquant que le juge ne pouvait pas « *charger l'expert de fixer les responsabilités, ou de rechercher le bien ou le mal fondé de la demande, ou encore de dire si le défendeur est redevable de la somme demandée* » (*V. Ch. Jarrosson, L'expertise juridique, in Mélanges Claude Raymond, Litec, 2004, p. 127, spec. p. 133*).

Cette règle s'applique également dans le cadre des procédures arbitrales où le tribunal arbitral ne peut pas déléguer à l'expert la mission juridictionnelle qui lui est confiée par les parties (*V. notamment l'ordonnance rendue dans l'affaire CCI n° 6057 (1990): JDI 1993, p. 1068, note D. H.*).

L'arbitre a invité l'expert à examiner si l'installation était défectueuse, à indiquer s'il y a eu des fautes dans la fabrication, l'installation ou la mise en service de la machine dans le cadre des spécifications contractuelles. L'arbitre a également demandé que l'expert examine, dans le cadre des travaux d'adaptation ou de réparation, « *s'il y a en matière une diminution de valeur ou une diminution de jouissance, le cas échéant les estimer* ».

On peut se demander si l'expert a dépassé sa mission purement technique quand il conclut que la demanderesse était « *responsable* » pour l'essentiel des défauts techniques. L'expert a néanmoins refusé ensuite de s'engager dans la discussion de l'application de l'article 43 des conventions Orgalime qui se « *situe sur le plan judiciaire et non sur le plan technique* ». L'expert a ainsi confirmé la portée technique de sa mission, même si le langage utilisé dans son rapport, aurait pu laisser croire qu'il a assumé mission juridique. Tel n'est pas le cas.

S'agissant d'une expertise technique, rappelons que l'avis de l'expert ne lie pas l'arbitre en vertu du principe général de la libre appréciation des preuves. L'expertise en est seulement un des moyens (*V. sentence CCI n° 2444: JDI 1977, p. 932-933; Paris, 1re Ch., 28 nov. 2002: Rev. arb. 2003, p. 445. — V. également Y. Derains et E. Schwartz, A Guide To The New ICC Rules of Arbitration, op. cit., p. 257 et s. — M. Bühler et S. Jarvin, The Arbitration Rules of the International Chamber of Commerce, in Practitioner's Handbook on International Arbitration, op. cit., p. 239. — E. Jolivet, Chronique de jurisprudence arbitrale de la Chambre de commerce internationale (CCI). Le recours à l'expertise dans la procédure d'arbitrage commercial international: Les Cahiers de l'Arbitrage, n° 2004/1, p. 3*). L'arbitre a suivi ce principe en motivant de façon extensive son opinion, surtout lorsqu'elle différait de celle de l'expert, afin de permettre aux parties de mieux comprendre son raisonnement dans le respect du principe du contradictoire et de celui d'être entendu (*V. J.-F. Poudret, S. Besson, Droit comparé de l'arbitrage international, Bruylant, LGDJ, Schulthess, 2002, spéc. p. 595*).

S. J.

Sentence rendue dans l'affaire n° 10982 en 2001

I. — Arbitrage international. — Droit applicable. — Clause d'élection d'un droit national. — Invocation d'un autre droit par les parties dans la procédure.

II. — Contrat. — Mandat. — Allégation de faux. — Fardeau de la preuve. — Renversement.

III. — Convention d'arbitrage. — Groupe de contrats.

IV. — Procédure d'arbitrage. — Formulation d'une demande reconventionnelle. — Soumission volontaire à la convention d'arbitrage.

V. — Contrat. — Mandat. — Apparence.

VI. — Contrat. — Consentement. — Dol. — Présomption de compétence professionnelle.

VII. — Contrat. — Clause d'exclusivité. — Violation. — Intention. — Réalisation.

VIII. — Arbitrage international. — Procédure. — Frais de procédure. — Répartition.

Un arbitre unique, siégeant à Paris, était saisi d'un litige opposant une société pétrolière d'un État africain A, demanderesse, tant à une société de Hongkong B qu'à une société chinoise C, défenderesses et demanderesses reconventionnelles.

Le litige concernait la conclusion et l'exécution d'un contrat, prévoyant l'arbitrage de la CCI et soumis au droit du pays de A, relatif à la cession par A à B de données sismiques de blocs pétroliers « off shore » pour un montant de US$ 7 000 000. Le contrat avait été signé par le directeur général de A et par Mme Y, en présence d'un dirigeant de B, M. X, et sur présentation d'un pouvoir écrit de C, l'autorisant à agir en son nom et au nom de « *sa joint venture* » B. Un acompte de US$ 50 000 avait été réglé par B lors de la signature du contrat, le solde devant être versé dans les dix jours suivant cette signature.

A prétendait n'avoir reçu qu'un montant de US$ 1 000 000 dans ce délai. Elle demandait donc que les défenderesses soient solidairement condamnées à lui payer le reliquat du prix de vente.

B contestait l'existence d'une joint venture entre elle et C, soulignait n'avoir jamais établi de pouvoir en faveur de Mme Y et niait avoir reçu les données sismiques, lesquelles auraient été remises à des préposés de Mme Y et transmises par cette dernière à C en vertu d'un contrat d'études géologiques conclu entre C et Mme Y, prétendant agir au nom de B. De plus, B estimait que A avait violé la clause d'exclusivité du contrat en se rapprochant d'une autre société de Hongkong B'. B demandait à l'arbitre d'annuler le contrat pour vice du consentement, subsidiairement d'en prononcer la résolution aux torts exclusifs de A. Elle sollicitait également la condamnation solidaire de A et de C à lui rembourser le montant de US$ 1.050.000 versés, plus intérêts et des dommages et intérêts de US$ 240 000.

C affirmait que le pouvoir présenté par Mme Y était un faux, qu'il n'existait pas de joint venture entre elle et B et objectait à la compétence de l'arbitre, indiquant ne pas être partie à la clause d'arbitrage. Elle reconnaissait être en possession des données sismiques qui lui auraient été remises en exécution d'un contrat d'études conclu avec B, en ajoutant qu'alors que l'étude avait été effectuée et remise à B, le prix ne lui en avait pas été payé. Elle demandait à l'arbitre de condamner A et B à lui verser US$ 5 000 000 « pour faux », plus US$ 100 000 000 pour atteinte à sa réputation.

L'arbitre se prononça tout d'abord sur le droit applicable dans les termes suivants:

« Bien que l'article (. . .) du [contrat] prévoie que le droit applicable est le droit [de l'État de A], les parties ne visent dans leurs écritures que le droit français et l'actuel Code civil français.

Est-ce parce que la Constitution [de l'État de A] a réaffirmé dans son article (. . .) le principe de la continuité législative, rendant ainsi le Code civil français applicable [dans l'État de A] dans toutes les matières qui ne sont pas régies par des dispositions spéciales du droit [de l'État de A], et que les articles du Code civil [de l'État de A] correspondent à cet égard très exactement à ceux du Code civil français?

Quoi qu'il en soit, compte tenu de la position unanime des parties sur ce point, l'arbitre unique ne recherchera pas davantage le contenu dit droit [de l'État de A] et appliquera le droit français en considérant, ce faisant, que les références qui seront faites au droit français et à sa jurisprudence sont applicables [dans l'État de A] ».

L'arbitre s'interrogea ensuite sur sa compétence à l'égard de C:

« [C] a soulevé (. . .) une exception d'incompétence, en déclarant qu'elle refusait d'être impliquée dans la procédure d'arbitrage au motif que [A] ne pouvait se prévalir d'aucune clause d'arbitrage à son encontre, puisqu'il n'existait aucune relation commerciale, ni aucun contrat ou convention liant ces deux sociétés.

Il est cependant admis en droit que l'on peut être lié par la clause compromissoire stipulée dans un contrat que l'on n'a pas conclu en personne, si l'on a été représenté au contrat par le biais d'un mécanisme de représentation parfaite, dont l'avatar le plus courant est le pouvoir.

Cela aurait été le cas en l'espèce, si [C] ne considérait pas que le pouvoir de représentation du (. . .) ayant autorisé Madame [Y] à agir en son nom était un faux, aux motifs (i) que le papier à en-tête de [C] sur lequel il aurait été rédigé ne serait en réalité pas un papier à en-tête de [C], et (ii) qu'il aurait été signé par une personne présentée comme le Président de [C] qui, à la date de la présente signature, était parti à la retraite depuis un an (. . .).

À l'appui de ses affirmations, [C] verse au dossier un modèle du sceau de [C] ne comportant pas les mots en hngue anglaise (. . .) figurant sur le papier à en-tête sur lequel a été tapé le pouvoir du (. . .), ainsi qu'un échantillon de la signature de l'ancien Président de [C] (. . .).

[A] et [B], à qui incombent à nouveau la charge de la preuve devant les indices de poids apportés par [C] n'ont cependant pas sérieusement tenté de démontrer ou de contredire les moyens avancés par [C] pour priver de tout effet le pouvoir du (. . .). L'arbitre unique estime dans ces conditions qu'aucune force probante ne peut être accordée à ce pouvoir du (. . .) pour établir que [B] a valablement représenté [C] à l'occasion de la signature du [contrat] contenant la clause d'arbitrage.

Certes, selon une jurisprudence française, et selon notamment un arrêt de la Cour d'appel de Paris du 7 décembre 1994, « dans le droit de l'arbitrage international, les effets de la clause compromissoire s'étendent aux parties directement impliquées dans l'exécution du Protocole dès lors que leur situation et leurs activités font présumer qu'elles avaient connaissance de l'existence et de la portée de cette clause afin que l'arbitre puisse être saisi de tous les aspects économiques et juridiques du litige ».

[C], *qui a admis être en possession des données sismiques (. . .) reconnaît en effet avoir effectué une étude géologique pour le compte de* [B], *aux termes d'un contrat du (. . .) qui aurait été négocié pour le compte de* [B] *non seulement par Madame* [Y] *mais également par deux autres représentants de [B] (. . .).*

[C] *reconnaît même n'avoir signé ce contrat d'étude géologique qu'après avoir eu connaissance de l'existence du* [contrat] *et de la lettre de* [A] *(. . .) donnant instruction à (. . .) de remettre les données sismiques à* [B].

Toutefois, si la signature du contrat du (. . .) aurait pu entraîner implicitement l'adhésion de [C] *aux dispositions du* [contrat], *il reste que les parties à ce contrat du (. . .) ont expressément entendu soumettre tout litige qui naîtrait de l'exécution du contrat à un mode d'arbitrage différent de celui qui est prévu à l'article (. . .) du* [contrat] *(. . .).*

En conséquence, l'argument selon lequel la signature par [C] *du contrat du (. . .) après avoir eu connaissance du [contrat] entraînerait l'adhésion implicite de* [C] *aux dispositions du* [contrat], *tombe de lui-même face à la présence d'une clause d'arbitrage spécifique dans le contrat du (. . .) qui n'est pas compatible avec les règles de conciliation et d'arbitrage de la CCI.*

Enfin, il convient de rejeter également l'argument de [A] *et de* [B] *selon lequel, tout en persistant à contester sa participation à l'arbitrage,* [C] *n'a eu de cesse (. . .) de faire part de son argumentation, communiquer ses pièces justificatives, et même formuler une demande reconventionnelle de 100 000 000 dollars US (. . .). Cet argument n'est pas convaincant car, en dernière analyse, les courriers susvisés de* [C] *n'avaient pour seul objectif que de dissuader* [A] *et* [B] *de la mettre en cause dans le présent arbitrage. Et s'il est vrai que* [C] *a formulé des demandes reconventionnelles, il s'agit en réalité plus d'esquisses virtuelles de demandes, plutôt que de demandes reconventionnelles réelles, s'apparentant davantage à des menaces faites par* [C] *qu'à une manifestation d'une volonté de participer à la présente procédure. Rappelons à cet égard que* [C] *ne s'est plus manifestée . . .* [ensuite] ».

L'arbitre estima que Mme Y avait pu valablement engager B :

« *Il n'est pas contesté qu'au cours de son séjour* [dans l'État de A] *avec Monsieur* [X] *et les autres membres de la délégation de* [B], *Madame* [Y] *a signé le (. . .), pour le compte de* [B], *un* [contrat] *rédigé en langue française aux termes duquel* [B] *s'engageait à acheter à* [A] *des données sismiques (. . .).*

[A] *verse au débat le pouvoir de représentation du (. . .) qui est rédigé sur un papier à en-tête qui est en apparence celui de* [C] *qui est signé par quelqu'un présenté comme le Président de* [C], *(. . .) et qui est revêtu du cachet de* [C]. [B] *et* [C] *contestent cependant à la fois la validité de ce pouvoir qui serait un faux, et l'existence d'une joint venture entre leurs deux sociétés (. . .).*

On peut certes s'étonner que [A], *société nationale d'opérations pétrolières, n'ait procédé à aucune vérification préalable approfondie pour s'assurer de l'identité de ses interlocuteurs et n'ait notamment pas cherché à vérifier l'authenticité du pouvoir qui lui avait été présenté par la délégation emmenée par Madame* [Y] *et Monsieur* [X], *alors qu'elle n'a eu de cesse d'affirmer dans ses écritures et au cours des auditions de témoins que* « *sans l'association de* [C] *avec* [B] [A] *ne serait jamais entrée en relations commerciales avec* [B], *société sans aucune réputation dans le milieu pétrolier ne présentant aucune garantie technique pour des opérations envisagées dans le* [contrat] ».

Cependant (. . .), il reste, ce qui n'est contesté par personne, que Madame [Y] *a signé le* [contrat] *en présence de Monsieur* [X], *sans qu'à aucun moment ce dernier ait manifesté une quelconque intention de le signer lui-même ou de refuser qu'il soit signé par Madame* [Y].

Monsieur [X] justifie, certes, sa position de retrait par le fait que deux demandes auraient été formulées en ce sens successivement par [un ministre de l'État de A et le Directeur général de A], *le contraignant ainsi à laisser le premier rôle à Madame* [Y].

Il ressort cependant de l'audition de Monsieur [X] *que ce dernier reconnaît qu'en acceptant que Madame* [Y] *signe le* [contrat], *il a pris un risque calculé: « Donc, dans cette situation, j'avais deux choix: soit de renoncer au contrat, soit d'accepter que ce soit Mme* [Y] *qui signe le contrat au nom de* [B]. *Ma réflexion, en tant que commerçant, à cette époque, était qu'en tant que commerçant, si je peux obtenir un contrat, c'est mon objectif principal, donc c'est en quelque sorte un succès. Bien sûr qu'au niveau du droit, Mme* [Y] *n'avait pas le droit de signer au nom de* [B]. *Mais comme j'avais envie que le contrat aboutisse, que j'obtienne le contrat, c'est ainsi que j'ai accepté que ce soit elle qui signe, parce que mon but est réalisé, quelle que soit la personne ».*

Ainsi, c'est donc avec l'accord de Monsieur [X], *et en vertu d'un pouvoir dont la révocation par* [B] *par un courrier du (...) confirme bien l'existence, que Madame* [Y] *a pu valablement engager* [B] *par la signature du* [contrat] *dont seuls* [A] *et* [B] *étaient les parties contractantes ».*

L'arbitre n'accepta pas que B ait été victime de manœuvres dolosives de la part de A:

« Dans son premier mémoire en réponse, [B] *invoque l'existence de manœuvres dolosives diligentées à son encontre par* [A] *et* [C] *pour demander l'annulation du* [contrat] *(...) pour vice du consentement aux torts exclusifs de* [A].

Aux termes de l'article 1116 du Code civil français, le dol est caractérisé par l'existence de manœuvres frauduleuses réalisées par l'un des cocontractants lors de la conclusion d'un contrat avec le dessein de tromper l'autre cocontractant et ayant pour effet de provoquer chez le cocontractant une erreur qui le détermine à contracter.

L'arbitre unique note à cet égard que la jurisprudence française est constante en matière de charge de la preuve, celle-ci incombant à la partie qui allègue le dol, et prévoit notamment que:

– les manœuvres frauduleuses doivent être prouvées;

– l'annulation fondée sur le dol ne peut être prononcée lorsque l'erreur de la victime est inexcusable.

Il incombe donc à l'arbitre unique d'examiner la demande d'annulation pour dol présentée par [B] *au regard des principes ci-dessus énoncés:*

(...) Monsieur [X] *a été présent aux cotés de Madame* [Y], *tout au long des négociations de (...) et jusqu'au moment de la signature du* [contrat] *(...). Monsieur* [X] *a fait à cet égard entièrement confiance à Madame* [Y] *bien que celle-ci ne fût pas en possession d'un mandat écrit en bonne et due forme de* [B]. *Monsieur* [X] *a reconnu, lors de son audition (...), que le processus de négociations « s'est déroulé d'une façon extraordinairement bien et assez rapide. C'est-à-dire qu'il n'y avait aucun obstacle entre les deux parties ».*

Il n'est pas davantage contesté que Madame [Y] *et Monsieur* [X] *ont entretenu des relations commerciales bien avant leur arrivée ensemble* [dans l'État de A] *(...).*

Ces relations ont débuté semble-t-il par la signature entre eux d'un contrat de bail (...). Puis ils ont développé ensemble un certain nombre de projets (...) « dans le domaine du bois, du diamant dans les pays africains comme le Congo, le Niger et le Bénin ». C'est d'ailleurs dans ce dernier cadre que Monsieur [X] *a décidé, au profit de Madame* [Y] *de « transformer une société appartenant à* [B], *qui était une société d'affaires, en* [B] *International Limited. C'est-à-dire changer de nom et le siège est transféré à l'adresse de Madame* [Y] ». *Cette dernière était d'ailleurs administrateur de ladite société à l'époque des faits (. . .) et l'est toujours aujourd'hui. Ces relations entre Monsieur* [X] *et Madame* [Y] *se sont également concrétisées par un contrat d'importation de jeeps* [dans l'État de A] *(. . .) signé par Madame* [Y] *pour le compte de* [B], *ainsi que par le détachement de deux des collaboratrices de Monsieur* [X] *(. . .), aux côtés de Madame* [Y], *respectivement en tant que représentante de* [B] *auprès de Madame* [Y] *et assistante personnelle de celle-ci.*

En outre, Monsieur [X] *est le Président d'un groupe Hongkongais dont les activités sont diversifiées et le chiffre d'affaires représente 20 milliards de dollars Hong Kong. Monsieur* [X], *qui se qualifie lui-même de tycoon, est donc nécessairement un homme d'affaires avisé et un opérateur rompu aux usages du commerce international. Par conséquent, si Monsieur* [X] *a pu être trompé et floué par Madame* [Y], *il paraît difficile d'accepter qu'il en rejette la responsabilité sur* [A].

Certes, Monsieur [X] *affirme ne comprendre ni l'anglais ni le français, mais les témoignages concordants qui ont été entendus au cours des auditions de témoins permettent de conclure que Madame* [Y] *et* [une secrétaire] *lui servaient d'interprètes. Monsieur* [X] *aurait en outre pu demander et obtenir que les différents contrats signés par Madame* [Y] *lui soient préalablement traduits in situ, de même qu'il aurait pu s'entourer de conseils ou d'avocats hongkongais, français ou de* [l'État de A], *pour l'assister dans ces négociations (. . .).*

Enfin, aucune conséquence particulière ne doit être attachée au fait que Madame [Y], *plutôt que Monsieur* [X] *a signé le* [contrat].

(. . .) il est établi que ce n'était pas la première fois que Madame [Y] *signait en lieu et place de Monsieur* [X]. *C'est ainsi un fait que Madame* [Y] *a signé dans le passé un* « *Financial Agreement* » *au nom et pour le compte d'une société (. . .) appartenant à Monsieur* [X] *(. . .).*

Enfin, et en tout état de cause, Monsieur [X] *a approuvé le fait que le* [contrat] *ait été signé par Madame* [Y]. *Il a en effet déclaré lors de son audition que* « *Avant d'arriver* [dans l'État de A], *nous sommes allés dans plusieurs pays africains où nous voulions traiter des affaires de bois et d'autres affaires, rien n'a abouti (. . .) C'était un peu dommage pour nous. Maintenant que Madame* [Y] *m'a dit que le contrat de pétrole est en bonne voie et qu'on va obtenir le contrat à la seule condition que ce soit elle qui signe le contrat au nom de* [B]. *Donc, dans cette situation, j'avais deux choix: soit renoncer au contrat, soit accepter que ce soit Madame* [Y] *qui signe le contrat au nom de* [B] *(. . .)* ». *L'acceptation de la signature du* [contrat] *par Madame* [Y] *au nom de* [B] *résulte donc d'un choix stratégique de Monsieur* [X].

En conclusion, l'Arbitre unique considère que [B] *n'a aucunement établi ni une quelconque intention de nuire de* [A], *ni que les conditions dans lesquelles le* [contrat] *a été négocié, puis signé, traduisent de quelconques manœuvres dolosives imputables à* [A], *ni enfin une éventuelle erreur excusable de Monsieur* [X] *ayant pu constituer un vice du consentement.* ».

L'arbitre constata que la clause d'exclusivité contenue au Contrat n'avait pas été violée par A:

« *[B] fait par ailleurs grief à* [A] *d'avoir cherché à l'évincer au profit d'une société* [B'], *société de droit hongkongais dirigée par Madame* [Y] *(. . .). Cette tentative d'éviction aurait été faite en violation de l'article 6 du* [contrat] *qui prévoit que* « *(. . .) s'engage pendant une période de 6 (0 à 6) mois à compter de la signature du présent* [contrat], *à n'entreprendre, avec des tiers, aucune action pouvant avoir pour effet de signer un contrat de partage de production relatif au bloc onshore objet du présent* [contrat] ».

Ont en effet été versés au dossier un certain nombre de courriers échangés entre [A] *et* [B']. *Parmi ceux-là, un courrier (. . .) dans lequel Madame* [Y] *transmit à* [A] *une lettre de* [C] *demandant un complément d'information sur la carte géographique de base (« base map ») de lignes sismiques et de puits (. . .), et une lettre de* [A] *(. . .) transmettant à Madame* [Y] *un plan de situation et les coordonnées géographiques desdites données (. . .).*

[B] *considère que la transmission de ces informations est une entorse à l'obligation d'exclusivité, alors que Monsieur* [dirigeant de A] *estime pour* [A] *que les informations en cause ne peuvent pas être considérées comme des informations confidentielles, dans la mesure où « la 'base map' n'est pas un document confidentiel C'est un document qui est joint aux données que l'on vend à toute société pétrolière ».*

L'arbitre unique considère que cet échange de correspondance n'établit pas une violation par [A] *de l'obligation d'exclusivité.*

Par ailleurs, par lettre du (. . .), Madame [Y] *a demandé pour la première fois à* [A] *d'accepter que son cocontractant soit dorénavant* [B'] *(. . .)*

On trouve cependant également une lettre du (. . .) signée par [le] *conseiller juridique de Madame* [Y], *réitérant la demande de changement de nom du cocontractant et priant instamment* [A] *« not accept any new offer from* [B] *and any acts made by* [B] *to be anything that gives* [B] *the position as a party who appropriately performs the agreement. We hope that our position as mentioned above will satisfy the agreement, your requirement and lays a good foundation for further co-operation between us » (. . .). Ce courrier révèle incontestablement une opposition d'intérêts entre* [B] *et* [B'] *qui n'a pu échapper à* [A]. *En proposant (. . .) que « the transfer of all rights and obligations from* [B] *to* [B'] *occurs upon confirmation of all payment pertaining to the seismic data and the 10% participating interest in bloc (. . .) », *[A] *semble bien avoir montré qu'elle était disposée, une fois qu'elle aurait été payée de la totalité des sommes qui lui étaient dues, à permettre le transfert à* [B'] *des droits que* [B] *tenait du* [contrat]. *Il reste cependant que cette télécopie (. . .) n'a pas été suivie d'effet et que l'on peut peut-être l'expliquer par l'exaspération ressentie par* [A] *devant les retards et reports successifs de paiement de* [B].

Mais, surtout, si on peut s'étonner aujourd'hui rétrospectivement de l'absence ou de l'ambiguïté des réactions de [A] *à ces différents courriers de* [B'], *on ne peut ne pas tenir compte de ce que ces courriers étaient faits tantôt sur le papier à en-tête de* [B'], *tantôt sur celui de* [B], *pour évoquer des questions intéressant* [B]; *que la dénomination sociale de* [B'] *pouvait prêter à confusion avec celle de* [B] *(. . .)* [et] *laisser croire qu'il s'agissait d'une société du groupe* [B] *d'autant plus que l'adresse de* [B'] *était identique à celle spécifiée pour* [B] *à l'article 10 du* [contrat]; *et enfin que le signataire de ces courriers était soit Madame* [Y], *représentant de* [B] *dans le cadre du* [contrat], *soit* [le] *conseiller juridique de Madame* [Y] *(. . .)*

L'affirmation de [A], *selon laquelle elle croyait avoir affaire au groupe* [B] *est donc parfaitement crédible et plausible (. . .) ».*

De même, l'arbitre estima qu'en remettant les données sismiques aux préposés de Mme Y, A avait rempli son obligation contractuelle:

« *Outre le non-respect de la clause d'exclusivité,* [B] *reproche à* [A] *de n'avoir pas exécuté une autre de ses obligations contractuelles consistant en la remise de la chose vendue. Elle demande en conséquence la résolution du* [contrat] *avec remboursement par* [A] *de la somme de 1 050 000 dollars US.*

Une remise des données sismiques aux mandataires de Madame [Y] « représentante de [B] » vaut-elle cependant remise à [B]?

*Malgré l'*întuitus personae *qui domine le mandat, la majorité de la doctrine et de la jurisprudence considèrent que la substitution de mandataire est licite, à moins qu'elle n'ait été expressément ou tacitement interdite. L'article 1994 du Code civil français, qui n'a pas envisagé la substitution non autorisée, organise même un régime de responsabilité du mandataire initial qui comporte une gradation selon l'intervention du mandant dans la substitution, et qui prévoit notamment qu'en l'absence pure et simple d'autorisation, la responsabilité du mandataire initial est particulièrement lourde puisqu'il « répond de celui qu'il s'est substitué dans sa gestion sans aucune restriction »*

Dès lors, la remise par [A] des données sismiques à Monsieur [Z] qui était dûment mandaté par Madame [Y], au nom et pour le compte de [B], par un pouvoir rédigé sur papier à en-tête [B] (. . .) valait bien remise de ces données à la disposition de [B]. Et ce même s'il s'avère que Monsieur [Z] les a ensuite remises à [C].

(. . .)

Que [B] ait été flouée par Madame [Y] est possible, voire vraisemblable, et il appartiendra à [B] d'en tirer les conséquences qui lui paraîtront s'imposer devant les juridictions appropriées.

Sauf à établir que le mandat consenti par elle à Madame [Y] avait bien été valablement révoqué, [B] n'est cependant pas fondée à imputer à [A] le fait que Madame [Y] se soit éventuellement révélée être une mandataire infidèle, comme [B] n'est pas davantage fondée à prétendre que l'infidélité éventuelle de son mandataire a eu pour résultat de priver de tout effet la remise des données sismiques par [A] aux délégués de son mandataire.

Il est vrai cependant que [B] soutient qu'elle a informé [A] et Madame [Y] (. . .) avant la remise des données à Monsieur [Z] de la révocation expresse du mandat ad hoc de cette dernière (. . .).

(. . .)

(. . .) l'arbitre unique considère que [B] n'a en aucune manière prouvé qu'elle avait notifié à [A] avant le (. . .) la remise des données par (. . .) aux délégués de Madame [Y], et donc de [B], ou que [A] avait eu connaissance avant cette date, de la révocation du mandat de Madame [Y]. L'arbitre unique considère donc que [A] a bien rempli ses obligations contractuelles en matière de mise des données sismiques à la disposition de [B] ».

L'arbitre donna donc gain de cause à A et se prononça comme suit sur la charge des frais de l'arbitrage:

« L'alinéa 1 de l'article 31 du Règlement CCI prévoit que « les frais de l'arbitrage comprennent les honoraires et frais des arbitres et les frais administratifs de la CCI fixés par la Cour, conformément au tableau de calcul en vigueur au moment de l'introduction de la procédure d'arbitrage, les honoraires et frais des experts nommés par le Tribunal arbitral ainsi que les frais raisonnables exposés par les parties pour leur défense à l'occasion de l'arbitrage », et l'alinéa 2 prévoit en outre que « la sentence définitive du tribunal arbitral liquide les frais de l'arbitrage et décide à laquelle des parties le paiement en incombe ou dans quelle proportion ils sont partagés entre elles ».

En ce qui concerne les frais proprement dits de l'arbitrage, y compris les frais administratifs de la CCI, mais non compris les honoraires des arbitres, il est généralement admis que la partie qui succombe au fond supporte l'intégralité ou une partie importante des frais de l'arbitrage. Une règle équivalente s'applique aux frais et honoraires raisonnables exposés par les parties pour leur défense, dans des proportions généralment fixées par les arbitres. En l'espèce, les frais et honoraires exposés par chacune des parties pour leur définse sont raisonnables et entrent dans le cadre de l'article 31 du Règlement.

Il reste cependant que ce litige ne serait peut-être pas né si [A] avait, quoi qu'elle en dise, procédé à la vérification de l'authenticité du pouvoir du (. . .) de la qualité de son prétendu signataire et de l'existence d'une joint venture entre [B] et [C]. [A] porte ainsi une part de responsabilité dans la genèse de ce litige.

Pour ces raisons, et bien que [A] ait triomphé sur sa demande principale, l'arbitre unique décide que:

S'agissant des frais d'arbitrage proprement dits, [B] supportera 75 % des frais, tandis que [A] en supportera 25 % (. . .).

S'agissant des autres frais et honoraires d'arbitrage, chacune des parties conservera à sa charge l'intégralité des frais qu'elle a exposés dans le cadre du présent arbitrage ».

OBSERVATIONS. — I. — Dans cette affaire rocambolesque, la détermination du droit applicable était probablement la seule question qui semblait simple. Non seulement une disposition contractuelle soumettait le contrat au droit de l'État de A, mais, dans la procédure, les parties s'étaient implicitement mises d'accord pour que soit appliqué au fond le droit français pour des raisons que l'arbitre ne cherche pas à élucider de façon précise. Il suppose que l'attitude des parties s'explique par l'identité du code civil français et de celui de l'État de A et le maintien de la référence au droit français dans cette ancienne colonie française pour toutes les matières qui ne sont pas régies par des dispositions spéciales. Mais peu importe finalement que cette supposition soit ou non fondée, puisque les parties sont libres de choisir le droit applicable au fond du litige au moment qui leur convient et de modifier un choix antérieur. Mais surtout, les arbitres considèrent qu'il n'y a lieu de trancher la question du droit applicable au fond que si les parties sont en désaccord sur ce point, (cf. la sentence rendue dans l'affaire CCI n° 3267 en 1979: *Recueil des sentences arbitrales de la CCI, 1974-1985, p. 76)*. Ceci, qu'il s'agisse de la détermination du droit à appliquer comme de son domaine. Il n'allait en effet pas de soi dans l'affaire ici rapportée que le droit applicable au contrat de cession de données sismiques, qu'il se confonde ou non avec le droit français, s'appliquait aussi au mandat apparemment conféré par une société chinoise à une personne privée en vue de conclure un contrat dans l'État de A avec une société de cet État. Mais, dans l'arbitrage international, la notion de droit applicable au fond du litige, sous tous ses aspects, lorsqu'il est choisi par les parties, prend le pas sur celle de droit applicable à une relation juridique particulière. En l'absence d'une *lex fori* de l'arbitre international, l'accord des parties sur le droit applicable au fond s'analyse mieux comme un accord sur une règle du jeu en vue de la solution d'un litige que comme l'appréhension d'une situation juridique par un système de droit déterminé.

II. — L'arbitrage international ne connaît pas de règles d'application stricte en matière de charge de la preuve. C'est ce que soulignait, dès 1975, dans les termes suivants, la sentence rendue dans l'affaire CCI n° 1434: « *En présence des allégations contradictoires des parties, il y a lieu de rappeler à qui incombe, d'une façon générale, le fardeau de la preuve sur ce point, encore que la pratique arbitrale ne soit pas tenue à une application aussi stricte que certaines juridictions étatiques des règles applicables en matière de preuve.* » (cf. *JDI 1976, p. 978, obs. Y. D'.).* Les adages « *actor incumbit probatio* » et « *reus in exipiendo fit actor* » n'en sont pas moins d'application systématique. C'est en effet au demandeur d'apporter la preuve des droits et des faits qu'il invoque à l'appui de sa demande, et au défendeur de prouver tout élément de fait ou de droit qu'il entend opposer au demandeur. Entre autres, la sentence qui vient d'être mentionnée l'illustre.

Ces principes généraux doivent être affinés lorsqu'une partie prétend qu'un document sur lequel l'autre fonde une prétention est entaché de faux. En présentant le document, la partie qui l'invoque a apporté la preuve à sa charge, formellement tout au moins, car il est encore nécessaire que le document ait la portée juridique prétendue. C'est alors à la partie qui excipe de l'exception de faux de prouver ses allégations. Mais, comme le montre la présente sentence, cette dernière n'est pas tenue d'apporter une preuve absolue de l'absence d'authenticité du document. Il lui suffit d'établir l'existence d'indices sérieux détruisant l'apparence d'authenticité. S'il est montré, *prima facie,* que l'on peut nourrir des doutes raisonnables à cet égard, le fardeau de la preuve est à nouveau renversé et c'est à la partie qui se prévaut du document de prouver que ces doutes sont infondés. Ainsi, dans la sentence ici rapportée, l'arbitre énumère un faisceau d'indices d'où il résulte que l'authenticité du pouvoir qu'aurait donné C à Mme Y était pour le moins douteuse: papier à en-tête de C non conforme, signature d'un ancien mandataire social retiré depuis un an . . . Dans ces circonstances, l'arbitre considère alors qu'il appartenait à A de dissiper le doute raisonnable qui résultait de ces éléments troublants. A ne l'ayant pas fait, il en conclut qu'A ne peut se prévaloir du pouvoir en faveur de Mme Y pour prétendre que C était partie au contrat contenant la convention d'arbitrage.

Bien sur, ce sont là des règles relatives à la charge de la preuve et non pas à son administration. En d'autres termes, il s'agit de déterminer laquelle des parties profite de l'incertitude et du doute subsistant à la suite de la production d'un élément présenté comme probant. La partie qui n'a pas la charge de la preuve serait bien imprudente d'attendre tranquillement que son adversaire ait réussi à en reporter sur elle le fardeau pour administrer les éléments nécessaires à dissiper le doute. Les renversements successifs de la charge de la preuve ne sont pas un ballet bien réglé où chacun des danseurs fait, tour à tour, quelques pas. Dans la réalité, les parties présentent leur preuves selon le calendrier de procédure fixé par les arbitres, lequel n'est pas strictement fonction de la répartition de la charge de la preuve de chacun des faits contestés.

C'est pourquoi la démarche adoptée par l'arbitre dans la sentence ici rapportée n'est qu'en apparence différente de celle retenue par le Tribunal irano-américain de La Haye, dans l'affaire n° 812 *(546-813-3),* qui a fait l'objet d'une sentence le 2 mars 1993 *(Yearbook International Arbitration, 1994, p. 421).* Dans cette affaire, en effet, alors que le défendeur prétendait qu'un acte sur lequel s'appuyait le demandeur était un faux, le Tribunal arbitral, tout en soulignant que le défendeur avait la charge de prouver l'inauthenticité de l'acte, déclara, dans les termes suivants, qu'il ne se préoccuperait de la question de savoir si cette preuve était rapportée qu'à condition que le demandeur ait présenté un document inspirant un minimum de confiance quant à son authenticité. Le demandeur doit démontrer, *prima facie,* que l'acte est authentique:

« *The Tribunal believes that the analysis of the distribution of the burden of proof in this Case should be centered around article 24, paragraph 1 of the Tribunal Rules which states that* « *[e]ach party shall have the burden of proving the facts relied on to support his claim or defence* ». *It was the Respondent who, at one point during the proceedings in this Case, raised the defence that the Deed is a forgery. Specifically, the Respondent has contended that the Deed, dated 15 August 1978, was in fact fabricated in 1982. Having made that factual allegation, the Respondent has the burden of proving it. However, the Tribunal need only concern itself with the question whether the Respondent has met that burden if the Claimant has submitted a document inspiring a minimally sufficient degree of confidence in its authenticity. It is therefore up to the Chimant first to demonstrate prima facie that the Deed is authentic.* ».

Dans la sentence ici rapportée, C, défenderesse, avait démontré que, *prima facie,* il y avait de sérieux doutes quant à l'authenticité du pouvoir en faveur de Mme Y. Le problème de savoir si elle s'était déchargée du fardeau de prouver l'absence d'authenticité du pouvoir ne se posait pas non plus pour l'arbitre, selon un raisonnement finalement bien proche de celui suivi par le Tribunal irano-américain.

III. — Le problème de l'extension d'une convention d'arbitrage à une partie qui ne l'a pas signée, mais qui est partie à un contrat lié économiquement à celui qui contient la convention d'arbitrage, est source de grandes difficultés.

Lorsque la partie non signataire invoque l'absence de convention d'arbitrage en début de procédure alors que le demandeur ne s'appuie que sur la notion de groupe de contrats, la Cour internationale d'arbitrage de la CCI déclare que l'arbitrage ne peut avoir lieu sur le fondement de l'article 6(2) de son règlement. Il n'est fait exception à cette règle que lorsque les parties signataires de chaque contrat appartiennent à deux groupes de sociétés, (cf. *A.-M. Whitesell et E. Silva Romero, L'arbitrage à pluralité de parties ou de contrats: l'expérience récente de la Chambre de Commerce Internationale in L'arbitrage complexe, Questions de procédure: Bulletin de la Cour internationale d'arbitrage de la CCI, Supplément spécial, 2003, p. 7).* On a pu d'ailleurs justement relever que « lorsque, appelées à statuer sur l'extension de la portée de la convention d'arbitrage à une partie non signataire du contrat la contenant, les sentences y répondent positivement, ce n'est pas sur le fondement de l'existence d'un groupe de contrats mais sur celle d'un groupe de sociétés. » *(D. Cohen, Arbitrage et groupes de contrats: Rev. arb. 1997, p. 471).* La sentence rendue dans l'affaire CCI n° 4131 en 1982 *(Dow Chemical: JDI 1983, p. 899, obs. Y. D.)* constitue une des illustrations les plus significatives de cette tendance. On peut également citer à cet égard la sentence rendue sous l'égide de la CCI le 27 janvier 1989, dans l'affaire *Kiss France cl Société Générale,* où, selon la Cour d'appel de Paris « le tribunal arbitral a, pour l'essentiel, retenu de l'analyse des conventions l'existence de deux groupes de sociétés et la réalisation d'une opération économique unique dans un ensemble contractuel associant étroitement les filiales des deux contractants. » *(Paris, 31 oct. 1989: Rev. arb. 1992, p. 90, note L. Aynès, p. 70 et note D. Cohen, p. 74).* Plus récemment, une sentence rendue dans l'affaire n° 8910 en 1998 *(JDI2000, p. 1085, obs. D. H.)* a retenu une analyse semblable. L'existence de groupes de sociétés permet de dégager, au-delà de personnalités juridiques multiples et de contrats distincts, la rencontre de consentements pour réaliser une opération économique intégrée dans un cadre juridique global, soumise à un mode de résolution des litiges unique.

En l'absence de groupes de sociétés, l'accord des volontés est beaucoup plus incertain. Cependant, s'appuyant sur la décision de la Cour d'appel de Paris dans l'affaire *Jaguar (CA Paris, 7 déc. 1994: Rev. arb. 1995, p. 245, note Ch. Jarrosson),* la sentence ici rapportée semble admettre le principe de l'extension de la convention d'arbitrage à une partie qui ne l'a pas signée, au sein d'un groupe de contrats, alors même que la notion de groupes de sociétés ne pouvait être invoquée. Il pourrait suffire, selon l'arbitre, que cette partie ait eu connaissance de la convention d'arbitrage contenue dans un contrat qu'elle n'a pas conclu mais qui constitue l'épicentre de l'opération économique intégrée à laquelle son propre contrat appartient, pour que cette convention lui soit opposable. Encore faut-il que son acceptation présumée de cette convention d'arbitrage ne soit pas démentie par l'existence d'une convention d'arbitrage différente dans le contrat qu'elle a conclu, incompatible avec un mode unique de résolution des litiges, comme c'était le cas en l'espèce (cf. en ce sens *Ph. Fouchard, E. Gaillard et B. Goldman: Traité de l'arbitrage commercial international, n° 521, p. 318).*

IV. — La position procédurale de C était pour le moins paradoxale. Elle contestait d'une part la compétence de l'arbitre en prétendant que le pouvoir, en vertu duquel Mme Y avait en son nom signé le contrat contenant la convention d'arbitrage, était un faux et, d'autre part, demandait à titre reconventionnel à l'arbitre de condamner A et B à lui verser US$ 5 000 000 « pour faux », plus US$ 100.000.000 pour atteinte à sa réputation. Le succès du principe même de cette demande reconventionnelle supposait que le faux allégué fut établi, fondement de son exception d'incompétence. On comprend alors que l'arbitre n'ait pas retenu la formulation de cette étrange demande reconventionnelle pour décider que C avait accepté la procédure arbitrale, d'autant plus que C ne s'était plus manifestée ultérieurement dans la procédure, se refusant même à signer l'acte de mission. De toutes façons, ce silence aurait permis à l'arbitre de conclure qu'elle avait abandonné sa demande reconventionnelle s'il s'était déclaré compétent sur le fondement de l'existence d'un groupe de contrats, indépendamment du débat sur l'authenticité du pouvoir présenté par Mme Y.

V. — En laissant Mme Y signer le contrat au nom de B, en sa présence, M. X, principal dirigeant de B, avait créé une apparence dont A pouvait se prévaloir pour prétendre que Mme Y avait valablement engagé B. Ce n'est pas la première fois qu'un arbitre du commerce international fonde une décision sur la notion de mandat apparent. On renverra sur ce point à la sentence rendue en 1987 dans l'affaire CCI n° 4667 en 1984 (cf. obs. Y. D. sous la sentence rendue dans l'affaire n° 5065 en 1986: *JDI 1987, p. 1039)* où, dans des circonstances de fait plus classiques, un tribunal arbitral estima que, selon les usages du commerce, « lorsqu'un directeur général est présent à une négociation, l'interlocuteur est fondé à croire que son représentant également présent dispose, lorsque le directeur général a quitté les lieux de la négociation après avoir vu l'ensemble des textes qui seront signés, d'un pouvoir de signature. ». Les effets du mandat apparent sont largement reconnus en droit comparé, ce qui a permis aux Principes d'Unidroit relatifs aux contrats du commerce international de les consacrer à leur article 2.2.5(2), confirmant ainsi que ces effets ont leur place parmi les règles bien établies de la *lex mercatoria*, même si le formalisme excessif de certains droits nationaux peut justifier quelque prudence (cf. la sentence rendue en 1988 dans l'affaire n° 5832: *JDI 1988, p. 1198, obs. G. A. A)*.

VI. — C'est pourquoi B pouvait difficilement soutenir avoir été victime de manœuvres dolosives de la part de A et de C qui justifieraient l'annulation du contrat. Pour être une cause de nullité du contrat en tant que vice du consentement, les manœuvres dolosives d'une partie doivent avoir déterminé l'autre à contracter. Or, aucune manœuvre dolosive de la part de A ayant suscité la conclusion du contrat par B n'était établie et l'exception de dol ne pouvait donc être favorablement accueillie. Il est possible que B ait été victime d'un dol, comme le relève par ailleurs l'arbitre, mais pas du fait de A. A côté de cette analyse classique, c'est surtout la présomption de compétence professionnelle de M. X, dont l'expérience ne permettait pas de croire qu'il ait pu être trompé lors de la conclusion du contrat, qui retient l'attention. Cette démarche est une des caractéristiques de la jurisprudence des arbitres du commerce international. La présomption de compétence professionnelle des opérateurs du commerce international fut utilisée dès 1966, dans l'affaire CCI n° 1307 (cf. obs. sur la sentence de 1972 dans l'affaire n° 1990: *JDI 1974, p. 897)*. Elle a été régulièrement confirmée depuis (cf. entre autres les sentences de 1975 dans les affaires n° 2438: *JDI 1976, p. 969*; n° 2281: *JDI 1980, p. 990*; dans les affaires n° 3380: *JDI 1981, p. 927 et n° 3130: JDI 1988, p. 932* et dans l'affaire n° 5346: *JDI 1991, p. 1060)*.

VII. — On comprend l'hésitation de l'arbitre avant de conclure qu'A n'avait pas violé la clause d'exclusivité du contrat en se montrant prête à transférer à B' les droits contractuels de B. Même si la similitude du nom des sociétés B et B' pouvait effectivement laisser penser qu'elles appartenaient au même groupe et, si l'intervention de Mme Y pour le compte de l'une et l'autre ne pouvait que confirmer cette présomption, l'obligation de compétence professionnelle qui vient d'être évoquée implique celle de se renseigner (cf. *P. Jourdain, Le devoir de se renseigner (contribution à l'obligation de renseignement): D. 1983, chron. p. 139)*. D'autant plus que le conflit d'intérêts entre B et B' ressortait clairement de la dernière correspondance de celle-ci, qui invitait A à ignorer les offres B, ce qui indiquait bien que, loin de se confondre avec B, le cocontractant de A, B' voulait la supplanter. Confrontée à cette invitation à violer la clause d'exclusivité contractuelle, A indiquait implicitement qu'elle n'y voyait pas d'inconvénient pour autant qu'elle y trouvât son intérêt. Seulement, cette intention n'a pas été suivie d'effet et elle ne suffisait donc pas à consommer la violation d'une obligation contractuelle. La faute suppose la violation d'une norme et ses conséquences peuvent être différentes selon qu'elle est intentionnelle ou non. Mais la simple intention non suivie de violation ne saurait constituer une faute contractuelle.

VIII. — Selon l'article 31(3) du règlement d'arbitrage de la CCI « *L'arbitre liquide les frais de l'arbitrage et décide à laquelle des parties le paiement en incombe ou dans quelle proportion ils sont partagés entre elles* ». Si les arbitres jouissent de la plus grande liberté dans ce domaine, comme l'a affirmé la sentence CCI rendue dans l'affaire n° 7006 en 1992 *(Yearbook Commercial Arbitration, 1993, p. 58)*, ils ont tendance à répartir la charge des coûts de la procédure en fonction du succès respectif des parties (cf. par exemple la sentence CCI rendue dans l'affaire n° 7986 en 1999: *JDI 2002, p. 1071, obs. Y.D.*). Cependant, ce principe général subit divers aménagements pour tenir compte des caractéristiques propres à chaque litiges. La sentence CCI rendue dans l'affaire n° 8486 en 1996 *(JDI 1998, p. 1047, obs. Y. D.)* reflétait la prise en compte par l'arbitre « de l'attitude des parties pendant la procédure », pour sanctionner celles qui font obstacle au bon déroulement de l'arbitrage et ainsi contribuent à en augmenter les coûts (dans ce sens, cf. également la sentence précitée dans l'affaire n° 7006). La sentence ici rapportée condamne A et B à supporter respectivement 25 % et 75 % des frais de l'arbitrage proprement dits, c'est-à-dire les honoraires et frais de l'arbitre et les frais administratifs de la CCI, laissant à chacune des parties la charge des frais qu'elle a directement exposée pour intervenir dans la procédure. La solution peut surprendre car A avait obtenu gain de cause sur l'essentiel. Comme il s'en explique, l'arbitre entend sanctionner la légèreté de A à qui est attribuée une part de responsabilité dans la genèse du litige. Si A s'était montrée plus prudente au moment de contracter, le litige aurait pu être évité. On constate ainsi que non seulement l'attitude des parties pendant la procédure peut influer sur la répartition de ses coûts, indépendamment de la solution qui est donnée au litige, mais encore leur comportement « à risque », avant la naissance de celui-ci.

Y.D.
B. D.

Sentence intérimaire sur la compétence rendue dans l'affaire CCI n° 10671

I. — Compétence du tribunal arbitral. — Qualification de l'objection soulevée par la partie défenderesse. — Objection à la compétence (oui). — Objection à la régularité de la constitution du tribunal arbitral (non). — Compétence *in abstracto* et compétence *in concrete* du tribunal arbitral. — Portée de l'article 6(2) du Règlement d'arbitrage de la CCI. — Portée du principe de la compétence. — Nature et effets juridiques de l'acte de mission.

II. — Convention d'arbitrage. — Droit applicable à l'interprétation de la convention d'arbitrage. — Notion de « jurisprudence arbitrate ». — Distinguishing. — Principes d'interprétation des conventions internationales d'arbitrage.

III. — Interprétation des contrats. — Méthodes subjective et objective d'interprétation contractuelle. — « Règlement de conciliation et d'arbitrage de la, Chambre de Commerce Internationale de Genève ». — Qualités des négociatcurs de la convention d'arbitrage. — Le sens du mot « International(e) ».

IV. — Frais de l'arbitrage. — « Usage » dans le système d'arbitrage de la CCI concernant la répartition entre les parties des frais de l'arbitrage. — Portée de l'article 31(2), *in fine,* du Règlement d'arbitrage de la CCI.

Le fond du litige n'éait pas particulièrement extraordinaire: une société suisse — partie défenderesse à la procédure arbitrale — avait confié à une société immatriculée au Panama — parde demanderesse — la réalisation d'une étude de marché en Grèce pour la vente de produits polycarbonate et polystyréne fabriquès par la première.

La partie demanderesse alléguait que la partie défenderesse n'avait pas réglé l'intégralité des prestations qu'elle lui avait fournies lors de la réalisation de l'étude de marché. Pour sa part, la partie défenderesse soulevait d'emblée des objections à la compétence administrative de la Cour internationale d'arbitrage de la Chambre de commerce internationale (« CCI ») pour organiser la procédure arbitrale (sur le contrat CCI d'organisation de l'arbitrage, cf. *Ph. Fouchard, Les institutions permanentes d'arbitrage devant le juge étatique (À propos d'une jurisprudence récente): Rev. arb 1987, n° 3, p. 225-274. — Th. Clay, L'arbiter: Dalloz, 2001, coll. Bibliothèque de thèses, spéc. p. 549 ets. — E. Silva-Romero, Les apports de la doctrine et de la jurisprudence françaises à l'arbitrage de la Chambre de commerce internationale: Rev. arb. 2005, n°2, p. 421-437)* et, par là même, s'opposait à ce qu'un tribunal arbitral constitué par et agissant sous l'égide de la Cour internationale d'arbitrage de la CCI (ci-après la « Cour ») tranche le litige au fond. Subsidiairement, la partie défenderesse alléguait que la partie demanderesse n'avait démontré ni le bien-fondé de sa créance ni le quantum de celle-ci.

L'objection de la partie défenderesse, qui fait l'objet de la sentence intérimaire sur la « compétence » rendue dans l'affaire CCI n° 10671 par un Tribunal arbitral composé par trois arbitres suisses, résultait de l'expression imprécise (sur la problématique de la « précision du consentement », cf. *E. Gaillard et J. Savage (éd.), Fouchard, Gaillard, Goldman in International Commercial Arbitration, La Haye; Kluwer Law International, 1999, spéc. p. 262-266)* du consentement des parties dans une clause compromissoire mal rédigée ou, selon la métaphore ou image médicale chère aux spécialistes en arbitrage, « pathologique » (sur la problématique des conventions d'arbitrage dites « pathologiques », cf. *F. Eisemann, La clause d'arbitrage pathologique in Essais in memoriam Eugenio Minoli, 1974, p. 129 et s. — B. Davis, Pathological Clauses — Frederic Eisemann's Still Vital Criteria, Arbitration International: Kluwer Law International, 1991, n° 7, p. 365 et s. — W. L. Craig, W. W. Park et J. Paulsson, International Chamber of Commerce Arbitration: Oceana Publications, Inc. et ICC Publishing SA, 2000, spéc. p. 85 et 86. — Y. Derains et E. Schwartz, A Guide to the New ICC Rules of Arbitration: Kluwer Law International, 1998, spéc. p. 89-92).*

La pathologie de la convention d'arbitrage découlait du texte suivant:

> « *Any dispute arising between* [la partie demanderesse] *and* [la partie défenderesse] *in connection with the Agreement or transactions carried out pursuant to the Agreement, which could not be settled in a friendly way, shall be finally settled under the Rules of Conciliation and Arbitration of the International Chamber of Commerce of Geneva by three arbitrators designated by* [la partie défenderesse] *and* [la partie demanderesse] *and they shall act in accordance with the above mentioned Rules in force at the time.*
> *The arbitration shall take place in Geneva, Switzerland* ».

Le Tribunal arbitral résume très clairement dans sa Sentence intérimaire les arguments des parties à l'égard de la pathologie de la clause compromissoire et du problème de la « compétence » de la manière suivante:

> « *17. Dans son mémoire du 15 janvier 2000, la défenderesse souligne que l'on est en présence d'une clause dite pathologique, dans la mesure où il est « constant qu'il n'existe pas de Chambre internationale de commerce à Genève, mais bien une Chambre de commerce et d'industrie qui est notamment organisée de telle sorte que des arbitrages se déroulent sous son auspice et qui a adopté un Règlement d'arbitrage* ».
>
> *Pour la défenderesse, l'intention des parties de se soumettre à un arbitrage de la CCIG [Chambre de commerce et d'industrie de Genève] résulte tant d'une interprétation subjective que d'une interprétation objective de la volonté des parties.*
>
> *18. D'un point de vue subjectif, la défenderesse considère que le rattachement des divers éléments du contrat et des qualités des parties elles-mêmes à Genève montre qu'elles « ont voulu soumettre leur litige à un système cohérent et qui leur était proche à toutes deux d'égale façon: application du droit suisse, siège à Genève, arbitrage CCIG; ce qui ne laisse aucune place à un arbitrage auprès de la CCI à Paris* ».
>
> *19. S'agissant de l'interprétation de la clause d'arbitrage selon la méthode objective, la défenderesse souligne l'importance accordée par la pratique arbitrale au fait que la clause pathologique vise un lieu déterminé.*
>
> *20. La demanderesse, quant à elle, relève que le contrat signé par les parties en décembre 1991 se réfère aux « Rules of Conciliation and Arbitration of the International Chamber of Commerce of Geneva » alors que le premier règlement d'arbitrage de la Chambre de commerce et d'industrie de Genève date du 1ᵉʳ janvier 1992. Les parties n'ont donc pas pu, pour la demanderesse, vouloir se soumettre à un règlement d'arbitrage qui n'existait pas encore.*
>
> *21. À l'audience de plaidoiries du 25 février 2000, les deux parties ont persisté dans leurs positions respectives.*
>
> *Répondant à l'argument de la demanderesse sur l'antériorité de la clause par rapport au Règlement de la CCIG, la défenderesse a souligné que le contrat ne précédait que d'une dizaine de jours l'entrée en vigueur dudit règlement, qui était par conséquent connu auparavant et auquel les parties pouvaient parfaitement s'être référées* ».

Dans le système d'arbitrage de la CCI, lorsqu'une des parties soulève un ou plusieurs moyens relatifs à l'existence, à la validité ou à la portée de la convention d'arbitrage, la Cour, conformément à l'article 6(2) du Règlement d'arbitrage de la CCI de 1998 (ci-après le « Règlement »), peut décider, sans préjuger de la recevabilité ou du bien-fondé de ce ou ces moyens, que l'arbitrage aura lieu si elle estime, *prima facie,* possible l'existence d'une convention d'arbitrage visant le Règlement. En l'espèce, la Cour a décidé, lors de sa session du 9 février 2000, que l'arbitrage devait avoir lieu (sur l'examen *prima facie* de la convention d'arbitrage par la Cour, cf. *W. L. Craig et al, op. cit., spéc. p. 155-161. — Y. Derains et al, op. cit., spéc. p. 79-102. — E. Silva-Romero, Les apports de la doctrine et de la jurisprudence françaises . . . , op. cit., spéc. p. 428-430. — E. Silva-Romero, ICC Arbitration and State Contracts: ICC International Court of Arbitration Bulletin, ICC Publishing SA, vol. 13, n° 1 — Spring 2002, spéc. p. 46-52).*

La décision de la Cour étant administrative (l'article 12 de l'Appendice II — Règlement intérieur de la Cour internationale d'arbitrage — du Règlement d'arbitrage de la CCI de 1988 disposait expressément que la décision de la Cour à l'issue de son analyse *prima facie* de la convention d'arbitrage était « de nature administrative »), il appartenait au Tribunal arbitral de prendre toute décision sur sa propre compétence. En l'espèce, la source du pouvoir du Tribunal arbitral de prendre toute décision quant à sa compétence ne résultait pas uniquement des dispositions de l'article 6(2) du Règlement et de la *lex arbitrii* (cf. l'article 183(1) de la loi suisse portant sur le droit international privé de 1987, ci-après « LDIP »). Elle provenait également de l'acte de mission signé par les parties qui, au chapitre consacré aux « Questions soumises au Tribunal arbitral — Sur la compétence », établissait ce qui suit:

> « *La défenderesse ayant, dans son mémoire sur exception d'incompétence et premier mémoire responsif du 15 janvier 2000, soulevé l'incompétence du Tribunal arbitral, celui-ci a, par Ordonnance n° 1 du 25 janvier 2000, imparti à la demanderesse un délai au 25 février 2000 pour le dépôt d'un mémoire de réponse sur exception d'incompétence.*
>
> *Le Conseil de la demanderesse s'est prononcé sur cette exception par courrier du 4 février 2000, concluant à la compétence du Tribunal et à l'application du Règlement de conciliation et d'arbitrage de la CCI.*
>
> *Parallèlement, la Cour internationale d'arbitrage de la CCI s'est saisie, en application de l'article 6(2) du Règlement d'arbitrage de la CCI, de la question de l'existence d'une convention d'arbitrage visant ledit règlement. Par décision du 9 février, la Cour a décidé que la procédure arbitrale aurait lieu conformément à l'article 6(2) du Règlement.*
>
> *Il incombe donc au Tribunal arbitral de statuer sur sa propre compétence, ce qu'il fera par une décision incidente (article 186 al. 3 LDIP)* ».

Après avoir examiné les écritures des parties et les avoir entendues lors d'une audience de plaidoiries, le Tribunal arbitral a rendue une Sentence intérimaire sur la « compétence » le 31 juillet 2000. Le raisonnement qui a conduit le Tribunal arbitral à sa décision mérite d'être transcrit intégralement:

> « *[. . .]*
>
> *22. Le Tribunal arbitral constate tout d'abord que la solution au problème posé doit être cherchée dans l'interprétation de la clause arbitrale controversée.*
>
> *23. L'examen de ladite clause montre que la question du siège de l'arbitrage est réglée indépendamment au deuxième alinéa (« The arbitration shall take place in Geneva, Switzerland »), de sorte que l'emploi du mot « Genève » dans le premier alinéa n'est pas en rapport avec la désignation du siège, mais seulement avec celle de l'institution sous l'égide de laquelle l'arbitrage devra se dérouler. Cette constatation est renforcée par le fait que référence est faite à l' « International Chamber of Commerce of Geneva » et non « in Geneva ». La mention de Genève*

est donc destinée à qualifier l'institution, non à situer le lieu où la procédure devra se dérouler.

24. La question se limite par conséquent à savoir si Us parties se sont trompées sur la dénomination de la Chambre de commerce et d'industrie de Genève, dont elles ont pensé qu'elle comportait le mot International, ou si elles ont erré quant à la localisation de la Chambre de commerce internationale, pensant que celle-ci avait à Genève son siège, voire un siège secondaire.

25. Le Tribunal arbitral observera préalablement que la défenderesse s'est à bon droit référée aux méthodes d'interprétation du droit suisse.

En effet, c 'est ce droit qui doit s'appliquer à l'interprétation de la clause arbitrale, tant en qualité de lex arbitrii du fait que le siège de l'arbitrage est à Genève, qu'au titre de droit choisi par les parties pour régir « in every » respect' le contrat lui-même (article 7 de la lettre-contrat du 20 décembre 1991).

26. Les indices de la volonté réelle des parties mentionnés par celles-ci dans leurs écritures et leurs plaidoiries n'aident guère à l'interprétation de la clause litigieuse.

Les liens des parties et de la cause avec Genève, sur lesquels la défenderesse insiste, ne sont nullement déterminants, cette localisation expliquant sans doute le choix de Genève comme lieu de l'arbitrage, ce qui fait l'objet de l'article 8 alinéa 2 du contrat, mais n'ayant que peu de portée quant au choix de l'institution d'arbitrage. Les arbitrages CCI avec siège à Genève sont en effet légion.

Le fait, invoqué par la demanderesse, que le Règlement d'arbitrage de la CCIG ne soit entré en vigueur que le 1er janvier 1992 alors que le contrat a été conclu en décembre 1991 n'exclut pas, à lui seul, le choix de ce Règlement. En effet, dix jours avant l'entrée en vigueur dudit Règlement, son texte était évidemment déjà connu des milieux de l'arbitrage. Il faut d'ailleurs relever que si ce texte est le premier qui porte le titre de Règlement, la Chambre de commerce et d'industrie de Genève possédait déjà des « Directives d'arbitrage » certes plus limitées dans leur objet puisqu'elles ne visaient que la désignation d'arbitres par la Chambre, mais néanmoins en vigueur depuis 1980. Il faut enfin observer que le contrat devait lui-même entrer en vigueur le 1er janvier 1992, soit en même temps que le nouveau Règlement d'arbitrage de la CCIG, de sorte qu'il était concevable que les parties s'y réfèrent.

On doit cependant souligner que les auteurs de la clause, qui étaient apparemment des organes ou employés de [la partie défenderesse] à Lugano, n'appartenaient à l'évidence pas aux milieux de l'arbitrage, à en juger par la rédaction de la clause pathologique, et encore moins aux milieux genevois de l'arbitrage. De sorte que si leur connaissance du nouveau Règlement de la CCIG n'est pas exclue, elle ne saurait être présumée. Deux arguments de texte tendent d'ailleurs à exclure une telle connaissance: d'une part, l'intitulé inexact du Règlement et de l'Institution qui l'a élaboré; d'autre part, le fait que, compte tenu de la nouveauté de ce texte qui n'était pas encore en vigueur, on se serait attendu à ce que les rédacteurs du contrat soient plus précis dans sa désignation.

27. Le Tribunal arbitral n'a donc d'autre solution que d'interpréter le contrat sur la base de son seul texte, en se demandant comment celui-ci pouvait et devait être compris par des parties présumées honnêtes, raisonnables et de bonne foi (voir P. Engel, Traité des obligations en droit suisse, 2e édition, Berne 1997, p. 237), ce qui rejoint la notion d'interprétation objective à laquelle recourt le Tribunal fédéral (notamment SJ 1996 p. 549, 552-553).

28. On remarquera tout d'abord que la référence aux « Rules of Conciliation and Arbitration » évoque la CCI. En effet, alors que le Règlement de la CCIG de 1992 est intitulé Arbitration Rules et ne contient qu'une disposition (l'article 21) autorisant le Tribunal arbitral à tenter de concilier les parties, la CCI a élaboré des Rules of Optional Conciliation et des Rules of Arbitration. À l'époque où le contrat a été conclu, ces deux règlements étaient présentés dans un fascicule portant le titre

*général « ICC Rules of Conciliation and Arbitration » et dont la couverture com-
portait en outre la mention « ICC International Chamber of Commerce », sans
indication de lieu de siège ni d'édition.*

*Certes, les mots Conciliation et Arbitration sont suffisamment associés dans
l'esprit des rédacteurs de contrats internationaux pour que leur usage ne constitue
pas nécessairement une référence à la CCI. Il n'empêche que l'expression « Rules
of Conciliation and Arbitration of the International Chamber of Commerce » évoque avec tant de précision et d'exactitude le Règlement de la CCI que l'ajout « of
Genève » ne dissipe pas l'impression que référence est faite à la CCI parisienne.*

*À l'inverse, cette formulation s'écarte de manière importante de la référence
correcte au Règlement d'arbitrage de la CCIG qui serait, en anglais: Arbitration
Rules of the Chamber of Commerce and Industry of Geneva. S'agissant tant du titre
du règlement d'arbitrage que de la dénomination de l'institution, la formulation du
contrat n'évoque un arbitrage CCIG que par la référence à Genève. On observera
que cette différence est particulièrement marquée du fait de la langue du contrat;
en français, compte tenu de l'ordre des mots, la différence est moins manifeste
entre Règlement de conciliation et d'arbitrage de la Chambre de Commerce Internationale et Règlement d'arbitrage de la Chambre de Commerce et d'Industrie de
Genève.*

29. En faveur de la CCIG, on peut arguer de ce que référence est faite à l'
*« International Chamber of Commerce of Geneva », ce qui paraît impliquer la
volonté de se rattacher à un organisme ayant son siège à Genève. Cet élément n'est
toutefois pas déterminant s'il n'est pas conforté par d'autres indices.*

*C'est ainsi qu'une jurisprudence constante considère une telle formule, que la
préposition utilisée soit à (in) ou de (of), comme prévoyant un arbitrage CCI avec
siège au lieu indiqué lorsque la détermination du siège ne fait pas, comme c'est le
cas en l'espèce à l'article 8 alinéa 2 du contrat, l'objet d'une clause contractuelle
particulière (notamment: Cour de Paris, 28.10.97, Revue de l'arbitrage 1998
pp. 399 ss, pour une référence à la « Chambre de commerce internationale de
Genève, conformément aux règles de l'arbitrage »; sentence CCI n° 4472 (1984),
Recueil des sentences arbitrales de la CCI, 1974-1985, p. 528, s'agissant de la
formule 'Internationale Handelskammer Zurich'; n° 5294 (1988), Recueil des
sentences 1986-1990, p. 182-183, pour la clause « arbitration under the rules of
conciliation and arbitration of the International Chamber of Commerce, Zurich,
Switzerland, in accordance with Swiss Law of the Canton of Zurich »).*

*Une sentence de 1977 (n° 2626, Recueil des sentences 1974-1985, p. 316, 317) a
également admis l'existence d'une clause en faveur de la CCI dans le cas d'une
référence à l'« International Chamber of Commerce in Geneva » alors que le siège
de l'arbitrage était fixé à Essen. Comme dans le présent cas, la mention de Genève
ne pouvait désigner le siège, mais servait uniquement à qualifier l'institution.
L'arbitre relève: « la désignation incorrecte du siège n'altère pas l'intention
des parties, qui apparaît clairement, d'attribuer compétence à la Cour d'arbitrage
de la C.C.I. de Paris ».*

*30. Il faut encore s'interroger sur la portée du mot « International » pour l'inter-
prétation d'une clause pathologique. Doctrine et jurisprudence arbitrale sont, à cet
égard, nuancées et démontrent que ce terme, à lui seul, n'est pas significatif et ne
permet pas d'exclure la compétence des institutions locales d'arbitrage. Ainsi, pour
Pierre A. KARRER (Pathological Arbitration Clauses, Malpractice, Diagnosis and
Therapy, in The International Practice of Law, Liber Amicorum for Thomas Bär and
Robert Karrer, 1998, pp. 109 ff. p. 122 and 123):*

*The word, « International » is not in itself sufficient to decide in favor of the
International Chamber of Commerce / Chambre de Commerce Internationale . . .
« International » is a generic term used also by other institutions such as the*

London, Copenhagen and Vienna Courts of International Arbitration, Belgium's CEPANI, the British Columbia and Quebec, Hong Kong, Channel Islands, Los Angeles Centers, the Milan and Singapore Chambers, the Mexican Academy. Most of these characterize the word, 'arbitration' as international. Even institutions that do not call themselves « international », such as the Zurich Chamber of Commerce, may have 'International Arbitration Rules'. Accordingly, it was held that arbitration under these rules was meant where the arbitration clause refined to the 'International Arbitration Court in Zurich' [Interim Award in ZHK 224/1993, point 28.4.], or to the « international trade arbitration organization in Zurich » [Interim Award in ZHK 245/1994, point 29.] (. . .)

(. . .) when an (institutional) chamber of commerce arbitration is selected for an international arbitration to be conducted in a town such as Zurich or Geneva, the reference to the institution must be understood to be a reference to the local Chamber of Commerce arbitration system which provides for international arbitration (. . .)

31. *La pratique arbitrale de la Chambre de commerce de Zurich est d'admettre la compétence de cette institution dès lors que les parties ont clairement prévu l'arbitrage, qu'elles se sont clairement prononcées pour un arbitrage institutionnel, et que la clause contient une claire référence à Zurich. Ont été ainsi admises comme se référant à la Chambre de commerce de Zurich (voir la sentence du 25 mars 1996, ZHK cas N° 287/95, Bull. ASA 1996 pp. 290 ss, 292) les appellations « Swiss Arbitration Court, Zurich » (ZHK cas n° 249/1994), « International Trade Arbitration Organization in Zurich, Switzerland » (ZHK cas n° 245/1994, Bull. ASA 1996 p. 303 ss, Yearbook Commercial Arbitration XXII (1997) p. 211 ss), « International Trade arbitration in Zurich (Switzerland) » (ZHK cas n° 260/1994), « International Arbitration Court in Zurich » (ZHK cas n° 224/1993).*

Quant à la CCIG, une sentence sur la compétence du 29 novembre 1996 (CCIG Arbitrage n° 117, Bull. ASA 1997 p. 534 ss) a admis la compétence de la Chambre de commerce et d'industrie de Genève dans une affaire où la clause litigieuse soumettait tout différend à « the Arbitration Court at the Swiss Chamber for Foreign Trade in Geneva, in accordance with the respective provisions of Rules and Buy [sic] Laws of th[e] said Arbitration Courts ». L'arbitre fonde sa décision sur le fait que l'interprétation du contrat démontrait la volonté des parties de soumettre leurs litiges à l'arbitrage sous l'auspices d'une institution suisse à Genève ayant adopté un règlement sur l'arbitrage international, ce qui ne pouvait désigner que la CCIG.

32. *Deux constatations s'imposent à la lecture des cas rapportés ci-dessus.*

La première est que la référence à une institution dont la dénomination erronée comporte le mot international ou une mention équivalente n'exclut pas nécessairement la compétence de la Chambre de commerce de Genève ou de Zurich dont le nom officiel n'inclut pas un tel qualificatif. C'est la volonté des parties d'avoir recours à une institution clairement située qui est prise en considération.

La deuxième constatation est que dans aucune de ces espèces, l'institution mal nommée ne comportait les mots Chambre de commerce internationale ou International Chamber of Commerce, suivis d'une indication de lieu. Il apparaît en effet que cette combinaison de mots correspond à une institution d'arbitrage connue et clairement identifiée, et que dès lors l'indication géographique qui la suit perd son caractère prépondérant pour l'identification de l'institution choisie. Selon les cas, le lieu devra être considéré soit comme désignant le siège de l'arbitrage, soit comme une erreur des rédacteurs sur le siège de la CCI. C'est ce qui résulte de la jurisprudence arbitrale citée sous chiffre 29 ci-dessus.

33. *Très subsidiairement, le Tribunal arbitral invoquera encore le principe* in dubio contra stipulatorem. *La rédaction de la clause litigieuse est due à la partie défenderesse. Elle ne saurait donc invoquer l'ambiguïté qu'elle a créée pour se*

soustraire à une demande d'arbitrage présentée devant l'institution que cette clause paraît prima facie désigner.

34. Après mûre réflexion, le Tribunal arbitral est ainsi arrivé à la conclusion que la clause compromissoire contenue dans la lettre-contrat du 20 décembre 1991 soumettait tout différend entre les parties à un arbitrage sujet au Règlement d'arbitrage de la Chambre de Commerce Internationale, le siège de l'arbitrage étant fixé à Genève.

Régulièrement désigné conformément à ce Règlement, le présent Tribunal arbitral se déclare donc compétent pour connaître au fond de la réclamation présentée par [la partie demanderesse] à l'encontre de [la partie défenderesse].

35. Conformément à l'usage, le Tribunal arbitral met à la charge de la défenderesse qui succombe les fiais de la procédure sur l'exception d'incompétence, dont le montant sera déterminé par le Tribunal arbitral à l'occasion de la sentence finale, par référence au montant globalement fixé par la Cour internationale d'arbitrage de la CCI conformément à l'article 31 du Règlement [. . .]».

OBSERVATIONS. — I. — La problématique de la « Sentence intérimaire sur la compétence » rendue le 31 juillet 2000 dans l'affaire arbitrale CCI n° 10671 (ci-après la « sentence ») nous invite d'abord à mettre, autant que faire se peut, les mots à leur place dans l'univers d'idées reçues de l'arbitrage commercial international (sur les mots et leur place, cf. E. Silva-Romero, *Wittgenstein et la philosophie du droit: PUF, Paris, 2002, coll. Droit, éthique, société*).

L'usage que la cour et le tribunal arbitral, y étant invités par les écritures et les plaidoiries des parties, ont fait du mot « compétence » serait, d'un certain point de vue, abusif.

La lecture de la sentence nous révèlerait qu'aucune des parties à la procédure arbitrale n'a soulevé d'objection générale et abstraite relative à l'existence, la validité ou la portée de la convention d'arbitrage. Aucune des parties, en d'autres termes, n'aurait véritablement contesté la compétence du Tribunal arbitral. La partie défenderesse n'a pas allégué, comme d'autres défenderesses l'ont fait dans des affaires arbitrales CCI similaires (cf. sentence rendue dans l'affaire n° 2626 en 1977: *JDI 1978, éd. techniques, n° 4, p. 981-985, obs. Y. Derains. —* sentence rendue dans l'affaire n° 3640 en 1980: *JDI 1981, éd. techniques, n° 4, p. 939-943, obs. Y. Derains. —* sentence rendue dans l'affaire n° 4023 en 1984: *JDI 1984, éd. techniques, n° 4, p. 950-952, obs. S. Jarvin. — CA Paris, Ire ch. civ., 14 févr. 1985: Rev. arb. 1987, n° 3, p. 325-334, note P. Level. —* sentence rendue dans l'affaire n° 5423 en 1987: *JDI 1987, éd. techniques, n° 4, p. 1048-1054, obs. S. Jarvin. —* sentence partielle rendue dans l'affaire n° 6709 en 1991: *JDI 1992, éd. techniques, n° 4, p. 998-1005, obs. D. Hascher. — CA Paris, Ire ch. civ., 28 oct. 1997: Rev. arb. 1998, n° 2, p. 399-47, note B. Leurent. — CCIG, Interim Award of 27 August 1999: Bull. ASA 2001, vol. 19, n° 2, p. 265-275*), que la convention d'arbitrage était inexistante ou nulle en raison de la dénomination incorrecte de l'institution arbitrale ou de son siège dans la clause compromissoire de l'espèce. La partie défenderesse s'est plutôt concrètement opposée à ce que la cour administre l'arbitrage et qu'un tribunal arbitral désigné par et agissant sous l'égide de celle-ci tranche le litige au fond. Selon elle, seulement la CCIG serait à bon droit appelée à organiser la procédure arbitrale, et un tribunal arbitral désigné par elle et agissant sous son égide serait juridiquement en mesure de trancher la controverse entre les parties.

La doctrine de l'arbitrage commercial international pourrait donc opérer une distinction entre compétence *in abstracto* et compétence *in concreto* du ou d'un tribunal arbitral.

D'un côté, la compétence *in abstracto **du*** tribunal arbitral serait contestée si l'une des parties mettait en cause l'existence, la validité ou la portée de la convention d'arbitrage. Ce serait, par exemple, le cas si l'une des parties alléguait que le litige que l'autre partie prétend soumettre à l'arbitrage n'est pas arbitrable conformément au droit applicable. En découlerait que tout tribunal arbitral agissant sous l'égide de n'importe quelle institution d'arbitrage serait en toute hypothèse incompétent pour trancher le litige et que seule une juridiction étatique pourrait s'en charger. En l'espèce, la partie défenderesse aurait soulevé une objection *in abstracto* à la compétence du tribunal arbitral si elle avait plaidé l'inexistence ou l'invalidité de la convention d'arbitrage sur la base du manque de précision de l'expression du consentement des parties dans celle-ci.

De l'autre, la compétence *in concreto d'un* Tribunal arbitral serait contestée si l'une des parties alléguait que le Tribunal arbitral désigné par une institution d'arbitrage et agissant sous son égide n'était pas compétent pour trancher le litige, mais qu'un autre Tribunal arbitral désigné autrement ou agissant sous les auspices d'une autre institution arbitrale serait tout à fait compétent pour en prendre la responsabilité. En fin de compte, une objection *in concreto* à la compétence d'un Tribunal arbitral poserait une question de régularité quant à la composition du Tribunal arbitral et non pas, *stricto sensu,* une question relative à sa compétence.

En résultent deux problèmes intéressants.

Le premier problème consiste en ce que la base juridique sur laquelle la Cour s'est saisie de la problématique proposée par la partie défenderesse n'est pas claire. L'article 6(2) du Règlement prévoit que la cour doit entreprendre un examen *prima facie* de la convention d'arbitrage si et seulement si (i) le défendeur ne répond pas à la demande comme il est prévu à l'article 5, ou (ii) lorsqu'une des parties soulève un ou plusieurs moyens relatifs à l'existence, à la validité ou à la portée de la convention d'arbitrage, c'est-à-dire relatifs à la compétence *in abstracto* du tribunal arbitral. Étant donné que l'objection de la partie défenderesse portait en l'espèce sur la compétence *in concreto* d'un tribunal arbitral, la cour aurait à notre avis pu se limiter à remettre le dossier au Tribunal arbitral et à lui renvoyer la problématique posée par la partie défenderesse pour résolution.

Cette solution permettrait d'éliminer le soupçon selon lequel un arbitre désigné par une institution arbitrale dont l'une des parties conteste la compétence administrative pour organiser l'arbitrage suivrait une tendance à confirmer la décision *prima facie* de celle-ci concluant que la dénomination de l'institution arbitrale dans la convention d'arbitrage peut bien la concerner.

Le second problème semblerait, du moins sur le plan théorique, beaucoup plus compliqué. Nul ne paraît mettre en doute qu'une problématique telle que celle du cas d'espèce doive être examinée et décidée, du moins dans un premier temps, par un tribunal arbitral. En l'espèce, le Tribunal arbitral lui-même invoque le sacro-saint principe de la compétence-compétence afin d'examiner et de résoudre l'objection à la compétence *in concreto* soulevée par la partie défenderesse. Néanmoins, s'il est vrai que l'objection de la partie défenderesse porte sur la régularité de la constitution du Tribunal arbitral et non sur sa compétence, il est légitime de se poser la question de savoir si la portée du principe de la compétence-compétence recouvre ce genre d'allégation et donne au tribunal arbitral le pouvoir de s'en occuper. En Suisse, l'article 183(1) LDIP ne semble pas recouvrir le cas d'une constitution irrégulière d'un Tribunal arbitral. Cette règle précise tout simplement que « Le tribunal arbitral statue sur sa propre compétence ». En France, en revanche, l'article 1466 du nouveau Code de procédure civile semble accorder aux arbitres la possibilité de trancher tout litige relatif à la régularité de leur désignation. Cet article dispose que « *Si, devant l'arbitre, l'une des parties conteste dans son principe ou son étendue le pouvoir juridictionnelle de l'arbitre, il appartient à celui-ci de statuer sur la validité ou les limites de son investiture* ».

Quoi qu'il en soit, les paragraphes ci-avant n'ont qu'une valeur théorique. En effet, en l'espèce, les parties, en signant l'acte de mission sans réserve avec la question soumise au Tribunal arbitral transcrite ci-avant, ont conclu une convention d'arbitrage CCI — un compromis — dont le seul objet était formé par la mission des arbitres de trancher le litige portant sur l'objection de la partie défenderesse à leur compétence *in concreto,* c'est-à-dire l'objection de la partie défenderesse portant sur la régularité de la constitution du Tribunal arbitral (sur la nature et les effets juridiques de l'acte de mission, cf. *E. Gaillard et al., op. cit., spéc. p. 672-674*). En découle le paradoxe que, même si la partie défenderesse ne voulait pas soumettre son litige à l'arbitrage CCI, la question sur la compétence *in concreto* du Tribunal arbitral a été confiée par les parties à des arbitres désignés dans le cadre d'un arbitrage CCI et agissant sous l'égide de la cour et que l'organisation de la procédure arbitrale limitée à la question de la régularité de la constitution du Tribunal arbitral a été confiée à celle-ci.

II. — Il est certainement dommage que, en l'espèce, aucun différend n'ait surgi quant aux règles juridiques applicables à l'interprétation de la convention d'arbitrage patholo-gique controversée, les deux parties ayant fondé leurs arguments sur le droit suisse. La sentence n'apporte donc pas de nouvelles lumières quant à savoir quel devrait être le critère de rattachement prépondérant pour déterminer les règles juridiques applicables à la convention d'arbitrage, y compris son interprétation (sur la problématique des règles de droit applicables à la convention d'arbitrage, cf. *H. Grigera-Naón, Choice-of-law Problems in International Commercial Arbitration: Recueil des cours de l'Académie de droit international de La Haye, Martinus Nijhoff Publishers, 2001, t. 289, spéc. p. 39-154*).

Malgré cette absence de controverse à l'égard du droit applicable, le Tribunal arbitral commence néanmoins par souligner que le droit suisse s'applique à l'interprétation de la convention d'arbitrage en l'espèce du fait de deux critères de rattachement, à savoir (i) le droit choisi par les parties comme droit applicable au contrat comprenant la clause com-promissoire en question, le droit suisse, et (ii) le siège de l'arbitrage, Genève, Suisse. Toutefois, le Tribunal arbitral ne souligne pas, car il n'en a pas besoin, lequel de ces critères devrait être prépondérant.

L'un des principaux intérêts théoriques de la sentence résulte paradoxalement du fait que le Tribunal arbitral a considéré que raisonner exclusivement d'après le droit suisse n'était pas suffisant et a ressenti le besoin d'avoir recours, et ce même si les parties n'ont pas présentés des arguments sur cette base, à la « jurisprudence arbitrale » (une décision récente sur la compétence du Tribunal arbitral dans une affaire CIRDI nous invite à mettre le mot « *jurisprudence* » entre guillemets. En effet, le Tribunal arbitral dans cette affaire affirme, au paragraphe 97 de sa décision, que « *[. . .] This raises a question whether, nonetheless, the present Tribunal should defer to the answers given by the SGS vs Pakistan Tribunal. The ICSID Convention provides only that awards rendered under it are « binding on the parties » (Article 53(1)), a provision which might be regarded as directed to the res judicata effect of awards rather than their impact as precedents in later cases. In the Tribunal's view, although different tribunals constituted under the ICSID system should in general seek to act consistently with each other, in the end it must be for each tribunal to exercise its competence in accordance with the applicable law, which will by definition be different for each BIT and each Respondent State. Moreover there is no doctrine of prec-edent in international law, if by precedent is meant a rule of the binding effect of a single decision. There is no hierarchy of international tribunals, and even if there were, there is no good reason for allowing the first tribunal in time to resolve issues for all later tribunals. It must be initially fir the control mechanisms provided for under the BIT and the ICSID Convention, and in the longer term for the development of a common legal opinion or jurisprudence constante, to resolve the difficult legal questions discussed by the SGS v. Pakistan Tribunal and also in the present decision* », (International Centre for the Settlement of Investment Disputes, Washington D.C., case n° ARB/02/6, « SGS Société Générale de Surveillance SA (Claimant) vs Republic of the Philippines (Respondent) » (ci-après l'affaire SGS vs Philippines): Decision of the Tribunal on Objections to Jurisdiction dated 29 January 2004, p. 37, disponible sur le site Internet du CIRDI, www.worlbank.org/icsid), à une certaine jurisprudence des cours étatiques françaises (cf. *CA Paris, l^{re} ch. civ., 28 oct. 1997, Sté Procédés de préfabrication pour le béton cl*

Libye: Rev. arb. 1998, n° 2, p. 399-407, note B. Leurent). Selon la Cour d'appel de Paris, la clause prévoyant « l'arbitrage de la Chambre de commerce internationale de Genève » ne peut être interprétée que comme désignant la CCI de Paris comme organisatrice de l'arbitrage, et Genève comme siège et même à la doctrine — notamment à l'article écrit par Pierre Karrer sur les conventions d'arbitrage pathologiques.

La Sentence contredit la position de ceux qui, suivant une perspective assez stricte (cf. la décision citée ci-avant dans l'affaire SGS vs Philippines), ne croient pas à l'existence d'une « jurisprudence arbitrale ». En l'espèce, le Tribunal arbitral analyse maintes sentences arbitrales portant sur la même question ou sur des questions similaires à celle qui lui est posée et, en utilisant la méthode anglo-saxonne du *distinguishing*, tient à définir les différences et ressemblances entre le cas qui lui a été confié et ceux examinés par d'autres tribunaux arbitraux avant lui. Force est donc de constater que, même si aucun tribunal arbitral n'est en principe obligé de faire sienne la décision d'un autre tribunal arbitral ayant décidé la même question ou une question similaire avant lui, certains tribunaux arbitraux apprécient et évaluent très sérieusement ce que d'autres tribunaux arbitraux ont précédemment dit. C'est dans ce sens qu'Yves Derains a bien identifié l'existence d'une « jurisprudence arbitrale CCI » (cf. *Y. Derains, L'obligation de minimiser le dommage dans la jurisprudence arbitrale in Revue de droit des affaires internationales: LGDJ 1987, Paris, n° 4, p. 375-382, spéc. p. 376; Les tendances de la jurisprudence arbitrale internationale: JDI 1993, éd. techniques, n° 4, p. 829-855, spéc. p. 829-831).*

En l'espèce, néanmoins, l'exercice du *distinguishing* nous démontre, avant tout, que chaque affaire est véritablement unique. Sa décision dépendra toujours de la rédaction particulière du contrat et de la convention d'arbitrage, des arguments soulevés par les parties et des règles de droit applicables. C'est le caractère unique de chaque affaire qui expliquerait, parmi d'autres choses, que, dans une affaire où la clause compromissoire faisait référence à la Chambre de Commerce Internationale de Genève sans déterminer dans un autre alinéa le siège de l'arbitrage, un arbitre unique suisse agissant sous les auspices de la CCIG ait donné, sur la base des déclarations des témoins présentés par les parties, plus d'importance au mot « Genève » qu'au mot « Internationale » et ait ainsi décidé que sa désignation par la CCIG était régulière et que la CCIG possédait compétence administrative pour organiser la procédure arbitrale (sf. sentence du 24 novembre 1999, cas CCIG n° 151, Arbitre unique: Paolo Michele Patoc-chi: *Bull. ASA 2003, vol. 21, n° 4, p. 754-780 — www.kluwerarbitration.com).*

Il est intéressant de noter que le Tribunal arbitral n'a pas considéré nécessaire de se référer à des principes d'interprétation contractuelle appartenant à la *lex mercatoria* telle qu'exprimée par la « jurisprudence arbitrale », à savoir, par exemple, le principe d'interprétation de bonne foi et le principe de l'effet utile (sur ces principes, cf. *E. Gaillard et al., op. cit., spéc. p. 254-262).*

III. — Malgré les références à la « jurisprudence arbitrale » et à la doctrine, la motivation de la Sentence n'est véritablement que l'application aux faits de l'espèce des deux méthodes d'interprétation des contrats citées par la partie défenderesse dans ses écritures, à savoir la méthode subjective et la méthode objective.

L'un des motifs donnés par le Tribunal arbitral échappe néanmoins à l'application de la méthode subjective. En effet, le Tribunal arbitral commence son raisonnement par préciser, sans se poser la question de savoir quelle a été la volonté réelle des parties à cet égard, que, étant donné que la question du siège de l'arbitrage se trouve réglée à l'alinéa 2 de la convention d'arbitrage, la référence à Genève du premier alinéa ne peut pas concerner le siège de l'arbitrage. La mention de Genève dans le premier alinéa de la clause compromissoire serait inexorablement liée à l'institution d'arbitrage. Le Tribunal arbitral aurait pu se demander si, du fait du va-et-vient des négociations contractuelles, les deux références à

Genève visaient à déterminer le siège de l'arbitrage. Il aurait également pu considérer que la référence à Genève dans le premier alinéa de la clause compromissoire visait, comme d'autres tribunaux arbitraux l'ont considéré (cf. sentence rendue dans l'affaire n° 2626 en 1977: *JDI 1978, p. 981-985, obs. Y. Derains*), le Comité national suisse de la CCI. En toute justice, il faut quand bien même souligner qu'aucune des parties n'a soulevé des tells arguments.

Le Tribunal arbitral conclut donc avec raison que les parties se sont trompées lors de la rédaction de la clause compromissoire. Ainsi le Tribunal arbitral précise-t-il très bien que « La question se limite par conséquent à savoir si les parties se sont trompées sur la dénomination de la Chambre de commerce et d'industrie de Genève, dont elles ont pensé qu'elle comportait le mot International, ou si elles ont erré quant à la localisation de la Chambre de commerce internationale, pensant que celle-ci avait à Genève son siège, voire un siège secondaire ». C'est d'ailleurs dans les mêmes termes que l'arbitre unique suisse définit la problématique dans la sentence arbitrale où il est arrivé à la conclusion inverse de celle du Tribunal arbitral de l'affaire CCI n° 10671 (cf. sentence du 24 novembre 1999, cas CCIG n° 151, *op. cit., spéc. § 80 et 81*).

L'article 18, alinéa l, du Code suisse des obligations consacre expressément la méthode dite subjective d'interprétation des contrats. Cette règle dispose que, « *Pour apprécier la forme et les clauses d'un contrat, il a lieu de rechercher la réelle et commune intention des parties, sans s'arrêter aux expressions ou dénominations inexactes dont elles ont pu se servir, soit par erreur, soit pour déguiser la nature véritable de la convention* ». Selon cette méthode, le Tribunal arbitral écarte deux arguments proposés par les parties.

D'une part, le Tribunal arbitral, avec raison, conclut que les liens des parties avec Genève ne sauraient à eux seuls indiquer que l'institution arbitrale choisie par les parties était la CCIG. « Les arbitrages CCI avec siège à Genève sont en effet légion ». En découle, cependant, une contradiction dans le raisonnement du Tribunal arbitral. En effet, les liens des parties avec Genève se refléteraient parmi d'autres dans l'expression du premier alinéa de la clause compromissoire, c'est-à-dire dans la phrase « *International Chamber of Commerce of Geneva* ». Néanmoins, le Tribunal arbitral soutient par ailleurs que cette référence ne peut pas viser le siège de l'arbitrage étant donné que le deuxième alinéa de la clause compromissoire règle cette question.

D'autre part, le Tribunal arbitral semblerait écarter également l'argument de la partie demanderesse selon lequel les parties n'auraient pu se mettre d'accord sur l'application du Règlement d'arbitrage de la CCIG car celui-ci n'était pas en vigueur au moment des négociations contractuelles. Néanmoins, le Tribunal arbitral, faisant application de la méthode subjective d'interprétation des contrats en droit suisse et tenant donc compte des qualités des parties contractantes, affirme dans sa sentence qu' « On doit cependant souligner que les auteurs de la clause, qui étaient apparemment des organes ou employés de [la partie défenderesse] à Lugano, n'appartenaient à l'évidence pas aux milieux de l'arbitrage, à en juger par la rédaction de la clause pathologique, et encore moins aux milieux genevois de l'arbitrage. De sorte que si leur connaissance du nouveau Règlement de la CCIG n'est pas exclue, elle ne saurait être présumée. Deux arguments de texte tendent d'ailleurs à exclure une telle connaissance: d'une part, l'intitulé inexact du Règlement et de l'institution qui l'a élaboré; d'autre part, le fait que, compte tenu de la nouveauté de ce texte qui n'était pas encore en vigueur, on se serait attendu à ce que les rédacteurs du contrat soient plus précis dans sa désignation ». Force est cependant de constater que le Tribunal arbitral considère que, à l'égard de l'argument ci-avant, l'application de la méthode subjective d'interprétation contractuelle s'avère insuffisante et a par conséquent recours à la méthode objective d'interprétation des contrats qui, de l'avis du Tribunal arbitral, coïnciderait en droit suisse avec l'analyse du langage utilisé dans la convention d'arbitrage. Il est à noter que l'analyse des qualités des négociateurs du contrat met à notre avis en évidence que la plupart des arguments des parties sur la pathologie de la convention d'arbitrage étaient élaborés pour l'arbitrage (*made-for-the-arbitration arguments*) et ne sauraient correspondre à la réalité des négociations contractuelles.

La méthode objective d'interprétation contractuelle aurait une origine prétorienne en droit suisse. Selon le Tribunal arbitral, « Le Tribunal arbitral n'a donc d'autre solution que d'interpréter le contrat sur la base de son seul texte, en se demandant comment celui-ci pouvait et devait être compris par des parties présumées honnêtes, raisonnables et de bonne foi (V. *P. Engel: Traité des obligations en droit suisse, 2e éd., Berne, 1997, p. 237*), ce qui rejoint la notion d'interprétation objective à laquelle recourt le Tribunal fédéral (notamment *SJ 1996, p. 549, 552-553*) ». Sur la base de cette seconde méthode d'interprétation contractuelle, le Tribunal arbitral élabore trois arguments qui lui permettent de conclure au rejet de l'objection soulevée par la partie défenderesse.

Tout d'abord, le Tribunal arbitral examine la dénomination du règlement d'arbitrage applicable et arrive à la conclusion que celle-ci fait nécessairement référence à la CCI. Cette conclusion nous semble incontestable.

Ensuite, par référence à la « jurisprudence arbitrale de la CCI », le Tribunal arbitral constate que l'expression CCI à Genève ou à Zurich a été interprétée par d'autres tribunaux arbitraux CCI comme spécifiant que la CCI est censée administrer l'arbitrage, et le siège de l'arbitrage est Genève ou Zurich (cf. sentence rendue dans l'affaire n° 2626 en 1977: *JDI 1978, n° 4, p. 981-984, obs. Y. Derains.* — sentence rendue dans l'affaire n° 3460 en 1980: *JDI 1981, p. 939-943, obs. Y. Derains.* — sentence rendue dans l'affaire n° 4023 en 1984: *JDI 1984, p. 950-952, obs. S. Jarvin.* — sentence finale dans l'affaire n° 5294 en 1988, S. Jarvin, Y. Derains et J.-J. Arnaldez: *Recueil des sentences arbitrales de la CCI 1986-1990, ICC Publishing, 1994, p. 180-189, spéc. p. 182-183.* — sentence partielle dans l'affaire n° 7920 en 1993, J.-J. Arnaldez, Y. derains et D. Hascher: *Recueil des sentences arbitrales de la CCI 1996-2000: ICC Publishing, 2003, p. 227-231.* — *CA Paru, Ire ch. civ., 28 act. 1997: Rev. arb. 1998, n° 2, p. 399-407 note B. Leurent*). Il constate également que, dans la plupart de ces affaires, la convention d'arbitrage ne comprenait pas un deuxième alinéa spécifiant le lieu de l'arbitrage. C'est la raison pour laquelle le Tribunal arbitral se réfère très spécialement à la sentence CCI n° 2626: « Une sentence de 1977 (*n° 2626: Recueil des sentences 1974-1985, p. 316 et 317*) a également admis l'existence d'une clause en faveur de la CCI dans le cas d'une référence à l'« International Chamber of Commerce in Geneva » alors que le siège de l'arbitrage était fixé à Essen. Comme dans le présent cas, la mention de Genève ne pouvait désigner le siège, mais servait uniquement à qualifier l'institution. L'arbitre relève: « la désignation incorrecte du siège n'altère pas l'intention des parties, qui apparaît clairement, d'attribuer compétence à la Cour d'Arbitrage de la CCI de Paris » ». En définitive, la sentence n° 2626 serait le seul véritable « précédent » auquel le Tribunal arbitral pourrait se référer.

Enfin, le Tribunal arbitral montre que des tribunaux arbitraux agissant sous l'égide de la CCIG ou de la Chambre de commerce de Zurich (ci-après « ZHK ») ont considéré que le mot « international » n'était pas suffisant pour écarter la compétence administrative de ces deux institutions arbitrales. Le Tribunal arbitral constate néanmoins que la terminologie utilisée dans les conventions d'arbitrage dans les affaires administrées par la CCIG et la ZHK n'était pas la même que celle utilisée dans le cas d'espèce (*distinguishing*) et arrive à la conclusion que la cour est compétente pour administrer la procédure arbitrale et que le Tribunal arbitral a été formé régulièrement. Un lecteur avisé pourrait soutenir que les décisions des tribunaux arbitraux dans les cas similaires au cas d'espèce dépendent considérablement de l'institution arbitrale qui a été saisie.

IV. — La décision du Tribunal arbitral quant aux frais de la phase juridictionnelle de la procédure arbitrale mérite, en dernier lieu, deux observations critiques.

D'une part, le Tribunal arbitral décide que la partie défenderesse doit supporter les frais de la procédure liée à la phase juridictionnelle sur la base d'un « *usage* » selon lequel la partie qui succombe devrait supporter les frais de l'arbitrage. L'existence de cet « *usage* » semble pour le moins très douteuse. L'examen de la « jurisprudence arbitrale CCI » nous révèle plutôt que les arbitres CCI jouissent d'une totale discrétion dans la prise de leur décision à l'égard de la répartition des frais de la procédure arbitrale entre les parties (cf. sentence finale rendue dans l'affaire n° 5285 en 1989: *Bull CCI 1993, Cour internationale d'arbitrage, ICC Publishing, vol. 4, n° 1, p. 37.* — sentence finale rendue dans l'affaire n° 5726: *Bull. CCI 1993, Cour internationale d'arbitrage, ICC Publishing, vol. 4, n° 1, p. 39.* — sentence finale rendue dans l'affaire n° 5896 en 1992: *Bull CCI 1993, Cour internationale d'arbitrage, ICC Publishing, vol. 4, n° 1, p. 40.* — sentence finale dans l'affaire n° 5987 en 1990: *Bull CCI 1993, Cour internationale d'arbitrage, ICC Publishing, vol. 4, n° 1, p. 43.* — sentence finale rendue dans l'affaire n° 6293: *Bull CCI 1993, Cour internationale d'arbitrage, ICC Publishing, vol. 4, n° 1, p. 46.* — sentence finale rendue dans l'affaire n° 7006 en 1992: *Bull CCI 1993, Cour internationale d'arbitrage, ICC Publishing, vol. 4, n° l, p. 58*). Ainsi l' « *usage* » en matière de répartition de frais de la procédure arbitrale CCI, s'il en existe un, serait-il plutôt que les arbitres distribuent librement ces frais entre les parties.

D'autre part, la décision quant aux frais du Tribunal arbitral semblerait porter sur tous les frais de la procédure (frais de l'arbitrage — honoraires, frais des arbitres et frais de la CCI — et frais d'avocat) et non pas seulement sur les frais d'avocat. Un lecteur avisé pourrait également s'interroger sur la légitimité de cette décision à la lumière de la disposition de l'article 31(2), *in fine*, du Règlement qui dispose que, « *À tout moment de la procédure, la tribunal arbitral peut prendre des décisions sur des frais autres que ceux fixés par la Cour* ».

Somme toute, la Sentence nous montre encore une fois que les mots ne sauraient être examinés et utilisés en droit d'une manière abstraite, c'est-à-dire isolée des affaires concrètes auxquelles ils sont censés s'appliquer. Le sens des mots juridiques dépend de leur usage dans le langage de chaque espèce. C'était sans doute en ce sens que Ludwig Wittgenstein disait que, « pour une large classe de cas où l'on use du mot « signification » — sinon pour tous les cas de son usage — on peut expliquer ce mot de la façon suivante: la signification d'un mot est son usage dans le langage [. . .] » (L. Wittgenstein, Tractatus Logico-Philosophicus suivi de Investigations Philosophiques, traduit de l'allemand par Pierre Klossowski: *Gallimard, coll. Tel, 1993, proposition 43, p. 135*).

E. S. R.

Sentence rendue dans l'affaire n° 9163 en 2001

I. — Procédure. — Loi du 25 janvier 1985. — Partie mise en redressement judiciaire avant l'instance. — Principe de suspension des poursuites individuelles. — Recevabilité de la demande d'arbitrage.

II. — Loi de police. — Prise en compte des règles de police qui se veulent directement et impérativement applicables.

Le Tribunal arbitral, siégeant à Genève, était saisi d'une action en responsabilité contractuelle engagée par A contre B, une société de droit français en redressement judiciaire après l'exécution du contrat. Le litige était soumis au droit français et le règlement d'arbitrage de la CCI applicable, parce qu'en vigueur à la date de la demande d'arbitrage, était celui de 1988. A, une société de transport maritime algérienne, avait confié à B la révision et la réparation d'un navire lors d'un arrêt technique de ce dernier dans un port français. Après qu'une défaillance de la grue, louée par la défenderesse auprès des autorités portuaires, ait provoqué un accident endommageant gravement le navire, la demanderesse a, dans un premier temps, demandé la nomination d'un expert judiciaire. Elle a ensuite procédé à une déclaration de créance, la défenderesse ayant entre temps feit l'objet d'un jugement d'ouverture de procédure collective. Puis, se fondant sur la clause compromissore figurant au contrat, elle a présenté une requête d'arbitrage aux fins de faire juger que la défenderesse était responsable de son entier préjudice et de fixer ce préjudice qu'elle décomposait en frais de réparation, frais d'immobilisation du navire, frais exposés en vue de réduire la durée d'immobilisation du navire et manque à gagner pour perte d'exploitation.

Dans sa réponse à la requête d'arbitrage, B a soutenu qu'étant en redressement judiciaire, aucune condamnation ne pouvait être présentée à son encontre. Elle participa ensuite à la constitution du Tribunal arbitral et à l'élaboration de l'acte de mission puis à la procédure arbitrale. Elle a alors changé de position et, dans son premier mémoire au fond ainsi que dans ses écritures ultérieures puis à l'audience, elle souleva une « exception d'irrecevabilité d'ordre public de la procédure arbitrale en soutenant que le litige relevait de la seule compétence du juge-commissaire de la procédure collective, dans le cadre de la vérification des créances » au motif que l'article 47 de la loi française de 1985, en interdisant postérieurement au jugement d'ouverture toute action en justice tendant à la condamnation du débiteur au paiement d'une somme d'argent sur le fondement d'une créance dont l'origine est antérieure au jugement d'ouverture, interdisait « toute action dont le but est, à terme, d'obtenir paiement », y compris une « action en constatation d'un fait générateur de responsabilité ». Après que le juge-commissaire se soit déclaré incompétent au profit du Tribunal arbitral sur demande conjointe des parties et que A ait engagé un nouvelle procédure arbitrale tendant aux mêmes fins, B, pour éviter de nouveaux frais de procédure, déclara renoncer à son exception d'irrecevabilité et accepta que le Tribunal arbitral statue au fond. Cette renonciation a fait l'objet d'une acceptation expresse de la demanderesse.

Bien que l'exception d'irrecevabilité ait fait l'objet d'une renonciation de la défenderesse acceptée par la demanderesse, le tribunal estime:

> *« qu'il lui appartient, en raison de h nature de l'exception soulevée par [la défenderesse] — tirée des règles d'ordre public du droit français de h faillite — et de l'intérêt qui s'attache à déterminer si et à quelles conditions une procédure arbitrale engagée après le jugement d'ouverture du règlement judiciaire du défendeur peut se poursuivre, de se prononcer sur le bien-fondé de l'exception soulevée par* [la défenderesse] *».*

Le tribunal se refuse à suivre la demanderesse en ce qu'elle soutient que l'exception d'irrecevabilité, soulevée après la signature de l'acte de mission, constituerait une demande nouvelle devant faire l'objet, conformément à l'article 16 du Règlement d'arbitrage alors en vigueur, d'un addendum à l'acte de mission signé des deux parties. Il note

« en effet, l'article V de l'acte de mission, définissant la mission du Tribunal arbitral, comporte un premier alinéa ainsi rédigé:

> « *Compte tenu de la procédure de redressement judiciaire dont* [la défenderesse] *est l'objet et des dispositions des articles 47 à 49 de la loi du 25 janvier 1985, le tribunal arbitral aura pour mission de répondre aux questions suivantes . . . ».*
>
> *Or ces trois articles constituent un paragraphe de la loi précisément intitulé* « *l'arrêt des poursuites individuelles* ». *L'incidence de ces règles dans la présente instance arbitrale était donc, dès ce moment, et complètement, 'dans le débat' et dans les limites de l'acte de mission* ».

Surtout, le tribunal estime devoir mettre en œuvre le principe de suspension des poursuites, indépendamment des demandes des parties, aussi bien au titre de la prise en compte des lois de police que dans un souci de respect de l'ordre public international français. Il observe à cet égard que:

> « *le Tribunal arbitral est tenu de respecter les règles de police qui se veulent directement et impérativement applicables à la situation litigieuse, lorsqu'elles sont édictées par la loi d'un État dont l'application en l'espèce est à la fois légitime, en raison des buts qu'elle poursuit et des intérêts qu'elle protège, et conforme à l'attente des parties. Il en est ainsi des dispositions de la loi française de 1985 sur l'arrêt des poursuites individuelles, non seulement parce que — comme le prétend* [la défenderesse] — *le droit français est applicable au fond du litige, mais aussi et surtout parce qu'elles doivent s'appliquer à la partie qui, établie en France, est soumise à une procédure de redressement judiciaire qui y a été régulièrement ouverte devant un tribunal français.*
>
> *La* lex concursus *présente alors tous les caractères d'une loi de police que le Tribunal arbitral s'estime tenu de prendre en considération, en raison des* « *liens étroits* » *qu'elle présente avec le litige et des* « *intérêts légitimes* » *qu'eue entend sauvegarder. Peu importent le lieu de l'arbitrage et la loi applicable au fond du litige ou à la procédure arbitrale. L'article 19 de la LDIP, qui retient ces critères pour permettre au juge suisse de prendre en considération une loi de police étrangère, n'interdirait pas au Tribunal arbitral de le faire* [références omises]. *Enfin, il incombe au Tribunal arbitral de veiller à ce que sa sentence* « *soit susceptible de sanction légale* » *(art. 26 du Règlement). À cette fin, il doit faire en sorte que l'exécution, le cas échéant, en France de la présente sentence ne soit pas contraire à l'ordre public international tel qu'il est entendu par le juge français (NCPC français, art. 1502, 5°, ci-après NCPC). Or, il est bien établi dans la jurisprudence française que les principes de suspension des poursuites individuelles et d'interruption de l'instance en matière de faillite sont d'ordre public international, et doivent en conséquence être respectés par les arbitres, quel que soit le pays dans lequel ils siègent* [références omises]. *Il en est de même du principe de l'égalité des créanciers* [références omises].
>
> *Dans plusieurs sentences, les arbitres ont tenu à respecter ces mêmes principes* [références omises], *bien que certains d'entre eux répugnent à suspendre l'instance arbitrale lorsqu'une procédure collective initiée à l'étranger affecte le défendeur* [références omises]. »
>
> *Même si les exigences du droit français paraissent, au regard du droit comparé et des besoins d'efficacité de l'arbitrage international, particulièrement*

rigoureuses [références omises], *le Tribunal arbitral estime qu'il doit, après avoir recueilli les explications des parties et dans le respect du principe du contradictoire, se prononcer sur l'incidence des règles françaises de la faillite dans le présent litige* ».

Selon le Tribunal arbitral, l'exception d'irrecevabilité ne saurait non plus être rejetée, contrairement à ce que soutenait A qui évoquait l'article 186 de la LDIP, en ce qu'elle constituerait une exception d'incompétence soulevée tardivement:

« *(. . .) d'une part, l'arrêt des poursuites individuelles dont s'est prévalue ultérieurement [la défenderesse] figurait déjà dans les questions que le Tribunal arbitral devait examiner, en raison des termes de l'acte de mission rappelés ci-dessus (. . .). D'autre part, les règles en cause étant d'ordre public international, le Tribunal arbitral aurait dû, au besoin d'office, en rechercher l'incidence sur la présente instance. Enfin, comme on le verra, et contrairement à ce prétend* [la défenderesse], *ces règles n'ont pas pour effet de rendre incompétent le Tribunal arbitral; la clause compromissoire reste valable et le litige n'est pas devenu inarbitrable (. . .). L'exception soulevée par* [la défenderesse] *porte sur la recevabilité (en l'état) de la demande de* [A], *plutôt que sur 'l'incompétence' du Tribunal arbitral, seule visée par l'article 186 de la LDIP* ».

Quant au bien-fondé de l'exception, le Tribunal rappelle qu'il est de jurisprudence constante que la validité de la clause compromissoire n'est pas affectée par l'ouverture d'une procédure de redressement judiciaire mais que le déroulement de l'instance arbitrale est perturbé par les règles d'ordre public et la suspension des poursuites individuelles. Il observe que l'article 48 de la loi du 25 janvier 1985, qui vise les instances antérieures au jugement d'ouverture ne peut être appliqué directement à l'espèce mais qu'il « *montre clairement le but dans lequel doit être réalisée la coordination des procédures collective et arbitrale* ». Or:

« *le but de ces règles est évident: laisser à son « juge naturel » en l'occurrence l'arbitre, le règlement du contentieux contractuel intéressant le débiteur, mais protéger ce dernier et surtout ses autres créanciers et la survie éventuelle de l'entreprise en rapportant au passif chirographaire de la procédure collective la créance qui sera ainsi fixée, sans conférer au demandeur la moindre préférence pour son paiement effectif, qui dépendra de l'issue de cette procédure et sera soumis à la loi du concours. Telle est exactement la mesure des exigences d'ordre public qu'il appartient à tout arbitre de respecter. On notera d'ailleurs que depuis la loi de 1985, l'interruption de l'instance est beaucoup plus brève qu'antérieurement, où elle se prolongeait jusqu'à l'arrêté de l'état des créances (P. Ancel, art. préc., spéc., p. 131)* ».

Le Tribunal s'interroge ensuite sur la portée de l'article 47 de la même loi qui « *semble interdire* » l'introduction d'une instance arbitrale après le jugement d'ouverture si elle tend à la condamnation du débiteur au paiement d'une somme d'argent.

« *Or, la demande d'arbitrage du* [date] *ne tendait qu'à l'établissement de la créance de* [la demanderesse]; *c'est l'objet même du litige tel que les parties l'ont défini dans l'acte de mission de* [date], *en présence des organes de la procédure collective de* [la défenderesse], *et donc avec leur accord; ces organes ont participé, dès* [date], *à la procédure arbitrale, dans laquelle le représentant des créanciers avait été mis en cause le* [date]. *En outre,* [la demanderesse] *avait déclaré sa créance le* [date] *auprès du représentant des créanciers, (. . .). Cette déclaration de créance ayant été contestée par [la défenderesse] et la représentant des créanciers (. . .), c'est tout naturellement devant le juge du contrat, c'est-à-dire le présent Tribunal arbitral, que les parties ont entendu débattre de la responsabilité éventuelle de [la défenderesse] et du préjudice de* [la demanderesse].

Compte tenu de l'objet particulier et limité de la demande d'arbitrage, et de la participation volontaire des organes de la faillite à la procédure arbitrale, il ne semble pas que l'article 47 conduise donc, en l'espèce, à juger que celle-ci ne devait pas commencer et donc que la demande est irrecevable.

C'est l'article 49 qui devrait plutôt trouver application en l'espèce, qui vise « les actions en justice (. . .) autres que celles visées à l'article 47 », et qui autorise leur poursuite après mise en cause de l'administrateur et du représentant des créanciers. Cette mise en cause, qui est régulièrement intervenue, implique que l'action visée par l'article 49 ait une incidence sur le patrimoine du débiteur, sans néanmoins tendre à sa condamnation, ce qui l'aurait fait régir par l'article 47. Dans ces conditions, le Tribunal arbitral estime que les parties ont pu lui soumettre cette mission de constatation qu'elles avaient définie dans l'acte de mission, et que la sentence qui se prononcera sur la responsabilité de [la défenderesse] *et évaluera le préjudice éventuellement réparable ne porte pas atteinte à l'ordre public interne ou international. En effet, les exigences fondamentales des règles françaises sur le redressement judiciaire ont été respectées: la créance a été déclarée; l'administrateur judiciaire devenu le commissaire à l'exécution du plan et le représentant des créanciers ont été mis en cause et ont participé à toute l'instance arbitrale; se bornant à fixer, le cas échéant, et dans des conditions régulières au regard de la loi de 1985, une créance de* [la demanderesse] *à l'égard de* [la défenderesse], *la présente ne portera pas atteinte à l'égalité des créanciers chirographaires et ne nuira en aucune façon à l'exécution du plan.*

Aucun principe fondamental ne s'oppose donc à ce qu'une demande d'arbitrage qui aurait été recevable si elle avait été présentée avant le [date], *ne le soit plus parce qu 'elle l'a été moins de 5 semaines plus tard ou 4 ans trop tôt. (. . .)*

Il est donc conforme à une bonne administration de la justice que la demande d'arbitrage de [la demanderesse] *ne soit pas déclarée irrecevable parce qu'elle aurait été notifiée 5 semaines trop tard, ou 4 ans trop tôt. En effet, si l'on suivait la thèse de [la défenderesse], c'est seulement après le* [date], *date à laquelle* [la défenderesse] *a été avisée que le juge-commissaire se déclarait incompétent, que celle-ci aurait pu présenter sa requête d'arbitrage, soit près de 5 ans après le sinistre (. . .) ».*

Le Tribunal s'interroge ensuite sur les conséquences de la décision d'incompétence prononcée par le juge-commissaire. Pour la défenderesse, la requête d'arbitrage, déposée après le jugement d'ouverture, n'en était pas moins irrecevable et la demanderesse n'avait que la possibilité d'introduire une nouvelle instance arbitrale dans les deux mois de la notification de la décision, conformément à l'article 102, al. 3, de la loi de 1985. Le Tribunal écarte cet argument:

« Malgré sa cohérence apparente, la position de [la défenderesse] *qui reconnaissait la compétence arbitrale mais déniait celle d'un Tribunal arbitral constitué d'un commun accord 4 ans plus tôt, présentait un caractère dilatoire certain. Pour le Tribunal arbitral, l'ordonnance du juge-commissaire ne pouvait que conforter la recevabilité de la demande dont il était saisi. Refuser de se prononcer sur l'acte de mission qu'il avait établi et que les parties avaient accepté aurait constitué de sa part un véritable déni de justice. Les modalités et délais de saisine prévus par l'article 102, al. 3 de la loi de 1985 ne sont applicables que si le juge ou l'arbitre compétent auquel renvoie le juge-commissaire n'a; pas encore été saisi. Le législateur exige alors qu 'il le soit très rapidement, car de sa décision dépendront l'établissement de l'état des créances (art. 103 à 105 de la même loi) et donc l'issue de la procédure collective. Puisqu'un Tribunal arbitral était déjà constitué et saisi en vertu de la convention d'arbitrage invoquée, il était*

parfaitement conforme à l'esprit et au but de la loi qu'il statue lui-même et qu'il n'y ait pas besoin d'en constituer un autre et de recommencer la procédure arbitrale ab initio *(. . .)* ».

Le Tribunal ayant ainsi déclaré la demande d'arbitrage recevable, il rappelle que ses pouvoirs:

« *n'en restent pas moins limités par les termes de l'acte de mission et les dispositions d'ordre public international du droit français des procédures collectives.*

Ce point n'étant pas contesté, il suffit de rappeler que le Tribunal arbitral ne peut, en application des articles 47, 48 et 49 de la loi de 1985, prononcer aucune condamnation pécuniaire d'un débiteur en état de redressement judiciaire pour des dettes dont l'origine est antérieure au jugement d'ouverture. C'est le cas des demandes portant tour à tour sur la responsabilité de [la défenderesse] *dans l'accident du* [date] *et sur la fixation du préjudice qui en est résulté pour* [la demanderesse].

En revanche, s'agissant des honoraires et des frais de toute nature supportés par les parties à l'occasion de la présente procédure arbitrale (. . .), et pour le cas où le Tribunal arbitral déciderait que ceux supportés par la demanderesse devraient en tout ou partie être mis à la charge de la défenderesse, il conviendrait de voir dans ces sommes des créances nées après le jugement d'ouverture et relevant de l'article 40 de la loi de 1985. À ce titre, et comme le soutient [la demanderesse] (. . .) elles pourraient donner lieu à condamnation dans la présente sentence ».

Après avoir constaté la responsabilité de B et évalué le préjudice réel supporté par la demanderesse, le Tribunal s'interroge sur les conséquences de la clause limitative de responsabilité figurant au contrat de réparation et stipulant que: « En cas de dépassement du délai contractuel, une pénalité égale à un montant de [. . .] par jour de retard sera payé par le chantier à l'armateur. Le montant total de la pénalité sera limitée *(sic)* à 8 % du montant du Contrat ». Pour le Tribunal:

« *Cette clause pénale, qui a aussi pour effet de fixer et de limiter conventionnellement un préjudice, ne vise que le dépassement du délai contractuel. Elle ne peut s'appliquer ni aux frais de réparation (. . .), ni aux frais de réduction de l'immobilisation du navire (. . .). Quant aux frais causés par l'immobilisation du navire (. . .), il s'agit de dépenses réellement supportées par l'armateur, et non d'une perte découlant du défaut d'exploitation de celui-ci. Seul ce dernier préjudice, pour un navire de l'importance et de la nature du* [nom du navire], *peut atteindre des montants considérables et difficiles à évaluer; c'est pour inciter le chantier naval à être diligent sans pour autant le pénaliser à une hauteur sans rapport avec l'intérêt économique de son intervention qu'une clause comme celle de l'article 21 vient limiter la réparation du manque à gagner.*

Pour le Tribunal arbitral, la clause pénale ou limitative de responsabilité ne peut donc s'appliquer qu'au calcul du préjudice résultant du défaut d'exploitation, c'est-à-dire du manque à gagner (. . .) ».

Mettant en œuvre le pouvoir modérateur que lui octroie l'article 1152 du Code civil français:

« *(. . .) le Tribunal arbitral constate tout d'abord que la peine prévue par jour de retard — [montant] — n'est ni excessive ni dérisoire. Son montant est d'ailleurs proche de celui du préjudice ci-dessus évalué par le Tribunal arbitral* [environ 80 %]. *En revanche, la limitation de ladite peine à 8 % du montant du contrat, soit* [montant] *correspond au préjudice effectif subi par la demanderesse pour un dépassement de délai contractuel de trois jours seulement. Ce montant, rapproché du préjudice subi par la demanderesse du fait de l'immobilisation de son navire*

pendant [. . .] jours, apparaît au Tribunal arbitral comme « manifestement déri-
soire » au sens de l'article 1152 du Code civil. Augmentant la peine convenue,
comme l'article 1152 lui en donne le pouvoir, le Tribunal arbitral estime justifié, en
l'espèce, d'appliquer le taux de pénalité par jour de retard (. . .) à la totalité du
retard subi par la demanderesse, soit [. . .] jours ».

En conséquence, le Tribunal dit que la demande d'arbitrage est recevable, que la défenderesse est responsable des conséquences dommageables de l'accident survenu au navire
de la demanderesse, fixe la créance de cette dernière, dit que cette somme produira intérêt
au taux légal français, qui a vocation à s'appliquer aussi bien parce que le droit français est
le droit applicable que parce que la débitrice a son siège en France, à compter de la date de
la demande d'arbitrage et jusqu'au paiement effectif et condamne la défenderesse à payer à
la demanderesse une certaine somme au titre des frais supportés pour sa défense.

OBSERVATIONS. — I. — La poursuite des procédures arbitrales en cours en dépit de
l'ouverture d'une procédure collective à l'encontre de l'une des parties semble être un
principe bien admis du droit de l'arbitrage international (sentence n° 7205 en 1993: *JDI
1995, p. 1031, obs.J.-J.A. et les sentences citées p. 1036).* Certaines sentences refusent
simplement toute incidence aux règles du droit de la faillite en invoquant le principe de la
territorialité de la faillite; ainsi des arbitres expliquent-ils que « quoi qu'il en soit de la loi
française, le tribunal arbitral, dont le siège a été fixé à Damas et qui doit appliquer le droit
syrien, considère que sa mission, (. . .) ne saurait être affectée par une jugement qui a été
rendu postérieurement en France et qui est inapte à produire sans autre son effet en Syrie
(. . .) » et condamnent-ils une partie mise en liquidation en France au paiement d'une
indemnité (sentence n° 6057 en 1991: *JDI 1993, p. 1016, obs. Y. D.).* D'autres sentences au
contraire, prennent en compte le droit de la faillite applicable au débiteur d'une part pour
vérifier que sa soumission à une procédure collective ne met pas fin à la compétence des
arbitres et d'autre part pour constater qu'il est interdit aux arbitres de prononcer une
condamnation à l'encontre du débiteur, et qu'ils peuvent seulement statuer sur le principe
et le montant de la créance (pour une société française mise en liquidation judiciaire en
cours d'instance, V. sentence n° 7205 précitée. — pour une société suédoise qui a été
déclarée « *bankrupt* » avant le dépôt de la demande d'arbitrage, V. sentence n° 7337 en
1996: *Yearbook Commercial Arbitration XXIVa (1999), p. 149).*

Ainsi que le rappelle la sentence commentée, les juridictions françaises admettent également sans ambiguïté le principe de la validité des clauses compromissoires et du maintien
de la compétence arbitrale en dépit de l'ouverture d'une procédure collective. Seuls y
échappent les litiges qui, selon les termes de l'article 174 du décret du 27 décembre
1985, « *concernent le redressement et la liquidation judiciaire* » et relèvent de la compétence exclusive du juge de la faillite. La limitation du pouvoir des arbitres résultant des
principes d'interdiction des poursuites individuelles et d'égalité des créanciers est également bien affirmé. La perturbation que des règles de la procédure collective apporte à la
procédure arbitrale pose plus de problèmes.

Il n'est pas douteux que, conformément à l'article L. 621-41 du Code de commerce
(l'article 48 de la loi de 1985), lorsque la procédure arbitrale est en cours au moment du
jugement d'ouverture, elle est suspendue et reprend de plein droit après que le créancier
poursuivant ait procédé à la déclaration de sa créance et que le représentant des créanciers,
et éventuellement l'administrateur, aient été mis en cause. C'est le principe que rappelle la
sentence.

Si, en revanche, la demande d'arbitrage n'a pas encore été formée lors du jugement
d'ouverture, il est généralement admis que l'article L. 621-40 *(ex-art. 47)* exige du
créancier qu'il déclare sa créance puis invoque l'existence de la clause compromissoire
devant le juge-commissaire qui, si elle est contestée, devra se déclarer incompétent pour
se prononcer sur le bien-fondé de la créance litigieuse. Le créancier dispose alors de deux

mois, à compter de la notification de cette décision d'incompétence, pour engager une procédure arbitrale. L'inconvénient est qu'il peut se dérouler un laps de temps extrêmement long, en l'espèce il était de près de quatre ans, entre la déclaration de créance et la décision du juge-commissaire, retardant sans raison pratique le début de la procédure arbitrale.

On comprend donc tout l'intérêt de la sentence qui refuse de faire application de l'article L. 621-40 au motif que, la demanderesse ne recherchant que la constatation de sa créance, son action ne tendrait pas « *à la condamnation du débiteur au paiement d'une somme d'argent* » et que peu importe qu'une demande d'arbitrage soit déposée quelques semaines avant ou quelques semaines après la déclaration de créance. On sait que la Chambre commerciale de la Cour de cassation a adopté une position contraire au visa de l'article 621-40, cassant sans renvoi, la décision d'une cour d'appel ayant fait droit à une demande de mise en œuvre de l'arbitrage postérieure à la mise en redressement judiciaire des débiteurs « *aux fins de fixation de la créance* » *(Cass. com., 2 juin 2004: Rev. arb. 2004, p. 593, note P. Ancel)*.

On relèvera enfin que le tribunal arbitral qualifie la créance résultant de la mise à la charge du débiteur des honoraires et frais supportés par la demanderesse à l'occasion de la procédure de créance née « après le jugement d'ouverture et relevant de l'article 40 de la loi de 1985 » pouvant faire à ce titre l'objet d'une condamnation. Cette décision tranche avec la sentence n° 7563 de 1993 *(JDI 1994, p. 1054, obs. Y. D.)* dans laquelle les arbitres ont au contraire considéré qu'une partie en redressement judiciaire ne pouvait « être condamnée au paiement des dépens » et se sont bornés à préciser que les parties succombantes (dont l'une était pourtant *in bonis*) étaient « conjointement et solidairement responsables des frais de l'arbitrage ». Il semble que la jurisprudence de la chambre commerciale de la Cour de cassation donne raison à cette seconde décision *(Cass. com., 9 dec. 1992 et 17 févr. 1998: D. 1998, jur. p. 381, note M. Pasturel)*.

II. — L'intérêt de la sentence ici rapportée porte également sur la notion de loi de police invoquée par le Tribunal arbitral pour motiver sa prise en compte du droit de la faillite français.

En des termes très généraux, le Tribunal arbitral se déclare « tenu de respecter les règles de police qui se veulent directement et impérativement applicables à la situation légitime, lorsqu'elles sont édictées par la loi d'un État dont l'application en l'espèce est à la fois litigieuse, en raison des buts qu'elle poursuit et des intérêts qu'elle protège et conforme à l'attente des parties ». Il devait donc « prendre en considération » la loi française de la faillite « en raison des « liens étroits » qu'elle présente avec le litige et des « intérêts légitimes » qu'elle entend sauvegarder (peu important) le lieu de l'arbitrage et la loi applicable au fond du litige ou à la procédure arbitrale ». Cette pétition de principe est d'autant plus forte qu'elle ne semble pas avoir été nécessaire au raisonnement. Le respect du droit de la faillite se justifiait en effet tant par la jurisprudence arbitrale que par le caractère d'ordre public international en France reconnu par la jurisprudence française au principe d'interdiction des poursuites individuelles et la nécessité de ne pas les violer afin que « la sentence soit susceptible de sanction légale » (art. 26 du Règlement CCI de 1988).

Les arbitres auraient également pu invoquer l'article 19 de la loi suisse de droit international privé.

On sait que la question a été largement débattue (cf. *Y. Derains, Les normes d'application immédiate dans la jurisprudence arbitrale internationale in Le droit des relations économiques internationales — Études offerts à Berthold Goldman: Litec 1982, p. 29-46. — L'ordre public et le droit applicable au fond du litige dans l'arbitrage international: Rev. arb. 1986, p. 375.* — cf. également *P. Mayer, Les lois de police étrangères: JDI 1981, p. 307 s. et L'interférence des lois de police: L'apport de la jurisprudence arbitrale, Dossiers de l'Institut du droit et des pratiques des affaires internationales, publication n° 440/1, 1986, ICC Publishing SA. — Fouchard, Gaillard, Goldman: Traité de l'arbitrage commercial international n° 1515 et s.).*

Si certains auteurs invitent les arbitres à tenir compte des lois de police n'appartenant pas à la *lex contractus (Y. Derains, art. préc. — P. Mayer, art. préc. — Ph. Fouchard, intervention au Comité français de droit international privé, journée du cinquantenaire: éd. du CNRS 1988, p. 115),* d'autres, au contraire, soutiennent que « la méthode de l'ordre public transnational demeure, plus que celle du recours à la théorie des lois de police n'appartenant pas à la *lex contractus,* conforme à la source transnationale du pouvoir de juger des arbitres » *(Fouchard, Gaillard et Goldman, n° 1525).*

Cependant, si la pétition de principe est claire, sa portée réelle semble plus limitée. En premier lieu, la loi de police considérée est le droit de la faillite qui, s'il y a un lien évident avec la situation économique en cause a peu de rapport avec le droit applicable au fond du litige. Il n'aurait donc pas été difficile de la prendre en considération même si le droit français n'avait pas été applicable au fond. De surcroît, la loi de police n'est prise en considération que si elle est édictée par la loi d'un État dont l'application en l'espèce est légitime en raison des buts qu'elle poursuit et des intérêts qu'elle protège et conforme à l'attente des parties. La sentence ne se différencie donc pas des nombreuses sentences qui ont refusé d'appliquer une norme d'application immédiate étrangère à la *lex contractus,* après l'avoir prise en considération, en raison de la faiblesse des liens qu'elle présente avec le litige ou du manque de légitimité des intérêts protégés (sentence n° 6294 en 1991: *JDI 1991, p. 1050, obs.J.-J. A.* — sentence n° 6320, *JDI 1995, p. 896, obs. D. H.* — sentence n° 7528 en 1993: *Yearbook Commercial Arbitration 1993 XXII (1997), p. 125).*

B. D.
Y. D.

Sintetice rendue dans l'affaire n° 9617 en 1999

I. — Procédure arbitrale. — Action en justice. — Action déclaratoire. — Recevabilité. — Intérêt légitime, né et actuel.

II. — Transaction. — Interprétation. — Nature. — Portée.

III. — *Culpa in contrabendo.*

Un tribunal arbitral siégeant à Paris était appelé — en application du Règlement d'arbitrage de la CCI de 1988 — à se prononcer sur un différend lié à un contrat de cession d'actions (la « Convention ») conclu en 1991 entre une société gabonaise (demanderesse A ou cessionnaire) et une société belge (défenderesse B ou cédant). Aux termes de la Convention, la demanderesse A a acquis de la défenderesse B la totalité des actions que celle-ci détenait dans la société X (non partie à l'arbitrage). La Convention comportait un certain nombre de dispositions, parmi lesquelles les suivantes:

«(. . .) — *L'article 3, alinéa 2. dispose ce qui suit c*
« *Comme indiqué dans l'Offering Memorandum le "périmètre cédé "exclut les séquelles dans le bilan de X relatives à la cession de l'activité azote à K et, plus généralement toutes responsabilités financières et juridiques extérieures à l'activité actuelle de X, celles-ci restent à la charge de B* » (. . .)
– *L'art. 8 al. 5 dispose:*
« *En outre, B prendra à sa charge toutes les conséquences financières des litiges en cours à la date du premier transfert des actions, et/ou dont le fait générateur serait antérieur à cette date. Elle garantit par ailleurs qu'elle-même ni aucune de ses filiales n'est sous le coup d'une assignation ou d'une procédure de nature à affecter durablement et substantiellement la valeur du "périmètre cédé",*
L'article 11 règle le sort des litiges entre les parties par l'institution d'une procédure arbitrale soumise au Règlement de conciliation et d'arbitrage de la Chambre de Commerce Internationale en application du droit belge (. . .)».

Comme la demanderesse A n'a pas souhaité assumer les risques et obligations liés aux activités non reprises par elle de la société X, la défenderesse B et la société X ont signé en 1991 un protocole (le « protocole ») aux termes desquels « *(. . .) B entend dégager X des risques et obligations qui ne sont pas directement liés aux opérations industrielles conduites par X et ses filiales, ainsi qu'il en a été convenu entre B et A* ». L'article 1 du protocole disposait en outre que la société X transférait à la défenderesse B « *l'universalité des dettes et des charges de la société X qui découlent de ses activités anciennes ou qui y sont liées, activités étrangères à son activité Sels & Oxydes Métalliques* ».

Dès la fin de 1991, un certain nombre de différends — nés des difficultés liées à l'exécution de la Convention — ont opposé d'une part les parties A et B, et d'autre part la défenderesse B et la société X et ses filiales. Ce dernier différend a fait l'objet d'une action judiciaire devant les tribunaux belges tandis que le différend entre les parties A et B a donné lieu à une procédure d'arbitrage introduite en 1992 à l'initiative de la partie A devant la CCI.

En 1993, les parties ont finalement transigé leurs deux différends et signé une transaction (la « transaction ») à cet effet. La transaction étais soumise au droit belge et le règlement des litiges étais soumis au Règlement d'arbitrage de la CCI.

Postérieurement à cette conclusion, la demanderesse A a découvert l'existence d'un litige judiciaire pendant devant les tribunaux belges depuis 1975 (« le litige ») où la société X a été citée en intervention et en garantie d'une de ses filiales par une société tiers. Par citation en date de 1997, et en se fondant sur le protocole signé avec la défenderesse B, la société X a cité celle-ci en intervention et garantie pour qu'elle soit tenue de « *toutes condamnations qui seraient prononcées contre elle* [la société X] *en principal, intérêt et frais* ».

L'existence de ce litige dans lequel les sociétés X et B sont pourtant impliquées, n'a pas été néanmoins porté à la connaissance de la demanderesse A au moment de la conclusion de la Convention et de la transaction. Celle-ci a alors décidé d'introduire contre la défenderesse B en 1997 une procédure d'arbitrage devant la CCI visant à faire constater que le litige n'était pas couvert par la transaction, et que la défenderesse B devait être par conséquent tenue de prendre en charge toutes les responsabilités afférentes à ce litige.

Aux termes de l'acte de mission signé avec les parties, les arbitres devaient se prononcer au préalable sur la recevabilité de l'action de la demanderesse A qui n'avait ni qualité ni intérêt pour obtenir une condamnation de la défenderesse B. Il y a répondu favorablement en estimant qu'il était saisi d'une action déclaratoire, la demanderesse A ayant un intérêt né et actuel à agir, et en tenant compte également du mécanisme de la cession d'actions.

« (. . .) *l'action déclaratoire est admise lorsque deux conditions sont réunies: le demandeur doit établir l'existence d'une menace grave et sérieuse au point de créer dès à présent un trouble précis et la déclaration judiciaire sollicitée doit être de nature à offrir au demandeur non point une satisfaction purement théorique, mais une utilité concrète et déterminée (. . .)*

Ces deux conditions sont en l'espèce réunies puisqu'il s'agit d'une procédure arbitrale diligentée à la suite de la brusque réapparition du Litige dans lequel la société cédé (société X) est partie. Cet événement justifie déjà la recevabilité de la présente action ne fût-ce qu'à titre déclaratoire.

Il faut ajouter, indépendamment de l'action admise à titre déclaratoire, que si l'intérêt dont la recevabilité de l'action en justice dépend doit être né dès l'introduction de l'action, il n'est pas requis qu'à ce moment la demanderesse ait subi un dommage ou ait payé une indemnité à un tiers (. . .) ».

Le tribunal arbitral a tranché ensuite la demande principale en faveur de la demanderesse A. Sur la base des éléments de fait et des témoignages, les arbitres ont estimé que les parties connaissaient en réalité l'existence du Litige mais à des degrés divers. Ils ont sanctionné néanmoins la défenderesse B qui a fourni une information erronée sur l'état de la société X en omettant de mentionner l'existence du litige dans l'offre de vente.

Les arbitres ont rappelé que la Convention avait pour objet de transférer la société X libérée de toutes responsabilités éventuelles liées à son activité antérieurement à sa cession à la demanderesse A. Il s'agissait d'une condition imposée par la demanderesse A qui était ainsi couvert dans le cadre de la garantie figurant à la Convention conclue avec la défenderesse B. La transaction conclue en 1993 ne mettait pas fin à l'obligation de garantie due par la défenderesse B.

« (. . .) *Cet oubli a déjà des répercussions à l'égards des tiers (. . .) Le public, destinataire de ce prospectus, est amené à penser que la restructuration produit pour effet d'éliminer définitivement les actifs et passif liés à la division C du bilan de X.*

Elle crée l'apparence erronée de la sortie des activités passées liées à la division C (. . .)

Dépositaire des actes relatifs à sa filiale, elle ne profite ni de la négociation de la cession de sa participation à A, ni de la négociation avec cette dernière de la transaction pour rectifier son erreur, qu'au contraire elle renouvelle. Ainsi, dans l'Offering memorandum, dans la Data room et dans la Convention et ses actes d'application, elle passe sous silence les risques liés à la division « menuiseries métalliques » (. . .) L'erreur est d'autant plus surprenante que B détient les documents relatifs à cette opération de restructuration et que M. D., quiparticipe à la restructuration et à la négociation de la cession de X, ne quitte la direction de B que le 12 avril 1992. Ainsi, tant une analyse des actes juridiques qu'une prise de conscience des acteurs directs de la restructuration auraient pu permettre à B d'éviter son erreur (. . .).

Dans la négociation de la Convention, A s'engage bien à acquérir des actions mais à la condition que les activités étrangères à celle des [qui sont reprises par A] *soient expurgées. (. . .)*

Pour parvenir au résultat convenu, les parties recourent à une garantie de passif mise en oeuvre par les articles 3, alinéa 2, et 8 de la Convention ainsi que par l'apport des activités indésirables de X à B ou à une société de son groupe. B s'engage à faire correspondre le « périmètre cédé » juridique au périmètre « cédé économique » (. . .)

Ainsi A peut raisonnablement se croire couverte pour toutes les activités passées de X par une double garantie stipulée aux articles 3 et 8 de la Convention. D'une part, les garanties de passif, d'autre part la garantie qui résulte de l'engagement de B de mettre en conformité le « périmètre cédé » juridique avec le « périmètre cédé » économique (. . .) ».

S'agissant de l'interprétation de la transaction, les arbitres se sont appuyés sur les dispositions du Code civil et de la doctrine belges pour décider qu'elle ne couvrait pas le litige. La transaction suppose trois éléments: un litige né ou à naître, l'intention des parties d'y mettre fin et l'acceptation de concessions réciproques. Or, le litige ne faisait l'objet d'aucun différend entre les parties à cette date.

«(. . .) Selon l'article 2044 du Code civil, « La transaction est un contrat par lequel les parties terminent une contestation née, ou préviennent une contestation à naître ». La doctrine a explicité cette définition (. . .)

H. de Page et R. Dekkers relèvent les trois éléments fondamentaux de la transaction, à savoir un litige né ou à naître, l'intention d'y mettre fin et l'existence de sacrifices réciproques (p. 483) (. . .)

Selon l'art. 2048 du Code civil, les transactions se renferment dans leur objet: la renonciation qui est faite à tous droits, actions et prétentions, ne s'entend que de ce qui est relatif au différend qui y a donné lieu.

L'article 2049 dispose que les transactions ne règlent que les différends qui s'y trouvent compris, soit que les parties aient manifesté leur intention par des expressions spéciales ou générales, soit que l'on reconnaisse cette intention par une suite nécessaire de ce qui est exprimé (. . .)

Les articles 2048 et 2049, compris dans le titre XV relatif aux transactions, reprennent la règle générale de l'interprétation des conventions contenues à l'art. 1156 du Code Civil: 'On doit dans les conventions rechercher quelle a été la commune intention des parties contractantes, plutôt que de s'arrêter au sens littéral des termes' (. . .)

le (sic) *transaction vise donc à régler les difficultés liées qu'ont rencontrées les parties dans l'exécution de la Convention, soit nécessairement des divergences apparues au sujet de problèmes concrets et en particulier les responsabilités liées à des questions environnementales mais également sur d'autres points. Or, le Litige n'a jamais fait l'objet d'aucune difficulté entre les parties que ce soit au sujet de la définition du "périmètre cédé" sont il ne faisait manifestement pas partie que des garanties à son sujet, indiscutablement à la charge de B aux termes des art. 3 al 2 et 8 al. 5 de la Convention (. . .) ».*

À titre surabondant, et pour démontrer que la responsabilité de la défenderesse B était engagée dans tous les cas, le Tribunal arbitral s'est fondé sur les dispositions de l'article 1382 et suivants du Code civil belge en application de la règle *culpa in contrahendo*. Ce moyen a été soulevé à titre subsidiaire par la demanderesse A, ce qui explique la démarche du Tribunal arbitral.

« (. . .) *la question ne se pose pas de savoir si elle* [la défenderesse B] *devait ou non fournir une information à son co-contractant lors de la négociation de la Convention mais celle de savoir si elle engage sa responsabilité en fournissant une information erronée (. . .) Le droit belge consacre cette règle sur le fondement de la responsabilité délictuelle ou quasi délictuelle qui trouve son siège aux articles 1382 et suivants du Code civil. Ainsi, la Cour de cassation belge a jugé que "celui qui par son comportement fautif lors de la conclusion d'une convention, a causé au cocontractant un dommage, a l'obligation de réparer celui-ci; que l'action qui en résulte ne se fonde toutefois pas sur une relation contractuelle, mais sur une faute quasi délictuelle commise par l'intéressé à l'occasion de son intervention au contrat" (. . .) Il faut donc rechercher si* [la défenderesse B] *a commis une faute lors des pourparlers, si* [la demanderesse A] *n'a pas contribué, par négligence, à la production de son propre dommage et si un lien de causalité existe entre la faute et le dommage (. . .)*

La doctrine belge enseigne que « *la communication d'informations erronées ou incomplètes, même de bonne foi, peut être sanctionné* » *(. . .) De même, J. Van Ryn et J. Heenen écrivent:* « *(. . .) La* culpa in contrahendo *existe dès lors que, soit sciemment, soit par imprudence ou par légèreté, une des parties a créé une fausse apparence de nature à tromper la légitime confiance du cocontractant* » *(Principes de droit commercial, t. III, Bruxelles, 1981, p. 30) (. . .)*

La faute consiste ici à omettre le Litige dans la liste des litiges établie lors de l'offre de cession de lu société X (. . .)

Mais il convient de encore de rechercher si [la demanderesse A] *n'a pas commis defaute (. . .) la théorie de la* culpa in conttahendo « *ne peut être invoquée par des personnes qui ne prennent pas les précautions normales et usuelles en contractant* » *(P. Van Ommeslaghe, Examen de jurisprudence (1974 à 1982), Les obligations: RCJB 1986, p. 153, n° 63) (. . .)*

Même si [la demanderesse A] *connaissait de manière générale l'existence du litige, (. . .) elle n'avait aucune raison d'effectuer des recherches relative à une responsabilité éventuelle de* [la société X] *du chef du litige au vu de l'affirmation péremptoire de l'Offering memorandum (. . .).* [La demanderesse A] *a pour sa part cherché à se protéger à la fois par une garantie du passif et par la purge des activités passées (. . .)*

En conclusion, une culpa in contrahendo *devrait en tout état de cause être retenue à la charge de* [la défenderesse B] *avec pour effet que les conséquences de cette faute, à savoir la prise en charge du dommage éventuel subi par* [la société X] *suite au litige, devaient de toute manière être supportées par* [la défenderesse B] *(. . .)* ».

OBSERVATIONS. — I. — La sentence examinée soulève une question de procédure préalable intéressante, à savoir la recevabilité de l'action de la demanderesse A. Elle offre ainsi aux arbitres l'occasion de rappeler les conditions nécessaires à une action en justice, soit l'existence d'un intérêt légitime, né et actuel à agir en justice. À défaut, l'action sera déclarée irrecevable en vertu du pouvoir d'appréciation des juges du fond selon un principe établi en jurisprudence « pas d'intérêt pas d'action » (V. par ex. Y. Desdevises, *Action en justice — Recevabilité — Conditions subjectives — Intérêt: J.-Cl. Procédure civile (1996), Fasc. 126-2. — S. Guinchard, Droit et pratique de la procédure civile: Dalloz, 2002-2003, p. 11 et s.).* Ce principe exclue donc en principe les actions préventives car le juge est appelé à trancher un litige qui est déjà né. En l'espèce, la demanderesse A n'avait pas *a priori* la qualité pour agir ni un intérêt particulier à obtenir au nom de la société X une condamnation de la défenderesse B. La requête d'arbitrage visait à obtenir une condamnation de la défenderesse B à indemniser la société X pour toutes les condamnations susceptibles d'être prononcées contre celle-ci dans le cadre du litige, objet d'une procédure judiciaire en cours — à laquelle la demanderesse A est étrangère — engagée par un tiers devant les tribunaux belges contre la société X qu'elle a reprise à l'occasion de la cession d'actions. La demanderesse A serait ainsi assurée de ne pas avoir à assumer les conséquences du litige qui seraient prononcées contre la société X qu'elle a rachetée.

Les arbitres ont répondu favorablement à cette requête en tenant compte du fait que la demanderesse A était juridiquement qualifiée pour défendre l'intérêt de la société X en sa qualité d'actionnaire unique.

Les arbitres ont ainsi admis la possibilité pour le cessionnaire d'introduire une demande préventive, soit une action déclaratoire dans le cadre particulier de la cession d'actions et de la clause de garantie du passif conclue. Cette conclusion est justifiée, sauf à préciser que le droit français n'admet pas la « pure action déclaratoire », à savoir celle qui vise à demander seulement « une simple consultation aux juges et qui serait totalement détachée de la notion d'intérêt » (V. *Y. Desdevises, op. cit., § 49. — L Ségur, L'action déchmtoire: Sirey 1965, I, 1902*). Tel n'est pas le cas en l'espèce puisque toute condamnation éventuelle de la société X dans le cadre de la procédure judiciaire a un impact sur son patrimoine, et a fortiori sur celui de la demanderesse A en sa qualité d'actionnaire unique de la société X, Or, la demanderesse A a voulu se protéger d'une telle éventualité en imposant à la défenderesse B l'acceptation d'une clause de garantie dans la convention.

En décidant ainsi, et pour éviter certainement toute ambiguïté, les arbitres ont pris soin de rappeler leur compétence qui découle de la clause compromissoire insérée dans la convention signée entre les parties A et B. Ils ont également indiqué l'absence de toute litispendance entre les instances judiciaire et arbitrale — les parties étant différentes — évitant ainsi toute discussion éventuelle sur l'opportunité d'un sursis à statuer. À supposer la question posée, on peut rappeler qu'il appartient au tribunal arbitral de décider ou non de suspendre la procédure arbitrale lorsqu'il lui semble opportun de le faire en considération des circonstances de l'affaire (V. sentence CCI n° 6610 (1991): *Recueil des sentences arbitrales de la CCI, vol. III, p. 277.* — sur la question de la litispendance, V. notamment *L. Cadiet, Répertoire de procédure civile: Dalloz, juin 2001*).

II. — La question principale soumise à l'examen des arbitres était de savoir dans quelles mesures les conséquences du litige dans le patrimoine de la société X étaient comprises ou non dans la transaction. En d'autres termes, la transaction mettait-elle un terme aux garanties données dans la convention et/ou le protocole? Dans l'affirmative, les conséquences du litige devraient être supportées par la demanderesse A. Dans le cas contraire, elles devraient être à la charge de la défenderesse B au titre des garanties données dans la convention.

Sur la base des correspondances échangées entre les parties, les arbitres constatent tout d'abord qu'elles étaient au courant de l'existence du litige. Chacune se croyait toutefois — à tort — déchargée de cette responsabilité en raison d'une interprétation divergente des garanties assumées par la défenderesse B dans la convention et de la transaction.

Ils rappellent ensuite l'objet des garanties insérées dans la convention qui était de transférer la société X purgée de toutes responsabilités éventuelles nées antérieurement à sa cession à la demanderesse A.

La transaction n'a pas mis un terme aux garanties assumées par la défenderesse B dans la convention ou le protocole en raison même de son objet. En effet, aux termes de l'article 2044 du Code civil belge « *La transaction est un contrat par lequel les parties terminent une contestation née, ou préviennent une contestation à naître* ». Une transaction suppose donc trois conditions: un litige né ou à naître, l'intention des parties d'y mettre fin et l'existence de concessions réciproques entre les intéressées (V. en ce sens la doctrine et jurisprudence belges citées par les arbitres, notamment, *J. de Gavre, Le contrat de transaction: Bruxelles, 1967, p. 78–79. — H. de Page et R. Dekkers, Les principaux contrats usuels, Traité élémentaire de droit civil belge, t. V: Bruxelles, 1975, p. 482. — Cass. 26 sept. 1974: Pas. 1995, I, p. 110. — Cass. 19 juin 1989: Pas. 1989, I, p. 1145.* — pour une identité des dispositions en droit belge et français, V. *P. Chauvel, Transaction: Rép. civ. Dalloz, sept. 2004. — Ch. Jarrosson, Les concessions réciproques dans la transaction: D. 1997, chron. p. 267).* En l'espèce, aucune des conditions citées n'était remplie car le litige n'existait tout simplement pas entre les parties au moment de la conclusion de la transaction. Chacune avait considéré qu'elle était tierce au litige. De ce fait, la responsabilité de la défenderesse B reste entière.

L'interprétation d'une transaction étant restrictive en raison de sa nature particulière, ses effets ne peuvent pas être étendus aux questions sur lesquelles les parties n'ont pas entendu s'accorder (V. en ce sens *P. Chauvel, op. cit., § 165-178).* Les arbitres soulignent ainsi toute l'importance des critères définis au Code civil belge, en particulier l'exigence de concessions réciproques sur un litige connu pour interpréter l'objet et la portée d'une transaction (sur l'importance des concessions réciproques, V. par analogie, les dispositions du Code civil italien, espagnol, portugais, hollandais, allemand, suisse cités par *Ch. Jarrosson, op. cit., p. 269 et seq.).*

III. — À titre surabondant, les arbitres ont examiné la question de savoir si la responsabilité de la défenderesse B pouvait être engagée au titre d'une faute précontractuelle sur la base de la règle *culpa in contrahendo.* Cette question a été soulevée à titre subsidiaire par la demanderesse A pour tenter de se protéger contre les conséquences financières d'une éventuelle condamnation judiciaire de la société X dans le cadre du litige, au cas où les arbitres auraient décidé qu'elle devait supporter les conséquences du litige.

Le tribunal arbitral a répondu favorablement à cette question en estimant que la défenderesse B « a engagé sa responsabilité en fournissant une information erronée » à la demanderesse A. L'obligation précontractuelle d'information est une obligation universelle du droit des affaires internationales que le droit belge sanctionne sur le fondement de la responsabilité délictuelle ou quasi-délictuelle *(C. civ. belge, art. 1382 et s.).*

On peut rappeler que la règle *culpa in contrahendo* et l'application des règles de la responsabilité qui en découlent ont été développées au IXXe siècle par Rudolf von Ihering (V. *De la* culpa in contrahendo *ou des dommages-intérêts dans les conventions nulles ou restées imparfaites: Œuvres choisies, trad. O. de Meulenaere, Paris, 1893, t. 2, p. 1).* Selon cet auteur, l'application de cette règle en droit allemand entraîne l'application des règles régissant la responsabilité contractuelle car la faute est de nature quasi-contractuelle. La phase précontractuelle oblige en effet les parties à faire preuve de diligence *(diligentia in contrahendo)* car le fait d'entrer en négociation ou de nouer un contact pour la conclusion éventuelle d'un contrat crée un rapport particulier entre les parties intéressées. C'est une « convention préalable » au contrat qui fonde l'obligation d'indemniser son cocontractant en cas de faute *(culpa)* dans la formation du contrat dans la mesure où les négociations ont fait légitimement espérer la conclusion du contrat. Le devoir de diligence s'impose au moment de la formation du contrat tout comme lors de sa conclusion ou de son exécution (plus généralement, V. *D. Deroussin,* Culpa in contrahendo. *L'indemnisation en cas d'annulation du contrat, du droit romain à la théorie classique des nullités: Rev. hist, droit, 82(2), avr.-juin 2004, p. 189-222).*

Le droit belge se différencie du droit allemand car il ne sanctionne pas une telle faute par l'application des règles de la responsabilité contractuelle. La solution appliquée en droit belge n'est pas une exception. Comme mentionné par le tribunal arbitral, le droit français applique les mêmes règles conformément aux dispositions des articles 1382 et suivants du Code civil français. Le recours à la théorie *culpa in contrahendo* entraîne l'application des règles de la responsabilité délictuelle car il s'agit d'une faute commise au stade précontractuel, au cours de la négociation (V. en ce sens *Rép. civ. Dalloz, 1988. — Cass. com., 13 févr. 1979: Bull. civ. n° 64, p. 49.* — V. également sentence CCI n° 5910 (1988): *JDI 1988, p. 1216 et Recueil des sentences arbitrales de la CCI, vol. II, p. 371.* — *J.-M. Loncle et J.-Y. Trochon, La phase des pourparlers dans les contrats internationaux — The negotiating phase of international contracts: RDAI/IBLJ 1997, n° 1, p. 32).* Le droit français a toujours ainsi refusé d'accueillir la solution allemande, qui voit dans la phase précontractuelle une situation qui oblige les parties à faire preuve de *diligentia in contrahendo.* À défaut de diligence, peut être retenue une faute commise au cours de la négociation, une *culpa in contrahendo,* fondement d'une responsabilité quasi-contractuelle. Le droit suisse applique également les principes de la responsabilité délictuelle pour sanctionner celui qui a causé des dommages à autrui, par négligence ou par imprudence (V. *C. civ. suisse, art. 4L* — V. également sentence CCI n° 2508 de 1976: *JDI 1977, p. 939 et Recueil des sentences arbitrales de la CCI, vol. I, p. 292:* « C'est un principe du droit suisse — *culpa in contrahendo* — conforme du reste à un principe général du droit — que celui qui cause un dommage à l'occasion d'une négociation, en manquant à ses devoirs de diligence ou à des devoirs dictés par la bonne foi ou l'équité, doit réparer le dommage; et cela que la négociation tende à un contrat proprement dit ou, comme en l'espèce, à une transaction pour liquider un litige. »). Le droit suédois — pourtant largement inspiré par le droit allemand — applique les mêmes règles de la responsabilité précontractuelle comme conséquence de la règle *culpa in contrahendo* (V. *Rodhe: Lärobok i obligationsrätt, 2ᵉ éd., Norstedts, Stockholm, 1969, p. 139 et seq.* — *Ramberg: Allmän avtalsrätt, 4ᵉ éd., Juristförlaget, Stockholm, 1996, p. 101).*

Le tribunal arbitral a fait sien de ce raisonnement puisqu'il reconnaît la responsabilité délictuelle de la défenderesse B dans le cadre des négociations et de la conclusion de la convention. Le fait que celle-ci n'ait pas révélé l'existence du litige dans l'offre de vente est une faute car la demanderesse A a acquis la société X sur la base d'une information erronée lors de la phase précontractuelle. En l'espèce, la condamnation de la défenderesse B ne se traduit pas par le paiement d'une somme d'argent fixée par le tribunal arbitral en faveur de la demanderesse A, mais par une condamnation de la défenderesse B à prendre à sa charge le dommage éventuel subi par la société X en cas de condamnation judiciaire de celle-ci dans le cadre du litige. Le résultat visé par le tribunal arbitral — et souhaité par la demanderesse A qui n'a pas demandé des dommages-intérêts ou l'annulation de la convention — est de garantir à la demanderesse A que le patrimoine de la société X ne serait pas affecté au cas où une condamnation judiciaire éventuelle serait prononcée contre cette dernière. Toutes les conséquences financières seront supportées par la défenderesse B. Une condamnation pécuniaire à un chiffre précis n'était pas de ce fait nécessaire.

Ainsi, en application de la règle *culpa in contrahendo,* une faute commise en amont de la conclusion d'un contrat peut être une source de responsabilité délictuelle au stade de son exécution.

S. J.
C. T.-N.

Sentence rendue dans l'affaire n° 10988 en 2003

Convention d'arbitrage, — Portée. — Responsabilité délictuelle. — Arbitrabilité. — Droit de la concurrence.

Groupe de sociétés. — Levée du voile social. — Responsabilité du fait d'une filiale. — Manque à gagner. — Calcul. — Perte de chance.

Le Tribunal arbitral est compétent pour connaître d'actes de concurrence déloyale dans la mesure où de tels actes sont intimement liés à l'inexécution ou à la mauvaise exécution d'un accord contractuel comportant une clause compromissoire.

L'arbitrabilité des litiges du droit de la concurrence est reconnue par bon nombre de juridictions, notamment par la jurisprudence suisse sous l'empire de la loi suisse d'arbitrage applicable à la présente procédure et, si les arbitres ne sauraient accorder une exemption individuelle en application de l'article 81 (3) du Traité CE, ils sont compétents pour constater que des contrats bénéficient d'une exemption par catégorie lorsqu'elle est prévue par les divers règlements de la Commission.

Des ventes réalisées par le licencié ou une de ses filiales en violation d'une interdiction figurant dans un contrat de licence valable constituent une faute contractuelle engageant la responsabilité du licencié qui est condamné à réparer le préjudice du donneur de licence, évalué sur la base de la perte de chance d'obtenir le marché.

Un tribunal arbitral de trois membres siégeant en Suisse a tranché, par application du droit italien, un litige portant sur des actes de concurrence déloyale entre une société franchise A et une société italienne B.

A avait concédé à B une licence exclusive d'usage de savoir-faire et de brevets (notamment un brevet français et un brevet européen) pour fabriquer dans les ateliers de B en Italie des produits identiques à ceux de A mais sous un habillage différent. B était de surcroît autorisée à céder à un tiers une sous-licence ou une licence pour la fabrication des produits ainsi définis, soit à l'issue du contrat si B avait effectivement fabriqué lesdits produits, soit dans le cas inverse, à l'issue d'une période de six ans (portée à dix par lettre séparée) à compter de la date d'entrée en vigueur du contrat. Par ailleurs, une licence de vente des produits dans le monde entier, à l'exception de certains pays dont la France, était concédée à B. À l'expiration du contrat, d'une durée initiale de cinq ans et prorogeable d'année en année sauf dénonciation avec préavis par l'une des parties, B « conservait le droit d'utiliser les informations techniques le savoir-faire et les brevets reçus (. . .) d'une façon illimitée dans le temps ».

Environ trois ans après l'expiration du contrat, A a engagé une procédure arbitrale contre B en invoquant la clause compromissoire figurant au contrat. Elle lui reprochait, d'une part, d'avoir concédé deux licences autorisant la fabrication des produits à des tiers dans deux pays extracommunautaires dont l'un figurait dans la liste des pays auxquels la licence de vente contractuelle ne s'étendait pas et, d'autre part, la participation de sa filiale française à un appel d'offres en France qui avait débouché sur la conclusions par cette filiale de deux contrats de fourniture de produits livrables en France. Pour A, ces opérations avaient été réalisées en violation du contrat et constituaient des actes de concurrence déloyale qui lui avaient causé un dommage dont elle demandait réparation.

B faisait valoir plusieurs moyens de défense. Elle soutenait en premier lieu que le Tribunal arbitral « n'est pas compétent et/ou (. . .) n'a pas la capacité juridique de juger par rapport aux demandes (. . .) visant la constatation de la commission d'actes de concurrence déloyale de la part de [B], et l'adoption relative de mesures de condamnation » au motif que « cela ne rentre pas dans le domaine d'application de la clause compromissoire (. . .) », laquelle portait sur « tous différends relatifs à l'interprétation et/ou l'exécution » du contrat. Le Tribunal rejette brièvement cet argument dans les termes suivants:

> « Le Tribunal arbitral relève, contrairement à ce que soutient la défenderesse, qu'il est compétent pour connaître d'actes de concurrence déloyale, soit d'actes illicites dans la mesure où de tels actes sont intimement liés à l'inexécution ou à la mauvaise exécution d'un accord contractuel comportant une clause compromissoire, ce qui est manifestement le cas ici (V. dans ce sens C. Reymond, Conflit de lois en matière de responsabilité délictuelle devant l'arbitre international in Travaux du Comité français de droit international privé, 1988-1989 p. 100 et s.) ».

Dans un second temps, le tribunal prend la peine, bien que cette question ne semble pas avoir été clairement soulevée par les parties, de confirmer l'arbitrabilité des litiges impliquant des questions de droit de la concurrence, et notamment de droit communautaire:

> « Au surplus et quand bien même la demanderesse paraît soutenir le contraire, l'arbitrabilité des litiges du droit de la concurrence est maintenant reconnue par bon nombre de juridictions, notamment par le Tribunal fédéral suisse dans un arrêt rendu sous l'empire de la LDIP, loi suisse d'arbitrage applicable à la présente procédure (cf. ATF 118 II 193).
>
> Il est vrai que les arbitres ne sauraient accorder une exemption individuelle en application de l'article 81 (3) du Traité CE (dans ce sens]. F. Poudret et S. Besson, Droit comparé de l'arbitrage international: Zurich/Bâle/Genève 2002, ad § 351, p. 319) mais la question ne se pose pas ici. En revanche, le Tribunal arbitral est compétent pour constater que des contrats peuvent bénéficier d'une exemption par catégorie lorsqu 'elle est prévue par les divers règlements de la Commission (dans ce sens, D. Hahn, L'arbitrage commercial international en Suisse face aux régies de concurrence de la CEE: Lausanne 1983, p. 95) ».

Sur le fond, B soutenait que le contrat devait s'analyser comme une cession différée de la technologie afférente au produit lui laissant toute latitude pour le fabriquer et le vendre après son expiration. Se fondant sur une interprétation littérale du contrat aussi bien que sur l'examen des conditions de sa négociation et de son équilibre éeonomique, le Tribunal rejette cette interprétation et décide que les limitations posées aux droits de B par le contrat survivent à son expiration. Le Tribunal juge ensuite que les actes reprochés à B, s'ils ne constituaient pas en fait des violations de la licence de fabrication concédée à B, dans la mesure où la partie interne des produits livrés, seule concernée par la licence de fabrication restait fabriquée en Italie conformément à cette dernière, pouvaient néanmoins constituer une violation de la licence de vente. En effet, cette dernière était limitée à certains territoires et, parce qu'elle était non cessible, n'autorisait de vendre qu'aux utilisateurs finaux du produit. Or, B soutenait que ces limites étaient contraires aux dispositions du droit communautaire et de l'article 2596 du Code civil italien car illimitées dans le temps. Le Tribunal est donc conduit à s'interroger sur leur validité.

Quant à l'article 2596, le Tribunal décide qu'il n'est pas applicable à l'espèce, la restriction litigieuse à la concurrence n'étant pas l'objet principal du contrat comme l'exige cette disposition, mais n'en constituant qu'une clause accessoire. Concernant le droit communautaire, le Tribunal distingue entre interdiction de vente dans des pays appartenant à la communauté européenne et ceux qui en étaient exclus à la date de conclusion des marchés litigieux:

> « En ce qui concerne maintenant le droit communautaire, les restrictions de concurrence prévues à l'article 3 du contrat litigieux relèvent, de l'avis du Tribunal arbitral, du Règlement CE n° 240/96 relatif à l'application de l'article 81 (ex-art. 85) du Traité CE à des catégories d'accords de transferts de technologie. En effet, les marchés conclus par la filiale française de la défenderesse avec EDF/GDF sont

postérieurs à l'entrée en vigueur dudit règlement, de sorte que c'est celui-ci qui s
'applique et non comme le voudrait la défenderesse, le règlement CE n° 2349/84 du
23 juillet 1984 qui précisément a été abrogé par le règlement CE n° 2410/96.

Or, et à teneur de l'article premier, paragraphe 4, de ce dernier règlement,
l'« exemption prévue aux paragraphes 1.1 à 5 s'applique pour les États membres
dans lesquels la technologie concédée est protégée par des brevets néssaires aussi
longtemps que le produit sous licence y est protégé par de tels brevets, lorsque la
durée de cette protection dépasse les périodes indiquées au paragraphe 3 » c'est-à-
dire dix ans à partir de la première mise en circulation du produit dans le commerce
communautaire par un des licenciés pour les accords de communication de savoir-
faire. Comme le souligne la doctrine, c'est donc la durée de protection la plus
avantageuse qui s'applique selon les cas: celle résultant de l'existence des brevets
ou la durée maximum de dix ans pour l'exemption des clauses stipulées dans des
accords purs de savoir-faire (cf. G. Bonnet, Le nouveau règlement d'exemption par
catégorie d'accords de transfert de technologie: JCP E 1996, étude 1, 544).

Force est alors de constater que là où le droit communautaire s'applique, ce qui
est le cas des marchés conclus avec EDF/GDF, les interdictions de l'article 3 du
contrat du 1ᵉʳ février 1998 ne sont nullement perpétuelles comme l'affirme la
défenderesse.

En revanche, le règlement CE de 1996 ne saurait viser des pays non membres de
la Communauté européenne, (. . .) de sorte que la question de savoir si l'on se
trouve en présence d'interdictions illimitées dans le temps pourrait alors se poser.

Également sur ce point, le Tribunal arbitral ne partage pas l'avis de la défen-
deresse et ce pour le motif suivant: il faut tout d'abord rappeler que la technologie
relative au [produit] *es protégée en Italie par la fraction italienne du brevet* [eur-
opéen] *(cf. Ann. B au contrat du (. . .)). Dès lors et si la défenderesse a été en*
mesure de livrer aux sociétés (. . .) et (. . .) la partie interne dudit compteur,
c'est parce qu 'érant au bénéfice de la licence de fabrication visée à l'article 2 du
contrat du 1ᵉʳ février 1988, elle était en droit de fabriquer cette partie interne dans
son usine de (. . .), soir en Italie. C'est dire que s'agissant des pays extracom-
munautaires, (. . .) la durée des interdictions de l'article 3 du contrat ne peut
dépendre que de la période de validité du brevet européen précité car une fois
celui-ci tombé dans le domaine public, la défenderesse pourra utiliser ladite tech-
nologie sans aucune restriction, la licence de fabrication visée à l'article 2 de
l'accord du 1ᵉʳ février 1988 n'ayant alors plus aucun fondement. Si donc c'est en
fonction de la validité du seul brevet (. . .) que doit être mesurée la durée des
limitations de concurrence concernant [les États extra-européens], *il importe peu,*
contrairement à ce que soutient la défenderesse, que dans l'intervalle, le titulaire
du brevet [obtenu dans l'un de ces pays] *ait été déchu de ses droits.*

Il est vrai que la licence conférée par le contrat du (. . .) pone également sur le
savoir-faire: toutefois, le Tribunal arbitral considère que ce savoir-faire qui ne vise
que la « fabrication et l'étalonnage des [produits] *» (cf. article 1.5. du contrat du*
1ᵉʳ février 1988) ne peut être qu'un accessoire du brevet de sorte qu 'il doit suivre
le sort de ce dernier et partant pourra être utilisé par tout un chacun à l'expiration
du brevet (dans ce sens, M. Pedrazzini, Die Vertragliche Behandlung des Behan-
dlung des Know-How: RSPI 1989, p. 183, 193). En d'autres termes, ce savoir-faire
ne saurait survivre au brevet (. . .), de sorte que c'est bien la durée de celui-ci qui
doit être prise en compte dans l'optique d'une limitation dans le temps des inter-
dictions prescrites à l'article 3 de l'accord du (. . .) ».

À la suite de cecte analyse, le Tribunal examine chacune des opérations critiquées par la
demanderesse. Il constate qu'elles ont toutes trois été réalisées alors que les brevets français
et européen de la demanderesse étaient en vigueur. Quant aux deux contrats conclus en
France, leur prohibition ne saurait être contraire au droit communautaire de la concurrence,

le Règlement faisant obligation au licencié de ne pas exploiter la technologie concédée dans le territoire du donneur de licence tant qu'il est protégé par un brevet. Peu importe que l'opération ait été réalisée par une filiale dans la mesure où, outre que des produits ont nécessairement été vendus par B à cette dernière en France, elle est sous la domination entière de B et où « *le principe de l'identité économique doit prévaloir sur celui de la dualité juridique* ». Quant aux opérations réalisées hors de la communauté, elles violent les termes de la licence de vente parce qu'elles n'ont pas été réalisées au profit d'utilisateurs finaux et pour l'une d'elles parce que l'acheteur est situé dans l'un des pays exclus du champ de la licence.

Le Tribunal quantifie ensuite le dommage subi par la demanderesse en se référant à l'article 1226 CCI dont il écrit qu'il « *permet au juge, donc à l'arbitre, de déterminer le préjudice subi de façon équitable* ». Il effectue le calcul en déduisant d'un prix de vente théorique par unité (selon les cas le prix de vente de la défenderesse ou celui qu'elle consent à sa filiale dans le pays concerné) un prix de revient établi par la demanderesse auquel il ajoute des frais de transport et de distribution qu'il estime « *faute d'indication plus précise à ce sujet et conformément à l'article 1226 CCI* » à 5 % du prix de revient. Après avoir appliqué le prix par unité ainsi obtenu aux quantités vendues par la défenderesse, le Tribunal examine l'argument de cette dernière selon lequel il était improbable que les marchés qui lui avaient été attribués l'auraient été à la demanderesse. Le Tribunal résout la difficulté en recourant à la théorie de la perte de chance et s'en explique ainsi:

> « *Dans ces conditions et en l'absence d'une preuve certaine dans un sens ou dans l'autre, le Tribunal arbitral résoudra cette question en application de la théorie de la perte d'une chance qui consiste à indemniser le lésé des chances perdues en fonction de leur probabilité de réalisation, théorie que la défenderesse invoque implicitement en citant un arrêt du Tribunal de Milan du 9 juin 1980 (cf. Giurisprudenza annotata di diritto industrial 1980, p. 475).*
>
> *Dans l'arrêt précité, ledit tribunal avait en effet jugé que s'agissant de déterminer le dommage subi par le titulaire d'un brevet contrefait, il était nécessaire de vérifier si tous les acquéreurs du produit se le seraient procurés auprès du breveté. Dans cette perspective, le Tribunal arbitral soulignera que la perte d'un chance — « perdita di un occasione » — est un concept auquel la jurisprudence italienne recourt fréquemment aux fins de déterminer le gain manqué du lésé dans le cadre d'une responsabilité précontractuelle (rupture abusive de pourparlers selon l'article 1337 CCI ou encore invalidité d'un contrat conclu par un représentant sans pouvoir ou excédent ses pouvoirs au sens de l'article 1398 CCI), voire dans d'autres cas (cf. Cass. 11.11.1997, n° 11126. — Cass. 21.05.1985, n° 3096), et surtout en matière de droit du travail (Cass. 07.03.199, 1 n° 2368: Foro it. 1991, I, 1793). C'est dire qu 'en appliquant la théorie de la perte d'une chance, le Tribunal arbitral se situe en droite ligne du droit italien qui régit le présent litige (V. aussi sur l'ensemble de la question A. Pinori, Il danno contrattuale: Principi generali e techniche di limitazione giuridiziale del risarcimento, Milan 1998, p. 67 et s.).*
>
> *Par nature, la perte d'une chance ne peut jamais être évaluée avec une exactitude mathématique, l'événement dont les conséquences doivent être appréciées ne s'étant en fait pas produit. De plus, les éléments fournis par les deux parties manquent de précision. Mais cela ne dispense pas le Tribunal arbitral de faire la meilleure évaluation possible à l'aide des éléments qui sont en sa possession* ».

En l'espèce, le Tribunal estime les chances qu'aurait eues la demanderesse d'obtenir les marchés concernés, pour des quantités similaires, à une sur trois et, en conséquence, réduit d'autant le montant de l'indemnité allouée.

Enfin, le Tribunal rejette les demandes qui lui sont faite de constater l'existence des violations contractuelles commises par la défenderesse et d'enjoindre à cette dernière de ne plus les commettre. Pour la première demande, le Tribunal observe que la condamnation de B impliquant constatation des violations alléguées par A, l'action en constatation lui est fermée. Pour la seconde, il décide en premier lieu que le brevet français de A étant tombé dans le domaine public, « *l'injonction sollicité serait contraire au droit communautaire, cela sous réserve d'une exemption individuelle que le Tribunal arbitral ne saurait toutefois accorder* ». Il ajoute que la demanderesse n'a pas établi que ses droits hors de la communauté étaient menacés par B, ce qui interdisait le prononcé de toute injonction.

À l'issue de sa décision, le Tribunal, rappelant ses pouvoirs discrétionnaires en la matière, décide que la défenderesse supportera les trois quarts des frais d'arbitrage, un quart restant à la charge de la demanderesse « *dès lors que si dans son principe sa réclamation en réparation du préjudice subi a été admise, elle n'obtient et de loin pas le quantum de ses prétentions* ». Les frais exposés par les parties pour leur défense restent à leur charge.

NOTE. — I. — Les arbitres sont fréquemment appelés à se prononcer sur leur compétence pour trancher des questions qui relèvent de la responsabilité extracontractuelle, notamment lorsqu'elles résultent d'actes de concurrence déloyale *(Sentence rendue dans l'affaire n° 5477 en 1988: JDI 1988, p. 1204, obs. G. Aguilar Alvarez)*. Le Tribunal répond ici à l'exception d'incompétence soulevée par la défenderesse de manière lapidaire mais très classique en observant « qu'il est compétent pour connaître d'actes de concurrence déloyale, soit d'acte illicites dans la mesure où de tels actes sont intimement liés à l'inexécution ou à la mauvaise exécution d'un accord contractuel comportant une clause compromissoire ». Encore faut-il que, l'investiture des arbitres trouvant sa source dans la clause compromissoire, que la rédaction de la clause permette aux arbitres de se saisir de la question. Cela ne semble pas devoir faire de doute en l'espèce où la clause avait pour objet « tous différends relatifs à l'interpretation et/ou l'exécution du présent Accord ». Le litige, portant sur les droits du licencié survivant à l'expiration du contrat, entrait certainement dans cette catégorie, et cela d'autant plus que le défendeur fondait sa défense sur une interprétation des dispositions pertinentes à cet égard tendant à lui donner les droits les plus larges sur la technologie licenciée. Au demeurant, le Tribunal conduit l'ensemble de sa motivation en termes strictement contractuels puisqu'il analyse les actes reprochés à la défenderesse à la mesure des droits qui lui sont concédés par le contrat, l'invocation des brevets de la demanderesse ne servant qu'à limiter dans le temps les interdictions de vente imposées au licencié. Ce sont donc bien des fautes contractuelles, pour lesquelles la compétence du Tribunal n'est pas contestable, qui justifient la condamnation de la défenderesse, ainsi que le Tribunal l'observe lorsqu'il écrit devoir « quantifier le dommage subi par la demanderesse du chef des violations contractuelles commises par la défenderesse ».

II. — La position adoptée par le Tribunal quant à l'arbitrabilité des litiges relevant du droit de la concurrence et notamment du droit communautaire de la concurrence est également des plus classiques. De très nombreuses sentences *(récemment, Sentence rendue dans l'affaire n° 8423 en 1998: JDI 2002, p. 1079, obs. J.-J. Arnaldez)*, confortée par la jurisprudence et la doctrine de nombreux pays, ont admis que les arbitres pouvaient trancher des litiges relevant d'une réglementation d'ordre public et notamment apprécier la conformité d'un accord restrictif de la concurrence au regard du droit communautaire. Les arbitres n'hésitent d'ailleurs pas à soulever la question d'office lorsque la situation se présente *(Sentence rendue dans l'affaire n° 7539 en 1995: JDI 1995, p. 1030, obs. Y. Derains. — Sentence rendue dans l'affaire n° 8423, préc)*.

Le tribunal, siégeant en Suisse, évoque uniquement la jurisprudence suisse et notamment l'arrêt du 28 avril 1992 du Tribunal fédéral *(Bull. ASA 1992, p. 368; Rev. arb. 1993, p. 124, note L. Idot)* dans lequel le Tribunal fédéral a annulé une sentence parce que l'arbitre s'y était à tort déclaré incompétent pour apprécier la validité d'un accord au regard de l'article 85 du

Traité. En effet, l'arbitrabilité du litige en Suisse est régie par l'article 177 LDIP, conçu comme une règle matérielle de droit international privé *(P. Lalive, J. F. Poudret et C. Reymond, Le droit de l'arbitrage interne et international en Suisse, p. 305)*, ce qui rendait inutile toute référence à la loi applicable au contrat. Au demeurant, la jurisprudence italienne semble admettre également l'arbitrabilité des questions de droit communautaire de la concurrence *(CA Bologne, 21 déc. 1991: YCA 1993, vol. XVIII, p. 422)*.

Le Tribunal avait donc non seulement le pouvoir, mais encore le devoir, de se prononcer sur la validité des clauses litigieuses. Certes, la jurisprudence suisse, contrairement à la jurisprudence française qui admet le caractère d'ordre public international du droit communautaire de la concurrence mais n'en sanctionne la violation par une sentence que s'il s'agit de violations « flagrantes, effectives et concrètes » *(CA Paris, 18 nov. 2004, SA Thales Air Défense cl GIE Euromissile: Juris-Data n° 2004-264585; JDI 2005, p. 357; Rev. arb. 2005, p. 751)* a-t-elle décidé que « les dispositions du droit de la concurrence, quel qu'il soit, ne font pas partie des valeurs essentielles et largement reconnues qui, selon les conceptions prévalant en Suisse, devraient constituer le fondement de tout ordre juridique. Par conséquent, la violation d'une disposition de ce genre ne tombe pas sous le coup de l'article 190, alinéa 2, *e* LDIP», lequel permet de sanctionner les sentences incompatibles avec l'ordre public *(Tribunal fédéral, 8 mars 2006: Bull. ASA 2006, p. 363)*. La même juridiction avait auparavant jugé qu'un arbitre chargé d'appliquer le droit suisse n'avait pas à soulever d'office les lois de police — en pratique l'article 85 du Traité — du droit normalement applicable *(Tribunal fédéral, 13 nov. 1998: Bull. ASA 1999, p. 529)*. Or, en l'espèce le contrat était soumis au droit italien qui incorpore le droit communautaire de la concurrence et la demanderesse soulevait l'incompatibilité avec ce dernier des clauses du contrat qu'il lui était reproché d'avoir violées. Envisageant des circonstances analogues, le Tribunal fédéral dans son même arrêt du 8 mars 2006 estime que l'arbitre qui « se déclare incompétent pour examiner l'application d'une loi de police étrangère, tel le droit européen ou italien de la concurrence, alors qu'une partie lui demande de le faire » viole l'article 190, alinéa 2, *e* LDIP « en liaison avec » l'article 187, alinéa 1, qui lui impose de statuer selon les règles de droit choisies par les parties.

On notera enfin l'observation par les arbitres que leur compétence se limite à apprécier la validité d'un accord au regard du droit communautaire de la concurrence, y compris au regard d'une exemption par catégorie, et qu'ils « ne sauraient accorder une exemption individuelle en application de l'article 81 (3) du Traité CE ». Le bien-fondé de cette affirmation, qui justifiera le refus par les arbitres d'enjoindre à la défenderesse de poursuivre ses opérations dans la communauté, ne fait en effet aucun doute. Les arbitres sont compétents pour tirer toutes conséquences civiles d'une violation du droit de la concurrence. Ils ne peuvent en revanche exercer des pouvoirs qui relève de la seule commission *(en ce sens J.-B. Racine, L'arbitrage commercial et l'ordre public: LGDJ 1999, p. 112)*.

III. — Le recours à la notion de groupe de société par les sentences arbitres est des plus fréquentes. Les arbitres l'invoquent le plus souvent, selon une jurisprudence bien connue initiée par la fameuse sentence *Isover St.-Gobain cl Dow Chemical (JDI 1983, p. 899)*, pour justifier l'extension de la force obligatoire d'une convention d'arbitrage à un tiers appartenant au même groupe de sociétés que l'une des parties lorsque les circonstances permettent de présumer le consentement dudit tiers. L'appartenance de ce dernier au groupe intervient alors comme un « commencement de preuve » *(J.-J. Amaldez, obs. sous sentent c̀ rendue dans l'affaire n° 10758 en 2000: JDI 2001, p. 1171)* ou un indice permettant d'envisager plus facilement l'extension de la convention d'arbitrage » *(Ch. Jarrosson, Conventions d'arbitrages et Groupes de sociétés, Groupes de sociétés: Contrats et responsabilités: LGDJ 1994, p. 53, cité par D. Hascher, obs. sous sentence rendue dans les affaires n° 7604 en 7610 en 1995: JDI 1998, p. 1027)*.

Ici, la notion intervient à un autre titre, non pas pour étendre la compétence du tribunal arbitral à la filiale de la défenderesse, ce qui n'avait d'ailleurs pas été demandé et n'aurait sans doute pas été possible faute de pouvoir établir la participation de cette dernière à la négociation et à la conclusion du contrat, mais pour rendre cette dernière responsable des actes de sa filiale. Le tribunal décide en effet que la défenderesse ne saurait se prévaloir de l'effet relatif des contrats et de la personnalité juridique de sa filiale pour s'exonérer de toute responsabilité du fait d'un acte de sa filiale, qui s'il avait été accompli par la défenderesse l'aurait été en violation de ses obligations contractuelles. Cette décision ne peut qu'être approuvée en l'espèce tant il est vrai que les préoccupations morales qui sous-tendent la notion d'abus et la levée du voile social ne sont pas inconnues de la jurisprudence arbitrale *(par ex. Sentence rendue dans l'affaire 8385 en 1995: JDI 1997, p. 1061, obs. Y, Detains)*. On peut néanmoins regretter que le tribunal ne cherche pas à la justifier plus avant en fait aussi bien qu'en droit. En fait, on ne sait rien de la nature et des modalités du contrôle exercé dont le tribunal nous apprend uniquement qu'il est entier. En droit, le tribunal aurait pu se fonder par exemple sur le principe de bonne foi, fréquemment invoqué par la juris-prudence arbitrale *(pour un exemple récent, V. Sentence rendue dans l'affaire 6317 en 1989: JDI 2003, p. 1156, obs. E. Jolivet)* qui est reconnu par le droit italien, notamment dans l'article 1375 du Code civil en ce qui concerne l'exécution de bonne foi des contrats. Il est vrai cependant qu'une motivation détaillée n'était pas nécessaire dès lors que la décision du tribunal s'appuyait également sur une faute personnelle de la défenderesse consistant en la vente directe des produits en France par cette dernière à sa filiale.

IV. — Ayant déterminé que les opérations litigieuses de la défenderesse était fautive, le Tribunal s'attache à calculer le dommage subi par la demanderesse à raison de chacune de ces opérations et calcule pour cela, dans un premier temps le gain que cette dernière aurait réalisé si les marchés obtenus par la défenderesse ou ses filiales lui avaient été attribués. On sait en effet que deux méthodes sont envisageables pour indemniser le titulaire d'un droit de propriété industrielle dont le droit a été violé: soit lui allouer une indemnisation d'un montant égal au bénéfice réalisé par l'auteur de la faute, soit calculer son gain manqué *(G. Viney et P. Jourdain, Traité de droit civil: les effets de la responsabilité: LGDJ 2ᵉ éd., n° 92)*. La première méthode est la plus dissuasive puisqu'elle retire au fautif l'intégralité de son gain mais seule la seconde est à même de permettre la réparation intégrale du préjudice subi qui est parfois présentée comme un principe général du droit du commerce international *(Ph. Fouchard, E. Gaillard et B. Goldman: Traité de l'arbitrage commercial international: Litec, n° 1492)*.

On ne pourra donc qu'approuver l'effort des arbitres pour calculer avec autant de pré-cision que le leur permet le dossier le gain que la demanderesse aurait réalisé si les marchés lui avaient été attribués. Ainsi que de nombreuses sentences l'ont déjà affirmé *(V. Sentence rendue dans l'affaire n° 10422 en 2001: JDI 2003, p. 1142, obs. E. Jolivet)*, celui-ci ne peut être identifié à la marge nette, comme la demanderesse le prétendait et le Tribunal s'attache donc avec raison à vérifier l'existence des coûts qu'elle aurait supporté en plus du prix de revient, quitte à procéder par estimation lorsque des informations suffisantes lui manquent.

On peut en revanche être plus hésitant sur le recours par le Tribunal à la notion de perte de chance. Certes les parties avaient discuté, à propos des opérations françaises, les chances de la demanderesse que les deux marchés lui soit attribués en l'absence de la participation de la filiale de la défenderesse à l'appel d'offre. On ne saurait donc reprocher au Tribunal arbitral une violation du principe du contradictoire. Mais la position de la demanderesse était que les marchés lui auraient certainement été attribués et elles demandaient donc la réparation d'un préjudice certain alors qu'en évaluant ses chances de succès à 30 %, le Tribunal répare un préjudice incertain. L'observation par le Tribunal que la théorie de la perte de chance a été invoquée implicitement par la défenderesse en citant une jurisprudence italienne montre d'ailleurs que les parties n'ont pas discuté la question. Il semble en réalité que le Tribunal ait cherché, par le biais de cette théorie, et cela est confirmé par l'application du même taux de 30 % aux deux autres marchés litigieux mais sans analyse cette fois de leur contexte commercial, à motiver sa détermination du montant de l'indemnité qui lui semblait justifiée par les circonstances de la cause, ce que l'article 1226 du Code civil italien, qui permet au juge de déterminer le préjudice subi de façon équitable, l'invitait à faire.

B. D.

Sentence intérimaire sur la responsabilité rendue dans l'affaire CCI n° 10671

Contrat *d'electio juris.* — Séparabilité de la clause d'*electio juris.* — Validité de la convention (oui). — Attitude des parties et pragmatisme juridique.

Simulation. — Nature du contrat. — « Cause juridique » de l'obligation / du contrat. — Véritables parties à l'arbitrage et compétence du Tribunal arbitral. - Validité du contrat simulé. — Fraude à la loi (non). — Évasion fiscale et contrariété aux bonnes mœurs du commerce international (non). — Détermination de la conception nationale des bonnes mœurs applicable à la simulation frauduleuse.

Lex mercatoria. — Bonne foi dans les affaires commerciales internationales. — Rapports entre « *nemo auditor propiam turpitudinem allegans* », « *ventre contra factum proprium* » et la bonne foi. — Opposabilité d'une simulation frauduleuse à l'une des parties y ayant participé (oui).

La sentence commentée établit qu'un contrat simulé, soumis au droit suisse, ayant pour cause de permettre à l'une des parties d'éviter le paiement d'impôts dans son pays, n'est contraire ni à l'ordre public international suisse ni aux bonnes mœurs du commerce international.

L'affaire CCI n° 10671 a donné lieu à quatre sentences arbitrales.

La première sentence intérimaire — portant sur la compétence *in concreto* du Tribunal arbitral — a déjà fait l'objet d'un commentaire au *Clunet (cf. E. Silva Romero, Cour internationale d'arbitrage de la Chambre de commerce internationale, Chronique de sentences arbitrales: JDI 2005, p. 1268 et s.).*

La deuxième sentence intérimaire a porté sur l'invitation faite par la demanderesse au Tribunal arbitral *« (. . .) à ordonner à la défenderesse de lui verser la part d'avance des frais d'arbitrage lui incombant selon le Règlement de la CCI. La défenderesse s'est (. . .) opposée à cette requête (. . .) Le Tribunal arbitral, statuant sur la requête de remboursement d'avance déposée le 14 août 2001 par la demanderesse, a rendue une Sentence partielle par laquelle il a: (. . .) 1. Condamné* [la partie défenderesse] *à rembourser à* [la partie demanderesse] *la somme de US$ 40'000. — avec intérêts à 5 % l'an dès le 23 mai 2000 (. . .) 2. Mis à la charge de la défenderesse (. . .) les frais de la procédure sur requête de remboursement par la défenderesse de la provision d'arbitrage, tels que ces frais seront fixés dans le cadre de la sentence finale ».*

Les questions théoriques et pratiques résultant de sentences telles que celle décrite ci-avant ont déjà été examinées *(cf. M. Secomb, Awards and Orders Dealing with the Advance on Costs in ICC Arbitration/ Theoretical questions and practical problems: Bulletin de la Cour internationale d'arbitrage de la CCI, vol. 14, n° l; ICC Publishing 2003, p. 59 et s.).*

La troisième sentence intérimaire (ci-après la « Sentence »), qui fait l'objet du présent commentaire, porte sur la responsabilité des parties.

Les faits de l'espèce doivent être rappelés. La société commerciale grecque X — SA — membre du groupe de la partie demanderesse — et la société Y — membre du groupe de la partie défenderesse — ont conclu un contrat dit « cadre » par lequel la société X devenait l'agent pour la Grèce de certaines sociétés du groupe de la société Y et devait conclure avec elles des contrats d'application. Les parties au contrat — cadre ont convenu que la commission en faveur de la société X serait de 4,85 % du prix CIF des produits livrés *(sur les Incoterms, cf. E. Jolivet, Les Incoterms. Étude d'une norme du commerce international: Litec, 2003).*

Le PDG de la société X, afin de rendre plus rentable l'opération commerciale pour son groupe, a néanmoins proposé — et le groupe de la partie défenderesse a accepté — (i) de limiter le pourcentage de la commission dans le contrat — cadre en faveur de la société X à 1,85 % et (ii) de conclure un contrat (en 1991) cette fois-ci entre la partie demanderesse, société off-shore du groupe X, et la partie défenderesse par lequel cette dernière s'engageait à verser une commission de 3 % à la partie demanderesse en paiement de services (une étude de marché) prétendument rendus par celle-ci en Grèce en faveur de la partie défenderesse.

Il a été démontré durant la procédure arbitrale que le but de conclure un contrat séparé entre la partie demanderesse et la partie défenderesse portant sur 3 % de la commission accordée par les deux groupes était d'éviter le paiement d'impôts en Grèce. Il s'agissait juridiquement d'une simulation. C'est en ce sens que le Tribunal arbitral souligne dans la Sentence que:

> « Le Tribunal arbitral considérera donc comme avéré le point de vue de la défenderesse, selon lequel la division de la commission globale de 4,85 % entre [la société X] et [la partie demanderesse] n'impliquait pour la demanderesse aucune obligation de rendre les services promis dans le contrat et [la partie demanderesse] n'a effectivement jamais réalisé l'étude de marché qui s'y trouve mentionnée ».

En 1993, la partie défenderesse a décidé de mettre fin au Contrat, et la partie demanderesse, pour sa part, a commencé l'arbitrage afin d'obtenir le paiement de commissions impayées.

Subsidiairement à son objection à la compétence *in concreto* du Tribunal arbitral — qui a été rejetée dans la première sentence intérimaire mentionnée ci-avant, « (. . .) la défenderesse a fait valoir que le contrat invoqué était nul car simulé et contraire aux mœurs, étant destiné à violer le droit fiscal grec (. . .) ».* C'est précisément les réflexions du Tribunal arbitral sur la simulation et la validité du Contrat qui se trouvent au cœur de la Sentence.

« IV. EN DROIT

47. Le Tribunal arbitral observe tout d'abord que les parties au présent arbitrage ont fait élection de droit, dans le contrat lui-même (art. 7), en faveur du droit suisse, choisi pour régir « in every respect » le contrat et son interprétation. Cette élection de droit, parfaitement valable, n'est en aucune manière remise en cause par les parties et c'est donc selon le droit suisse que le Tribunal arbitral statuera.

a) De la simulation

48. La défenderesse allègue que le contrat de 1991 est un acte simulé, donc nul, l'acte dissimulé consistant à détourner une partie de la commission due à [la société X] sur une société off-shore, en violation des règles du droit des sociétés, voire du droit pénal, en tout cas du droit fiscal grecs. Cette violation du droit étranger rendrait l'acte dissimulé nul comme contraire aux mœurs (art. 20 al. 1 CO) [Code suisse des obligations].

49. Le contrat du 20 décembre 1991 prévoit que [la partie demanderesse] s'engage à réaliser en Grèce une étude de marché dont la défenderesse allègue qu'il n'était pas dans l'intention des parties d'en poursuivre l'exécution, que la demanderesse eût d'ailleurs été incapable de fournir. Le Tribunal arbitral a admis que cette interprétation de la volonté des parties, corroborée par les témoins [T] et [N], correspondait bien à la réalité.

Le contrat constate l'engagement [de la partie défenderesse] *de verser à* [la partie demanderesse], *en rémunération de ses services, une commission de 3 % des ventes réalisées en Grèce par* [la partie défenderesse]. *Sous réserve du fait qu'il s'agit en réalité des ventes faites par* [la société Y], *cet engagement correspond à la volonté réelle des parties, confirmée par une exécution spontanée apparemment sans faille* [par la partie défenderesse] *jusqu'au 30 juin 1993, et même au-delà puisque les derniers paiements sont intervenus en septembre 1993.*

On peut donc en conclure que le contrat du 20 décembre 1991 est effectivement simulé, dans la mesure où il attribue à l'engagement de la défenderesse de payer une commission à la demanderesse une cause qui ne correspond pas à la volonté réelle des parties. La véritable cause juridique de cet engagement réside dans les services rendus en Grèce par [la société X] *à* [la société Y] *et dont il était admis entre les parties que la rémunération normale était une commission de 4,85 %, correspondant, d'après le témoin* [T], *aux conditions du marché.*

L'acte dissimulé par le langage du contrat du 20 décembre 1991, et correspondant à la réelle et commune intention des parties (art. 18, al. 1, CO) était donc un engagement de [la partie défenderesse] *de payer à* [la partie demanderesse] *une commission de 3 % sur les ventes en Grèce de* [la société Y], *sans contrepartie de la part de* [la partie demanderesse]. *La conséquence de principe devrait donc être l'obligation de la défenderesse de payer cette commission sur toutes les opérations réalisées jusqu'au 30 juin 1993, sans pouvoir exiger de* [la partie demanderesse] *une prestation en échange, ni arguer de l'absence de prestation pour refuser le paiement.*

Sauf si, comme le soutient la défenderesse, son engagement est frappé de nullité.

b) De la validité du contrat du 20 décembre 1991

50. [La partie défenderesse] *allègue tout d'abord que l'accord en question constitue une fraude au droit fiscal grec car il tend à détourner de la société grecque* [X] *une rémunération lui revenant, pour l'attribuer à une société off-shore dans laquelle elle échappera à l'impôt grec qui aurait normalement dû la frapper.*

Certes, la vie des affaires montre que le versement à une société [off shore] *d'une rémunération correspondant à des services rendus par une société ayant son siège dans un pays à fiscalité élevée peut être un moyen d'éviter le paiement des impôts normalement dus dans ce pays. Mais l'utilisation de telles structures est trop répandue, et parfois pour de bonnes raisons commerciales, pour que l'on puisse a priori et sans aucune preuve admettre une intention frauduleuse de la part des parties.*

La défenderesse a affirmé que [la partie demanderesse] *appartenait* [au PDG de la société X] *ou à lui et ses proches, sans que l'actionnariat et les structures d'un groupe* [X], *si un tel groupe existe, soient clairement établis. Rien n'exclut — ni ne prouve — que les bénéfices réalisés par* [la partie demanderesse] *apparaissent au niveau consolidé dans des comptes de groupe ou soient déclarés comme dividendes par un ou plusieurs actionnaires.*

51. *Quelle serait cependant la situation si l'on voulait, par hypothèse, retenir comme vraisemblable la volonté des parties de soustraire à l'imposition en Grèce une part substantielle de la commission à laquelle il apparaît que* [la société X] *pouvait prétendre ? Cette volonté passant par la mise au point d'un contrat simulé, l'opération serait sans doute, selon le droit grec, constitutive de fraude fiscale. D'où une violation du droit étranger susceptible de rendre le contrat immoral, et donc nul, au regard de l'article 20, alinéa 1er CO.*

Il est admis en doctrine et en jurisprudence que la finalité du contrat sur laquelle les parties étaient d'accord peut être assimilée à l'objet du contrat au sens de l'article 20, alinéa 1er CO: une finalité illicite ou contraire au mœurs peut donc avoir pour conséquence la nullité d'un contrat dont l'objet au sens étroit ne serait pas vicié. « Le but du contrat doit *se comprendre comme étant le but commun aux deux parties: les bonnes mœurs sont violées si la finalité immorale du contrat en est la base pour l'un des cocontractants et si l'autre le sait ou doit le savoir » (P. Engel, Traité des obligations en droit suisse, 2ᵉ éd., Berne, 1997, p. 293).*

Si la finalité du contrat est la violation du doit étranger, le contrat n'est pas illicite, mais il peut être contraire aux mœurs. Pour qu'il en soit ainsi, la loi étrangère violée doit protéger « des intérêts individuels ou sociaux d'une importance fondamentale, des biens juridiques que l'éthique et le respect de la dignité humaine placent au-dessus de la liberté contractuelle; tel serait le cas d'un contrat relatif à la traite des femmes ou au commerce des stupéfiants, mais non pas celui qui enfreint des mesures de politique commerciale ou de contrôle des changes (ATF [Arrêt du Tribunal fédéral] n° 76/1950, II p. 33 s.) » (P. Engel, op. cit., p. 275. — V. aussi Gauch/Schluep/Schmid/Rey, Schweizerisches Obligationenrecht. Allgemeiner Teil, 7. Aufl., N. 675. — E. A. Kramer, Berner Kommentar ad Art. 19-20 OR, N. 162). Si cette conception peut sembler aujourd'hui trop restrictive, il paraît en tout cas justifié de ne frapper de nullité un contrat, par ailleurs soumis au droit suisse, que s'il viole une norme étrangère dont la violation serait sanctionnée par la nullité si une telle norme était édictée par le législateur suisse ou résultait de la conception suisse des bonnes mœurs. Ce critère est dans la logique qui inspire l'article 19 LDIP [Loi fédérale sur le droit international privé], aux termes duquel la prise en considération d'une norme imperative de droit étranger non directement applicable suppose que cette norme mette en cause « des intérêts légitimes et manifestement prépondérants au regard de la conception suisse du droit ».

Or, et quel que soit par ailleurs le sort réservé en droit grec à un contrat ayant pour but la violation d'obligations fiscales à l'égard du fisc grec, il n'est pas évident que la sanction d'un contrat conclu pour frauder le fisc soit toujours, en droit suisse, la nullité civile. Il est sans doute significatif que le Commentaire bernois (E. A. Kramer, loc. cit., N. 137) ne cite qu'un exemple, au demeurant fort ancien (ATF 48 II 270), de nullité d'un contrat ayant pour but unique une soustraction d'impôt. À travers des critères qui lui sont propres, tels que les notions d'opération insolite, de prestation appréciable en argent, etc., le droit fiscal suisse a les moyens de rétablir à seules fins fiscales ce qui lui apparaît comme la réalité économique, sans porter atteinte à la structure juridique voulue par les parties, sans toucher à leurs obligations contractuelles.

Le Tribunal arbitral estime donc que même si le contrat du 20 décembre 1991 était contraire au droit fiscal grec, il ne pourrait pour cette seule raison être considéré comme nul au regard du droit suisse.

52. La défenderesse allègue également que le contrat avec [la partie demanderesse] *violerait le droit grec des sociétés du fait que la convention en cause aboutirait au « détournement de sommes destinées à une personne morale valablement constituée et qui a été ainsi dépouillée d'une partie de son patrimoine » (. . .). Elle ajoute qu'il y aurait là une violation « de l'ordre public international », qui imposerait la prise en considération du droit grec sur la base de l'article 19 LDIP.*

La défenderesse ne cite cependant aucune disposition de droit grec qui serait ainsi violée. Elle ne prouve en rien non plus que l'opération violerait « le principe que les animateurs ou organes d'une personne morale valablement constituée ne sont pas autorisés à disposer librement et à leur profit exclusif des biens faisant partie du patrimoine distinct de la personne morale ou devant lui échoir ». Il convient de rappeler, en effet, qu'aucune information précise n'a été apportée au Tribunal arbitral au sujet des rapports entre [la société X] *et* [la partie demanderesse], *de l'actionnariat de ces deux sociétés, de leur éventuelle appartenance à un même groupe, de l'existence possible de comptes de groupe, etc. toutes circonstances dont il peut parfaitement résulter qu'au niveau consolidé, le contrat de décembre 1991 n'ai rien changé.*

En l'absence de précisions tant sur ces points de fait que sur les normes du droit grec éventuellement méconnues, rien ne permet de soutenir que des « animateurs ou organes » de [la société X] *auraient disposé « à leur profit exclusif » de biens de cette société. Il n'est donc nullement prouvé que la société ait subi un dommage.*

Il apparaît en tout cas que la société [X] *a poursuivi normalement son activité et qu'elle est encore (ou était bien après juin 1993)* in bonis, *de sorte que l'on ne saurait prétendre que le contrat avec* [la partie demanderesse] *était passé en fraude des droits des créanciers de la société grecque. Il n'est du reste pas allégué que ses créanciers aient subi un quelconque préjudice.*

Dans la mesure où le détournement allégué par la partie défenderesse n'est pas prouvé à satisfaction de droit et où il n'est pas allégué qu'il ait eu une quelconque incidence sur la vie sociale de la société grecque et les intérêts de ses créanciers, rien ne permet de conclure, sur cette base, à l'illicéité du contrat.

53. Même si la nullité de principe du contrat devait être admise, son invocation par la défenderesse n'apparaîtrait pas conforme à la bonne foi en affaires.

En effet, elle admet avoir signé ce contrat en parfaite connaissance de cause et sans avoir jamais attendu de la demanderesse qu'elle rende les services qui y étaient spécifiés. Elle a ensuite payé, à huit reprises d'après les pièces produites, les commissions contractuellement prévues, en dernier lieu le 22 septembre 1993, soit après la fin du contrat avec la demanderesse. Ce faisant, elle a clairement manifesté à la demanderesse sa volonté de respecter le contrat qu'elle avait signé.

Ce n'est que face aux réclamations subséquentes de [la partie demanderesse], *et plus particulièrement dans le cadre du présent arbitrage, que la défenderesse a soulevé la nullité du contrat, pour éviter de payer le solde dû sur des commissions dont elle avait précédemment admis le bien-fondé puisqu'elle les avait payées conformément aux engagements pris. Ce faisant, elle adoptait une attitude contradictoire* (Venire contra factum proprium) *contraire à la bonne foi. En invoquant, pour se soustraire à des obligations librement acceptées, la violation du droit étranger à laquelle elle affirme avoir participé, la défenderesse méconnaît également le principe* Nemo auditur propriam turpitudinem allegans.

La jurisprudence du Tribunal fédéral montre qu'il peut y avoir abus de droit à invoquer une nullité absolue. S'agissant d'un contrat affecté d'un vice de forme, le Tribunal fédéral refuse de prendre en considération l'invalidité en résultant et tient « son invocation pour inadmissible lorsqu'elle viole les règles de la bonne foi et constitue un abus de droit manifeste au sens de l'article 2, alinéa 2 CC [Code civil suisse]. *Le juge décide si tel est le cas en tenant compte de toutes les circonstances du cas concret. Le Tribunal fédéral a ainsi jugé que la partie, qui a exécuté le contrat volontairement, sans erreur et au moins pour l'essentiel, viole les règles de la bonne foi lorsqu'elle refuse l'exécution en invoquant le vice de forme (ATF 116 II 700 c. 3b; 1212 II 330 c. 2, 107 c. 3c. 3c) » (TF 7 janvier 1999, SJ 2000 p. 534 s., 536). Il est vrai que le juge ne valide pas pour autant le contrat, mais accorde une prétention en exécution du solde fondée sur l'article 2 alinéa 2 CC (ATF 112 II 107 c. 3c), sur la responsabilité fondée sur la confiance (SJ 2000 précité), voire sur l'article 41 CO (question laissée ouverte par l'arrêt SJ 2000 précité).*

En l'espèce, on retiendra que s'agissant d'un cas où la nullité de principe du contrat est pour le moins douteuse, la défenderesse ne saurait l'invoquer, et que même si le Tribunal arbitral croyait devoir la constater d'office, la défenderesse ne saurait se fonder sur cette nullité pour refuser de payer le solde des commissions qu'elle s'est, librement et en toute connaissance de cause, engagée à payer.

54. En tout état, le Tribunal arbitral considère que la moralité en matière commerciale ne se trouverait pas satisfaite par la nullité du contrat.

La constatation de la nullité du contrat en cause dans le cadre du présent arbitrage aurait pour seule conséquence de permettre à la défenderesse de se dispenser de payer un solde de commissions relatives aux livraisons facturées par [la société Y] *jusqu'au 30 juin 1993. Or, il résulte sans ambiguïté des explications de la défenderesse et des témoins issus du groupe* [de la partie défenderesse] *qu'une commission totale de 4,85 % était due par le groupe* [de la partie défenderesse] *au groupe* [de la partie demanderesse], *que cette commission a été divisée entre* [la société X] *et* [la partie demanderesse] *pour la période du 1ᵉʳ janvier 1992 au 30 juin 1993, et qu'elle a été versée en totalité à la société grecque à compter du 30 juin 1993. Monsieur* [T] *a ainsi déclaré devant le Tribunal arbitral :*

« *Je précise que la commission de 4,85 % correspondait au marché et que pour nous elle a toujours été versée. En juin 1993, nous avons voulu en changer les modalités mais non le montant. À mon avis, la commission globale de 4,85 % devait être versée* [au groupe X] *avant comme après le 30 juin 1993 dans la mesure où les ventes avaient été effectuées et payées.* ».

Même si le montant exact des commissions impayées donne lieu à discussions entre les parties, la défenderesse reconnaît que plus de 400 millions de lires de commissions relatives à des factures établies avant le 30 juin 1993 n'ont été payées ni à [la partie demanderesse], *ni à* [la société X]. *Devant le Tribunal arbitral, le témoin* [N] *a déclaré :*

« *La décision a été prise par la société mère de ne pas effectuer ces paiements. La société* [Y] *nous a expressément dit qu'elle n'entendait plus payer ces commissions.* ».

Loin de sauvegarder les intérêts du fisc grec ou de [la société X], *la reconnaissance par le Tribunal arbitral de la nullité du contrat du 20 décembre 1991 ne profiterait qu'à la défenderesse, ou du moins au groupe auquel elle appartient.*

55. Le Tribunal arbitral s'est ainsi convaincu qu'une éventuelle violation du droit grec n'entraînerait pas nécessairement la nullité du contrat du 20 décembre 1991, et que la défenderesse n'est, en tout état, pas recevable à invoquer cette prétendue nullité pour se soustraire à son obligation de régler les commissions impayées. Aussi a-t-il décidé d'admettre la validité du contrat, et l'obligation en résultant pour la défenderesse de payer à la demanderesse les commissions non versées sur les factures [de la société Y] *antérieures au 1ᵉʳ juillet 1993.*

Le Tribunal arbitral a enfin réservé sa décision quant au quantum des commissions impayées pour la sentence finale (quatrième sentence arbitrale dans cette affaire).

NOTE. — I. — La problématique de la « *Sentence intérimaire sur la responsabilité* » rendue le 30 juillet 2001 nous invite d'abord à rendre explicite l'une des conclusions que le Tribunal arbitral à décidé de garder implicite dans la Sentence. Au début de sa motivation « en droit » transcrite ci-avant, le Tribunal arbitral écrit : « Le Tribunal arbitral observe tout d'abord que les parties au présent arbitrage ont fait élection de droit, dans le contrat lui-même *(art. 7),* en faveur du droit suisse, choisi pour régir « in every respect » le contrat et son interprétation. Cette élection de droit, parfaitement valable, n'est en aucun manière remise en cause par les parties et c'est donc selon le droit suisse que le Tribunal arbitral statuera ».

L'expression « parfaitement valable » suscite une interrogation. En l'espèce, la partie défenderesse arguait que le contrat était nul car il violait le droit fiscal grec et par la même les mœurs reconnues par le droit suisse. Se posait à notre avis donc la question de savoir si l'article 7 (comprenant le contrat d'*electio juris* des parties) du contrat relatif au droit applicable à celui-ci était également frappé de nullité. Le Tribunal arbitral répond implicitement à cette question sur la base de deux fondements.

D'une part, il semblerait que le Tribunal arbitral soutient que le contrat d'*electio juris* doit être considéré comme étant juridiquement autonome ou séparable du contrat principal — en l'espèce le contrat — qui le comprend. Autrement, il serait impossible d'expliquer, en bonne logique, comment le Tribunal arbitral, avant même d'examiner la validité de ce contrat principal — en l'espèce le contrat -, est arrivé à la conclusion que la clause de droit applicable incorporée dans celui-ci est « parfaitement valable ». Il est intéressant à cet égard de noter que l'autonomie ou séparabilité du contrat d'*electio juris* n'est pas aussi souvent mentionnée que la très célèbre autonomie ou séparabilité de la convention d'arbitrage *(cf. P. Mayer, Les limites de la séparabilité de la clause compromissoire: Rev. arb. 1998, n° 2, p. 359 à 368. — C. Duquenne, L'autonomie de la clause compromissoire en droit du commerce international, Thèse Université McGill (Montréal), Institute of Comparative Law, 2000. — J.-C. Dubarry et E. Loquin, Les parties peuvent-elle écarter l'application des règles matérielles françaises de validité de la clause compromissoire internationale en soumettant expressément la clause à une loi étatique étrangère?: RTD com. 2003, n°3, p. 443 et 445. — C. Blanchin et H. Gaudemet-Tallon, L'autonomie de la clause compromissoire: un modèle pour la clause attributive de juridiction?: LGDJ 1995 — cf. les commentaires de Y. Derains à la sentence arbitrale CCI n° 1507 de 1970: JDI 1974, n° 4, p. 913 à 921. — F. Klein, Du caractère autonome de la clause compromissoire en matière d'arbitrage international: Rev. crit. DIP 1961, vol. 50 p. 449 à 552).* Pourrait-on en fin de comptes affirmer que la « jurisprudence arbitrale de la CCI » au sens établi par Yves Derains *(cf. Y. Derains, L'obligation de minimiser le dommage dans la jurisprudence arbitrale: RD aff. int. 1987, n° 4, p. 375 à 382, spéc. p. 376; Les tendances de la jurisprudence arbitrale internationale:JDI 1993, n° 4, p. 829 à 855, spéc. p. 829 à 831)* a bien posé le principe de la autonomie ou séparabilité du contrat d'*electio juris*?

La difficulté de donner une réponse tranchée à la question ci-avant a, à notre avis, invité le Tribunal arbitral à ajouter, d'autre part, que le contrat d'*electio juris* est « parfaitement valable » étant donné qu'aucune des parties ne l'a mis expressément en cause lors de l'arbitrage. La Sentence, néanmoins, n'offre aucun développement sur la possible contestation indirecte, voire implicite — par le biais de la mise en cause de la validité du Contrat — de la validité du contrat d'*electio juris*.

En définitive, nous ne pouvons qu'approuver le pragmatisme *(cf. L. Menand, Pragmatism: Vintage Books 1997)* adopté par le Tribunal arbitral pour affirmer l'applicabilité du droit suisse aux problèmes de la simulation et de la validité du contrat. Si l'applicabilité du droit suisse n'avait pas été retenue, le Tribunal arbitral aurait probablement dû faire application du droit grec (droit du lieu d'exécution de la prestation caractéristique) et sa décision quant à la simulation et la validité du contrat aurait pu être très différente.

II. — Quant au problème de la simulation, il est intéressant de souligner que le cas d'espèce nous donne un exemple parfait, voire un cas d'école, de celle-ci: deux parties acceptent de simuler un contrat pour que l'une d'entre elles puisse ainsi éviter le paiement de certains impôts *(cf. D. Veaux, Recevabilité des différents procédés de preuve: J. -Cl. Civil Code, Fasc. 30, § 41 et s. — cf. par ex. Cass. 3ᵉ civ., 25 févr. 2004: Bull. civ. 2004, III, n° 42, p. 39; RTD civ. 2004, n° 2, p. 279 et 280, note J. Mestre et B. Fages).*

L'analyse des faits relatifs au problème de la simulation transcrite ci-avant est faite par le Tribunal arbitral à l'abri de l'article 18, alinéa 1, dudit code, c'est-à-dire de la règle générale, voire le principe, d'interprétation des contrats en droit suisse. L'article 18, alinéa 1, du Code suisse des obligations prévoit: « *Pour apprécier les formes et les clauses d'un contrat, il y a lieu de rechercher la réelle et commune intention des parties, sans s'arrêter aux expressions ou dénominations inexactes dont elles ont pu se servir, soit par erreur, soit pour déguiser la nature véritable de la convention* » (nous soulignons). Il va sans dire que, en l'espèce, le Tribunal arbitral, sur la base notamment de la preuve par témoins entendue dans l'arbitrage — ce qui démontre l'importance capitale des audiences dans l'arbitrage commercial international *(P. Griffin, Recent Trends in the Conduct of International Arbitration — Discovery Procedures and Witness Hearings: Journal of*

International Arbitration, 2000, vol. 17, n° 2, p. 19 à 30. — M. Roth, False Testimony at International Arbitration Hearings Conducted in England and Switzerland — A Comparative View: Journal of International Arbitration, 1994, vol. 1, n° 1, p. 5 à 42), arrive clairement et logiquement à la conclusion que le contrat « est effectivement simulé, dans la mesure où il attribue à l'engagement de la défenderesse de payer une commission à la demanderesse une cause qui ne correspond pas à la volonté réelle des parties. La véritable cause juridique de cet engagement réside dans les services rendus en Grèce par la [société X] à [la société Y] et dont il était admis entre les parties que la rémunération normale état une commission de 4,85 %, correspondant, d'après le témoin [T], aux conditions du marché ».

Il est aussi intéressant de remarquer la référence du Tribunal arbitral à la « cause juridique » de l'obligation de payer la commission *(cf. Ch. Larroumet, Droit civil, Les obligations, Le contrat: Économica, 5ᵉ éd., 2003, n° 449 et s. — H., L. et J. Mazeaud, Leçons de droit civil, t. II, 1ᵉʳ vol., Obligations: Montchrestien, 1998, 9ᵉ éd., par F. Chabas, n° 256 et 258. — F. Terré, Ph. Simler et Y. Lequette, Les obligations: Dalloz, 2003, 9ᵉ éd., n° 331 et s. — Ph. Simler, Cause: J.-CL Civil Code, art. 1131 à 1133, Fasc. 10).* C'est dans son analyse implicite de la cause juridique du contrat que le Tribunal arbitral tranche ensuite le point litigieux (le Code civil du Québec explique, dans son article 1410, que « *La cause du contrat est la raison qui détermine chacune des parties à le conclure. Il n'est pas nécessaire qu'elle soit exprimée » [cf. en France Ch. Larroumet, op. cit., n° 482 et s. — F. Terré, Ph. Simler et Y. Lequette, op. cit., n° 351 et s. — J. Rochfeld, Cause et type de contrat: LGDJ 1999. — J. Binet, De la fausse cause: RTD civ. 2004, p. 655 à 672. — Cass. 3ᵉ civ., 4 mai 2000, n° 98-19.806: Juris-Data n° 2000-001851; Bull. civ. 2000, III, n° 95, p. 64. — T. com. Paris, ch. 18, 19 mai 1993: Juris-Data n° 1993-042145. — Cass. soc., 21 mars 1990, n° 87-44.173]).*

Nous croyons enfin que la conclusion du Tribunal arbitral sur la simulation pose automatiquement un problème relatif à la compétence *rationae personae* du Tribunal arbitral que les parties n'auraient pas débattu après l'établissement de l'acte de mission, et le Tribunal arbitral n'aurait par conséquent pas examiné. En effet, la constatation de la simulation suppose que les « véritables » parties à l'opération « réelle » étaient la société X et la société Y. À notre connaissance, toutefois, la société X et la société Y n'ont pas souscrit le contrat comprenant la clause compromissoire donnant une base juridique à l'arbitrage, et aucune des parties n'a avancé d'arguments visant à étendre les effets de ladite clause à la société X et à la société Y. Deux observations critiques s'imposent.

D'un côté, le silence de la Sentence sur cette question et le compréhensible pragmatisme y afférant du Tribunal arbitral nous semblent tout à fait justifiés. Néanmoins, à la lecture de l'acte de mission établi dans cette affaire, se pose en tous les cas la question de savoir si le Tribunal arbitral était véritablement compétent pour trancher le litige « réel » opposant la société X à la société Y. D'autant plus que, dans le résumé de la position de la partie défenderesse incorporé dans l'acte de mission, il est précisé qu'elle soutenait à ce stade de la procédure que « les parties à la convention dissimulée ne sont pas les parties à l'arbitrage ».

De l'autre, force est de constater que la simulation révèle l'une des limites à la séparabilité de la clause compromissoire *(cf. P. Mayer, Les limites de la séparabilité de la clause compromissoire: Rev. arb. 1998, p. 359 à 368).*

III. — Les passages de la Sentence consacrés à l'analyse de la validité du contrat sont sans nul doute ceux qui revêtent le plus grand intérêt juridique. Le Tribunal arbitral y répond aux deux arguments principaux soulevés par la partie défenderesse.

La partie défenderesse soutenait d'abord que le contrat simulé opérait une fraude au droit fiscal grec et était donc contraire aux mœurs reconnues par l'article 20, alinéa 1, du Code suisse des obligations. Ledit article dispose: « *Le contrat est nul s'il a pour objet une chose impossible, illicite ou contraire aux mœurs* ».

Le Tribunal arbitral, après avoir noté, de façon pragmatique, que « cause » et « objet » sont — malgré l'histoire de la philosophie (métaphysique et logique) — mystérieusement assimilées par la jurisprudence suisse et que l'intention frauduleuse des parties n'a pas été prouvée par la partie défenderesse, adopte successivement deux points de vues différents pour rejeter le premier argument avancé par celle-ci.

D'une part, le Tribunal se place sur le plan de la société marchande internationale — milieu exigeant et impitoyable — et se limite à constater une réalité sans la qualifier moralement:

« Certes, la vie des affaires montre que le versement à une société [off shore] d'une rémunération correspondant à des services rendus par une société ayant son siège dans un pays à fiscalité élevée peut être un moyen d'éviter le paiement des impôts normalement dus dans ce pays. Mais l'utilisation de telles structures est trop répandue, et parfois pour de bonnes raisons commerciales, pour que l'on puisse *a priori* et sans aucune preuve admettre une intention frauduleuse de la part des parties ».

Le Tribunal arbitral a néanmoins considéré que sa référence à une « vie normale des affaires » n'était pas suffisante pour rejeter le premier argument de la partie défenderesse. La « normalité des affaires » n'est pas nécessairement morale, c'est-à-dire en accord avec les mœurs désignées par l'article 20, alinéa 1, du Code suisse des obligations. C'est la raison pour laquelle le Tribunal arbitral décide, d'autre part, d'assumer qu'une fraude au droit fiscal grec s'est produite et d'entreprendre une analyse du premier argument de la partie défenderesse sur la base du droit suisse des obligations et des contrats. Selon cette optique, le Tribunal arbitral conclut que le Contrat devrait être déclaré contraire aux mœurs reconnues par l'article 20, alinéa 1, du Code suisse des obligations « *s'il viole une norme étrangère dont la violation serait sanctionnée par la nullité si une telle norme était édictée par le législateur suisse ou résultait de la conception suisse des bonnes mœurs* ». Ce critère est dans la logique qui inspire l'article 19 LDIP, aux termes duquel la prise en considération d'une norme impérative de droit étranger non directement applicable suppose que cette norme met en cause « *des intérêts légitimes et manifestement prépondérants au regard de la conception suisse du droit* ».

L'article 19 de la loi suisse sur le droit international privé dispose:

> « *1 Lorsque des intérêts légitimes et manifestement prépondérants au regard de la conception suisse du droit l'exigent, une disposition impérative d'un droit autre que celui désigné par la présente loi peut être prise en considération, si la situation visée présente un lien étroit avec ce droit.*
> *2 Pour juger si une telle disposition doit être prise en considération, on tiendra compte du but qu'elle vise et des conséquences qu'aurait son application pour arriver à une décision adéquate au regard de la conception suisse du droit* ».

Il en résulte que, selon le Tribunal arbitral, un tribunal arbitral siégeant en suisse et appliquant le droit suisse doit adopter la conception suisse des bonnes mœurs même si leur prétendue violation a été portée dans un autre État. En Suisse, la violation du droit fiscal ne constitue automatiquement ni une violation des mœurs ni la nullité civile. En l'espèce, le Tribunal arbitral ne s'est donc pas intéressé à examiner les faits portés à son attention sur la base de la conception grecque des bonnes mœurs. Aurait-il dû adopter une conception réellement internationale des bonnes mœurs ? Le Tribunal arbitral nous répond implicitement que la méthode utilisée par les parties dans le contrat est courante dans la « vie des affaires ».

Par ailleurs, la partie défenderesse alléguait que le contrat violait « (. . .) le droit grec des sociétés du fait que la convention en cause aboutirait au "détournement de sommes destinées à une personne morale valablement constituée et qui a ainsi été dépouillée d'une parie de son patrimoine" (. . .) Elle [ajoutait] qu'il y aurait là une violation "de l'ordre public international'', qui imposerait la prise en considération du droit grec sur la base de l'article 19 LDIP ».

À cet égard, le lecteur de la Sentence reste sur sa faim car le Tribunal arbitral se limite à constater que la prétendue violation du droit grec des sociétés n'a pas été prouvée.

IV. — Le Tribunal arbitral ne se contente pas d'examiner et de rejeter les deux arguments soulevés par la partie défenderesse. Il se place à la fin de la sentence sur le terrain de la *lex mercatoria* telle que reconnue et établie par la « jurisprudence arbitrale de la CCI » *(cf. E. Jolivet, La jurisprudence arbitrale de la CCI et la lex mercatoria: Cah. arb. 2002, p. 253 à 260)* et ajoute que, « même si la nullité de principe du contrat devait être admise, son invocation par la défenderesse n'apparaîtrait pas conforme à la bonne foi en affaires ».

Il est très intéressant de noter que le Tribunal arbitral considère que les maximes « *venire contra factum proprium* » et « *nemo auditur propriam turpitu-dinem allegans* » découlent du principe de la bonne foi qui gouverne les relations commerciales *(cf. E. Gaillard, L'interdiction de se contredire au détriment d'autrui comme principe général du droit du commerce international: Rev. arb. 1985, p. 241 et s. — Sentence rendue dans l'affaire CCI n° 6294 en 1991: JDI 1991, p. 1052. — Sentence du 19 août 1988 dans l'affaire CCI n° 5622: Rev. arb. 1993, p. 327 à 342. — Sentence finale dans l'affaire CCI n° 9333 de 1998: Bull. ASA 2001, vol. 19, n° 4, p. 757 à 780. — Partial Award on Jurisdiction and Admissibility in ICC case n° 6474 of 1992: Yearbook of Commercial Arbitration, 2000, vol. XXV, p. 432. — Interim Award of June 2002, ICC Arbitration n° 10947: Bull. ASA 2004, vol. 22, n° 2, p. 308 à 332).*

Nous ne pouvons qu'approuver la conclusion du Tribunal arbitral à cet égard. Il est incontestable en l'espèce que la partie défenderesse connaissait parfaitement la finalité réelle du contrat et qu'elle a, malgré cette parfaite connaissance, conclu celui-ci en toute liberté. Il ne serait pas juste que cette même partie puisse, d'une manière opportuniste et à l'occasion d'un litige, soulever la contrariété aux mœurs et la nullité d'un contrat auquel elle a librement consenti. C'est par ailleurs dans ce sens que nous avons soutenu que la règle de l'article 177 (2) de la loi suisse sur le droit international privé a des limites *(cf. E. Silva Romero, Requiem for the Rule of Article 177(2) of the Swiss Private International Law Act? in Global Reflections on International Law, Commerce and Dispute Resolution: Liber Amicorum in honour of Robert Briner, ICC Publishing, 2005, p. 825 et s.).*

Enfin, cette dernière partie de la motivation du Tribunal arbitral nous rappelle la célèbre sentence dans l'affaire CCI n° 1110 dans laquelle l'arbitre unique a décliné sa compétence après avoir constaté que le contrat à l'origine du litige avait pour objet des pots-de-vin, en s'appuyant pour ce faire sur la violation manifeste des bonnes mœurs et de l'ordre public international et ajoutant que, par conséquent et en application du principe « *nemo auditur propriam turpitu-dinem allegans* », aucune des deux parties n'avait le droit de faire valoir leurs obligations contractuelles *(Award of 1963 in ICC Case n° 1110: Arbitration International 1994, vol. 10, n° 3, p. 282 à 294).*

Nous pourrions commenter en conclusion et encore une fois le pragmatisme du Tribunal arbitral. Nous préférons souligner que la grande vertu de cette sentence arbitrale — remarquablement claire et convaincante — est que son lecteur reste persuadé qu'elle devrait être exécutée spontanément par les parties.

E. S. R.

Sentence finale rendue dans l'affaire n° 11277 en 2003 (original en langue française)

Droit applicable. — Convention de Genève relative au transport international de marchandises par route du 19 mai 1956 (CMR). — Application. — Convention de Rome du 19 juin 1980 sur la loi applicable aux obligations contractuelles. — Article 4 (4).

Prescription extinctive. Délai. — Point de départ.

La sentence se prononce de façon classique sur la détermination du droit applicable par le tribunal arbitral conformément à l'article 17 du Règlement d'arbitrage de la CCI. S'agissant d'un contrat de transport international de marchandises par route, la CMR s'applique directement sans que le tribubal arbitral ait besoin de se référer aux mécanismes des conflits de lois. L'application de la CMR n'exclut pas pour autant l'application des dispositions du droit interne résultant de l'article 4(4) de la Convention de Rome de 1980. Le droit interne s'applique à titre supplétif en cas de silence de la CMR.

Le tribunal arbitral a rejeté la demande de prescription des demandes principales sur la base de l'article 32 de la CMR. Le tribunal rappelle le champ d'application de cet article qui vise les actions en justice liées de manière générale aux transports plutôt qu'aux contrats de transport. Le tribunal arbitral a pu ainsi retenir librement la date de la lettre de voiture qui matérialise le contrat de transport plutôt que la date de livraison des marchandises ou encore celle du contrat-cadre.

En date du 5 août 1998, une société française X (le « demandeur ») avait signé avec une société italienne Y (le « défendeur ») un contrat pour le transport de wagons de métro de l'Italie vers la Grèce (le « contrat »). Une partie du transport avait été sous-traitée à une société française Z (non partie à l'arbitrage) par le défendeur sur proposition du demandeur. Les wagons étaient ainsi chargés depuis l'Italie par la société Z pour être transportés jusqu'en Grèce. Après le dernier transport des wagons, le défendeur avait refusé de libérer les remorques en exigeant d'être payé d'abord par le demandeur.

La société Z ayant pris des mesures judiciaires contre le demandeur pour la non-restitution de ses matériels, ce dernier décida d'introduire une requête d'arbitrage contre le défendeur devant la Cour internationale d'arbitrage de la CCI aux fins d'obtenir, entre autres, le paiement de dommages-intérêts et le remboursement des sommes qu'il avait dû verser à la société Z.

Après avoir rendu une sentence partielle sur la compétence, l'arbitre unique, siégeant à La Haye, devait se prononcer sur le fond. Il devait se déterminer préalablement sur la question du droit applicable et ensuite sur la prescription des demandes principales.

Sur la question du droit applicable, l'arbitre avait déclaré applicable la Convention de Genève relative au transport international de marchandises par route du 19 mai 1956 (la « CMR ») et le droit italien en vertu de la Convention de Rome du 19 juin 1980 sur la loi applicable aux obligations contractuelles (la « Convention de Rome de 1980 ») dans les termes suivants:

> « *LE DROIT APPLICABLE*
> *Le contrat ne contient pas de choix du droit applicable.*
> *Le contrat concerne un transport de voitures de métro, chargées sur remorques, de [lieu 1], Italie, à [lieu 2], Grèce, donc un transport international par route. Les conditions de la Convention de Genève relative au contrat de transport international de marchandises par route du 19 mai 1956 (entrée en vigueur le 2*

juillet 1961, la « CMR ») sont applicables. Le fait que pour une partie du parcours les remorques avec les voitures ont été chargées sur un navire n'empêche pas l'application de la CMR. En effet, l'article 2.1 de la CMR dispose:

« Si le véhicule contenant les marchandises est transporté par mer, chemin de fer, voie navigable intérieure ou air sur une partie du parcours, sans rupture de charge sauf, éventuellement, pour l'application des dispositions de l'article 14, la présente Convention s'applique, pour l'ensemble du transport (. . .) ».

Les parties s'accordent sur ce point.

L'application des conditions CMR se limite au transport de marchandises. Au reste s'applique le droit italien, en vertu de la Convention de Rome du 19 juin 1980 sur la loi applicable aux obligations contractuelles (entrée en vigueur le 1ᵉʳ avril 1991). L'article 4 dispose:

Loi applicable à défaut de choix

« 1. Dans la mesure où la loi applicable au contrat n'a pas été choisie conformément aux dispositions de l'article 3, le contrat est régi par la loi du pays avec lequel il présente les liens les plus étroits (. . .)

2. Sous réserve du paragraphe 5, il est présumé que le contrat présente les liens les plus étroits avec le pays où la partie qui doit fournir la prestation caractéristique a, au moment de la conclusion du contrat, sa résidence habituelle ou, s'il s'agit d'une société, association ou personne morale, son administration centrale (. . .)

3. (. . .)

4. Le contrat de transport de marchandises n'est pas soumis à la présomption du paragraphe 2. Dans ce contrat, si le pays dans lequel le transporteur a son établissement principal au moment de la conclusion du contrat est aussi celui dans lequel est situé le lieu de chargement ou de déchargement ou l'établissement principal de l'expéditeur, il est présumé que le contrat a les liens les plus étroits avec ce pays (. . .) »

L'élément central des prestations devant être fournies par les parties se trouvait chez Y à [lieu 1], en Italie. Son établissement principal au moment de la conclusion du contrat et le lieu de chargement se trouvaient en Italie. Donc le droit italien est applicable au reste en vertu de la Convention de Rome.

Les parties s'accordent sur ce point. (. . .) ».

S'agissant de la prescription des demandes principales soulevée par le défendeur en vertu de l'article 32 de la CMR, l'arbitre avait rejeté la prétention aux motifs suivants:

« PRESCRIPTION

Se référant à l'article 32 de la CMR, Y allègue qu'il y a prescription quant aux réclamations de X.

Le paragraphe 1 de cet article dispose:

« Les actions auxquelles peuvent donner lieu les transports soumis à la présente Convention sont prescrites dans le délai d'un an. Toutefois, dans le cas de dol ou de faute considérée, d'après la loi de la juridiction saisie, comme équivalente au dol, la prescription est de trois ans. La prescription court:

Dans le cas de perte partielle, (. . .)

Dans le cas de perte totale, (. . .)

Dans tous les autres cas, à partir de l'expiration d'un délai de trois mois à dater de la conclusion du contrat de transport.

Le jour indiqué ci-dessus comme point de départ de la prescription n'est pas compris dans le délai. »

(Note de l'arbitre: les points a. et b. ne s'appliquent pas à ce cas, parce que les réclamations de X ne portent pas sur une perte mais sur le refus de Y de libérer les remorques.)

Pour juger de la prescription alléguée par Y, il faut d'abord que soit établi quel jour le délai de prescription a débuté, et ensuite, siXa saisi l'arbitrage de ses réclamations à l'intérieur de ce délai.

Y a négligé d'indiquer quel jour, à son avis, commençait le délai de prescription. Elle a seulement allégué — non pas dans l'arbitrage mais dans les conclusions déposées par elle au Tribunal de commerce de Nanterre auxquelles elle s'est référée dans sa lettre du 6 février 2001 à la CCI ci-dessus mentionnée — « que la prise en charge à [lieu 1] a eu lieu le 30 janvier 1999 ». Ce faisant, elle considérait évidemment le début du transport de voitures de métro comme point de départ du délai de prescription.

Y ne renvoie pas à la date du contrat conclu le 5 août 1998. En effet ce contrat n 'est que le contrat cadre. Au cours de l'exécution de ce contrat cadre, des transports ont été conclus pour les envois individuels, confirmés chaque fois par une lettre de voiture. L'article 4 de la CMR dit « Le contrat de transport est constaté par une lettre de voiture ». L'arbitre est d'avis que la date de la lettre de voiture d'un envoi sert de date visée par l'article 32, par. 1, sous c. et que le délai de prescription d'un an débute à partir de l'expiration de trois mois.

Serait-il autrement, et si h date du contrat cadre était la date pertinente, la prescription aurait débuté avant le transport du dernier envoi de wagons. Comme il apparaît dans la pièce 62 annexée aux conclusions ci-dessus mentionnées, il y a eu encore en novembre 1999 des wagons transportés de [lieu 1] à [lieu 2] (départ de [lieu 1] le 28 novembre 1999 d'après la pièce 62). Une telle interprétation de l'article 32, par. 1, sous c. conduirait donc à un résultat absurde.

L'arbitre n'a pas pu établir si la pièce 62 concerne le dernier envoi. Il se peut qu'il y ait eu des envois suivants. Le point à retenir est qu'il y a eu un envoi en novembre 1999. L'arbitrage a été initié par X oar une lettre du 8 novembre 2000 à k CCI, reçue par la CCI le 10 novembre 2000, par conséquent dans le délai d'un an à partir de l'expiration d'un délai de trois mois à dater de la conclusion du contrat de transport pour l'envoi de novembre 1999.

L'arbitre rejette le recours en prescription,

(. . .)

Y n'a pas allégué qu'il y avait prescription des réclamations de X en vertu du droit italien; en alléguant la prescription en vertu de la CMR mais pas une éventuelle prescription en vertu du droit italien, elle a perdu le droit au recours en prescription en vertu du droit italien. ».

NOTE. — I. — Conformément à l'article 17 (1) du Règlement d'arbitrage de la CCI, à défaut de choix par les parties des règles de droit applicables, l'arbitre appliquera les règles de droit qu'il juge appropriées. La référence aux règles de droit appropriées est importante car elle permet au tribunal d'exposer seulement les principes qui l'ont conduit à considérer justifiée l'application d'une loi plutôt qu'une autre, sans avoir besoin de se référer à un système de conflit de lois préexistant.

En l'espèce, l'arbitre a déclaré applicable la CMR sur la base des éléments définis à l'article 1 de la CMR:

C'est un contrat de transport de marchandises effectué sur route sur des remorques;

C'est un transport à caractère international car les marchandises étaient prises en charge en Italie pour être livrées en Grèce. Le critère du franchissement géographique défini par l'article 1 (1) de la CMR était donc rempli;

L'Italie et la Grèce ont par ailleurs ratifié la CMR, respectivement le 3 avril 1961 et le 24 mai 1977.

En d'autres termes, la CMR s'applique de plein droit car le transport routier est effectué entre deux lieux situés dans deux pays différents dont l'un au moins a ratifié la convention. En tant que convention portant loi uniforme, elle prime sur les dispositions des droits nationaux, et le juge tout comme l'arbitre est tenu de l'appliquer d'office sans que les parties puissent y déroger directement ou indirectement (article 41 de la CMR: « *1. Sous réserve des dispositions de l'art. 40, est nulle de nul effet toute stipulation, qui directement ou indirectement, dérogerait aux dispositions de la présente Convention. La nullité de telles stipulations n'entraîne pas la nullité des autres dispositions du contrat* ») *(V. généralement, L. Peyrefitte, Transports terrestres internationaux — Transports internationaux par route:J.-Cl. Droit international, Fase. 565-B-20, § 40 et s.; Diet. perm. Droit des affaires, Transports terrestres, 2 mai 2005, n°3101 et s. — V. également F.-J. Sanchez-Gamborino, La CMR en tant que loi applicable au transport national in Études offertes à Barthélemy Mercadal: éd. Francis Lefebvre 2002, p. 513. — V. également, Ph. Delebecque, Le nouveau droit international des transports in Mélanges Jacques Béguin: Litec, 2005, p. 261. — M. A. Clarke, International Carriage of Goods by Road: CMR, LLP, 4th edition, 2003).* Il s'ensuit que les contrats de transports internationaux de marchandises par route échappent généralement aux mécanismes des conflits de lois. C'est seulement au cas où les questions posées ne seraient pas réglées par la CMR qu'il convient de déterminer la loi applicable au contrat susceptible de s'appliquer. Le recours à la Convention de Rome est classique et la démarche de l'arbitre doit être approuvée. Elle s'inscrit dans la logique de l'article 4 (4) de la Convention de Rome qui précise que le contrat de transport de marchandises est présumé avoir les liens les plus étroits avec le pays dans lequel le transporteur a son établissement principal et où est situé le lieu de chargement ou de déchargement. On peut en déduire que l'application de la CMR n'exclut pas l'application d'une règle matérielle interne pas plus que celle-ci n'exclut l'application de la CMR. La CMR prime sur le droit national dès lors que la question posée entre dans son champ d'application. À défaut, ce sont les dispositions du droit interne qui s'appliquent. Le rôle supplétif du droit interne s'explique par le fait que la CMR n'a pas prévu le(s) cas où elle présenterait des lacunes. Cette position est différente de cille adoptée par d'autres conventions internationales portant loi uniforme, telle que la Convention de Vienne du 11 avril 1980 sur la vente internationale de marchandises (« CVIM »). L'article 7 (2) de la CVIM indique en effet que les questions qui « *ne sont pas expressément tranchées par elle seront réglées selon les principes généraux dont elle s'inspire ou, à défaut de ces principes, conformément à la loi applicable en vertu des règles du droit international privé* » *(V. notamment H. Slim, Transports internationaux: les lacunes de la CMR et les exigences de la justice matérielle. À propos de l'arrêt Société Transports Collomb Muret Auto SA vs Société Panini France SA, Cass. com., 24 mars 2004, n° 02-16.573: Rev. Lamy Dr. civ. 2005, n°13, p. 15 et n° 14, p. 13).*

II. — Le défendeur avait allégué que les demandes principales étaient prescrites en application de l'article 32 de la CMR sans indiquer la date de départ du délai de prescription. La détermination du point de départ revenait ainsi à l'arbitre en considération de la formulation de l'article 32 de la CMR qui est très large. Elle vise en effet « les transports » et non pas « les contrats de transport ». De ce fait, la prescription de l'article 32 de la CMR s'applique à toutes les actions en justice liées d'une manière quelconque au transport international de marchandises par route régi par la CMR *(V. L. Peyrefitte, op. cit., § 118)*. L'arbitre a finalement décidé de retenir la date de la lettre de voiture qui matérialise le contrat de transport (articles 4 et 32 (1) (c) de la CMR). Il n'a pas retenu la date de livraison des marchandises ou encore celle du contrat conclu en août 1998. S'agissant d'un contrat cadre, il implique la conclusion de contrats d'application, à savoir les contrats de transports conclus pour chaque envoi des marchandises. À supposer applicable la date du contrat cadre, elle aurait conduit à un résultat absurde en application du délai d'un an de l'article 32 de la CMR: la demande principale aurait été déjà prescrite alors même que le contrat était en cours d'exécution *(sur la notion de contrat cadre, V. notamment S. Andrieu, Le contrat cadre en droit international privé, DEA de droit international privé, Université Panthéon-Assas Paris II, 2002-2003).*

L'arbitre a conclu en indiquant que le défendeur avait perdu le droit d'invoquer une éventuelle prescription des demandes principales en vertu du droit italien du fait qu'il avait invoqué seulement les dispositions de la CMR. L'arbitre donne le sentiment d'être dispensé d'examiner la question de la prescription en droit italien parce qu'elle n'avait pas été invoquée par le défendeur. Cette impression est inexacte. En effet, à supposer même que le défendeur avait soulevé ce moyen, l'arbitre n'aurait pas eu besoin de se référer au droit italien puisque la question de la prescription était couverte par la CMR. Comme indiqué précédemment, en raison du caractère impératif de la CMR, ses dispositions priment d'office sur celles du droit applicable qui n'a qu'un rôle supplétif. C'est seulement aux cas où la CMR est « muette » sur la question posée que l'arbitre doit alors consulter le droit applicable au fond. Les deux corps de règles coexistent, ce qui explique la démarche adoptée par l'arbitre lorsqu'il s'était prononcé sur la détermination du droit applicable. Il avait d'abord admis l'application de la CMR et le droit italien ensuite *(V. en ce sens l'arrêt Transports Collomb Muret auto, préc., comm, H. Slim, op. cit. — Ph. Delebecque, La loi applicable à l'action en paiement direct du transporteur routier de marchandises: lex contractus ou CMR?: JCP G 2004, II, 10078).* Dans cet arrêt, la Cour de cassation française a distingué la question de l'action directe en paiement des prestations du transporteur contre le destinataire de son régime. Si la question de l'action directe doit être réglée conformément au droit français du fait du silence de la CMR à ce sujet, le problème de la prescription de cette action relève de la CMR conformément à l'article 32. Ce n'est que dans son silence qu'il est possible de se reporter au droit applicable.

S. J.
C. T.-N.

Sentence finale rendue dans l'affaire n° 12045 en 2003 (original en langue française).

Droit applicable. — Choix des parties. — Dispositions du contrat. — Directive n° 86/653/CEE du 18 décembre 1986 concernant les agents commerciaux indépendants. — Remise en cause. — Loi belge du 13 avril 1995 sur l'agence commerciale.

Contrat d'agence commerciale. — Résiliation unilatérale avec effet immédiat. — Manquements contractuels graves. — Représentation de produits concurrents. — Obligation de loyauté et de bonne foi. — Principe général du droit commercial international.

La sentence rappelle le principe de l'autonomie de la volonté des parties dans le choix du droit applicable au fond. À l'argument que le choix de la directive européenne n° 86/653/CEE du 18 décembre 1986 sur l'agence commerciale n'implique pas une élection du droit applicable, le tribunal arbitral répond qu'il est lié par la volonté claire et expresse des parties en l'absence de toute fraude à la loi ou contrariété à l'ordre public international. La loi belge du 13 avril 1995 sur l'agence commerciale n'est pas applicable en l'espèce.

La sentence rappelle également le caractère a minima de la directive de 1986 qui vise seulement certains aspects de la relation d'agence. S'agissant des clauses de non-QJ;concurrence, l'article 20 de la directive de 1986 couvre la question seulement dans le cadre d'une violation post-contractuelle. Cet article ne vise pas les cas où la violation de la clause de non-concurrence a lieu en cours d'exécution du contrat. Dans une telle hypothèse, il incombe au tribunal arbitral de caractériser les faits susceptibles de justifier une résiliation unilatérale avec effet immédiat en tenant compte du principe de bonne foi et de loyauté dans l'exécution du contrat en tant que principe général du droit.

L'arbitre unique siégeant à Paris était appelé à se prononcer sur la validité de la résiliation unilatérale d'un contrat d'agence commerciale conclu en décembre 1995 entre une société demanderesse X (Belgique) (ci-dénommée « l'agent » ou le demandeur) et une société défenderesse Y (Espagne) (ci-dénommée le « commettant » ou le défendeur). Aux termes du contrat qui était conclu pour un an renouvelable par tacite reconduction, l'agent devait promouvoir les ventes au Bénélux des vêtements de prêt-à-porter féminins produits par le commettant.

Le contrat avait été résilié en juillet 1999 par le défendeur avec effet immédiat pour manquement grave de l'agent. Celui-ci avait violé l'article 4 du contrat qui lui interdisait, sauf autorisation préalable écrite du commettant, de représenter, fabriquer ou distribuer directement ou à travers des tiers, des produits qui seraient concurrents à ceux du commettant pendant la durée du contrat.

L'agent avait contesté la validité de la résiliation pour les motifs indiqués devant la Cour internationale d'arbitrage de la CCI aux fins d'obtenir la réparation du préjudice subi. Il avait invoqué à cet effet l'application du droit belge ayant considéré que le fait pour les parties d'avoir stipulé l'application de la directive européenne n° 86/653/CEE du 18 décembre 1986 sur l'agence commerciale (la « directive de 1986 ») n'impliquait nullement une élection du droit applicable.

Le défendeur avait refusé l'application du droit belge au fond en s'appuyant sur l'article 21 du contrat qui excluait l'application des lois nationales au profit des dispositions du contrat et la directive de 1986:

« *Tout désaccord dérivé ou en relation avec le présent contrat, sera tranché définitivement, conformément aux dispositions de conciliation et d'arbitrage de la CCI par un ou plusieurs arbitres nommés, conformément aux dites dispositions.*

Les arbitres appliqueront les dispositions obligatoires contenues dans la directive CEE 86/653 du 18/12/86. ».

Conformément aux dispositions de l'acte de mission signé par les parties, l'arbitre devait se prononcer sur les règles de droit applicable et sur le manquement contractuel grave allégué par le mandant à l'encontre de son agent.

S'agissant de la question du droit applicable, l'arbitre avait fait prévaloir la volonté claire des parties pour appliquer les dispositions du contrat et, à défaut celles de la directive de 1986. L'arbitre avait rejeté l'application de loi belge, sollicité par le demandeur, dans les termes suivants:

« *47. Les parties, aux termes de l'article 21 du contrat, ont clairement stipulé que les arbitres appliqueront les dispositions du présent contrat et, à défaut, les dispositions obligatoires contenues dans la directive CEE 86/653 du 18 décembre 1986.*

48. Le Tribunal Arbitral constate qu 'à la date de la signature du contrat, et donc de la clause d'arbitrage quis'y trouve incluse, les législateurs belges et espagnols avaient transposé dans leur droit interne, les dispositions de la directive CEE 86/653, par une loi du 13 avril 1995 en Belgique et par une loi du 27 mai 1995 en Espagne.

49. Dès lors, le Tribunal Arbitral considère que les parties, en soumettant leur différend à la loi du contrat et, à défaut, aux dispositions obligatoires dans la directive CEE 86/653, ont souhaité écarter l'application des lois nationales auxquelles ils leur étaient loisibles de se référer, si telle avait été leur volonté, préférant dépendre directement des règles de droit proposées par ladite directive.

50. Le Tribunal Arbitral qui puise ses pouvoirs dans la volonté des parties, doit donner le pas à cette volonté, dans la mesure où elle s'est clairement exprimée, notamment sur le choix des règles de droit applicables et dans la mesure où ce choix, comme en l'espèce, n'est pas contraire à l'ordre public international, qu'il permet la résolution du litige, et qu'il n'est pas constitutif d'une fraude à la loi, étant également rappelé qu'un arbitre n'a pas pour mission de sauvegarder les règles d'un for quel qu'il soit.

51. Le Tribunal Arbitral, relève par ailleurs, que l'article 27 de la loi belge du 13 avril 1995 ne stipule pas que celle- ci a vocation à s'appliquer nonobstant les textes internationaux auxquels la Belgique a adhéré, mais que bien au contraire si cet article stipule effectivement que toute activité d'un agent commercial ayant son établissement principal en Belgique relève de la loi belge et de la compétence des tribunaux belges c'est « sous réserve de l'application des conventions internationales auxquelles la Belgique est partie ».

52. À cet égard, le Tribunal de commerce de Dendermonde — Division de Sint-Niklaas dans son jugement en date du 16 mars 2001, après avoir rappelé les dispositions de la Convention Européenne sur l'Arbitrage International, retient pour se déclarer incompétent, que l'article 27 de la loi sur les contrats d'agence commerciale belge ne déroge pas à l'application des traités internationaux que la Belgique a conclu, et juge d'une part que la directive CEE 86/653 ne s'oppose pas à la possibilité d'arbitrage du litige, et d'autre part que concernant le droit d'application, le législateur belge, ne s'oppose pas à ce que le conflit soit réglé conformément aux dispositions de la directive européenne 86/653. ».

S'agissant du deuxième point en litige, l'arbitre s'était appuyé sur les dispositions du contrat et avait analysé le comportement des parties pour conclure que l'agent avait commis effectivement une faute grave justifiant la résiliation immédiate du contrat par le commettant.

« 72. *Conformément à l'article 1 du contrat, le Demandeur a été nommé agent commercial du Défendeur pour promouvoir les ventes au Bénélux de produits de prêt-à-porter féminin.*

73. *L'article 3 de ce même contrat stipule au titre des obligations du Demandeur que celui-ci s'engage à vendre les produits fabriqués par le Défendeur, en se conformant aux instructions raisonnables du demandeur et à Défendre ses intérêts avec diligence.*

74. *L'article 4 du contrat stipule une clause de non-concurrence, aux termes de laquelle, sauf accord préalable écrit du Défendeur, le Demandeur s'engage à ne pas représenter, fabriquer ou distribuer, directement ou à travers des tiers, quels qu'ils soient, des produits concurrents du Défendeur pendant la durée du contrat.*

75. *La lecture de ces articles fait ressortir que les parties, en soumettant à une autorisation préalable écrite du Défendeur, la possibilité pour le Demandeur de représenter des produits concurrents, ont entendu donner un relief tout particulier à l'obligation de non-concurrence durant le contrat, soulignant un des aspects de l'obligation de loyauté et de bonne foi, principe général du droit commercial international, qui doit colorer l'exécution des conventions.*

76. *Les parties au contrat ont également pris soin de définir à l'article 18 dudit contrat la notion de manquement grave justifiant une résiliation à effet immédiat, en retenant que toute inexécution par un des contractants de tout ou partie de ses obligations, qui cause à l'autre un préjudice, tel que ce dernier est privé de manière substantielle de ce qu'il était en droit d'attendre du présent contrat, sera considéré comme un manquement grave au regard des effets de la présente clause.*

77. *La combinaison des articles 1, 3, 4, et 18, du contrat, pemet de considérer qu'une violation de la clause de non-concurrence stipulée par l'article 4 du cnntrnt, si elle était avérée, constituerait incontestablement un manquement grave au sens de l'article 18 du contrat, puisqu'elle priverait le Défendeur d'une des attentes substantielles du contrat signé, à savoir l'assurance de voir les produits concurrents écartés des gammes de vêtements représentées par le demandeur.*

78. *Le Demandeur ne conteste d'ailleurs pas le principe suivant lequel la représentation de produits concurrents constituerait bien un manquement grave à ses obligations contractuelles justifiant une résiliation immédiate du contrat.*

79. *En revanche, le Demandeur conteste formellement que les produits de la marque C dont le Défendeur lui reproche d'avoir accepté la représentation, soient des produits concurrents des produits fabriqués par le Demandeur.*

80. *Le débat doit dès lors se concentrer autour du point de savoir si les produits de la marque C, que le Demandeur admet avoir distribués, peuvent être regardés ou non comme étant concurrents des produits fabriqués par le Défendeur.*

81. *Du point de vue juridique, les activités concurrentes sont celles qui satisfont des demandes de produits ou de services, identiques ou proches, c'est-à-dire qui s'adressent à une même clientèle, et qui susceptibles d'être préférés les uns par rapport aux autres, peuvent être considérés comme substituables.*
(. . .)

104. *De tout ce qui précède, et après analyse des éléments de fait et de droit, le Tribunal Arbitral considère que le simple fait d'avoir distribué des produits de prêt-à-porter féminins autres que ceux du Défendeur, aurait dû inciter le Demandeur, dans un esprit de loyauté et de bonne foi, et sans délai, à aviser le Défendeur de cette situation.*

105. *L'argument développé par le Demandeur et consistant à expliquer que de bonne foi il pensait ne pas contrevenir au contrat doit être considéré comme inopérant.*

106. En effet, d'une part, les produits sont très proches les uns des autres, et les différences avancées par le Demandeur, pour la plupart inexactes, n'autorisent pas à considérer que la société Z et le Défendeur soient, s'agissant de leurs gammes de produits destinées aux femmes, autre chose que des concurrents.

107. D'autre part, l'attitude du Demandeur lui-même tend à démontrer qu'il avait une claire conscience des difficultés liées à la concurrence (. . .)

108. À cet égard, le Tribunal Arbitral ne peut retenir l'argument du Demandeur suivant lequel, la production du catalogue du salon (. . .) par le Défendeur serait la démonstration de la connaissance qu'il avait de la représentation par le Demandeur de la marque C, alors même, ainsi que l'établissent les pièces versées par le Défendeur (. . .), que le Demandeur lors de la rencontre de [lieu], le 23 juillet 1999, s'employait à distiller des informations contradictoires et erronées sur la réalité de cette représentation, et que le Défendeur indique, sans pouvoir être contredit sur ce point, avoir obtenu le catalogue (. . .) postérieurement aux déclarations contradictoires et inquiétantes du Demandeur lors de la réunion de [lieu].

109. Le Tribunal Arbitral retient également qu'il est avéré, à travers les attestations versées aux débats par les deux parties, que les produits concernés sont distribués, dans les mêmes magasins, et donc visent par définition une même clientèle fréquentant lesdits magasins, et que les fournisseurs des marques du Défendeur et de la société Z, soit prennent le soin de leur assurer une exclusivité absolue, soit s'emploient à leur fournir des dessins différent: et des qualités différentes, afin d'éviter des difficultés précisément liées à la concurrence. (. . .)

116. Le Tribunal Arbitral considère donc que le Demandeur a manqué à une obligation contractuelle en représentant des produits concurrents de ceux du Défendeur, méconnaissant ainsi les dispositions de l'article 4 du contrat, et que ce manquement est grave au regard de la définition donnée par les parties elles-mêmes de la gravité dans l'article 18 du contrat, justifiant ainsi la résiliation immédiate du contrat par le Défendeur (. . .). ».

NOTE. — I. — Conformément à la volonté des parties, les règles de droit applicables en cas de litige étaient celles qui résultaient du contrat, et à défaut les dispositions impératives de la directive européenne n° 86/653/CEE du 18 décembre 1986 relative à la coordination des États membres concernant les agents commerciaux indépendants *(Dir n° 86/653/CEE, 18 déc. 1986: JOCE n° L 382, 31 déc. 1986, p. 17).* L'arbitre devait néanmoins se prononcer sur la question des règles de droit applicables à la requête du demandeur dans le cadre de la réparation de son préjudice. Celui-ci avait sollicité l'application de la loi belge du 13 avril 1995 sur l'agence commerciale (« loi de 1995 ») ayant estimé que la référence à la directive de 1986 n'impliquait nullement une élection du droit applicable. Elle reflétait simplement la volonté des parties de bénéficier au moins de la protection de la directive en cas de différend. Selon le demandeur, qui exerçait son activité sur le territoire belge, le droit belge était applicable en vertu des dispositions de l'article 27 de la loi de 1995 qui indiquent que « *Sous réserve de l'application des conventions internationales auxquelles la Belgique est partie, toute activité d'un agent ayant son établissement principal en Belgique relève de la loi belge et de la compétence des tribunaux belges* ». Il avait invoqué également l'article 4 (1) et (2) de la Convention de Rome 19 juin 1980 sur la loi applicable aux obligations contractuelles (« Convention de Rome de 1980 ») pour affirmer l'application du droit belge. Le défendeur avait rejeté l'application du droit belge en se fondant sur la volonté des parties qui avaient « volontairement soumis les différends aux dispositions du contrat "loi INTERPARTES" et aux dispositions obligatoires de la directive précitée (. . .). À défaut et dans l'hypothèse où l'arbitre estime que la loi belge du contrat d'agence est applicable, éventualité niée par le Défendeur, elle devrait se limiter à compléter, en tant que de besoin, les concepts d'indemnité prévus au contrat et dans la directive ». L'arbitre avait fait droit à cette argumentation en deux temps. Il avait affirmé tout d'abord la primauté de la volonté des parties qui avaient souhaité écarter l'application des lois nationales en soumettant leur différend à la loi du contrat et aux dispositions impératives de la directive de 1986. Il avait ensuite validé leur choix en l'absence de fraude ou de contrariété à l'ordre public pour conclure à la prééminence de la directive de 1986, l'arbitre n'ayant pas pour mission de sauvegarder les règles d'un *for* quel qu'il soit. Conformément à l'article 27 de la loi de 1995, celle-ci s'applique seulement « *sous réserve de l'application des conventions internationales auxquelles la Belgique est partie* ». La décision de l'arbitre est correcte et n'appelle pas de commentaires particuliers. Elle est toutefois intéressante car le droit applicable choisi par les parties n'est pas une loi étatique mais une directive européenne qui présente la particularité d'être une directive *a minima.*

Conçue pour remédier à la diversité des textes nationaux, la directive de 1986 a fixé seulement un régime de protection minimale de l'agent sur certains aspects essentiels de la relation d'agence. Elle a laissé une grande liberté aux États membres de la compléter pour renforcer la protection de l'agent lors de sa transposition dans leur législation nationale *(V. J.-M. Leloup, Agents commerciaux — Statuts juridiques — Stratégies professionnelles, Dehnas 2005, 6 éd., n° 233, p. 34. — C. Diloy, Le contrat d'agence commercial en droit international, LGDJ 2000, n° 259, p. 221. — Th. Steinmann, Ph. Kenel et I. Bilione, Le contrat d'agence commerciale en Europe, Bruylant, LGDJ, Schulthess 2005, p. 6 et p. 141).*

La Belgique qui ne connaissait pas de réglementations particulières en ce domaine a usé de la faculté laissée par la directive de 1986 pour adopter la loi de 1995 accordant ainsi à l'agent commercial un véritable statut protecteur en considération de sa position de faiblesse économique *(V. Th. Steinmann et Ph. Kenel, I. Billotte, op. cit., p. 9. — P. Crahay, La loi relative au contrat d'agence commerciale: résiliation et indemnité d'éviction, Revue de droit commercial belge 1995, p. 825. — P. Kileste, La loi belge du 13 avril 1995 relative au contrat d'agence commerciale transposant en droit interne la directive européenne 86/653, RDAI/IBLJ 1995, n° 7, p. 801).* À cette occasion, le législateur a affirmé le caractère impératif de la loi de 1995 sauf dispositions expresses contraires *(Th. Steinmann, Ph. Kenel et I. Billette, op. cit., p. 10 et le rapport parlementaire, Sénat, SE 1991-1992, n° 355-3, p. 14:* « *Le ministre confirme une fois de plus que toutes les dispositions ont un caractère impératif, à moins qu'il n'en soit expressément stipulé autrement. Le groupe de travail conclut donc que toutes les dispositions sont de droit impératif sauf celles où il est expressément mentionné que les dérogations sont possibles* »). Le champ d'application de la loi de 1995 étant plus large et plus important que celui de la directive de 1986, le législateur belge a voulu favoriser l'application du droit belge en adoptant l'article 27 qui indique que « *Sous réserve de l'application des conventions internationales auxquelles la Belgique est partie, toute activité d'un agent commercial ayant son établissement principal en Belgique relève de la loi belge et de la compétence des tribunaux belges* ». La formulation est maladroite car l'application impérative du droit belge est faite en réalité « *sous réserve de l'application des conventions internattonales auxquelles la Belgique est partie* ». La loi de 1995 est donc plutôt une loi d'ordre public interne, comme semble le reconnaître d'ailleurs les juges belges eux-mêmes (V. le jugement du 16 mars 2001 du Tribunal de Dendermonde cité par l'arbitre). Elle ne prime pas sur la directive de 1986 qui est assimilable à une loi de police communautaire en raison de l'objectif poursuivi: le renforcement de l'ordre public européen de protection de l'agent.

Le caractère impératif de la directive de 1986 s'impose aux État membres car bien qu'elle laisse aux instances nationales la compétence quant à la forme et aux moyens, elle lie tout État membre destinataire quant aux résultats à atteindre *(V. Traité CE, art. 249 (3)).* Plus généralement, la directive de 1986 s'impose sur tout le territoire de la Communauté européenne. Elle est ainsi opposable à un commettant non communautaire quel que soit le droit applicable au fond dès lors que l'agent commercial « *exerce son activité à l'intérieur de la Communauté* ». L'agent a normalement droit à une indemnisation à l'issu de la cessation de son contrat par application des dispositions impératives de la directive de 1986 *(art. 17 à 19) (V. en ce sens CJCE, 9 nov. 2000, aff. C-381/98, Ingmar GB Ltd vs Eaton Leonard Technologies Inc.: Ree. CJCE 2000, I, p. 8035; Rev. crit. DIP 2001, p. 90, note L. Idot. — K.J. Hopt, L'entreprise et le droit européen: Rev. sociétés 2001, p. 301. — J.-M. Leloup, op. cit., n° 1806, p. 305 — dans un sens inverse, V. Cass. com., 28 nov. 2000, n° 98-11.335, Allium SA vs Alfin Inc et Groupe Inter Parfums: Juris-Data n° 2000-007123; JCP E 2001, p. 997, note L. Bernardeau; Cah. dr. entr. 2001 n° 2, p. 12, note J. Raynard).* La Cour de cassation française a refusé l'application de la loi du 25 juin 1991 transposant la directive n° 86/653/CEE à un contrat, soumis au droit américain, conclu entre un commettant américain et un agent établi en France et exerçant son activité en Europe et en Israël. Selon la Cour de cassation, « la loi du 25 juin 1991, codifiée dans les articles L. 134-1 et suivants du Code de commerce, loi protectrice d'ordre public interne, applicable à tous les contrats en cours à la date du 1er janvier 1994, n'est pas une loi de police applicable dans l'ordre international ». La portée de la décision française reste encore à confirmer si on veut bien se rappeler les coïncidences malheureuses des calendriers. L'arrêt *Ingmar* du 9 novembre 2000 était rendu par la Cour de justice entre le délibéré et le prononcé de l'arrêt de la Cour de cassation française. Voir en ce sens les critiques de J.-M. Leloup *(op. cit., n° 1806, p. 306)* qui a estimé le motif erroné. Selon cet auteur, pour toute l'exécution du contrat sur le territoire de l'Union européenne, le rapport de droit en cause n'était pas dans l'ordre international mais dans l'ordre communautaire et il appartenait à la Cour de cassation d'interpréter la loi nationale conformément au texte et à la finalité de la directive. On devrait alors admettre le droit à indemnité pour la partie du contrat exécutée sur le territoire des États membres et à le rejeter pour le surplus *(dans un sens opposé, V. J. Eraw. The Law Applicable to Distribution Agreements in Arbitration and Commercial Distribution: Reports on the Colloquium of CEPANI, November 17, 2005, p. 61).*

Les dispositions de la directive de 1986 doivent d'autant plus s'appliquer si elle a été désignée comme droit applicable par les parties. Ce choix est d'ailleurs validé par l'article 3 de la Convention de Rome de 1980 à laquelle la Belgique fait partie et le Règlement d'arbitrage CCI *(art. 17).* L'agent peut donc décider de bénéficier de la protection minimale préconisée par la directive n° 86/653/ CEE en renonçant à la protection plus importante que lui offrirait la loi de 1995 *(V. F. Bortolotti, Le contrat international d'agent commercial dans l'arbitrage de la CCI: Bull. CCI, vol. 12, n° 1, 1er semestre, p. 52 et p. 59 — V. également l'affaire CCI n° 8817 selon laquelle l'application de la directive de 1986 par le tribunal arbitral qui a considéré que les « dispositions communes au Danemark et à l'Espagne, sont celles de la directive (. . .) » et l'affaire CCI n° 9032 où le tribunal arbitral a affirmé le principe selon lequel « les parties privées restent libres de choisir une directive ». — V. également J.-M. Leloup, op. cit., n° 233, p. 34. — Th. Steinmann, Ph. Kenel et I. Billotte, op. cit., p. 149. — C. Diloy, op. cit., n° 332 et 337, p. 282 et 284. — C. Ferry, Contrat international d'agent commercial et lois de police: JDI 1993, p. 299).*

De ce qui précède, on peut constater les limites de la directive de 1986. L'harmonisation est partielle au sein des États membres car la réglementation est partielle dans la directive de 1986 elle-même qui, dans certains cas, propose seulement des options. De ce fait, les divergences nationales demeurent en raison des choix laissés aux États membres dans la transposition de la directive de 1986 et en fonction de leur tradition juridique (V. par ex. l'article 17 en matière de compensation financière. — plus généralement, *V. C. Diloy, op. cit., n° 268, p. 227).*

II. — D'une manière générale, l'agent a pour mission principale de promouvoir les affaires du commettant, de veiller à ses intérêts et de s'abstenir de promouvoir des produits concurrents. La représentation de produits concurrents est une question délicate car le mandant risque de voir son agent donner la préférence à d'autres produits dans le cadre de son activité. Ce risque est d'autant plus important s'il a accordé à son agent le bénéfice d'une exclusivité territoriale. Comme indiqué par J.-M. Leloup dans son ouvrage *(op. cit., n° 312, p. 46)*, « Le fait de concurrence est précisément délicat à cerner: l'identité physique des produits peut s'effacer devant les différences de prix, de présentation et de mise en marché. Il en résulte des appréciations délicates et changeantes ». C'était précisément le problème posé à l'arbitre. Le demandeur avait estimé que les produits vestimentaires de la marque C étaient différents de ceux fabriqués par son commettant compte tenu de leur style, de la coupe, des couleurs, du prix et de la clientèle. Le défendeur, quant à lui, avait fait valoir que les deux produits étaient bien des produits concurrents. Il s'agissait de types de vêtements très similaires, qui couvraient la même partie du marché et dirigés vers une clientèle de femmes qui s'identifiaient aux deux produits.

L'arbitre avait analysé minutieusement les éléments de fait et de droit pour reconnaître le manquement du demandeur et valider la résiliation faite par le défendeur. Sur le plan matériel, l'arbitre s'était fondé sur les attestations des deux parties, les catalogues, et en particulier sur un tableau comparatif des produits visés établi par un expert pour conclure que « les produits concernés sont distribués, dans les mêmes magasins, et donc visent pas définition une même clientèle fréquentant lesdits magasins, et que les fournisseurs des marques du défendeur et de la société C prennent le soin de leur assurer une exclusivité absolue, soit s'emploient à leur fournir des dessins différents et des qualités différentes, afin d'éviter des difficultés précisément liées à la concurrence ». L'effort fait par l'arbitre de rechercher si les produits matériellement étaient ou non concurrents mérite d'être souligné car son approche s'aligne sur la conception restrictive adoptée par la jurisprudence, notamment française, donnant ainsi une base légale à sa décision (sur la nécessité de comparer les produits concurrents, V. par ex. *Cass. com., 6 juill. 1982: http://www.legifrance.gouv.fr*: « Attendu qu'en statuant ainsi, sans rechercher si les blocs portes coupe-feu des établissements Placal pouvait être assimilés aux blocs portes équipés d'une porte coupe-feu fabriqués par la Sami, alors qu'elle avait relevé que la société Métalbois ne pouvait, sans accord de son mandant, commercialiser pour le compte de tiers des produits similaires du contrat, la cour d'appel n'a pas donné de base légale à sa décision. ». — V. également *Cass. com., 16 mars 1993, n° 91-11.194: Juris-Data n° 1993-000495; Bull. civ. 1993, IV, n° 109, p. 75)*.

Toute faute du mandataire ne justifiant pas une résiliation du contrat, l'arbitre avait pris soin de s'appuyer sur les dispositions contractuelles et de rappeler la nécessité d'un comportement loyal des parties lors de l'exécution des contrats. En l'espèce, les parties avaient précisé dans leur contrat plusieurs points importants: le champ d'activité de l'agent (la distribution de produits de prêt-à-porter au Bénélux, article 1), ses obligations (l'engagement de vendre les produits fabriqués selon les instructions du commettant, article 3), le respect de la clause de non-concurrence, sauf dérogation expresse acceptée par le commettant (article 4), et la sanction de la faute grave (résiliation à effet immédiat, article 18). De ce fait, l'arbitre avait pu constater que « La combinaison des articles 1, 3, 4, et 18, du contrat, permet de considérer qu'une violation de la clause de non-concurrence stipulée par l'article 4 du contrat, si elle était avérée, constituerait incontestablement un manquement grave au sens de l'article 18 du contrat, puisqu'elle priverait le défendeur d'une des attentes substantielles du contrat signé, à savoir l'assurance de voir les produits concurrents écartés des gammes de vêtements représentées par le demandeur (. . .) le simple fait d'avoir distribué des produits de prêt-à-porter féminins autres que ceux du défendeur, aurait dû incirer le demandeur, dans un esprit de loyauté et de bonne foi, et sans délai, à aviser le défendeur de cette situation (. . .) ».

La précision contractuelle faite par les parties est particulièrement utile à plusieurs égards. Elle comble le silence de la directive de 1986 sur les clauses de non-concurrence « pendant » la durée du contrat. L'article 20 de la directive de 1986 vise uniquement les clauses de non-concurrence « après » la cessation du contrat contrairement à certaines législations nationales qui interdisent expressément l'exercice par l'agent d'activités concurrentes pendant la durée du contrat (V. notamment l'article 3 de la loi française de 1991, l'article 1743 du Code civil italien, l'article 4 du décret-loi portugais du 3 juillet 1986). Même en l'absence d'une interdiction contractuelle expresse, on peut toutefois soutenir raisonnablement que l'agent est tenu d'une obligation de loyauté ou de bonne foi vis-à-vis du commettant en raison des intérêts qui les lient. En effet, le fait pour un agent de nouer des relations avec un concurrent du commettant risque de créer une confusion pour la clientèle à propos des deux marques concurrentes. L'article 3 (1) de la directive de 1986 rappelle d'ailleurs que « *l'agent commercial, doit, dans l'exercice de ses activités, veiler aux intérêts du commettant et agir loyalement et de bonne foi* ». Affirmé au niveau européen, le principe de bonne foi ou de coopération est également reconnu dans la pratique arbitralo en tant que principe général du commerce international *(V. les nombreuses références citées dans l'affaire CCI n° 6673 (1992) in Recueil des sentences arbitrales de la CCI de 1991-1995, vol. III: Kluwer/ICC n° 533, p. 434, note D. H. — Th. Steinmann, Ph. Kenel et I. Bilhtte, op. cit., p. 228. — C. Diloy, op. cit., n° 90, p. 85. — plus généralement V. S. Jarvin, L'Obligation de coopérer de bonne foi in L'apport de la jurisprudence arbitrale: ICC 1986, n° 1434, p. 168. — C. Truong, Les différends liés à la rupture des contrats internationaux de distribution dans les sentences arbitrales CCI: Litec, 2002, n° 279, p. 238).* L'arbitre a fort justement sanctionné le comportement déloyal du demandeur qui n'avait pas hésité à distiller des informations contradictoires et erronées en cours d'exécution du contrat *(V. notamment Cass. com., 30 nov. 2004, n° 02-17.414, Sté Sorimer vs Sté Condensa conducciones y derivados: Juris-Data n° 2004-025988. — Cass. com., 22 janv. 2002, n° 99-14.150, GmbH Bultel Bekleidungswerke vs M. Marc Malka. — Cass. com., 16 oct. 2001, n° 99-11.932, Sté Rifobois vs Sté Belipa: RJDA 2002, n° 149).*

S. J.
C. T.-N.

Sentence arbitrale finale dans l'affaire CCI n° 11426

Procédure arbitrale. — Confidentialité. — Recevabilité de certaines pièces dans un arbitrage commercial international (oui). — Critères formels pour établir le caractère confidentiel d'un document.

Principe d'efficacité des contrats. — Protection de la partie la plus faible. — « Justice distributive ».

Dommage (lien de causalité). — Pluralité de causes du dommage et cause prépondérante. — Droit de la responsabilité civile et droit des assurances. — *Lex mercatoria.* — Présomption d'égalité des commerçants internationaux et présomption de compétence professionnelle des opérateurs du commerce international. — « Justice corrective ».

Frais de l'arbitrage. — « Usage » dans le système d'arbitrage de la CCI concernant la répartition entre les parties des frais de l'arbitrage. — Pouvoir discrétionnaire des arbitres pour répartir les frais de l'arbitrage (oui). — Critères utilisés pour répartir les frais de l'arbitrage.

La sentence commencée, à l'occasion d'un litige découlant d'un contrat d'assurance relatif au lancement d'un satellite, examine la causalité en droit français et nous rappelle que l'arbitre international doit se placer sur le terrain de la « justice corrective » de la société marchande internationale afin d'accomplir la mission que les parties — commerçants internationaux compétents, professionnels et avisés — lui ont confiée.

Le fond du litige tranché par la sentence arbitrale finale rendue dans l'affaire CCI n° 11426 comporte deux éléments qui surprendront immédiatement le lecteur: la controverse entre les parties (i) découle d'un contrat d'assurance et (ii) porte sur le préjudice causé par le retard de lancement d'un satellite du fait de son endommagement. Il n'est en effet pas très courant de trouver des clauses compromissoires insérées dans de contrats d'assurance *(cf. I. Hunter, L'arbitrage relatif à l'assurance et à la réassurance dans le système du Common law: questions pratiques, Supplément Spécial: Bull. CCI 2000, Cour internationale d'arbitrage, ICC Publishing, publication n° 627, p. 43. — pour une vue plus nuancée, V. J. Bigot, Arbitrage et assurance, sous l'angle du droit français, op. cit., p. 33. — V. également la liste des litiges selon leur objet portés devant la cour d'appel de Paris de 1981 à 1990, S. Crépin, Le contrôle des sentences arbitrales par la cour d'appel de Paris depuis les réformes de 1980 et 1981: Rev. arb. 1991, n° 4, p. 533).* L'arbitrabilité du contrat d'assurance a été discutée aux États-Unis *(cf. United States Court of Appeals, 1st Circuit, 31 janv. 2000, n° 1 A/C, Francesco DiMercurio vs Sphere Drake Insurance PLC: Yearbook Commercial Arbitration, 2000, vol. XXV, p. 641 à 1164).* Il existe toutefois quelques exemples d'arbitrages portant sur un contrat d'assurance *(Sentence rendue dans l'affaire CCI n° 7563 en 1993: JDI 1994, p. 1055 à 1060. — Sentence du 17 novembre 1994 (arbitrage CNUDCI), Banque arabe et internationale d'investissement et al. cl Inter-Arab Investment Guarantee Corporation: Yearbook Commercial Arbitration, 1996, vol. XXI, p. 13 à 39. — TGI Paris, ord. réf., 26 mars 1986, Sté Scoa et P. Galbois cl Les Assurances générales de France (AGF): Rev. arb. 1987, n° 2, p. 179 et s., note Ph. Fouchard)* ainsi que de les utiliser dans le secteur si pointu des satellites *(cf. A. Mourre, La résolution des litiges dans les contrats spatiaux in Le droit des activités spatiales à l'aube du XXIᵉ siècle, L. Ravillon (dir.), actes du colloque des 10 et 11 juin 2004 à Dijon, travaux du CREDIMI, vol. 25: Litec, 2005, p. 197 à 227).*

Le Tribunal arbitral résume remarquablement bien les faits de l'espèce comme suit:

En [année N] [la partie demanderesse], *« opérateur de télécommunications par satellite, et les Assureurs* [parties défenderesses] *ont conclu un contrat d'assurance « Satellite All Risks Pre-Launch and Consequential Loss Insurance Policy ».*

La construction du satellite en question (. . .) avait été confiée par [la partie demanderesse] *à la société* [A]. *Le lancement devait être effectué à partir de la base* [B] *(. . .) à l'aide d'une fusée* [X] *».*

Le [date 1, année N + 4], *« l'ordinateur de bord du satellite en question fut endommagé. Avant cette* (sic) *endommagement du satellite, la date de lancement programmée du satellite était le* [date 2 un mois après la date du sinistre].

Le [date 3], *quelques jours après l'endommagement du satellite, un incident majeur est intervenu lors du lancement d'un autre satellite sur une fusée* [X] *entraînant une suspension du programme de lancement* [X] *jusqu'à environ fin* [date un mois après la date de lancement initialement prévue].

Une nouvelle suspension du programme de lancement des fusées [X] *est intervenue le* [date trois mois après la date de lancement initialement prévue] *à la suite d'un autre incident technique lors du lancement d'un autre satellite. Cette seconde suspension a duré jusqu'au mois de (. . .)* [sept mois après la date de lancement initialement prévue].

Le satellite [en question], *qui faisait l'objet du contrat d'assurance litigieux, a finalement été lancé le* [date, neuf mois après la date de lancement initialement prévue].

Les parties sont en désaccord sur les conditions d'acquisition de la garantie et sur la mise en jeu de la police d'assurance (. . .) ».

En bref, la partie demanderesse alléguait que la cause de son préjudice était l'endommagement du satellite — risque qui était bel et bien couvert par la police d'assurance objet du litige — alors que les parties défenderesses soutenaient que la cause du préjudice — s'il y en avait véritablement eu un — était la suspension du programme de lancement — risque qui, à son tour, n'était pas couvert par la police d'assurance.

Selon la partie demanderesse, son préjudice consistait dans le manque à gagner résultant du retard de lancement du satellite.

Le Tribunal arbitral précise la difficulté de cet arbitrage ainsi:

« La difficulté de cet arbitrage vient de l'intervention des deux événements suivants:

Le [date 1], *le satellite fut endommagé rendant impossible son lancement à la date du* [date 2] *(– date de lancement prévue juste avant l'endommagement du satellite –);*

Le [date 3], *lors du lancement d'un autre satellite, une fusée* [X] *a explosé ce qui a conduit les autorités de* [B], *sur le territoire duquel se trouve le champ de tir* [B], *à suspendre le programme de lancement avec fusées* [X].

Le fait que chacun des deux événements ait été auto-suffisant pour rendre impossible le lancement prévu pour le [date 2] *».*

Le Tribunal arbitral analyse préalablement le point litigieux de la recevabilité de certaines pièces qui, selon la partie demanderesse, n'auraient pas dû être produites dans la procédure du fait de leur nature transactionnelle et donc confidentielle.

À cer égard, la sentence dispose:

« Aucune de ces pièces ne comporte la mention « confidentielle » et aucune de ces pièces n'émane ou n'a été adressée à un professionnel soumis à des obligations déontologiques de confidentialité. Tout au contraire, ces documents s'insèrent dans un échange tout à fait classique entre un assuré et son assureur. Le fait que [la partie demanderesse], *à cette époque, ne réclamait aux assureurs qu'environ 50 % de la somme réclamée maintenant dans le cadre de cet arbitrage, et le fait que* [la partie demanderesse] *se serait apparemment, à cette époque, contentée*

d'un tel payement, témoigne peut-être d'une incertitude quant au bien-fondé de sa demande ou d'une demande supérieure, mais ne confere aucunement à ces documents un « caractère transactionnel » ou « confidentiel » qui permettrait de les écarter maintenant des débats.

Dans ces conditions, il n'est pas nécessaire d'approfondir la question — purement théorique — de savoir si la question d'une éventuelle confidentialité serait régie par le droit français ou le droit anglais car les deux droits arrivent en l'espèce manifestement au même résultat, à savoir la non-confidentialité de ces pièces ».

Plus loin dans la sentence, néanmoins, le Tribunal arbitral ajoute:

« (. . .) Sans remplir les conditions pour être qualifié de document confidentiel, ces pièces montrent un « esprit de transaction », peut-être parce que [la partie demanderesse] *n'était pas sûr[e] de sa position en droit vu les questions — en effet très difficiles — de causalité (endommagement du satellite d'une part et suspension du programme de lancement d'autre pert) (. . .) ».*

Le Tribunal arbitral procède ensuite à examiner le cœur du litige opposant les parties, à savoir la question de la causalité ainsi que celle de la portée du préjudice.

Le Tribunal arbitral détermine d'abord que le litige entre les parties porte avant tout sur le problème du lien de causalité entre l'endommagement du satellite ou la suspension du programme de lancement et le retard de lancement du satellite. Il écrit en ce sens dans la sentence que:

« (. . .) le point soulevé par les Assureurs touche au problème plus général de la causalité, à savoir s'il faut donner, dans le cadre du contrat d'assurance en question, la priorité à l'endommagement du satellite du [date 1] *ou à la suspension du programme de lancement du* [date 3] *(. . .) ».*

Les parties défenderesses cherchaient à se faire exonérer de toute responsabilité sur la base de certaines dispositions du contrat d'assurance.

Le Tribunal arbitral rejette cet argument de la manière suivante:

« Ce document [le contrat d'assurance] *ne permet certainement pas d'écarter par le biais d'une interprétation de la police d'assurance, la responsabilité des assureurs. En effet, du moins sur le plan purement factuel, l'endommagement du satellite était une cause auto-suffisante du retard de lancement. Même s'il n'y avait pas eu de suspension du programme de lancement* [X], *le satellite n'aurait pas pu être lancé le* [date 2] *à cause de son endommagement (. . .).*

Si l'analyse juridique devait s'arrêter là, c'est-à-dire si on devait se limiter aux termes de la police d'assurance et de son interprétation, le Tribunal arbitral serait enclin de faire droit à la demande [de la partie demanderesse] *plutôt que de la rejeter. Un événement envisagé au contrat d'assurance, l'endommagement du satellite, s'est produit. Cet événement était, sur le plan factuel, une cause « auto-suffisante » du dommage.* [La partie demanderesse] *a payé et les assureurs ont reçu la prime d'assurance convenue qui était destinée à compenser justement ce risque qui s'est réalisé. Dans ces conditions, placé devant le choix entre « le tout ou rien », le Tribunal arbitral considère que le principe d'efficacité des contrats commande de retenir l'événement prévu au contrat plutôt que de privilégier un autre événement non prévu au contrat qui, sur le plan factuel, est — au mieux — équivalent (. . .) ».*

Néanmoins, étant donné, parmi d'autres raisons (cf. II ci-après), que les parties ont largement fondé leurs plaidoiries sur la causalité en droit français, le Tribunal arbitral procède à l'analyse des faits de l'espèce à la lumière de celle-ci. Les passages de la sentence sur cette question méritent d'être transcrits *in extenso:*

« C. LA CAUSALITÉ EN DROIT FRANÇAIS

Subsidiairement à leurs premiers arguments fondés sur les termes même de la police d'assurance, [la partie demanderesse] *ainsi que les assureurs se sont expliqués, de manière approfondie, sur la question de causalité en droit français.*

Selon [la partie demanderesse] *il convient d'appliquer le droit français de la responsabilité civile (voir par exemple mémoire* [de la partie demanderesse] *n° . . .) selon lequel, en cas de pluralité de faits à l'origine d'un même dommage, la victime est libre de se fonder sur l'un ou l'autre d'entre eux pour obtenir l'indemnisation. Selon l'opinion exprimée par le Professeur* [P] *dans son opinion juridique versée aux débats par* [la partie demanderesse] *(pièce* [de la partie demanderesse] *n°]):*

« *(. . .) un principe fondamental du droit civil français qui ne comporte que de rares exceptions impose de choisir la 'cause' qui permet l'indemnisation.* »).

Ce principe fondamental s'appliquerait dans tous les types de concours de « *causes* » *de dommage, qu 'ils 'agisse d'un phénomène d'enchaînement, d'un cumul de causes ou de causes concurrentes. Dans tous ces cas le droit français retiendrait la cause ou les causes qui permet(tent) l'indemnisation de la victime. En conclusion de son opinion juridique, le Professeur* [P] *(p. [n° J) parle du* « *principe général qui impose en cas de concours des 'causes' d'un même dommage, le choix de celle des 'causes' concurrentes qui permet l'indemnisation de ce dommage* ».

Selon les assureurs la réponse du droit français doit être trouvée non pas dans le droit de la responsabilité civile, mais dans le droit des assurances (voir par exemple mémoire des assureurs n° . . . , p. . . . ainsi que la consultation juridique du Professeur [B] *(pièce Assureurs n° . . . , p. . . .).*

Le Tribunal arbitral partage, sur ce point, l'opinion des assureurs. En effet, le principe privilégiant la cause ou les causes permettant l'indemnuation du dommage se justifie et se comprend parfaitement en matière de responsabilité civile où le droit privilégie à juste titre les intérêts de la victime aux intérêts d'un (co-)auteur de dommage. Il n'y a pas lieu, selon l'avis du Tribunal arbitral, de transposer ce principe et cette finalité juridique aux intérêts des parties à un contrat d'assurance. Il n'y a pas de principe général, ni dans le droit général des contrats ni en matière de contrats d'assurance, qui permettrait de privilégier les intérêts d'une partie contractante par rapport à ceux du co-contractant.

Il faut donc rechercher la causalité telle que définie par le droit français en matière d'assurance.

Déjà dans son premier mémoire en défense les assureurs ont parlé de « *cause directe et immédiate (proximate cause)* » *(n° . . . , p. . . .) ou encore de* « *cause profonde, durable et adéquate* » *(n° . . . , p. . . .).*

Dans leur mémoire en défense n° (. . .) les assureurs parlent d'une cause « *effective* » *(« il faut, . . . qu'un endommagement ait effectivement affecté le satellite, qu'un retard de lancement ait effectivement été constaté et que ce retard ait effectivement trouvé sa cause dans ledit endommagement du satellite* » *(p. . . .).*[2]

Le Professeur [B], *dans sa consultation juridique parle de la nécessité de rechercher la* « *cause déterminante* » *(p. . . .) ou* « *cause prépondérante* » *(p. . . .).*

Dans sa note additive (pièce Assureurs n° . . .) le Professeur [B] *utilise également, manifestement de manière synonyme, le terme* « *cause adéquate* » *(p. . . .).*

Le Tribunal arbitral ne peut que souscrire à cette analyse. En effet, comme il a été montré par le Professeur [B] *dans sa note additive, en application de la jurisprudence concernant les assurances de choses, il faut* « *établir la cause prépondérante* ». *Cela résulte notamment de l'arrêt de la Cour de cassation du 2 juillet 1996 (Cass. civ., 2 juill. 1996: RGDA 1997, 931). Les demandeurs dans cette*

---

2. *Les assureurs ont également invoqué, dans le contexte de la causalité, le principe indemnitaire. Or, ce principe n'a rien à voir avec le problème de causalité qui se pose en l'espèce. Il n'a de rôle à jouer qu'en ce qui concerne le quantum.*

affaire avaient conclu un contrat d'assurance couvrant les dommages causés aux bâtiments et aux récoltes par l'action du vent dû à la tempête en excluant ceux causés par la grêle. Un certain jour, comme l'arrêt l'indique, « des chut's de grêle accompagnées de vent ont endommagé des biens de l'assuré ». La cour d'appel débouta les demandeurs et la Cour de cassation rejeta le pourvoi en cassation pour le motif suivant:

« attendu, ensuite, que, lorsque le vent et la grêle sont associés, il appartient aux juges du fond de rechercher lequel de ces phénomènes météorologiques a été déterminant dans la réalisation des dommages; que la cour d'appel appréciant souverainement, et sans se contredire, les éléments de preuve soumis à son examen, a constaté que le vent n'avait pas joué un rôle déterminant dans la réalisation du sinistre affectant les biens [des demandeurs]; (. . .) »

En d'autres termes, les demandeurs auraient eu gain de cause si le vent (– contre lequel les demandeurs étaient assurés –) et non pas la grêle (– qui était exclue de la police d'assurance-) avait joué « un rôle déterminant dans la réalisation du sinistre ». L'arrêt semble admettre que l'assurance aurait même dû payer si le vent avait joué un rôle déterminant, même si le vent n'avait pas, à lui seul, suffit à provoquer le sinistre. Il doit en être de même lorsque, malgré la coïncidence du vent et de la grêle, le vent à lui seul aurait suffit à provoquer le sinistre. C'est exactement dans cette situation que l'on se trouve dans le litige qui oppose [la partie demanderesse] *aux assureurs. Chacun des deux événements était « autosuffisant » pour causer le dommage.*

On peut, par ailleurs, toujours dans le cadre des assurances des choses, faire référence à l'article L. 125.1 du Code des assurances qui, bien que pour l'assurance des risques de catastrophes naturelles, parle de « cause déterminante ». Le Professeur [B] *parle dans ce contexte de « causalité adéquate » et cite Leduc, JurisClasseur Resp. civ. et Ass., Fascicule 525. n° 31, qui parle d' « antécédent [c'est-à-dire cause] déterminant, prépondérant » (note additive, pièce Assureurs n° . . . , . . .).*

En somme, le Tribunal arbitral approuve ce que dit le Professeur [B] *au point 3 de la conclusion de sa consultation (pièce Assureurs n° . . . , p. . . .) à savoir qu'il convient de rechercher*

« la cause prépondérante de cette perte et de n'accorder d'indemnité que si et dans la mesure où cette cause prépondérante serait l'incident technique, visé dans la clause de garantie, et non la suspension des lancements [X], *pour les conséquences desquelles l'assuré ne s'est pas garanti ».*

Il va de soi que la solution à la question posée est le résultat d'une analyse et d'une appréciation juridique et non pas le résultat d'un raisonnement en pure science naturelle. [La partie demanderesse] *a, à juste titre, insisté sur ce point:*

*« La **seule véritable question** qui se pose au Tribunal est dès lors de savoir si le lien de causalité entre le sinistre du* [date 1] *et l'impossibilité de réaliser le tir du* [date 2] *ne se trouve pas rompu par la survenance, entre ces deux dates, d'un autre événement, également de nature à rendre impossible le lancement prévu.*

Une telle question ne peut être traitée comme une question de fait, dès lors qu'il n'est pas contesté que chacun des deux événements en cause suffisait à rendre impossible le lancement prévu le [date 2].

Si on s'interroge sur le point de savoir ce qui a été la cause de l'impossibilité de réaliser le tir du [date 2], *on ne peut, en fait, privilégier l'un ou l'autre événement. Chacun d'eux a, dans une égale mesure, rendu ce tir impossible.*

La question est donc une question de droit: une question de causalité. »

Il [le Tribunal arbitral] doit trancher une question de droit et non pas un problème de physique (d'ailleurs parfaitement insoluble puisque, sur le plan qui est celui des faits, toutes les « causes » du retard de lancement sont, en tant que telles, équivalentes).

Il lui faut trancher cette question de droit en appliquant des règles juridiques car seul des règles juridiques peuvent lui permettre de choisir entre les « causes » factuellement équivalentes des pertes éprouvées par l'assuré. » (opinion juridique du Professeur [P], pièce [de la partie demanderesse] n° . . . , p. . . .).

Ce point fut confirmé par le Professeur [B] dans sa note additive (pièce Assureurs n° . . .):

« La causalité n'est pas une simple question de faits mais également une question de droit. Parmi les différentes notions de causalité (causa proxima), équivalence des causes, causa sine qua non', cause adéquate, il faut d'abord rechercher celle qui est applicable dans la cadre d'une assurance de choses (question de droit) puis la solution qui s'en évince sur la base de cette notion (question de fait). » (p. . . .)».

Une fois les critères fixés, le Tribunal arbitral se livre à la détermination de la cause dite « *prépondérante* » du retard de lancement et donc du préjudice subi par la partie demanderesse. Après une analyse très détaillée des faits de l'espèce, le Tribunal arbitral conclut:

« Le Tribunal arbitral est donc amené à conclure sur ce point que la « cause prépondérante » était l'endommagement du satellite et non pas la première et/ou la seconde suspension du programme de lancement.

À titre complémentaire, voir superfétatoire, le Tribunal arbitral rappelle qu'il n'y avait pas une seule période de suspension continue mais deux périodes de suspension et que — sans l'endommagement du [date 1] — le satellite aurait pu être lancé après la première et avant la seconde suspension ».

Le Tribunal arbitral procède enfin à déterminer le quantum de la condamnation contre les parties défenderesses et à prendre sa décision quant aux frais de l'arbitrage.

La motivation du Tribunal arbitral concernant les frais de l'arbitrage mérite d'être transcrite:

« Tout en admettant qu'il est en général justifié de tenir compte dans le cadre de la décision sur les frais, surtout du résultat de la procédure, c'est-à-dire du degré de réussite de chaque partie, le Tribunal arbitral considère que ce principe doit être pondéré en l'espèce.

Tout d'abord, la question centrale de cette affaire, la question de la causalité, était difficile en fait aussi bien qu'en droit. Chaque partie a présenté sa thèse de bonne foi et de manière brillante. Chacune des thèses sur la causalité, celle [de la partie demanderesse] et celle des Assureurs, était défendable. Il ne serait donc pas justifié aux yeux du Tribunal arbitral, de faire supporter la totalité des frais aux Assureurs. À cela s'ajoute le fait [que la partie demanderesse] n'a pas eu gain de cause dans l'incident de procédure soulevé par elle au sujet de la prétendue confidentialité de certaines pièces communiquées par les Assureurs.

Tentant compte de tous ces éléments et usant du pouvoir d'appréciation donné aux arbitres en matière de répartition des frais de procédure, le Tribunal Arbitral décide que les Assureurs devront verser à [la partie demanderesse] au titre de frais et honoraires d'avocat la somme de . . . (H. T.). Les frais d'arbitrage au sens strict (frais de l'institution arbitrale et frais et honoraires du Tribunal Arbitral) devront être supportés à hauteur de deux tiers par les Assureurs et à hauteur d'un tiers par [la partie demanderesse] ».

NOTE. — I. — Le caractère confidentiel de certaines pièces produites et leur recevabilité dans un arbitrage commercial international reste l'un des sujets ambigus pour lequel le rôle de la méthode des conflits de lois et donc la diversité des droits applicables en la matière conservent encore tout leur intérêt. La sentence pose le problème juridique mais — hélas — ne le résout point.

Le Tribunal arbitral opère d'abord implicitement une distinction entre « documents transactionnels/confidentiels » et « documents à esprit transactionnel/non confidentiels » qui n'est pas tout à fait convaincante. Le Tribunal arbitral adopte en effet une optique foncièrement formaliste et considère que rentrent seulement dans la première catégorie les pièces comportant la mention « confidentielle » ou les pièces qui émanent ou ont été adressées à un professionnel soumis à des obligations déontologiques de confidentialité. En l'espèce, le Tribunal arbitral conclut qu' « aucune de ces pièces ne comporte la mention « confidentielle » et aucune de ces pièces n'émane ou n'a été adressée à un professionnel soumis à des obligations déontologiques de confidentialité ».

Force est de constater qu'en la matière — du moins, selon le Tribunal arbitral, en droits français et anglais — la forme l'emporterait sur le fond. En résulte l'évidence que, si l'on désire préserver la caractère confidentiel d'un document, encore faudrait-il le marquer clairement comme étant « confidentiel ».

La décision du Tribunal arbitral concernant les pièces mentionnées n'a en fin de comptes pas eu de grandes conséquences quant à sa décision sur le fond étant donné qu'il a fait droit aux prétentions de la partie demanderesse. Ladite décision a toutefois eu des conséquences quant aux frais de l'arbitrage (cf. IV ci-après).

II. — Le Tribunal arbitral affirme que, s'il limitait son analyse juridique à l'interprétation de la police d'assurance, il arriverait — sur le fondement du principe dit d'efficacité des contrats — à la conclusion que la partie demanderesse doit l'emporter.

Le Tribunal arbitral affirme que « le principe d'efficacité des contrats commande de retenir l'événement prévu au contrat plutôt que de privilégier un autre événement non prévu au contrat qui, sur le plan factuel, est — au mieux — équivalent ».

Le principe d'efficacité des contrats viserait à faire prévaloir l'application des clauses d'un contrat même en dépit des règles supplétives du droit des obligations s'y opposant *(cf. V. Avena-Robardet, Le cédé ne peut se prévaloir d'une clause d'agrément du contrat de base pour s'opposer à la cession Dailly: Recueil Dalloz, 2001, n° 1, p. 123. — – D. Mazeaud, Le groupe de contrats: LPA 2000, p. 64 et s. — D. Mazeaud, La révision du contrat: LPA 2005, p. 4 et s.).*

Nous ne pouvons pas nous empêcher de voir dans le raisonnement du Tribunal arbitral une idée de « protection de la partie faible de la relation contractuelle », à savoir — dans la relation assureur — assuré, l'assuré. Or, cette idée de « protection » découle-t-elle du principe d'efficacité des contrats? Le principe d'efficacité des contrats ne pourrait-il pas indiquer plutôt que la suspension du programme de lancement devrait être retenue comme cause du retard de lancement? Nous demeurons convaincu que, quelque soit son contenu, le principe d'efficacité des contrats ne saurait privilégier la position de l'une des parties au détriment de la position de la partie adverse.

Le Tribunal arbitral, lors de son interprétation de la police d'assurance, semblerait vouloir appliquer une « justice distributive » *(cf. Aristote, Éthique à Nicomaque, traduction J.-F. Voilquin: GF-Flammarion, 1992, p. 139 et s. — Ch. Perelman, Logique juridique. Nouvelle rhétorique: Dalloz, 1999, p. 100, § 49)* visant avant tout à garantir que la victime d'un préjudice soit toujours indemnisée.

La sentence révèle néanmoins que le Tribunal arbitral et les parties n'étaient pas tout à fait à l'aise avec la possibilité d'une décision rendue sur l'unique base de l'interprétation de la police d'assurance et qu'ils ont tous choisi d'analyser les faits de l'espèce sur la base de la causalité en droit français.

III. — Quant à la causalité en droit français, le Tribunal abandonne son optique de « justice distributive » décrite ci-avant et adopte une optique correspondant à la « justice corrective » *(cf. Aristote, op. cit., p. 141).*

La « justice corrective » suppose que les parties en litige soient considérées de manière égalitaire et que le rôle du juge ou de l'arbitre se limite à rétablir l'équilibre perdu de la relation entre les parties.

En l'espèce, cette approche conduit le Tribunal arbitral à rejeter la définition de « causalité » soutenue par la partie demanderesse et par son expert juridique et à adopter celle proposée par les parties défenderesses et par leur expert juridique.

La partie demanderesse s'est placée sur le plan de la « justice distributive « et a soutenu que:

« (. . .) en cas de pluralité de faits à l'origine d'un même dommage, la victime est libre de se fonder sur l'un ou l'autre d'entre eux pour obtenir l'indemnisation. Selon l'opinion exprimée par le Professeur [P] dans son opinion juridique versé aux débats par [la partie demanderesse] (pièce [de la partie demanderesse] n° . . .):

« (. . .) un principe fondamental du droit civil français qui ne comporte que de rares exceptions impose de choisir la "cause" qui permet l'indemnisation. » (p. . . .) ».

Les parties défenderesses, pour leur part, se sont placées sur le plan « de la justice corrective » et de la présomption de l'égalité des parties participant au commerce international (cf. Sentence rendue dans l'affaire CCI n° 1990 en 1972: JDI 1974, p. 897. — Sentence rendue dans l'affaire CCI n° 5346 en 1988: JDI 1991, p. 1081) et ont allégué que la causalité telle que définie par le droit des assurances — et non pas par le droit civil de la responsabilité — devait être retenue.

Le Tribunal arbitral accepte — avec raison — la position des parties défenderesses quant à la causalité en droit français applicable au cas d'espèce. Il affirme à cet égard que « le Tribunal arbitral partage, sur ce point, l'opinion des assureurs. En effet, le principe privilégiant la cause ou les causes permettant l'indemnisation du dommage se justifie et se comprend parfaitement en matière de responsabilité civile où le droit privilégie à juste titre les intérêts de la victime aux intérêts d'un (co-)auteur de dommage. Il n'y a pas lieu, selon l'avis du Tribunal arbitral, de transposer ce principe et cette finalité juridique aux intérêts des parties à un contrat d'assurance. Il n'y a pas de principe général, ni dans le droit général des contrats ni en matière de contrats d'assurance, qui permettrait de privilégier les intérêts d'une partie contractante par rapport à ceux du co-contractant. Il faut donc rechercher la causalité telle que définie par le droit français en matière d'assurance ».

Il n'appartiendrait donc pas aux arbitres internationaux de protéger certains marchands internationaux au détriment d'autres commerçants internationaux mais de rétablir l'équilibre perdu des relations juridiques entre commerçants internationaux qui son présumés être des égaux. La lex mercatoria comprend bien en ce sens un principe selon lequel les marchands internationaux sont tous présumés être compétents et professionnels (cf. Sentence rendue dans l'affaire CCI n° 1512 de 1971: JDI 1974, p. 905. — Sentence rendue dans l'affaire CCI n° 2438 de 1975: JDI 1976, p. 969 et s. — Sentence rendue dans l'affaire CCI n° 3380 de 1980: JDI 1981, p. 928 et s. — Sentence rendue dans l'affaire CCI n° 5346 de 1988: JDI 1991, p. 1080 et s.).

Selon le Tribunal arbitral, la notion de « cause prépondérante » satisferait aux besoins de la « justice corrective ».

Nous ne pouvons qu'approuver l'application de la « justice corrective » au cas d'espèce. La sentence montre bien que les parties au litige étaient toutes les deux des marchands internationaux bien avisés. La présomption de leur égalité nous semble donc correcte. Nous osons néanmoins espérer que les arbitres internationaux appliqueront la « justice corrective » avec prudence dans les affaires où il s'avère que l'une des parties est de toute évidence dans une position plus forte que sa partie adverse.

En définitive, il est souhaitable que les tribunaux arbitraux internationaux fassent application du pragmatisme (cf. L. Menand, Pragmatism: Vintage Books, 1997) raisonné dont le

Tribunal arbitral de l'espèce a fait preuve au lieu d'analyser l'affaire sur la base d'idéologies qui mettent en relief la justice sociale en dépit de la justice du cas concret dont l'arbitre international est en même temps le serviteur et le maître.

IV. — Nous avons déjà signalé que la décision du Tribunal arbitral quant au caractère confidentiel (ou non) de certaines pièces versées au dossier a été importante à l'égard de sa décision quant à la répartition des frais de l'arbitrage entre les parties. La décision du Tribunal arbitral quant aux coûts de l'arbitrage mérite deux commentaires supplémentaires.

D'une part, le Tribunal arbitral, tel que l'avait fait un tribunal arbitral dans une sentence intérimaire que nous avons commentée *(cf. E. Silva Romero, Cour internationale d'arbitrage de la Chambre de commerce internationale, Chronique de sentences arbitrales: JDI 2005, p. 1268 et s.)*, semble affirmer que la règle de répartition des frais de procédure entre les parties est que la partie qui succombe devrait supporter les frais de l'arbitrage. La « jurisprudence arbitrale de la CCI » nous montre que l'existence d'une telle règle est — pour le moins — douteuse. Ladite « jurisprudence » nous révèle plutôt que les arbitres CCI jouissent d'une totale discrétion dans la prise de leur décision à l'égard de la répartition des frais de la procédure entre les parties *(cf. Sentence finale rendue dans l'affaire n° 5285 en 1989: Bull. CCI 1993, Cour internationale d'arbitrage: ICC Publishing, vol. 4, n° 1, p. 37. — Sentence finale rendue dans l'affaire n° 5726, op. cit., p. 39. — Sentence finale rendue dans l'affaire n° 5896, en 1992, op. cit., p. 40. — Sentence finale dans l'affaire n° 5987 en 1990, op. cit., p. 43. — Sentence finale rendue dans l'affaire n° 6293, op. cit., p. 46. — Sentence finale rendue dans l'affaire n° 7006' en 1992, op. cit., p. 58)*. Ainsi, la règle en matière de répartition de frais de la procédure arbitrale CCI, s'il en existe une, serait-elle plutôt que les arbitres distribuent librement ces frais entre les parties.

De l'autre, il est toujours intéressant, car ils sont d'habitude peu connus, de souligner les critères suivis par le Tribunal arbitral pour prendre sa décision quant à la répartition des frais de procédure entre les parties. En l'espèce, le Tribunal arbitral a tenu compte (i) du degré de réussite de chaque partie, (ii) de la difficulté de la question centrale de l'affaire, à savoir le problème de la causalité, (iii) du fait que les positions des deux parties quant à la causalité étaient défendables, (iv) de la bonne foi des parties à cet égard et des brillantes prestations des conseils des parties sur le thème de la causalité et (v) de la défaite de la partie demanderesse au sujet de l'incident sur le caractère « confidentiel » de certaines pièces versées au dossier.

La sentence, par le biais de sa brillante analyse de la causalité en droit français, nous rappelle que l'arbitre international doit se placer sur le terrain de la « justice corrective » de la société marchande internationale afin d'accomplir la mission que les parties — commerçants internationaux compétents, professionnels et avisés — lui ont confié.

E. S. R.

Décision rendue dans l'affaire 12711 en 2004

Procédure arbitrale. — Ordonnance de procédure. — Répartition entre l'acte de mission et les décisions de procédure.

Taxe sur la valeur ajoutée sur les honoraires des arbitres. — Article 2(9) de l'appendice III du règlement CCI.- Calcul. — Paiement. — Solidarité passive (non) — Création d'un compte séquestre. — Consignation d'une provision. — Avance sur provision.

Face au risque de non-paiement par les parties de la TVA sur leurs honoraires, les arbitres assujettis à cette taxe recherchent diverses solutions. L'une d'entre elle consiste pour ceux-ci à appeler et consigner une provision pour TVA établie en fonction du montant supposé des honoraires. Cette provision, réévaluée en cours d'instance selon la fluctuation du montant en litige et des honoraires qui pourraient être versés par la CCI aux arbitres, est liquidée par le tribunal arbitral en fin de procédure. Le mécanisme d'appel de la provision et sa gestion peuvent être fixés par le tribunal arbitral dans une ordonnance de procédure.

Procedural Order n° 6

Deposit for VAT

1. The ICC letter of [date 1], by which the advance on costs was raised due to the new amount in dispute has as a consequence that also new deposits for VAT are due in follow-up to Procedural Orders n° 2 and n° 4.

2. In that context, the Tribunal recalls again Section [X] of the Terms of Reference signed by the Parties and the Tribunal:

> « *Art. 2(9) of Appendix III of the ICC Arbitration Rules provide that the Parties have a duty to pay any possible value added taxes (VAT) and that the respective payment arrangements shall be made directly between the Parties and the Arbitrators. In its letter of* [date 2], *the ICC drew attention to this provision. Accordingly, the Parties shall, as the advances due to the ICC under Art. 30 of the Rules, pay at the request of the Tribunal a deposit on the applicable VAT to the trust account of the Chairman of the Tribunal from which the VAT shall be paid once the ICC has set the fees of the Arbitrators, remaining amounts to be reimbursed to the Parties.* »

3. Of the deposit of [sum 1] for fees and expenses newly set by the ICC Court as mentioned above, according to the ICC Arbitration Cost Calculator, the new amount in dispute of [sum 2] leads to [sum 3] as the amount set aside for total average fees of the members of the Tribunal.

4. On this amount, it is presently expected that VAT in the total amount of [sum 4] will have to be paid 50 % of which are due from each Party, *i.e.* [sum 5].

5. The Tribunal notes, that each Party has transferred the amount requested in Procedural Order n° 4, *i.e.* [sum 6] thus leaving an outstanding amount of [sum 7]. Therefore, in application of Section 2 above, each Party is now requested to transfer, by [date 3], [sum 7] to the trust account of the Chairman of the Tribunal:

(. . .)

NOTE. — I. — L'ordonnance de procédure rapportée présente une grande originalité quant aux choix opérés par le tribunal arbitral, et plus particulièrement son président, dans la conduite de l'instance. Il est en effet exceptionnel qu'un tribunal arbitral use de la faculté qui lui est tacitement accordée par le règlement d'arbitrage de la CCI de se prononcer sur les questions de taxe sur la valeur ajoutée par voie d'ordonnance. Lorsque ces questions sont abordées par les tribunaux arbitraux, la pratique consiste à les évoquer et les régler dans l'acte de mission ainsi que dans de simples lettres. L'acte de mission pose alors le principe général retenu par le tribunal arbitral en matière de TVA. Il s'agit le plus souvent d'un rappel de l'article 2 (9) de l'appendice III du règlement et parfois des termes de la lettre de saisine des arbitres émanant du secrérariat de la Cour internationale d'arbitrage et attirant l'attention des arbitres et des parties sur cet article. Les lettres fixent ensuite les modalités pratiques détaillées de mise en œuvre du principe, qu'il s'agisse du calcul de la somme due au titre de la TVA ou de son paiement.

En l'espèce, le président du tribunal arbitral adopte une démarche particulièrement précautionneuse en matière de TVA. L'acte de mission contenait des dispositions relativement plus détaillées que ce qui est communément prévu dans un tel document. Ces dispositions ont ensuite fait l'objet non de simples lettres mais de plusieurs ordonnances de procédure rendues par le seul président du tribunal arbitral, en fonction de l'évolution financière du dossier, à savoir les réévaluations de la provision pour frais d'arbitrage et l'acquittement des paiements dus à ce titre par les parties.

Au moins deux explications peuvent être avancées pour expliquer l'approche retenue.

D'une part, régler les questions de TVA par ordonnance confere aux décisions prises une solennité que n'auraient pas de simples lettres.

D'autre part, éviter de compliquer l'acte de mission par l'ajout de dispositions précises dont la discussion par les parties pourrait susciter certaines difficultés procédurales, peut s'avérer judicieux. C'est notamment le cas lorsque l'attitude des parties laisse planer une incertitude quant à leur volonté de signer l'acte de mission ou dans les hypothèses où le tribunal arbitral entrevoit de longues discussions sur les points mentionnés. Aux termes de l'article 18 (3) du règlement d'arbitrage, le refus de signature de l'acte de mission a pour conséquence la nécessité de le faire approuver la cour. Cette dernière est généralement opposée, par principe, à l'adoption d'un tel acte qui contiendrait des expressions tendant à faire accroire à l'existence d'un accord des parties, ce dernier faisant précisément défaut du fait d'un refus de signature. L'opportunité de préciser que les dispositions de l'acte de mission ne lient que les parties signataires est discutable en ce qu'une telle formule souligne clairement, par une interprétation *a contrario,* que les parties non signataires ne seraient pas tenues par les obligations stipulées. Traiter les questions délicates dans un document non soumis à l'approbation des parties peut donc être un facteur de célérité de la procédure et contribuer à préserver une égalité de traitement entre les parties.

En l'espèce, les rappels qui ont été faits à l'acte de mission dans plusieurs ordonnances de procédure prises par le président du tribunal arbitral après signature de ce document insistent sur l'acceptation de ses termes par les parties. La démarche suivie par le président du tribunal tend à renforcer les droits des arbitres au paiement de la TVA sur leurs honoraires. En effet, aux termes de l'article 33 du règlement d'arbitrage, toute contestation tardive du principe du paiement de la taxe, alors que ce dernier aurait été répété dans des actes de procédure en cours d'instance sans soulever d'objection des parties, ne saurait remettre en cause l'obligation d'acquittement de la taxe dont les parties sont débitrices.

II. — De manière habituelle, le président du tribunal arbitral vise expressément l'article 2 (9) de l'appendice III du règlement définissant les rôles respectifs des parties, des arbitres et de l'institution d'arbitrage en matière de paiement de TVA sur les honoraires des arbitres. Constituant une exception au principe implicite d'interdiction de relation financière directe entre les parties prévue par le règlement d'arbitrage, cet article dispose expressément que le « *recouvrement [de la TVA] est seulement affaire entre l'arbitre et les parties* ». Deux remarques découlent de cette affirmation.

D'une part, la CCI refusait traditionnellement (et encore à la date de la présente ordonnance de procédure) d'agir en tant que collecteur de TVA et ne satisfaisait pas aux demandes des parties tendant à la création d'un compte séquestre administré par l'institution pour la TVA due sur les honoraires des arbitres. Cette approche est désormais abandonnée. La CCI a accepté la création d'un tel compte, chaque arbitre qui en fait la demande à la CCI ayant la possibilité d'ouvrir un compte sur lequel les sommes dues part les parties au titre de la TVA sur les honoraires des arbitres seraient consignées. Chaque arbitre a donc l'initiative de l'ouverture du compte et, en cas d'ouverture de compte, l'initiative du moment et de la fixation du montant de tout versement de sommes d'argent au crédit du compte et de tout paiement au débit du compte.

D'autre part, c'est aux parties et aux arbitres qu'il revient d'organiser contractuellement leurs relations en matière de TVA dans le respect de la législation fiscale qui leur est applicable. Il ne rentre pas dans la mission de l'institution d'arbitrage et *a fortiori* dans ses obligations de veiller au respect par les parties et les arbitres de leurs obligations en matière de TVA et plus généralement en toute matière fiscale.

L'organisation de ces relations doit notamment tenir compte du fait qu'au sein d'un tribunal arbitral tous les arbitres ne seront pas nécessairement assujettis à la TVA et que le taux de la taxe varie selon les pays. Concernant le premier point, les arbitres adoptent des approches vaiiées. Ils rappellent parfois en termes généraux que la TVA sur les honoraires serait due par les parties, dans la mesure où le paiement d'une telle taxe incomberait aux arbitres en application du droit applicable. Certains arbitres retiennent une formule plus précise consistant à mentionner le numéro d'article de la loi fiscale ou du code des impôts applicable, voire à les citer *in extenso*. Quelques rares tribunaux arbitraux constitués d'arbitres domiciliés ou exerçant dans l'Union européenne ont expressément indiqué que la source d'une telle obligation de paiement de la TVA résultat de l'interprétation de la 6ᵉ directive *(Dir. n° 77/388/CEE, 17 mai 1977: JOCE n° L 145, 13 juin 1977, p. 1)* par la Cour de justice des Communautés européennes *(CJCE, 16 sept. 1997, affi. C-145/96, Von Hoffmann: Rec. CJCE 1997, I, p. 4857).*

En l'espèce et au regard de la pratique arbitrale, l'ordonnance s'avère relativement complète. Tant les modalités de calcul de la taxe que celles afférentes à son paiement sont énoncées.

Le président du tribunal arbitral rappelle opportunément que la TVA est payable sur les honoraires perçus par les arbitres et fixés par la cour en fonction du montant en litige. Le montant définitif des honoraires n'est connu qu'en fin de procédure lorsque la cour liquide les frais de l'arbitrage en application de l'article 31 du règlement. Certains arbitres acceptent de différer intégralement le paiement de la TVA par les parties jusqu'à la liquidation finale des frais de l'arbitrage. Cette approche peut les conduire à acquitter le paiement de la TVA auprès de leurs autorités fiscales, par exemple, en cas d'avance sur honoraires versée par la cour, alors que les sommes correspondant à ce montant de TVA n'ont pas été payées par les parties. De plus, le risque de non-paiement de la taxe tend à croître si l'une des parties pressent qu'elle n'obtiendra pas gain de cause ou a reçu notification d'une sentence lui étant défavorable.

Faute de paiement additionnel de la TVA par les parties, certains arbitres ont parfois considéré que la TVA serait incluse dans la somme payée par la CCI au titre des honoraires. Une telle interprétation est contraire à l'esprit du règlement. Les arbitres ne souhaitant pas différer ainsi le moment du paiement du montant de la taxe par les parties peuvent recourir à la méthode des paiements échelonnés en fonction des versements d'avances sur honoraires opérés par la cour à la demande du tribunal arbitral. Dans cette hypothèse également, le tribunal arbitral réclamera le paiement aux parties après fixation de l'avance par la cour. Le montant de TVA dû par les parties sera calculé sur la somme allouée par la cour. Or, il se peut que l'étape significative de la procédure donnant lieu à une avance sur honoraires mécontente une partie qui refusera de payer la TVA.

Certains tribunaux arbitraux on tenté de remédier à ce risque de non-paiement en stipulant dans l'acte de mission que la communication de la sentence arbitrale est subordonnée au paiement de la TVA aux arbitres. Cette démarche pose un certain nombre de difficultés pratiques tenant notamment à son ambiguïté et au risque d'impliquer la cour ou son secrétariat dans l'exécution de l'obligation de paiement de la TVA aux arbitres par les parties, en contravention au règlement d'arbitrage. Pour ces raisons, elle doit être écartée.

Une deuxième réponse aux risques de non-paiement de la TVA en fin de procédure consiste pour le tribunal arbitral ou les seuls arbitres assujettis à la TVA à fixer une provision séparée destinée à couvrir le montant de la TVA due par les parties aux arbitres *(en ce sens, en droit français, V.J.-P. Le Gall, Note explicative sur l'assujettissement des arbitres à la TVA sous l'empire de l'article 259 du Code général des impôts: Rev. arb. 2006, p. 554).* C'est cette technique qui est retenue en l'espèce. Naturellement, la licéité d'une telle approche devra impérativement être vérifiée par chaque arbitre assujetti à la TVA au regard du droit fiscal qui lui est applicable. Cette obligation de vérification est *intuitu personae,* elle pèse sur chaque arbitre assujetti à la TVA et ne saurait être transmise à l'institution d'arbitrage administrant la procédure. En effet, l'article 2 (9) de l'appendice III du règlement d'arbitrage de la CCI laisse aux parties et aux arbitres concernés la charge de déterminer le régime applicable au recouvrement *lato sensu* de la TVA. La détermination de ce régime recouvre donc deux aspects, d'une part, l'identification du droit fiscal applicable à la situation et, d'autre part, la fixation des modalités contractuelles du recouvrement en conformité avec le droit fiscal applicable.

Une troisième réponse possible au risque de non-paiement de la TVA due aux arbitres par les parties tient à l'existence ou non de la solidarité entre celles-ci.

La mention expresse d'une telle solidarité passive permet de limiter le risque de défaut de paiement de l'intégralité de la TVA sur leurs honoraires réclamée par les arbitres concernés, que la somme à payer représente la totalité de la TVA due au terme de la procédure arbitrale ou seulement une partie de celle-ci. En l'espèce commentée, aucune solidarité passive n'était prévue ou invoquée par les arbitres.

Selon l'approche suivie en l'espèce, en début de procédure, le tribunal détermine quel serait le montant moyen des honoraires qui pourraient être versés aux arbitres. La connaissance du montant en litige permet aisément de connaître ce montant par l'application du barème des honoraires publié dans l'appendice III du règlement d'arbitrage. La tâche est encore simplifiée lorsque le tribunal arbitral recourt au calculateur de coûts sur le site Internet de la cour *(www.iccarbitration.org)* plutôt que d'effectuer manuellement les calculs.

Sur la base du montant moyen des honoraires, le tribunal arbitral calcule le montant de TVA qui serait dû par les arbitres si ces honoraires venaient à être payés. C'est ensuite l'intégralité ou une partie seulement de ce montant qui est réclamée de manière anticipée aux parties par le tribunal et consignée. La formulation de cet appel de fonds (versement d'une avance, acompte, paiement de garantie, etc.) n'étant pas toujours neutre au regard du régime fiscal applicable, les arbitres devraient systématiquement effectuer les vérifications nécessaires afin de retenir la qualification juridique pertinente en l'espèce *(V. pour le droit français, G. Blanluet, La fiscalité des rémunérations des arbitres, actes du colloque Arbitrage et fiscalité, Dijon, 6 oct. 2000: Rev. arb. 2001, p. 357. — S. Lazareff et J.-P. Le Gall, op. cit., p. 543 et 544).*

Le montant en litige étant susceptible de fluctuations, le tribunal arbitral devrait réviser le montant de la provision séparée pour TVA en conséquence.

En fin d'arbitrage, le montant définitif des honoraires des arbitres ayant été fixés par la cour, le tribunal arbitral est à même de solder la provision séparée consignée et le plus souvent rembourser le trop-perçu. Le cas échéant il peut demander un paiement complémentaire au titre de la TVA lorsque le montant de la provision initiale a été sous-estimé. Si l'obligation de remboursement aux parties du trop-perçu par le tribunal arbitral est parfois expressément spécifiée dans l'acte de mission, la pratique de la cour est de ne pas admettre qu'une décision relative au paiement de la TVA aux arbitres figure dans le dispositif des sentences. Si la cour considère que le dispositif des sentences doit rester vierge de toute mention de la TVA sur les honoraires des arbitres, elle a parfois accepté qu'une décision sur la répartition de la charge financière de la TVA figure dans les motifs de la sentence, cette charge financière entrant alors dans les coûts globaux de l'arbitrage aux termes de l'article 31 *in fine*.

Sur un plan comptable et fiscal, il peut être judicieux pour les arbitres de prendre la précaution de gérer les sommes perçues au titre de la TVA sur un compte distinct de celui auquel sont affectés les honoraires versés et les remboursements de frais effectués au titre de l'arbitrage considéré. L'existence d'un tel compte séquestre est portée à la connaissance des parties par les arbitres. Ainsi sont-elles informées du nom de l'organisme professionnel ou bancaire tenant le compte et de ses coordonnées. En revanche, il n'en est généralement pas de même des modalités d'ouverture et de fonctionnement du compte, les arbitres ne communicant pas nécessairement aux parties la convention de compte ou une explication sur ces points.

En pratique, les arbitres semblent appeler les sommes devant être consignées soit dans une facture, *pro forma* ou non *(sur la pratique en droit français, V. S. Lazareff et J.-P. Le Gall, op. cit., p. 544),* soit dans de simples lettres. Certains arbitres ont, dans cette dernière situation, considéré que la fourniture possible et prévue à l'acte de mission d'un simple récépissé de paiement de la TVA serait de nature à aider les parties à récupérer le montant de la taxe acquitté auprès des autorités fiscales compétentes. Les arbitres doivent en cette matière aussi veiller au strict respect des dispositions fiscales applicables.

Une autre considération pratique intéressante tient à la répartition de la somme due par les débiteurs de l'obligation de paiement de la TVA. Il arrive, par exemple en cas d'arbitrage multipartite, que le montant de la TVA due par les demandeurs d'une part et les défendeurs d'autre part soit réparti en fonction du nombre de demandeurs et de défendeurs. Ainsi, 50 % de la TVA due pourrait être mis à la charge de l'unique demandeur alors que chacun des deux défendeurs serait tenu de verser 25 % de la somme due.

Dans plusieurs affaires, les tribunaux arbitraux ont soumis le paiement du montant de TVA due au résultat de l'instance. Les parties étaient alors tenues de payer la TVA dans les proportions définies par le tribunal arbitral pour le paiement des frais de l'arbitrage.

La présente ordonnance illustre un développement pratique récent du droit de l'arbitrage. Les tribunaux arbitraux abordent dorénavant de plus en plus fréquemment les questions de paiement de la TVA sur les honoraires des arbitres. La clarté de l'explication fournie aux parties dans l'affaire rapportée est exemplaire. Le traitement des questions de TVA de manière explicite et transparente dans l'instance arbitrale, en tenant compte des spécificités de chaque affaire et notamment du cadre fiscal applicable, contribuerait vraisemblablement à limiter les incompréhensions voire les contentieux surgissant entre les parties et les arbitres en cette matière.

E. J.

Sentence rendue dans l'affaire n° 11776 en 2002

Procédure arbitrale. — Procédure de référé arbitral. — Relations. — Procédure arbitrale. — Frais de l'arbitrage. — Réparation.

Contrat. — Distribution. — Distribution sélective. — Obligations contractuelles. — Violation. — Absence de conséquence dommageable. — Sanction (non). — Obligation de concertation. — Notion. — Sanction.

Une procédure de référé pré-arbitral selon le règlement de la CCI peut être initiée après le déclenchement d'une procédure d'arbitrage. La décision du tiers sur la charge des frais de la procédure de référé pré-arbitral n'est pas remise en cause par le Tribunal arbitral à l'issue de la procédure d'arbitrage.

Le principe de bonne justice commande que la partie qui succombe supporte les frais de l'arbitrage, dans la proportion où la partie adverse obtient gain de cause.

La nature propre d'un contrat peut justifier l'existence d'une obligation de concertation qui ne se confond pas avec l'obligation de coopérer de bonne foi traditionnellement consacrée par la jurisprudence arbitrale. C'est un instrument de gestion courante, nécessaire en raison de l'incidence des décisions prises par une partie sur les activités de l'autre. Sa sanction trouve sa source dans le droit commun de la responsabilité.

La violation d'une obligation contractuelle qui ne cause aucun préjudice ne saurait justifier la résiliation d'un contrat.

La demanderesse A, société française et trois sociétés française et suisses du groupe C, défenderesses, ont conclu un contrat de licence mondiale et exclusive (ci-après « le contrat ») ayant pour objet la création, la fabrication, la distribution, le marketing, la publicité et la vente de vêtements et d'autres produits de marque C (ci-après « la marque ») par la demanderesse, y compris le droit exclusif pour celle-ci d'exploiter des boutiques (ci-après « les boutiques ») qui commercialisent essentiellement des vêtements, et quelques autres produits (ci-après « les autres produits ») distribués sous la marque.

La demanderesse soutenait que, selon le contrat, elle avait le seul contrôle des produits distribués sous la marque dans les boutiques et que les licenciés des autres produits (c'est-à-dire autres que des vêtements), ayant contracté directement avec les défenderesses, ne pouvaient imposer la vente directe de ceux-ci dans les boutiques sans passer par l'intermédiaire de la demanderesse.

Après la conclusion du contrat, les défenderesses et des fabricants d'autres produits (ci-après les « autres licenciés ») avaient conclu divers contrats de licence mondiale et exclusive pour la fabrication et la distribution sous la marque de ces produits.

Les autres licenciés se voyaient reconnaître le droit de vendre directement d'autres produits dans les boutiques.

La demanderesse estimait que les droits concédés par les défenderesses aux autres licenciés étaient incompatibles avec les droits exclusifs qu'elle tenait du contrat.

Elle engagea donc une procédure arbitrale pour faire constater qu'en contractant avec les autres licenciés, les défenderesses avaient notamment manqué à leurs obligations contractuelles de coordination et de concertation et porté atteinte à son exclusivité.

Elle demandait que soit reconnue l'étendue de ses droits consacrés par le contrat

Les défenderesses sollicitaient le rejet des prétentions de la demanderesse et présentait diverses demandes reconventionnelles.

Le contrat était soumis au droit français. Il contenait une clause d'arbitrage disposant entre autres:

> « Tous différends découlant du présent contrat ou en relation avec celui-ci seront tranchés définitivement suivant le Règlement d'arbitrage de la Chambre de commerce internationale par un ou plusieurs arbitres nommés conformément à ce règlement.
>
> Nonobstant ce qui est stipulé à (. . .) ci-dessus, les parties pourront recourir au Règlement de référé pré-arbitral de la Chambre de commerce internationale et seront liées par les dispositions dudit règlement ».

Moins d'un mois après le dépôt de la demande d'arbitrage, les défenderesses ont introduit une procédure de référé pré-arbitral selon le Règlement de la Chambre de commerce internationale, qui a donné lieu au prononcé par le tiers de deux premières ordonnances:

– constatant l'existence, à titre préalable et *prima facie,* d'un droit d'accès direct au profit d'un des autres licenciés aux boutiques de ses sous-licenciés ou distributeurs exclusifs;

– ordonnant à tout le moins la poursuite de la vente des produits de maroquinerie C dans les espaces de vente vêtements C;

– ordonnant à A, à titre provisoire, pour un an, et tous droits réservés quant au fond du litige, de donner accès aux boutiques aux produits de maroquinerie C;

– ordonnant à A de s'abstenir de tout acte, quel qu'il soit, de nature à aggraver le différend qui l'oppose au Groupe C.

Environ une semaine après le prononcé de ces ordonnances mais avant la remise du dossier au Tribunal arbitral, A, à son tour, saisit le tiers pour lui demander de constater que les projets de contrats qu'elle avait adressés au groupe C à la suite de ces ordonnances étaient conformes aux dispositifs de celles-ci.

Par une nouvelle ordonnance rendue après la saisine du Tribunal arbitral, le tiers constata cette conformité.

A prétendait que les dispositions du contrat de licence consacraient une volonté de stratégie commune et un principe de concertation entre les parties pour conduire cette stratégie de manière ordonnée, et que le groupe C avait méconnu ces principes à l'occasion de la négociation et de la conclusion d'un contrat avec un des autres licenciés.

Il s'agissait, selon A, d'une concertation préalable afin de permettre, dans l'intérêt de tous les opérateurs concernés et de la marque, d'analyser objectivement un projet d'ouverture, de fournir au groupe C toutes les informations sur les points de vente qui préexistaient dans la zone et y commercialiser les mêmes autres produits et d'identifier ensemble les risques potentiels de conflits.

Le groupe C estimait que le contrat n'avait pas fixé de principe général de concertation d'où résulterait une obligation de co-décision en matière de vêtement ou d'autres produits et que chaque'partie pouvait conduire souverai-nement la stratégie relevant de son domaine propre et se serait seulement engagée avec l'autre à échanger des informations sur leurs domaines respectifs de responsabilités.

Le Tribunal arbitral statua ainsi sur cette question:

> « Les parties ne parvenant pas à s'entendre sur le sens de leur convention, il appartient au tribunal arbitral de l'interpréter et pour cela de rechercher leur commune volonté.
>
> L'Annexe (. . .) [du contrat] énonce les moyens stratégiques de parvenir au but commun que se sont assigné les deux parties: « le développement de [C] (. . .) ».

Elle précise les choix de cette stratégie commune pour chacune des activités [C] *existantes: évolution des collections des vêtements* [C] *(. . .), organisation du système d'approvisionnement des vêtements* [C] *(. . .), évolution de la distribution des vêtements* [C] *(. . .), évolution de la communication (. . .), et sous le titre « Autres activités » (. . .), la convention souligne tout particulièrement « l'importance, tant pour l'image* [C] *que sur le plan financier, de la poursuite du développement des lignes de produits autres que les vêtements* [C] *(. . .), et la nécessité de « rechercher toutes synergie possibles dans le domaine de la distribution et de la communication, entre les vêtements* [C] *et les autres produits, notamment chaque fois que les conditions de vente et la taille des points de vente le permettent » (. . .).*

Un tel texte ne peut être réduit à une simple délimitation de deux domaines d'activité, autonomes et indépendants l'un de l'autre, entre lesquels n'existerait qu'une passerelle consistant en un échange d'informations (. . .). Il est manifeste au contraire qu'après avoir défini: « le développement de [C] *», les parties se sont mises d'accord sur les options stratégiques à retenir pour tenter de l'atteindre. Ces options sont décrites pour les articles (. . .) à (. . .). À l'intérieur de chacune des (. . .) rubriques, ont été précisées les « évolutions » nécessaires pour atteindre les « objectifs énumérés », ces évolutions devant être conduites « de faç on ordonnée ».*

En d'autres termes, l'Annexe (. . .) fixe les buts qu'il faut chercher à atteindre par des évolutions qu'il convient de conduire de façon ordonnée, de concert.

Ainsi, et même si le terme n'est pas utilisé dans les textes rédigés par les parties, il n'est pas contestable que le dernier paragraphe de l'Annexe (. . .) recèle **une obligation de concertation** *qu'appelle d'ailleurs la nature coopérative des conventions signées entre les parties. Ce principe de concertation mérite trois précisions relatives à* **sa consistance,** *à* **son étendue** *et* **aux conséquences de son non-respect éventuel***.*

(a) Quant à sa consistance, les lexicographes généraux définissent généralement la concertation comme le fait de s'entendre pour agir de concert, ce qui pourrait suggérer une obligation de co-décision que conteste radicalement le groupe [C] *et que ne réclame pas* [A]. *La définition donnée par le Vocabulaire Juridique Capitani par G. Cornu est plus juridique et plus fine: « Recherche en commun, par les personnes dont les intérêts sont convergents, complémentaires ou même opposés, d'un accord tendant à l'harmonisation de leurs conduites respectives ».* **Il apparaît alors clairement qu'une obligation de concertation consiste à rechercher un accord, mais n'oblige pas à y parvenir.** *Une telle décision n'est pas neutre. Elle exclut toute idée de co-décision sans pour autant vider l'obligation de son contenu: en contraignant au dialogue elle facilite la conduite « de façon ordonnée » des évolutions procédant de la poursuite des objectifs communs. (. . .)*

Les parties sont tenues de se concerter avant de prendre individuellement et librement les décisions relevant de leur sphère de compétence propre.

Une telle concertation est d'autant plus nécessaire que la diversité des environnements économiques dans lesquels interviennent les réseaux [C] *— qui sont mondiaux — fait qu'une décision peut être bonne dans un pays donné et ne pas correspondre, dans un autre pays, au paysage économique local. S'il n'est pas possible de se mettre d'accord une fois pour toutes sur tel ou tel sujet, il devient indispensable de se concerter pays par pays ou région par région, sur la meilleure façon de tendre vers les buts communs.*

L'obligation de se concerter pourrait être de nature à ralentir le processus décisionnel appartenant respectivement aux parties, mais ce ralentissement, à le supposer avéré, ne serait pas pour autant un inconvénient dans les rapports entre les parties. Pour réussir les évolutions de fond visées par l'Annexe (. . .), il paraît en effet plus efficace de se préoccuper de la qualité des projets, qui passent par leur maturation concertée, que de s'assurer de leur rapidité d'exécution, dès lors que la construction en commun de plusieurs réseaux mondiaux cohérents entre eux (dans chaque pays et entre chacun de ces pays) et destinés au développement de la marque [C], requiert un travail de fond et de coopération. La communauté d'intérêts reconnue par les parties dans l'Annexe (. . .) procède en effet de ce que cette marque et les produits commercialisés sous cette marque sont indissociablement liés. Économiquement, le produit crée la marque autant que la marque crée le produit.

*(b) **L'étendue de l'obligation de concertation est identique à celle du champ contractuel des conventions qui recèlent l'Annexe (. . .) ou qui s'y réfèrent.** En conséquence, elle porte aussi bien sur les rapports d'actionnaires (changement de dirigeant, par exemple) que sur la politique de diversification ou la distribution des autres produits dans les boutiques (. . .). Elle s'applique aussi à la création par des licenciés autres produits de réseaux de distribution de leurs propres produits. L'article (. . .) de l'Annexe (. . .) faisant aux parties l'obligation de « rechercher toutes synergies possibles dans le domaine de la distribution et de la communication, entre les vêtements [C] et les autres produits (. . .) », l'implantation de points de vente autres produits sans concertation préalable avec [A] constituerait une violation de l'obligation de concertation que [C] pourra toujours répercuter sur ses licenciés autres produits si elle l'estime opportun.*

*(c) **Quant à la sanction du non-respect éventuel de l'obligation de concertation, les conventions des parties sont muettes.***

*La concertation contractuellement prévue vise à la seule recherche d'une solution harmonieuse, et non à l'accord sur sa définition. **La violation de l'obligation de concertation par l'une des parties consisterait donc dans le simple fait pour elle de négliger de recourir au dialogue lorsque celui-ci devient nécessaire, et certainement pas dans le fait de ne pas s'accorder sur une solution au terme de cette concertation.***

C'est pourquoi l'Annexe (. . .) ne stipule pas que le recours à la concertation devrait nécessairement précéder toute décision prise par les parties dans leurs domaines d'activités propres. Au contraire, le recours à la concertation n'est prévu que « aussi souvent que nécessaire » (Annexe . . .).

La définition du seuil de déclenchement de cette nécessité est laissée à l'appréciation des parties, sous leur seule responsabilité. Elle n'est pas précisée par la convention. En l'absence d'organisation contractuelle, la violation du principe de concertation ne sera sanctionnable qu'en application des principes du droit commun de la responsabilité contractuelle, ce qui suppose la démonstration d'une faute, d'un préjudice résultant de l'absence ou de l'insuffisance de concertation, et d'un lien de causalité entre cette faute et ce préjudice ».

Le Tribunal estima ensuite que le groupe C avait effectivement violé son obligation de concertation en concluant un contrat de licence avec un de ses distributeurs d'autres produits D. Il releva ce qui suit:

« Historiquement, les activités [C] en sacs de loisir et de sport, en maroquinerie et en bagages, ont été considérées par les parties comme étant différents.

Ainsi, l'annexe (. . .) du [contrat] qui identifie les autres produits mentionne ces activités de manière distincte. Cette distinction se retrouve aussi dans les ordres du jour des conseils d'administration de (. . .).

Avant la conclusion de la licence [D], les lignes sacs et maroquinerie étaient vendues dans l'ensemble du réseau vêtements (. . .).

Le point sur ces activités, et notamment sur la « licence bagages [C] », a fait l'objet d'informations fournies par le groupe [C] au cours des comités d'associés ou en conseil d'administration de [C] depuis (. . .), mais ces informations

étaient pour ainsi dire squelettiques et maintenaient la distinction entre les trois lignes.
(. . .)

Lorsque les négociations avec [D] *furent évoquées succinctement le (. . .), mais uniquement au niveau des activités maroquinerie/ bagages,* [un représentant de A] *a souligné toute l'importance qu 'il y avait à bien définir dans le contrat le principe de la distribution sélective car la présence de* [D] *dans les hypermarchés était très importante.*

[Ensuite un représentant du groupe C] *déclara que dans le dossier bagages et maroquinerie (l'activité sacs de loisir et de sport n'étant pas mentionnée), les négociations étaient en cours, que de « bonnes nouvelles » pourraient peut-être être données dans « quelques semaines », mais que le dossier était un peu compliqué par les exigences que* [C] *maintenait à propos de la distribution sélective.*

Aucune information ne sera cependant donnée lors de la réunion du [une **semaine après]** *alors que la licence* **[D]** *allait être signée à peine six jours plus tard.*

Ces informations, **ou plutôt bribes d'informations,** *se concilient mal avec les intentions déclarées par* [C] *à* [D], *les . . . et . . . , de faire approuver le projet de licence et les produits concernés lors des conseils d'administration de* [C] *des (. . .), réunions au cours desquelles ces sujets n'ont pas été abordés.*

[A], *qui en sa capacité d'actionnaire minoritaire (mais important) de* [C], *était représentée au conseil d'administration de celle-ci, n'avait donc pas de raison particulière de penser que la licence* [D] *qu 'on lui présentait comme étant centrée sur les bagages, aurait en réalité un objet beaucoup plus étendu et recouvrirait l'activité distincte en sacs de loisir et de sport.* [A] *continuait d'ailleurs d'intégrer cette activité,* [dans son budget de l'année suivante].

Il s'avère que, dans le même temps, **[C]** *envisageait expressément l'intégration chez* **[D]** *des trois lignes d'activités concernées, et notamment l'activité sacs de loisir et de sport exploitée par* **[A]**, *qu'il présentait pourtant comme un « partenariat actuel très valable » (. . .).*

L'absence de toute concertation avec [A] *à propos de ces négociations apparaît comme étant délibérée de la part du groupe* [C] *puisque celui-ci devait nécessairement savoir que* [A] *comprendrait mal l'arrivée de* [D] *dans la distribution de* [C] *tels que les sacs de loisir et de sport (. . .).*

Cette absence de concertation est également confirmée, mais implicitement cette fois, par la lettre de [C] **dans laquelle il informait celle-ci de la conclusion de la licence [D],** *information qui eut été superflue si les parties s'étaient concertées en vue des négociations et la conclusion du contrat.*

(. . .)

Les conditions dans lesquelles le groupe [C] *a mené les négociations avec* [D], *(. . .) ont violé le principe de concertation, et cette violation suffit par elle-même à justifier la mesure demandée, à savoir l'obligation par* [C] *de respecter à l'avenir le principe de concertation lors de toute nouvelle conclusion, ou de tout renouvellement, d'un contrat de licence d'autres produits ».*

De son côté, le groupe C reprochait, entre autres, à A d'avoir violé ses obligations contractuelles en ne concluant pas de contrats avec les commerçants qui composent son réseau de distribution de vêtements [C] en Allemagne. Or, un article du contrat indiquait que A, autant que possible, serait contractuellement liée aux détaillants qui composent le système de distribution sélective [C]. C, au cours de la procédure arbitrale, avait donc mis en demeure A de remédier à cette situation, en application d'une disposition contractuelle permettant à une partie de résilier le contrat dans le cas où l'autre ne respecterait pas l'une quelconque de ses obligations essentielles, six mois après mise en demeure.

C demandait au Tribunal arbitral de constater qu'il avait valablement mis en demeure A tout en suspendant les effets de cette mise en demeure jusqu'au prononcé de la sentence arbitrale.

Le Tribunal arbitral répondit comme suit:

> « Le Tribunal arbitral estime qu'il n'est pas établi que la lettre de mise en demeure du (. . .) réponde à une préoccupation légitime du groupe [C] compte tenu de sa date, des antécédents de la situation qu'elle dénonce, et de l'absence de conséquences dommageables causées par les griefs retenus.
>
> La dénonciation de la situation manque donc de la bonne foi requise pour valider la mise en demeure litigieuse.
>
> Si ZGmbH est en effet une filiale de [A], il est tout aussi constant qu'elle était également, et depuis [plus de 20 ans] déjà, le distributeur direct en Allemagne de [C] (. . .). Après la conclusion du [contrat], ZGmbH s'est contentée de maintenir le réseau allemand qu'elle avait organisé [dès l'origine] conformément aux principes contractuels de distribution sélective convenue directement entre elle et [C]. Or, le groupe [C] ne produit aucun document établissant que cette situation ne correspondait pas à l'image de marque qu'il avait chargé [Z] de défendre en Allemagne depuis [l'origine] ni que le réseau créé par ZGmbH ne correspondait pas au système de distribution sélective qui lui imposait l'article (. . .) du contrat de distribution, ni que le marché allemand avait manqué d'étanchéité ou généré des problèmes de distribution parallèle, ni surtout que cette situation préexistante aurait effectivement gêné, avant ou après la conclusion du [contrat] la conclusion de contrats par les autres licenciés [C] sur ce territoire.
>
> La lettre [de mise en demeure] paraît donc avoir été adressée pour des raisons de pure opportunité, d'autant que dans un territoire comparable ou à tout le moins proche tel que l'Italie, le groupe [C] avait expressément dispensé son distributeur principal de son obligation de conclure de tels contrats (. . .).
>
> Pour ces raisons, la lettre de mise en demeure du (. . .) doit être considérée comme dénuée de tout effet ».

Ayant accueilli l'essentiel des demandes de [A] et rejeté les demandes reconventionnelles de [C], le Tribunal Arbitral se prononça sur la répartition des frais de l'arbitrage dans les termes suivants:

> « Le principe de bonne justice veut que la partie qui succombe supporte les frais de l'arbitrage, du moins dans la proportion où la sentence donne raison à la partie adverse.
>
> En l'espèce, le Tribunal arbitral, tout en faisant droit à la grande majorité des demandes de [A] et en déboutant le groupe [C] de ses demandes reconventionnelles, constate la complexité de l'objet du litige et admet que les défenses et les demandes du groupe [C] ont été présentées (à la seule exception de sa lettre de mise en demeure du (. . .)) de bonne foi.
>
> Il décide donc de laisser à la charge du groupe [C] la totalité de ses propres frais de défense, et de ne lui faire supporter que les trois quarts des frais d'arbitrage (. . .) et les trois quarts des frais de défense exposés par [A].
>
> Le Tribunal arbitral estime toutefois qu'il y a lieu de faire exception à ce principe en ce qui concerne les frais de la procédure de référé pré-arbitral, et de maintenir à cet égard les précisions prises par le tiers à ce sujet dans ses ordonnances des (. . .) telles qu'elles ont été au demeurant exécutées par les parties ».

NOTE. I. — Comme l'a relevé la Cour d'appel de Paris dans son arrêt du 29 avril 2003 *(CA Paris, 29 avr. 2003: Juris-Data n° 2003-213825; Rev. arb. 2003, p. 1296, note Ch. Jarrosson)*, le règlement de référé pré-arbitral de la CCI « répond à un besoin spécifique:

celui de recourir à très bref délai à un tiers — « le tiers statuant en référé » — habilité à ordonner des mesures provisoires revêtant un caractère d'urgence ». Comme en témoigne la sentence ici présentée, ces mesures tendent à fournir une solution aux difficultés d'ordre juridique qui doivent être résolues de façon urgente, ce qui était l'objectif poursuivi par la CCI lorsqu'elle initia en 1980 les travaux qui aboutirent à l'adoption de son règlement de référé pré-arbitral *(cf. notamment Y. Derains, Expertise technique et référé pré-arbitral: Rev. arb. 1982, p. 239)*. Cependant, à l'époque, la CCI envisageait que ce soit un arbitre qui prenne les mesures urgentes nécessaires. C'est ainsi que lors de sa session d'octobre 1980, la Commission de l'arbitrage international de la CCI décida de créer un groupe de travail « avec la mission de mettre au point un système de référé arbitral qui permette aux parties d'obtenir la désignation immédiate d'un arbitre pour que cet arbitre puisse prendre des mesures provisoires ou provisionnelles et éventuellement conservatoires dans l'attente d'une procédure au fond ». Or, contrairement à la solution adoptée par le Netherlands Arbitration Institute aux articles 42 et suivants de son règlement d'arbitrage, ce n'est finalement pas la désignation d'un arbitre que permet le règlement de référé pré-arbitral de la CCI, mais d'un tiers dont la décision, comme l'a dit judicieusement la Cour d'appel de Paris dans l'arrêt précité, n'a que l'autorité « de la chose convenue », par opposition à l'autorité de la chose jugée. Cette qualification, qui exclut tout recours en annulation de la décision du Tiers a fait couler beaucoup d'encre et il est inutile d'y revenir *(cf. entre autres, en plus de la note de Ch. Jarrrosson mentionnée ci-avant J. Béguin, L'arbitrage international: les voies de recours: JCP E 2004, p. 1816. — Th. Clay, Chronique de jurisprudence: Référé pré-arbitral: Dalloz, 2003, n° 36, p. 2478 et 2479. — B. Davis, The ICC Pre-arbitral referee procedure in context with technical expertise, conciliation and arbitration: Intl. Const. Law Review, 1992, p. 218 et s. — E. Gaillard et Ph. Pinsolle, The ICC pre-arbitral Referee, First Practical Experiences: Arbitration International, 2004, n° 1 (à paraître). — E. Loquin, De la nature juridique du référé pré-arbitral de la CCI: RTD com. 2003, n° 3, p. 482 à 487. — A. Mourre, Référé pré-arbitral de la CCI: to be or not to be a judge . . . : Gaz. Pal. mai-juin 2003, p. 1484)*.

En revanche, la sentence ici rapportée fournit un exemple des modalités d'articulation de la procédure de référé pré-arbitral et d'une procédure d'arbitrage. On aura noté que dans la présente affaire, le déclenchement de la seconde est antérieur à l'initiation de la première. On ne se trouve pas dans l'hypothèse classique à laquelle pensaient les auteurs du règlement de référé pré-arbitral lorsqu'ils envisageaient des mesures conservatoires « dans l'attente d'une procédure au fond », où les mesures conservatoires demandées sont le prélude d'une action arbitrale. Ici, ce sont les parties défenderesses à l'arbitrage qui, au vu du contenu de la demande d'arbitrage, cherchent à se voir confirmer par le tiers, jusqu'à l'issue de la procédure d'arbitrage, le droit de poursuivre l'exécution du contrat comme elles l'entendent et contrairement à l'interprétation que la demanderesse cherche à faire consacrer par le Tribunal arbitral. Il suffit de prendre connaissance des demandes présentées au tiers par les défenderesses à l'arbitrage pour constater que les mesures auraient tout aussi bien pu être prises par le Tribunal arbitral, à titre provisoire. En effet, l'article 23 (1) du règlement d'arbitrage de la CCI dispose qu' « *à moins qu'il n'en ait été convenu autrement par les parties, le tribunal arbitral peut, dès remise du dossier, à la demande de l'une d'elles, ordonner toute mesure conservatoire ou provisoire qu'il considère appropriée* ». Mais, pour cela, encore eût-il fallu qu'il fût constitué. En effet, il s'écoule nécessairement un certain délai entre la saisine de la Cour internationale d'arbitrage de la CCI et la constitution d'un Tribunal arbitral, délai rarement inférieur à deux mois.

Il est donc particulièrement utile aux parties, pendant cette période qui se situe déjà dans la procédure arbitrale mais sans qu'un arbitre puisse intervenir, de pouvoir disposer d'une procédure non étatique capable de statuer au provisoire. Bien sûr, dès que le Tribunal arbitral est saisi du dossier, il doit pouvoir exercer la totalité de ses prérogatives en matière de mesures provisoires et conservatoires. Le règlement de référé pré-arbitral en déduit que le tiers, sauf s'il a été précédemment saisi, n'a plus de rôle à jouer. En effet, son article 2.4.1 indique que:

> « À l'exception du cas prévu à l'article 2.4 ci-dessus, la juridiction compétente, une fois saisie de l'affaire, peut seule, en vertu des règles qui lui sont applicables, ordonner toute autre mesure provisoire ou conservatoire qui s'avèrerait nécessaire. La juridiction compétente, si son règlement le permet, est à cet effet réputée avoir obtenu des parties l'autorisation d'exercer les pouvoirs conférés par l'article 2.1 au tiers statuant en référé ».

L'exception visée est celle qui, dans l'affaire ici rapportée, a permis au tiers de prendre sa seconde ordonnance sur le fondement de l'article 2.4 du règlement de référé pré-arbitral:

> « Si la juridiction compétente est saisie de l'affaire après la nomination du tiers statuant en référé, ce tiers conserve néanmoins le pouvoir d'ordonner des mesures dans les délais prévus à l'article 6.2, sauf accord contraire des parties ou décision contraire de la juridiction compétente ».

Il apparaît donc que le règlement de référé pré-arbitral part du principe que les pouvoirs du tiers et du Tribunal arbitral ne sauraient être concurrents. On peut s'interroger sur le bien-fondé de cette solution. Après tout, la remise du dossier à l'arbitre n'interdit pas aux parties de demander des mesures provisoires ou conservatoires à une autorité judiciaire « dans des circonstances appropriées », ainsi que le souligne l'article 23 (2) du règlement d'arbitrage de la CCI. Mais ces circonstances appropriées sont sans doute celles où le secours de l'*imperium* du juge est nécessaire. Quoi qu'il en soit, l'articulation des pouvoirs des arbitres et de ceux du tiers qui résultent du règlement de référé pré-arbitral de la CCI justifierait une intégration totale de ce dernier dans le règlement d'arbitrage, à l'instar du règlement du Netherlands Arbitration Institute. Ainsi, il suffirait aux parties d'insérer une clause d'arbitrage CCI dans leur contrat pour bénéficier des avantages du système de référé pré-arbitral. La CCI a fait un pas important en ce sens en publiant depuis peu dans la même brochure les deux règlements et en proposant une clause type contenant une référence aux deux procédures. Il reste à espérer que le pas suivant interviendra à l'occasion d'une prochaine révision du Règlement d'arbitrage.

II. — La jurisprudence arbitrale fait peser sur les opérateurs du commerce international une obligation de coopérer de bonne foi *(cf. S. Jarvin, L'obligation de coopérer de bonne foi, exemple d'application au plan de l'arbitrage international* in *l'Apport de la jurisprudence arbitrale, les Dossiers de l'Institut du droit et des pratiques des affaires internationales, p. 157)*. On en donnera pour exemple la sentence rendue en 1987 dans l'affaire n° 4761 *(JDI 1987, p. 1012, obs. S. Jarvin)* et, peut-être plus significative encore, celle rendue dès 1975, dans l'affaire n° 2443 (citée dans les observations d'Yves Derains sous la sentence rendue dans l'affaire n° 2291: *JDI 1976, p. 989)*, dans laquelle le tribunal arbitral déclarait: « les parties (. . .) devaient être parfaitement conscientes que seule une collaboration loyale, totale et constante entre elles pouvait éventuellement permettre de résoudre, au-delà des difficultés inhérentes à l'exécution de tout contrat les nombreux problèmes résultant de l'extrême complexité dans la formulation et l'enchevêtrement des engagements litigieux ». Le Tribunal arbitral ajoutait: « cette obligation de coopération, qu'à juste titre la doctrine moderne retrouve dans la bonne foi qui doit gouverner l'exécution de toute convention, s'impose ». On a pu voir dans l'obligation de coopération un des principes généraux de la *lex mercatoria (F. Osman, Les principes généraux de la lex mercatoria, p. 135 et s.)* et l'article 5.1.3. des principes d'Unidroit relatifs aux contrats du commerce international, dans leur texte de 2004. dispose avec plus de timidité, il est vrai: « *Les parties ont entre elles un devoir de collaboration lorsque l'on peut raisonnablement s'y attendre dans l'exécution de leurs obligations.* ». La version anglaise se référant à une « cooperation », il est clair que c'est l'obligation de coopération que les principes UNIDROIT visent.

L'obligation de concertation que la sentence ici rapportée consacre s'y rattache mais ne se confond pas avec elle. Cette obligation de concertation se justifie par « la nature coopérative des conventions signées entre les parties » indique le Tribunal arbitral. Mais elle a une fonction différente de l'obligation de coopération. Comme l'a relevé M. Fontaine, cette dernière correspond à une obligation d'assistance mutuelle pour surmonter en commun, de façon constructive, les difficultés apparues en cours d'exécution *(M. Fontaine, Les contrats internationaux à long terme* in *Études offertes à Roger Houin, p. 270).* L'obligation de concertation mise à la charge des parties par la présente sentence est un instrument de gestion courante, nécessaire en raison de l'incidence des décisions prises par chaque partie dans le domaine qui lui est propre sur les activités de l'autre. Il s'agit de ne prendre aucune décision susceptible d'avoir un tel effet à moins de s'être préalablement efforcé de le faire d'un commun accord, sans qu'un tel accord doive nécessairement être trouvé. C'est évidemment la notion de bonne foi qui éclaire l'obligation de concertation et qui permet d'apprécier son exécution. Au-delà d'une absence de discussion, comme en l'espèce, une discussion sans volonté sérieuse d'aboutir ne répondrait pas à ses exigences.

La sanction d'une violation de l'obligation de concertation se trouve, selon la sentence, faute de sanction expressément prévue au contrat, dans le droit commun de la responsabilité. Elle suppose donc un préjudice causé par l'absence de recherche d'un accord de bonne foi sur une décision à prendre. Selon la nature et la portée de celle-ci, il n'est pas à exclure que ce préjudice puisse être important.

III. — C'est également sur la notion de bonne foi que repose la décision par laquelle les arbitres se refusent à reconnaître toute légitimité à la lettre de mise en demeure des défenderesses qui, constatant une violation réelle de la lettre du contrat, devait automatiquement conduire à sa résiliation. La sentence considère en effet que la mise en demeure, notifiée en cours d'arbitrage, n'avait d'autre but que d'exercer une pression sur la demanderesse, d'autant plus que la violation de l'obligation contractuelle que dénonçaient les défenderesses perdurait depuis des années sans objection de leur part, ne leur causait aucun préjudice et était acceptée par les défenderesses s'agissant d'un autre distributeur. On peut à cette occasion invoquer un autre des principes d'UNIDROIT qui figure à leur article 1.8 et qui consacre l'interdiction de se contredire. Mais surtout, la sentence se situe dans la droite ligne de celle rendue en 1975 dans l'affaire 2520 *(JDI 1976, p. 992, obs. Y. Derains),* d'où il découlait que le non-respect d'une prompte dénonciation d'une inexécution contractuelle valait renonciation à s'en prévaloir de la part du créancier de l'obligation inexécutée *(cf. également Sentence de 2001 dans l'affaire n° 10422: JDI 2003, p. 1142).*

IV. — Selon l'article 31 (3) du règlement d'arbitrage de la CCI « *L'arbitre liquide les frais de l'arbitrage et décide à laquelle des parties le paiement en incombe ou dans quelle proportion ils sont partagés entre elles* ». Comme l'a souligné la sentence de 1992, dans l'affaire n° 7006 *(Yearbook of Commercial Arbitration, 1993, p. 58):* « L'arbitre jouit d'une entière liberté pour répartir les coûts comme il l'estime approprié et, à cet effet, il peut prendre en compte non seulement l'issue de l'affaire mais aussi l'attitude des parties en rapport avec la procédure, car elles peuvent, dans certains cas, avoir inutilement fait augmenter les coûts. Dans la plupart des cas, cependant, à moins que cette attitude ne présente un facteur tempérant en faveur de la partie perdante, la partie gagnante devra être remboursée de ses frais. C'est, après tout, la partie perdante qui a occasionné les coûts soit en déposant une demande d'arbitrage injustifiée, soit en la contestant de façon injustifiée ». La sentence ici rapportée partage de toute évidence ce point de vue puisque le tribunal arbitral déclare que « Le principe de bonne justice veut que la partie qui succombe supporte les frais de l'arbitrage, du moins dans la proportion où la semence donne raison à la partie adverse ». Une telle approche peut être critiquable dans certains cas (cf. à cet égard les observations judicieuses d'Eduardo Silva Romero sur la sentence de 2000 dans l'affaire 10671: *JDI 2005, p. 1269).* Surtout, les arbitres devraient plus souvent faire savoir aux parties, dès le début de la procédure, que leur succès respectif ne sera pas le seul critère pour décider de la répartition des frais et qu'une partie qui augmente à l'excès le coût et la durée de l'arbitrage en présentant des preuves documentaires ou testimoniales sans nécessité réelle risque d'être sanctionnée sur ce plan, même si elle obtient finalement gain de cause.

Enfin, on notera avec intérêt que le tribunal arbitral se refuse à inclure dans les frais de l'arbitrage ceux exposés dans la procédure de référé pré-arbitral. Cette décision est justifiée s'agissant de deux procédures indépendantes, le tiers s'étant déjà prononcé sur la charge de ces coûts. La solution devrait probablement être reconsidérée si la procédure d'arbitrage et celle de référé étaient un jour intégrées.

Y. D.

Sent. arb. finale rendue dans l'affaire CCI n° 12167 en 2002 (original langues française et anglaise)

Convention d'arbitrage. — Portée. — Demande reconventionnelle. — Responsabilité délictuelle.

Frais de l'arbitrage. — Répartition. — Pouvoir discrétionnaire des arbitres. — Critères d'appréciation.

La sentence arbitrale commentée rappelle la compétence des arbitres à examiner une demande reconventionnelle fondée sur une question de responsabilité quasi délictuelle à partir du moment où la convention d'arbitrage est rédigée de manière suffisamment large pour refléter la volonté des parties de soumettre à l'arbitrage le règlement de tout litige qui « découle » ou qui est « en relation » avec le contrat.

La sentence rappelle également le pouvoir des arbitres de répartir librement le coût total de l'arbitrage entre les parties.

En date du 9 mai 2001, une société hollandaise X (le « demandeur »), désireuse de développer son réseau de distribution de produits pharmaceutiques en France, a conclu deux contrats de cession d'actions (les « contrats ») avec une société française Y (le « défendeur n° 1 ») et un individu français Z (le « défendeur n° 2 ») pour l'acquisition d'une société française A (non partie à l'arbitrage). La société A est détenue à 75 % par le défendeur n° 1 et 25 % par le défendeur n° 2.

Aux termes de l'article 6.4.6 des deux contrats, les parties ont convenu que les coûts des travaux de mise en conformité technique de la société A sollicités par les autorités administratives françaises compétentes seraient supportés par les défendeurs à titre de garantie.

Le demandeur a ainsi invoqué les dispositions de cet article pour obtenir que les défendeurs exécutent à leurs propres frais les travaux imposés par l'administration française, soit l'Agence française de sécurité sanitaire des produits de santé (« AFSSaPS »). À défaut, les défendeurs devraient rembourser les frais avancés par le demandeur à cet effet. À l'appui de sa demande, X a produit un rapport d'inspection de l'AFSSaPS.

Devant le refus de ses cocontractants qui ont contesté l'interprétation de l'article 6.4.6 des contrats, le demandeur a introduit une requête d'arbitrage devant la Cour internationale d'arbitrage de la CCI en vue d'obtenir du tribunal arbitral qu'il fasse droit à sa demande.

Dans leur réponse à la requête d'arbitrage, les défendeurs ont conclu au rejet de l'ensemble des demandes principales. À titre reconventionnel, ils ont sollicité la condamnation du demandeur au paiement de 500 000 € à titre de dommages-intérêts dans la proportion de 75 % et de 25 % au profit de Y et Z respectivement en réparation du préjudice causé par la démarche procédurale abusive du demandeur. Selon les défendeurs, l'abus aurait consisté dans le fait que le demandeur a « *tenté par une interprétation totalement contraire tant aux textes des conventions qu'à la volonté des parties qui y est clairement exprimée, de s'approprier des sommes qui n'entrent nullement dans quelque garantie ou obligation dont les vendeurs seraient débiteurs; d'autre part, X se serait permis de "notifier ses réclamations fantaisistes à la banque de Y et Z, démarche destinée à jeter le discrédit des vendeurs auprès de leur partenaire financier habituel"* ». Les défendeurs ont également demandé la condamnation de X au paiement de l'ensemble des frais d'arbitrage et de conseils, y compris une compensation pour les heures passées par les services internes de Y au traitement du contentieux.

En réponse à la demande reconventionnelle, le demandeur a soulevé l'incompétence du tribunal arbitral. Selon le demandeur, il s'agit d'une question de responsabilité quasi délictuelle qui n'est pas rattachée au contrat principal. Par ailleurs, la preuve du dommage allégué n'a pas été rapportée par les défendeurs.

C'est dans ce contexte que le tribunal arbitral, siégeant à Genève, a été appelé à se prononcer sur le différend qui oppose les parties. Aux termes de l'acte de mission signé par les parties, le tribunal devait d'abord interpréter l'obligation de garantie des défendeurs résultant de l'article 6.4.6 des contrats. Il devait ensuite se prononcer sur sa compétence à examiner la demande reconventionnelle qui est fondée sur la responsabilité quasi délictuelle du demandeur sur la base de la clause compromissoire ainsi rédigée dans les deux contrats:

> « All disputes arising out of or in connection with this Agreement shall be finally settled by arbitration at law under the rules of the international Chamber of Commerce, in Geneva, Switzerland, by three (3) arbitrators (hereafter, « Arbitrators ») appointed in accordance with said rules. The arbitration proceedings shall follow the rules of the International Chamber of Commerce and will be conducted in the French and/or English language. »
>
> Traduction libre des auteurs: « Tous différends découlant ou en relation avec ce Contrat seront tranchés définitivement par arbitrage en droit suivant le règlement d'arbitrage de la Chambre de Commerce Internationale, à Genève, Suisse, par trois (3) arbitres (ci-dénommés, « Arbitres ») nommés conformément à ce Règlement. La procédure d'arbitrage sera conduite en application du règlement d'arbitrage de la Chambre de Commerce Internationale, en langue française et/ou anglaise. »

En se fondant sur le droit français, droit applicable au fond prévu dans les contrats, le tribunal arbitral a rejeté la demande principale en tenant compte des circonstances et des négociations menées par les parties avant la signature définitive des contrats. Celles-ci avaient clairement accepté que l'obligation de garantie des défendeurs s'appliquait uniquement aux travaux rendus « obligatoires » par une décision « exécutoire » de l'autorité administrative compétente. Tel n'est pas le cas du rapport d'inspection de l'AFSSaPS produit le demandeur. Selon les dispositions du Code de la santé publique française, que les conseils du demandeur ne pouvaient pas ou n'auraient pas dû ignorer, un tel rapport a la valeur d'un simple avis. Il n'acquiert une force contraignante que s'il est suivi d'abord d'une mise en demeure et, ensuite, d'une décision du Directeur général de l'AFSSaPS qui, seule, a force exécutoire et peut être frappée d'un recours devant la juridiction administrative. Or, aucune décision n'est intervenue pour rendre obligatoires les travaux suggérés par le rapport d'inspection.

S'agissant de la demande reconventionnelle et de la responsabilité quasi délictuelle alléguée du demandeur, le tribunal arbitral a admis sa compétence après avoir analysé la portée de la clause compromissoire dans les termes suivants:

> « 4. Le présent arbitrage est, en vertu de la volonté des parties exprimée dans la clause compromissoire, régi quant à la procédure par le Règlement d'arbitrage de la Chambre de commerce internationale (SPA, art. 11.13).
>
> Aux termes de l'article 15.1 de ce Règlement, en cas de silence de celui-ci sur une règle de procédure, il pourra être fait application de "any rules which the parties or, failing them, the Arbitral Tribunal may settle on, whether or not reference is thereby made to the rules of procedure of a national law to be applied to the arbitration".
>
> 5. En, vertu de la clause compromissoire, le siège du Tribunal arbitral a été fixé à Genève. Cela a été confirmé au paragraphe V. de l'acte de mission. En outre, il a été précisé dans celui-ci: "This arbitration is therefore governed by chapter 12 of the Swiss Private International Law Act of 18 December 1987 (SPILA)".
>
> 6. Ni le Règlement d'arbitrage de la CCI, ni le chapitre 12 de la loi fédérale suisse sur le droit international privé (LDIP) ne contiennent de dispositions relativement à la compétence d'un tribunal arbitral, régulièrement saisi d'une demande principale d'arbitrage, pour statuer à l'égard d'une demande

reconventionnelle. Dans leur commentaire de l'article 186 de la LDIP suisse relatif à la 'compétence-compétence' du tribunal arbitral, note 7, p. 382, les professeurs Lalive, Poudret et Reymond écrivent:

"L'arbitre a également qualité pour statuer sur sa compétence à l'égard d'une demande reconventionnelle. Il lui appartient notamment de trancher la question de savoir si la demande reconventionnelle doit entrer dans les prévisions de la convention d'arbitrage sur la base de laquelle il a été saisi par la partie demanderesse, le cas échéant dans celles d'une autre convention d'arbitrage qui pourrait lier les parties. Il devra également résoudre la question de savoir s'il faut et s'il suffit que la demande reconventionnelle ait un lien de connexité *avec la demande principale, comme le prévoit l'article 8 LDIP pour la demande reconventionnelle portée devant les tribunaux étatiques. Il est rare que ces questions soient réglées par la législation ou le règlement régissant la procédure d'arbitrage (v. cependant l'article 19.3 du Règlement CNUDCI). À ce défaut, il appartiendra à l'arbitre de décider, vu l'autonomie que lui confère l'art.182, s'il estime devoir exiger un lien de connexité entre les deux demandes ou non."*

7. Pour leur part, Fouchard, Gaillard et Goldman considèrent, dans leur Traité de l'arbitrage commercial international (n° 1222) que, "contrairement à la règle admise devant les tribunaux français, un lien de connexité ou, dans la terminologie du nouveau code de procédure civile, un lien suffisant entre dans la demande principale et la demande reconventionnelle n'est pas nécessaire, dès lors que celle-ci repose sur la convention d'arbitrage qui a fondé la demande initiale."

8. Ces opinions relativement convergentes conduisent le Tribunal arbitral à fonder sa compétence en l'espèce sur le libellé de la clause compromissoire. Or celle-ci a pour objet et pour effet de lui donner compétence pour statuer sur "all disputes arising out or in connection with this Agreement."

Ainsi les parties ont-elles voulu clairement investir le tribunal arbitral du pouvoir de statuer sur "all disputes", c'est-à-dire n'importe quel litige, sans autre condition de qualification, qui, même ne résultant pas directement du contrat, serait né en tout cas en relation avec celui-ci.

En pareil cas, il a été jugé maintes fois que même si elle est fondée sur une faute extracontractuelle reprochée à une partie au contrat, l'examen d'une demande est susceptible d'entrer dans la compétence de l'arbitre si cette faute a été commise en relation avec le contrat (Fouchard, Gaillard et Goldman, op.cit, n° 524 et jurisprudence citée en note 241, V. aussi Cl. Reymond, Conflits de lois en matière de responsabilité délictuelle devant l'arbitre international: Trav. Comité fi: DIP 1988-1989; Poudret et Besson, Droit comparé de l'arbitrage international, n° 307, p. 287).

9. On pourrait considérer qu'en l'espèce, la demande reconventionnelle ne découle pas ("arising out") du contrat, dès lors que le moyen allégué se réfère au comportement de X dans la procédure et au caractère soi-disant tendancieux de son interprétation de la clause de garantie litigieuse, ayant pour objet de se faire attribuer un avantage indu par le Tribunal arbitral.

Mais d'une part, il n'en demeure pas moins que la faute alléguée, si elle avait été commise, l'aurait été en relation avec ("in connection with") le contrat. D'autre part, elle s'y rattacherait d'autant plus qu'elle aurait consisté précisément dans le fait d'interpréter le contrat d'une manière fautive.

Dès lors, à supposer nécessaire la démonstration d'une connexité, ou d'un "lien suffisant", le Tribunal arbitral considère que la preuve de celle-ci a été suffisamment rapportée par les défendeurs.

10. Cette conclusion s'étend sans difficulté au grief de notification à la banque des défendeurs de la demande d'arbitrage. Il suffit ici de relever que cette banque s'était portée caution des obligations des défendeurs envers X relativement à la garantie contractuelle qui fait l'objet du litige. Ici encore, à supposer qu'il y ait eu faute quasi-délictuelle, celle-ci se rattachait suffisamment au contrat pour que l'examen de la demande reconventionnelle entre dans la compétence du tribunal arbitral.

11. Quant à la prétention des défendeurs à une compensation pour les dépenses internes de leurs services contentieux, soit un montant de 115 000 € (inclus dans la demande globale de 500 000 €), d'une part, elle apparaît plutôt comme une conclusion accessoire de la défense à la demande principale, et dans cette mesure ne peut susciter de controverse juridictionnelle; d'autre part, à supposer que ces dépenses aient été causées ou accrues à raison de la commission par X de la faute délictuelle qui lui est reprochée, elle n'en tomberait pas moins dans la notion de demande (reconventionnelle) "arising in connection with the contract".

Le Tribunal est donc compétent à tous égards. »

La demande reconventionnelle a été finalement rejetée par le tribunal pour défaut de preuves suffisantes rapportées par les défendeurs.

Les frais de l'arbitrage ont été fixés ensuite par le tribunal arbitral dans la proportion de 75 % à la charge du demandeur et de 25 % pour les défendeurs (ce quart étant lui-même à supporter à raison de 75 % par Y et de 25 % par Z, pourcentages correspondant aux participations et demandes respectives de Y et Z). Le demandeur a été en outre condamné à supporter les frais de défense des défendeurs dans la même proportion de 75 % et de 25 % entre eux. Selon les arbitres, cette pondération est justifiée en considération des circonstances de l'espèce.

« 1. Le Tribunal estime en premier lieu que les parties ont déployé, pour soutenir leurs intérêts, des efforts d'une ampleur comparable. Il constate en second lieu qu'elles ont succombé l'une et l'autre dans toutes leurs prétentions. Néanmoins, il constate que le poids spécifique de la demande principale dans laquelle X a succombé a été sans commune mesure avec celui de la demande reconventionnelle. Il constate également que X a succombé aussi dans son exception d'incompétence. Cela étant, le Tribunal estime que l'application pure et simple de la règle d'après laquelle les dépens doivent être supportées par la partie qui succombe, ce qui devrait, à la lettre, conduire à les faire supporter en l'espèce par les deux parties à égalité, dès lors que chacune d'elle a été déboutée, ne serait pas justifié. Une pondération s'impose et c'est pourquoi il y a lieu de décider (. . .) »

NOTE. — I. — L'arbitrage porte généralement sur le règlement des différends de nature contractuelle. Toutefois, il est acquis que l'arbitrage peut également se porter sur des litiges de nature délictuelle ou extracontractuelle. Dans tous ces cas, la compétence du tribunal arbitral est justifiée par une analyse de la portée de la convention d'arbitrage signée par les parties. Les termes de cette convention doivent être suffisamment larges et généraux pour englober tous les litiges qui « découlent » (« arising out of ») ou qui sont « en relation » (« in connection with ») avec le contrat en cause (V. notamment *J.-F. Poudret et S. Besson, Comparative Law of International Arbitration: Thomson/Sweet&Maxwell, 2007, 2nd ed., § 307; p. 266. — A. Redfern et M. Hunter, Law and Practice of International Commercial Arbitration: Thomson/Sweet&Maxwell, 2004, 4th ed., § 3-39, p. 154. — F. Gonzales, La responsabilité délictuelle dans les sentences arbitrales de la Chambre de commerce internationale: Bull. CCI, vol. 13, n° 2, 2e trimestre 2002, p. 41. — C. Reymond, Conflits de lois en matière de responsabilité délictuelle devant l'arbitre international in Travaux comité fr. DIP 1988-1989, Paris, CNRS 1991, p. 97).*

En l'espèce, la demande reconventionnelle et le moyen allégué qui repose sur une faute extracontractuelle du demandeur sont couverts par le libellé de la convention d'arbitrage insérée dans les contrats conclus entre les parties. Comme indiqué par le tribunal arbitral, les parties ont voulu investir les arbitres « du pouvoir de statuer sur "all disputes", c'est-à-dire n'importe quel litige, sans autre condition de qualification, qui, même ne résultant pas directement du contrat, serait né en tout cas en relation avec celui-ci ». La demande reconventionnelle, qui vient se greffer sur la demande principale sans laquelle elle ne peut exister, vise à obtenir un avantage autre que le simple rejet de cette demande principale. Dans le cas présent, elle tombe dans le champ d'application de la convention d'arbitrage car elle tend précisément à obtenir du tribunal arbitral l'interprétation d'une clause litigieuse des contrats. Quant au moyen tiré du comportement fautif du demandeur, à savoir le dénigrement fait par X auprès des banques de Y et Z, il entre également dans le cadre de la convention d'arbitrage car ces banques se sont précisément portées cautions des obligations des défendeurs envers X relativement à l'obligation de garantie contractuelle qui est l'objet du litige. La réponse apportée par les arbitres à la question est classique et mérite d'être suivie d'autant plus que la demande reconventionnelle figurait bien dans l'acte de mission.

On appréciera la démarche du tribunal qui a permis de pallier au fait que le Règlement d'arbitrage de la CCI et le Chapitre 12 de la LDIP suisse ne contiennent pas de dispositions relatives à la compétence d'un tribunal arbitral régulièrement saisi d'une demande principale. On constatera surtout que l'exigence d'un « lien de connexité » ou encore du « caractère suffisant » qui unit les demandes principales et reconventionnelles — qui est soumis à l'appréciation souveraine des tribunaux judiciaires — est atténué par les arbitres dont la compétence repose sur la convention d'arbitrage qui a fondé la demande principale (V. en ce sens *Fouchard-Gaillard-Goldman, Traité de l'arbitrage commercial international: Litec, 1996, § 1222, p. 670.* — *M. Douchy-Oudot, Demande reconventionnelle in Rép. Pr. civ. Dalloz, sept. 2003.* — V. également *sentence partielle CCI n° 12363, 23 déc. 2003: Bull. ASA 2006, p. 462* qui traite de la compétence du tribunal arbitral, siégeant en Suisse, à examiner une demande reconventionnelle sollicitant des dommages-intérêts contre le demandeur principal pour l'obtention injustifiée de mesures provisoires devant les tribunaux étatiques: « According to the leading trend of the doctrine, there is a presumption that in case of doubt, an arbitral tribunal has ''all-encompassing jurisdiction'' (see W. Wenger: In International arbitration in Switzerland, Basel/Geneva/Munich 2000, ad art.178, note 51, p. 348). Indeed, it had been decided by the Federal Tribunal that as long as an arbitration agreement does not contain any restriction in this respect, it must be assumed that the parties wish for an ''all-embracing jurisdiction'' of the Arbitral Tribunal, given that they have concluded an arbitration agreement (ATF 116 la 56 and foll). In other words, it is the view of Swiss law that in the absence of any express limitation contained in the arbitration clause, a broad interpretation of the same should prevail upon a narrow one, contrary to Claimant's contention ». — V. également *Cass. Iʳᵉ civ., 6 déc. 1988, Sté Navimpex Centrala Navala v. Wiking Trader: Rev. Arb. 1989, p. 641, note B. Goldman.* — *CA Paris, 11 déc. 1981, Bureau de recherches géologiques et minières (BRGM) et a. cl Sté Patino International NV: Rev. Arb. 1982, p. 311, note J. Rubellin-Devichi.* — plus généralement, sur une distinction entre les demandes reconventionnelles, demandes croisées (« cross-claims ») et compensation et la compétence des arbitres, V. *Claims, Counterclaims, Cross Claims and Set-off Claims: ICC, Dossier n° 685, à paraître).*

II. — Le coût total d'un arbitrage CCI comprend les frais fixés par la Cour internationale d'arbitrage de la CCI (ou les « frais proprement dits de la CCI ») mais aussi les frais engagés par les parties pour se défendre (ou les « frais des parties »). Dans le premier cas, il s'agit des frais administratifs de la CCI, des honoraires des arbitres fixés par la Cour internationale d'arbitrage et des dépenses du tribunal arbitral. Dans le second cas, il s'agit notamment des frais de conseils des parties, des frais d'expertise, des coûts liés aux déplacements des rémoins ou encore des frais internes des parties. Conformément aux dispositions de l'article 31(3) du Règlement d'arbitrage de la CCI, le tribunal arbitral *« liquide les frais de l'arbitrage et décide à laquelle des parties le paiement en incombe ou dans quelle proportion ils sont partagés entre elles ».* Le Règlement d'arbitrage de la CCI ne donne aucune règle ou critère particulier à suivre par les arbitres qui sont donc libres de rendre la décision qu'ils souhaitent sous réserve de la motiver. De ce fait, l'existence d'une pratique homogène ou encore moins d'un usage dans ce domaine ne peut être affirmé *(V. sentence CCI n° 10671: JDI 2006, p. 1453, note E. Silva Romero).*

Plusieurs critères sont pris en compte par les arbitres parmi lesquels l'issue de l'arbitrage: une partie qui perd son procès, doit en principe supporter les coûts de la procédure. Le comportement des parties en cours de procédure ou encore leur bonne foi peut également avoir une influence sur la décision des arbitres (V. notamment *M. W. Bühler et Th. H. Webster, Handbook of ICC Arbitration — Commentary, Precedents, Materials, Thomson/Sweet&Maxwell, 2005, 1st ed., § 31-41, p. 368. — R. Kreindler, Fin. il Ruling On Costs: Loser Pays All? » in ASA Special Series n° 26, July 2006; Best Practices in International Arbitration: ASA Conference of January 27, 2006, Zurich, p. 41. — M. Bühler, Awarding Costs in International Commercial Arbitration: an Overview: Bull. ASA 2004, p. 249).*

Dans l'espèce commentée, le tribunal arbitral a refusé de condamner les parties à supporter par moitié le coût total de l'arbitrage nonobstant le fait que les demandes principales et reconventionnelles ont été toutes rejetées. Le tribunal a jugé néanmoins que l'échec du demandeur a été prépondérant puisqu'il a perdu non seulement dans ses prétentions initiales mais aussi dans l'exception d'incompétence qu'il a soulevée devant les arbitres. Le demandeur a été condamné en conséquence à supporter 75 % des frais proprement dits de l'arbitrage CCI et une partie des dépenses des défendeurs. En laissant 25 % des frais à la charge des défendeurs, le tribunal a probablement voulu les sanctionner également. Y et Z n'ont pas en effet rapporté la preuve de la mauvaise foi alléguée contre le demandeur dans l'exercice de son droit à se prévaloir de l'application de l'article 6.4.6 des contrats. Ils n'ont pas prouvé davantage le préjudice résultant du dénigrement abusif fait par le demandeur auprès de leurs banques. L'introduction de la demande reconventionnelle a non seulement élargi l'objet du litige mais augmenté certainement le coût de la procédure. C'est aussi peut-être dans cet esprit que le tribunal a rejeté la demande de remboursement des frais internes des défendeurs en se fondant sur le fait qu'ils ont basé leur prétention sur un abus de procédure du demandeur lequel a été finalement déclaré non fondé par les arbitres.

S. J.
C. T.-N.

Sent. arb. finale rendue dans l'affaire CCI n° 12193 en 2004 (original en langue française)

Droit applicable. — Méthode cumulative. — Méthode de la voie directe. — Principes généraux du droit. — Application de la loi du lieu de la prestation caractéristique. — Contrat de distribution.

Arbitrabilité. — Compétence exclusive de tribunaux étatiques. — Lois de police.

Préavis. — Forme. — Lettre simple. — Lettre recommandée. — Régularisation ultérieure.

Préjudice. — Stocks. — Gain manqué. — Perte de clientèle. — Concurrence déloyale. — Obligation de minimiser le dommage.

Le tribunal arbitral décide qu'en l'absence de clause d'electio juris, la loi applicable au contrat de distribution exclusive est la loi du lieu d'exécution de la prestation caractéristique, c'est-à-dire le lieu d'établissement du distributeur. Le tribunal arbitral fait application à la fois de la méthode cumulative et de la méthode de la voie directe.

Le tribunal estime également que le litige est arbitrable quand bien même la loi libanaise applicable au litige réserve une compétence exclusive aux tribunaux du lieu d'établissement du distributeur pour se prononcer sur les litiges relatifs aux contrats de distribution.

Le tribunal accorde au demandeur une indemnisation au titre du gain manqué, de la perte de clientèle et de la concurrence déloyale mais rejette les réclamations relatives aux stocks et aux licenciements de certains employés.

L'affaire commentée oppose un commerçant libanais, M. X, exerçant sous l'enseigne A, à une société allemande B. A et B sont liés depuis 1971 par un contrat de distribution exclusive portant sur la promotion et la distribution de produits laitiers au Liban. Des difficultés sont apparues à la suite de la résiliation du contrat par le concédant (B) au prétexte de fautes commises par le distributeur (A). B reproche notamment à A son manque de performance et son manque de pénétration du marché. Les parties n'ayant pu résoudre amiablement leur litige, le demandeur A saisissait la Cour internationale d'arbitrage de la CCI afin d'obtenir réparation pour la rupture du contrat de distribution, qu'il juge abusive. Le contrat cadre contenait en effet une clause aux termes de laquelle: *« Le lieu d'exécution et de compétence juridique est la Chambre de commerce Internationale de Bâle, pour tous les litiges éventuels résultant du présent contrat, y compris les actions de change »*. Malgré la rédaction hasardeuse de cette clause, la compétence du tribunal n'était pas contestée.

La sentence consacre d'importants développements à la question de la loi applicable. Le contrat ne contenait en effet pas de clause *d'electio juris* et les parties étaient en désaccord sur la loi applicable au contrat. Le demandeur prétendait que le contrat était, par application des règles de conflit de loi suisses, lieu du siège de l'arbitrage, soumis au droit libanais, la prestation caractéristique du contrat étant exécutée au Liban. La défenderesse était elle d'avis que la loi applicable au contrat était la loi suisse, comme cela résultait selon elle de l'intention des parties exprimée dans le contrat. Le tribunal se prononce sur cette question dans les termes suivants:

« C — Discussion

21. Les témoignages écrits versés aux débats et les déclarations des témoins ne permettent pas de déceler avec certitude quelle a été la véritable intention des parties telle qu'elle est exprimée dans la clause (. . .) du Contrat, dont la rédaction maladroite et ambiguë ne permet certainement pas d'affirmer que cette clause traduit l'expression d'un choix clair et non équivoque des parties en faveur du droit suisse. Il est, notamment, difficile de conclure que les expressions "lieu d'exécution" et "compétence juridique", utilisées par les négociateurs et signataires du Contrat, qui n'étaient pas juristes de formation, aient pu vouloir signifier une référence précise au droit suisse, alors que la Suisse n'est même pas expressément mentionnée en tant que telle, seule la ville de Bâle l'étant. En effet, s'il est généralement admis, en droit international privé comparé, qu'un accord explicite des parties n'est pas nécessaire quant au droit applicable, encore faut-il que l'accord de volontés soit certain, ce qui n'est pas le cas en l'espèce. Le seul choix du lieu de l'arbitrage ne saurait s'analyser en un choix du droit applicable au Contrat litigieux (V. Fouchard Gaillard Goldman, Traité de l'arbitrage commercial international: Litec, 1996, p. 800, n° 1428). De même, le Tribunal arbitral, sur la base des témoignages recueillis de part et d'autre, n'est pas convaincu qu'en désignant le lieu d'exécution comme étant situé à Bâle alors qu'en réalité le Contrat s'exécutait au Liban, les parties ont voulu manifester leur intention de soumettre le Contrat au droit suisse.

22. En l'absence de volonté clairement exprimée dans le Contrat, il appartient, dès lors, au Tribunal arbitral de déterminer le droit applicable selon les méthodes qui sont à sa disposition à cette fin. À cet égard, il est de principe que les règles de conflit du siège de l'arbitrage ne s'imposent pas au Tribunal arbitral et encore moins les règles matérielles, ce qui exclut l'application automatique du droit suisse. Quant à la pratique des sociétés allemandes, invoquée par la Défenderesse, outre que la preuve de cette pratique n'est pas suffisamment rapportée, les déclarations des témoins ne permettent pas d'affirmer que le Demandeur était d'accord sur l'application du droit suisse. Le Tribunal arbitral considère que la preuve n'est pas établie d'un accord implicite des parties pour appliquer ce droit à leur Contrat.

23. L'application cumulative des règles de conflit en présence, à savoir, d'une part celles des États dont les parties sont ressortissantes (le Liban et l'Allemagne) et, d'autre part, celles du siège de l'arbitrage (la Suisse), permet de vérifier qu'elles convergent vers l'application du droit libanais. En effet, en premier lieu, l'article 4 du décret-loi libanais n° 34/67 du 10 août 1967 relatif à l'agence commerciale, mais applicable également, selon son article 1er alinéa 2, à la distribution commerciale, impose de façon impérative les dispositions de ce texte en cas de non renouvellement du contrat de distribution à l'arrivée de son terme ou, par assimilation, en cas de résiliation. En second lieu, la solution est identique si l'on applique la règle de conflit allemande, qu'il s'agisse de celle qui était applicable à la date de la signature du Contrat (1971) ou de celle qui serait actuellement, depuis l'entrée en vigueur en Allemagne de la Convention de Rome du 19 juin 1980 sur la loi applicable aux obligations contractuelles.

24. Avant la ratification par l'Allemagne de la Convention de Rome, la détermination du droit applicable au contrat se faisait en utilisant une échelle d'analyse à quatre niveaux. En l'absence d'une indication expresse du droit applicable par les parties (premier niveau), le deuxième niveau consistait à rechercher un accord implicite au moyen de divers indices dégagés par la doctrine et la jurisprudence: un accord exprès relatif à la compétence juridictionnelle, à la compétence arbitrale (Bâle), au lieu d'exécution (Bâle), à la langue ou à la monnaie du contrat notamment. La plupart de ces indices, notamment celui relatif à la compétence arbitrale et celui relatif au lieu d'exécution choisi par les parties et distinct de leurs sièges respectifs ainsi que des lieux d'exécution effectifs des obligations découlant du contrat, sont des indices forts. Leur mise en œuvre conduirait donc plutôt à conclure à l'applicabilité du droit suisse. Toutefois, la volonté des parties, même implicite, doit être certaine, or ce n'est pas le cas ici. Il est donc nécessaire de procéder à l'analyse au troisième niveau. Pour ce troisième niveau, on ne recherche plus l'expression d'une volonté implicite, qui n'a, par définition, pas pu être dégagée lors de l'analyse au deuxième niveau, mais le plus fort lien de rattachement du contrat avec un droit national. Les mêmes indices qu'au deuxième niveau sont utilisés, outre, éventuellement, le lieu de conclusion du contrat ou le siège des parties. Une volonté non équivoque des parties n'est plus exigée à ce niveau. Là encore, la mise en œuvre de ces indices tendrait plutôt à désigner le droit suisse. Une partie de la doctrine prenait toutefois déjà en considération la prestation caractéristique du type de contrat en cause lors de l'analyse au troisième niveau, analyse plus conforme aux tendances actuelles. Dans le cas d'un contrat de distribution exclusive, la prestation caractéristique est considérée comme étant celle du distributeur exclusif. Le siège de la partie exécutant la prestation caractéristique déterminant le droit applicable, il s'agirait alors du droit libanais, ce qui dispense, dès lors, d'appliquer le quatrième niveau d'analyse. Le Tribunal arbitral, dans le cadre de cet examen, estime qu'il convient de suivre ladite doctrine relative à la prestation caractéristique, et ceci notamment en raison du fait que cette doctrine a par la suite été consacrée lors de l'adoption par l'Allemagne de la Convention de Rome du 19 juin 1980. La solution qu'elle permet de dégager, conforme au droit allemand applicable au moment de la formation du contrat est donc, par ailleurs, en harmonie avec la solution qui résulterait de l'application du droit allemand actuel.

25. En effet, la règle de conflit allemande, telle qu'elle résulte de l'article 4 alinéa 1er de la Convention de Rome, désigne la loi du pays ayant les liens les plus étroits avec le contrat. Il en va de même de la loi suisse, selon l'article 187 alinéa 1er de la LDIP. S'agissant des contrats de distribution exclusive, en dépit de certaines divergences, la jurisprudence et la doctrine allemandes et suisses s'accordent généralement à considérer que la prestation caractéristique est la prestation du distributeur plutôt que la fourniture du produit par le fabricant (TF 10 décembre 1974, Asbrink Eiker: ATF 100 II 450; JDI 1976, p. 712, chron. P. Lalive. — F. Vischer, Internationales Vertragsrecht, 2e ed. 2000, n° 667 et s.). En droit allemand le contrat-cadre de distribution est on principe régi par la loi du lieu du distributeur (OLG Düsseldorf, 11 juill. 1996: Recht der internationalen Wirtschaft, 1996, p. 958; Revue suisse de droit international et de droit européen, 1996, p. 139. — V. Reithmann-Martiny, Internationales Vertragsrecht, 6e éd., 2004, n° 2050. — Martiny in München-er Kommentar, 3e éd., t. 10, 1998. Art. 28, n° 159; von Bar, Internationales Privatrecht, t. 2, 1991, n° 499). Cette solution est conforme à l'analyse économique du contrat de distribution, qui vise à la conquête et à l'exploitation d'un marché particulier (V. Marie-Elodie Ancel, La prestation caractéristique du contrat: Economica, 2002, p. 176 et s.). Selon le Tribunal Fédéral suisse, dans l'arrêt Asbrink Eiker, lorsque le volume du chiffre d'affaires n'est pas fixé à l'avance, il dépend du dynamisme du représentant exclusif, ce qui permet d'identifier clairement la prestation caractéristique, « la prestation [du distributeur] ayant une importance fondamentale et économique plus grande que celle du fournisseur ».

26. C'est également la solution assez généralement admise par la jurisprudence arbitrale internationale. Ainsi, plusieurs sentences arbitrales CCI, appliquant la méthode cumulative, ont désigné la loi de l'établissement du distributeur comme loi applicable (V. sentence CCI n° 7319/1992: Recueil des sentences arbitrales de la CCI, vol. IV, 1996-2000, p. 300. — sentence CCI n° 7250/1992: Bull. CCI, vol. 7, mai 1996, p. 93). Dans la sentence n° 8195/1996 relative à un contrat de distribution conclu entre un fabricant français et un distributeur libanais, l'arbitre unique, siégeant à Paris, après s'être référé aux principes généraux du droit (dont, notamment, l'article 4, alinéa 2, de la Convention de Rome), et avoir appliqué les règles de conflit française et libanaise, selon l'article 813 du Code de procédure civile libanais qui dispose que « l'arbitre tranche les litiges conformément aux règles de droit choisies par les parties et, à défaut d'un tel choix, conformément aux règles qu'il estime appropriées. Il tient compte, dans tous les cas, des usages commerciaux », est parvenu à la conclusion que le droit libanais présentait les liens les plus étroits avec le contrat, la prestation caractéristique du contrat (la distribution de produits pharmaceutiques) étant localisée au Liban où le distributeur était par ailleurs établi *(sentence inédite, citée par Corinne Truong; in Les différends liés à la rupture des contrats internationaux de distribution dans les sentences arbitrales CCI: Litec, Paris, 2002, p. 165 n° 172, Préface de Philippe Fouchard).*

27. La méthode de la voie directe, suggérée par la Défenderesse, conduit au même résultat. Selon cette méthode, il s'agit, pour l'arbitre, de procéder directement au rattachement du contrat, sans passer par la règle de conflit, afin d'appliquer à la relation contractuelle litigieuse qui lui est soumise la loi qu'il juge la plus appropriée, ainsi que l'y invite l'article 17 alinéa 1er du Règlement d'arbitrage CCI. S'agissant des contrats internationaux de distribution, la jurisprudence arbitrale retient communément comme critère déterminant le lieu d'exécution de la prestation caractéristique du contrat. Ainsi, dans la sentence CCI n° 6500/1992, qui présente une grande analogie avec la présente affaire, le tribunal arbitral, siégeant en Suisse, ayant à connaître d'un litige relatif à un contrat de distribution exclusive conclu entre une société suisse (fabricant), filiale d'une société américaine, et une société libanaise (distributeur), après avoir écarté la loi suisse en l'absence de tout rattachement déterminant, a décidé d'appliquer la loi libanaise en tant que *"loi de la partie qui devait et a mené les activités qui étaient l'objet du contrat. C'est, comme on le dit souvent en droit international privé, la loi du pays où le centre de gravité du contrat est situé. Quand un contrat implique l'exécution d'activités par l'une des parties, qui résultent dans la réalisation du but et objet du contrat, la loi applicable est celle du pays où de telles activités sont effectuées" (sentence CCI n° 6500/1992: JDI 1992, p. 1015, n° 55, note J.-J. A.; Revue libanaise de l'arbitrage, n° 9, p. 32). La sentence CCI n° 8606/1997,* relative à un contrat de concession exclusive conclu entre un concédant français et un concessionnaire libanais a également retenu l'application du droit libanais aux motifs qu' *" en l'absence de volonté des parties sur le choix de la loi applicable, les contrats de représentation commerciale, de commission ou de concession, doivent être régis par la loi du lieu d'exécution du contrat . . . c'est, en effet, au Liban que s'exécutent les principales obligations du distributeur . . ." (sentence CCI n° 8606/1997, Revue libanaise de l'arbitrage,. n° 9, p. 20 et s.).* Le recours à la méthode de la voie directe conduit ainsi à l'application du droit libanais, droit du lieu d'exécution du Contrat.

28. À titre subsidiaire, la Défenderesse demande au Tribunal arbitral d'appliquer les principes généraux du droit, tels qu' ils résultent notamment des Principes UNIDROIT, autrement dit, la lex mercatoria. Le Tribunal arbitral considère que si celle-ci était applicable, elle ne le serait éventuellement qu'à titre complémentaire du droit libanais et qu'il n'existe aucun intérêt à l'appliquer en écartant le droit libanais car elle contient des dispositions analogues à celui-ci. Le recours à la lex mercatoria n'est pas justifié, dans l'hypothèse où il existe, comme dans la présente affaire, des liens étroits entre le Contrat et une loi nationale déterminée. Il pourrait éventuellement en être autrement si le distributeur exerçait ses activités dans plusieurs pays, ce qui n'est pas le cas de M. [X]. La lex mercatoria pourrait encore se concevoir si le droit libanais ne prévoyait aucun droit à dommages-intérêts en cas de résiliation du contrat de distribution, ce qui n'est pas le cas non plus, ainsi que cela sera exposé ci-après. La jurisprudence arbitrale admet qu'en cas de rupture fautive d'un contrat de distribution, le contractant qui subit la rupture a droit à des dommages-intérêts (V., notamment, la sentence CCI n° 2103/1972: Recueil des sentences arbitrales de la CCI, 1974-1975, p. 204, obs. Y. D. — C.

Truong, Les différends liés à la rupture des contrats internationaux de distribution dans les sentences arbitrales CCI, préc, p. 199 et s. — Behar-Touchais et Virassamy, Les contrats de la distribution: LCDJ 1999, p. 452) et l'article 7-4.1 des Principes UNIDROIT contient un principe général de droit à indemnisation en cas d'inexécution du contrat. L'application de la lex mercatoria au présent litige n'apparaît pas, dès lors, appropriée en tant que telle. Son contenu permet cependant de vérifier que le droit libanais des contrats d'agence et de distribution n'est pas en opposition avec elle.

29. Un auteur particulièrement bien informé a d'ailleurs observé que, quelle que soit la méthode adoptée par les arbitres statuant sous l'égide de la CCI (application cumulative des règles de conflit intéressées au litige, application des règles de conflit du siège de l'arbitrage ou encore recours aux principes généraux du droit), la tendance générale est de choisir la règle de conflit de lois qui est en faveur de l'application du lieu de la distribution (V. C. Truong, Le droit applicable au fond dans les contrats internationaux de distribution: analyse des sentences arbitrales de la CCI: Bull. CCI, vol. 12 n° 1, 2001, p. 40 et s. — adde, du même auteur, Les différends liés à la rupture des contrats internationaux de distribution dans les sentences arbitrales CCI, préc, p. 66). »

Après s'être prononcé sur le droit applicable, il revenait au tribunal arbitral de se prononcer sur l'argument de la défenderesse selon lequel le litige ne serait arbitrable car le droit libanais réserve une compétence exclusive à certains tribunaux pour se prononcer sur les litiges relatifs aux contrats de distribution. Le tribunal arbitral rejette cet argument dans les termes suivants:

« *30. Il reste à examiner l'argument de la Défenderesse selon lequel le droit libanais en vigueur à l'époque de la signature du Contrat prohibait le recours à l'arbitrage dans les contrats d'agence et de distribution commerciale. Selon la Défenderesse le décret-loi libanais n° 34/67 attribue une compétence exclusive aux tribunaux du lieu d'exercice de l'agent ou du distributeur, c'est-à-dire aux tribunaux libanais. L'article 5 dudit décret-loi dispose en effet que: ''nonobstant toute disposition contraire, sont compétents pour trancher les conflits résultant du contrat de représentation commerciale, les tribunaux du lieu ou le représentant de commerce exerce son activité''.*

31. Selon ce texte, les litiges relatifs aux contrats de représentation commerciale seraient inarbitrables. Cependant, la jurisprudence et la doctrine libanaises apparaissent divisées sur cette question. Ainsi, en 1988, la Cour de cassation libanaise a admis la validité de la clause compromissoire au motif que la convention d'arbitrage est régie par le principe d'autonomie dans les termes suivants: ''Attendu que la teneur de l'article 5 du décret-loi du 5 août 1967 impose d'interpréter l'expression ''nonobstant toute convention contraire'' comme étant exclusivement relative à l'accord qui donne compétence à un tribunal qui n'est pas celui désigné par le texte du décret, qui relève, elle, de l'autonomie de la volonté, ce qui permet aux cocontractants, non seulement de convenir de l'autorité arbitrale, mais encore du droit applicable (article 767 du Code de procédure civile) ainsi que de donner toute liberté à l'arbitre pour le choix du droit ou de la coutume applicables ou les plus appropriés à la solution du litige, ce d'autant plus que l'article 767 a énoncé que les parties peuvent convenir de recourir à l'arbitrage pour trouver une solution au litige même si un tribunal en est déjà saisi [. . .]. Attendu que la convention d'arbitrage se situant en dehors du champ de l'Article 5 précité, l'accord des parties sur l'arbitrage n'est pas contraire à l'ordre public de même que la sentence arbitrale rendue en conséquence, ni aux principes de droit [. . .]'' (C. cass., 7 juill. 1988: Rec. Hatem, fasc. 197, p. 417; Rev. al-Adl, 1992, p. 32, note N. Diab; Revue libanaise de l'arbitrage, n° 1, p. 56 et 80, ibid n° 3, p. 17; cité également par C. Truong in Les différends liés à la rupture des contrats internationaux de distribution dans les sentences arbitrales CCI, précité, p. 94 et 95). Cette analyse est partagée par la doctrine la plus autorisée, qui estime que ce texte "n'a statué que pour fixer la compétence des tribunaux les uns par rapport aux autres. Pour exclure la procédure extra judiciaire de l'arbitrage, il aurait fallu une disposition expresse de la loi" (cf. E. Tyan, Droit commercial, t. 2, 1970, p. 476, n° 1314). Selon cette analyse, l'article 5 du décret-loi doit donc être interprété comme interdisant les clauses attributives de compétence à des juridictions autres que libanaises et non comme prohibant les clauses compromissoires.

32. D'autres décisions des juridictions libanaises ont cependant annulé des clauses compromissoires insérées dans des contrats de représentation commerciale, en considérant que l'article 5 dudit décret-loi 34/67 est une loi de police excluant non seulement la compétence des juridictions étrangères mais également le recours à l'arbitrage. Selon cette jurisprudence, la compétence exclusive des juridictions libanaises se justifierait par l'idée selon laquelle elles seules seraient en mesure d'appliquer les dispositions impératives du droit libanais résultant du décret-loi 34/67, dont l'objectif est d'assurer la protection du représentant libanais, notamment en ce que ce texte lui accorde une indemnité en cas de rupture du contrat. La nullité de la clause compromissoire, ou l'inarbitrabilité du litige, seraient ainsi fondées sur le risque de non application du droit libanais par un tribunal arbitral.

33. Cette conception, qui revient, à limiter la compétence de l'arbitre aux matières ne relevant pas des lois de police ou de l'ordre public, apparaît aujourd'-hui largement dépassée (cf. Ch. Jarrosson et I. Idot, L'arbitrabilité: Revue de Jurisprudence commerciale, 1995, p. 1 et s. — Ch. Séraglini, Lois de police et justice arbitrale internationale: Dalloz, 2001, p. 77 et s — B. Hanotiau, L'arbitrabilité: Recueil des Cours de l'Académie de droit international de La Haye, 2002, p. 62 et s.). Il est en effet, généralement admis, en droit comparé de l'arbitrage commercial international, que l'arbitre doit appliquer les lois de police de la lex cause (V. Fouchard Gaillard Goldman, Traité de l'arbitrage commercial international, p. 861, n° 1517. — Poudret et Besson, Droit comparé de l'arbitrage international, p. 647, n° 706. — Ch. Séraglini, Lois de police et justice arbitrale internationale: Dalloz, 2001, not. p. 215 et s. — J.-B. Racine, L'arbitrage commercial international et l'ordre public: LGDJ 1999, p. 248 et s. — P. Cannage. L'arbitre et les lois de police et de sûreté: Revue libanaise de l'arbitrage, 1996, n° 3, p. 14). Cette obligation est d'autant plus évidente que la loi de police en cause est destinée à assurer la protection de la partie faible, ce qui est précisément le but poursuivi par le décret-loi 34/67. C'est la raison pour laquelle la doctrine libanaise distingue, en ce qui concerne la reconnaissance de la sentence arbitrale par les juridictions libanaises, selon que les arbitres ont accordé une indemnité au représentant ou au distributeur libanais en vertu du droit libanais ou d'un droit équivalent, ou qu'ils ont méconnu la protection assurée à la partie faible par l'un ou l'autre de ces droits (V. Issa El Khoury, Conditions relatives à la reconnaissance au Liban d'une sentence arbitrale internationale rendue en matière de représentation commerciale: Revue libanaise de l'arbitrage, 1996, n° 3, p. 17).

34. Le décret-loi 34/67 ayant pour objet une double protection — juridictionnelle et législative — du distributeur libanais, celui-ci a la faculté de renoncer à la protection juridictionnelle dès lors que le droit libanais (ou un droit équivalent) est appliqué par le tribunal arbitral. Cette solution a été admise par le tribunal arbitral dans la sentence CCI n° 8606/1997 précitée. Dans cette affaire, le tribunal arbitral, saisi par un distributeur libanais en vertu de la clause compromissoire insérée dans le contrat litigieux, après avoir rappelé l'arrêt de la Cour de cassation libanaise du 7 juillet 1988, qui permet au distributeur de renoncer à la protection de l'article 5 du décret-loi 34/67 lorsqu'il n'est plus en état d'infériorité, a estimé que "tel est le cas, semble-t-il, du distributeur qui, postérieurement à la signature du contrat de repré-sentation commerciale accepte de s'en remettre à l'arbitrage aux termes d'un com-promis d'arbitrage''. Cette solution peut, selon le Tribunal arbitral, être étendue à la clause compromissoire lorsque, comme dans la présente espèce, les parties ont signé un Acte de mission ne comportant aucune réserve sur la validité de la clause d'arbitrage ou sur la compétence du tribunal arbitral. En introduisant la procédure d'arbitrage et en signant l'Acte de mission, M. [X] a librement et clairement mani-festé son intention de renoncer à la protection juridictionnelle que lui accorde la loi libanaise. On pourrait ajouter qu'à cette date il n'était plus sous la dépendance économique de la société [B], et que cette protection n'était donc plus nécessaire.

35. Cela étant, dès lors que le siège du Tribunal arbitral est situé à Bâle, le présent arbitrage est régi par le droit suisse, conformément aux dispositions de l'article 176 LDIP. L'arbitrabilité étant régie par la loi du siège de l'arbitrage, il convient donc de déterminer si le litige est arbitrable au regard du droit suisse.

36. Aux termes de l'article 177 LDIP ''toute cause de nature patrimoniale peut faire l'objet d'un arbitrage''. Selon le Tribunal fédéral suisse, l'arbitrabilité est ''régie par la lex arbitrii sans égard aux dispositions peut-être plus strictes de la lex causae ou de la loi nationale des parties, ce qui peut entraîner des conséquences quant à la reconnaissance à l'étranger d'une sentence rendue en Suisse'' (Arrêt du 28 avril 1992, ATF 118 II 193: Revue suisse de droit international et de droit européen, 1994, p. 108). Dans un autre arrêt, du 23 juin 1992, le Tribunal fédéral a jugé que ''le législateur ayant choisi un critère d'arbitrabilité dépendant de la nature de la cause et non du droit qui la régit, il n'y a, en principe, pas lieu de tenir compte des restrictions et prohibitions du droit étranger relatives à l'arbitrabilité de la cause'' (ATF 118 II 353, Revue suisse de droit international et de droit européen, 1994, p. 111). Ainsi, même si un contrat est nul, par exemple parce qu'il violerait l'ordre public international, il s'agit là d'un problème de fond et non pas d'arbitrabilité. L'ordre public ''ne pourrait avoir de l'importance que s'il exigeait impérativement que la prétention litigieuse soit soumise à une autorité étatique. En revanche, le fait que ladite prétention touche à l'ordre public ne suffirait pas, en soi, à exclure l'arbitrabilité de la cause''. Interprétant cette der-nière réserve, le Tribunal fédéral estime que l'exigence de soumission d'une pré-tention litigieuse à une autorité étatique exclusivement ne peut être acceptée que de façon tout à fait exceptionnelle. Il l'a refusée dans l'arrêt précité, relatif à la validité d'un contrat portant sur la livraison d'armes à l'Irak antérieurement aux Résolutions de l'ONU de 1990 et 1991 interdisant toute activité commerciale avec l'Irak. Le Tribunal fédéral ajoute que ''cet état de chose [ne peut] déboucher sur la constatation de l'inarbitrabilité des prétentions déduites de ces contrats, et à plus forte raison de celles issues de contrats connexes comme le contrat d'agence sur lequel l'intimé assoit ses prétentions. On ne voit pas, en particulier, quels principes juridiques fondamentaux établiraient un monopole de la juridiction éta-tique pour régler les différends portant sur des prétentions de nature civile influ-encées par des règles de droit international public''.

37. C'est dire que, même si le droit libanais devait réserver aux autorités judiciaires libanaises l'exclusivité du règlement des différends concernant un dis-tributeur libanais, cette règle ne porterait pas atteinte à l'arbitrabilité du différend dès lors que, comme en l'espèce, le tribunal arbitral a son siège en Suisse.

38. Sur un plan plus général, il convient d'observer que l'idée selon laquelle l'arbitrabilité peut être circonscrite par des règles de compétence exclusive réser-vant à une autorité étatique particulière la connaissance de certains litiges, tend de plus en plus à être interprétée de façon très restrictive. Ainsi, par exemple, en Allemagne la doctrine considère qu'une règle de compétence excluant l'arbitrabil-ité d'un litige patrimonial (V. § 1030, al. 1 ZPO) ne devrait être admise que de façon tout à fait exceptionnelle (cf. Jean-François Poudret et Sébastien Besson, Droit comparé de l'arbitrage international, Schultess 2002, p. 312; Raeschke-Kessler, H. Berger K.P., Recht und Praxis des Schieldsverfa-brens, 3ᵉ éd., Cologne 1999, p. 164). De la même façon, les systèmes juridiques qui, traditionnellement, ont voulu protéger le distributeur considéré comme la partie faible dans un contrat de distribution, ont également tendance à renoncer à la compétence exclusive des tribunaux du domicile du distributeur.

39. Selon la doctrine la plus autorisée, à propos de la loi belge, analogue au décret-loi libanais 34/67, "il est permis d'espérer que les juridictions arbitrales chargées de se prononcer sur l'arbitrabilité de la rupture des contrats de conces-sions exclusives [. . .] reconnaîtront cette arbitrabilité au regard des seules con-ceptions généralement admises dans le commerce international conformément à une démarche qui correspond à un fondement international de leur compétence" (V. Fouchard Gaillard Goldman, op. cit. p. 372, n° 588; adde, C. Truong, op. cit., p. 92 et s., spéc. p. 99). La jurisprudence belge est d'ailleurs en voie d'évolution (V. à ce sujet, Bernard Hanotiau, Panorama de jurisprudence belge, in les Cahiers de l'arbitrage, Gazette du Palais, n° 2001/1, pp. 59.62).

40. L'admission de l'arbitrabilité pour ce type de contrats a ainsi été consacrée par la sentence arbitrale CCI précitée n° 8606/1997 rendue à Paris à l'occasion d'un litige opposant un distributeur libanais à un laboratoire français de produits phar-maceutiques, et ce dans les termes suivants: "Il appartient donc à l'arbitre unique de faire prévaloir la règle d'autonomie de la clause compromissoire consacrée par le droit international privé. Ainsi, l'arbitre se doit d'apprécier la validité de la con-vention d'arbitrage, indépendamment des règles de conflit de droits internes en présence, voire des dispositions substantielles des droits concernés. L'arbitre n'appartenant à aucun ordre juridique interne, il est en droit de faire application d'un corps de règles transnationales plutôt que des ordres juridiques internes qui n'ont pas à s'imposer à lui" (Revue libanaise de l'arbitrage, n° 9, p. 20, spéc. p. 24).

41. Pour l'ensemble des motifs exposés ci-dessus, le Tribunal arbitral considère que les dispositions impératives du décret-loi libanais 34/67 ne font obstacle ni à l'arbitrabilité du litige ni à la compétence du Tribunal arbitral. »

Ayant déterminé que le litige était soumis au droit libanais et que celui-ci était arbitrable, le tribunal arbitral étudie une à une les demandes du distributeur au fond.

Le demandeur considère en effet que la résiliation du contrat est à la fois irrégulière et injustifiée et que la défenderesse a violé la clause d'exclusivité du contrat. Il fait ainsi remarquer que la lettre de préavis lui est parvenue par simple courrier et non par lettre recommandée comme cela était prévu au contrat. La défenderesse prétend au contraire que la résiliation est régulière mais également justifiée par la faiblesse des résultats financiers, le caractère obsolète de la stratégie du distributeur ainsi que par l'absence de structures appropriées.

Le tribunal arbitral commence par constater que « *les dispositions claires et non équi-voques de l'article 12 du Contrat n'ont, à l'évidence, pas été respectées, ni en ce qui concerne la forme — par lettre ordinaire — de la résiliation, ni en ce qui concerne le préavis de six mois contractuellement prévu* ». Le tribunal considère par ailleurs que la tentative de régularisation postérieure de la défenderesse — qui a adressé une seconde lettre de résiliation sept mois après la première — est inopérante et que c'est donc à la date de la première lettre de résiliation qu'il convenait de se placer pour apprécier les effets et la régularité de la résiliation. Le tribunal repousse également les motifs de résiliation avancés par la défenderesse et constate que les résultats financiers du distributeur étaient plus qu'honorables dans un contexte difficile et que « *les témoignages recueillis par le tribunal ne démontrent pas le contraire* ». Il en conclut donc que la défenderesse ne pouvait se fonder sur ces motifs pour mettre fin au contrat.

Le tribunal rappelle cependant que, s'agissant d'un contrat à durée déterminée se renouvelant par tacite reconduction, la défenderesse était libre d'y mettre fin, à condition de respecter les règles contractuelles. Le tribunal constate à cet égard que la défenderesse a, par le biais d'une société sœur, violé la clause d'exclusivité prévue au contrat en entrant en contact avec un autre distributeur local et en cessant de livrer ses produits au demandeur. Le tribunal en conclut que la défenderesse a mis fin au contrat de manière irrégulière et injustifiée et qu'elle a violé la clause d'exclusivité, *« obligation essentielle dudit contrat »*. Il ajoute que *« les conditions du droit à réparation du Demandeur — absence de faute et de motif légitime — étant réunies selon le droit libanais applicable, il convient dès lors, d'examiner les demandes relatives aux différents préjudices allégués »*.

Au titre du préjudice, le demandeur réclame réparation pour: (1) les marchandises invendables en stock, (2) les frais liés à l'enregistrement des produits, (3) les frais liés aux licenciements des employés, (4) le gain manqué, et (5) l'indemnité pour la clientèle et le fonds de commerce ainsi que le dommage subi du fait de la concurrence déloyale. Le demandeur réclame également le paiement d'intérêts au taux légal sur ces sommes.

Le tribunal rejette la demande du demandeur au titre des stocks de marchandises invendables. Il considère en effet que la décision du demandeur de détruire les stocks sans laisser le temps à la défenderesse de les racheter et sans établir d'inventaire contradictoire *« apparaît non seulement intempestive mais encore infondée »*. Le tribunal ajoute qu' *« en procédant à la destruction du stock, le Demandeur a failli à son obligation de minimiser le dommage »*.

Le tribunal rejette également la demande d'indemnisation pour les frais d'enregistrement des produits pour deux raisons. Premièrement, le tribunal constate qu'il manque d'éléments probants sur la réalité et le montant du préjudice. Au demandeur, qui faisait valoir qu'il avait demandé la production d'un certain nombre de pièces à cet égard à la défenderesse, le tribunal répond: *« contraindre la défenderesse à produire des pièces que le demandeur aurait dû conserver conduirait à renverser la charge de la preuve qui incombe au demandeur »*. Deuxièmement, le tribunal constate que la rémunération prévue au contrat couvre toutes les revendications résultant des engagements pris en vertu du contrat et que les obligations d'enregistrement figurent en tête des engagements souscrits par le demandeur. Le demandeur ne pouvait donc pas demander l'indemnisation d'un préjudice pour une prestation qui avait déjà été rémunérée en vertu du contrat.

Le tribunal rejette encore les demandes relatives aux licenciements des salariés, faute de preuves convaincantes à cet égard et de preuve du lien de causalité entre la résiliation du contrat et lesdits licenciements. Le tribunal fait ainsi valoir qu'il *« n'aurait pu, en tout état de cause, ne retenir que les indemnités versées aux employés licenciés immédiatement à la suite de la résiliation du contrat »*.

Le tribunal accorde cependant une indemnité au demandeur au titre du gain manqué, indemnité dont il évalue le montant de la façon suivante: *« le tribunal arbitral usant de son pouvoir souverain d'appréciation que lui confère le droit libanais applicable, retiendra donc le bénéfice net moyen réalisé sur les trois dernières années ayant précédé la rupture du Contrat en tenant compte de l'ancienneté des relations contractuelles (plus de 25 ans), des circonstances économiques difficiles, ainsi que de la gravité de la faute commise par la défenderesse dans la rupture du contrat »*.

Enfin, le tribunal estime que le demandeur est en droit de recevoir une indemnité de clientèle car *« il serait inéquitable, dès lors que le distributeur n'a commis aucune faute et que la résiliation a été jugée irrégulière et injustifiée, de permettre à la défenderesse de conserver sans compensation la clientèle constituée et fidélisée par les efforts et soins du Demandeur »*. Le tribunal considère également que la défenderesse a commis des actes de concurrence déloyale en livrant des produits à un concurrent du demandeur alors que le contrat était toujours en vigueur et que ces actes déloyaux ont nécessairement causé au demandeur un préjudice. Le tribunal accorde par conséquent au demandeur une somme forfaitaire à ce titre.

Conformément à ses demandes, le tribunal accorde au demandeur des intérêts au taux légal libanais. Le tribunal ordonne également à la défenderesse de supporter la charge des frais de conseil du demandeur à hauteur de 50% de leur montant « *le tribunal n'ayant pas fait droit à toutes les demandes du demandeur* » et les frais d'arbitrage à hauteur de 60%.

NOTE. — I. — Le raisonnement du tribunal arbitral concernant la loi applicable au contrat de distribution exclusif est d'une particulière richesse. Le tribunal fait en effet une application rigoureuse et méthodique des différentes méthodes de détermination du droit applicable pour déterminer la loi applicable au contrat.

Le tribunal commence par répondre aux arguments de la défenderesse, qui prétend que les parties auraient implicitement désigné le droit suisse comme applicable au contrat dans la mesure où la clause compromissoire stipulait: « Le lieu d'exécution et de compétence juridique est la Chambre de commerce Internationale de Bâle, pour tous les litiges éventuels résultant du présent contrat, y compris les actions de change ».

Le tribunal constate que cette clause ne peut être interprétée comme renfermant une désignation du droit applicable, qu'elle soit explicite ou implicite. Un tel choix implicite aurait pu notamment résulter du fait que les parties ont plaidé conformément à un même droit national (V. dans ce sens *Sentence rendue dans l'affaire CCI n° 10264 en 2000: JDI 2004, p. 1256, obs. S. Jarvin.* — V. aussi *Sentence partielle dans l'affaire CCI n° 8113 en 1995: Recueil des sentences arbitrales de la CCI, vol. IV: ICC Publishing, 2003, p. 385).* Dans le cas présent, on ne peut que partager l'opinion du tribunal arbitral tant la clause visée par la défenderesse est confuse.

Le tribunal arbitral entreprend ensuite la détermination de la loi applicable par application des différentes méthodes de conflits susceptibles de s'appliquer à l'affaire: droit allemand et droit libanais (droits des États dont les parties sont ressortissantes) et droit suisse (droit du siège de l'arbitrage).

Le tribunal constate également que les règles de conflit allemandes n'étaient pas les mêmes au jour de la signature du contrat et au jour où le tribunal statue, l'Allemagne ayant ratifié la Convention de Rome sur la loi applicable aux obligations contractuelles du 19 juin 1980 entre-temps.

La méthode cumulative utilisée par le tribunal consiste à faire simultanément application des règles de conflit de tous les systèmes présentant un rattachement avec la cause. Elle a été appliquée par de nombreux tribunaux arbitraux siégeant sur le fondement du règlement d'arbitrage de la CCI (sur cette méthode, V. *E. Gaillard, Arbitrage commercial international — Sentence arbitrale — Droit applicable au fond du litige: J.-Cl. Procédure civile, Fasc. 1070-1, § 128, et les références citées, notamment Y. Derains, L'application cumulative par l'arbitre des systèmes de conflit de lois intéressés au litige: Rev. arb. 1972, p. 99. — Sentence rendue dans l'affaire CCI n° 4996: JDI 1986, p. 1131. obs. Y. Derains. — Sentence rendue dans l'affaire CCI n° 3043:JDI 1979, p. 1000, obs. Y. Derains. — Sentence rendue dans l'affaire CCI n° 5717 [1988]: Bull. CCI, vol. I, n° 2. 1990, p. 22 — Sentence rendue dans l'affaire CCI n° 6281 [1989]: JDI 1991, p. 1054, obs. D. Hascher; Yearbook 1990, p. 96. — Sentence rendue dans l'affaire CCI n° 6283 [1990]: Yearbook 1992, p. 178 — Sentence rendue dans l'affaire CCI n° 6149 [1990]: Yearbook 1995, p. 41).* Selon Filali Osman, l'application de la règle cumulative procède d'un esprit d'apaisement car elle montre aux parties qu'il existe une communauté de règles de conflit conduisant à l'application de la même loi *(F. Osman, Les principes généraux de la lex mercatoria: LGDJ, Bibliothèque de droit privé, t. 224, p. 368).*

Faisant application de la méthode cumulative, le tribunal arbitral constate que la loi applicable au contrat de distribution est la loi du lieu dans lequel la prestation caractéristique a été exécutée. Le tribunal constate également qu'en matière de contrat de distribution, il est généralement reconnu par la jurisprudence suisse et allemande, mais également par la « jurisprudence arbitrale internationale », que la prestation caractéristique est celle du disiributeur et par conséquent que la loi applicable est celle du lieu d'établissement de celui-ci. Il est cependant intéressant de noter que cette conception n'est pas partagée universellement. La Cour de cassation française a en effet eu par deux fois l'occasion d'affirmer que la prestation caractéristique dans un contrat de distribution exclusive est la prestation de fourniture, et donc que la loi applicable est la loi du lieu d'établissement du fournisseur. Selon la Cour de cassation, « pour un contrat de distribution, la fourniture du produit est la prestation caractéristique » *(Cass. 1ʳᵉ civ., 15 mai 2001: Juris-Data n° 2001-009552; JCP G 2001, II, 10634, note J. Raynard; Rev. crit. DIP 2002, p. 86, note P. Lagarde. — Cass. 1ʳᵉ civ., 25 nov. 2003: Juris-Data n° 2003-021050; Cah. dr. entr. 2004, n° 3, p. 28, obs. D. Mainguy. — M. Behar-Touchais et G. Virassamy, Les contrats de la distribution: LGDJ 1999, p. 399)*. La Court of Appeals of England and Wales partageait d'ailleurs la position de la Cour de cassation dans une décision *Print Concept GmbH c/ GEW (EC) Ltd (2 mars 2001, [2001] FWCA Civ 352)* dans laquelle la Cour décidait qu'un contrat de distribution conclu entre un producteur anglais et un distributeur allemand était régi par le droit anglais car, selon la Cour, les opérations de vente réalisées constituaient *« the real meat »* du contrat.

Le tribunal fait également, à la demande de la défenderesse, application de la méthode dite de la voie directe. Cette méthode consiste pour l'arbitre à choisir le droit applicable sans avoir à se préoccuper d'une règle de conflit quelconque *(E. Gaillard, op. cit., § 133. — M. de Boisséson, Le droit français de l'arbitrage interne et international: GLN Joly 1990, p. 597)*. Le choix peut être dicté par les rattachements existants entre la cause et le droit choisi, comme dans la méthode conflictuelle, mais aussi par le contenu du droit choisi. Les arbitres peuvent en effet estimer que l'application d'une loi est plus adéquate que l'application d'une autre dans un litige particulier en raison des effets iniques que l'application de celle-ci pourrait avoir au cas d'espèce. C'est ainsi que les arbitres peuvent, en l'absence de choix de la loi applicable par les parties, décider de ne pas retenir la loi dont l'application conduirait à l'annulation du contrat *(Sentence rendue dans l'affaire CCI n° 4145 [1984]: JDI 1985, p. 985, obs. Y. Derains. — Sentence rendue dans l'affaire CCI n° 4996: JDI 1986, p. 1132, obs. Y. Derains. — Sentence rendue dans l'affaire CCI n° 4132: JDI 1983, p. 891, obs. Y. Derains. — Sentence rendue dans l'affaire CCI n° 2694. — Sentence rendue dans l'affaire CCI n° 3880: JDI 1983, p. 897, obs. Y. Derains et S. Jarvin. — Sentence rendue dans l'affaire CCI n° 6840: JDI 1992, p. 1030, obs. Y. Derains)*. L'application de la voie directe s'analyse parfois simplement en une dispense de motiver le choix de la méthode ou du critère de rattachement retenu par les arbitres pour déterminer le droit applicable *(Sentence rendue dans l'affaire CCI n° 6719: JDI 1994, p. 1071)*.

Le tribunal arbitral décide finalement qu'il n'y a pas lieu de faire application des principes généraux du droit à la présente affaire dans la mesure où le litige comprend des liens de rattachement forts avec la loi d'un État déterminé et que la substance des principes généraux ne diffère pas de manière significative de la loi applicable au litige. Telle n'a pas toujours été la position des tribunaux arbitraux internationaux, certains ayant appliqué de manière combinée un système juridique national et la *lex mercatoria (Sentence CCI rendue dans l'affaire n° 1512: JDI 1974, p. 905. — Sentence CCI rendue dans l'affaire n° 3130: Recueil des sentences arbitrales de la CCI, vol. I, p. 413)*. Le tribunal constate ainsi de manière incidente que les principes généraux du droit reconnaissent au distributeur un droit à des dommages et intérêts en cas de rupture fautive du contrat de distribution *(sentence, § 28)*. Le tribunal arbitral ajoute également que l'application des principes généraux du droit ou la *lex mercatoria* pourraient être appliqués pour pallier les lacunes du droit national désigné par les règles de conflit, notamment si celui-ci ne prévoyait aucun droit à dommages-intérêts. Le raisonnement du tribunal arbitral démontre que la méthode directe contenue à l'article 17(1) du Règlement d'arbitrage de la CCI de 1998 est en fin de compte une méthode indirecte. En effet, n'importe quel tribunal souhaitant faire application de la méthode de la voie directe devra néanmoins se justifier dans le choix du droit applicable et, pour ce faire, il lui faudra toujours rechercher les critères de rattachement qui renverront inexorablement à la soit disant « méthode indirecte » archaïque.

II. — Cette affaire soulevait également une question intéressante en matière d'arbitrabilité. La question se posait en effet de savoir si le tribunal arbitral pouvait se prononcer sur le litige alors que la loi libanaise attribue une compétence exclusive aux tribunaux du lieu d'exercice du distributeur pour les litiges relatifs au contrat de distribution. Le tribunal arbitral commence par retenir que « cette conception, qui revient à limiter la compétence de l'arbitre aux matières ne relevant pas des lois de police ou de l'ordre public apparaît aujourd'hui largement dépassée » *(sentence, § 33)* et qu' « il est généralement admis, en droit comparé de l'arbitrage international, que l'arbitre doit appliquer les lois de police de la *lex cause* » (V. au sujet de l'application des lois de police de la *lex cause*, en sus des références citées dans la sentence, *1'. Mayer, Droit international privé: Domat, 8ᵉ éd., § 127 — B. Audit, Droit international privé. 3ᵉ éd., § 117).* Le tribunal ajoute que cette obligation est d'autant plus évidente quand la loi de police en cause a pour objet d'assurer la protection d'une partie faible (V. à ce sujet *K. Sachs, La protection de la partie faible en arbitrage, 2007(2), Cahiers de l'arbitrage: Gaz. Pal. 13-17 juill. 2007).* Le tribunal constate enfin que la protection conférée au distributeur par la loi libanaise revêt une double nature, à la fois juridictionnelle et substantielle. Le tribunal en conclut que le distributeur peut renoncer à la protection juridictionnelle, qui est prévue dans son seul intérêt, dès lors que le droit libanais est appliqué par le tribunal arbitral. Le raisonnement du tribunal est certes intéressant, néanmoins nous sommes d'avis que celui-ci aurait pu se limiter à faire application de l'article 177(1) de la LDIP.

III. — La forme du préavis retient également l'attention du tribunal. Celui-ci fait en effet remarquer que « les dispositions claires et non équivoques de l'article 12 du Contrat n'ont, à l'évidence, pas été respectées, ni en ce qui concerne la forme — par lettre ordinaire — de la résiliation » ni en ce qui concerne la durée du préavis. Or on aurait pu penser que la forme de la notification importait peu dans la mesure où le but de celle-ci était atteint et que le débiteur reconnaissait avoir été informé de la résiliation. Comme l'écrivait Berthold Goldman: « S'agissant enfin de la forme des actes, on est fondé à penser que les instruments de communication modernes (télex, télécopie) de plus en plus souvent utilisés dans les rapports économiques internationaux, seront considérés, par une règle de la *lex mercatoria*, comme suffisants pour la formation et la preuve des contrats qui sont l'instrument juridique de ces rapports » *(B. Goldman, Festschrift P. Lalive, p. 241-249).* On peut donc s'étonner que le tribunal ait attaché une importance particulière au fait que la lettre de résiliation devait être une lettre recommandée avec accusé de réception.

IV. — Le tribunal arbitral passe ensuite en revue les différents chefs de préjudice invoqués par le distributeur. La question de la détermination du préjudice à la suite de la résiliation d'un contrat de distribution a déjà fait l'objet de nombreuses sentences. Ainsi, dans une sentence datée de 1987, un tribunal arbitral statuant sur le fondement du droit hongrois a accordé au distributeur le gain manqué du fait de la rupture *(Sentence rendue dans l'affaire CCI n° 5418 en 1987: Recueil des sentences arbitrales de la CCI, vol. II, p. 123).* Un arbitre unique statuant sur le fondement du droit français a accordé à un distributeur les pertes directes ainsi que le gain manqué résultant de la résiliation, mais a exclu d'indemniser le préjudice commercial *(Sentence rendue dans l'affaire CCI n° 7006 en 1992: Recueil des sentences arbitrales de la CCI, vol. III, p. 199. — V. également Sentence rendue dans l'affaire CCI n° 1250 en 1964: Recueil des sentences arbitrales de la CCI, vol. I, p. 32).* Dans le cas présent, le tribunal refuse d'accorder au distributeur le remboursement des marchandises invendables en stock, faute de preuve de ce préjudice. Le tribunal constate également qu'en procédant à la destruction des biens en question sans rechercher un autre débouché à ceux-ci et sans laisser au fournisseur un temps raisonnable pour les racheter, le distributeur avait failli à son obligation de minimiser le dommage *(Y. Derains, L'obligation de minimiser le dommage dans la jurisprudence arbitrale: RDAI 1987, p. 375. — A. S. Komarov, Mitigation of damages in Evaluation of Damages in International Arbitration, publication de la CCI n° 668, 2006, p. 37 et seq. Y. Tanigucbi, The obligation to mitigate damages in Evaluation of Damages in International Arbitration, publication de la CCI n° 668, 2006, p. 79).* Cette obligation a été reconnue par de nombreux tribunaux arbitraux *(Sentence rendue dans l'affaire CCI n° 2142: Yearbook 1976, p. 132. — Sentence rendue dans l'affaire CCI n° 2404: JDI 1976, p. 995-996. — Sentence rendue dans l'affaire CCI n° 2478: Yearbook 1978, p. 222-223. — Sentence rendue dans l'affaire CCI n° 3344: JDI 1982, p. 978-983. — Sentence rendue dans l'affaire CCI n° 4761: JDI 1987, p. 1012-1017. — Sentence rendue dans l'affaire CCI n° 5514: JDI 1992, p. 1022-1024. — Sentence rendue dans l'affaire CCI n° 5721: JDI 1990, p. 1019-1025. — Sentence rendue dans l'affaire CCI n° 5865: JDI 1998, p. 1008-1013. — Sentence rendue dans l'affaire CCI n° 5885: Yearbook 1991, p. 91-95. — Sentence rendue dans l'affaire CCI n° 5910: JDI 1988, 1216-1219. — Sentence rendue dans l'affaire CCI n° 6840: JDI 1992, 1030-1034; Sentence rendue dans l'affaire CCI n° 7110, 10 Bull. CCI n° 2, 1999, p. 39-57. — Sentence rendue dans l'affaire CCI n° 8817, 10: Bull. CCI n° 2, 1999, p. 75-77).* Le principe de l'obligation de minimiser le dommage est l'un des principe les mieux établi de la *lex mercatoria,* alors même qu'il n'est pas reconnu en tant que tel dans tous les États *(Fouchard, Gaillard, Goldman on International Commercial Arbitration, § 832).* Certains tribunaux avaient déjà par le passé fait application de ce principe sans faire référence à des droits nationaux quelconques *(W. L. Craig, W. Park et J. Paulsson, International Chamber of Commerce Arbitration: Oceana Publications, 3ᵉ éd., p. 646).* Ce principe prend diverses formes et requiert de la victime d'un préjudice qu'elle adopte différentes attitudes. Ainsi la victime doit elle accepter certaines révisions du contrat manifestement déraisonnables pour minimiser son dommage *(Sentence rendue dans l'affaire CCI n° 2478: Yearbook 1978, p. 222-223).* Dans le cas présent, le tribunal donne une nouvelle illustration de ce principe, qui implique donc que le distributeur mette en œuvre des moyens raisonnables pour revendre les stocks restants à la suite de la résiliation du contrat de distribution. La seconde sentence commentée ci-dessous *(Sentence rendue dans l'affaire CCI n° 11855: JDI 2007, p. 1283)* donne une autre illustration de ce principe: un distributeur doit accepter de payer son fournisseur comptant pour recevoir la marchandise si, du fait d'impayés récurrents, celui-ci refuse de lui faire crédit. L'application de ce principe à la présente affaire peut malgré tout sembler surprenante dans la mesure où le tribunal avait indiqué qu'il ne ferait pas application des principes généraux de la *lex mercatoria* et qu'il ne fait pas référence à des dispositions spécifiques de la loi libanaise. Cette application, sans référence à une loi déterminée ou à un principe quelconque, pourrait donc participer à la consécration de ce principe, dont les arbitres font application sans nécessairement en détailler les raisons, alors même qu'il n'est pas reconnu en tant que tel universellement. C'est ainsi qu'en droit français l'obligation de minimiser le dommage constitue plus un souhait qu'une réalité *(S. Reifegerste, Pour une obligation de minimiser le dommage: PUAM 2002. — S. Pimont, Remarques complémentaires sur le devoir de minimiser son propre dommage: Rev. Lamy Droit civil, 2004, n° 9, p. 15).*

Le tribunal rejette également la demande liée aux frais d'enregistrement des produits estimant que ceux-ci ont déjà été rémunérés selon le contrat. Le tribunal écarte ainsi une double indemnisation d'un même dommage. Le tribunal rejette aussi la demande relative aux licenciements de certains salariés, faute de preuve du lien de causalité existant entre la résiliation du contrat et le licenciement de ceux-ci. Le tribunal arbitral accorde cependant au distributeur une somme forfaitaire pour le gain manqué et la perte de clientèle, en rappelant que le distributeur avait activement participé à la conquête du marché libanais. À cet égard, le tribunal, faisant usage du pouvoir souverain d'appréciation que lui confère le droit libanais, retient trois critères pour déterminer l'indemnité à allouer au distributeur:

(1) l'ancienneté des relations entre les parties; (2) les circonstances économiques prévalant lors de l'exécution du contrat, et (3) la gravité de la faute du fournisseur. Il est intéressant de noter que le tribunal tient compte de la gravité de la faute dans la fixation du dommage dans le cadre d'un litige soumis à un droit romano-germanique. Le tribunal fait donc application de manière incidente de la notion de sanction civile ou « *punitive damages* » (V. entre autres J. *Werner, Punitive and exemplary damages in international arbitration* in *Evaluation of Damages in International Arbitration: publication de la CCI n° 668, 2006, p. 101 et seq. — Y. Derains, Intérêts moratoires, dommages-intérêts compensatoires et dommages punitifs devant l'arbitre international in Études offertes à Pierre Bellet: Litec, Paris, 1991).* Ceci est d'autant plus intéressant que la gravité de la faute n'est pas prise en compte dans certaines juridictions, notamment en France *(J-Cl. Civil code, Fasc. 202-1-1, par M. Perier).*

E. S.R.

Sent. arb. finale rendue dans l'affaire CCI n° 11855 en 2003 (original en langue française)

Exception d'inexécution. — Non-paiement de certaines factures. — Refus de livraison. — Impossibilité de livrer le client final. — Obligation de minimiser le dommage.

Enrichissement sans cause. — Caractère subsidiaire. — Préjudice. — Préjudice moral. — Dénigrement. — Atteinte à l'image. — Intervention volontaire. — Accord des parties. — Intérêts. — Taux légal. — Taux contractuel. — Pouvoir de l'arbitre de fixer l'intérêt.

Intervention volontaire. — Accord des parties.

Le tribunal estime que le fournisseur était en droit de suspendre ses livraisons au distributeur en raison d'impayés récurrents et injustifiés de celui-ci.

Le tribunal arbitral refuse d'accorder à la demanderesse d'indemnité quelle qu'elle soit sur le fondement de la théorie de l'enrichissement sans cause, dans la mesure où celle-ci à un caractère subsidiaire et ne saurait prospérer lorsqu'il existe un contrat entre les parties.

Le tribunal estime que le distributeur a subi un préjudice moral dans la mesure où le fournisseur a informé les clients finaux de la rupture de leur contrat et du fait que le distributeur n'avait pas payé certaines factures.

La sentence rendue dans cette affaire a trait à un litige opposant la société suisse A à son distributeur espagnol B et sa filiale C, intervenant volontaire à l'instance. A a confié la représentation de l'essentiel de sa gamme de matériel ferroviaire à B en Espagne depuis 1993. Les relations entre les parties ont fait l'objet de plusieurs contrats: (1) un contrat de représentation commerciale, (2) un contrat de développement industriel, et (3) un contrat de concession de distribution. Ultérieurement, les parties ont également conclu un avenant au contrat de distribution et confié à B des missions d'agent. Le contrat de concession était un contrat à durée déterminée de sept ans, renouvelable par tacite reconduction pour des périodes successives de deux années sauf dénonciation par lettre recommandée avec avis de réception avec un préavis de six mois. Le contrat ne prévoyait aucun dédommagement en cas de non reconduction mais prévoyait toutefois qu'en cas de résiliation pour quelque motif que ce soit, les commandes devaient être normalement exécutées.

Le 14 décembre 1999, A signifiait par lettre recommandée avec accusé de réception à B sa volonté de ne pas reconduire le contrat à son échéance. Le litige ne porte cependant pas sur la décision de rupture elle-même mais sur la manière dont le concédant s'est comporté pendant la période de préavis et postérieurement à la rupture des relations contractuelles. B reproche notamment à A: (1) le débauchage de l'un de ses salariés, (2) le détournement de certaines commandes, (3) l'augmentation abusive du prix de certains produits au cours de la période de préavis, (4) des retards de livraison au cours du préavis et le refus de livrer certaines références, (5) la création d'une *« illusion de renégociation »* d'un nouveau contrat, et (6) le dénigrement de B par A et l'atteinte portée à son image. C, intervenue volontairement à l'instance, forme des demandes strictement similaires à celle de B. B et C demandent que A soit condamnée à indemniser indifféremment l'une ou l'autre, afin de leur laisser ainsi la liberté de répartir entre elles les sommes allouées par le tribunal. De son côté, la défenderesse forme une demande reconventionnelle et demande la condamnation du demandeur à lui payer plusieurs factures non réglées. A demande également au tribunal d'ordonner la compensation entre les différentes condamnations.

Les parties n'ayant soulevé aucune exception de procédure, le tribunal arbitral, siégeant à Genève sur le fondement du droit français, traite immédiatement les demandes de la demanderesse au fond.

Le tribunal examine dans une première partie la demande principale, qui elle-même se divise en demandes relatives à l'inexécution du contrat de distribution pendant la période de préavis et en griefs relatifs à la résiliation du contrat d'agence, avant de traiter des demandes fondées sur l'enrichissement sans cause, puis des préjudices et enfin de la demande reconventionnelle et des demandes annexes, telles que la compensation et les frais de procédure.

En ce qui concerne l'augmentation des prix au cours de la période de préavis, le tribunal estime que « *c'est sans aucune intention malveillante que A a augmenté dans certains cas le prix des pièces de rechange fournies à B ou a, dans certains cas, augmenté le prix au titre du service après vente. Toutefois, sur ce dernier point, le Tribunal Arbitral considère que c'est de façon injustifiée que A a procédé à cette augmentation* ». Le tribunal constate que l'augmentation du prix des pièces de rechange n'avait pas été généralisée, était limitée à certaines pièces, ne portait que sur de faibles montants et que « *l'augmentation du prix des pièces a été clairement expliquée au cours des témoignages* ». Le tribunal, après une analyse détaillée des raisons de l'augmentation, rappelle que selon lui cette augmentation ne relève pas d'une intention malveillante et rejette les demandes du distributeur à cet égard.

Le tribunal aborde ensuite les demandes relatives aux prétendus retards et refus de livraison. Le tribunal estime non fondées les demandes du distributeur à cet égard dans les termes suivants:

> « *66. Le Tribunal Arbitral a examiné attentivement les tableaux fournis par [B] tendant à établir l'existence d'importants retards de livraison dans le chef de [A] après la fin de la période de préavis contractuel. Il estime que ces tableaux ne constituent pas une preuve suffisante d'une politique délibérée, en ce que notamment ils n'établissent pas la nature du retard (et notamment la question de savoir si celui-ci porte sur une pièce ou sur cinquante pièces). Et en tout état de cause, ces retards sont dûment contestés par [A]. Le Tribunal Arbitral ne peut dès lors considérer que la preuve des retards a été établie à suffisance de fait par [B], à l'exception de la partie de la commande [client final D] qui a été livrée.*
>
> *67. En ce qui concerne l'annulation par [D] d'une partie de ses commandes, le Tribunal arbitral estime que la responsabilité contractuelle de [A] n'est aucunement engagée à ce titre. Il est incontestable qu'en janvier 2001, de nombreuses factures adressées à [B] demeuraient impayées. Le problème était d'ailleurs récurrent. Pour nombre de factures, [B] ne pouvait avancer aucune explication valable. Tel est le cas par exemple lorsqu'elle invoquait à l'appui du non paiement la fermeture de ses bureaux pendant les périodes de vacances ou l'augmentation injustifiée des prix des pièces de rechange, grief que le Tribunal Arbitral a jugé non fondé. Force est d'ailleurs de constater que sur l'ensemble des factures dont [A] réclame aujourd'hui le paiement à [B], seules quatre d'entre elles sont encore contestées. [A] — dont la bonne foi ne peut être mise en cause — avait donc le droit d'invoquer en janvier 2001 l'exceptio non adimpleti contractus. Le fait que le contrat prévoyait le paiement d'intérêts en cas de retard est sans pertinence. De manière positive, [A] a d'ailleurs proposé à plusieurs reprises à [B] de lui livrer contre paiement comptant. Le Tribunal Arbitral estime que quel que soit le bien-fondé de sa contestation des factures impayées, [B] aurait pu, de façon à minimiser le dommage, éviter tout problème en payant comptant. Ne l'ayant pas fait, elle ne saurait donc en réclamer réparation, quand bien même [A] serait responsable, ce qui n'est pas le cas.*

> *68. En conclusion, le Tribunal Arbitral estime non fondée la demande d'indem-*
> *nité postulée par [B] au titre des retards de livraison et du manque à gagner qu'elle*
> *a subi au titre de l'annulation par [D] d'une partie de ses commandes. »*

Il était cependant établi que A avait livré en retard certains produits au client final D car toutes les formalités administratives n'avaient pas été effectuées dans les délais et que A n'avait pas assuré le suivi du respect de ces formalités. D avait par conséquent imposé des pénalités de retard à B, qui demandait au tribunal de condamner A à supporter ces pénalités. Le tribunal estime que:

> *« [A] doit supporter les conséquences du non respect des délais de livraison et*
> *payer les indemnités de retard. En revanche, dés lors que les conditions générales*
> *applicables dans les relations A — B ne prévoient pas l'application systématique*
> *des pénalités de retard imposées par le client final, en l'occurrence la société [D],*
> *les pénalités dont [A] est redevable devraient être en principe calculées conformé-*
> *ment à l'article 8.4 des conditions générales de [A] lequel prévoit que "[c]haque*
> *semaine complète de retard donne droit à un dédommagement s'élevant au*
> *maximum 1/2%. Le total de ces dédommagements est limité à 5%. Ces taux sont*
> *appliqués au prix convenu dans le contrat correspondant à la partie tardive de la*
> *livraison. Les deux premières semaines de retard ne donnent droit à aucun*
> *dédommagement."»*

Le tribunal, constatant que le montant réclamé par le demandeur était inférieur au montant auquel aurait conduit l'application des conditions générales, estime la demande bien fondée.

Les raisonnements suivants du tribunal sont dévolus au détournement de clientèle. Le distributeur faisait en effet valoir que A aurait engagé sa responsabilité contractuelle en procédant à la livraison directe aux clients de commandes passées au cours de l'exécution du contrat. Le tribunal rejette cette demande, estimant que la demanderesse n'établissait aucunement le détournement de clientèle au mépris de la clause d'exclusivité figurant au contrat. Le tribunal constate cependant que l'une des commandes a été passée avant l'expiration du délai de préavis et accorde donc au distributeur sa marge sur cette commande.

Il revient ensuite au tribunal de se prononcer sur les demandes relatives à la concurrence déloyale. Cette demande se décompose en plusieurs « sous demandes » que le tribunal examine successivement.

Tout d'abord, le tribunal se penche sur la demande du distributeur concernant le prétendu débauchage de l'un de ses cadres. Selon la demanderesse, ce débauchage est le fruit d'une manœuvre qui a permis au nouveau distributeur des produits de A (la société E) d'embaucher l'un des principaux cadres commerciaux de B. Le tribunal décide que le cadre en question « *avait parfaitement le droit d'entrer au service de [E], dès lors que [B] perdait la distribution des produits [A]. Il considère d'autre part que [B] n'apporte aucunement la preuve de manœuvres déloyales et, partant de débauchage, dans le chef de [A].* »

Le tribunal étudie ensuite la demande relative à l'installation d'un nouveau distributeur E par A au cours de la période de préavis. Le tribunal rejette cette demande dans la mesure où « *le Tribunal Arbitral estime que [A] n'a commis aucune faute dans l'installation de [E] et n'a aucunement tenté de détourner la clientèle de [B].* »

Vient ensuite la discussion relative à l' « *illusion de renégociation* » que A aurait laissé se créer au détriment de B. Une fois encore, le tribunal rejette cette demande au motif que:

> *« aucune pièce du dossier n'établit que de manière fautive ou malveillance, [A]*
> *aurait fait abusivement miroiter à [B] une intention prétendue de renouveler le*
> *contrat de distribution. De façon tout à fait habituelle, [A] n'a pas exclu d'établir*

de nouvelles relations avec [B], sans doute de nature différente, après la résiliation du contrat de concession. Elle y a cependant renoncé en fin de compte vu la situation de concurrence existant entre les parties sur certains marchés. »

Le distributeur B reprochait également au fournisseur A des actes de dénigrement. A avait, selon elle, manifestement eu pour objectif de discréditer B sur son marché national en procédant unilatéralement à des augmentations de prix abusives et en empêchant délibérément B de livrer certains clients dans les délais convenus. B reproche également à A d'avoir adressé deux courriers à ses clients afin de les informer de la rupture des relations entre les parties. Le tribunal revient sur les termes des courriers adressés par A à B dans lesquels celle-ci informait le distributeur qu'elle n'effectuerait plus de livraison tant que les factures échues n'étaient pas réglées et qu'elle informerait les clients de ce fait. Le tribunal constate ensuite qu'il n'est pas certain que A ait mis ces menaces à exécution et ait informé les clients des retards de paiement de B, sauf en ce qui concerne le client final D. Le tribunal reconnaît que le marché concerné est un marché restreint et par conséquent que « *le fait d'informer [D] est une initiative malheureuse et regrettable. Le Tribunal Arbitral estime donc partiellement justifiée la demande de B et lui octroie, au titre de dommage moral, la somme de 150 euros.* »

En sus de sa demande pour préjudice moral, le distributeur présente une demande au titre de l'atteinte à son image, atteinte qui serait directement liée aux actes qu'elle reproche à A au titre de la violation de ses obligations contractuelles. Le tribunal tranche la question de la façon suivante:

> *96. Le Tribunal Arbitral considère que [B] ne prouve pas au-delà des violations contractuelles et des actes de dénigrement qu'elle reproche à [A] et qui ont été examiné plus haut, l'existence de griefs spécifiques d'atteinte à l'image ayant engendré un préjudice spécifique. Le seul cas dans lequel [A] peut avoir porté atteinte à l'image de [B] a été traité ci-avant, dans le contexte du grief de dénigrement et a donné lieu à l'octroi d'une indemnisation appropriée.*

Après avoir traité des demandes relatives à l'inexécution du contrat de distribution au cours de la période de préavis, le tribunal consacre une deuxième partie de son examen de la demande principale à la résiliation du contrat d'agence. Selon la demanderesse, la non reconduction du contrat de distribution exclusive a entraîné la résiliation du contrat d'agence qui lui était lié. La demanderesse réclame donc une indemnité compensatoire du préjudice subi et rappelle qu'elle a favorisé le développement des produits A sur son marché national de sorte que A bénéficiera pendant de nombreuses années du développement commercial qu'elle a réalisé. A prétend que cette demande constitue une demande nouvelle au sens de l'article 19 du Règlement CCI et n'est donc pas recevable, faute d'autorisation spécifique du tribunal. Le tribunal rejette cet argument et estime que la demande n'est pas nouvelle dans la mesure où « *l'indemnité sollicitée par B est une indemnité de clientèle due au titre de la résolution du contrat, telle que figurant à l'Acte de Mission, sous le libellé "Indemnité de clientèle résultant de la résiliation du contrat d'agence commerciale pour les produits [A] non indus dans le contrat de distribution exclusif."* ». Le tribunal étudie ensuite la doctrine et la jurisprudence fournies par la demanderesse aux termes desquelles l'indemnité due à l'agent s'évalue en fonction de plusieurs critères (dont la perte de commissions auxquelles l'agent pouvait légitimement prétendre, la perte ou la réduction du bénéfice qu'il pouvait retirer des investissements réalisés) mais est généralement fixée à deux années de commissions. Tenant compte de cette jurisprudence et de cette doctrine, le tribunal estime que l'octroi d'une indemnité de deux ans est justifié en l'espèce « *compte tenu de l'activité déployée par [B] et de la circonstance que du fait de la rupture, elle a perdu Là clientèle espagnole (. . .)* ».

Le tribunal arbitral s'étant prononcé sur toutes les demandes de nature contractuelle, celui-ci se penche désormais sur les demandes du distributeur/agent fondées sur l'enrichissement sans cause. B estime en effet que, nonobstant le fait que le contrat de distribution ait été résilié par A conformément aux termes des dispositions contractuelles, cette résiliation la prive des fruits du travail effectué pendant des années pour développer certains produits pour A. Elle réclame à ce titre la marge qu'elle aurait pu obtenir sur les équipements qui ont été vendus par A après la résiliation du contrat. B fonde sa demande sur la théorie de l'enrichissement sans cause. Le tribunal rejette cette demande et décide que:

> « 116. C'est à juste titre que [A] fait valoir que l'action basée sur l'enrichissement sans cause a un caractère subsidiaire. Lorsqu'il y a un contrat, la volonté des parties doit prévaloir. En l'espèce, les parties avaient prévu qu'il pouvait être mis fin au contrat moyennant un préavis de six mois. [B] a marqué son accord sur ces modalités lors de la signature de la convention. Elle est donc tenue par ses termes. Accorder à [B] l'indemnité qu'elle postule au titre des ventes réalisées après la fin du contrat, voire des ventes aléatoires et en tout cas, non encore réalisées, aboutirait à anéantir la volonté des parties et serait par conséquent une violation du principe pacta sunt servanda.
>
> 117. L'activité qu'a déployée [B] et la rémunération y afférente trouvent leur source et leur cause dans le contrat, lequel prévoit à l'article 4.4 que [B] devait obtenir les autorisations administratives nécessaires. C'est sur le contrat que [B] doit se fonder pour postuler une rémunération. En l'occurrence, aucune rémunération n'est prévue après la fin du contrat. La demande de [B] doit donc être rejetée (. . .). »

Le tribunal récapitule ensuite dans une sous section distincte l'ensemble de ses décisions sur les demandes de la demanderesse et les dommages accordés. Le tribunal accorde d'autre part à la demanderesse, conformément à ses demandes, le paiement d'intérêts au taux légal français en vigueur au jour de la sentence. Le tribunal ne précise cependant pas la date à laquelle les intérêts sont amenés à courir.

Le tribunal se penche ensuite sur la demande de condamnation à payer conjointement les co-demandeurs B et C. En effet, ceux-ci demandent au tribunal d'ordonner le paiement des sommes dues par A à B et C indifféremment, leur laissant la liberté de se répartir ces sommes comme elles l'entendent. Le tribunal se prononce de la façon suivante:

> « 128. Le Tribunal Arbitral note que les demandes ont été formulées au nom de [B], même si [C] a indiqué que ses demandes étaient identiques. Par ailleurs, les postes pour lesquels la Tribunal Arbitral a accordé des sommes à [B] concernent celle-ci directement, sinon à titre exclusif. Le Tribunal Arbitral estime dès lors justifié de porter les condamnations au bénéfice de [B], ce qui n'empêche pas [B] et [C] de répartir certaines sommes entre elles si elles le souhaitent. L'on rappellera d'ailleurs que la mise en cause de [C] était essentiellement justifiée par le fait qu'elle restait devoir des sommes importantes à [A]. »

Après s'être prononcé sur l'ensemble des demandes du distributeur B, le tribunal aborde les demandes reconventionnelles du fournisseur A, qui réclame le paiement de certaines factures. Le tribunal passe méthodiquement en revue l'ensemble des factures dont le paiement est demandé, en commençant par les factures dues par B, puis en étudiant celles dues par C. Il constate qu'une grande majorité d'entre elles sont justifiées, à l'exception de certaines dont l'origine n'est pas établie, la défenderesse n'ayant pu fournir la preuve des commandes en question. Le tribunal fait donc droit aux demandes reconventionnelles du fournisseur qu'il réduit cependant à concurrence des demandes non étayées par des éléments probatoires suffisants. Le tribunal décide également, conformément aux demandes du fournisseur, que les montants impayés porteront l'intérêt de 12% prévu au contrat à compter de la date d'échéance des factures jusqu'au jour du paiement.

Les parties demandaient au tribunal d'ordonner la compensation entre les sommes qui leur étaient respectivement dues. Le tribunal ordonne donc la compensation entre les sommes dues entre A et B mais estime qu'il n'y a pas lieu de prononcer la compensation pour les sommes dues entre A et C.

Enfin, le tribunal se prononce sur les frais d'arbitrage et de conseil dans les termes suivants:

> « [v]u les décisions rendues par le Tribunal Arbitral, celui-ci considère que les frais de l'arbitrage, fixés par la Cour d'arbitrage de la Chambre de Commerce Internationale à US$ [XXX], avancés pour moitié par les demanderesses, d'une part, et la défenderesse, d'autre part, doivent être supportés à concurrence de 60% par [B], 20% par [C] et 20% par [A]. »

Le tribunal estime également que B et C devront supporter les frais qu'elles ont exposés pour leur défense et que les frais de conseil de la défenderesse seront supportés à 60% par B, 20% par C et 20% par A elle-même.

NOTE. — I. — Dans cette affaire, une filiale de la société demanderesse B est intervenue volontairement. Le tribunal accepte cette intervention et souligne que l'intervention de la société C avait été acceptée par les deux parties. Cette affaire rappelle donc que l'intervention volontaire de tiers dans un arbitrage est toujours possible dès lors que les autres parties acquiescent à cette demande. La situation est cependant bien plus compliquée quand toutes les parties ne sont pas d'accord sur ce point (V. à ce sujet A. M. Whitesell et E. Silva Romero, Multiparty and Multicontract Arbitration: Recent ICC Experience in Complex Arbitrations Perspectives on their Procedural Implications, Supplément spécial 2003: Bulletin de la Cour internationale d'arbitrage de la CCI).

II. — L'exception d'inexécution a déjà fait l'objet d'application par les arbitres, qui la présentent souvent sous sa dénomination latine exceptio non adimpleti contractus (Sentence CCI rendue dans l'affaire n° 7539 [1995]: JDI 1996, p. 1030, note Y. Derains. — Sentence CCI rendue dans l'affaire n° 8365 [1996]: JDI 1997, p. 1078. — Sentence CCI rendue dans l'affaire n° 1795: YCA 1999, p. 196. — Sentence CCI rendue dans l'affaire n° 2583: JDI 1977, p. 950. — Sentence CCI rendue dans l'affaire n° 4761: JDI 1987, p. 1012. — Sentence CCI rendue dans l'affaire n° 8365: JDI 1997, p. 1078. — Sentence CCI rendue dans l'affaire n° 9797, Bull. ASA 2000, p. 514). Certaines sentences qualifient même le droit pour l'une des parties de suspendre l'exécution de ses obligations en cas de violation de ses obligations par l'autre partie de principe du droit du commerce international (Sentence CCI rendue dans l'affaire n° 3540 en 1980, citée dans Fouchard, Gaillard, Goldman, op. cit., § 1496). L'exercice de cette prérogative par le créancier est toutefois généralement conditionnée par la gravité de la violation de ses obligations par le débiteur et la proportionnalité entre l'obligation suspendue et la violation de l'adversaire (en droit français, V. N. Cuzacq, La notion de riposte proportionnée en matière d'exception d'inexécution: LPA n° 91, 7 mai 2003). C'est ainsi que, dans l'affaire CCI n° 4269 opposant un maître de l'ouvrage à un entrepreneur, le tribunal arbitral a mis en avant le fait que l'obligation pour le maître de l'ouvrage de mettre à disposition de l'entrepreneur un site dans un état permettant les travaux était une obligation essentielle, « of utmost importance », et par conséquent que l'entrepreneur était en droit de suspendre ses obligations tant que le maître de l'ouvrage ne mettait pas à disposition le site en question (Sentence rendue dans l'affaire CCI n° 4629 en 1989: Recueil des sentences arbitrales de la CCI, vol. III, p. 152). Dans l'affaire CCI n° 8365, le tribunal arbitral, faisant application de lex mercatoria, insistait également sur le fait que « les règles applicables de la lex mercatoria devraient comprendre des principes tels (. . .) qu'une partie est en droit de se considérer comme déchargée de ses obligations si l'autre partie a commis une violation du contrat, mais seulement si celle-ci est substantielle » (Sentence CCI rendue dans l'affaire n° 8365: JDI 1997, p. 1078). Dans le cas présent, le tribunal arbitral n'étudie pas en détail l'exacte proportionnalité entre l'obligation suspendue et la violation de ses obligations par le distributeur ni la gravité de la violation. Le tribunal constate cependant que les défauts de paiement étaient récurrents et n'étaient pas justifiés par de raisons quelconques. Le tribunal confirme ainsi que l'exercice de l'exception d'inexécution est justifié en l'espèce.

III. — Le tribunal arbitral était d'autre part saisi d'une demande fondée sur l'enrichissement sans cause. Le tribunal arbitral rejette cette demande sans ambages et rappelle que la demande fondée sur l'enrichissement sans cause n'a qu'un caractère subsidiaire et qu'elle ne saurait être invoquée en présence d'un contrat entre les parties. Le tribunal estime en effet que dans ce cas, les relations entre les parties sont définies et réglementées par les stipulations du contrat et qu'accepter une demande fondée sur l'enrichissement sans cause reviendrait à porter atteinte au principe *pacta sunt servanda*. La question de l'enrichissement sans cause se pose souvent aux arbitres en termes de compétence: ceux-ci doivent décider si la clause compromissoire leur donne compétence pour se prononcer sur des demandes quasi-contractuelles. Il est généralement admis que les arbitres retiendront leur compétence si les termes de la clause compromissoire sont suffisamment larges, ce qui sera le cas si la clause ne se limite pas exclusivement aux différends trouvant leur origine dans l'exécution du contrat (*J.-F. Poudret et S. Besson, Droit comparé de l'arbitrage international, p. 282, n° 307. — V. également Sentence CCI rendue dans l'affaire n° 12167 [2002]: JDI 2007, p. 1261*). Une fois résolue la question de la compétence, les arbitres, saisis d'une question relative à l'enrichissement sans cause au fond, doivent se prononcer sur la recevabilité de celle-ci sur la base du droit applicable au litige, en l'espèce le droit français. Or il est établi en droit français que l'action fondée sur l'enrichissement sans cause a une nature subsidiaire (*F. Terré, Ph. Simler et Y. Lequette, Les obligations: Dalloz, 2002, n° 1062*). C'est donc à juste titre que le tribunal rejette cette demande.

IV. — Le tribunal accorde au demandeur une indemnité au titre du préjudice moral, estimant que « le fait d'informer [D] est une initiative malheureuse et regrettable. Le Tribunal Arbitral estime donc partiellement justifiée la demande de B et lui octroie, au titre de dommage moral, la somme de 150 euros». Certains arbitres ont, par le passé, reconnu que le dommage moral d'une partie était indemnisable. C'est ainsi qu'un tribunal siégeant sur le fondement du règlement d'arbitrage de la chambre de commerce internationale de Roumanie a décidé d'attribuer au défendeur des dommages et intérêts pour préjudice moral (*Sentence n°33: Yearbook 1998, p. 113*). Le tribunal appliquait le droit roumain mais avait constaté que celui-ci était similaire au droit français en matière d'indemnisation du dommage. Le tribunal se fondait donc sur la doctrine française pour estimer que le préjudice moral devait être réparé. Le tribunal rappelait que l'objet de la loi était de réparer le dommage, et non de le faire disparaître, et par conséquent que le dommage moral pouvait être indemnisé sous forme monétaire. Il reconnaissait toutefois que l'évaluation du préjudice moral est une tâche délicate, mais que cette difficulté ne pouvait, à elle seule, justifier que le dommage moral ne soit pas réparé. Cette affirmation est partagée par la doctrine. Selon le Dr J. Ortscheidt: « Si la fonction de la réparation est de rétablir la victime dans la situation qui eut été la sienne en l'absence d'événement dommageable, il importe d'indemniser cette atteinte à l'image et à la réputation commerciale *(. . .)*. La reconnaissance d'un droit à l'indemnisation à l'atteinte à l'image et à la réputation commerciale, en dehors de toute référence à une norme étatique en ce sens, résulte très clairement de la sentence CCI n°3131 rendue en 1979 dans l'affaire *Norsolor. (. . .)* Les difficultés d'évaluation de l'aspect purement moral de l'atteinte à la réputation commerciale n'ont donc pas conduit les arbitres à écarter la demande d'indemnisation de ce chef de préjudice. » (*J. Ortscheidt, La réparation du dommage dans l'arbitrage commercial international: Dalloz 2001, p. 78. — sur Norsolor, V. Rev. arb. 1983, p. 525*). Les demandes relatives au dommage moral sont cependant souvent rejetées, faute de preuve du préjudice (*V. Sentence CCI rendue dans l'affaire n° 6379: Yearbook 1992, p. 212. — Sentence CCI rendue dans l'affaire n° 6283 [1990]: Yearbook 1992, p. 178. — V.*

également sur le préjudice extrapatrimonial *Sentence CCI rendue dans l'affaire n° 4972 [1989]: JDI, 1989, p. 1101. — Sentence CCI rendue dans l'affaire n° 5639 [1987]: JDI 1987, p. 1054*). Le tribunal ajoutait également que l'image et la crédibilité d'une entreprise étaient d'une importance majeure dans le commerce international car celui-ci requiert l'honnêteté, le prestige et la crédibilité. Dans la présente affaire, le tribunal arbitral devait faire face à la même difficulté d'évaluation du préjudice moral. Celui-ci avait en effet admis que le distributeur avait souffert d'un dommage moral du fait du fournisseur, qui avait intempestivement informé des clients finaux des retards de paiement du distributeur. Le tribunal accordait donc une somme forfaitaire au distributeur pour l'indemniser de ce préjudice moral. La sentence suggère également que le tribunal ne distingue pas le préjudice moral de l'atteinte à l'image, celui-ci décidant que le seul cas dans lequel le fournisseur avait pu porter atteinte à l'image du fournisseur avait été traité dans le cadre du raisonnement sur le dénigrement et avait donné lieu à l'octroi d'une indemnisation appropriée (V., de manière générale sur le sujet en droit français, *V. Wester-Ouisse, Le préjudice moral des personnes morales: JCP G 2003, I, 145*).

V. — Dans cette affaire, le tribunal arbitral accorde à la demanderesse des intérêts au taux légal français en vigueur au jour de la sentence et accorde à la défenderesse des intérêts à un taux contractuel de 12% sur les sommes dues en vertu des factures impayées. Le tribunal arbitral s'en est donc tenu aux demandes des parties et n'a pas fait usage du pouvoir discrétionnaire qui lui est largement reconnu en matière de fixation des intérêts dans la jurisprudence de la CCI. Dans l'affaire CCI n° 6219, le tribunal arbitral décidait ainsi: « Dans le cadre d'un arbitrage international, cette détermination [du taux d'intérêt] n'est pas gouvernée par des règles rigoureuses et précises. La tendance générale qui se dégage, en doctrine et dans la pratique arbitrale, est de laisser à l'arbitre une grande liberté dans la fixation de ce taux [. . .] Celui-ci n'est pas tenu de se référer aux taux légal d'un système juridique national, qu'il s'agisse de celui de la loi contractuelle ou de celui du lieu de l'arbitrage » (*Sentence CCI rendue dans l'affaire n° 6219: Recueil des sentences arbitrales de la CCI, vol. II, p. 429. — V. à ce sujet M. Secomb et L. Hammoud, Les intérêts dans les sentences CCI: introduction et commentaires: Bull. CCI 2004, p. 54*). Il a en effet été décidé à de nombreuses reprises qu'un tribunal arbitral n'est pas tenu de se référer à une législation précise quand il se prononce sur les intérêts (*Sentence CCI rendue dans l'affaire n° 5904: Recueil des sentences arbitrales de la CCI, vol. II, p. 389. — Sentence CCI rendue dans l'affaire n° 6219: Recueil des sentences arbitrales de la CCI, vol. II, p. 429-430; Sentence CCI rendue dans l'affaire n° 5030: Recueil des sentences arbitrales de la CCI, vol. III, p. 483. — Sentence CCI rendue dans l'affaire n° 6962, Recueil des sentences arbitrales de la CCI, vol. III, p. 307. — Sentence CCI rendue dans l'affaire n° 7331: Recueil des sentences arbitrales de la CCI, vol. III, p. 597*). Il a cependant été décidé par la Cour de cassation que, si l'arbitre n'a pas statué sur ce point et qu'il ne peut plus être saisi, la loi applicable aux intérêts moratoires postérieurs à la sentence, qui s'attachent de plein droit à la décision de condamnation, est la loi du lieu de la procédure d'exécution (*Cass., 1re civ., 30 juin 2004 Juris-Data n° 2004-024344; JCP E 2004, 1860, note G. Chabot*). Le tribunal arbitral n'a toutefois pas précisé la date à laquelle les intérêts alloués au distributeur devaient commencer à courir. On peut raisonnablement penser que ces intérêts devaient courir à compter du jour du dépôt de la demande d'arbitrage, comme cela était notamment le cas dans une affaire qui a fait l'objet d'un recours devant la cour d'appel de Paris. Cette affaire devait donner l'occasion à la cour de rappeler que « le droit applicable à la cause étant le droit français, [l'article 1153-1 du Code civil] autorisait donc les arbitres à accorder les intérêts des sommes allouées à partir de la demande d'arbitrage, sans avoir à motiver spécialement leur décision sur ce point » (*CA Paris, 25 mars 2004: Rev. arb. 2004, p. 671, note Ortscheidt. — V. cependant CA Paris, 30 juin 2005: Cah. arb. 2005/2. — V. P. Raoul-Duval, Intérêts moratoires: vers une mise en cause du pouvoir des arbitres?: Cah. arb. 2005, p. 49*). Dans l'affaire CCI n° 5082, le tribunal décidait également que les intérêts devaient commencer à courir à compter de la date du dépôt de la demande d'arbitrage, en l'absence de mise en demeure préalable (*Sentence CCI rendue dans l'affaire n° 5082: Bull. CCI, vol. 15, n° 1, p. 65*).

M^{es} remerciements vont à Romain Dupeyré pour son aide dans la préparation de cette chronique.

E.S.R.

Sent. rendue dans l'affaire CCI n° 12551 en 2004

Compétence. — Convention d'arbitrage par référence. — Clause pathologique. — Portée *rattorte personae* de la Convention d'arbitrage.

Procédure arbitrale. — Demandes nouvelles — Frais de l'arbitrage — Répartition entre les parties.

Dans une affaire où une société s'était substituée à une autre, en liquidation et appartenant au même groupe, pour l'exécution d'un contrat d'assistance commerciale, un arbitre unique statuant à Paris, après avoir obtenu la confirmation de sa compétence par les parties dans l'acte de mission, décide que le cocontractant de la seconde société défaillante n'est pas lié vis-à-vis de la première à défaut d'avoir accepté la cession ou la rénovation de son contrat, son silence ne pouvant valoir acceptation dans les circonstances de l'espèce où elle n'a pas répondu à une offre de signature d'un contrat, ni payé aucune des factures qui lui étaient adressées. Son silence a néanmoins concouru à l'existence du litige et justifie que les frais de l'arbitrage soient mis à sa charge.

Un arbitre unique, siégeant à Paris, s'est prononcé sur les prestations d'une société A qui demandait la condamnation de la société B au paiement de factures, plus intérêts, émises au titre de prestations qu'elle alléguait avoir rendues à B dans un cadre contractuel liant cette dernière à une société C et à une personne physique, X.

Initialement, B avait conclu avec X un contrat, dénommé « Convention de Conseiller » aux termes duquel X devait assister B « en qualité de conseiller, dans le cadre de [son] action commerciale en vue de la conclusion de contrats » dans un pays étranger. Le contrat stipulait que :

> « *Tous différends découlant de la présente convention seront tranchés définitivement à Paris, suivant le règlement de conciliation et d'arbitrage de la Chambre de Commerce Internationale (ou Tribunal de Commerce), par un ou plusieurs arbitres nommés conformément à ce règlement et avec application du droit français* ».

X a ensuite été engagé par la société française C qui admettait que le co-contractant de B reste X et s'engageait vis-à-vis de X à recruter ses collaborateurs dans le pays cible.

Après qu'un accord portant sur un projet d'exploitation et de maintenance d'une usine ait été conclu entre B, C et une ville du pays cible, B et C ont conclu un Avenant n° 1 à la Convention de Conseiller liant B à X, portant sur des « prestations d'études et d'assistance pour » différents projets dont celui mentionné ci-dessus et dont les dispositions « s'intègrent aux dispositions générales de la Convention de Conseiller . . . ».

Il semble que les négociations du projet se soient normalement poursuivies jusqu' à ce que C rencontre des difficultés financières. X, à titre personnel, a alors indiqué à B que ses activités au titre de la Convention de Conseiller se poursuivraient dans le cadre de la société A, appartenant au même groupe que C, et lui a proposé un Avenant n° 2 aux termes similaires à ceux de l'Avenant n° 1 mais devant être conclu entre A et B. Après le dépôt de bilan de C, il lui a à nouveau adressé le même avenant déjà signé par A mais cette fois en sa qualité de Directeur général adjoint de B.

Cet Avenant n'a pas été signé et A a adressé à B, dans le courant de l'année suivante, 4 factures pour ses prestations, pour un montant forfaitaire identique à celui qui aurait été dû à C conformément aux stipulations de l'Avenant n° 1. Ces factures se référaient expressément à l'Avenant n° 1, la dernière d'entre elles étant expressément émise à titre de solde pour tout compte.

Aucune de ces factures n'a été payé et, après une tentative de transaction infructueuse, A s'est tournée vers les juridictions françaises qui, au regard de la clause compromissoire figurant à la Convention de Conseiller, se sont déclarées incompétentes. Devant l'arbitre, elle a demandé notamment le paiement de ces factures. Après la signature de l'acte de mission, elle a ajouté à ses prétentions une demande de paiement d'intérêts sur le principal ainsi que le remboursement de ses frais de procédure devant le Tribunal de commerce et la Cour d'appel.

L'arbitre unique observe en premier lieu que:

« *l'Avenant n° 1 a été signé par [C] et non par [A] et, sauf preuve du contraire, ne liait pas [B] à cette dernière.*

Il s'agit donc de déterminer si [A] peut se prévaloir de cet Avenant et de ces factures à l'encontre de [B].

À titre préliminaire, il convient d'observer qu 'aucun élément du dossier n 'indique que, par effet de la loi ou d'une décision de justice, l'Avenant n° 1 ait été automatiquement transféré à [A] dans le cadre de la liquidation de [C], et ce, même à supposer possible un tel transfert sans le consentement de [B] (. . .). Il convient donc de déterminer si [B] a consenti à être liée à [A] par les termes de l'Avenant n° 1 ou autrement, d'une manière justifiant l'émission et le règlement des factures litigieuses.

En effet, en droit, pour créer un effet obligatoire entre des parties, une convention doit être légalement formée, ce qui implique, comme condition essentielle, le consentement de la partie qui s'oblige (Articles 1134 et 1108 du Code Civil). En particulier, que l'opération soit analysée sous l'angle de la cession de contrat ou de la novation, le consentement de la partie cédée, en l'occurrence [B], est requis (Cass. com., 6 mai 1997: D. 1997.588; Rép. civ. Dalloz. V° Cession de Contrat, n° 6).

Ce consentement peut être exprès ou tacite ».

Après avoir constaté qu'il n'existe pas de consentement exprès en l'espèce, l'arbitre unique ajoute que:

« *Si, en droit, un consentement peut être tacite, il n'en doit pas moins être évident et certain. Ainsi, la Cour de cassation a jugé que "l'acceptation d'un contrat, si elle peut être tacite, ne peut résulter que d'actes démontrant avec évidence l'intention de la partie d'accepter le contrat proposé" (Cass. 2ᵉ civ., 21 janv. 1981: Bull. civ. 1981, n° 14).*

L'article 1273 du Code civil dispose: lla novation ne se présume point; il faut que la volonté de l'opérer résulte clairement de l'acte". La Cour de cassation a jugé "qu 'il n 'est pas nécessaire que l'intention de nover soit exprimée en termes formels dès lors qu'elle est certaine" (Cass. 3ᵉ civ., 15 janv. 1975: Bull. civ. 1975, III, n° 16), et que l'intention de nover doit être "certaine" ou "non équivoque" et "résulter clairement des faits et actes intervenus entre les parties" (Cass. com., 19 mars 1979: Bull. civ. 1979, IV, n° 105. — Cass. com., 31 janv. 1983: Bull. civ. 1983, IV, n° 44).

Il appartient donc à ce Tribunal de rechercher si, par ses actes, le Défendeur a démontré avec évidence son intention d'être lié à [A]. La charge de la preuve de cette intention incombe à la partie qui l'invoque, à savoir [A] (Article 1315 du Code civil, premier alinéa. — Cass. com. 17 févr. 1965: Bull. civ. 1965, III, n° 130. — Cass. com., 11 janv. 1983: Bull. civ. 1983, IV, n° 13. — Cass. com., 18 juin 1991: Bull. civ. 1991, IV, n° 228) ».

Or, une telle intention est douteuse dès lors que la Convention de Conseiller faisait dépendre la rémunération de M. X. de la conclusion de contrats dans le pays cible, et excluait le remboursement de ses frais « sauf accord spécifique à conclure ponctuellement » tel que l'Avenant n° 1. Pour l'arbitre, « ceci suggère une approche particulièrement prudente quant au constat d'une éventuelle acceptation par [B] de supporter de tels frais » et cela d'autant plus qu'elle s'est refusée à signer l'Avenant n° 2 et les factures présentées par A.

L'arbitre unique observe néanmoins qu'un « consentement implicite de [B] pouvait résulter de la fourniture, à la supposer avérée, de prestations par [A], et dont [B] aurait effective-ment bénéficié sans objection ». Or, l'examen du dossier l'amène à conclure que les salariés de C visés à l'Avenant n° 1 et dont les contrats avaient été repris par B, soit n'appartenaient plus au personnel de A pendant la période considérée, soit ne travaillaient pas, ou peu sur les projets intéressant [B]. De plus, il constate que « en dehors des courriers relatifs à la visite de (. . .) [laquelle a été tenue sans la participation de B qui en a postérieurement critiqué l'organisation], les diverses lettres adressées par [C] et [A] à [B] [pendant la période litigieuse] et concernant la poursuite des prestations abordent ce sujet d'une manière très générale, sans préciser la nature de ces prestations ». L'arbitre ajoute qu'on ne saurait conclure, du seul fait qu'un des projets envisagés à l'Avenant n° 1 ait abouti deux années plus tard à un contrat, que « [A] ait effectivement fourni, en [. . .], des prestations dont [B] aurait bénéficié ».

L'arbitre unique s'interroge ensuite sur la portée du « silence et [de] l'absence d'oppo-sition et de réaction officielle de [B] face [aux] interpellations concernant la poursuite des relations ». Il admet que :

> « Ceci étant, l'absence de réaction écrite de [B] tout au long de l'année 1995 est effectivement frappante. [B] n'a pas écrit à [A] qu'elle s'opposait au transfert de l'Avenant N° 1 ou déclinait son offre de prestations, pas plus d'ailleurs qu'elle n'a écrit les accepter.
>
> Ce silence de [B] est certes troublant et a manqué de transparence et de spon-tanéité. Mais, ce Tribunal rappelle qu'il doit trancher ce litige conformément aux règles de droit français (Acte de mission, Section VII), et les parties ne lui ont pas conféré la mission de statuer comme amiable compositeur. Or, en droit, le silence ne vaut en principe pas acceptation. La Cour de Cassation a posé le principe que "le silence de celui qu'on prétend obligé ne peut suffire, en l'absence de toute autre circonstance, pour faire preuve contre lui de l'obligation alléguée" (Cass. 25 mai 1870: D. 1870.1.257; S. 1870.1341).
>
> À cet égard, le Professeur Jacques Ghestin relève que, exceptionnellement, "lorsque les circonstances donnent au silence la signification objective d'une acceptation dépourvue d'équivoque, il constitue un moyen d'expression qui a valeur de consentement (. . .) Il appartient naturellement à celui qui s'en prévaut d'établir que le silence gardé par le destinataire de l'offre avait bien la significa-tion objective d'une acceptation, ce qui implique qu'il devait au moins être com-pris comme tel par les deux parties" (Traité de Droit Civil, la formation du contrat: LGDJ, 3ᵉ éd., n° 405).
>
> Il apparaît à ce Tribunal que les circonstances exposées plus haut, lesquelles sont marquées par l'absence de signature du projet d'Avenant n° 2 et de paiement des factures par [B] et par sa demande à M. [X] dès le (. . .) de suspendre les contacts avec la partie [du pays cible] dans l'affaire (. . .), puis ses remontrances concernant la visite d'une délégation de [ville du pays cible] organisée par lui, ne sont pas de nature à conférer au silence de [B] la signification d'un consentement de sa part. Toutefois, ce Tribunal tient à observer que compte tenu de l'antériorité des relations de [B] avec [C] (société du même groupe que [A]) de la poursuite de la Convention de Conseiller et du transfert de Monsieur [X] et de son équipe restant au sein de [A], [B] en conservant un tel silence prolongé face aux interpellations de [A], paraît s'être placée à la limite extrême de la protection que peut conférer la règle selon laquelle le silence ne vaut pas en principe acceptation, et ce, d'autant plus que rien en apparence n'eut été plus simple pour [B] que de fixer par écrit [A] sur son refus.
>
> Mais ce Tribunal, tenu par l'application des règles de droit, ne peut que con-stater que, si ce silence manifeste un manque de transparence et de spontanéité à l'égard de la société [A], il n'a pas pour autant valeur de consentement implicite de la part de [B] ».

Peu importe donc que A ait supporté des frais liés aux activités de M. X. dans le cadre de l'exécution de la Convention de Conseiller, A ne rapportant pas la preuve d'un consentement exprès ou tacite de B d'être liée à A, ni celle des prestations alléguées. Elle est donc déboutée de sa demande de paiement des factures et par voie de conséquence, de sa demande de paiement d'intérêts. Elle est également déboutée de sa demande de communication d'informations, qui apparaissent inutiles à l'instruction de l'affaire. Sa demande de remboursement de ses frais engagés devant les juridictions nationales est également rejetée, A ayant « pris l'initiative d'intenter son action devant les juridictions étatiques plutôt que de la soumettre en premier lieu à l'arbitrage et [parce] qu'il ne serait donc pas juste de faire supporter au Défendeur les conséquences de cette décision ».

Bien que A soit déboutée de l'ensemble de ses demandes, l'arbitre unique ne met pas à sa charge les frais de la procédure arbitrale. Il observe que, certes, A:

> « *n'ayant pas gain de cause, il n'eut pas été inhabituel de mettre tout ou la majorité de ces frais à sa charge.*
>
> *Toutefois, ce Tribunal a relevé le caractère troublant, à l'époque des faits, de l'absence prolongée de réaction écrite de [B] face aux interpellations de [A] relatives à la poursuite des relations qui existaient antérieurement avec [C]. Si, en droit et compte tenu des circonstances analysées plus haut, ce silence de [B] ne vaut pas consentement de sa part et ne permet pas de donner gain de cause à [A], il n'en demeure pas moins qu'il a concouru à l'existence du présent arbitrage. En effet, une simple lettre de [B] à [A] à l'époque des faits, l'informant officiellement de son refus, aurait fixé [A] et pu permettre d'éviter le présent arbitrage.*
>
> *En conséquence, ce Tribunal décide, en vertu des pouvoirs discrétionnaires que lui confère l'article 31-3 du Règlement CCI, que [B] supportera l'intégralité des frais visés à l'article 30(2).*
>
> *Enfin, étant observé que [A] a choisi de ne pas être représentée par un avocat, ce Tribunal décide, en vertu des mêmes pouvoirs, que chaque partie supportera les autres frais qu'elle a exposés pour sa défense à l'occasion de cet arbitrage* ».

NOTE. — I. — La compétence de l'arbitre unique ne présentait aucun doute en l'espèce, si ce n'est comme on le verra ci-après à l'égard d'une demande qui excédait peut-être la portée de la convention d'arbitrage, puisque les parties avaient confirmé dans l'acte de mission leur volonté de soumettre à l'arbitrage le litige qui en faisait l'objet. Sans cette précaution, elle aurait accumulé les obstacles tenant tant à la rédaction déficiente de la convention d'arbitrage qu'à la détermination des parties à qui elle était opposable, de nature à ralentir le déroulement de la procédure arbitrale ou même à la paralyser.

En premier lieu, la clause compromissoire qui pouvait justifier la compétence de l'arbitre ne figurait pas dans le document contractuel invoqué par la Demanderesse (« l'Avenant n° 1 ») — c'est-à-dire la convention conclue entre la Défenderesse et la société sœur de la Demanderesse à laquelle elle prétendait se substituer — mais dans un contrat conclu entre la Défenderesse et un tiers. Cependant, l'Avenant n° 1 était justement présenté comme un avenant à cette dernière convention. De surcroît, son article 3 stipulait que « *Les dispositions du présent Avenant s'intègrent aux dépositions générales de la [convention principale]* ». Le droit français admet très largement les conventions d'arbitrage par référence, à tout le moins en matière internationale, dès lors qu'elles traduisent la volonté des parties de compromettre, puisque selon les termes de l'arrêt *Prodexport (Cass. 1ʳᵉ civ., 3 juin 1997: Juris-Data n° 1997-002451; Bull. civ. 1997, I, n° 177; Rev. arb. 1998, p. 537, et chron. X. Boucobza, La clause compromissoire par référence en matière d'arbitrage international, p. 495; Rev. crit. DIP 1999, p. 92, note P. Mayer),* « la clause compromissoire par référence à un document qui la stipule est valable lorsque la partie à laquelle on l'oppose en a eu connaissance au moment de la conclusion du contrat et qu'elle a, fût-ce par son silence, accepté cette référence » (pour un état récent de la question, V. *C. Legros, Chronique de jurisprudence française: Rev. arb, 2003, p. 1341.* — pour une application récente, V. *CA Paris, 25 janv. 2007: Rev. arb. 2007, p. 137).* En l'espèce les deux partie à l'Avenant n° 1 avaient nécessairement connaissance des termes du contrat principal, auquel l'une était d'ailleurs parties, et de la clause compromissoire y figurant, puisque l'Avenant avait justement pour objet l'exécution du contrat principal et l'assistance que l'autre partie s'engageait à apporter au signataire du contrat principal dont elle était devenue l'employeur. Il semble donc ne faire aucun doute quant à leur volonté d'être liées par la clause. Mais encore fallait-il qu'elle soit valable et qu'elle soit opposable à la défenderesse.

II. — À cet égard, la référence au Tribunal de commerce figurant dans une clause compromissoire qui par ailleurs reprenait presque intégralement les termes de la clause type proposée par la CCI — « Tous différends découlant de la présente convention seront tranchés définitivement à Paris, suivant le règlement de conciliation et d'arbitrage de la Chambre de commerce internationale (ou Tribunal de commerce), par un ou plusieurs arbitres nommés conformément à ce règlement . . . » — n'allait pas sans problème. Les parties à cette clause, plutôt que soumettre tous leurs litiges futurs à l'arbitrage, ne voulaient-elles pas ouvrir une option entre un recours à l'arbitrage ou la juridiction nationale? S'agissait-il au contraire d'une simple erreur matérielle dans la désignation de la Cour d'arbitrage de la CCI? Doit-on au contraire y voir une incompréhension des parties quant à la nature de l'arbitrage qui conduirait à remettre en doute la réalité de leur consentement? On ne sait pas si la question s'est posée devant le Tribunal de commerce initialement saisi par la Demanderesse, la sentence nous indiquant uniquement qu'il « s'est déclaré incompétent au profit de la juridiction arbitrale ». Quand bien même cela aurait été le cas, le Tribunal ne pouvait que juger en ce sens, la clause n'étant pas « manifestement nulle » au sens de l'article 1458, alinéa 2, du Nouveau Code de procédure civile. Quoi qu'il en soit, le principe de l'effet utile, largement reconnu par la jurisprudence française et arbitrale (V. par ex. *Sentence rendue dans l'affaire n° 6709 en 1991: JDI 1992, p. 998, note D. Hascher),* conduit à interpréter les clauses pathologiques dans le sens qui leur fait produire un effet, plutôt que dans celui qui ne leur en donne aucun, et donc de donner effet à la volonté des parties de recourir à l'arbitrage. On sait en particulier qu'en France, « la jurisprudence s'est systématiquement efforcée en cas de contradiction apparente entre une clause compromissoire et une clause attributive de juridiction de faire prévaloir la première sur la seconde » *(Ph. Fouchard, B. Gaillard et E. Goldman, Traité de l'arbitrage commercial international: Litec, 1996, n° 490).* Elle cherche également à sauver les clauses dont la référence à l'institution d'arbitrage choisie par les parties est maladroite. Cependant, en l'espèce, il n'y avait pas véritablement contradiction entre deux attributions de compétence concurrentes, ni référence maladroite à la CCI, mais plutôt insertion dans la clause compromissoire d'une référence au Tribunal de commerce que le reste de la disposition, portant sur la désignation des arbitres, rendait difficilement compréhensible. Certes, même en l'absence de confirmation de la compétence de l'arbitre unique par les parties, il semble que le principe de l'effet utile aurait suffi pour sauver la clause devant les arbitres et la juridiction de contrôle mais la déficience de sa rédaction aurait pu compliquer la procédure arbitrale si l'une des parties en avait fait état.

III. — En second lieu, en admettant que la Défenderesse et son cocontractant à l'Avenant n° 1 soient liés par la clause compromissoire figurant au contrat principal, cette clause était-elle opposable à la Demanderesse? Aucune réponse à cette question ne peut être déduite de la décision des juridictions françaises puisque, conformément à l'effet négatif du principe de compétence-compétence, elles ne pouvaient, dès lors que la clause compromissoire était invoquée par une partie, que se déclarer incompétentes, laissant ainsi à l'arbitre la possibilité de se prononcer en premier sur la compétence, sous le contrôle du juge de l'annulation. Or, la Défenderesse avait en effet fait valoir l'existence d'une clause compromissoire par référence dans l'Avenant n° 1 mais elle soutenait en même temps que la Demanderesse n'était jamais devenue partie à cet Avenant. Le paradoxe n'est qu'apparent si on raisonne en termes de cession de contrat dans le contexte du droit français de l'arbitrage international. On sait en effet que pour la jurisprudence, la clause compromissoire est transmise automatiquement en cas de cession de contrat *(CA Paris, 28 janv. 1988: Rev. arb. 1988, p. 565)* et cela, « quelle que soit la validité de la transmission des droits substantiels » *(Cass. 1re civ., 28 mai 2002: Juris-Data n° 2002-014482; Rev. arb. 2003, p. 397, note D. Cohen)*. La nullité de la cession en l'absence de l'accord du cocontractant cédé était donc sans effet sur la transmission de la clause compromissoire. Peu importe également que la cession de contrat, valable ou non, n'ait semble-t-il jamais eu lieu, le cocontractant initial en liquidation n'ayant jamais manifesté de volonté en ce sens. Dès lors que les prétentions de la Demanderesse étaient fondées sur l'avenant n° 1 auquel elle soutenait être partie, la clause compromissoire figurant dans celui-ci, fût-ce indirectement, lui était opposable.

Mais il n'en aurait pas été de même dans l'hypothèse, également envisagée par l'arbitre, où ces prétentions auraient été fondées sur une novation du contrat par changement de débiteur. Certains auteurs ont en effet soutenu que ce type de novation (par opposition à la novation objective) entraînant « l'extinction de l'obligation et la naissance d'une nouvelle obligation liant des personnes différentes, on voit mal comment on pourrait faire jouer la clause compromissoire à l'égard du nouveau débiteur ou du nouveau créancier » *(P. Ancel, Arbitrage et novation: Rev. arb. 2002, p. 3. —* dans le même sens, V.*J -L. Goutal, L'arbitrage et les tiers: le droit des contra's rapports général: Rev. arb. 1988, p. 439. — Ch. Jarrosson, note sous Cass. 1re civ., 10 mai 1988: Rev. arb. 1988, p. 639)*. La clause compromissoire ne survit alors que si le nouveau débiteur a voulu être tenu dans les mêmes conditions que le débiteur initial. À défaut d'une acceptation de sa compétence dans l'acte de mission par les parties, l'arbitre unique n'aurait donc pas pu se prononcer sur l'existence ou l'absence d'un nouvel accord entre les parties se substituant à l'Avenant n° 1 et aurait dû se déclarer incompétent à cet égard, sauf à établir que les parties avaient entendu soumettre les litiges nés de ce nouvel accord à l'arbitrage dans des conditions équivalentes à celles stipulées par l'accord initial.

IV. — L'arbitre unique, après avoir déclaré admissibles deux demandes qu'il qualifie de demandes nouvelles, les rejette au fond: une demande de condamnation du Défendeur au paiement d'intérêts sur le montant des factures et une demande de réparation de ses frais devant les juridictions nationales. Cette décision d'admissibilité appelle deux commentaires. L'article 19 du Règlement d'arbitrage dispose qu'après la signature de l'acte de mission, « les parties ne peuvent formuler de nouvelles demandes, reconventionnelles ou non, hors des limites de l'acte de mission, sauf autorisation du tribunal arbitral qui tiendra compte de la nature de ces nouvelles demandes principales ou reconventionnel-les, de l'état d'avancement de la procédure et de toutes autres circonstances pertinentes ». Le Règlement cependant ne définit pas les demandes nouvelles et si cette qualification semble appropriée s'agissant d'une demande de remboursement de frais, il en va différemment de la demande d'intérêts de retard. Plusieurs sentences ont en effet considéré qu'une « demande d'intérêt est une demande accessoire directement liée à la demande principale [et qu'elle] ne peut donc être considéré comme une nouvelle demande hors des limites de l'acte de mission » *(Sentence rendue dans l'affaire CCI n° 11424, cité par E. Schwartz, Les « nouvelles demandes »: s'orienter au sein de l'article 19 du règlement d'arbitrage de la CCI: Bull. CCI, 2006, p. 70)*. Au contraire, une autre sentence a qualifié une demande d'intérêts de demande nouvelle, parce que constituant « une demande d'intérêts séparée » mais, comme l'arbitre unique dans la présente sentence, l'a jugée admissible *(affaire n° 10578, également citée par E. Schwartz)*. Si la qualification n'a en principe pas d'importance pratique dès lors que le tribunal arbitral autorise la demande, on peut se demander s'il en va toujours ainsi dans l'hypothèse, qui est peut-être celle de l'espèce, où la compétence des arbitres ne repose pas sur une clause compromissoire visant l'ensemble des différends nés de leur relation contractuelle mais d'un compromis figurant à l'acte de mission et limité au différend visé dans cet acte de mission. Dès lors que la demande nouvelle est « hors des limites de l'acte de mission », n'excède-t-elle pas la portée de la convention d'arbitrage?

V. — L'observation par l'arbitre que la Demanderesse « n'ayant pas gain de cause, il n'eut pas été inhabituel de mettre tout ou la majorité [des frais de l'arbitrage] à sa charge » fait référence à une longue série de décisions qui affirment implicitement que les frais de l'arbitrage doivent être mis à la charge de la partie qui succombe (V. récemment *Sentence rendue dans l'affaire n° 11426: JDI 2006, p. 1443, note E. Silva Romero. — Sentence rendue dans l'affaire n° 11776: JDI 2006, p. 1460, note Y. Derains).* L'existence même de cette règle est contestée par certains *(E. Silva Romero, préc.)* ou son contenu à tout le moins tempéré par d'autres *(Y. Derains, préc),* qui observent qu'aux termes de l'article 31(3) du Règlement, les arbitres ont toute latitude pour répartir les frais de l'arbitrage et devraient prendre en considération d'autres éléments que le résultat de l'affaire, comme l'attitude procédurale de chaque partie et son effet sur la durée et les coûts de la procédure. C'est d'ailleurs en l'espèce ce que fait l'arbitre unique, qui ne mentionne une règle de répartition des frais que pour ne pas la suivre, en conformité avec un certain nombre de sentences publiées (voir la jurisprudence arbitrale citée par E. Silva Romero). La sentence commentée mérite cependant d'être remarquée en ce qu'elle va jusqu'à renverser la règle en mettant l'intégralité des frais à la charge de la partie qui a intégralement gain de cause et lui laisse la charge de ses frais de représentation.

B. D.

Keyword Index

Index des mots clés

Keyword Index (English)

Keyword in English	Corresponding notion in French
Calculation of damages	Préjudice
Changed circumstances	Changement de circonstances
Claim	Demande
Company	Société
Competence of arbitrator	Compétence de l'arbitre
Competence-competence	Compétence-compétence
Competition	Concurrence
Concordat on Arbitration	Concordat suisse sur l'Arbitrage
Concurrent Court proceedings	Connexité, litispendance
Conflict of law rules	Conflit de lois
Construction contract	Contrat de construction
Contract	Contrat
Costs of Arbitration	Frais de l'arbitrage
Damages	Dommages-intérêts, préjudice
Delay	Retard
Delivery	Livraison
Depreciation	Dévalorisation
Devaluation	Dévaluation
Dissolution of party during arbitration	Faillite d'une partie à l'arbitrage, liquidation
Distributorship contract	Contrat de distribution, de représentation
Engineer	FIDIC
Equity	Amiable composition
Error *in contrahendo*	*Culpa in contrahendo*
Estoppel	*Venire contra factum proprium (Nemo auditur turpitudinem suam allegans)*
European Economic Community	Traité de la CEE
Ex æquo et bono	*Ex æquo et bono*
Exception non adimpleti contractus	*Exception non adimpleti contractus*
Exchange losses	Risque de change
Expatriate staff	Personnel
Expert	Expert technique
Fait du Prince	Fait du Prince
FIDIC	FIDIC
First demand guarantee	Garantie bancaire
Force majeure	Force majeure, "Frustration"

818

Keyword in English	Corresponding notion in French
Foreign exchange regulations	Contrôle des changes
Frustration	*Force majeure*, "Frustration"
General conditions (of sale)	Conditions générales (de ventes)
General principles of Law	Principes généraux du Droit
General principles of International Law	Principes de portée internationale
Geneva Convention	Convention européenne de Genève
Good Faith	Bonne foi; obligation de coopérer, d'informer, de négocier
Group of companies	Groupe de sociétés
Guarantee	Garantie
Hague Convention	Convention de La Haye
Hostilities	Hostilités, conflit armé
ICC rules	Règlement de la CCI
– article 8.3	– *Prima facie*
ICSID Convention	Convention de Washington
Immunity	Immunité
Indexation clause	Clause d'indexation
Injunction	Injonction
Interest	Intérêt
Interim measures	Mesures provisoires/conservatoires
International Commerce	Commerce international
International trade usages	Usages du commerce international
Interpretation of	Interprétation de
Joint venture	Consortium, contrat d'association
Jurisdiction	Compétence (juridiction)
Letter of credit	Crédit documentaire
Lex fori	*Lex fori*
Lex loci solutionis	*Lex loci solutionis*
Lex Mercatoria	*Lex Mercatoria*
Liability	Responsabilité
Licence contract	Licence (contrat de)
Limitation	Prescription
Liquidated damages	"Liquidated damages", pénalités contractuelles
Lis pendens	Litispendance, connexité
Loss of profit	Perte, préjudice

Keyword in English	Corresponding notion in French
Merchantability	Conformité des marchandises
Mitigation of damages	Obligation de minimiser les pertes
Multiparty arbitration	Arbitrage multipartite
Nationalization	Nationalisation
New York Arbitration Convention (1958)	Convention de New York (1958)
Notice	Réclamation
Nullity of contract	Nullité du contrat
Oil	Pétrole
Ordre public	Ordre public
Pacta sunt servanda	*Pacta sunt servanda*
Parallel Court proceedings	Connexité/litispendance
Partial award	Sentence partielle
Party	Partie
Performance Bond	Garantie de bonne fin
Personnel	Personnel
Place of arbitration	Lieu de l'arbitrage
Price	Prix, révision de prix
Proof	Preuve, *Actori incumbit probatio*
Proper law of the contract	"Proper law of the contract"
Public policy	Ordre public
Rebus sic stantibus	*Rebus sic stantibus*
Renvoi	Renvoi
Res judicata	Autorité de la chose jugée
Sales/purchase contract	Contrat d'achat/vente
Scrutiny of the draft award by the ICC Court of Arbitration	Examen du projet de sentence, Règlement CCI (article 21)
Set-off	Compensation
Settlement	Transaction
Sovereign immunity	Immunité
Stabilization clause	Clause de stabilisation
State	État
Stay of arbitral proceedings	Sursis à statuer
Subcontract	Sous-traitance
Technical expertise	Expert technique
Termination	Résiliation, annulation

Keyword in English	*Corresponding notion in French*
Terms of reference	Acte de mission
Time limit	Prescription, délai
Tort	Responsabilité délictuelle
Trade usages	Usages du commerce
Treaty of Rome	Traité de la CEE
ULIS	Loi uniforme sur la vente internationale
Uniform Customs and Practices for Documentary Credits	Règles et usances uniformes relatives aux crédits documentaires
Vienna Sales Convention	Convention de Vienne
Voie directe	"Voie directe"
Waiver	Renonciation
War	Conflit armé, hostilités
Warranty	Garantie, conformité des marchandises

Index des mots clés (Français)

Mot clé (Français)	Notion ou rubrique correspondante (Anglais)
Centre international d'expertise de la CCI	ICC International Centre for Expertise
Chambre de Commerce Internationale	International Chamber of Commerce
Change	Exchange losses / Foreign Exchange Regulations
Changement de circonstances	Changed circumstances / *Rebus sic stantibus*
Chose jugée	*Res judicata*
Clause d'arbitrage	Arbitral clause / Arbitration agreement
Clause d'indexation	Indexation clause
Clause résolutoire	Termination of contract
Clause de révision de prix	Price revision
Commerce international	International commerce
Commission de la CEE	Commission of the European Economic Community
Compensation	Set-off
Compétence de l'arbitre	Competence of arbitrator / Jurisdiction
Compétence-compétence	Competence-competence
Concession de distribution exclusive	Distributorship contract
Concordat suisse sur l'arbitrage	Concordat on Arbitration, Swiss
Concurrence	Antitrust Law / Competition
Conditions générales	General conditions
Conflit de lois	Conflict of law rules
Conflit armé	War, Hostilities
Conformité des marchandises	Merchantability / Warranty
Connexité (exception de ~)	Concurrent . . . / Parallel Court proceedings / *Lis pendens*
Consortium	Joint venture
Contrat	Contract
Contrat d'adhésion	Adhesion contract
Contrat d'agence commerciale	Agency contract
Contrat d'association	Joint venture
Contrat de construction	Construction contract
Contrat de distribution	Distributorship contract
Contrat de fourniture de longue durée	Long term delivery contract

Mot clé (Français)	Notion ou rubrique correspondante (Anglais)
Contrat de licence	Licence contract
Contrat de représentation	Agency contract, Distributorship
Contrat de sous-traitance	Sub-contract
Contrat de travaux publics	Construction contract
Contrat de vente	Sales/purchase contract
Contravention essentielle au contrat	Breach of contract
Contrôle des changes	Foreign exchange regulations
Convention européenne de Genève	Geneva Convention of 1961
Convention de La Haye	Hague Convention
Convention de New York	New York Arbitration Convention
Convention de Vienne	Vienna Sales Convention
Convention de Washington, CIRDI	ICSID Convention
Corruption	Bribery
Crédit documentaire	Letter of credit
Culpa in contrahendo	*Culpa in contrahendo*
Délai	Time-limit
Délai de dénonciation des vices cachés	Notice
Délai de réclamation	Notice
Demande nouvelle	Amendment of claim
Dévalorisation	Depreciation
Dévaluation	Devaluation
Devoir de limiter le préjudice	Mitigation of damages
Dommages-intérêts	Damages
Droit applicable	Applicable law
– à la convention d'arbitrage	– to validity of arbitration agreement
– au fond	– to substance
– à la procédure	– to procedure
État	State
État souverain	Sovereign State
Évaluation du préjudice	Calculation of damages
Ex æquo et bono	*Ex æquo et bono*
Exceptio non adimpleti contractus	*Exceptio non adimpleti contractus*
Expert technique	Expert / Technical expertise
Faillite d'une partie à l'arbitrage	Dissolution of party during arbitration
Fait du prince	*Fait du prince*

Mot clé (Français)	Notion ou rubrique correspondante (Anglais)
FIDIC	FIDIC / Engineer
Force majeure	*Force majeure*, Frustration
Frais de l'arbitrage	Costs of arbitration
Frustration	Frustration
Garantie bancaire	Bank guarantee / First demand guarantee
Garantie de bonne fin	Performance bond
Garantie contractuelle	Guarantee
Garantie de performance/ d'exécution	Performance bond
Groupe de sociétés	Group of companies
Hostilités	Hostilities / War
Immunité de juridiction	Immunity
Indexation	Indexation
Injonction	Injunction
Intérêts	Interest
Interprétation de la clause compromissoire	Interpretation of arbitration clause
Lex fori	*Lex fori*
Lex loci solutionis	*Lex loci solutionis*
Lex Mercatoria	*Lex Mercatoria*
Licence	Licence
Lieu de l'arbitrage	Place of arbitration
Liquidated damages	Liquidated damages
Limitation de responsabilité	Limitation / Liability
Litispendance	Parallel Court proceedings / *Lis pendens*
Liquidation	Dissolution
Livraison	Delivery
Loi applicable	Applicable law
Loi uniforme sur la vente internationale	ULIS
Mesures provisoires/conservatoires	Interim measures
Modifications des circonstances	Changed circumstances

Mot clé (Français)	Notion ou rubrique correspondante (Anglais)
Monnaie étrangère	(Foreign) Currency
Multipartite	Multiparty
Nationalisation	Nationalization
Nemo auditur turpitudinem suam allegans	Estoppel
Nomination d'arbitre	Appointment of arbitrator
Normes anationales	Anational rules
Nullité du contrat	Nullity of contract
Obligation de coopérer/d'informer/ de négocier	Good faith
Obligation de minimiser les pertes	Mitigation of damages
Ordre public	*Ordre public* / Public policy
Ordre public international	*Ordre public* / Public policy
Pacta sunt servanda	*Pacta sunt servanda*
Partie	Party
Pénalité contractuelle	Liquidated damages
Personnel	Personnel / Expatriate Staff
Perte	Damages / Loss of profit
Pétrole	Oil
Préjudice	Damages / Calculation of damages
Prescription	Time Limit
Preuve	Proof
Prima facie	ICC Rules (article 8.3)
Principes généraux du droit	General principles of law
Principes de portée internationale	General principles of international law
Prix	Price
Procédure arbitrale	Procedure
Proper law of the contract	Proper law of the contract
Rebus sic stantibus	*Rebus sic stantibus*
Réclamation	Notice
Règlement CCI	ICC Rules
Règlement d'Expertise de la CCI	ICC Rules for Expertise
Règles et usances uniformes (CCI) relative aux crédits documentaires	Uniform customs and practices for documentary credits

Mot clé (Français)	Notion ou rubrique correspondante (Anglais)
Renvoi	*Renvoi*
Résiliation (d'un contrat)	Termination of contract / Rescission
Résiliation unilatérale	Termination of contract / Rescission
Responsabilité	Liability
Responsabilité delictuelle	Tort / Liability
Retard	Delay
Révision du prix	Revision of price / Price
Risque de change	Exchange losses
Sentence	Award
Sentence partielle	Partial award
Société	Company
Sous-traitance	Subcontract
Stabilisation	Stabilization clause
Succession	Succession
Traité de la CEE	European Economic Community
Transaction	Settlement
Travaux publics	Construction contract
Usages du commerce	Trade usages
Usages du commerce international	International trade usages
Venire contra factum proprium	Estoppel
Vente	Sales, purchase contract
Violation du contrat	Breach of contract
Visa	Visa
Voie directe	*Voie directe*

Table of Cross-Referenced Cases

Table de correspondence des références

CASE/ AFFAIRE	Award rendered in/ Sentence rendue en	REFERENCE: (JDI: "Journal du Droit International") (YB: "Yearbook Commercial Arbitration") (I.C.L.R.: "International Construction Law Review")	Obs.	Collection of ICC Awards/ Recueil: (Volume/ page)	
n° 369	1932	JDI 1974, 902	YD	I	204
n° 519	1932	JDI 1974, 892	YD	I	193
n° 536	1933	JDI 1974, 901	YD	I	203
n° 953	1956	YB III (1978) 214		I	17
n° 1110	1963	JDI 1984, 921	YD	I	498
	1963	YB XXI (1996) 47		IV	1
n° 1250	1964	YB V (1980) 168		I	30
n° 1350	1968	JDI 1975, 931,	YD	I	239
n° 1397	1966	JDI 1974, 879,	YD	I	179
n° 1422	1966	JDI 1974, 884,	YD	I	185
n° 1434	1975	JDI 1976, 978,	YD	I	263
n° 1455	1967	YB III (1978) 215		I	18
n° 1507	1970	JDI 1974, 913,	YD	I	215
n° 1512	1967	YB V (1980) 170		I	33
	1970	YB V (1980) 174		I	37
	1971	YB I (1976) 128		I	3
		JDI 1974, 905,	YD	I	207
n° 1526	1968	JDI 1974, 915,	YD	I	218
n° 1581	1971	JDI 1974, 887,	YD	I	188
n° 1598	1971	YB III (1978) 216		I	19
n° 1641	1969	JDI 1974, 888,	YD	I	189
n° 1675	1969	JDI 1974, 895,	YD	I	197
n° 1677	1975	YB III (1978) 217		I	20
n° 1689	1970	JDI 1974, 886,	YD	I	186
n° 1703	1971	JDI 1974, 894,	RT	I	195
		YB I (1976) 130		I	6
n° 1704	1977	JDI 1978, 977,	YD	I	312
n° 1717	1972	JDI 1974, 890,	YD	I	191
n° 1759	1972	JDI 1974, 886,	YD	I	186
n° 1776	1970	JDI 1974, 886,	YD	I	186
n° 1782	1973	JDI 1975, 923,	YD	I	230
n° 1784	1975	YB II (1977) 150		I	10

CASE/ AFFAIRE	Award rendered in/ Sentence rendue en	REFERENCE: (JDI: "Journal du Droit International") (YB: "Yearbook Commercial Arbitration") (I.C.L.R.: "International Construction Law Review")	Obs.	Collection of ICC Awards/ Recueil: (Volume/ page)
n° 1803	1972	YB V (1980) 177		I 40
n° 1837	1971	JDI 1979, 988,	YD	I 346
n° 1840	1972	YB IV (1979) 209		I 27
n° 1850	1972	JDI 1974, 910,	YD	I 213
n° 1939	1971	JDI 1974, 919,	YD	I 222
n° 1990	1972	JDI 1974, 897,	YD	I 199
		YB III (1978) 217		I 20
n° 2068	1973	JDI 1974, 892,	YD	I 193
n° 2073	1972	JDI 1975, 932,	YD	I 240
n° 2074	1973	JDI 1975, 924,	YD	I 232
n° 2090	1976	YB VI (1981) 131		I 56
n° 2096	1972	JDI 1974, 886,	YD	I 186
n° 2103	1972	JDI 1974, 902,	YD	I 204
		YB III (1978) 218		I 21
n° 2119	1978	JDI 1979, 997,	YD	I 355
n° 2129	1972	YB III (1978) 219		I 23
n° 2136	1974	JDI 1982, 993,	YD	I 456
n° 2138	1974	JDI 1975, 934,	YD	I 242
n° 2139	1974	JDI 1975, 929,	YD	I 237
		YB III (1978) 220		I 23
n° 2142	1974	JDI 1974, 892,	RT	I 194
		YB I (1976) 132		I 7
n° 2216	1974	JDI 1975, 917,	YD	I 224
n° 2249	1973	JDI 1974, 924,	YD	I 231
n° 2272	1975	YB II (1977) 151		I 11
n° 2291	1975	JDI 1976, 989,	YD	I 274
n° 2321	1974	JDI 1975, 938,	YD	I 246
		YB I (1976) 133		I 8
n° 2347	1979	JDI 1980, 961,	YD	I 376
n° 2374	1972	JDI 1978, 997,	YD	I 333
n° 2375	1975	JDI 1976, 973,	YD	I 257
n° 2376	1976	JDI 1977, 949,	YD	I 303
n° 2391	1976	JDI 1977, 949,	YD	I 302

CASE/ AFFAIRE	Award rendered in/ Sentence rendue en	REFERENCE: (JDI: "Journal du Droit International") (YB: "Yearbook Commercial Arbitration") (I.C.L.R.: "International Construction Law Review")	Obs.	Collection of ICC Awards/ Recueil: (Volume/ page)	
n° 2404	1975	JDI 1976, 995,	YD	I	280
n° 2438	1975	JDI 1976, 969,	YD	I	253
n° 2443	1975	JDI 1976, 991,	YD	I	276
n° 2444	1976	JDI 1977, 932,	YD	I	285
n° 2462	1974	JDI 1975, 925,	YD	I	232
n° 2476	1976	JDI 1977, 936,	YD	I	289
n° 2478	1974	JDI 1975, 925,	YD	I	233
		YB III (1978) 222		I	25
n° 2502	1977	JDI 1978, 989,	YD	I	325
n° 2508	1976	JDI 1977, 939,	YD	I	292
n° 2520	1975	JDI 1976, 992,	YD	I	278
n° 2521	1975	JDI 1976, 997,	YD	I	282
n° 2540	1976	JDI 1977, 943,	YD	I	296
n° 2546	1976	JDI 1977, 945,	YD	I	299
n° 2558	1976	JDI 1977, 952,	YD	I	306
n° 2559	1976	JDI 1977, 949,	YD	I	302
n° 2583	1976	JDI 1977, 950,	YD	I	304
n° 2585	1977	JDI 1978, 998,	YD	I	334
n° 2602	1976	JDI 1977, 949,	YD	I	303
n° 2605	1977	JDI 1978, 989,	YD	I	325
n° 2626	1977	JDI 1978, 981,	YD	I	316
n° 2637	1975	YB II (1977) 153		I	13
n° 2654	1976	JDI 1977, 949,	YD	I	303
n° 2673	1976	JDI 1977, 947,	YD	I	301
n° 2680	1977	JDI 1978, 997,	YD	I	334
n° 2689	1977	JDI 1978, 998,	YD	I	335
n° 2694	1977	JDI 1978, 985,	YD	I	320
n° 2730	1982	JDI 1984, 914,	YD	I	490
n° 2734	1972	JDI 1978, 997,	YD	I	333
n° 2735	1976	JDI 1977, 947,	YD	I	301
n° 2745	1977	JDI 1978, 990,	YD	I	326
n° 2762	1977	JDI 1978, 990,	YD	I	326
n° 2763	1980	YB X (1985) 43		I	157

CASE/ AFFAIRE	Award rendered in/ Sentence rendue en	REFERENCE: (JDI: "Journal du Droit International") (YB: "Yearbook Commercial Arbitration") (I.C.L.R.: "International Construction Law Review")	Obs.	Collection of ICC Awards/ Recueil: (Volume/ page)
n° 2795	1977	YB IV (1979) 210		I 28
n° 2801	1976	JDI 1977, 949,	YD	I 303
n° 2811	1978	JDI 1979, 984,	YD	I 341
n° 2879	1978	JDI 1979, 989,	YD	I 346
n° 2886	1977	JDI 1978, 996,	YD	I 332
n° 2930	1982	YB IX (1984) 105		I 118
n° 2977	1978	YB VI (1981) 133		I 58
n° 2978	1978	YB VI (1981) 133		I 58
n° 3031	1977	JDI 1978, 999,	YD	I 335
n° 3033	1978	YB VI (1981) 133		I 58
n° 3043	1978	JDI 1979, 1000,	YD	I 358
n° 3055	1980	JDI 1981, 937,	YD	I 422
n° 3086	1977	JDI 1978, 996,	YD	I 332
n° 3093	1979	JDI 1980, 951,	YD	I 365
n° 3099	1979	YB VII (1982) 87		I 67
n° 3100	1979	JDI 1980, 951,	YD	I 365
		YB VII (1982) 87		I 67
n° 3130	1980	JDI 1981, 932,	YD	I 417
n° 3131	1979	JDI 1981, 922,	YD	I 407
		YB IX (1984) 109		I 122
n° 3202	1978	JDI 1979, 1003,	YD	I 362
n° 3226	1979	JDI 1980, 959,	YD	I 374
n° 3235	1980	JDI 1981, 925,	YD	I 410
n° 3243	1981	JDI 1982, 968,	YD	I 429
n° 3267	1979	JDI 1980, 962,	YD	I 376
		YB VII (1982) 96		I 76
	1984	YB XII (1987) 87		II 43
n° 3281	1981	JDI 1982, 990,	YD.	I 453
n° 3292	1980	JDI 1981, 924,	YD	I 409
n° 3316	1979	JDI 1980, 970,	YD	I 385
		YB VII (1982) 106		I 87
n° 3327	1981	JDI 1982, 971,	YD	I 433
n° 3344	1981	JDI 1982, 978,	YD	I 440

CASE/ AFFAIRE	Award rendered in/ Sentence rendue en	REFERENCE: (JDI: "Journal du Droit International") (YB: "Yearbook Commercial Arbitration") (I.C.L.R.: "International Construction Law Review")	Obs.	Collection of ICC Awards/ Recueil: (Volume/ page)	
n° 3380	1980	JDI 1981, 928,	YD	I	413
		YB VII (1982) 116		I	96
n° 3383	1979	JDI 1980, 978,	YD	I	394
		YB VII (1982) 119		I	100
n° 3460	1980	JDI 1981, 939,	YD	I	425
n° 3472	1982	JDI 1983, 895,	YD	I	461
n° 3493	1983	YB IX (1984) 111		I	124
		YB VII (1982) 124		I	105
n° 3572	1982	YB XIV (1989) 110		II	154
n° 3742	1983	JDI 1984, 910,	YD	I	486
n° 3779	1981	YB IX (1984) 124		I	138
n° 3790	1983	JDI 1983, 910,	SJ	I	476
		YB IX (1984) 119		II	3
		(1983) 1 I.C.L.R. 372	SJ	II	447
n° 3820	1981	YB VII (1982) 134		I	115
n° 3879	1984	YB XI (1986) 127		II	11
n° 3880	1983	JDI 1983, 897,	YD/SJ	I	462
		YB X (1985) 44		I	159
n° 3881	1984	JDI 1986, 1096,	SJ	II	257
n° 3894	1981	JDI 1982, 987,	YD	I	449
n° 3896	1982	JDI 1983, 914,	SJ	I	481
		YB X (1985) 47		I	161
n° 3902	1984	(1984) 2 I.C.L.R. 49	SJ	II	452
n° 3913	1981	JDI 1984, 920,	YD	I	497
n° 3916	1982	JDI 1984, 930,	SJ	I	507
n° 3938	1982	JDI 1984, 926,	SJ	I	503
n° 3987	1983	JDI 1984, 943,	YD	I	521
n° 4023	1984	JDI 1984, 950,	SJ	I	528
n° 4126	1984	JDI 1984, 934,	SJ	I	511
n° 4131	1982	JDI 1983, 899,	YD	I	465
		YB IX (1984) 131		I	146
n° 4132	1983	JDI 1983, 891,	YD	I	456
		YB X (1985) 49		I	164

CASE/ AFFAIRE	Award rendered in/ Sentence rendue en	REFERENCE: (JDI: "Journal du Droit International") (YB: "Yearbook Commercial Arbitration") (I.C.L.R.: "International Construction Law Review")	Obs.	Collection of ICC Awards/ Recueil: (Volume/ page)
n° 4145	1983	YB XII (1987) 97		II 53
	1984	JDI 1985, 985,	YD	I 559
		YB XII (1987) 97		II 53
	1986	YB XII (1987) 97		II 53
n° 4156	1983	JDI 1984, 937,	SJ	I 515
n° 4187	1982	JDI 1983, 895,	YD	I 460
n° 4237	1984	YB X (1985) 52		I 167
n° 4265	1984	JDI 1984, 922,	YD	I 499
n° 4338	1984	JDI 1985, 982,	YD	I 555
n° 4367	1984	YB XI (1986) 134		II 18
n° 4381	1986	JDI 1986, 1103,	YD	II 264
n° 4392	1983	JDI 1983, 907,	YD	I 473
n° 4402	1983	YB IX (1984) 138		I 153
n° 4415	1984	JDI 1984, 952,	SJ	I 530
n° 4416	1985	JDI 1985, 969,	SJ	I 542
		(1986) 3 I.C.L.R. 67	SJ	II 462
n° 4434	1983	JDI 1983, 893,	YD	I 458
n° 4462	1985	YB XVI (1991) 54		III 3
	1987	YB XVI (1991) 54		III 3
n° 4467	1984	JDI 1984, 924,	X	I 501
n° 4504	1985	JDI 1986, 1118,	SJ	II 279
	1986	JDI 1986, 1118,	SJ	II 279
n° 4555	1985	JDI 1985, 964,	SJ	I 536
		YB XI (1986) 140		II 24
n° 4567	1984	YB XI (1986) 143		II 27
	1985	YB XI (1986) 143		II 27
n° 4589	1984	YB XI (1986) 148		II 32
		(1985) 2 I.C.L.R. 298	SJ	II 456
n° 4604	1984	JDI 1985, 973,	YD	I 546
n° 4629	1989	YB XVIII (1993) 11		III 152
n° 4650	1985	YB XII (1987) 111		II 67
n° 4667	1984	JDI 1987, 1047,	YD	II 338
	1985	JDI 19886, 1136,	YD	II 297

CASE/ AFFAIRE	Award rendered in/ Sentence rendue en	REFERENCE: (JDI: "Journal du Droit International") (YB: "Yearbook Commercial Arbitration") (I.C.L.R.: "International Construction Law Review")	Obs.	Collection of ICC Awards/ Recueil: (Volume/page)
n° 4695	1984	YB XI (1986) 149		II 33
n° 4707	1986	(1986) 3 I.C.L.R. 470	SJ	II 479
n° 4761	1984	JDI 1986, 1137,	SJ	II 298
	1987	JDI 1987, 1012,	SJ	II 302
		(1989) 6 I.C.L.R. 330	SJ	II 521
n° 4840	1986	(1986) 3 I.C.L.R. 277	SJ	II 467
n° 4862	1986	JDI 1987, 1018,	SJ	II 309
		(1989) 6 I.C.L.R. 44	SJ	II 510
n° 4972	1989	JDI 1989, 1101,	GAA	II 380
n° 4975	1988	YB XIV (1989) 122		II 165
n° 4996	1985	JDI 1986, 1132,	YD	II 293
n° 4998	1985	JDI 1986, 1139,	SJ	II 300
n° 5029	1986	YB XII (1987) 113		II 69
		(1986) 3 I.C.L.R. 473	SJ	II 482
n° 5030	1992	JDI 1993, 1004,	YD	III 475
n° 5065	1986	JDI 1987, 1039,	YD	II 330
n° 5073	1986	YB XIII (1988) 53		II 85
n° 5080	1985	YB XII (1987) 124		II 80
n° 5103	1988	JDI 1988, 1207,	GAA	II 361
n° 5117	1986	JDI 1986, 1113,	YD	II 274
n° 5118	1986	JDI 1987, 1027,	SJ	II 318
n° 5195	1986	YB XIII (1988) 69		II 101
n° 5269	1986	JDI 1987, 1029,	SJ	II 320
n° 5277	1987	YB XIII (1988) 80		II 112
n° 5294	1988	YB XIV (1989) 137		II 180
n° 5314	1988	YB XXI (1995) 35		III 309
n° 5333	1986	(1987) 4 I.C.L.R. 321	SJ	II 497
n° 5346	1988	JDI 1991, 1060,	YD	III 414
n° 5418	1987	YB XIII (1988) 91		II 123
n° 5423	1987	JDI 1987, 1048,	SJ	II 339
n° 5428	1988	YB XIV (1989) 146		II 189
n° 5460	1987	YB XIII (1988) 104		I 136
n° 5477	1988	JDI 1988, 1204,	GAA	II 358

CASE/ AFFAIRE	Award rendered in/ Sentence rendue en	REFERENCE: (JDI: "Journal du Droit International") (YB: "Yearbook Commercial Arbitration") (I.C.L.R.: "International Construction Law Review")	Obs.	Collection of ICC Awards/ Recueil: (Volume/ page)
n° 5485	1987	YB XIV (1989) 156		II 199
n° 5514	1990	JDI 1992, 1022	YD	III 459
n° 5548	1988	YB XVI (1991) 79		III 28
N° 5617	1989	JDI 1994, 1041	DH	III 537
n° 5622	1988	YB XIX (1994) 105		III 220
n° 5625	1987	(1987) 4 I.C.L.R. 239	SJ	II 486
n° 5634	1988	JDI 1994, 1034	DH	III 530
n° 5639	1987	JDI 1987, 1054	SJ	II 345
		(1989) 6 I.C.L.R. 417	SJ	II 528
n° 5649	1987	YB XIV (1989) 174		II 217
n° 5650	1989	YB XVI (1991) 85		III 34
n° 5713	1989	YB XV (1990) 70		II 223
n° 5721	1990	JDI 1990, 1020,	JJA	II 400
n° 5730	1988	JDI 1990, 1029,	JJA	II 410
n° 5759	1989	YB XVIII (1993) 34		III 175
n° 5779	1988	JDI 1988, 1206,	GAA	II 360
n° 5832	1988	JDI 1988, 1198,	GAA	II 352
		(1990) 7 I.C.L.R. 421	GAA	II 535
n° 5864	1989	JDI 1997, 1073	YD	IV 485
n° 5865	1989	JDI 1998, 1008	DH	IV 493
n° 5885	1989	YB XVI (1991) 91		III 40
n° 5904	1989	JDI 1989, 1107,	GAA	II 387
n° 5910	1988	JDI 1988, 1216,	YD	II 371
n° 5943	1990	JDI 1996, 1014	DH	IV 431
n° 5946	1990	YB XVI (1991) 97		III 46
n° 5953	1989	JDI 1990, 1056,	YD	II 437
n° 5961	1989	JDI 1997, 1051	DH	IV 465
n° 5989	1989	YB XV (1990) 74		II 227
	1989	JDI 1997, 1046	DH	IV 461
n° 6057[2]	1991	JDI 1993, 1016,	YD	III 487
n° 6076	1989	YB XV (1990) 83		II 236
n° 6142	1990	JDI 1990, 1039,	YD	II 420
n° 6162	1990	YB XVII (1992) 153		III 75

CASE/ AFFAIRE	Award rendered in/ Sentence rendue en	REFERENCE: (JDI: "Journal du Droit International") (YB: "Yearbook Commercial Arbitration") (I.C.L.R.: "International Construction Law Review")	Obs.	Collection of ICC Awards/ Recueil: (Volume/ page)
n° 6197	1995	YB XXIII (1998) 13		IV 164
n° 6219	1990	JDI 1990, 1047,	YD	II 427
n° 6230	1990	YB XVII (1992) 164		III 86
n° 6233	1992	YB XXI (1995) 58		III 332
n° 6248	1990	YB XIX (1994) 124		III 239
n° 6268	1990	YB XVI (1991) 119		III 68
n° 6281	1989	JDI 1989, 1114,	GAA	II 394
		JDI 1991, 1054,	DH	III 409
		YB XV (1990) 96		II 249
n° 6283	1990	YB XVII (1992) 178		III 100
n° 6286	1991	YB XIX (1994) 141		III 256
n° 6294	1991	JDI 1991, 1050,	JJA	III 405
n° 6309	1991	JDI 1991, 1046	JJA	III 401
n° 6317	1989	JDI 2003, 1156	SJ	V 623
n° 6320	1992	JDI 1995, 986	DH	III 577
		YB XXI (1995) 62		III 336
n° 6363	1991	YB XVII (1992) 186		III 108
n° 6378	1991	JDI 1993, 1018,	DH	III 489
n° 6379	1990	YB XVII (1992) 212		III 134
n° 6474	1992	YB XXV (2000) 279		IV 341
n° 6497	1994	YB XXIVa (1999) 71		IV 232
n° 6500	1992	JDI 1992, 1015,	JJA	III 452
n° 6503	1990	JDI 1995, 1022	YB	III 613
n° 6515	1994	YB XXIVa (1999) 80		IV 241
n° 6516	1994	YB XXIVa (1999) 80		IV 241
n° 6519	1991	JDI 1991, 1065,	YD	III 420
n° 6527	1991	YB XVIII (1993) 44		III 185
n° 6531	1991	YB XVII (1992) 221		III 143
n° 6535	1992	JDI 1993, 1024,	DH	III 495
n° 6560	1990	YB XVII (1992) 226		III 148
n° 6573	1991	YB XXI (1995) 110		III 382
n° 6610	1991	YB XIX (1994) 162		III 277
n° 6648	1992	YB XXIII (1998) 30		IV 180

CASE/ AFFAIRE	Award rendered in/ Sentence rendue en	REFERENCE: (JDI: "Journal du Droit International") (YB: "Yearbook Commercial Arbitration") (I.C.L.R.: "International Construction Law Review")	Obs.	Collection of ICC Awards/ Recueil: (Volume/ page)
n° 6653	1993	JDI 1993, 1040	JJA	III 512
		JDI 1993, 1053	JJA	III 525
n° 6670	1992	JDI 1992, 1010,	JJA	III 447
n° 6673	1992	JDI 1992, 992,	DH	III 429
n° 6709	1991	JDI 1992, 998,	DH	III 435
n° 6719	1991	JDI 1994, 1071	JJA	III 567
n° 6733	1992	JDI 1994, 1038	DH	III 534
n° 6752	1991	YB XVIII (1993) 54		III 195
n° 6754	1993	JDI 1995, 1009	YD	III 600
n° 6769	1991	JDI 1992, 1019,	YD	III 456
n° 6829	1992	YB XIX (1994) 167		III 282
n° 6840	1991	JDI 1992, 1031,	YD	III 467
n° 6850	1992	YB XXIII (1998) 37		IV 187
n° 6932	1992	JDI 1994, 1064	YD	III 560
n° 6955	1993	YB XXIVa (1999) 107		IV 267
n° 6962	1992	YB XIX (1994) 184		III 299
n° 6998	1994	YB XXI (1996) 54		IV 7
n° 7006	1992	YB XVIII (1993) 58		III 199
n° 7047	1994	YB XXI (1996) 79		IV 32
n° 7063	1993	YB XXII (1997) 87		IV 75
n° 7081	1994	JDI 2003, 1132	SJ	V 599
n° 7105	1993	JDI 2000, 1062	YD	IV 548
n° 7139	1995	JDI 2004, 1272	YD-BD	V 647
n° 7146	1992	YB XXVI (2001) 119		V 3
n° 7153	1992	JDI 1992, 1006,	DH	III 442
n° 7154	1993	JDI 1994, 1059	YD	III 555
n° 7155	1993	JDI 1996, 1037	JJA	IV 451
n° 7181	1992	YB XXI (1996) 99		IV 52
n° 7197	1992	JDI 1993, 1029,	DH	III 500
n° 7205	1993	JDI 1995, 1031	JJA	III 622
n° 7263	1994	YB XXII (1997) 92		IV 80
n° 7301	1993	YB XXIII (1998) 42		IV 192
n° 7314	1995	YB XXIII (1998) 49		IV 198

CASE/ AFFAIRE	Award rendered in/ Sentence rendue en	REFERENCE: (JDI: "Journal du Droit International") (YB: "Yearbook Commercial Arbitration") (I.C.L.R.: "International Construction Law Review")	Obs.	Collection of ICC Awards/ Recueil: (Volume/ page)
n° 7319	1992	YB XXIVa (1999) 141		IV 300
n° 7331	1994	JDI 1995, 1001	DH	III 592
n° 7337	1996	YB XXIVa (1999) 149		IV 308
n° 7385	1992	YB XVIII (1993) 68		III 209
n° 7402	1992	YB XVIII (1993) 68		III 209
n° 7453	1994	YB XXII (1997) 107		IV 94
n° 7518	1994	JDI 1998, 1034	YD	IV 516
n° 7528	1993	YB XXII (1997) 125		IV 112
n° 7539	1995	JDI 1996, 1030	YD	IV 445
n° 7544	1995	JDI 1999, 1062	DH	IV 533
n° 7563	1993	JDI 1994, 1054	YD	III 550
n° 7585	1994	JDI 1995, 1015	YD	III 606
n° 7604	1995	JDI 1998, 1027	DH	IV 510
n° 7626	1995	YB XXII (1997) 132		IV 119
n° 7639	1994	YB XXIII (1998) 66		IV 214
n° 7645	1995	YB XXVI (2001) 130		V 15
n° 7661	1995	YB XXII (1997) 149		IV 135
n° 7710	1995	JDI 2001, 1148	YD	V 513
n° 7722	1999	YB XXXII (2007) 13		V 437
n° 7792	1994	JDI 1995, 993	DH	III 583
n° 7893	1994	YB XXVII (2002) 139		V 67
n° 7920	1993	YB XXIII (1998) 80		IV 227
n° 7929	1995	YB XXV (2000) 312		IV 373
n° 7983	1996	JDI 2002, 1085	SJ	V 567
n° 7986	1999	JDI 2002, 1071	YD	V 553
n° 8032	1995	YB XXI (1996) 113		IV 66
n° 8035	1995	JDI 1997, 1040	DH	IV 455
n° 8113	1995	YB XXV (2000) 324		IV 385
n° 8128	1995	JDI 1996, 1024	DH	IV 440
n° 8324	1995	JDI 1996, 1019	DH	IV 435
n° 8331	1996	JDI 1998, 1041	YD	IV 522
n° 8362	1995	YB XXII (1997) 164		IV 150
n° 8365	1996	JDI 1997, 1078	JJA	IV 489

CASE/ AFFAIRE	Award rendered in/ Sentence rendue en	REFERENCE: (JDI: "Journal du Droit International") (YB: "Yearbook Commercial Arbitration") (I.C.L.R.: "International Construction Law Review")	Obs.	Collection of ICC Awards/ Recueil: (Volume/ page)
n° 8385	1995	JDI 1997, 1061	YD	IV 474
n° 8420	1996	YB XXV (2000) 328		IV 389
n° 8423	1994	YB XXVI (2001) 153		V 39
	1998	JDI 2002, 1079	JJA	V 561
n° 8445	1996	YB XXVI (2001) 167		V 53
n° 8486	1996	YB XXIVa (1999) 162		IV 321
	1996	JDI 1998, 1047	YD	IV 527
n° 8501		JDI 2001, 1164	EJ	V 529
n° 8528	1996	YB XXV (2000) 341		IV 402
n° 8547	1999	YB XXVIII (2003) 27		V 115
n° 8626	1996	JDI 1999, 1073	JJA	IV 543
n° 8694	1996	JDI 1997, 1056	YD	IV 470
n° 8742	1996	JDI 1999, 1066	DH	IV 536
n° 8782	1997	YB XXVIII (2003) 39		V 127
n° 8790	2000	YB XXIX (2004) 13		V 155
n° 8817	1997	YB XXV (2000) 355		IV 415
n° 8855	1997	JDI 2000, 1070	JJA	IV 555
n° 8873	1997	JDI 1998, 1017	DH	IV 500
n° 8891	1998	JDI 2000, 1076	DH	IV 561
n° 8910	1998	JDI 2000, 1085	DH	IV 569
n° 8938	1996	YB XXIVa (1999) 174		IV 333
n° 9163	2001	JDI 2005, 1283	YD-BD	V 703
n° 9302	1998	YB XXVIII (2003) 54		V 141
n° 9333	1998	JDI 2002, 1094	SJ	V 575
n° 9427	1998	YB XXVII (2002) 153		V 81
n° 9443	1998	JDI 2002, 1106	EJ	V 589
n° 9466	1999	YB XXVII (2002) 170		V 97
n° 9608	1998 et 1998	JDI 2004, 1294	SJ	V 669
n° 9613	1999	YB XXXII (2007) 42		V 463
n° 9617	1999	JDI 2005, 1291	SJ-CTN	711
n° 9667	1998	JDI 2000, 1096	DH	IV 579
n° 9762	2001	YB XXIX (2004) 26		V 167

CASE/ AFFAIRE	Award rendered in/ Sentence rendue en	REFERENCE: (JDI: "Journal du Droit International") (YB: "Yearbook Commercial Arbitration") (I.C.L.R.: "International Construction Law Review")	Obs.	Collection of ICC Awards/ Recueil: (Volume/page)
n° 9771	2001	YB XXIX (2004) 46		V 187
n° 9781	2000	YB XXX (2005) 22		V 273
n° 9787	1998	YB XXVII (2002) 181		V 107
n° 9800	2000	JDI 2004, 1284	YD-BD	V 659
n° 9839	1999	YB XXIX (2004) 66		V 207
n° 10060	1999	YB XXX (2005) 42		V 291
n° 10264	2000	JDI 2004, 1256	SJ	V 629
n° 10274	1999	YB XXIX (2004) 89		V 229
n° 10329	2000	YB XXIX (2004) 108		V 249
n° 10377	2002	YB XXXI (2006) 72		V 341
n° 10422	2001	JDI 2003, 1142	EJ	V 609
n° 10526	2000	JDI 2001, 1179	SJ	V 545
n° 10527	2000	JDI 2004, 1263	EJ	V 637
n° 10596	2000	YB XXX (2005) 66		V 315
n° 10671		JDI 2005, 1269	ESR	V 689
		JDI 2006, 1417	ESR	V 727
n° 10758	2000	JDI 2001, 1171	JJA	V 537
n° 10904	2002	YB XXXI (2006) 95		V 363
n° 10973	2001	YB XXX (2005) 77		V 327
n° 10982	2001	JDI 2005, 1256	YD-BD	V 677
n° 10988	2003	JDI 2006, 1406	BD	V 719
n° 11277	2003	JDI 2006, 1429	SJ-CTN	V 737
n° 11333	2002	YB XXXI (2006) 117		V 383
n° 11426		JDI 2006, 1443	ESR	V 751
n° 11440	2003	YB XXXI (2006) 127		V 393
n° 11443	2001	YB XXX (2005) 85		V 335
n° 11663	2003	YB XXXII (2007) 60		V 479
n° 11776	2002	JDI 2006, 1460	YD	V 767
n° 11849	2003	YB XXXI (2006) 148		V 413
n° 11855	2003	JDI 2007, 1292	ESR	V 797
n° 12045	2003	JDI 2006, 1434	SJ-CTN	V 743
n° 12167	2002	JDI 2007, 1270	SJ-CTN	V 777

CASE/ AFFAIRE	Award rendered in/ Sentence rendue en	REFERENCE: (JDI: "Journal du Droit International") (YB: "Yearbook Commercial Arbitration") (I.C.L.R.: "International Construction Law Review")	Obs.	Collection of ICC Awards/ Recueil: (Volume/ page)
n° 12172	2003	YB XXXII (2007) 85		V 503
n° 12193	2004	JDI 2007, 1277	ESR	V 783
n° 12551	2004	JDI 2007, 1301	BD	V 807
n° 12711	2004	JDI 2006, 1454	EJ	V 761

BD :   Bertrand Derains
CTN : Corinne Truong-Nguyen
EJ :   Emmanuel Jolivet
ESR : Eduardo Silva Romero
DH :   Dominique Hascher
GAA : Guillermo Aguilar Alvarez
JJA : Jean-Jacques Arnaldez
RT :   Robert Thompson
SJ :   Sigvard Jarvin
YD :   Yves Derains